UNIVERSITY CASEBOOK SERIES

EVIDENCE

THIRD EDITION

by

GEORGE FISHER
Judge John Crown Professor of Law
Stanford Law School

1 New York Plaza, 34th Floor
New York, NY 10004
Phone Toll Free 1–877–888–1330
Fax 646–424–5201
foundation–press.com

Printed in the United States of America

ISBN 978–1–60930–060–9

Mat #41181422

For Lu and Dick.

PREFACE

My aim in writing this book has been above all to create an evidence book students will love. And if this goal has proved past my reach, I hope the book at least grabs and holds students' interest. The challenge has been to present the law's gritty details in a way students find intellectually compelling and sometimes even fun. I've followed several strategies—some substantive, some stylistic, some purely pedagogical:

Focus on the Criminal Context: Courtrooms come alive when examined through a criminal law lens. Criminal cases seem earthier, more vital than mill-run civil actions. The pages ahead therefore focus on criminal cases and scenarios. But because some evidence rules operate mainly on the civil side and because I've aimed to cover every important evidence topic, some civil cases join the mix. Still, whenever the doctrine has let me choose, I feature the rough-and-tumble of the criminal process.

Emphasize History: Most evidence casebooks add intellectual content by exploring the epistemology of proof. Though the goal is worthy, the approach seems doubtful. Epistemology never grabbed students in my day, and I suspect it would work no better today. But the history of evidence law sometimes simply fascinates. Consider how the racial politics of the Civil War era stalled the inevitable collapse of many old and unrelated witness competency rules. (*See* pages 364–71.) Or take the back story of *Mutual Life Insurance Co. v. Hillmon* of 1892, a grisly tale of dirty dealings on the frontier. (*See* pages 522–31.) And the history of the 1960s classic, *People v. Collins*, reveals the hidden hand of a future legal legend, then a 25-year-old law clerk, who ghostwrote much of the famous opinion. (*See* pages 75–79.) History is not just for fun, of course. Studying the stories behind the law strengthens students' grasp of the principles that drive our evidence rules and deepens understanding of how the law works today.

Make It Timely: Rich in history, evidence law is also a happening field. Since launching the *Crawford* revolution in 2004, the Supreme Court has decided nine major cases in a quixotic quest to define how tightly the Sixth Amendment Confrontation Clause constrains admission of hearsay against criminal defendants. Chapter 8 details the latest skirmishes among the Court's warring factions, struggling to make this chaotic doctrine more predictable. Meanwhile the National Academy of Sciences lit a brushfire with its 2009 report scorching the methods and standards of the so-called forensic "sciences." Suddenly it was thinkable that courts might yield to timeworn defense demands, now girded by the NAS report, to bar or limit expert testimony about fingerprint or handwriting identification or hair or firearms analysis. Chapter 9 traces the defense bar's rising hopes, largely disappointed, of undermining these familiar techniques. Amid this strife in the courts, change came too from the rule writers. In

September 2010 the U.S. Judicial Conference approved a full-scale restyling of the Federal Rules of Evidence. As of December 2011, when the newly restyled evidence rules took effect, virtually every rule has a new text, and some rules have new numbering schemes. Confrontation law upended; forensic sciences attacked; evidence rules recast—these seismic events demanded this new edition, which strives to make students masters of the latest rules and caselaw.

Mix It Up: But rules and caselaw are not all of law. Other sources—news articles, journal articles, behavioral and scientific studies—inform law and are informed by it. Exploring the doctrine from many perspectives helps students see how evidence law suits (or doesn't suit) our whole system of justice. Moreover, many students like flowcharts, diagrams, and tables because visual images of the law often reveal its structure more clearly than any verbal description. The occasional map, photo, cartoon, or poem can enlighten analysis or reflect the force of the law in action. Cases, too, remain a critical component. Real-world disputes breathe life into law, and disagreements among parties challenge students to flex their advocacy skills. And case-based narratives stick in the mind. Wrapping a rule's tangled verbiage inside a memorable story makes that rule easier to remember and apply later.

Use Real–Life Problems: Problems also are essential, but pose hazards. Students seem to resent the hidden hand of the law professor, guiding them toward supposedly spontaneous moments of intellectual discovery. There are many forms of this pedagogical device, though rhetorical questions and elaborate hypotheticals are the two most obvious. I've avoided rhetorical questions almost entirely. As for hypotheticals, I think the best problems spring from life. So whenever possible, I have based problems on facts quoted from cases or news articles, complete with citations. My hope is that students will ask themselves, "How would a good lawyer attack this problem?" rather than "What is the professor driving at?"

Help Students Swim: I never have succeeded in teaching all of the Rules' intricacies through caselaw and commentary—and I doubt even the best student could learn evidence law without some straightforward guidance through doctrinal labyrinths. So at many critical junctures in the book, I've laid out the details of doctrine as clearly as I can. The introductions to propensity evidence and hearsay, which address some of the toughest territory in evidence law, aim to give students a firm base on which to build the unwieldy doctrines of these two realms. They are just two of dozens of areas where I've felt a quick, treatise-like interjection could resolve confusions.

Fight the Bulge: A malady strikes casebooks as they age into later editions. New cases come along, and new studies and news stories follow. Earnest authors add them to the mix. Older cases, meanwhile, past their prime, somehow elude the author's sharpened pencil and survive into the next edition. Page counts swell, margins shrink, and smaller fonts strain students' eyes and patience. I've resolved to fight the bulge, erasing one old case for each new case and resisting temptations to cover every topic. But with confrontation caselaw in disarray and forensic sciences under assault, the book has thickened to my regret. I will continue to fight the bulge and hope the book will remain as I intended it—one that lets professors assign and students enjoy every page.

These have been my strategies. Over the years they have worked for my students and me. I hope they will work for you. But if I have taken a misguided course or missed a fruitful one, I trust that you (both students and professors) will let me know. The next edition will profit from your thoughts.

—GF

ACKNOWLEDGMENTS

I begin with a confession: No matter how many pages I consume and names I mention, I will leave out too many people who deserve thanks. Countless friends and helpful strangers have sent ideas and citations and the best sorts of criticisms. There are too many such folks for me to remember, much less to list. I regret any I leave unacknowledged.

I have leaned on no one so heavily as the small army of student research assistants, paid and unpaid, who have dug out forgotten cases and obscure articles and cite-checked, proofread, and indexed. They have assembled fifty-state surveys of odd aspects of evidence law, and they have offered student-sensitive insights, warning me when my drafts are confusing or arcane or dull. As if by magic they have converted hand-drawn charts and diagrams into blueprint-quality art forms. To say that collectively they have been indispensable is no exaggeration, and several can claim that distinction independently. The list is long: My thanks to Billy Abbott, Stephanie Alessi, Matt Alexander, Justin Barnard, Fred Bloom, Binyamin Blum, Jake Gardener, Christine Hwang, Vivek Kothari, Steve Mansell, Katherine McCarron, Duane Pozza, Anitha Reddy, Karen Saah, Zoe Scharf, and Anthony Sun. To Gabe Schlabach goes credit not only for making unnumbered contributions to this volume, but for engineering the rulebook that accompanies this edition. Mark Menzies likewise has done dual duty, enriching this text and suffering production of the index, a task that brooks no imprecision.

Helping both students and me in myriad ways are the endlessly resourceful members, past and present, of our law library. Among those who have saved us more than once from ignorance and error are Alba Holgado, Sonia Moss, Rich Porter, Rachael Samberg, Kate Wilko, George Wilson, and Sarah Wilson. And Bobbi Dufek has performed miraculous administrative feats, keeping our gears in motion when deadlines loomed.

From colleagues who have used or reviewed the book, I've received many thoughtful suggestions and sharp-eyed corrections. With a repeated apology to those I'm forgetting, I will attempt a list: Michael Ariens, Michael Avery, Charles Baron, Norman Bay, Jeff Bellin, Judge Isaac Borenstein, Mark Brodin, Rosanna Cavallaro, Ed Cheng, Katherine Darmer, Ingrid Eagly, Jeff Fisher, Bill Fortune, John Garvey, Mark Godsey, Michael Gottesman, Lisa Griffin, Erica Hashimoto, Bruce Hay, David Kaye, Kate Kruse, Lash LaRue, Melanie Leslie, Andy Levy, Craig Lewis, Lane Liroff, Kevin McMunigal, Miguel Méndez, Deborah Merritt, Colin Miller, Jennifer Mnookin, Joïle Moreno, Ann Murphy, Dale Nance, Deirdre O'Connor, Katherine Pearson, Judge Paul Plunkett, Richard Polenberg, Phil Pucillo, Judge Timothy Rice, Mark Rienzi, Tanina Rostain, Rick Underwood, Si Wasserstrom, Marianne Wesson, Dan Williams, and Tom Workman. Dan Capra and John Rabiej hold the clue to every recent and forthcoming change in the Federal Rules and have shared their knowledge generously and patiently.

Many kind folks scattered across the country have added color and depth to important cases. Gene Talerico of the Lackawanna County District Attorney's Office and André Stuart of 21st Century Forensic Animations helped secure the animation featured in *Commonwealth v. Serge* (page 49). Jake Ersland of the National Archives at Kansas City dug out and scanned the photos that accompany *Mutual Life Insurance Co. v. Hillmon* (page 529). David Mark of the Bristol County District Attorney's Office helped gain access to the 911 call examined in *Commonwealth v. Nesbitt* (page 643). And Christopher Holm of Lucasfilm Ltd. bestowed permission to reprint the famous image at issue in *Seiler v. Lucasfilm* (page 921).

To the exceptionally talented and astonishingly patient production crew at Foundation Press goes all credit for the handsomely proportioned pages, the easy-reading text, and the meticulous error detection. Tessa Boury, Sharon Pizzi, and Greg Olson suffered the headaches caused by my many missed deadlines with seemingly bottomless patience and complete professionalism. Backing them and bearing the brunt of my delays were Christina Eschbach, Laura Holle, Cathy Lundeen, Holly Saari, Jennifer Schlagel, and Bekke Schneider. Paul Thomson has supplied essential support day in, day out, year after year. And Editor-in-Chief John Bloomquist, with sheer competence and understated command, has steered to print two editions of this book, never hinting when I have needed his time that mine is just one of many books he oversees. Together these good people have given corporate headquarters an unusually homey name.

I owe a special thanks to Professor David Leonard, who together with Professor Rosanna Cavallaro read the entire manuscript of the first draft of this book. Though David had his own casebook in the works, he offered his wise counsel on page after page of mine. David died much too young early in 2010. He has been spoken of in death exactly as he was in life—as one of the nicest guys any of us has known.

Thanks finally to my Aunt Lu and Uncle Dick, who have lent moral support as long as I can remember. Their generous spirits and open minds have been lifelong inspirations. I have dedicated this volume to them.

—GF

SUMMARY OF CONTENTS

TABLE OF CONTENTS

CHAPTER 3 CHARACTER EVIDENCE 145

TABLE OF CASES

Principal cases are in bold type. Non-principal cases are in roman type. References are to Pages.

TABLE OF SECONDARY AUTHORITIES

Books and Treatises

Articles

EVIDENCE

THIRD EDITION

INTRODUCTION

Evidence law is about the limits we place on the information juries hear. The chapters ahead examine these limits, their boundaries, their ambiguities, and how they work in practice. Mastering the Federal Rules of Evidence will occupy much of our time. It is essential to know what the rules say and how judges enforce them. It is just as important to know when the meaning of a rule is unclear and on what grounds courts decide close calls. But behind these rule-bound and case-focused inquiries lies a more fundamental question: Why have evidence rules anyway?

Why should we limit the information juries hear? Some reasons are clear enough. To begin with, trials have to *end*, so judges must restrict pointless, bloated, or repetitive evidence. Moreover, the Supreme Court has barred use of some evidence obtained in violation of the Constitution. And we as a society have chosen to protect the privacy of certain communications—between wife and husband, lawyer and client, for example—even at the expense of good evidence. These are examples of evidence rules that serve discrete and identifiable goals. The great majority of evidence rules, however, serve a more elusive goal.

That goal has something to do with achieving, at trial, the *right* result. We want juries to return the right verdict, and by that we may mean the *truthful* verdict, the one that accords with *what happened*. Charles Nesson has argued that we do not want truthful verdicts so much as verdicts that will *seem* truthful and therefore will gain legitimacy and stability. *See* Charles Nesson, *The Evidence or the Event? On Judicial Proof and the Acceptability of Verdicts*, 98 Harv. L. Rev. 1357 (1985). But whether the goal is truth or virtual truth, we still can wonder why external limits on the flow of information help achieve that goal.

One reason, of course, is that in many cases only one lawyer is advocating the "right" result. So we cannot count on lawyers to present only sound and helpful evidence. Still, since juries surely know what lawyers are up to, can't we count on juries to separate wheat evidence from chaff? Evidence rules presume otherwise. They presume that certain evidence will distract juries from their search for truth and produce wrong results.

Yet our mistrust of juries' fact-finding powers is not uniform. Sometimes we place great and arguably unjustified faith in the power of juries to see the truth. Once a witness has testified before a jury, for example, we grant the jury unreviewable power to say whether the witness was truthful. At other times our faith in jury fact-finding is perhaps unreasonably low. We worry that autopsy photos may impassion juries to convict regardless of guilt. We fear that juries may misuse evidence of a person's past behavior, so we often forbid such evidence in court. We typically deem juries unable to judge the credibility of persons who are not in court. And when it comes to expert witnesses, we are so afraid juries will take charlatans at their word that we establish judges as gatekeepers to guard against unsound evidence.

Much of our task ahead is to plot the crooked line that separates evidence we think the jury can evaluate reasonably (and therefore is admissible) from evidence we think will distract the jury from its search for truth (and therefore is not admissible). Examine this line critically. After all, the notion that we can get more truth from less evidence must have strict limits. If *you* would find a particular piece of evidence useful, why keep it from the jury?

The inconstancy of our faith in juries' power to judge the truth is one source of irregularity in our evidence rules, but there are others. Various public policy goals have shaped the rules in ways that are not wholly predictable. Moreover, the rules of evidence are largely the product of centuries of common-law contrivance and compromise. At times we will trace the common-law sources of the rules, if only to highlight the difficulty of finding consistent attitudes and uniform principles.

Hard as it may be to identify themes that unify the rules of evidence, it is not hard to organize the rules loosely according to function. The Contents Summary on pages xi through xiii suggests that the great bulk of the federal evidence scheme addresses either the relevance or the reliability of the information going before the jury. Rules of relevance seek to focus the parties and the jury on the issues at hand. They guard against digression and distraction. Rules of reliability seek to ensure that the evidence the jury hears is as good as it purports to be—or at least that its defects are apparent to the jury. These broad bodies of rules occupy Units I and II and most of the book. Unit III addresses privileges, which exclude evidence that is both relevant and reliable to serve other societal interests. These three categories are rough and overlapping, but they should help give shape to the book.

You should note that the book addresses only those evidence rules that limit the kind of information that reaches the jury and the uses the jury may make of that information. I will not deal with the mechanics of getting that information to the jury—the proper form of a question, the way to offer an exhibit. These topics seem more suited to a course in trial practice. Nor will I address questions of the sufficiency of evidence, the effect of presumptions, or the allocation of burdens of proof. These topics fall on the cusp of evidence, procedure, and substantive lawmaking. They are rich in theory and would reward your curiosity, but I think they would distract us from the study of the flow of information to the jury.

The Federal Rules of Evidence

This book centers around the Federal Rules of Evidence, which govern in the great majority of federal judicial proceedings. At last count forty-four states and Puerto Rico have adopted or mimicked the Federal Rules in whole or greater part, sometimes adding state rules that have no federal counterpart.* Even the six states that have adopted distinct evidence codes or have not codified their evidence law—California, Kansas, Massachusetts, Missouri, New York, and Virginia—adhere to similar evidence principles. Hence I often use state cases to illustrate the operation of the Federal Rules. Underlying almost all American evidence law is the common-law tradition, and the Federal Rules borrow heavily from that tradition.

Enacted by Congress in 1975, the rules are fundamentally statutes and may be interpreted in light of their history. In a formal sense that history began in 1965, when Chief Justice Earl Warren appointed an advisory committee of judges, practitioners, and academics, who drafted the original slate of proposed rules. Guided principally by its reporter, Professor Edward W. Cleary, the advisory committee drew not only from the common law but also from earlier codification efforts, including the Model Code of Evidence of 1942 and the Uniform Rules of Evidence of 1953. The committee delivered its proposed rules to the Supreme Court in November 1972. The Court approved the rules essentially without change and sent them on to Congress.

Occasionally you will see suggestions that the Supreme Court "promulgated" the rules. But as Justice Douglas wrote in dissent when the Court transmitted the rules to Congress, the Court's role was "merely perfunctory":

> [T]his Court does not write the Rules, nor supervise their writing, nor appraise them on their merits, weighing the pros and cons. The Court concededly is a mere conduit. Those who write the Rules are members of a Committee....

Rules of Evidence for United States Courts and Magistrates, 56 F.R.D. 183, 185 (1972) (Douglas, J., dissenting). Years later the whole Court acknowledged it had served "in truth merely [as] a conduit." *United States v. Abel*, 469 U.S. 45, 49 (1984).

Congress proved in contrast to be a tough and discriminating audience. The House and Senate Judiciary Committees aggressively scrutinized the proposed rules and amended many of them. The full Congress amended a few more. Most strikingly, Congress scrapped thirteen proposed privilege rules and replaced them with a single rule, FRE 501,

* I thank Professors Michael Ariens, Mark Brodin, and Colin Miller and research assistants Anthony Sun and Mark Menzies for their help in compiling, checking, and supplementing this list. The 44 adopting states include Connecticut, which has rules largely similar to the Federal Rules. The list does not include Massachusetts. Late in 2008 the Supreme Judicial Court "recommend[ed] the use" of a newly prepared *Massachusetts Guide to Evidence*, updated each year since. Though the *Guide* adopts the numeration and much of the language of the Federal Rules, it aims only to compile existing Massachusetts evidence law and has no authoritative force.

which abdicated the entire matter of privileges to the courts. Over the years Congress has amended the Federal Rules several times and has added new rules. The most significant additions have been Rule 412, passed in 1978, which created a federal rape shield provision, and Rules 413 through 415, enacted in 1994, which generally admit evidence of a criminal or civil defendant's propensity to commit certain sexual offenses.

The Evidence Rules Restyling Project

Several years ago the advisory committee undertook a full-scale restyling of the whole slate of federal evidence rules. The restyling project, led mainly by Professor Joseph Kimble, was part of a larger venture to apply uniform conventions of style and usage across all of the federal rules. Earlier restyling efforts had targeted the rules of appellate, criminal, and civil procedure. The restyled evidence rules were released for public comment in 2009 and won approval from the Supreme Court early in 2011. They became law on congressional inaction on December 1, 2011.

True to its name, the restyling project aimed to improve style, not alter substance. After each of the refashioned rules the advisory committee appended a standard note, varying only slightly from rule to rule:

> **Committee Note**
>
> The language of Rule [___] has been amended as part of the restyling of the Evidence Rules to make them more easily understood and to make style and terminology consistent throughout the rules. These changes are intended to be stylistic only. There is no intent to alter any result in any ruling on evidence admissibility.

In the rulebook I have omitted this standard note to avoid repetition, but you may wish to test its accuracy. The old and restyled rules appear side by side in the rulebook beginning at page 380. Consider whether the committee accurately captured the meaning of the old rules, printed on the left, in the restyled text, printed on the right in shaded boxes.

As this casebook goes to press, little caselaw has grown up around the restyled rules. Many of the cases you read therefore will incorporate the now-obsolete language of the unrestyled rules. Where the old language differs substantially from the new, I've added a footnote to clarify the change.

In the rulebook at pages 375 to 378 you will find more details on the restyling project and on Professor Kimble's conventions of good English prose and sound rule writing.

Interpreting the Federal Rules

In his introduction to the Federal Rules, Professor Cleary wrote that although "[t]he language of [a] rule itself should be taken as the prime source of meaning," the rule should be read in the light of its "legislative history, which on occasion may even override an apparently plain and unmistakable meaning of the words of the rule." So it is important to read the legislative history that follows the text of each rule in your rulebooks. You'll see that if Congress amended a rule as submitted by the Supreme Court, the rule's legislative history generally includes a report from the House or Senate Judiciary Committee or excerpts from floor debate. Occasionally a conference committee report reflects a compromise struck between competing House and Senate versions of a rule. If Congress has amended a rule since 1975, the legislative history of the amendment follows the original rule's history in the rulebook.

The significance of the Advisory Committee's Note that accompanies each rule is a matter of some dispute. Professor Cleary recommended that whenever Congress adopted a rule as written by the advisory committee and submitted by the Court, the committee's note "should be taken as the equivalent of a congressional committee report as representing the thinking of Congress." In 1995 Justice Scalia rejected Cleary's suggestion and declared that the Advisory Committee's Notes "bear no special authoritativeness as the work of the draftsmen." *Tome v. United States*, 513 U.S. 150, 167 (1995) (Scalia, J., concurring). You will see, though, that the great majority of justices, judges, and courts follow Cleary's advice and turn often to the committee's notes for guidance.

When a rule's language and history both fail to make its meaning clear, Cleary said to look to the common law for guidance. "No common law of evidence in principle remains under the rules," he wrote. Still, "the common law remains as a source of guidance in identifying problems and suggesting solutions, within the confines of the rules." *See also* Edward W. Cleary, *Preliminary Notes on Reading the Rules of Evidence*, 57 NEB. L. REV. 908 (1978) (offering more detailed principles of construction for interpreting the rules). As you read *Tanner v. United States*, 483 U.S. 107 (1987) (page 8), note how the majority and dissent both employ (or manipulate?) the legislative history of Rule 606(b) to support their positions.

Two Notes on Using This Book

Now and then you will see a boldfaced notice of the sort that appears on page 8: "*Focus on* FRE 606(b)." I hope you will turn at this point to the rulebook and read the cited rule along with any related legislative history. Page references to the rulebook appear with the abbreviation "RB."

The casebook presents many problems challenging you to apply rules or caselaw. Sometimes I have based these problems on published cases and included case cites for your reference. Though you may find it useful to refer to the cited cases, you should not assume that they reach the "right" result or even that they address the same issue raised in the problem. If a problem has no case cite, its facts are fictional.

TANNER V. UNITED STATES: *Historical Prelude*

Before we proceed to the heart of the book—the rules of relevance, reliability, and privilege—let us take a short digression. As I said at the outset, evidence rules aim to limit the information juries hear. The tangled rules that make up this course betray deep and long-held suspicions about the talents and limits of jurors. Yet this systemic mistrust all but vanishes at the moment the jury renders its verdict. At that moment the system proclaims a blind faith in the judgment of the jury. After all, the jury deliberates in secret and renders its verdict inarticulately, in one or two words—"guilty" or "not guilty." *Tanner* stands for the system's unwillingness to look past the jury's verdict to expose whatever flaws in reasoning or understanding might lie behind the curtain of the deliberation room.

Our reluctance to examine what juries do with the evidence they hear perhaps highlights the importance of monitoring what they hear in the first place. If we are to exercise virtually no review of the jurors' skill and fairness in evaluating evidence, perhaps we need to be especially vigilant to ensure the evidence they hear is useful and fair. So instead of beginning with the many ways in which we mistrust juries, it may be revealing to start with that final moment of blind trust. That blind trust is the theme of *Tanner* and of Federal Rule 606(b). A glance backward at the jury's early history may help set our stage.

The Criminal Jury Trial: A Brief History of the Early Days

Although the jury's origins lie hidden in Dark Ages rituals, we can trace the origins of one sort of jury—the criminal trial jury, which is at issue in *Tanner*—with something like pinpoint accuracy: The first true criminal jury trial seems to have taken place at Westminster in 1220.[1]

The cause of the sudden birth of trial by jury was the sudden death of trial by ordeal. Before 1215 criminal trials had proceeded by ordeal or by battle. In the ordeal of cold water the accused was tossed into a pool with a rope tied around his hips. If he sank, he was hauled out an innocent person, for the purity of the water had accepted him. But if the water repelled him and he floated, he was condemned. In the ordeal of

1. *See* Roger D. Groot, *The Early–Thirteenth–Century Criminal Jury*, *in* TWELVE GOOD MEN AND TRUE: THE CRIMINAL TRIAL JURY IN ENGLAND, 1200–1800, at 3, 17–18 (J.S. Cockburn & Thomas A. Green eds., 1988). Much of the material in this prelude originally appeared in George Fisher, *The Jury's Rise as Lie Detector*, 107 YALE L.J. 575, 585–87, 600–01 (1997).

hot iron the accused walked barehanded with a hot iron bar. Three days later, when her bandages were removed, her healing hands revealed her fate: If the wounds were healing cleanly, she was absolved; if corruptly, condemned.[2] In all events the judgment was God's.

But in 1215 the Church forbade priests to officiate at ordeals and suddenly stripped these rituals of their divine imprimatur. When the Church decertified ordeals, it wrecked them, for the system no longer could claim that God—and not some mere human agency—had decreed the accused's guilt and authorized punishment. English and other European justice systems soon abandoned the ordeal in criminal cases. The countries of Continental Europe embraced forms of proof that exalted the power of sworn eyewitness testimony and the accused's confession, often coerced through torture. The English turned to trial by jury.

Lacking any claim to divine legitimacy, the jury eventually found a remarkable source of systemic legitimacy in the secrecy of its deliberation room. The jury's private and usually unexplained decisionmaking generally has protected it from embarrassing public failures. At least within the system's formal bounds the jury's verdict has been almost immune from contradiction. There never has been a mechanism by which the defendant or anyone outside the system could command the jury to reveal its decisionmaking processes. The jury's secrecy is arguably an aid to legitimacy, for the privacy of the jury box shrouds the shortcomings of the jury's methods.

In modern times the law has gone to great lengths to protect the privacy of the deliberation process. In 1954 several law professors associated with the Chicago Jury Project won permission from the judges of the Tenth Circuit to make secret recordings of jury deliberations in the district court in Wichita. The next year a Senate Subcommittee on Internal Security summoned Chicago Dean (and future Attorney General) Edward Levi and Professor Harry Kalven to Washington. Lumping the "bugging" of jury rooms with the Communist bugaboos of the day, senators cast the law professors as a threat to national security. Of Levi the subcommittee's chairman asked, "Now, do you not realize that to snoop on a jury, and to record what they say, does violence to every reason for which we have secret deliberations of a jury?" Of Kalven the committee counsel asked, "Did you write a letter to President Truman, asking clemency for the atomic spies, Rosenbergs?" *See* JAY KATZ, EXPERIMENTATION WITH HUMAN BEINGS 67, 84–91 (1972). A year later Congress made it a crime to record, listen to, or observe any federal jury deliberation. *See* Act of Aug. 2, 1956, ch. 879, § 1, 70 Stat. 935 (codified as amended at 18 U.S.C. § 1508 (2012)).

Yet efforts to shield jury deliberations from scrutiny are not a dim memory of a McCarthyite past. As the Supreme Court's ruling in *Tanner*

2. *See* THOMAS ANDREW GREEN, VERDICT ACCORDING TO CONSCIENCE: PERSPECTIVES ON THE ENGLISH CRIMINAL TRIAL JURY, 1200–1800, at 8 n.18 (1985).

shows, secret deliberations are an established feature of the common-law tradition and remain a central element of our trial system.

Focus on FRE 606(b)

TANNER v. UNITED STATES

483 U.S. 107 (1987).

■ O'CONNOR, J., delivered the opinion for a unanimous Court with respect to Parts III and IV and the opinion of the Court with respect to Parts I and II, in which REHNQUIST, C. J., and WHITE, POWELL, and SCALIA, JJ., joined. MARSHALL, J., filed an opinion concurring in part and dissenting in part, in which BRENNAN, BLACKMUN, and STEVENS, JJ., joined.

■ JUSTICE O'CONNOR delivered the opinion of the Court. Petitioners William Conover and Anthony Tanner were convicted of conspiring to defraud the United States and of committing mail fraud. . . . Petitioners argue that the District Court erred in refusing to admit juror testimony at a post-verdict hearing on juror intoxication during the trial. . . .

I

. . . The day before petitioners were scheduled to be sentenced, Tanner filed a motion . . . seeking continuance of the sentencing date, permission to interview jurors, an evidentiary hearing, and a new trial. According to an affidavit accompanying the motion, Tanner's attorney had received an unsolicited telephone call from one of the trial jurors, Vera Asbul. Juror Asbul informed Tanner's attorney that several of the jurors consumed alcohol during the lunch breaks at various times throughout the trial, causing them to sleep through the afternoons. The District Court continued the sentencing date, ordered the parties to file memoranda, and heard argument on the motion to interview jurors. The District Court concluded that juror testimony on intoxication was inadmissible under Federal Rule of Evidence 606(b) to impeach the jury's verdict. The District Court invited petitioners to call any nonjuror witnesses, such as courtroom personnel, in support of the motion for new trial. Tanner's counsel took the stand and testified that he had observed one of the jurors "in a sort of giggly mood" at one point during the trial but did not bring this to anyone's attention at the time.

Earlier in the hearing the judge referred to a conversation between defense counsel and the judge during the trial on the possibility that jurors were sometimes falling asleep . . . :

"MR. MILBRATH [defense counsel]: But, in any event, I've noticed over a period of several days that a couple of jurors in particular have been taking long naps during the trial.

"THE COURT: Is that right. Maybe I didn't notice because I was—

"MR. MILBRATH: I imagine the Prosecutors have noticed that a time or two.

"THE COURT: What's your solution?

"MR. MILBRATH: Well, I just think a respectful comment from the Court that if any of them are getting drowsy, they just ask for a break or something might be helpful.

"THE COURT: Well, here's what I have done in the past—and, you have to do it very diplomatically, of course: I once said, I remember, 'I think we'll just let everybody stand up and stretch, it's getting a little sleepy in here,' I said, but that doesn't sound good in the record.

"I'm going to—not going to take on that responsibility. If any of you think you see that happening, ask for a bench conference and come up and tell me about it and I'll figure out what to do about it, and I won't mention who suggested it.

"MR. MILBRATH: All right.

"THE COURT: But, I'm not going to sit here and watch. . . . [C]ome up and let me know and I'll figure how—either have a recess or—which is more than likely what I would do."

As the judge observed during the hearing, despite the above admonitions counsel did not bring the matter to the court again.

The judge also observed that in the past courtroom employees had alerted him to problems with the jury. "Nothing was brought to my attention in this case about anyone appearing to be intoxicated," the judge stated, adding, "I saw nothing that suggested they were."

Following the hearing the District Court filed an order stating that "on the basis of the admissible evidence offered I specifically find that the motions for leave to interview jurors or for an evidentiary hearing at which jurors would be witnesses is not required or appropriate." The District Court also denied the motion for new trial.

While the appeal of this case was pending before the Eleventh Circuit, petitioners filed another new trial motion based on additional evidence of jury misconduct. In another affidavit, Tanner's attorney stated that he received an unsolicited visit at his residence from a second juror, Daniel Hardy. Despite the fact that the District Court had denied petitioners' motion for leave to interview jurors, two days after Hardy's visit Tanner's attorney arranged for Hardy to be interviewed by two private investigators. The interview was transcribed, sworn to by the juror, and attached to the new trial motion. In the interview Hardy stated that he "felt like ... the jury was on one big party." Hardy indicated that seven of the jurors drank alcohol during the noon recess. Four jurors, including Hardy, consumed between them "a pitcher to three pitchers" of beer during various recesses. Of the three other jurors who were alleged to have consumed alcohol, Hardy stated that on several occasions he observed two jurors having one or two mixed drinks during the lunch recess, and one other juror, who was also the foreperson, having a liter of wine on each of three occasions. Juror Hardy also stated that he and three other jurors smoked marijuana quite regularly during the trial. Moreover, Hardy stated that during the trial he observed one juror ingest cocaine five times and another juror ingest cocaine two or three times. One juror sold a quarter pound of marijuana to another juror during the trial, and took marijuana, cocaine, and drug paraphernalia into the courthouse. Hardy noted that some of the jurors were falling asleep during the trial, and that one of the jurors described himself to Hardy as "flying." Hardy stated that before he visited Tanner's attorney at his residence, no one had contacted him concerning the jury's conduct, and Hardy had not been offered anything in return for his statement. Hardy said that he came forward "to clear my conscience" and "because I felt ... that the people on the jury didn't have no business being on the jury. I felt ... that Mr. Tanner should have a better opportunity to get somebody that would review the facts right."

The District Court ... denied petitioners' motion for a new trial.

The Court of Appeals for the Eleventh Circuit affirmed. 772 F.2d 765 (1985). We granted certiorari to consider whether the District Court was required to hold an evidentiary hearing, including juror testimony, on juror alcohol and drug use during the trial....

II

Petitioners ... assert that, contrary to the holdings of the District Court and the Court of Appeals, juror testimony on ingestion of drugs or alcohol during the trial is not barred by Federal Rule of Evidence 606(b). Moreover, petitioners argue that whether or not authorized by Rule 606(b), an evidentiary hearing including juror testimony on drug and alcohol use is compelled by their Sixth Amendment right to trial by a competent jury.

By the beginning of this century, if not earlier, the near-universal and firmly established common-law rule in the United States flatly prohibited the admission of juror testimony to impeach a jury verdict.

Exceptions to the common-law rule were recognized only in situations in which an "extraneous influence," Mattox v. United States, 146 U.S. 140, 149 (1892), was alleged to have affected the jury. In *Mattox*, this Court held admissible the testimony of jurors describing how they heard and read prejudicial information not admitted into evidence. The Court allowed juror testimony on influence by outsiders in Parker v. Gladden, 385 U.S. 363, 365 (1966) (bailiff's comments on defendant), and Remmer v. United States, 347 U.S. 227, 228–30 (1954) (bribe offered to juror). *See also* Smith v. Phillips, 455 U.S. 209 (1982) (juror in criminal trial had submitted an application for employment at the District Attorney's office)....

Lower courts used this external/internal distinction to identify those instances in which juror testimony impeaching a verdict would be admissible. The distinction was not based on whether the juror was literally inside or outside the jury room when the alleged irregularity took place; rather, the distinction was based on the nature of the allegation. Clearly a rigid distinction based only on whether the event took place inside or outside the jury room would have been quite unhelpful. For example, under a distinction based on location a juror could not testify concerning a newspaper read inside the jury room. Instead, of course, this has been considered an external influence about which juror testimony is admissible. Similarly, under a rigid locational distinction jurors could be regularly required to testify after the verdict as to whether they heard and comprehended the judge's instructions, since the charge to the jury takes place outside the jury room. Courts wisely have treated allegations of a juror's inability to hear or comprehend at trial as an internal matter.

Most significant for the present case, however, is the fact that lower federal courts treated allegations of the physical or mental incompetence of a juror as "internal" rather than "external" matters. In United States v. Dioguardi, 492 F.2d 70 (2d Cir. 1974), the defendant Dioguardi received a letter from one of the jurors soon after the trial in which the juror explained that she had "eyes and ears that ... see things before [they] happen," but that her eyes "are only partly open" because "a curse was put upon them some years ago." Armed with this letter and the opinions of seven psychiatrists that the letter suggested that the juror was suffering from a psychological disorder, Dioguardi sought a new trial or in the alternative an evidentiary hearing on the juror's competence. The District Court denied the motion and the Court of Appeals affirmed. The Court of Appeals noted "the strong policy against any post-verdict inquiry into a juror's state of mind," and observed:

> "The quickness with which jury findings will be set aside when there is proof of tampering or *external* influence, ... parallel the reluctance of courts to inquire into jury deliberations when a verdict is valid on its face.... Such exceptions support rather than undermine the rationale of the rule that possible *internal* abnormalities in a jury will

> not be inquired into except 'in the gravest and most important cases.' "

... Substantial policy considerations support the common-law rule against the admission of jury testimony to impeach a verdict. As early as 1915 this Court explained the necessity of shielding jury deliberations from public scrutiny:

> "Let it once be established that verdicts solemnly made and publicly returned into court can be attacked and set aside on the testimony of those who took part in their publication and all verdicts could be, and many would be, followed by an inquiry in the hope of discovering something which might invalidate the finding. Jurors would be harassed and beset by the defeated party in an effort to secure from them evidence of facts which might establish misconduct sufficient to set aside a verdict. If evidence thus secured could be thus used, the result would be to make what was intended to be a private deliberation, the constant subject of public investigation—to the destruction of all frankness and freedom of discussion and conference." McDonald v. Pless, 238 U.S. at 267–68.

... There is little doubt that postverdict investigation into juror misconduct would in some instances lead to the invalidation of verdicts reached after irresponsible or improper juror behavior. It is not at all clear, however, that the jury system could survive such efforts to perfect it. Allegations of juror misconduct, incompetency, or inattentiveness, raised for the first time days, weeks, or months after the verdict, seriously disrupt the finality of the process. *See, e.g.*, Government of the Virgin Islands v. Nicholas, 759 F.2d 1073, 1081 (3d Cir. 1985) (one year and eight months after verdict rendered, juror alleged that hearing difficulties affected his understanding of the evidence). Moreover, full and frank discussion in the jury room, jurors' willingness to return an unpopular verdict, and the community's trust in a system that relies on the decisions of laypeople would all be undermined by a barrage of postverdict scrutiny of juror conduct. . . .

Petitioners . . . argue that substance abuse constitutes an improper "outside influence" about which jurors may testify under Rule 606(b). In our view the language of the Rule cannot easily be stretched to cover this circumstance. However severe their effect and improper their use, drugs or alcohol voluntarily ingested by a juror seems no more an "outside influence" than a virus, poorly prepared food, or a lack of sleep.

In any case, whatever ambiguity might linger in the language of Rule 606(b) as applied to juror intoxication is resolved by the legislative history of the Rule. . . . The House Judiciary Committee described the effect of the version of Rule 606(b) transmitted by the Court as follows:

> "As proposed by the Court, Rule 606(b) limited testimony by a juror in the course of an inquiry into the validity of a verdict or indict-

ment. He could testify as to the influence of extraneous prejudicial information brought to the jury's attention (e.g., a radio newscast or a newspaper account) or an outside influence which improperly had been brought to bear upon a juror (e.g., a threat to the safety of a member of his family), but he could not testify as to other irregularities which occurred in the jury room. Under this formulation a quotient verdict* could not be attacked through the testimony of juror, *nor could a juror testify to the drunken condition of a fellow juror which so disabled him that he could not participate in the jury's deliberations.*" (Emphasis supplied.)

The House Judiciary Committee, persuaded that the better practice was to allow juror testimony on any "objective juror misconduct," amended the Rule** ... and the House passed this amended version.

The Senate ... decided to reject the broader House version and adopt the narrower version approved by the Court. The Senate Report explained:

"[The House version's] extension of the ability to impeach a verdict is felt to be unwarranted and ill-advised.

"The rule passed by the House ... would have the effect of opening verdicts up to challenge on the basis of what happened during the jury's internal deliberations, for example, where a juror alleged that the jury refused to follow the trial judge's instructions or that some of the jurors did not take part in deliberations....

"Public policy requires a finality to litigation. And common fairness requires that absolute privacy be preserved for jurors to engage in the full and free debate necessary to the attainment of just verdicts. Jurors will not be able to function effectively if their deliberations are to be scrutinized in post-trial litigation. In the interest of protecting the jury system and the citizens who make it work, rule 606 should not permit any inquiry into the internal deliberations of the jurors."

The Conference Committee Report reaffirms Congress' understanding of the differences between the House and Senate versions of Rule

* [*Black's Law Dictionary* explains that in reaching a *quotient verdict*, "[e]ach juror reaches the sum he wishes to award by the verdict; these amounts are all added together, and the total is divided by twelve." The jury then awards the resulting average. BLACK'S LAW DICTIONARY 1422 (4th ed. 1968).—GF]

** The House version ... read as follows:

"Upon an inquiry into the validity of a verdict or indictment, a juror may not testify concerning the effect of anything upon his or any other juror's mind or emotions as influencing him to assent to or dissent from the verdict or indictment or concerning his mental processes in connection therewith. Nor may his affidavit or evidence of any statement by him indicating an effect of this kind be received for these purposes." H. R. 5463, 93d Cong., 2d Sess. (1974).

606(b): "The House bill allows a juror to testify about objective matters occurring during the jury's deliberation, such as the misconduct of another juror or the reaching of a quotient verdict. The Senate bill does not permit juror testimony about any matter or statement occurring during the course of the jury's deliberations." The Conference Committee adopted, and Congress enacted, the Senate version of Rule 606(b).

Thus, the legislative history demonstrates with uncommon clarity that Congress specifically understood, considered, and rejected a version of Rule 606(b) that would have allowed jurors to testify on juror conduct during deliberations, including juror intoxication. This legislative history provides strong support for the most reasonable reading of the language of Rule 606(b)—that juror intoxication is not an "outside influence" about which jurors may testify to impeach their verdict. . . .

Petitioners also argue that the refusal to hold an additional evidentiary hearing at which jurors would testify as to their conduct "violates the sixth amendment's guarantee to a fair trial before an impartial and *competent* jury."

This Court has recognized that a defendant has a right to "a tribunal both impartial and mentally competent to afford a hearing." Jordan v. Massachusetts, 225 U.S. 167, 176 (1912). . . .

Petitioners' Sixth Amendment interests in an unimpaired jury . . . are protected by several aspects of the trial process. The suitability of an individual for the responsibility of jury service, of course, is examined during *voir dire*. Moreover, during the trial the jury is observable by the court, by counsel, and by court personnel. *See* United States v. Provenzano, 620 F.2d 985, 996–97 (3d Cir. 1980) (marshal discovered sequestered juror smoking marijuana during early morning hours). Moreover, jurors are observable by each other, and may report inappropriate juror behavior to the court *before* they render a verdict. *See* Lee v. United States, 454 A.2d 770 (D.C. App. 1982), *cert. denied sub nom.* McIlwain v. United States, 464 U.S. 972 (1983) (on second day of deliberations, jurors sent judge a note suggesting that foreperson was incapacitated). Finally, after the trial a party may seek to impeach the verdict by nonjuror evidence of misconduct. *See* United States v. Taliaferro, 558 F.2d 724, 725–26 (4th Cir. 1977) (court considered records of club where jurors dined, and testimony of marshal who accompanied jurors, to determine whether jurors were intoxicated during deliberations). Indeed, in this case the District Court held an evidentiary hearing giving petitioners ample opportunity to produce nonjuror evidence supporting their allegations.

In light of these other sources of protection of petitioners' right to a competent jury, we conclude that the District Court did not err in deciding, based on the inadmissibility of juror testimony and the clear insufficiency of the nonjuror evidence offered by petitioners, that an additional postverdict evidentiary hearing was unnecessary. . . .

■ JUSTICE MARSHALL, with whom JUSTICE BRENNAN, JUSTICE BLACKMUN, and JUSTICE STEVENS join, concurring in part and dissenting in part. . . .

II

. . . I readily acknowledge the important policy considerations supporting the common-law rule against admission of jury testimony to impeach a verdict, now embodied in Federal Rule of Evidence 606(b): freedom of deliberation, finality of verdicts, and protection of jurors against harassment by dissatisfied litigants. It has been simultaneously recognized, however, that "simply putting verdicts beyond effective reach can only promote irregularity and injustice." If the above-referenced policy considerations seriously threaten the constitutional right to trial by a fair and impartial jury, they must give way.

In this case, however, we are not faced with a conflict between the policy considerations underlying Rule 606(b) and petitioners' Sixth Amendment rights. Rule 606(b) is not applicable to juror testimony on matters *unrelated* to the jury's deliberations. By its terms, [unrestyled] Rule 606(b) renders jurors incompetent to testify only as to three subjects: (i) any "matter or statement" occurring during deliberations; (ii) the "effect" of anything upon the "mind or emotions" of any juror as it relates to his or her "assent to or dissent from the verdict"; and (iii) the "mental processes" of the juror in connection with his "assent to or dissent from the verdict." . . .

The Court's analysis of legislative history confirms the inapplicability of Rule 606(b) to the type of misconduct alleged in this case. As the Court emphasizes, the debate over two proposed versions of the Rule—the more restrictive Senate version ultimately adopted and the permissive House version—focused on the extent to which jurors would be permitted to testify as to what transpired *during the course of the deliberations themselves.* Similarly, the Conference Committee Report, quoted by the Court, compares the two versions solely in terms of the admissibility of testimony as to matters occurring during, or relating to, the jury's deliberations: "The House bill allows a juror to testify about objective matters occurring during the jury's deliberation, such as the misconduct of another juror or the reaching of a quotient verdict. The Senate bill does not permit juror testimony about any matter or statement occurring *during the course of the jury's deliberations.*" (Emphasis added.) The obvious conclusion . . . is that *both* versions of Rule 606(b) would have permitted jurors to testify as to matters not involving deliberations. The House Report's passing reference to juror intoxication during deliberations is not to the contrary. Reflecting Congress' consistent focus on the deliberative process, it suggests only that the authors of the House Report believed that the Senate version of Rule 606(b) did not allow testimony as to juror intoxication during deliberations.

In this case, no invasion of the jury deliberations is contemplated. Permitting a limited postverdict inquiry into juror consumption of alcohol and drugs *during trial* would not "make what was intended to be a private deliberation, the constant subject of public investigation—to the destruction of all frankness and freedom of discussion and conference." McDonald v. Pless, 238 U.S. at 267–68. . . .

Even if I agreed with the Court's expansive construction of Rule 606(b), I would nonetheless find the testimony of juror intoxication admissible under the Rule's "outside influence" exception. As a commonsense matter, drugs and alcohol *are* outside influences on jury members. . . . The Court suggests that, if these are outside influences, "a virus, poorly prepared food, or a lack of sleep" would also qualify. Distinguishing between a virus, for example, and a narcotic drug is a matter of line-drawing. Courts are asked to make these sorts of distinctions in numerous contexts; I have no doubt they would be capable of differentiating between the intoxicants involved in this case and minor indispositions not affecting juror competency. . . .

III

The Court acknowledges that "postverdict investigation into juror misconduct would in some instances lead to the invalidation of verdicts reached after irresponsible or improper juror behavior," but maintains that "[i]t is not at all clear . . . that the jury system could survive such efforts to perfect it." Petitioners are not asking for a perfect jury. They are seeking to determine whether the jury that heard their case behaved in a manner consonant with the minimum requirements of the Sixth Amendment. If we deny them this opportunity, the jury system may survive, but the constitutional guarantee on which it is based will become meaningless. . . .

Problem I.1

"They cause all the trouble."

Consider the facts of *United States v. Villar*, 586 F.3d 76 (1st Cir. 2009), *cert. denied*, 131 S. Ct. 2167 (2011)*:

> After a jury trial, Defendant-appellant Richard Villar, a Hispanic man, was convicted of bank robbery. Hours following his conviction, defense counsel received an e-mail message from [Juror No. 66] . . . :
>
> > I felt compelled to send this to you. I don't know if I should even be doing this but I don't care. I know it's

* My thanks to Professors Lisa Griffin and Richard Underwood and Judge Timothy Rice, all of whom pointed me to *Villar*.

> late but I want you to know that there were at least 3 people on that jury who actually listened to the testimony with an open mind. We tried to make the rest pay attention. We made them go through every piece of evidence and every witness. . . . We finally decided to not prolong that young man's hope any longer. We could have stayed there for another week. Their minds were made up from the first day. *Here's one example, A man said "I guess we're profiling, but they cause all the trouble."* Well I won't keep you longer. Again I am sorry we couldn't do more. You know if I thought he would have gotten a different kind of jury the next time I think [I] would have kept them there. . . .
>
> [D]efense counsel moved to set aside the jury's verdict, arguing that there was the possibility of bias and prejudice on the part of at least one juror based upon Villar's Hispanic ethnicity.

In light of Rule 606(b) and *Tanner*, should the court permit Juror No. 66 to testify that another juror said during deliberations, "I guess we're profiling, but they cause all the trouble"?

TANNER V. UNITED STATES: *Afterthoughts*

The jury resolves our most heated social conflicts privately and without explanation. In 1920 Professor Edson Sunderland explained how hidden jury deliberations protect the reputation of the justice system by concealing any possible source of error. The system's need for legitimacy, Sunderland wrote, demands that "[t]he record . . . be absolutely flawless, but such a result is possible only by concealing, not by excluding mistakes." Edson R. Sunderland, *Verdicts, General and Special*, 29 YALE L.J. 253, 262 (1920). The jury's hidden decisionmaking process and its one-or two-word verdicts leave all mistakes and causes for criticism locked in the black box of the jury room. The jury's inscrutability, in Sunderland's marvelous imagery,

> covers up all the shortcomings which frail human nature is unable to eliminate from the trial of a case. . . . [C]oncrete details are swallowed up, and the eye of the law, searching anxiously for the realization of logical perfection, is satisfied. . . . It serves as the great procedural opiate, which draws the curtain upon human errors and soothes us in the assurance that we have attained the unattainable.

Id. But what does this have to do with evidence law?

Our long tradition of secret jury deliberations, as embodied today in Rule 606(b), means our justice system engages in very little quality control at the back end. Though the system provides for review of procedural errors and judicial errors of law, errors in the way juries interpret evidence are virtually undetectable, much less correctable. With so little quality control at the back end of our trial process, it may be wise to have quality control at the front end. That is, since we don't scrutinize the deliberative process, we have to scrutinize and regulate the quality of the evidence fed into that process. *See* John H. Langbein, *The Criminal Trial Before the Jury*, 45 U. CHI. L. REV. 263, 289 (1978).

The Supreme Court has never addressed whether our resolution to shield deliberations from view holds firm even when racial or ethnic bias infects the jury room. Over the past decades many state and lower federal courts have asked whether Rule 606(b) and its various state counterparts, all rooted in centuries of common-law precedents, can constitutionally bar juror testimony about racist comments uttered during deliberations. Or must the usual rule yield in the face of such evidence to the defendant's Sixth Amendment right to an impartial jury? The question has split courts roughly into three groups:

- A few courts have dodged the constitutional quandary by deeming a juror's racism to be an "outside influence . . . improperly brought to bear" on the juror. Rule 606(b) therefore raises no bar against testimony by fellow jurors about that juror's racist comments during deliberations. *See, e.g., Tobias v. Smith*, 468 F. Supp. 1287, 1290 (W.D.N.Y. 1979); *State v. Bowles*, 530 N.W.2d 521, 536 (Minn. 1995).

- A second, larger group of courts have ruled that racism is no more an external influence than the drugs and alcohol at issue in *Tanner*, yet strict application of Rule 606(b) in the face of claims of racial bias would violate a defendant's rights to an impartial jury and to due process. Courts taking this view have cast doubt on the four protections hailed by Justice O'Connor in *Tanner*. Though these protections may help expose juror intoxication, they may work less well against racism. Pretrial voir dire, the First Circuit reasoned, "has shortcomings because some jurors may be reluctant to admit racial bias." Visual observation, whether by court or counsel, is "unlikely to identify jurors harboring racial or ethnic bias." And "non-jurors are more likely to report . . . alcohol or drug use," which they can see, "than racial statements uttered during deliberations," which they cannot hear. Only pre-verdict disclosures by fellow jurors of a colleague's racist comments can guard against such bias—and such disclosures, so often lacking, afford too thin a shield against so great a threat to fairness. *United States v. Villar*, 586 F.3d 76, 87 (1st Cir. 2009); *accord Mason v. Mitchell*, 320 F.3d 604, 636 (6th Cir. 2003); *Commonwealth v. Laguer*, 571 N.E.2d 371, 376 (Mass. 1991).

- A third contingent of courts have held unyieldingly to Rule 606(b)'s bar. These courts have forbidden testimony by fellow jurors about a juror's racial or ethnic comments and have rejected arguments that the Constitution demands that Rule 606(b) bend to permit such testimony. Leading this contingent, the Tenth Circuit acknowledged a systemic interest in purging racial and ethnic bias from the jury room. But "[w]here the attempt to cure defects in the jury process . . . entails the sacrifice of structural features in the justice system that have important systemic benefits, it is not necessarily in the interest of overall justice" to work such a cure. The court expressed faith that the four protections listed in *Tanner* would have some force in exposing juror racism. "These protections might not be sufficient to eliminate every partial juror," the court allowed, "just as in *Tanner* they proved insufficient to catch every intoxicated juror, but jury perfection is an untenable goal." *United States v. Benally*, 546 F.3d 1230, 1234–40 (10th Cir. 2008), *cert. denied*, 130 S. Ct. 738 (2009); *accord Williams v. Price*, 343 F.3d 223, 230, 234–36 (3d Cir. 2003).

Even in the face of racial injustice, then, courts wrangle about whether the systemic protections of Rule 606(b) must yield.* Beyond such fraught social turf, the centuries-old rule stands strong, a monument to our systemic faith in the wisdom of twelve common persons gathered together.

There is an irony here: Because our system invests such enormous trust in jurors' decisions, we need a system of evidence rules that betrays deep mistrust of jurors' ability to cull good evidence from bad. Because we apparently do not trust jurors to cast off and disregard meaningless, misleading, and unreliable evidence, we screen out such evidence before they ever hear it. This screening process—the quality control we exercise over the information juries hear—is the realm of evidence law.

* For more detail on this topic see Jessica L. West, *12 Racist Men: Post-Verdict Evidence of Juror Bias*, 27 HARV. J. RACIAL & ETHNIC JUSTICE 165 (2011); Andrew C. Helman, Comment, *Racism, Juries, and Justice: Addressing Post-Verdict Juror Testimony of Racial Prejudice During Deliberations*, 62 ME. L. REV. 327, 348 (2010).

UNIT I: RELEVANCE

CHAPTER 1

GENERAL PRINCIPLES OF RELEVANCE

A. PROBATIVENESS AND MATERIALITY

Let us begin with the Federal Rules' very simple approach to relevance. Almost all of the material in Unit I, spanning Chapters 1 through 5, derives from Rules 401, 402, and 403. Together these three rules consume just four sentences of text. Rule 402 establishes the basic principle that evidence is not admissible if not relevant, but typically admissible if relevant. Rule 403 presents the first of many exceptions to the fundamental norm that relevant evidence is admissible. It says "[t]he court may exclude relevant evidence" if that evidence poses problems that "substantially outweigh[]" its probative value. Most of the material in Unit I amplifies Rule 403's prejudice-versus-probativeness standard.

But we start with the most fundamental rule of all. Rule 401 defines *relevance*:

> Evidence is relevant if:
>
> **(a)** it has any tendency to make a fact more or less probable than it would be without the evidence; and
>
> **(b)** the fact is of consequence in determining the action.

This rule wraps together two definitions. First, evidence must be *probative*—it must tend to *prove* or *disprove* a fact by making it "more or less probable than it would be without the evidence." At common law this concept of probativeness took the name "relevancy," a usage that can cause understandable confusion given the text of Rule 401. Some authorities use the expression "logical relevance." Any of these terms will do, so long as you do not merge the issue of probativeness with the second component of relevance as defined by Rule 401.

That component concerns *materiality*. Evidence is *material* if it bears on a fact "of consequence in determining the action." Let's say the prosecutor in a murder case seeks to offer evidence of the victim's lost earning potential. The defense lawyer justifiably will object that the evidence is *immaterial*. Whether a murder victim had a lucrative job is typically of no consequence to the defendant's guilt or innocence. But in a civil wrongful death suit arising out of the same attack, the victim's lost earnings would be a material fact. Similarly, in a civil suit about a dog bite, questions addressing the dog owner's negligence in failing to leash the dog would be material in a state that conditions liability for dog bites on negligence—but probably not in a state that makes dog owners strictly liable for injuries inflicted by their pets.

Whether evidence is material therefore turns on what issues are at stake in the proceeding, which often turns on the substantive law of the jurisdiction. To decide whether an issue is material, don't look to the evidence rules for an answer, but to the substantive law.

A simple diagram captures the two components of relevance as defined by Rule 401—probativeness and materiality:

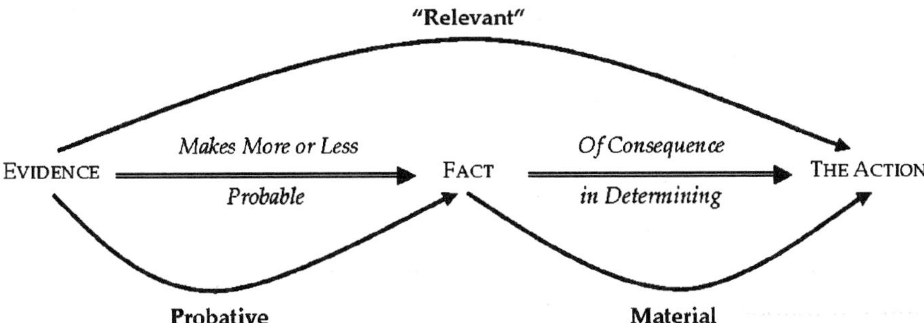

Note that Rule 401 permits courtroom lawyers in the heat of trial to abandon the old distinction between a materiality objection and one rooted in probativeness. In logic the distinction remains: testimony from an employer about a murder victim's salary is *probative* of earning potential, but not *material* to the defendant's guilt or innocence. Yet the opposing lawyer may object simply that the evidence is *irrelevant*.

It would be hard to devise a more lenient test of probativeness than Rule 401's "any tendency" standard. To be probative, evidence need not *prove* anything conclusively. It merely must have some *tendency* to make a fact more or less probable. Evidence will be probative if it contributes just one brick to the wall of proof built by a party. Or as Professor Charles McCormick said, "A brick is not a wall." Advisory Committee's Note (ACN) to FRE 401 (RB 38) (quoting McCormick).

Rule 401's very lenient standard of probativeness is part of what the Supreme Court has called the "liberal thrust" of the Federal Rules. *See, e.g., Daubert v. Merrell Dow Pharmaceuticals, Inc.*, 509 U.S. 579, 588 (1993); *Beech Aircraft Corp. v. Rainey*, 488 U.S. 153, 169 (1988). Here "liberal" means a preference for more rather than less evidence. On the whole the Federal Rules have a liberal, evidence-friendly reputation. As we work through the course, consider whether the Rules earn their liberal stripes.

Deeper exploration of what it means for evidence to be probative of a fact—the nature of knowledge, for example, and the distinction between deductive and inductive reasoning—would make for good reading but not perhaps for a more solid understanding of Rule 401. So among the many admirable studies of these questions, only one appears here—a classic treatment by George F. James of what it means to have *any tendency* to make a material fact more or less probable.

Focus on **FRE 401 & 402**

---

1. PROBATIVENESS

George F. James

Relevancy, Probability and the Law

29 CALIF. L. REV. 689 (1941).

Reprinted by Permission.

* * *

Relevancy, as the word itself indicates, is not an inherent characteristic of any item of evidence but exists as a relation between an item of evidence and a proposition sought to be proved. If an item of evidence tends to prove or disprove any proposition, it is relevant to that proposition. If the proposition itself is one provable in the case at bar, or if it in turn forms a further link in a chain of proof the final proposition of which is provable in the case at bar, then the offered item of evidence has probative value in the case. Whether the immediate or ultimate proposition sought to be proved is provable in the case at bar is determined by ... the substantive law governing the case.... [A]n offered item of evidence may be excluded as "irrelevant" for either of these two quite distinct reasons: because it is not probative of the proposition at which it is directed, or because that proposition is not provable in the case.[6] ...

[To flesh out what it means to be "probative of" a proposition, consider an argument discussed by Wigmore:] "Men's fixed designs are probably carried out; A had a fixed design to kill B; therefore, A probably did kill B." ... We know that we are interested in the probability of execution of a fixed design of a particular kind: to commit murder. There may be variation in the probability of execution of fixed designs on various subjects. As an initial criticism, therefore, the primary generaliza-

6. Henceforth, for brevity, propositions of ultimate fact properly provable in a case under the pleadings and substantive law will be referred to as 'material propositions'....

tion should be "Men's fixed designs to kill are probably carried out." In this form we have a valid, quasi-syllogistic argument based upon the limited data available. Still, is the premise sound?

"Men's fixed designs to kill are probably carried out," as a major premise in this argument, must mean that they are carried out more often than not.... Persons who are unwilling to agree that men's fixed designs (at least in case of murder) are "probably" carried out—or, even conceding the fact of murder, that proof of A's fixed design to kill B establishes A, more likely than not, as B's killer—still agree that somehow this bit of evidence does have some tendency to indicate A's guilt. What form of general statement can reconcile these views? Perhaps something like this: "Men having such a fixed design are more likely to kill than are men not having such a fixed design." Those who contend that even fixed designs to kill are more often abandoned or thwarted than carried out can and doubtless will still concede that enough such designs are carried to execution so that the percentage of murderers is higher among persons entertaining such a fixed design than among the general public. Obviously this proposed generalization does not lead us from A's fixed design to kill B to the conclusion that A probably did kill B. There is nothing disturbing in this. This conclusion simply does not follow from the evidence of design.... In fact, no useful conclusion about A's guilt can be drawn from design or intent alone. On the basis of an acceptable generalization we are able only to place A in a class of persons in which the incidence of murder is greater than among the general public. We cannot now say that A is probably guilty, but we can say that *the apparent probability of his guilt is now greater than before the evidence of design was received.* This is logical relevancy—the only logical relevancy we can expect in dealing with practical affairs where strict demonstration is never possible....

Problem 1.1

"Show me the body."

Consider these facts from *Commonwealth v. Zagranski,* 408 Mass. 278, 558 N.E.2d 933 (1990), in which the defendant was charged with the murder of a man with whom he had engaged in business dealings:

> [Three days after the victim's disappearance, police officers visited the defendant's home. When called as witnesses by the prosecutor, the officers testified to these facts:]
>
> Immediately after the defendant admitted the officers to the kitchen through the back door, they handcuffed him and advised him of his rights. His wife then entered the kitchen and, very excitedly, asked what was going on. A

> State police sergeant answered that her husband was under arrest for murder. She then yelled, "Murder? Where is the body? Show me the body. Where is the body if there's a murder?" Another arresting officer testified that the defendant's wife, very agitated, shouted "Where's the body? Where's the body? I challenge you to tell me where the body is." . . .
>
> . . . At this time, the police had not discovered the victim's body. . . .

If defense counsel objects that evidence of the wife's statements to the police is not relevant, how should the prosecutor respond? By what chain of inferences might this evidence be relevant to the defendant's guilt?

Problem 1.2
Brotherhood

At the defendant's trial on a robbery charge, a government witness, Ehle, testified that the defendant had taken part in the crime. The defendant later called a witness, Mills, who testified that Ehle had told Mills in prison that Ehle intended to implicate the defendant falsely. On cross-examination, the prosecutor then asked Mills if he and the defendant were members of a "secret type of prison organization" that had a creed requiring members to lie and kill for each other.

If the defendant objects to the prosecutor's question of Mills as irrelevant, how should the court rule? By what chain of inferences might this evidence be relevant to the defendant's guilt? *See United States v. Abel*, 469 U.S. 45 (1984).

Problem 1.3
Polygraph Consent

The defendant, charged with murder, claimed that he was alone and in bed at the time of the crime. Two months before trial his lawyer hired a polygraph expert to quiz the defendant about the night of the crime. Although the defendant sought to offer the polygraph examiner's testimony about the results of the examination, the trial court excluded all testimony about the polygraph exam itself.

At trial defense counsel called the polygraph examiner as a witness. The judge permitted the examiner to testify as follows: At the beginning of her meeting with the defendant she explained the polygraph equipment and her methodology. She told the defendant that in the past she had achieved a very high degree of success in detecting whether her subjects were lying. Then, adhering to her usual protocol in preparing subjects for an examination, she asked the defendant if he wished to proceed. He responded, "Go ahead, Doc, hook me up." The examiner testified that the defendant spoke these words "firmly and unhesitatingly." She did not testify about the examination itself.

How should the court have ruled on the prosecutor's objection that this testimony was irrelevant? *Cf. United States v. Scheffer*, 523 U.S. 303, 331–32 (1998) (Stevens, J., dissenting).

---

2. MATERIALITY

Problem 1.4
Knowledge

The defendant is charged in federal court with a violation of 18 U.S.C. § 922(g)(1). The only language in that statute that bears on this case reads as follows:

> (g) It shall be unlawful for any person—
>
> (1) who has been convicted in any court of a crime punishable by imprisonment for a term exceeding one year . . . to ship or transport in interstate or foreign commerce, or possess in or affecting commerce, any firearm or ammunition. . . .

The defendant was found to be carrying a loaded handgun as she drove a truck filled with farm goods across the Wisconsin–Illinois border. At trial the prosecutor presented evidence that the defendant previously had been convicted in Massachusetts of assault and battery and sentenced to three months in prison. The prosecutor offered proof that under Massachusetts law, assault and battery carries a penalty of up to two and one-half years in prison.

In her defense the defendant testified that she did not know until her arrest in this case that assault and battery is punishable in Massachusetts by more than a year's confinement. If the prosecutor objects to this testimony as irrelevant, how should the court rule?

Problem 1.5

Voluntary Intoxication

Consider these facts from *Montana v. Egelhoff*, 518 U.S. 37 (1996):

> In July 1992, while camping out in the Yaak region of northwestern Montana to pick mushrooms, [the defendant, Egelhoff,] made friends with Roberta Pavola and John Christenson, who were doing the same. On Sunday, July 12, the three sold the mushrooms they had collected and spent the rest of the day and evening drinking, in bars and at a private party in Troy, Montana. Some time after 9 p.m., they left the party in Christenson's 1974 Ford Galaxy station wagon. The drinking binge apparently continued, as [Egelhoff] was seen buying beer at 9:20 p.m. and recalled "sitting on a hill or a bank passing a bottle of Black Velvet back and forth" with Christenson.
>
> At about midnight that night, officers of the Lincoln County, Montana, sheriff's department, responding to reports of a possible drunk driver, discovered Christenson's station wagon stuck in a ditch along U.S. Highway 2. In the front seat were Pavola and Christenson, each dead from a single gunshot to the head. In the rear of the car lay [Egelhoff], alive and yelling obscenities. His blood-alcohol content measured .36 percent over one hour later. On the floor of the car, near the brake pedal, lay [Egelhoff's] .38 caliber handgun, with four loaded rounds and two empty casings; [Egelhoff] had gunshot residue on his hands.
>
> [Egelhoff] was charged with two counts of deliberate homicide, a crime defined by Montana law as "purposely" or "knowingly" causing the death of another human being. MONT. CODE ANN. § 45–5–102 (1995). A portion of the jury charge, uncontested here, instructed that "[a] person acts purposely when it is his conscious object to engage in conduct of that nature or to cause such a result," and that "[a] person acts knowingly when he is aware of his conduct or when he is aware under the circumstances his conduct constitutes a crime; or, when he is aware there exists the high probability that his conduct will cause a specific result."

Montana law provides that voluntary intoxication "may not be taken into consideration in determining the existence of a mental state which is an element of [a criminal] offense." MONT. CODE ANN. § 45–2–203 (1995). If the defendant, at trial, offers evidence of his high blood alcohol level to show that he could not have acted "purposely" or "knowingly" when he shot Pavola and Christenson, and if the prosecution objects on relevance grounds, how should the court rule? Why?

UNITED STATES v. JAMES

169 F.3d 1210 (9th Cir. 1999) (en banc).

■ NOONAN, CIRCUIT JUDGE: Ernestine Audry James appeals her conviction of aiding and abetting manslaughter. . . .

FACTS AND PROCEEDINGS

James met her boyfriend, David Ogden (the victim), . . . in Seattle. He was nice sober, nasty drunk. Ogden had boasted to her about once killing a man and getting away with it. He told her he had sold another man a fake watch, and when the man complained, had stabbed him in the neck with a ball point pen. Ogden told James that "it was pretty funny watching a guy with a pen dangling out of his neck." He also bragged that he had once "ripped a side view mirror off the car and beat a man unconscious with it," and that, in yet another incident, he had robbed an old man by holding him down with a knife in his face and threatening to cut his eyes out.

James had seen Ogden's violence with her own eyes and suffered it. . . . On [one] occasion when Ogden wanted to have sexual intercourse with James and she had refused, he came into the room where she and her daughter Jaylene Jeffries were and started yelling at James and calling her names. Jaylene got up and held Ogden at knife point with a carving knife until James ordered them both to desist. . . .

Jaylene, the daughter, had beaten Ogden on three occasions. . . . Ogden would never fight back against her. He acted scared of her, even though she was only fourteen. . . .

. . . On the day Ogden was killed, [Ogden, James, Jaylene, and Jaylene's boyfriend, Michas Tiatano] had been together at a party. . . . When James decided to leave the party, her van got stuck on a fishnet lying on the ground. She and Jaylene were sitting in the van, when Jaylene heard Tiatano say, "Oh man," and fall down. Ogden had just punched Tiatano in the face, possibly with some object in his hand, so hard that he broke his nose and knocked him unconscious. . . .

[Shortly afterward, Jaylene shot and killed Ogden with a gun James handed her. James was charged with aiding and abetting the killing and faced trial before the U.S. District Court for the Western District of Washington, which had territorial jurisdiction.]

James testified that after Ogden had "cold cocked" Tiatano, Jaylene chased him for awhile. According to James, the following ensued:

> *A.* Jaylene came . . . back to the van and she was breathing heavy, like she was running. She was very upset and she just started begging me for the gun. She said, mom, please give me the gun, give me the gun. She said it several times.
>
> *Q.* And what did you do when she begged you for the gun?
>
> *A.* I just grabbed for my purse and got the gun and handed it to her. . . .
>
> *Q.* At that moment when Jaylene asked you for the gun and you reached in and gave it to her, why did you give it to her?
>
> *A.* I gave it to her to protect herself and the family members.
>
> *Q.* What did you expect her to do with the gun when you gave it to her?
>
> *A.* I just expected her to fend David off. I didn't want her to shoot him. It was just to scare him away from the property.
>
> *Q.* Why did you want her to scare him away from the property?
>
> *A.* Because I knew how violent he was and I knew that he wouldn't stop at just one punch and he wanted to continue being violent. . . .

Defense counsel argued self-defense. He pointed out to the jury that James, his client, was charged with aiding and abetting the daughter by handing her the gun, so James had to be judged by what she knew at the moment. . . . He argued that because the mother knew Ogden was drunk, vicious when drunk, and usually carried a knife in his sock, it was not grossly negligent to give "the gun to her daughter so that Jaylene could protect herself in that one moment when [the mother] had that decision, the split second decision to make."

The jury heard all the evidence discussed above. In the pretrial skirmishing, the court had ruled that James and Jaylene could testify about prior violent misconduct they had known about when James handed Jaylene the gun, but could not introduce extrinsic evidence of which they had no knowledge at that time. This appeal is about four exhibits that the mother's attorney was not allowed to show the jury. He had . . . court documents setting forth detailed findings on the robbery of a 58–year old man, in which Ogden sat on the man and held a knife at his throat and at his eyes while threatening to blind him. . . .

The jury sent out a number of questions during its deliberations. One read as follows:

Dear Judge,

The jury would like to know if it is a "fact" that:

1) Ogden did stab an "old man" and was sentenced to 20 yrs & on parole
2) did he really stab someone with a pen
3) did he really murder a man . . . ?

Are there police or court documents to prove this or is it "brag?"

Thanx.

Robert Reedy

Foreman

The judge declined to supplement the evidence.

The district judge further explained why he had excluded the evidence. In his ruling on defendant's motion for a new trial, he explained that "evidence of every past violent act by Ogden, known to the defendant, was placed before the jury" . . . The extrinsic evidence was not such evidence, because "the only relevant facts concerning Ogden's past were the ones defendant knew about; only to that extent could her state of mind at the time of the shooting have been affected by Ogden's past misconduct." The district judge noted that if the court records had in fact been to the contrary, and proved that Ogden had been exaggerating and was not really so violent as he claimed, the court would have sustained a defense objection, "because the court record, never seen by defendant, could not have affected her state of mind. The result should be no different when the defendant offers the extraneous record."

James was convicted and sentenced to five years' probation. She appealed, and a divided panel of this court affirmed her conviction. We then took the case en banc.

ANALYSIS

. . . Ernestine Audry James's only defense was that she believed that she and her daughter were in danger of grievous bodily harm or death from Ogden. Essential to that defense was her belief in Ogden's stories of previous acts of vicious violence committed by him. These stories were of such a remarkable character of atrocity that one might doubt that he had told them of himself or doubt that they had really occurred. Hence the question raised by the jurors as to Ogden's stabbing of an old man; Ogden's stabbing of another person with a pen; and Ogden's murdering a man: "Are there police or court documents to prove this or is it 'brag'?"

For the defense the records, if admitted, would have . . . corroborate[d] Ernestine James's own testimony that she had heard Ogden tell her these things. . . .

The district court thought the only function of the evidence would have been to show Ernestine James's state of mind and that, since she had not seen the records, the documents proved nothing as to her state of mind. That interpretation of the proffered evidence was too narrow. It was absolutely necessary to her defense for the jury to believe . . . that she wasn't making up the stories. . . . The records proved that [Ogden] had done [these terrible things] so that the stories of his wild exploits would have had the ring of truth to her, and the records proved that what Ernestine James testified to had actually taken place. The records corroborated her testimony, and the records corroborated her reason to fear.

Because the crux of James's defense rested on her credibility and because her credibility could be directly corroborated through the excluded documentary evidence, exclusion of the documents was prejudicial and more probably than not affected the verdict.

For the reasons stated, the judgment of the district court is *reversed.*

■ KLEINFELD, CIRCUIT JUDGE, dissenting. . . .

UNITED STATES v. JAMES: *Afterthoughts*

The Materiality of the Excluded Documents

James presents a classic materiality problem. Proof that Ogden really had robbed an "old man" at knifepoint surely seems probative of *something*. But of what? How was that evidence *material* to James's claim of self-defense? James said she reasonably believed that at the time she handed Jaylene the gun, Ogden posed an imminent threat to her and Jaylene. The issue, therefore, was James's state of mind at that moment. As the district judge said, "the only relevant facts concerning Ogden's past were the ones defendant knew about; only to that extent could her state of mind at the time of the shooting have been affected by Ogden's past misconduct. . . . [T]he court record [tending to prove Ogden had robbed the 'old man'], never seen by defendant, could not have affected her state of mind."

The appeals court concluded that the trial judge was wrong—that the excluded documents did help prove James's fearful state of mind though she had no idea they existed. But how could they do that?

The Probative Value of the Excluded Documents

The crux of the appeals court's reasoning lies in this single sentence: "For the defense the records, if admitted, would have . . . corroborate[d]

Ernestine James's own testimony that she had heard Ogden tell her these things. . . ." Exactly how does evidence that Ogden committed certain vicious acts corroborate James's claim that he had bragged to her about them? In *Knapp v. State*, 168 Ind. 153 (1907), the Supreme Court of Indiana considered the converse of the situation in *James*. There, the defendant complained that the trial court had permitted the state to prove that the stories the defendant claimed to have heard were *not* true. This factual difference notwithstanding, the two cases have much in common:

> Appellant, as a witness in his own behalf, offered testimony tending to show a killing in self-defense. He afterwards testified, presumably for the purpose of showing that he had reason to fear the deceased, that before the killing he had heard that the deceased, who was the marshal of Hagerstown, had clubbed and seriously injured an old man in arresting him, and that he died a short time afterwards. On appellant's being asked, on cross-examination, who told him this, he answered: "Some people around Hagerstown there. I can't say as to who it was now." The State was permitted, on rebuttal, to prove by a physician, over the objection and exception of the defense, that the old man died of senility and alcoholism, and that there were no bruises nor marks on his person. Counsel for appellant contend that it was error to admit this testimony; that the question was whether he had, in fact, heard the story, and not as to its truth or falsity. . . .
>
> . . . One of the first principles of human nature is the impulse to speak the truth. "This principle," says Dr. Reid, . . . "has a powerful operation, even in the greatest liars; for where they lie once they speak truth a hundred times." Truth speaking preponderating, it follows that to show that there was no basis in fact for the statement appellant claims to have heard had a tendency to make it less probable that his testimony on this point was true. Indeed, . . . we do not perceive how . . . the State could be denied the opportunity to meet in the manner indicated the evidence of the defendant as to what he had heard, where he, cunningly perhaps, testifies that he cannot remember who gave him the information. The fact proved by the State tended to discredit appellant, since it showed that somewhere between the fact and the testimony there was a person who was not a truth speaker, and with appellant unable to point to his informant, it must, at the least, be said that the testimony complained of had a tendency to render his claim as to what he had heard less probable.

168 Ind. at 155–57.

Just as Knapp's unnamed sources were more likely to say the old man was clubbed to death if he really was, so Ogden was more likely to say he had robbed an old man at knifepoint if he really did. That Ogden in fact had committed such a crime therefore made it more likely that

James was telling the truth when she said Ogden had told her about the crime.

Something to Ponder

Assume the appeals court was correct in *James*—and evidence that Ogden had committed certain vicious acts tended to corroborate James's claim that he had bragged about those acts. Does that mean the trial court should have admitted the evidence of Ogden's past acts? Or could the government have raised other objections to the evidence besides irrelevance? You might begin to think ahead to arguments under Rule 403, which we take up shortly.

Problem 1.6
Violin Case

Chicago, 1924. A city police officer faced manslaughter charges in the shooting death of Johnny Coker. The officer claimed self-defense—that he acted in reasonable fear for his life at the time he shot Coker.

At trial the officer testified that in the aftermath of a bloody gangland slaying on the city's South Side, he was searching for suspects in the dark alleyways leading from the crime scene. Working alone, he suddenly encountered Coker emerging from a speakeasy at the end of the alley. Coker was carrying a violin case in his right hand.

The officer dropped to his knees, aimed his revolver at Coker, and shouted, "Drop the case!" Instead, he said, Coker suddenly raised the violin case to his shoulder and "aimed" it at the officer. The officer testified that, fearing the case concealed a sawed-off shotgun, he shot and killed Coker.

In rebuttal, the prosecution sought to prove that a search after Coker's death revealed the violin case contained $40,000 in cash, but no gun. Over the defendant's objection that evidence of the absence of a gun was irrelevant, how should the court have ruled? How could the prosecution argue that absence of a gun was material to the defendant's claim of self-defense? *Cf. Sherrod v. Berry*, 856 F.2d 802, 809–11 (7th Cir. 1988) (Cummings, J., dissenting); *id.* at 813–14 (Flaum, J., dissenting).

B. Conditional Relevance

Focus on FRE 104(b)

Problem 1.7
Threat to Disclose

Consider the following news account:

Fitzhugh Case: Judge Allows Paternity Motive

Bill D'Agostino

Palo Alto Weekly, June 22, 2001

Jurors will be permitted to hear evidence concerning Kenneth Fitzhugh's possible motive for murdering his wife, Kristine, in their Palo Alto home last year, according to a Wednesday ruling issued by Santa Clara County Superior Court Judge Franklin Elia.

In a motion filed last week, prosecutor Michael Fletcher stated he will argue Fitzhugh killed Kristine because she planned to tell her oldest son, Justin, that Fitzhugh was not his father.

Fletcher wrote that family friend Robert Brown "had a long-term, intimate relationship with the victim" in the 1970s, around the time Justin Fitzhugh was conceived. He also noted that a DNA test has established that Brown, who will be a witness in the case, is Justin Fitzhugh's father.

Brown, according to the district attorney, is planning to testify that in January 2000, Kristine told him over the phone that she was planning to tell Justin about his real father after her son graduated from college.

Kristine Fitzhugh, 53, was murdered in her home on May 5, 2000, approximately two weeks before Justin graduated from the University of the Pacific in Stockton. . . .

Defense attorney Thomas Nolan wrote in his own motion that "unless the district attorney can show that Mr. Fitzhugh knew of the facts that constituted a possible motive, it cannot be a motive."

In his response, Fletcher gave no proof that Fitzhugh was told of Kristine's alleged plans to tell her son. Instead, he wrote that "It is a fair and reasonable inference that the victim would not tell her son this critical information without first telling her husband, especially since she did tell Mr. Brown. In this circumstance, it is reasonable to infer that the victim did, in fact, tell the [defendant] her plan." . . .

Fletcher wrote that the issue of Justin Fitzhugh's paternity came up accidentally while Kenneth Fitzhugh was being interviewed the day of the murder. Palo Alto Police Detective Michael Denson was questioning Fitzhugh, who referred to Justin as "her older son" rather than "our older son."

"Her older son graduates from college in a couple of weeks," Fitzhugh said, according to the prosecution's motion....

When Denson asked, "You said 'her older son.' Is he not your son?" Fitzhugh responded, "No. He's our son."

Assume this case is governed by the Federal Rules of Evidence. Was the trial judge right to admit the prosecutor's evidence of motive? What are the best arguments for both sides?

COX v. STATE

Supreme Court of Indiana.
696 N.E.2d 853 (Ind. 1998).

■ BOEHM, JUSTICE. In this direct appeal from a conviction for murder, Patrick E. Cox contends that ... the trial court erred by admitting certain testimony, the relevance of which depended upon Cox's knowledge of the content of the testimony....

FACTUAL BACKGROUND

In the early morning hours of September 22, 1995, James and Patricia Leonard were asleep in the ground floor bedroom of their home. At about 3:00 a.m. Patricia ... was awakened by a single "loud pop sound," and quickly realized that James had been shot in the eye. James was rushed to the hospital but died three days later.

Bullet holes were found in the bedroom window and its screen, and a bullet casing was outside beneath the window. An officer who was called to the scene that night had a clear view of the inside of the bedroom from immediately outside the window. A firearms expert testified that the pattern of discoloration on the screen could have been produced only by a shot fired within six inches of the screen.

Police questioned Cox on the morning of the shooting. Cox denied any involvement in the crime and said he returned home from a nearby friend's house at about 1:00 a.m. However, later that morning one of Cox's friends told police that Cox had said that he had looked into the Leonards' window, fired a shot, and fled. Cox also told him that "Leonards probably ain't gonna have a dad after last night." ... In addition, Angela Bowling, a friend of Cox's, testified that she bought bullets for Cox at his request the night of the shooting and that she and a few other friends were with him at the home of Helen Johnson until Cox left between 3:30 and 4:00 a.m.

Johnson was the mother of Cox's close friend, Jamie Hammer.... The State contended that Cox killed Leonard as an act of retaliation because Hammer was in prison pending the resolution of charges filed against him by the Leonards for molesting their young daughter. The jury convicted Cox of murder....

III. RELEVANCE OF EVIDENCE CONDITIONED ON A FACT

At trial, Cox objected to testimony by David Puckett, a deputy prosecutor in Madison County. Puckett testified that four days before the murder he had represented the State of Indiana at a bond reduction hearing for Cox's close friend Jamie Hammer. He testified that: (1) he had informed the court at the hearing that three class B felony charges were to be filed against Hammer, in addition to a single pending charge, for alleged acts of child molestation of Leonard's daughter; (2) Helen Johnson, Hammer's mother, testified at the hearing; and (3) Hammer's bond was not reduced as a result of the hearing. Cox contends that this testimony was inadmissible because it could be relevant only if Cox knew what happened at the hearing and the State was unable to prove conclusively that Cox had that knowledge. The trial court admitted the evidence, concluding that because Hammer's mother knew about the denial of Hammer's bond reduction and the additional charges to be filed, "other persons in [Hammer's] circle reasonably are likely to know about it."

The admissibility of Puckett's testimony is governed by Indiana Evidence Rule 104(b), "Relevancy Conditioned on Fact," although neither party cites this rule. The Indiana Rule is identical to [unrestyled] Federal Rule of Evidence 104(b). It provides: "When the relevancy of evidence depends upon the fulfillment of a condition of fact, the Court shall admit it upon, or subject to, the introduction of evidence sufficient to support a finding of the fulfillment of the condition." Here, the relevance of Puckett's testimony depends upon a condition of fact—whether Cox knew about what happened at the bond reduction hearing. If Cox knew of the latest developments in Hammer's case, then the information was relevant and extremely probative of the State's theory that Cox killed Leonard—the father of Hammer's victim—because of Hammer's plight. If Cox was ignorant of these developments, then Puckett's testimony would be irrelevant and unfairly prejudicial.

We have not yet had occasion to set out the standard for questions under Rule 104(b). Under its terms, the court may admit the evidence only after it makes a preliminary determination that there is sufficient evidence to support a finding that the conditional fact exists. As Weinstein commented, "these issues are, for the most part, simple factual questions to be decided on the basis of common sense, and the Rules [of Evidence] assume that the jury is as competent to decide them as the judge." We adopt the prevailing federal standard that "the judge must determine only that a reasonable jury could make the requisite factual determination based on the evidence before it." *See, e.g.,* United States v. Beechum, 582 F.2d 898, 913 (5th Cir. 1978) (en banc) ("the preliminary fact can be decided by the judge against the proponent only where the jury could not reasonably find the preliminary fact to exist"). The trial court is not required to weigh the credibility of the evidence or to make a finding. *See* Huddleston v. United States, 485 U.S. 681, 690 (1988).

Here, the State introduced evidence that Cox spent almost every day at the Hammer house where Hammer's mother lived both before and after the bond reduction hearing and up to the time of the shooting. Hammer and Cox were close friends and Hammer's mother attended the hearing. This evidence is sufficient to support the inference that Cox had learned what transpired at the hearing. Accordingly, the trial court did not abuse its discretion by admitting the evidence. . . .

COX V. STATE: *Afterthoughts*

The Problem of Conditional Relevance

Both *Fitzhugh* (Problem 1.7, page 35) and *Cox* seem to present problems of conditional relevance. In each case there is evidence that *might* be relevant, but only if some other condition is met. Kristine Fitzhugh's apparent intention to tell her son that Kenneth Fitzhugh was not his father *might* have given Kenneth Fitzhugh a motive to kill her, but only if he had heard of her intention. And the new charges lodged against Patrick Cox's friend, Jamie Hammer, in the case involving the Leonard daughter *might* have given Cox a motive to kill James Leonard, but only if Cox had heard of the new charges.

In each case Rule 104(b) tells us that the contested evidence—Kristine Fitzhugh's apparent intention to disclose her son's paternity or the new charges lodged against Jamie Hammer—is admissible only if "proof [is] introduced sufficient to support a finding that the [conditional] fact does exist." The theory behind the rule is that the chain of inferences leading from the contested fact to the conclusion of the defendant's guilt is simply *severed* if the conditional fact—that Fitzhugh had learned of his wife's intentions or that Cox had learned of the new charges—is not established. The rule therefore requires that there be sufficient evidence to support a jury finding of the conditional fact.

One can imagine similar problems of conditional relevance. The advisory committee suggests that "if a letter purporting to be from Y is relied upon to establish an admission [of fault] by him, it has no probative value unless Y wrote or authorized it." (RB 14.) By the same reasoning, a ballistics expert's opinion that a particular bullet was shot from the defendant's gun would have no relevance unless the bullet the expert examined is the one that struck the victim (or is otherwise connected with the crime). And a chemist's opinion that a particular bag of white powder contains cocaine would have no relevance without evidence that the defendant at some point possessed or was otherwise connected with the bag.

Such problems—or apparent problems—of conditional relevance seem obvious enough. In fact it is fairly easy to imagine chains of inference that depend on conditional facts. It is far harder, however, to imagine a chain of inferences *free* of any problem of conditional relevance. That is our next challenge.

Conditional Relevance: Is There a There There?

How will we know that a piece of evidence presents *no* problem of conditional relevance? The Advisory Committee's Note to Rule 104(b) gives some guidance. It suggests that there is no problem of conditional relevance with "evidence in a murder case that accused on the day before purchased a weapon of the kind used in the killing." The note adds that such evidence is "treated in Rule 401." (RB 14.)

Is there really no problem of conditional relevance buried within evidence that the defendant bought a weapon of the sort used on the day before the killing? In an article titled, "The Myth of Conditional Relevancy," Professor Vaughn Ball writes: "It seems to me safe to say that instead of some, virtually all offers of evidence can raise problems of conditional relevancy...." Vaughn C. Ball, *The Myth of Conditional Relevancy,* 14 GA. L. REV. 435, 456 (1980). And Professor Dale Nance adds: "Indeed, the only limit on the number of conditioning facts pertaining to each proffer is one's imagination." Dale A. Nance, *Conditional Relevance Reinterpreted,* 70 B.U. L. REV. 447, 452 (1990). Take Ball's and Nance's claims as a challenge: Can you identify "conditioning facts" that must be proved before we can feel confident that "evidence in a murder case that accused on the day before purchased a weapon of the kind used in the killing" is relevant? More than likely you can.

Here is another example. Several pages back, Problem 1.3 presented a scenario in which the defendant agreed to undergo a polygraph examination. The judge excluded the results of the test. The defendant then sought to offer evidence that he had agreed to be tested even after he was warned that the technique accurately detected deceit. The relevance of the defendant's consent to the examination was that it tended to prove his *consciousness of innocence.* The chain of inferences had four links: (1) the defendant consented to the test despite the expert's warning; (2) therefore he must have been prepared to tell the truth; (3) therefore he must have been confident the truth could not hurt him; (4) therefore he must be innocent.

But was there no possible missing link in this chain of inferences? One could imagine at least a couple. For example, the reasoning assumes the defendant truly *believed* the polygraph test would detect any attempt to lie. What if the defendant felt certain he could beat the test and lie without detection? In that event his consent to the examination would have had no relevance in proving his innocent state of mind. Likewise, the chain of inferences depends on the defendant's belief that the results of the test could somehow end up in the hands of authorities. What if the defendant in fact believed that if the test came out badly, he could keep the whole thing to himself and his lawyer? In that event the defendant's confidence in undergoing the test might be evidence not of his consciousness of innocence, but of his certainty that the results, if unfavorable, would never become evidence against him. In either event the defendant's consent to the polygraph would cease to be relevant evidence of innocence.

Most experts agree with Professors Ball and Nance that there is no *separate* problem of conditional relevance. "[A]ll cases of relevancy are cases of conditional relevancy." Ronald J. Allen, *The Myth of Conditional Relevancy*, 25 LOY. L.A. L. REV. 871, 879 (1992); *accord* Craig R. Callen, *Rationality and Relevancy: Conditional Relevancy and Constrained Resources*, 2003 MICH. ST. L. REV. 1243, 1256 ("[T]he relevancy of an item of evidence is always dependent on the other information we have."). That is, within *any* logical chain of inferences, a clever lawyer could spot a missing link without which the chain breaks apart. Those lawyers sharp enough to spy the missing link and articulate a conditional relevance objection may force the judge to analyze the problem under Rule 104(b). Less resourceful lawyers will not. And where no conditional relevance objection is made, the judge likely will admit the proffered evidence if it surmounts the bare relevance standard of Rule 401.

The difference in this circumstance between having a sharp lawyer and having a slacker amounts to this: In the one case, the judge will test the opponent's evidence against Rule 104(b)'s conditional relevance standard. In the other, she will apply only Rule 401's bare relevance standard. But is this a difference that makes a difference?

And if There's No There There . . .

The answer depends on how much harder it is to surmount the 104(b) standard than the 401 standard. Consider again the facts of *Cox*. How much easier would it have been to admit Prosecutor Puckett's proposed testimony under a bare relevance standard than under the conditional relevance standard imposed by the court? Under a bare relevance standard, the trial judge would have asked simply whether the outcome of Jamie Hammer's bond reduction hearing had any tendency to make it more probable that Cox had a motive to kill (and therefore did kill) James Leonard. The answer, presumably, would have been yes, as long as there was *any* non-negligible chance that Cox had heard about the outcome of the hearing. Under the 104(b) standard, evidence of the bond-reduction hearing could come in only if the prosecutor introduced "sufficient [evidence] to support a finding" that Cox had heard about the hearing.

But now we've raised another question: sufficient to support *what kind* of finding? There are several possibilities—a finding beyond a reasonable doubt, a finding by clear and convincing evidence, or a finding by a mere preponderance of the evidence. The rule writers did not specify the standard. The Supreme Court, however, has resolved this question by choosing the most lenient option: Rule 104(b) requires that the proponent introduce sufficient evidence that "the jury could reasonably find the conditional fact . . . by a preponderance of the evidence." *See Huddleston v. United States*, 485 U.S. 681 (1988) (excerpted below at page 201).

This is not the last we will see of Rule 104(b)—or of its sibling rule, 104(a), which we take up in Chapter 7. I will look at the distinction between these two rules in some detail at pages 427 to 429. For now, you should mull this muddled state of affairs: In erecting a distinct standard to govern questions of conditional relevance, the rule writers almost surely made a logical error. *Every* chain of inferences has potential missing links. The consequence of this error is that when the missing link is obvious enough—or the opposing lawyer is canny enough to spot it—the judge will admit the challenged evidence only if the proponent introduces sufficient evidence of the conditional fact (the missing link) that the jury could reasonably find by a preponderance of the evidence that the link is established. But when the missing link is less apparent—or the opposing lawyer less resourceful—the judge will test the proffered evidence against only the bare relevance standard.

This state of affairs is surely somewhat troubling. But in practice it seems to prompt little concern or confusion. In part that is because lawyers simply do not make many conditional relevance objections. And in part it is because the conditional relevance standard, though higher than the bare relevance standard, is not *much* higher. The difference between *Huddleston*'s standard of conditional relevance (sufficient evidence that "the jury could reasonably find the conditional fact . . . by a preponderance of the evidence") and Rule 401's bare relevance standard (evidence having "any tendency to make a fact more less probable") amounts to little in the rough-and-tumble of real-world fact-finding.

On Condition of Later Proof

Rule 104(b) says that the trial judge "may admit the proposed evidence on the condition that the proof be introduced later." Consider the *Cox* case again. Assume prosecutor Puckett has taken the stand, ready to testify about the new charges lodged against Jamie Hammer. If there already is enough evidence in the record to support an inference that Patrick Cox had heard of the new charges at the time of Leonard's murder, Puckett's testimony may be admitted without further ado. If such evidence is not already in the record, the judge may permit Puckett to testify "on the condition" of connection. The prosecution still must introduce evidence that connects the new charges against Hammer with Cox's alleged motive to kill. If the prosecution fails to do so, the judge will instruct the jury to disregard Puckett's testimony about the bail reduction hearing.

The advisory committee's explanation of this mechanism is hardly a model of clarity. To make matters worse, there is a small but significant error in the committee's note to Rule 104(b). Here are the note's concluding sentences:

> If after all the evidence on the issue is in [i.e., all evidence about whether Cox had heard of the new charges] . . . , the jury could reasonably conclude that fulfillment of the condition is **not** established, the issue [i.e., the import of Puckett's testimony about the new charges] is for them [the jury]. If the evidence is not such as to allow a finding [that Cox had heard of those charges], the judge withdraws the matter from their consideration.

(RB 15.) That boldfaced "not" is a mistake. These two sentences make (somewhat) more sense without it.

C. PROBATIVENESS VERSUS THE RISK OF UNFAIR PREJUDICE

Focus on FRE 403

RULE 403, PHRASE BY PHRASE

Rule 403 is short, but its simplicity is deceptive. Almost every phrase of the rule deserves scrutiny:

> The court may exclude relevant evidence if its probative value is substantially outweighed by a danger of one or more of the following: unfair prejudice, confusing the issues, misleading the jury, undue delay, wasting time, or needlessly presenting cumulative evidence.

It is worth taking a moment to master the mechanics of Rule 403. Virtually every piece of evidence admitted at trial must survive this rule's probativeness-versus-risk-of-unfair-prejudice weighing test. Some evidence must survive a stricter screening. But only the narrow class of evidence defined by Rule 609(a)(2), which we take up in Chapter 4, is altogether exempt from Rule 403 scrutiny.

"The court may exclude ...": The operative word here is "may." Decisions whether to exclude evidence under Rule 403 are committed to the trial judge's discretion and are reviewable on appeal only for abuse of discretion. Although abuse-of-discretion review acts as "a virtual shield from reversal," ROGER PARK ET AL., EVIDENCE LAW § 12.01, at 540–41 & n.6 (1998), reversals are not unheard of. One example is *Old Chief v. United States*, 519 U.S. 172 (1997), excerpted below at page 82.

"... relevant evidence ...": The rule writers anticipated that Rule 403 often would result in exclusion of relevant evidence.

"... if its probative value is substantially outweighed by ...": Note that Rule 403 is a *liberal* evidence rule in the sense that it is friendly toward admission of evidence. If the evils of a particular piece of evidence (say, its potential to confuse the jury) exactly offset the probative value of the evidence, Rule 403 grants the trial judge no discretion to exclude. Even if such evils actually outweigh probative value, though only slightly, the rule still grants no permission to exclude. Only if these evils "substantially outweigh[]" the probative value of the evidence does Rule 403 give the judge discretion to exclude the evidence.

"... a danger of ... unfair prejudice ...": Here the operative word is "unfair." "Relevant evidence is inherently prejudicial; but it is only *unfair* prejudice, *substantially* outweighing probative value, which permits exclusion of relevant matter under Rule 403." *United States v. McRae*, 593 F.2d 700, 707 (5th Cir.), *cert. denied*, 444 U.S. 862 (1979). The next several cases—*Bocharski, Serge, James, Myers*, and *Collins*—explore different sorts of potential *unfair* prejudice. These cases hardly exhaust the imaginable varieties.

"... a danger of ... confusing the issues, misleading the jury ...": Distracting the jury from the task at hand also may supply grounds for excluding evidence under Rule 403.

"... a danger of ... [1] undue delay, [2] wasting time, or [3] needlessly presenting cumulative evidence.": Even sheer time waste may justify exclusion—"a concession," as Holmes said, "to the shortness of life." *Reeve v. Dennett*, 145 Mass. 23, 28, 11 N.E. 938 (1887). Conceding

nothing on this score, the rule writers spelled out the problem of time waste three times.

---

1. PHOTOS AND OTHER INFLAMMATORY EVIDENCE

STATE V. BOCHARSKI

Supreme Court of Arizona.
22 P.3d 43 (Ariz. 2001).

■ ZLAKET, CHIEF JUSTICE. Defendant Phillip Alan Bocharski moved from Michigan to Arizona with Frank Sukis in November 1994. The two settled just outside the small town of Congress. The defendant initially stayed with Sukis, but in December moved to a well-populated campsite on Ghost Town Road. Around Christmas, Sukis gave the defendant a Kabar knife, slightly smaller than one he kept for himself. This knife was described by Bocharski as his "pride and joy," and he was frequently seen with it.

In April 1995, Sukis moved to a location near the defendant. Shortly thereafter, an eighty-four year old woman named Freeda Brown established a campsite between Bocharski and Sukis....

On May 10, Sukis picked up Bocharski at the latter's tent. The two of them saw Brown polishing her truck.... Sukis later testified that ... the defendant suggested "maybe he should offer [*sic*] or get rid of [Brown], on account of her arthritis, 'cause she was complaining all the time, she was praying God he'd take her out of her misery." ...

On May 13, Duane Staley noticed that Freeda Brown's dog had no water and its leash was wrapped around a tree. He had not seen Brown in a while and grew concerned. He knocked on her trailer door and tried to open it. He then obtained help from Sukis, who got inside and found Brown's body on the bed, covered by a blanket....

The officer who arrived at the trailer observed that the woman's body had already begun to decompose. He concluded that her death was due to natural causes.... [But a] subsequent autopsy disclosed that Brown had perished as a result of at least sixteen stab wounds to the head....

... [O]fficers searched around a mine and a nearby cemetery in hopes of finding Bocharski's Kabar knife, which was last seen by any witness three months before the killing. The knife was never located. In fact, no murder weapon was ever found.... Two of [Bocharski's] fingerprints were found on the door of the deceased's trailer, but could not be dated.

The defendant ... was convicted of first-degree felony murder and first-degree burglary.... Bocharski was sentenced to twenty-one years' imprisonment on the burglary charge and to death for the murder. We review this case on direct, automatic appeal....

TRIAL ISSUES

A. Gruesome Photographs

The trial court allowed six photographs into evidence over defense counsel's objection that they were gruesome, highly inflammatory, and unduly prejudicial:

Exhibit 42:	the victim's clothed body, showing gross marbling of the skin, discoloration of the face, and fluid coming from both the nose and mouth;
Exhibit 43:	a closeup of the victim's face in profile before it was cleaned
Exhibit 44:	the victim's torso and face after the body had been washed and her head had been shaved to make the wounds more visible;
Exhibit 45:	a closeup of the victim's hand and finger; and
Exhibits 46, 47:	views of the victim's skull, the top and its contents having been removed, with a metal rod going through an opening to the inside.

Relevant photographs may be received in evidence even though they "also have a tendency to prejudice the jury against the person who committed the offense." State v. Chapple, 135 Ariz. 281, 287–88 (1983). This does not mean, however, that every relevant photograph should automatically be admitted. If a photograph "is of a nature to incite passion or inflame the jury," *id.*, the court must determine whether the danger of unfair prejudice substantially outweighs the exhibit's probative value. ARIZ. R. EVID. 403. A trial court's decision in this regard will generally not be disturbed unless we find a clear abuse of discretion.

Bocharski concedes that the photographs of the victim's body were relevant. We agree. [Unrestyled] Rule 401 declares that evidence which has "*any tendency* to make the existence of any *fact that is of consequence* to the determination of the action more probable or less probable than it would be without the evidence" is relevant. ARIZ. R. EVID. 401 (emphasis added). We have previously recognized that the state has the burden of proving every element of first-degree murder. We have also suggested that photographs of a homicide victim's body are generally admissible because "the fact and cause of death are always relevant in a murder case." State v. Harding, 141 Ariz. 492, 499 (1984).

However, if a defendant does not contest the "fact that is of consequence," ARIZ. R. EVID. 401, then a relevant exhibit's probative value may be minimal. Under such circumstances, gruesome photographs may "have little use or purpose except to inflame," *Chapple*, 135 Ariz. at 288, and their prejudicial effect can be significant. In the present case, the photographs introduced by the state went to largely uncontested issues. The defense did not challenge the fact of the victim's death, the extent of her injuries, or the manner of her demise.

Exhibits 42 and 43 depict both the state of the body's decomposition and facial wounds. There was some question about how long the victim had been dead before she was found. This was discussed by the medical examiner and a forensic pathologist who performed the autopsy. The witnesses could not ascertain an exact time of death, only coming within a few days in their estimates. Moreover, while diagrams were available to depict the size and location of the deceased's most profound injuries, the state introduced Exhibit 44 to show superficial head wounds, and Exhibit 45 to show a cut on the victim's finger. Testimony indicated that the latter was not a defensive wound, making its significance marginal at best.

Nevertheless, we do not conclude that the trial court abused its discretion by admitting Exhibits 42–45. The state "cannot be compelled to try its case in a sterile setting." *Chapple*, 135 Ariz. at 289–90. We are, however, concerned about the admission of Exhibits 46 and 47. Their admission was unnecessary and quite risky. The state contends that these photos were required to show the angles and depths of the penetrating wounds. According to the state, this information was important because a juror asked the medical examiner about it. The defense argues that the photographs had no probative value; the manner of the victim's death was not in issue and the photographs failed to show that the defendant's missing knife caused the wounds.

The trial judge originally allowed Exhibits 46 and 47 to be admitted for the purpose of showing the angles of the wounds. However, the prosecutor did not elicit testimony concerning these angles or their significance. Indeed, there was no testimony at trial rendering Exhibits 46 and 47 particularly meaningful. The photographs do not reveal what type of knife was used, nor did the prosecutor refer to them when examining witnesses regarding a possible murder weapon. Although the pictures met the bare minimum standard of relevance . . . they had little tendency to establish any disputed issue in the case. Accordingly, we are left to conclude that they were introduced primarily to inflame the jury.

Let us again make clear that not every relevant photograph is admissible. Trial courts have broad discretion in admitting photographs. However, judges also have an obligation to weigh the prejudice caused by a gruesome picture against its probative value. ARIZ. R. EVID. 403. In the present case, the record reflects that the trial judge conducted a Rule 403 weighing. In our view, however, he reached the wrong conclusion with regard to Exhibits 46 and 47. These two photos should not have been admitted....

[Having concluded that the trial court erred, the court then considered whether the error affected the jury's verdict:]

Here, the photographs of the corpse were startling, as evidenced by the jurors' visible reactions to them. In particular, two jurors showed physical signs of distress upon seeing Exhibits 42, 43, and 44, with one of them apparently trying to prevent herself from hyperventilating. The judge noted on the record that after seeing these reactions to the first group of photographs, he "watched [the jurors] closely as they passed around Forty-six and Forty-seven." His observation that "they seemed to take them in stride" is uncontroverted. Bocharski has not shown that Exhibits 46 and 47 had a particularly adverse effect on this jury....

... Nothing before us suggests that the jurors' thoughtful consideration of the evidence was hampered by the objectionable photographs. Their verdict reflects careful attention to detail. Indeed, they chose felony murder instead of premeditated murder—a distinction that might easily have been overlooked if the verdict had been attributable to outrage or emotion generated by the gruesome pictures.... Accordingly, we find ... that the error in admitting Exhibits 46 and 47 did not contribute to or affect the jury's verdict....

DISPOSITION

We affirm the defendant's convictions....

■ MARTONE, JUSTICE, concurring in the judgment. I join the court in affirming the convictions.... I write separately to express my disapproval of parts of the opinion.

I. PHOTOGRAPHS

Bocharski conceded the relevance of all the admitted photographs. The question then is simply whether the trial court abused its discretion in weighing probative value against prejudicial effect under Rule 403, Ariz. R. Evid. As evidenced by the majority's sua sponte speculation here, appellate courts are not in a very good position to second guess such judgments.... Murder is a grisly business and is likely to involve grisly photographs. Absent egregious error, we should not disturb Rule 403 weighing by the trial judge. There was no appeal to emotion, sympathy, or horror here.

One's view on the exclusion of otherwise relevant evidence is influenced by one's view of the jury system. I do not believe that jurors need to be protected from themselves. In my experience, jurors quite properly separate the wheat from the chaff.... I do not believe that we should be paternalistic with our jurors. The trial court did not err in admitting any of the photographs....

■ McGREGOR, JUSTICE, specially concurring....

Problem 1.8
Photo of Guns

Consider these facts from *United States v. Hitt*, 981 F.2d 422 (9th Cir. 1992):

> Dale Lee Hitt was convicted of possessing an unregistered machine gun in violation of 26 U.S.C. § 5861(d). The government alleged he had altered a semiautomatic rifle so it would discharge more than one shot per trigger pull—the defining characteristic of a machine gun....
>
> The key question ... was whether the rifle would in fact rapid-fire. The government and Hitt each had their own experts test-fire it: In the government's test, the rifle did fire more than one shot per trigger pull, but when Hitt's expert (witnessed by two police officers) tested it, it didn't. Hitt's expert suggested the gun may have fired automatically in the government's test because of a malfunction, perhaps because the internal parts were dirty, worn or defective. In response, the government introduced a photograph of the rifle which, it argued, showed the rifle was neither dirty, worn nor defective.
>
> Unfortunately, the photograph showed nothing of the gun's interior. All the jury could see was the outside, and not very well at that, as the gun occupied only a small part of the 4″ × 6″ photograph. The rest was taken up by about a dozen other weapons—nine other guns, including three that looked like assault rifles, and several knives—all belonging to Hitt's housemate.

Was the photograph relevant? Should the trial court have admitted it over Hitt's objection?

This Tyco Videotape Has Been Edited for Content

Andrew Ross Sorkin

New York Times, Oct. 28, 2003, at C1

. . . The most salacious scenes in the video of L. Dennis Kozlowski's multimillion-dollar birthday party for his second wife, Karen, on the island of Sardinia were ordered cut yesterday from a version to be shown to jurors in the trial of Mr. Kozlowski, who is accused of helping loot Tyco International of $600 million.

Judge Michael J. Obus left on the cutting room floor scenes of the ice sculpture of Michelangelo's "David" urinating Stolichnaya vodka into crystal glasses and Mrs. Kozlowski's birthday cake in the shape of a woman's body with sparklers protruding from her breasts.

"While I am hesitant to make this trial any less entertaining than it already has been," Judge Obus said, he told both sides that he had to agree with Mr. Kozlowski's lawyers, who argued that the scenes could prejudice the jury. "Whether an ice sculpture was at this party couldn't matter less," Judge Obus said. The point, he said, is that "there is no doubt this was a lavish party."

Prosecutors contend that Mr. Kozlowksi, the former chairman and chief executive of Tyco, and Mark H. Swartz, the firm's chief financial officer, looted the company of $600 million by secretly making Tyco foot the bill for their expensive tastes.

The Roman Empire-themed birthday party—part of a six-day event that cost $2.1 million—may be the most vivid example of a list of high-price items that prosecutors contend Mr. Kozlowksi bought with money from Tyco, which picked up half the tab. . . . Mr. Kozlowski contends that the event was in large part a business function.

Prosecutors had planned to show an uncut version of the party videotape yesterday, but were blocked when the judge ordered that certain scenes be removed. The jury is scheduled to see the edited version today.

Among the other scenes that have been ordered deleted, described by Mr. Kozlowski's lawyer, include a guest "mooning the camera," a waitress feeding grapes to male guests and "dancers who may be viewed as somewhat erotic." Another scene in which Mrs. Kozlowksi is carried around by models dressed as gladiators was also cut. . . .

Commonwealth v. Serge

Supreme Court of Pennsylvania.
586 Pa. 671, *cert. denied*, 549 U.S. 920 (2006).

■ Madam Justice Newman. . . . On the morning of January 15, 2001, Michael Serge (Appellant) shot his wife, Jennifer Serge (Victim), three times, killing her inside their home in Scott Township, Lackawanna County. Appellant was arrested that morning and charged with one count of first-degree murder.

On June 18, 2001, prior to trial, the Commonwealth filed a Motion in limine, seeking to present the prosecution's theory of the fatal shooting through a computer-generated animation (CGA) based on both forensic and physical evidence.[1] On September 14, 2001, following an evidentiary hearing, the trial court granted the Commonwealth's Motion in limine provided that certain evidentiary foundations were established at trial. The trial court required the Commonwealth to authenticate the animation as both a fair and accurate depiction of expert reconstructive testimony and exclude any inflammatory features that may cause unfair prejudice. To safeguard against potential prejudice, the trial court required the pre-trial disclosure of the CGA.

At his jury trial held January 29, 2002, to February 12, 2002, Appellant alleged that he had acted in self-defense as his wife attacked him with a knife.... The Commonwealth countered ... that Appellant, a former Lieutenant of Detectives with the Scranton Police Department, "used his decades of experience as a police officer to tamper with the crime scene to stage a self-defense setting." In particular, the Commonwealth asserted that Appellant had moved his wife's body and strategically positioned her near a knife that he had placed on the floor, as depicted in the CGA.

On February 7, 2002, during its case-in-chief, the Commonwealth presented a CGA as demonstrative evidence to illustrate the expert opinions of its forensic pathologist, Gary W. Ross, M.D., and crime scene reconstructionist, Trooper Brad R. Beach. The CGA showed the theory of the Commonwealth based upon the forensic and physical evidence, of how Appellant shot his wife first in the lower back and then through the heart as she knelt on the living room floor of their home....

On February 12, 2002, the jury found Appellant guilty of first-degree murder and the trial court immediately sentenced him to life imprisonment.... [W]e granted allowance of appeal limited solely to the issue of whether the admission of the CGA depicting the Commonwealth's theory of the case was proper....

DISCUSSION

... [H]ad the Commonwealth's experts ... used traditional methods, they may have drawn chalk diagrams or sketches on a blackboard to help explain the basis for their opinions. Instead, they used a CGA to more concisely and more clearly present their opinion. The difference is

1. A CGA [consists of drawings] created by a computer that, when assembled frame by frame, produce the image of motion. The image is merely a graphic representation depicting the previously formed opinion of a witness or witnesses, in this case the Commonwealth experts.... Accordingly, a CGA is only as credible as the underlying testimony that it represents....

one of mode, not meaning. The law does not, and should not, prohibit proficient professional employment of new technology in the courtroom. This is, after all, the twenty-first century....

[D]espite the relative novelty of CGA evidence, the evaluation of its admissibility relates back to [the] longstanding evaluation of probative value versus prejudicial value.... [A] CGA should be deemed admissible as demonstrative evidence if it: (1) is ... a fair and accurate representation of the evidence it purports to portray; (2) is relevant pursuant to Pa. R. Evid. 401 and 402; and (3) has a probative value that is not outweighed by the danger of unfair prejudice pursuant to Pa. R. Evid. 403....

[C]onspicuously absent among the factors to be considered in determining the relevancy and prejudice of evidence is the potency of the evidence. Thus, although the use of illustrative demonstrative evidence by an expert, such as a CGA, may help explain his or her opinion and make the testimony more persuasive than it otherwise might have been, it is not proper grounds for excluding this relevant evidence....

Randy Matzkanin, the Director of Operations for 21st Century Forensic Animations, ... described the process employed in making the animation and testified that it was a strict depiction of the Commonwealth's forensic evidence and ... expert opinions provided by Trooper Beach and Dr. Ross.... [He] discussed both the computer software and hardware that created the three-dimensional CGA drawings.... Matzkanin ... specified that many changes were made to ensure that the CGA conformed to the opinions of Trooper Beach and Dr. Ross....

Appellant contends that the CGA was littered with choices unsupported by either the record or the opinions of Trooper Beach and Dr. Ross. These alleged liberties taken by the Commonwealth included ... depicting the victim as kneeling during one of the gun shots ... [and] the combat-style crouch by Appellant.... Matzkanin testified that the poses, although not guaranteed to be 100% accurate, were within the confines of the ... expert opinions of both Dr. Ross and Trooper Beach. Specifically, Dr. Ross testified that ... as a result of the first shot, the victim would have collapsed to the floor in a kneeling position.... [H]e was able to surmise that the victim was kneeling and facing Appellant because of an abrasion on her left cheek consistent with falling onto her eyeglasses from a distance of approximately eighteen to twenty-four inches....

As stated by the Superior Court, "The animation's relevance under Pa. R. Evid. 401 lay in its clear, concise, and accurate depiction of the Commonwealth's theory of the case, which included the rebuttal of Appellant's self-defense theory...." ... Accordingly, we must turn to the [question of unfair] prejudice....

[T]he content of the CGA was neither inflammatory nor unfairly prejudicial. Any prejudice ... resulted not from the on-screen depiction of the Commonwealth's theory, but rather [from] the reprehensible act of murder.... In particular, the CGA did not include: (1) sounds; (2) facial expressions; [or] (3) evocative or even life-like movements.... Instead, much like a two-dimensional hand drawing of bullet trajectories, the CGA merely highlighted the trajectory of the three bullets fired, concluding from ballistics and blood splatter that the body had been moved after the victim died as part of Appellant's attempt to stage his self-defense. The CGA was devoid of drama so as to prevent the jury from improperly relying on an emotional basis....

Within his argument concerning prejudice, Appellant ... additionally raises the issue that ... a CGA ... costs between $10,000 and $20,000 to make. He notes that his entire defense fund, provided by the Commonwealth due to his *in forma pauperis* status, was limited to $10,000.... Precedent exists concerning the admission of expert testimony that is beyond the means of an indigent defendant.... [I]n Ake v. Oklahoma, 470 U.S. 68, 70 (1985), the U.S. Supreme Court held "that when a capital defendant's mental health is at issue, 'the Constitution requires that an indigent defendant have access to the psychiatric examination and assistance necessary to prepare an effective defense.'" However, this Court [has] limited access to those funds to circumstances where the defendant's sanity at the time of the offense was a significant factor at trial.... [A] defendant does not have an absolute right to a court-appointed investigator based on *Ake*. "'Traditionally' the appointment of an investigator has been a matter vested in the discretion of the court." Commonwealth v. Bardo, 551 Pa. 140, 149, *cert. denied*, 525 U.S. 936 (1998).... Similarly, there can be no obligation to provide the defendant the finances necessary to create a CGA of his or her own.

Chief Justice Cappy's concurring Opinion accurately summarizes the ultimate concerns regarding the economic disparity between the Commonwealth and an indigent defendant. *See* Concurring Opinion (Cappy, C.J.) ("... This monetary disparity between the Commonwealth and defense in obtaining a CGA is a relevant factor when considering the prejudice to the defense.") Thus, we ultimately conclude that the relative monetary positions of the parties are relevant for the trial court to consider when ruling on whether or not to admit a CGA into evidence.... [T]he trial court sitting with all facts before it, including the monetary disparity of the parties, must determine if the potentially powerful effect of the CGA and the inability of a defendant to counter with his or her own CGA should lead to its preclusion....

It is argued that the uniquely dangerous aspect of a CGA is in its visual appeal to a jury resulting in an acceptance of the CGA as fact. However, ... the trial court safeguarded against ... potential prejudice by supplying a thorough and extensive cautionary instruction before playing the CGA ...:

> Members of the jury, parties in a case are permitted to use photographs, drawings and other exhibits to illustrate a point they are attempting to make in a case. This is what we refer to as demonstrative evidence . . . since it is offered merely to demonstrate or illustrate a point rather than as actual proof of that point.
>
> . . . You heard testimony from Dr. Gary Ross and Trooper Brad Beach that the computer-generated animation, which will now be shown to you, is a fair and accurate illustration of the opinions that they formed as to how this shooting allegedly occurred. . . .
>
> Please understand that what you are about to view is an animation. . . . You should not confuse art with reality and should not view the animation as a definitive recreation of the actual incident. The series of pictures which have been drawn by the computer and transferred onto the tape for your review are no different from a witness sketching a series of drawings on paper and then fanning those pages to portray moving images of his or her opinion.
>
> Remember, the demonstrative animation is only as good as the underlying testimony, data, assumptions, and opinions that serve as the basis for its images, and the computer maxim, "garbage in, garbage out," applies equally to computer animations. Like all other evidence in the case, you may accept it or reject it . . . in whole or in part. . . . Always bear in mind that the Commonwealth must still meet its burden of proving all of the elements of the offense charged beyond a reasonable doubt.

. . . [S]uch cautionary instructions limit the prejudice or confusion that could surround a CGA . . . by insisting that the jury not . . . mistake it for fact . . . [and] rely upon it [only] to the extent they credited the underlying testimony.

CONCLUSION

. . . [T]he admission of a CGA depicting the theory of the Commonwealth in this case was proper. Accordingly, we affirm the decision of the Superior Court. . . .

■ MR. CHIEF JUSTICE CAPPY. I join the majority opinion. . . . I agree with the majority that the admission of the CGA will be guided by the considerations that normally govern demonstrative evidence, including authentication, relevancy, and weighing the probative value versus the prejudicial impact of that evidence. In reviewing the probative/prejudice prong, I emphasize that the trial court needs to consider whether giving the defendant the opportunity to present his own CGA will mitigate the prejudicial impact of the evidence. . . . This monetary disparity between the Commonwealth and defense in obtaining a CGA is a relevant factor when considering the prejudice to the defense. . . .

■ MR. JUSTICE CASTILLE: I concur in the result.... As with all human endeavors, the process of creating a CGA offers an opportunity for coloring and manipulating the end-product.... In a case where both parties are well-funded, each will have the resources available to hire the computer professionals necessary to challenge the accuracy of a proffered CGA or to generate a competing animation. In contrast, in a criminal case involving an indigent defendant, the cost of assuring that the defense is able to adequately assess the accuracy of a Commonwealth CGA, or to produce a competing CGA of its own ..., would have to be borne by the state. If such funding is denied, the burden will fall upon appointed counsel to attempt to school himself in a field in which he most likely is not expert....

[G]iven the limited value of this sort of evidence, the wisest course for the trial judge might be to exclude such evidence entirely in those situations where the defense cannot secure an equivalent production....

■ MR. JUSTICE EAKIN. I concur with the result of the majority.... I write separately as I think the court's discussion of this irrelevant area [of finances] is dangerous.

Admissibility of evidence is not a function of finances of the parties. If one side chooses to develop evidence, of this or any type, its admissibility cannot rest on a determination of the relative resources of the other party. Relevance, not money, is what makes something admissible. If a defendant feels the need for unaffordable evidence, such as these animations, an expert, or testing of any kind, he has but to ask the court, which will determine the entitlement under existing principles. The remedy is not to ignore the rules of evidence or to preclude the other side from introducing relevant evidence. Suggesting that disparate resources can comprise a reason to exclude evidence presages the triumph of social sensitivity over legal reason....

UNITED STATES V. JAMES

169 F.3d 1210 (9th Cir. 1999) (en banc).

[For the facts and the majority ruling in this case, see the earlier excerpt at pages 29 to 32.]

■ KLEINFELD, CIRCUIT JUDGE, dissenting: ... Defense counsel had to deal with a problem regarding his self-defense theory. The daughter shot an unarmed man who was standing with his hands up, and she testified that she did not fear him. The mother gave her daughter a gun while the daughter was chasing the man. The mother's defense attorney dealt with the problem by reminding the jury that the mother was on trial, not the daughter, and the mother had to be judged by her state of mind, what she knew and thought, at the moment she gave her daughter the gun. The judge accordingly let in every bit of evidence with any bearing on what the mother knew at that moment. All he kept out was what the mother did not then know, that there were papers corroborating what the victim allegedly had said about the vicious things he had done. Because the mother had not known of the papers and had never seen them, the trial judge concluded that the papers could not have had any effect on her state of mind. That makes sense, and I do not think so sensible a decision can properly be characterized as an abuse of discretion.

The majority is correct, that the papers were nevertheless relevant in another sense. Evidence that the victim really had killed a man, and had stabbed another in the throat with a pen, made it more probable that the victim had told the mother that he had done these things. For that reason, it would not have been an abuse of discretion for a judge to have admitted the documents. But admissibility does not suffice to make exclusion an abuse of discretion.

There were good reasons to keep the documents out. The documents were somewhat remote corroboration, not direct evidence of anything relevant. They showed nothing directly about the mother's state of mind, because she had never seen them. And the risk of unfair prejudice to the prosecution was considerable. The victim was a bad man. Some people would say, in private and out of court, that "he deserved it," or "he needed killing." But no one says such things in a courtroom, because the law does not permit murder, even of very bad people.

The jury's questions—"did he really stab someone with a pen," "Are there police or court documents to prove this or is it 'brag?' "—may mean that the jury was asking the wrong question, whether the victim deserved to be shot. The majority says that the evidence went to the mother's credibility, not the victim's character. But the jury's questions suggest that jurors were wondering whether the victim really did what he claimed, as opposed to whether Ms. James believed him. And the trial judge who, unlike us, was there, may have seen that coming. Plenty of evidence lends itself both to permissible and impermissible uses, and trial judges have to weigh the risks as the trial proceeds.

I concede the possibility that the truth of what the victim allegedly had told the mother gave his remarks the "ring of truth," as the majority suggests. But this is pretty remote. This relevant purpose could be outweighed by the inappropriate purpose to which the jury might put the documents. The defendant was supposed to be on trial, not the victim.

A district judge is supposed to exclude evidence if its probative value "is substantially outweighed by the danger of unfair prejudice." Fed. R. Evid. 403 [unrestyled]. . . . Rule 403 does not limit "unfair prejudice" to one side. "Unfair prejudice" means, at its most serious, "an undue tendency to move the tribunal to decide on an improper basis, commonly, though not always, an emotional one." McCORMICK ON EVIDENCE § 185, at n.31 (2d ed. 1972); *see* FED. R. EVID. 403, 1972 Advisory Committee Note. While a defendant is fully entitled to prove self-defense, a defendant is not entitled to persuade a jury by evidence "justifying the deliberate destruction by private hands of a detested malefactor." 2 WIGMORE ON EVIDENCE § 246, at 57. . . .

. . . There is [a parallel between this case and] Cohn v. Papke, 655 F.2d 191 (9th Cir. 1981). A man who had been arrested for soliciting sex from male police officers brought a civil rights suit for police brutality. We held that the trial judge had abused his discretion by admitting the defendants' evidence that the man was homosexual, because the man's sexuality was of limited relevance, and the relevance was outweighed by the risk of unfair prejudice. . . .

United States v. Burks, 470 F.2d 432, 437 (D.C. Cir. 1972), [which held that evidence of the victim's past violent acts should have been admitted] . . ., strikes me as an anomaly not deserving to be followed decades later in another circuit. In *Burks*, the victim was late paying the defendant for a truck that he had bought. After they argued about it, the defendant went to a friend's house, got a gun, and came back and shot his debtor dead. *Burks* held that the killer was entitled to prove that the victim had killed his own six-year-old son some years earlier, in order to corroborate his self-defense claim that he was scared of the man. The possibility that a man would feel that he needed a gun to argue about a debt with a man who had beaten a six-year-old to death strikes me as pretty unlikely. The trial judge made a reasonable decision in *Burks* that the risk of unfair prejudice, because of any juror's natural feelings about a man who had beaten his six-year-old son to death, would outweigh the probative value toward showing which man started the deadly confrontation, and it is surprising that it was not affirmed.

The more typical result is the one that the Eighth Circuit reached in United States v. Driver, 945 F.2d 1410 (8th Cir. 1991). The defendant had shot a man in the head, and wanted to prove that the victim was being investigated for child abuse. He claimed that this evidence would help prove his self-defense theory. The Eighth Circuit of course held that the "evidence of the child abuse investigation involving the victim would have served merely to portray him as a bad person, deserving to be shot, but did not relate to Driver's claim of self-defense." *Id.* at 1416. We should follow *Driver*, not *Burks*.

We did not try Ms. James's case. When a trial judge makes a sensible decision to admit or exclude evidence, well within the range of what is ordinary, for a sensible reason, as the trial judge did in this case, we should let it alone. Ms. James got a fair trial.

Excerpts from the Ruling on the Fuhrman Tapes

N.Y. Times, Sept. 1, 1995, at A16

LOS ANGELES. Following are excerpts from the ruling yesterday by Judge Lance A. Ito of Superior Court allowing the jury in the O.J. Simpson murder trial to hear two examples of racial epithets by Detective Mark Fuhrman in conversations with Laura Hart McKinny but barring examples of Mr. Fuhrman's boasting of misconduct:

The Fuhrman tapes and transcripts raise a number of complex and compelling issues. This court's focus, however, is legally restricted to just two issues: 1) Is Orenthal James Simpson guilty of the murders of Ronald L. Goldman and Nicole Brown Simpson, and 2) How should these tapes impact upon the testimony by and about now retired Los Angeles Police Department Detective Mark Fuhrman.

A key part of the defense case is the allegation that Fuhrman, motivated by hatred of blacks/African Americans and interracial couples, transported a bloody leather glove from the Bundy crime scene to the defendant's Rockingham residence for the purpose of placing the blame upon the defendant for the savage murders of Ronald L. Goldman and Nicole Brown Simpson....

During the course of the presentation of the prosecution's case in chief, Fuhrman testified without objection that he had not used a particular racial epithet in the past 10 years....

On cross-examination the defense was allowed to question Fuhrman as to his biases against African Americans.

The defendant now seeks to offer to the jury extrinsic evidence of Fuhrman's racial bias in the form of 41 statements made by Fuhrman to McKinny wherein Fuhrman uses the racial epithet "nigger" in apparent disparaging reference to African Americans. The court has reviewed each of the 41 uses of the racial epithet in question either by reference to the transcript(s), audio tapes or both. The court finds that each involves Fuhrman's use of the subject racial epithet in a disparaging manner within the time frame posed by the cross-examination and in contradiction to his testimony before the jury. It is therefore relevant and admissible as impeachment....

Having found Fuhrman's use of the subject racial epithet to be relevant and admissible, the court must then analyze each usage under Evidence Code Section 352 [California's counterpart to Federal Rule 403]: "The court may exclude evidence if its probative value is substantially outweighed by the probability that its admission will (a) necessitate undue consumption of time or (b) create substantial danger of undue prejudice, of confusing the issues, or of misleading the jury." The specific racial epithet at issue is perhaps the single most insulting, inflammatory and provocative term in use in modern day America. The court's examination of these 41 uses reveals not only the racial epithet itself, but a context that only adds to the insulting and inflammatory nature....

The probative value of the evidence of Fuhrman's use of racial epithets comes from the fact that he has testified that he has not used the term in the last 10 years, thereby impacting his credibility. Because of Fuhrman's discovery of a bloody glove at the Rockingham residence and its scientific significance, he is a significant although not essential witness against the defendant. As such, the defendant is entitled to effectively cross-examine him. However, as noted above, the court retains some discretion in controlling the inquiry. The defense may present McKinny's testimony as follows: ... That ... between 1985 and 1986 Fuhrman used the term "nigger" in a disparaging manner 41 times [during tape-recorded conversations with McKinny].

The defense may play and display the following excerpts [from the tapes] as impeachment:

> 8: "We have no niggers where I grew up."
>
> 13: Q. "Why do they live in that area?"
>
> A. "That's where niggers live."
>
> ...

The court finds the probative value of the remaining examples to be substantially and overwhelmingly outweighed by the danger of undue prejudice....

2. Evidence of Flight

United States v. Myers

550 F.2d 1036 (5th Cir. 1977), *cert. denied*, 439 U.S. 847 (1978).

■ CLARK, CIRCUIT JUDGE.... On June 13, 1974, at approximately two o'clock in the afternoon, a branch of the First Federal Savings and Loan Association of Largo, located in Clearwater, Florida, was robbed by a lone gunman. He escaped with an estimated $1500. After changing cars at a nearby motel, the robber disappeared. There is no dispute about how the robbery was committed; the central issue in this case, despite two eyewitnesses and hundreds of still photographs taken by an automatic camera, is by whom. The government has proceeded on the theory that it was [Larry Allen] Myers who entered the bank brandishing a revolver, ordered a teller to place the contents of her cash drawer in a flimsy brown paper bag, and fled. Myers has steadfastly maintained that it was not.

... The government's task in prosecuting Myers on these charges was complicated when a friend of Myers' named Dennis Coffie, who bears a remarkable physical resemblance to Myers, pled guilty to having been the lone gunman in the Florida robbery.[2] . . . Myers has been tried twice. The first trial ended with the declaration of a mistrial after the jury announced its inability to reach a verdict. A fortnight later, a second jury found Myers guilty as charged. The district court sentenced him to ten years' imprisonment on February 17, 1976. . . .

FLIGHT INSTRUCTION

Myers . . . argues that the district court erred in instructing the jury concerning the proper use of evidence indicating that he fled from FBI agents on two occasions (one in Florida, the other in California) subsequent to the commission of the robbery. He does not ask us to approve or disapprove of the charge as an abstract statement of legal principles; instead he contends that the instruction should not have been given because there was insufficient evidence to support it. . . .

The . . . text of the challenged instruction is as follows:

> The intentional flight of a defendant immediately after the commission of a crime or after he is accused of a crime that has been committed is not, of course, sufficient evidence in itself to establish his guilt, but is a fact which, if proved, may be considered by the jury in the light of all other evidence in the case in determining . . . guilt or innocence[.] [W]hether or not evidence of flight shows a consciousness of guilt and the significance to be attached to any such evidence are matters exclusively within the province of the jury. In considering any evidence of flight, the jury should consider the motive which prompted it.

The only account of the circumstances surrounding the Florida incident was supplied by Debra Dunn, whose apartment Myers shared for three to four months preceding the robbery. She testified that during the weeks following the robbery Special Agents Shields and Miller of the FBI tried to contact Myers through her on several occasions, but he was not at home when they called. According to Dunn, the only reason Shields and Miller gave for wanting to contact Myers was to determine the whereabouts of Coffie. When she reported these attempts to Myers he indicated that he did not wish to speak with the agents.

Approximately three weeks after the robbery, Myers called Dunn on the telephone and asked her to bring some of his clothing to the Fashion Square Mall in Orlando, Florida. After she arrived at the shopping center she noticed Agents Shields and Miller in plain clothes waiting nearby. When they asked her whether she intended to meet Myers, she lied, but they guessed her true purpose. A few minutes later they spotted him some distance off, and after one of Dunn's daughters revealed Myers'

2. Coffie also pled guilty to charges that he committed an armed bank robbery in Warren, Pennsylvania, on July 29, 1974. Myers too, was indicted in connection with the Pennsylvania robbery. He pled not guilty, but was convicted on February 10, 1975.

identity, Agent Miller ran toward him without identifying himself in any way. Myers bolted into the shopping center and disappeared.

At some time during the three weeks following this incident, Myers left Florida and traveled to Pennsylvania. Although it is known that he was in Warren, Pennsylvania, on July 29, 1974, and . . . testimony indicates that he remained there for approximately two weeks, the date on which he left Florida cannot be determined from the record.

Special Agent Hanlon of the FBI testified at the second trial concerning the circumstances surrounding the arrest of Coffie and Myers in Laguna Beach, California, which occurred on August 12, 1974, approximately two months after the Florida robbery. The agents decided to close in while Coffie and Myers were riding a motorcycle. The sequence of events culminating in their arrest began when Special Agent Callie, who was approaching Coffie and Myers from the opposite direction in an unmarked car, suddenly crossed over into their lane of travel and drove straight at them. Coffie swerved but was unable to avoid a slight collision. The motorcycle came to a stop approximately one hundred feet past Callie's car. Immediately thereafter, Hanlon, who was not in uniform and had been following Coffie and Myers in another unmarked car, pulled up alongside the motorcycle. He testified that as he arrived Coffie moved "about three feet" to the front of the motorcycle and that Myers moved a similar distance to the rear. Hanlon then emerged from his car with his gun drawn, identified himself as an FBI agent, and informed Coffie and Myers that they were under arrest. He also testified that he believed that Coffie and Myers were beginning to flee at the time of his arrival "because they were—I would say approximately fifty feet from where they alighted and moving—one was moving in one direction and one was moving in the other direction and my own interpretation at this point would be that they were moving away from the bike."

On cross-examination the defense introduced portions of Hanlon's testimony from Myers' trial on the Pennsylvania charges which are inconsistent with the account of the arrest outlined above. During the Pennsylvania trial Hanlon had testified that when he arrived on the scene "Mr. Coffie was putting the stand down so that the bike wouldn't fall over." And when asked whether Coffie or Myers attempted to flee, he had responded: "I was not aware that anyone did."

The only other testimony concerning the circumstance of the arrest was furnished by Coffie. He merely stated that when he swerved to avoid the oncoming car he had no idea that it contained police or federal agents.

Analytically, flight is an admission by conduct. Its probative value as circumstantial evidence of guilt depends upon the degree of confidence with which four inferences can be drawn: (1) from the defendant's behavior to flight; (2) from flight to consciousness of guilt; (3) from consciousness of guilt to consciousness of guilt concerning the crime charged; and (4) from consciousness of guilt concerning the crime charged to actual guilt of the crime charged. The use of evidence of flight has been criticized on the grounds that the second and fourth inferences are not supported by common experience and it is widely acknowledged that evidence of flight or related conduct is "only marginally probative as to the ultimate issue of guilt or innocence." United States v. Robinson, 475 F.2d 376, 384 (D.C. Cir. 1973).

Nevertheless, in United States v. Ballard, 423 F.2d 127 (5th Cir. 1970), we stated: " 'It is today universally conceded that the fact of an accused's flight, escape from custody, resistance to arrest, concealment, assumption of a false name, and related conduct, are admissible as evidence of consciousness of guilt, and thus of guilt itself.' " *Id.* at 133 (quoting 2 J. WIGMORE, EVIDENCE § 276, at 111 (3d ed. 1940)).

Applying these principles to the California incident initially, it is apparent that the events do not support the first of the four inferences. The only evidence that Myers or Coffie attempted to flee from the arresting officers was furnished by Agent Hanlon. But Hanlon's testimony was inconclusive. He first stated that Myers and Coffie were three feet from the motorcycle; then that they were fifty feet from it. In addition, Hanlon's testimony below conflicted with statements he made at Myers' trial on the Pennsylvania charges. There he testified that neither Myers nor Coffie had attempted to flee. Indeed, it seems unlikely that they would get off of the motorcycle if their purpose was to avoid capture. For a jury to find that Myers fled from federal agents prior to his arrest in California would require conjecture and speculation. It was error to instruct the jury that they could infer consciousness of guilt from an alleged flight which was without support in the record.

The evidentiary basis for the instruction regarding the California incident is also deficient in another respect. Even assuming that Myers did attempt to flee, giving a flight instruction would still be improper because the third inference upon which the probative value of flight as circumstantial evidence of guilt depends, from consciousness of guilt to consciousness of guilt concerning the crime charged, cannot be drawn. Since it is known that Myers committed an armed bank robbery in Pennsylvania between the date on which the Florida robbery occurred and the date of his arrest in California, the hypothesis that he fled solely because he felt guilty about the Pennsylvania robbery cannot be ruled out. The theory under which evidence of flight is admitted presumes that consciousness of guilt concerning the Pennsylvania robbery could be a sufficient cause of flight. Without knowing whether Myers committed the Florida robbery it is impossible to say whether the California flight resulted from feelings of guilt attributable to the Florida and Pennsylvania robberies or from consciousness of guilt about the Pennsylvania robbery alone. Therefore, even if Myers did flee from the federal agents in California, no inference that he is guilty of the Florida robbery is possible, and it was error for this reason also to instruct the jury that they could draw such an inference. *Cf.* State v. Whitney, 43 Idaho 745 (1927) (attempted escape by prisoner awaiting trial for two [distinct] offenses not relevant to show that he is guilty of either).

Because of the inherent unreliability of evidence of flight, and the danger of prejudice its use may entail, a flight instruction is improper unless the evidence is sufficient to furnish reasonable support for all four of the necessary inferences. The evidence relating to the California incident did not meet that standard.[20]

Turning next to the Florida incident, the evidence, though somewhat stronger, was likewise insufficient to support the flight instruction given. The version of Myers' conduct in Florida most favorable to the prosecution's case is that federal agents were unable to contact him at his usual place of residence for three weeks after the robbery, that he had his girlfriend bring his clothing from her house to a rendezvous point in a shopping center, that he fled when an unidentified man ran toward him at the shopping center, and that he left the state between three and six weeks after the date of the robbery. . . . *Compare* United States v. Rowan, 518 F.2d 685, 691 (6th Cir. 1975) (flight instruction not improper where defendant left the community within 36 hours of the time at which the charged crime was committed) *with* United States v. White, 488 F.2d 660, 662 (8th Cir. 1973) (instruction improper where five months had elapsed between the date of the charged offense and the attempted arrest). . . . It is the instinctive or impulsive character of the defendant's behavior, like flinching, that indicates fear of apprehension and gives evidence of flight such trustworthiness as it possesses. The more remote in time the alleged flight is from the commission or accusation of an offense, the greater the likelihood that it resulted from something other than feelings of guilt concerning that offense. Under the evidence adduced it was error to instruct the jury that they could infer from the Florida incident that Myers committed the crime with which he is charged.

During oral argument, counsel for the government conceded that the evidence in this case was so evenly balanced that if the district court erred . . . , the error could not be viewed as harmless. . . . [I]t follows that judgment and conviction appealed from must be

Reversed.

UNITED STATES V. MYERS: *Afterthoughts*

The *Myers* court's sole explicit reference to Rule 403 appears in footnote 20: "The prejudicial effect of Hanlon's testimony so far out-

20. The prejudicial effect of Hanlon's testimony so far outweighs its probative value that it should not be admitted on retrial. *See* FED. R. EVID. 403.

weighs its probative value that it should not be admitted on retrial." Note that this invocation of Rule 403 omits the essential modifier "unfairly" before the words "prejudicial effect." That the prosecution's evidence may be prejudicial to the defendant is in itself no vice. Yet what was *unfairly* prejudicial about evidence of flight in this case?

At times the court suggests that evidence of flight was simply *weak*—that it was " 'only marginally probative as to the ultimate issue of guilt or innocence.' " (Page 61.) Evidence of Myers's alleged flight from agents in California was particularly weak: It was not clear Myers *did* flee, the court suggests, and if he did, it was not clear he fled because of the Florida robbery at issue in his trial.

There is however no rule against weak or ambiguous evidence. Rule 401 requires only minimal probative force. It is true that some relevant evidence may be so nearly pointless and so cumbersome to present that a court may exclude it under Rule 403 as time wasting. Typically, though, Rule 403 bars evidence because the risk of unfair prejudice substantially outweighs probative value. How does weak, ambiguous evidence of flight unfairly prejudice the defendant? After all, defense counsel typically can counter weak evidence either by offering contrary evidence or by exposing weaknesses to jurors in closing argument.

Several courts have suggested that the trouble with evidence of flight is that it often bears innocent interpretation. In a case you'll read shortly, District Judge Jack B. Weinstein wrote, "Because a person may leave a jurisdiction for any number of innocent reasons, courts are often reluctant to admit evidence of flight." *United States v. Jackson*, 405 F.Supp. 938, 944 (E.D.N.Y. 1975) (page 81). But why exclude evidence just because it may have an innocent explanation? As Maryland's highest court has observed, "Where the defendant possesses an innocent explanation that does not risk prejudicing the jury against him, it would be expected that the defendant would present his purported reasons for his flight to the jury." *Thompson v. State*, 393 Md. 291, 315 (2006).

With this conundrum in mind—what is the *unfairly* prejudicial nature of evidence of flight?—consider the next problem:

Problem 1.9
Fleeing Trouble I

Defendant Rex Dewayne Cutchall was charged with the 1989 murder of Cathern Young. Over the defendant's objection, the trial court permitted the prosecutor to offer evidence that the defendant had fled from the scene of the crime. When the defendant took the stand, his lawyer questioned him as follows:

Q: [*by defense counsel*]: Why did you just leave the Young household [after finding Cathern Young injured and apparently dead in the laundry room]?

A: [*by defendant*]: Because I was scared.

Q: Why, Rex, were you scared?

A: Because I was afraid I'd be arrested.

Q: Why?

A: Mainly because of my priors.

Q: By "priors" what do you mean?

A: Prior convictions I had.

Q: Did you go to prison before?

A: Yes, I had.

Q: When?

A: I went in '77, in December.

Q: What was that for?

A: Unarmed robbery.

Q: And how long did you stay in prison?

A: I was in prison for six years.

People v. Cutchall, 200 Mich. App. 396, 418–19 (1993).

Cutchall was convicted. As defense counsel on appeal, how would you articulate the unfair prejudice caused by the prosecution's evidence of flight? As prosecutor, how would you defend against the appeal?

Problem 1.10

Fleeing Trouble II

On February 3, 2003, Shante Powell was shot as she walked toward a convenience store in Chester, Pennsylvania. She told police that her attacker was Jamar Johnson. Weeks earlier, Powell had testified against Johnson's brother in a murder prosecution.

At about 8:00 p.m. on February 4, 2003, police spotted Johnson on the street. As officers walked toward him, he began to back away. When ordered to get on the ground, he "fled the scene and discarded a [small] jar before stopping three blocks away." The jar contained marijuana.

Johnson was charged with attempted murder and several other crimes related to Powell's shooting. At his trial and over his objection, the prosecution offered evidence of his flight as detailed above. Because Johnson was not charged with possession of the marijuana, prosecution witnesses did not mention the jar he discarded as he ran. Johnson was convicted of attempted murder and related crimes.

On appeal he "contend[ed] that the evidence of flight should not have been admitted because it forced him to present evidence of a bad act, namely, possession of marijuana, to rebut the inference that he fled out of a fear of apprehension for the shooting."

What are the strongest arguments in support of Johnson's claim? What are the prosecution's strongest rebuttals? Are Johnson's arguments for exclusion stronger or weaker than Cutchall's (the topic of the last problem)? *See Commonwealth v. Johnson*, 910 A.2d 60 (Pa. Super. 2006).

Problem 1.11
Staying Put

A local businessman stands charged with the murder of a young woman. For seven weeks before her body was found, her disappearance had been a matter of mystery and great concern about town. The local paper ran many stories on efforts to find her and reported the latest theories of her whereabouts. The paper repeated town gossip linking her and the defendant in a romantic affair and hinting that he was involved in her disappearance. Under pressure to find the woman, police officials publicized various investigative steps that focused on the defendant and his ties with the young woman and repeatedly interviewed him about the matter. Yet he was not arrested and charged until after her body was found.

At trial, the defendant seeks to offer evidence that even while suspicions of his guilt mounted—and despite ample cash reserves to fund a getaway—he made no attempt to flee the community. If the prosecutor objects, should the judge allow the evidence? What are the best arguments on both sides?

3. PROBABILITY EVIDENCE

PEOPLE v. COLLINS

Supreme Court of California.
68 Cal. 2d 319 (1968).

■ SULLIVAN, J. We deal here with the novel question whether evidence of mathematical probability has been properly introduced and used by the prosecution in a criminal case. While we discern no inherent incompatibility between the disciplines of law and mathematics and intend no general disapproval or disparagement of the latter as an auxiliary in the fact-finding processes of the former, we cannot uphold the technique employed in the instant case. As we explain in detail, the testimony as to mathematical probability infected the case with fatal error and distorted the jury's traditional role of determining guilt or innocence according to long-settled rules. Mathematics, a veritable sorcerer in our computerized society, while assisting the trier of fact in the search for truth, must not cast a spell over him. We conclude that on the record before us defendant should not have had his guilt determined by the odds and that he is entitled to a new trial. We reverse the judgment.

A jury found defendant Malcolm Ricardo Collins and his wife, defendant Janet Louise Collins, guilty of second-degree robbery. Malcolm appeals from the judgment of conviction. Janet has not appealed.[1]

On June 18, 1964, about 11:30 a.m. Mrs. Juanita Brooks, who had been shopping, was walking home along an alley in the San Pedro area of the City of Los Angeles. She was pulling behind her a wicker basket carryall containing groceries and had her purse on top of the packages. She was using a cane. As she stooped down to pick up an empty carton, she was suddenly pushed to the ground by a person whom she neither saw nor heard approach. She was stunned by the fall and felt some pain. She managed to look up and saw a young woman running from the scene. According to Mrs. Brooks the latter appeared to weigh about 145 pounds, was wearing "something dark," and had hair "between a dark blond and a light blond," but lighter than the color of defendant Janet Collins' hair as it appeared at trial. Immediately after the incident, Mrs. Brooks discovered that her purse, containing between $35 and $40 was missing.

About the same time as the robbery, John Bass, who lived on the street at the end of the alley, was in front of his house watering his lawn.

1. Hereafter, the term "defendant" is intended to apply only to Malcolm, but the term "defendants" to Malcolm and Janet.

His attention was attracted by "a lot of crying and screaming" coming from the alley. As he looked in that direction, he saw a woman run out of the alley and enter a yellow automobile parked across the street from him. He was unable to give the make of the car. The car started off immediately and pulled wide around another parked vehicle so that in the narrow street it passed within 6 feet of Bass. The latter then saw that it was being driven by a male Negro, wearing a mustache and beard. At the trial Bass identified defendant as the driver of the yellow automobile. However, an attempt was made to impeach his identification by his admission that at the preliminary hearing he testified to an uncertain identification at the police lineup shortly after the attack on Mrs. Brooks, when defendant was beardless.

In his testimony Bass described the woman who ran from the alley as a Caucasian, slightly over 5 feet tall, of ordinary build, with her hair in a dark blonde ponytail, and wearing dark clothing. He further testified that her ponytail was "just like" one which Janet had in a police photograph taken on June 22, 1964.*

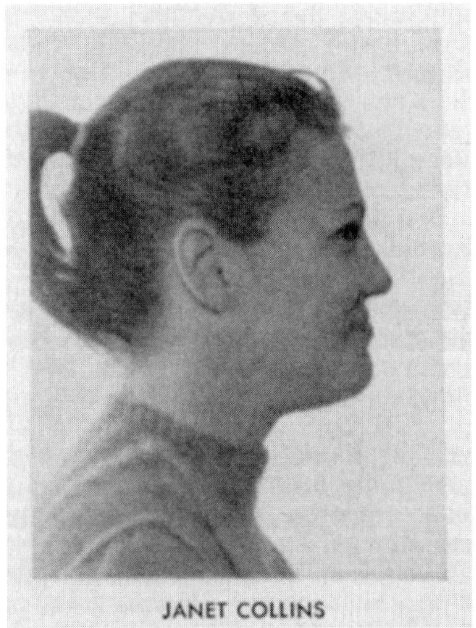

JANET COLLINS

WARD SHARRER

HUSBAND MALCOLM ON PRISON PROJECT

On the day of the robbery, Janet was employed as a housemaid in San Pedro. Her employer testified that she had arrived for work at 8:50 a.m. and that defendant had picked her up in a light yellow car[2] about 11:30 a.m. On that day, according to the witness, Janet was wearing her hair in a blonde ponytail but lighter in color than it appeared at trial.[3]

* [Photographs are reproduced from *Trial by Mathematics*, TIME, Apr. 26, 1968, at 41.—GF]

2. Other witnesses variously described the car as yellow, as yellow with an off-white top, and yellow with an egg-shell white top. The car was also described as being medium to large in size. Defendant drove a car at or near the times in question which was a Lincoln with a yellow body and a white top.

3. There are inferences which may be drawn from the evidence that Janet at-

There was evidence from which it could be inferred that defendants had ample time to drive from Janet's place of employment and participate in the robbery. Defendants testified, however, that they went directly from her employer's house to the home of friends, where they remained for several hours. . . .

At the seven-day trial the prosecution experienced some difficulty in establishing the identities of the perpetrators of the crime. The victim could not identify Janet and had never seen defendant. The identification by the witness Bass, who observed the girl run out of the alley and get into the automobile, was incomplete as to Janet and may have been weakened as to defendant. There was also evidence, introduced by the defense, that Janet had worn light-colored clothing on the day in question, but both the victim and Bass testified that the girl they observed had worn dark clothing.

In an apparent attempt to bolster the identifications, the prosecutor called an instructor of mathematics at a state college. Through this witness he sought to establish that, assuming the robbery was committed by a Caucasian woman with a blond ponytail who left the scene accompanied by a Negro with a beard and mustache, there was an overwhelming probability that the crime was committed by any couple answering such distinctive characteristics. The witness testified, in substance, to the "product rule," which states that the probability of the joint occurrence of a number of *mutually independent* events is equal to the product of the individual probabilities that each of the events will occur.[8] *Without presenting any statistical evidence whatsoever in support of the probabilities for the factors selected,* the prosecutor then proceeded to have the witness *assume*[9] probability factors for the various characteristics which he deemed to be shared by the guilty couple and all other couples answering to such distinctive characteristics.[10]

tempted to alter the appearance of her hair after June 18. Janet denies that she cut, colored or bleached her hair at any time after June 18, and a number of witnesses supported her testimony.

8. In the example employed for illustrative purposes at the trial, the probability of rolling one die and coming up with a "2" is 1/6, that is, any one of the six faces of a die has one chance in six of landing face up on any particular roll. The probability of rolling two "2's" in succession is 1/6 × 1/6, or 1/36, that is, on only one occasion out of 36 double rolls (or the roll of two dice), will the selected number land face up on each roll or die.

9. His argument to the jury was based on the same gratuitous assumptions or on similar assumptions which he invited the jury to make.

10. Although the prosecutor insisted that the factors he used were only for illustrative purposes—to demonstrate how the probability of the occurrence of mutually independent factors affected the probability that they would occur together—he nevertheless attempted to use factors which he personally related to the distinctive characteristics of defendants. In his argument to the jury he invited the jurors to apply their own factors, and asked defense counsel to suggest what the latter would deem as reasonable. The prosecutor himself proposed the individual probabilities set out in the table below. . . .:

Applying the product rule to his own factors the prosecutor arrived at a probability that there was but one chance in 12 million that any couple possessed the distinctive characteristics of the defendants. Accordingly, under this theory, it was to be inferred that there could be but one chance in 12 million that defendants were innocent and that another equally distinctive couple actually committed the robbery. Expanding on what he had thus purported to suggest as a hypothesis, the prosecutor offered the completely unfounded and improper testimonial assertion that, in his opinion, the factors he had assigned were "conservative estimates" and that, in reality, "the chances of anyone else besides these defendants being there, ... having every similarity, ... is something like one in a billion."

Objections were timely made to the mathematician's testimony on the grounds that it was immaterial, that it invaded the province of the jury, and that it was based on unfounded assumptions. The objections were "temporarily overruled" and the evidence admitted subject to a motion to strike. When that motion was made at the conclusion of the direct examination, the court denied it, stating that the testimony had been received only for the "purpose of illustrating the mathematical probabilities of various matters, the possibilities for them occurring or re-occurring."

Both defendants took the stand in their own behalf. They denied any knowledge of or participation in the crime and stated that after Malcolm called for Janet at her employer's house they went directly to a friend's house in Los Angeles where they remained for some time. According to this testimony defendants were not near the scene of the robbery when it occurred. Defendants' friend testified to a visit by them "in the middle of June" although she could not recall the precise date....

Defendant [claims] ... that the introduction of evidence pertaining to the mathematical theory of probability and the use of the same by the prosecution during the trial was error prejudicial to defendant....

As we shall explain, the prosecution's introduction and use of mathematical probability statistics injected two fundamental prejudicial errors into the case: (1) The testimony itself lacked an adequate foundation both in evidence and in statistical theory; and (2) the testimony and the manner in which the prosecution used it distracted the jury from its proper and requisite function of weighing the evidence on the issue of guilt, encouraged the jurors to rely upon an engaging but logically irrelevant expert demonstration, foreclosed the possibility of an effective defense by an attorney apparently unschooled in mathematical refine-

	Characteristic	**Individual Probability**
A.	Partly yellow automobile	1/10
B.	Man with mustache	1/4
C.	Girl with ponytail	1/10
D.	Girl with blond hair	1/3
E.	Negro man with beard	1/10
F.	Interracial couple in car	1/1000

ments, and placed the jurors and defense counsel at a disadvantage in sifting relevant fact from inapplicable theory.

We initially consider the defects in the testimony itself. As we have indicated, the specific technique presented through the mathematician's testimony and advanced by the prosecutor to measure the probabilities in question suffered from two basic and pervasive defects—an inadequate evidentiary foundation and an inadequate proof of statistical independence. First, as to the foundational requirement, we find the record devoid of any evidence relating to any of the six individual probability factors used by the prosecutor and ascribed by him to the six characteristics as we have set them out in footnote 10, *ante*. To put it another way, the prosecution produced no evidence whatsoever showing, or from which it could be in any way inferred, that only one out of every ten cars which might have been at the scene of the robbery was partly yellow, that only one out of every four men who might have been there wore a mustache, that only one out of every ten girls who might have been there wore a ponytail, or that any of the other individual probability factors listed were even roughly accurate.[12]

The bare, inescapable fact is that the prosecution made no attempt to offer any such evidence. Instead, ... having perfunctorily elicited from the witness the response that the latter could not assign a probability factor for the characteristics involved,[13] the prosecutor himself suggested what the various probabilities should be and these became the basis of the witness' testimony (see fn. 10, *ante*). It is a curious circumstance of this adventure in proof that the prosecutor not only made his own assertions of these factors in the hope that they were "conservative" but also in later argument to the jury invited the jurors to substitute their "estimates" should they wish to do so. We can hardly conceive of a more fatal gap in the prosecution's scheme of proof. A foundation for the admissibility of the witness' testimony was never even attempted to be laid, let alone established. His testimony was neither made to rest on his own testimonial knowledge nor presented by proper hypothetical questions based upon valid data in the record. *See* State v. Sneed, 76 N.M. 349 (1966). In the

12. We seriously doubt that such evidence could ever be compiled since no statistician could possibly determine after the fact which cars, or which individuals, "might" have been present at the scene of the robbery; certainly there is no reason to suppose that the human and automotive populations of San Pedro, California, include all potential culprits—or, conversely, that all members of these populations are proper candidates for inclusion. Thus the sample from which the relevant probabilities would have to be derived is itself undeterminable.

13. The prosecutor asked the mathematics instructor: "Now, let me see if you can be of some help to us with some independent factors, and you have some paper you may use. Your specialty does not equip you, I suppose, to give us some probability of such things as a yellow car as contrasted with any other kind of car, does it? ... I appreciate the fact that you can't assign a probability for a car being yellow as contrasted to some other car, can you? *A.* No, I couldn't."

Sneed case, the court reversed a conviction based on probabilistic evidence, stating: "We hold that mathematical odds are not admissible as evidence to identify a defendant in a criminal proceeding *so long as the odds are based on estimates, the validity of which have [sic] not been demonstrated.*" (Italics added.)

But, as we have indicated, there was another glaring defect in the prosecution's technique, namely an inadequate proof of the statistical independence of the six factors. No proof was presented that the characteristics selected were mutually independent, even though the witness himself acknowledged that such condition was essential to the proper application of the "product rule" or "multiplication rule." *See* Note, *Evidence: Admission of Mathematical Probability Statistics Held Erroneous for Want of Demonstration of Validity* (1967) DUKE L.J. 665, 669–70 n.25.[14] To the extent that the traits or characteristics were not mutually independent (e.g., Negroes with beards and men with mustaches obviously represent overlapping categories[15]), the "product rule" would inevitably yield a wholly erroneous and exaggerated result even if all of the individual components had been determined with precision.

In the instant case, therefore, because of the aforementioned two defects—the inadequate evidentiary foundation and the inadequate proof of statistical independence—the technique employed by the prosecutor could only lead to wild conjecture without demonstrated relevancy to the issues presented. It acquired no redeeming quality from the prosecutor's statement that it was being used only "for illustrative purposes" since, as we shall point out, the prosecutor's subsequent utilization of the mathematical testimony was not confined within such limits.

We now turn to the second fundamental error caused by the probability testimony. Quite apart from our foregoing objections to the specific technique employed by the prosecution to estimate the probability in question, we think that the entire enterprise upon which the prosecution embarked and which was directed to the objective of measuring the likelihood of a random couple possessing the characteristics allegedly distinguishing the robbers, was gravely misguided. At best, it

14. It is there stated that: "A trait is said to be independent of a second trait when the occurrence or nonoccurrence of one does not affect the probability of the occurrence of the other trait. The multiplication rule cannot be used without some degree of error where the traits are not independent."

15. Assuming *arguendo* that factors B and E (see fn. 10, *ante*), were correctly estimated, nevertheless it is still arguable that most Negro men with beards *also* have mustaches (exhibit 3 herein, for instance, shows defendant with both a mustache and a beard, indeed in a hirsute continuum); if so, there is no basis for multiplying 1/4 by 1/10 to estimate the proportion of Negroes who wear beards *and* mustaches. Again, the prosecution's technique could *never* be meaningfully applied, since its accurate use would call for information as to the degree of interdependence among the six individual factors. Such information cannot be compiled, however, since the relevant sample necessarily remains unknown.

might yield an estimate as to how infrequently bearded Negroes drive yellow cars in the company of blonde females with ponytails.

The prosecution's approach, however, could furnish the jury with absolutely no guidance on the crucial issue: *Of the admittedly few such couples, which one, if any, was guilty of committing this robbery*? Probability theory necessarily remains silent on that question, since no mathematical equation can prove beyond a reasonable doubt (1) that the guilty couple *in fact* possessed the characteristics described by the People's witnesses, or even (2) that only *one* couple possessing those distinctive characteristics could be found in the entire Los Angeles area.

As to the first inherent failing we observe that the prosecution's theory of probability rested on the assumption that the witnesses called by the People had conclusively established that the guilty couple possessed the precise characteristics relied upon by the prosecution. But no mathematical formula could ever establish beyond a reasonable doubt that the prosecution's witnesses correctly observed and accurately described the distinctive features which were employed to link defendants to the crime. Conceivably, for example, ... the driver of the car might have been wearing a false beard as a disguise; or the prosecution's witnesses might simply have been unreliable.[16]

The foregoing risks of error permeate the prosecution's circumstantial case. Traditionally, the jury weighs such risks in evaluating the credibility and probative value of trial testimony, but the likelihood of human error or of falsification obviously cannot be quantified; that likelihood must therefore be excluded from any effort to assign a *number* to the probability of guilt or innocence. Confronted with an equation which purports to yield a numerical index of probable guilt, few juries could resist the temptation to accord disproportionate weight to that index; only an exceptional juror, and indeed only a defense attorney schooled in mathematics, could successfully keep in mind the fact that the probability computed by the prosecution can represent, *at best*, the likelihood that a random couple would share the characteristics testified to by the People's witnesses—*not necessarily the characteristics of the actually guilty couple.*

As to the second inherent failing in the prosecution's approach, even assuming that the first failing could be discounted, the most a mathematical computation could *ever* yield would be a measure of the probability that a random couple would possess the distinctive features in question. In the present case, for example, the prosecution attempted to compute the probability that a random couple would include a bearded Negro, a

16. In the instant case, for instance, the victim could not state whether the girl had a ponytail, although the victim observed the girl as she ran away. The witness Bass, on the other hand, was sure that the girl whom he saw had a ponytail. The demonstration engaged in by the prosecutor also leaves no room for the possibility, although perhaps a small one, that the girl whom the victim and the witness observed was [not], in fact, the same girl.

blonde girl with a ponytail, and a partly yellow car; the prosecution urged that this probability was no more than one in 12 million. Even accepting this conclusion as arithmetically accurate, however, one still could not conclude that the Collinses were probably *the* guilty couple. On the contrary, as we explain in the Appendix, the prosecution's figures actually imply a likelihood of over 40 percent that the Collinses could be "duplicated" by at least *one other couple who might equally have committed the San Pedro robbery*. Urging that the Collinses be convicted on the basis of evidence which logically establishes no more than this seems as indefensible as arguing for the conviction of X on the ground that a witness saw either X or X's twin commit the crime.

Again, few defense attorneys, and certainly few jurors, could be expected to comprehend this basic flaw in the prosecution's analysis. Conceivably even the prosecutor erroneously believed that his equation established a high probability that *no* other bearded Negro in the Los Angeles area drove a yellow car accompanied by a ponytailed blonde. In any event, although his technique could demonstrate no such thing, he solemnly told the jury that he had supplied mathematical proof of guilt.

Sensing the novelty of that notion, the prosecutor told the jurors that the traditional idea of proof beyond a reasonable doubt represented "the most hackneyed, stereotyped, trite, misunderstood concept in criminal law." He sought to reconcile the jury to the risk that, under his "new math" approach to criminal jurisprudence, "on some rare occasion . . . an innocent person may be convicted." "Without taking that risk," the prosecution continued, "life would be intolerable . . . because . . . there would be immunity for the Collinses, for people who chose not to be employed to go down and push old ladies down and take their money and be immune because how could we ever be sure they are the ones who did it?"

In essence this argument of the prosecutor was calculated to persuade the jury to convict defendants whether or not they were convinced of their guilt to a moral certainty and beyond a reasonable doubt. Undoubtedly the jurors were unduly impressed by the mystique of the mathematical demonstration but were unable to assess its relevancy or value. Although we make no appraisal of the proper applications of mathematical techniques in the proof of facts, we have strong feelings that such applications, particularly in a criminal case, must be critically examined in view of the substantial unfairness to a defendant which may result from ill conceived techniques with which the trier of fact is not technically equipped to cope. We feel that the technique employed in the case before us falls into the latter category.

. . . [W]e think that under the circumstances the "trial by mathematics" so distorted the role of the jury and so disadvantaged counsel for the defense, as to constitute in itself a miscarriage of justice. . . . The judgment against defendant must therefore be reversed. . . .

APPENDIX

If "Pr" represents the probability that a certain distinctive combination of characteristics, hereinafter designated "C," will occur jointly in a random couple, then the probability that C will *not* occur in a random couple is (1–Pr). Applying the product rule (see fn. 8, *ante*), the probability that C will occur in *none* of N couples chosen at random is $(1–Pr)^N$, so that the probability of C occurring in *at least one* of N random couples is $[1–(1–Pr)^N]$.

Given a particular couple selected from a random set of N, the probability of C occurring in that couple (i.e., Pr), multiplied by the probability of C occurring in none of the remaining N–1 couples (i.e., $(1–Pr)^{N–1}$), yields the probability that C will occur in the selected couple and in no other. Thus the probability of C occurring in any particular couple, and in that couple alone, is $[(Pr) \times (1–Pr)^{N–1}]$. Since this is true for each of the N couples, the probability that C will occur in precisely *one* of the N couples, without regard to which one, is $[(Pr) \times (1–Pr)^{N–1}]$ added N times, because the probability of the occurrence of one of several *mutually exclusive* events is equal to the *sum* of the individual probabilities. Thus the probability of C occurring in *exactly one* of N random couples (*any* one, but *only* one) is $[(N) \times (Pr) \times (1–Pr)^{N–1}]$.

By subtracting the probability that C will occur in *exactly one* couple from the probability that C will occur in *at least one* couple, one obtains the probability that C will occur in *more than one* couple: $[1–(1–Pr)^N]–[(N) \times (Pr) \times (1–Pr)^{N–1}]$. Dividing this difference by the probability that C will occur in at least one couple (i.e., dividing the difference by $[1–(1–Pr)^N]$) then yields *the probability that C will occur more than once in a group of N couples in which C occurs at least once.*

Turning to the case in which C represents the characteristics which distinguish a bearded Negro accompanied by a ponytailed blonde in a yellow car, the prosecution sought to establish that the probability of C occurring in a random couple was 1/12,000,000—i.e., that Pr = 1/12,000,000. Treating this conclusion as accurate, it follows that, in a population of N random couples, the probability of C occurring *exactly once* is $[(N) \times (1/12{,}000{,}000) \times (1–1/12{,}000{,}000)^{N–1}]$. Subtracting this product from $[1–(1–1/12{,}000{,}000)^N]$, the probability of C occurring in *at least one* couple, and dividing the resulting difference by $[1–(1–1/12{,}000{,}000)^N]$, the probability that C will occur in at least one couple, yields the probability that C will occur more than once in a group of N random couples of which at least one couple (namely, the one seen by the witnesses) possesses characteristics C. In other words, the probability of *another* such couple in a population of N is the quotient A/B, where A designates the numerator $[1–(1–1/12{,}000{,}000)^N]–[(N) \times (1/12{,}000{,}000) \times (1–1/12{,}000{,}000)^{N–1}]$, and B designates the denominator $[1–(1–1/12{,}000{,}000)^N]$.

N, which represents the total number of all couples who might conceivably have been at the scene of the San Pedro robbery, is not determinable, a fact which suggests yet another basic difficulty with the use of probability theory in establishing identity. One of the imponderables in determining N may well be the number of N-type couples in which a single person may participate. Such considerations make it evident that N, in the area adjoining the robbery, is in excess of several million; as N assumes values of such magnitude, the quotient A/B computed as above, representing the probability of a second couple as distinctive as the one described by the prosecution's witnesses, soon exceeds 4/10. Indeed, as N approaches 12 million, this probability quotient rises to approximately 41 percent. We note parenthetically that if 1/N = Pr, then as N increases indefinitely, the quotient in question approaches a limit of (e–2)/(e–1), where "e" represents the transcendental number (approximately 2.71828) familiar in mathematics and physics.

Hence, even if we should accept the prosecution's figures without question, we would derive a probability of over 40 percent that the couple observed by the witnesses could be "duplicated" by at least one other equally distinctive interracial couple in the area, including a Negro with a beard and mustache, driving a partly yellow car in the company of a blonde with a ponytail. Thus the prosecution's computations, far from establishing beyond a reasonable doubt that the Collinses were the couple described by the prosecution's witnesses, imply a very substantial likelihood that the area contained *more than one* such couple, and that a couple *other* than the Collinses was the one observed at the scene of the robbery.

People v. Collins: *Historical Postscript*

"It is a curious circumstance of this adventure in proof," the *Collins* court wrote, that the prosecutor himself suggested probabilities for each of the characteristics that allegedly distinguished the Collinses as the guilty couple. "We can hardly conceive of a more fatal gap in the prosecution's scheme of proof."

How could the prosecutor have blundered so badly? Decades later, prosecutor Ray Sinetar is eager to explain. He was young then, just two years out of UCLA Law School and only nine months a deputy district attorney in Long Beach. His trial strategy in *Collins*, he says, was hardly the product of long deliberation.

One morning in November 1964 Sinetar was assigned a second-degree robbery trial set to begin that afternoon.[1] It was a simple purse-snatching—a straightforward but flawed case. Though the elderly victim

1. Ray Sinetar kindly supplied these and other details of his work on the *Collins* case in a telephone interview on June 30, 2005, and in later, follow-up interviews. Much of this historical postscript draws from George Fisher, *Green Felt Jungle: The Story of* People v. Collins, *in* Evidence Stories 7–27 (Richard Lempert ed., 2006).

was sure to win jurors' sympathy, Juanita Brooks could not identify Janet Collins as her attacker and never saw the yellow car or its driver. Her neighbor Mr. Bass identified Malcolm Collins in court as the getaway driver. But he had seen the driver only fleetingly as the yellow car rolled by—and Bass had been wearing his reading glasses.

As Sinetar lay in bed after the first day of testimony, he had the nagging sense he was not connecting with the jury. For him, what clinched the Collinses' guilt was the sheer unlikelihood that any other couple in the area of the robbery could match Brooks's and Bass's descriptions of the robbers and their car. After all, that's how the Collinses were caught. Shortly after the crime, Mrs. Brooks's son canvassed neighborhood gas stations asking attendants if they knew a matching couple. One replied, "Sure, they come in here for gas all the time." Police then followed the attendant's lead. Sinetar lay in bed wondering how he could get the jury to see what he and Mrs. Brooks's son saw so plainly—that the Collinses, even if not one of a kind, were of an exceedingly rare kind.[2]

Then Sinetar fixed on a strategy. There was a mathematician in his family—his brother-in-law Edward Thorp, whose popular 1962 book, *Beat the Dealer*, had taught blackjack sharps how to use the laws of probability to beat the house. Sinetar realized he could bring the principles of probability to bear on the Brooks robbery.[3]

Acting on that inspiration early the next morning, he called the math department at Cal State Long Beach, just across town from the courthouse. He left a message explaining he was mid-trial and needed a witness—a mathematician who specialized in probability. Then he set about collecting some figures to plug into the mathematician's theory. He strode down the hall to the secretaries' office and asked one office veteran her estimates: What were the odds that a randomly chosen car would be partly yellow? that a randomly chosen woman would be blond? that a randomly chosen couple would be mixed race? Other secretaries offered their views as Sinetar jotted notes. His survey complete, he made up a chart and headed to court.

Later that morning a casually dressed, bookish man appeared in the courtroom. At twenty-six, Assistant Professor Daniel Martinez was only two months into his teaching career at Cal State Long Beach. That morning he had arrived at work to learn that a local prosecutor had phoned for an expert in probability, a subject Martinez was teaching. "I

2. *See* Jerry Cohen, *Justice Invokes Science: Law of Probability Helps Convict Couple*, L.A. TIMES, Dec. 11, 1964, at 1; David McCord, *A Primer for the Nonmathematically Inclined on Mathematical Evidence in Criminal Cases:* People v. Collins *and Beyond*, 47 WASH. & L. L. REV. 741, 766–67 (1990) (reporting Sinetar's nighttime deliberations based on an earlier interview).

3. *See* EDWARD O. THORP, BEAT THE DEALER: A WINNING STRATEGY FOR THE GAME OF TWENTY-ONE (1962); Bob Schmidt, *Justice by Computer*, [Long Beach] INDEPENDENT-PRESS-TELEGRAM, Nov. 29, 1964, at A-1.

had a chance to perform a civic duty," he recalled decades later. "So I went right to court." But when he saw the crowded courtroom, he took pause. "I had an inkling that I was stepping into something I really shouldn't."[4]

Neither the Collinses' lawyer nor the jurors quite understood what happened next. The California Supreme Court was right to worry that defense counsel was "unschooled in mathematical refinements." Though attorney Don Ellertson objected valiantly as Sinetar and Martinez moved through their analysis, he didn't entirely understand it. "I was not a mathematician myself," he later confessed, "and I was a little bewildered...." One of the trial jurors made a similar confession: "I don't remember our discussing the professor much when we deliberated. Maybe we were overwhelmed by the numbers." Other jurors reported that they disregarded Martinez's testimony and found the Collinses guilty based on other witnesses' accounts.[5]

Though jurors perhaps ignored the probabilistic evidence, the press did not. Five days after the verdict, a local paper ran a story about the case under the headline, "Justice by Computer." It quoted a longtime prosecutor who felt "like the horse that just saw his first Ford." Two weeks later the story hit the front page of the *Los Angeles Times*. "Justice Invokes Science," the headline proclaimed, "Law of Probability Helps Convict Couple." Within a month the news went national. *Time* magazine heralded "a totally new test of circumstantial evidence." The Collinses were convicted, *Time* said, "because Prosecutor Ray Sinetar, 30, cannily invoked ... the laws of statistical probability."[6]

In time Sinetar would meet his undoing—and at the hands of a man even younger and less experienced. At age sixteen Laurence Tribe had entered Harvard as a math prodigy, finishing *summa cum laude* in algebraic topology. He enrolled in a doctoral program, but soon abandoned it for Harvard Law School. By the time Malcolm Collins's appeal reached the California Supreme Court in April 1967, Tribe was clerking for Justice Mathew Tobriner—and still only twenty-five years old.

Tribe saw in Collins's appeal the chance to express long-nagging concerns about courtroom misuse of mathematical evidence. He worried that the magic of math overwhelmed mushy but meaningful facts that resist quantification—and that by expressing guilt in quantifiable terms, prosecutors invited jurors to dismiss a certain probability of innocence as an acceptable risk of modern justice and crime control. Tribe revered the

4. The last several paragraphs draw from phone interviews with Sinetar on June 30, 2005, and with Professor Daniel Martinez on July 6, 2005.

5. Defense counsel Don Ellertson and I spoke on July 19, 2005. A trial juror (who asked not to be named) and I spoke on August 15, 2005. Reporter Bob Schmidt interviewed jurors shortly after the trial. *See* Schmidt, *supra* note 3.

6. Schmidt, *supra* note 3; Cohen, *supra* note 2; *Trials: The Laws of Probability*, Time, Jan. 8, 1965, at 42.

exacting standards of our criminal justice system, requiring proof beyond a reasonable doubt, for they advertised our insistence on *moral certainty*, the fullest proof human affairs allow. But Tribe had no need to rehearse his general misgivings about mathematical evidence in his memo to Justice Tobriner, for in Tribe's view, Sinetar had simply mangled the math. His memo spelled out for Tobriner the errors in Sinetar's probability-based argument—the same errors the California Supreme Court later condemned.[7]

In exposing Sinetar's gaffes, Tribe got little guidance from Collins's appellate counsel. True, attorney Rex DeGeorge rightly highlighted the risk of interdependence among various characteristics of the guilty couple. But DeGeorge's speculation about the nature of that interdependence was too goofy to copy:

> The Court is invited to take judicial notice of the following: . . .
>
> There is a dependency between blonds and intermarriage. Blonds and redheads tend to be more adventuresome, more daring, and more likely to choose to be [in a mixed marriage]. . . .
>
> There is a dependency between the way a woman would normally wear her hair and how she would fix it when she goes to carry on a robbery.

Petition for Hearing (Cal. Sup. Ct., 2d Cr. No. 10819 (Apr. 24, 1967)), at 21–22.

Tribe persuaded Justice Tobriner of the importance of declaring the non-probabilistic nature of the reasonable-doubt standard. Tobriner in turn persuaded Chief Justice Roger Traynor and Justice Raymond Sullivan, who was assigned to write the court's opinion. After Sullivan asked Tobriner's help in drafting the ruling, Tobriner recruited Tribe to keep a hand in the process even after he left to clerk for Justice Potter Stewart. The more mathematical parts of Justice Sullivan's opinion and particularly the mathematical appendix drew heavily from Tribe's work.

Malcolm Collins eventually walked free. After the high court reversed his conviction and the case was set for retrial, Sinetar confessed he could not regather his witnesses, and the trial court dismissed the case. Janet Collins had absconded from parole even as Malcolm's appeal wended its way through the system. Later she apparently was recaptured and returned to prison.

Outside the courtroom the *Collins* ruling sparked an academic firestorm. Threatened by the court's anti-math rhetoric, mathematicians and statisticians rushed to defend their disciplines. They insisted all proof is probabilistic, and we ought to be upfront about it and help jurors

7. Professor Tribe described his role in *Collins* in email correspondence with me on April 28, 2003, and February 15, 2004. My thanks to Professor Lewis Henry LaRue,

measure probabilities intelligently. Indeed only one academic voice spoke prominently and powerfully in the *Collins* court's defense. Under the title "Trial by Mathematics," borrowed from his own virtually ghostwritten opinion, Laurence Tribe rose to defend his unattributed work.[8] By then a young assistant professor at Harvard, he went largely unsuspected as counsel in his own defense.

Collins's *Legacy*

Despite the California court's memorable rhetoric, the enduring lesson of *Collins* is not that math always "cast[s] a spell" over the trier of fact. As the court wrote, math also can "assist[] the trier . . . in the search for truth." (Page 66.) In condemning math done badly, the justices did not reject the utility of math done well. Hence today we often hear prosecutors say that only one man in a billion—or trillion or quadrillion—matches the killer's and the defendant's genetic markers. Today DNA evidence counters any claim that *Collins* forever banished the sorcerer mathematics from criminal courtrooms.

For DNA analysis is fundamentally probabilistic. Aided by an expert, a prosecutor seeking to identify the source of blood found at a crime scene begins by listing *alleles*, shown by DNA analysis of the bloodstain to lie at specific chromosomal sites. Then the expert testifies that the defendant's DNA reveals those same alleles at the same sites. To each such match the expert assigns a probability. The expert then applies the product rule, multiplying the probability of each allelic match to arrive at a one-in-billions chance that a different person, randomly picked, would share all the same alleles.

The difference between DNA identification evidence and Sinetar's sorcerer math is not the mathematical principle, but the rigor of the math and the quality of the underlying data. Today's jurors may be no better schooled in math than those who judged Janet and Malcolm Collins. But because courts and scientists now are confident of the math and data behind DNA analysis, DNA test results typically prove admissible, however magical they may seem. Not long back the California Supreme Court approved a DNA analysis showing that the probability that a random person other than the defendant could be the source of crime-scene evidence was one in 930 sextillion. *See People v. Nelson*, 185 P.3d 49 (Cal.), *cert. denied*, 555 U.S. 926 (2008).

That is not to say such results are *right*. Just as Sinetar's witnesses could have erred in describing the guilty couple—they could have mistaken a false beard for a real one, as the *Collins* court suggested, or brown hair for dark blond—human error can distort DNA analysis. Careless or corrupt police can contaminate crime scenes, and chemists can

who first suggested to me Professor Tribe's possible involvement in *Collins*.

8. *See* Laurence H. Tribe, *Trial by Mathematics: Precision and Ritual in the Legal Process*, 84 HARV. L. REV. 1329 (1971) (discussing *Collins* but not Tribe's role).

cross samples in the lab. Such risks of human fault or fraud, however, typically do not justify excluding DNA test results, for jurors understand the risks and can assess them.[9]

So it appears that the difference between casting a spell and casting a light turns on the soundness of the math, the accuracy of the underlying facts, and the ability of jurors to assess defects beyond the math. The lesson of *Collins* is that probabilistic evidence poses a risk of unfair prejudice when it is *wrong*—when it rests on either false data or mistaken mathematical principles—and when jurors and defense counsel can't spy those flaws.

---

4. EFFECT OF STIPULATIONS

UNITED STATES V. JACKSON

405 F. Supp. 938 (E.D.N.Y. 1975).

■ WEINSTEIN, DISTRICT JUDGE. Defendant, accused of robbing a bank at gunpoint, has made pretrial motions for [an advance ruling that] the evidence that he used a false name on being arrested in Georgia shortly after the robbery is inadmissible because its probative value is outweighed by the risk of unfair prejudice. The [motion is] granted on conditions designed to prevent the defendant from gaining any unfair advantage from exclusion. . . .

II. MOTION TO EXCLUDE BECAUSE OF PREJUDICE

. . . Defendant's motion raises a complex Rule 403 question, rich in factual nuances. The bank robbery took place on August 23, 1971. Defendant was arrested in Georgia on November 7, 1971, when a local policeman thought defendant and his passengers were acting suspiciously in an area where an armed robbery had just taken place. Stopped for a traffic check, defendant had no license but did have false identification. The defendant was arrested for driving without a license. Guns were found in the car. Subsequently, defendant escaped from the local jail.

Presence in another jurisdiction is arguably proof of flight resulting from consciousness of guilt. Use of a false name increases the probative force of this circumstantial line of proof.

9. *See, e.g.,* Dale A. Nance & Scott B. Morris, *Juror Understanding of DNA Evidence: An Empirical Assessment of Presentation Formats for Trace Evidence with a Relatively Small Random–Match Probability*, 34 J. LEG. STUD. 395, 433 (2005) (showing that experimental jurors have fairly accurate intuitions about the likelihood of lab error).

Because a person may leave a jurisdiction for any number of innocent reasons, courts are often reluctant to admit evidence of flight. *See, e.g.*, Wong Sun v. United States, 371 U.S. 471, 483 n.10 (1963) ("[We] have consistently doubted the probative value in criminal trials of evidence that the accused fled the scene of an actual or supposed crime.").

The probability that defendant left New York to escape arrest for the bank robbery is somewhat reduced by the fact that at the time of his departure he had been indicted by the state for the assault which ultimately led to [a felony assault conviction]. It seems improbable, however, that if he were fleeing it was from the earlier assault since the indictment had been handed up in July 1971, and the evidence will apparently show that the defendant remained in New York until just after the bank robbery in August.

The probative value of defendant's conduct is heightened by the posture of the government's proof. It is apparent that the surveillance photographs and the eye-witness testimony are not likely to make out a completely positive identification of defendant. The government, therefore, has legitimate need for corroborative evidence. On balance, then, the Georgia events have significant probative value.

The other side of the coin under Rule 403 is the possibility that defendant will be unfairly prejudiced. The Georgia patrolman's testimony will acquaint the jury with the fact of defendant's unrelated arrest and surrounding uncomplimentary circumstances. This revelation will necessarily impinge on the protective policy of Rule 404(b) of the Federal Rules of Evidence which excludes other crimes when their primary use is to show generalized propensity to violate the law. Even if the fact that defendant and his companions were heavily armed and subsequently escaped from the local Georgia jail were concealed, the jury might well infer from the Georgia events that defendant was engaged in a nationwide crime spree. Beyond all this, the government's argument—flight, therefore guilty mind respecting the bank robbery, therefore guilt of that robbery—cannot be fairly evaluated without revelation of the state court indictment. This would acquaint the jury with the assault incident that resulted in a conviction....

In sum, the government's offer of proof entails the risk that unrelated crimes will be brought to the attention of the jury. At the very least, the jury might well be confused if it is called upon to resolve conflicting interpretations of what is essentially a collateral event. The question of whether the risk of inaccurate fact-finding by the jury will be increased more by reception than by exclusion of the evidence is thus a close one.

Still other considerations must be accorded some weight in determining admissibility under Rule 403. Among these is the delay in the completion of the trial which will necessarily be occasioned by the calling of at least one additional witness, the patrolman, who may be subjected to extended cross-examination. There is also a complex of issues respecting the legality of the Georgia arrest—though the court, after a preliminary hearing, has held the arrest valid and denied a motion to suppress on Constitutional grounds.

With the evidentiary and pertinent policy considerations in such an ambiguous posture, it is apparent that a ruling that the government's proof is either wholly admissible or wholly [in]admissible would not be completely satisfactory. Accordingly, we hold that the evidence relating to defendant's arrest in Georgia will be inadmissible at trial, provided that defendant enter into a stipulation to the effect that he was in Georgia shortly after the robbery and that while there he used a false name.

... [A] conditional ruling of this sort is justified by Rule 102 of the Federal Rules of Evidence. Rule 403, read in the light of Rule 102, contemplates a flexible scheme of discretionary judgments by trial courts designed to minimize the evidentiary costs of protecting parties from unfair prejudice. Conditioning exclusion of proof of the arrest upon the entry of a stipulation is a practical solution to that problem here. Elimination of all references to the Georgia apprehension effectively removes the risk that the jury will perceive the defendant as a national crime figure. At the same time, the stipulation will afford the jury a concrete basis for the inference that defendant left New York to escape capture for the bank robbery. Any remaining ambiguity may be intelligently evaluated by the jury in light of the other evidence....

There are, of course, dangers when a trial is so hedged with restrictions and somewhat misleading presentations to the jury. Witnesses, counsel and the court have to be wary lest some forbidden fact slip out. The jurors, who tend to be extremely sensitive to courtroom nuances, may get the impression—wholly accurate in most cases—that they are not getting the entire story and they may let their imaginations fill in the gaps to the prejudice of one side or another. Moreover, it is disquieting to be trying a carefully constructed and sanitized version of life—a kind of two dimensional cartoon rendition of the three dimensional world. But trials are not designed to get at the total truth in all its mystery; they only allow decision of narrow issues of fact and law within the limitations of a moderately effective litigation system. Given those limits, the conditions imposed in this case are justifiable....

OLD CHIEF v. UNITED STATES

519 U.S. 172 (1997).

■ JUSTICE SOUTER delivered the opinion of the Court. Subject to certain limitations, 18 U.S.C. § 922(g)(1) prohibits possession of a firearm by anyone with a prior felony conviction, which the government can prove by introducing a record of judgment or similar evidence identifying the previous offense. Fearing prejudice if the jury learns the nature of the earlier crime, defendants sometimes seek to avoid such an informative disclosure by offering to concede the fact of the prior conviction. The issue here is whether a district court abuses its discretion if it spurns such an offer and admits the full record of a prior judgment, when the name or nature of the prior offense raises the risk of a verdict tainted by improper considerations, and when the purpose of the evidence is solely to prove the element of prior conviction. We hold that it does.

I

In 1993, petitioner, Old Chief, was arrested after a fracas involving at least one gunshot. The ensuing federal charges included not only assault with a dangerous weapon and using a firearm in relation to a crime of violence but [also] violation of 18 U.S.C. § 922(g)(1). This statute makes it unlawful for anyone "who has been convicted in any court of[] a crime punishable by imprisonment for a term exceeding one year" to "possess in or affecting commerce, any firearm. . . ." . . .

The earlier crime charged in the indictment against Old Chief was assault causing serious bodily injury. Before trial, he moved for an order requiring the Government "to refrain from . . . offering into evidence or soliciting any testimony from any witness regarding the prior criminal convictions of the Defendant, *except* to state that the Defendant has been convicted of a crime punishable by imprisonment exceeding one (1) year." He said that revealing the name and nature of his prior assault conviction would unfairly tax the jury's capacity to hold the Government to its burden of proof beyond a reasonable doubt on current charges of assault, possession, and violence with a firearm, and he offered to "solve the problem here by stipulating, agreeing and requesting the Court to instruct the jury that he has been convicted of a crime punishable by imprisonment exceeding one (1) year[]." He argued that the offer to stipulate to the fact of the prior conviction rendered evidence of the name and nature of the offense inadmissible under Rule 403 of the Federal Rules of Evidence, the danger being that unfair prejudice from that evidence would substantially outweigh its probative value. He also proposed this jury instruction: . . .

> "[I] hereby instruct you that Defendant JOHNNY LYNN OLD CHIEF has been convicted of a crime punishable by imprisonment for a term exceeding one year."

The Assistant United States Attorney refused to join in a stipulation, insisting on his right to prove his case his own way, and the District Court agreed, ruling orally that, "If he doesn't want to stipulate, he doesn't have to." At trial, over renewed objection, the Government introduced the order of judgment and commitment for Old Chief's prior conviction. This document disclosed that on December 18, 1988, he "did knowingly and unlawfully assault Rory Dean Fenner, said assault resulting in serious bodily injury," for which Old Chief was sentenced to five years' imprisonment. The jury found Old Chief guilty on all counts, and he appealed.

The Ninth Circuit [affirmed].... We now reverse the judgment of the Ninth Circuit.

II

A

As a threshold matter, there is Old Chief's erroneous argument that the name of his prior offense as contained in the record of conviction is irrelevant to the prior-conviction element, and for that reason inadmissible under Rule 402 of the Federal Rules of Evidence. [Unrestyled] Rule 401 defines relevant evidence as having "any tendency to make the existence of any fact that is of consequence to the determination of the action more probable or less probable than it would be without the evidence." FED. R. EVID. 401 (unrestyled). To be sure, the fact that Old Chief's prior conviction was for assault resulting in serious bodily injury rather than, say, for theft was not itself an ultimate fact, as if the statute had specifically required proof of injurious assault. But its demonstration was a step on one evidentiary route to the ultimate fact, since it served to place Old Chief within a particular sub-class of offenders for whom firearms possession is outlawed by § 922(g)(1). A documentary record of the conviction for that named offense was thus relevant evidence in making Old Chief's § 922(g)(1) status more probable than it would have been without the evidence.

Nor was its evidentiary relevance under Rule 401 affected by the availability of alternative proofs of the element to which it went, such as an admission by Old Chief that he had been convicted of a crime "punishable by imprisonment for a term exceeding one year" within the meaning of the statute. The 1972 Advisory Committee Notes to Rule 401 make this point directly:

> "The fact to which the evidence is directed need not be in dispute. While situations will arise which call for the exclusion of evidence offered to prove a point conceded by the opponent, the ruling should be made on the basis of such considerations as waste of time and undue prejudice (see Rule 403), rather than under any general requirement that evidence is admissible only if directed to matters in dispute." Advisory Committee's Notes on FED. R. EVID. 401 [RB 38–39].

If, then, relevant evidence is inadmissible in the presence of other evidence related to it, its exclusion must rest not on the ground that the other evidence has rendered it "irrelevant," but on its character as unfairly prejudicial, cumulative or the like, its relevance notwithstanding.

B

* * *

1

The term "unfair prejudice," as to a criminal defendant, speaks to the capacity of some concededly relevant evidence to lure the factfinder into declaring guilt on a ground different from proof specific to the offense charged. So, the Committee Notes to Rule 403 explain, " 'Unfair prejudice' within its context means an undue tendency to suggest decision on an improper basis, commonly, though not necessarily, an emotional one." Advisory Committee's Notes on FED. R. EVID. 403 [RB 42].

Such improper grounds certainly include the one that Old Chief points to here: generalizing a defendant's earlier bad act into bad character and taking that as raising the odds that he did the later bad act now charged (or, worse, as calling for preventive conviction even if he should happen to be innocent momentarily). As then-Judge Breyer put it, "Although . . . 'propensity evidence' is relevant, the risk that a jury will convict for crimes other than those charged—or that, uncertain of guilt, it will convict anyway because a bad person deserves punishment—creates a prejudicial effect that outweighs ordinary relevance." United States v. Moccia, 681 F.2d 61, 63 (1st Cir. 1982). Justice Jackson described how the law has handled this risk:

> ". . . The state may not show defendant's prior trouble with the law, specific criminal acts, or ill name among his neighbors, even though such facts might logically be persuasive that he is by propensity a probable perpetrator of the crime. The inquiry is not rejected because character is irrelevant; on the contrary, it is said to weigh too much with the jury and to so overpersuade them as to prejudge one with a bad general record and deny him a fair opportunity to defend against a particular charge. The overriding policy of excluding such evidence, despite its admitted probative value, is the practical experience that its disallowance tends to prevent confusion of issues, unfair surprise and undue prejudice." Michelson v. United States, 335 U.S. 469, 475–76 (1948).

[Unrestyled] Rule of Evidence 404(b) reflects this common-law tradition by addressing propensity reasoning directly: "Evidence of other crimes, wrongs, or acts is not admissible to prove the character of a person in order to show action in conformity therewith." FED. R. EVID. 404(b) (unrestyled).* There is, accordingly, no question that propensity would be an "improper basis" for conviction and that evidence of a prior conviction is subject to analysis under Rule 403 for relative probative value and for prejudicial risk of misuse as propensity evidence. *Cf.* 1 J. STRONG, MCCORMICK ON EVIDENCE 780 (4th ed. 1992) (Rule 403 prejudice may occur, for

* [We will address Rule 404 in considerably more detail in Chapter 3.—GF]

example, when "evidence of convictions for prior, unrelated crimes may lead a juror to think that since the defendant already has a criminal record, an erroneous conviction would not be quite as serious as would otherwise be the case.").

As for the analytical method to be used in Rule 403 balancing, two basic possibilities present themselves. An item of evidence might be viewed as an island, with estimates of its own probative value and unfairly prejudicial risk the sole reference points in deciding whether the danger substantially outweighs the value and whether the evidence ought to be excluded. Or the question of admissibility might be seen as inviting further comparisons to take account of the full evidentiary context of the case as the court understands it when the ruling must be made. This second approach would start out like the first but be ready to go further. On objection, the court would decide whether a particular item of evidence raised a danger of unfair prejudice. If it did, the judge would go on to evaluate the degrees of probative value and unfair prejudice not only for the item in question but for any actually available substitutes as well. If an alternative were found to have substantially the same or greater probative value but a lower danger of unfair prejudice, sound judicial discretion would discount the value of the item first offered and exclude it if its discounted probative value were substantially outweighed by unfairly prejudicial risk. As we will explain later on, the judge would have to make these calculations with an appreciation of the offering party's need for evidentiary richness and narrative integrity in presenting a case, and the mere fact that two pieces of evidence might go to the same point would not, of course, necessarily mean that only one of them might come in. It would only mean that a judge applying Rule 403 could reasonably apply some discount to the probative value of an item of evidence when faced with less risky alternative proof going to the same point. Even under this second approach, as we explain below, a defendant's Rule 403 objection offering to concede a point generally cannot prevail over the Government's choice to offer evidence showing guilt and all the circumstances surrounding the offense.

The first understanding of the rule is open to a very telling objection. That reading would leave the party offering evidence with the option to structure a trial in whatever way would produce the maximum unfair prejudice consistent with relevance. He could choose the available alternative carrying the greatest threat of improper influence, despite the availability of less prejudicial but equally probative evidence. The worst he would have to fear would be a ruling sustaining a Rule 403 objection, and if that occurred, he could simply fall back to offering substitute evidence. This would be a strange rule. It would be very odd for the law of evidence to recognize the danger of unfair prejudice only to confer such a degree of autonomy on the party subject to temptation, and the Rules of Evidence are not so odd.

Rather, a reading of the companions to Rule 403, and of the commentaries that went with them to Congress, makes it clear that what counts as the Rule 403 "probative value" of an item of evidence, as distinct from its Rule 401 "relevance," may be calculated by comparing evidentiary alternatives. The Committee Notes to Rule 401 explicitly say that a party's concession is pertinent to the court's discretion to exclude evidence on the point conceded. Such a concession, according to the Notes, will sometimes "call for the exclusion of evidence offered to prove [the] point conceded by the opponent. . . ." Advisory Committee's Notes on FED. R. EVID. 401 [RB 38–39]. As already mentioned, the Notes make it clear that such rulings should be made not on the basis of Rule 401 relevance but on "such considerations as waste of time and undue prejudice (see Rule 403). . . ." *Ibid.* The Notes to Rule 403 then take up the point by stating that when a court considers "whether to exclude on grounds of unfair prejudice," the "availability of other means of proof may . . . be an appropriate factor." Advisory Committee's Notes on FED. R. EVID. 403 [RB 43]. The point gets a reprise in the Notes to Rule 404(b), dealing with admissibility when a given evidentiary item has the dual nature of legitimate evidence of an element and illegitimate evidence of character: "No mechanical solution is offered. The determination must be made whether the danger of undue prejudice outweighs the probative value of the evidence in view of the availability of other means of proof and other facts appropriate for making decision[s] of this kind under 403." Advisory Committee's Notes on FED. R. EVID. 404 [RB 47]. Thus the notes leave no question that when Rule 403 confers discretion by providing that evidence "may" be excluded, the discretionary judgment may be informed not only by assessing an evidentiary item's twin tendencies, but by placing the result of that assessment alongside similar assessments of evidentiary alternatives. *See* 1 MCCORMICK 782 & n.41 (suggesting that Rule 403's "probative value" signifies the "marginal probative value" of the evidence relative to the other evidence in the case); 22 C. WRIGHT & K. GRAHAM, FEDERAL PRACTICE AND PROCEDURE § 5250, at 546–47 (1978) ("The probative worth of any particular bit of evidence is obviously affected by the scarcity or abundance of other evidence on the same point.").

2

In dealing with the specific problem raised by § 922(g)(1) and its prior-conviction element, there can be no question that evidence of the name or nature of the prior offense generally carries a risk of unfair prejudice to the defendant. That risk will vary from case to case, for the reasons already given, but will be substantial whenever the official record offered by the Government would be arresting enough to lure a juror into a sequence of bad character reasoning. Where a prior conviction was for a gun crime or one similar to other charges in a pending case the risk of unfair prejudice would be especially obvious, and Old Chief sensibly worried that the prejudicial effect of his prior assault conviction, significant enough with respect to the current gun charges alone, would take on added weight from the related assault charge against him.

The District Court was also presented with alternative, relevant, admissible evidence of the prior conviction by Old Chief's offer to stipulate, evidence necessarily subject to the District Court's consideration on the motion to exclude the record offered by the Government. Although Old Chief's formal offer to stipulate was, strictly, to enter a formal agreement with the Government to be given to the jury, even without the Government's acceptance his proposal amounted to an offer to admit that the prior-conviction element was satisfied, and a defendant's admission is, of course, good evidence. *See* FED. R. EVID. 801(d)(2)(A).

Old Chief's proffered admission would, in fact, have been not merely relevant but seemingly conclusive evidence of the element. The statutory language in which the prior-conviction requirement is couched shows no congressional concern with the specific name or nature of the prior offense beyond what is necessary to place it within the broad category of qualifying felonies, and Old Chief clearly meant to admit that his felony did qualify, by stipulating "that the Government has proven one of the essential elements of the offense." As a consequence, although the name of the prior offense may have been technically relevant, it addressed no detail in the definition of the prior-conviction element that would not have been covered by the stipulation or admission. Logic, then, seems to side with Old Chief.

3

There is, however, one more question to be considered before deciding whether Old Chief's offer was to supply evidentiary value at least equivalent to what the Government's own evidence carried. In arguing that the stipulation or admission would not have carried equivalent value, the Government invokes the familiar, standard rule that the prosecution is entitled to prove its case by evidence of its own choice, or, more exactly, that a criminal defendant may not stipulate or admit his way out of the full evidentiary force of the case as the Government chooses to present it. The authority usually cited for this rule is Parr v. United States, 255 F.2d 86, 88 (5th Cir.), *cert. denied*, 358 U.S. 824 (1958), in which the Fifth Circuit explained that the "reason for the rule is to permit a party 'to present to the jury a picture of the events relied upon. To substitute for such a picture a naked admission might have the effect to rob the evidence of much of its fair and legitimate weight.' "

This is unquestionably true as a general matter. The "fair and legitimate weight" of conventional evidence showing individual thoughts and acts amounting to a crime reflects the fact that making a case with testimony and tangible things not only satisfies the formal definition of an offense, but tells a colorful story with descriptive richness. Unlike an abstract premise, whose force depends on going precisely to a particular step in a course of reasoning, a piece of evidence may address any number of separate elements, striking hard just because it shows so much at once; the account of a shooting that establishes capacity and causation may tell just as much about the triggerman's motive and intent. Evidence thus has force beyond any linear scheme of reasoning, and as its pieces come together a narrative gains momentum, with power not only to support conclusions but to sustain the willingness of jurors to draw the inferences, whatever they may be, necessary to reach an honest verdict. This persuasive power of the concrete and particular is often essential to the capacity of jurors to satisfy the obligations that the law places on them. Jury duty is usually unsought and sometimes resisted, and it may be as difficult for one juror suddenly to face the findings that can send another human being to prison, as it is for another to hold out conscientiously for acquittal. When a juror's duty does seem hard, the evidentiary account of what a defendant has thought and done can accomplish what no set of abstract statements ever could, not just to prove a fact but to establish its human significance, and so to implicate the law's moral underpinnings and a juror's obligation to sit in judgment. Thus, the prosecution may fairly seek to place its evidence before the jurors, as much to tell a story of guiltiness as to support an inference of guilt, to convince the jurors that a guilty verdict would be morally reasonable as much as to point to the discrete elements of a defendant's legal fault.

But there is something even more to the prosecution's interest in resisting efforts to replace the evidence of its choice with admissions and stipulations, for beyond the power of conventional evidence to support allegations and give life to the moral underpinnings of law's claims, there lies the need for evidence in all its particularity to satisfy the jurors' expectations about what proper proof should be. Some such demands they bring with them to the courthouse, assuming, for example, that a charge of using a firearm to commit an offense will be proven by introducing a gun in evidence. A prosecutor who fails to produce one, or some good reason for his failure, has something to be concerned about. "If [jurors'] expectations are not satisfied, triers of fact may penalize the party who disappoints them by drawing a negative inference against that party." Saltzburg, *A Special Aspect of Relevance: Countering Negative Inferences Associated with the Absence of Evidence*, 66 Calif. L. Rev. 1011, 1019 (1978) (footnotes omitted).[9] Expectations may also arise in jurors' minds simply from the experience of a trial itself. The use of witnesses to describe a train of events naturally related can raise the prospect of learning about every ingredient of that natural sequence the same way. If suddenly the prosecution presents some occurrence in the series differ-

9. *Cf.* Green, *"The Whole Truth?": How Rules of Evidence Make Lawyers Deceitful*, 25 Loyola (LA) L. Rev. 699, 703 (1992) ("Evidentiary rules . . . predicated in large measure on the law's distrust of juries [can] have the unintended, and perhaps ironic, result of encouraging the jury's distrust of lawyers. The rules do so by fostering the perception that lawyers are deliberately withholding evidence.").

ently, as by announcing a stipulation or admission, the effect may be like saying, "never mind what's behind the door," and jurors may well wonder what they are being kept from knowing. A party seemingly responsible for cloaking something has reason for apprehension, and the prosecution with its burden of proof may prudently demur at a defense request to interrupt the flow of evidence telling the story in the usual way.

In sum, the accepted rule that the prosecution is entitled to prove its case free from any defendant's option to stipulate the evidence away rests on good sense. A syllogism is not a story, and a naked proposition in a courtroom may be no match for the robust evidence that would be used to prove it. People who hear a story interrupted by gaps of abstraction may be puzzled at the missing chapters, and jurors asked to rest a momentous decision on the story's truth can feel put upon at being asked to take responsibility knowing that more could be said than they have heard. A convincing tale can be told with economy, but when economy becomes a break in the natural sequence of narrative evidence, an assurance that the missing link is really there is never more than second best.

4

This recognition that the prosecution with its burden of persuasion needs evidentiary depth to tell a continuous story has, however, virtually no application when the point at issue is a defendant's legal status, dependent on some judgment rendered wholly independently of the concrete events of later criminal behavior charged against him. As in this case, the choice of evidence for such an element is usually not between eventful narrative and abstract proposition, but between propositions of slightly varying abstraction, either a record saying that conviction for some crime occurred at a certain time or a statement admitting the same thing without naming the particular offense. The issue of substituting one statement for the other normally arises only when the record of conviction would not be admissible for any purpose beyond proving status, so that excluding it would not deprive the prosecution of evidence with multiple utility; if, indeed, there were a justification for receiving evidence of the nature of prior acts on some issue other than status (i.e., to prove "motive, opportunity, intent, preparation, plan, knowledge, identity, or absence of mistake or accident," FED. R. EVID. 404(b) [unrestyled]), Rule 404(b) guarantees the opportunity to seek its admission. Nor can it be argued that the events behind the prior conviction are proper nourishment for the jurors' sense of obligation to vindicate the public interest. The issue is not whether concrete details of the prior crime should come to the jurors' attention but whether the name or general character of that crime is to be disclosed. Congress, however, has made it plain that distinctions among generic felonies do not count for this purpose; the fact of the qualifying conviction is alone what matters under the statute. "A defendant falls within the category simply by virtue of past conviction for any [qualifying] crime ranging from possession of short lobsters to the most aggravated murder." United States v. Tavares, 21 F.3d 1, 4 (1st Cir. 1994). The most the jury needs to know is that the conviction admitted by the defendant falls within the class of crimes that Congress thought should bar a convict from possessing a gun, and this point may be made readily in a defendant's admission and underscored in the court's jury instructions. Finally, the most obvious reason that the general presumption that the prosecution may choose its evidence is so remote from application here is that proof of the defendant's status goes to an element entirely outside the natural sequence of what the defendant is charged with thinking and doing to commit the current offense. Proving status without telling exactly why that status was imposed leaves no gap in the story of a defendant's subsequent criminality, and its demonstration by stipulation or admission neither displaces a chapter from a continuous sequence of conventional evidence nor comes across as an officious substitution, to confuse or offend or provoke reproach.

Given these peculiarities of the element of felony-convict status and of admissions and the like when used to prove it, there is no cognizable difference between the evidentiary significance of an admission and of the legitimately probative component of the official record the prosecution would prefer to place in evidence. For purposes of the Rule 403 weighing of the probative against the prejudicial, the functions of the competing evidence are distinguishable only by the risk inherent in the one and wholly absent from the other. In this case, as in any other in which the prior conviction is for an offense likely to support conviction on some improper ground, the only reasonable conclusion was that the risk of unfair prejudice did substantially outweigh the discounted probative value of the record of conviction, and it was an abuse of discretion to admit the record when an admission was available.[10] What we have said shows why this will be the general rule when proof of convict status is at issue, just as the prosecutor's choice will generally survive a Rule 403 analysis when a defendant seeks to force the substitution of an admission for evidence creating a coherent narrative of his thoughts and actions in perpetrating the offense for which he is being tried.

10. There may be yet other means of proof besides a formal admission on the record that, with a proper objection, will obligate a district court to exclude evidence of the name of the offense. A redacted record of conviction is the one most frequently mentioned. Any alternative will, of course, require some jury instruction to explain it (just as it will require some discretion when the indictment is read). A redacted judgment in this case, for example, would presumably have revealed to the jury that Old Chief was previously convicted in federal court and sentenced to more than a year's imprisonment.... The Government might, indeed, propose such a redacted judgment for the trial court to weigh against a defendant's offer to admit, as indeed the government might do even if the defendant's admission had been received into evidence.

The judgment is reversed, and the case is remanded to the Ninth Circuit for further proceedings consistent with this opinion.

■ JUSTICE O'CONNOR, with whom THE CHIEF JUSTICE, JUSTICE SCALIA, and JUSTICE THOMAS join, dissenting. The Court today announces a rule that misapplies Federal Rule of Evidence 403 and upsets, without explanation, longstanding precedent regarding criminal prosecutions. I do not agree that the Government's introduction of evidence that reveals the name and basic nature of a defendant's prior felony conviction in a prosecution brought under 18 U.S.C. § 922(g)(1) "unfairly" prejudices the defendant within the meaning of Rule 403. Nor do I agree with the Court's newly minted rule that a defendant charged with violating § 922(g)(1) can force the Government to accept his concession to the prior conviction element of that offense, thereby precluding the Government from offering evidence on this point. I therefore dissent.

I

... Certainly, Rule 403 does not permit the court to exclude the Government's evidence simply because it may hurt the defendant. As a threshold matter, evidence is excludable only if it is "unfairly" prejudicial, in that it has "an undue tendency to suggest decision on an improper basis." Advisory Committee's Note on FED. R. EVID. 403; Dollar v. Long Mfg., N.C., Inc., 561 F.2d 613, 618 (5th Cir. 1977) ("Virtually all evidence is prejudicial or it isn't material. The prejudice must be 'unfair.' "), *cert. denied*, 435 U.S. 996 (1978). The evidence tendered by the Government in this case—the order reflecting petitioner's prior conviction and sentence for assault resulting in serious bodily injury—directly proved a necessary element of the § 922(g)(1) offense, that is, that petitioner had committed a crime covered by § 921(a)(20). Perhaps petitioner's case was damaged when the jury discovered that he previously had committed a felony and heard the name of his crime. But I cannot agree with the Court that it was *unfairly* prejudicial for the Government to establish an essential element of its case against petitioner with direct proof of his prior conviction....

... In the same vein, consider a murder case. Surely the Government can submit proof establishing the victim's identity, even though, strictly speaking, the jury has no "need" to know the victim's name, and even though the victim might be a particularly well loved public figure. The same logic should govern proof of the prior conviction element of the § 922(g)(1) offense. That is, the Government ought to be able to prove, with specific evidence, that petitioner committed a crime that came within § 922(g)(1)'s coverage.

The Court never explains precisely why it constitutes "unfair" prejudice for the Government to directly prove an essential element of the § 922(g)(1) offense with evidence that reveals the name or basic nature of the defendant's prior conviction. It simply notes that such evidence may lead a jury to conclude that the defendant has a propensity to commit crime, thereby raising the odds that the jury would find that he committed the crime with which he is currently charged....

Yes, to be sure, [unrestyled] Rule 404(b) provides that "evidence of other crimes, wrongs, or acts is not admissible to prove the character of a person in order to show action in conformity therewith." But ... [i]n a prosecution brought under § 922(g)(1), the Government does not submit evidence of a past crime to prove the defendant's bad character or to "show action in conformity therewith." It tenders the evidence as direct proof of a necessary element of the offense with which it has charged the defendant....

Any incremental harm resulting from proving the name or basic nature of the prior felony can be properly mitigated by limiting jury instructions. [Unrestyled] Federal Rule of Evidence 105 provides that when evidence is admissible for one purpose, but not another, "the court, upon request, shall restrict the evidence to its proper scope and instruct the jury accordingly." Indeed, on petitioner's own motion in this case, the District Court instructed the jury that it was not to " 'consider a prior conviction as evidence of guilt of the crime for which the defendant is now on trial.' " The jury is presumed to have followed this cautionary instruction, *see* Shannon v. United States, 512 U.S. 573 (1994), and the instruction offset whatever prejudice might have arisen from the introduction of petitioner's prior conviction.

II

The Court also holds that, if a defendant charged with violating § 922(g)(1) concedes his prior felony conviction, a district court abuses its discretion if it admits evidence of the defendant's prior crime that raises the risk of a verdict "tainted by improper considerations." Left unexplained is what, exactly, it was about the order introduced by the Government at trial that might cause a jury to decide the case improperly. The order offered into evidence (which the Court nowhere in its opinion sets out) stated, in relevant part:

> "And the defendant having been convicted on his plea of guilty of the offense charged in Count II of the indictment in the above-entitled cause, to-wit: That on or about the 18th day of December 1988, at Browning, in the State and District of Montana, ... JOHNNY LYNN OLD CHIEF ... did knowingly and unlawfully assault Rory Dean Fenner, said assault resulting in serious bodily injury, in violation of Title 18 U.S.C. §§ 1153 and 113(f)."

The order went on to say that petitioner was sentenced for a term of 60 months' imprisonment, to be followed by two years of supervised release.

Why, precisely, does the Court think that this item of evidence raises the risk of a verdict "tainted by improper considerations"? Is it because the jury might learn that petitioner assaulted someone and caused serious bodily injury? If this is what the Court means, would evidence that petitioner had committed some other felony be admissible, and if so, what sort of crime might that be? Or does the Court object to the order because it gave a few specifics about the assault, such as the date, the location, and the victim's name? Or perhaps the Court finds that introducing the order risks a verdict "tainted by improper considerations" simply because the § 922(g)(1) charge was joined with counts charging petitioner with using a firearm in relation to a crime of violence and with committing an assault with a dangerous weapon? Under the Court's nebulous standard for admission of prior felony evidence in a § 922(g)(1) prosecution, these are open questions.

More troubling still is the Court's retreat from the fundamental principle that in a criminal prosecution the Government may prove its case as it sees fit. The Court reasons that, in general, a defendant may not stipulate away an element of a charged offense because, in the usual case, "the prosecution with its burden of persuasion needs evidentiary depth to tell a continuous story." The rule has, however, "virtually no application when the point at issue is a defendant's legal status, dependent on some judgment rendered wholly independently of the concrete events of later criminal behavior charged against him." Thus, concludes the Court, there is no real difference between the "evidentiary significance" of a defendant's concession and that of the Government's proof of the prior felony with the order of conviction. Since the Government's method of proof was more prejudicial than petitioner's admission, it follows that the District Court should not have admitted the order reflecting his conviction when petitioner had conceded that element of the offense.

On its own terms, the argument does not hold together. A jury is as likely to be puzzled by the "missing chapter" resulting from a defendant's stipulation to his prior felony conviction as it would be by the defendant's conceding any other element of the crime. The jury may wonder why it has not been told the name of the crime, or it may question why the defendant's firearm possession was illegal, given the tradition of lawful gun ownership in this country....

III

... Like it or not, Congress chose to make a defendant's prior criminal conviction one of the two elements of the § 922(g)(1) offense. Moreover, crimes have names; a defendant is not convicted of some indeterminate, unspecified "crime." Nor do I think that Federal Rule of Evidence 403 can be read to obviate the well accepted principle, grounded in both the Constitution and in our precedent, that the Government may not be forced to accept a defendant's concession to an element of a charged offense as proof of that element. I respectfully dissent.

CHAPTER 2

THE SPECIALIZED RELEVANCE RULES

Rules 407 through 411 stand in a class of their own. Each applies only in narrow circumstances. Yet in terms of concept, structure, and rationales, they share much in common.

Each of these five rules reflects the rule writers' judgment that, as a matter of law, the evidence it governs fails a Rule 403 weighing test. *See* MUELLER & KIRKPATRICK, EVIDENCE § 4.11, at 186 n.8 (5th ed. 2012). Take a brief look at perhaps the clearest example, Rule 411. That rule declares that evidence of a party's liability insurance is not admissible to show "the person acted negligently or otherwise wrongfully." In the typical case the rule makes simple good sense. After all, how can a party's being insured (or not) bear on her negligence? Do we really think an insured motorist is (much) more likely to drive carelessly than an uninsured motorist? And as difficult as it is to see the probativeness of insurance in the typical case, it is easy to see how evidence of insurance could risk unfair prejudice. Jurors naturally might impose damages on the party who can best afford them, regardless of fault.

Like Rule 411, each of these rules concerns evidence of rather low probative power. Not all, however, address evidence posing such obvious risks of unfair prejudice. Rule 409, for example, excludes evidence of a person's promise to pay medical expenses if offered to prove liability for the underlying injury. Such a promise supplies weak evidence of fault. As the advisory committee suggests, "'humane impulses'" rather than a guilty conscience may be at work. (RB 67.) Yet it is hard to spot the source of unfair prejudice in admitting such offers to pay. The exclusionary principle of Rule 409 may spring instead from certain public-policy goals. By excluding evidence of offers to pay medical expenses, we may encourage people to make such offers. Moreover, we avoid the unseemly spectacle of punishing parties for their humanity. All five of these rules serve similar public-policy concerns. The chart on page 97 explores the dual rationales lying behind each rule—rationales based on the balance between probativeness and unfair prejudice and those rooted in public policy.

Most of these rules share a common structure. The chart on the next page explores their text and form. Note that Rules 407, 408, 409, and 411 all prohibit *only certain uses* of the evidence they govern, while permitting

SPECIALIZED RELEVANCE RULES: *Analytical Charts*

THE TEXT OF THE RULES

FRE 407 *Subsequent Remedies*

BARS **subsequent remedial measures** TO PROVE negligence, culpable conduct, product defect, or need for warning	BUT MAY BE ADMITTED for another purpose "SUCH AS" impeachment or, *if disputed*, proving ownership, control, or feasibility

FRE 408 *Compromise*

BARS **compromise / attempt to compromise** a *disputed claim* **and conduct / statements in negot'ns** TO PROVE validity or amount of the claim	BUT MAY BE ADMITTED for another purpose "SUCH AS" proving witness bias, lack of undue delay, or efforts to obstruct criminal investigation

FRE 409 *Medical Expenses*

BARS
offer or payment of medical costs
TO PROVE
liability

FRE 410 *Pleas*

BARS (against the defendant) (1) **guilty plea later withdrawn** (2) **nolo contendere plea** (3) **statements in plea proceedings** (4) **statements in plea talks *with prosecutor***	BUT MAY BE ADMITTED (i) to complete partial account of plea discussions or (ii) in a perjury prosecution if statement under oath, on record, and in counsel's presence

FRE 411 *Liability Insurance*

BARS **liability insurance or lack of it** TO PROVE negligence / wrongful action	BUT MAY BE ADMITTED for another purpose "SUCH AS" proving witness bias or agency, ownership, or control

RATIONALES **[RB = Rule Book]**

(1) = Rationale Based on Limited Probative Value or Risk of Unfair Prejudice
(2) = Rationale Based on Other Public Policy

<table>
<tr>
<td>

FRE 407 *Subsequent Remedies*

(1) Evidence of later remedy is often weak evidence of negligence. "[T]he rule rejects the notion that 'because the world gets wiser as it gets older, therefore it was foolish before.'" (ACN (quoting Bramwell), RB 57.)

BUT "the inference [of negligence] is . . . a possible one" because repair "tend[s] to show consciousness that the situation called for additional safety-precautions." (ACN, RB 57; MCCORMICK, EVIDENCE § 77 (1954).)

(2) To encourage remedies:

= the "more impressive" ground for exclusion. (ACN, RB 57.)

</td>
<td>

FRE 408 *Compromise*

(1) Compromise "may be motivated by a desire for peace rather than from any concession of weakness of position." (ACN, RB 60.)

This is especially true if the settlement amount is small.

[BUT *statements* made during negotiations may mean more.]

(2) To encourage compromise:

= the "more consistently impressive ground." (*Id.*)

FRE 409 *Medical Expenses*

(1) Offer is "'usually made from humane impulses.'" (ACN, RB 67.)

(2) Admitting evidence "'would tend to discourage assistance.'" (*Id.*)

</td>
</tr>
<tr>
<td>

FRE 410 *Pleas*

(1) A defendant, although not guilty, might offer a plea to avoid the risk of loss after trial and an even greater penalty. (Note the absence of any such argument in the Advisory Committee's Notes.)

(2) Exclusion promotes plea bargaining. (ACN, RB 70.)

</td>
<td>

FRE 411 *Liability Insurance*

(1) (a) It is unlikely that the insured are more careless or the uninsured more careful. (ACN, RB 78.)

(b) The jury might otherwise seek deep (insured) pockets or reduce recoveries to insured plaintiffs.

= the "[m]ore important" ground for exclusion. (*Id.*)

(2) Exclusion encourages insuring and avoids a windfall for the opponent of an insured party.

</td>
</tr>
</table>

SPECIALIZED RELEVANCE RULES

ROUTE OF ADMISSIBILITY

(Taking evidence of subsequent remedy as example.)

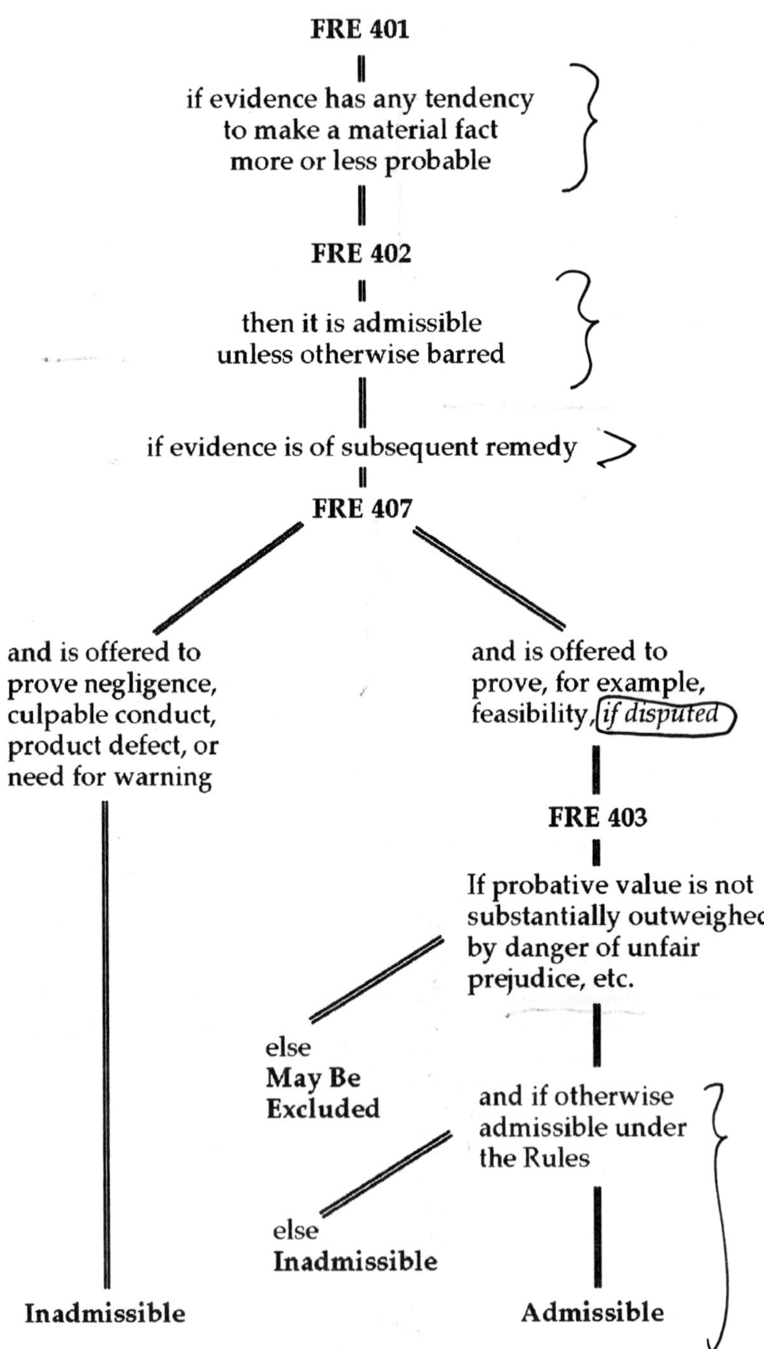
FRE 401
if evidence has any tendency to make a material fact more or less probable
FRE 402
then it is admissible unless otherwise barred
if evidence is of subsequent remedy
FRE 407
and is offered to prove negligence, culpable conduct, product defect, or need for warning
Inadmissible
and is offered to prove, for example, feasibility, if disputed
FRE 403
If probative value is not substantially outweighed by danger of unfair prejudice, etc.
else May Be Excluded
and if otherwise admissible under the Rules
else Inadmissible
Admissible

all other uses. On this score Rule 410 is a distinct outlier. That rule bars evidence of aborted pleas of guilty or no contest *for all purposes* and specifies only two narrow windows of admissibility. As you work through this chapter, consider why the rule writers imposed a stricter exclusionary regime on evidence of aborted pleas of guilty than on any other kind of evidence governed by these rules.

A. Subsequent Remedial Measures

Focus on FRE 407

Problem 2.1
Wolf Attack

Consider the facts of *Mahlandt v. Wild Canid Survival & Research Ctr., Inc.*, 588 F.2d 626, 628–29 (8th Cir. 1978):

> On March 23, 1973, Daniel Mahlandt, then 3 years, 10 months, and 8 days old, was sent by his mother to a neighbor's home on an adjoining street to get his older brother.... Daniel's path took him along a walkway adjacent to the Poos' residence. Next to the walkway was a five foot chain link fence to which Sophie had been chained with a six foot chain. In other words, Sophie was free to move in a half circle having a six foot radius on the side of the fence opposite from Daniel.

> . . . Kenneth Poos, as Director of Education for the Wild Canid Survival and Research Center, Inc., had been keeping [the wolf] at his home. . . . Sophie was chained because the evening before she had jumped the fence and attacked a beagle who was running along the fence and yapping at her.
>
> A neighbor . . . heard a child's screams and went to his window, where he saw a boy lying on his back within the enclosure, with a wolf straddling him. The wolf's face was near Daniel's face. . . .
>
> [Hurt but alive,] Daniel had lacerations of the face, left thigh, left calf, and right thigh, and abrasions and bruises of the abdomen and chest. . . .

Assume both the beagle's owner and Daniel (through his parents) sue Kenneth Poos for damages caused by the wolf. And assume each plaintiff, at separate trials, attempts to introduce evidence that Poos chained the wolf after learning of Sophie's attack on the beagle. If Poos objects to admission of this evidence at both trials, how should each court rule? What policy benefits might justify the answers Rule 407 gives to this question?

TUER V. MCDONALD

Court of Appeals of Maryland.
347 Md. 507 (1997).

■ WILNER, J. This is a medical malpractice action filed by Mary Tuer, the surviving spouse and personal representative of her late husband, Eugene, arising from Eugene's death at St. Joseph's Hospital on November 3, 1992. . . . [W]e are concerned here only with the action against Mr. Tuer's two cardiac surgeons, Drs. McDonald and Brawley, and their professional association. A jury in the Circuit Court for Baltimore County returned a verdict for those defendants, the judgment on which was affirmed by the Court of Special Appeals. We granted certiorari to consider whether the trial court erred in excluding evidence that, after Mr. Tuer's death, the defendants changed the protocol regarding the administration of the drug Heparin to patients awaiting coronary artery bypass surgery. The court's ruling was based on Maryland Rule 5–407, which renders evidence of subsequent remedial measures inadmissible to prove negligence or culpable conduct. . . .

FACTUAL BACKGROUND

. . . Mr. Tuer, 63, had suffered from angina pectoris for about 16 years. In September 1992, his cardiologist, Dr. Louis Grenzer, recommended that he undergo coronary artery bypass graft (CABG) surgery and referred him to the defendants for that purpose. The surgery was initially scheduled for November 9, 1992. On October 30, however, Mr. Tuer was admitted to St. Joseph's Hospital after suffering chest pains the night before, and the operation was rescheduled for the morning of November 2.

After a second episode of chest pain following Mr. Tuer's admission, Dr. Grenzer prescribed . . . Heparin, an anti-coagulant, to help stabilize the angina. The Heparin was administered intravenously throughout the weekend, and . . . it achieved its purpose; there were no further incidents of chest pains or shortness of breath. The defendants assumed responsibility for Mr. Tuer on November 1. Dr. McDonald was to perform the operation, with Dr. Brawley assisting.

The operation was scheduled to begin between 8:00 and 9:00 a.m. on November 2. In accordance with the protocol then followed by the defendants and by St. Joseph's Hospital, an anesthesiologist caused the administration of Heparin to be discontinued at 5:30 that morning. That was done to allow the drug to metabolize so that Mr. Tuer would not have an anticoagulant in his blood when the surgery commenced.

Both Mr. Tuer and Dr. McDonald prepared for the 9:00 a.m. surgery. Shortly before the surgery was due to begin, however, Dr. McDonald was called to deal with an emergency involving another patient, whose condition was more critical than that of Mr. Tuer, and that required a three- to four-hour postponement of Mr. Tuer's operation. Mr. Tuer was taken to the coronary surgery unit (CSU) in the meanwhile, where he could be closely monitored. Dr. McDonald considered restarting the Heparin but decided not to do so.

Dr. McDonald next saw Mr. Tuer just after 1:00 p.m., when he was summoned to the CSU and found his patient short of breath and with arrhythmia and low blood pressure. Quickly thereafter, Mr. Tuer went into cardiac arrest. Appropriate resuscitation efforts, including some seven hours of surgery, were undertaken, and, although Mr. Tuer survived the operation, he died the next day. Following Mr. Tuer's death—apparently because of it—the defendants and St. Joseph's Hospital changed the protocol with respect to discontinuing Heparin for patients with unstable angina. Under the new protocol, Heparin is continued until the patient is taken into the operating room; had that protocol been in effect on November 2, 1992, the Heparin would not have been discontinued at 5:30 a.m., and no issue would have arisen as to restarting it. . . .

The admissibility of the change in protocol first came before the court through the defendants' motion *in limine* to exclude any reference to the change in practice. At a hearing on that motion, the plaintiff took alternative positions with respect to the admissibility of the evidence. First, she contended that, because the defendants were claiming that the protocol in place on November 2 was a correct one, consistent with the applicable standard of care, the new protocol was not really a remedial measure and, for that reason, did not fall under the Rule. The court rejected that approach, concluding that a defendant did not have to admit wrongdoing in order for a subsequent change to be regarded as remedial. The plaintiff has not pressed that argument in this appeal. She also asserted that the evidence would be admissible to show that restarting the Heparin was "feasible," to which the court responded that it would allow the evidence for that purpose if the feasibility of restarting the Heparin was denied by the defendants. The defendants made clear that they did not intend to assert that the new protocol was not feasible and that they had no problem with the plaintiff asking Dr. McDonald whether Heparin could have been restarted. The court granted the motion subject to revisiting it "because of the way the trial goes."

The Heparin issue first arose at trial when the plaintiff called Dr. McDonald as an adverse witness. In direct examination, Dr. McDonald stated that he approved discontinuation of the Heparin at 5:30 so that it would metabolize before the scheduled surgery. That decision, he said, was taken to minimize the risk attendant to an inadvertent puncture of the carotid artery by the anesthesiologist. . . . A puncture of the carotid artery, he said, could produce a serious bleeding problem, and it was for that reason that the protocol called for patients not to have an anticoagulant in their blood when the surgery commenced. . . .

[Dr. McDonald testified] that he had considered restarting the Heparin once the surgery was postponed and elected not to do so because he did not want the drug in Mr. Tuer's blood when the surgery commenced. [Plaintiff's counsel] asked whether it was "feasible to restart Heparin for Mr. Tuer after your decision to postpone the surgery," but the court sustained an objection to that question.* Counsel then inquired whether it was Dr. McDonald's contention "that it would have been *unsafe* to restart Mr. Tuer's Heparin after your decision to postpone his surgery," (emphasis added) to which the witness responded in the affirmative, for the reason already given.

With that answer, plaintiff urged that she was entitled to ask about the change in protocol for impeachment purposes—presumably to show that it is not unsafe to bring a patient into surgery with Heparin in his or her system. The court again rejected that argument, distinguishing between the situation presented, of the doctor changing his mind about the relative safety of the protocol, apparently as a result of the unfortunate death of Mr. Tuer, and the case of the doctor not really believing at the time that it would have been unsafe to restart the Heparin. The latter, the court concluded, would constitute grounds for impeachment, but not the former: "In order to impeach his opinion that it was unsafe on November the 1st, 1992, there need be evidence that he didn't think it was unsafe on November the 1st, 1992, not what he thought in January or February of 1993." . . .

The defendants produced three expert witnesses who supported Dr. McDonald's decision not to restart the Heparin. . . . They each opined that a reasonably competent cardiovascular surgeon would not have restarted the Heparin in anticipation of a three- to four-hour delay in the surgery. Dr. Fortuin, in particular, recounted what he regarded as "logistical" difficulties in recommencing the drug. He stated that, to get the benefit of the Heparin, a large dose would have had to be administered, which would take several hours to dissipate, and expressed concern over the "roller coaster" effect of stopping and starting the drug or not knowing when to stop it in order to allow the drug to metabolize prior to surgery. Seizing on the statement that it would be logistically difficult to have restarted the Heparin, the plaintiff inquired of Dr. Fortuin on cross-

* [One basis for this objection may have been that because *feasible*, as used in Rule 407, is a legal term of art, the question sought the witness's legal opinion. Also see note 10 at pages 108 to 109 below.—GF]

examination whether it would have been "feasible" to restart the drug, but the court, as it did when that question was put to Dr. McDonald, sustained an objection.

DISCUSSION

Prior to the adoption of Maryland Rule 5–407, Maryland followed the common law with respect to the admissibility of subsequent remedial measures. We first adopted that law principally as articulated by the Supreme Court in Columbia v. Hawthorne, 144 U.S. 202 (1892)—a pre-workers' compensation era negligence action by an employee against his employer for injuries sustained when a pulley fell on him. The employer, who lost in a territorial trial court, complained about the allowance of evidence regarding measures undertaken after the accident to make the pulley more secure.

The Supreme Court held that the evidence was inadmissible and reversed. The Court regarded it as "settled" that "the evidence is incompetent, because the taking of such precautions against the future is not to be construed as an admission of responsibility for the past, has no legitimate tendency to prove that the defendant had been negligent before the accident happened, and is calculated to distract the minds of the jury from the real issue, and to create a prejudice against the defendant." *Columbia*, 144 U.S. at 207. In this regard, the Court quoted with approval from Morse v. Minneapolis & St. Louis Railway Co., 30 Minn. 465, 468–69 (1883):

> "... A person may have exercised all the care which the law required, and yet, in the light of his new experience, after an unexpected accident has occurred, and as a measure of extreme caution, he may adopt additional safeguards. The more careful a person is, the more regard he has for the lives of others, the more likely he would be to do so; and it would seem unjust that he could not do so without being liable to have such acts construed as an admission of prior negligence. We think such a rule puts an unfair interpretation upon human conduct, and virtually holds out an inducement for continued negligence."

... The Federal Advisory Committee on Rules of Evidence, which drafted Fed. R. Evid. 407, offered two justifications for excluding evidence of subsequent remedial measures to prove culpability: first, that the subsequent conduct "is not in fact an admission, since the conduct is equally consistent with injury by mere accident or through contributory negligence," and second, the "social policy of encouraging people to take, or at least not discouraging them from taking, steps in furtherance of added safety." Although some commentators have since questioned the efficacy of the "social policy" argument, it was significant to the Advisory Committee and, together with the relevance argument, was sufficiently persuasive to cause the Federal rule to be proposed by the Supreme Court and adopted by Congress.[8] . . .

The plaintiff offers two grounds for the admissibility of the change in procedure adopted after her husband's death, both hinging on Dr. McDonald's testimony and that of his expert witnesses regarding the risk associated with taking patients into CABG surgery with Heparin in their blood. That testimony, she urges, effectively controverted the feasibility of protecting patients with Heparin until taken into the operating room, which she was then entitled to establish through evidence of the revised protocol. That evidence was also admissible, she claims, to impeach Dr. McDonald's statement that restarting the drug would have been "unsafe." Although these arguments overlap, we shall deal with them separately.

Feasibility

Rule 5–407 . . . exempts subsequent remedial measure evidence from the exclusionary provision of [the rule] when it is offered to prove feasibility, if feasibility has been controverted. That raises two questions: what is meant by "feasibility" and was feasibility, in fact, controverted? These two questions also tend to overlap and are often dealt with together; whether a defendant has controverted feasibility may well depend on how one defines the term.

The exception allowing subsequent conduct evidence to show feasibility has been a troublesome one, especially in negligence cases, for, as Judge Weinstein points out, "negligence and feasibility [are] often indistinct issues. The feasibility of a precaution may bear on whether the defendant was negligent not to have taken the precaution sooner." 2 WEINSTEIN'S FEDERAL EVIDENCE, § 407.04[3] (Matthew Bender 2d ed. 1997). The Court of Special Appeals noted that two seemingly divergent approaches have been taken in construing the feasibility exception. Some courts have construed the word narrowly, disallowing evidence of subsequent remedial measures under the feasibility exception unless the defendant has essentially contended that the measures were not physically,

8. Criticism of the "social policy" argument centers on the notion that an exclusionary rule is not necessary to impel corrective action—that a defendant who is able to do so would likely take corrective action even in the absence of such a rule. Professor Saltzburg offers a modified social policy argument in favor of the rule—that people who take post-accident safety measures are doing exactly what good citizens should do and that, so long as the relevance of those measures is not great, which he does not believe it is, courts should not sanction procedures which appear to punish praiseworthy behavior. LEMPERT & SALTZBURG, A MODERN APPROACH TO EVIDENCE 194 (2d ed. 1982). He and his co-authors Martin and Capra see far more force in the relevance basis of the rule, urging that "subsequent remedial measures are of marginal relevance in assessing the defendant's culpability or fault, and that this marginal relevance is almost always substantially outweighed by the risk of jury confusion created by the introduction of a subsequent remedial measure." 1 SALTZBURG, MARTIN & CAPRA, FEDERAL RULES OF EVIDENCE MANUAL 482 (6th ed. 1994). . . .

technologically, or economically possible under the circumstances then pertaining. Other courts have swept into the concept of feasibility a somewhat broader spectrum of motives and explanations for not having adopted the remedial measure earlier, the effect of which is to circumscribe the exclusionary provision.

Courts in the first camp have concluded that feasibility is not controverted—and thus subsequent remedial evidence is not admissible under the Rule—when a defendant contends that the design or practice complained of was chosen because of its perceived comparative advantage over the alternative design or practice; or when the defendant merely asserts that the instructions or warnings given with a product were acceptable or adequate and does not suggest that additional or different instructions or warnings could not have been given; or when the defendant urges that the alternative would not have been effective to prevent the kind of accident that occurred.

Courts announcing a more expansive view have concluded that "feasible" means more than that which is merely possible, but includes that which is capable of being utilized successfully. In Anderson v. Malloy, 700 F.2d 1208 (8th Cir. 1983), for example, a motel guest who was raped in her room and who sued the motel for failure to provide safe lodging, offered evidence that, after the event, the motel installed peepholes in the doors to the rooms. The appellate court held that the evidence was admissible in light of the defendant's testimony that it had considered installing peepholes earlier but decided not to do so because (1) there were already windows next to the solid door allowing a guest to look out, and (2) based on the advice of the local police chief, peepholes would give a false sense of security. Although the motel, for obvious reasons, never suggested that the installation of peepholes was not possible, the court, over a strident dissent, concluded that, by [implying] that the installation of peepholes would create a lesser level of security, the defendant had "controverted the feasibility of the installation of these devices." *See also* Kenny v. Southeastern Pennsylvania Transp., 581 F.2d 351, 356 (3d Cir. 1978) ("when the defendant opens up the issue by claiming that all reasonable care was being exercised at the time, then the plaintiff may attack that contention by showing later repairs which are inconsistent with it"); Reese v. Mercury Marine Div. of Brunswick Corp., 793 F.2d 1416 (5th Cir. 1986) (evidence of new warning in manufacturer's revised manual admissible in light of defense that such warning by manufacturer, as opposed to dealer, would not have been effective to alert ultimate customer to potential danger).

The apparent divergence indicated by these cases may, at least to some extent, be less of a doctrinal division than a recognition that the concept of practicability is implicit in the notion of feasibility and allows some leeway in the application of the rule. Part of the problem is that dictionaries, which are often resorted to by the courts, contain several definitions of the word "feasible." *Webster's New Universal Unabridged Dictionary* (2d ed. 1983), for example, contains three definitions: (1) "that may be done, performed, executed, or effected; practicable; possible"; (2) "likely; reasonable; probable; as, a feasible story"; (3) "that may be used or dealt with successfully; as, land feasible for cultivation." Each of those definitions embod[ies], to some extent, the concept of practicability. Some courts have tended to follow the first definition and have thus articulated the notion of feasibility in terms of that which physically, technologically, or economically is capable of being done; others, like the Eighth Circuit in *Anderson v. Malloy*, have latched on to the third definition, which brings more into play the concepts of value, effectiveness, and overall utility.

. . . As Saltzburg, Martin, and Capra point out, if a remedial measure has, in fact, been taken that could have been taken earlier, the defendant is not likely to claim that the measure was not possible or practicable, and, indeed, defendants often are willing to stipulate to feasibility in order to avoid having the subsequent remedial evidence admitted. 1 SALTZBURG, MARTIN & CAPRA, FEDERAL RULES OF EVIDENCE MANUAL 486 (6th ed. 1994). The issue arises when the defendant offers some other explanation for not putting the measure into effect sooner—often a judgment call as to comparative value or a trade-off between cost and benefit or between competing benefits—and the plaintiff characterizes that explanation as putting feasibility into issue. To the extent there can be said to be a doctrinal split among the courts, it seems to center on whether that kind of judgment call, which is modified later, suffices to allow the challenged evidence to be admitted.

That is essentially what occurred in this case. At no time did Dr. McDonald or any of his expert witnesses suggest that the Heparin could not have been restarted following the postponement of Mr. Tuer's surgery. Indeed, they indicated quite the opposite; Dr. McDonald, in fact, made clear that, had Mr. Tuer exhibited signs of renewed unstable angina, he would have restarted the Heparin. The only fair reading of his testimony and that of his supporting experts is that the protocol then in effect was the product of a professional judgment call that the risk to Mr. Tuer of having CABG surgery commence while there was a significant amount of Heparin in his blood outweighed the prospect of harm accruing from allowing him to remain Heparin-free for several hours.

Dr. McDonald's brief response to one question that, at the time, he regarded it as "unsafe" to restart the Heparin cannot be viewed in isolation but has to be read in the context of his whole testimony. Under any reasonable view of the meaning of feasibility, a flat assertion by a physician that the remedial measure was inappropriate because it was medically "unsafe" would ordinarily be tantamount to asserting that the measure was not feasible and would thus suffice to controvert the feasibility of the measure. In a medical context at least, feasibility has to include more than mere physical possibility; as we have so sadly learned from history, virtually anything can physically be done to the human body. The practice of medicine is quintessentially therapeutic in nature. Its purpose is to comfort and to heal, and a determination of whether a practice or procedure is feasible has to be viewed in that light. The assertion that a given course would be unsafe, in the sense that it would likely cause paramount harm to the patient, necessarily constitutes an assertion that the course would not be feasible. Dr. McDonald was not asserting, however, in any absolute sense, that restarting the Heparin would have been unsafe but only that, given the complications that could have arisen, and that, in other cases had arisen, from an inadvertent puncture of the carotid artery, weighed against Mr. Tuer's apparently stable condition at the time and the intensive monitoring he would receive during the waiting period, there was a relative safety risk that, at the time, he and the hospital believed was not worth taking. That does not, in our view, constitute an assertion that a restarting of the Heparin was not feasible. It was feasible but, in their view, not advisable.

Impeachment

The exception in the Rule for impeachment has created some of the same practical and interpretive problems presented by the exception for establishing feasibility. As Saltzburg, Martin, and Capra point out, "almost any testimony given by defense witnesses could be contradicted at least in some minimal way by a subsequent remedial measure. If the defendant's expert testifies that the product was safe, a subsequent remedial measure could be seen as contradicting that testimony. If the defendant is asked on cross-examination whether he thinks that he had taken all reasonable safety precautions, and answers in the affirmative, then a subsequent remedial measure can be seen as contradicting that testimony." 1 SALTZBURG, MARTIN & CAPRA, *supra*, 487.

The prevailing, and pragmatically necessary, view is that the impeachment exception cannot be read in so expansive a manner. As Wright and Graham note, even at common law it would likely have been impermissible for the plaintiff to "have called the defendant to the stand, asked him if he thought he had been negligent, and impeached him with evidence of subsequent repairs if he answered 'no.' " 23 WRIGHT & GRAHAM, FEDERAL PRACTICE AND PROCEDURE § 5289, at 145 (1980).[10] . . .

10. The plaintiff has not made a separate issue of the court's disallowance of her question to Dr. McDonald and Dr. Fortuin of whether restarting the Heparin would have been feasible, although she has asked rhetorically what harm would have ensued from allowing the answer if feasibility was not being controverted. Although we need not answer that question, we do note, in the context of the impeachment issue, the view of the Alabama Supreme Court that "to impeach the credibility of a witness through the introduction of a subsequent remedial measure, the testimony providing grounds for impeachment must have been initiated by the witness." Because, the court said, the exception was created "to protect a plaintiff from an aggressive defendant attempting to manipulate the exclusionary nature of the rule for his own advantage, it

To some extent, that begs the question; whether the evidence is allowed for impeachment seems to depend more on the nature of the contradiction than on the fact of it. In Muzyka v. Remington Arms Co., 774 F.2d 1309, 1313 (5th Cir. 1985), for example, where a defense witness asserted that the challenged product constituted "perhaps the best combination of safety and operation yet devised," a design change made after the accident but before the giving of that testimony was allowed as impeachment evidence, presumably to show either that the witness did not really believe that to be the case or that his opinion should not be accepted as credible. In Dollar v. Long Mfg., N.C., Inc., 561 F.2d 613 (5th Cir. 1977), the court allowed evidence of a post-accident letter by the manufacturer to its dealers warning of "death dealing propensities" of the product when used in a particular fashion to impeach testimony by the defendant's design engineer, who wrote the letter, that the product was safe to operate in that manner. In these circumstances, the subsequent remedial measure falls neatly within the scope of classic impeachment evidence and directly serves the purpose of such evidence—to cast doubt on the credibility of the witness's testimony; it is not a mere pretext for using the evidence to establish culpability. Compare, however, Davenport v. Ephraim McDowell Mem. Hosp., 769 S.W.2d 56 (Ky. App. 1988) (evidence that, after the decedent's death, the defendant reactivated alarms on heart monitoring machines held admissible to impeach defense testimony that the alarms had been made inoperative at the time of the event because they went off unnecessarily on false readings and were distracting to the nursing staff).

Consistent with the approach taken on the issue of feasibility, however, subsequent remedial measure evidence ha[s] been held inadmissible to impeach testimony that, at the time of the event, the measure was not believed to be as practical as the one employed, or that the defendant was using due care at the time of the accident.

Largely for the reasons cited with respect to the feasibility issue, we do not believe that the change in protocol was admissible to impeach Dr. McDonald's brief statement that restarting the Heparin would have been unsafe. As we observed, that statement must be read in context, and, when so read, would not be impeached by the subsequent change in protocol. It is clear that Dr. McDonald made a judgment call based on his knowledge and collective experience at the time. He had read about and, in 5% to 10% of the cases had experienced, problems arising from an inadvertent puncture of the carotid artery; he had not experienced a patient in Mr. Tuer's circumstances dying from the lack of Heparin during a four-hour wait for surgery. He was aware that the same protocol, of allowing the Heparin to metabolize, was used at Johns

follows that a plaintiff who is on the offensive should not be allowed to manipulate the impeachment exception in order to introduce evidence for purposes otherwise inadmissible."

Hopkins Hospital. The fact that the protocol was changed following Mr. Tuer's death in no way suggests that Dr. McDonald did not honestly believe that his judgment call was appropriate at the time. The only reasonable inference from his testimony, coupled with counsel's proffer as to why the protocol was changed, was that Dr. McDonald and his colleagues reevaluated the relative risks in light of what happened to Mr. Tuer and decided that the safer course was to continue the Heparin. That kind of reevaluation is precisely what the exclusionary provision of the Rule was designed to encourage.

Affirmed.

Problem 2.2

Wood Chipper I

In *Wood v. Morbark Industries*, 70 F.3d 1201 (11th Cir. 1995), a woman whose husband was killed by a wood chipper sued the machine's maker. In response to a defense motion, the court ruled before trial that Rule 407 barred the plaintiff from offering evidence that the defendant later lengthened the infeed chutes of its wood chippers, which originally were seventeen inches long, to make such accidents less likely. Consider what happened at trial:

> In his opening statement to the jury, Morbark's counsel [made the following statement]:
>
> > COUNSEL FOR MORBARK: As a matter of fact, the evidence will indicate that after Hurricane Andrew the Army Corps of Engineers ordered thirty machines just like the one that is involved in this case, for disposing of the debris down there.
>
> During his cross-examination of [John] Infinger, [the deceased's coworker,] Morbark's counsel [posed the following questions]:
>
> > *Q:* (COUNSEL FOR MORBARK): Mr. Infinger, are you still actively employed by the City of DeFuniak Springs?
> >
> > *A:* Yes, I am.
> >
> > *Q:* And do you still work in the same capacity as street maintenance?
> >
> > *A:* Yes, I am.
> >
> > *Q:* And you still have that Morbark chipper machine?
> >
> > *A:* Yes, it's still there.

If plaintiff now seeks to offer evidence that the defendant has modified its wood chippers, including those sold to the Army

Corps of Engineers and in use in DeFuniak Springs, should the court change its pretrial ruling and admit the evidence? Why?

Problem 2.3

Wood Chipper II

As the trial in *Wood v. Morbark Industries, supra,* drew to a close, plaintiff's counsel had the following exchange with Norvel Morey, Morbark's president and the designer of the wood chipper that killed the plaintiff's husband:

> *Q:* (COUNSEL FOR WOOD): [Isn't it true that your design did not protect workers against accidentally catching their gloves in the blades?]
>
> *A:* (MR. MOREY): That's what the control bar is for, is if there's a problem, if they get their glove caught or any of their clothes caught they can stop [the machine] instantly.
>
> *Q:* So you think that the control bar takes care of any of the problems this short chute poses as a danger to the user?
>
> *A:* I've said it once and a thousand times, it's the safest length chute you could possibly put on the machine.
>
> *Q:* Yet you're selling them to the Army Corps of Engineers longer?
>
> *COUNSEL FOR MORBARK:* Objection.

Wood, 70 F.3d at 1205. How should plaintiff's counsel respond to the defense objection? How should the court rule?

NOTES ON RULE 407: *Subsequent Remedial Measures*

THIRD–PARTY REPAIRS

Does Rule 407 exclude evidence of subsequent remedies carried out by someone *other* than the defendant in this litigation? Rule 407 is written in the passive voice ("When measures are taken. . . .") and therefore seems to apply to repairs made by anyone. The public policy of the rule, however, supplies no reason to exclude evidence of third-party repairs. After all, most third parties will not be dissuaded from making repairs just because evidence of those repairs might be offered against *someone else*. Most courts follow this latter reasoning and admit the evidence. In 2007 the Eleventh Circuit Court of Appeals "join[ed] the seven Circuits that have agreed that such evidence [of third-party repair] is not barred" by Rule 407. *See Millennium Partners, L.P. v. Colmar Storage, LLC*, 494 F.3d 1293, 1302–03 (11th Cir. 2007) (citing cases from the Third, Fourth, Fifth, Seventh, Eighth, Ninth and Tenth Circuits); *Raymond v. Raymond Corp.*, 938 F.2d 1518, 1524 (1st Cir. 1991) (taking the same stance); MUELLER & KIRKPATRICK, EVIDENCE § 4.23, at 237 (5th ed. 2012).

But how can another party's later repair be *relevant* to this defendant's negligence? That's a hard question. The probative value of most subsequent remedies is that they amount to an admission by the defendant that its previous conduct was unsafe. Some courts have found that evidence of third-party repairs, although not barred by Rule 407, has too little probative force to get past Rule 403. See the court's handling of this issue in *Werner v. Upjohn Co.*, 628 F.2d 848, 859 (4th Cir. 1980) ("[W]hen a third party has required the change the relevance of the evidence is one more step removed from the central issue in the case. . . ."), *cert. denied*, 449 U.S. 1080 (1981), as well as in *Raymond*, *supra*, 938 F.2d at 1524–25 (holding that later repair by a third party "has little bearing" on the defendant's liability).

STRICT LIABILITY

A 1997 amendment to Rule 407 made it clear that the rule applies in strict liability (defective product) lawsuits. Before the amendment courts had split on the issue. Their disagreement stemmed from differing interpretations of the public policy of the rule:

One Interpretation:

Rule 407 SHOULD NOT apply in defective product cases: The typical defendant in a negligence suit, one might argue, is an individual or small business that faces few such suits. Such a defendant is likely to be most concerned about losing *this* lawsuit and will not make a repair if evidence of that repair may be admitted in the present case. In lawsuits involving such defendants, Rule 407 advances the public policy of encouraging repair.

Most product makers, in contrast, operate on a large scale and can anticipate many future lawsuits if their defective products are not fixed now. Acting in their own economic interests, such product makers will make repairs even at the risk of losing the present lawsuit. For them the protection of Rule 407, barring evidence of repair in the present case, comes as a windfall. See Justice Mosk's argument for the California Supreme Court in *Ault v. International Harvester Co.*, 13 Cal. 3d 113, 119–21 (1974).

The Contrary Interpretation:

Rule 407 SHOULD apply in defective product cases: One needn't accept this portrait of the typical product manufacturer. Even large-scale product makers might be deterred from making repairs if evidence of such repairs could be used against them. *See Grenada Steel Indus., Inc. v. Alabama Oxygen Co.*, 695 F.2d 883, 887 (5th Cir. 1983):

> Voluntary change to improve a product and reduce the possible hazard to a user should be encouraged. While there is no evidence concerning whether admission of evidence of change would deter such action by manufacturers, the assumption in the rule that it might have a deterrent effect is not demonstrably inapplicable to manufacturers upon whom strict liability is imposed.

"IF DISPUTED"

The qualifier, "if disputed," applies to ownership, control, *and* feasibility. *See* MUELLER & KIRKPATRICK, *supra*, § 4.24, at 241. Rule 407, as newly restyled, eliminates an ambiguity in the old rule, which had seemed to demand "controver[sion]" only for proof of feasibility. (*See* RB 398–99.)

B. COMPROMISE OFFERS AND PAYMENT OF MEDICAL EXPENSES

Focus on FRE 408 & 409

BANKCARD AMERICA, INC. V. UNIVERSAL BANCARD SYSTEMS, INC.

203 F.3d 477 (7th Cir.), *cert. denied*, 531 U.S. 877 (2000).

■ EVANS, CIRCUIT JUDGE. Football fans know the sickening feeling: your team scores a big touchdown but then a penalty flag is tossed, wiping out the play. Universal Bancard Systems, Inc. knows that feeling firsthand after seeing not one, but two big touchdowns called back. The referee who waved off the first—a $7.8 million verdict—and then the second—a $4.1 million jury verdict after a second trial—was the Honorable Richard A. Posner, the circuit's chief judge who in this case was wearing, by designation, the robe of a district judge. Like the instant replay official, we now review the decisions of our colleague. . . .

It's obvious that Universal Bancard Systems, Inc. fared wonderfully in this litigation with juries, but terribly with Judge Posner. At the first trial, in 1996, a jury found that Bankcard America, Inc. breached its contract with Universal. . . . When District Judge Brian Barnett Duff, who presided over the first trial, moved to senior status, the case was reassigned to Judge Posner. . . . Citing errors at the first trial, Judge Posner threw out the verdict and ordered a new trial, at which he presided.

At the second trial, in 1998, the jury . . . again concluded that Bankcard breached the contract, this time awarding Universal $4.1 million on that claim. But Judge Posner got rid of that verdict, too, entering judgment for Bankcard because the evidence of damages was insufficient. That left Universal, after nearly a decade of litigation, with nary a penny, an outcome they appeal.

Though the average consumer is oblivious to such arrangements, a customer who slaps down her credit card to make a purchase triggers a chain of financial transactions. The merchant usually keeps about 98 percent of the total, with the remaining 2 percent divided between the credit card company (such as MasterCard), the cardholder's bank (the friendly folks who fill your mailbox every day with credit card offers), and the merchant's bank that processes credit card transactions. Credit card processing banks generally contract with independent sales organizations (ISOs), who sign up merchants on behalf of the bank and provide the merchant with the necessary equipment (such as the nifty little machine through which credit cards are swiped). Big ISOs, in turn, often contract with sub-ISOs to do some of this same work of signing up merchants and servicing the accounts. Once the merchant's credit card processing bank gets its share, it pays the ISO its cut, and the ISO then pays the sub-ISO its portion (the "residuals").

At least that's the way it's supposed to work. Things never are quite so tidy in real life, of course, and in this case a contract signed in late 1991 by ISO Bankcard and sub-ISO Universal already had come asunder by early 1993. Bankcard went to court first, suing Universal for breach of contract. . . . Universal counterclaimed against Bankcard for breach of contract and RICO violations. . . . [At the first trial] the jury slogged through it all and returned a favorable verdict for Universal. . . .

[Among the errors Judge Posner identified in ordering a new trial was the improper admission at the first trial of testimony about settlement talks. Universal challenges this reason on appeal.]

. . . Rule 408 of the Federal Rules of Evidence . . . forbids the admission of statements made during settlement negotiations to prove liability or the lack of liability. The rule does not require exclusion when the evidence is offered for another purpose, such as proving the bias or prejudice of a witness. Because settlement talks might be chilled if such discussions could later be used as admissions of liability at trial, the rule's purpose is to encourage settlements.

Under the Bankcard–Universal contract, for one year after the termination of the contract Universal was forbidden to steer merchants it had signed up to Bankcard competitors. Bankcard terminated the contract in March 1993. In the next few months Universal rolled over a number of accounts to United Jersey Bank, one of Bankcard's competitors, with whom Universal also had a contract. Bankcard claimed that Universal thereby breached the contract and that Universal should not be allowed to recover on its breach of contract counterclaim because it had failed to comply with all material terms of the contract. Universal, however, said that it rolled over the accounts at a time when it thought it had reached a settlement with Bankcard that allowed the rollovers. Of course, no settlement was ever made final or this case would not be before us. Judge Duff initially thought Rule 408 should bar evidence that Universal thought it had reached a settlement that allowed it to convert the accounts before the one-year ban expired. Upon further consideration, however, Judge Duff allowed in the evidence to explain why Universal had rolled over the accounts. Judge Duff warned Universal not to go into the terms of the purported settlement and not to use the terms "negotiation" or "settlement."

Richard Rothberg, Universal's president, testified that he thought it was "okay" to convert certain merchant accounts from Bankcard to United Jersey Bank during the one-year period because he "was led to believe that based upon the discussions that had ensued with Mr. Hamman [Bankcard's attorney] and Mr. Jacobs [Universal's attorney at the time] that these accounts were ours to move over, that there was an understanding. When I was told that the arrangements between the two of them had changed, that there was a change of heart on the side of ABC [Bankcard], we ceased to do this anymore because it was going back into a litigation situation." Bankcard filed suit in April 1993, was granted its motion to dismiss the case in May 1993 while settlement talks were underway, and was granted its motion to reinstate the case in June 1993 after the settlement talks broke down. Rothberg testified that Bankcard "dropped the lawsuit" and then later "decided to go forward with the lawsuit and there was no agreement reached in the final stages."

In closing argument, Bankcard's counsel said there never was any "agreement" and that it was a "blatant breach of contract" for Universal to go "out ahead early" and convert the merchant accounts. During rebuttal, Universal's counsel said: "You heard in the testimony that there was a suit that was filed. This suit was filed, and this suit was dismissed voluntarily by BAI [Bankcard], and later it was refiled. It was after the—after the conversations going on among the attorneys in which this suit was dismissed voluntarily that Mr. Rothberg, as he had testified, came to the understanding that it was okay for him to take those accounts and roll them over or convert them, which he did at that time. And he also testified that when he was informed by his attorney that no, that was a misunderstanding, now they were going to refile the suit and they were going to go on with the litigation, he stopped."

Rule 408 is not an absolute ban on all evidence regarding settlement negotiations. The rule permits evidence that is ... offered for a purpose other than establishing liability....

It would be an abuse of Rule 408 to allow one party during compromise negotiations to lead his opponent to believe that he will not enforce applicable time limitations and then object when the opponent attempts to prove the waiver of time limitations. Similarly, it would be an abuse of Rule 408 to let Bankcard lull Universal into breaching the contract and then prevent Universal from explaining its actions because the lulling took place around the settlement table. Rothberg's testimony was admitted to show his state of mind and to explain why Universal converted accounts. In hindsight, Universal could have avoided this evidentiary quandary by waiting until a settlement was final before relying on Bankcard's word that converting certain accounts would be OK. Nonetheless, to counter Bankcard's argument that Universal had violated the contract, Judge Duff correctly allowed Universal to explain that it converted accounts because it thought a settlement had been reached.

Rule 408's spirit and purpose must be considered in its application. The purpose of Rule 408 is to encourage settlements. Settlements will not be encouraged if one party during settlement talks seduces the other party into violating the contract and then, when a settlement ultimately is not reached, accuses the other party at trial of violating the contract. To use Rule 408 to block evidence that the violation of the contract was invited would be unfair. The need for Universal to explain it thought a settlement had been reached allowing it to roll over accounts—without allowing any details about the settlement talks or even use of the word "settlement"—outweighed any potential for discouraging future settlements and did nothing to undermine the purpose and spirit of Rule 408. The admission of Rothberg's testimony that touched on settlement negotiations was not, in our view, grounds for ordering a new trial....

So we come to the final score.... We ... reverse [Judge Posner's] grant of a new trial on the breach of contract claim following the first trial.... We hold that the second trial on the breach of contract claim, considering our reinstatement of the verdict the first time around, was a nullity....

... The case is remanded to the district court for the entry of an amended judgment.

So ordered.

Problem 2.4
Hotel Inspection

Consider the facts of *Ramada Development Co. v. Rauch*, 644 F.2d 1097 (5th Cir. 1981):

> On December 13, 1972, Martin Rauch signed a contract in which the Ramada Development Company agreed to design, furnish, and construct a 160–unit Ramada Inn Motor Hotel and Restaurant in Venice, Florida....
>
> [In early 1974] ... Rauch occupied most of the motel using the restaurant and renting rooms.... But at some time Rauch became dissatisfied with the motel or the furnishings and supplies. Although the contract demanded that the final payment was due upon "substantial completion," Rauch admittedly refused to make the final payment....
>
> ... Ramada brought this diversity action against Rauch for the balance due under the contract.... The defendant answered, denying liability and alleging a counterclaim against Ramada for failure to perform according to the contract....
>
> [Under Rule 408, the district court excluded a document] referred to as the Goldsmith Report. Goldsmith was an architect employed by Ramada in 1974 to study the defects that Rauch had alleged at that time. Rauch claims that he sought to introduce this report as "a part of his case in chief," because it confirmed the majority of the alleged defects....
>
> ... Goldsmith was commissioned by Ramada to prepare a report that would function as a basis of settlement negotiations.... The report was to identify arguable defects that could then be discussed in monetary terms in the negotiations [with Rauch]....

Was the district judge right to exclude the Goldsmith Report?

NOTES ON RULE 408: *Compromise and Offers to Compromise*

"CLAIM"

Rule 408 does not protect offers to compromise made before a "claim" of some sort has been made. A lawsuit is clearly a claim, and courts will sometimes deem informal oral or written demands to be claims. But "[e]ven if it is obvious that one party has caused injury to another under circumstances that might result in liability, the 'implicit' or potential claim does not mean that all offers of aid or compensation are necessarily covered by FRE 408." MUELLER & KIRKPATRICK, EVIDENCE § 4.25, at 247 (5th ed. 2012).

"DISPUTED AS TO VALIDITY OR AMOUNT"

"The policy considerations which underlie [Rule 408] do not come into play when the effort is to induce a creditor to settle an admittedly due amount for a lesser sum. Hence the rule requires that the claim be disputed as to either validity or amount." (Advisory Committee's Note, RB 60.)

OPERATION IN CRIMINAL CASES

Plea discussions and plea agreements in criminal cases are treated in Rule 410, not Rule 408. But Rule 408 addresses the admission *at criminal trials* of conduct and statements made in *civil* compromise talks. Except in one fairly narrow circumstance, "statements made during compromise negotiations of . . . disputed [civil] claims are not admissible in subsequent criminal litigation, when offered to prove liability for, invalidity of, or amount of those claims." ACN to 2006 Amendment to FRE 408 (RB 64). The advisory committee explains that admission at criminal trials of statements made in civil settlement talks "could lead to parties refusing to admit fault, even if by doing so they could favorably settle the private matter." *Id.*

In one circumstance, however, Rule 408 poses no bar to admission at criminal trials of conduct or statements made in civil compromise negotiations—"when the negotiations related to a claim by a public office in the exercise of its regulatory, investigative, or enforcement authority." FRE 408(a)(2). The advisory committee explains:

> Where an individual makes a statement in the presence of government agents, its subsequent admission in a criminal case should not be unexpected. The individual can seek to protect against subsequent disclosure through negotiation and agreement with the civil regulator or an attorney for the government.

ACN to 2006 Amendment to FRE 408 (RB 63).

MAY EVIDENCE OF COMPROMISE AND OF STATEMENTS BE USED TO IMPEACH?

Before the 2006 amendment to Rule 408, courts had split on whether settlement attempts and statements made in settlement talks were admissible to impeach later trial testimony. Now the matter is settled: No and yes.

No

As amended in 2006 and restyled in 2011, Rule 408(a) bars evidence of compromise attempts and of conduct or statements made in settlement talks when offered "to impeach by a prior inconsistent statement or a contradiction." Without such a bar, Rule 408 would offer little meaningful protection. During negotiations a party could utter a carelessly worded conciliatory statement—"I regret your injuries" or "I regret my role in this incident"—that others interpret as an admission of fault. If such artless statements could be used to impeach a party's later denial of wrongdoing at trial, parties would be reluctant to negotiate, and the purpose of the rule would be frustrated. Even an offer of a cash settlement could be seen to contradict a later denial of wrongdoing at trial. Hence the rule forbids impeachment by "prior inconsistent statement or contradiction."

Yes

Rule 408(b) permits evidence of compromise negotiations and of conduct and statements made in such negotiations when offered to "prov[e] a witness's bias or prejudice." As we will see in Chapter 4, evidence of a witness's interest in the outcome of a case tends to show the witness has a *motive to lie*—and hence may be lying. Only in rather narrow contexts will evidence of settlement talks or of statements made in such talks tend to show a witness's bias. Say that a car accident injured two persons, A and B, both of whom sue the defendant. If the defendant settles generously with A, and A later testifies against B on the defendant's behalf, B could offer evidence of A's handsome settlement to show her bias toward the defendant. By permitting evidence of compromise and of related statements in such narrow circumstances, Rule 408 probably does not greatly undermine its purpose of encouraging settlement.

COMPROMISES WITH THIRD PARTIES

Virtually every federal circuit court has puzzled over this question: Does Rule 408 limit its exclusionary reach to compromises and payments between the two parties in *this lawsuit*—or does the rule also bar evidence that one of the parties settled with *someone else* if that evidence is offered to prove liability for or invalidity of the claim contested in the present suit? This question has exposed a troubling tension between the rule's language and its rationale.*

Strictly read, Rule 408 seems to apply only to the present parties and only to the claim at issue in their suit: "[T]o prove or disprove the validity or amount of a disputed claim," the rule says, evidence

* I thank Professor Mark Rienzi for pointing out courts' nuanced approaches toward this question.

of "compromising or attempting to compromise *the* claim" is not admissible. (FRE 408 (emphasis added). "*[T]he* claim" refers back to "a disputed claim"—the claim contested by the parties before the court.

Though several federal circuit courts have rehearsed this semantic exercise—and though scattered rulings have relied on this exercise in admitting evidence of third-party compromises—it seems *not one* circuit court has ruled that such evidence always or even generally eludes Rule 408's exclusionary force. At least nine circuit courts have addressed the question, and *all* have ruled or declared in dictum that trial judges may apply Rule 408 to bar evidence of compromises with third parties when doing so advances the public policy favoring settlement that informs the rule.*

The Tenth Circuit Court of Appeals has addressed squarely the tension between the rule's strict language and its more expansive rationale. A 1987 ruling made the point with pith:

> Rule 408 is limited in its application to evidence concerning the settlement or compromise of "a claim" when such evidence is offered to prove liability or validity of "*the* claim" (emphasis added) or its amount. Read literally, the rule does not appear to cover compromise and compromise offers that do not involve the dispute that is the subject of the suit, even if one of the parties to the suit was also a party to the compromise.

The court nonetheless added, albeit in dicta, that if the compromised claims arose out of the same undertaking that prompted the present lawsuit, they may be "similar enough to the claim sued upon in this case to be relevant." This factor, "combined with the strong policy interest in encouraging the settlement of disputes without resort to litigation, is sufficient to bring the evidence concerning the [earlier] compromises and settlements under the umbrella of Rule 408." *Bradbury v. Phillips Petroleum Co.*, 815 F.2d 1356, 1363 (10th Cir. 1987).

A decade later the Tenth Circuit still perceived the rule with ambivalence. "Rule 408 does not require the exclusion of evidence regarding the settlement of a claim different from the one litigated, though admission of such evidence may nonetheless implicate the same concerns of prejudice and deterrence of settlements which

* *McInnis v. A.M.F., Inc.*, 765 F.2d 240, 248–49 (1st Cir. 1985); *Banker v. Nighswander, Martin & Mitchell*, 37 F.3d 866, 872 (2d Cir. 1994); *Fiberglass Insulators, Inc. v. Dupuy*, 856 F.2d 652, 654–55 (4th Cir. 1988) (dictum); *Branch v. Fid. & Cas. Co. of N.Y.*, 783 F.2d 1289, 1294 (5th Cir. 1986); *Quad/Graphics, Inc. v. Fass*, 724 F.2d 1230, 1235 (7th Cir. 1983); *Williams v. Fermenta Animal Health Co.*, 984 F.2d 261, 264 (8th Cir. 1993); *United States v. Contra Costa Cnty. Water Dist.*, 678 F.2d 90, 92 (9th Cir. 1982); *Bradbury v. Phillips Petroleum Co.*, 815 F.2d 1356, 1363 (10th Cir. 1987) (dictum); *Lampliter Dinner Theater, Inc. v. Liberty Mut. Ins. Co.*, 792 F.2d 1036, 1042 (11th Cir. 1986).

underlie Rule 408." *Towerridge, Inc. v. T.A.O., Inc.,* 111 F.3d 758, 770 (10th Cir. 1997).

The Seventh Circuit likewise has straddled Rule 408's fence. In its often-cited ruling in *Zurich Am. Ins. Co. v. Watts Indus., Inc.,* 417 F.3d 682 (7th Cir. 2005), the court held that Rule 408 did not bar evidence of an attempt to compromise a claim related to but distinct from the claim then before the court. At the same time the court announced a formula permitting the rule's broader application in other cases. "In deciding whether Rule 408 should be applied to exclude evidence," the court wrote, "courts must consider the spirit and purpose of the rule and decide whether the need for the settlement evidence outweighs the potentially chilling effect on future settlement negotiations." *Id.* at 689.

This "chilling effect" depends on the parties' expectations at the time of settlement negotiations. If they or their lawyers foresee a future dispute in which evidence of the present negotiations could harm their interests, the "spirit and purpose" of Rule 408 demand that evidence of those negotiations be barred in resolving that future dispute. The parties' expectations—and the foreseeability of that future dispute—in turn depend on the relationship between the present and future disputes. Consider for example a gas explosion that has damaged thirty homes. The responsible utility company likely anticipates dozens of similar claims for the costs of repair. The company's willingness to settle with any one homeowner therefore might depend on its confidence that no other homeowner can offer evidence of that agreement to prove the company's fault in a future lawsuit. As Judge John Minor Wisdom wrote decades ago, "the incentive for parties to settle cases involving many plaintiffs would be undermined if their settlement with one victim could come back to haunt them in later suits." *McHann v. Firestone Tire & Rubber Co.,* 713 F.2d 161, 167 (5th Cir. 1983).

Such reasoning has prompted several courts to endorse a "common event" or "same transaction" principle, holding in Judge Jack B. Weinstein's words that Rule 408 bars "attempted use of a completed compromise of a claim arising out of the same transaction between a third person and a party to the suit being litigated." 2 J. WEINSTEIN, WEINSTEIN'S EVIDENCE, § 408[04], at 408–27 (1986).* Most federal circuit

* *See, e.g., McInnis,* 765 F.2d at 248–49 (in a suit against a motorcycle manufacturer arising out of a traffic accident and injury, deeming inadmissible plaintiff's settlement with the driver who struck plaintiff's motorcycle); *Fiberglass Insulators,* 856 F.2d at 655 ("Essentially, the trial judge determined that this case arose out of the same transaction, i.e., the breakup of the business association. The present claims are related to the dissolution of that relationship, just as much as were the claims pursued in the prior lawsuits between the same parties."); *Branch,* 783 F.2d at 1294 (in a negligence suit against a petroleum company arising from an oil rig accident that killed two workers and injured a third, deeming inadmissible plaintiffs' settlement with the workers' third-party employer).

courts have not, however, *limited* Rule 408's exclusionary force to cases in which the contested claim and the settled claim arose out of the same transaction or common event. Courts instead have excluded evidence of settlement with a third party whenever admission of that evidence likely would deter future settlements in similar circumstances. "Our application of Rule 408," the Fifth Circuit wrote in 2010, "has been and remains fact-specific, and tethered to the rationales underlying the rule." *Lyondell Chem. Co. v. Occidental Chem. Co.*, 608 F.3d 284, 298 (5th Cir. 2010). Here the Fifth Circuit is typical of federal courts of appeals, which generally have elevated Rule 408's aim of encouraging settlement over a narrowly literal limitation of its scope to compromises of "the" claim presently contested.

Despite this general trend toward broad application of Rule 408 to evidence of compromises with third parties, bear in mind that the rule excludes such evidence only when offered "to prove or disprove the validity or amount of a disputed claim or to impeach by a prior inconsistent statement or a contradiction." When evidence of a compromised claim is introduced instead to prove a witness's bias, for example, Rule 408 poses no bar. *See* FRE 408(a), (b); *Zurich*, 417 F.3d at 689 ("Evidence coming out of settlement negotiations is obviously admissible to show bias or prejudice of a witness."). Mueller and Kirkpatrick elaborate:

> Subject to FRE 403, evidence of prior settlements or offers to compromise is admissible to show that a witness was biased or prejudiced, as might happen if a witness has settled her own claim against one of the parties and thus may be disposed (or perhaps feel obliged as a matter of human impulse or feeling) to testify favorably for that party. Sometimes nearly the opposite situation arises: A witness who tried unsuccessfully to settle might be inclined to slant her testimony against the party who rejected her overtures. Some settlement agreements formally obligate a person to testify in a case, although it is illegal to seek to bind a person to a particular version of events.

MUELLER & KIRKPATRICK, EVIDENCE § 4.26, at 251 (5th ed. 2012).

"I'm Sorry": Why Is That So Hard for Doctors to Say?

Kevin B. O'Reilly

53 AMERICAN MEDICAL NEWS 14, 14–15 (2010)

When you hurt someone, saying "sorry" may seem like the least you can do. But when the hurt occurs in the medical arena, offering an apology is not so easy.

Thirty-five states have laws offering some kind of legal protection for physicians who express regret or empathy to patients who experience an adverse event. But laws vary in what they protect from admissibility in court.* Most insurers discourage doctors from apologizing for fear it could hurt them in court, and lawyers often advise against it.

Hospitals are required to tell patients about serious mistakes. But it is unclear to what extent disclosure policies are followed, and these disclosures may not be accompanied by apologies.

More than a decade since studies first showed that openness and apology might work, "I'm sorry" is still rarely uttered in medicine. Indeed, it has been more than two decades since the Lexington Veterans Affairs Medical Center in Kentucky decided to change how it reacted in the aftermath of adverse events.

The move came in 1987 after the hospital paid more than $1.5 million in damages in two liability lawsuits. Under its policy, the hospital investigates and discloses the results, even if findings show the adverse event was the result of an error. An apology is offered when appropriate, along with a financial settlement.

The physician who managed the disclosure program, and who talked to the patients and families, was Steve S. Kraman, MD. . . .

Dr. Kraman and his colleagues at the Lexington VA believed that

---

* [Two scholars recently surveyed state apology statutes and reported their findings:

> Most of these laws apply to "any statements, gestures, or expressions of apology, benevolence, sympathy, or commiseration made by a health care provider to an alleged victim of an unanticipated outcome or the victim's relative or representative". . . . But even while encouraging expressions of sympathy, some state legislatures distinguish an apology from a statement of fault, which is admissible. For instance, Maine's apology law specially notes that "[n]othing in this section prohibits the admissibility of a statement of fault," and the Louisiana legislation states, "A statement of fault, however, which is part of, or in addition to, any such communication shall not be made inadmissible pursuant to this Section." Nebraska, Virginia, Vermont, Louisiana, Maryland, South Dakota, Indiana, Hawaii, California, Florida, Tennessee, Illinois, Missouri, New Hampshire, Idaho, and the District of Columbia also contain legislation in which a statement of fault is admissible separate from an inadmissible apology.

Nicole Marie Saitta & Samuel D. Hodge, Jr., *Is It Unrealistic to Expect a Doctor to Apologize for an Unforeseen Medical Complication?—A Primer on Apologies Laws*, 82 PA. BAR ASSN Q. 93, 102–03 (2011). *See also id.* at 101: "[I]n 2005, then Senators Hillary Rodham Clinton and Barack Obama co-sponsored the National Medical Error Disclosure and Compensation Act, a measure which would have implemented a national-level apology law, but the bill never passed."—GF]

being honest with patients, apologizing for mistakes and offering financial compensation was both the right thing to do and financially sound. But how did their costs compare with those of other VA hospitals? . . .

From 1990 to 1996, the Lexington VA had 88 claims and paid an average $15,622 per claim, compared with a $98,000 average at VA hospitals without "I'm sorry" policies. . . .

"Initially, I thought this was a good idea, and as soon as it's publicly known, it probably will be a quick change." Dr. Kraman said. "I was naive. In most places, it's not changed—it's business as usual."

There has been some movement.

. . . In 2002, . . . the University of Michigan Health System adopted a disclosure, apology and compensation policy, cutting litigation costs by $2 million a year and new claims by more than 40%.

Medical centers affiliated with the University of Illinois at Chicago, Stanford University, Johns Hopkins University and Harvard University also have adopted "I'm sorry" policies. So have Kaiser Permanente's medical centers, the Catholic Healthcare West system, and the Children's Hospitals and Clinics of Minnesota. . . .

Rick Boothman is chief risk officer at the University of Michigan Health System. . . . He said the reason other doctors and hospitals have been slow to say "I'm sorry" is simple.

"What holds us back is fear . . . ," Boothman said. . . .

The change has been frustratingly slow, said Michael S. Woods, MD, CEO of Civility Mutual Educational Services, which offers training on apology and disclosure.

"This is something that's been on the radar now for 10 years, and we aren't seeing huge changes," said Dr. Woods, author of *Healing Words: The Power of Apology in Medicine*. "There are pockets where there's incredible success. But if we had the same evidence for a new diabetes treatment that we have for the success of apology and truth-telling, people would go out and change their treatment of diabetes tomorrow. That's how compelling the data are."

Legal, insurance barriers

Physicians may have good reasons to steer clear of apologizing, some lawyers say.

"If [the apology] becomes an admission that's usable in a malpractice case, it could affect the ability to defend the case," said Steven I. Kern, a senior partner at Kern Augustine Conroy & Schoppmann, a Bridgewater, N.J.–based law firm that specializes in representing physicians. "Most insurance companies say that if you as the insured do something that affects our ability to defend the case, we're not going to cover it. Going out and saying 'I'm sorry' not only is going to adversely impact any ability to defend the case, but may well relieve you of that insurance coverage."

David Harlow, a health lawyer in the Boston area, said doctors nationally are contractually required to notify their liability insurers of potential claims. Taking a more active approach, including apologizing when appropriate, could help avoid court, he said.

"I teach preventive law to my clients," Harlow said. "Hopefully, that resonates with people who believe in preventive medicine. It's equally applicable. For short-term money up front, you can address issues before they mushroom into something much bigger."

Some medical liability insurers are open to the idea of doctors apologizing.

"We encourage our insureds to disclose any error or any process that occurred that caused injury to patients," said Robin Diamond, senior vice president of patient safety at The Doctors Co., a physician-owned carrier. But, she added, the company wants to make sure everyone agrees about what happened first.

"Disclosure doesn't always equal saying 'I'm sorry,'" Diamond said. "Apologies are very appropriate in certain situations. But physicians who are very familiar with 'I'm sorry' programs sometimes say 'I'm sorry' too quickly.... We still have the American justice system to contend with." ...

COMPARING RULES 408 (*Compromise*) AND 409 (*Medical Expenses*)

CONDUCT AND STATEMENTS IN COMPROMISE NEGOTIATIONS

Rule 408 generally excludes evidence of conduct or statements made during compromise negotiations when offered to prove liability for a claim. If parties to a suit are sitting around a conference table with their lawyers in the course of settlement talks, they can be fairly confident their careless words will not return to haunt them at trial. Rule 409 extends no such protection to statements surrounding offers to pay medical expenses; the rule excludes only the offer. Say a driver leaps out of his car after a traffic accident and exclaims in sudden remorse, "Gosh, I'm sorry I ran the light—let me take care of your treatment!" Rule 409 will bar evidence of the driver's "humane impulse[]" to pay the other's medical bills—but his unguarded impulse to apologize and admit fault will come in against him.

This difference in the scope of Rules 408 and 409 is not easy to explain. And the advisory committee's reasoning is not immediately satisfying:

> Communication is essential if compromises are to be effected, and consequently broad protection of statements is needed [under Rule 408]. This is not so in cases of payments or offers or promises to pay medical expenses, where factual statements may be expected to be incidental in nature. [RB 67.]

The committee's rationale leaves us wondering why settlement of claims under Rule 408 requires so much more protection than offers to pay medical expenses under Rule 409. If we focus on the two rationales that underlie Rule 409 (see page 97), we might find some basis for the rule's failure to exclude statements associated with offers to pay:

The Relevance–Based Rationale

The statement, "Let me take care of your treatment," may be entirely the product of "humane impulses" and therefore not probative of negligence. (ACN to Rule 409 (RB 67)). In contrast, the statement, "I'm sorry I ran the light—let me take care of your treatment," sounds like a genuine admission of fault that may be highly probative of negligence. But doesn't this same reasoning apply in the Rule 408 context?

The Public–Policy Rationale

Rule 408 aims in part to encourage settlement and avoid a lawsuit. Rule 409 aims in part to encourage offers to assist, which likewise may avoid a lawsuit. Despite this apparent symmetry, encouraging settlement of "a claim" under Rule 408 may require broader protection than encouraging a simple offer to pay medical expenses under Rule 409.

Consider the position of the average driver involved in an accident. She probably is not a lawyer and may not be weighing how her words could be used against her at trial. She probably is unaware of Rule 409 and the scope of its protection. So a more protective rule—one that excluded her words of apology and admission of fault—would have little impact on whether she utters that apology and admission. Any excess protection offered by the rule therefore comes as a windfall to her, depriving the justice system of evidence of her fault without serving any public goal.

Contrast the situation governed by Rule 408. After a "claim" has been made and lawyers perhaps have become involved, Rule 408's broad protection might be essential to foster compromise negotiations. The lawyers would know of the risk of careless statements and, absent the protection offered by the rule, would advise their clients to keep quiet even if their silence frustrates successful negotiations.

C. LIABILITY INSURANCE

Focus on

FRE 411

WILLIAMS v. MCCOY

Court of Appeals of North Carolina.
145 N.C. App. 111 (2001).

■ TIMMONS-GOODSON, JUDGE. Joanne C. Williams ("plaintiff") appeals from a judgment entered pursuant to a jury's verdict finding Mia McCoy ("defendant") negligent and awarding plaintiff $3000 in damages....

Plaintiff filed an action against defendant claiming personal injury resulting from a 1997 automobile accident between the two litigants. Based upon a pre-trial motion by defendant, the trial court instructed plaintiff not to testify "that there was liability insurance, reference any conversations or contact with liability insurance adjusters, et cetera[,] pursuant to [North Carolina Rule of Evidence] 411." Plaintiff objected to the court's pre-trial ruling. Plaintiff informed the court that she first hired an attorney "after meeting [defendant's] claims adjuster." Plaintiff contended that restricting her testimony pursuant to Rule 411 was prejudicial, arguing that she would not be allowed to explain why she hired an attorney if defendant so inquired. The court reserved ruling based upon plaintiff's objections until such time as the question was raised at trial.

... [P]laintiff testified concerning the facts surrounding the alleged automobile accident. Plaintiff further testified that she visited and was subsequently released from the emergency room immediately following the accident. According to plaintiff, at the urging of her husband, she visited a chiropractor four days after being released from the emergency room. Plaintiff explained that she did not visit the doctor sooner because he was unavailable....

On cross-examination, defense counsel questioned plaintiff extensively concerning the timing of her visit to the chiropractor, the symptoms she related to the emergency room staff, and why she did not return to the emergency room although her condition worsened. At some point in plaintiff's testimony, defense counsel inquired, "Would you agree that you retained your attorney prior to going to the chiropractor?" Plaintiff objected to the defense's inquiry, but the court overruled the objection and ordered plaintiff to answer. Plaintiff then responded, "No." Defense counsel further inquired, "You dispute that[,]" to which plaintiff answered, "No, in fact, I was told not to talk about insurance." Again, the attorney inquired, "I asked you a question and that is did you retain your attorney prior to going to the chiropractor during which time you said your condition—," and plaintiff responded, "I don't remember."

Following the aforementioned exchange, the court excused the jury and reiterated to plaintiff that she was not to testify concerning insurance. Plaintiff's attorney requested permission to allow plaintiff to explain why she hired an attorney, arguing that defense counsel was attempting to prejudice plaintiff by suggesting that she was litigious. Plaintiff's attorney explained that defense counsel was "building his whole case" around plaintiff's alleged litigious nature. Plaintiff's attorney then quoted the following from defense counsel's opening statement: "We're going to show you that she's here for profit and that she stated it by hiring an attorney before she went to see a doctor." According to plaintiff's attorney, "that [was defendant counsel's] whole theme. He led her into that. As a matter of fact, you hired a lawyer before you went to a chiropractor."

The court subsequently allowed plaintiff to explain her answer on *voir dire*, outside the presence of the jury. Plaintiff offered the following explanation as to why she hired an attorney:

> [Defendant's claims adjuster] came to my house. And he tried to persuade me to take some money. And he told me that because I had had an injury in '76 that I was wasting my time and that I needed money and let them settle with me so that I can get medical help.

The court again refused to allow plaintiff's testimony and further instructed plaintiff that if she mentioned "insurance" again, he would declare a mistrial and hold her in contempt of court.

Following the presentation of evidence, arguments from counsel, and jury instructions, the jury returned its verdict, finding defendant negligent and awarding plaintiff $3000 in damages. The court denied a subsequent motion by plaintiff for a new trial and entered judgment based upon the jury's verdict, taxing the cost of the action to plaintiff. From this judgment, plaintiff appeals....

... [P]laintiff contends that the trial court erred in not permitting her to explain her answer when asked whether she hired an attorney prior to visiting the doctor. Plaintiff argues that her explanation was admissible for a purpose other than to prove the existence of liability insurance and that the court abused its discretion in not admitting it as such. With plaintiff's arguments, we agree.

Rule 411 of our Rules of Evidence provides: "Evidence that a person was or was not insured against liability is not admissible upon the issue of whether he acted negligently or otherwise wrongfully." Rule 411 represents a narrow exception providing for the exclusion of otherwise admissible and relevant evidence.... As such, the Rule does not absolutely bar the admission of evidence concerning liability [insurance] when that evidence is "offered for another purpose, such as proof of agency, ownership, or control, or bias or prejudice of a witness." *Id.* The [permissible uses] listed in the Rule are nonexclusive, as Rule 411 *only* excludes insurance evidence "as an independent fact, i.e., solely on the issue of negligent or wrongful conduct" but not if it "is offered to achieve [another] purpose," Carrier v. Starnes, 120 N.C. App. 513, 516 (1995).

In reviewing whether to admit or exclude evidence under Rule 411, the trial court must consider the mandate of North Carolina Rule of Evidence 403. Rule 403 specifies, in pertinent part, that relevant evidence "may be excluded if its probative value is substantially outweighed by the danger of unfair prejudice, confusion of the issues, or misleading the jury. . . ." . . .

It is clear to this Court that Rule 411 did not bar plaintiff's explanation as to why she hired an attorney. . . . [D]efense counsel knew plaintiff would testify that her motivation for hiring an attorney was a negative encounter with defendant's insurance adjuster. It appears that during opening statements, defense counsel then argued that plaintiff hired an attorney prior to seeing the doctor. Plaintiff's explanation as to defense counsel's subsequent question did not bear directly on defendant's liability or wrongful conduct, but . . . simply explained the somewhat confusing answer solicited by the defense. We therefore find that plaintiff's examination should not have been excluded per Rule 411.

Concerning Rule 403, our review of the transcript reveals that the court did not consider or balance the risk of unfair prejudice to defendant's case with the above-noted probative value of plaintiff's explanation. . . . Certainly, we recognize, as pointed out by defendant, that had plaintiff been allowed to explain why she hired an attorney, it may have had some prejudicial effect on defendant. However, this prejudice does not outweigh the probative value of plaintiff's testimony and the prejudice she suffered in not being allowed to explain her answer. This is true especially in light of the clear implication that plaintiff only visited her doctor after seeking an attorney's advice, the fact that the extent of plaintiff's injuries was a major issue at trial, and the apparent trial strategy by defendant to characterize plaintiff as blatantly seeking profit. In fact, we wholeheartedly agree with plaintiff: "Without [] being allowed to explain herself, the total weight of [defendant's] attack . . . fell on [plaintiff] and affected the verdict. The [trial court's] denying her explanation allowed the jury to assume the worst, that she had an improper motive in hiring an attorney, was litigious, and therefore lacked credibility."

Furthermore, in assessing the prejudice to defendant which may have resulted from plaintiff's testimony, we note the realities of what the jury already assumes about defendants in motor vehicle cases. The jurors, who more than likely drive automobiles, would also more than "likely [] know that in all probability there is insurance, that the matter has been investigated by the insurer's claim agent or attorney, and that insurer has employed the trial counsel." 1 KENNETH S. BROUN, BRANDIS & BROUN ON NORTH CAROLINA EVIDENCE § 108, at 333 (5th ed. 1998). More importantly, having taken *voir dire* testimony of plaintiff's explanation, the court could have further limited any prejudice to defendant by restricting the import of plaintiff's testimony and giving a limiting instruction, if so requested. *See* Rule 105 ("When evidence which is admissible as to one party or for one purpose but not admissible as to another party or for another purpose is admitted, the court, upon request, shall restrict the evidence to its proper scope and instruct the jury accordingly."). Because none of the aforementioned was considered by the trial court, we find its decision to exclude plaintiff's explanation unsupported by reason. We therefore conclude that the trial court abused its discretion in failing to admit plaintiff's explanatory testimony, and considering the obvious prejudice suffered by plaintiff, the court's abuse of discretion constituted reversible error.

. . . Accordingly, the judgment of the trial court is reversed, and we remand the case for a new trial.

Problem 2.5

Claims Adjuster

Consider the facts of *Lacher v. Anderson*, 526 N.W.2d 108 (N.D. 1994):

> On March 3, 1986, Joan Lacher attended a bridge club gathering at the Andersons' home. While looking for a bathroom, Joan opened a door, stepped into the darkness, and fell down a flight of stairs. . . .
>
> On March 11, . . . Bob Smith, an adjuster for the Andersons' insurer, visited Joan in the hospital. Joan voluntarily gave a tape-recorded statement describing her recollection of the accident.
>
> The Lachers brought this action for personal injuries and loss of consortium caused by the Andersons' negligence. . . . The case was tried to a jury, which returned a verdict finding the Andersons had not been negligent. . . .
>
> The Lachers assert the trial court erred in refusing to allow them to present evidence that Bob Smith . . . was employed by the Andersons' insurance company. The Andersons used the [tape-recorded] statement to impeach Joan at trial. Smith did not testify before the jury. . . .
>
> The Lachers argue evidence of Smith's employment by the Andersons' liability insurer was relevant to show his bias and prejudice in taking Joan's statement. . . . [At trial] Joan assert[ed], upon recollection, she was mistaken in some particulars when she made the statement to Smith in the hospital. Specifically, she . . . dispute[d] part of the statement where she said she had been in the Andersons' house "at least a dozen times" before the accident. . . .

Was the trial judge right to exclude evidence of Smith's employment? What are the best arguments on both sides?

Problem 2.6

Malpractice Insurer

Consider the facts of *Roberson v. Netherton*, 1994 WL 164153 (Tenn. App. Ct. 1994):

> On June 7, 1989, the plaintiffs brought a medical malpractice suit against the defendant, Cynthia Netherton, M.D. . . . Through pre-trial discovery, the plaintiffs learned that the defendant and her expert witnesses Larry T. Arnold, M.D., and Tom Nesbitt, M.D. were insured by the same medical malpractice liability mutual insurance carrier.
>
> The defendant filed a pre-trial motion in limine seeking to exclude from evidence that portion of Dr. Larry Arnold's video deposition in which he was questioned regarding his medical malpractice insurance coverage with State Volunteer Mutual Insurance Company. . . .
>
> The trial court granted the defendant's motion in limine. Therefore, the plaintiffs were precluded from presenting evidence that the defendant and her expert witnesses, Dr. Arnold and Dr. Nesbitt, were insured by the same medical malpractice liability mutual insurance carrier. . . .
>
> . . . Mr. Ashworth, the plaintiffs' attorney, asked Dr. Arnold the following questions in his deposition:
>
> *Q:* Doctor who carries your malpractice coverage?
>
> *A:* State Volunteer.
>
> *Q:* Do you know who carries Cynthia Netherton's?
>
> *A:* I wouldn't be surprised if it was the same.
>
> *Q:* State Volunteer is a mutual insurance company isn't it?
>
> *A:* I think so. I am not sure what that means.
>
> *Q:* Doctor, doesn't it mean that everybody spreads the profits and spreads the losses?
>
> *A:* I don't know. I don't understand mutuals and stocks. I don't understand all that stuff. . . .

Was the trial judge right to exclude evidence of this portion of Dr. Arnold's deposition?

Problem 2.7

Failure to Report

The owner of a children's daycare center faces prosecution under a statute making it a misdemeanor to fail to report instances of child abuse that come to the attention of daycare providers. The prosecution alleges that the defendant learned that one of the children who attended her daycare center was abused on the premises by one of the center's employees, who is being prosecuted separately.

The defendant denies she knew anything about the alleged acts of abuse. At her trial, she seeks to offer evidence that the daycare center maintained a liability insurance policy that covered claims brought by families of children who alleged abuse on the premises. She argues that the policy is evidence she lacked a motive to conceal abuse taking place on the daycare center's grounds. The prosecutor objects to the admission of evidence of the insurance policy.

How should the court rule?

Shari Seidman Diamond & Neil Vidmar

Jury Room Ruminations on Forbidden Topics

87 VA. L. REV. 1857 (2001).

* * *

II. BLINDFOLDING AND ADMONITIONS AS METHODS OF JURY CONTROL

One of the most commonly employed techniques for controlling juror decisionmaking is blindfolding, that is, withholding certain information from the jury. Ordinarily, juries cannot be told about . . . subsequent remedial measures taken in the wake of an accident . . . [or] settlement between original parties to the suit. . . .

Some blindfolding efforts probably succeed in preventing jurors from considering forbidden topics. If the jury has no reason to make assumptions or speculate about an issue unless it is mentioned at trial . . ., avoiding any mention of the topic eliminates any possibility that it will affect the jury. Blindfolding attempts, however, are not always successful.

Failures can arise in three common situations. First, the topic may be introduced at trial because an attorney is able to argue persuasively that it is being offered for a legally acceptable purpose.... Courts then must rely on a limiting instruction to tell jurors how they are permitted to use the information. Thus, the jury is given the psychologically challenging, and probably impossible, task of using the [evidence only for the permissible purpose]....

Blindfolding attempts may also fail when a witness mentions a subject in front of the jury even though the rules of evidence prohibit it. The party who is potentially disadvantaged by the introduction of a legally inappropriate topic must then determine whether or not to make an immediate objection and request either an instruction to disregard or a mistrial. The potential cost of an objection is that it may draw increased attention to the witness's statement that an instruction to disregard will not overcome. Researchers have examined the effect on mock jurors of simple admonitions that instruct the jury to disregard psychologically compelling but inadmissible testimony. The results provide support for practitioner intuitions: Simple admonitions often fail to unring the bell.... Professor Daniel Wegner's theory of ironic mental processes predicts that individuals who attempt to suppress specific thoughts may fail precisely because of the effort they engage in to suppress those thoughts....

... The third and perhaps most common situation in which a blindfolding attempt may fail occurs when the jurors' pretrial experiences, attitudes, or beliefs provide them with a foundation of potentially relevant information that makes the forbidden topic likely to come to mind....

... We have been able to assess the success of blindfolding by observing the conversations of a sample of real deliberating civil juries in Arizona....

III. A Look Inside the Jury Room

A. The Arizona Jury Project

... To study the discussion and deliberation process directly, the Arizona Supreme Court sanctioned a videotaping project in Pima County (where Tucson is the major city).... In [fifty civil cases, with the jurors' consent], we videotaped the entire trial from the opening statements to the closing arguments and jury [deliberations].... The final sample consists of twenty-six motor vehicle tort cases (52%), seventeen non-motor vehicle tort cases (34%), four medical malpractice cases (8%), and three contract cases (6%).... The results discussed in this article are based primarily on [forty of these] tort cases....

B. Juror Talk About Insurance

1. Evidentiary Constraints: Rules of evidence generally preclude parties from introducing evidence that a person carried liability insurance for the purpose of establishing whether the person acted negligently or wrongly. Although insurance, or lack of insurance, may affect the care that a person is likely to take and therefore may have probative value, the exclusion reflects a concern that jurors will use the information to decide cases on improper grounds. . . . Rules mandating the exclusion of testimony about insurance are predicated on assumptions about what jurors will do with the information if it is revealed (that is, that they will use it inappropriately in reaching their verdict) and what they will do if no evidence on the existence or absence of insurance is presented (that is, they will not consider it in reaching their verdict). These rules assume that blindfolding will prevent jurors from considering the forbidden topic.

2. ***The Prevalence of Talk about Insurance:*** For a topic that is ostensibly irrelevant or forbidden and generally entitled to little or no attention from jurors, talk about insurance was a strikingly common occurrence in the jury room. Conversations about insurance occurred in 85% of all cases. On average, jurors in these trials referred to insurance at least four times during deliberations. . . .

3. ***Mention of Insurance by a Witness at Trial:*** . . . An inappropriate reference to insurance at trial produced a judicial instruction in . . . two . . . cases in this group. In the first case, due to the mention of a workman's compensation hearing during the trial, the judge instructed the jurors to "ignore the existence, if any, of alleged proceeds from a workman's compensation hearing referred to at trial. The court and not the jury will decide this." Jurors referred to the issue later and disagreed about what to do about it, but the ambiguity about the existence and amount of previous compensation signaled in the judge's instruction seemed to offer support for the jurors who wanted to put the issue aside:

> Juror #2: [The plaintiff] may have made a million dollars, or he may have made nothing, but it doesn't matter.
>
> Juror #3: We aren't to speculate one way or another.

Near the end of deliberations, as the jurors were converging on a final award, one of the jurors characterized the defendant as "coming off cheaply." Another juror defended the award as sufficient in light of the fact that, "maybe we shouldn't discuss it, but there was an industrial compensation." Several jurors responded by chiding the juror for revisiting the forbidden issue.

In the second case that spawned a judicial instruction, the plaintiff mentioned insurance when describing what happened at the accident scene. The plaintiff said that the defendant made a statement to someone about wanting to exchange insurance numbers and get going because the defendant was in a hurry. The defense attorney, out of the presence of the jury, asked for a mistrial based on a violation of Federal Rule of Evidence 411, claiming that the reference was willful and that the plaintiff had been warned not to mention insurance. The judge agreed to admonish the jury to ignore the issue of insurance and warned the plaintiff's counsel that another violation would result in a mistrial. In their deliberations, the jurors . . . , without referring to the particular disclosure, . . . discussed insurance at length. . . . The jurors speculated about whether the defendant's insurance would cover an award, and whether the plaintiff's insurance had already paid the medical expenses. . . . At least one juror expressed the view that the plaintiff suffered a long time and he would base his award on the doctors and insurance. In the conversation that followed, four different jurors reiterated that they weren't supposed to think about insurance, and the jury produced a $2225 award designed to cover what the jurors decided was the amount that would pay for a reasonable number of doctor's visits, one-eighth of what the plaintiff asked for to compensate for lost wages and medical expenses, nothing for pain or inconvenience, and nothing for other general damages. . . .

4. *Summary: The Connection Between Trial Mentions and Juror Talk:* . . . In . . . twenty-five cases, jurors did not require prompting from inadvertent or planned disclosures about insurance to consider whether one of the parties did or did not have insurance or how much the insurance had paid or would pay. Although many of the comments were not directly linked to verdict preferences, all of these juror speculations introduced legally inappropriate considerations into the discussions. Moreover, the other jurors were not in a position to evaluate the accuracy of many of the pronouncements in the particular case. . . . Thus, the jurors were left on their own to determine whether to accept, reject, or ignore their fellow juror's speculations [about the existence and impact of insurance]. . . .

The juror [discussions of insurance] are revealing in another way. According to traditional lore, the focus of juror interest in insurance is on the defendant. Nondisclosure regarding insurance is viewed as necessary so that jurors will not be tempted to find for the plaintiff even if the defendant is not liable because a "deep pocket" insurance company is available to pay for the injuries of an accident victim. The juror [discussions] in the Arizona Jury Project tell a different story. . . . [Jurors showed far more interest in whether the plaintiff was insured. T]his focus on the plaintiff appeared to arise from the jurors' concern that the plaintiff may have already been compensated wholly or in part for any injuries. . . . In fifteen cases, at least one juror explicitly raised concerns about double recovery or argued that the plaintiff did not need to be paid or paid the full amount because insurance had probably already paid some or all of the plaintiff's expenses:

> Juror #5: His insurance paid all his doctor's bills. He's not really out anything. . . .
>
> Juror #3: Insurance usually covers chiropractic care. Why should we give her above and beyond what she is probably going to get on her insurance? . . .

Although jurors frequently mentioned insurance (in 34/40 of the cases or 85%), in many cases (45%) their conversation was casual or perfunctory, or it could not have affected the verdict (for example, the jurors mentioned that the defendant was probably insured, but found for the defendant). In the remaining cases in which insurance was mentioned (40%), the discussion was substantial enough that an effect on the verdict could not be ruled out. . . .

The current system of blindfolding juries, or attempting to blindfold them, on the topic of insurance breeds the variations revealed in these cases in how juries handle the issue of insurance. To the extent that jurors enter the courtroom unsure about the role that insurance should play and to the extent that courts decline to address the issue, the ground is laid for juries to rely on their own assumptions in determining how to treat the issue of insurance. . . .

IV. A Behaviorally Informed Approach to Blindfolding

. . . When the forbidden topic is unlikely to be raised spontaneously by the jury, it is an appropriate subject for blindfolding. . . . [Another] situation that favors a blindfolding approach occurs when jurors are unlikely to have expectations about information. . . . Subsequent remedial measures and settlement efforts fall in this category. . . . In none of the three slip and fall cases in our sample did jurors assume that the premises were or were not altered following the alleged accident. The topic simply did not come up. . . . Occasionally, the jurors . . . were curious about whether [settlement] negotiations might have occurred, but were unable to pursue that interest because they received no information about it and could not rely on their own experience to form an impression of what the settlement talks might have revealed.

When is blindfolding both futile and potentially unnecessary? When jurors come to the trial with experiences that reliably lead them to speculate about an issue. . . . Ignoring their attention to the issue is tantamount to behaving like an ostrich. . . . Juror talk about insurance . . . is common, and these references occur not in the process of deciding how the injury took place or how much damage the plaintiff suffered from the event itself, but rather in assessing how much it will take to compensate the plaintiff who has gone to trial. Under these conditions, alternative strategies may be both necessary and available.

V. Minimizing Deleterious Effects When Blindfolding Is Not a Plausible Strategy

. . . [A] reasoned approach would recognize the jury's predisposition to speculate about matters like insurance. . . . [A] modified jury instruction offers the possibility of persuading jurors that they are wasting their time in speculating about the parties' insurance coverage. . . . Here is a proposed instruction for a standard motor vehicle case:

> In reaching your verdict, you should not consider whether any party in this case . . . was or was not covered by insurance. As you

> may know, some plaintiffs are covered and some are not, and some have various forms of partial coverage. The same is true for defendants. The law does not allow the parties to present any evidence about insurance or lack of insurance or amount of insurance, and there is no way that you can accurately determine whether any party in this case has insurance coverage or, if they have it, how much insurance they have.
>
> More importantly, insurance or lack of insurance has no bearing on whether the defendant . . . was or was not negligent or on how much damage, if any, the plaintiff . . . has suffered.

The instruction not only admonishes the jurors to avoid speculating about insurance, it also accurately informs them that what they think the facts are (for example, the plaintiff has medical insurance or the large corporation has sufficient insurance to cover any award they choose to give) may be inaccurate or incomplete (for example, the policies have limits or do not cover all types of accidents). . . . The . . . strategy of routinely incorporating the instruction in the jurors' normal instruction package promises to be the most effective way to combat misinformation about, and inappropriate influence from, jury discussions about insurance. . . .

D. Pleas in Criminal Cases

Focus on FRE 410

(The legislative history of Rule 410 is rather complex. The rulebook includes the history of the rule's original adoption and of amendments in 1975 and 1980. (See RB 68–78) As you read this legislative history, it is useful to bear in mind that Rule 410 and Fed. R. Crim. P. 11(e)(6) used to be almost identical. Today Fed. R. Crim. P. 11(f) simply incorporates FRE 410 by reference.)

Problem 2.8
Prosecutor's Offer

As the defendant's trial for first-degree murder approached, the prosecutor offered to permit the defendant to plead guilty to second-degree murder. The defendant spurned the offer.

In her opening statement at trial the prosecutor promised the jury she would prove that the defendant premeditated the killing and is therefore guilty of first-degree murder. During the defense case the defendant sought to offer evidence of the prosecutor's earlier proposed deal. The prosecutor objected. When the judge asked defense counsel to explain the relevance of the evidence, he said he offered it to show:

1. The prosecutor herself perceived weaknesses in the government's case; and

2. The defendant displayed his consciousness of innocence in rejecting the government's offer—that is, a guilty person might have taken the deal.

Should the trial judge admit evidence of the prosecutor's offer for either of these purposes?

UNITED STATES v. BIAGGI

909 F.2d 662 (2d Cir. 1990), *cert. denied sub nom.* Simon v. United States, 499 U.S. 904 (1991).

■ NEWMAN, CIRCUIT JUDGE. This is an appeal by six defendants, including a former United States Congressman, from convictions arising out of the affairs of the Wedtech Corporation, a manufacturing company located in New York City that received contracts from the Defense Department. The defendants [include] former Congressman Mario Biaggi . . . [and] the former chief executive officer of Wedtech, John Mariotta. . . .

IV. CONDUCT OF THE TRIAL

* * *

B.

Evidence of Mariotta's "Consciousness of Innocence." Mariotta contends that it was error to exclude evidence of immunity negotiations that he contends was admissible to prove his "consciousness of innocence." Specifically, Mariotta sought to prove that the Government had offered him immunity if he would give what the Government regarded as truthful information regarding wrongdoing by other Wedtech officers and various public officials, and that Mariotta, in response to this offer, denied knowledge of any such wrongdoing, thereby "rejecting" immunity. The Government does not dispute that it made the offer, but contended before the District Court that the prosecution had rejected immunity for Mariotta after reaching the conclusion that the testimony he would give, based on his denial of knowledge of wrongdoing, was not credible. . . .

. . . The distinction is of no moment. Even on the Government's view of the matter, it rejected immunity because Mariotta did not come forward with incriminating evidence about Wedtech officers and public officials. But that is precisely the point Mariotta wanted the jury to know: that he had a chance to gain immunity for himself if he told the Government about the wrongdoing of Wedtech officers, and that he denied knowledge of such wrongdoing at a time when admitting he had such knowledge would have assured him immunity. The available inference is that he really lacked such knowledge, as he claimed throughout the trial. The inference is the same whether the immunity offer is viewed as "rejected" by Mariotta's inability to satisfy the Government's condition or "rejected" by the Government's assessment that its condition was not satisfied.

The Government also contends that evidence of immunity negotiations should be excluded because of the same considerations that bar evidence of plea negotiations. Preliminarily, we note that plea negotiations are inadmissible "against the defendant," FED. R. EVID. 410, and it does not necessarily follow that the Government is entitled to a similar shield. More fundamentally, the two types of negotiations differ markedly in their probative effect when they are sought to be offered against the Government. When a defendant rejects an offer of immunity on the ground that he is unaware of any wrongdoing about which he could testify, his action is probative of a state of mind devoid of guilty knowledge. Though there may be reasons for rejecting the offer that are consistent with guilty knowledge, such as fear of reprisal from those who would be inculpated, a jury is entitled to believe that most people would jump at the chance to obtain an assurance of immunity from prosecution and to infer from rejection of the offer that the accused lacks knowledge of wrongdoing. That the jury might not draw the inference urged by the defendant does not strip the evidence of probative force.

Rejection of an offer to plead guilty to reduced charges could also evidence an innocent state of mind, but the inference is not nearly so strong as rejection of an opportunity to preclude all exposure to a conviction and its consequences. A plea rejection might simply mean that the defendant prefers to take his chances on an acquittal by the jury, rather than accept the certainty of punishment after a guilty plea. We need not decide whether a defendant is entitled to have admitted a rejected plea bargain. *Cf.* United States v. Verdoorn, 528 F.2d 103, 107 (8th Cir. 1976) (approving exclusion of a rejected plea bargain offered by a defendant to prove prosecutor's zeal, rather than defendant's innocent state of mind). The probative force of a rejected immunity offer is clearly strong enough to render it relevant. As Dean Wigmore has written:

> Let the accused's whole conduct come in; and whether it tells for consciousness of guilt or for consciousness of innocence, let us take it for what it is worth, remembering that in either case it is open to varying explanations and is not to be emphasized. Let us not deprive an innocent person, falsely accused, of the inference which common sense draws from a consciousness of innocence and its natural manifestations.

2 WIGMORE ON EVIDENCE § 293, at 232 (J. Chadbourn rev. ed. 1979).

It is a closer question whether the District Judge exceeded her discretion under Fed. R. Evid. 403 to bar relevant evidence whose probative value is outweighed by the danger of unfair prejudice, confusion, or delay. On this point we note first that the District Judge appears to have excluded the evidence primarily, if not entirely, on the ground that the evidence was not relevant, that it contributed no probative force beyond the defendant's entry of a "not guilty" plea. But Rule 403 concerns may well have influenced the exclusion ruling; the Court at one point inquired whether a hearing would be necessary to determine if an immunity offer had been made, though Mariotta's basic claim concerning the offer was not disputed. Though we recognize the latitude of a district judge in making Rule 403 determinations, we conclude that in this case, the exclusion of Mariotta's state of mind evidence denied him a fair trial....

With the credibility of the accusations about Mariotta's knowledge of wrongdoing seriously challenged, evidence of his denial of such knowledge in response to an opportunity to obtain immunity by admitting it and implicating others became highly significant to a fair presentation of his defense. The unfairness of preventing his presentation of evidence of his consciousness of innocence was exacerbated when the Government presented evidence of his consciousness of guilt. This consisted primarily of the action of his wife, shortly after the cooperating witnesses pled guilty, in withdrawing $3.5 million from a joint account she and her husband maintained and using it to purchase gold bars and other investments in her own name.

Where evidence of a defendant's innocent state of mind, critical to a fair adjudication of criminal charges, is excluded, we have not hesitated to order a new trial....

Problem 2.9
Mariotta's Retrial

Assume that at his new trial, Mariotta successfully introduced the evidence at issue in *Biaggi*: When offered immunity in exchange for information about wrongdoing by other Wedtech officers and certain public officials, Mariotta denied knowledge of such wrongdoing, and the government withdrew its immunity offer. Later, in its rebuttal case, the government sought to prove that when he denied knowledge of others' wrongdoing, Mariotta explained to prosecutors, "I'd rather face you guys at sentencing than those guys up some dark alley."

If Mariotta claims that Rule 410 bars admission of this statement, what is the government's best response? How should the court rule?*

NOTES ON RULE 410: *Pleas, Plea Discussions, and Related Statements*

BREADTH OF EXCLUSION

As I noted at the outset of this chapter, the exclusion of Rule 410 is fundamentally different from that of each of the other specialized relevance rules. Rule 408, for example, bars evidence of compromise attempts and statements made during compromise negotiations only when that evidence is offered "to prove or disprove the validity or amount of a disputed claim or to impeach by a prior inconsistent statement or a contradiction." Rule 408 permits such evidence to be used for *any other purpose*, including *but not limited to* "proving a witness's bias or prejudice, negating a contention of undue delay, or proving an effort to obstruct a criminal investigation or prosecution." Likewise, Rules 407, 409, and 411 all exclude evidence only when offered to prove certain specified things, while admitting it *on any other issue*. Rule 410 operates differently. The evidence it addresses is *always* barred *except where specifically permitted.*

MAY EVIDENCE OF STATEMENTS BE USED TO IMPEACH?

Statements the defendant makes during plea negotiations with the prosecutor may not be used to impeach her should she later testify differently at trial. The legislative history of Rule 410 makes plain that Congress, in writing the present form of the rule, intended to bar such impeachment. As first enacted, Rule 410 provided that it would *not* exclude "voluntary and reliable statements made in court on the record in connection with [an offer to plead guilty] where offered for impeachment purposes." (RB 69). The rule had barely taken effect, however, when Congress eliminated this provision. (RB 72).

* I thank Professor Mark Godsey for suggesting this problem.

The rationale for the change is clear: If defendants worried that any statements they make during plea negotiations might be used to impeach them at trial, they might not enter plea negotiations. Of course, Rule 410 does permit certain statements by defendants to be used against them at later perjury prosecutions—an exception that "may discourage defendants from being completely candid and open during plea negotiations." (Report of House Committee on the Judiciary, RB 73.) Moreover, the Supreme Court has held that prosecutors may, as a precondition to any plea negotiations, demand that defendants agree that any statements they make during negotiations may be used to impeach contradictory testimony they give at trial. *See United States v. Mezzanatto*, 513 U.S. 196 (1995). The Court noted that a "criminal defendant may knowingly and voluntarily waive many of the most fundamental protections afforded by the Constitution," *id.* at 201—and there was no reason to assume Congress intended the protection of Rule 410 to be nonwaivable.

Extending the principles of *Mezzanatto*, federal prosecutors more recently have demanded that defendants engaging in plea negotiations agree that if negotiations fail and the case goes to trial, any statements defendants make during negotiations are admissible against them in the government's case-in-chief—and not merely to impeach defendants' testimony. Courts of appeals have relied on *Mezzanatto* in deeming such agreements valid. *See, e.g., United States v. Mitchell*, 633 F.3d 997, 998, 1004–06 (10th Cir. 2011); *United States v. Sylvester*, 583 F.3d 285, 289–90 (5th Cir. 2009), *cert. denied*, 130 S.Ct. 1313 (2010).

EXPLAINING RULE 410's ABSOLUTE PROTECTION

How can we explain Rule 410's unusually broad protection against evidence of plea negotiations and related statements?

The advisory committee points to the justice system's strong desire to encourage plea bargaining: " 'Effective criminal law administration in many localities would hardly be possible if a large proportion of the charges were not disposed of by such compromises.' " (RB 70 (quoting McCormick on Evidence § 251, at 543).) Not only is plea bargaining essential to efficient case management, it also helps win an accused's cooperation in prosecuting his cohorts.

Many criminal defendants might simply refuse to engage in plea negotiations were it not for the broad protection of Rule 410. Criminal defendants are, after all, negotiating with their liberty and may be an especially risk-averse group. For that matter, the rule's protectiveness may simply express a common understanding that criminal defendants are the legal system's most vulnerable litigants. You will see that various evidence rules extend them special solicitude.

PLEA NEGOTIATIONS WITH THE PROSECUTOR

The protection offered by paragraph (a)(4) of Rule 410 reaches only statements "made during plea discussions." If the defendant unilaterally offers information without first establishing that he is seeking a concession, a court may determine that no "plea discussions" had begun and that the defendant's statements therefore are admissible against him.

Paragraph (a)(4), moreover, shields only discussions with *prosecutors*. If a prosecutor has designated a police officer to act as an agent for purposes of plea discussions, statements made to the police officer will fall within the rule's protection. But defendants speak at their peril to police officers who merely *appear* to have authority to negotiate pleas. In *United States v. Greene*, 995 F.2d 793 (8th Cir. 1993), for example, the Eighth Circuit affirmed a district judge's finding that a DEA agent had no actual or apparent authority to negotiate a plea with the defendant, although the agent had advised the defendant that he would make any "cooperation known to [the prosecutor] and the Court" and had told the defendant that if his "attorney wanted some information, he could ... call" either the prosecutor or the DEA agent himself. *Id.* at 799–800. Because the agent had no authority to negotiate, the court held that Rule 410 did not exclude the defendant's statements to the agent. (*See also* ACN to 1980 Amendment to Rule 410, RB 75–76).

Believing it unfair for defendants to be trapped by Rule 410's formal categories, other courts have interpreted the rule more generously. For instance, the Fifth Circuit held in *United States v. Robertson*, 582 F.2d 1356, 1366 (5th Cir. 1978), that Rule 410 should exclude the defendant's statements if she "exhibited an actual subjective expectation to negotiate a plea" and that "expectation was reasonable given the totality of the objective circumstances." *Accord United States v. Sitton*, 968 F.2d 947, 957 (9th Cir. 1992) (adopting *Robertson*'s two-part test), *cert. denied*, 507 U.S. 929 (1993).

EVIDENCE OFFERED AGAINST THE PROSECUTOR

Rule 410 bars evidence of pleas and plea discussions only when offered "against the defendant." By its terms, the rule does not prevent the defendant from presenting evidence that the prosecutor offered to drop a charge during plea discussions. *See* Problem 2.8 (*Prosecutor's Offer*), at page 137; *United States v. Biaggi*, at page 139. But since admitting such evidence would discourage prosecutors from negotiating pleas and thereby would frustrate the purpose of the rule, courts generally have ignored the strict language of the rule and have barred the evidence. *See* ACN to 1980 Amendment to Rule 410, RB 78 (citing *United States v. Verdoorn*, 528 F.2d 103, 107 (8th Cir. 1976)).

THE SPECIALIZED RELEVANCE RULES: *Afterthoughts*

After wending your way through the mazelike terms of the five specialized relevance rules, you might wonder whether all this is necessary. The advisory committee writes in its Note to Rule 403 that "[t]he rules which follow in this Article are concrete applications evolved for particular situations." (RB 42.) If these rules merely apply Rule 403's probativeness-versus-unfair-prejudice weighing test, why not simply authorize judges to deal with matters of later remedy, compromise talks, offers to pay, insurance, and pleas through discretionary application of Rule 403? No doubt this technique would produce better results in many individual cases, especially those that somehow fall outside the norm imagined by the rule writers.

Anticipating this objection (though in a different context), the advisory committee predicted five unappealing consequences of so broad an application of Rule 403. (*See* ACN to Article VIII, RB 191.) Replacing specific exclusionary rules with multiple ad hoc decisions of the trial judge, first of all, would vastly expand judicial discretion. Broad discretion could breed arbitrary and biased decisionmaking. And it could spur forum shopping, as litigants sought out judges whose evidence rulings most nearly suited their needs.

Second, the loss of specific exclusionary rules would spell a loss of predictability. Unable to foresee which evidence would come in and which stay out, litigants could not reliably predict trial outcomes—and therefore could not reach informed settlements ahead of trial. And a loss of predictability would frustrate the substantive policies behind Rules 407 through 410, designed to promote repairs and settlement. Without more reliable guarantees against admission of evidence, wary litigants might avoid taking actions that could be offered against them at trial

Third, trial preparation would grow more complex as litigants tried to anticipate all possible outcomes of the judge's discretionary weighing tests. Fourth—and relatedly—court business would slow as "the already over-complicated congeries of pretrial procedures" were supplemented by long lists of in limine motions brought to secure evidence rulings in advance of trial.

And finally, because criminal defendants have rights that might be left unprotected by ad hoc rulemaking, there probably would have to be different rules for criminal and civil litigation.

Consider each of these arguments carefully. As we are just beginning our long trek through the tangle of evidence rules, you have plenty of time to ponder the comparative goods and ills of a less rule-bound system.

CHAPTER 3

CHARACTER EVIDENCE

A. THE CHARACTER–PROPENSITY RULE

Focus on FRE 404(a)(1)

(For now, you may skip the balance of Rule 404.)

Man, Girl Sought in Street Fight Fatal to Youth

Victim Is Shot by Friend of Woman He Was Alleged to Have Insulted—Flee in Car

BROOKLYN DAILY EAGLE, Nov. 11, 1929, at 19

Detectives under Capt. Raymond Honan today are searching for a well-dressed young man about 24 years old who early yesterday shot and killed Frank Capola, 21, of 72 Scholes St., who is alleged to have passed an insulting remark to a pretty brunette, a friend of the man sought. Police also are looking for the girl, who fled with her companion in his machine.

Shortly after 2 o'clock Sunday morning young Capola, a clerk employed by the Edison Company, and three friends were repairing their machine in front of 73 Devoe St. A few minutes later the girl came along and hesitated as she reached the machine. Capola, according to his friends, asked her what she wanted. They denied any of them made an insulting remark.

The girl ran back to the corner of Lorimer St., where her friend was seated in his machine watching her.

The man came back to the machine with the girl. He walked up to Capola.

"You're a fresh guy, aren't you?" shouted the man, and, drawing a gun, he fired pointblank at Capola. The bullet struck him in the chest and penetrated his heart. As he fell the girl and man ran back to their machine and escaped.

Capola's friends rushed him to the Greenpoint Hospital, where he was pronounced dead. A canvass of the neighborhood by police failed to reveal the identity of either the girl or the man. Capola's friends were unable to give an accurate description of the pair.

Girl Wife Held with Husband in Fatal Shooting

Fancied Insult Caused Killing, Police Assert—Third Person Quizzed

BROOKLYN DAILY EAGLE, Jan. 8, 1930, at 12

A man and his wife, charged with homicide, ... were questioned today by the District Attorney concerning the shooting of a Brooklyn man.

Joseph Zackowitz, 25, of 105 Devoe St., and his wife, Irene, 17, were arrested last night by Detectives Dempsey, Clauer, Hart and Winderberg of the 14th Detective Bureau....

[Police also] found three revolvers and a device resembling a fountain pen which is both a revolver and a tear gas gun.

Zackowitz and his wife are charged with killing Frank Coppola, 21, of 72 Scholes St.

Coppola was one of four men repairing an automobile tire in front of 73 Devoe St. that night when Mrs. Zackowitz, passing by, heard the men curse and thought the remarks were directed at her. The woman told her husband.

Detectives say Zackowitz told them he was drunk when his wife told him of the incident. He thought that his wife had been insulted. He accosted the four men and shot one, detectives say, and tossed the gun in the East River....

Zackowitz Goes to Death Chair Week of May 5

Slayer, Before Sentence, Tells Judge Nova He Did Not Have a Fair Trial

BROOKLYN DAILY EAGLE, March 25, 1930, at 3

County Judge Algeron L. Nova today sentenced Joseph Zackowitz, 24, of 105 Devoe St., to death in the electric chair the week of May 5. The sentence followed conviction of the defendant on a charge of first degree murder last Friday. He was taken immediately to Sing Sing Prison.

Zackowitz was not to have been sentenced until next Friday. Judge Nova, however, advanced the date of pronouncement to today after Zackowitz escaped from a prison van and ran several blocks through the streets of the borough before being caught after the verdict of the jury became known last week....

Asked before pronouncement of sentence whether he had anything to say, Zackowitz declared: "I never had a fair trial." ...

People v. Zackowitz

Court of Appeals of New York.
254 N.Y. 192 (1930).

■ Cardozo, J., joined by Lehman, Kellogg, and O'Brien, JJ. On November 10, 1929, shortly after midnight, the defendant in Kings county shot Frank Coppola and killed him without justification or excuse. A crime is admitted. What is doubtful is the degree only.

Four young men, of whom Coppola was one, were at work repairing an automobile in a Brooklyn street. A woman, the defendant's wife, walked by on the opposite side. One of the men spoke to her insultingly, or so at least she understood him. The defendant, who had dropped behind to buy a newspaper, came up to find his wife in tears. He was told she had been insulted, though she did not then repeat the words. Enraged, he stepped across the street and upbraided the offenders with words of coarse profanity. He informed them, so the survivors testify, that "if they did not get out of there in five minutes, he would come back and bump them all off." Rejoining his wife, he walked with her to their apartment house located close at hand. He was heated with liquor which he had been drinking at a dance. Within the apartment he induced her to tell him what the insulting words had been. A youth had asked her to lie with him, and had offered her two dollars. With rage aroused again, the defendant went back to the scene of the insult and found the four young men still working at the car. In a statement to the police, he said that he had armed himself at the apartment with a twenty-five calibre automatic pistol. In his testimony at the trial he said that this pistol had been in his pocket all the evening. Words and blows followed, and then a shot. The defendant kicked Coppola in the stomach. There is evidence that Coppola went for him with a wrench. The pistol came from the pocket, and from the pistol a single shot, which did its deadly work. The defendant walked away and at the corner met his wife who had followed him from the home. The two took a taxicab to Manhattan.... On the way the defendant threw his pistol into the river. He was arrested on January 7, 1930, about two months following the crime.

At the trial the vital question was the defendant's state of mind at the moment of the homicide. Did he shoot with a deliberate and premeditated design to kill? Was he so inflamed by drink or by anger or by both combined that, though he knew the nature of his act, he was the prey to sudden impulse, the fury of the fleeting moment? If he went forth from his apartment with a preconceived design to kill, how is it that he failed to shoot at once? How to reconcile such a design with the drawing of the pistol later in the heat and rage of an affray? These and like questions the jurors were to ask themselves and answer before measuring the defendant's guilt. Answers consistent with guilt in its highest grade can reasonably be made. Even so, the line between impulse and deliberation is too narrow and elusive to make the answers wholly clear. The sphygmograph records with graphic certainty the fluctuations of the pulse. There is no instrument yet invented that records with equal certainty the fluctuations of the mind. At least, if such an instrument exists, it was not working at midnight in the Brooklyn street when Coppola and the defendant came together in a chance affray. With only the rough and ready tests supplied by their experience of life, the jurors were to look into the workings of another's mind, and discover its capacities and disabilities, its urges and inhibitions, in moments of intense excitement. Delicate enough and subtle is the inquiry, even in the most favorable conditions, with every warping influence excluded. There must be no blurring of the issues by evidence illegally admitted and carrying with it in its admission an appeal to prejudice and passion.

Evidence charged with that appeal was, we think, admitted here. Not only was it admitted, and this under objection and exception, but the changes were rung upon it by prosecutor and judge. Almost at the opening of the trial the People began the endeavor to load the defendant down with the burden of an evil character. He was to be put before the jury as a man of murderous disposition. To that end they were allowed to prove that at the time of the encounter and at that of his arrest he had in his apartment, kept there in a radio box, three pistols and a tear-gas gun. There was no claim that he had brought these weapons out at the time of the affray, no claim that with any of them he had discharged the fatal shot. He could not have done so, for they were all of different calibre. The end to be served by laying the weapons before the jury was something very different. The end was to bring persuasion that here was a man of vicious and dangerous propensities, who because of those propensities was more likely to kill with deliberate and premeditated design than a man of irreproachable life and amiable manners. Indeed, this is the very ground on which the introduction of the evidence is now explained and defended. The District Attorney tells us in his brief that the possession of the weapons characterized the defendant as "a desperate type of criminal," a "person criminally inclined." The dissenting opinion, if it puts the argument less bluntly, leaves the substance of the thought unchanged. "Defendant was presented to the jury as a man having dangerous weapons in his possession, making a selection therefrom and going forth to put into execution his threats to kill." The weapons were not brought by the defendant to the scene of the encounter. They were left in his apartment where they were incapable of harm. In such circumstances, ownership of the weapons, if it has any relevance at all, has relevance only as indicating a general disposition to make use of them thereafter, and a general disposition to make use of them thereafter is without relevance except as indicating a "desperate type of criminal," a criminal affected with a murderous propensity.

We are asked to extenuate the error by calling it an incident: what was proved may have an air of innocence if it is styled the history of the crime. The virus of the ruling is not so easily extracted. Here was no passing reference to something casually brought out in the narrative of the killing, as if an admission had been proved against the defendant that he had picked one weapon out of several. Here in the forefront of the trial, immediately following the statement of the medical examiner, testimony was admitted that weapons, not the instruments of the killing, had been discovered by the police in the apartment of the killer; and the weapons with great display were laid before the jury, marked as exhibits, and thereafter made the subject of animated argument. Room for doubt there is none that in the thought of the jury, as in that of the District Attorney, the tendency of the whole performance was to characterize the defendant as a man murderously inclined. The purpose was not disguised. From the opening to the verdict, it was flaunted and avowed.

If a murderous propensity may be proved against a defendant as one of the tokens of his guilt, a rule of criminal evidence, long believed to be of fundamental importance for the protection of the innocent, must be first declared away. Fundamental hitherto has been the rule that character is never an issue in a criminal prosecution unless the defendant chooses to make it one. In a very real sense a defendant starts his life afresh when he stands before a jury, a prisoner at the bar. There has been a homicide in a public place. The killer admits the killing, but urges self-defense and sudden impulse. Inflexibly the law has set its face against the endeavor to fasten guilt upon him by proof of character or experience predisposing to an act of crime. The endeavor has been often made, but always it has failed. At times, when the issue has been self-defense, testimony has been admitted as to the murderous propensity of the deceased, the victim of the homicide, but never of such a propensity on the part of the killer. The principle back of the exclusion is one, not of logic, but of policy. There may be cogency in the argument that a quarrelsome defendant is more likely to start a quarrel than one of milder type, a man of dangerous mode of life more likely than a shy recluse. The law is not blind to this, but equally it is not blind to the peril to the innocent if character is accepted as probative of crime. "The natural and inevitable tendency of the tribunal—whether judge or jury—is to give excessive weight to the vicious record of crime thus exhibited, and either to allow it to bear too strongly on the present charge, or to take the proof of it as justifying a condemnation irrespective of guilt of the present charge" (1 WIGMORE, EVIDENCE § 194, and cases cited).

A different question would be here if the pistols had been bought in expectation of this particular encounter. They would then have been admissible as evidence of preparation and design. A different question would be here if they were so connected with the crime as to identify the perpetrator, if he had dropped them, for example, at the scene of the affray. They would then have been admissible as tending to implicate the possessor (if identity was disputed), no matter what the opprobrium attached to his possession. Different, also, would be the question if the defendant had been shown to have gone forth from the apartment with all the weapons on his person. To be armed from head to foot at the very moment of an encounter may be a circumstance worthy to be considered, like acts of preparation generally, as a proof of preconceived design. There can be no such implication from the ownership of weapons which one leaves behind at home.

The endeavor was to generate an atmosphere of professional criminality. It was an endeavor the more unfair in that, apart from the suspicion attaching to the possession of these weapons, there is nothing to mark the defendant as a man of evil life. He was not in crime as a business. He did not shoot as a bandit shoots in the hope of wrongful gain. He was engaged in a decent calling, an optician regularly employed, without criminal record, or criminal associates. If his own testimony be true, he had gathered these weapons together as curios, a collection that interested and amused him. Perhaps his explanation of their ownership is false. There is nothing stronger than mere suspicion to guide us to an answer. Whether the explanation be false or true, he should not have been driven by the People to the necessity of offering it. Brought to answer a specific charge, and to defend himself against it, he was placed in a position where he had to defend himself against another, more general and sweeping. He was made to answer to the charge, pervasive and poisonous even if insidious and covert, that he was a man of murderous heart, of criminal disposition. . . .

The judgment of conviction should be reversed, and a new trial ordered.

■ POUND, J. (dissenting, joined by CRANE and HUBBS, JJ.). . . . The People may not prove against a defendant crimes not alleged in the indictment committed on other occasions than the crime charged as aiding the proofs that he is guilty of the crime charged unless such proof tends to establish (1) motive; (2) intent; (3) absence of mistake or accident; (4) a common scheme or plan embracing the commission of two or more crimes so related to each other that proof of the one tends to establish the other; (5) the identity of the person charged with the commission of the crime on trial. These exceptions . . . may not be all-inclusive. None of them apply here nor were the weapons offered under an exception to the general rule. They were offered as a part of the transaction itself. The accused was tried only for the crime charged. The real question is whether the matter relied on has such a connection with the crime charged as to be admissible on any ground. If so, the fact that it constitutes another distinct crime does not render it inadmissible. . . . It was "a part of the history of the case" having a distinct relation to and bearing upon the facts connected with the killing.

As the District Attorney argues in his brief, if defendant had been arrested at the time of the killing and these weapons had been found on his person, the People would not have been barred from proving the fact, and the further fact that they were nearby in his apartment should not preclude the proof as bearing on the entire deed of which the act charged forms a part. Defendant was presented to the jury as a man having dangerous weapons in his possession, making a selection therefrom and going forth to put into execution his threats to kill; not as a man of a dangerous disposition in general, but as one who, having an opportunity to select a weapon to carry out his threats, proceeded to do so. . . .

The judgment of conviction should be affirmed.

PEOPLE V. ZACKOWITZ: *Afterthoughts**

Justice Cardozo's opinion in *Zackowitz* stands for certain fundamental principles in the law of character evidence. But a cynical reader might sense that something besides evidence law was going on here. After all, Justice Cardozo sounds oddly well disposed toward Zackowitz. In Cardozo's account of the crime a disembodied "pistol came from the pocket, and from the pistol a single shot, which did its deadly work." Where was Zackowitz in all this?

Professor Richard Polenberg argues that "Cardozo's decision . . . was based largely on his assessment of the defendant's character." Richard Polenberg, *Law and Character: The "Saintly" Cardozo: Character and the Criminal Law*, 71 U. COLO. L. REV. 1311, 1311 (2000). As Polenberg notes, Cardozo emphasized that Zackowitz killed while enraged at an insult to his wife's honor. And Cardozo took pains to say "that, apart from the suspicion attaching to the possession of these weapons, there is nothing to mark the defendant as a man of evil life."

In one of the opinion's most remarkable passages Justice Cardozo wrote that Zackowitz was "engaged in a decent calling, an optician regularly employed." But Zackowitz's employment status was not so straightforward:

> [I]n April 1929 . . . Zackowitz was then employed in manufacturing eyeglass frames for an optical firm. He left that job in August, starting an automobile wrecking business with a friend, buying used cars and selling the parts. In October, however, Zackowitz quit to try to open his own wrecking establishment. In November, when Copolla was murdered, Zackowitz was still unemployed, living on savings.

Polenberg, *supra*, at 1315. Justice Pound's dissent makes no mention of this inconsistency in the record. Yet one suspects that Pound's offhand remark, omitted above, that the "defendant, aged twenty-four, [had a]

* I'm grateful to Richard Polenberg for sharing his thoughts and materials on the *Zackowitz* case with me.

seventeen-year-old wife 'Fluff' " aimed to counterbalance Cardozo's praise of Zackowitz's character.

Cardozo wrote, "Not only was [evidence of the other weapons] admitted, ... but the changes were rung upon it by prosecutor and judge." Indeed the presiding judge played a less than neutral role:

> The trial judge, Algeron I. Nova, ... questioned [Zackowitz] aggressively: "What is an automatic, Zackowitz?" "I can't describe it, your Honor." "Is it one of those guns that when you put your finger on the trigger it shoots and keeps on shooting?" "Don't it do that?" the judge persisted, even as the defense attorney futilely objected. Later, Judge Nova intervened once again: "An automatic is a gun that has a magazine that you stick in the handle of it where the bullets are loaded, isn't that so?" "Yes, sir," Zackowitz answered. "And then when you press your finger on the trigger and the shot goes off and the fire comes out, the shell releases itself; right?" "Yes." The judge naturally overruled objections to his own line of questioning.

Polenberg, *supra*, at 1316–17. If Cardozo had reason to feel sympathy for Zackowitz, Judge Nova's behavior surely deepened his sense that an injustice was done.

Professor Andrew Kaufman gives Cardozo's decision a more legalistic, less emotional cast. In a speech delivered not long before his decision in *Zackowitz*, Cardozo condemned the law's definition of an act done with premeditation and deliberation—any act that was not "the result of immediate or spontaneous impulse"—as a "mystifying cloud of words." Kaufman reasons that "[s]ince Cardozo thought that the test of premeditation and deliberation was difficult for the jury to apply, it was not surprising that he viewed quite seriously any trial error affecting the issue that might have tipped the balance against the defendant." ANDREW L. KAUFMAN, CARDOZO 397 (1998).

Even if Cardozo's opinion did not *reflect* sympathy toward Zackowitz's character, it nonetheless *exploited* such sympathy by casting the defendant in a light more rosy than real. Though Cardozo feared jurors would give "excessive weight" to evidence showing Zackowitz to be "a man of vicious and dangerous propensities," he perhaps hoped his readers would overweigh Zackowitz's "engage[ment] in a decent calling." Cardozo apparently felt that even in denouncing the dangers of character evidence, he had to rehabilitate Zackowitz's character. He knew that character evidence, a dangerous thing in a jury's hands, could be very useful to a judge aiming to persuade readers that the court's ruling was just.*

---

* My thanks to Duane Pozza for suggesting this last point.

THE PROPENSITY BOX

Evidence that a person has a particular character trait generally is not admissible to show that the person acted in accordance with that trait at a particular time. This was the rule at common law, and it remains in force today in the guise of Rule 404. In *Zackowitz* the court found that the prosecutor's purpose in offering evidence of the defendant's weaponry was to prove him "a man of vicious and dangerous propensities, who because of those propensities was more likely to kill with deliberate and premeditated design than a man of irreproachable life and amiable manners." That is, the prosecutor's aim was exactly what the rule forbids: The state was trying to show that Zackowitz had a propensity to act in a particular way to prove that he acted in that way on the night of the shooting.

The problem with such evidence is not that it is not relevant. "There may be cogency in the argument that a quarrelsome defendant is more likely to start a quarrel than one of milder type. . . ." (Page 149.) Rather, the problem is that such evidence can cause unfair prejudice.

This unfair prejudice takes two forms. The first is the risk that the jury will "give *excessive weight* to the vicious record of crime thus exhibited, and . . . allow it to bear too strongly on the present charge. . . ." (Page 149 (emphasis added).) Assigning the right weight to character evidence is enormously hard. Let's say the evidence shows Zackowitz to be generally violent. How much weight should the jury give this evidence when deciding if he shot Coppola with premeditation at the fatal moment? How could a jury begin to resolve that question? The danger of giving too much weight to evidence of character is especially great because litigants sometimes seek to prove a person's character with evidence of his specific acts. Those acts, such as Zackowitz's possession of "three pistols and a tear-gas gun," laid "with great display . . . before the jury," are often colorful and memorable.

The second form of unfair prejudice that can flow from character evidence threatens greater danger. Cardozo worried that the jury might "take proof of [character] as justifying a condemnation irrespective of guilt of the present charge." That is, the jury might punish Zackowitz simply for being a man of vicious and dangerous propensities, on the theory that this sort of person is better kept off the streets even if not guilty of the crime charged. Alternatively—and perhaps more dangerous still—the jury might punish Zackowitz for having possessed his small arsenal, on the theory that this offense deserves punishment even if he is not guilty of the crime charged. In a much later opinion, Justice Souter characterized these last two dangers as forms of "preventive conviction," which the jury considers justified even if the defendant "should happen to be innocent momentarily." *Old Chief v. United States*, 519 U.S. 172, 180–81 (1997) (page 85).

Beyond these dangers of unfair prejudice, evidence of a person's character carries other risks. The specific acts used to prove character normally are not the focus of the present case. Evidence about them could confuse and distract the jury. And once one litigant offers evidence that someone committed certain specific acts, the other side will want to offer evidence that she didn't. The mini-trial that ensues could consume loads of time.

When conducting a balancing test under Rule 403, a trial judge normally must weigh the risk of all of these harms—unfair prejudice, juror confusion, and waste of time—against the probative value of the evidence. Rule 404 reflects the judgment of Congress that *as a matter of law* the probative value of propensity evidence is substantially outweighed by the risk it poses of unfair prejudice, juror confusion, and waste of time. *Cf.* MUELLER & KIRKPATRICK, EVIDENCE § 4.11, at 186 n.8 (5th ed. 2012).

Diagramming the Propensity Ban

The line of reasoning that Rule 404 forbids may be represented this way:

The step in this chain of inferences barred by Rule 404 is the one in the box. Evidence is not admissible to show a person's character "to prove that on a particular occasion the person acted in accordance with the character or trait." In general, a litigant may not lead the jury on a chain of inferences that goes through the propensity box.

Routes Around the Propensity Box

There are, however, many ways to get *around* the propensity box. Justice Cardozo discussed a few of these in *Zackowitz*. For now let's focus on just one of Cardozo's examples:

Assume Zackowitz had raised a *different* defense. Instead of admitting he shot Coppola, he claimed someone else killed Coppola and Zackowitz was never there. Now say the police found three pistols "at the scene of the affray" rather than in Zackowitz's apartment. Assume finally the prosecutor could prove—perhaps with testimony from the person who sold Zackowitz the weapons—that the three pistols were his. Cardozo noted that this scenario would present "[a] different question." (Page 149.) That is because in this scenario the chain of inferences that makes evidence of the three pistols relevant travels *around* rather than *through* the propensity box:

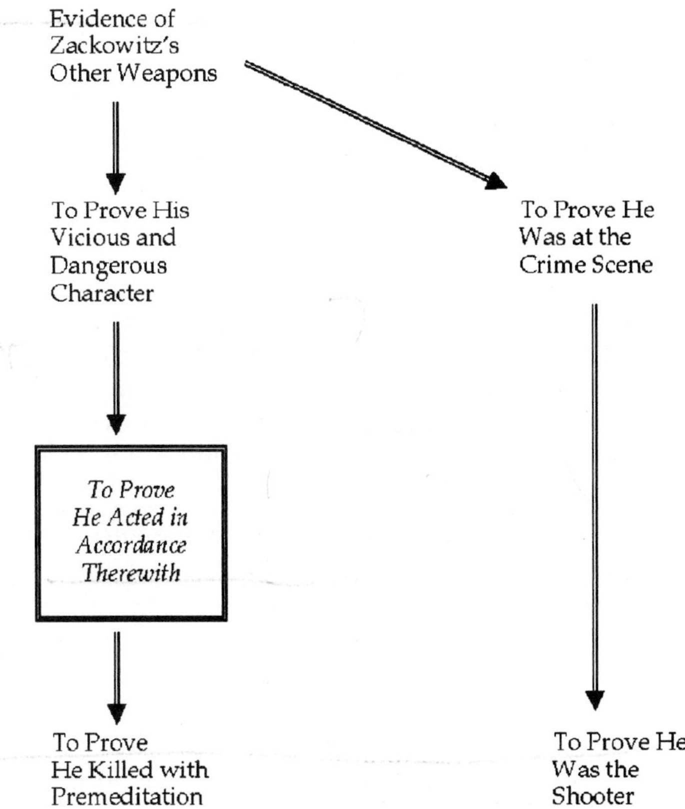

Evidence of the pistols, if offered to prove identity via the alternate route on page 155, would not invite the jury to conclude anything about the defendant's general character. Rather the prosecutor would argue simply that the person most likely to have dropped Zackowitz's guns at the crime scene was Zackowitz. Rule 404 therefore would not forbid this alternate use of the evidence of the guns. The guns would not be, in the words of the rule, "[e]vidence of a person's character or character trait . . . [offered] to prove that . . . the person acted in accordance with the character or trait."

This is not to say the judge necessarily should admit evidence that police found Zackowitz's guns at the crime scene. There is after all a risk that the jury would use evidence of Zackowitz's gun ownership as something *other* than proof he was at the crime scene. The jury could hear that Zackowitz owned several guns and conclude on its own he is "a man of vicious and dangerous propensities" who acted in accordance with that trait in shooting Coppola.

In such situations Rule 105 directs the trial judge, at the defendant's request, to deliver a limiting instruction to the jury: "If . . . evidence . . . is admissible against a party or for a purpose—but not against another party or for another purpose—the court, on timely request, must restrict the evidence to its proper scope and instruct the jury accordingly." The judge's instruction should explain in clear terms the permitted, around-the-box purpose for which the evidence of other acts is being admitted. If the defendant wishes, the judge should spell out as well the forbidden, through-the-box purpose to make clear to jurors how they are *not* supposed to use the evidence. The instruction could take this form:

> Members of the jury, the evidence of guns found at the crime scene is admitted for exactly one purpose. You may use this evidence in deciding whether Mr. Zackowitz was at the crime scene on the night Frank Coppola was shot. You are not to use this evidence to draw any general inference about the defendant's character. Nor are you to consider whether possession of these weapons would amount to a separate offense under the law. Mr. Zackowitz has not been charged with possession of these weapons and is not on trial for any such offense.

Such a limiting instruction cannot ensure the jury will not use evidence of other acts in the forbidden, through-the-box way. Recall that the Advisory Committee's Note to Rule 403 says one of the factors a judge should consider when weighing the risk of unfair prejudice is "the probable effectiveness or lack of effectiveness of a limiting instruction." (RB 43.) If the judge believes the jury will not abide by the limiting instruction, she may choose to exclude the evidence under Rule 403.

Sometimes the defendant may not want the judge to give a limiting instruction—or may not want the judge to give so *full* an instruction. That is, the judge's admonitions not to draw general inferences about the defendant's character and not to consider whether possession of the three guns was itself a crime could put those very ideas in the jury's mind. Defense counsel therefore must make a strategic choice. As with many such choices facing both advocates throughout the trial, this one turns on a lawyer's best guess about the unseen workings of the jurors' minds.

Focus on
FRE 404(b)

Close-up of Rule 404(b)

Rule 404(b) specifically recognizes several permissible routes around the propensity box:

> **(1) Prohibited Uses.** Evidence of a crime, wrong, or other act is not admissible to prove a person's character in order to show that on a particular occasion the person acted in accordance with the character.
>
> **(2) Permitted Uses**. . . . This evidence *may be admissible for another purpose, such as* proving motive, opportunity, intent, preparation, plan, knowledge, identity, absence of mistake, or lack of accident.

(Emphasis added.) This deceptively simple rule causes both courts and advocates much confusion. Focusing on a few aspects of the rule may lend clarity.

First, the phrase "crime, wrong, or other act" refers to *any* act other than those directly at issue in the case. Zackowitz's ownership of weapons other than the murder weapon was an "other act," distinct from his shooting of Coppola. This other act need not have been a crime—and it could have taken place either before or after the crime charged.

Second, Rule 404(b)(1)'s statement that such evidence "is not admissible to prove a person's character in order to show that . . . the person acted in accordance with the character" is superfluous. This provision merely restates the substance of Rule 404(a)(1). Likewise, Rule 404(b)(2)'s instruction that evidence of other acts "may be admissible for another purpose" is superfluous. Because Rule 404(a)(1) bans only one thing—evidence of a character trait offered to prove action in accordance therewith—it necessarily does not ban the other purposes contemplated by Rule 404(b)(2). Moreover, the list of possible other purposes presented in the rule is unnecessary. Evidence of a person's other acts may be used for *any* purpose other than the one purpose forbidden by the rule—to prove character to show action in accordance therewith. In this sense Rule 404(b)(2)'s list of possible other purposes is merely *illustrative,* not *exhaustive.* At bottom, then, it appears that almost *all* of Rule 404(b) is superfluous. It merely clarifies the meaning of Rule 404(a)(1).

Third, Rule 404(b)(2) does not *require* that trial judges admit evidence of other acts whenever such evidence does not violate the propensity evidence ban. Rather, the rule says only that the evidence "*may* be admissible for another purpose." (Emphasis added.) The word *may* indicates that admission of such evidence remains within the court's discretion. Typically judges will evaluate the evidence under Rule 403 and exclude it if its probative value is substantially outweighed by the risk of unfair prejudice, confusion of the issues, or undue delay.

Fourth, the permitted purposes listed in Rule 404(b)(2) are not "exceptions" to Rule 404(a)(1). They are merely possible uses of other-acts evidence *not banned* by Rule 404(a)(1). An advocate has no need for an "exception" to Rule 404(a)(1) to build a chain of inferences that goes *around* the propensity box. That is because Rule 404(a)(1) bans only trips *through* the box.

Genuine "exceptions" to Rule 404(a)(1) do exist. In certain circumstances these exceptions specifically authorize trips through the propensity box—they admit evidence of character traits precisely to show action in accordance therewith on a specific occasion. There are seven such exceptions:

- FRE 404(a)(2)(A);
- FRE 404(a)(2)(B);
- FRE 404(a)(2)(C);
- FRE 404(a)(3), as elaborated by FRE 607, 608, and 609;
- FRE 413;
- FRE 414; and
- FRE 415.

We will study each of these rules in time, but they do not concern us now. For now it is important to note only that Rule 404(b)(2) is not one of these exceptions.

It is true that judges often *call* the permitted purposes listed in FRE 404(b)(2) "exceptions" to Rule 404(a)(1). But all such references are in error. Such mistakes help explain why Rule 404(b) "generates more published opinions than any other provision of the Rules." Edward J. Imwinkelried, *An Evidentiary Paradox: Defending the Character Evidence Prohibition by Upholding a Non–Character Theory of Logical Relevance, the Doctrine of Chances*, 40 U. RICHMOND L. REV. 419, 433 (2006).

Sometimes the error of calling these other purposes "exceptions" to the propensity evidence ban can lead a court to the wrong result. Suppose for example that Zackowitz had denied he shot Coppola and thereby had made the killer's identity an issue in the case. Now suppose the prosecutor offered evidence of the weapons found hidden in Zackowitz's apartment to prove "identity," a purpose specifically authorized by Rule 404(b)(2). If challenged to explain how weapons found in the defendant's apartment could help prove his identity as Coppola's killer, the prosecutor might set out this chain of inferences:

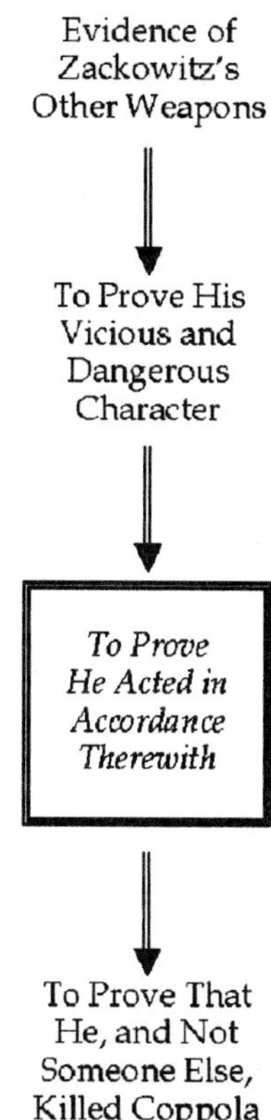

The problem with this proposed chain of inferences is not that it is logically incoherent. Evidence that Zackowitz possessed several deadly weapons indeed makes it somewhat more likely he is a vicious and dangerous person. And evidence he is a vicious and dangerous person makes it somewhat more likely he is the person who shot Coppola. Hence this chain of inferences helps prove Zackowitz's *identity* as Coppola's shooter.

But just as clearly, this chain of inferences leads the jury straight through the propensity box. In Justice Cardozo's earlier scenario, in which weapons found at the crime scene were offered to prove Zackowitz was there, the intended chain of inferences went around rather than through the propensity box. Here the probative value of the evidence depends directly on the forbidden inference that Zackowitz acted on this occasion in accordance with his violent nature.

Now we can see how thinking of the permitted purposes listed in Rule 404(b)(2) as "exceptions" to the propensity evidence ban can lead a court astray. If proof of identity were an exception to the rule, the prosecutor's proposed chain of inferences, pictured above, would be permissible. But evidence of other acts, even when offered to prove identity, is not admissible if the chain of inferences leads through the propensity box. Rule 404(b)(2) simply does not grant litigants permission to invite the jury through the propensity box. And while this last example was fairly obvious, clever lawyers devise more subtle ways to sneak the jury through the propensity box. Be on the watch for them!

One last point about Rule 404 and the propensity box: Although most of the fact patterns I have discussed so far derive from *Zackowitz*, the rule does not apply only in criminal cases. Nor does it apply only to proof of the *defendant's* character. True, the *exceptions* spelled out in Rules 404(a)(2), which we take up later, function only in criminal cases. But the general propensity evidence ban of Rule 404 operates fundamentally the same way in all cases.

Where We Go from Here

There is a good deal left to say about character evidence, a topic that will occupy us for some time. The flowchart on the next page may give you a sense of the territory we have left to cover. This chart, together with another flowchart I'll present a little later, illustrates the various rules that fall under the general heading of character evidence. Don't try to traverse the flowchart all in one stride. For now it is enough to focus on a few points.

You will see that the propensity box, which appears toward the top left of the flowchart, seems insignificantly small. Don't be fooled. That small box drives the entire chart and the entire dynamic of the character evidence rules. The general ban against going *through* the propensity box helps explain the elaborate routes around the box that consume all but the left-hand edge of the flowchart.

Our discussion so far has focused on the vertical line that falls third from left. It depicts the various around-the-box routes recognized in Rule 404(b)(2). After we have thoroughly explored such uses of other-acts evidence, we will proceed to consider each of the other routes of admissibility depicted on the chart.

CHARACTER EVIDENCE

ROUTES OF ADMISSIBILITY

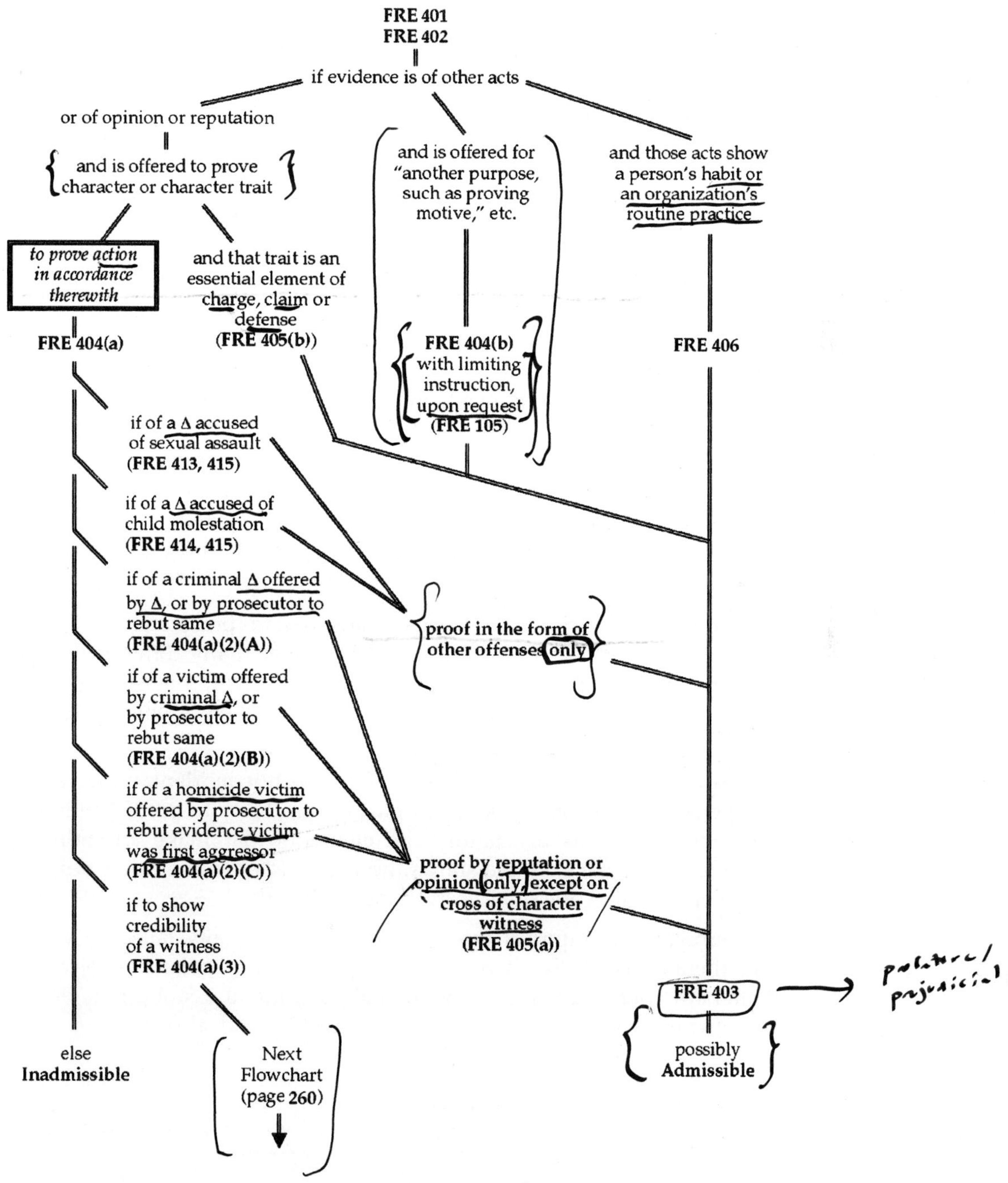
FRE 401
FRE 402
if evidence is of other acts
or of opinion or reputation
and is offered to prove character or character trait
to prove action in accordance therewith
FRE 404(a)
and that trait is an essential element of charge, claim or defense
(FRE 405(b))
and is offered for "another purpose, such as proving motive," etc.
FRE 404(b) with limiting instruction, upon request (FRE 105)
and those acts show a person's habit or an organization's routine practice
FRE 406
if of a Δ accused of sexual assault (FRE 413, 415)
if of a Δ accused of child molestation (FRE 414, 415)
if of a criminal Δ offered by Δ, or by prosecutor to rebut same (FRE 404(a)(2)(A))
if of a victim offered by criminal Δ, or by prosecutor to rebut same (FRE 404(a)(2)(B))
if of a homicide victim offered by prosecutor to rebut evidence victim was first aggressor (FRE 404(a)(2)(C))
if to show credibility of a witness (FRE 404(a)(3))
proof in the form of other offenses only
proof by reputation or opinion only, except on cross of character witness (FRE 405(a))
FRE 403
possibly Admissible
else Inadmissible
Next Flowchart (page 260)

Miguel A. Méndez

Character Evidence Reconsidered: "People Do Not Seem to be Predictable Characters."

49 HASTINGS L.J. 871, 877–80 (1998)

* * *

PERSONALITY THEORY

... Early psychologists believed that certain attributes or mental structures called "traits" comprised the personality and that it was a unique combination of these traits that set one personality apart from all others. Allport, one of the most influential founders of trait theory, believed that traits were the most fundamental "dispositions" or constituents of personality.[20] Whether viewed as constructs created for explanatory convenience or as mental structures that exist in people, trait theorists came to believe "that traits are relatively stable and enduring predispositions" that exert sufficient influence to produce generally consistent behavior across widely divergent situations.[21]

The application of trait theory to the trait for honesty illustrates their view of how the theory operates:

> The unidimensional approach holds that a person is, or strongly tends to be, consistent in his behavior over many different kinds of situations. Thus a person who lies in one situation is not only likely to lie in other situations, but is also highly likely to cheat, steal, not feel guilty, and so on.[22]

The focus on the predictive value of traits was not accidental: the value of any personality theory depends in part on its ability to predict individual behavior as well as to identify the elements that make an individual personality. As the example shows, trait theorists assumed that traits and their behavioral expressions corresponded directly.

Subsequent empirical research, however, not only failed to validate trait theory, especially its predictive attributes, but generally rejected it. Walter Mischel in particular found that "the initial assumptions of trait-state theory were logical, inherently plausible, and also consistent with

20. G.W. ALLPORT, PERSONALITY—A PSYCHOLOGICAL INTERPRETATION 286 (1937). He defined a trait as "a generalized and focalized neuropsychic system (peculiar to the individual), with the capacity to ... initiate and guide consistent (equivalent) forms of adaptive and expressive behavior." *Id.* at 295.

21. WALTER MISCHEL, PERSONALITY AND ASSESSMENT 6 (1968).

22. Burton, *Generality of Honesty Reconsidered*, 70 PSYCHOL. REV. 481, 482 (1963).

common sense and intuitive impressions about personality. Their real limitation turned out to be empirical—they simply have not been supported adequately." Instead, research conducted for much of [the twentieth] century showed that behavior is largely shaped by specific situational determinants that do not lend themselves easily to predictions about individual behavior. Mischel, who became a leading exponent of the new theory of situational specificity, explains:

> First, behavior depends on stimulus situations and is specific to the situation: response patterns even in highly similar situations often fail to be strongly related. Individuals show far less cross-situational consistency in their behavior than has been assumed by trait-state theories. The more dissimilar the evoking situations, the less likely they are to lead to similar or consistent responses from the same individual. *Even seemingly trivial situational differences may reduce correlations to zero.*[24]

To me, these findings undermine not only "common sense" or intuitive notions of the predictive value of personality traits; they threaten also the law's assumption about the probative value of character evidence. If, as a scientific matter, even trivial situational differences can render behavioral predictions invalid, then in my judgment, character evidence should not serve as the basis for in-court predictions by experts or jurors about whether an individual engaged in specified behavior on a given occasion or was truthful as a witness.

Recent research by Mischel and his colleague, Yuichi Shoda,[25] has not changed my opinion. Although Mischel generated much of the empirical evidence that individual differences in social behaviors tend to be surprisingly variable across different situations, he nonetheless did not conclude that all the assumptions underlying trait theory were false. Instead, after conducting additional research, Mischel and Shoda have proposed a new theory of personality that attempts to reconcile the paradoxical findings on the invariance of personality and the variability of behavior across situations. Their review of the empirical data convinces them that the very variability of behavior observed across situations reflects, rather than denies, "some of the essence of personality coherence."

In their new theory, Mischel and Shoda still reject Allport's theory that discrete predispositions or traits acting alone explain why individuals engage in certain behaviors across situations. Instead, they embrace and extend a competing theory that holds that personality is "a system of mediating processes, conscious and unconscious, whose interactions are manifested in predictable patterns of situation—behavior relations." . . .

24. MISCHEL, *supra* note 21, at 177 (emphasis added).

25. *See* Walter Mischel & Yuichi Shoda, *A Cognitive–Affective System of Personality: Reconceptualizing Situations, Dispositions, Dynamics, and Invariance in Personality Structure*, 102 PSCYHOL. REV. 246 (1995).

If, for example, one wants to know whether a subject who cheats his clients is likely to understate his income, one would need to know how the subject perceives the two situations (cheating clients and cheating the government) psychologically: how he categorizes and encodes them cognitively and emotionally, and how those encodings activate and interact with other cognitions and affects in the subject's personality system. One would need to discover the active psychological ingredients in the two situations to begin to arrive at a valid personality profile or "if . . . then . . ." signature for the defendant. Only by constructing such a personality profile could one predict with some confidence the likelihood that a particular defendant who cheats his clients also cheats on his taxes.

Mischel and Shoda acknowledge that their work is but a contribution toward a new conception of personality in which distinctive and stable patterns of behavioral variability are seen as reflecting essential expressions of an underlying stable personality system. It is thus doubtful that their findings can meet the tests for admitting expert testimony in a given case. More importantly, as intriguing as their findings may be, they do not make the case for repealing the ban on the use of character evidence. In its current stage of development, their theory cannot justify such a profound change. . . .

Updating the Research: Looking back at a decade of psychological research following Professor Méndez's 1998 article, Professor Edward Imwinkelried concluded in 2008 that the late-twentieth-century trend toward "interactionism"—the belief that behavior is a function of "the interactive interplay of character traits and situational cues"—had solidified. "Interactionism is no passing fancy." Imwinkelried reported that the most recent behavioral studies "consistently yielded the finding that predictions [of behavior] based on interactions are more accurate than predictions based solely on either trait or situation." Despite some dissenters, "[t]here is a growing consensus that an integrative model . . . is preferable." He quoted one researcher's 2006 hyperbole: " 'Nowadays, everybody is an interactionist.' " Edward J. Imwinkelried, *Reshaping the "Grotesque" Doctrine of Character Evidence: The Reform Implications of the Most Recent Psychological Research*, 36 SW. U. L. REV. 741, 754–55, 768 (2008) (quoting David C. Funder, *Towards a Resolution of the Personality Triad: Persons, Situations, and Behaviors*, 40 J. RES. IN PERSONALITY 21, 22 (2006)).

Professors Lee Ross and Donna Shestowsky agree. Social psychologists do not claim, they write, "that individual differences are nonexistent or unimportant in determining behavior" or "that all actors will respond similarly to a given situation or set of incentives and disincentives." But "laboratory and field studies *have* demonstrated . . . [that] seemingly small and subtle manipulations of the social situation often have much larger effects on behavior than most lay observers would predict"—effects that "are likely to 'swamp' the impact of . . . individual differences in personality, values, or temperament." Lee Ross & Donna Shestowsky, *Two Social Psychologists' Reflections on Situationism and the Criminal Justice System*, *in* IDEOLOGY, PSYCHOLOGY, AND LAW (Jon Hanson ed., 2012).

B. ROUTES AROUND THE BOX

Now we embark on a tour of several of the permitted uses of other-acts evidence, some explored through cases and some through problems. Remember that Rule 404(b)(2)'s list of permitted routes around the box is not exhaustive—some of those we are about to study appear on the list, some do not. And remember that Rule 404 bars only one thing—the forbidden inference of action on a particular occasion in accordance with a character trait.

---

1. PROOF OF KNOWLEDGE

Problem 3.1

Hacker

In February 2012 a Silicon Valley computer maker shipped several dozen desktop computers to the Ronald Reagan High School in San Francisco. Then it discovered San Francisco has no Ronald Reagan High School. An investigation revealed that a hacker had penetrated the computer maker's encryption system and placed the order directly with the shipping department, bypassing the sales department and customary credit checks.

In March, while the investigation was ongoing, the computer maker discovered an order had been placed for fourteen laptops to be delivered to a nonexistent accounting office in Las Vegas. Whoever placed this order also had managed to penetrate the company's encryption system. Delivery was scheduled for March 23 to a Las Vegas warehouse. Police staked out the location. When the defendant, who proved to be a seventeen-year-old high school senior from Boise, signed for the delivery, police arrested him.

The defendant was charged in separate federal indictments with two counts of interstate wire fraud, one relating to the February incident and one to the March incident. He pled guilty to the latter charge, but insisted he was not guilty of the earlier theft. Before the defendant's upcoming trial on the February charges, the prosecution gave notice to defense counsel that it would seek to offer evidence of the later theft. If the defendant now brings a pretrial motion to exclude the evidence, how should the court rule?

Problem 3.2
Drug Seller

An hour after witnessing a drug transaction from a lookout point, police arrested Davis and charged him with drug distribution. One of the officers posted at the lookout site identified Davis as the seller in the observed transaction. Davis claims the police caught the wrong man. No evidence of drug activity was found on his person at the time of his arrest.

At trial the government seeks to offer proof that Davis was convicted once before of distributing drugs. The government argues that the past conviction is evidence of Davis's knowledge of the drug trade—and therefore of his identity as the seller in the transaction just described.

Admissible? *Cf. United States v. Crowder*, 87 F.3d 1405 (D.C. Cir. 1996), *vacated*, 519 U.S. 1087 (1997).

Problem 3.3
Train Crash

In *Baltimore & Ohio R.R. Co. v. Henthorne*, 73 F. 634 (6th Cir. 1896), the plaintiff, Henthorne, was a brakeman for the defendant railroad. Henthorne was badly injured in a train crash. He alleged the crash was caused by the negligence of a drunken engineer, John Harrison, or by that of Harrison's employer, the Baltimore & Ohio Railroad. After Henthorne offered evidence "that Harrison's drunken condition was the cause of the accident," the trial continued:

> Plaintiff introduced further evidence to show that Harrison had a general reputation . . . [at] the terminal stations of his run, as well as among the railroad men along the line of the division, of being addicted to the excessive use of intoxicating liquor. The plaintiff introduced the depositions of a former superintendent, one Britton, and a former master mechanic, one Lowther, both of whom had left the company before the collision, who stated that Harrison had been

discharged from the employ of the company while they were connected with it for negligence and drunkenness. The plaintiff also introduced a witness who had been in the employ of the defendant company, who testified that when, as conductor of a train, with Harrison as his engineer, he was about to leave Chicago Junction, Fitzgerald, the yard-master of the defendant company at Chicago Junction, cautioned him concerning Harrison's intoxicated condition, and directed him to keep watch to prevent accidents.

On what theory might this evidence have been admitted against the defendant railroad? How would you complete the judge's limiting instruction:

> COURT: The plaintiff [may] not attempt to prove that Harrison was drunk at this particular time by offering evidence as to his general bad reputation. . . .
>
> JUROR: If your honor please, we do not understand the last instruction.
>
> COURT: You [may] not look to the general bad reputation as establishing drunkenness at this particular time. It was not offered by the plaintiff for that purpose. They claim it for the purpose of showing that his reputation was so generally bad that—

---

2. Proof of Motive

Problem 3.4
US v. Peltier I

Consider these facts from *United States v. Peltier*, 585 F.2d 314 (8th Cir. 1978), *cert. denied*, 440 U.S. 945 (1979):

> On June 26, 1975, two Special Agents of the Federal Bureau of Investigation, Jack Coler and Ronald Williams, were murdered [in South Dakota]. . . . Leonard Peltier [and three others] were charged with the murders. . . .
>
> Shortly before noon on June 26, Special Agent Williams, driving a 1972 Rambler, and Special Agent Coler, driving a 1972 Chevrolet, . . . were following three individuals [including Peltier] riding in a red and white van. . . . The van stopped at a fork in the road. . . . The agents stopped at the

> bottom of a hill. Williams advised Coler on the radio that the occupants of the van were about to fire on them. Firing commenced.... [The agents were struck and killed.]
>
> At the trial, the [government seeks to prove] the following facts: On November 22, 1972, Peltier was charged with attempted murder in Milwaukee, Wisconsin. He was arrested, pleaded not guilty, and was released on bond. On July 29, 1974, he failed to appear for trial on the charge, his bond was forfeited, and a bench warrant was issued for his arrest. Peltier was aware of the outstanding arrest warrant for attempted murder....

Assume Peltier is tried alone. What is the government's best argument for admitting against him evidence of his attempted murder charge in Wisconsin? What are Peltier's best arguments against admission?

Problem 3.5

Streetcar Mishap

Tillie Moss sued the United Railways Company of St. Louis for injuries she suffered when thrown from one of the defendant's streetcars. The jury returned a verdict for the defendant railway, and Mrs. Moss appealed. Consider the opinion of the Missouri Supreme Court:

> The plaintiff testified: That she desired to stop at Twentieth street. That she rang the bell for the conductor to stop there, but he failed to do so. Then she rang the bell for him to stop at Nineteenth street, which he also failed to do. (On motion of defendant, this testimony was stricken from the record.) Plaintiff then testified: That as she approached Eighteenth street, she again rang the bell, and the car stopped at the proper place on Eighteenth street to allow her to get off. That she stepped safely from the platform of the car to the step leading to the street, but as she was in the act of alighting from the step to the ground, and before her foot reached the ground, the car suddenly started rapidly forward without warning and threw her to the pavement and injured her....
>
> The ruling of the court in striking out plaintiff's testimony that she rang the bell for the conductor to stop at Twentieth street, and again at Nineteenth street, and that he failed to heed her signal, is urged as error, for the reason that it tended to prove that the conductor ... negligently

> started the car forward without giving plaintiff a reasonable time to alight at Eighteenth street. We think the court committed error in striking out such testimony.
>
> The fact that the conductor would not stop at all, when plaintiff rang the bell at Twentieth and Nineteenth streets, is potent evidence to show that he would not or did not stop long enough for her to safely alight at Eighteenth street.

Was the Supreme Court right? By what reasoning, other than propensity reasoning, could the jury conclude that the conductor's failing to stop at the two previous stops was "potent evidence ... that he ... did not stop long enough ... at Eighteenth street"? *See Moss v. Wells*, 249 S.W. 411 (Mo. 1923).

---

3. Proof of Identity

Problem 3.6
US v. Peltier II

Review the facts stated in Problem 3.4 (*US v. Peltier I*) at page 167. At Peltier's trial, the government also sought to prove these facts:

> On November 14, 1975, Oregon State Police stopped two vehicles near Ontario, Oregon: a motor home and a Plymouth station wagon. Peltier was one of the occupants of the motor home.... Upon searching both vehicles, Oregon authorities recovered from the motor home Special Agent Coler's revolver in a paper bag bearing Peltier's thumbprint, and from the station wagon several shell casings that had been fired from Coler's revolver. [The authorities also found] fourteen firearms, eight of which had obliterated serial numbers, and numerous boxes of shells; tool boxes containing wiring, pocket watches with wires leading out of them, tools, pliers, and empty shell casings; pieces of paper ... upon which were written code numbers and words as follows: #510 bomb; #54 pigs; #527 ammo; #529 cops; #528 dynamite; #524 roadblock; ... [and] nine hand grenades. According to the doctor who performed the autopsies, the agents were shot with a high velocity, small caliber weapon. Peltier's AR–15, [which was found in the

motor home,] the civilian counterpart of the M–16, [is a high velocity, small caliber weapon].

The defendant objected to admission of all evidence of the Oregon incident and of the items found in the vehicles. How should the judge have ruled?

Problem 3.7
Lottery Lists

Consider these facts from *United States v. Jones*, 28 F.3d 1574 (11th Cir. 1994), *vacated*, 516 U.S. 1022 (1995):

> . . . [O]n July 19, 1991, the Atlanta police department executed a search warrant at 138 Griffin Street. . . . The officers found cocaine in the kitchen, along with . . . small bags of the kind used to package cocaine. . . . The police seized from the apartment several pieces of paper with lottery numbers and lists of bets written on them. . . .
>
> [At Gregory Jones's trial on narcotics charges, it was disputed whether he was the occupant of the apartment.] Lists of lottery numbers and bets made in illegal street lotteries, which had been found in the apartment, were admitted into evidence along with . . . evidence of Jones's 1987 conviction for commercial gambling. The government argues that this evidence tends to show that: the occupant of the apartment in July 1991 was involved in illegal commercial gambling; because Jones had been convicted of illegal commercial gambling in 1987 . . ., it was more likely that Jones was involved in such gambling in July 1991; and, therefore, it was more likely that Jones was the one who occupied the apartment in July 1991.

Admissible?

Problem 3.8
Cycling Brochures

Imagine a case very much like *Jones*, just discussed in Problem 3.7 (*Lottery Lists*). On searching the apartment, police again found cocaine and packaging supplies. But instead of finding gambling slips, they discovered various recently published brochures for bicycle-racing equipment. Though no fingerprints were found on the brochures, the prosecution hopes to link them to the defendant by offering evidence that three years ago he was known to be an avid bicycle racer. Hence the prosecution's argument parallels that made in the last problem: Whoever occupied the apartment at the time of the police search was involved in bicycle racing; because the defendant was a bicycle racer several years ago, it is more likely he was involved in bicycle racing at the time police searched the apartment; therefore it is more likely the defendant was the occupant of the apartment at the time the police searched it.

Admissible?

Proof of Modus Operandi: One way to prove guilt when identity is in dispute is to show that the crime matches the defendant's "M.O." If we know the defendant committed a particular crime in the past, and the present offense matches that crime in idiosyncratic ways, we may infer that the defendant committed the present offense as well. The permitted inference is *not* that "this is the defendant's kind of crime"—that would amount to the crassest form of propensity reasoning. Rather the idea is "this could not be *anyone else's* crime." For this route around the propensity box to be legitimate, the similarities between the two crimes must be so distinctive that the inference that *nobody else* could have committed this crime overcomes the jury's temptation to engage in propensity reasoning pure and simple. Consider the next case:

UNITED STATES V. TRENKLER

61 F.3d 45 (1st Cir. 1995).

■ STAHL, CIRCUIT JUDGE. . . . On October 28, 1991, a bomb exploded at the Roslindale home of Thomas L. Shay ("Shay Sr."), killing one Boston police officer and severely injuring another. The two officers, members of the Boston Police Department Bomb Squad, had been dispatched to Shay Sr.'s home to investigate a suspicious object located in Shay Sr.'s driveway. Shay Sr. had earlier reported that, while backing his 1986 Buick Century into the street the day before, he had heard a loud noise emanating from beneath the floorboard of his automobile. Shay Sr. added that, subsequently, he found the suspicious object resting near the crest of his driveway.

Following the explosion, a massive investigation ensued involving a variety of federal, state and local law-enforcement agencies. On June 24,

1993, this investigation culminated with the return of a three-count indictment charging Alfred Trenkler and Thomas A. Shay ("Shay Jr."), Shay Sr.'s son, with responsibility for the Roslindale bombing. Trenkler filed a successful severance motion, and the government tried the two defendants separately. . . .

At Trenkler's trial, the thrust of the government's case was that Trenkler had built the Roslindale bomb for Shay Jr. to use against his father. To establish Trenkler's identity as the builder of the bomb, the government offered, *inter alia*, evidence that Trenkler had previously constructed a remote-control device, the Quincy bomb, which exploded in Quincy, Massachusetts, in 1986. The government contended that unique similarities in design, choice of components, and overall modus operandi between the two bombs compelled the conclusion that Trenkler had designed and built both devices. Prior to trial, the government filed a motion in limine seeking to admit the "similarity" evidence. Following a day-long evidentiary hearing, the district court ruled the evidence admissible, finding that it was relevant on the issues of identity, skill, knowledge, and intent. Although Trenkler did not testify at trial, his counsel stipulated at the evidentiary hearing that Trenkler had built the Quincy bomb.[3]

1986 QUINCY BOMB

Trenkler constructed the Quincy bomb in 1986 for a friend, Donna Shea. At the time, Shea was involved in a dispute with the owners of the Capeway Fish Market, and she wanted the bomb to use as a means to intimidate them. At her request, Trenkler assembled a remote-control, radio-activated explosive device. The device was later attached to the undercarriage of a truck belonging to the Capeway Fish Market and detonated in the middle of the night. The resulting bomb blast caused no injuries and little property damage.

In building the Quincy bomb, Trenkler used as the explosive material a military flash simulator typically utilized to mimic gunfire in combat exercises. To provide remote-control capabilities, Trenkler employed a radio-receiver he had removed from a small toy car. Trenkler wrapped the bomb in duct tape and attached a large donut-shaped speaker magnet to enable the bomb to adhere to the undercarriage of the truck. Other components Trenkler used included a "double throw" toggle switch, four AA batteries, two six-volt batteries, an electric relay, solder, various wires, and a slide switch.

Testimony at trial established that Trenkler purchased some of the electrical components for the Quincy bomb from a Radio Shack store. On

3. During the original 1986 investigation of the Quincy bombing, Trenkler admitted building the bomb. In 1987, the Commonwealth of Massachusetts brought charges against Trenkler for his involvement in the Quincy bombing, but the charges were dismissed.

one occasion, Trenkler sought to obtain needed components by sending Shea's eleven-year-old nephew into a Radio Shack store with a list of items to purchase while Trenkler remained waiting outside. Shea's nephew, however, was unable to find all of the items, and Trenkler eventually came into the store to assist him.

1991 Roslindale Bomb

The government contended that Trenkler built the Roslindale bomb at Shay Jr.'s request. . . .

Testimony from government investigators and Shay Sr. established that the Roslindale bomb was a remote-control, radio-activated device with an explosive force supplied by two or three sticks of dynamite connected to two electrical blasting caps. A black wooden box weighing two or three pounds and measuring approximately eight to ten inches long, five to six inches wide and one to two inches deep housed the bomb. A large donut-shaped magnet and several smaller round magnets attached to the box were used to secure the device to the underside of Shay Sr.'s automobile. Other components used in the construction of the bomb included duct tape, a "single throw" toggle switch, four AA batteries, five nine-volt batteries, a Futaba radio receiver, solder, various wires, and a slide switch.

According to the government's experts and Shay Sr., the bomb was originally attached to the undercarriage of Shay Sr.'s automobile directly beneath the driver's seat. The government's explosives expert testified that if the bomb had exploded while still attached to the car, it probably would have killed or at least seriously injured any individual sitting in the driver's seat.

The government also asserted that Trenkler used Shay Jr. to purchase the electronic components used in the bomb. In support of this assertion, the government introduced a sales receipt for a toggle switch purchased in October 1991 at a Radio Shack store located across the street from where Trenkler, at the time, was installing a satellite dish. Agents from the Bureau of Alcohol, Tobacco and Firearms ("ATF") recovered from the debris of the Roslindale bomb a switch identical to the one purchased. Shay Jr. admitted purchasing the switch during a taped television interview, portions of which the government introduced at trial. Furthermore, a sales clerk at the Radio Shack testified that, prior to purchasing the switch, the person who bought it had browsed in the store for several minutes, appearing to shop for items written on a list. . . .

Both the government and Trenkler elicited testimony from their respective explosives experts explaining the similarities and differences between the two bombs. Both experts testified at length concerning the electronic designs, the choice of components and the method of construction. The government's expert opined that the two incidents shared many similar traits and characteristics, evincing the "signature" of a single bomb maker. He further stated that he had no doubt "whatsoever" that the same person built both bombs. Trenkler's expert, on the other hand, stated that too many dissimilarities existed to conclude that the same person built both bombs. Moreover, Trenkler's expert testified that the similarities that existed lacked sufficient distinguishing qualities to identify the two bombs as the handiwork of a specific individual.

EXIS COMPUTER DATABASE EVIDENCE

To support the inference that Trenkler built both bombs, the government offered testimony . . . concerning information retrieved from an ATF computer database of explosives and arson incidents. Stephen Scheid, an Intelligence Research Specialist with ATF, testified that the database, known as EXIS, contains information taken from reports submitted to ATF by various federal, state and local law-enforcement agencies. Scheid further testified that he had been personally responsible for maintaining the database since 1977. Scheid stated that he reviews submitted incident reports, culling from them information describing the characteristics of each bombing or arson episode. Scheid added that he then encodes the extracted information on a standardized worksheet, which he or a data-entry person in turn uses to enter the information into the database.

Scheid testified that, through the use of a computer program, he then produces investigatory leads by retrieving all incidents entered in the database that are listed as possessing a specific component or characteristic. Scheid further testified that, in an effort to identify the builder of the Roslindale bomb, he performed a series of computer queries, focusing on characteristics of the Roslindale bomb. This series of inquiries narrowed the field of reported incidents in the database from 40,867 to seven.[6] The seven remaining incidents included both the Roslindale and Quincy bombs. Scheid stated that he subsequently conducted a manual analysis of the remaining incidents and was able to identify several additional characteristics common to only the Roslindale and Quincy bombs.[7] . . .

The jury returned a guilty verdict on all counts of the indictment. Subsequently, the district court sentenced Trenkler to concurrent terms of life imprisonment on the counts of receipt of explosive materials and

6. The computer queries and the total number of resulting incidents are listed below. The queries are successive.

All incidents in database	—40,867
Bombings and attempted bombings	—14,252
Involving cars and trucks	—2,504
Under vehicles	—428
Remote-control	—19
Using Magnets	—7

7. Scheid testified that, of the seven remaining incidents, only the Roslindale and the Quincy bomb were reported as possessing all of the additional features: duct tape, soldering, AA batteries, toggle switches, and "round" magnets.

attempted malicious destruction of property by means of explosives and sixty months on the count of conspiracy. Trenkler now appeals.

II. DISCUSSION

On appeal, Trenkler assigns error to the admission of the Quincy bomb evidence, contending primarily that the incident was not sufficiently similar to the Roslindale bomb to be relevant on the issue of identity. . . .

1. *Fed. R. Evid. 404(b): Other Act Evidence*

In general, Rule 404(b) proscribes the use of other bad-act evidence solely to establish that the defendant has a propensity towards criminal behavior. Rule 404(b)'s proscription, however, is not absolute: the rule permits the use of such evidence if it bears on a material issue such as motive, knowledge or identity. In this Circuit, we have adopted a two-part test for determining the admissibility of Rule 404(b) evidence. First, the district court must determine whether the evidence has some "special relevance" independent of its tendency simply to show criminal propensity. Second, if the evidence has "special relevance" on a material issue, the court must then carefully conduct a Rule 403 analysis to determine if the probative value of the evidence is not substantially outweighed by the danger of unfair prejudice. As with most evidentiary rulings, the district court has considerable leeway in determining whether to admit or exclude Rule 404(b) evidence. Accordingly, we review its decision only under the lens of abuse of discretion.

2. *Identity . . .*

a. *Rule 404(b) Evidence: Special Relevance:* When, as in this case, Rule 404(b) evidence is offered because it has "special relevance" on the issue of identity, we have required, as a prerequisite to admission, a showing that there exists a high degree of similarity between the other act and the charged crime. Indeed, the proponent must demonstrate that the two acts exhibit a commonality of distinguishing features sufficient to earmark them as the handiwork of the same individual. This preliminary showing is necessary because

> [a] defendant cannot be identified as the perpetrator of the charged act simply because he has at other times committed the same commonplace variety of criminal act except by reference to the forbidden inference of propensity. The question for the court[, therefore, must be] whether the characteristics relied upon are *sufficiently idiosyncratic* to permit an inference of pattern for purposes of proof.

United States v. Pisari, 636 F.2d 855, 858–59 (1st Cir. 1981) (emphasis added). . . .

Trenkler contends that the array of similarities between the two incidents amounts to no more than a collection of "prosaic commonalit[ies that] cannot give rise to an inference that the same person was involved in both acts without reference to propensity." United States v. Garcia–Rosa, 876 F.2d 209, 225 (1st Cir. 1989). However, in resolving whether the evidence supports an inference that the two incidents are "sufficiently idiosyncratic," we have cautioned that "an exact match is not necessary." United States v. Ingraham, 832 F.2d 229, 232 (1st Cir. 1987). The test must focus on the "totality of the comparison," demanding not a "facsimile or exact replica" but rather the " 'conjunction of several identifying characteristics *or* the presence of some highly distinctive quality.' " *Id.* at 232–33 (emphasis added); *see also* United States v. Myers, 550 F.2d 1036, 1045 (5th Cir. 1977) ("[A] number of common features of lesser uniqueness, although insufficient to generate a strong inference of identity if considered separately, may be of significant probative value when considered together."). In this case, we think the balance of the evidence tilts sufficiently towards admission to satisfy the first step of the Rule 404(b) analysis. Accordingly, we believe that the district court did not abuse its discretion in determining that the numerous similarities in components, design, and technique of assembly, combined with the similar modus operandi and the closeness of geographic proximity between the two events, sufficiently support the inference that the same person built both bombs.

We begin by noting that the government's explosives expert, Thomas Waskom, testified that his analysis of the similarities shared by the two incidents left him with no doubt "whatsoever" that the same individual built both bombs. Our own review of the record reveals that the two bombs did indeed share a number of similar components and characteristics. Both bombs were remote-controlled, radio-activated, electronic explosive devices. Both were homemade mechanisms, comprising, in general, electronic components easily purchased at a hobby store. Both had similar, though not identical, firing and fusing circuits with separate battery power supplies for each. Both had switches in their fusing circuits to disconnect the radio receivers. To energize their respective radio receivers, both devices utilized similar power supplies, consisting of four AA batteries. Both employed many similar components such as batteries, duct tape, toggle switches, radio receivers, antennas, solder, electrical tape, and large round speaker magnets. Moreover, both used a distinctive method (i.e., twisting, soldering, and taping) to connect some, though not all, of the wires used.[14] Though we hardly find any of these factors by themselves to be "highly distinctive," the coalescence of them is fairly persuasive.[15] Indeed, even Trenkler's expert witness, Denny Kline, testi-

14. Though it is unclear from a close reading of the record just how many of the wires in each bomb employed this connection method, it is apparent that at least some did. More interestingly, we note that, before learning that both bombs had wires that were joined in this fashion, Trenkler's explosives expert stated that such a method is a "singularly unique method[] of assembly which individual bomb makers are very likely to repeat."

15. On the other hand, Trenkler argues that the differences between the two bombs are more significant. Some of the differences that Trenkler cites include:

fied at the pretrial hearing that, in light of these similarities, "there is a possibility, a *probability*, that maybe *there is a connection* between the maker of these two bombs." (Emphasis added.)

Moreover, we note that, in refusing to conclude "beyond a reasonable doubt"[16] that the same person built both bombs, Trenkler's expert Kline eschewed reliance on any factors except the physical evidence. The appropriate test for sufficient similarity, however, is not so limited. ". . . [T]he trial court must consider all evidence presented to the jury."

Accordingly, we believe some significance is properly attributed to the simple fact that both incidents are bombings. A bombing, in and of itself, is, arguably, a fairly distinctive method for intimidating or killing an individual. *Cf.* United States v. Patterson, 20 F.3d 809, 813 (10th Cir. 1994) (in a hijacking case, uniqueness of crime itself has significance in Rule 404(b) similarity analysis); *Pisari*, 636 F.2d at 858 ("Much more is demanded than the mere repeated commission of crimes of the same class, such as repeated burglaries or thefts. The device used must be so unusual and distinctive as to be like a signature."). In addition, both incidents involved not simply bombs, but remote-control bombs that were placed underneath automotive vehicles.

In both instances, the bombs were constructed and used to benefit a friend of the builder. Trenkler built the Quincy bomb for Donna Shea to use to intimidate the owners of the Capeway Fish Market, and the evidence supported the inference that the person who constructed the Roslindale bomb built it for Shay Jr. to use against his father. Furthermore, in both instances the builder attempted to conceal his or her

Roslindale Bomb	Quincy Bomb
Two or three sticks of dynamite rewrapped in a magazine page and electrical blasting caps which killed one officer and severely injured another	Military flash simulator used which produced only minor damage
Futaba remote control system which used a small electrical servo motor	Radio receiver taken from toy car
"Single throw" toggle switch used to send power to dynamite	Relay allowed power to be sent to explosives; "double throw" toggle switch used as safety
Five nine-volt batteries provided power to firing system	Two six-volt batteries supplied power to firing system
Device was housed in a black wooden box	Device was wrapped in silver duct tape

16. As the district court correctly noted in its ruling, the government is not required to establish "beyond a reasonable doubt" that the same person built the two bombs. *See* Huddleston v. United States, 485 U.S. 681, 690 (1988).

participation by using a third party to purchase the electronic components used in the explosive device. In 1986, Trenkler initially waited in his car while sending Donna Shea's nephew into the electronics store with a list to purchase the needed components. Similarly, the evidence supports the inference that the builder of the Roslindale bomb used Shay Jr. to purchase the needed components. Finally, the fact that both bombings occurred within a relatively close geographic proximity must be given some weight in the analysis.

In United States v. Pisari, 636 F.2d 855, 859 (1st Cir. 1981), we reversed the district court's decision to admit evidence of a prior robbery solely on the issue of identity, where the only similarity between it and the charged offense was that a knife was used. Similarly, in *Garcia–Rosa*, 876 F.2d at 224–25, we refused to sanction the admission of a prior drug transaction where the only characteristic linking it to the charged drug deal was the characteristic exchange of a sample of drugs prior to the sale. In *Garcia–Rosa*, we held that a single "prosaic commonality" was insufficient "to give rise to an inference that the same person was involved in both acts without reference to propensity." *Id.* at 225. *See also* United States v. Benedetto, 571 F.2d 1246, 1249 (2d Cir. 1978) (no signature where shared characteristic is merely "a similar technique for receiving the cash: the passing of folded bills by way of a handshake").

In the present case, however, the government presented more than a single "prosaic commonality." Indeed, the government propounded a laundry list of similarities in design, component selection, construction and overall modus operandi. On the other hand, Trenkler offered a fairly impressive list of differences between the two incidents. In the absence of one or more highly distinctive factors that in themselves point to idiosyncra[s]y, we must examine the combination of all the factors. Had Trenkler been unable to point to any significant differences, we suspect he would have had little chance in establishing an abuse of discretion in allowing the evidence. Similarly, had the government found but three or four common characteristics to establish sufficient similarity, we doubt that the admission of the evidence would have been granted or sustained. Here, in the middle, with substantial evidence on either side and conflicting expert opinions, [we hold the district court did not abuse its discretion in admitting the evidence]. *See Ingraham*, 832 F.2d at 233 (admitting evidence) ("Given the host of important comparables, the discrepancies—though themselves not unimportant—go to the weight of the challenged evidence, not to its admissibility.").[17]

17. As we explain *infra* in Part II.A., we believe that the district court erred in admitting the EXIS database evidence on the issue of idiosyncratic similarity. Our review of the record, however, convinces us that the EXIS evidence did not weigh significantly in the court's decision to admit the evidence of the Quincy bomb.

[The court's ruling that the EXIS evidence was wrongly admitted was based on hearsay law, not the law of character evi-

b. *Rule 404(b) Evidence: Probative Value and Unfair Prejudice:* Resolving that the district court did not abuse its discretion [in finding that the Quincy bomb had "special relevance" on the issue of identity] . . . does not end the analysis. We must also review the trial court's determination that the probative value of the evidence was not substantially outweighed by the risk of unfair prejudice. Several factors weigh heavily in this balancing, such as the government's need for the evidence, the strength of evidence establishing the similarity of the two acts, the inflammatory nature of the evidence, and the degree to which it would promote an inference based solely on the defendant's criminal propensity.

We believe the district court acted well within its broad discretion in admitting the evidence. First, the evidence was important to the government's case. . . . Second, although the evidence of similarity could have been more compelling, it was nonetheless substantial: Indeed, the government's explosives expert testified that he had no doubt "whatsoever" that the same person designed and constructed both bombs.

On the other hand, we disagree with the district court that the evidence did not pose any risk of unfair prejudice.[18] As with all "bad act" evidence, there is always some danger that the jury will use the evidence not on the narrow point for which it is offered but rather to infer that the defendant has a propensity towards criminal behavior. Nonetheless, outside the context of propensity, the evidence was not unduly inflammatory. The Quincy bomb did not kill or injure any individual and caused little property damage. Moreover, the district court minimized any risk of unfair prejudice by carefully instructing the jury not to use the evidence of the Quincy bombing to infer Trenkler's guilt simply because he was a bad person or because the fact he had a built a bomb in the past made it more likely he had built the bomb in this case. In sum, we believe that the district court did not abuse its discretion in determining that the probative value of the Quincy bomb evidence was not substantially outweighed by the risk of unfair prejudice.[19] . . .

III. CONCLUSION

For the foregoing reasons, we affirm Trenkler's conviction.

dence. We will take up hearsay in Chapter 7.—GF]

18. In ruling on the evidence, the district court stated, *inter alia*, "The evidence of the [Quincy] bomb is without question prejudicial in the sense that it will likely harm the defendant. That is not the test, however, the question is whether it is unfairly prejudicial. It is not."

19. Trenkler also contends that the district court abused its discretion in admitting the Quincy bomb evidence to prove knowledge [and] skill. . . . [W]e find little merit in Trenkler's argument. Obviously, the fact that Trenkler had in the past built a remote-control bomb has some relevance on whether he possessed the skill and knowledge necessary to build the Roslindale bomb. Furthermore, because the evidence was otherwise admissible to show identity, allowing the government to use it to show skill and knowledge posed no additional risk of unfair prejudice. . . .

■ TORRUELLA, CHIEF JUDGE, (Dissenting).... [There is] a potentially ... pernicious problem concerning the EXIS-derived evidence. The ... database entry for the Roslindale incident lists approximately twenty-two characteristics describing that incident, but Scheid, inexplicably, chose only to query ten of those characteristics.[34] ... Scheid offers no reason why he chose to query only certain generic characteristics instead of the more specific characteristics of the Roslindale bomb, which would be more evincing of a "signature." For example, the Quincy device would not have been a match if Scheid had queried any of the following characteristics of the Roslindale bombing: Futaba antenna, Rockstar detonator, use of dynamite, nails, glue, 6–volt battery, slide switch, paint, magazine page, or black electrical tape. The majority leaves the implication unspoken. I will not be so discreet. The obvious implication is that Scheid chose the particular characteristics in an attempt to find a match with the Quincy device. This implication is enforced by the fact that, according to Scheid's own testimony, the Quincy incident was not entered into the database until after the Roslindale incident. That is, government agents brought the Quincy bombing to Scheid's attention when they asked him to investigate the Roslindale bombing....

The EXIS-derived evidence is also misleading because it focuses the jury's attention on the trees instead of the forest. By focusing on similar minor aspects between the two devices—e.g., duct tape, magnets and soldering—the majority completely brushes aside the fact that the central and most important ingredient in the two devices is fundamentally different. The central ingredient in a bomb, one would think, is the explosive content (in much the same way that the central ingredient in a high-performance car is the engine). The Roslindale bomb used two to three sticks of dynamite—a very powerful explosive. The Quincy device used an M–21 Hoffman artillery simulator, which is a device used by the military to simulate, in a safe fashion, the flash and noise of artillery. The simulator is, in effect, a firecracker-like device; it has nowhere near the strength of dynamite. In stark contrast to dynamite, a simulator is not designed to cause physical or property damage. Indeed, while the Roslindale device created an explosion large enough to kill, the Quincy device caused no visible damage to the truck it was placed under. Equating the two devices is like equating a BB gun with a high caliber rifle.[38] ...

---

34. The queried characteristics were 1) bombings and attempted bombings; 2) involving cars or trucks; 3) with bomb placed under the car or truck; 4) using remote-control; and 5) magnets. EXIS listed seven incidents which included these characteristics. Scheid testified that he then performed a manual query of the seven incidents using other characteristics of the Roslindale bombing. He checked the other incidents to see if they involved 1) duct tape; 2) soldering; 3) AA batteries; 4) a toggle switch; and 5) round magnets. Scheid did not check all 14,252 bombings and attempted bombings for these latter characteristics, only the seven.

38. Federal authorities apparently did not deem the Quincy incident serious

UNITED STATES v. STEVENS

935 F.2d 1380 (3d Cir. 1991).

■ BECKER, CIRCUIT JUDGE. . . . At about 9:30 p.m. on April 15, 1989, a damp and chilly Saturday evening, two white Air Force police officers, Jane Smith[1] and Tony McCormack, were strolling back to their dormitories at Fort Dix, New Jersey, after having seen a movie at a nearby shopping mall. Because a light rain was falling, the officers decided to sit and chat under a glass-enclosed bus shelter.

A few minutes later, a black male, wearing a wool cap and a tan nylon jogging suit, entered the shelter, paused for a moment about ten feet away from the officers, and then asked them who they were. Both officers stood, but neither responded to the inquiry. The man approached the officers and, standing just a few feet away, reached his right hand into the small of his back and drew a small, silver handgun from his pants. Pointing the gun at McCormack's chest, the man demanded McCormack's wallet. McCormack handed over his wallet, which contained an unsigned $100 money order. To assure himself that McCormack was not withholding any cash, the man quickly frisked him; once satisfied, he told McCormack to sit down.

The man then turned his attention, and his gun, to Smith. He asked for her money, but she had none. After patting down Smith's pockets, the man [sexually assaulted Smith].

. . . The man told McCormack [and Smith] to leave the bus shelter and run across an adjacent field. . . . The two ran to the nearest building, the non-commissioned officers' club, where they telephoned the military police. Within five minutes, two military police officers arrived and escorted Smith and McCormack to the Fort Dix military police station.

At the station, Smith and McCormack met Christine Amos, a military police investigator. . . . Amos invited Smith and McCormack to take a look at the wanted board on the wall and to see if anyone resembled their assailant. This wanted board consisted of eight posters, containing mostly composite sketches but also some photographs. McCormack rose, approached the wanted board, and almost immediately focused upon a photograph of the defendant, Richard Stevens. McCormack said: "This is him. This is the man." Smith agreed that the photograph resembled their attacker, but thought that it made him appear a bit heavier. When Amos returned, Smith and McCormack informed her that they had identified a photograph of their assailant. Amos removed the poster of Stevens from

enough to warrant bringing charges against Trenkler pursuant to 18 U.S.C. § 844(i) (malicious destruction of property by means of an explosive), one of the statutes at issue in this case. State charges stemming from the Quincy incident were dismissed.

1. We have used a pseudonym to preserve this victim's anonymity.

the wall and then accompanied Smith to Walson Army Community Hospital....

Five days later, Smith and McCormack returned to the police station to view a lineup. The lineup, which consisted of seven individuals, was prepared and conducted by Agent James Maxwell of the Federal Bureau of Investigation. Smith and McCormack viewed the lineup separately and, without consulting with one another, each identified Stevens as their assailant. Both stated that they were positive that Stevens was the man who had robbed and assaulted them at the roadside bus stop....

In January of 1990, Stevens was tried before a jury, which ultimately became deadlocked, so a mistrial was declared. Stevens was retried in March of 1990 on the same charges. Following a four-day trial, this jury convicted Stevens on both counts [of robbery and sexual assault]....

VI. THE "REVERSE 404(b)" ISSUE

To shore up his theory that Smith and McCormack misidentified him as the perpetrator, Stevens sought to introduce under Fed. R. Evid. 404(b) the testimony of Tyrone Mitchell, the victim of a similar crime at Fort Dix. Three days after Smith and McCormack were assaulted, Mitchell, a black man, was robbed at gunpoint by another black man who, according to Mitchell's description, resembled Smith's and McCormack's attacker. Unlike Smith and McCormack, however, Mitchell stated that Stevens was not his assailant. Stevens reasons that Mitchell's failure to identify him tends to establish that he did not assault Smith and McCormack. The syllogism goes as follows. In view of the many parallels between the two crimes, one person very likely committed both; and because Stevens was exonerated by Mitchell, a black man whose identification (or lack thereof) is arguably more reliable than that of the two white victims, Stevens was not that person. The critical question is, of course, one of degree of similarity.

The similarities between the Mitchell robbery and the Smith and McCormack robbery/sexual assault are significant. Both crimes: (1) took place within a few hundred yards of one another; (2) were armed robberies; (3) involved a handgun; (4) occurred between 9:30 p.m. and 10:30 p.m.; (5) were perpetrated on military personnel; and (6) involved a black assailant who was described similarly by his victims. Indeed, based on these similarities, the United States Army Criminal Investigation Division came to believe, initially, that the same person had committed both crimes. Agent Jackson, the CID officer assigned to investigate the instant crime, reported that:

> This office is currently investigating a second Armed Robbery that occurred on the night of 18 Apr. 89, at the NCO Academy. The suspect in the second armed robbery matches the physical description in the Armed Robbery/Forced Sodomy.

He further remarked:

> [The Mitchell] Robbery has a lot of similarities with . . . ([the Smith] and McCormack Robbery/Sodomy) excluding the sexual aspects. The subject, in both files, had a gun, stole wallets and rummaged through the victims pockets and were in the same areas on post.

Stevens, as a result, quickly became the CID's leading suspect in the Mitchell robbery, as well as the Smith and McCormack robbery/sexual assault. CID Agent Bronisz stated: "Dix CID is certain that STEVENS robbed MITCHELL of his ID." The FBI, cognizant of this fact, thus had Mitchell view Stevens in the same lineup and on the same day that Smith and McCormack viewed him. Mitchell, however, did not identify Stevens as his assailant.

An additional, and even more striking, parallel subsequently developed which made the similarities between the two crimes more difficult to dismiss as mere coincidence. Mitchell was robbed of various items, including his military identification card. This card later was used to cash two stolen checks at the Fort Meade exchange in Maryland. Significantly, McCormack's stolen money order, like Mitchell's identification, also ended up near Fort Meade: it was cashed by someone other than Stevens at the Odenton Pharmacy located across the street from Fort Meade. That the fruits of the Mitchell and McCormack robberies, which occurred within days of one another at Fort Dix, New Jersey, both surfaced near Fort Meade, Maryland, is undoubtedly probative that the same individual committed both offenses.

The analytical basis for Stevens's proffer of Mitchell's testimony was a rarely used variant of Rule 404(b), known as "reverse 404(b)." In contrast to ordinary "other crimes" evidence, which is used to incriminate criminal defendants, "reverse 404(b)" evidence is utilized to exonerate defendants. As Wigmore's treatise points out:

> It should be noted that ["other crimes"] evidence may be also available to negative the accused's guilt. E.g., if A is charged with forgery and denies it, and if B can be shown to have done a series of similar forgeries connected by a plan, this plan of B is some evidence that B and not A committed the forgery charged. This mode of reasoning may become the most important when A alleges that he is a victim of mistaken identification.

Despite its rarity, several cases discuss "reverse 404(b)" evidence at length. . . . [T]hese cases . . . illuminate how "reverse 404(b)" evidence has been used in the past.

In Commonwealth v. Murphy, 282 Mass. 593 (1933), there was no evidence connecting the defendant to the offenses except for the victims' identifications. To offset these identifications, the defendant offered evidence of three similar crimes, one of which occurred while he was in custody. He also sought to introduce evidence that two of the victims of the other crimes had stated that he looked somewhat like (but was not)

the assailant, and that the third victim had admitted to misidentifying him as the assailant. On appeal, the Supreme Judicial Court of Massachusetts reversed the trial court's exclusion of this evidence, emphasizing that the jury was entitled to consider it in evaluating the victims' identifications: "No one, we think, will deny that if the evidence offered is the truth it well might shake confidence in the identifications upon which alone this conviction rests." *Id.* at 596–97. . . .

[A] New Jersey [case is] also helpful. In State v. Garfole, 76 N.J. 445 (1978), the defendant, who was charged with sexually molesting two children, sought to introduce evidence that he had been indicted on charges arising out of five similar episodes; that the charges arising out of four of those episodes had been dismissed; and that he had an alibi for all but two of the episodes. *Id.* at 448. The trial court rejected this proffer, stating that it was irrelevant to the specific charge at issue.

The New Jersey Supreme Court disagreed, noting that the evidence clearly had some relevance to the case. *Id.* at 451. The Court then turned to the question whether the other crimes were sufficiently relevant (i.e., similar) to outweigh countervailing considerations such as undue consumption of time and confusion of the issues. The Court observed, in this regard, that the trial court had imposed on the defendant the same standard of similarity that would have applied if the State had offered the evidence, in essence requiring that the other crimes be so distinctive as to constitute "signature" crimes. This, the Court held, was error:

> We are of the view . . . that [less] similarity of offenses may justly be required of a defendant using other-crime evidence defensively than is exacted from the State when such evidence is used incriminatorily. . . . Other-crimes evidence submitted by the prosecution has the distinct capacity of prejudicing the accused. . . . Therefore a fairly rigid standard of similarity may be required of the State if its effort is to establish the existence of a common offender by the mere similarity of the offenses. But *when the defendant is offering that kind of proof exculpatorily, prejudice to the defendant is no longer a factor, and simple relevance to guilt or innocence should suffice as the standard of admissibility. . . .*

Id. at 452–53 (emphasis added).[25] The Court thus instructed the trial court to rebalance the probative value of the evidence against the countervailing considerations, keeping in mind that prejudice to the defendant is not a factor when the defendant offers the other crimes evidence. . . .

The precise rationale for the district court's exclusion of Stevens's "reverse 404(b)" evidence is difficult to glean from the record. It appears

25. The Court stated that the application of a lower standard of similarity to the defendant's proffer "is additionally justified by the consideration that the defendant need only engender reasonable doubt of his guilt whereas the State must prove guilt beyond a reasonable doubt." *Garfole*, 76 N.J. at 453.

that the court barred the evidence on relevancy grounds, holding that the Mitchell robbery was a "separate offense . . . not directly related or tied . . . to this defendant." . . .

The government defends the district court's exclusion by asserting that a defendant may avail himself of Rule 404(b) in only three "constrained" circumstances, none of which apply to the instant case. First, the government submits, the defense may introduce evidence that the government induced others to commit crimes in order to show that the defendant was induced to commit the charged offense. This usage obviously has no bearing on Stevens's case. Second, the government argues, Rule 404(b) permits a defendant to introduce evidence that another person committed a similar crime, and that he (the defendant) was misidentified as the perpetrator of that similar crime. . . . *Murphy*, the government contends, [is an example] of this line of cases, which, the government asserts, is unavailable to Stevens because Mitchell never misidentified him as the assailant. Finally, the government states, defendants may invoke Rule 404(b) to admit evidence of other crimes "where those other crimes were sufficiently numerous and similar in their execution as to form a clear pattern." This is the so-called "signature" crime exception. The government maintains that this use, which supposedly is typified by . . . *Garfole*, is also unavailable to Stevens, because Stevens has proffered evidence of only one other crime, and because that crime was dissimilar in that there was no sexual assault.

Based on our survey of the case law, we believe that the district court imposed too stringent a standard of similarity on Stevens, and that the government has unnecessarily compartmentalized the permissible uses of "reverse 404(b)" evidence. "It is well established that a defendant may use similar 'other crimes' evidence defensively if in reason it tends, alone or with other evidence, to negate his guilt of the crime charged against him." State v. Williams, 214 N.J. Super. 12, 20 (App. Div. 1986). In our view, the most persuasive treatment of "reverse 404(b)" evidence is found in *Garfole, supra,* wherein the New Jersey Supreme Court observed that a lower standard of similarity should govern "reverse 404(b)" evidence because prejudice to the defendant is not a factor. We agree with the reasoning of *Garfole* and with its holding that the admissibility of "reverse 404(b)" evidence depends on a straightforward balancing of the evidence's probative value against considerations such as undue waste of time and confusion of the issues. Recasting this standard in terms of the Federal Rules of Evidence, we therefore conclude that a defendant may introduce "reverse 404(b)" evidence so long as its probative value under Rule 401 is not substantially outweighed by Rule 403 considerations.

Given the flexible contours of the above equation, we reject the government's attempt to impose hard and fast preconditions on the admission of "reverse 404(b)" evidence. More specifically, the defendant, in order to introduce other crimes evidence, need not show that there has been more than one similar crime, that he has been misidentified as the assailant in a similar crime, or that the other crime was sufficiently similar to be called a "signature" crime. These criteria, although relevant to measuring the probative value of the defendant's proffer, should not be erected as absolute barriers to its admission. Rather, a defendant must demonstrate that the "reverse 404(b)" evidence has a tendency to negate his guilt, and that it passes the Rule 403 balancing test.

Here, Mitchell's testimony, in conjunction with [the] comments [of Dr. Steven Penrod, an expert witness,] about the suspect nature of cross-racial identifications, easily satisfies the Rule 401 threshold. The government's case against Stevens rested entirely on two white victims' identifications of him as the assailant. To rebut the natural force of these identifications, Stevens attempted to mount a two-pronged defense. He began by offering Dr. Penrod's expert testimony that cross-racial identifications are notoriously unreliable. Then, to ground more concretely Dr. Penrod's opinion in the facts of this case, Stevens sought to introduce evidence that Mitchell, a black victim of a similar crime, had failed to identify him as the assailant.

The similarities between the Mitchell robbery and the Smith and McCormack robbery/sexual assault are demonstrated amply, in our view, by the facts that the CID was convinced that the same person had committed both crimes, and that the fruits of both robberies (i.e., McCormack's money order and Mitchell's military identification) ended up in Fort Meade. That the Mitchell robbery lacked a sexual element, we think, is not fatal to Stevens's proffer, because Mitchell, unlike McCormack, did not have a female companion. While we readily concede that the two attacks are by no means "signature" crimes, this is simply not the test. All that is necessary is that the evidence satisfy the relevancy standard of Rule 401. Having determined that Stevens's "reverse 404(b)" proffer was relevant under Rule 401 (i.e., it had a tendency to make Stevens's guilt less probable), we turn now to the countervailing Rule 403 considerations.

Under the circumstances of this case, the potential for waste of time or for misleading the jury, if the "reverse 404(b)" evidence were admitted, was minimal. Although the government objected to Mitchell's testimony, it agreed to stipulate to all of the essential facts regarding the Mitchell robbery in the event that his testimony were admitted. Stevens maintains that, as a result of this stipulation, Mitchell would have been a "fifteen-minute" witness, who simply would have testified regarding the details of the robbery and his viewing of the lineup. In addition, Stevens probably would have asked CID Agent Jackson and FBI Agent Maxwell some questions on cross-examination about the similarities between the Mitchell robbery and the Smith and McCormack robbery/sexual assault and about the government's initial suspicion that Stevens had robbed Mitchell.

Thus, even if Stevens's estimate of "fifteen minutes" was overly optimistic, there was no appreciable risk that Stevens's presentation of "reverse 404(b)" evidence would have degenerated into a mini-trial about whether or not Stevens had robbed Mitchell. Nor was there any real danger that Stevens's portrayal of the parallels between the two crimes would have obstructed the orderly progress of the trial or would have distracted the jurors' attention from the real issues in this case. The government, in fact, does not dispute seriously these points. The thrust of its challenge to Stevens's "reverse 404(b)" evidence was that it did not pass muster under Rule 401, not Rule 403. We thus conclude that the probative value of the Mitchell robbery was not substantially outweighed by the prospect of undue delay or confusion of the issues.

. . . To garner an acquittal, the defendant need only plant in the jury's mind a reasonable doubt. Had Stevens been allowed to adduce at trial evidence of the similarities between the Mitchell robbery and the Smith and McCormack robbery/sexual assault—including the Fort Meade connection—the jury might have determined that it was possible that another person had committed both crimes, thereby giving rise to a reasonable doubt. We do not know, of course, how a jury would weigh this evidence, but we do think that, at the very least, Stevens was entitled to have the jury consider the evidence and draw its own conclusions.

VII. HARMLESS ERROR

The government contends that we should affirm Stevens's conviction because the district court's errors were harmless under Fed. R. Crim. P. 52(a). If the evidence against Stevens were overwhelming, we could adopt such an approach, but that is not the case here. As mentioned above, Stevens's first trial ended in a mistrial because the jury was unable to reach a verdict. Given the apparent closeness of the evidence, we think it possible that the admission of evidence about the Mitchell robbery might have swayed the jury toward acquittal. . . . We therefore decline to affirm on harmless error grounds.

VIII. CONCLUSION

. . . [T]he judgment of sentence will be reversed and the case remanded for a new trial.

***Afterthought on* United States v. Stevens:** The *Stevens* court held that "because prejudice to the defendant is not a factor . . . the admissibility of 'reverse 404(b)' evidence depends on a straightforward balancing of the evidence's probative value against considerations such as undue waste of time and confusion of the issues." (Page 185.) Note that the court did not raise the possibility of unfair prejudice *to the government*. That is not because the government may *never* complain that evidence offered by the defendant poses a risk of unfair prejudice to the government. Rather, the court simply recognized that the evidence Stevens offered here—that someone else committed a crime similar to the crime with which he was charged—posed no such risk. After all, the danger of similar-crimes evidence when offered by the government is that the jury will punish the defendant for his *other* crimes or because of his propensity to commit this act. But when the defendant offers reverse-404(b) evidence of the sort at issue in *Stevens*, these forms of unfair prejudice simply pose no danger to the government.

The next problem addresses a different, quite common misreading of *Stevens*:

Problem 3.9
Misreading Stevens

Consider the facts of *United States v. Williams*, 458 F.3d 312 (3d Cir. 2006):

> . . . Defendant Richard Williams was convicted of possession of a firearm by a felon after police discovered a semi-automatic handgun in the bedroom in which he was apprehended. At trial, Williams sought to introduce evidence that another individual with whom he was arrested, Andre Urlin, had previously been convicted of possessing a firearm. The evidence was offered to show that the weapon found in the bedroom belonged to Urlin rather than Williams. [There was no evidence that Urlin's prior conviction involved the same gun, or even the same type of gun.] The District Court excluded the evidence. On appeal, Williams contends that the District Court erred and that, pursuant to our holding in United States v. Stevens, 935 F.2d 1380 (3d Cir. 1991), evidence of crimes or bad acts committed by persons other than the defendant ("reverse Rule 404(b) evidence") is admissible so long as its probative value is not substantially outweighed by the risk of unfair prejudice, undue delay or confusion of the issues. . . .
>
> [Williams] argues that Urlin's prior conviction "rationally tends to disprove [Williams's own] guilt"—the import of the conviction being that Urlin has a propensity to possess firearms and that, therefore, the gun recovered from under the mattress was likely Urlin's.
>
> Williams misreads *Stevens*. . . .

How has Williams misread *Stevens*?

4. Narrative Integrity (Res Gestae)

Problem 3.10
Russian Roulette

In *United States v. Hite,* 364 F.3d 874 (7th Cir. 2004), *vacated on other grounds,* 543 U.S. 1103 (2005), William Hite was charged with possession of a revolver with an obliterated serial number. Authorities found the gun in a backpack in Hite's bedroom during a February 2001 search of his grandmother's home. Hite claimed the gun was his cousin's. Before trial the government disclosed that to prove Hite's possession of the weapon, it intended to call his ex-fiancée, Patricia Stuart, who "would testify that in the early part of 1998, Hite played 'Russian roulette' with her. Specifically, . . . Hite pointed a revolver at her head, inserted one round, showed the inserted round to her, spun the chamber, and pulled the trigger a 'few times,' until she convinced him to stop."

In a pretrial in limine motion heard in March 2002, Hite asked the trial judge to exclude Stuart's testimony under Rules 403 and 404. The judge "instructed counsel that Stuart could testify that the defendant possessed a revolver, placed a bullet in it, spun the barrel and pulled the trigger. However, Stuart was told that, at no time, was she to characterize the event as 'Russian roulette,' nor was she to testify that the gun was pointed at her face or head." At trial Stuart testified as follows:

> *Q* [BY THE PROSECUTOR]: And what were the circumstances by which you saw Government Exhibit 5 [the revolver found in the backpack]?
>
> *A:* He had it in his hand.
>
> *Q:* And what did you observe about Government Exhibit 5 when he had it in his hand?
>
> *A:* He's [*sic*] showed me that there was a bullet in the chamber, spun it—
>
> *Q:* Let me stop you there. How did he show you there was a bullet in the chamber?
>
> *A:* He opened up the chamber and showed it to me.

Q: And then what?

A: He spun the chamber and pulled the trigger a few times.

Q: Now, did—was a shot ever fired?

A: No.

Q: Did this cause you any concern?

A: Yes.

Q: Did he stop pulling the trigger?

A: Yes.

Q: And why did he stop pulling the trigger?

A: I had convinced him to stop.

Under what theory might the judge have admitted this evidence? Was the court right to forbid references to Russian roulette and to bar testimony that Hite pointed the gun at Stuart's head? Why not simply limit Stuart to saying Hite showed her the gun in early 1998?

United States v. DeGeorge

380 F.3d 1203 (9th Cir. 2004).

■ Gibson, J. . . . The government alleged that [Rex K.] DeGeorge participated in a scheme to defraud by purchasing a yacht, inflating its value through a series of sham transactions, obtaining insurance on the yacht at the inflated value, scuttling it off the coast of Italy, and attempting to collect the insurance proceeds. . . .

Facts

DeGeorge, an attorney,* contracted with an Italian firm in June 1992 for the construction of a 76–foot yacht, later named the *Principe di Pictor,* for $1.9 million. In late July of that year, DeGeorge assigned his rights in the construction contract to Continental Pictures Corp., which in turn sold its interest in the yacht to Polaris Pictures Corp. for $3.6 million in October. DeGeorge himself continued throughout this time to make payments to the Italian builder.

* [DeGeorge appeared once before in this book, as appellate counsel to Malcolm Collins. (*See* page 78.)—GF]

Polaris had been formed by DeGeorge, and its President at the time of the yacht's purchase was Paul Ebeling, who was later indicted as a co-conspirator and who eventually testified as a government witness at trial. Polaris ostensibly financed its purchase of the yacht through notes issued by U.S. Inbanco, Ltd., a corporation formed by DeGeorge and incorporated on the same day that Polaris bought the yacht from Continental. Ebeling testified that the name "Inbanco" was designed to give the appearance that the corporation was a bank. Inbanco was given a security interest in the yacht in exchange for the notes. With the exception of DeGeorge's original contract with the Italian builder, no money changed hands in any of these transactions....

DeGeorge disguised his connection with Polaris by engaging in a stock swap with Tridon Corporation about two weeks before Continental sold the yacht to Polaris. DeGeorge traded all his shares of Polaris to Tridon Corporation, whose CEO was Ebeling, in exchange for two million shares of Tridon stock.... Ebeling testified that, to his knowledge, no money ever actually changed hands between Inbanco, Tridon, and Polaris.

The net effect of these transactions was to make Tridon, and not DeGeorge, the owner of Polaris, which now owned the *Principe*, which now appeared to have a market value of $3.6 million.

Tridon's ownership of Polaris was necessary for insurance purposes. DeGeorge had a rather extensive history of boat losses, including three instances—one alleged theft and two alleged sinkings—where he was fully compensated by insurance companies. Ebeling testified that DeGeorge was concerned that his loss history would prevent him from obtaining insurance in his own name. Whether this evidence of prior losses was admissible was a contested issue at trial, and the district court ultimately allowed the government to show only that three prior vessels owned by DeGeorge were insured; that he claimed the vessels were lost at sea; and that the vessels were not recovered. The government was not permitted to elicit details of the incidents themselves or the fact that DeGeorge had collected insurance proceeds on the losses.

Polaris purchased insurance from Cigna Property and Casualty Insurance Company in late October 1992. The insurance application listed $3.675 million as the purchase price of the yacht, made no mention of DeGeorge whatsoever, and listed U.S. Inbanco, Ltd. as the loss payee. Cigna issued an insurance policy binder to Polaris on October 22, insuring the yacht for $3.5 million.

... DeGeorge, Ebeling, and a third associate, Gabriel Falco, set out from Viareggio, Italy, on November 4, 1992, for the maiden voyage of the *Principe*.... [On the night of November 6, according] to testimony from Ebeling and Falco, ... DeGeorge instructed Falco to take the power tools they had purchased a few days earlier and begin cutting holes in the boat. For the next six or seven hours, DeGeorge, Falco, and Ebeling took turns cutting holes and trying to do anything else necessary to sink the *Principe,* including smashing equipment and opening vents in the engine room to make the boat take on more water.... Despite their efforts, ... the *Principe* refused to sink.

Sometime after daybreak, Italian authorities patrolling the coast spotted the yacht and began to approach.... Falco and Ebeling testified that ... DeGeorge devised a story for the three men to explain how they ended up off the coast of Italy with a scuttled yacht.

DeGeorge's story went as follows: he, Ebeling, and Falco had been in Naples looking for a captain. A man named Captain Libovich, who resembled Robert Redford and claimed to be a former Russian submarine captain, heard of their search and offered his services, along with those of his two crewmen. The six men took the yacht out from Naples for what was ostensibly to be a test drive. The captain and his men each brought aboard two large black duffel bags.

After several hours at sea, the captain and his crewmen overpowered the others and forced them into the cabin of the yacht. The captain and crew then set about cutting holes in the yacht so that it would sink. Sometime near dawn, a black speed boat pulled up next to the yacht. Libovich and his men unloaded their six bags onto the boat, jumped aboard, and sped off.

DeGeorge, Ebeling, and Falco recited this story to the Italian authorities.... Ebeling, acting in his capacity as Polaris's president and at the behest of DeGeorge, submitted a claim to Cigna on February 17, 1993, seeking payment under the insurance policy. The request repeated the Libovich story.... DeGeorge was indicted in January 1999 on charges including mail fraud, wire fraud, and perjury.... The case eventually went to trial, where DeGeorge was convicted....

VI.

... The district court allowed the government to introduce evidence that DeGeorge had previously lost three insured vessels at sea. The court reasoned that the prior losses were "inextricably intertwined" with the facts giving rise to the indictment against DeGeorge and therefore admissible [despite] Rule 404(b) of the Federal Rules of Evidence. In particular, the court believed the prior loss history was necessary to assist the jury in understanding why DeGeorge had maneuvered to distance himself from the boat's ownership.... The court did not permit the government to introduce evidence that DeGeorge had collected insurance proceeds on those vessels or to discuss any further details surrounding those incidents....

We have recognized two categories of evidence that may be considered "inextricably intertwined" with a charged offense.... *See* United States v. Vizcarra–Martinez, 66 F.3d 1006, 1012 (9th Cir. 1995). First, evidence of prior acts may be admitted if the evidence "constitutes a part of the transaction that serves as the basis for the criminal charge." Second, prior act evidence may be admitted "when it was necessary to do so in order to permit the prosecutor to offer a coherent and comprehensible story regarding the commission of the crime." *Id.* at 1012–13.

Contrary to the government's assertion, the evidence of DeGeorge's prior marine losses does not appear to fit into the first category. The prior losses are too far removed in both time and circumstance to be linked with the alleged fraud in this case as part of a "single criminal episode."

The prior loss evidence does, however, fit into the second category. The concealment of DeGeorge's prior losses had an important factual connection to several counts contained in the indictment.... The government specifically alleged that DeGeorge's scheme included sham transactions to hide his ownership of the boat.... The government presented evidence, including Ebeling's testimony, to support this allegation. The jury would not have understood the relevance of the transactions and concealment without hearing at least some explanation for why DeGeorge could not obtain insurance in his own name. *See* Vizcarra–Martinez, 66 F.3d at 1013 ("The jury cannot be expected to make its decision in a void—without knowledge of the time, place, and circumstances of the acts which form the basis of the charge."). Thus, the district court did not err in concluding that the prior loss evidence was "inextricably intertwined" with the underlying offense.

Moreover, the district court's limitations on the evidence are sufficient to convince us that the court did not abuse its discretion under Rule 403. While we agree with DeGeorge that the prior loss evidence could imply a propensity to defraud insurance companies, the district court prevented the government from presenting evidence that DeGeorge had collected under the previous insurance policies. Instead, the court limited the use of the prior loss evidence to correspond with the issue to which it was relevant: DeGeorge's non-disclosure of prior losses. The court's conclusion that the probative value of this limited evidence [was not substantially] outweighed [by] the danger of unfair prejudice was not an abuse of discretion....

In sum, we AFFIRM DeGeorge's convictions in all respects....

---

5. Absence of Accident

Problem 3.11
Cleaning His Gun

The defendant, charged with shooting his wife, testified at trial he was cleaning his hunting rifle when it accidentally discharged. After the defendant testified, the prosecutor sought to admit evidence that three years earlier the defendant had shot and killed his first wife. At the time of the earlier shooting the defendant claimed he had been cleaning his hunting rifle when it accidentally discharged. He was never charged in connection with this incident.

If the defendant objects to the prosecutor's proposed evidence, how should the judge rule? What purpose can the prosecutor articulate for the evidence of the earlier event other than proof of the defendant's violent propensity?

Problem 3.12
Cruelty to Dogs

Rebuttal OKd if Burnett Testifies That Leo Bit Him

Witness Says He Beat Another Dog to Death

Alan Gathright

SAN FRANCISCO CHRONICLE, June 15, 2001

If Andrew Douglas Burnett testifies that he reflexively tossed Leo the dog onto the street—but not to his death—after it bit him, prosecutors can call a witness who claims Burnett clubbed a stray dog to death in the Navy, a San Jose judge ruled yesterday.

During a hearing without the jury, Santa Clara County Superior Court Judge Kevin J. Murphy tentatively ruled he will allow testimony from the defendant's former Navy supervisor who said Burnett admitted while working as a naval base guard in Puerto Rico in 1995 that he beat a mutt to death with a police baton "to put the dog out of its misery because it was a stray."

"It wasn't a big deal," Burnett supposedly told his supervisor, Audrey Warren, according to Murphy's recounting of a sworn statement by the potential witness. Warren, who now lives in San Antonio, was not present in court yesterday.

Warren will only be called as a rebuttal witness if testimony by Burnett or other defense witnesses next week echoes assertions by defense attorney Marc Garcia that his client was instinctively reacting to a bite and didn't fling [Leo] the dog into traffic in anger over a fender-bender with the pet's owner last year. In opening remarks to the jury, Garcia implied that a startled Burnett simply dropped the tiny white dog onto the road and it scampered under the wheels of a passing car.

Was the judge's ruling right? Assume the Federal Rules of Evidence control this case. *Cf. People v. Burnett*, 110 Cal. App. 4th 868, 879–82 (2003).

6. DOCTRINE OF CHANCES

A Note on the Next Case: *Rex v. Smith*, 11 Cr. App. R. 229, 84 L.J.K.B. 2153 (1915), is an evidence law classic, a topic of much study and debate. The appellate report of the case is unfortunately spare and unhelpful. *Smith* is better viewed through the eyes of those who watched the trial unfold in the *Times* of London:

THE BRIDES CASE

Prisoner on Trial at the Old Bailey.

The Death of Miss Mundy.

THE TIMES, June 23, 1915, at 5

George Joseph Smith . . . was placed on his trial before Mr. Justice Scrutton . . . yesterday, upon the indictment charging him with the wilful murder of Bessie Constance Annie Mundy on July 13, 1912. . . .

THE OPENING SPEECH.

Mr. Bodkin [the prosecutor] described how [Smith] . . . made the acquaintance of Miss Mundy at a boarding-house at Clifton at the beginning of August [1910], and on the 26th of that month went through the form of marriage with her at Weymouth. Miss Mundy had inherited from her father, a bank manager, a little over £2,500. . . .

THE FATAL BATH.

. . . Mr. Bodkin went on to describe how the prisoner had taken Miss Mundy to Dr. French, saying she had had a fit, how he had sent for the doctor saying she had had another fit. . . . Then he told how on the morning of July 13 a little after 8 o'clock, a note was handed to Dr. French, "Can you come at once? I am afraid my wife is dead"; how Dr. French found the prisoner in a downstairs room, how they went up together and saw the body of Miss Mundy lying face upwards in the bath, . . . the mouth under the water. . . .

AFTER THE DEATH.

On July 17 the prisoner . . . called at the office of the landlord . . . and, putting his face in his hands on the clerk's desk, wept. He said to the clerk:—"My wife is dead. . . . Wasn't it a jolly good job I got her to make her will." . . .

A QUESTION OF EVIDENCE.

At this point the Judge asked the jury to leave the Court while a discussion took place as to the admissibility of evidence which Mr. Bodkin proposed to adduce in respect to the cases of Miss Burnham and Miss Lofty, to both of whom the prisoner was married, and who both died in baths.

Mr. Justice Scrutton admitted the evidence, but told the jury that they must not use it for the purpose of saying "He is a man of bad character, and therefore is very likely to have murdered Miss Mundy." It was admissible only for the purpose of helping the jury to draw an inference as to whether the death of Miss Mundy was accidental or designed by the prisoner—in other words, as evidence to show whether he had a system of murdering women with whom he went through the form of marriage in order to obtain their money.

Mr. Bodkin then went on to mention the circumstances surrounding the deaths of Miss Burnham and Miss Lofty. Both of them made, he said, their wills, leaving everything to the prisoner.... Mr. Bodkin remarked that it was all very well to talk about a person having a fainting fit and getting drowned in a bath, but it was an extraordinarily unlikely thing to happen.... To a police officer the prisoner said, "I admit the two deaths form a phenomenal coincidence, but that is my hard luck. You may think it strange, but it was the irony of fate that my two wives died in that way." The death of Miss Lofty, said [Bodkin], was not then known. There were numerous points of similarity in the three cases which justified the grave assertion that the prisoner was out to make money out of the drowning of people with whom he went through the form of marriage....

BRIDES IN BATHS

Prisoner Sentenced to Death.

The Closing Scenes

THE TIMES, July 2, 1915, at 4

* * *

THE SUMMING-UP.

Mr. Justice Scrutton, in summing up, said ... that the way in which [Mundy's] body was found, [and] the circumstances in which the woman appeared to have died, might seem to the jury to be quite consistent, or very nearly quite consistent, with accident or design. And it might be that even then the jury were not sure whether it was accident or design—and then came in the purpose, and the only purpose, for which they were allowed to consider the evidence as to the other deaths. If they found an accident which [monetarily] benefited a person, and they found that that person had been sufficiently fortunate to have that accident happen to him a number of times, benefiting him each time, they [would draw] a very strong and frequently an irresistible inference that the occurrence of so many accidents benefiting him was such a coincidence that it could only have happened by design.

INFERENCE OF DESIGN.

... He might illustrate his point by an imaginary incident in a game of cards. Supposing they found in the pocket of one of the players the ace of trumps they might regard the matter with suspicion. But cards had a way of falling about, and perhaps on an isolated case they would not form a definite opinion. Supposing, however, they heard that on several other occasions the ace of trumps had been found in that man's pocket they would draw from that series of fortunate accidents the inference of design. The matter depended on the unusualness of the occurrence and the number of times it was repeated. Each additional case increased the improbability of accident. It was for that purpose only that they must consider this evidence....

VERDICT AND SENTENCE.

The jury retired to consider their verdict at eight minutes to 3 o'clock. They returned at 10 minutes past 3, and, in reply to the Clerk of the Court, the foreman said they found the prisoner *Guilty*....

REX V. SMITH: *Afterthoughts*

The Doctrine of Chances

At the *Smith* trial both Justice Scrutton and the prosecutor suggested a number of around-the-box theories that might—or might not—have justified Scrutton's decision to admit evidence of Burnham's and Lofty's deaths. Scrutton instructed the jury at the outset that the evidence was admissible to help "the jury to draw an inference as to whether the death of Miss Mundy was accidental or designed by the prisoner." Rule 404(b) lists "proof of ... absence of mistake or accident" as one of the "other purposes" for which evidence of other acts may be used. Refer again to Problem 3.11, *Cleaning His Gun*, at page 193. Could a good defense lawyer distinguish that case from *Smith* in terms of the probative power of the past deaths in showing absence of accident?

Justice Scrutton also advised the jurors that they could use the evidence of Burnham's and Lofty's deaths when considering whether the defendant "had a system of murdering women with whom he went through the form of marriage in order to obtain their money." Here Scrutton alludes to proof of both "motive" and "plan"—also listed in Rule 404(b). Again, could a good defense lawyer argue that using the other deaths in this case to prove motive or plan does not in fact evade the propensity evidence ban? Or are these winning arguments for the prosecution?

Scrutton's final theory, illustrated with his imaginary card game, has made this case famous. The jury could, Scrutton said, "draw from that series of fortunate accidents the inference of design. The matter depended on the unusualness of the occurrence and the number of times it was repeated." Scrutton's insight—the sheer improbability that Smith's three wives all could die in their tubs without foul play—has become known as the *doctrine of chances*, recognized in some quarters as an around-the-box use of other-acts evidence.

The Court of Criminal Appeal upheld Smith's conviction of murdering Bessie Mundy. *See Rex v. Smith*, 11 Cr. App. R. 229, 84 L.J.K.B. 2153 (1915). The court noted that Justice Scrutton "was very careful to point out to the jury the use they could properly make of the evidence" of the deaths of Burnham and Lofty. But Lord Chief Justice Reading's opinion was not particularly clear about which of Scrutton's theories the appellate court accepted. At oral argument Reading observed that "[i]t must be remembered that it is only in very abnormal circumstances that people die in baths." *Drowned Brides Case*, THE TIMES, July 30, 1915, at 3. Perhaps, then, the appellate court embraced the doctrine of chances.

Scholars at Odds

Does the doctrine of chances avoid forbidden propensity reasoning? Or does it somehow—if covertly—lead the jury through the propensity box? On this fundamental question evidence scholars differ.

Professor Edward Imwinkelried insists the doctrine of chances articulates "a valid, noncharacter theory of admissibility" of other-acts evidence. He cites as a "paradigmatic case" *United States v. Woods*, 484 F.2d 127 (4th Cir. 1973), *cert. denied*, 415 U.S. 979 (1974). Martha Woods, charged with infanticide after the cyanosis-related death of a foster son, claimed his suffocation was accidental. The prosecution rebutted with evidence that over a twenty-five-year period, children in the defendant's custody or care suffered at least twenty episodes of cyanosis resulting in seven deaths. Responding to defense counsel's claim that this history amounted to evidence of the defendant's bad character, the prosecution cited the doctrine of chances.

Defending the prosecutor's stance, Imwinkelried distinguishes simple propensity reasoning and the doctrine of chances. Under both, the jury begins with evidence of the defendant's uncharged crimes. But from there the chain of inferences diverges widely. A jury engaged in character reasoning must first decide "whether to infer from the evidence that the accused has a personal bad character." Propensity reasoning therefore forces jurors to "address ... the type of person the accused is" and tempts them to punish the defendant for her past bad acts or general bad character.

"In contrast," Imwinkelried says, "under the doctrine of chances, the trier need not focus on the accused's subjective character." Rather "the initial decision facing the trier is whether the uncharged incidents are so numerous that it is objectively improbable that so many accidents would befall the accused." He elaborates:

> Assume arguendo that statistics compiled by the United States Public Health Service indicate that during a twenty-five year period, only two percent of American children experienced an accidental cyanotic episode. Contrast that figure with the incidence of cyanotic episodes experienced by the children in Ms. Woods' custody. Suppose, for example, that during the same twenty-five year period, twenty percent of those children had cyanotic episodes. The frequency of the episodes among those children far exceeds the national average for such episodes. The episodes are so recurrent among those children that it is objectively implausible to assume that all those episodes were accidental.

"Either one or some of those episodes were caused by human intervention," he concludes, "or Ms. Woods is one of the most unlucky people alive."

Imwinkelried allows that the doctrine does not avoid all risk of character reasoning. Though jurors need not address the defendant's character traits, "[t]here is an undeniable probability that on their own motion" they will do so. But because "the doctrine of chances does not compel the jurors to focus on the accused's subjective disposition, . . . the doctrine significantly reduces the risk of a decision on an improper basis." And just as it reduces the risk that jurors will punish the defendant for her *other* acts or her bad character, the doctrine of chances avoids another form of unfair prejudice commonly linked with character evidence—the danger that jurors will overweigh the probative value of other-acts evidence. "The doctrine invites the trier to compare the accused's experience with statistical data or the trier's knowledge of everyday, human experience. We commonly accept the trier's knowledge of 'the ways of the world' as a trustworthy basis for legal reasoning." Edward J. Imwinkelried, *The Use of an Accused's Uncharged Misconduct to Prove Mens Rea: The Doctrines Which Threaten to Engulf the Character Evidence Prohibition*, 51 OHIO ST. L.J. 575, 585–92 (1990).

Eyeing the doctrine of chances more warily, Professor Paul Rothstein doubts that Imwinkelried has evaded the propensity box. Rothstein begins by restating the doctrine's driving question: "What are the chances that an innocent person would be charged falsely so many times?" If the answer is *rarely*, "it is safe to infer that the person is not innocent." Paul Rothstein, *Intellectual Coherence in an Evidence Code*, 28 LOY. L.A. L. REV. 1259, 1262–63 (1995).

Rothstein does not deny the obvious force of this argument. Rather he claims that its force derives from unspoken character reasoning. If there is a disparity between the (small) probability that an innocent person could face multiple similar criminal charges and the (larger) probability that a guilty person could do so, "it is only because a guilty person would have the propensity to repeat the crime. If it were not for the propensity to repeat, . . . the probability that an innocent person and a guilty person would be charged repeatedly would be identical." Hence the effort to avoid propensity reasoning "has failed."

Rothstein alleges other shortcomings in the doctrine of chances. The doctrine does not say "how many [similar events] are needed and how similar must they be," though these factors influence the likelihood of innocent misfortune. Nor does the doctrine say *how* unlikely innocent misfortune must be before an inference of guilt will follow.

A Thought Experiment

The doctrine of chances relies on the belief that multiple misfortunes, if similar enough and rare enough, suggest guilt *only* because of the unlikelihood of innocent coincidence. Rothstein counters that the force of the doctrine also draws from the perceived likelihood of guilty contrivance. He finds an ally in the British Royal Statistical Society. Commenting on a case of multiple SIDS deaths, the group observed in an October 2001 press release: "Two deaths by SIDS or two murders are each quite unlikely, but one has apparently happened in this case. What matters is the relative likelihood of the deaths under each explanation [innocent and guilty], not just how unlikely they are under one [innocent] explanation."

Rothstein and the Royal Statistical Society agree that the force of the evidence of three bathtub deaths in *Smith* does not depend solely on the unlikelihood of repeated—and rare—misfortunes. The inference of Smith's guilt depends as well, they believe, on an unspoken understanding that some men, including perhaps Smith, batter and even kill successive spouses as an expression of their violent or controlling natures.

To test the suspicion that propensity reasoning explains the persuasive force of the evidence in *Smith*, imagine a different factual scenario and an equally phenomenal coincidence: Imagine that instead of summoning his doctor on discovering his wife's lifeless body in the tub, Smith had called the police and reported his name and the apparent drowning. Just as the call ended, the dispatcher's phone rang again. A second man named George Smith was calling to report the bathtub drowning of his wife, also named Bessie. When the dispatcher insisted they had just spoken, the caller insisted they had not. On investigation the police learned that two George Smiths had lost wives named Bessie in almost simultaneous bathtub deaths. More phenomenally still, the two Smiths shared the same birthday!

A coincidence? The odds against it seem astronomical. Should we therefore declare one or both Smiths guilty of murder? And if not, why not?

In the story of two George Smiths the inference of innocent happenstance seems farfetched—but so does the inference of guilty plan. Why on earth would two men named Smith scheme to kill their wives by a common method at the same time? Because no theory of guilt comes to mind, we are prepared to attribute the coincidental deaths, however amazing, to chance. In the real *Smith* case, in contrast, the inference of guilt comes naturally to mind. Is that because the inference of Smith's violent or controlling or greedy nature seems so plausible? If so, we have reason to question whether the doctrine of chances truly evades the propensity box. *Cf.* Michael Redmayne, *"A Likely Story,"* 19 OXFORD J. LEGAL STUD. 659, 662–63 (1999).

C. THE *HUDDLESTON* STANDARD

HUDDLESTON V. UNITED STATES

485 U.S. 681 (1988).

■ REHNQUIST, C.J., delivered the opinion [for a unanimous] Court.... Petitioner, Guy Rufus Huddleston, was charged with one count of selling stolen goods in interstate commerce, and one count of possessing stolen property in interstate commerce. The two counts related to two portions of a shipment of stolen Memorex video cassette tapes that petitioner was alleged to have possessed and sold, knowing that they were stolen.

The evidence at trial showed that a trailer containing over 32,000 blank Memorex video cassette tapes with a manufacturing cost of $4.53 per tape was stolen from the Overnight Express yard in South Holland, Illinois, sometime between April 11 and 15, 1985. On April 17, 1985, petitioner contacted Karen Curry, the manager of the Magic Rent-to-Own in Ypsilanti, Michigan, seeking her assistance in selling a large number of blank Memorex video cassette tapes. After assuring Curry that the tapes were not stolen, he told her he wished to sell them in lots of at least 500 at $2.75 to $3 per tape. Curry subsequently arranged for the sale of a total of 5,000 tapes, which petitioner delivered to the various purchasers—who apparently believed the sales were legitimate.

There was no dispute that the tapes which petitioner sold were stolen; the only material issue at trial was whether petitioner knew they were stolen. The District Court allowed the Government to introduce evidence of "similar acts" under Rule 404(b), concluding that such evidence had "clear relevance as to [petitioner's knowledge]." The first piece of similar act evidence offered by the Government was the testimony of Paul Toney, a record store owner. He testified that in February 1985, petitioner offered to sell new 12″ black and white televisions for $28 a piece. According to Toney, petitioner indicated that he could obtain several thousand of these televisions. Petitioner and Toney eventually traveled to the Magic Rent-to-Own, where Toney purchased 20 of the televisions. Several days later, Toney purchased 18 more televisions.

The second piece of similar act evidence was the testimony of Robert Nelson, an undercover FBI agent posing as a buyer for an appliance store. Nelson testified that in May 1985, petitioner offered to sell him a large quantity of Amana appliances—28 refrigerators, 2 ranges, and 40 icemakers. Nelson agreed to pay $8,000 for the appliances. Petitioner was arrested shortly after he arrived at the parking lot where he and Nelson had agreed to transfer the appliances. A truck containing the appliances was stopped a short distance from the parking lot, and Leroy Wesby, who was driving the truck, was also arrested. It was determined that the appliances had a value of approximately $20,000 and were part of a shipment that had been stolen.

Petitioner testified that the Memorex tapes, the televisions, and the appliances had all been provided by Leroy Wesby, who had represented that all of the merchandise was obtained legitimately. Petitioner stated that he had sold 6,500 Memorex tapes for Wesby on a commission basis. Petitioner maintained that all of the sales for Wesby had been on a commission basis and that he had no knowledge that any of the goods were stolen.

In closing, the prosecution explained that petitioner was not on trial for his dealings with the appliances or the televisions. The District Court instructed the jury that the similar acts evidence was to be used only to establish petitioner's knowledge, and not to prove his character. The jury convicted petitioner on the possession count only.

A divided panel of the United States Court of Appeals for the Sixth Circuit initially reversed the conviction, concluding that because the Government had failed to prove by clear and convincing evidence that the televisions were stolen, the District Court erred in admitting the testimony concerning the televisions. 802 F.2d 874 (1986).[1] The panel subsequently granted rehearing to address the decision in United States v. Ebens, 800 F.2d 1422 (6th Cir. 1986), in which a different panel had held: "Courts may admit evidence of prior bad acts if the proof shows by a preponderance of the evidence that the defendant did in fact commit the act." *Id.* at 1432. On rehearing, the court affirmed the conviction. "Applying the preponderance of the evidence standard adopted in *Ebens*, we cannot say that the district court abused its discretion in admitting evidence of the similar acts in question here." 811 F.2d 974, 975 (1987). The court noted that the evidence concerning the televisions was admitted for a proper purpose and that the probative value of this evidence was not outweighed by its potential prejudicial effect.

1. "The government's only support for the assertion that the televisions were stolen was [petitioner's] failure to produce a bill of sale at trial and the fact that the televisions were sold at a low price." 802 F.2d at 876 n.5.

We granted certiorari to resolve a conflict among the Courts of Appeals as to whether the trial court must make a preliminary finding before "similar act" and other Rule 404(b) evidence is submitted to the jury. We conclude that such evidence should be admitted if there is sufficient evidence to support a finding by the jury that the defendant committed the similar act.

Federal Rule of Evidence 404(b)—which applies in both civil and criminal cases—generally prohibits the introduction of evidence of extrinsic acts that might adversely reflect on the actor's character, unless that evidence bears upon a relevant issue in the case such as motive, opportunity, or knowledge. Extrinsic acts evidence may be critical to the establishment of the truth as to a disputed issue, especially when that issue involves the actor's state of mind and the only means of ascertaining that mental state is by drawing inferences from conduct. The actor in the instant case was a criminal defendant, and the act in question was "similar" to the one with which he was charged. Our use of these terms is not meant to suggest that our analysis is limited to such circumstances.

Before this Court, petitioner argues that the District Court erred in admitting Toney's testimony as to petitioner's sale of the televisions.[3] The threshold inquiry a court must make before admitting similar acts evidence under Rule 404(b) is whether that evidence is probative of a material issue other than character. The Government's theory of relevance was that the televisions were stolen, and proof that petitioner had engaged in a series of sales of stolen merchandise from the same suspicious source would be strong evidence that he was aware that each of these items, including the Memorex tapes, was stolen.[4] As such, the sale of the televisions was a "similar act" only if the televisions were stolen. Petitioner acknowledges that this evidence was admitted for the proper purpose of showing his knowledge that the Memorex tapes were stolen. He asserts, however, that the evidence should not have been admitted because the Government failed to prove to the District Court that the televisions were in fact stolen.

Petitioner argues from the premise that evidence of similar acts has a grave potential for causing improper prejudice. For instance, the jury may choose to punish the defendant for the similar rather than the charged act, or the jury may infer that the defendant is an evil person inclined to violate the law. Because of this danger, petitioner maintains, the jury ought not to be exposed to similar act evidence until the trial court has

3. Petitioner does not dispute that Nelson's testimony concerning the Amana appliances was properly admitted under Rule 404(b).

4. The Government also argues before this Court that the evidence concerning the televisions is relevant even if the jury could not conclude that the sets were stolen. We have found nothing in the record indicating that this theory was suggested to or relied upon by the courts below, and in light of our ruling, we need not address this alternative theory.

heard the evidence and made a determination under Federal Rule of Evidence 104(a) that the defendant committed the similar act. [Unrestyled] Rule 104(a) provides that "preliminary questions concerning the qualification of a person to be a witness, the existence of a privilege, or the admissibility of evidence shall be determined by the court, subject to the provisions of subdivision (b)." According to petitioner, the trial court must make this preliminary finding by at least a preponderance of the evidence.[5]

We reject petitioner's position, for it is inconsistent with the structure of the Rules of Evidence and with the plain language of Rule 404(b).... [That rule] protects against the introduction of extrinsic act evidence when that evidence is offered solely to prove character. The text contains no intimation, however, that any preliminary showing is necessary before such evidence may be introduced for a proper purpose. If offered for such a proper purpose, the evidence is subject only to general strictures limiting admissibility such as Rules 402 and 403.

Petitioner's reading of Rule 404(b) as mandating a preliminary finding by the trial court that the act in question occurred not only superimposes a level of judicial oversight that is nowhere apparent from the language of that provision, but it is simply inconsistent with the legislative history behind Rule 404(b). The Advisory Committee specifically declined to offer any "mechanical solution" to the admission of evidence under 404(b). (ACN on FRE 404(b).) Rather, the Committee indicated that the trial court should assess such evidence under the usual rules for admissibility: "The determination must be made whether the danger of undue prejudice outweighs the probative value of the evidence in view of the availability of other means of proof and other factors appropriate for making decisions of this kind under Rule 403." *Ibid.; see also* S. Rep. No. 93–1277, p. 25 (1974) ("It is anticipated that with respect to permissible uses for such evidence, the trial judge may exclude it only on the basis of those considerations set forth in Rule 403, *i.e.* prejudice, confusion or waste of time.").

Petitioner's suggestion that a preliminary finding is necessary to protect the defendant from the potential for unfair prejudice is also belied by the Reports of the House of Representatives and the Senate. The House made clear that the version of Rule 404(b) which became law was

5. In his brief, petitioner argued that the Government was required to prove to the trial court the commission of the similar act by clear and convincing proof. At oral argument, his counsel conceded that such a position is untenable in light of our decision last Term in Bourjaily v. United States, 483 U.S. 171 (1987), in which we concluded that preliminary factual findings under Rule 104(a) are subject to the preponderance-of-the-evidence standard. Petitioner now asserts that although the Sixth Circuit correctly held that the Government must prove the similar act by preponderant evidence before it is admitted, the court erred in applying that test to these facts. We consider first what preliminary finding, if any, the trial court must make before letting similar acts evidence go to the jury.

intended to "place greater emphasis on admissibility than did the final Court version." H.R. REP. No. 93–650, p. 7 (1973). The Senate echoed this theme: "The use of the discretionary word 'may' with respect to the admissibility of evidence of crimes, wrongs, or other acts is not intended to confer any arbitrary discretion on the trial judge." S. Rep. No. 93–1277, at 24. Thus, Congress was not nearly so concerned with the potential prejudicial effect of Rule 404(b) evidence as it was with ensuring that restrictions would not be placed on the admission of such evidence.

We conclude that a preliminary finding by the court that the Government has proved the act by a preponderance of the evidence is not called for under Rule 104(a).[6] This is not to say, however, that the Government may parade past the jury a litany of potentially prejudicial similar acts that have been established or connected to the defendant only by unsubstantiated innuendo. Evidence is admissible under Rule 404(b) only if it is relevant. "Relevancy is not an inherent characteristic of any item of evidence but exists only as a relation between an item of evidence and a matter properly provable in the case." (ACN on FRE 401.) In the Rule 404(b) context, similar act evidence is relevant only if the jury can reasonably conclude that the act occurred and that the defendant was the actor. In the instant case, the evidence that petitioner was selling the televisions was relevant under the Government's theory only if the jury could reasonably find that the televisions were stolen.

Such questions of relevance conditioned on a fact are dealt with under Federal Rule of Evidence 104(b). [Unrestyled] Rule 104(b) provides:

> "When the relevancy of evidence depends upon the fulfillment of a condition of fact, the court shall admit it upon, or subject to, the introduction of evidence sufficient to support a finding of the fulfillment of the condition."

In determining whether the Government has introduced sufficient evidence to meet Rule 104(b), the trial court neither weighs credibility nor makes a finding that the Government has proved the conditional fact by a preponderance of the evidence. The court simply examines all the evidence in the case and decides whether the jury could reasonably find the conditional fact—here, that the televisions were stolen—by a preponderance of the evidence. The trial court has traditionally exercised the broadest sort of discretion in controlling the order of proof at trial, and we see nothing in the Rules of Evidence that would change this practice.

6. Petitioner also suggests that in performing the balancing prescribed by Federal Rule of Evidence 403, the trial court must find that the prejudicial potential of similar acts evidence substantially outweighs its probative value unless the court concludes by a preponderance of the evidence that the defendant committed the similar act. We reject this suggestion because Rule 403 admits of no such gloss and because such a holding would be erroneous for the same reasons that a preliminary finding under Rule 104(a) is inappropriate. We do, however, agree with the Government's concession at oral argument that the strength of the evidence establishing the similar act is one of the factors the court may consider when conducting the Rule 403 balancing.

Often the trial court may decide to allow the proponent to introduce evidence concerning a similar act, and at a later point in the trial assess whether sufficient evidence has been offered to permit the jury to make the requisite finding. If the proponent has failed to meet this minimal standard of proof, the trial court must instruct the jury to disregard the evidence.

We emphasize that in assessing the sufficiency of the evidence under Rule 104(b), the trial court must consider all evidence presented to the jury. "Individual pieces of evidence, insufficient in themselves to prove a point, may in cumulation prove it. The sum of an evidentiary presentation may well be greater than its constituent parts." Bourjaily v. United States, 483 U.S. 171, 179–80 (1987). In assessing whether the evidence was sufficient to support a finding that the televisions were stolen, the court here was required to consider not only the direct evidence on that point—the low price of the televisions, the large quantity offered for sale, and petitioner's inability to produce a bill of sale—but also the evidence concerning petitioner's involvement in the sales of other stolen merchandise obtained from Wesby, such as the Memorex tapes and the Amana appliances. Given this evidence, the jury reasonably could have concluded that the televisions were stolen, and the trial court therefore properly allowed the evidence to go to the jury.

We share petitioner's concern that unduly prejudicial evidence might be introduced under Rule 404(b). We think, however, that the protection against such unfair prejudice emanates not from a requirement of a preliminary finding by the trial court, but rather from four other sources: first, from the requirement of Rule 404(b) that the evidence be offered for a proper purpose; second, from the relevancy requirement of Rule 402—as enforced through Rule 104(b); third, from the assessment the trial court must make under Rule 403 to determine whether the probative value of the similar acts evidence is substantially outweighed by its potential for unfair prejudice; and fourth, from Federal Rule of Evidence 105, which provides that the trial court shall, upon request, instruct the jury that the similar acts evidence is to be considered only for the proper purpose for which it was admitted.

Affirmed.

Problem 3.13
Past Acquittal

Consider these facts of *Dowling v. United States*, 493 U.S. 342 (1990):

> On the afternoon of July 8, 1985, a man wearing a ski mask and armed with a small pistol robbed the First Pennsylvania Bank in Frederiksted, St. Croix, Virgin Islands....

> During [Dowling's trial for this crime], the Government, over [his] objection, called a woman named Vena Henry to the stand. Ms. Henry testified that a man wearing a knitted mask with cutout eyes and carrying a small handgun had, together with a man named Delroy Christian, entered her home in Frederiksted approximately two weeks after the First Pennsylvania Bank robbery. Ms. Henry testified that a struggle ensued and that she unmasked the intruder, whom she identified as Dowling. Based on this incident, Dowling had been charged under Virgin Islands law with burglary, attempted robbery, assault, and weapons offenses, but had been acquitted after a trial held before his . . . trial in the bank robbery case.
>
> The Government assertedly elicited Henry's testimony for two purposes. First, it believed that Henry's description of Dowling as wearing a mask and carrying a gun similar to the mask worn and the gun carried by the robber of the First Pennsylvania Bank strengthened the Government's identification of Dowling as the bank robber. Second, the Government sought to link Dowling with Delroy Christian, the other man who entered Henry's home [and who had apparent links to the bank robbery].

Did Dowling's acquittal in the offense against Vena Henry bar the government from offering her testimony against him at the bank robbery trial?

D. PROPENSITY EVIDENCE IN SEXUAL ASSAULT CASES

2-7-34

Focus on
FRE 413, 414, & 415

Rules 413, 414, and 415 lead our inquiry into the true *exceptions* to the propensity evidence ban. These three rules, enacted as part of the Violent Crime Control and Law Enforcement Act of 1994, permit prosecutors and civil plaintiffs to offer evidence of the defendant's other acts of sexual assault or child molestation "on any matter to which it is relevant." As Representative Susan Molinari, the principal House sponsor of legislation authorizing the rules, noted, "This includes the defendant's propensity to commit sexual assault or child molestation offenses. . . ." Refer again to the character evidence flowchart on page 161. Rules 413 to 415 appear on the far left, just under the propensity box. That is, we are about to begin our first (sanctioned) trip through the box.

The next three cases—*Lannan v. State*, 600 N.E.2d 1334 (Ind. 1992), *State v. Kirsch*, 139 N.H. 647, 662 A.2d 937 (1995), and *United States v. Guardia*, 135 F.3d 1326 (10th Cir. 1998)—all bear on our discussion of Rules 413 to 415. Only *Guardia*, however, actually addresses application of the rules, which took effect in 1995. In *Lannan* the Indiana Supreme Court rejected a common-law rule that, in many states, once permitted the kind of evidence now allowed in federal courts by Rules 413 to 415. *Kirsch* stems from a child sex abuse prosecution in New Hampshire, which had no such permissive rule. Governed by the state's equivalent of FRE 404, the New Hampshire Supreme Court rebuffed the prosecution's arguments that evidence of the defendant's other acts of sexual molestation did not violate Rule 404(a)(1)'s propensity ban.

Note that Rules 413 to 415 now save federal prosecutors the effort of having to justify evidence of other sexual offenses under Rule 404. Are these three rules an improvement?

LANNAN V. STATE

Supreme Court of Indiana.
600 N.E.2d 1334 (Ind. 1992).

■ SHEPARD, CHIEF JUSTICE. A jury convicted appellant Donald Lannan of molesting young V.E., after hearing testimony from another girl who said Lannan had molested her in the past and testimony from the victim regarding several other instances of molestation which were not charged. Lannan's petition for transfer asks this Court to abandon the so-called "depraved sexual instinct" exception under which evidence about these uncharged acts was admitted. We grant transfer to reexamine the exception, its rationales, and whether they remain compelling enough to justify its continued application. Counsel for the parties and for amicus have presented us with excellent briefs on this question. We have concluded that Rule 404(b) of the Federal Rules of Evidence provides a better basis for testing the admissibility of this sort of evidence than our existing caselaw provides.

I. HISTORY OF THE EXCEPTION

It has long been settled that in prosecutions for incest, sodomy, criminal deviate conduct or child molesting, evidence of certain kinds of prior sexual conduct is admissible under Indiana's depraved sexual instinct exception to the general rule of inadmissibility of prior bad acts.

See State v. Robbins, 221 Ind. 125 (1943); State v. Markins, 95 Ind. 464 (1884). This exception has been carved out of the general rule for two reasons. First, the exception has been based on a recidivist rationale: " 'Acts showing a perverted sexual instinct are circumstances which with other circumstances may have a tendency to connect an accused with a crime of that character.' " Kerlin v. State, 255 Ind. 420, 424 (1970). Second, the exception has been based on the need to bolster the testimony of victims: to lend credence to a victim's accusations or testimony which describe acts which would otherwise "seem improbable standing alone." Stwalley v. State, 534 N.E.2d 229, 231 (Ind. 1989).

The desire to level the playing field by bolstering the testimony of a solitary child victim-witness (recounting unspeakable acts, often in embarrassing detail in the intimidating forum of a courtroom while subject to aggressive cross-examination) was central to the holding in *Robbins,* the forerunner in a long line of modern era cases developing the depraved sexual instinct exception. In *Robbins,* the defendant was the superior court judge in Vincennes during the late 1930s. He was indicted on two counts of sodomy with a twelve-year-old girl. The case might fairly have been characterized as a credibility contest between a child and a pillar of the community. To even up this contest, the State sought to introduce testimony from other children regarding other instances of sexual misconduct committed by the defendant against children. The trial court excluded the evidence; this Court held that the testimony of the other children should have been allowed.

Indiana has not stood alone in fashioning exceptions to the rules of evidence in cases where children are victims of sexual abuse. Approximately twenty other states have or have had such exceptions. Some, such as Missouri and Kansas, explicitly recognize a depraved sexual instinct exception or allow evidence of prior bad acts to prove defendant's "lustful disposition or nature." Others, such as Illinois, South Dakota and Wisconsin, follow rules similar to Federal Rule of Evidence 404(b), but stretch the definition of the common scheme and plan doctrine to allow prior occurrences of sexual misconduct into evidence, in effect to prove proclivity. One court has likened this contortion of the traditional 404(b) exceptions to "forcing a square peg into a round hole."

The Supreme Court of Wisconsin has been particularly forthright in explaining the justification for what has come to be known in that state as the "greater latitude" doctrine. The justification is, quite simply, protection of children, the most sexually vulnerable in society. Like our Court in *Robbins,* Wisconsin has sought to level the playing field in service to the desirable social end of convicting child molesters:

> Because of immaturity, fear and embarrassment, sexually abused children find it difficult to testify. It is for this reason that much is being written of late about the necessity of support activities to make the taking of a statement less traumatic. Among these proposals are

video taping their examinations and cross-examinations and allowing appropriate support persons to be present to make the ordeal of reliving and reciting their exploitation less difficult.

These are among the reasons why a more liberal admission of other crimes evidence is the rule in Wisconsin on sex crime cases.

State v. Friedrich, 135 Wis. 2d 1, 30–31 (1987) (emphasis added).

II. THE RECIDIVISM RATIONALE

Implicit in the application of our exception and those applied across the country under different names is the assumption that sexual offenders repeat their crimes more often than other criminals. "To a person of normal, social and moral sensibility, the idea of the sexual exploitation of the young is so repulsive that it's almost impossible to believe that none [*sic*] but the most depraved and degenerate would commit such an act." *Friedrich*, 135 Wis. 2d at 27. The Indiana Association of Criminal Defense Lawyers, amicus curiae, calls such a belief "ignorant" and "founded on myth," yet we are inclined to accept the conclusion that recidivism among sexual deviates is quite high.[6] This alone, however, cannot justify continued adherence to the depraved sexual instinct exception. We have no doubt that recidivism among those who violate drug laws, for instance, is extraordinarily high. We do not allow the State to introduce previous drug convictions in its case-in-chief in a prosecution for selling illegal drugs, however, even though it can hardly be disputed that such evidence would be highly probative.... If a high rate of recidivism

6. An Emory University psychiatrist who has accumulated data on more than 500 sexual offenders reports that the average number of sex crimes committed by the adult offender is usually in the hundreds. *See Discovering and Dealing with Deviant Sex*, PSYCHOLOGY TODAY (April 1985), at 8, 10. Conversely, defendant and amicus argue that those convicted of sex crimes have a lower rate of recidivism than those convicted of most other crimes. *See* amicus brief at 17 (citing BLINDER, PSYCHIATRY IN THE EVERYDAY PRACTICE OF LAW 213 (2d ed. 1982 & 1991 supp.)). We believe studies which show a low recidivism rate among sex offenders are of questionable value, since often they utilize arrest and conviction rates, which are inadequate measures of recidivism due to the low number of cases which actually make it that far into the system. *See* A. Nicholas Groth, Robert E. Longo & J. Bradley McFadin, *Undetected Recidivism among Rapists and Child Molesters*, 28 CRIME & DELINQUENCY 450 (1982):

> It is generally true that most criminals get away with more crimes than they are convicted of, but it would appear that this is especially true of offenders who commit sexual assaults. The low recidivism rate generally attributed to such offenders can be understood due to the low visibility of such offenses. Although the sexual offender's behavior is repetitive, most of his recidivism goes undetected....
>
> Then, too, there is a wide variety of factors that serve to deter many victims of sexual assault from reporting their victimization. Even if the offense is reported, in the majority of cases, no suspect is apprehended; few of the cases in which a suspect is apprehended reach trial level, and still fewer result in conviction.

Id. at 457–58.

cannot justify a departure from the propensity rule for drug defendants, logic dictates it does not provide justification for departure in sex offense cases.

III. THE BOLSTERING RATIONALE

We turn then to the second rationale frequently offered for the depraved sexual instinct exception—that allowing such evidence lends credence to a victim's testimony describing acts which would otherwise seem improbable standing alone. This rationale has its origins in an era less jaded than today. When the accusations were brought in *Robbins*, in the late 1930s, the idea that an adult male who occupied a position of responsibility in the community would force himself sexually upon a child bordered on the preposterous. Sadly, it is our belief that fifty years later we live in a world where accusations of child molest[ation] no longer appear improbable as a rule. This decaying state of affairs in society ironically undercuts the justification for the depraved sexual instinct exception at a time when the need to prosecute is greater.

Indeed, there remains what might be labeled the "rationale behind the rationale," the desire to make easier the prosecution of child molesters, who prey on tragically vulnerable victims in secluded settings, leaving behind little, if any, evidence of their crimes. Nearly four decades ago, the *Minnesota Law Review*, noting the trend toward admissibility of depraved sexual instinct-type evidence, attributed it to a feeling "that handicapping the state in the prosecution of criminals is undesirable. It is also likely that a realization of the difficulty of obtaining proof of sexual offenses has been partially responsible for the trend." Note, *Evidence of Similar Transactions in Sex Crime Prosecutions: A New Trend Toward Liberal Admissibility*, 40 MINN. L. REV. 694, 704 (1956). The emotional appeal of such an argument is powerful, given the special empathy that child victims of sexual abuse evoke. But even this cannot support continued application of an exception which allows the prosecution to accomplish what the general propensity rule is intended to prevent.

In the interest of aiding the prosecution, we could of course expand the exception and abrogate the general rule. After all, our empathy for victims of all crimes is considerable. But the general rule prohibiting the state from offering character evidence merely to show the defendant is a "bad guy" and therefore probably committed the crime with which he is charged remains as fundamental today as ever. "We indeed live in a vulgar age," Lee v. Weisman, 505 U.S. 577, 637 (1992) (Scalia, J., dissenting), when recidivists flout the law and routinely violate the behavioral norms of civilized society. We have not yet reached the point, though, where we are prepared to abandon a basic tenet of criminal evidence law older than the republic itself,[9] however desirable the social end may be.

9. *See* Commonwealth v. Boulden, 179 Pa. Super. 328, 333–34 (1955) (quoting 1 WIGMORE ON EVIDENCE 646 (3d ed. 1940)): "[F]or nearly three centuries, ever since the liberal reaction which began with the Restoration of the Stuarts, this poli-

As we said in Penley v. State, 506 N.E.2d 806, 808 (Ind. 1987), "The notion that the State may not punish a person for his character is one of the foundations of our system of jurisprudence. . . ."

IV. DISADVANTAGES OF PRESENT RULE

We do not wish to imply that the rationales put forth on behalf of the depraved sexual instinct exception are entirely without merit. They are not. Each retains some measure of validity. Yet it seems to us that any justification for maintaining the exception in its current form is outweighed by the mischief created by the open-ended application of the rule. . . .

[T]his Court has allowed evidence of extremely remote instances of sodomy, molest[ation] or sexual assault, under the theory that remoteness goes to weight and not admissibility. *See* Lawrence v. State, 464 N.E.2d 923 (Ind. 1984) (evidence of sexual crime committed twenty-two years earlier admitted to show depraved sexual instinct); Kerlin v. State, 255 Ind. 420 (1970) (in prosecution for sodomy with fifteen-year-old boy, evidence admitted showing defendant committed sodomy with two adult males seven and eight years before). The *Kerlin* decision drew a strong dissent from Justice DeBruler, who wrote:

> There was no connection between the [prior acts] and the offense being tried. This testimony was not offered as bearing on an issue such as motive, intent, identity; nor could it evince any common scheme or plan, etc. This evidence was offered for the purpose of showing the appellant's character was bad and that he had a tendency to commit acts of sodomy. As such it was inadmissible. . . .

255 Ind. at 427. Twenty-two years later, Justice DeBruler has carried the day. His reasoning tracks the language of Federal Rule of Evidence 404(b), which we hereby adopt in its entirety, effective from this day forward.

V. USE OF RULE 404(b)

We hasten to add that abandoning the depraved sexual instinct exception does not mean evidence of prior sexual misconduct will never be admitted in sex crimes prosecutions. It means only that such evidence will no longer be admitted to show action in conformity with a particular character trait. It will continue to be admitted, however, for other purposes such as proof of motive, opportunity, intent, preparation, plan, knowledge, identity, or absence of mistake. . . .

cy of exclusion, in one or another of its reasonings, has received judicial sanction, more emphatic with time and experience. It represents a revolution in the theory of criminal trials, and is one of the peculiar features, of vast moment, which distinguishes the Anglo-American from the Continental system of Evidence."

For example, this Court has on occasion approved the admission of evidence of prior sexual crimes . . . "to demonstrate the common plan or scheme of criminal activity from which the accused originated the charged crime." Malone v. State, 441 N.E.2d 1339, 1346 (Ind. 1982). Thus, as explained in *Malone*:

> The test to bring evidence of other offenses within the common plan or scheme exception is not whether the other offenses have certain elements in common with the charged crime, but whether the other offenses tend to establish a preconceived plan . . . [and are] so related in character, time and place of commission as to establish some plan which embraced both the prior and subsequent criminal activity and the charged crime.

441 N.E.2d at 1347. . . .

In Penley v. State, 506 N.E.2d 806 (Ind. 1987), we upheld admission of prior sexual assaults under the modus operandi exception. That is, the State may prove identity by showing that the similarities between the prior offense and the crime charged are so strong and the method so clearly unique that it is highly probable that the perpetrator of both is the same person. "However, the repeated commission of similar crimes is not enough to qualify for the exception to the general rule. The acts or methods employed must be so similar, unusual, and distinctive as to earmark them as the acts of the accused." Willis v. State, 268 Ind. 269, 272 (Ind. 1978). It is also important to note that such evidence may be admitted only where identity is an issue in the case.

. . . Further examples are sure to come before this Court with the adoption of Federal Rule of Evidence 404(b), as this rule has generated more reported decisions than any other rule. . . .

■ DEBRULER, DICKSON, and KRAHULIK, JJ., concur.

■ GIVAN, J., concurring in the result [which ultimately affirmed Lannan's conviction because the impact on the jury of the wrongly admitted evidence of other acts of molestation "was not of sufficient weight to require reversal"]. . . . I strongly disagree with the majority's abolition of the depraved sexual instinct rule. The majority opinion very accurately has set forth the reasons for the adoption of this rule and the long history of its usage in this State. . . . Suffice it to say that based upon those reasons given, I believe the necessity to protect children from the devastating harm of molestation justifies the invocation of the rule.

I fully recognize, as stated by the majority, that in most cases the evidence of prior conduct probably will come in under accepted rules which the majority leaves intact. However, I do not believe this fact justifies the abrogation of the rule. I believe a jury is entitled to know that a defendant in a child molesting case has a history of sexual deviate conduct because of the heinous nature of the crime and the possible unbelievability of a small child. To me, the abrogation of this rule is an erosion, albeit small, of the protection of children. I would not diminish that protection one iota....

STATE v. KIRSCH

Supreme Court of New Hampshire.
139 N.H. 647 (1995).

■ BATCHELDER, J. The defendant, David W. Kirsch, ... was tried on thirteen indictments charging sexual assaults on three young girls between 1984 and 1987. In addition to the three victims named in the indictments, three other young women testified, pursuant to Rule 404(b), about sexual abuse committed against them by the defendant from the late 1970s to the mid–1980s. With minor variations, each young woman testified to similar activity and association with the defendant. During that time period, the defendant led pre-teen church groups at the Granite State Baptist Church in Salem, occasionally driving the church bus that transported the children from their homes to the church.... [T]he defendant was one of several church staff members who monitored sleep-overs at the church. He also hosted church sleep-overs at his home in Salem and, later, at his home in Plaistow. Each of the victim/witnesses testified to having been approximately seven to ten years old when she met the defendant through her association with the church and to having become close to him through the church groups she attended. Each rode on the bus or in his van with the defendant and spent the night at the church or at his home. Some remembered sitting in the defendant's lap, and all remembered the defendant's inappropriate touching [and sexual acts].

Of the thirteen indictments on which the defendant was tried, seven were dismissed at the close of the State's case. The six remaining indictments all involved the same victim, Karen G., and were comprised of three counts each of aggravated felonious sexual assault and felonious sexual assault. The defendant was found guilty of all six charges....

The defendant ... argues that the trial court erred in permitting the State to introduce evidence of other bad acts committed by the defendant. Prior to trial the State moved to introduce evidence of other uncharged sexual assaults as evidence of the defendant's motive, intent, and common plan or scheme. *See* N.H. R. EVID. 404(b). According to the State's proffer to the trial court, the evidence would show that the defendant "selected and seduced each victim by always choosing as his victims young girls, who lived well below the poverty line, in dysfunctional households, without any real father figure." It would further show, according to the State, that the defendant "positioned himself," through his role in the church, as a trusted father figure who occasionally fed and clothed them and "then seduced each of the little girls in the same manner." After a hearing, the trial court ruled that the evidence was relevant to prove motive, intent, and common plan or scheme, that there was clear proof the defendant committed the acts, and that the probative value of the evidence was not substantially outweighed by prejudice to the defendant. . . .

[N.H.] Rule 404(b) provides:

> Evidence of other crimes, wrongs, or acts is not admissible to prove the character of a person in order to show that the person acted in conformity therewith. It may, however, be admissible for other purposes, such as proof of motive, opportunity, intent, preparation, plan, knowledge, identity, or absence of mistake or accident.*

. . . The burden is on the State to articulate to the trial judge the precise evidentiary purpose for which it seeks to introduce the other crimes evidence and the purported connection between the evidence and the stated purpose. The State proffered, and the trial court found, three evidentiary purposes for the other bad acts evidence; namely, motive, intent, and common plan or scheme. We examine each in turn.

Motive is generally understood to refer to the "reason that nudges the will and prods the mind to indulge the criminal intent," State v. Bassett, 139 N.H. 493, 497 (1995), or what prompts a defendant to engage in a particular criminal activity. The State argued below that the evidence of the uncharged assaults would show the defendant's "motive in selecting these particular victims," and argues on appeal that the evidence showed "the motive with which the defendant acted when he involved himself in the church's pre-teen program, and subsequently in the lives of each of these girls." . . . The crux of the State's argument appears to be that the other incidents show the defendant's desire for sexual activity with a certain type of victim. This, however, "is proof of propensity, not motive." State v. Whittaker, 138 N.H. 524, 527 (1994). . . .

The second reason advanced by the State for admitting the other acts was that they were probative of the defendant's intent. "To be relevant to intent, evidence of other bad acts must be able to support a reliable inference, not dependent on the defendant's character or propensity, that the defendant had the same intent on the occasions of the charged and uncharged acts." *Bassett*, 139 N.H. at 499.

In the trial court, the State put forth essentially the same argument with respect to relevance to prove intent as it did to prove motive. Focusing on the number and similarity of the assaults and the defendant's mode of seduction, the State argued that "these actions on the part of the defendant show how he purposely selected and seduced his

* [This language of N.H. R. Evid. 404(b) is almost identical to the unrestyled language of FRE 404(b). *See* RB 394.—GF]

victims. As such this type of evidence bears directly on the defendant's intent. . . ."

This argument is indistinguishable from one that would seek to use the evidence to show the defendant's propensity to sexually assault young girls and therefore to imply his intent to commit the charged assaults. *See id.* at 500. "The only connection is the putative similarity of the activity," State v. Richardson, 138 N.H. 162, 167 (1993), and to argue that evidence of the defendant's other similar assaults tends to prove his guilt of the charged offenses is to seek to show "propensity, pure and simple; calling it relevant to prove 'state of mind' does not make it so." *Id.* at 168.

With respect to the State's common plan or scheme rationale for relevance, the State argued to the trial court that the defendant's "routine used in assaulting any one of the victims is similar, if not identical, to the manner in which he assaulted other victims." The common plan exception to the Rule 404(b) prohibition requires more. "A pattern or systematic course of conduct is insufficient to establish a plan." *Whittaker*, 138 N.H. at 528. Rather, to be admissible as evidence showing the defendant's plan, other bad acts must be constituent parts of some overall scheme. "Therefore, it is not enough to show that each crime was 'planned' in the same way; rather, there must be some overall scheme of which each of the crimes is but a part." *Id.* Showing that the defendant had a preexisting "plan" to gain the trust of young girls from deprived homes in order to seduce and sexually assault them does not demonstrate a common plan or scheme as we have thus defined it in *Whittaker*. It is merely proof of the defendant's penchant or propensity for committing the same offense repeatedly; this is "the precise purpose, under Rule 404(b), for which it may not be used," *id.*

Whether nominally labeled motive, intent or common plan, the ostensible purpose for which the prosecution sought to admit evidence of a multitude of other uncharged sexual assaults was to show the defendant's predilection for molesting young females over whom he was able to gain control through engendering trust. At most, this is evidence of the defendant's disposition to commit the offenses with which he was charged, impermissible under Rule 404(b). Because it was not relevant for a permissible purpose, the evidence should have been excluded, and its introduction was an abuse of discretion. . . .

Reversed and remanded.

■ THAYER, J., with whom HORTON, J., joined, concurred in part and dissented in part; HORTON, J., concurred in part and dissented in part; the others concurred.

■ THAYER, J., concurring in part and dissenting in part: . . . . [T]he prior bad acts alleged by the State and recounted by the majority were offered to show the defendant's plan, and they do so. The majority's narrow reading of the common plan exception essentially requires the State to show the defendant's state of mind before he started on his spree of criminal conduct, limiting the exception to a mutually dependent series of events.... [T]he rule should not be so limited. Furthermore, even under the standard set forth by the majority, the State can show, by circumstantial evidence, that the defendant's plan was to obtain a position of authority and then select his victims utilizing, as the trial court found, a common set of criteria. Unlike *Whittaker,* in which the defendant allegedly committed two otherwise unrelated sexual assaults in a somewhat similar manner over a five-year period, here there was evidence of the defendant's common scheme to use his position to sexually assault young girls. *See* State v. Bennett, 36 Wash. App. 176, 180 (1983) (evidence that defendant offered food and shelter to other vulnerable teenagers in exchange for sex relevant under Rule 404(b) to demonstrate defendant's plan, making it more probable that sexual intercourse occurred with victims). In my view, the evidence was clearly relevant for that purpose.

Problem 3.14

Common Plan and Domestic Violence

In *Kirsch* the New Hampshire court held that if the state wishes to use past acts to show the defendant's "common plan or scheme," the state must do more than simply "show that each crime was 'planned' in the same way; rather, there must be some overall scheme of which each of the crimes is but a part." Can this common-plan route around the propensity box play a role in domestic violence prosecutions? Consider Professor Myrna Raeder's argument:

> ... The defendant does not necessarily hate his wife; rather, he is obsessed with her. It is his jealousy and fear of abandonment that drives him to dominate his wife. When the murder is committed during estrangement, the prior bad acts demonstrate how the defendant previously controlled his victim by nonlethal violence. The failure of such acts to prevent her from leaving precipitates the defendant to commit murder as the final act of control....
>
> [M]ost domestic violence evidence fits within traditional plan theory. The evidence forms a linked-acts or chain plan in which each crime is a means to the overarching end—links in a chain ultimately leading to the accomplishment of the overall objective.
>
> In domestic violence cases, this translates to individual acts of abuse forming a blueprint that details how to control the victim, even though the acts may differ in type and

> severity. Therefore, intimidation, stalking, assault and property crimes are all integral to the grand design.
>
> Myrna S. Raeder, *The Admissibility of Prior Acts of Domestic Violence:* Simpson *and Beyond*, 69 S. CAL. L. REV. 1463, 1495 (1996).
>
> Assume you are defending a man accused of murdering his wife. If the prosecutor offers evidence of past battering incidents under Raeder's theory that they form part of an overarching plan to gain and keep control of his wife, how will you argue against admission? How should the judge rule?

NOTES ON RULES 413, 414, AND 415

Lannan and *Kirsch* are examples of how state courts struggled to deal with evidence of past sexual misconduct in regimes otherwise governed by equivalents of Federal Rule 404. By enacting Rules 413, 414, and 415 in 1994, Congress sought to ensure that federal trial judges could admit evidence of past sexual misconduct in sexual assault and child molestation cases without having to stretch the meaning of "intent," "motive," and "plan" in the ways rejected by the New Hampshire court in *Kirsch*. *See also* Karen M. Fingar, *And Justice for All: The Admissibility of Uncharged Sexual Misconduct Evidence Under the Recent Amendment to the Federal Rules of Evidence*, 5 S. CAL. REV. L. & WOMEN'S STUD. 501, 514–30 (1996) (discussing the contrivances used to admit evidence of past sexual misconduct despite rules barring propensity evidence).

Of course few sexual assault or child molestation cases are tried in federal courts. In fiscal year 2011 federal prosecutors initiated only 679 cases alleging sexual assault or abuse of either minors or adults. *See* JUDICIAL BUSINESS OF THE UNITED STATES COURTS—FY 2011, tbl.D–2. State courts will remain the primary battlefields of this particular evidentiary war. But Congress's adoption of Rules 413 to 415 has led to parallel action in some state legislatures, and others may yet follow. *See People v. Falsetta*, 21 Cal. 4th 903, 912 (1999) (noting that California Evidence Code "Section 1108 was modeled on rule 413 of the Federal Rules of Evidence"). As this book goes to press toward the end of 2012, at least fifteen states have adopted rules or statutes similar to FRE 413 or FRE 414 or both: Alaska, Arizona, Arkansas, California, Florida, Georgia, Illinois, Kansas, Louisiana, Michigan, Nebraska, Oklahoma, Tennessee, Texas, and Utah.*

* *See* ALASKA R. EVID. 404(b)(2), 404(b)(3) (2012); ARIZ. R. EVID. 404(c) (2012); ARK. CODE ANN. § 16–42–103 (2012); CAL. EVID. CODE § 1108 (2012); FLA. STAT. §§ 90.404(2)(b), 90.404(2)(c) (2012); CODE GEO. ANN. §§ 24–4–413, 24–4–414, 24–4–415 (eff. Jan. 1, 2013); 725 ILL. COMP. STAT. 5/115–7.3 (2012); KAN. STAT. ANN. § 60–455(d) (2011); LA. CODE EVID.

A glance at the legislative history of Rules 413, 414, and 415 may help clarify several of their more ambiguous passages.

Floor Statement of the Principal House Sponsor, Representative Susan Molinari, Concerning the Prior Crimes Evidence Rules for Sexual Assault and Child Molestation Cases

(140 CONG. REC. H8991–92, Aug. 21, 1994)

Mr. Speaker, the revised conference bill contains a critical reform that I have long sought to protect the public from crimes of sexual violence—general rules of admissibility in sexual assault and child molestation cases for evidence that the defendant has committed offenses of the same type on other occasions. The enactment of this reform is first and foremost a triumph for the public—for the women who will not be raped and the children who will not be molested because we have strengthened the legal system's tools for bringing the perpetrators of these atrocious crimes to justice. . . .

The new rules will supersede in sex offense cases the restrictive aspects of Federal Rule of Evidence 404(b). In contrast to Rule [404(b)(1)]'s general prohibition of evidence of character or propensity, the new rules for sex offense cases authorize admission and consideration of evidence of an uncharged offense for its bearing "on any matter to which it is relevant." This includes the defendant's propensity to commit sexual assault or child molestation offenses, and assessment of the probability or improbability that the defendant has been falsely or mistakenly accused of such an offense.

Art. 412.2 (2012); MICH. COMP. LAWS § 768.27a (2012); NEB. REV. STATS. §§ 27–413, 27–414, 27–415 (2012); 12 OKLA. STAT. §§ 2413, 2414 (2012); TENN. CODE ANN. § 40–17–124 (2012); TEX. CODE CRIM. PROC. art 38.37 (2012); UTAH R. EVID. 404(c) (2012).

In addition, Oregon's evidence code generally provides that "[i]n criminal actions, evidence of other crimes, wrongs or acts by the defendant is admissible if relevant" with exceptions not applicable here. *See* ORE. REV. STAT. § 40.170(4) (2011).

The Kansas equivalent of Rules 413 and 414—Kan. Stat. Ann. § 60–455(d) (2011)—recently has been called in doubt by a state court of appeals. The court reasoned that if evidence of the defendant's past sex offenses is not probative of motive, modus operandi, plan, or any of the other non-propensity purposes listed in the state's equivalent of FRE 404(b)—Kan. Stat. Ann. § 60–455(b) (2011)—the risk of unfair prejudice triggered by admission of evidence of the past acts necessarily will substantially outweigh the small probative value of the evidence. Hence the law pertaining to past sex offenses is redundant of § 60–455(b) and has no independent application. Review of the appeals court's judgment is pending before the state supreme court. *See State v. Hart*, 44 Kan. App. 2d 986, 1018–19, 242 P.3d 1230 (2010), *review granted, State v. Hart* (Kan. May 16, 2011).

I thank Anthony Sun for initially compiling this list and Mark Menzies for checking and updating it.

In other respects, the general standards of the rules of evidence will continue to apply, including the restrictions on hearsay evidence and the court's authority under Evidence Rule 403 to exclude evidence whose probative value is substantially outweighed by its prejudicial effect. Also, the government (or the plaintiff in a civil case) will generally have to disclose to the defendant any evidence that is to be offered under the new rules at least 15 days before trial.

The proposed reform is critical to the protection of the public from rapists and child molesters, and is justified by the distinctive characteristics of the cases it will affect. In child molestation cases, for example, a history of similar acts tends to be exceptionally probative because it shows an unusual disposition of the defendant—a sexual or sado-sexual interest in children—that simply does not exist in ordinary people. Moreover, such cases require reliance on child victims whose credibility can readily be attacked in the absence of substantial corroboration. In such cases, there is a compelling public interest in admitting all significant evidence that will illumine the credibility of the charge and any denial by the defense.

Similarly, adult-victim sexual assault cases are distinctive, and often turn on difficult credibility determinations. Alleged consent by the victim is rarely an issue in prosecutions for other violent crimes—the accused mugger does not claim that the victim freely handed over his wallet as a gift—but the defendant in a rape case often contends that the victim engaged in consensual sex and then falsely accused him. Knowledge that the defendant has committed rapes on other occasions is frequently critical in assessing the relative plausibility of these claims and accurately deciding cases that would otherwise become unresolvable swearing matches.

The practical effect of the new rules is to put evidence of uncharged offenses in sexual assault and child molestation cases on the same footing as other types of relevant evidence that are not subject to a special exclusionary rule. The presumption is in favor of admission. The underlying legislative judgment is that the evidence admissible pursuant to the proposed rules is typically relevant and probative, and that its probative value is normally not outweighed by any risk of prejudice or other adverse effects.

In line with this judgment, the rules do not impose arbitrary or artificial restrictions on the admissibility of evidence. Evidence of offenses for which the defendant has not previously been prosecuted or convicted will be admissible, as well as evidence of prior convictions. No time limit is imposed on the uncharged offenses for which evidence may be admitted; as a practical matter, evidence of other sex offenses by the defendant is often probative and properly admitted, notwithstanding very substantial lapses of time in relation to the charged offense or offenses. *See, e.g.,* United States v. Hadley, 918 F.2d 848, 850–51 (9th Cir.

1990), *cert. dismissed*, 506 U.S. 19 (1992) (evidence of offenses occurring up to 15 years earlier admitted); State v. Plymate, 345 N.W.2d 327 (Neb. 1984) (evidence of defendant's commission of other child molestations more than 20 years earlier admitted).

Finally, the practical efficacy of these rules will depend on faithful execution by judges of the will of Congress in adopting this critical reform. To implement the legislative intent, the courts must liberally construe these rules. . . .

REPORT OF THE JUDICIAL CONFERENCE OF THE UNITED STATES ON THE ADMISSION OF CHARACTER EVIDENCE IN CERTAIN SEXUAL MISCONDUCT CASES

(Submitted to Congress, Feb. 9, 1995)

I. INTRODUCTION

. . . After careful study, the Judicial Conference urges Congress to reconsider its decision on the policy questions underlying the new rules for reasons set out in Part III below. . . .

II. BACKGROUND

. . . [I]n preparation for its consideration of the new rules, the Advisory Committee on Evidence Rules sent out a notice soliciting comment on new Evidence Rules 413, 414, and 415. The notice was sent to the courts, including all federal judges, about 900 evidence law professors, 40 women's rights organizations, and 1000 other individuals and interested organizations.

III. DISCUSSION

On October 17–18, 1994, the Advisory Committee on Evidence Rules met in Washington, D.C. It considered the public responses, which included 84 written comments, representing 112 individuals, 8 local and 8 national legal organizations. The overwhelming majority of judges, lawyers, law professors, and legal organizations who responded opposed new Evidence Rules 413, 414, and 415. The principal objections expressed were that the rules would permit the admission of unfairly prejudicial evidence and contained numerous drafting problems not intended by their authors.

The Advisory Committee['s January 1995] . . . report was unanimous except for a dissenting vote by the representative of the Department of Justice. The advisory committee believed that the concerns expressed by Congress and embodied in new Evidence Rules 413, 414, and 415 are already adequately addressed in the existing Federal Rules of Evidence. In particular, Evidence Rule [404(b)(2)] now allows the admission of evidence against a criminal defendant of the commission of prior crimes, wrongs, or acts for specified purposes, including to show intent, plan, motive, preparation, identity, knowledge, or absence of mistake or accident.

Furthermore, the new rules, which are not supported by empirical evidence, could diminish significantly the protections that have safeguarded persons accused in criminal cases and parties in civil cases against undue prejudice. These protections form a fundamental part of American jurisprudence and have evolved under long-standing rules and case law. A significant concern identified by the committee was the danger of convicting a criminal defendant for past, as opposed to charged, behavior or for being a bad person.

In addition, the advisory committee concluded that, because prior bad acts would be admissible even though not the subject of a conviction, mini-trials within trials concerning those acts would result when a defendant seeks to rebut such evidence. . . .

It is important to note the highly unusual unanimity of the members of the Standing and Advisory Committees, composed of over 40 judges, practicing lawyers, and academicians, in taking the view that Rules 413–415 are undesirable. Indeed, the only supporters of the Rules were representatives of the Department of Justice. . . .

Baggage Check; How Far Should We Go?

Sally Quinn

WASHINGTON POST, Feb. 28, 1999, at B1

. . . Perhaps no one has gotten entangled in the sexual harassment laws of this country more thoroughly or more embarrassingly than our president. And the irony is that he was partly responsible for one of the recent legislative changes that gave ammunition to Paula Jones and her lawyers—and has made many other defendants wary. In 1994, Bill Clinton signed into law new Federal Rules of Evidence, including Rule 415, which makes elements of a defendant's sexual history admissible in civil cases involving sexual assault and child molestation. This rule, with its broad definition of assault that includes the sort of unwanted touching often found in sexual harassment cases, was cited by Judge Susan Webber Wright as one of the reasons why she allowed Jones's lawyers to look into Clinton's sexual history. (Jones had, in effect, accused Clinton of sexual assault because, she said, he had placed his hand on her thigh.)

When the legislation was enacted, many legal scholars, lawyers and judges objected that the new rule was unfair, but nobody could have known five years ago how it might affect the nation's most prominent sexual misconduct case. Asked recently if he could have foreseen how Clinton's support of these rules might come back to haunt him, Leon Panetta, then the president's chief of staff, answered, with a burst of laughter, "Hell, no!" And former Republican congresswoman Susan Molinari, one of the bill's sponsors, says she had no idea that her legislation, which was designed to increase the prosecution and conviction of child molesters, might be interpreted as allowing lawyers greater latitude in probing the alleged harasser's sexual history. "I didn't connect," she says....

Since its passage in 1994, Rule 415 has met with resistance in the civil courtroom.... Jane Harris Aiken, a professor at Washington University School of Law, says many judges have simply not been comfortable with the notion of admitting evidence about the defendant's character at trial.... Historically, of course, American courts have stood by a basic principle of Anglo-Saxon jurisprudence in both criminal and civil cases: A person is tried for specific acts, not for his or her character.... But in cases where the evidence is reduced to a swearing contest—a battle of "he said, she said"—how do you break the deadlock?

One logical approach is to look for patterns of behavior—of either defendant or plaintiff. (How can you not think about Jones, Kathleen Willey and Monica Lewinsky when you hear about Juanita Broaddrick?)* Hence, the situation that used to pertain in rape cases in which lawyers often looked into the sexual history of the plaintiff to try to settle the issue of consent: Was she the type to invite the defendant's actions?

Accusing women of being [promiscuous], as UCLA law professor Susan Estrich has pointed out, is the oldest defense in the book: "The woman goes on trial instead of the defendant; her state of mind, her motives, her sexual past become the focus of the inquiry instead of his." The 1978 rape shield law, which was extended to civil cases in 1994, has helped to protect plaintiffs from having their private sex lives exposed in sexual misconduct cases. Now, the passage of Rule 415 raises the chances that it will be the defendants' backgrounds—usually men's—that will become more vulnerable to investigation....

* [Jones, Willey, and Broaddrick all accused Clinton of sexual aggression toward them.—GF]

Katharine K. Baker

Once a Rapist? Motivational Evidence and Relevancy in Rape Law

110 HARV. L. REV. 563 (1997)

* * *

Advocates of Rule 413 . . . unabashedly and without proof suggest that rapists are more likely than other criminals to repeat their acts. The evidence that we have is to the contrary. A 1989 Bureau of Justice Statistics recidivism study found that only 7.7% of released rapists were rearrested for rape. In contrast, 33.5% of released larcenists were rearrested for larceny; 31.9% of released burglars were rearrested for burglary; and 24.8% of drug offenders were rearrested for drug offenses. Only homicide had a lower recidivism rate than rape.* It is true that released rapists are more likely than other released prisoners to be rearrested for rape, but that rapists are more likely than others to rape again does not distinguish rapists from other criminals. Larcenists are twenty-five percent more likely to be rearrested for larceny than rapists are to be rearrested for rape.[81] Arguing from the statistics, a crime-based prior act exception is better suited to larcenists and drug offenders than to rapists.

Admittedly, there are a number of reasons to believe that the recidivism rate for rape is higher than the Bureau of Justice Statistics suggests. Many women choose not to report that they have been raped even if they acknowledge that they were raped. Other women do not even consider illegal and are therefore highly unlikely to report acts that clearly qualify as sexual assault. Studies show that rapists in jail have usually raped two or three times before getting caught. Proponents of Rule 413 who suggest that these kind[s] of problems with recidivism statistics are limited to sexual assault crimes are simply wrong, however. Other crimes, particularly consensual crimes like gambling, prostitution, and drug offenses, are notoriously underreported. Nor are rapists alone

* [Studies issued by the Bureau of Justice Statistics in 2002 and 2003 update these statistics based on prisoners released in 1994. The figures below represent the percentage of convicts who were rearrested for the same crime within three years of release:

Drug offenses:	41.2%
Larceny/Theft:	33.9
Burglary:	23.4
Robbery:	13.4
Rape or sexual assault:	5.3
Child molestation:	3.3
Rape:	2.5
Homicide:	1.2

BUREAU OF JUSTICE STATISTICS, RECIDIVISM OF PRISONERS RELEASED IN 1994, at 9 tbl.10 (2002); BUREAU OF JUSTICE STATISTICS, RECIDIVISM OF SEX OFFENDERS RELEASED FROM PRISON IN 1994, at 1–3 (2003). A new BJS recidivism study, based on offenders released from prison in 2005, is set for release in 2013.—GF]

81. Pedophiles may constitute their own special class of particularly recidivistic rapists, *see* Lawrence Wright, *A Rapist's Homecoming*, NEW YORKER (Sept. 4, 1995), at 56, 68–69, but the prior sexual acts of pedophiles would be treated under new Federal Rule of Evidence 414, not Rule 413.

in being apprehended and convicted only after they have repeatedly engaged in comparable illegal conduct.[87]

If the rule against prior act admissibility is meant to guard against any one particular evil, that evil is the tendency of the jury to interpret prior act evidence as propensity evidence. Yet propensity theory is precisely what advocates of Rule 413 invoke: "It would be quite a coincidence if a person who just happened to be a chronic rapist was falsely or mistakenly implicated in a later crime of the same type."[89] There are two significant problems with this invocation of coincidence. First, as discussed above, proponents cannot justify the use of the word "chronic" to describe rapists. There is simply no proof that someone who has raped is a chronic rapist, any more than someone who has robbed a bank is a chronic bank robber. Second, the facially attractive appeal to coincidence ignores the reality of police processes. It is not so strangely coincidental for one who has been previously apprehended to be charged again if the universe of perpetrators from which the victim identifies her attacker is limited to photographs supplied by the police. Mug shot identifications are standard practice for stranger rapes. They are also notoriously unreliable and overvalued by juries. This process will only become more unreliable and further riddled with prejudice if prior acts become admissible. Chances of conviction will increase if the prior act evidence is admissible because juries will overvalue it; police will therefore have significantly more incentive than they already do to convince a victim that the man who raped her is the man in the picture—a man whom the police know to have been involved in a previous rape. The prior actor is easier for police to find (because they know who he is), easier for the victim to identify (because his picture is placed in front of her), and easier for the jury to convict (because the prior act evidence makes it more comfortable in finding him guilty).

In fairness to the proponents of Rule 413, their assumptions about who rapes find support in many state court opinions. These courts have developed what is known as the "lustful disposition" or "depraved sexual instinct" exception to the general prohibition on prior act evidence. Not all courts accept this exception, but those that do rest the exception on the previously discussed misconceptions that rapists are rare and particularly recidivistic, and on a belief that the private nature of the act

87. Despite underreporting problems, 24.8% of drug offenders, who commit victimless crimes, were rearrested. The problem of addiction readily explains recidivism among drug offenders and might justify a prior act exception for this offense. There is no comparable physiological or psychological evidence that most rapists are addicted to rape.

89. David J. Karp, *Evidence of Propensity and Probability in Sex Offense Cases and Other Cases*, 70 CHI.-KENT L. REV. 15, 20 (1994). [Mr. Karp, who served as Senior Counsel at the Office of Policy Development at the Department of Justice, apparently drafted Rules 413–415. *See Johnson v. Elk Lake Sch. Dist.*, 283 F.3d 138, 154 (3d Cir. 2002); Edward J. Imwinkelried, *Some Comments about Mr. David Karp's Remarks on Propensity Evidence*, 70 CHI.-KENT L. REV. 37, 37 (1994).—GF]

justifies letting in prior act evidence due to the absence of corroborating witnesses.... [But the] private nature of sex crimes hardly distinguishes them from other criminal acts: thieves and murderers rarely commit their criminal activity in plain view of potential witnesses. Nor can gang rapes be considered private.... Nonetheless, the belief that rape is different from other crimes continues....

If this "common sense" assumption is actually misguided and rapists are no more likely than others to repeat their acts, then the evidentiary rule should cut in the opposite direction of the lustful disposition exception and Rule 413: courts should be particularly careful to exclude prior sexual act evidence because jurors are particularly likely to believe (inappropriately) in a rapist's psychopathologically induced tendency to repeat his acts....

Those who endorse Rule 413 as a means of overcoming the harms that rape perpetuates need to recognize the inferences that are likely to accompany a prior act exception. Admitting prior act evidence may increase the chance of conviction, but such admissions will also increase the risk that a jury will punish the defendant for acts other than those for which he is on trial ... [and] that may not have been proven beyond a reasonable doubt.... [And] in a world in which prior acts of rape are admissible, a recidivism theory may become the norm. If jurors come to expect prior act evidence, jurors may start to view the absence of prior acts as evidence cutting against the likelihood that the accused is a "rapist." ... [J]urors will be less likely to believe that he did it.

Rule 413 is also likely to ... perpetuate stereotypes of the chronic rapist. As discussed above, Rule 413 gives police an added incentive to arrest men who have allegedly been involved in rapes before.... Police are more likely to be aware of the histories of men who have already encountered the criminal justice system—a class of men that is overwhelmingly poor and minority ... [and] least likely to have access to high quality legal counsel.... Poor, minority men with an alleged prior record will be much more likely to be falsely identified, improperly tried, and wrongfully convicted for ... rapes that they did not commit.... [And this change will come] at the expense of women who are assaulted by nonpoor, nonminority men.... Thus, the legal system will fail to reflect precisely what feminist scholarship has fought to establish: that rape is a crime across all classes, among all races, and by all sorts of men....

UNITED STATES v. GUARDIA

135 F.3d 1326 (10th Cir. 1998).

■ TACHA, CIRCUIT JUDGE. On September 5, 1996, a federal grand jury in New Mexico returned an indictment charging defendant David Guardia with two counts of sexual abuse.... The indictment is based upon the complaints of two alleged victims who contend that Dr. Guardia sexually abused them in the course of gynecological procedures that he conducted at Kirtland [Air Force Base]. Both complainants, Carla G. and Francesca L., allege that during an examination Dr. Guardia engaged in ... contact that exceeded the bounds of medically appropriate examination techniques and constituted sexual abuse.... Neither of the examinations occurred in the presence of a chaperon.

In addition to offering the testimony of Carla G. and Francesca L., the government moved to introduce, under Rule 413, the testimony of four women who allege that Dr. Guardia abused them during gynecological examinations in a manner similar to the alleged abuse of Carla G. and Francesca L....

[Dr. Guardia moved in limine to exclude the testimony of the other four women.] After considering the nature and content of the testimony proffered under Rule 413, the district court applied Rule 403 and excluded the evidence [finding that the risk of jury confusion substantially outweighed probative value]. The government appeals the district court's determination....

I. Requirements of Rule 413

... [E]vidence offered under Rule 413 must meet three threshold requirements before a district court can admit it. A district court must first determine that "the defendant is accused of an offense of sexual assault." *Cf.* Fed. R. Evid. 413(d) [unrestyled] (defining an "offense of sexual assault"). Second, the court must find that the evidence proffered is "evidence of the defendant's commission of another offense of ... sexual assault." Fed. R. Evid. 413(a) [unrestyled]. The district court implicitly recognized these requirements in its hearing on the motion *in limine* and in its written opinion.

The third requirement, applicable to all evidence, is that the evidence be relevant. *See* Fed. R. Evid. 402 [unrestyled] ("Evidence which is not relevant is not admissible."). The rules define relevant evidence as evidence that "has any tendency to make the existence of any fact that is of consequence to the determination of the action more probable or less probable than it would be without the evidence." Fed. R. Evid. 401 [unrestyled]. A defendant with a propensity to commit acts similar to the charged crime is more likely to have committed the charged crime than another. Evidence of such a propensity is therefore relevant. *See* Old Chief v. United States, 519 U.S. 172, 181 (1997) ("[P]ropensity evidence is relevant...."); Michelson v. United States, 335 U.S. 469, 475–76 (1948) (noting the "admitted probative value" of propensity evidence).

In most cases, though not in Rule 413 cases, the court must exclude propensity evidence despite its acknowledged relevance. [Unrestyled] Rule 404(b) prohibits the use of prior acts of a person "to prove the character of a person in order to show action in conformity therewith." Under [unrestyled] Rule 413, however, evidence of a defendant's other sexual assaults may be admitted "for its bearing on *any* matter to which it is relevant." Thus, Rule 413 supersedes Rule 404(b)'s restriction and allows the government to offer evidence of a defendant's prior conduct for the purpose of demonstrating a defendant's propensity to commit the charged offense....

If believed, the Rule 413 evidence in this case would demonstrate that the defendant has a propensity to take advantage of female patients by touching them in a salacious manner and making comments while doing so. Because the defendant's propensity is to engage in conduct which closely matches that alleged in this case, the evidence is probative of his guilt.... The evidence proffered in this case, therefore, satisfies Rule 413's three threshold requirements.

II. THE APPLICABILITY OF RULE 403

... [Unrestyled] Rule 403 allows a district court to exclude evidence "if its probative value is substantially outweighed by the danger of unfair prejudice" or other enumerated considerations, including confusion of the issues or undue delay. Rule 403 applies to all evidence admitted in federal court, except in those rare instances when other rules make an exception to it. *See, e.g.*, FED. R. EVID. 609(a)(2) (mandating that prior conviction of a witness be admitted for impeachment purposes if prior crime involved dishonesty)....

[A]fter the district court resolves the three threshold issues, including a finding that the proffered evidence is relevant, it must proceed to balance the probative weight of the Rule 413 evidence against "the danger of unfair prejudice, confusion of the issues, or misleading the jury, or ... considerations of undue delay, waste of time, or needless presentation of cumulative evidence." FED. R. EVID. 403 [unrestyled]. We hold that a court must perform the same 403 analysis that it does in any other context, but with careful attention to both the significant probative value and the strong prejudicial qualities inherent in all evidence submitted under 413.

A. *Legal Principles:* Rule 413 marks a sea change in the federal rules' approach to character evidence, a fact which could lead to at least two different misapplications of the 403 balancing test. First, a court could be tempted to exclude the Rule 413 evidence simply because character evidence traditionally has been considered too prejudicial for admission. *Cf. Old Chief*, 519 U.S. at 181 (stating that Rule 404(b) merely "reflects ... common law tradition"). Second, a court could perform a restrained 403 analysis because of the belief that Rule 413 embodies a legislative judgment that propensity evidence regarding sexual assaults is never too prejudicial or confusing and generally should be admitted. *See* United States v. LeCompte, 131 F.3d 767 (8th Cir. 1997).

We find both interpretations illogical. With regard to the first position, we note that this court refrains from construing the words and phrases of a statute—or entire statutory provisions—in a way that renders them superfluous. Rule 413 allows for evidence that otherwise would be excluded to be admitted. If Rule 413 evidence were always too prejudicial under 403, Rule 413 would never lead to the introduction of evidence. Therefore, Rule 413 only has effect if we interpret it in a way that leaves open the possibility of admission.

This interpretation harmonizes with the Supreme Court's comment in *Old Chief* and similar statements in the advisory committee's notes to Rules 401 and 403 that the ban on character evidence is merely an application of Rule 403 to a recurring issue. *See Old Chief*, 519 U.S. at 182. All of the rules in Article IV of the Federal Rules of Evidence, not just Rule 404, are "concrete applications [of rules 402 and 403] evolved for particular situations." FED. R. EVID. 403 advisory committee's note [RB 42]. The fact that Congress created Rule 413 can only mean that Congress intended to partially repeal the "concrete application" found in 404(b) for a subset of cases in which Congress found 404(b)'s rigid rule to be inappropriate. That conclusion is not surprising, given the fact that propensity evidence has a unique probative value in sexual assault trials and that such trials often suffer from a lack of any relevant evidence beyond the testimony of the alleged victim and the defendant. Rule 413 is a refinement, and it exemplifies the type of evolution of Rules 402 and 403 that one can expect to find in Article IV.

While Rule 413 removes the per se exclusion of character evidence, courts should continue to consider the traditional reasons for the prohibition of character evidence as "risks of prejudice" weighing against admission. For example, a court should, in each 413 case, take into account the chance that "a jury will convict for crimes other than those charged—or that, uncertain of guilt, it will convict anyway because a bad person deserves punishment." *Old Chief*, 519 U.S. at 181. A court should also be aware that evidence of prior acts can have the effect of confusing the issues in a case. These risks will be present every time evidence is admitted under Rule 413. The size of the risk, of course, will depend on the individual case.

With regard to the second potential misapplication of Rule 413, the government urges us to approve a lenient 403 balancing test. We agree that Rule 413, like all other rules of admissibility, favors the introduction of evidence. *See* 140 CONG. REC. H8968–01, H8991 (Aug. 21, 1994) (statement of S. Molinari) ("The presumption is in favor of admission."). Rule 413, however, contains no language that supports an especially lenient application of Rule 403. Furthermore, courts apply Rule 403 in undiluted form to Rules [404(a)(2)(A)–(C) and 404(a)(3)], the other exceptions to the ban on propensity evidence. Those rules allow a criminal defendant to use character evidence of himself, his victim, or in limited circumstances, of other witnesses, in order to "prove action in conformity therewith." Like Rule 413, these rules carve out exceptions to Rule [404(a)(1)] and reflect a legislative judgment that certain types of propensity evidence should be admitted. Courts have never found, however, that because the drafters made exceptions to the general rule of [404(a)(1)], they tempered 403 as well.

Similarly, under Rule 404(b), evidence of a person's prior acts can be used for ... purposes other than proving character. Despite Rule 404(b)'s legislative judgment in favor of admission, Rule 403 applies with all its vigor to Rule 404(b) evidence. *See* Huddleston v. United States, 485 U.S. 681, 687–88 (1988) (noting that rules of admissibility in Article IV are subject to "general strictures ... such as Rules 402 and 403").

When balancing Rule 413 evidence under 403, then, the district court should not alter its normal process of weighing the probative value of the evidence against the danger of unfair prejudice. In Rule 413 cases, the risk of prejudice will be present to varying degrees. Propensity evidence, however, has indisputable probative value. That value in a given case will depend on innumerable considerations, including the similarity of the prior acts to the acts charged, the closeness in time of the prior acts to the charged acts, the frequency of the prior acts, the presence or lack of intervening events, and the need for evidence beyond the testimony of the defendant and alleged victim. Because of the sensitive nature of the balancing test in these cases, it will be particularly important for a district court to fully evaluate the proffered Rule 413 evidence and make a clear record of the reasoning behind its findings.

B. *Balancing in the Present Case:* The decision to exclude evidence under Rule 403 is within the sound discretion of the trial court, and will be reversed only upon a showing of a clear abuse of that discretion. During the motion hearing and in its written decision, the district court made clear that its overriding, if not exclusive, concern was the danger that the proffered testimony would confuse the issues in the case, thereby misleading the jury. The district court properly exercised its discretion in determining that the potential for confusion of the issues substantially outweighed the probative value of the proffered testimony.

We must consider the trial court's ruling in light of the unusual nature of this case. This trial undoubtedly will focus upon whether the manner in which Dr. Guardia examined the complaining patients was medically appropriate. Unlike other sexual assault cases, resolution of credibility issues alone will not enable the jury to decide whether Dr. Guardia's act was proper. Rather, the jury will be required to evaluate expert testimony regarding the medical propriety of each examination to determine whether Dr. Guardia acted within the scope of his patients' consent.

Because so much depends upon the medical propriety of Dr. Guardia's conduct towards Carla G. and Francesca L., the fact that Dr. Guardia treated the four additional witnesses under similar but distinct circumstances creates a substantial risk of jury confusion. Admission of the testimony would transform the trial of two incidents into the trial of six incidents, each requiring description by lay witnesses and explanation by expert witnesses. The subtle factual distinctions among these incidents would make it difficult for the jury to separate the evidence of the uncharged conduct from the charged conduct.

Expert testimony explaining the propriety of Dr. Guardia's conduct as to each witness would exacerbate the risk of confusion by multiplying conflicting and overlapping testimony. Although the evidence proffered under Rule 413 is probative of Dr. Guardia's disposition and supports the testimony of the complaining witnesses, we cannot conclude that the district court exceeded the bounds of permissible choice by excluding the evidence under the circumstances of this case.

Finally, we reject the government's contention that the district court erred by failing to engineer a method of presenting the evidence to minimize the risk of jury confusion. In Hill v. Bache Halsey Stuart Shields Inc., 790 F.2d 817, 826–27 (10th Cir. 1986), we held that the district court abused its discretion under Rule 403 because it excluded evidence that had a high probative value even though its prejudicial effect could have been minimized through a "less elaborate" method of presentation. In this case, however, the evidence that the district court excluded is not realistically susceptible to any less elaborate presentation than that proposed by the government. Thus, the district court did not abuse its discretion by failing to require such a presentation.

CONCLUSION

... Given the deference due district courts in making Rule 403 determinations, we find that the district court did not abuse its discretion in concluding under Rule 403 that the risk of jury confusion substantially outweighed the probative value of the Rule 413 evidence proffered by the government. Therefore, the decision of the district court is affirmed.

Postscript to* United States v. Guardia*: In a part of Judge Tacha's opinion I've omitted, she considered whether Rule 413 had "create[d] an exception for itself to the Rule 403 balancing test." 135 F.3d at 1329. This question arose because of an ambiguity that once infected Rules 413, 414, and 415. As enacted, all three had provided that evidence of past sexual assaults "is admissible" if the rules' other terms were met. (RB 408, 410, 412.) In its scathing report on the these rules, excerpted earlier, the

Judicial Conference of the United States noted commentators' concerns that

> the Rules, as drafted, were mandatory—that is, such evidence had to be admitted regardless of other rules of evidence such as the hearsay rule or the Rule 403 balancing test. The [evidence advisory] committee believed that this position was arguable because Rules 413–415 declare without qualification that such evidence "is admissible." In contrast, the new Rule 412, passed as part of the same legislation, provided that certain evidence "is admissible if it is otherwise admissible under these Rules."

REPORT OF THE JUDICIAL CONFERENCE OF THE UNITED STATES ON THE ADMISSION OF CHARACTER EVIDENCE IN CERTAIN SEXUAL MISCONDUCT CASES (submitted to Congress, Feb. 9, 1995), *reprinted at* 159 F.R.D. 51, 51–54 (1995).

Joining virtually every court and commentator, Judge Tacha concluded that despite the new rules' imprecision, their application is subject to Rule 403's balancing test. This conclusion seems consistent with congressional intent. In her floor statement supporting Rules 413 through 415, principal House sponsor Susan Molinari noted that "the general standards of the rules of evidence will continue to apply, including the restrictions on hearsay evidence and the court's authority under Evidence Rule 403 to exclude evidence whose probative value is substantially outweighed by its prejudicial effect." (Page 220 above.)

In the excerpts of *Guardia* and the Judicial Conference's report presented above, I deleted reference to this controversy because the Evidence Rules Restyling Project has swept it away. Rules 413 through 415 no longer contain the worrisome words, "is admissible." Instead they provide that if the other conditions of those rules are met, "the court *may admit* evidence that the defendant [or civil party] committed any other" sexual assault. (RB 409, 411, 413 (emphasis added).) Throughout the Federal Rules the phrase "may admit" serves as code that the trial judge retains discretion to exclude the evidence, normally under Rule 403.

A Note on the Next Case: At Alvin Mound's trial on several charges of sexual abuse and assault, the government offered evidence under Rule 413 of two other acts of sexual abuse. Mound argued on appeal that Rule 413 violates the Due Process Clause of the Fifth Amendment because it "authorizes the jury to overvalue character evidence, to punish a defendant for past acts and to convict the defendant for who he is, rather than for what he has done." Rejecting that challenge, Judge Richard S. Arnold wrote for a panel of the Eighth Circuit Court of Appeals that because evidence admitted under Rule 413 must survive a Rule 403 weighing test, the evidence is not " 'so extremely unfair that its admission violates fundamental conceptions of justice.' " United States v. Mound, 149 F.3d 799, 801 (8th Cir. 1998) (quoting Dowling v. United States, 493 U.S. 342, 352 (1990)). Other Circuit Courts of Appeals have agreed that application of Rule 403 to Rules 413 and 414 " 'should always result in the exclusion of evidence' that is so prejudicial as to deprive the defendant of his right to a fair trial. . . ." United States v. LeMay, 260 F.3d 1018, 1027 (9th Cir. 2001), *cert. denied*, 534 U.S. 1166 (2002) (quoting United States v. Castillo, 140 F.3d 874, 883 (10th Cir. 1998)). The Tenth Circuit has dismissed the notion that the long pedigree of the rule against propensity evidence makes it sacrosanct: "That the practice is ancient does not mean it is embodied in the Constitution." United States v. Enjady, 134 F.3d 1427, 1432 (10th Cir.), *cert. denied*, 525 U.S. 887 (1998).

After losing his appeal, Mound asked the Eighth Circuit for rehearing en banc. The court declined. Judge Morris Sheppard Arnold, Richard Arnold's brother, dissented:

UNITED STATES v. MOUND

157 F.3d 1153 (8th Cir. 1998), *cert. denied*, 525 U.S. 1089 (1999).

■ The suggestion for rehearing *en banc* is denied. . . .

■ MORRIS SHEPPARD ARNOLD, CIRCUIT JUDGE, dissenting, joined by MCMILLIAN, WOLLMAN, and BEAM, CIRCUIT JUDGES. Because this case seems to me to involve "a question of exceptional importance," I dissent from the order denying the suggestion for rehearing *en banc*.

Fed R. Evid. 413 runs counter to a centuries-old legal tradition that views propensity evidence with a particularly skeptical eye. The common law, of course, is not embodied in the Constitution, but the fact that a rule has recommended itself to generations of lawyers and judges is at least some indication that it embodies " 'fundamental conceptions of justice,' " Dowling v. United States, 493 U.S. 342, 352 (1990). It also cannot be irrelevant that the members of two committees, consisting of 40 persons in all, and appointed by the Judicial Conference of the United States to examine Fed. R. Evid. 413 before its passage, all but unanimously urged that Congress not adopt the rule because of deep concerns about its fundamental fairness. Members of the committees worried that the new rule would displace "essential 'protections [that have] formed a fundamental part of American jurisprudence and have evolved under long-standing rules and case law.' " *See* M.A. Sheft, *Federal Rules of Evidence 413: A Dangerous New Frontier*, 33 AM. CRIM. L. REV. 57, 73 (1995) (quoting *Report of the Judicial Conference of the United States on the Admission of Character Evidence in Certain Sexual Misconduct Cases*, at 2 (1995)).

It seems to me that the *en banc* court ought to consider, as one commentator has put it, whether Fed R. Evid. 413 "presents [so] great a risk that the jury will convict a defendant for his past conduct or unsavory character" that it violates due process. Sheft, *Frontier*, at 76. We might well conclude that the common-law rule against propensity evidence has as distinguished a legal pedigree as, say, the rule that guilt must be proved beyond a reasonable doubt. Our resolution of the relevant constitutional questions would necessarily involve us in an examination of the ultimate rationality of Fed R. Evid. 413. There is a great deal of evidence that the prognosticative power of past sexual behavior is quite low; in fact, the recidivism rate for rape is lower than that for any major crime other than murder. While the kind of review that I think we ought to undertake would require us to consider matters that Congress has already presumably weighed, that is inevitable when fairness (a necessary component of which is rationality) is the subject of judicial inquiry. . . .

E. PROOF OF THE DEFENDANT'S AND THE VICTIM'S CHARACTER

Focus on
FRE 404(a)(2)(A), 404(a)(2)(B), & 405

MICHELSON v. UNITED STATES

335 U.S. 469 (1948).

■ MR. JUSTICE JACKSON delivered the opinion of the Court. In 1947 petitioner Michelson was convicted of bribing a federal revenue agent. The Government proved a large payment by accused to the agent for the purpose of influencing his official action. The defendant, as a witness on his own behalf, admitted passing the money but claimed it was done in response to the agent's demands, threats, solicitations, and inducements that amounted to entrapment. It is enough for our purposes to say that determination of the issue turned on whether the jury should believe the agent or the accused.

On direct examination of defendant, his own counsel brought out that, in 1927, he had been convicted of a misdemeanor having to do with trading in counterfeit watch dials. On cross-examination it appeared that in 1930, in executing an application for a license to deal in second-hand jewelry, he answered "No" to the question whether he had theretofore been arrested or summoned for any offense.

Defendant called five witnesses to prove that he enjoyed a good reputation. Two of them testified that their acquaintance with him extended over a period of about thirty years and the others said they had known him at least half that long. A typical examination in chief was as follows:

"*Q.* Do you know the defendant Michelson?

"*A.* Yes.

"*Q.* How long do you know Mr. Michelson?

"*A.* About 30 years.

"*Q.* Do you know other people who know him?

"*A.* Yes.

"*Q.* Have you had occasion to discuss his reputation for honesty and truthfulness and for being a law-abiding citizen?

"*A.* It is very good.

"*Q.* You have talked to others?

"*A.* Yes.

"*Q.* And what is his reputation?

"*A.* Very good."

These are representative of answers by three witnesses; two others replied, in substance, that they never had heard anything against Michelson.

On cross-examination, four of the witnesses were asked, in substance, this question: "Did you ever hear that Mr. Michelson on March 4, 1927, was convicted of a violation of the trademark law in New York City in regard to watches?" This referred to the twenty-year-old conviction about which defendant himself had testified on direct examination. Two of them had heard of it and two had not.

To four of these witnesses the prosecution also addressed the question the allowance of which, over defendant's objection, is claimed to be reversible error:

"Did you ever hear that on October 11, 1920, the defendant, Solomon Michelson, was arrested for receiving stolen goods?"

None of the witnesses appears to have heard of this.

The trial court asked counsel for the prosecution, out of presence of the jury, "Is it a fact according to the best information in your possession, that Michelson was arrested for receiving stolen goods?" Counsel replied that it was, and to support his good faith exhibited a paper record which defendant's counsel did not challenge.

The judge also on three occasions warned the jury, in terms that are not criticized, of the limited purpose for which this evidence was received.[3]

3. In ruling on the objection when the question was first asked, the Court said:

"... I instruct the jury that what is happening now is this: the defendant has called character witnesses, and the basis for the evidence given by those character witnesses is the reputation of the defendant in the community, and

Defendant-petitioner challenges the right of the prosecution so to cross-examine his character witnesses. The Court of Appeals held that it was permissible. The opinion, however, points out that the practice has been severely criticized and invites us, in one respect, to change the rule.[4] Serious and responsible criticism has been aimed, however, not alone at the detail now questioned by the Court of Appeals but at common-law doctrine on the whole subject of proof of reputation or character. It would not be possible to appraise the usefulness and propriety of this cross-examination without consideration of the unique practice concerning character testimony, of which such cross-examination is a minor part.

Courts that follow the common-law tradition almost unanimously have come to disallow resort by the prosecution to any kind of evidence of a defendant's evil character to establish a probability of his guilt. Not that the law invests the defendant with a presumption of good character,

since the defendant tenders the issue of his reputation the prosecution may ask the witness if she has heard of various incidents in his career. I say to you that regardless of her answer you are not to assume that the incidents asked about actually took place. All that is happening is that this witness' standard of opinion of the reputation of the defendant is being tested. Is that clear?"

4. Footnote 8 to that court's opinion reads as follows:

"Wigmore, *Evidence* (3d ed. 1940) § 988, after noting that 'such inquiries are almost universally admitted,' not as 'impeachment by extrinsic testimony of particular acts of misconduct,' but as means of testing the character 'witness' grounds of knowledge,' continues with these comments: 'But the serious objection to them is that practically the above distinction—between rumors of such conduct, as affecting reputation, and the fact of it as violating the rule against particular facts—cannot be maintained in the mind of the jury. The rumor of the misconduct, when admitted, goes far, in spite of all theory and of the judge's charge, towards fixing the misconduct as a fact upon the other person, and thus does three improper things,—(1) it violates the fundamental rule of fairness that prohibits the use of such facts, (2) it gets at them by hearsay only, and not by trustworthy testimony, and (3) it leaves the other person no means of defending himself by denial or explanation, such as he would otherwise have had if the rule had allowed that conduct to be made the subject of an issue. Moreover, these are not occurrences of possibility, but of daily practice. This method of inquiry or cross-examination is frequently resorted to by counsel for the very purpose of injuring by indirection a character which they are forbidden directly to attack in that way; they rely upon the mere putting of the question (not caring that it is answered negatively) to convey their covert insinuation. The value of the inquiry for testing purposes is often so small and the opportunities of its abuse by underhand ways are so great that the practice may amount to little more than a mere subterfuge, and should be strictly supervised by forbidding it to counsel who do not use it in good faith.'

"Because, as Wigmore says, the jury almost surely cannot comprehend the judge's limiting instruction, the writer of this opinion wishes that the United States Supreme Court would tell us to follow what appears to be the Illinois rule, *i.e.*, that such questions are improper unless they relate to offenses similar to those for which the defendant is on trial. *See* Aiken v. People, 183 Ill. 215 (1899); *cf.* People v. Hannon, 381 Ill. 206 (1942)."

but it simply closes the whole matter of character, disposition and reputation on the prosecution's case-in-chief. The state may not show defendant's prior trouble with the law, specific criminal acts, or ill name among his neighbors, even though such facts might logically be persuasive that he is by propensity a probable perpetrator of the crime. The inquiry is not rejected because character is irrelevant; on the contrary, it is said to weigh too much with the jury and to so overpersuade them as to prejudge one with a bad general record and deny him a fair opportunity to defend against a particular charge. The overriding policy of excluding such evidence, despite its admitted probative value, is the practical experience that its disallowance tends to prevent confusion of issues, unfair surprise and undue prejudice.

But this line of inquiry firmly denied to the State is opened to the defendant because character is relevant in resolving probabilities of guilt. He may introduce affirmative testimony that the general estimate of his character is so favorable that the jury may infer that he would not be likely to commit the offense charged. This privilege is sometimes valuable to a defendant, for this Court has held that such testimony alone, in some circumstances, may be enough to raise a reasonable doubt of guilt and that in the federal courts a jury in a proper case should be so instructed. Edgington v. United States, 164 U.S. 361 (1896).

When the defendant elects to initiate a character inquiry, another anomalous rule comes into play. Not only is he permitted to call witnesses to testify from hearsay, but indeed such a witness is not allowed to base his testimony on anything but hearsay. . . . The witness may not testify about defendant's specific acts . . .; nor can he testify that his own acquaintance, observation, and knowledge of defendant leads to his own independent opinion that defendant possesses a good general or specific character, inconsistent with commission of acts charged.* The witness is, however, allowed to summarize what he has heard in the community, although much of it may have been said by persons less qualified to judge than himself. The evidence which the law permits is . . . only as to the shadow his daily life has cast in his neighborhood. This has been well described in a different connection as "the slow growth of months and years, the resultant picture of forgotten incidents, passing events, habitual and daily conduct, presumably honest because disinterested, and safer to be trusted because prone to suspect. . . . It is for that reason that such general repute is permitted to be proven. It sums up a multitude of trivial details. It compacts into the brief phrase of a verdict the teaching of many incidents and the conduct of years. It is the average intelligence drawing its conclusion." Finch, J., in Badger v. Badger, 88 N.Y. 546, 552 (1882).

* [FRE 405(a) modified this aspect of evidence law by permitting character witnesses to testify about their opinion of the defendant's character as well as about the defendant's reputation.—GF]

While courts have recognized logical grounds for criticism of this type of opinion-based-on-hearsay testimony, it is said to be justified by "overwhelming considerations of practical convenience" in avoiding innumerable collateral issues which, if it were attempted to prove character by direct testimony, would complicate and confuse the trial, distract the minds of jurymen and befog the chief issues in the litigation. People v. Van Gaasbeck, 189 N.Y. 408, 419 (1907).

Another paradox in this branch of the law of evidence is that the delicate and responsible task of compacting reputation hearsay into the "brief phrase of a verdict" is one of the few instances in which conclusions are accepted from a witness on a subject in which he is not an expert. However, the witness must qualify to give an opinion by showing such acquaintance with the defendant, the community in which he has lived and the circles in which he has moved, as to speak with authority of the terms in which generally he is regarded. . . .

Thus the law extends helpful but illogical options to a defendant. Experience taught a necessity that they be counterweighted with equally illogical conditions to keep the advantage from becoming an unfair and unreasonable one. The price a defendant must pay for attempting to prove his good name is to throw open the entire subject which the law has kept closed for his benefit and to make himself vulnerable where the law otherwise shields him. The prosecution may pursue the inquiry with contradictory witnesses to show that damaging rumors, whether or not well-grounded, were afloat—for it is not the man that he is, but the name that he has which is put in issue. Another hazard is that his own witness is subject to cross-examination as to the contents and extent of the hearsay on which he bases his conclusions, and he may be required to disclose rumors and reports that are current even if they do not affect his own conclusion. It may test the sufficiency of his knowledge by asking what stories were circulating concerning events, such as one's arrest, about which people normally comment and speculate. Thus, while the law gives defendant the option to show as a fact that his reputation reflects a life and habit incompatible with commission of the offense charged, it subjects his proof to tests of credibility designed to prevent him from profiting by a mere parade of partisans.

To thus digress from evidence as to the offense to hear a contest as to the standing of the accused, at its best opens a tricky line of inquiry as to a shapeless and elusive subject matter. At its worst it opens a veritable Pandora's box of irresponsible gossip, innuendo and smear. In the frontier phase of our law's development, calling friends to vouch for defendant's good character, and its counterpart—calling the rivals and enemies of a witness to impeach him by testifying that his reputation for veracity was so bad that he was unworthy of belief on his oath—were favorite and frequent ways of converting an individual litigation into a community contest and a trial into a spectacle. Growth of urban conditions, where one may never know or hear the name of his next-door neighbor, have tended to limit the use of these techniques and to deprive them of weight with juries. The popularity of both procedures has subsided, but courts of last resort have sought to overcome danger that the true issues will be obscured and confused by investing the trial court with discretion to limit the number of such witnesses and to control cross-examination. . . .

Wide discretion is accompanied by heavy responsibility on trial courts to protect the practice from any misuse. The trial judge was scrupulous to so guard it in the case before us. He took pains to ascertain, out of presence of the jury, that the target of the question was an actual event, which would probably result in some comment among acquaintances if not injury to defendant's reputation. He satisfied himself that counsel was not merely taking a random shot at a reputation imprudently exposed or asking a groundless question to waft an unwarranted innuendo into the jury box.

The question permitted by the trial court, however, involves several features that may be worthy of comment. Its form invited hearsay; it asked about an arrest, not a conviction, and for an offense not closely similar to the one on trial; and it concerned an occurrence many years past.

Since the whole inquiry, as we have pointed out, is calculated to ascertain the general talk of people about defendant, rather than the witness' own knowledge of him, the form of inquiry, "Have you heard?" has general approval, and "Do you know?" is not allowed.

A character witness may be cross-examined as to an arrest whether or not it culminated in a conviction, according to the overwhelming weight of authority. This rule is sometimes confused with that which prohibits cross-examination to credibility by asking a witness whether he himself has been arrested.

Arrest without more does not, in law any more than in reason, impeach the integrity or impair the credibility of a witness. It happens to the innocent as well as the guilty. Only a conviction, therefore, may be inquired about to undermine the trustworthiness of a witness.

Arrest without more may nevertheless impair or cloud one's reputation. False arrest may do that. Even to be acquitted may damage one's good name if the community receives the verdict with a wink and chooses to remember defendant as one who ought to have been convicted. A conviction, on the other hand, may be accepted as a misfortune or an injustice, and even enhance the standing of one who mends his ways and lives it down. Reputation is the net balance of so many debits and credits that the law does not attach the finality to a conviction, when the issue is reputation, that is given to it when the issue is the credibility of the convict.*

The inquiry as to an arrest is permissible also because the prosecution has a right to test the qualifications of the witness to bespeak the community opinion. If one never heard the speculations and rumors in which even one's friends indulge upon his arrest, the jury may doubt whether he is capable of giving any very reliable conclusions as to his reputation.

In this case the crime inquired about was receiving stolen goods; the trial was for bribery. The Court of Appeals thought this dissimilarity of offenses too great to sustain the inquiry in logic, though conceding that it is authorized by preponderance of authority. It asks us to substitute the Illinois rule which allows inquiry about arrest, but only for very closely similar if not identical charges, in place of the rule more generally adhered to in this country and in England. We think the facts of this case show the proposal to be inexpedient.

The good character which the defendant had sought to establish was broader than the crime charged and included the traits of "honesty and truthfulness" and "being a law-abiding citizen." Possession of these characteristics would seem as incompatible with offering a bribe to a revenue agent as with receiving stolen goods. The crimes may be unlike, but both alike proceed from the same defects of character which the witnesses said this defendant was reputed not to exhibit. It is not only by comparison with the crime on trial but by comparison with the reputation asserted that a court may judge whether the prior arrest should be made subject of inquiry. By this test the inquiry was permissible. It was proper cross-examination because reports of his arrest for receiving stolen goods, if admitted, would tend to weaken the assertion that he was known as an honest and law-abiding citizen. The cross-examination may take in as much ground as the testimony it is designed to verify. To hold otherwise would give defendant the benefit of testimony that he was honest and law-abiding in reputation when such might not be the fact; the refutation was founded on convictions equally persuasive though not for crimes exactly repeated in the present charge.

The inquiry here concerned an arrest twenty-seven years before the trial. Events a generation old are likely to be lived down and dropped from the present thought and talk of the community and to be absent from the knowledge of younger or more recent acquaintances. The court in its discretion may well exclude inquiry about rumors of an event so remote, unless recent misconduct revived them. But two of these witnesses dated their acquaintance with defendant as commencing thirty years before the trial. Defendant, on direct examination, voluntarily called

* [Impeachment of witnesses with evidence of their past convictions is governed by Rule 609, which we address in Chapter 4. *See* pages 276–307.—GF]

attention to his conviction twenty years before. While the jury might conclude that a matter so old and indecisive as a 1920 arrest would shed little light on the present reputation and hence propensities of the defendant, we cannot say that, in the context of this evidence and in the absence of objection on this specific ground, its admission was an abuse of discretion.

We do not overlook or minimize the consideration that "the jury almost surely cannot comprehend the judge's limiting instruction," which disturbed the Court of Appeals. The refinements of the evidentiary rules on this subject are such that even lawyers and judges, after study and reflection, often are confused, and surely jurors in the hurried and unfamiliar movement of a trial must find them almost unintelligible. However, limiting instructions on this subject are no more difficult to comprehend or apply than those upon various other subjects; for example, instructions that admissions of a co-defendant are to be limited to the question of his guilt and are not to be considered as evidence against other defendants. . . .* A defendant in such a case is powerless to prevent his cause from being irretrievably obscured and confused; but, in cases such as the one before us, the law foreclosed this whole confounding line of inquiry, unless defendant thought the net advantage from opening it up would be with him. Given this option, we think defendants in general and this defendant in particular have no valid complaint at the latitude which existing law allows to the prosecution to meet by cross-examination an issue voluntarily tendered by the defense.

We end, as we began, with the observation that the law regulating the offering and testing of character testimony may merit many criticisms. England and some states have overhauled the practice by statute. But the task of modernizing the longstanding rules on the subject is one of magnitude and difficulty which even those dedicated to law reform do not lightly undertake.

The law of evidence relating to proof of reputation in criminal cases has developed almost entirely at the hands of state courts of last resort, which have such questions frequently before them. This Court, on the other hand, has contributed little to this or to any phase of the law of evidence, for the reason, among others, that it has had extremely rare occasion to decide such issues, as the paucity of citations in this opinion to our own writings attests. It is obvious that a court which can make only infrequent sallies into the field cannot recast the body of case law on this subject in many, many years, even if it were clear what the rules should be.

* [The Supreme Court long ago lost confidence in jurors' ability and willingness to consider a codefendant's confession in relation to his guilt alone and to ignore it when weighing the guilt of jointly tried accomplices named in his confession. *See* *Bruton v. United States*, 391 U.S. 123 (1968) (pages 694–703).—GF]

We concur in the general opinion of courts, textwriters and the profession that much of this law is archaic, paradoxical and full of compromises and compensations by which an irrational advantage to one side is offset by a poorly reasoned counterprivilege to the other. But somehow it has proved a workable even if clumsy system when moderated by discretionary controls in the hands of a wise and strong trial court. To pull one misshapen stone out of the grotesque structure is more likely simply to upset its present balance between adverse interests than to establish a rational edifice.

The present suggestion is that we adopt for all federal courts a new rule as to cross-examination about prior arrest, adhered to by the courts of only one state and rejected elsewhere. The confusion and error it would engender would seem too heavy a price to pay for an almost imperceptible logical improvement, if any, in a system which is justified, if at all, by accumulated judicial experience rather than abstract logic.

The judgment is

Affirmed.

■ MR. JUSTICE FRANKFURTER, concurring....

■ MR. JUSTICE RUTLEDGE, with whom MR. JUSTICE MURPHY joins, dissenting.... [I]n the guise of "testing the standards of the witness" when he speaks to reputation, the door has been thrown wide open to trying the defendant's whole life, both in general reputation and in specific incident. What is worse, this is without opportunity for the defendant to rebut either the fact or the innuendo.... Hardly any incident, however remote or derogatory, but can be drawn out by asking the witness who testifies to the defendant's good character, "Have you heard this" or "Have you heard that." And many incidents, wholly innocent in quality, can be turned by the prosecutor, through an inflection or tone, to cast aspersion upon the defendant by the mere asking of the question, without hope of affirmative response from the witness....

[In this case, after the prosecutor asked about Michelson's 1920 arrest, the trial] court solemnly instructed the jury that they were not to consider that the incident took place.... [But the] very form of the question was itself notice of the fact to the jury. They well might assume, as men of common sense, that the court would not allow the question if the fact were only fiction. And why "on October 11th, 1920," rather than merely "in 1920" or "Have you ever heard of the defendant's being arrested, other than for the trademark violation?" Why also "for receiving stolen goods"? In my opinion the only answers to these questions are, not that the prosecution was "testing the witness' standard of opinion of reputation," but that it was telling the jury what it could not prove directly and what the petitioner had no chance to deny, namely, that he had been so arrested; and thereby either insinuating that he had been convicted of the crime or leaving to the jury to guess that this had been the outcome. The question was a typical abuse arising from allowing this type of inquiry. It should have been excluded. There is no way to tell how much prejudice it produced. . . .

MICHELSON V. UNITED STATES: *Afterthoughts*

Proving Character Under Rules 404(a)(2)(A) and 404(a)(2)(B)

Rule 404(a)(2)(A) permits criminal defendants to offer proof of pertinent traits of their own character. This was Michelson's course: he aimed to show he had an honest character, inconsistent with the charge that he had bribed a revenue agent. Rule 404(a)(2)(B) permits criminal defendants to offer proof of pertinent traits of the alleged victim's character. Defendants most often deploy Rule 404(a)(2)(B) when pleading self-defense against a charge of violence. The defendant typically aims to prove that the victim is a violent person who, acting in accordance with this violent propensity, was the first aggressor in the encounter with the defendant. Both Rule 404(a)(2)(A) and Rule 404(a)(2)(B) specifically permit the defendant to lead the jury through the propensity box. Hence in the flowchart on page 161 they are depicted on the far left as exceptions to the propensity evidence ban.

Both rules give the defendant the sole option to open the character inquiry. In Justice Jackson's words, the law "simply closes the whole matter of character, disposition and reputation on the prosecution's case-in-chief." Outside the context of sexual offenses, addressed by Rules 413 through 415, the government may initiate propensity-based proof of guilt in its case-in-chief in only one narrow circumstance: In homicide cases Rule 404(a)(2)(C) permits the prosecution to offer evidence of the victim's peaceful character if the defendant has offered evidence (even *non*character evidence) that the victim was the first aggressor.

Rules 404(a)(2)(A) and 404(a)(2)(B), by their terms, give only *criminal* defendants the option to open the character inquiry. As enacted in 1975, the forebears of these rules stated this limitation clearly, but not *so* clearly that every court honored it. A few courts held that when the allegations in a civil suit were "in nature criminal," the defendant should share a criminal defendant's prerogative to defend against the "stigma" of the charge with character evidence. *See, e.g., Perrin v. Anderson*, 784 F.2d 1040, 1044–45 (10th Cir. 1986). Rebuking this judicial innovation, the advisory committee crafted a 2006 amendment to the rules to "clarify that in a civil case evidence of a person's character is never admissible to prove that the person acted in conformity with the character trait." (ACN to 2006 Amendment to FRE 404(a) (RB 50.))

Rules 404(a)(2)(A) and 404(a)(2)(B) permit defendants to prove only *pertinent* traits of character. Although Michelson could offer evidence of his honesty, he could not have offered evidence of his peacefulness, since he faced no charge of violence.

Whenever the defendant offers evidence of her own character under Rule 404(a)(2)(A) or of the alleged victim's character under Rule 404(a)(2)(B), the manner of proof is controlled by Rule 405(a). The boldfaced type in the bottom middle of the flowchart on page 161 notes this constraint. Rule 405(a) permits the character witness to testify in the form of opinion or reputation *only*. The rule preserves the common-law bar against proving character with evidence of specific acts. The advisory committee acknowledged that specific instances of conduct are "the most convincing" way to prove character. But proof of specific acts also "possesses the greatest capacity to arouse prejudice, to confuse, to surprise, and to consume time." (ACN to FRE 405 (RB 52.))

Rule 405(a) does, however, permit "inquiry into relevant specific instances of . . . conduct" *on cross-examination* of the character witness. This feature of the common law gave rise to the facts of *Michelson*. Cross-examination about specific acts is *not*, under Rule 405(a), a means of proving or disproving that the defendant (or victim) actually has the character trait in question. Rather the litigant may ask about specific acts only to test the character witness's knowledge of the defendant's reputation (if the witness has offered reputation evidence) or her familiarity with the defendant (if she has offered opinion evidence). Hence the trial judge in *Michelson* took care to limit how the jury could use the prosecutor's inquiries about Michelson's old arrest:

> [W]hat is happening now is this: the defendant has called character witnesses, and the basis for the evidence given by those character witnesses is the reputation of the defendant in the community, and since the defendant tenders the issue of his reputation the prosecution may ask the witness if she has heard of various incidents in his career. I say to you that regardless of her answer you are not to assume that the incidents asked about actually took place. *All that is happening is that this witness' [knowledge] of the reputation of the defendant is being tested.* Is that clear?

Michelson, pages 235–36 n.3 (emphasis added).

One wonders if the trial judge intended his closing line—"Is that clear?"—as judicial irony. *Of course* the instruction was not clear. Wigmore himself, quoted in note 4 of the Court's opinion, declared that the distinction the judge was drawing "cannot be maintained in the mind of the jury." (Page 236.) Even Justice Jackson admitted that "jurors in the hurried and unfamiliar movement of a trial must find [such instructions] almost unintelligible." (Page 241.) Despite the trial judge's admonition, the jury very possibly interpreted questions about Michelson's old arrest as proof he really was arrested and was consequently a man of bad character. This was Justice Rutledge's point in dissent. The risk of such disobedience by the jury is of course one species of unfair prejudice and must be considered by the court when conducting a Rule 403 weighing test.

The Common Law and the Federal Rules Compared

Though he seemed to share Justice Rutledge's concerns, Justice Jackson hewed meticulously to the received common law of character evidence. The authors of the Federal Rules displayed almost as much fidelity to the old texts. Rules 404(a)(2)(A), 404(a)(2)(B), and 405(a) generally perpetuate the traditional common-law principles at work in *Michelson.*

These rules diverge from the common law in only two significant ways. First, Rule 405(a) provides that whenever proof of character is allowed under Rule 404(a)(2)(A) or Rule 404(a)(2)(B), that proof may take the form of *either* reputation *or opinion* evidence. The common law permitted proof only by reputation. "[T]he whole inquiry," Justice Jackson wrote, "is calculated to ascertain the general talk of people about defendant, rather than the witness' own knowledge of him. . . ." (Page 239.) The defendant's character witness therefore could not "testify that his own acquaintance, observation, and knowledge of defendant leads to his own independent opinion that defendant possesses a good . . . character. . . ." (Page 237.) Today, a character witness may offer precisely that sort of testimony.

And second, Congress amended Rule 404(a) in 2000 to provide that if the defendant offers evidence of an alleged victim's character under what is now Rule 404(a)(2)(B), the prosecution may offer evidence that the defendant shares this same trait of character, *even if the defendant has not put his own character in issue.* Rule 404(a)(2)(B)(ii) now captures this provision. There was no corresponding principle at common law. If the defendant did not open the matter of his character, neither could the prosecution.

For Criminal Defendants Only

A 2006 amendment to Rule 404 made it emphatically clear that only criminal defendants may open the matter of character under Rules 404(a)(2)(A) and 404(a)(2)(B). Why impose this limit? This simple question divides in two: Why deny *prosecutors* the option to open character?—and why deny that option to *civil litigants*?

McCormick's answer addressed both questions: Permission to offer character evidence about defendants and their alleged victims "was a special dispensation to criminal defendants whose life or liberty were at hazard." MCCORMICK ON EVIDENCE § 192, at 459–60 (2d ed. 1972). Before 2006 not every court marched in step with this message. In *Perrin v. Anderson,* 784 F.2d 1040 (10th Cir. 1986), the Tenth Circuit Court of Appeals reviewed a civil § 1983 lawsuit against state troopers alleged to have used excessive force against a suspect, causing his death. "A verdict against the defendants . . . would be tantamount to finding that they killed Perrin without cause," the court wrote. "The resulting stigma warrants giving them the same opportunity to present a defense that a criminal defendant could present." 784 F.2d at 1044–45. But reasonable people could deny that reputational harm—even reputational harm carrying money damages and job loss—falls in the same category as imprisonment or possible execution. After the 2006 amendment to what are now Rules 404(a)(2)(A) and 404(a)(2)(B), the *Perrin* doctrine is dead.

A second possible justification for limiting the character-evidence option to criminal defendants is one Justice Jackson hinted at in *Michelson.* All parties agree that character evidence typically has little probative power. It is of little use to a litigant who bears a substantial burden of proof. But criminal defendants bear the slightest "burden" of any litigant. They go free if, after all the evidence is in, the jury is left with a reasonable doubt of guilt. Now recall Justice Jackson's words: a criminal defendant's evidence "that the general estimate of his character is . . . favorable" may "alone . . . be enough to raise a reasonable doubt of guilt. . . ." (Page 237.) Hence character evidence may mean a great deal to criminal defendants, for whom such evidence can be enough to win.

There is another reason character evidence may mean more for criminal defendants than for other litigants. A prosecutor's argument that the defendant has a generally violent character and therefore must have committed *this* particular violent crime is weak on its face. In contrast, the defendant's argument that she is a generally peaceful person who could never have committed this—*or any*—violent crime has real probative power. Now, this argument does not clearly distinguish criminal defendants from civil defendants, at least where the civil suit concerns a violent act. More typically, though, civil suits concern acts of negligence, contractual breach, and so on. And it is easy to see the weakness in the argument that the defendant is a generally careful person who *never* could have committed this particular negligent act. Careful persons are occasionally careless—but law-abiding persons typically *never* commit serious crimes. That is a fortunate fact of life. There is no other context in which character evidence carries such persuasive probative force.

A final reason to limit the character-evidence option to criminal defendants is that character evidence about an accused creates an asymmetrical risk of unfair prejudice. A prosecutor's evidence of the defendant's bad character could prompt the jury, even if unconvinced of his guilt in the present case, to punish the defendant for his past bad acts or for his general bad character. When the accused offers evidence of his *good* character, however, there is little risk of unfair prejudice to the government. Perhaps the jury could resent the government's decision to prosecute so good and worthy a person, but the risk of such resentment seems slight.

Note that this focus on unfair prejudice cannot explain why we give criminal defendants the option to offer evidence of the alleged *victim's* bad character. When a defendant claiming self-defense presents evidence that the alleged victim had a violent nature, the prosecutor faces a very real risk of unfair prejudice. Even if convinced of the defendant's guilt, the jury could choose to deny the law's protection to so unsavory a victim. Recall Judge Kleinfeld's concern in his dissenting opinion in *United States v. James*: "The victim was a bad man. Some people would say, in private and out of court, that 'he deserved it,' or 'he needed killing.' " (Page 55.) Note too that this focus on unfair prejudice does not explain why the rules deny *civil* defendants the option to offer evidence of their own good character. There is again little risk the jury will resent the plaintiff for having sued the good and worthy defendant.

Distinguishing Proof of Character Under Rules 413 to 415

Rule 405(a)'s requirement that proof be by reputation or opinion does not apply to Rules 413, 414, and 415. These rules *require* proof by specific acts. The prosecutor must offer "evidence that the defendant committed any other sexual assault" or "any other child molestation." Refer again to the flowchart on page 161. The boldfaced type in the middle of the chart distinguishes the manner of proof under Rules 413 to 415 from that under Rule 405(a).

There is a risk that proof and counterproof of other sexual offenses under Rules 413 to 415 could swell into a trial within a trial, distending the proceedings and distracting the jury from the crime at hand. In *United States v. Guardia*, 135 F.3d 1326 (10th Cir. 1998), the appeals court worried that permitting other alleged victims of the defendant to testify "would transform the trial of two incidents into the trial of six incidents, each requiring description by lay witnesses," and "would make it difficult for the jury to separate the evidence of the uncharged conduct from the charged conduct." Moved by such considerations, the appeals court found no abuse of discretion in the district judge's decision to exclude, under Rule 403, the prosecutor's proposed evidence of the defendant's other alleged acts of sexual assault. *Id.* at 1332.

Distinguishing Proof of Character Under Rule 405(b)

Rule 405(b) provides:

> When a person's character or character trait is an essential element of a charge, claim, or defense, the character or trait may also be proved by relevant specific instances of the person's conduct.

This little rule causes much confusion. *Cf. Perrin*, 784 F.2d at 1045 n.4 (confessing error in applying Rule 405(b)).

Most of the confusion stems from an overly broad conception of what it means for a character trait to be "an essential element of a charge, claim, or defense." Consider, first, a case in which Rule 405(b) does *not* apply. Defendants charged with violent crimes often claim that the alleged victim was the first aggressor and that the defendant therefore acted in self-defense. To persuade the jury that the victim attacked first, a defendant often offers evidence of the victim's violent character, a course permitted by Rule 404(a)(2)(B). The desired chain of inferences is that the victim is a generally violent person who, on the night in question, acted in accordance with his violent character and attacked the defendant.

Because one step in this chain of inferences requires evidence that the victim has a violent character, it is tempting to conclude that the victim's violent character is "an essential element of" the defendant's claim of self-defense. But that conclusion is mistaken. To see why, consider the standard that typically governs a claim of self-defense. The question is whether the defendant reasonably feared for her life or safety at the time she attacked the alleged victim. The *essential* element here is that the defendant have been reasonably in fear—*not* that the victim have been a violent person. Acting in self-defense simply is not defined as "attacking someone of violent character."

True, evidence of the victim's violent character may help the defendant prove her fear was reasonable. Here the desired chain of inferences is that the victim is a violent person who, acting in accordance with his violent nature, attacked first, *thereby placing the defendant in reasonable fear.* But the defendant need not follow this particular chain of reasoning. Instead she may simply testify that the victim attacked her first. For that matter, she may testify that she *feared* the victim would attack her first. If the jurors believe her claim and believe her fear was reasonable, they presumably will sustain her claim of self-defense. The defendant need not present any evidence of the victim's character.

So when *does* Rule 405(b) apply? Only when the *existence* of the character trait—and not conduct in accordance with the trait—is the thing to be proved. This circumstance arises rarely. Here are perhaps the three most common specimens of this very scarce breed:

(1) ***Rebutting an Entrapment Defense:*** When alleging entrapment, a defendant claims a government agent induced her to commit a crime she otherwise would not have committed. In many jurisdictions the prosecutor may rebut this claim by showing the defendant was "predisposed" to commit the crime in question. That is, the government may show that the defendant had a thievish (or corrupt or drug-dealing) disposition. The government need not prove the defendant was acting in accordance with this disposition at the time of the alleged offense. The *existence* of the predisposition is the critical thing.

(2) ***Proving or Rebutting a Defense of Truth in a Libel or Slander Action:*** A defendant's public accusation that the plaintiff is a thief (or bully or liar) could give rise to an action for libel or slander. If the defendant claims in defense that her accusation was truthful, the trial will focus on whether the plaintiff is indeed a thief, bully, or liar. In that event the *existence* of the character trait is the critical thing.

(3) ***Resolving a Parental Custody Dispute:*** In custody disputes in most jurisdictions, the judge must determine which of the parties is the better parent. Here each litigant's *character* as a good or bad parent is the critical thing.

These three situations have one fact in common: The litigant's aim is to prove the *existence* of the character trait, not action in accordance with that trait. Look again at the flowchart at page 161. The step in the reasoning process that involves a trip through the propensity box is the inference from a general character trait to action in accordance with that trait at a specific time. But when Rule 405(b) applies, the litigant never takes this inferential step. Hence the branch of the flowchart that deals with proof via Rule 405(b)—the second from left on the chart—never goes through the propensity box. Rule 405(b) simply makes explicit what is always true: If a chain of inferences does not go through the propensity box, Rule 405(a)'s special constraints on proof of character don't apply. Proof therefore may take any form otherwise permitted by the evidence rules, including, of course, proof of specific acts.

Problem 3.15

"I wouldn't shoot anybody."

Niki Lynn Martinez was charged with killing John Lentz in a drive-by shooting. At her trial she testified that she fired the gun only when James Cusick, an acquaintance who was riding in the car with her, told her to do so. During her direct examination, the following exchange took place between Martinez and her lawyer:

Q. [BY DEFENSE COUNSEL]. As you sit here today, Niki, if you had this to do over again, would you shoot Mr. Cusick, or would you shoot [at someone] out of the car?

A. *I wouldn't shoot anybody*. But if I had to, it would be Mr. Cusick.

Q. And why would you shoot Mr. Cusick, Niki?

A. Because of the type of person that he was.

Q. Were you afraid of Mr. Cusick?

A. Yes.

During cross-examination, the prosecutor asked Martinez about her statement to the police that she had shot at people in the past:

> *Q.* [BY PROSECUTOR]: You've shot at other people before, haven't you?
>
> *A.* No, I haven't.
>
> *Q.* In your interview with the detectives, you told the detectives you had shot at people before, though, didn't you?
>
> *A.* Yes.

Assume the Federal Rules of Evidence governed this proceeding. If Martinez's lawyer had objected to the prosecutor's first question—"You've shot at other people before, haven't you?"—how should the judge have ruled? What would be the best arguments for and against admission? *Cf. People v. Martinez*, 51 Cal. App. 4th 537, 542–43 (1996).

Problem 3.16

Character of Victim I

Ronald Keiser is charged with shooting and paralyzing Victor Romero. Keiser claims he acted in self-defense. During a break in the trial, Romero encounters Keiser's brother in the courthouse hallway and shouts to his friends, "There's his brother. I want you to remember his face, remember his face."

Keiser's lawyer now seeks to offer testimony about this incident as evidence of Romero's violent nature. If the prosecutor objects, how should the court rule? *See United States v. Keiser*, 57 F.3d 847 (9th Cir.), *cert. denied*, 516 U.S. 1029 (1995).

Problem 3.17

Character of Victim II

Recall the defendant's testimony in *United States v. James*, 169 F.3d 1210 (9th Cir. 1999) (page 29), a homicide case in which the defendant pled self-defense:

> [The defendant, Ernestine James, testified that David] Ogden had boasted to her about once killing a man and getting away with it. He told her he had sold another man a

fake watch, and when the man complained, had stabbed him in the neck with a ball point pen. Ogden told James that "it was pretty funny watching a guy with a pen dangling out of his neck." He also bragged that he had once "ripped a side view mirror off the car and beat a man unconscious with it," and that, in yet another incident, he had robbed an old man by holding him down with a knife in his face and threatening to cut his eyes out.

If the prosecutor had objected to this testimony as improper character evidence, how should the court have ruled? Should the result here be the same as in *Keiser*, the topic of the last problem?

Problem 3.18

Character of Victim III

Charged with murder, the defendant claimed he acted in self-defense. The jury nonetheless found him guilty. On appeal, he complained that the trial court wrongly excluded the expert testimony of James Merikangas, a toxicologist:

> In an offer of proof outside the presence of the jury, the defendant offered the testimony of Merikangas. Merikangas had examined the hospital records of the treatment of the victim following the fatal encounter. On the basis of those records, Merikangas ... testified that at the time of the incident, the victim's body contained cocaine, morphine and alcohol, and that the victim had [used] five or six bags of heroin and [had drunk] a six pack of beer [that day]. Merikangas linked the morphine found in the victim's system with his heroin use by testifying that heroin "tests as morphine." Merikangas testified further that: the effect of the combination of cocaine, morphine and alcohol "is to prolong the effect of the cocaine ... so that the cocaine high lasts longer than it would" otherwise; the effect of "simultaneous use of opiates like morphine with cocaine" is to make the intravenous drug user "get high and feel good at the same time"; and the use of these substances increases "the likelihood that [the victim] was the aggressor" because "alcohol reduces one's impulse control ... and cocaine, particularly, acutely causes violence...."

State v. Shabazz, 246 Conn. 746 (1998), *cert. denied*, 525 U.S. 1179 (1999).

Assume the Federal Rules of Evidence apply. Was the trial court right to exclude Merikangas's testimony as improper evidence of the victim's character? What are the best arguments for and against exclusion?

F. EVIDENCE OF HABIT

Focus on FRE 406

HALLORAN v. VIRGINIA CHEMICALS INC.

Court of Appeals of New York.
41 N.Y.2d 386 (1977).

■ BREITEL, CHIEF JUDGE. . . . Plaintiff Frank Halloran, an automobile mechanic, obtained a verdict in his favor, after a jury trial on the issue of liability only, for injuries he sustained while using a can of refrigerant packaged and sold by the chemical company. . . .

On June 1, 1970, the day of the accident, Frank Halloran, a mechanic for 15 years, had been employed by the Hillcrest Service Station for over three years. Among his duties was the servicing and charging of automobile air-conditioning units. . . . The particular task involved that day was the changing of the air-conditioning compressor on a 1967 Chrysler automobile. Plaintiff testified that he had emptied the system, removed the old compressor, and installed a new one. He then began to charge the unit.

The first two cans of the refrigerant, Freon, flowed into the system without difficulty. By the time he was emptying the third can, however, plaintiff found it necessary to accelerate the flow of the refrigerant. The mechanic described how he filled an empty two-pound coffee tin with warm tap water, used a thermometer to determine that the water temperature was about 90 to 100 degrees, and inserted into the coffee tin the third can of Freon. Having a similar problem with the flow of the fourth can, Halloran again dropped the Freon into the warm water. Noticing that his low pressure gauge showed a rapid increase in the pressure, and aware that "something was wrong," Halloran reached down to remove the can from the water, but was too late. The can exploded before he could touch it.

Neither the thermometer Halloran claimed to have used nor the bottom of the exploded can of Freon was produced at trial. Halloran knew that excessive heating of the can would cause damage, and that the warnings on the can specified 130 degrees as the maximum permissible safe temperature.... [H]e proved no particular defect in the can, its contents, or in so much of the exploded can which was produced at the trial. Having worked alone that day, Halloran was the only eyewitness to the explosion.

Defendant Virginia Chemicals, on cross-examination of Halloran and on its defense, sought to establish that it was Halloran's "usage and practice" to use an immersion coil to heat the water in which the Freon was placed. Halloran denied ever making such use of an immersion coil. But defendant offered a witness prepared to testify not only that he had seen Halloran on previous occasions using an immersion coil to heat Freon, but that he had warned plaintiff of the danger as well. Plaintiff ... objected to the admissibility of such testimony. The Trial Judge sustained the objection.

Of course, had an immersion heating coil been used at the time of the accident the unexplained and thus far unexplainable explosion would have been fully explained....

To be sure, Halloran's practice prior to June 1, 1970, is not conclusive proof of the method he employed in working on the 1967 Chrysler.... [But l]ogically probative it is and ought to be. While courts of this State have in negligence cases traditionally excluded evidence of carefulness or carelessness as not probative of how one acted on a particular occasion, in other cases evidence of a consistent practice or method followed by a person has routinely been allowed....

Because one who has demonstrated a consistent response under given circumstances is more likely to repeat that response when the circumstances arise again, evidence of habit has, since the days of the common-law reports, generally been admissible to prove conformity on specified occasions. Hence, a lawyer, to prove due execution of a will, may testify that he always has wills executed according to statutory requirements. So too, to prove that notice is mailed on a specified day of the month, one is allowed to testify that he is in the habit of being home on that day of the month to transact such business....

At least, as in this kind of case, where the issue involves proof of a deliberate and repetitive practice, a party should be able, by introducing evidence of such habit or regular usage, to allow the inference of its persistence, and hence negligence on a particular occasion....

... Halloran, in the course of his work as a mechanic, had serviced "hundreds" of automobile air conditioners and had used "thousands" of cans of Freon. From his testimony at trial it seems clear that in servicing these units he followed, as of course he would, a routine. If, indeed, the use of an immersion coil tended to be part of this routine whenever it was necessary to accelerate the flow of the refrigerant, as he indicated was often the case, the jury should not be precluded from considering such evidence as an aid to its determination.

Of course, to justify introduction of habit or regular usage, a party must be able to show on *voir dire*, to the satisfaction of the Trial Judge, that he expects to prove a sufficient number of instances of the conduct in question (*see* FED. R. EVID. 406; 2 WIGMORE, EVIDENCE § 376 (3d ed. 1940)). If defendant's witness was prepared to testify to seeing Halloran using an immersion coil on only one occasion, exclusion was proper. If, on the other hand, plaintiff was seen a sufficient number of times, and it is preferable that defendant be able to fix, at least generally, the times and places of such occurrences, a finding of habit or regular usage would be warranted and the evidence admissible for the jury's consideration. . . .

Accordingly, the order of the Appellate Division should be modified by reversing so much of the order as affirmed the award of judgment to plaintiffs. . . .

HALLORAN V. VIRGINIA CHEMICALS INC.: *Afterthoughts*

The *Halloran* court, in a passage I omitted, distinguished evidence of past conduct generally from evidence of habit: "Evidence of habit or regular usage, if properly defined and therefore circumscribed, involves more than unpatterned occasional conduct, that is, conduct however frequent yet likely to vary from time to time depending upon the surrounding circumstances; it involves a repetitive pattern of conduct and therefore predictable and predictive conduct."

The key word here is "predictive." Remember that propensity evidence of the sort barred by Rule 404(a)(1) poses two risks of unfair prejudice. One is the danger the jury will overweigh evidence of other acts. Because it is more predictive than other propensity evidence, evidence of habit is harder to overweigh. When a person performs the same conduct over and over again the same way, as Halloran was alleged to have done, we can predict with some confidence how that person will perform that act next time. The more predictive the evidence of other acts is, the more probative it is of present conduct.

Wigmore defined habit as behavior of "invariable regularity." (Quoted in ACN to FRE 406 (RB 55).) Our most invariable actions are those we do automatically and almost without volition. Few of us think about putting on a seatbelt, yet many of us do so *every single time* we drive. Lack of volition is therefore one sign that behavior qualifies as a habit. But the true touchstone of habitual behavior is regularity and hence predictability.

Something else may be at work in distinguishing habits from character-based propensities. The second form of unfair prejudice posed by propensity evidence is the risk that the jury will punish the actor for his past (bad) acts or simply for having a bad character. Is there less risk that a jury will punish someone for his (bad) habits than for his other propensities?

Perhaps there is. It is rare that someone *invariably* acts badly. True, there are many "bad" habits. Cigarette smoking is one. But while smoking is incontestably bad for one's health and offends many people, it is hard to imagine that a jury would punish someone for her past cigarettes or for being a smoker.

But can't a person be habitually violent? In commenting on Rule 406, the advisory committee says that "evidence of other assaults is inadmissible to prove the instant one." (RB 55.) And indeed, while it is easy to think of people who commit repeated violent acts, it is far harder to identify someone who (almost) always, in a frequently recurring set of circumstances, lashes out. Even in the domestic violence context, which most nearly approaches this form, violence might be very frequent yet far from invariable.

The advisory committee also suggests that regular drinking does not qualify as a habit under Rule 406. (RB 54.) Yet surely some people take a daily drink as predictably as others buckle their seat belts. Courts therefore occasionally admit evidence of habitual drinking, especially when the drinking in question is precisely defined. But unlike smoking, regular drinking—especially regular heavy drinking—can spark contempt and moral condemnation. *See* MUELLER & KIRKPATRICK, EVIDENCE § 4.21, at 230–31 (5th ed. 2012). The advisory committee's judgment that regular drinking does not qualify as habit is therefore some evidence that the committee meant to extend the category of habit only to relatively innocuous behavior.

In the end there is no clear and straight line separating "habits" from the sort of character-based "propensities" that are regulated by Rule 404. Even if we could decide where to draw that line, human behavior rarely conforms to human categorizations. Lying between the realms of regular and rather innocuous behavior at one end of the spectrum and intermittent, socially despised behavior at the other is a vast span of human conduct. When judging the admissibility of conduct in this middle realm, a court perhaps can do no better than revert to the principle that underlies Rule 404's ban against propensity evidence—the probativeness-versus-unfair-prejudice weighing test of Rule 403.

Because proof of habit does not (at least in theory) involve drawing inferences from general "trait[s] of character," it falls outside Rule 404(a)(1)'s bar against evidence of character offered to show action in accordance therewith. On the flowchart at page 161, proof of habit therefore appears as a route around the propensity box. This last leg of the flowchart—the one pictured at the far right—completes our study of the topics addressed by the chart. As is true of all routes that evade the propensity box, proof of habit need not take any particular form. Rule 406 therefore permits proof by evidence of specific acts. In *Halloran*, if the trial court found on remand that Frank Halloran habitually used an immersion coil to help speed the flow of refrigerant, the court presumably would have permitted the defendant's proposed witness to testify at a new trial "that he had seen Halloran on previous occasions using an immersion coil to heat Freon. . . ." From this evidence of *habit*, the jury would have been permitted to infer that Halloran used an immersion coil on the day the can exploded.

Problem 3.19

Steroids

Consider the facts of *Weil v. Seltzer*, 873 F.2d 1453 (D.C. Cir. 1989):

> On March 27, 1984, Martin Weil died unexpectedly at the age of 54 years. Weil's treating physicians could not explain the cause of his death nor could they account for a series of recent medical problems which he suffered from prior to his death. An autopsy . . . and a subsequent investigation into the treatment that Weil received from his allergist, Dr. Seltzer, were very revealing.
>
> Dr. Seltzer had treated Weil for more than twenty years, and over the course of this treatment Dr. Seltzer regularly prescribed medication which Weil was led to believe were antihistamines. After Weil's death, however, it was determined that Dr. Seltzer had been prescribing a drug called prednisone, which is a steroid. . . . It became apparent that Weil's illnesses were attributable to his long-term ingestion of steroids prescribed by Dr. Seltzer. . . .
>
> Weil's estate filed suit against Dr. Seltzer. . . . [The] estate then contacted eight of Dr. Seltzer's former patients and learned that each had been treated by Dr. Seltzer for many years and they were prescribed pills which Dr. Seltzer represented to be antihistamines and decongestants. All of the patients later learned that the pills prescribed by Dr. Seltzer were in fact steroids. . . .

Assume that Seltzer's defense at trial is that he never prescribed steroids to Weil and that Weil must have received them from another of his many doctors. If plaintiff (Weil's estate), over Seltzer's objection, seeks to offer evidence that Seltzer prescribed steroids to the eight other patients, how should the court rule?

CHAPTER 4

IMPEACHMENT AND CHARACTER FOR TRUTHFULNESS

A. MODES OF IMPEACHMENT

A lawyer *impeaches* a witness by casting doubt on the witness's accuracy or trustworthiness. Impeachment can take several forms. Let's begin by dividing those that demand little evidentiary analysis from those that require mastery of the character evidence rules.

"That's an Error!" vs. "That's a Lie!"

Distinguish first between allegations of mistake and of mendacity. A lawyer can call a witness *mistaken* by casting doubt on her powers of *perception, memory,* or *narrative accuracy.* Questions about the witness's eyesight or hearing or the lighting at the crime scene challenge her perception. Questions about passage of time or (more delicately) the witness's age may go to her memory. And suggestions that the witness misspoke go to her powers of narration.

Character evidence rules impose no constraint on these modes of calling a witness *mistaken.* A lawyer typically may ask a witness about her perception, memory, or narrative skills and may offer other witnesses or exhibits bearing on these issues, as long as the evidence is relevant under Rule 401 and can survive a Rule 403 weighing test. Because feeble eyesight, failing memory, and poor narrative skills are not traits of *character,* a lawyer may cast doubt on these capacities without regard to the character evidence rules. Beware, though, that some rules we encounter later—those governing hearsay and expert testimony and privileges, for example—can constrain these (and other) modes of impeachment.

"You're Lying!" vs. "You're a Liar!"

Just as there are several ways to call a witness mistaken, there are several ways to say she deceived. Begin by separating character from noncharacter modes of impeachment.

Noncharacter Impeachment: A lawyer's suggestion that a witness is lying *now* may say little about the witness's *general* tendency to tell the truth. Consider these three forms of noncharacter impeachment:

- *Contradiction by Conflicting Evidence:* A lawyer can impeach Witness A's claim that a traffic signal was red by calling Witness B to say it was green. Or the lawyer can offer a bystander's video showing a green light at the relevant moment. Or the lawyer can contrast A's claim with the common experiences of life, which in light of other facts might render her testimony implausible. Note that such *contradiction* can expose not only lies, but also mistakes of perception, memory, or narration.
- *Contradiction by Past Inconsistent Statement:* Evidence that Witness A once before said the light was green tends to impeach her trial testimony that it was red. The theory of this form of impeachment is that the witness has said different things at different times about the color of the light and therefore shouldn't be believed *on this point.* Again, such inconsistency could trace not only to lying, but also to misperception or poor memory or bad narrative skills. Absent such an explanation, however, inconsistent statements of fact invite suspicion that the witness has sought to deceive. We will address this form of impeachment again in Chapter 7. (*See* pages 435 to 452.)
- *Evidence of Bias:* Bias "describe[s] the relationship between a party and a witness which might lead the witness to slant . . . his testimony in favor of or against a party." It comprehends not only the witness's "like, dislike, or fear of a party," but also his self-interest in preferring one outcome in the lawsuit over another. *United States v. Abel*, 469 U.S. 45, 52 (1984). We could call *corruption*—lying for fee or other gain—a form of bias. Bias in all its forms is a close kin of *motive,* treated under Rule 404(b). Like motive, bias typically describes a noncharacter-based reason for acting.

None of these impeachment modes depends on the inference that the witness is *generally* a liar. Contradiction typically exposes one lie at a time. It is *consistent* with the claim that the witness generally lies, but does not compel that inference. And bias typically implies a reason to lie *in this case,* not a general disposition to lie. That is, neither of these impeachment modes depends on the claim that the witness has a *bad character for truthfulness.* Hence a lawyer usually may impeach a witness by any of these techniques without reference to the character evidence rules. Rules 402 and 403 of course constrain such evidence, as may rules governing hearsay, expert testimony, and privileges.

Character–Based Impeachment: Sometimes a lawyer seeks to cast doubt on a witness's words by showing she is, by trait, *a liar* and lied in conformity with that trait. Although Rule 404(a)(1) would seem to bar such propensity-based reasoning, Rule 404(a)(3) specifically permits propensity evidence "of a witness's character" as provided in Rules 607, 608, and 609:

- *Rule 607: Either* party may attack a witness's credibility, including the party that sponsored the witness. Litigants sometimes need to call an unfriendly witness because only that person can give certain essential testimony. Rule 607 makes it clear that the sponsoring party may, if otherwise appropriate under the Rules, attack its own witness's credibility.

- *Rule 608(a):* Either party may offer evidence of a witness's character for untruthfulness. The opponent may then rebut with evidence of the witness's character for truthfulness. In either event the evidence must take the form of opinion or reputation. The permitted inference is that the witness has a bad (or good) character for truthfulness and therefore is more (or less) likely to have lied in this case.
- *Rule 608(b):* On cross-examination a party may ask a witness about "specific instances of a witness's conduct . . . if they are probative of . . . character for truthfulness or untruthfulness. . . ." Here the permitted inference is that the person's past lies (or deceptive conduct) are evidence of her general bad character for truthfulness and that, acting in accordance with that character trait, she is lying now.
- *Rule 609:* Either party may seek to impeach a witness by showing her past conviction of a sufficiently serious or deceptive crime. The permitted inferential chain now seems less natural: The past crime is evidence of general immorality or lawlessness and, acting in conformity with that trait, the witness is lying now.

These three forms of character-based impeachment pose far greater challenges than the noncharacter impeachment modes noted above. All of them are a bit more complex than these capsule summaries suggest. The balance of this chapter examines them in detail.

Impeachment Evidence Flowchart

On the next page is a new character evidence flowchart depicting the many modes of impeachment. It lays out the paths this chapter will track.

Note first the three noncharacter forms of impeachment at the top right. Evidence of contradiction or bias typically doesn't call in question a witness's character for truthfulness. Hence the lines of inference running from these impeachment modes do not (usually) lead through a propensity box, and Rules 608 and 609 do not constrain the forms of proof. If evidence of contradiction or bias survives scrutiny under Rules 402 and 403 and other rules we have not yet addressed, it will be admitted. As I discuss a bit later, though, impeachment by contradiction is sometimes so broad that it amounts to a general attack on the witness's truthful character. The dashed lines on the chart represent this possibility.

Now focus on the *other* half of the flowchart—the left half. The single line at the top left leads from the earlier character evidence flowchart on page 161. This line has traveled through Rule 404(a)(3), which authorizes evidence of a witness's character for truthfulness as permitted by Rules

IMPEACHMENT EVIDENCE

ROUTES OF ADMISSIBILITY

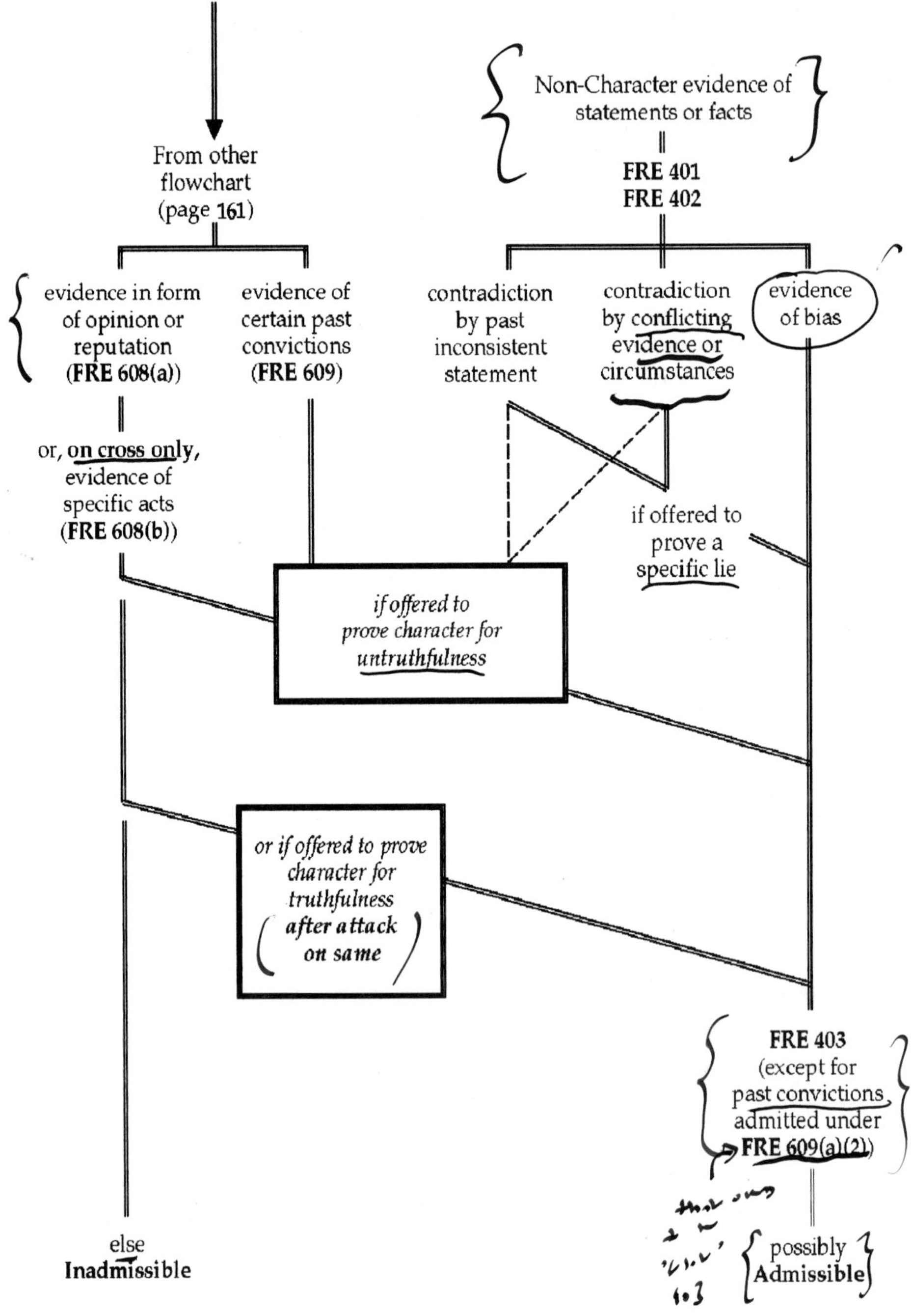

607, 608, and 609. The two vertical lines beneath depict the rather complicated forms of impeachment addressed in Rules 608 and 609.

There is no need to master this chart now. We spend the balance of the chapter tracing its routes. After addressing impeachment under Rule 608 in the next unit, we turn to use of past convictions under Rule 609.

B. IMPEACHMENT BY OPINION, REPUTATION, AND CROSS-EXAMINATION ABOUT PAST LIES

Focus on FRE 404(a)(3), 607, & 608

UNITED STATES V. WHITMORE

359 F.3d 609 (D.C. Cir. 2004).

■ KAREN LECRAFT HENDERSON, *CIRCUIT JUDGE*: Gerald F. Whitmore was convicted by a jury on firearm and drug charges. He appeals the firearm conviction on the ground that the district court committed reversible error in preventing him at trial from attacking the credibility of the arresting officer. . . .

I. BACKGROUND

. . . Viewed in the light most favorable to the government, the evidence at trial established that on the evening of November 1, 2001, Officer Bladden Russell of the District of Columbia Metropolitan Police Department (MPD), while patrolling the Fort Davis neighborhood in Southeast Washington, directed a crowd gathered at a bus stop to disperse. The crowd, with the exception of Whitmore, complied. Russell exited his car to approach Whitmore and Whitmore fled. Russell pursued him on foot and noticed that Whitmore, while running, held his right hand close to his body at his waist and the right side pocket of his jacket.

Whitmore successfully eluded Russell, but MPD Officer Efrain Soto, Jr., who was also patrolling the neighborhood in his police cruiser, spotted Whitmore and gave chase, first in his car and then on foot. Soto also noticed Whitmore's right hand holding the right side of his jacket. . . . Soto saw Whitmore throw a gun towards an apartment building next to an alley Whitmore ran into. Shortly thereafter, Soto apprehended Whitmore. Once Russell caught up to assist, Soto found a gun in a window well of the apartment building. The weapon (with four rounds of ammunition, one of which was chambered) showed signs that it had been recently thrown against the building: a piece of brick was stuck in its sight, there were scuff marks on it and it was covered with masonry dust. The police found nothing in the right pocket of Whitmore's jacket but did discover a small bag of cocaine base in his left pocket.

At trial [in late 2002] Whitmore defended on the ground that Soto had fabricated the story about the gun and had planted the gun in the window well. Soto provided, almost exclusively,[1] the evidence connecting Whitmore to the gun, and Whitmore therefore sought to attack Soto's credibility in several ways. He first attempted to call three defense witnesses—Jason Cherkis, Bruce Cooper and Kennith Edmonds—to testify regarding Soto's "character for truthfulness" under Fed. R. Evid. 608(a). Cherkis, a reporter with the *City Paper*, wrote an article in January 2000 reporting that Soto and three other MPD officers were the target of multiple complaints from residents of the MPD's Sixth District, the district in which Whitmore was arrested. According to Whitmore, Cherkis would testify, based on conversations he had with his sources for the article, that Soto had a reputation as a liar. . . .

Bruce Cooper was a local criminal defense counsel who, Whitmore claimed, would testify regarding both Soto's reputation for untruthfulness within what he called the "court community" and Cooper's own opinion that Soto was untruthful. Whitmore proffered that Cooper would testify that several defense counsel thought Soto was a liar and that Cooper had the same opinion based on having tried many cases in which Soto was a government witness. . . .

Kennith Edmonds, whom Whitmore also sought to call as both a reputation and opinion witness, was an acquaintance of Soto who used to live in the neighborhood where Soto worked and who saw Soto regularly until roughly five years before the trial, when Edmonds moved away. Whitmore proffered that Edmonds would say that he still saw Soto a few times each week when Edmonds returned to his old neighborhood to visit his mother and still maintained contacts with others in the neighborhood who knew Soto. Edmonds's proffered opinion evidence was based on two incidents: (1) Soto had participated in the arrest of a friend of his and, when Edmonds attempted to collect his friend's property from the police, Edmonds was told that there was no property to collect; and (2) Soto and other officers wrongly arrested Edmonds for drug possession in 1995. . . .

In addition to these three character witnesses, Whitmore also sought to impeach Soto by cross-examining him on . . . the suspension of Soto's driver's license and Soto's failure to report the suspension to his supervisors [and on] Soto's failure to pay child support. . . . [A] state document manifest[ed] that Soto's Maryland driver's license had been suspended from 1998 to 2000 for failure to pay child support. MPD regulations require all officers to maintain a valid driver's license and to notify their

1. Although Officer Russell testified that Whitmore held his right hand close to his right side as he fled, Russell did not see him throw anything.

supervisor of any change in status. Whitmore invoked ... Fed. R. Evid. 608(b) ... in support of cross-examination on these subjects: ... Soto's alleged failure to report his suspended license and to make child support payments would reveal his inclination to dissemble and evade the law.... The district court prohibited cross-examination on both subjects....

In light of the trial court's rulings, Whitmore presented no evidence in his defense and was limited to cross-examining the government witnesses about inconsistencies in their trial testimony. The jury convicted Whitmore on both counts....

II. DISCUSSION

* * *

1. Character Witnesses

Fed. R. Evid. 608(a) allows a party to attack the credibility of a witness through reputation and opinion evidence of his character for truthfulness.... In order to offer reputation evidence under this rule, a party must establish that the character witness is qualified by having an "acquaintance with [the witness]," his "community," and "the circles in which he has moved, as to speak with authority of the terms in which generally [the witness] is regarded." *Michelson v. United States,* 335 U.S. 469, 478 (1948). With regard to Cherkis, Whitmore relied on the interviews that Cherkis had conducted for the 2000 article and on the holding in *Wilson v. City of Chicago,* 6 F.3d 1233, 1239 (7th Cir. 1993), in which the Seventh Circuit reversed a district court's exclusion of a reporter's reputation testimony.... [But] neither Cherkis nor Edmonds had had direct contact with Soto or his community for some time. The district court found the proposed testimony of both Cherkis and Edmonds as to Soto's alleged reputation for truthfulness "too remote" in time from the time of trial. *See United States v. Lewis,* 482 F.2d 632, 640 n.44 (D.C. Cir. 1973) (witness's "reputation for testimonial honesty ... is to be established by evidence of his community reputation at the time of trial and during a period not remote thereto"). Finally, with regard to Cooper's testimony—and leaving aside the troublesome issue whether the "court community" represents a cognizable community for the purpose of a law enforcement officer's reputation—the district court found the foundation for his testimony weak because it relied on Cooper's conversations with only a few other criminal defense counsel, a subset of the proposed "community." *See Williams v. United States,* 168 U.S. 382, 397 (1897) (reputation evidence inadmissible because foundation was few individuals in one building ...); *see also* 28 CHARLES ALAN WRIGHT & VICTOR JAMES GOLD, FEDERAL PRACTICE AND PROCEDURE § 6114, at 63 (1993) ("The community must not be so parochial that there is a risk that each member of that community forms opinions as to character based on the same set of biases."). We conclude that the district court did not abuse its discretion in excluding the reputation evidence of these witnesses.[3]

While recognizing that the foundational requirement for *opinion* evidence regarding a witness's character for truthfulness is less stringent than that for *reputation* evidence, the district court nonetheless rejected both Cooper's and Edmonds's proposed opinion evidence. It concluded that both opinions lacked sufficiently supportive factual information to be credible and thus would be unfairly prejudicial under Fed. R. Evid. 403. *See United States v. Cortez*, 935 F.2d 135, 139–40 (8th Cir. 1991) (rejecting opinion testimony by police officers because officers had only minimal, post-arrest contacts with witness and their testimony "merely expresses their belief in the story he told them"). The foundation for Cooper's opinion that Soto was untruthful was limited to his observation that Soto had testified falsely against his clients; the facts underlying Edmonds's opinion did not provide a reasonable basis from which the jury could conclude that Soto was even directly involved in the events, much less indicate that he was untruthful about them. *United States v. Dotson*, 799 F.2d 189, 193 (5th Cir. 1986) ("An opinion ... may be excluded if it amounts to no more than a conclusory observation....").

... The district court did not abuse its discretion in excluding this evidence under Fed. R. Evid. 608—the foundational defects *were* serious—and [under] Fed. R. Evid. 403, on the ground that its value would have been substantially outweighed by the unfair prejudice to the government and by needlessly occupying the time of the jury and the court.

2. Cross–Examination of Soto

Fed. R. Evid. 608(b) allows a party to attack the credibility of a witness by cross-examining him on specific instances of past conduct. Cross-examination pursuant to Fed. R. Evid. 608(b) is not confined to prior criminal convictions—they are governed by Fed. R. Evid. 609—but the conduct must be probative of the witness's character for truthfulness....

Whitmore contends that the district court erroneously prevented him from cross-examining Soto under Fed. R. Evid. 608(b) regarding ... the 1998 suspension of Soto's Maryland driver's license and his failure to

3. The district court also excluded Cherkis's and Cooper's testimony because neither lived in Soto's community. Courts have rejected the notion, however, that reputation testimony is confined to the witness's residential community or that the character witness must physically reside in that community. *See, e.g., Wilson*, 6 F.3d at 1239 (admitting reporter's testimony about witness's reputation among people with whom he had worked and among his family because "a community doesn't have to be stable in order to qualify under the rule"); *United States v. Mandel*, 591 F.2d 1347, 1370 (4th Cir. 1979) (noting that expansion of community to include witness's professional environment reflects "the realities of our modern, mobile, impersonal society"); *United States v. Lewin*, 467 F.2d 1132, 1140 (7th Cir. 1972) (rejecting notion that "an identity of residence is essential" for reputation testimony).

report the suspension to his supervisors; and Soto's failure to make child-support payments. . . .

The trial court precluded cross-examination on those matters on the ground that there was "no basis" for the cross-examination because Whitmore's only support for them—the record from the Maryland Motor Vehicle Administration—was inadmissible hearsay. Counsel, however, need only have "'a reasonable basis for asking questions on cross-examination which tend to incriminate or degrade the witness,'" and "the general rule in such situations is that 'the questioner must be in possession of some facts which support a genuine belief that the witness committed the offense or the degrading act to which the question relates.'" *United States v. Lin*, 101 F.3d 760, 768 (D.C. Cir. 1996). The copy of Soto's Maryland driving record provided sufficient basis for such cross-examination, and defense counsel readily acknowledged that he did not seek to admit the record itself and would be bound by Soto's answers. The court apparently assumed, however, that Soto would simply deny that his license had been suspended, leaving the jury with a bare denial of a damaging accusation. *See United States v. Brooke*, 4 F.3d 1480, 1484 (9th Cir. 1993) (Fed. R. Evid. 608(b) prohibits extrinsic evidence on cross-examination, and thus cross-examiner is "stuck with whatever response" witness gives). We pass over the fact that this assumption implied that Soto would intentionally lie under oath. The court lacked a basis for such an assumption, however, because it failed to conduct any voir dire. The knowledge that he could be charged with perjury would encourage Soto to respond truthfully, even if he thought that Whitmore's counsel could not impeach him further. Accordingly, in excluding cross-examination on these matters . . . , the district court abused its discretion.

3. Error Not Harmless

. . . Soto provided the sole and critical eyewitness evidence to support Whitmore's firearm conviction. We are hard-pressed to understand the government's claim that the proposed cross-examination would have "had only marginal evidentiary value," and we cannot ignore the potential impact of such . . . [an] attack on Soto's character for truthfulness.

But the government argues that the court's rulings, if erroneous, were harmless because Soto's testimony was "amply corroborated by the other officers involved in the arrest" and Whitmore's "defense theory was incredible." The government finds no safe harbor in either argument. First, the fact that Officer Russell testified that Whitmore ran when confronted by Russell is of little importance in light of the cocaine base he was carrying. That another officer testified the gun showed signs it had been recently thrown against the wall of a nearby building does not say anything about who threw it. There were no fingerprints on the weapon. In fact, the only independent piece of evidence corroborating Soto's testimony connecting Whitmore to the gun was Russell's testimony that

Whitmore was holding the right side of his jacket as he fled. Standing alone, this evidence would hardly sustain Whitmore's conviction....

III. CONCLUSION

... The cumulative effect of prohibiting all ... proposed lines of cross-examination was to deprive Whitmore of any genuine opportunity to challenge the credibility of the only witness who testified that he possessed the gun in question. We cannot conclude that the error was harmless. We therefore vacate the judgment of conviction [for being a] felon in possession of a firearm and remand for a new trial on that charge. Whitmore's conviction [for] simple possession of a controlled substance remains unaffected....

H. Richard Uviller

Credence, Character, and the Rules of Evidence: Seeing Through the Liar's Tale

42 DUKE L.J. 776, 789–93 (1993).

* * *

C. Character as a Source of Impeachment

Of the several methods for the recognition of truth, one of the most impressive and most troublesome is ... character. In the realms of ordinary life, we accord great weight to our appraisal of character in judging behavior. To conclude that a person did or did not do a critical act, we want to know what kind of a person our subject is: Is that the sort of conduct one would expect from a person of that character? Specifically, on the issue of credence, it is extremely helpful to know whether the character of the witness reveals a respect for truth and the obligations of fair and accurate recital.

In the law of evidence—code and common law—the character trait of veracity or mendacity is, in a sense, anomalous. Despite (or maybe because of) its strong inferential link, evidence of a personality trait consistent with the [primary wrongdoing alleged in the case] will generally be excluded from the factfinder's consideration. Yet evidence of the trait of truthfulness (or dishonesty) will generally be admitted to prove the secondary conduct of a witness in testifying truthfully (or untruthfully) from the witness stand.[27] For instance, the character trait of dishonesty

27. The original Advisory Committee Note to Rule 608 is quite explicit on the allowance of character to prove propensity to falsehood. It states:

(or a prior conviction for fraud) will not be received as evidence that the defendant embezzled funds as charged in the indictment, but if the defendant should testify that he did not steal from his employer, the same evidence will be admitted to prove he is lying on the stand. The framers of the Federal Rules of Evidence acknowledge—and uncritically perpetuate—the curious discontinuity in the theory of the common law (if the common law can be said to have a "theory") relating to evidence of character.

In allowing character evidence on the issue of credence, the law postulates several factual axioms:

1. *Dishonest People Are More Likely To Lie in Any Given Situation than Honest People.* Lack of respect for truth is a pervasive trait that affects testimonial veracity in all situations, regardless of other interests. Thus, for example, a bystander who once falsified an unrelated insurance claim is more likely to lie about whether the getaway car contained two blacks or two whites than is a witness of unblemished career. And a defendant with no criminal record is more likely to tell the truth on the stand about his commission of the crime (though he had committed it) than is a defendant with a record (though he is as innocent as the judge). Moreover, unlike the personality traits that may dispose a person to commit the conduct charged in the indictment, the predisposition to render a truthful or untruthful account from the stand is generally of sufficient reliability and discernibility to be entrusted to the evaluation of the jury.

2. *The Character Trait of Veracity/Mendacity Is Detectable by Casual Observers in the Community, and the Community Consensus Is Accurately Transmitted among Acquaintances.* Those who reside or work in the same location as the subject are likely to learn of her reputation among neighbors and associates with regard to the specific attribute of "truth and veracity" (as it is usually termed). Commonly a subject of discussion among these casual acquaintances, reputation is a trustworthy distillation of a broad behavioral history in various circumstances and hence a fair reflection of character. More recently, this preeminent index of character has accommodated discernment by personal experience.[29] Thus, by a series of interactions, a person may form a general opinion of another's characteristic mode of dealing with the events of his life. And from the

> In Rule 404(a) the general position is taken that character evidence is not admissible for the purpose of proving that the person acted in conformity therewith, subject, however, to several exceptions, one of which is character evidence of a witness as bearing on his credibility. The present rule develops that exception.

FED. R. EVID. 608 advisory committee note.

29. As a reflection of the usual practice of calling character witnesses who had dealings with the witness on which an opinion could be formed rather than reporters of community gossip, the framers originally intended to replace reputation with personal opinion. As promulgated, however, the Federal Rules allow evidence in either form. FED. R. EVID. 608(a); *see id.* advisory committee note.

opinion of a casual acquaintance, as well as from the rumor and report that qualifies as evidence of reputation, the trait of scrupulous regard for truth—or its absence—may be reliably inferred.

3. *Ordinary People, Properly Instructed as Jurors, Will Appreciate the Distinction Between an Inference from Dishonest Character to Untruthful Testimony and an Inference from Dishonest Character to Criminal Conduct.* Further, their understanding will allow them to use such character evidence strictly for the evaluation of testimonial veracity without allowing it to color their judgment regarding the critical behavior at issue in the trial. For example, evidence that a testifying witness was known as a liar and a cheat will not influence the jury to conclude that the witness was part of a conspiracy to defraud investors, but will be narrowly applied to discredit the witness's testimony as to the point that he had no dishonest intentions.

It is not difficult to expose the weakness in these axioms and postulates. Thus stated in all their naked naïveté, they reflect a view of human nature more suitable to the nursery than the courtroom. It is remarkable that a set of assumptions so far from the lessons of experience could support a fully developed and widely observed structure of litigation law. We all know that the inclination toward mendacity is a complex and subtle process. With the possible exception of a few sick minds, people generally tell mostly the truth to most people most of the time, and make more or less critical adjustments to a number of others some of the time, depending on the subject, the circumstances, and the stakes. Neither truthtelling nor lying can be called a pervasive trait like a quick temper or a pessimistic outlook. Moreover, in my circles at least, friends and co-workers rarely discuss one another's characteristic respect for verity with each other. The idea is little short of ludicrous that I could report a reliable consensus on the subject, emerging from ordinary conversation, such that a rational prediction might be made concerning the truthfulness or falsity of some sworn declaration.

Those who hold to a rational predicate for modern law must find their minds casting about for alternatives; the ones here cannot be the true underlying premises of the law of character and credence. They are certainly the ostensible premises; but perhaps there is some covert predicate, something a bit more realistic. The best alternative I have been able to discover is hardly a model of rational precision. It grows from the need to put a more human face on the two-dimensional witness performing a well-rehearsed part in a professionally crafted persona in the witness box. It is, in effect, a rule founded on rebellion among the pragmatic judiciary against the controlled presentation of human recollection called for by courtroom protocol. An actor, detached from his personal history, retains no individuality by which to judge credibility. My surmise is that the artificiality of testimony constitutes such a dense barrier to recognition of the individual human traits on which we depend in life at large that some tunnel must be bored through it. However crude, the history of a witness living among his peers in the real world, the traces of character discernible in repute or personal opinion, afford some glimpse of the human being lurking behind the polished and wary figure in the witness box. . . .

Problem 4.1

Bar Fight

Election night at the Golden Tap turned ugly. In its aftermath Connor Larken sued Eric Parker for injuries he claimed Parker inflicted. At the resulting civil trial Larken called Deborah Rice, who testified she saw Parker strike Larken with a pool cue. As his next witness, Larken called one of Rice's neighbors, who testified as follows:

1. "Rice's reputation in the neighborhood for peacefulness is good."
2. "Rice's reputation in the neighborhood for truthfulness and veracity is good."

If Parker objected to both lines of testimony, how should the court have ruled?

During the defense case Parker called a longtime coworker of Rice, who testified as follows:

3. "When Rice sold me her old car, she told me she had just replaced the brake pads, but she was lying."
4. "My opinion, based on all my dealings with Ms. Rice, is that she's a liar."

If Larken objected to both lines of testimony, how should the court have ruled?

Assume the court permitted the coworker to testify as in paragraph 4. On cross-examination of the coworker, Larken asked:

5. "Isn't it true that you were expelled from college for a semester for trashing your dorm room in a drunken rage?"
6. "Didn't you lie on your medical school application about whether you had any disciplinary offenses during college?"

On Parker's objection to both questions, how should the court have ruled?

CHARACTER AND CREDIBILITY: STUDY GUIDE (PART I)

Fundamentals

As you know, evidence of a person's character, if offered to prove action in accordance therewith, is generally barred. There are seven exceptions to this general rule of exclusion:

(1) FRE 413:	Similar offenses in a sexual assault prosecution;
(2) FRE 414:	Similar offenses in a child molestation prosecution;
(3) FRE 415:	Similar offenses in a civil action concerning sexual assault or child molestation;
(4) FRE 404(a)(2)(A):	Character of a criminal defendant, offered by the accused;
(5) FRE 404(a)(2)(B):	Character of a victim, offered by a criminal defendant;
(6) FRE 404(a)(2)(C):	Character of a homicide victim's peaceful character, offered by the prosecutor to rebut evidence that the victim attacked first;
(7) FRE 404(a)(3):	Character of a witness.

The final exception—proof of the character of a witness—concerns us now.

Rule 404(a)(3) says such evidence may be admitted under Rules 607, 608, and 609. In general Rules 608 and 609 say that once a witness has offered testimony, the opposing lawyer may use character evidence to attack the witness's credibility. The witness's sponsor then may use character evidence to support her credibility.

All character evidence, to be relevant, must bear on a "pertinent trait." This is the language of Rules 404(a)(2)(A) and (a)(2)(B). A person charged with a crime of violence, for example, may offer evidence of her character for peacefulness under Rule 404(a)(2)(A). That same evidence, offered in an embezzlement case, would be excluded because the defendant's peacefulness no longer would be pertinent. Evidence of the character of a *witness*, to be pertinent, must bear on the witness's character for truth-telling.

Rules 608 and 609 constrain when and how a party may offer evidence about a witness's character for truthfulness. You should note two ways in which these rules permit more liberal proof of character than the rules governing evidence of the character of the accused (Rule 404(a)(2)(A)) and evidence of the character of a victim (Rules 404(a)(2)(B) and (a)(2)(C)). First, the latter three rules apply by their terms only in criminal cases, whereas the rules governing evidence of a witness's character apply in both criminal and civil cases. Second, Rules 404(a)(2)(A) and (a)(2)(B) permit only the criminal *defendant* to initiate the use of character evidence. Outside the narrow confines of Rules 404(a)(2)(C), 413, and 414, a prosecutor may not offer character evidence until after the accused has put his own or the victim's character in issue. In contrast Rules 608 and 609 permit either party to initiate an attack on a witness's character for truthfulness.

An Ordering Principle

Return for a moment to the flowchart on page 260. Note the two propensity boxes in the middle of the page. In general an advocate may attack a witness's character for truthfulness (by going through the first box) or support a witness's character for truthfulness (by going through the second) only as permitted by Rules 608 and 609, which are depicted on the left side of the chart. By arranging the two boxes one above the other, I have attempted to capture an important ordering principle imposed by Rule 608(a): A party may *support* a witness's character for truthfulness (by going through the second box) only after the other party has attacked that character (by going through the first). I address this limitation in more detail in the section on rehabilitation at pages 308 to 309.

Rules 608(a) and 608(b)

As we saw in *Whitmore,* Rule 608(a) permits a litigant to offer evidence of a witness's "character for truthfulness or untruthfulness" in the form of opinion or reputation. The evidence must pertain to truthfulness or untruthfulness, not peacefulness, temperance, or anything else.

As *Whitmore* also showed, Rule 608(b) permits a party to ask on cross-examination about "specific instances of a witness's conduct." Rules 608(b)(1) and (b)(2) address two separate contexts in which such inquiry may be made. Assume, for example, that Witness Jones saw a shooting. Because she can testify substantively about the crime (and not merely about another witness's character), we call her a *principal* witness. Assume further that Witness Jones lied to the police about an unrelated matter. Rule 608(b) would, with certain limitations, permit inquiry about that lie:

(1) during cross-examination of Witness Jones (the principal witness); *and*

(2) during cross-examination of a *character* witness who has offered testimony about Witness Jones's character for truthfulness or untruthfulness.

Rule 608(b) therefore allows more liberal use of specific instances of conduct than does Rule 405(a), which governs the forms of character evidence offered under Rules 404(a)(2)(A), 404(a)(2)(B), and 404(a)(2)(C). Consider again Rule 405(a), italicized to emphasize this difference:

> When evidence of a person's character or character trait is admissible, it may be proved by testimony about the person's reputation or by testimony in the form of an opinion. On cross-examination *of the character witness*, the court may allow an inquiry into relevant specific instances of the person's conduct. [Emphasis added.]

That is, Rule 405(a) permits inquiry into specific instances of conduct during cross-examination *of the character witness*, but not during cross-examination of any other person, including the person about whom the character witness is testifying. Hence the prosecutor could ask an accused murderer's character witness, who has testified to the defendant's reputation as a peaceful man, about a violent incident in the defendant's past. This is the sort of cross-examination we saw in *Michelson*. But if the defendant himself took the stand, cross-examination about his past violence would remain off-limits unless:

- evidence of the past incident had a valid non-propensity purpose under Rule 404(b);
- the defendant has made himself his own character witness by vouching for his peaceful nature (*cf.* Problem 3.15 (*"I wouldn't shoot anybody."*), page 249); or
- the past incident resulted in a conviction of a serious crime and survives the weighing test set out in Rule 609(a)(1)(B).

Limitations on FRE 608(b)(1)

Rule 608(b)(1) exposes every witness who takes the stand to possible cross-examination about "specific instances of [the] witness's conduct." Absent meaningful limits, cross-examination could degrade into a smear campaign. Someone who simply answered a subpoena to appear as a witness could find her reputation dirtied. Happily the Rules and caselaw limit such cross-examination in several ways.

Rule 608(b) itself imposes two limits: The specific instance of conduct must be "probative of . . . truthfulness or untruthfulness." And it "may not be proved by extrinsic evidence." The ban on extrinsic evidence means the lawyer must accept the witness's answer to the question. If the lawyer asks about a past lie the witness told in an unrelated matter and the witness denies it, that is the end of the matter. As Whitmore's counsel acknowledged in seeking to cross-examine Officer Soto about his past deception, counsel "would be bound by Soto's answers." The lawyer could not call a second witness to prove that the first witness really told the lie in question.

A third limitation is implicit in Rule 608(b)'s use of the word *may*—"the court may" allow such cross-examination. This reference to the court's discretion suggests the inquiry must survive a Rule 403 weighing test.

A fourth limitation emerged in Justice Jackson's discussion of an analogous line of questioning in the *Michelson* case. Jackson noted that the prosecutor advised the trial court that his inquiry about Michelson's previous arrest was rooted in fact. "[A]nd to support his *good faith* [the prosecutor] exhibited a paper record which defendant's counsel did not challenge." (Page 235 (emphasis added).) In general a lawyer may not ethically ask about specific instances of bad conduct without having a good-faith basis for believing they took place. That is, the lawyer must have in his possession "information that reasonably leads him to believe that the acts of conduct . . . have in fact been committed. . . ." *People v. Pic'l*, 114 Cal. App. 3d 824, 891 (1981), *disapproved of on other grounds by People v. Kimble*, 44 Cal. 3d 480, 496–98 (1988). The same limiting principle appeared in *Whitmore*, though the terminology differed: Counsel must have " 'a reasonable basis for asking questions on cross-examination which tend to incriminate or degrade the witness,' " and "the general rule in such situations is that 'the questioner must be in possession of some facts which support a genuine belief that the witness committed the offense or the degrading act to which the question relates.' " *Whitmore*, page 265 (quoting *United States v. Lin*, 101 F.3d 760, 768 (D.C. Cir. 1996)).

Rule 611(a)(3) imposes a fifth limitation on cross-examination under Rule 608(b)(1): "The court should exercise reasonable control over the mode and order of examining witnesses . . . so as to . . . protect witnesses from harassment or undue embarrassment."

Finally, because Rule 609 prescribes very particular limits for admission of evidence of past convictions, many courts will not permit a lawyer to use Rule 608(b) to offer evidence that is *of a type* covered by Rule 609, but is excluded by Rule 609. For example, if a lawyer tried to use an eleven-year-old conviction, excluded by Rule 609(b), as a "specific instance[ ] of a witness's conduct" under Rule 608(b), many courts would exclude the evidence. Rule 608(b) is not a back door for admission of evidence not admissible under Rule 609.

Practice

Look again at Problem 4.1 (*Bar Fight*), at page 269. Here are some suggested answers:

(1) *Inadmissible.* Larken has offered testimony of Rice's reputation for "peacefulness." No such evidence is admissible under Rule 404(a)(2)(A) or (a)(2)(B) because this is a civil case and because Rice is neither accused nor victim. Nor is such evidence admissible under Rule 608(a) because it does not concern Rice's "character for truthfulness or untruthfulness."

(2) *Inadmissible.* Rule 608(a) says that "evidence of truthful character is admissible only after the witness's character for truthfulness has been attacked," and Rice's character for truthfulness has not yet suffered attack. If, however, defense counsel cross-examined Rice concerning her past lies under Rule 608(b)(1) or presented evidence of her conviction of a crime punishable by more than a year in prison under Rule 609(a)(1)(A), the attack on her truthful character would justify a character-based defense.

(3) *Inadmissible.* Parker has attempted to impeach Rice by asking a coworker about a lie Rice once told. That is, Parker is offering evidence of a specific instance of Rice's untruthful conduct. Rule 608(a) would not allow this inquiry because it permits proof only by reputation or opinion evidence. And although Rule 608(b) permits cross-examination about specific instances of conduct, here the coworker is testifying on direct. As we'll see a little later when we turn to the topic of extrinsic evidence, this scenario also offends Rule 608(b)'s ban on such evidence.

(4) *Admissible.* Rule 608(a) permits an opponent to attack a witness's character for truthfulness by opinion or reputation evidence. Here the coworker offers her opinion that Rice is a liar—which is just a shorthand way of stating her opinion that Rice has a bad character for truthfulness. Given their longtime acquaintance, the coworker apparently is competent to offer this opinion.

(5) *Inadmissible.* Larken has attempted to impeach the coworker by asking on cross-examination about a drunken rage during college. Although Rule 608(b)(1) permits inquiry about the witness's specific acts, those acts must be "probative of . . . truthfulness or untruthfulness." This incident does not qualify.

(6) *Admissible.* Larken now attempts to impeach the coworker by asking on cross-examination about a lie she told in a semi-official context. Although the underlying dormitory incident did not reflect on the coworker's character for truthfulness, her later lie about that same incident does. Rule 608(b)(1) therefore permits the question.

Problem 4.2

Lawyer's Lies

Character to Be a Major Issue in Tyco Trial

Jonathan D. Glater

NEW YORK TIMES, May 6, 2004, at C1

The trial of yet another former Tyco International executive begins today, and the outcome may well turn more on what jurors think about his character than on the facts.

The former chief counsel at Tyco, Mark A. Belnick, is charged with stealing money from Tyco in the form of unauthorized bonuses and loans, and with failing to disclose payments he received. In hearings, prosecutors have indicated that they hope to introduce evidence that they believe shows that Mr. Belnick has lied repeatedly—to get out of jury duty, to get a new driver's license and to help his boss's daughter get into business school, for example—to try to illustrate what kind of person he is. The judge has said that if Mr. Belnick testifies, prosecutors may question him about such past conduct, posing a problem for the defense.

Mr. Belnick's case has transfixed the New York legal community because Mr. Belnick was a prominent lawyer at the top of the profession before joining Tyco in 1998. Mr. Belnick's lawyers have argued that he has not committed a crime because he believed that the money he received was properly approved and disclosed, and that he did not know of any wider fraud at the company.

Whether Mr. Belnick has a history of telling falsehoods matters because to prove the charges against him, prosecutors must show that he knew he was doing something wrong. If jurors believe that Mr. Belnick is a chronic liar, it could be easier for prosecutors to convince them that he tried to conceal the money Tyco paid him....

[P]rosecutors want to be able to ask, for example, about a letter Mr. Belnick sent to the New York County Clerk in late summer 2000, asking to be excused from jury duty in New York on the grounds that he had moved to Park City, Utah.

... Amy Schwartz, an assistant district attorney, told Justice Obus ... [that] according to records kept by Mr. Belnick's accountant, Mr. Belnick did not become a Utah resident until the following year.... [And] Mr. Belnick said in a sworn statement a week before the letter's date that he lived in New York City....

Prosecutors also asked to be able to tell jurors about Mr. Belnick's application for a Utah driver's license in 2001, in which Mr. Belnick denied that his driving privileges had been suspended or revoked in the last 10 years, Ms. Schwartz said. A New York driver's record showed that Mr. Belnick's license was revoked. . . .

Prosecutors in addition have requested that the judge let them ask about a letter of recommendation that Mr. Belnick wrote for the daughter of [L. Dennis] Kozlowski, who hired him at Tyco. Prosecutors contended that Sandy Kozlowski asked for the letter to help her get into Columbia Business School and that Mr. Belnick, in writing the letter, helped her to create the false impression that she had worked at Tyco steadily for two years. . . .

Assume the Federal Rules of Evidence control this case. Was the trial judge right to rule that if Belnick testifies, the prosecutors may question him about these three alleged lies? What arguments should the defense have made?

C. IMPEACHMENT WITH PAST CONVICTIONS

Focus on FRE 609

1. THE THEORY AND HISTORY OF RULE 609

H. Richard Uviller

Credence, Character, and the Rules of Evidence: Seeing Through the Liar's Tale

42 DUKE L.J. 776, 813, 815 (1993)

* * *

D. The Disposition To Lie Under Oath

The theoretical discontinuity perpetuated by Rule 609 is a major wrench to reason: No inference to the [alleged wrongdoing at issue in the case] may be based on the predisposition of character, but disposition to lie under oath may be inferred from a variety of prior convictions. If anything, this ancient precept of the law of evidence is the reverse of common experience. Resolution of the question of whether a criminal defendant committed the bank robbery charged is materially assisted by knowledge that he robbed several others just like it—he has the personality to which that sort of conduct belongs. Knowing his predatory character and penchant for banks, a jury could reasonably find an elevated likelihood that the defendant as compared with the world at large committed the act in issue. But the issue of whether a person (criminal defendant or other) is lying on the witness stand is very slightly illuminated, if at all, by data that the person had, on a previous occasion, misappropriated rent receipts. Testifying as a witness is such rare behavior, the trial such a unique occasion, that the honesty or dishonesty of the witness's testimony cannot be said to be consistent with a pattern of predictable behavior. Simply put, it is extremely unlikely that any person testifies dishonestly because of a trait of dishonesty manifested by dishonest behavior in other, very different, circumstances. . . .

There is one line of reasoning by which certain prior convictions can be made truly relevant to testimonial veracity. But it is decidedly a bootleg inference, and (unlike the Federal Rules) it applies only when prejudice is highest—when the witness is a criminal defendant and the prior crime is very similar to the charge on trial. By ordinary probability—and contrary to the Rules of Evidence—a person who has previously committed a certain type of crime is more likely to have committed another like it than a person who has not. One street mugger may be no more likely than another to have committed the mugging charged. But by the laws of personality and behavior, either is substantially more likely to have committed the mugging in question than a person drawn at random from those who have never committed a robbery. And the more probably guilty person (viz., the one with the record) who gives exculpatory testimony is more likely to be lying than is a more likely innocent person, since truthful testimony will help acquit the innocent but will surely convict the guilty. Thus, testifying criminal defendants with records, especially for the same sort of crime, are more likely to be lying on the stand than those without records, because they are more likely to be guilty.

But however this line of reasoning may accord with logic and experience, it is utterly repugnant to basic premises of the trial process. Adamantly excluding direct use of evidence of propensity, this dogma would never tolerate indirect use of evidence of propensity by an inference to self-protective perjury. Moreover, discrediting the exculpatory testimony of the one felon on trial may convict him on evidence that offers no basis whatsoever for selecting him over thousands of others with similar records. . . .

RULE 609 AND DEFENDANT TESTIMONY: *Historical Prelude*

Rule 609 permits impeachment of witnesses with evidence of their past crimes. The rule has a long and eye-opening history.

An older provision of the common law, probably dating to the early seventeenth century, simply barred all convicted felons from the witness stand. Pioneering evidence scholar Jeffrey Gilbert explained the old rule this way: "[W]here a Man is convicted of Falshood and other Crimes against the common Principles of Honesty and Humanity, his Oath is of no Weight." [JEFFREY GILBERT], THE LAW OF EVIDENCE 159 (London, Henry Lintot 1756).* Writing about a century later, Thomas Starkie agreed that felons have no credibility: "[I]t cannot reasonably be expected that such a person would regard the obligation of an oath." 1 THOMAS STARKIE, A PRACTICAL TREATISE ON THE LAW OF EVIDENCE 83 (Boston, Wells & Lilly 1826).

In England and in most American jurisdictions the rule barring felons from the witness stand was abolished in the mid-nineteenth century. Legislators replaced it with a new rule permitting felons to testify but also permitting the opposing party to impeach such witnesses with evidence of their past crimes. An 1852 Massachusetts law, for example, abolished the rule against testimony by felons and also declared that "the conviction of any crime may be shown to affect the credibility of any person testifying." *See* Act of May 22, 1852, ch. 312, § 60, 1852 Mass. Acts 235, 235.

Richard Uviller may have been right when he said that "the issue of whether a person (criminal defendant or other) is lying on the witness stand is very slightly illuminated, if at all, by data that the person had, on a previous occasion, misappropriated rent receipts." No doubt he would have found the old rule, which conclusively presumed that all felons are liars, even harder to defend.

But the aspect of Rule 609's operation that Uviller attacked most pointedly never arose under the old rules. He argued that "the question of whether a criminal defendant committed the bank robbery charged is materially assisted by knowledge that he robbed several others just like it." Yet evidence of earlier bank robberies may *not* be used to show a penchant for robbing banks, while such evidence often may be used to show a penchant to lie. And this is true *even when the witness being impeached is the defendant charged with bank robbery.* If the judge admits evidence of the past robberies to impeach the defendant's testimony, she normally instructs the jurors that they may use the evidence to assess the defendant's character as a liar, not his character as a thief. The law generally presumes that the jury obeys this counterintuitive command.

* Gilbert died in 1726 and therefore must have written his treatise several decades before it was first published in 1756. Much of the material in this prelude appeared in a somewhat different form in George Fisher, *Plea Bargaining's Triumph,* 109 YALE L.J. 857, 977–81 (2000).

The old rules never challenged logic in this way. That is because until the last half of the nineteenth century, criminal defendants simply could not testify under oath. Because they could not testify, they could not be impeached with evidence of their past crimes. So trial judges never had to instruct jurors that evidence of the witness's past crimes, offered only to impeach, could not be used to judge his guilt of the crime charged.

That the common law barred criminal defendants from testifying perhaps shouldn't surprise us. Common-law judges believed the ban against testimony by convicted felons served to keep likely liars from the witness stand. No doubt those same judges thought the most likely liars of all were criminal defendants, who had by far the strongest motivations to lie. As Justice Francis North told an accused traitor in 1681, "Why if yours or any man's word in your case should go for truth, no man that stands at a bar, could be convicted: For every man will say he is an honest man. . . ." *The Trial of Stephen Colledge*, 8 HOWELL'S STATE TRIALS 549, 681 (1681). Uviller apparently believed North was on the mark. "All guilty defendants who choose to testify," he wrote, "will lie on the stand about anything that might improve their chances and about which they imagine they can be persuasive." Uviller, *supra*, at 813.

Despite such suspicions, the old rules barring defendants from testifying began to fall in the last half of the nineteenth century. In 1864 Maine became the first jurisdiction in the common-law world to allow persons accused of serious crimes to give evidence under oath in their defense. *See* Act of Mar. 25, 1864, ch. 280, § 1, 1864 Me. Laws 214, 214. Other states soon followed course. By the end of 1880 all but seventeen states and territories allowed defendant testimony. *See Ferguson v. Georgia*, 365 U.S. 570, 577 n.6 (1961).

Perceptive observers soon saw that the new laws permitting defendants to testify, no doubt intended by legislators to help assure fair trials, instead exposed defendants to damaging cross-examination about past wrongdoings. In 1867, only a year after Massachusetts opened the witness stand to criminal defendants, Judge Seth Ames of the Massachusetts Superior Court scoffed at the notion that the new law would aid criminal defendants. Ames argued that the law left an accused with two unpleasant alternatives. First he could choose silence and face almost inevitable conviction. True, the law declared that the defendant could testify "at his own request, but not otherwise" and guaranteed that "neglect or refusal to testify shall not create any presumption against" him. But these were "fallacious and idle" words, Ames wrote. "The statutes might as well prohibit the tide from rising. . . ." After all, "the jurors all know that the defendant has the privilege (as it is called) of making himself a witness if he sees fit; and they also know that he would if he dared." If the defendant "should decline to make himself a witness, the jury would convict him without leaving their seats." And so this law permitting defendants to testify "will inevitably *compel* the defendant to testify, and will have substantially the same effect as if it did not go through the mockery of saying that he might testify if he pleased." [Seth Ames], *Testimony of Persons Accused of Crime*, 1 AM. L. REV. 443, 444–47 (1866–1867) (emphasis added); *see* Act of May 26, 1866, ch. 260, 1866 Mass. Acts 245, 245.

Yet if the defendant did as he must and took the stand, Ames continued, he faced a second unpleasant alternative: Those defendants who had criminal records would be "torn to pieces by cross-examination"—presumably because their past convictions could be offered to impeach them. [Ames], *supra*, at 447. Ames himself, sitting as a trial judge shortly after Massachusetts enacted its defendant-testimony law, permitted a prosecutor to impeach a defendant with evidence he previously had pled guilty to forgery. Ruling on appeal in that case, the Supreme Judicial Court (which Ames would join shortly) wrote that "[t]he defendant . . . offered himself as a witness, and the rules of evidence affecting the competency or credibility of witnesses were all applicable to him in that character." *Commonwealth v. Gorham*, 99 Mass. 420, 421 (1868).

Today Rule 609(a)(1) and the law of evidence in many states give criminal defendants stronger protections against impeachment by past crimes than are accorded most witnesses. Note the extra-protective weighing test that Rule 609(a)(1)(B) erects for criminal defendants. Defendants who chose to testify in nineteenth-century Massachusetts enjoyed no such special protection. In 1867 the Supreme Judicial Court reviewed a trial judge's ruling admitting evidence of the defendant's past crimes "to affect his credibility as a witness, but for no other purpose." The defendant's counsel complained on appeal "that it is a subtlety beyond the capacity of jurors" to confine such evidence to its impeachment value rather than "regarding it as affecting his character generally." To this the high court curtly replied, "The statute does not exempt [the defendant] from cross-examination, and impeachment as a witness; and there is no reason why he should be exempt from it." *Commonwealth v. Bonner*, 97 Mass. 587, 589 (1867).

Judge Ames did not try to predict the consequences of a law that gave any defendant with a criminal record the options of being convicted on her silence or convicted on her testimony. Several decades later New York prosecutor Arthur Train took Ames's analysis further. Train first of all confirmed the two halves of Ames's dilemma. On the one hand those defendants who "do not testify . . . will probably pay the usual penalty" for their silence. "Three jurors out of five," Train declared, "will convict any man who is unwilling to offer an explanation of the charge against him." He "ha[d] heard more than one [juror] say, in discussing a verdict, 'Of course we couldn't take it against him, but we *knew* he was guilty because he was afraid to testify.' "

On the other hand those who do testify "are more than likely to be convicted 'on their records.' " That is because "[a]n affirmative answer to the simple question, 'Have you ever been convicted?' is, in three cases out of five, equivalent to a plea of guilty." So any defendant with a criminal record "generally throws up his hands and stolidly takes his medicine"— and "dickers for the lowest plea he can get." ARTHUR TRAIN, THE PRISONER AT THE BAR 148, 161, 164 (1906).

The upshot, in Train's eyes, was that a law that purported to grant defendants a new right to testify at trial instead deprived those defendants who had criminal records of the right to any meaningful trial. The law left them with little alternative but to seek the best plea bargain they could get.

Back to the Future—Testing the Impact of Evidence of Past Convictions: About a century after Train wrote, Professors Theodore Eisenberg and Valerie Hans examined how state rules similar to FRE 609 affect the trial strategy of those few criminal defendants who choose to go to trial rather than plead guilty.

Theodore Eisenberg & Valerie P. Hans

Taking a Stand on Taking the Stand: The Effect of a Prior Criminal Record on the Decision to Testify and on Trial Outcomes

94 CORNELL L. REV. 1353 (2009)

This Article uses unique data from over 300 criminal trials in four large counties to study the relations between the existence of a prior criminal record and defendants' testifying at trial, between defendants' testifying at trial and juries' learning about criminal records, and between juries' learning about criminal records and their decisions to convict or acquit. . . .

INTRODUCTION

. . . Not testifying in one's own defense may influence a trial's outcome notwithstanding the Fifth Amendment's prohibition against self-incrimination. Prosecutors [in some jurisdictions], until prohibited from doing so, argued that a defendant's failure to testify was evidence of guilt. In a less direct violation of the Fifth Amendment, prosecutors may argue that the defendant failed to rebut particular evidence, even if the only reasonable way to do so was through the defendant's testifying. . . . [A] principal reason defendants decline to testify is the existence of prior criminal records.

All U.S. jurisdictions allow the use of some criminal convictions to impeach the credibility of a witness. . . .

II. DATA DESCRIPTION

. . . Four sites participated in the data collection: The Central Division, Criminal, of the Los Angeles County Superior Court, California; the Maricopa County Superior Court (Phoenix), Arizona; the Bronx County Supreme Court, New York; and the Superior Court of the District of Columbia. [Dates of data collection were 2000 and 2001.] . . .

III. DEFENDANT TESTIMONY AND JURIES' LEARNING OF CRIMINAL RECORD

. . . Table 1 shows the relation between . . . the existence of a prior criminal record and whether the defendant testified at trial. . . . Forty-five percent of defendants with prior records testified, compared to 62% of defendants without known prior records. . . .

TABLE 1
DEFENDANT TESTIMONY AND [CRIMINAL RECORD]

Defendant had—	*Number Not Testifying*	*Number Testifying*	*Percent Testifying*
Prior record	137	114	45.4
No prior record	30	49	62.0*

* indicates $p < 0.05$ [statistically significant]

. . . To assess whether juries learn of criminal records, we limit the sample to those cases in which the defendant had a prior record. . . . Table 4 shows . . . the association between whether the defendant testified and the jury's learning of the prior record. . . . About 52% of juries learned of a defendant's record if the defendant testified. In contrast, juries learned about criminal record if defendants did not testify in less than 9% of cases. . . .

TABLE 4
DEFENDANT TESTIMONY AND JURY KNOWLEDGE OF CRIMINAL RECORD

Defendant—	*Jury Did Not Learn of Criminal Record (N)*	*Jury Learned of Criminal Record (N)*	*Percent Learning of Criminal Record*
Testified	55	59	51.8
Did not testify	125	12	8.8***

*** indicates $p < 0.001$ [highly statistically significant]

IV. THE EFFECT OF JURIES' LEARNING OF CRIMINAL RECORDS

. . . [J]ury knowledge of prior criminal history is significantly associated with conviction in weak cases and not significantly associated with conviction in strong cases. . . .

The magnitude of the effect of knowledge of criminal record can be strikingly large. In . . . cases that round to evidentiary value three [based on juror's assessments of evidentiary strength on a one-to-seven scale], the marginal effect of knowledge of criminal conviction in the District of Columbia is to increase the probability of conviction by 0.36. The corresponding increase is 0.30 in Los Angeles, 0.32 in Maricopa, and 0.10 in the Bronx. As the overall probability of conviction at evidentiary level three without a criminal record is just below 0.20, the presence of a criminal record increases the probability of conviction from less than 20% to about 50% or greater. . . .

Together, these results suggest that in . . . weak cases, cases with evidence less than or equal to 3.5, the dominant tendency is not to convict. But, in the strongest of weak cases, the existence of a prior criminal record can prompt a jury to convict. The prior record effectively leverages the existing evidence over the threshold needed to support conviction.

TABLE 10
JURY KNOWLEDGE OF PRIOR CRIMINAL RECORD AND CONVICTION

	Number Not Convicted	*Number Convicted*	*Percent Convicted*
EVIDENCE STRENGTH ≤ 3.5			
Jury did not learn of record	32	7	18.0
Jury learned of record	12	9	42.9*
EVIDENCE STRENGTH > 3.5			
Jury did not learn of record	11	109	90.8
Jury learned of record	3	41	93.2

* indicates significance < 0.05 using mid-p exact test

The results . . . help identify the cases in which the shifted conviction threshold has most effect. A prior record plays little role in cases with strong or even average (value four) evidence. . . . Nor does prior criminal record often play an outcome-determinative role in cases with evidence too far below the conviction threshold of about four. Hence [there is a] small difference at evidence value two between cases with and without juror knowledge of criminal records and the low conviction rates for both classes of cases. But for cases with evidentiary value close to, but below, the threshold of four, a prior criminal record can lead to conviction.

One could view a prior record as "making up" for evidentiary deficiencies. Or one might view the prior record as evidence tending to suggest guilt. Under either view, the prior record makes a difference. . . .

CONCLUSION

. . . The criminal-record effect could be even stronger than we have found in these analyses; the experimental work suggests that having a record for a similar offense creates the most bias, and we had information only about the presence of a defendant's criminal record, not its type. . . .

The enhanced conviction probability that prior record evidence supplies in close cases may well contribute to erroneous convictions. . . . [P]rosecutors making charging decisions and judges considering the prejudicial effect of prior records should take into account the dramatic effect that knowledge of criminal record can have in close cases. Similarly, criminal defense attorneys should think long and hard about having clients testify in what they believe juries might regard as close cases.

2. RULE 609 IN FORCE

Problem 4.3
Impeachment Modes

At his trial on charges of grand theft in 2012, the defendant took the stand and testified he was hundreds of miles away at the time of the crime. The prosecutor then attempted several modes of impeachment:

(1) She asked the defendant on cross-examination whether he shot a man in the arm during a drunken barroom brawl in 2006.

(2) She called a witness to testify that he saw the defendant shoot a man in the arm during a drunken barroom brawl in 2006.

(3) She offered evidence that the defendant was convicted of assault and battery by means of a dangerous weapon and sentenced to serve five years in state prison for

having shot a man in the arm during a drunken barroom brawl in 2006.

(4) She asked the defendant on cross-examination whether he was convicted of turnstile jumping and sentenced to three months in county jail in 2006.

(5) She offered evidence that the defendant was convicted of lying to a federal investigator and sentenced to two years in a federal penitentiary in 1998.

On the defendant's objection to each of these modes of impeachment, how should the trial judge have ruled? What policy concerns can explain the differing answers the rules give to these questions?

UNITED STATES V. BREWER

451 F. Supp. 50 (E.D. Tenn. 1978).

■ TAYLOR, DISTRICT JUDGE ... This criminal action wherein defendant stands charged by the Grand Jury with one count of kidnapping and one count of transporting a stolen motor vehicle (from Jellico to Valdosta, Georgia) is set for trial on Wednesday, March 15, 1978....

MOTION

The defendant has moved to suppress the Government's proposed introduction of certain past convictions as impeachment evidence if the defendant takes the stand. While the defendant filed the motion, Rule 609 places upon the Government the burden of persuading the Court that the convictions are admissible....

The four convictions which the Government wants to introduce to impeach the defendant's testimony, should he take the stand, all ... meet the first requirement under [FRE 609(a)(1)(B)], *i.e.*, they were punishable by death or imprisonment in excess of one year. Thus, the only requirement to be met before these convictions are admissible for impeachment, is the requirement that the Court determine that the probative value of admitting the evidence of these convictions outweighs the prejudicial effect to the defendant.

Before discussing the standards used by the Courts in determining whether the probative value outweighs the prejudicial effect, it must be noted that defendant's attorney argues that the special provisions of 609(b), dealing with convictions over ten years old (computed under the standard provided by 609(b)) should apply to all four convictions. For the reasons stated below, the special provisions of subpart (b) of Rule 609 do not appear to apply to any of the convictions.

TIME LIMIT IN 609(b)

Under subpart (b) of [unrestyled] Rule 609, when a conviction is offered as impeachment evidence and it is over ten years old, it is *not* admissible *unless*:

> [T]he Court determines, in the interests of justice, that the probative value of the conviction *supported by specific facts and circumstances substantially outweighs its prejudicial effect*. [Emphasis added.]

609(b) also requires the Government to give advance notice of its intention to use such evidence.[1]

The Government argues that the more stringent test of 609(b) does not apply to these convictions because, under the formula provided in the Rule for determining how old a conviction is, none of these convictions is over ten years old.

[Unrestyled] Rule 609(b) states that it shall apply when "more than ten years has elapsed since the date of the conviction or of the release of the witness from the confinement imposed for that conviction, whichever is the later date. . . ."

The convictions in question are as follows:

Date of Conviction			
10–20–60	Kidnapping	E.D. Kentucky	10 years
1–6–68	Rape	Greene County, Ohio (State Court)	3–20 years
1–6–68	Aggravated Assault	Greene County, Ohio (State Court)	1–[3] years
1–6–68	Assault with a deadly weapon	Greene County, Ohio (State Court)	1–15 years (the three Ohio convictions were consecutive)

The relevant date obviously is the date the defendant was released from the confinement imposed for each conviction. While the three 1968 Ohio state convictions were rendered slightly over ten years ago, the minimum sentence of one year on each conviction means that whichever he served first, the one-year minimum set his release date *for that*

1. The Government, realizing that there might be some debate as to whether 609(b) applied, wisely filed advance notice as required under that subsection.

conviction within the last ten years. Defendant was not actually sentenced until March 22, 1968, less than ten years ago. Therefore, March 22, 1969, would have been the earliest release date on either the 1–3 years or 1–15 years sentences, and that release date is unquestionably within the last ten years.

As to the federal kidnapping charge, although the conviction occurred over seventeen years ago, the release date is the determinative date. Defendant was first released from federal custody on June 27, 1967, and placed on parole. If this were the *only* release date, it would have occurred over ten years ago, and the special provisions of 609(b) would apply. However, while on federal parole, defendant was convicted of the above mentioned state crimes on January 6, 1968. After serving time on the state convictions, defendant was *recommitted to federal confinement* for violation of parole on the kidnapping conviction. He was released on February 9, 1976, and again placed on parole. This second release date is well within the last ten years, and thus 609(b) does not apply.

Defendant argues that release from "confinement imposed for that conviction" means the initial release and not subsequent releases following reconfinement for parole violations. While no case addressing this issue has been cited by either side, and the Court has found none, the Court is of the opinion that reconfinement pursuant to parole violation is "confinement imposed for [the original] conviction," and therefore the release date from that second confinement is the one used in computing time under Rule 609(b).

It should be noted that, even without the intervening 5–1/2 years state incarceration, *i.e.,* had defendant immediately been returned to federal confinement upon conviction of the state crimes, his release date (assuming an identical period of federal incarceration of over two years) would have been in April 1970, also well within the last ten years. Having ruled that none of these convictions requires the application of the stringent standards of 609(b), the Court must now determine if the Government has met the standard applicable under 609(a).

BALANCING TESTS UNDER 609(a)

Application by the Courts of the 609(a) requirement that a determination be made that the probative value of admitting the evidence outweighs its prejudicial effect has generally followed the formula developed in the D.C. Circuit in a string of cases starting with Judge McGowan's opinion in Luck v. United States, 348 F.2d 763 (D.C. Cir. 1965), and including an often quoted opinion by then Judge Burger in Gordon v. United States, 383 F.2d 936 (D.C. Cir. 1967), *cert. denied,* 390 U.S. 1029 (1968). . . .

The five factors discussed by Judge Burger in *Gordon* are:

(1) the nature of the crime;

(2) the time of conviction and the witness' subsequent history;

(3) similarity between the past crime and the charged crime;

(4) importance of defendant's testimony; and

(5) the centrality of the credibility issue.

(1) *The Nature of the Crimes.* The nature of these crimes is that of violent action against individuals. In *Gordon*, Judge Burger noted, "Acts of violence on the other hand, which may result from a short temper, a combative nature, extreme provocation, or other causes, generally have little or no direct bearing on honesty and veracity." 383 F.2d at 940. Thus, the nature of these four convictions is a factor against admitting them for impeachment purposes.

(2) *The Time of Conviction and the Witness' Subsequent History.* While the time elapsed since the actual convictions at issue here range[s] from ten to seventeen years, the defendant's conduct following release from custody has been less than would be expected of a rehabilitated individual. Not only did the defendant commit the three previously mentioned, serious state crimes while on federal parole in 1968, after his release on parole from federal custody in February 1976, he was convicted of another crime in Ohio and was reconfined again for violation of his federal parole. The Court is of the opinion that the defendant's continued conflict with the law, even while on parole, is a factor supporting admission of the convictions for impeachment purposes.

(3) *The Similarity Between the Past Crime and the Charged Crime.* The principle involved here was explained by Judge Burger in *Gordon*:

> A special and even more difficult problem arises when the prior conviction is for the same or substantially the same conduct for which the accused is on trial. Where multiple convictions of various kinds can be shown, strong reasons arise for excluding those which are for the same crime because of the inevitable pressure on lay jurors to believe that "if he did it before he probably did so this time." As a general guide, those convictions which are for the same crime should be admitted sparingly; one solution might well be that discretion be exercised to limit the impeachment by way of a similar crime to a single conviction and then only when the circumstances indicate strong reasons for disclosure, and where the conviction directly relates to veracity.

383 F.2d at 940.

This principle would apply only to the prior kidnapping conviction. If the Court should admit any of the four convictions, a limiting instruction would be given to the jury emphasizing that they are admitted only to impeach the credibility of the defendant as a witness. The question is whether, even with a limiting instruction, the evidence of a prior conviction for the same crime might, nevertheless, allow the jury to engage in the impermissible assumption that "if he did it before he probably did so this time." . . .

Based on the principle stated in *Gordon*, the Court is of the opinion that there is a strong argument to keep the prior kidnapping conviction from the jury's knowledge.

(4) & (5) *Final Factors.* Factors four and five seem to counterbalance each other in this case. While defendant's testimony may be of some importance, a factor favoring nonadmission, at the same time his credibility may be a central issue in the case, a factor favoring admission.

CONCLUSION

Although the Court, at the hearing on this motion, initially ruled that all four convictions were admissible, further consideration has convinced the Court that the probative value of the prior kidnapping conviction on the issue of defendant's truthfulness, should he take the stand, does not outweigh the prejudicial effect knowledge of such conviction could have on the jury. Admission of the other three convictions, all involving serious crimes, should sufficiently serve the purpose of impeaching the defendant's credibility. The addition of one more conviction would seem to add little to the Government's attempt to impeach the defendant's credibility. . . . Rather than allow this "overkill" at the risk of prejudicial error, the Court is of the opinion, and holds, that the prior kidnapping conviction is inadmissible under Rule 609(a). As for the three other convictions, the Court holds that the Government has established that the probative value of these three convictions for impeachment purposes outweighs the prejudicial effect that admission of such evidence would have on the jury.

Order Accordingly.

CHARACTER AND CREDIBILITY: STUDY GUIDE (PART II)

Rule 609 permits a litigant to impeach a witness with evidence that the witness has been convicted of a crime. Opposing counsel often presents such evidence during cross-examination of the witness. The inquiry takes the following form:

> Q: Are you the same Leslie Stephens who, on June 8, 2008, in Sullivan County Superior Court, was convicted of armed robbery and sentenced to four years in state prison?

The evidence also may take the form of a court document reflecting the conviction. Inquiry into the underlying details of the crime generally is barred. Some judges, however, permit the witness to explain the circumstances of the crime or the conviction. *See* C. MUELLER & L. KIRKPATRICK, EVIDENCE § 6.34, at 528–29 (5th ed. 2012).

The district court's careful decision in *United States v. Brewer*, excerpted above, suggests an important lesson for practitioners: While judges are sometimes careless in enforcing such mushy standards as Rule 403's probativeness-versus-unfair-prejudice test and Rule 404(a)'s propensity bar, judges rigorously enforce the very specific time standards of Rule 609(a)(1) and Rule 609(b).

The following notes highlight other important issues in the application of Rule 609. Please refer to the rule as you read.

Rule 609(a)(1)

Rule 609(a)(1) is written in terms of the *available* penalty, not the penalty actually assessed. The requirement that the penalty must be more than one year means, in most jurisdictions, that the crime must be a felony, not a misdemeanor. The language of the rule makes it clear, however, that the potential penalty—not the designation "felony" or "misdemeanor"—controls.

Note that evidence of a past conviction offered to impeach a witness other than a criminal defendant must survive a Rule 403 weighing test. A stricter weighing test governs evidence of the accused's past conviction. Only if probative value outweighs the potential to cause unfair prejudice to the defendant can such evidence gain admission. The *Brewer* court (at pages 287 to 288) laid out five factors, drawn from then Judge Burger's opinion in *Gordon v. United States*, 383 F.2d 936, 940–41 (D.C. Cir. 1967), *cert. denied*, 390 U.S. 1029 (1968), which generally govern this weighing test:

(1) the nature of the crime;

(2) the time of conviction and the witness's subsequent history;

(3) similarity between the past crime and the charged crime;

(4) the importance of the defendant's testimony; and

(5) the centrality of the credibility issue.

The *Brewer* court suggested that the fourth standard, the "importance of the defendant's testimony," means that the more critical the defendant's testimony is to his case, the more hesitant a trial court should be to admit the impeaching evidence. Other courts have spelled out this thought more completely. In *United States v. Paige*, 464 F. Supp. 99 (E.D. Pa. 1978), the district judge noted that "[i]n this case, it is especially important that the defendant feel free to testify, and this also weighs heavily against allowing the impeachment use of the prior similar conviction." After explaining how the facts and law of the case made the defendant's testimony critical to his defense, the judge concluded: "Thus, his defense will be prejudiced severely if he is deterred from testifying from fear that he will be convicted on the basis of a prior crime. Therefore, . . . justice requires that use of the prior conviction be disallowed unless the government shows strong justification." *Id.* at 100–01.

Trial judges have discretion under Rule 403 to admit evidence of a past conviction while withholding from jurors the nature of that conviction. Jurors in such cases learn only of a witness's "felony" conviction or her conviction "of a crime punishable by imprisonment in excess of one year" and the date of conviction. In *United States v. Ford*, 17 F.3d 1100 (8th Cir. 1994), the Eighth Circuit Court of Appeals upheld the district judge's exercise of discretion in admitting under the label "felony" a witness's past conviction of a sexual offense against a minor. "The introduction of [the witness's] specific felony," the court wrote, "could easily have distracted the jury from its task without adding any real probative information to their deliberations." *Id.* at 1103.

In general, however, trial courts permit jurors to learn the nature of the past crime. In *United States v. Estrada*, 430 F.3d 606 (2d Cir. 2005), *cert. denied sub nom. DeJesus v. United States*, 547 U.S. 1048 (2006), the Second Circuit rejected a district court's practice of routinely stripping the crime's identity from evidence of past convictions. The appeals court held that this "conviction-only" method ignored the teaching of *Gordon* that different crimes have different probative power in showing untruthful character: *Gordon* "distinguished between crimes that reflect adversely on a person's integrity, and which therefore bear on honesty—such as those involving deceit, fraud, and theft—and acts of violence, 'which may result from a short temper, a combative nature, extreme provocation, or other causes, [and] generally have little or no direct bearing on honesty and veracity.'" *Estrada*, 430 F.3d at 617–18 (quoting *Gordon*, 383 F.2d at 940). *Accord United States v. Howell*, 285 F.3d 1263, 1268 (10th Cir. 2002) ("We therefore conclude that the district court erred in adopting a blanket rule that the nature of the government witnesses' felony convictions was categorically inadmissible."); *United States v. Burston*, 159 F.3d 1328, 1335 (11th Cir. 1998) (holding that the probative value of past convictions "necessarily varies with their nature and number").

Rule 609(a)(2)

Rule 609(a)(2) carves out a class of convictions as particularly probative of untruthful character and declares that they "*must* be admitted" regardless of punishment. (Emphasis added.) The Conference Committee's Report interprets this command to mean that "admission of prior convictions involving dishonesty and false statements is not within the discretion of the [trial] Court. Such convictions . . . *are always to be admitted.*" (RB 137 (emphasis added).) Alone in the evidentiary universe, evidence admitted under Rule 609(a)(2) escapes balancing under Rule 403 or any other weighing test unless Rule 609(b), (c), or (d) applies.*

Because such impeachment evidence is to be "automatically admitted," the all-important question is *which* convictions the rule covers. (ACN to 2006 Amendment, RB 145.) As amended in 2006 and restyled in 2011, the rule applies only when "the court can readily determine that estab-

* My thanks to Professor Charles Baron and his RWU students for suggesting clarifications to this material.

lishing the elements of the crime required proving—or the witness's admitting—a dishonest act or false statement." The Advisory Committee's Note to the 2006 Amendment confirmed earlier suggestions in the rule's legislative history that crimes requiring proof or admission of "a dishonest act or false statement" are those

> "crimes such as perjury, subornation of perjury, false statement, criminal fraud, embezzlement, or false pretense, or any other offense in the nature of *crimen falsi*, the commission of which involves some element of deceit, untruthfulness, or falsification bearing on the [witness's] propensity to testify truthfully."

(ACN to 2006 Amendment (quoting original Conference Report), RB 145.) "Historically," the advisory committee said, "offenses classified as *crimina falsi* have included only those crimes in which the ultimate criminal act was itself an act of deceit." (RB 145.)

In its note to the 1990 amendment to Rule 609, the committee put a helpful gloss on the reference to *crimen falsi*. It wrote that this language "provides sufficient guidance to trial courts . . . , notwithstanding some decisions that take *an unduly broad view* of 'dishonesty,' admitting convictions such as for bank robbery or bank larceny." (RB 144 (emphasis added).) This passage suggests that bank robbery and bank larceny are *not* typically crimes of dishonesty because they are not "in the nature of *crimen falsi*." Another remnant of the rule's original legislative history adds color to this conclusion. During the Senate's consideration of Rule 609(a)(2), Arkansas Senator John Little McClellan remarked:

> There is no deceit in armed robbery. You take a gun, walk out, and put it in a man's face and say, "Give me your money," or walk up to the counter of the cashier and say, "this is a holdup; give me your money." There is no deceit in that. They are not lying. They mean business. They will murder you if you do not do it.

120 CONG. REC. S19,913 (daily ed. Nov. 22, 1974).

Just as violent robbery typically would not qualify as *crimen falsi*, neither would most simple thefts. In a decades-old ruling that seems valid today, the District of Columbia Circuit distinguished those crimes covered by Rule 609(a)(2) from simple theft by noting that one is characterized by deceit, the other by mere stealth. *See United States v. Fearwell*, 595 F.2d 771, 776 & n.8 (D.C. Cir. 1978). That is, the rule uses "dishonest[y]" in a narrow sense. Though the word could mean, broadly, "a breach of trust, a 'lack of . . . probity or integrity in principle,' [a] 'lack of fairness,' or a 'disposition to . . . betray,'" the rule instead uses "dishonest[y]" to mean only "deceitful behavior, a 'disposition to defraud . . . [or] deceive,' or a 'disposition to lie, cheat, or defraud.'" *United States v. Brackeen*, 969 F.2d 827, 829 (9th Cir. 1992) (quoting WEBSTER'S THIRD NEW INTERNATIONAL DICTIONARY 650 (1986 unabridged ed.); BLACK'S LAW DICTIONARY 421 (5th ed. 1979)).

The 2006 amendment to the rule aimed to ban the practice, once common in some courts, of holding "'mini-trial[s]' in which the court plumbs the record of the previous proceeding to determine whether the crime was in the nature of *crimen falsi*." (RB 146.) The amended rule, as recently restyled, applies only "if the court *can readily determine* that establishing the elements of the crime required proving—or the witness's admitting—a dishonest act or false statement." (Emphasis added.) The advisory committee's note to this amendment lists a bare handful of sources that "readily" could support the court's finding:

- the statutory elements of the charged crime;
- the face of the trial court's judgment;
- the indictment;
- a statement of admitted facts (if any); or
- jury instructions (if any).

A statement of admitted facts may exist if the witness pled guilty to the past crime. It would state those facts that the witness admitted to be true in pleading guilty. The committee's note suggests that a transcribed change-of-plea colloquy, in which the defendant orally admitted facts, also would qualify. (*See* RB 145–46.)

The committee apparently did not intend this list to exhaust the means for making the ready determination called for by the rule. The list simply illustrates a few ways to assess the past crime's nature as *crimen falsi*. The important thing is that there be no mini-trial. Unless the judge can find a requirement of proof of dishonesty or false statement on the surface of the paper record, evidence of a conviction will be inadmissible under Rule 609(a)(2) even if "the witness exhibited dishonesty or made a false statement in the process of the commission of the [past] crime." (RB 144.)

Although evidence of dishonesty or false statement generally must be admitted without a discretionary weighing test, such evidence is subject to the constraints imposed by Rules 609(b), (c), and (d). If a witness has a fourteen-year-old perjury conviction, for example, Rule 609(b) will impose a demanding weighing test that may trump Rule 609(a)(2)'s command that the evidence "must be admitted."

Rule 609(b)

When the conviction is more than ten years old, it will be admitted only if "its probative value, supported by specific facts and circumstances, substantially outweighs its prejudicial effect." This reverse–403 weighing test is stricter than those called for in Rules 609(a)(1) and 609(a)(2). In effect Rule 609(b) establishes a rebuttable presumption against admission of old convictions. Note the remark of the Senate Judiciary Committee, included in the legislative history, that "[i]t is intended that convictions over ten years old will be admitted very rarely and only in exceptional circumstances." (RB 139.)

Earlier I mentioned the *Brewer* court's unusual care in measuring the ten-year span. Mueller and Kirkpatrick offer thoughts on pinpointing the end of the span:

> The end point . . . could be the date of [the present] indictment, the date trial begins, or the date the witness testifies. The date of indictment seems preferable. There is little chance the government will rush an indictment to beat the ten-year period, and any incentive to act quickly seems good rather than bad. Defining the date of trial or testimony by the witness as the end point might add to defense incentives to delay, which seems undesirable.

MUELLER & KIRKPATRICK, *supra*, § 6.36, at 533.

Rule 609(d)

Juvenile adjudications are never admissible in civil cases or to impeach the testimony of criminal defendants. Even when used against other witnesses in a criminal case, they must survive the strictest standard of any prescribed in Rule 609. They are admissible only if "an adult's conviction for that offense would be admissible to attack the adult's credibility; and . . . admitting the evidence is necessary to fairly determine guilt or innocence."

The Various Standards of Admission

The various subparts of Rule 609 set out a bewildering jumble of standards to govern admission of past convictions to attack a witness's character for truthfulness. Here are the different standards, arrayed from most permissive to most restrictive:

1. *Rule 609(a)(2):* Conviction of "any crime . . . must be admitted if the court can readily determine that establishing the elements of the crime required proving—or the witness's admitting—a dishonest act or false statement," subject only to the limits imposed by Rules 609(b), 609(c), and 609(d).
2. *Rule 609(a)(1)(A):* If the witness is not the accused in a criminal case, conviction of a crime "punishable by death or by imprisonment for more than one year . . . must be admitted, subject to Rule 403."
3. *Rule 609(a)(1)(B):* If the witness is the accused in a criminal case, conviction of a crime "punishable by death or by imprisonment for more than one year . . . must be admitted . . . if the probative value of the evidence outweighs its prejudicial effect to that defendant."

4. *Rule 609(b):* "[I]f more than 10 years have passed since the witness's conviction or release from confinement for it, whichever is later," evidence of a conviction "is admissible only if . . . its probative value, supported by specific facts and circumstances, substantially outweighs its prejudicial effect."
5. *Rule 609(d):* Evidence of a juvenile adjudication is never admissible in a civil case or to impeach the accused in a criminal case, but may be admitted to impeach another witness in a criminal case if the evidence otherwise qualifies under Rule 609 and "admitting the evidence is necessary to fairly determine guilt or innocence."

This mad variety of standards has a method. The rule's drafters apparently intended the various subsections of Rule 609 to reflect a number of discrete Rule 403–style weighing tests. Behind several of Rule 609's components lie judgments about the varying *probativeness* of the evidence they govern:

- *Rule 609(a)(1):* More serious crimes suggest greater readiness to lie under oath. This rule therefore generally requires that crimes used to impeach have been punishable by death or more than a year in prison.
- *Rule 609(a)(2):* Crimes involving deceit are especially probative of one's propensity to lie and are therefore made "automatically" admissible. (RB 145.)
- *Rule 609(b):* Older crimes are less probative of present character and so are less readily admitted.
- *Rule 609(c):* A person's successful rehabilitation diminishes the probativeness of past crimes, and a later "finding of innocence" would reduce probativeness to near zero.
- *Rule 609(d):* If the witness was a juvenile at the time of her past offense, there is a greater chance her character has changed and perhaps improved.

Some of Rule 609's subsections likewise reflect judgments about the varying risk of unfair *prejudice* posed by evidence of past convictions. Most prominently, the rule guards against unfair prejudice toward criminal defendants. Unlike an ordinary witness, a criminal defendant faces the very real risk that the jury will use evidence of her past crimes, admitted only to impeach her character for truthfulness, to draw more general conclusions about her criminal propensities. And unlike a civil party, when a criminal defendant suffers from a jury's wayward propensity reasoning, she faces the ultimate penalties of imprisonment or execution. Rules 609(a)(1)(B) and 609(d) therefore extend greater protection to criminal defendants who take the stand than to civil parties or ordinary witnesses. Rule 609(a)(1)(B) imposes a stricter-than-usual weighing test on prosecutors seeking to use evidence of past convictions against criminal defendants. And Rule 609(d) altogether bars evidence of a defendant's juvenile adjudications.

Practice

Look again at Problem 4.3 (*Impeachment Modes*), at page 284. Here are some suggested answers:

(1) *Inadmissible.* Because there is no mention of a conviction, we must analyze this problem under Rule 608(b) rather than Rule 609. That the defendant shot someone during a brawl is not so "probative of [his] character for truthfulness or untruthfulness" that it could be asked about under Rule 608(b).

(2) *Inadmissible.* Again, because there is no mention of a conviction, we must analyze this problem under Rule 608 rather than Rule 609. If the question is posed on direct examination, Rule 608(a) limits the prosecutor to opinion or reputation evidence, whereas here she asks about specific acts. Moreover, Rule 608(a) limits the prosecutor to questions bearing on character for truthfulness or untruthfulness.

(3) *Maybe admissible.* Rule 609(a)(1)(B) will permit this question "if the probative value of the evidence outweighs its prejudicial effect to that defendant." The probative value of a six-year-old crime of violence in showing the defendant's present character for untruthfulness is perhaps not great. The crime is not particularly recent, and it is unclear how a violent act bears on truthfulness. On the other hand shooting someone is a serious crime. And the risk of unfair prejudice to the defendant is moderated by the dissimilarity of the old crime (involving violence) to the present charges (alleging theft).

(4) *Probably inadmissible.* If turnstile jumping is punishable by more than a year in prison, which seems unlikely, and if the judge finds that the probative value of the evidence outweighs the danger of unfair prejudice, the evidence may be admitted under Rule 609(a)(1)(B). If either of these conditions is not met, the only possible routes of admission are Rules 609(a)(2) and 608(b). Rule 609(a)(2) doesn't apply because turnstile jumping does not involve false statement. And most judges would not regard a conviction of turnstile jumping to be "probative of . . . character for truthfulness or untruthfulness," as required by Rule 608(b). Moreover, since the evidence is of a type governed by Rule 609, yet is excluded by the terms of Rule 609 (if not punishable by more than a year), many judges would not permit a backdoor admission under Rule 608(b). Even if the evidence were admitted under Rule 608(b), there still would be the problem of getting past Rule 403.

(5) *Possibly admissible.* Because of the age of the conviction, it is presumptively inadmissible under Rule 609(b): It is not admissible unless "its probative value, supported by specific facts and circumstances, substantially outweighs its prejudicial effect" (and unless the notice provi-

sions of Rule 609(b)(2) have been met). Still, the evidence seems rather probative—if not for its age, the conviction of lying to a federal investigator would have been automatically admissible under Rule 609(a)(2). And the evidence poses only a moderate risk of unfair prejudice because the present charges of theft bear little similarity to the old conviction of lying to an investigator. Some judges would take the defendant's more recent criminal record into account. If the defendant recently has been involved in other criminal matters, this old conviction may be more probative of his present character for truthfulness than if he has been out of trouble for a while. See, for example, Judge Taylor's opinion in *Brewer* at page 288, above (discussing factor 2 of the *Gordon* test).

Problem 4.4
Weighing Tests

Consider the facts of *United States v. Valencia*, 61 F.3d 616 (8th Cir. 1995), in which the defendant appealed his conviction of distributing cocaine:

> Appellant first contends the district court erred when it admitted, for impeachment purposes, a prior conviction of the appellant for unlawful possession for sale and purchase for sale of [cocaine]. Previously, in its case in chief, the government had offered the prior conviction pursuant to Fed. R. Evid. 404(b). The district court denied the use of the previous conviction during the government's case in chief, finding that the balancing required under Fed. R. Evid. 403 militated against admission....
>
> Later in the trial the appellant testified in his own defense.... On cross-examination, the government offered a certified copy of the appellant's prior conviction.... Over the appellant's objection, the copy of the prior conviction was admitted under Fed. R. Evid. 609 for impeachment purposes....
>
> ... The appellant contends that Rule [609(a)(1)(B)]'s internalized balancing test is stricter in terms of admissibility in that a prior conviction is not admissible against the accused for impeachment purposes unless the probative value of the evidence outweighs its prejudicial effect. Appellant's argument is that after finding that the prejudice of the prior conviction *substantially* outweighed the probative value under 404(b), the district court abused its discretion in admitting the same evidence under Rule 609, where it

would be excluded if the prejudice *merely* outweighed its probative effect.

Is the appellant right?

Problem 4.5
Meter Fixing

Gary A. sued his former employer, Borden Confectionary Company, alleging that Borden fired him because of his age in violation of the Age Discrimination in Employment Act. After an October 2012 trial, a jury found for Borden. On appeal A. complains that the trial judge permitted defense counsel to impeach his testimony by asking on cross-examination, "Mr. A., in 2002 you were convicted of the crime of tampering with electric meters of Commonwealth Edison, weren't you?"—to which A. replied, "Yes."

A.'s 2002 crime fell under the general heading of misdemeanor theft as defined by Illinois law. The relevant parts of the governing statute read as follows:

Theft. (a) A person commits theft when he or she knowingly:

(1) Obtains or exerts unauthorized control over property of the owner; or

(2) Obtains by deception control over property of the owner; or

(3) Obtains by threat control over property of the owner....

Cf. 720 ILL. COMP. STAT. ANN. 5/16–1 (2012).

Assume that A.'s 2002 crime carried a maximum penalty of six months' confinement. Assume, too, that A. pled guilty to the 2002 charge and that his plea agreement included a statement of admitted facts. That document, signed by A., stated that he "tamper[ed] with electric meters of Commonwealth Edison," but supplied no other details. When Borden's counsel sought to impeach A. with this conviction, Borden's counsel advised the trial judge, "Apparently what happened is that A. helped several McDonald's franchisees in the Chicago area to alter the electric meters in their restaurants, in order to reduce their electric bills."

Should the trial judge have admitted evidence of the conviction? What are the best arguments on both sides? *Cf. Altobello v. Borden Confectionary Products, Inc.*, 872 F.2d 215 (7th Cir. 1989).

RULE 609: CASE NOTES ON APPELLATE REVIEW

Rule 609 puts criminal defendants who take the stand in a peculiarly vulnerable position. A defendant may justly worry that the jury will use evidence of past convictions offered only to impeach as evidence that the defendant is not merely a liar, but also a thief (or assailant or drug dealer).

Aware of this risk of unfair prejudice, the rule writers made Rule 609 especially protective of criminal defendants. If the trial judge disregards the Rule's safeguards and wrongly admits evidence of past convictions to impeach a defendant, the defendant normally may appeal. The Supreme Court has ruled, however, that a defendant may not appeal from the trial judge's ruling unless two conditions are met: First, the defendant must have testified at trial. Second, the prosecutor must have introduced evidence of the contested conviction. The Court set down these conditions in *Luce v. United States*, 469 U.S. 38 (1984), and *Ohler v. United States*, 529 U.S. 753 (2000).

Luce v. United States

469 U.S. 38 (1984).

Editor's Note: The defendant asked the trial judge to determine in advance whether the prosecutor would be permitted to impeach the defendant with evidence of his past convictions should he choose to testify. The judge tentatively ruled that the convictions would be admissible. The defendant therefore chose not to testify. He was convicted and appealed. The Supreme Court ruled unanimously that the defendant's failure to testify barred his appeal. The Court reasoned that because the defendant did not testify, it was impossible for a reviewing court to measure how badly the challenged evidence would have harmed the defendant's case. It was impossible to know even whether the challenged evidence would have been admitted. Chief Justice Burger explained:

> . . . Any possible harm flowing from a district court's *in limine* ruling[2] permitting impeachment by a prior conviction is wholly speculative. The ruling is subject to change when the case unfolds, particularly if the actual testimony differs from what [the defense counsel led the trial judge to expect]. Indeed even if nothing unexpected happens at trial, the district judge is free, in the exercise of sound judicial discretion, to alter a previous *in limine* ruling. On a

2. *"In limine"* has been defined as "[on] or at the threshold; at the very beginning; preliminarily." BLACK'S LAW DICTIONARY 708 (5th ed. 1979). We use the term in a broad sense to refer to any motion, whether made before or during trial, to exclude anticipated prejudicial evidence before the evidence is actually offered.

record such as here, it would be a matter of conjecture whether the District Court would have allowed the Government to attack petitioner's credibility at trial by means of the prior conviction.

When the defendant does not testify, the reviewing court also has no way of knowing whether the Government would have sought to impeach with the prior conviction. If, for example, the Government's case is strong, and the defendant is subject to impeachment by other means, a prosecutor might elect not to use an arguably inadmissible prior conviction.

Because an accused's decision whether to testify "seldom turns on the resolution of one factor," New Jersey v. Portash, 440 U.S. 450, 467 (1979) (BLACKMUN, J., dissenting), a reviewing court cannot assume that the adverse ruling motivated a defendant's decision not to testify....

Concurring, Justice Brennan emphasized that "[t]he careful weighing of probative value and prejudicial effect that Rule [609(a)(1)(B)] requires of a district court can only be evaluated adequately on appeal in the specific factual context of a trial as it has unfolded."

Ohler v. United States

529 U.S. 753 (2000).

Editor's Note: The government brought a pretrial in limine motion to determine whether evidence of the defendant's past conviction would be admissible to impeach her testimony should she take the stand. The trial judge ruled the evidence would be admissible. The defendant chose to testify anyway. During direct examination her lawyer questioned her about the past conviction. She was convicted and appealed, claiming the judge wrongly deemed her past conviction admissible. The Supreme Court ruled five to four that by offering evidence of the past conviction herself, the defendant had waived any right to complain about its admission:

■ CHIEF JUSTICE REHNQUIST delivered the opinion of the Court.... Generally, a party introducing evidence cannot complain on appeal that the evidence was erroneously admitted. *Cf.* 1 J. STRONG, MCCORMICK ON EVIDENCE § 55, at 246 (5th ed. 1999) ("If a party who has objected to evidence of a certain fact himself produces evidence from his own witness of the same fact, he has waived his objection."). Ohler seeks to avoid the consequences of this well-established commonsense principle....

Rule 609(a) is ... unavailing for Ohler.... The Rule originally provided that admissible prior conviction evidence could be elicited from the defendant or established by public record during cross-examination, but it was amended in 1990 to clarify that the evidence could also be introduced on direct examination.* According to Ohler, it follows from this amendment that a party does not waive her objection to the *in limine* ruling by introducing the evidence herself. However, . . . Rule 609(a) simply does not address this issue. There is no question that the Rule authorizes the eliciting of a prior conviction on direct examination, but it does no more than that.

Next, Ohler argues that it would be unfair to apply such a waiver rule in this situation because it compels a defendant to forgo the tactical advantage of preemptively introducing the conviction in order to appeal the *in limine* ruling. She argues that if a defendant is forced to wait for evidence of the conviction to be introduced on cross-examination, the jury will believe that the defendant is less credible because she was trying to conceal the conviction. The Government . . . argues that it is debatable whether jurors actually perceive a defendant to be more credible if she introduces a conviction herself. Second, even if jurors do consider the defendant more credible, the Government suggests that it is an unwarranted advantage because the jury does not realize that the defendant disclosed the conviction only after failing to persuade the court to exclude it.

Whatever the merits of these contentions, they tend to obscure the fact that both the Government and the defendant in a criminal trial must make choices as the trial progresses. . . . The Government, . . . in a case such as this, must make a choice. If the defendant testifies, it must choose whether or not to impeach her by use of her prior conviction. Here the trial judge had indicated he would allow its use,[3] but the Government still had to consider whether its use might be deemed reversible error on appeal. This choice is often based on the Government's appraisal of the apparent effect of the defendant's testimony. If she has offered a plausible, innocent explanation of the evidence against her, it will be inclined to use the prior conviction; if not, it may decide not to risk possible reversal on appeal from its use. . . .

Petitioner's submission would deny to the Government its usual right to decide, after she testifies, whether or not to use her prior conviction against her. She seeks to short-circuit that decisional

* [Note the advisory committee's explanation of this change: "It is common for witnesses to reveal on direct examination their convictions to 'remove the sting' of the impeachment." (ACN to 1990 Amendment to FRE 609, RB 141.)—GF]

3. The District Court ruled on the first day of trial that Ohler's prior conviction would be admissible for impeachment purposes, and the court likely would have abided by that ruling at trial. However, *in limine* rulings are not binding on the trial judge, and the judge may always change his mind during the course of a trial. *See* Luce v. United States, 469 U.S. 38, 41–42 (1984). Ohler's position, therefore, would deprive the trial court of the opportunity to change its mind after hearing all of the defendant's testimony.

process by offering the conviction herself (and thereby removing the sting) and still preserve its admission as a claim of error on appeal.

But here petitioner runs into the position taken by the Court in a similar, but not identical, situation in Luce v. United States, 469 U.S. 38 (1984), that "any possible harm flowing from a district court's *in limine* ruling permitting impeachment by a prior conviction is wholly speculative." . . .

■ JUSTICE SOUTER, with whom JUSTICE STEVENS, JUSTICE GINSBURG, and JUSTICE BREYER join, dissenting. . . . In requiring testimony and actual impeachment before a defendant could appeal an *in limine* ruling to admit prior convictions, . . . *Luce* . . . merely acknowledged the incapacity of an appellate court to assess the significance of the ruling for a defendant who remains silent.

This case is different, there being a factual record on which Ohler's claim can be reviewed. She testified, and there is no question that the *in limine* ruling controlled her counsel's decision to enquire about the earlier conviction; defense lawyers do not set out to impeach their own witnesses, much less their clients. Since analysis [on appeal] is made no more difficult by the fact that the convictions came out on direct examination, not cross-examination, the case raises none of the practical difficulties on which *Luce* turned, and *Luce* does not dictate today's result. . . .

[Today's result will unfairly prejudice those defendants who face Ohler's choices.] The jury may feel that in testifying without saying anything about the convictions the defendant has meant to conceal them. The jury's assessment of the defendant's testimony may be affected not only by knowing that she has committed crimes in the past, but by blaming her for not being forthcoming when she seemingly could have been. Creating such an impression of current deceit by concealment is very much at odds with any purpose behind Rule 609, being obviously antithetical to dispassionate fact-finding in support of a sound conclusion. The chance to create that impression is a tactical advantage for the Government, but only in the majority's dismissive sense of the term; it may affect the outcome of the trial, but only if it disserves the search for truth. . . .

Postscript to* Ohler v. United States:* *Ohler* does not bar state courts from allowing appeals by defendants who preemptively offer evidence of their past convictions after a judge's pretrial ruling that such evidence would be admissible to impeach them. Several state supreme courts have taken this more permissive approach. *See, e.g., Zola v. Kelley*, 149 N.H. 648, 652 (2003) ("We therefore decline to follow *Ohler* and conclude that when a trial judge makes a definitive pretrial ruling that evidence of a prior conviction is admissible, a party's preemptive introduction of that evidence does not automatically waive the issue for appellate review."); *State v. Gary*, 270 Wis.2d 62, 76, 676 N.W.2d 475 (2004) (similar); *State v. Daly*, 623 N.W.2d 799, 801 (Ia. 2001) (similar).

In *Daly* the Iowa Supreme Court quoted the exchange between Daly and his counsel at trial:

> *Q*. Let's get one thing out right now, Mr. Daly. You've been convicted of crimes in the past, haven't you?
>
> *A*. Yes.
>
> *Q*. What crimes were you convicted of?
>
> *A*. Possession with intent to deliver methamphetamine. . . .
>
> *Q*. When was that?
>
> *A*. 1993.
>
> *Q*. Found guilty by a jury?
>
> *A*. No, I pleaded guilty.

Daly, 623 N.W.2d at 800. Note how Daly's counsel used this disclosure to *enhance* Daly's credibility. Not only did Daly tell jurors about his old conviction with apparent frankness, he specified that he *pled guilty* to the old crime. The implication is that Daly demanded trial of the present charge because *this time* he's innocent.

Rule 609 in Force: A Last Look at the Evidence: Recall Professor Richard Uviller's suspicions that jurors can't distinguish between the (permitted) inference that past convictions reflect badly on the defendant's truthfulness and the (forbidden) inference that they reflect badly on his general character. (*See* pages 276–77.) In a 1985 study that yielded some of the best available evidence on the subject, Roselle Wissler and Michael Saks tested whether such suspicions are justified:

Roselle L. Wissler & Michael J. Saks

On the Inefficacy of Limiting Instructions: When Jurors Use Prior Conviction Evidence to Decide on Guilt

9 LAW & HUM. BEHAVIOR 37 (1985)

INTRODUCTION

According to [unrestyled] Rule 609(a) of the Federal Rules of Evidence, evidence that an individual has been previously convicted of a crime may be admitted during a trial "for the purpose of attacking the credibility of a witness." When such evidence is admitted for a defendant testifying on his or her own behalf, the judge instructs the jury that the defendant's prior record should be used solely to assess the credibility of the defendant ... and not to determine the defendant's propensity to commit the present crime or to determine guilt....

Several courts and legal commentators have expressed concern, however, that the cautionary instructions may not enable the jury "to restrict the impact" of prior conviction evidence "to the issue of credibility." ... A 1968 survey indicated that 98 percent of the lawyers and 43 percent of the judges questioned expressed the belief that jurors are not able to follow an instruction to use prior conviction evidence only for assessing credibility....

While ... previous studies ... generally support the notion that evidence of a prior criminal record increases the likelihood of conviction and that judges' instructions do not prevent people from using such evidence to determine guilt, the possibility remains that subjects are using the information in a legally acceptable way. That is, the higher conviction rates in prior record conditions may be merely a consequence of the defendant's testimony being discounted by his decreased credibility. The present study attempted to rule out that possibility by using previous convictions of several different crimes: one which bears directly on the believability of the defendant's testimony (i.e., perjury) and others which relate to the defendant's propensity to commit the particular crime and not necessarily to his or her disposition to tell the truth. If the law's rationale is correct, more convictions would result when the prior conviction is for perjury; but if jurors are misusing the information, more convictions would result from a prior conviction for the same crime; and an intermediate number of convictions would result from a prior conviction for a dissimilar crime.

METHOD

* * *

Subjects

Subjects were 160 adult men and women who were approached at laundromats, supermarkets, airports, bus terminals, and private homes in the metropolitan Boston area and agreed to participate in the study....

Cases

Written, two-page descriptions of two hypothetical cases, one involving auto theft and one involving murder, were given to the subjects. These case summaries included various facts of the case, the testimony of the defendant and several other witnesses, and instructions as to the elements which would be necessary in order to find the defendant guilty beyond a reasonable doubt. Through pilot testing, the cases were designed in such a way that the guilt or innocence of the accused was ambiguous. Four prior record conditions accompanied each case: no mention of the defendant's prior record, previous conviction for the same crime, previous conviction for a dissimilar crime (murder in the auto theft case and auto theft in the murder case), and previous conviction for perjury.... Included in the case summaries of subjects in the latter three conditions were instructions by the judge that they were not to consider the evidence of the defendant's prior record as indicating that the defendant has criminal tendencies or dispositions but to use this evidence solely to assess the believability of his testimony.[5]

Procedure

... After they had read the case summary, subjects were given a questionnaire which asked them to indicate: (1) whether they thought the accused person was guilty or not guilty of the charge; (2) how certain they were of their verdict on a ten-point scale; (3) the credibility of each witness, including the defendant, on a ten-point scale; (4) the major reasons they reached their decision in the case; [and] (5) how much the defendant's prior conviction had influenced their guilty/not guilty verdict on a seven-point scale....

RESULTS

The findings pertaining to the defendant's credibility are presented in Table 1. The credibility ratings of the defendant did not vary as a function of prior conviction or case.... It is particularly important to note that the defendant's credibility was not significantly higher with no prior conviction [or] significantly lower with a prior conviction for perjury, indicating that the evidence of prior convictions did not affect ratings of the defendant's credibility. In addition, the credibility rating of the defendant was significantly lower than that of the other witnesses in each case. On a scale from 0 (not at all credible) to 10 (completely credible), the average credibility rating of the defendant in the auto theft and murder cases, respectively, was 3.58 and 3.18, while the average credibility rating of the [other] witnesses in each case was 7.52 and 7.30.

Conviction rates varied as a function of prior conviction (see Table 2).... Combining both cases, ... defendants with no prior record had a significantly lower conviction rate than defendants with any of the three types of prior convictions. Conversely, defendants previously convicted of

5. The instructions used in the case summaries are a shortened version of the actual instructions to jurors on the use of prior conviction evidence typically used in Massachusetts.

TABLE 1
MEAN RATINGS OF THE DEFENDANT'S CREDIBILITY

	Case		
Prior Conviction	*Auto Theft*	*Murder*	*Mean*
None	4.45	2.95	3.70
Same	3.40	2.90	3.15
Dissimilar	3.20	4.20	3.70
Perjury	3.25	2.65	2.95

TABLE 2
PERCENT OF JURORS VOTING TO CONVICT

	Case		
Prior Conviction	*Auto Theft*	*Murder*	*Mean*
None	35%	50%	42.5%
Same	80	70	75.0
Dissimilar	70	35	52.5
Perjury	70	50	60.0

the same crime had a significantly higher conviction rate than defendants previously convicted of perjury or a dissimilar crime. . . .

. . . [F]ifty-six percent of the subjects reported they felt that the evidence of the defendant's prior conviction increased the likelihood that he was guilty, while thirty-eight percent reported that it did not influence the likelihood of the defendant's guilt. . . Thirteen percent of the subjects who found the defendant guilty stated that the prior conviction was the critical factor in reaching their verdict. Two-thirds of these subjects were in the same-prior-conviction condition while only one-third were in the perjury condition. . . .

DISCUSSION

. . . If prior convictions were used to make only credibility judgments, we reasoned, the prior conviction for perjury would have done the most to vitiate the defendant's credibility. In fact, credibility judgments were unaffected by prior conviction condition. . . . The defendant's credibility is already so much lower than that of the other witnesses (because it obviously is in the defendant's self-interest to give testimony which favors his or her position) that the admission of prior convictions does not reduce the credibility of the defendant further. . . .

Although the defendant's credibility did not vary by prior record condition, conviction rates *did* vary as a function of the existence and type of prior record.... Note that ... perjury prior convictions do not increase conviction rates more than the other prior convictions do.... Therefore, it appears that the mock jurors used the prior conviction evidence to help them judge the likelihood that the defendant committed the crime charged. Also interesting to note is that the subjects were willing to state that the prior conviction evidence increased the likelihood of the defendant's guilt and was the reason they found him guilty, even though they had been instructed not to use the information for that purpose. The key finding, then, is that, at least for these mock jurors, prior conviction evidence does not have its impact on verdicts by way of an intervening impact on perceptions of credibility....

D. REHABILITATION

Problem 4.6

Rehabilitating the Witness

The defendant is standing trial for bank robbery. After the prosecution rests, the defendant calls Louise Johnson as an alibi witness. On direct examination by defense counsel, Johnson testifies that at the time of the bank robbery, she and the defendant were having a late lunch at the Circle Deli. Consider each of the following scenarios separately:

1. On cross-examination of Johnson, the prosecutor asks, "Aren't you in business with the defendant's father?" and Johnson answers, "Yes." May the defendant now call a witness to testify that Johnson's reputation for truthfulness and veracity is good?

2. On cross-examination of Johnson, the prosecutor asks, "Isn't it true that, on the day of the bank robbery, the Circle Deli was closed for a religious holiday?" Johnson answers, "That's right—I forgot. We had to eat next door at Rosie's instead." May the defendant now call a witness to testify that Johnson's reputation for truthfulness and veracity is good?

3. On cross-examination of Johnson, the prosecutor asks, "Didn't you state in an application for a bank loan that you had no outstanding debt, when in fact you still owed $82,000 in student loans?" Johnson answers, "Yes." May the defendant now call a witness to testify that Johnson's reputation for truthfulness and veracity is good?

4. After Johnson completes her testimony, the prosecutor offers evidence that six years earlier she was convicted of armed

robbery and sentenced to serve four years in state prison. The defendant then calls Johnson's neighbor, who testifies that he has known Johnson for eight years and that, in his opinion, she is a truthful person. On cross-examination of the neighbor, may the prosecutor ask, "Do you know that Ms. Johnson stated in an application for a bank loan that she had no outstanding debt, when in fact she still owed $82,000 in student loans?"

CHARACTER AND CREDIBILITY: STUDY GUIDE (PART III)

Rehabilitating the Credibility of a Witness

This section and the next, Extrinsic Evidence, add little new law. They simply explore the consequences of rules we already have studied.

"Rehabilitation" concerns a party's attempts to *support* a witness's character for truthfulness. As the second sentence of Rule 608(a) makes clear, one party may rehabilitate its own witness's character for truthfulness *only after the other party has attacked* the witness's character for truthfulness. The tricky issue is determining what constitutes an attack on the witness's character for truthfulness. Any of the forms of attack provided in Rules 608 and 609 clearly qualifies. Therefore if one party has:

(1) offered opinion or reputation testimony of the witness's bad character for truthfulness (Rule 608(a)); or

(2) elicited on cross-examination evidence of specific acts of the witness probative of untruthful character (Rule 608(b)); or

(3) offered evidence of a past conviction of the witness (Rule 609),

the other party may use any of the techniques permitted in Rule 608 to rehabilitate the witness's character for truthfulness.

Can an attack on the truthfulness of a witness's testimony *in this proceeding* constitute an attack on the witness's *general character for truthfulness*? Recall that there are at least three ways to attack the truthfulness of a witness's testimony in this proceeding: evidence of bias, contradiction by past inconsistent statement, and contradiction by conflicting evidence. The Advisory Committee's Note to Rule 608(a) decrees flatly that "[e]vidence of bias or interest does not" qualify as an attack on the witness's character for truthfulness under Rule 608(a). (RB 127–28.) Reasonable people could disagree with the advisory committee on this point. One could argue for example that Detective Mark Fuhrman's racism went not merely to his bias in the O.J. Simpson case, but to his general character for truthfulness. It is probably wise, however, to accept the Advisory Committee's Note as authoritative.

Evidence that contradicts a witness's specific testimony *may* call in question the witness's general character for truthfulness. The advisory committee writes: "Whether evidence in the form of contradiction is an attack upon the character of the witness must depend upon the circumstances." (RB 128.) The Advisory Committee's Note offers no further guidance on this point, but one thing seems clear: If the contradicted testimony can be explained as a *mistake* of perception, memory, or narration and might not be a lie at all, the contradiction would *not* qualify as an attack on character for truthfulness. If, on the other hand, the contradicting evidence suggests the witness has lied intentionally and pervasively, the evidence might well constitute an attack on character for truthfulness. Trial courts must in good judgment decide whether an attack in the form of contradiction has taken this pervasive, broad-based form.

Refer again to the impeachment evidence flowchart at page 260, which attempts to capture this evidentiary scheme. A litigant may attack a witness's character for truthfulness—and hence pass through the first propensity box—as permitted by Rules 608 and 609. Occasionally, as represented by the dashed lines on the right, contradictory evidence amounts to an attack on truthful character. Once a litigant has attacked the witness's character for truthfulness, the opposing lawyer may support the witness's character for truthfulness—and hence go through the second propensity box—as permitted by Rule 608.

The truthfulness of a witness's testimony *in this proceeding* may be corroborated by *non*character evidence without regard to the constraints imposed by Rule 608. That is, if a witness has testified that the light was red, a litigant may offer any kind of evidence otherwise permitted by the rules to show that the light indeed was red. This evidence may take the form of a photograph, the testimony of another eyewitness, or the testimony of an expert about the way the traffic signal was functioning at the relevant moment. The litigant need not wait for the opposing party to attack the first witness's testimony or her character for truthfulness. Because the evidence is being offered to prove the color of the light—not to support the first witness's character for truthfulness—it is not constrained by any of the character evidence rules. The court may, however, exclude the evidence under Rule 403 as cumulative (i.e., time wasting) or under other rules we have not yet studied.

Practice

Look again at Problem 4.6 (*Rehabilitating the Witness*), at page 307. Here are some suggested answers:

(1) *Inadmissible.* Evidence of Johnson's bias is not an attack on her character for truthfulness. (ACN to FRE 608(a), RB 127–28.) Rule 608(a) therefore forbids evidence in support of Johnson's character for truthfulness.

(2) *Probably inadmissible.* Rule 608(a) permits evidence in support of Johnson's character for truthfulness only after that character has been attacked. Evidence that specifically contradicts one aspect of Johnson's testimony probably does not amount to an attack on her character for truthfulness, especially as Johnson might have been merely mistaken (and not intentionally untruthful) in her original testimony about where she and the defendant ate. As the advisory committee wrote, "Whether evidence in the form of contradiction is an attack upon the character of the witness must depend upon the circumstances." (ACN to FRE 608(a), RB 128.) Here the circumstances are a single contradiction exposing a possible memory lapse and hence no attack on character.

(3) *Admissible.* The prosecutor's question about the loan application appears to be an acceptable way under Rule 608(b)(1) to attack Johnson's character for truthfulness. Now that her character for truthfulness has been attacked, Rule 608(a) permits the defendant to offer opinion or reputation evidence in support of Johnson's character for truthfulness.

(4) *Admissible.* Evidence of Johnson's armed robbery conviction appears to be an acceptable way under Rule 609(a)(1)(A) to attack her character for truthfulness. Now that Johnson's character for truthfulness has been attacked, Rule 608(a) permits the defendant to call Johnson's neighbor to support her character for truthfulness with opinion or reputation evidence. Rule 608(b)(2) in turn permits the prosecutor to cross-examine the neighbor about "specific instances" of Johnson's conduct "to attack . . . [her] character for truthfulness." The point of the prosecutor's question is to test whether the neighbor's opinion of Johnson's credibility is both well informed and well considered.

Problem 4.7

Bolstering

Angelita Kettles was the government's chief witness at the trial of Vernon Bonner, charged with swindling Kettles out of her Veterans Administration (VA) benefit payments. Trial ended in Bonner's conviction. On appeal he challenged the admission of testimony by two character witnesses who told jurors of their high opinion of Kettles's honesty.

Rejecting Bonner's complaint, the Seventh Circuit Court of Appeals wrote:

> "Witness bolstering," or "offering evidence solely for the purpose of enhancing a witness's credibility before that credibility is attacked," is impermissible. . . . Once the credibility of the witness has been challenged, however, such evidence may be offered to rehabilitate a witness in the eyes of the jury. *See* [unrestyled] FED. R. EVID. [608(a)] ("evidence

of truthful character is admissible only after the character of the witness for truthfulness has been attacked"). The district court found that Angelita's character had been challenged and thus that rehabilitation evidence was proper.

Bonner disagrees. . . . [W]e find ample evidence in the record to support the district court's view. In his opening statement, after setting out his version of the events, Bonner's counsel stated: "Now, I don't expect Ms. Kettles to agree to that, because now she is receiving government benefits again, and she had been cut off in the past." He also suggested that Angelita would not confirm Bonner's story because she had recently been cleared of the investigation [into the disappearance of her VA benefits]. On cross-examination, Angelita was questioned by the defense about her receipt of money from the VA in connection with the fact that she "would have to testify against Mr. Bonner." These were all statements that implied that Angelita might have gained some advantage from cooperating with the government's case, and as such, they are precisely the kind that allow for testimony aimed at rehabilitation of the witness's character. Given these attacks on her credibility, the district court did not err in admitting the evidence Bonner has challenged.

Do you agree? *See United States v. Bonner*, 302 F.3d 776, 780–81 (7th Cir. 2002).

E. USE OF EXTRINSIC EVIDENCE

Problem 4.8
Offering Proof

1. On cross-examination of Louise Johnson, the defendant's alibi witness, the prosecutor asks, "Didn't you state on an application for a bank loan that you had no outstanding debt, when in fact you still owed $82,000 in student loans?" Johnson answers, "No." May the prosecutor now call the bank's loan officer to testify that Johnson indeed claimed she had no outstanding debt as well as a record-keeper from the student loan agency to testify about the status of her student loans?

2. On cross-examination of Johnson, the prosecutor asks, "Aren't you in business with the defendant's father?" Johnson

answers, "No." May the prosecutor now call a witness to testify that Johnson is in business with the defendant's father?

CHARACTER AND CREDIBILITY: STUDY GUIDE (PART IV)

Extrinsic Evidence

There is a common-law principle that *extrinsic evidence will not be admitted on a collateral matter.* Exactly what constitute "extrinsic evidence" and a "collateral matter" depends somewhat on circumstances. Perhaps it is best to focus on the two specific contexts in which the issue arises. As you read the next few pages, note that a clear understanding of the meaning of "extrinsic evidence" and "collateral matter" is *not* essential to a correct understanding of the relevant rules of admissibility.

In the Context of Character Evidence

There are two points in the rules governing character evidence where the litigant reaches a dead end. First, under Rule 405(a) the litigant may ask a character witness on cross-examination whether that witness has heard of a specific act committed by the person about whose character the witness is testifying (*cf. Michelson*). Regardless of the witness's answer, the lawyer may present no other evidence (i.e., no *extrinsic* evidence) regarding the act.

Second, under Rule 608(b) the litigant may cross-examine a witness about specific instances of conduct that bear on character for truthfulness. But the rule explicitly states that "[e]xcept for a criminal conviction under Rule 609, extrinsic evidence is not admissible to prove specific instances of a witness's conduct." If the witness denies having done (or having heard of) the specific act, the lawyer may present no other evidence about it. "Thus, there is an inescapable irony associated with Rule 608(b) impeachment—it works only when the witness is honest enough to acknowledge the prior impeaching acts." *Behler v. Hanlon*, 199 F.R.D. 553, 559 (D. Md. 2001).

In both of these circumstances the litigant must "take the answer of the witness" to the question posed on cross-examination. C. MUELLER & L. KIRKPATRICK, EVIDENCE § 6.27, at 506–07 (5th ed. 2012). The matter in question (the defendant's character in the first case, a witness's character in the second) is deemed "collateral," not directly probative of the issues in dispute. And evidence of specific acts beyond what may be learned on cross-examination is deemed "extrinsic," meaning (somewhat circularly) "more than" or "outside of" what can be learned on cross-examination.

Extrinsic evidence that tends to prove *both* a collateral matter *and something else* may well be admissible. As the advisory committee writes, Rule 608(b) "impose[s] an absolute bar on extrinsic evidence only if the *sole* purpose for offering the evidence was to prove the witness' character for veracity." (ACN to 2003 Amendment to FRE 608(b), RB 130 (emphasis added).) That's the lesson of *United States v. Abel*, 469 U.S. 45 (1984), and *United States v. Pisari*, 636 F.2d 855 (1st Cir. 1981). In *Abel* the defendant called Witness A, who testified helpfully for the defendant. On cross-examination the prosecutor asked Witness A if he and the defendant belonged to a secret organization whose members were supposed to lie, steal, or kill on one another's behalf. That evidence was arguably admissible for either of two purposes:

(1) Witness A's membership in an organization that subscribed to lying was a specific instance of conduct that tended to show Witness A's character for untruthfulness under Rule 608(b)(1); and

(2) Witness A's membership, together with the defendant, in an organization that required its members to lie on one another's behalf tended to show Witness A's *bias* toward the defendant.

Witness A denied knowledge of the organization. The prosecutor then called Witness B to testify that Witness A and the defendant indeed were members of the organization.

The question before the Supreme Court was whether Witness B's testimony was properly admitted. If the only basis for the original question posed to Witness A had been the first one stated above, any further evidence on the point would have been inadmissible, because Rule 608(b) forbids extrinsic evidence about specific instances of conduct that bear only on character for truthfulness. But as we have seen, evidence of bias is not character evidence governed by Rule 608, so a witness's bias is not deemed collateral. In the words of a Massachusetts court, "evidence tending to show a witness's bias, prejudice, or motive to lie is so significant that it is not considered a mere collateral matter but is deemed exculpatory evidence that may be established by extrinsic proof as well as by impeachment through cross-examination." *Commonwealth v. O'Neil*, 51 Mass. App. Ct. 170, 178 (2001). Hence the prosecutor in *Abel* was free to offer Witness B's testimony to contradict Witness's A's testimony on the question of bias. That is, although Witness B's testimony was inadmissible as to purpose (1), it was admissible as to purpose (2). As Justice Rehnquist wrote (somewhat cryptically) for the Court, "It would be a strange rule of law which held that relevant, competent evidence which tended to show bias on the part of a witness was nonetheless inadmissible because it also tended to show that the witness was a liar." 469 U.S. at 56.

Pisari presented a similar problem, but different facts compelled the opposite result. On cross-examination of the defendant, charged with robbery at knifepoint, the prosecutor asked, "In late 1977, did you commit any robberies by knife?" The defendant denied any such robbery, albeit hesitantly:

> *Q*: In late 1977, did you commit any robberies by knife?
>
> *A*: In 1977? By knife? Did I commit any robberies?
>
> [DEFENSE COUNSEL]: I object to that, your Honor.
>
> THE WITNESS: No.
>
> THE COURT: He said no. All right.
>
> THE WITNESS: No. I didn't, wait a minute. 1977? Did I commit any robberies?
>
> *Q*: Late 1977, any robberies by knife?
>
> *A*: I—no. I have not committed any robberies by knife in 1977.

636 F.2d at 857. The prosecutor then called an ATF agent to testify that the defendant had told him he committed a knife robbery in 1977.

The question before the court was the admissibility of the ATF agent's testimony. The answer turned on the purpose for which the prosecutor initially asked about the 1977 robbery. The defendant had not been *convicted* of the knife robbery or even prosecuted for it, so the evidence could not come in under Rule 609. Nonetheless, evidence of the crime was arguably admissible for either of two purposes:

(1) as a specific instance of conduct tending to show the defendant's character for untruthfulness under Rule 608(b); and

(2) as evidence of a previous act so similar to the knife robbery with which the defendant stood charged that it tended to show identity and was therefore admissible under Rule 404(b).

Had the original question posed to the defendant been permissible under Rule 404(b) (the second purpose listed above), the ATF agent's testimony would have been admissible under the reasoning of *Abel.* Because evidence that comes in for some "other purpose" under Rule 404(b) is not character evidence, it is not constrained by the rules governing character evidence. The Court of Appeals ruled, however, that evidence of the previous knife robbery was not admissible under Rule 404(b) because the similarities between the two robberies were not "so distinctive as to give rise to an inference that the same person was involved in both."

That ruling left only one possible route of admissibility for the original question asked on cross-examination—to show character for untruthfulness under Rule 608(b)(1). It is hardly clear that an old knife-point robbery would have been "probative of [Pisari's] truthfulness or untruthfulness" as required by that rule.* But even if the prosecutor's

* I thank Professor John Garvey for raising this point.

initial inquiry was proper, Rule 608(b) clearly barred the follow-up questioning of the ATF agent, which constituted extrinsic evidence. The prosecutor therefore had no further recourse once the defendant denied the earlier robbery (except perhaps to prosecute the defendant for perjury). Because neither of the two theories of admissibility permitted the testimony of the ATF agent, the Court of Appeals reversed the defendant's conviction.

An important lesson of this segment is that Rule 608(b)'s bar against extrinsic evidence applies only to evidence offered to show a witness's general *character for truthfulness*. The rule places no restriction on extrinsic evidence offered to show that a witness lied about noncharacter matters *in this case*. A lawyer therefore may offer any sort of evidence otherwise permitted by the rules to prove that a witness is biased or to contradict a witness's testimony.

In the Context of Contradicting Specific Testimony

In a case involving a collision at an intersection, it is essential to know what color the traffic light was. Therefore, if a witness says the light was green, a lawyer may call another witness to say it was red. The matter is not collateral, so extrinsic evidence is allowed.

If, however, the first witness says that a car parked on the far side of the intersection was red, the actual color of the car might be a collateral point in the sense that it is not probative of the color of the light. Still, one might argue that the true color *of the car* is a way to test the accuracy of the witness's perception and memory of the color *of the light*.

So could a lawyer call another witness to testify about the car's color? Under the common-law *Hitchcock* rule the answer probably would have been no. That rule held that a litigant could offer extrinsic evidence on a particular subject to contradict a witness only if that subject had "such a connection with the issue [in dispute], that [the litigant] would be allowed to give it in evidence" independent of its value in contradicting the witness. *Attorney General v. Hitchcock*, 1 Exch. 91, 99 (Eng. 1847). Because the color of the car became relevant only after an opposing witness testified about it and is relevant now only to test that witness's perception and memory, the litigant initially could not have offered evidence about it. Note, however, that the litigant could cross-examine the witness about the color of the car—"Isn't it true that the car was blue and not red as you have testified?"—because cross-examination is not deemed extrinsic evidence.

But one can easily imagine a situation in which the witness's lies or mistakes, although all about matters that would be deemed collateral under the *Hitchcock* rule, are so pervasive that it would seem unfair to deny the opposing party the chance to expose them. For that reason, the mechanical *Hitchcock* rule has given way to the more flexible, fact-bound approach of Rule 403:

> The better approach—and one in accord with the structure of the federal rules—would be to eliminate mechanical application of the "collateral" test in favor of the balancing approach mandated by Rule 403. Evidence at which the collateral test is primarily directed, which is relevant solely because it suggests that the witness may have lied about something in the past, would generally be excluded because of its low probative value and its tendency to prejudice the jury. Evidence of higher probative value would be assessed in terms of its impact on the jury in light of the particular circumstances presented.

3 WEINSTEIN, EVIDENCE § 607[06], at 607–71–72 (1978). Mueller and Kirkpatrick are more succinct: "Counterproof is admissible if it contradicts on a matter that counts, but not otherwise." MUELLER & KIRKPATRICK, *supra*, § 6.47, at 565. *Accord United States v. Fonseca*, 435 F.3d 369, 374–77 (D.C. Cir. 2006), *cert. denied* 552 U.S. 829 (2007).

The advisory committee has endorsed this more modern approach. The committee's note to the 2003 amendment to Rule 608(b) says that "the amendment leaves the admissibility of extrinsic evidence offered for [noncharacter-based] grounds of impeachment (such as contradiction, prior inconsistent statement, bias and mental capacity) to Rules 402 and 403." (RB 130.)

Practice

Look again at Problem 4.8 (*Offering Proof*), at page 311. Here are suggested answers:

1. *Inadmissible.* There is no indication Johnson was convicted of anything, so Rule 609 does not apply. The false claim on the loan application probably qualifies as a specific instance of conduct probative of untruthfulness under Rule 608(b). But that rule specifically bars extrinsic evidence of such conduct.

2. *Admissible.* The prosecutor's question went to Johnson's bias. Because bias is not deemed a collateral matter, extrinsic evidence to prove bias is allowed. *See Abel.*

Problem 4.9
Selfish Lies

At Thomas Hall's trial for conspiracy to run a clandestine drug lab, Brenda Schriner testified that Hall permitted her and a third person to operate the lab in Hall's home. Schriner already had pled guilty to operating the lab. Prosecutors promised her probation if she testified against all others involved in the crime.

Before trial Hall advised the judge that he intended to call as witnesses John David Parker and Jim Mikolash. As summarized by the Wyoming Supreme Court, Parker would testify that Schriner once had "falsely accused him of possessing methamphetamine in order to divert the authorities' attention from her to Parker." Mikolash would say "that Schriner threatened to report him to the Division of Criminal Investigation [for drug-related crimes] if he refused to fix her car."

"Hall's theory," the Wyoming high court wrote in reviewing the case, "was that Schriner was a methamphetamine addict who used such threats to gain one sort of advantage or another, thus to promote her own self-interest. Furthermore, the purport of the evidence was in part to demonstrate her lack of truthfulness, but of equal importance was that it also demonstrated her propensity to report to authorities if it served to further her self-interest." The court added later that "Hall's theory was that Schriner had a motive to slant her testimony, so as to implicate him in the clandestine laboratory operation, in order to achieve her desired goal of being placed on probation—i.e., her self-interest gave her a motive to lie or exaggerate."

Assume the Federal Rules of Evidence apply. Should the trial judge have permitted Mikolash and Parker to testify as Hall proposed? What are the best arguments for both sides? *See Hall v. State*, 109 P.3d 499 (Wyo. 2005).

CHAPTER 5

THE RAPE SHIELD LAW

A. HISTORICAL BACKDROP

PEOPLE V. ABBOT

Supreme Court of Judicature of New York.
19 Wend. (N.Y.) 192 (1838).

By the Court, COWEN, J.... The question to the prosecutrix herself, whether she had not had previous criminal connection with other men, was, I think, proper.... In [a rape] case the material issue is on the willingness or reluctance of the prosecutrix—an act of the mind. These offenses, as well as the kindred moral crime of mere seduction, to which, on examination, they often dwindle down, are, in their very nature, committed under circumstances of the utmost privacy. The prosecutrix is usually, as here, the sole witness to the principal facts, and the accused is put to rely for his defense on circumstantial evidence. Any fact tending to the inference that there was not the utmost reluctance and the utmost resistance, is always received. That there was not an immediate disclosure, that there was no outcry, though aid was at hand and that known to the prosecutrix, that there are no indications of violence to the person, are put as among the circumstances of defense; not as conclusive, but as throwing distrust upon the assumption that there was a real absence of assent, 1 HALE, P.C. 633. A mixed case will not do; the connection must be absolutely against the will; and are we to be told that previous prostitution shall not make one among those circumstances which raise a doubt of assent?—that the triers should be advised to make no distinction in their minds between the virgin and a tenant of the stew?—between one who would prefer death to pollution, and another who, incited by lust and lucre, daily offers her person to the indiscriminate embraces of the other sex? And how is the latter case to be made out? How more directly and satisfactorily than by an examination of the prosecutrix herself? ...

On a question of *scienter* you may show other acts, as in passing counterfeit money or bills. Why? Because in the practiced vender of bad coin or bad bills we more readily infer a guilty knowledge than in the novice. And will you not more readily infer assent in the practiced Messalina, in loose attire, than in the reserved and virtuous Lucretia?

Both knowledge and assent are affections of the mind, and the mode of proving both, rests on the same principle in the philosophy of evidence.

I am fully aware of the two cases of *Rex v. Hodgson*, Russ. & R. Cr. Cas. 211, and *Rex v. Clarke*, 2 Stark. 241, in which it was held that you shall not be permitted to inquire of the prosecutrix's connection with other men. It is with a view to those cases that I have thought it my duty to consider the question *a priori;* and I must say that they appear to me entirely anomalous, not only when compared with the cases in respect to circumstantial evidence generally, but with adjudications in respect to evidence receivable on trials for this very crime. It seems, in the first place, to be perfectly agreed that you may prove the prosecutrix to be in fact (not merely by general reputation, but in fact) a common prostitute; because, say Mr. East and Mr. Roscoe, that is a proper circumstance to be submitted to the jury. 1 EAST C.L. 444, 445; ROSCOE, CR. EV. 708. It has been repeatedly adjudged that, in the same view, you may also show a previous voluntary connection between the prosecutrix and the prisoner. *Rex v. Aspinwall*, 2 Stark. Ev. 700; *Rex v. Martin*, 6 Carr. & P. 562. Why is this? Because there is not so much probability that a common prostitute or the prisoner's concubine would withhold her assent, as one less depraved; and may I not ask, does not the same probable distinction arise between one who has already submitted herself to the lewd embraces of another, and the coy and modest female, severely chaste and instinctively shuddering at the thought of impurity? Shall I be answered that both are equally under the protection of the law? That I admit, and so are the common prostitute and the concubine. If either have, in truth, been feloniously ravished, the punishment is the same, but the proof is quite different. It requires that stronger evidence be added to the oath of the prosecutrix, in one case than in the other. Shall I be answered that an isolated instance of criminal connection does not make a common prostitute? I answer, yes; it only makes a prostitute, and I admit introduces a circumstance into the case of less moment; but the question is not whether it be of more or less persuasive force; it is one of competency; in other words, whether it be of any force at all....

There must at least be a retrial....

Afterthoughts on **People v. Abbot:** Judge Cowen's suggestion that we "more readily infer assent in the practiced Messalina, in loose attire, than in the reserved and virtuous Lucretia" is among the most notorious passages in all American law. But where does it fit in the realm of evidence?

Imagine a world governed by the Federal Rules of Evidence as you know them, but without the rape shield provision now embodied in Rule 412. Under what rule could a defendant charged with sexual assault offer evidence of the complainant's alleged prostitution? Assume there is no evidence that the defendant and the complainant had engaged in an act of prostitution. Rather, assume the defendant wished to show that the complainant had taken money from other men for sex. Under the Federal Rules, would Judge Cowen have been correct to say that the defendant "may prove the prosecutrix to be in fact (not merely by general reputation, but in fact) a common prostitute"?

STATE V. SIBLEY

Supreme Court of Missouri
131 Mo. 519 & 132 Mo. 102 (1895).

■ BURGESS, J.—From a conviction and sentence to imprisonment in the penitentiary for a term of two years for defiling, debauching, and carnally knowing one Lula Hawkins, a female under the age of eighteen years, who was charged to have been confided to his care and protection, defendant appealed.

Lula is the daughter of defendant's wife, Roxie, by a former husband, and at the time of her mother's marriage with defendant was about nine years of age.... She testified that when she was between twelve and thirteen years of age, and about the first of July, 1887, ... during the absence of her mother from home, defendant had criminal connection with her by force and against her will. That ... after that time defendant had criminal connection with her on different occasions, for as many as thirty-five to forty times.... That from this intercourse with defendant she became pregnant, and in about eight months thereafter, in the city of St. Louis, where she had gone to be confined, ... she was delivered of a stillborn child of which defendant was the father. That during her pregnancy defendant gave her medicine to produce an abortion....

Defendant testified as a witness in his own behalf, and denied ever having any improper relations with Lula, ... or that he was the father of her child.

The evidence as to defendant's character for morality and chastity, truth and veracity, was conflicting. He had been twice elected justice of the peace, and had at one time been a member of the county court of Scott county....

Witnesses were permitted over the objection of defendant to testify that his general character for chastity and virtue was bad. This evidence was, of course, introduced for the purpose of impeaching him as a witness, and not for the purpose of assailing his character as a party defendant, though it is doubtful if its effect was not more disastrous in its application to him in his character as defendant than as witness. No evidence had been offered by him to sustain his character as defendant, and until that was done it could not be directly attacked as such by the state.

In *State v. Grant*, 79 Mo. 113 (1883), it was held that the rule in this state permitting a witness to be impeached by proof of general reputation for unchastity has been confined to females. . . . The more recent decisions of this court, however (*State v. Rider*, 95 Mo. 474 (1888), and *State v. Shroyer*, 104 Mo. 441 (1891)), hold that the rule applies alike to both sexes, and that such reputation may be shown to discredit a male as well as a female witness.

The writer adheres to the rule first stated, and is of the opinion that such evidence is inadmissible in any case for the purpose of impeaching the character of a male witness, and especially in a case like the one in hand, where the defendant's character for chastity is directly involved. It is a matter of common knowledge that the bad character of a man for chastity does not even in the remotest degree affect his character for truth, when based upon that alone, while it does that of a woman. It is no compliment to a woman to measure her character for truth by the same standard that you do that of man's predicated upon character for chastity. What destroys the standing of the one in all the walks of life has no effect whatever on the standing for truth of the other.* Thus in *Bank v. Stryker*, 1 Wheel. Crim. Cas. 332, it is said: "Adultery has been committed openly by distinguished and otherwise honorable members [of the bar] as well in Great Britain as in our own country, yet the offending party has not been supposed to destroy the force of the obligation which they feel from the oath of office." . . . And so Macaulay said, respecting the weakness of Lord Byron for sexual pleasure, "that it was an infirmity he shared with many great and noble men, Lord Somers, Charles James Fox, and others." . . .

The judgment is reversed and the cause remanded. . . . BARCLAY, J., concurs in the result. SHERWOOD, J., . . . [and] ROBINSON, J., concur[ ].

■ GANTT, J.— . . . I dissent from so much of the opinion of the court as discredits and overrules *State v. Rider*, 95 Mo. 474 (1888), and *State v. Shroyer*, 104 Mo. 441 (1891).

I do not consider that *State v. Grant*, 79 Mo. 113 (1883), is authority for the distinction made between the impeachment of male and female witnesses. . . . The case of *Comm. v. Murphy*, 14 Mass. 387 (1817), cited as authority in the *Grant* case, drew no such distinction. . . .

It is important to get at the reason underlying the decision, [which permitted evidence that a female witness was a prostitute,] and the Massachusetts court put it upon the ground of the loss of moral principle. This testimony is admitted upon the ground that the prostitute, by her life of vice, has so impaired her moral sense that the obligation to speak the truth is no longer binding, or has become more or less lax. If this be

* [For a similar view, see *Sharon v. Hill*, 26 F. 337, 360 (C.C.D. Cal. 1885): "[A]s the world goes and is, the sin of incontinence in a man is compatible with the virtue of veracity, while in the case of a woman, common opinion is otherwise."—GF]

true of the female, why not true of her habitual companions; and why, though there be degrees in the vice, may not a man's disregard of the laws of chastity, which compel[s] his association with the prostitute, be shown as tending to prove a disposition to lightly regard the obligations of his oath[?] The rule only admits the evidence when it has ripened into a general reputation for the vice. For my part, I think it rests upon the same foundation whether the witness be male or female. . . .

For these reasons I most respectfully dissent from the views of JUDGE BURGESS on this point. BRACE, C. J., and BARCLAY and MACFARLANE, JJ., concur with me on this proposition.

Afterthoughts on **State v. Sibley:** Judge Burgess wrote for the court that "[w]itnesses were permitted over the objection of defendant to testify that his general character for chastity and virtue was bad. This evidence was, of course, introduced for the purpose of impeaching him as a witness. . . ." Imagine again a world governed by the Federal Rules of Evidence as you know them, but without the rape shield provision now embodied in Rule 412. What rule would have permitted this line of proof?

John Henry Wigmore

A TREATISE ON THE ANGLO-AMERICAN SYSTEM OF EVIDENCE IN TRIALS AT COMMON LAW

(3d ed. 1940, Vol. 3)

§ 924a. **Woman Complainant's Chastity in a Charge of Sexual Crime**

There is . . . at least one situation in which chastity may have a direct connection with veracity, viz. when a *woman or young girl testifies* as complainant against a man charged with a sexual crime. . . . Modern psychiatrists have amply studied the behavior of errant young girls and women coming before the courts in all sorts of cases. Their psychic complexes are multifarious, distorted partly by inherent defects, partly by diseased derangements or abnormal instincts, partly by bad social environment, partly by temporary physiological or emotional conditions. One form taken by these complexes is that of contriving false charges of sexual offences by men. The unchaste (let us call it) mentality finds incidental but direct expression in the narration of imaginary sex-incidents of which the narrator is the heroine or the victim. On the surface the narration is straightforward and convincing. The real victim, however, too often in such cases is the innocent man; for the respect and sympathy naturally felt by any tribunal for a wronged female helps to give easy credit to such a plausible tale. . . .

The modern realist movement having insisted on removing the veil of romance which enveloped all womanhood since the days of chivalry, it is now allowable for judges to look at the facts. The facts are that there exist occasionally female types of excessive or perverted sexuality, just as there are such male types; and that these are often accompanied by a testimonial plausibility which should not be taken at its face value. Only an inquiry into the social and mental history will reveal the degree of credibility. This inquiry the law of Evidence ought to permit to the fullest extent, rejecting the hindrance of rules that were framed without an understanding of these facts.

No judge should ever let a sex-offence charge go to the jury unless the female complainant's social history and mental makeup have been examined and testified to by a qualified physician.

It is time the Courts awakened to the sinister possibilities of injustice that lurk in believing such a witness without careful psychiatric scrutiny. . . .

In 1937–38 this subject was one of twenty placed on the program of the American Bar Association's Committee on the Improvement of the Law of Evidence. . . . The relevant part of their Report is as follows:

> Today it is *unanimously* held (and we say 'unanimously' advisedly) by experienced psychiatrists that the complainant woman in a sex offense should *always* be examined by competent experts to ascertain whether she suffers from some mental or moral delusion or tendency, frequently found especially in young girls, causing distortion of the imagination in sex cases. . . .

B. THE SHIELD LAW

Susan Estrich

REAL RAPE

(1987)

In May 1974 a man held an ice pick to my throat and said: "Push over, shut up, or I'll kill you." I did what he said, but I couldn't stop crying. When he was finished, I jumped out of my car as he drove away.

I ended up in the back seat of a Boston police car. I told the two officers I had been raped by a man who came up to the car door as I was getting out in my own parking lot (and trying to balance two bags of groceries and kick the car door open). He took the car, too.

They asked if he was a crow. That was their first question. A crow, I learned that day, meant to them someone who is black. That was the year the public schools in Boston were integrated.

They asked me if I knew him. That was their second question. They believed me when I said I didn't. Because, as one of them put it, how would a nice (white) girl like me know a crow?

Now they were really listening. They asked me if he took any money. He did; but though I remember virtually every detail of that day and night, I can't remember how much. It doesn't matter. I remember their answer. He did take money; that made it an armed robbery. Much better than a rape. They got right on the radio with that.

We went to the police station first, not the hospital, so I could repeat my story (and then what did he do?) to four more policemen. When we got there, I borrowed a dime to call my father. They all liked that.

By the time we went to the hospital, they were really on my team. I could've been one of their kids. Now there was something they'd better tell me. Did I realize what prosecuting a rape complaint was all about? Did I think I could handle it, I seemed like a nice girl, what a defense lawyer could do....

Late that night, I sat in the Police Headquarters looking at mug shots. I was the one who had insisted on going back that night. My memory was fresh. I was ready. They had four or five to "really show" me; being "really shown" a mug shot means exactly what defense attorneys are afraid it means. But it wasn't any one of them. After that, they couldn't help me very much.... It was late. I didn't have a great description of identifying marks or the like: no one had ever told me that if you're raped, you should not shut your eyes and cry for fear that this is really happening, but should keep your eyes open and focus so you can identify him when you survive. After an hour of looking, I left the police station. They told me they'd get back in touch. They didn't.

A clerk called one day to tell me that my car had been found minus all its tires and I should come sign a release and have it towed.... The women from the rape crisis center called me every day, then every other day, then every week. The police detectives never called at all....

[U]nder the best circumstances, prosecuting a rape case has unique costs for the victim. And many jurisdictions have made it harder still, by imposing unique obstacles in rape cases.... Three centuries ago the English Lord Chief Justice Matthew Hale warned that rape is a charge "easily to be made and hard to be proved, and harder to be defended by the party accused, tho' never so innocent." If it is so difficult for the man to establish his innocence, far better to demand that a woman victim prove hers; under Hale's approach, the one who so "easily" charges rape must first prove her own lack of guilt. That has been the approach of the law. The usual procedural guarantees and the constitutional mandate that the government prove the man's guilt beyond a reasonable doubt have not been considered enough to protect the man accused of rape. The crime has been defined so as to require proof of actual physical resistance by the victim, as well as substantial force by the man. Evidentiary rules have been defined to require corroboration of the victim's account, to penalize women who do not complain promptly, and to ensure the relevance of a woman's prior history of unchastity....

The reform of these rules has been a primary goal of feminist efforts in recent years, and for good reasons. The rules all too often resulted in the victim's being violated a second time—by the criminal justice system. Formally, most of these rules have now been repealed. In practice, many of them are still applied, if not quite as often in the opinions of appellate courts, then in the day-to-day workings of the system.

I am interested in these evidentiary rules not so much as an example of the law of evidence gone awry, but for the light they shed on how the crime of rape has been understood in the courts. Here, as with the definition of the crime itself, the underlying theme is distrust of women; ... the evidentiary rules, like the resistance requirement, serve to enforce the "no means yes" philosophy of social relations and to assure men broad sexual access....

The requirement that the victim's testimony be corroborated in order to support a conviction was, in its heyday, formally applied in a significant minority of American jurisdictions. In practice, it continues to be a critical factor in determining the disposition of rape charges even today. The justification for the formal rule was, quite explicitly, that women lie....

The evidentiary rules relating to the relevance of a woman's sexual past have been even more controversial than the corroboration requirement.... [U]nchastity was relevant both to the issue of consent and to the woman's credibility as a witness.... Some courts restricted evidence of the victim's sexual relations with men other than the defendant to testimony of general reputation; witnesses could be asked if the victim had a "bad" reputation for chastity in the community. Others allowed cross-examination, and even direct evidence, relating to "specific immoral and unchaste acts," so long as not too remote in time. When the woman took the stand to testify, defense counsel could cross-examine her as to the details of any of these past relations with other men. In some states the men themselves might be called as witnesses. As the Nebraska Supreme Court explained it in 1949, evidence of past specific acts must be available, "not only for the purpose of being considered by the jury in deciding the weight and credibility of [the victim's] testimony generally, but for the purpose of inferring the probability of consent and discrediting her testimony relating to force or violence used by the defendant in accomplishing his purpose and her claimed resistance thereto." The court termed this "the modern realist rule," and "the better one." It certainly was the better one for the male defendant. . . .

If a defendant knew of a woman's sexual history, an argument might be made that such knowledge is relevant to determining what he thought at the time of the intercourse, whether he believed that she was consenting to his advances. Even in that case one might conclude that the prejudice of the evidence exceeded its very limited probative value. But the admission of evidence of a woman's sexual history was not limited to cases where the defendant himself knew his victim's reputation or history. The defendant lucky enough to find out, albeit later, that his victim was sexually experienced could and would try to hide behind that fact at trial, if she was willing even to proceed to trial. . . .

The cautionary instruction is a final example of the institutionalization of the law's distrust of women victims through rules of evidence and procedure. Juries are always told that they must be convinced beyond a reasonable doubt of the defendant's guilt. In rape cases, since the nineteenth century they have also been told, sometimes in Hale's own words, that they must be especially suspicious of the woman victim. In a fairly typical version of the instruction, the jury is told "to evaluate the testimony of a victim or complaining witness with special care in view of the *emotional involvement* of the witness and the *difficulty of determining the truth* with respect to alleged sexual activities carried out in private."[102] All women who are forced to have sex therefore have an "emotional involvement" in the event and are not to be totally trusted in their recounting of it. The force of the instruction is, not unintentionally I think, likely to be greatest in those cases where there is some prior "involvement," if not emotion, between the man and the woman. . . .

Focus on
FRE 412

---

102. Model Penal Code and Commentaries § 213.6(5), at 412 (emphasis added).

Sherry F. Colb

"Whodunit" Versus "What Was Done": When to Admit Character Evidence in Criminal Cases

79 N.C. L. REV. 939 (2001)

* * *

No one has yet adequately defended the distinction between a victim's violent character in a self-defense assault (or homicide) case—fair game for the defense—and a victim's sexual predisposition or character in a consent-defense rape case—off-limits to the defense.... After all, most behavior can be classified along a continuum, and knowing where an individual falls along that continuum generally helps us predict what that individual will do on a particular occasion. If X (female) and Y (male) went out on a date, for example, and we wished to place bets on whether X decided to have sex with Y on this date, the knowledge that X regularly decides to have sex with each new man whom she dates would help us calculate the odds, even if we passed no normative judgments upon either X or Y.

If sexual predisposition is a meaningful construct, then why not admit it against the victim in consent-defense rape cases? The answer is that once there is a rape prosecution, we have a piece of information whose significance overwhelms any relevance that the sexual propensity data would have—the victim swears that, on the occasion in question, she did not consent. Consider what this means....

... [W]e would not expect a person—regardless of whether she is sexually active—to claim falsely that a consensual sexual act in which she participated was actually a rape.... To make a rape accusation falsely thus represents an act of significant treachery and dishonesty. The false rape accuser is accordingly a bad (and deviant) actor not for having had consensual sex in the first place, but for having later made a false accusation about it....

To put it differently, it is no more likely that a sexually active woman would carry out such a scurrilous act of false rape accusation than that a woman less sexually experienced would do so. The informative value of an inclination to consent to sexual activity thus vanishes once a woman has leveled an accusation of rape against a man.... [T]he fact of that accusation becomes salient and the relevant propensities become her propensity for making false accusations about rape or about other serious matters and the defendant's propensity for committing rapes. Any evidence suggesting a predisposition to engage in sexual activity would accordingly be irrelevant....[107]

107. Arguably, this should hold true even under the circumstances covered by the existing exception to the rape shield law for evidence about a victim's previous con-

One might defend the use of such evidence . . . on the ground that its relevance is not absolutely zero. If the victim tried to rule out even the possibility of consent by arguing, for example, that she would never agree to have sex . . ., evidence [that a woman has chosen to have sex with men in the past] would surely be relevant. If there is an inclination and therefore a potential for consent, the victim's consent to sex . . . is not ruled out. There is at least a theoretical plausibility to the defendant's story that there simply would not be if consent were utterly out of the question.

. . . The presence of such a propensity, however, is nonetheless virtually irrelevant when there has been a rape charge. That is, it is irrelevant except to the extent that it allows for the possibility of consent, a possibility that the victim in most cases does not deny. She does not, in other words, say that she could not have consented but swears instead that on this occasion, she did not consent. Under such circumstances, the relevance of an inclination to consent is vanishingly small. For this reason, I speak of it as irrelevant. . . .

Harriett R. Galvin

Shielding Rape Victims in the State and Federal Courts: A Proposal for the Second Decade

70 MINN. L. REV. 763 (1986)

* * *

AN ALTERNATIVE LEGISLATIVE SOLUTION

The response of state legislatures to advocates of rape-shield legislation was swift and far-reaching. By 1976, over half of the states had enacted statutes governing the admissibility of sexual conduct evidence in rape trials. At present, forty-eight states, the federal government, and the military have such provisions. . . . *

sensual relationship with the defendant. Her having consented to have sex with him in the past does not make her more likely to be leveling a false rape accusation against him on this occasion. Evidence about a preexisting relationship between the defendant and the victim may be a necessary part of providing the context for the events in question, but specifying that their relationship was sexual need not be. The suggestion, implicit in the rule, that consent on prior occasions makes the victim's complaint less likely to be true, is therefore flawed, for the same reasons as I outline in criticizing the notion that sexual propensity evidence is relevant to rape cases generally.

* [At the time of Galvin's article Utah had no rape-shield law, and Arizona limited evidence of a victim's other sexual conduct

[B]efore the enactment of rape-shield laws, evidence of the complaining witness's sexual conduct was treated as a species of character proof. Evidence that a complainant had engaged in sexual relations outside of marriage was admissible to establish unchaste character, from which the inference of consent on a particular occasion could be drawn. The purpose and effect of the rape-law reform movement was to highlight the sexist assumptions behind this evidentiary doctrine. Reformers convincingly demonstrated that the concept of unchastity as a character trait, from which consent could be inferred, was simply outmoded in light of contemporary sexual mores and the changed status of women in our society. Empirical data showed that the world of women does not neatly divide into the chaste and the unchaste, or those "who don't" and those "who do."

The appropriate legislative response to this new outlook would have been simply to abolish the outmoded, sexist-based use of sexual conduct evidence while permitting other uses of such evidence to remain. Two of those other uses [are] evidence of prior sexual conduct between the complainant and the accused to prove consent, and evidence of prior sexual conduct between the complainant and others to provide an alternative explanation for the physical consequences of the alleged rape.... [Neither of these] evidentiary uses rests on the anachronistic and invidious inference of unchaste character, that is, "if she consented with one man, she probably consented with others." Moreover, such noncharacter uses of sexual conduct evidence may be essential to the establishment of a defense. Therefore, to prohibit them might violate the accused's sixth amendment rights.

The invidious unchaste-character inference could have been abolished simply by amending the rule that permits the accused to elicit evidence of a pertinent trait of the victim's character. Such an amendment might take the following form:

> In a prosecution for rape, evidence that the victim has engaged in consensual sexual conduct with persons other than the accused is not admissible to support the inference that a person who has previously engaged in consensual sexual conduct is for that reason more likely to consent to the sexual conduct with respect to which rape is alleged. Evidence of consensual sexual conduct on the part of the victim may, however, be admissible for other purposes.

This proposed amendment is nothing more than a specialized application of the long-standing doctrine, now codified in [unrestyled] Rule 404(b) of the Federal Rules of Evidence, that prohibits using evidence of a person's "other crimes, wrongs, or acts" to prove that person's bad character as the basis for inferring conduct on a specific occasion.... Rule 404(b)

by judicial decision and not by statute. Both states since have enacted rape-shield statutes. *See* ARIZ. REV. STAT. ANN. § 13–1421 (1998); UTAH R. EVID. 412 (1994).—GF]

permits evidence of other crimes, wrongs, or acts for other than propensity purposes, such as to prove identity, opportunity, common plan or scheme, and for other purposes not specifically mentioned in the rule. . . .

Of course, the court must determine, on a case-by-case basis, whether the probative value of the evidence in proving the permissible inference is substantially outweighed by the danger that the jury will use it for the impermissible inference. . . . [U]nder the statute proposed above, the court would balance the probative value of the evidence in proving any noninvidious inference against the danger that the jury would rely on the invidious inference of consent.

Finally, regarding the minority of states that permitted evidence of unchastity for the purpose of impeaching the rape complainant's credibility, this sexually discriminatory use could have been barred by a simple rule or amendment to the rule permitting character evidence to impeach credibility. Such a provision might read as follows:

> In a prosecution for rape, evidence that the victim has engaged in consensual sexual conduct is not admissible to support the inference that a person who has previously engaged in consensual sexual conduct is for that reason less worthy of belief as a witness.[234]

Such a rule would be analogous to Rule 610 of the Federal Rules of Evidence, which similarly puts to rest the archaic practice of allowing parties to introduce evidence of a witness's religious belief or opinions "for the purpose of showing that by reason of their nature [the witness's] credibility is impaired or enhanced." Now, for example, proof that a witness is an atheist may not be offered to show that such witness is unworthy of belief. The Advisory Committee Notes make clear, however, that other uses of such evidence are still permitted, such as to show interest or bias on the part of the witness based upon a church affiliation. Similarly, evidence of the complainant's previous sexual conduct with someone other than the accused may be relevant to show her motive for fabricating the charge or to specifically rebut elements of her testimony. These examples of attacks on the complainant's credibility are distinct from reliance on the inference that merely because the complainant is unchaste, she is more likely to lie under oath.

The basic problem with existing rape-shield legislation is its failure to distinguish between benign and invidious uses of sexual conduct evidence. This failure stems from a misperception by the drafters of the precise wrong to be redressed by reform legislation. The result is not merely bad evidence law; in many instances, the result is constitutional problems that stem from unnecessarily broad enactments. These various problems could have been avoided . . . [if] legislators had clearly under-

234. This proposal . . . [could be added] to Rule 608 of the Federal Rules of Evidence.

stood the underlying evidentiary concepts and had properly incorporated those concepts in the rape-shield statutes.[239] . . .

C. THE LAW IN FORCE

1. PAST SEXUAL BEHAVIOR WITH THE ACCUSED

Problem 5.1

Emails

The defendant, Oliver Jovanovic, and the complainant had dinner together—their first date—on the evening of November 22, 1996. The date followed weeks of online conversations and email correspondence.

At Jovanovic's trial for rape, kidnapping, and assault, the complainant testified that after dinner she and the defendant went to his apartment. The defendant played a pornographic videotape. Then he tied the complainant's arms and legs to his bed frame, dripped hot wax on her body, bit her, and sodomized her. The defendant admitted these acts took place, but claimed they were part of a consensual sadomasochistic encounter.

Although the trial judge admitted much of the email correspondence that preceded the events of November 22, he excluded evidence of certain communications offered by the defendant. In one of these, an email of November 19, the complainant told the defendant about a man she was dating: "He was a sadomasochist and now I'm his slave and [it's] painful, but the fun of telling my friends 'hey I'm a sadomasochist' more than outweighs the torment."

In an email of November 20, also excluded by the court, Jovanovic wrote the complainant: "You're submissive sometimes? Should have told me earlier." The complainant replied,

239. This is not to say that the reformers were unable to grasp the fundamentals of evidence law. It may be more fair to state that they lacked confidence in a predominantly male judiciary to apply fairly a rule that allowed the judiciary considerable discretion. *See* Amsterdam & Babcock, *Proposed Position on Issues Raised by the Administration of Laws Against Rape: Memorandum for the ACLU of Northern California, reprinted in* B. BABCOCK, A. FREEDMAN, E. NORTON & S. ROSS, SEX DISCRIMINATION AND THE LAW 843 (1975) ("We are . . . loath to leave determinations of general 'relevancy' to judges who are too frequently male and too frequently imbued with unread and insensitive attitudes toward women's sexual attitudes and experiences.").

"[Y]es, I'm what those happy pain fiends at the Vault call a 'pushy bottom'." (The appeals court, in its opinion, explained: "The Vault is a club catering to sadomasochists, and a 'pushy bottom' is a submissive partner who pushes the dominant partner to inflict greater pain.")

If this case had been tried in federal court under the Federal Rules of Evidence as they stand today, would the trial judge have been right to exclude these emails? What are the defendant's best arguments for admission? What are the prosecutor's best arguments against? *See People v. Jovanovic*, 700 N.Y.S.2d 156 (App. Div., 1st Dept. 1999).

---

2. Explaining the Source of Physical Evidence

Problem 5.2
Fingerprints

The defendant, charged with rape, worked as the complainant's accountant. The complainant testified that the defendant had never been in her apartment before January 11, 2012, the night of the alleged attack. At about 8:00 p.m. that evening the defendant dropped by to leave some documents for the complainant's signature. She testified he then sexually assaulted her.

The prosecution offered evidence that the defendant's fingerprints were found on the complainant's bedroom bureau. During his testimony the defendant claimed he never visited the complainant on the night of the alleged attack. To explain the presence of his fingerprints in her bedroom, the defendant testified—over the prosecutor's objection—that a month before the alleged attack, he and the complainant had a consensual sexual encounter in her apartment. The defendant offered expert testimony that his fingerprints could have remained intact a month later.

Was the trial judge right to admit the defendant's testimony about the alleged earlier encounter?

---

3. Past Allegedly False Accusations

State v. Smith

Supreme Court of Louisiana.
743 So. 2d 199 (La. 1999).

■ Traylor, Justice. Eual Howard Smith, Jr., was convicted of attempted indecent behavior with a juvenile and sentenced to three years' imprisonment at hard labor. The sentence was suspended and defendant was placed on five years' probation subject to serving three months in parish jail. We granted certiorari to consider defendant's assertion that the trial court improperly precluded him from introducing evidence of prior false allegations of molestation made by the victim. . . .

Facts and Procedural History

During the summer of 1996, the alleged victim, who was twelve years old at the time, told her mother's friend that the defendant, her grandmother's husband, had touched her in inappropriate places, on and off, for several years. . . . Because the victim did not claim the defendant attempted penetration in any manner, there was no physical evidence of abuse, and the outcome of trial rested entirely on her credibility.

During trial, defense counsel cross-examined the victim's mother's friend, Julie, regarding similar accusations the victim had made against her cousin and allegedly subsequently recanted. The State thereafter moved to prevent any further such questioning in accordance with La. C.E. art. 412, the so-called "rape shield statute." In response, defense counsel argued the evidence was not barred by Article 412 because the allegation was false and not of prior sexual behavior, but rather evidence of the victim's state of mind.

Relying on this court's decision in *State v. Allen*, 693 So. 2d 728 (La. 1997), the trial judge held a hearing outside the presence of the jury "under Code of Evidence Article 412" to determine whether the victim actually made the allegations and, if so, whether such allegations were false. The defense first called the victim's mother who testified that the victim made allegations of molestation against her cousin, T.S. When asked whether the victim later retracted those allegations, the witness stated, "Not to me, no." Furthermore, she stated she had no reason to believe those allegations were false. The defense then called the victim, who claimed the accusations were true and denied retracting them. Finally, the defense called the younger brother of T.S., who was also the victim's cousin. The younger brother, M.S., testified that he, T.S., and the victim played together on a regular basis. M.S. testified that when they were rollerblading, the victim said that T.S. had "touched her and all" when she spent the night with her cousins. M.S. stated T.S. denied touching the victim and the victim skated away, but returned and told T.S. she was just joking. After hearing the testimony presented, the trial judge ruled as follows:

> All right. Based on the testimony that we just heard in this hearing under Code of Evidence Article 412, I find that there were no prior false allegations of sexual molestation by the victim. And pursuant to Article 412, if there were, in fact, incidents of sexual molestation, I find that specific instances of the victim's past sexual behavior are not admissible and that the exceptions of their inadmissibility under [La. C.E. art. 412,] Paragraph[s] B–1 and 2 do not apply in this case. Therefore, I will not permit any evidence of prior sexual misconduct, nor will I allow the cross-examination of the victim or evidence of prior false allegations at the trial.

The trial resumed, and defendant was subsequently convicted of attempted indecent behavior with a juvenile.

The court of appeal affirmed defendant's conviction, finding there was no abuse of discretion in the trial court's refusal to permit the presentation of evidence concerning the allegedly false prior allegations of molestation. The court stated:

> *Allen* gives a defendant the right to cross-examine the victim and to present evidence regarding prior false allegations of sexual molestation by the victim, *in the event the court determines there are prior false allegations of sexual molestation by the victim.* In the instant case, the trial court dutifully complied with the hearing requirements as set forth by *Allen* and concluded that any prior accusations of molestation made by the victim were not false.

State v. Smith, 713 So. 2d 1220, 1226 (La. App. 1998) (emphasis in original).

We granted certiorari to address defendant's argument that defense counsel should have been allowed to present to the jury testimony and cross-examination of witnesses regarding the allegations of prior molestation, which were subsequently allegedly recanted, to impeach the victim's credibility at trial.

DISCUSSION

. . . La. C.E. art. 412 bars the introduction of evidence of the victim's past sexual behavior, except that evidence of the victim's past sexual behavior with persons other than the accused . . . is admissible to challenge the source of semen or injury, and evidence of past sexual behavior with the defendant is admissible to show the victim consented to the behavior.[1] . . .

1. Federal Rule of Evidence 412 includes the two exceptions that are found in La. C.E. art. 412. Additionally, [unrestyled] F.R.E. [412(b)(1)(C)] provides that evidence

This court recently addressed the admissibility of prior allegations of sexually assaultive behavior in *State v. Allen*. There, defendant was charged with sexual molestation of his fourteen-year-old niece.... Prior to trial, defendant filed an Article 412 motion seeking to introduce evidence that the victim had previously alleged she had been sexually molested by her maternal grandfather and that the victim's own father avoids his home because he fears being accused of molesting the victim. Additionally, defendant wanted to introduce evidence that the victim had been accused of molesting younger males. The trial judge, who is coincidentally the same judge involved in the instant appeal, denied defendant's motion without a hearing. The trial court held evidence that the victim had been accused of molesting other persons and was involved with persons other than the defendant was barred by La. C.E. art. 412. The court of appeal denied defendant's writ application. Subsequently, this court, recognizing that the trial court failed to specifically address defendant's argument regarding the admissibility of prior allegations of molestation, granted in part defendant's application for certiorari in a per curiam opinion. The opinion states in its entirety:

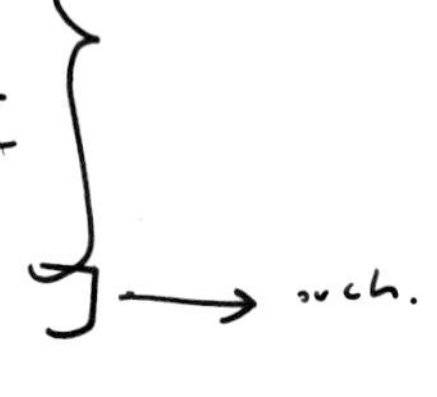

> Granted in part, otherwise denied. The ruling of the trial court is vacated in part. The case is remanded to the trial court for a pre-trial evidentiary hearing on the issue of prior false allegations made by the victim. In the event the court determines there are prior false allegations of sexual molestation by the victim, the defendant shall be allowed to cross-examine the victim and to present evidence regarding same at trial.

State v. Allen, supra.

Thus, in the instant case, when accusations of prior false allegations surfaced, the trial judge, mindful of this court's earlier decision in *Allen*, held a hearing "under Code of Evidence Article 412" to determine whether prior false allegations of sexual molestation had, in fact, been made by the victim. Defendant argues that La. C.E. art. 412 is inapplicable to the instant situation as evidence that the victim had previously accused another male of molesting her and then quickly retracted those accusations is not evidence of past sexual behavior of the victim, but rather impeachment evidence used to attack the victim's credibility. We agree.

As previously discussed, Article 412 prevents the introduction of evidence of the victim's past sexual behavior, with certain limited exceptions. The statute defines "past sexual behavior" as "sexual behavior

of a victim's past sexual behavior is admissible when such evidence is "constitutionally required to be admitted." Although La. C.E. art. 412 does not specifically contain this exception, the official comments recognize this additional exception in the Federal Rules of Evidence and state that La. C.E. art. 412, "like every Article in this Code is necessarily subject to constitutional requirements, and it has not been the general practice of this Code specifically to refer to them." La. C.E. art. 412, Comment (b).

other than the sexual behavior with respect to which the offense of sexually assaultive behavior is alleged." La. C.E. art. 412(F). It has also been described as "sexual history," although not limited to sexual intercourse. State v. Everidge, 702 So. 2d 680 (La. 1997). Here, by attempting to introduce evidence that the victim had accused her cousin of molestation and then retracted the accusation, defendant was not seeking to prove that the victim had engaged in prior sexual behavior or that she had an unchaste character. Rather, defendant sought to prove for impeachment purposes that the victim had, in the past, made false allegations regarding sexual activity. Because the evidence defendant attempted to introduce did not concern the victim's prior sexual behavior, history or reputation for chastity, we conclude that prior false allegations of sexual assault by the victim do not constitute "past sexual behavior" for purposes of our rape shield statute.[2] We hold, therefore, that Article 412 is inapplicable in sexual assault cases where defendant seeks to question witnesses regarding the victim's prior false allegations concerning sexual behavior for impeachment purposes. Consequently, no Article 412 hearing is required when defendant seeks to introduce such evidence. To the extent *State v. Allen* suggests otherwise, it is hereby overruled.

In this case, because the rape shield statute was inapplicable, an Article 412 hearing to determine whether the evidence of prior false allegations of molestation made by the victim was admissible should not have been held.[3] Instead, . . . this evidence directly concerning the victim's credibility could have been admitted provided the trial court determined it met all other standards for admissibility.[4]

CONCLUSION

. . . Because the outcome of this case rested entirely upon the jury's perception of the victim's veracity, the trial court's ruling regarding the victim's prior false allegations of sexual molestation cannot be said to be harmless. Therefore, because defendant has been prejudiced by the confused and erroneous state of the law applied in his case and because his right to a fair trial has been impeded, we must reverse the conviction and remand the case to the trial court for a new trial to be held.

Reversed and remanded.

2. Such a conclusion is in accord with those reached in a number of other jurisdictions. *See also* F.R.E. 412, Advisory Committee Notes to the 1994 Amendments ("Evidence offered to prove allegedly false prior claims by the victim is not barred by Rule 412.") [RB 82].

3. We recognize that the trial judge held the Article 412 hearing because he read *State v. Allen* to require such a hearing although he personally (and correctly) believed Article 412 was inapplicable to the situation at hand: "Well, in *Allen*, . . . I thought that it didn't fall under the requirements of 412 and they ordered me to have a hearing anyway."

4. Of course, the introduction of such evidence is still subject to the requirements of La. C.E. arts. 403, 404, 607, 608 and 613. [Each of these is similar to its counterpart in the Federal Rules.—GF]

■ VICTORY, J., dissents. In my view the evidence should have been excluded under article 403 of the La. Code of Evidence.

Problem 5.3

Smith on Remand

The *Smith* court ruled that "this evidence directly concerning the victim's credibility could have been admitted provided the trial court determined it met all other standards for admissibility." In footnote 4 the court noted that these other requirements of the evidence code include the constraints imposed by Rules 403, 404, and 608. These Louisiana rules are similar to their federal counterparts. Assume the federal rules themselves govern this case:

(1) Would the defendant's proposed inquiries survive scrutiny under Rules 403, 404, and 608? Recall that the defendant in *Smith* hoped "to present to the jury testimony and cross-examination of witnesses regarding the allegations of prior molestation, which were subsequently allegedly recanted, to impeach the victim's credibility at trial." *See* Denise R. Johnson, *Prior False Allegations of Rape:* Falsus in Uno, Falsus in Omnibus? 7 YALE J.L. & FEMINISM 243, 273–75 (1995).

(2) Before the defendant elicits evidence of the victim's past allegations, must he first establish that she made the earlier allegations and that they were false? Was the *Smith* court correct in ruling that the defendant must satisfy the *Huddleston* standard (*see* page 205 above) concerning the falsity of past complaints? In a passage I have deleted, the *Smith* court wrote:

> [W]hen considering the admissibility of such evidence, the question for the trial court is not whether it believed the prior allegations were false, but whether reasonable jurors could find, based on the evidence presented by defendant, that the victim had made prior false accusations. *See* Huddleston v. United States, 485 U.S. 681 (1988) (in ruling on the admissibility of other crimes evidence, the district court "neither weighs credibility nor makes a finding that the Government has proved the conditional fact by a preponderance, [but] simply examines all the evidence in the case and decides whether the jury could reasonably find the conditional fact ... by a preponderance of the evidence").

If the *Huddleston* standard does not control, what rule or standard does determine whether a defendant may inquire about a victim's allegedly false past claim of molestation?

Problem 5.4
Old Accusation

Consider these facts of *State v. Alvey*, 458 N.W.2d 850 (Iowa 1990), *abrogated by State v. Baker*, 679 N.W.2d 7 (Iowa 2004):

> Complainant is twenty-one years old. . . . The offense occurred in March of 1988. The complainant met defendant in a tavern and accepted his invitation to go to his home to meet defendant's daughter. . . . Defendant stopped his car at a secluded spot [and allegedly raped her]. . . .
>
> Defendant sought to . . . [offer] evidence that, in 1984, the complainant had stated she had been raped after engaging in consensual sexual intercourse. . . . [Defense counsel advised the court that] a witness would testify
>
>> I was sitting at the kitchen table at [the victim's cousin's] house. [John] lived there also. I had been staying there for, oh, a month or so and [the complainant] had gone to bed with [John], late hours, early morning hours, whatever. We were all sitting at the kitchen table still partying and visiting and having our fun. And [the complainant] came running out of the bedroom and she said, 'he raped me; he raped me; he raped me.' And she was a little bit upset, but all of us there at the table we knew she hadn't been raped. I mean her sisters . . . sat right there, you know, and chuckled about it.
>
> . . . Both the victim herself and the alleged partner in the past conduct denied the incident.

(1) Assume Iowa's rape shield law is identical to FRE 412. If the prosecutor objected to the defendant's proposed evidence, should the trial judge nonetheless have admitted it? How might the prosecutor have distinguished this case from *Smith*?

(2) Assume the defendant, instead of offering a separate witness to testify about this incident, proposed merely to cross-examine the complainant about it. Would your ruling on admissibility change?

---

4. 404(b)–Style Uses of Evidence of Past Sexual Behavior

The balance of this chapter explores Harriett Galvin's suggestion that Congress should have cast Rule 412 in the mold of Rule 404(b), rather than in the more strongly exclusionary form of the present rule. (*See* pages 329–30 above.) Galvin would have barred evidence of a victim's past sexual behavior only when offered to support the sort of propensity reasoning traditionally banned by Rule 404—that is, when offered "to support the inference that a person who has previously engaged in consensual sexual conduct is for that reason more likely to consent to the sexual conduct with respect to which rape is alleged" (or "is for that reason less worthy of belief as a witness"). Her proposed rule, like Rule 404(b), would provide that "[e]vidence of consensual sexual conduct on the part of the victim may ... be admissible for other purposes."

In what situations would Galvin's proposed rule produce different results from those reached under Rule 412? The next several cases consider various purposes for which defendants have attempted to offer evidence of a victim's past sexual behavior: to prove the victim's bias or motive to lie, to maintain the narrative integrity of the defendant's account, and to show his state of mind at the time of offense. In each context a 404(b)-style rule of the sort Galvin proposes probably would have permitted the defendant's line of proof. In only one of these three contexts, however, is Rule 412 likely to supply the same result—and it does so only because the defendant's constitutional right to confront his accuser overcomes the rule's exclusionary text.

So is Galvin right? Or are we better off with a more strictly exclusionary rule?

---

a. PROOF OF BIAS

OLDEN V. KENTUCKY

488 U.S. 227 (1988).

■ PER CURIAM: Petitioner James Olden and his friend Charlie Ray Harris ... were indicted for kidnaping, rape, and forcible sodomy. [The complainant testified that after the attack, and at] her request, the men then dropped her off in the vicinity of Bill Russell's house....

Russell, who also appeared as a State's witness, testified that on the evening in question he heard a noise outside his home and, when he went out to investigate, saw the complainant* get out of Harris's car. She

* [In both this case and *Stephens v. Miller*, which follows, I have replaced the victim's name with either pronouns or "the complainant." For ease of reading, I have not bracketed these changes.—GF]

immediately told Russell that she had just been raped by petitioner and Harris. . . . Petitioner and Harris asserted a defense of consent. . . .

Although the complainant and Russell were both married to and living with other people at the time of the incident, they were apparently involved in an extramarital relationship. By the time of trial the two were living together, having separated from their respective spouses. Petitioner's theory of the case was that the complainant concocted the rape story to protect her relationship with Russell, who would have grown suspicious upon seeing her disembark from Harris's car. In order to demonstrate the complainant's motive to lie, it was crucial, petitioner contended, that he be allowed to introduce evidence of her and Russell's current cohabitation. Over petitioner's vehement objections, the trial court nonetheless granted the prosecutor's motion *in limine* to keep all evidence of the complainant's and Russell's living arrangement from the jury. Moreover, when the defense attempted to cross-examine the complainant about her living arrangements, after she had claimed during direct examination that she was living with her mother, the trial court sustained the prosecutor's objection.

Based on the evidence admitted at trial, the jury acquitted Harris of being either a principal or an accomplice to any of the charged offenses. Petitioner was likewise acquitted of kidnaping and rape. However, in a somewhat puzzling turn of events, the jury convicted petitioner alone of forcible sodomy. He was sentenced to 10 years' imprisonment.

Petitioner appealed, asserting, *inter alia*, that the trial court's refusal to allow him to impeach the complainant's testimony by introducing evidence supporting a motive to lie deprived him of his Sixth Amendment right to confront witnesses against him. The Kentucky Court of Appeals upheld the conviction. . . .

The Kentucky Court of Appeals failed to accord proper weight to petitioner's Sixth Amendment right "to be confronted with the witnesses against him." That right, incorporated in the Fourteenth Amendment and therefore available in state proceedings, Pointer v. Texas, 380 U.S. 400 (1965), includes the right to conduct reasonable cross-examination. Davis v. Alaska, 415 U.S. 308, 315–16 (1974).

In *Davis v. Alaska*, we observed that, subject to "the broad discretion of a trial judge to preclude repetitive and unduly harassing interrogation . . . , the cross-examiner has traditionally been allowed to impeach, i.e., discredit, the witness." *Id.* at 316. We emphasized that "the exposure of a witness's motivation in testifying is a proper and important function of the constitutionally protected right of cross-examination." *Id.* at 316–17. Recently, in Delaware v. Van Arsdall, 475 U.S. 673 (1986), we reaffirmed *Davis*, and held that "a criminal defendant states a violation of the Confrontation Clause by showing that he was prohibited from engaging in otherwise appropriate cross-examination designed to show a prototypical form of bias on the part of the witness, and thereby 'to expose to the jury the facts from which jurors . . . could appropriately draw inferences relating to the reliability of the witness.' " 475 U.S. at 680 (quoting *Davis*, *supra*, at 318).

In the instant case, petitioner has consistently asserted that he and the complainant engaged in consensual sexual acts and that she—out of fear of jeopardizing her relationship with Russell—lied when she told Russell she had been raped and has continued to lie since. It is plain to us that "[a] reasonable jury might have received a significantly different impression of [the witness'] credibility had [defense counsel] been permitted to pursue his proposed line of cross-examination." *Delaware v. Van Arsdall*, *supra*, at 680. . . .

Here, the complainant's testimony was central, indeed crucial, to the prosecution's case. Her story, which was directly contradicted by that of petitioner and Harris, was corroborated only by the largely derivative testimony of Russell, whose impartiality would also have been somewhat impugned by revelation of his relationship with the complainant. . . .

[T]he judgment of the Kentucky Court of Appeals is reversed, and the case is remanded for further proceedings not inconsistent with this opinion.

It is so ordered.

■ JUSTICE MARSHALL, dissenting [from the summary disposition of the case]. . . .

OLDEN V. KENTUCKY: *Afterthoughts*

Both *Olden* and its principal precedent, *Davis v. Alaska*, 415 U.S. 308 (1974), protect a defendant's Sixth Amendment right to cross-examine an accuser "to show a prototypical form of bias on the part of the witness." (*Olden*, page 340.) The Supreme Court held in *Davis* that a defendant charged with burglary had the right to confront the prosecution's chief eyewitness with questions about the witness's probationary status. As the witness was on probation for burglary, he arguably had an interest in pleasing prosecutors and in denying his own guilt of the crime he pinned on Davis.

As we saw in the last chapter, bias-based impeachment suggests that the witness has a motive to lie *in this case*, not that he has a bad character for truthfulness. (*See* pages 258, 308.) Neither *Davis* nor *Olden* nor any other Supreme Court opinion addresses whether the Confrontation Clause also protects a defendant's right during cross-examination to make a general, character-based attack on a prosecution witness's credibility. This question arises in rape prosecutions in those states with rape-shield laws that, unlike FRE 412, bar inquiry into a victim's past allegedly false complaints of sexual assault. (*Cf.* ACN to 1994 Amendment to FRE 412, RB

82 ("Evidence offered to prove allegedly false prior claims by the victim is not barred by Rule 412.").) If not for such rape-shield provisions, state rules modeled after FRE 608(b) typically would permit a defendant to cross-examine his accuser about past false complaints and to argue that these past lies show her general propensity to lie about rape.

Federal courts of appeals have reached no consensus about a defendant's right on cross-examination to expose a victim's past false complaints. In *Boggs v. Collins*, 226 F.3d 728 (6th Cir. 2000), *cert. denied*, 532 U.S. 913 (2001), the Sixth Circuit reviewed an Ohio rape prosecution in which the trial judge had barred such inquiry. Rejecting the defendant's claim that this ruling frustrated his confrontation right, the circuit court noted that *Davis* "distinguished between a 'general attack' on the credibility of a witness—in which the cross-examiner 'intends to afford the jury a basis to infer that the witness's character is such that he would be less likely than the average trustworthy citizen to be truthful in his testimony'—and a more particular attack on credibility 'directed toward revealing possible biases, prejudices, or ulterior motives as they may relate directly to issues or personalities in the case at hand.'" *Boggs*, 226 F.3d at 736 (quoting *Davis*, 415 U.S. at 316). The *Boggs* court noted that Justice Stewart's concurrence in *Davis* "underscored that the Confrontation Clause was implicated only because Davis was seeking to show bias or prejudice." It quoted Stewart's insistence that *Davis* "'neither holds nor suggests that the Constitution confers a right in every case to impeach the general credibility of a witness through cross-examination.'" *Boggs*, 226 F.3d at 737 (quoting *Davis*, 415 U.S. at 321 (Stewart, J., concurring)).

In an opinion that same year by Judge Richard Posner, the Seventh Circuit agreed, albeit in dictum, that the Confrontation Clause does not protect attacks on a witness's character for truthfulness. Judge Posner wrote that the probative value "of evidence that a person has lied in the past to show that she is lying now is questionable, quite apart from rape-shield laws, since very few people, other than the occasional saint, go through life without ever lying, unless they are under oath." *Redmond v. Kingston*, 240 F.3d 590, 593 (7th Cir. 2001). The Fourth Circuit likewise acknowledged that *Davis* does not protect a defendant's "attacks on the general credibility of the witness," but only "a more particular attack on credibility" focused on the witness's "potential bias or motive to fabricate charges." *Quinn v. Haynes*, 234 F.3d 837, 845 (4th Cir. 2000), *cert. denied*, 532 U.S. 1024 (2001).

Other courts of appeals have defined constitutionally protected cross-examination more expansively. In *Fowler v. Sacramento Cnty. Sheriff's Dep't*, 421 F.3d 1027 (9th Cir. 2005), the Ninth Circuit asked broadly "whether the [defendant's] proffered cross-examination [about the victim's past complaints of sexual molestation] sufficiently bore upon [her] reliability or credibility such that a jury might reasonably have questioned it." The court relied on a plurality opinion in *Pennsylvania v. Ritchie*, 480 U.S. 39

(1987), in which Justice Powell asserted for himself and three other justices that "[o]f course, the right to cross-examine includes the opportunity to show that a witness is biased, *or that the testimony is exaggerated or unbelievable.*" *Id.* at 51–52 (Powell, J.) (emphasis added). "[T]here can be no doubt," the *Fowler* court concluded, that the forbidden cross-examination could have prompted the jury to doubt the victim's story. The trial judge's refusal to permit such inquiry triggered reversal. *Fowler*, 421 F.3d at 1035, 1038–40, 1043–44.

In *White v. Coplan*, 399 F.3d 18 (1st Cir.), *cert. denied sub nom. Cattell v. White*, 546 U.S. 972 (2005), the First Circuit deftly straddled those courts that grant special constitutional status to bias-based cross-examination and those that extend Sixth Amendment protection to character-based attacks too. White, charged with sexual assault, had sought to question his two accusers about charges of sexual assault they had made—allegedly falsely—in the past. Acknowledging that "'general credibility' evidence . . . , under Confrontation Clause standards, may have a lower status," the court said it was "dealing here with something far more potent." Though a victim's "motive may be unknown, . . . if the prior accusations are similar enough to the present ones and shown to be false, a motive can be inferred and from it a plausible doubt or disbelief as to the witness's present testimony." 399 F.3d at 26. Hence past false accusations can *themselves* be evidence of bias, the court said, so defendants have a Sixth Amendment right to ask about them.

Following the First Circuit's lead, the Seventh Circuit recently reached a similar result on similar reasoning. The defendant, charged with sexual abuse of a third-grader whom he mentored at school, wished to cross-examine the boy and offer other evidence about the boy's earlier, seemingly false allegations of sexual abuse by his father. The defendant was "not attempting simply to expose another incident of [the boy's] lack of truthfulness," the court wrote. Citing evidence that the boy resented his father's absence and had leveled his earlier accusation to get his father's attention, the court noted that the boy alleged abuse by his schoolhouse mentor after the boy had moved away and was seeing less of the mentor:

> The jury reasonably could have concluded that [the boy] was prone to use allegations of sexual abuse against father figures as a means either of gaining their attention or . . . of punishing them for abandoning him. . . . In short, "[w]e are dealing here with something far more potent than 'general credibility' evidence which, under confrontation clause standards, may have a lower status." *White v. Coplan*, 399 F.3d at 26. We are addressing evidence that exposes a motive to fabricate a specific kind of lie under a specific set of circumstances and, therefore, directly implicates [the defendant's] rights under the Confrontation Clause.

Sussman v. Jenkins, 636 F.3d 329, 356–57 (7th Cir.), *cert. dismissed*, 132 S.Ct. 68 (2011).

Even the Sixth Circuit has retreated from its holding in *Boggs* that the Confrontation Clause does not protect cross-examination targeting a witness's character for truthfulness. The court held that a murder defendant had a Sixth Amendment right to impeach an important prosecution eyewitness with evidence of his past convictions, which the trial court had barred because of a technical peculiarity in Michigan's version of Rule 609(a). The circuit court criticized its holding in *Boggs* for "unquestioningly accept[ing] Justice Stewart's attempt to commandeer the majority opinion in *Davis*." And it distinguished *Boggs* as a "rape-shield case where the Confrontation Clause arguably provides defendants less protection than in other cases." Noting the important interests underlying rape-shield laws, the court cited longstanding caselaw stating that the confrontation right is not absolute and " 'may, in appropriate cases, bow to accommodate other legitimate interests in the criminal trial process.' " *Vasquez v. Jones*, 496 F.3d 564, 573 (6th Cir. 2007) (quoting *Chambers v. Mississippi*, 410 U.S. 284, 295 (1973)).

At bottom, then, whether a defendant has a Sixth Amendment right to cross-examine his accusers about their past lies depends on where he is and on the facts of his case. Until the Supreme Court clears this judicial thicket, the constitutional status of defense attacks on accusers' truthful character will vary from circuit to circuit.

Problem 5.5
Bryant's Accuser

Bryant Defense Goes on Offense

Attorneys Say Woman Accusing Laker Guard of Rape Had Sex with Two Prosecution Witnesses, and Had Sex Hours After Encounter with Bryant.

Steve Henson

LOS ANGELES TIMES, March 2, 2004, at D1

EAGLE, COLO. Kobe Bryant's attorneys went on the offensive Monday, making controversial allegations about the sexual activity of the woman who has accused the Laker star of rape.

The defense claimed during a pretrial hearing and in a court filing that the woman has had sex with two prosecution witnesses and that she also had intercourse only hours after her encounter with Bryant.

Defense attorney Hal Haddon told Judge Terry Ruckriegle that swabs of semen taken from the ... 19–year–old accuser during an examination 15 hours after the alleged rape were from a man other than Bryant.

Eagle County Dist. Atty. Mark Hurlbert objected.... Haddon did not mention the woman's sexual conduct again, but in a court document filed over the weekend and made public Monday ... he offered several reasons why it is relevant and should be an exception to the rape-shield law....

The woman says she was assaulted on the night of June 30 at the Edwards, Colo., resort where she worked. Bryant, 25, says they had consensual sex....

Haddon said the defense had established: ...

- [T]he woman's sexual acts with other men ... show the "accuser's knowledge, intent, common plan, pattern and modus operandi with respect to whether she consented to having sex with Bryant." ...
- There is evidence that the woman had sexual relationships with two prosecution witnesses. A source close to the prosecution said the men are the woman's ex-boyfriend, Matt Herr, and hotel bellman Bobby Pietrack. The woman called Herr on her cellphone while driving home from her encounter with Bryant. Pietrack followed her home in his car. The sexual history between the woman and those witnesses is relevant to their credibility, Haddon said. Pietrack's testimony is especially important because he is the first person the woman spoke to after leaving Bryant's hotel room.
- [E]vidence of sexual conduct soon after the alleged rape should be admissible to rebut a contention by prosecutors that the woman was diagnosed with post-traumatic stress disorder....

Assume the Federal Rules of Evidence govern this case. How should the judge rule on each of the defendant's three bulleted claims? If you think the defendant should prevail on any of these claims, in what form may the defendant offer the challenged evidence? What additional facts, if any, would the judge need before ruling?

The Shield That Failed

Dahlia Lithwick

NEW YORK TIMES, Aug. 8, 2004, § 4, at 11

The case against Kobe Bryant may end before it begins. Anyone surprised? The prosecution has lost its bid to exclude evidence of the accuser's sexual history from the trial. The courthouse in Eagle, Colo., is more porous than a sea sponge. And the accuser is no longer certain she wants to testify.... Underlying the entire mess is one simple, largely unacknowledged fact: The legal system is inadequate to the task of resolving acquaintance rape cases, and the media actually exacerbates the original injustice—be that a rape, or a false accusation of rape....

With [the defendant's] right to a fair trial and [his accuser's] right to be spared a second assault on a collision course, the role of the media becomes absolutely lethal. In the Bryant case, by insisting on its constitutional right to act as watchdog, the press gained access to the most lurid details of the accuser's intimate life. Consequently, high-profile rape trials allow the media to do far more damage than rape shield laws ever tried to mitigate.

When the national media expose a woman's sexual history, it means the difference between shaming her in her community, and doing so worldwide.... [B]y detailing the sexual conduct of Mr. Bryant's accuser in the 72-hour period surrounding her rape, the press will eviscerate the entire purpose of the Colorado rape shield law....

For Mr. Bryant's part, ... from the moment the district attorney peered into the flashbulbs and labeled him a rapist, his life was over, whether he was convicted or acquitted.... And so [he] found in the media an eager handmaid to help him around the rape shield problem, clearing him through leaks, insinuations and repeated use of his accuser's name. In that one sense rape law is not unlike campaign finance reform law—block one path and the sludge just oozes elsewhere.

Enacted with the best of intentions, rape shield laws don't work, particularly in high-profile cases. These laws either don't protect victims, or undermine defendants' rights to a fair trial.... Add the press to the mix and you have a perfect storm—with either accuser or accused twice victimized. There is a class of cases that are simply beyond the ability of the legal system to resolve, both because some truths are ultimately unknowable, and because it isn't "justice" when everyone emerges from a trial so damaged that it hardly matters who won. *Colorado v. Bryant* is one of those cases.

b. NARRATIVE INTEGRITY (RES GESTAE)

STEPHENS v. MILLER

13 F.3d 998 (7th Cir.), *cert. denied*, 513 U.S. 808 (1994).

■ En Banc. Before POSNER, CHIEF JUDGE, CUMMINGS, BAUER, CUDAHY, COFFEY, FLAUM, EASTERBROOK, RIPPLE, MANION, KANNE, and ROVNER, CIRCUIT JUDGES.

■ BAUER, CIRCUIT JUDGE. ... On the night of March 17, 1987, Lonnie Stephens went to the complainant's trailer. At trial, Stephens and the complainant told vastly different stories about what happened after Stephens arrived. The events of that evening began after Stephens and David Stone finished drinking. Stone drove Stephens to the complainant's trailer and dropped him off. Stephens and the complainant knew each other as casual acquaintances. She was asleep on the couch when Stephens arrived, and her sister and brother-in-law were asleep in the guest room. The complainant's son and nephew were asleep in another bedroom.

According to the complainant, she did not lock the door before she fell asleep. She awoke and found Stephens standing in front of the door inside the trailer. Stephens sat down next to her and attempted to kiss her. She told Stephens of the others who were asleep in the trailer and called out for her sister. Stephens hesitated but, after a moment, continued his advances. The complainant yelled one more time for her sister, but her sister again did not respond. Stephens went to the bathroom and, when he returned, angrily told the complainant that she lied to him about the others being in the trailer. He threw her down on the couch and covered her mouth with his hand to prevent her from screaming. Stephens pressed his body against hers, undid her bra, and tore a button from her shirt. Next, Stephens reached down to undo his pants. The complainant pushed Stephens off of her and ran screaming into the bedroom occupied by her sister and brother-in-law.

Stephens ran out the door to the nearby home of his friends, Jeff and Lisa Strait. Stephens told the Straits that he had been at a local Pic a Pac Store. Later, Stephens told that same story to the police officer who investigated the incident. Stephens directed Stone to say, if he were asked, that Stone dropped him off at the Pic a Pac. At trial, Stone first repeated the Pic a Pac story, then admitted on cross-examination that he dropped Stephens off at the complainant's trailer. Stone also admitted that he told the Pic a Pac story pursuant to directions from Stephens.

Stephens testified at trial and painted a quite different picture of the evening's events. He claimed that the complainant invited him into her trailer after Stone dropped him off. Stephens stated that when he entered the trailer, the complainant's son was asleep on the couch. Stephens carried him to one of the bedrooms and the complainant explained that her sister, brother-in-law, and their child were also asleep in the bedroom. All three slept through Stephens' visit to the trailer. Stephens and the complainant talked in the living room, and she told Stephens he could kiss her. One thing led to another, according to Stephens, until the two of them ended up on the floor as two consenting adults engaged in sexual intercourse.

Stephens stated in an offer of proof that the two of them were "doing it doggy fashion" when he said to her "don't you like it like this? ... Tim Hall said you did." Stephens also asserted that he said something to the complainant about "switching partners." The trial court excluded these statements pursuant to the Indiana Rape Shield Statute.[1] The court did, however, allow Stephens to testify that he said something to the complainant that angered her and led her to fabricate the attempted rape charge. Stephens testified that after he made these statements, she ordered him to stop and leave. Stephens claimed that he did as she asked, got dressed, and left.

The jury returned a guilty verdict against Stephens on the attempted rape charge. The Indiana Supreme Court affirmed his conviction and the district court denied his petition for writ of habeas corpus.

II.

Stephens contends that the Indiana trial court erred when it excluded the proffered testimony. First, he ... claims that the court's application of the Indiana Rape Shield Statute violated his constitutional right to testify in his own defense. [And he] argues that the excluded testimony should be admissible as the res gestae of the attempted rape....

B. Constitutionality of the Indiana Rape Shield Statute as Applied Here

... [Although] the principle of rape shield statutes has been held constitutional, both by this court and the Supreme Court in *Michigan v. Lucas*, 500 U.S. 145 (1991), the constitutionality of the law as applied remains subject to examination on a case by case basis. Stephens claims that Indiana unconstitutionally applied its Rape Shield Statute in this case. His primary argument is that Indiana denied him his constitutional right to testify in his own defense when it did not allow him to tell his version of the events, in their entirety and in his own words, about what happened on March 17, 1987, at the complainant's trailer. Stephens argues that the Indiana court violated the federal constitution when it excluded his statements about "doggy fashion" sexual intercourse and partner switching.

The Supreme Court has interpreted the Constitution to provide a criminal defendant, like Stephens, with an implicit right to testify in his or her own defense.... A criminal defendant's right to testify, however, is not unlimited and may bow to accommodate other legitimate interests in

1. [Here the court reprinted the Indiana rape shield statute, which is substantially similar to Rule 412.—GF]

the criminal trial process. *Lucas*, 500 U.S. at 149; Rock v. Arkansas, 483 U.S. 44, 55 (1987). There is, for example, no constitutional right to commit perjury. Furthermore, numerous procedural and state evidentiary rules control the presentation of evidence and do not offend a criminal defendant's right to testify. *Rock*, 483 U.S. at 55 n.11; Chambers v. Mississippi, 410 U.S. 284, 302 (1973).

Rape shield statutes fall into the category of procedural and evidentiary rules referred to in *Rock* and *Chambers*. Rape shield statutes, like Indiana's, represent the valid legislative determination that victims of rape and, as here, attempted rape deserve heightened protection against surprise, harassment, and unnecessary invasions of privacy. *Lucas*, 500 U.S. at 149. These statutes also protect against surprise to the prosecution. Restrictions imposed by rape shield statutes, especially as they relate to a criminal defendant's right to testify, may not, however, be arbitrary or disproportionate to the purposes they are designed to serve. Rather, the state is required to evaluate whether the interests served by the rule justify the limitation imposed on the criminal defendant's right to testify.

In this case, Stephens was allowed to give his entire version of the facts, except for the excluded evidence. The Indiana court allowed Stephens to testify in front of the jury that he said something to the complainant that angered her and caused her to fabricate the attempted rape charge. The court did nothing arbitrary or disproportionate to the purposes the Indiana Rape Shield Statute was designed to serve when it excluded the "doggy fashion" and "partner switching" statements. The Indiana Rape Shield Statute was enacted to prevent just this kind of generalized inquiry into the reputation or past sexual conduct of the victim in order to avoid embarrassing her and subjecting her to possible public denigration. Its application to exclude references here to "doggy fashion" sexual intercourse and partner switching effectuate[d] its purpose. The Indiana trial court properly balanced Stephens' right to testify with Indiana's interests because it allowed him to testify about what happened and that he said something that upset the complainant. The Constitution requires no more than this. The interests served by the Indiana Rape Shield Statute justify this very minor imposition on Stephens' right to testify.

We note also that Stephens and the complainant told drastically different stories of what happened and that Stephens directed David Stone to commit perjury. The jury was entitled to credit the complainant's story, discount Stephens' account, and return a guilty verdict. Testimony about the complainant's alleged sexual preferences would have served no other purpose than to embarrass and humiliate her. Accordingly, the Indiana trial court properly balanced the state's interests with Stephens' right to testify when it excluded the testimony at issue here....

C. Res Gestae

Stephens raises one other argument: that the excluded testimony was evidence concerning the res gestae of the offense and therefore should have been admitted. Literally "the thing done," the res gestae of a particular offense under Indiana law is admissible and is defined as evidence of happenings near in time and place which complete the story of a crime. There are two problems with Stephens' res gestae argument.

First, we do not accept Stephens' res gestae argument because to do so would effectively gut rape shield statutes and violate the principle established in *Lucas*. If Stephens' res gestae argument were correct, as a matter of constitutional law, criminal defendants could always circumvent rape shield statutes by claiming that they said something near in time and place to the alleged rape or attempted rape about the victim's past sexual history or reputation.

Second, Stephens offers nothing, probably because nothing exists, to support his res gestae argument as a constitutional violation. In fact, the use of the term res gestae, for purposes of federal law, is essentially obsolete. The Federal Rules of Evidence, adopted in 197[5], govern evidentiary questions in federal court, and, more significantly given the issue here, no court has ever held that res gestae is a concept with any constitutional significance. Other federal courts have described the phrase res gestae as useless, harmful, and almost incapable of a definition. Simply put, as a federal matter, "the old catchall, 'res gestae,' is no longer part of the law of evidence." Miller v. Keating, 754 F.2d 507, 509 (3d Cir. 1985).

We observe only that for purposes of the Constitution and federal law, the term res gestae is without significance. Indiana and the other states are, of course, free to keep the res gestae concept as part of their law of evidence. But here, as we have said, we ask only whether the Indiana court denied Stephens any right guaranteed to him by the Constitution. It did not.

III.

Nothing in the Constitution prohibited the exclusion of the testimony at issue in this case. The district court's decision to deny Stephens' petition for writ of habeas corpus is therefore

Affirmed.

■ FLAUM, CIRCUIT JUDGE, joined by ROVNER, CIRCUIT JUDGE, concurring. . . .

■ ROVNER, CIRCUIT JUDGE, concurring. . . .

■ CUMMINGS, CIRCUIT JUDGE, joined by CUDAHY and MANION, CIRCUIT JUDGES, dissenting. Lonnie Stephens claims that on the night of March 17, 1987, he made comments to the complainant that caused her to end their consensual sexual encounter, send Stephens immediately from her home, wake her sister, and the next day to file a groundless charge of attempted rape. The content of the offending statement—a cornerstone of Stephens' case—was never presented to the jury, the trial judge having ruled that the proposed testimony was barred by the Indiana Rape Shield Statute. The exclusion of this evidence indisputably gives rise to a colorable claim that the application of an evidentiary rule, the rape shield statute, has interfered with the defendant's right to present his defense. When a defendant presents such a colorable claim, the task of the court is to balance the exculpatory import of the excluded evidence against the interest of the state manifested in the rule at issue.

The interests served by the Indiana [Rape Shield Statute] are obvious—and substantial. The . . . Statute furthers laudable and pragmatic goals. It protects victims from needless exposure of their past sexual conduct; ensures that the focus of rape trials remains the guilt or innocence of the accused rather than the sexual history of the complainant; and, by reducing the embarrassment and anguish of trial, encourages victims to report rapes. Without the protection provided by rape shield statutes, victims may find trial an ordeal not worth enduring. *Cf.* 124 Cong. Rec. H.11944 (1978) (statement of Rep. Holtzman); FED. R. EVID. 412 cmt. (1993) ("Many [rape victims] find trial almost as degrading as the rape itself. . . ."). Moreover, Indiana has the power to pursue these goals through evidentiary rules—it is each state's "sovereign prerogative" to regulate the presentation of evidence in its courts. McMorris v. Israel, 643 F.2d 458, 460 (7th Cir. 1981). Indiana's rape shield statute is a valid legislative determination that rape victims deserve heightened protection from harassment and unnecessary explorations into their personal life, and exceptions to it should not be carved out liberally. Nonetheless, the desire to shield rape victims from harassment must yield in certain cases to another vital goal, the accused's right to present his defense. Sending the innocent to jail, or depriving the guilty of due process, is not a price our Constitution allows us to pay for the legitimate and worthy ambition to protect those already victimized from additional suffering. Though relevant and competent evidence may properly be excluded to accommodate other legitimate interests, Chambers v. Mississippi, 410 U.S. 284, 295 (1973), evidence with genuine exculpatory potential must be admitted. *See* Sharlow v. Israel, 767 F.2d 373, 377–78 (7th Cir. 1985) (critical evidence may not be excluded); *cf. Chambers*, 410 U.S. at 302. In the end then, what matters here—and what must be weighed against Indiana's policy choice—is the significance of the contested evidence to Lonnie Stephens' case.

The jury in this case heard conflicting accounts of the events that occurred at the complainant's house trailer: she testified that Lonnie Stephens was an unwelcome guest who attempted to rape her; Stephens testified that he and the complainant were engaging in consensual sex, but that in response to statements he made during intercourse she became angry, ended the encounter, ordered him to leave and fabricated a rape allegation in retaliation. The prosecution offered physical and testimonial evidence tending to corroborate complainant's version. Stephens' account consisted primarily of his own testimony. The plausibility of Stephens' defense turned in substantial part on whether the jury could be persuaded that something Stephens had said to the complainant could have so enraged her that she would have responded in the manner he alleged. Central to Stephens' case then are the words he claims to have said that night, words the jury never heard. Stephens proposed to testify that while he and the complainant were engaged in intercourse "doggy fashion," he said to her "Don't you like it like this? . . . T[i]m Hall said you did." Stephens instead was permitted only to testify without elaboration that he had said something that angered the complainant. The judge required Stephens to convince the jury of the truth of his story without allowing him to reveal the fragments on which its plausibility turned. He was asked to counter the detailed and vivid depiction offered by the prosecution with a version whose essential elements had been expunged. The jury might well have disbelieved Stephens' testimony even if he had testified fully; however, it is hard to imagine his story being believed absent this evidence.

The majority is dismissive of the significance of Stephens' statements to his defense—the exclusion is but a "very minor burden" on Stephens. Stephens, according to the majority, is not harmed by the exclusion because he "was allowed to give [the rest of] his [] version of the facts" and little was expurgated. That Stephens was allowed to present the rest of his defense, however, is irrelevant to the question of whether the excluded evidence was in itself important. At issue is not whether Stephens was allowed to present some defense, but whether the Sixth Amendment requires that he be allowed to present the specific evidence excluded. Since the majority has failed to explore the exculpatory significance of the excluded evidence, it is not surprising that it concludes that the exclusion of Stephens' testimony is not "disproportionate to the purposes [of] the Indiana Rape Shield Statute"—the majority has weighed only one of the issues to be balanced.

Moreover, I do not believe that allowing the evidence at issue would undermine the operation of the Indiana Rape Shield Statute. The statute may, consistent with the Sixth Amendment, operate to exclude a significant body of evidence—likely, the type of evidence with which the drafters of the legislation were most concerned. Prohibited still is evidence suggesting that because of an alleged victim's past sexual conduct she probably consented this time or "asked" to have intercourse or other argument that seeks to explain or excuse a rape based on the victim's past behavior. . . . Admittedly, allowing Stephens' testimony would create an exception to the statute, but the exception is a narrow one. That Stephens allegedly uttered these comments during the evening in question is not alone sufficient to compel admission. The Sixth Amendment does not create a broad res gestae exception to rape shield statutes. Neither does the Sixth Amendment require that the statements be admitted because they have some tendency to aid Stephens' defense. *Chambers*, 410 U.S. at 295 (relevant and competent evidence may be excluded). Rather, Stephens' statements must be admitted here because they are central to his defense.

This is not to say that the purpose of the rape shield statute would not be frustrated at all by the admission of Stephens' offered testimony. Although admitting Stephens' statement is unlikely to transform the trial into an inquiry into the complainant's private life, she would undoubtedly suffer some anguish and embarrassment—anguish and embarrassment from which Indiana, in the cause of encouraging victims to report assaults, has an interest in protecting her. However, the state's interest in allowing rape victims to testify "free of embarrassment and with [their] reputation unblemished must fall before the right of [the defendant] to seek out the truth in the process of defending himself.... The State cannot ... require [the defendant] to bear the full burden of vindicating the State's interests...." Davis v. Alaska, 415 U.S. 308, 320 (1974).

Allowing Stephens' testimony acknowledges that because the protection of defendants' rights is fundamental to our system, at times other interests may be impaired. Given the significance of the excised testimony to his case, Indiana's interests must yield to Stephens' fundamental constitutional right to present his defense. I, therefore, respectfully dissent.

■ CUDAHY, CIRCUIT JUDGE, dissenting....

■ COFFEY, CIRCUIT JUDGE, dissenting....

■ RIPPLE, CIRCUIT JUDGE, dissenting....

Afterthought on **Stephens v. Miller:** In his opinion for the court in *Stephens*, Judge Bauer wrote that if Stephens prevailed here, "criminal defendants could always circumvent rape shield statutes by claiming that they said something near in time and place to the alleged rape or attempted rape about the victim's past sexual history or reputation." How important to the court's reasoning is the possibility that Stephens never really asked the complainant, "[D]on't you like it like this? ... Tim Hall said you did." Assume for a moment that Stephens in fact spoke those words during a consensual sexual encounter with the complainant. Do you think his statement could explain why she ran screaming into her sister's bedroom and later accused Stephens (falsely) of rape?

---

c. DEFENDANT'S STATE OF MIND

UNITED STATES v. KNOX

1992 WL 97157 (U.S.A.F. Ct. Mil. Rev. 1992), *aff'd*, 41 M.J. 28 (Ct. Mil. App. 1994), *cert. denied*, 513 U.S. 1153 (1995).

■ HODGSON, SENIOR JUDGE: . . . [The appellant, Bobby L. Knox, and] the prosecutrix, Theresa, . . . worked in the same shop at Kadena Air Base, Japan. . . .

On 28 April 1989, a Friday, . . . members of [the appellant's] shop gathered outside Theresa's dormitory to celebrate the end of the week and a favorable dorm inspection. After drinking three or so beers, Theresa went to her room for a shower. . . . After her shower, the appellant invited her and [Lu] Castonguay [her boyfriend] to his room. While she was there and sitting on Castonguay's lap, the appellant kept running his hands up and down her legs. She told him to "knock it off." By then she was sipping on her sixth beer. . . .

About 2245 or so, the appellant left the room. . . . Theresa sat on the bed, undressed, rolled over next to Castonguay and began "hugging and kissing" him. . . . That's the last thing she remembered as she fell asleep. She does not remember having sex with Castonguay that evening, and she thinks she would have remembered if she had.

When she awoke she was on her stomach, and someone was having sexual intercourse with her. There was a comforter over her head, and "some hands were on [her] back." In the process of waking up, she assumed her partner was Castonguay. . . . Later, she thought "there was something funny going on," and looked over her shoulder and saw the appellant "having sex with [her]." She started crying and said, "Lu [Castonguay], get him the hell out of here." The appellant . . . jumped off the bed. As he jumped off, he said, . . . "Lu, we're in trouble," and "Lu, I didn't know that she didn't know." She heard Castonguay say, "It's okay, Bobby, she'll be okay in a minute." She screamed for both of them to leave the room so she could get dressed which they did. Later, the appellant approached Theresa and said, "we're really sorry; we're really sorry and we feel so bad about this; we discussed it and we're ready to face the consequences for what we did." She subsequently called the Rape Intervention Crisis Center at the Kadena Clinic. She said she did not consent to having sexual intercourse with the appellant. . . .

Theresa's and the appellant's testimony are essentially in agreement as to what happened up to the point where the appellant left [his room]. It is here that the two versions of the event part company. The appellant testified that when he returned to his room a second time, Theresa and Castonguay were [having sex]. . . . Theresa looked at [the appellant] and he interpreted her "suggestive looks and motions" as an invitation to join the sexual encounter. He did so and had sexual intercourse with her. . . .

He said that while Theresa made no noise during the episode, she was awake and not asleep....

He denied saying, ... "Lu, we're in trouble," and "Lu, I didn't know that she didn't know." He also denied saying, "We're ready to turn ourselves in and face the consequences." ...

Here, the issue before the court members was clear and succinct: Which version of the events of 28 April was to be believed—Theresa's or the appellant's? In his opening statement, the trial defense counsel concisely identified the paramount matter to be settled when he observed: "[The] issue you decide is was [Theresa] awake [when the sexual intercourse occurred] and is making up a story or was she not awake?" Thus, the credibility of each participant is the crucial factor.

Theresa's version of what happened cannot be reconciled with the appellant's. She testified that she passed out on a bed with her boyfriend, and when she awoke her boyfriend had his hands on her shoulders and the appellant was having sexual intercourse with her. She said she did not consent to this. She further stated that the appellant's reaction to her anger over what had happened was one of concern and fear for what might happen to him as a result of the incident. Additionally, Theresa testified that both the appellant and Castonguay expressed remorse for what they had done and were willing to accept the consequences for their actions....

The appellant, on the other hand, maintained that Theresa was awake and freely consented to having sexual relations with him in a group setting....

MIL. R. EVID. 412

Mil. R. Evid. 412 is intended to protect victims of sexual assaults from embarrassing and degrading cross-examination and evidence presentations that are common to the prosecution of such offenses. Yet, this rule of evidence is not an absolute bar to offering evidence relating to the purported victim's past sexual experience if it is relevant and "constitutionally required."

At trial the appellant served notice under Mil. R. Evid. 412(c)(1) that he intended to "offer evidence of specific incident and reputation evidence of the [complainant's] past sexual behavior." The appellant claims "he thought [the complainant] was awake and by her actions was consenting to his advances." Thus, [he claims] evidence as to his *state of mind* was constitutionally required.

In his offer of proof under Mil. R. Evid. 412(c)(2), the appellant stated he would testify that the prosecutrix had the reputation of being a "bimbo" who liked to "party," was sexually promiscuous, and "very easy"; he had also been told that she had taken "her top off" in a downtown bar; several co-workers had stated to him that they had cont[r]acted a sexually transmitted disease from her in the fall of 1988; and that in July 1988, at a beach party, she engaged in various sex acts in the presence of others—the appellant was not at the party, but was told about the incident.

The trial judge admitted some portions of the appellant's proposed testimony, but excluded any reference to individual acts of sexual conduct by the prosecutrix. He concluded that neither those individual acts nor her reputation, either known or believed by the appellant, had any tendency to make the existence of any fact more or less probable than it would [be] without the evidence. . . .

We find no fault with that ruling. The key issue in this case is clear-cut: the prosecutrix testified she was asleep when the appellant had sexual intercourse with her, and the appellant maintained she was a wide-awake, consenting partner in the encounter. The fact-finders received two distinct, and widely divergent, accounts of the event which posed a factual issue of consent, unfettered by any true possibility of mistake. They resolved this question of fact by believing the victim.

The appellant sought to do what Mil. R. Evid. 412 seeks to prevent: portray an alleged rape victim as a bad person who got no more than she deserved. . . .

For the reasons stated, the findings of guilty and the sentence are

Affirmed.

UNITED STATES V. KNOX: *Afterthoughts*

In *Knox* the accused airman wanted to offer evidence that he previously had heard of the victim's reputation for promiscuity and of specific acts of her sexual behavior. This evidence, he said, would explain why he was reasonably mistaken about whether she consented to have sex with him on the night in question. Because he could not fit such evidence under either of the narrowly defined exceptions to Rule 412—Rule 412(b)(1)(A) or 412(b)(1)(B)—he claimed instead that excluding this evidence would violate the Constitution, a possibility addressed by Rule 412(b)(1)(C). (The Military Rules of Evidence are patterned after the Federal Rules.) Although the court's opinion did not elaborate on Knox's constitutional claim, presumably he relied on one of three constitutional principles: the Fifth Amendment's Due Process Clause and its implied guarantee of a fair trial; the Sixth Amendment's Compulsory Process Clause and its implied guarantee of the right to mount a full defense; or (relatedly) the right to testify in one's own defense, discussed in *Stephens v. Miller* and derived from various constitutional provisions.

As we will see when we take up *Chambers v. Mississippi*, 410 U.S. 284 (1973), in Chapter 8, the Supreme Court has suggested that criminal defendants may have a right under either the Fifth or Sixth Amendment to offer evidence that is "critical" to their defense even if it violates the evidence rules. But the Court has never granted criminal defendants a right to disregard the rules altogether. It made clear in *Chambers* that the defendant's right to put on evidence "may, in appropriate cases, bow to accommodate other legitimate interests in the criminal trial process." 410 U.S. at 295. The purposes that underlie Rule 412—encouraging victims to report rape and protecting victims' privacy—surely constitute such "legitimate interests."

The *Knox* court concluded that given the glaring conflict between the complainant's and the defendant's stories, Knox could make no believable claim of reasonable mistake. Either the defendant or the complainant was lying—there was no genuine possibility of simple mistake. Evidence supporting such a strained defense could hardly be deemed *critical* to Knox—the standard imposed by *Chambers*. The Constitution therefore did not guarantee him the right to support this defense with otherwise inadmissible evidence.

Professor Rosanna Cavallaro has attacked the assumption that such polar differences between the defendant's and the victim's stories rule out the possibility of reasonable mistake. Writing about a California case similar to *Knox*, Cavallaro argued that this reasoning "does not allow for the possibility that a jury may find the 'truth' to be somewhere between" the two accounts. Rather than choose between "the testimony of the complainant and defendant as two entireties, . . . a jury might accept portions of each witness's testimony and reject other portions":

> [A] jury might not credit that portion of a complainant's testimony that described the use of force, although crediting her ultimate assertion that she did not consent. Conversely, a jury might reject that portion of a defendant's testimony that suggests positive enthusiasm by the complainant, concluding instead that the complainant exhibited only that amount of passive acquiescence sufficient to permit the defendant to form a good faith and reasonable belief as to consent. . . .

Rosanna Cavallaro, *A Big Mistake: Eroding the Defense of Mistake of Fact About Consent in Rape*, 86 J. CRIM. L. & CRIMINOLOGY 815, 848–51 (1996).

Professor Cavallaro believes that in the course of constructing the truth from pieces of each person's testimony, jurors could find it useful to know that the defendant had heard of the victim's reputation for promiscuity and of her other sexual acts. This information might persuade them to construct an account in which the defendant was reasonably mistaken about the victim's consent. Still, it is not enough for Cavallaro to show that evidence of what Knox had heard was *relevant* to the possibility of reasonable mistake. Rather, Knox's constitutional claim depended on his showing that such evidence was *critical* to his defense. The jarring differences between his story and the complainant's account arguably made his claim of reasonable mistake so implausible that evidence supporting it could not be deemed critical to his defense. And without mounting that constitutional hurdle, Knox could not overcome Rule 412's bar.

At least one court has held, however, that Rule 412 poses no bar to evidence of the sort Knox hoped to offer. Like Knox, the accused in *Doe v. United States*, 666 F.2d 43 (4th Cir. 1981), wanted to support his defense of reasonable mistake with evidence that he previously had heard of specific sexual acts by the complainant and of her reputation for promiscuity. As in *Knox*, the court rebuffed the defendant's claim of a constitutional right to present this evidence. But the *Doe* court nonetheless ruled that the defendant could offer evidence he had heard of the complainant's reputation and of certain sexual acts by her to support his defense of reasonable mistake:

> [Defendant] Black's knowledge, acquired before the alleged crime, of the victim's past sexual behavior is relevant on the issue of Black's intent. *See* 2 WEINSTEIN AND BERGER, EVIDENCE ¶ 412(01). . . .
>
> The legislative history [of Rule 412] discloses that reputation and opinion evidence of the past sexual behavior of an alleged victim was excluded because Congress considered that this evidence was not relevant to the issues of the victim's consent or her veracity. There is no indication, however, that this evidence was intended to be excluded when offered solely to show the accused's state of mind. Therefore, its admission is governed by the Rules of Evidence dealing with relevancy in general.

666 F.2d at 48. Hence the *Doe* court read Rule 412 as though the rule had taken the form Harriett Galvin proposed earlier. (*See* pages 329–30.) Like Rule 404(b), *Doe*'s version of Rule 412 would bar evidence of the victim's reputation or other sexual behavior to prove a propensity to consent or to lie, but would permit such evidence for any other purpose.

It appears no other federal appeals court has followed the Fourth Circuit in this line of reasoning. Even the Fourth Circuit seems to have had second thoughts. In *United States v. Saunders*, 943 F.2d 388 (4th Cir. 1991), *cert. denied*, 502 U.S. 1105 (1992), the court frankly noted the disfavor *Doe* has found:

> *Doe* has been criticized for reading an exception into the flat prohibition of Fed. R. Evid. 412(a), when relevant to the defendant's state of mind. *See* Spector & Foster, *Rule 412 and the* Doe *Case: The Fourth Circuit Turns Back the Clock*, 35 OKLA. L. REV. 87, 96–97 (1982):
>
>> The court arrogated to itself the authority to declare that the categorical mandate expressed in the rule did not fully articulate Congress' intent. Furthermore, the court fashioned and propounded its own exception to the rule's explicit ban on previous sexual behavior, an exception unauthorized by legislative fiat that is of such magnitude that its very existence threatens to . . .

> vitiate the utility of Rule 412 as a means of implementing the federal legislative purposes motivating its enactment....

Id. at 391 n.1. The *Saunders* court wrote that Rule 412, far from permitting evidence of the victim's reputation to prove the defendant's reasonable mistake, "manifests the policy that it is unreasonable for a defendant to base his belief of consent on the victim's past sexual experiences with third persons, since it is intolerable to suggest that because the victim is a prostitute, she automatically is assumed to have consented with anyone at any time." *Id.* at 392.

Knox's claim of reasonable mistake—and hence his evidence of the victim's reputation and other sex acts—would have been entirely immaterial if proof of rape required no culpable mental state on his part. The federal statute defining aggravated sexual abuse requires proof that the defendant "*knowingly* cause[d] another person to engage in a sexual act ... by using force against that other person" or "by threatening or placing that other person in fear" of violence. 18 U.S.C. § 2241(a) (2012) (emphasis added). But at least eight states appear to demand no such proof of the man's mental state.* The Massachusetts rape law, for

* Those eight are Illinois, Indiana, Iowa, Massachusetts, Michigan, Virginia, Washington, and Wisconsin. *See People v. Mangiaracina*, 98 Ill. App. 3d 606, 609 (1981) ("[W]hether the defendant intended to commit the offenses without the victim's consent is not relevant; the critical question being whether the victim did, in fact, consent."); *Tyson v. State*, 619 N.E.2d 276, 293 n.19 (Ind. Ct. App. 1993) ("[E]vidence that the defendant reasonably believed that the alleged victim consented to the sexual conduct is irrelevant."); *State v. Christensen*, 414 N.W.2d 843, 846 (Iowa Ct. App. 1987) ("[A] defendant's knowledge of his or her partner's lack of consent is not an element of section 709.4(1) [the statute defining sexual abuse in the third degree]."); *Commonwealth v. Guisti*, 434 Mass. 245, 249 (2001) (quoting *Commonwealth v. Cordeiro*, 401 Mass. 843, 851 (1988)) ("[T]o prove a charge of rape against the defendant, the Commonwealth need not prove 'either that the defendant intended the sexual intercourse be without consent or that he had actual knowledge of the victim's lack of consent.' "); *People v. Hale*, 142 Mich. App. 451, 453 (1985) ("No Michigan case law requires the trial court to define consent in terms of a defendant's reasonable and honest belief."); *Gonzales v. Comm.*, 45 Va. App. 375, 382 (2005) ("[T]he crime of rape does not require proof that the defendant harbor a specific intent to have intercourse without the victim's consent, only the general intent evidenced by the act of committing the offense itself. The lack of consent required for rape involves the victim's mental state, not the defendant's."); *State v. Higgins*, 168 Wash. App. 845, 855 (2012) (quoting *State v. Elmore*, 54 Wash. App. 54, 57 n.5 (1989)) (" '[I]t makes sense that the Legislature would focus on the issue of the victim's consent, or rather lack thereof, rather than the perpetrator's subjective assessment of the situation. To do otherwise would lead to the ludicrous result that a perpetrator could be exonerated simply by arguing that he did not know the victim's expressed lack of consent was genuine or that he did not intend to have nonconsensual sexual intercourse with the victim.' "); *Hagenkord v. State*, 100 Wis. 2d 452, 483 n.9 (1981) ("The new sexual assault law ... omits the use of any such words [signifying intent]. The new jury instructions assert that criminal intent, therefore, continues to be absent as a required element of the crime, creating a type of 'strict liability.' ").

I thank Professor Norman Bay for prompting me to reexamine this topic and

example, penalizes anyone who "has sexual intercourse ... with a person, and compels such person to submit by force and against his will...." GEN. LAWS ch. 265, § 22 (2012). Massachusetts caselaw appears to confirm the absence of a state-of-mind requirement. The Supreme Judicial Court has held that "to prove a charge of rape against the defendant, the Commonwealth need not prove 'either that the defendant intended the sexual intercourse be without consent or that he had actual knowledge of the victim's lack of consent.'" *Commonwealth v. Guisti*, 434 Mass. 245, 249 (2001) (quoting *Commonwealth v. Cordeiro*, 401 Mass. 843, 851 (1988)). Moreover, the prosecution need not prove that the defendant "'did not act pursuant to an honest and reasonable belief that the victim consented.'" *Commonwealth v. Lopez*, 433 Mass. 722, 725 (2001) (quoting *Commonwealth v. Ascolillo*, 405 Mass. 456, 463 (1989)).

Beyond the eight states that define rape without a state-of-mind requirement bearing on the victim's consent, another fifteen states appear to lack clear law on the question. Only about half the states, therefore, demand proof of the defendant's knowledge of the victim's lack of consent to sustain a rape charge. Hence even if rape-shield laws did not exist, a defendant in Knox's shoes often could not claim that his earlier knowledge of the complainant's reputation or other acts explains his reasonable mistake in thinking she consented.

---

5. A Glance at Civil Cases

Problem 5.6
Jones v. Clinton

President's Accuser May Be Questioned on Her Sexual Past

Neil A. Lewis

NEW YORK TIMES, June 2, 1997, at A1

WASHINGTON. President Clinton's personal lawyer today threatened to make an issue of Paula Corbin Jones's sexual history if she goes ahead with her plan to take Mr. Clinton to trial on charges of sexual harassment and damaging her reputation.

my research assistants Gabriel Schlabach and (now Professor) Binyamin Blum for meticulously compiling state rape statutes and caselaw.

The pointed warning from the lawyer, Robert S. Bennett, came in response to comments from Ms. Jones's lawyers, who confirmed on television interview programs today that they would probably seek testimony from other women who might have been sexually propositioned by Mr. Clinton when he was the Governor of Arkansas. Ms. Jones's lawyers also said they could seek testimony from state troopers who might have asked women to meet with Mr. Clinton in that time.

"You know this is a two-way street," Mr. Bennett responded moments later on the NBC News program "Meet the Press." "If Paula Jones insists on having her day in court and her trial, and she really wants to put her reputation at issue, as we hear, we are prepared to do that."

In fact, lawyers working with Mr. Bennett acknowledged that they spent several hours on Saturday questioning a man who said he had an intimate relationship with Ms. Jones. The man, whom they declined to identify, was flown to Washington and put up in a hotel by the lawyers, who said he provided a sworn statement about her behavior....

Mr. Bennett said in his television appearance that he hoped exposure of the sexual past of both parties could be avoided.

He said the trial judge, Susan Webber Wright, might be persuaded to say in a ruling: "This is not about Paula Jones's past sex life; this is not about the President and what if anything ever occurred in the past. Let's get on with what happened on that particular day." ...

Could Bennett have followed through on his threat to make an issue of Paula Jones's reputation? Is evidence of the sexual history of the two parties really "a two-way street"? Why do the rules sometimes treat defendants' and plaintiffs' sexual histories differently?

UNIT II: RELIABILITY

CHAPTER 6

Competency of Witnesses

Historical Prelude: *Rules of Witness Competency and the Clash Between North and South**

At the beginning of the nineteenth century a law school evidence course (had there been such a thing) would have devoted weeks to the topic of witness competency. A broad array of competency rules dictated who could and could not testify in court. These rules barred from the witness stand all parties to the proceeding—both plaintiff and defendant in a civil suit and all criminal defendants. They excluded spouses of parties, persons with a financial interest in the case, convicted felons, and atheists. In effect competency rules labeled certain witnesses liars as a matter of law.

Exactly when the rules evolved is unclear. Wigmore traced the rule barring civil parties to the sixteenth century and that barring all other interested persons to the mid-seventeenth century. *See* 2 John Henry Wigmore, A Treatise on the Anglo-American System of Evidence in Trials at Common Law § 575, at 679–80 (3d ed. 1940). But it seems these dates merely mark the earliest examples Wigmore could find—the rules may well be older.

There is no doubt about the rules' rationale. All sources agree they sought to keep from the witness stand anyone whose temptation or inclination to lie was greater than the norm. Competency rules therefore served two purposes: They ensured juries would base their verdicts (mostly) on truthful evidence; and they protected the souls of witnesses who otherwise might have been tempted to commit the mortal sin of perjury. Jeffrey Gilbert, writing in the early eighteenth century, uttered the most famous statement of these principles:

> Men are generally so short-sighted, as to look at their own private Benefit which is near to them, rather than to the Good of the World that is more remote; therefore ... the Law removes them from Testimony, to prevent their sliding into Perjury; and it can be no

* Much of the material in this section appeared earlier in a somewhat different form in George Fisher, *The Jury's Rise as Lie Detector*, 107 Yale L.J. 575, 669–74, 684–85, 693–96 (1997).

> Injury to Truth, to remove those from the [hearing of the] Jury, whose Testimony may hurt themselves, and can never induce any rational belief.

[JEFFREY GILBERT], THE LAW OF EVIDENCE 122 (London, Henry Lintot 1756).[1]

Today an evidence teacher in a hurry can get through the topic of witness competency in half an hour—or less. Virtually all of the old competency rules are gone, and those few that remain arise rarely and affect rather few witnesses. But while competency rules themselves warrant little of our attention, the story of their undoing is worth a longer look. As it happens, the downfall of one of the most important of the old rules—the rule barring testimony by parties in civil suits—overlaps with the history of race relations in the United States.

Table 1 (page 366) shows when the first thirty-six American states passed laws to abolish the old rule and permit testimony by civil parties. This list includes all those states that joined the Union (and perhaps later the Confederacy) before the end of the Civil War. The most striking thing about this table is the segregation of the Southern states—almost all are clustered on the right. With the exception of Mississippi, not a single member of the Confederacy (marked with an asterisk) had dropped its ban against testimony by civil parties before the end of the Civil War. Yet within nine years of the War's end, all ten of the remaining Confederate states had abolished the old rule. Among the four border states (marked with a double asterisk), only Maryland permitted parties to testify before the end of the Civil War, while the three others permitted civil parties to testify within seven years of the War's end. For some reason, the general reticence of Southern states to permit civil parties to testify ended abruptly in 1866.

The two maps on page 367 show the same list of states. The top map shades those states that permitted civil parties to testify before the Civil War ended in 1865. The bottom map shades those that still forbade such testimony at War's end. The segregation of most Southern and border states in the second map is plain. Could such a marked North–South split, remarkably like today's splintering of Blue and Red America, be coincidence? Or is it possible that this arrangement owes something to the racial politics of the Civil War era?

1. As I mentioned in Chapter 4, Gilbert died in 1726 and must have written his treatise long before its first publication in 1756.

TABLE 1
STATUTES PERMITTING TESTIMONY BY CIVIL PARTIES[2]

STATE	DATE	STATE	DATE
Connecticut	1848	**Maryland	1864
Minnesota	1851	*Florida	1866
Vermont	1852	*Virginia	1866
Ohio	1853	*North Carolina	1866
Maine	1856	*South Carolina	1866
Rhode Island	1857	*Georgia	1866
*Mississippi	1857	**Missouri	1866
New York	1857	*Alabama	1867
Massachusetts	1857	Illinois	1867
New Hampshire	1857	*Louisiana	1867
Kansas	1858	**West Virginia	1868
Wisconsin	1858	*Tennessee	1868
New Jersey	1859	Nevada	1869
Iowa	1860	Pennsylvania	1869
Michigan	1861	*Texas	1871
Indiana	1861	**Kentucky	1872
Oregon	1862	*Arkansas	1874
California	1863	Delaware	1881

It is likely the Southern states' initial reluctance to permit party testimony, as well as their sudden conversion after the War, had something to do with their old attachment to a wholly different and seemingly unconnected competency rule—a rule that barred testimony by nonwhite persons. Such racial exclusion laws took various forms. Some barred testimony by all nonwhites. Some barred testimony only by African Americans and persons of mixed black-white blood. Some barred all testimony by the specified class, while some permitted such testimony when not offered against whites. And Louisiana did not have a racial exclusion law per se, but rather provided that nonwhite status could be used to impeach a witness. "The circumstance[] of the witness being . . . a free colored person," the Louisiana law declared, "is not a sufficient cause to consider the witness as incompetent, but may, according to the circumstances, diminish the extent of his credibility." LA. CIV. CODE. ANN. art. 2261 (1857).

2. My thanks to Alexis Haller and Binyamin Blum for collecting the state laws represented in Tables 1 and 2.

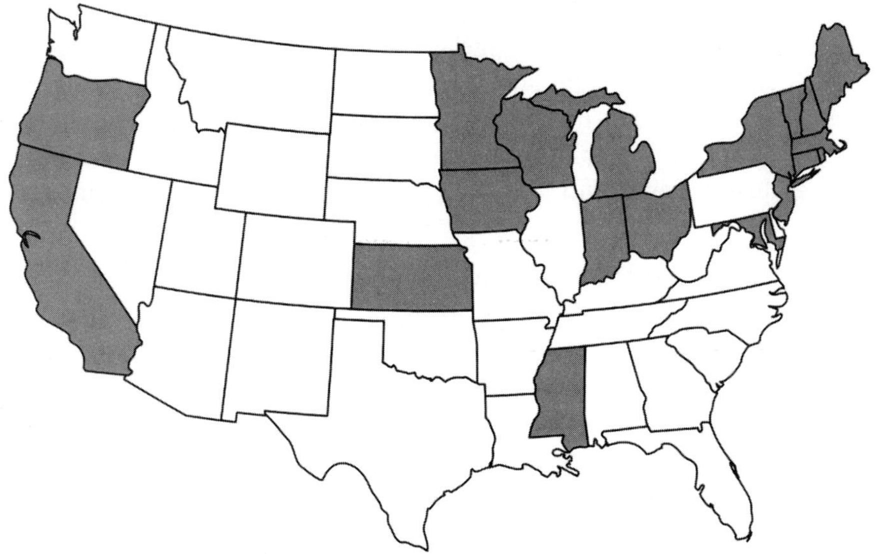

STATES PERMITTING TESTIMONY BY CIVIL PARTIES BEFORE THE CIVIL WAR'S END

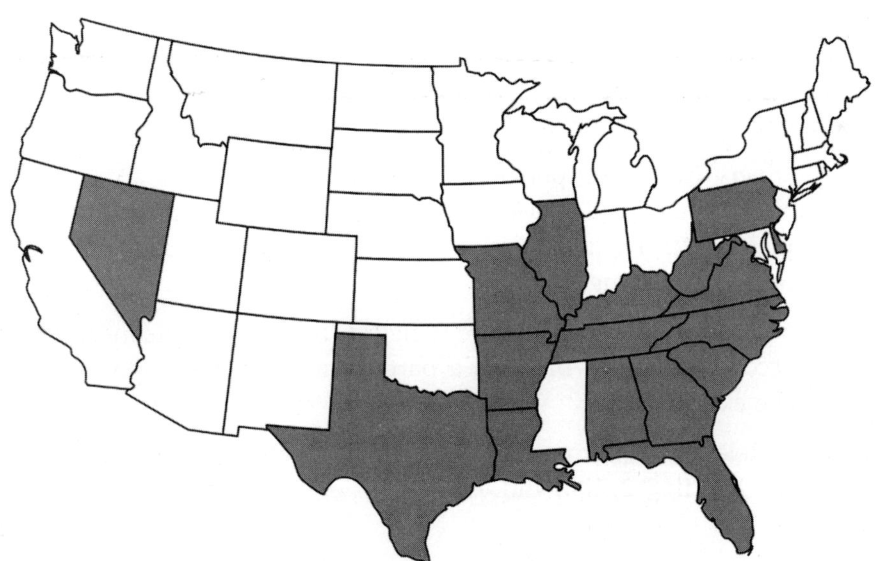

STATES BARRING TESTIMONY BY CIVIL PARTIES AT THE CIVIL WAR'S END

Now consider Table 2 on page 369, which lists all those states in Table 1 that at one time had racial exclusion laws. Note that Table 2 includes almost every state shaded in the second map as well as a few others. Note too that not all states with racial exclusion laws were Southern. This table explores the relationship between the abolition of racial exclusion laws and the end of competency rules barring civil parties.

I have arranged the states that once had racial exclusion laws in three groups. States in the first group, which make up almost half of the total, abolished their racial exclusion laws and their laws barring civil parties at exactly the same—or almost the same—moment. States in the second group abolished their racial exclusion laws first and repealed their civil parties ban during the next several years. In only three of these twenty-four states did the civil parties bar fall first.

If we focus on the three anomalous states—Indiana, Maryland, and Mississippi—we perhaps can discover why states that had racial exclusion laws generally clung to their laws barring civil parties. Each of these three states made civil parties competent to testify while still excluding nonwhites from the witness stand. In doing so, they had to address this question: What happens when a party is not white? Would that person be permitted to testify as a party or be barred as nonwhite?

Indiana's 1861 statute resolved this difficulty in a surprising way:

> Every free white person of competent age shall be a competent witness in any civil cause or proceeding, and no person shall be disqualified as a witness ... because such person is a party in said action or proceeding.
>
> ... Provided, That where a negro, Indian, or person excluded on account of mixed blood is a party to a cause, his opponent shall also be excluded....

An Act in Relation to Witnesses and to Repeal Section 238 of Article 13 of the Act, ch. XXVII, § 2, 1861 Ind. Acts 51, 52.

TABLE 2
ABOLITION OF RULES AGAINST TESTIMONY BY NONWHITES AND CIVIL PARTIES

STATE	RACIAL EXCLUSION ABOLISHED[3]	CIVIL PARTIES ALLOWED
Iowa	Mar. 29/30, 1860	Same
Kansas	Feb. 12, 1858	Same
Kentucky	Jan. 30, 1872	Same
Louisiana	Mar. 13, 1867	Same
Nevada	Mar. 8, 1869	Same
Oregon	Oct. 11, 1862	Same
North Carolina	Mar. 10, 1866	2 Days Later
South Carolina	Sept. 21, 1866	2 Days Earlier
Virginia	Feb. 28, 1866	2 Days Later
California	Mar. 16, 1863	6 Weeks Later
Florida	Oct. 25, 1865	3 Months Later
Alabama	Dec. 9, 1865	Feb. 14, 1867
Arkansas	Feb. 6, 1867	1874
Delaware	?	April 6, 1881
Georgia	Dec. 15, 1865	Dec. 15, 1866
Illinois	Feb. 7, 1865	Feb. 19, 1867
Missouri	July 4, 1865	Mar. 20, 1866
Ohio	Feb. 10, 1849	Mar. 11, 1853
Tennessee	Jan. 25, 1866	Mar. 13, 1868
Texas	Oct. 8, 1866	May 19, 1871
West Virginia	Feb. 27, 1866	Feb. 7, 1868
Indiana	Dec. 20, 1865	Mar. 17, 1861
Maryland	July 2, 1866	Mar 2, 1864
Mississippi	Nov. 25, 1865	1857

3. Just as racial exclusion laws took many forms, so did the laws that repealed those exclusions. Many such repeals were incomplete. California's 1863 repeal was particularly incomplete, granting African Americans the right to testify while retaining the bar against other nonwhites. *See* 1863 CAL. STAT., ch. 68, at 60 (Act of Mar. 16, 1863).

The state of Indiana apparently was willing to take inequality only so far. Although it barred nonwhites from testifying, it balked at pitting a nonwhite litigant who could not speak at trial against a white adversary who could. Hence if one party was not white, neither party could testify. Maryland and Mississippi did not take such care to assure a fair fight. Each state made civil parties competent and, within the same statute, made clear that the state's racial exclusion law would trump. Therefore nonwhites, even when parties, would be incompetent to testify, while their white opponents could testify against them. *See* Act of Mar. 2, 1864, ch. 109, § 1.1, 1864 Md. Laws 136, 136–37; An Act to Establish Circuit Courts, to Define Their Jurisdictions, and to Regulate the Practice Therein (adopted 1857) (codified at MISS. REV. CODE ch. LXI, § 17, arts. 190–93 (1857)).

As for the other twenty-one states in this table, they apparently maintained the old bar against civil parties because their lawmakers saw no good way to reconcile testimony by parties with their racial exclusion laws. That is, they rejected both the Maryland–Mississippi solution and the Indiana solution. Even in an otherwise unfair world, lawmakers may have recoiled from the Maryland–Mississippi solution and the spectacle of permitting a white party to testify against an African–American opponent who was silenced. As for the Indiana solution, lawmakers may have seen a different problem: Under that state's law white parties had the right to testify unless their opponent happened to be nonwhite. Perhaps the image of a world in which white parties could testify against white adversaries but must sit silently when facing African–American foes was too discordant for Southern tastes.

After the North's victory in 1865 Southern states acted quickly to grant African Americans the right to testify at least in certain circumstances. They did so not entirely voluntarily. Federal authorities had established Freedmen's Courts throughout the South. Officials of the Union Army, claiming they spoke for the President, declared that Freedmen's Courts would not surrender jurisdiction to Southern authorities until Southern states made African Americans competent to testify.

By and large, Southern states did what they had to do to rid themselves of the Freedmen's Courts, though they did no more. Only four Southern states—Arkansas, Louisiana, South Carolina, and Tennessee—removed all distinctions of color from the qualification of witnesses during the 1860s. Each of the rest granted African Americans the right to testify only in those cases in which an African American was a party or, in a criminal case, the victim. More strikingly, the North Carolina law required that "whenever a person of color shall be examined as a witness, the court shall warn the witness to declare the truth." Ch. 40, § 10, 1866 N.C. Pub. Laws Stat. 99, 102.

At the very least, though, these new laws put nonwhite parties on roughly the same footing as white parties. That meant Southern states now could make civil parties competent to testify without facing the question they once had found so awkward—how to deal with nonwhite parties. The evidence therefore points to one conclusion: In states with racial exclusion laws, legislators avoided a clash between those laws and rules permitting testimony by civil parties simply by resisting the latter as long as they retained the former.

In fact, once Southern states abolished their racial exclusion laws, they had an incentive to permit civil parties to testify—and to do so quickly. Otherwise, they would have faced a circumstance many in the South would have found unsettling: White parties would have had to sit silently even as African-American witnesses testified against them. Hence when South Carolina first permitted African Americans to testify in certain cases in 1865, it provided at the same time that "[t]he accused, in *such* a criminal case, and the parties, in every *such* civil case, may be witnesses. . . ." An Act to Establish District Courts, § 30, 1865 S.C. Stat. 25, 25 (emphasis added). Likewise, neighboring North Carolina made non-whites competent in certain cases in 1866 and, by the same law, provided that "no person shall be deemed incompetent to bear testimony in *such* cases, because of being a party to the record." An Act Concerning Negroes and Persons of Color or of Mixed Blood, ch. 40, § 9, 1866 N.C. Pub. Laws 99, 102 (emphasis added). And when Alabama made African Americans competent in a limited group of cases in 1865, it provided at the same time that "in all cases . . . in which a freedman . . . is a witness against a white person, or a white person against a freedman . . . the parties shall be competent witnesses." An Act to Protect Freedmen in Their Rights of Person and Property in This State, No. 86, 1866 Ala. Acts 98 (adopted Dec. 9, 1865).

It is very likely that this same impulse—to avoid the spectacle of freedmen testifying against white parties who could not speak—is what moved the other states that appear in the first group in Table 2 to make civil parties competent at virtually the same moment they made non-whites competent.

The upshot is that the overt racism that marked the evidence codes of many states before the Civil War stunted the modernization of those codes in other ways. Long after the first Northern states stepped toward the future by permitting civil parties to testify, almost every Southern state held back. Had the victorious North not demanded that the South give up its racial exclusion laws, the old Confederate states might have clung even longer to obsolete rules barring civil parties.

Focus on
FRE 601, 602, 603, & 610

COMPETENCY RULES TODAY

Today there is little left of the old competency rules. The Federal Rules' treatment of the topic seems almost offhand. Rule 601 declares, "Every person is competent to be a witness unless these rules provide otherwise." But the rules do little by way of providing otherwise. Rule 602 requires lay witnesses to testify from "personal knowledge"; Rule 603 requires all witnesses to swear or affirm to tell the truth. That's about it in the way of general restrictions on witness competency. Addressing more specialized matters, Rule 605 makes the presiding judge incompetent to testify, and Rule 606, as we saw earlier (at pages 8 to 19), limits testimony by jurors.

Caselaw likewise dwells rarely on competency disputes. A few exotic cases deal with witnesses who offer to testify about events long forgotten, now remembered by aid of hypnosis or otherwise. Most prominently, *Rock v. Arkansas*, 483 U.S. 44 (1987), held that a state rule barring *all* hypnotically refreshed testimony could not be applied in a per se manner to bar criminal defendants from the witness stand. "[R]estrictions of a defendant's right to testify," the Supreme Court ruled, "may not be arbitrary or disproportionate to the purposes they are designed to serve." To prevent a defendant's testimony based on her hypnotically refreshed memory, the state first would have "to show that [the] testimony in [this] particular case is so unreliable that exclusion is justified." *Id.* at 55–56, 61.

Despite the prominence of *Rock*, cases of recovered memory and hypnotically refreshed memory generally keep a low profile on the legal landscape. Instead the issue of witness competency arises most commonly when very young children take the stand. The factors that determine a child's competency vary from jurisdiction to jurisdiction, but generally include:

- whether the child can perceive and remember events accurately;
- whether she can communicate them intelligibly;
- whether she understands the difference between truth and falsehood and the obligation to tell the truth; and
- whether she can respond intelligently to questions posed on cross-examination.

When there is doubt about the child's capacity along any of these dimensions, the trial court normally will hold a competency hearing before permitting the child to testify.

One such hearing took place in *State v. Swan*, 114 Wash. 2d 613, 790 P.2d 610 (1990), *cert. denied*, 498 U.S. 1046 (1991). The Washington Supreme Court recounted the testimony given at the competency hearing by the three-year-old victim of alleged sexual abuse:

> ... R.T. said that her birthday was in "higher June." She also said she had been in the courtroom 40 times (she had never been

> there before) and that it was Saturday, although it was not. When asked if she recognized anyone, she pointed to defense counsel and said she had seen him 4 days ago, which she had not. She did not say that she recognized her father or the defendants, who also were in the courtroom. When the court asked R.T. if she knew the difference between the truth and a lie, R.T. said "not telling the truth" is telling a lie. The court then asked R.T. if it would be the truth or a lie if she said she was wearing a pink dress. Though her dress was pink, R.T. said it would be a lie because her dress was long. R.T. then said her dress was "blue, sort of, but it's pink." The court excused R.T. and found her incompetent to testify on the basis she did not understand the obligation to tell the truth on the witness stand and because she did not have a sufficient memory to speak truly about past events.

114 Wash.2d at 646. The Washington Supreme Court held the trial court had not abused its discretion in finding R.T. incompetent to testify.

Not all states encourage or even permit such close judicial scrutiny of children's capacity as witnesses. Alabama, Connecticut, and Utah all declare child victims of physical or sexual abuse to be competent as a matter of law. In the words of the relevant Connecticut statute, "any child who is a victim of assault, sexual assault or abuse shall be competent to testify without prior qualification. The weight to be given the evidence and the credibility of the witness shall be for the determination of the trier of fact." CONN. GEN. STAT. § 54–86h (2012). Laws in Alabama and Utah are similar. *See* ALA. CODE ANN. § 15–25–3(e) (2012); UTAH CODE ANN. § 76–5–410 (2012).

Congress has proved only slightly less welcoming toward victims' testimony in child abuse cases. A 1990 statute created a rebuttable presumption that children are competent witnesses. Trial courts may conduct competency hearings only on finding "that compelling reasons exist"—and "[a] child's age alone is not a compelling reason." The act requires that questions asked of the child at these hearings "shall focus on determining the child's ability to understand and answer simple questions." *See* 18 U.S.C. § 3509(c)(4), (8) (2012).

There is no need to linger on the matter of witness competency. Far more common and complex problems lie ahead. Foremost among them is hearsay. You will see there is an important link between the rather obscure matter of witness competency and the hugely pervasive problem of hearsay: Each is prominently concerned with a party's ability to test a witness through cross-examination, deemed by Wigmore the "greatest legal engine ever invented for the discovery of truth." 6 JOHN HENRY WIGMORE, A TREATISE ON THE ANGLO-AMERICAN SYSTEM OF EVIDENCE IN TRIALS AT COMMON LAW § 1838, at 463 (James H. Chadbourn ed., 1976).

CHAPTER 7

THE RULE AGAINST HEARSAY

A. HISTORICAL PRELUDE

THE TRIAL OF SIR WALTER RALEIGH, KNT. AT WINCHESTER, FOR HIGH TREASON (1603)

Reprinted in 2 T.B. HOWELL, A COMPLETE COLLECTION OF STATE TRIALS 1 (1816); 1 D. JARDINE, CRIMINAL TRIALS 400 (1832)*

... The general points of treason laid in the Indictment were these;—

> That he did conspire, and go about to deprive the king of his Government; to raise up Sedition within the realm; to alter religion to bring in the Roman Superstition and to procure foreign enemies to invade the kingdom. The overt acts charged were, that, on the 9th of June, Sir Walter Raleigh had conferred with Lord Cobham about advancing Arabella Stuart [an aunt of the King, James I] to the Crown of England, and dispossessing the King; that it was then arranged that Lord Cobham should go to the King of Spain ... for the purpose of supporting Arabella Stuart's title....
>
> To the Indictment, Sir Walter Raleigh pleaded Not Guilty....

[Because defendants in treason cases had no right to counsel, Raleigh represented himself. He repeatedly complained that although his alleged coconspirator, Cobham, did not testify in court, Cobham's confession was admitted against Raleigh:]

The Lord Cobham's Examination.

Then was read the Declaration of Lord Cobham, dated the 20th July:—

"He confesseth, he [Cobham] had a Passport to go into Spain, intending to go to the Archduke to confer with him about these Practices.... At the first beginning, he breathed out oaths and exclamations against Raleigh, calling him Villain and Traitor; saying he [Cobham] had

* [These two accounts of Raleigh's trial are not identical. I have drawn some passages from one and some from the other.—GF]

never entered into these courses, but by [Raleigh's] instigation, and that [Raleigh] would never let him alone...."

Raleigh. Let me see the Accusation: This is absolutely all the Evidence can be brought against me; poor shifts! ... I claim to have my accuser brought here face to face to speak.... If you proceed to condemn me ... upon a paper accusation, you try me by the Spanish Inquisition....

Attorney General [Sir Edward Coke].... Cobham saith, he would never have entered into these courses, but by your instigation, and that you would never let him alone....

Raleigh. All this is but one Accusation of Cobham's, I hear no other thing.... I beseech you, my lords, let Cobham be sent for; let him be charged [i.e., sworn] upon his soul, upon his allegiance to the King, and if he will then maintain his accusation to my face, I will confess myself guilty.... The Proof of the Common Law is by witness and jury: let Cobham be here, let him speak it. Call my accuser before my face, and I have done....

Lord Chief Justice. This thing cannot be granted, for then a number of Treasons should flourish: the Accuser may be drawn by practise [i.e., may be led along by artful examination], whilst he is [testifying] in person....

Raleigh.... But it is strange to see how you press me still with my Lord Cobham, and yet will not produce him; ... he is [a prisoner] in the house hard by and may soon be brought hither.... Susanna had been condemned, if Daniel had not cried out, "Will you condemn an innocent Israelite, without examination or knowledge of the truth?" ... [For Cobham] to accuse me is my certain danger, and it may be a means to excuse himself. [That is, Cobham may be accusing Raleigh to exculpate himself.] ...

Good my Lords, let my accuser come face to face, and be deposed. Were the case but for a small copyhold, you would have witnesses or good proof to lead the jury to a verdict; and I am here for my life!

Lord Chief Justice. You have no law for it: God forbid any man should accuse himself upon his oath! [That is, by testifying against Raleigh, Cobham necessarily would have to incriminate himself.] ...

Raleigh.... [B]y this means you may have any man's life in a week; and I may be massacred by mere hearsay.... You say, that Brooke told Watson what Cobham told Brooke, that I had said to him;—what proof is this? ...

Attorney General. I shall now produce a witness *viva voce* ["with the living voice"—i.e., in person. He then produced one Dyer, a boat pilot]:

Dyer. I came to a merchant's house in Lisbon ...; there came a gentleman into the house, and enquiring what countryman I was, I said, an Englishman. Whereupon he asked me, if the king was crowned? And I answered, No, but that I hoped he should be so shortly. Nay, saith he, he shall never be crowned; for Don Raleigh and Don Cobham will cut his throat ere that day come.

Raleigh. This is the saying of some wild Jesuit or beggarly Priest; but what proof is it against me?

Attorney General. It . . . shows that your treason had wings. . . .

[Later, engaging now in a hearsay war, Raleigh produced his own letter from Cobham:]

Here Raleigh pulled a Letter out of his pocket, which the lord Cobham had written to him . . .; the effect of it was as follows:

> Seeing myself so near my end, for the discharge of my own conscience, and freeing myself from your blood, which else will cry vengeance against me; I protest upon my salvation I never practised with Spain by your procurement; God so comfort me in this my affliction, as you are a true subject for any thing that I know . . . So God have mercy upon my soul, as I know no Treason by you.

["Here was much ado," the reporter wrote. "Mr. Attorney [Coke] alledged, that his last Letter was politicly and cunningly urged from the lord Cobham, and that the first was simply the truth. . . ." The reporter then continued:]

This was the last Evidence: whereupon a marshal was sworn to keep the Jury private. The Jury departed, and staid not a quarter of an hour, but returned, and gave their verdict, Guilty. . . .

B. Defining Hearsay

1. The Basic Rule

Focus on
FRE 801(a)–(c) & 802

Hearsay: An Introduction

Sometimes a lawyer asks a witness what she *heard* someone *say*. Hence we have the problem of *hearsay*. But very often, when a witness says what she heard someone say, the testimony is not hearsay at all. So our first challenge is definitional: What exactly is hearsay? This introduction and a later segment on assertions will offer some guidance.

It helps to begin by recognizing that the hearsay rule is about the *reliability* of the evidence the jury hears. Let's look for a moment at normal, nonhearsay testimony. Such testimony has four possible sources of unreliability. When a witness testifies, "Then I saw John pull the trigger," we worry about a failure of one or more of the four *testimonial capacities*:

Perception:	The witness saw *Tom* pull the trigger, but mistook him for John.
Memory:	The witness saw and recognized Tom, but now *thinks* it was John.
Narration:	The witness *means* to say Tom, but says John.
Sincerity:	The witness means to deceive.

The problem can be represented this way:

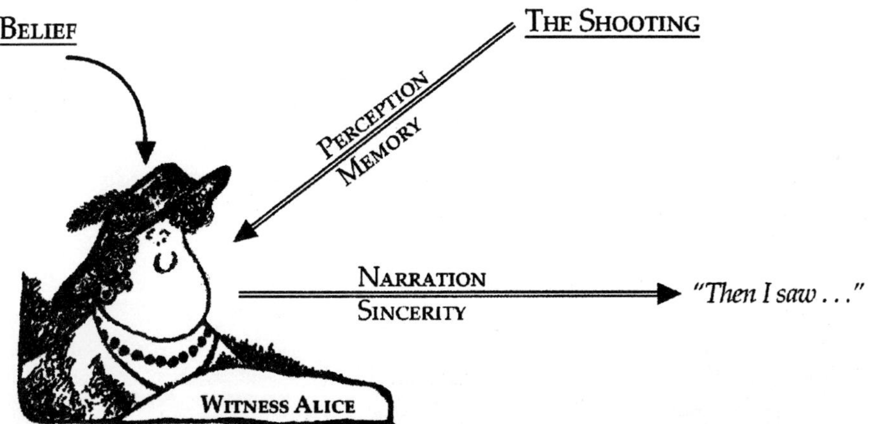

Alice, our witness, sees an event (a shooting), forms a belief about it, and relates that belief to the jury. Her belief accurately reflects the event only if she perceived and remembers the event accurately. Her testimony accurately reflects her belief only if she narrates accurately and truthfully. The information the jury hears about the shooting is accurate only if all four of the witness's testimonial capacities are sound.

Despite these potential infirmities, we regularly permit witnesses to testify about facts they have observed. We feel reasonably confident about the accuracy of such testimony because it is tested by three courtroom tools:

The Oath:	Witnesses must swear or affirm they will tell the truth. Those witnesses not impressed by a wrathful deity may heed the penalties of perjury. Penalties aside, the solemnity of the ritual prompts sincerity and care.
Demeanor Evidence:	Jurors scrutinize faces and mannerisms, watch for signs of stress, and judge intellect, precision, and trustworthiness.
Cross–Examination:	The opposing lawyer probes for deficiencies in perception, memory, narration, and sincerity. In criminal cases, the witness normally must answer questions while facing the accused.

Beyond the force of these truth-testing tools, witnesses may be less likely to lie in court because they have to testify in view of opposing parties and the public—or because the dignity of the courtroom makes it unseemly to lie.

Why Bar Hearsay?

Now consider the problem of hearsay. Assume that witness Alice, who said she saw John pull the trigger, does not come to court. Instead the state calls witness Bill, who testifies, "Alice told me she saw John pull the trigger." Our diagram is now considerably more complicated:*

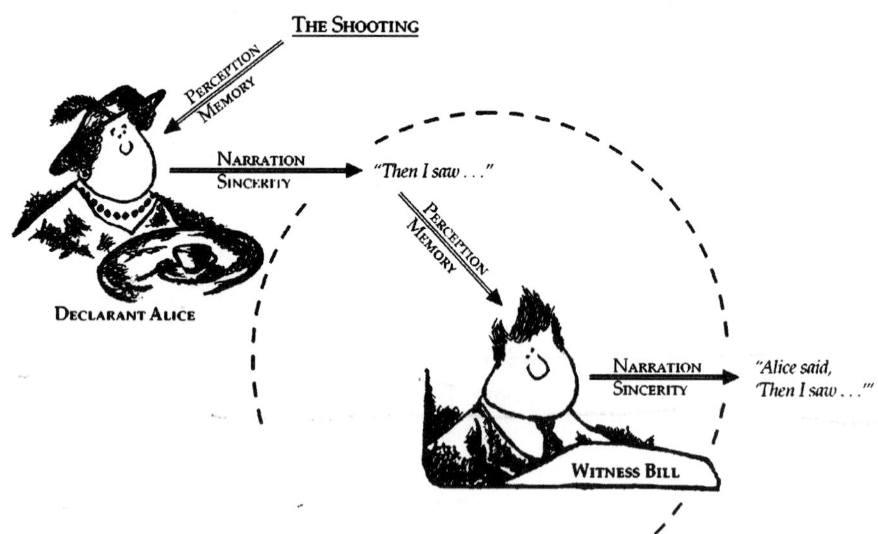

* Compare this diagram to Laurence Tribe's hearsay triangle and Michael Graham's hearsay stickpersons. *See* Laurence Tribe, *Triangulating Hearsay*, 87 HARV. L. REV. 957, 957–61 (1974); Michael H. Graham, *"Stickperson Hearsay": A Simplified Approach to Understanding the Rule Against Hearsay*, 1982 U. ILL. L. REV. 887, 895–96 (1982).

The truth of Bill's testimony—that he heard Alice say she saw John pull the trigger—depends on all four of his testimonial capacities. The jury is able to assess his testimonial capacities if Bill testifies in court. But for the jury to conclude *that John in fact pulled the trigger*, it must rely on all four of Bill's testimonial capacities *and* all four of Alice's testimonial capacities. Because Alice is not in court, however, she cannot be sworn or cross-examined, and the jury cannot observe her demeanor as she speaks. The probative powers of the oath, demeanor evidence, and cross-examination (represented in the diagram by the circle) therefore reach only as far as the reliability of Bill's testimony about what Alice said. To get from that testimony to the truth of Alice's assertion (and thus to the conclusion that John pulled the trigger), we must rely on Alice's *untested* testimonial capacities.

Defining Hearsay

If you refer now to Rule 801, you will see that Alice's claim about what she saw is a "statement" as defined in Rule 801(a). Alice herself is a "declarant" as defined in Rule 801(b). And Bill's testimony about Alice's statement, *if offered by a litigant to prove John pulled the trigger*, is "hearsay" by the terms of Rule 801(c). Unless spared by one of the many exceptions to the hearsay rule (which we will study in time), Alice's statement will be excluded by Rule 802.

Hearsay is an out-of-court statement offered by a litigant to prove what the declarant asserted. The rule writers could have clarified Rule 801(c)'s definition of hearsay by adding the italicized words:

> **Rule 801. DEFINITIONS . . .**
>
> **(c) Hearsay.** "Hearsay" means a statement that:
>
> **(1)** the declarant does not make while testifying at the current trial or hearing; and
>
> **(2)** a party offers in evidence to prove the truth of the matter asserted in the statement *by the declarant*.

Absent the italicized words, one could think the rule applies to out-of-court statements a party offers to prove the truth of the matter asserted *by the party*. That misreading could lead to the conclusion that almost *every* out-of-court statement is hearsay. After all, lawyers typically offer evidence to prove the truth of their own assertions.

Note that the rule's cumbersome phrase—"a statement that . . . the declarant does not make while testifying at the current trial or hearing"—typically may be replaced by the shorthand "an out-of-court statement":

> "Hearsay" means [an out-of-court] statement that . . . a party offers in evidence to prove the truth of the matter asserted in the statement *by the declarant*.

Hence under Rule 801(c), we must ask two questions to decide whether any particular out-of-court statement is hearsay:

(1) Is the party offering the statement to prove (the truth of) what it says or was meant to say?

(2) Did the declarant assert—that is, did she mean to communicate—that fact?

The second question is the subject of the next segment, "Defining Assertions," and especially pages 392 to 400. For now, we should concentrate on the first question. Remember—unless the answer to both questions is yes, the statement is not hearsay.

Nonhearsay Uses of Out-of-Court Statements

Answering the first question requires us to know or surmise why a litigant is offering the out-of-court statement. Often lawyers offer statements for reasons other than proving their truth. There are several common *nonhearsay* purposes for evidence of an out-of-court statement. We begin with these three:

- To prove the statement's impact on someone who heard it;
- To prove a legal right or duty triggered by—or an offense caused by—uttering the statement; and
- To impeach the declarant's later, in-court testimony.*

As we consider each of these categories, bear in mind that the important question is whether the litigant is offering the statement to prove what it says or was meant to say. If not, the statement is not hearsay.

Words Offered to Prove Their Effect on the Listener: Assume that Bill, pictured on page 378, is now our defendant, charged with having shot a man named Joey. Assume too that he is claiming self-defense—that he shot Joey because he reasonably feared Joey otherwise might kill him. To establish that his fear was reasonable, Bill might want to offer evidence that Alice had warned him of Joey's ill intentions. Hence Bill might testify, "The day before I had the run-in with Joey, Alice told me, 'Watch out for Joey. He's looking for you, and he has a gun.'" Our diagram now looks simpler:

* My thanks to Judge Paul Plunkett for suggesting this approach to nonhearsay uses of out-of-court statements.—GF

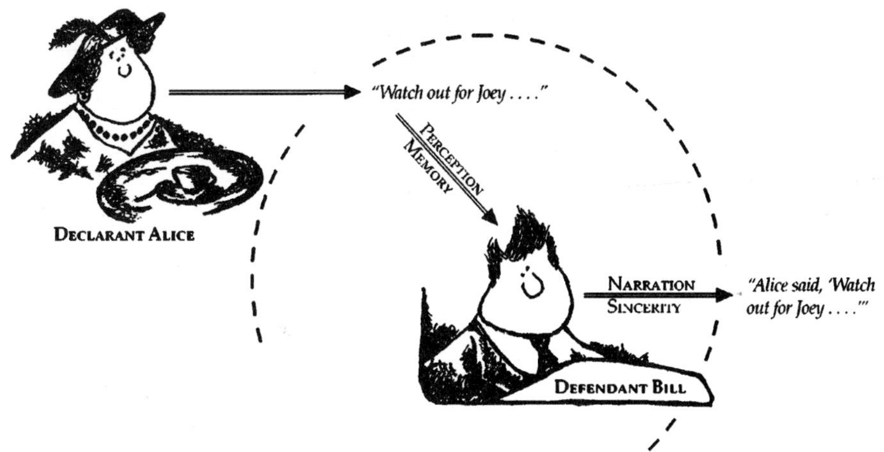

If Bill had offered evidence of Alice's statement to prove Joey really was looking for him and really had a gun, Alice's statement would be hearsay. The truth of those facts depends on the soundness of Alice's testimonial capacities.

Alice's statement would *not* be hearsay, however, if offered to prove the defendant had reason to fear Joey at the time of the attack. In that case the defendant would not be offering Alice's statement to prove the truth of what it asserts. Alice's warning gave the defendant reason to fear Joey even if what she said was completely false. Put differently, the evidentiary significance of Alice's words, when offered to prove the defendant's reasonable fear of Joey, does *not* depend on the soundness of her testimonial capacities. All we need to know is that she *said* the words ("Watch out for Joey. . . . [H]e has a gun.") and that the defendant *heard* (and believed) them. The defendant's testimony about these facts therefore would not be hearsay.

Because it does not matter whether Alice's testimonial capacities were sound, it does not matter that the opposing lawyer can't subject Alice to the courtroom tests of the oath, presence before the jury, and cross-examination. That is why the rule does not exclude as hearsay those statements offered only to show their effect on the listener.

Legally Operative Words (Verbal Acts): Simply by uttering certain words, a declarant can trigger a legal right or duty or commit an offense. Treatises often refer to such legally operative words as *verbal acts* because they have legal force independent of the speaker's intended meaning. The substantive law of the jurisdiction typically determines the legal force of spoken or written words. If other conditions are met, saying "I accept" after an offer can create a contract. Saying "I do" at the altar makes a marriage. Saying "I will kill you" constitutes a threat. And saying "He's a thief" in public can be slander.

All these statements operate independently of the speaker's belief or intended meaning. The soundness of her testimonial capacities therefore doesn't matter, so there is no reason to exclude her words as hearsay.

Inconsistent Statements Offered to Impeach: Lawyers often seek to impeach (or prove false) a witness's courtroom testimony with evidence that she once said something different. The theory of such impeachment is *not* that the out-of-court statement is true, so the present testimony must be false. Instead the theory is that the out-of-court statement proves that the witness has said different things at different times about this fact, so her testimony on this point can't be trusted. Under this theory the truth of the out-of-court statement is irrelevant. Evidence of inconsistent statements offered only to impeach therefore is not hearsay.

We return to this form of impeachment later in the chapter, at pages 435 to 452, and consider it in more detail then.

The Hearsay Flowchart

One feature is common to these three categories of nonhearsay: In offering an out-of-court statement for these purposes, the proponent does *not* rely on the *belief* of the declarant when she uttered the out-of-court words. The lawyer is *not* suggesting to the jury, "The declarant believed the stated fact to be true; therefore you should too." From the proponent's perspective what matters is simply that the words *were spoken*. Hence the declarant's testimonial capacities are irrelevant.

Now consider the hearsay flowchart on the next page. The first branch toward the top distinguishes statements offered to prove the truth of the declarant's belief, which may be hearsay, from *all other statements, which are not hearsay*. At this first branch ask yourselves, "Does the lawyer's purpose in offering this statement depend on the truth of the declarant's belief?" If so, we need to descend to the next branch of the flowchart, which we examine more closely in the segment on defining assertions at pages 388 to 403. If not, the statement is not hearsay.

Whenever out-of-court words are offered for a reason other than proving their truth, the opponent may worry that jurors will simply believe the words and use them for the forbidden hearsay purpose of proving their truth. Rule 105 requires the judge, if asked, to give a limiting instruction confining jurors to the permitted, nonhearsay use of the words. As always, the chance that jurors will not or cannot obey this instruction poses a risk of unfair prejudice weighed by the judge under Rule 403. (See ACN to FRE 403, RB 43.)

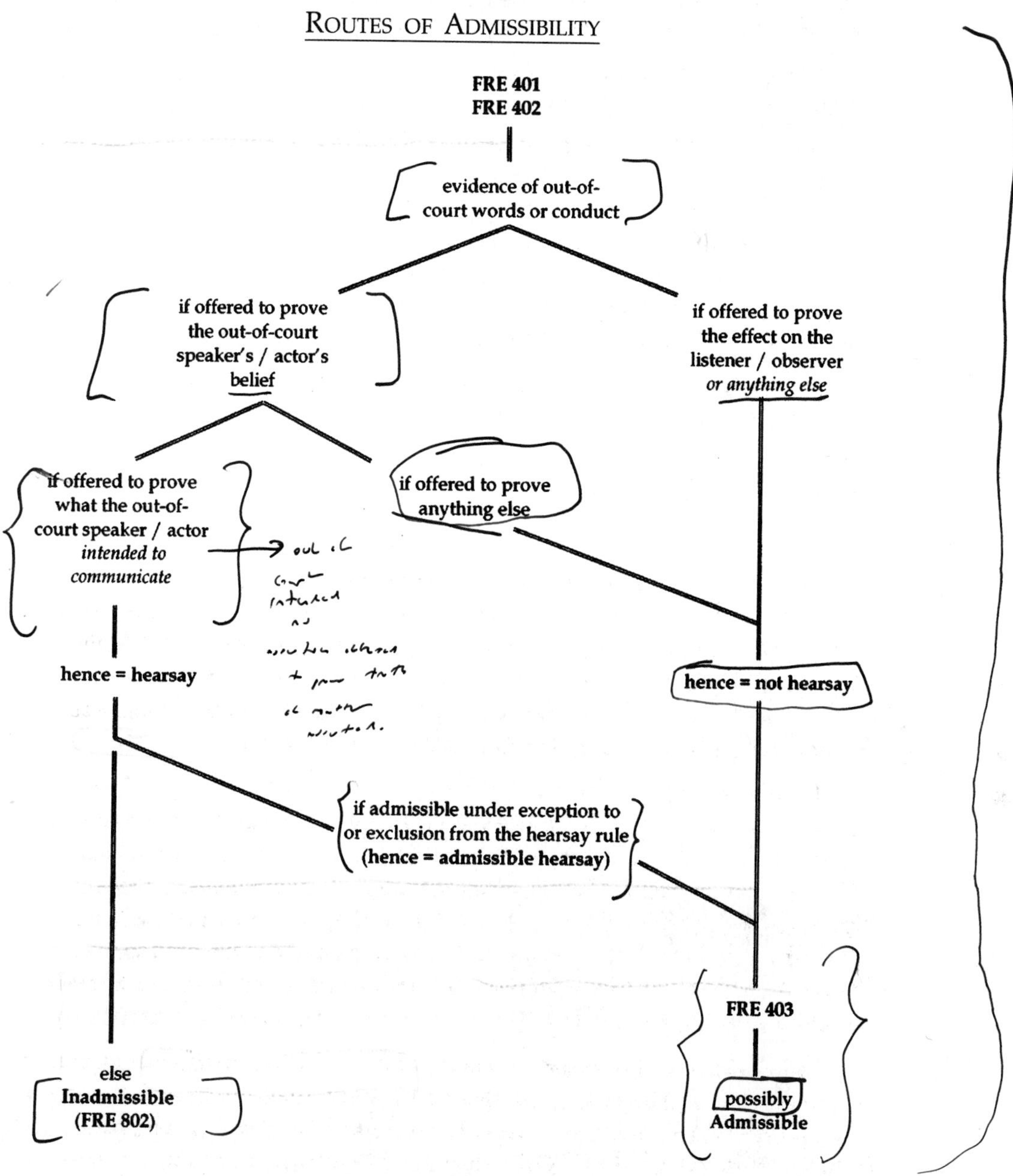

Problems

Problems 7.1 through 7.8 ask you to distinguish hearsay, as defined by Rule 801(c), from nonhearsay statements. The first four problems focus on the definitions of "statement" and "declarant." The last four call on you to decide whether a statement is offered to prove the truth of the declarant's belief. Begin by asking why the lawyer offers the statement. Then ask whether the lawyer's claim depends on the truth of the declarant's belief. If a statement has a valid nonhearsay purpose, consider what limiting instruction the judge should give on request.

Note that no problem addresses the out-of-court statements of animals. Rule 801's definitions of "statement" and "declarant" confine hearsay to statements of a "person." Presumably the rule writers weren't concerned that animals lie in the ordinary sense. Or perhaps they thought juries can assess the reliability of bloodhounds without seeing them in court. Litigants may challenge the accuracy of an animal's signals under Rule 403. And under Rule 702, the focus of Chapter 9, litigants may contest the expertise of human handlers who interpret a bark or hiss. But unless an animal's signals simply responded to human commands, as when a dog barks on order, a hearsay objection will not avail.

Problem 7.1
Affidavit

A large group of individuals injured in rollover crashes of a particular SUV brought a class action lawsuit against the automaker. Fearing that the plaintiffs' chief witness, who was ill, would die before trial, plaintiffs' counsel secured an affidavit from her. Her affidavit stated that she had watched rollover crash tests of the same model SUV conducted by the automaker two years before the first fatal crash. In those tests employees of the automaker had induced explosions in tires of SUVs traveling at normal highway speeds. The explosions caused many of the vehicles to roll over. The witness signed the affidavit "under the pains and penalties of perjury."

The witness died before trial. At trial plaintiffs' counsel offers the affidavit to prove that the automaker's own tests had demonstrated the rollover hazard. Is the affidavit hearsay?

Problem 7.2
Gesture

To prove that Jeffrey was short on cash in March 2012, the prosecution calls one of his friends as a witness. She testifies that sometime in March she asked Jeffrey, "Why don't you replace that beat-up carcass of a bicycle?" According to the witness, Jeffrey said nothing in response. Instead he held up his right hand and rubbed his thumb together with his index and middle fingers—a gesture the witness recognized to mean money.

Is the witness's testimony about the gesture hearsay?

Problem 7.3
Quoting Herself

To prove the defendant was the person who robbed Marilyn, the prosecutor examined Marilyn on the witness stand as follows:

Q: What did you do at the police station?

A: The detective had me look at a lineup of eight men.

Q: Did you see the man who robbed you in that lineup?

A: Yes.

Q: What did you say to the detective?

A: I said, "He's number three."

Is this evidence hearsay? You may assume the detective will testify for the prosecution that "number three" was the defendant.

Problem 7.4
Blood Test

After his arrest on a charge of driving under the influence of alcohol or drugs, Washington agreed to give a blood sample for testing. A nurse drew a vial of his blood, which the arresting officer sent for analysis to the Armed Forces Institute of Pathology.

Using a gas chromatograph and computers with ChemStation software, lab technicians subjected the blood to various tests. The machine generated a printout stating that "the sample of blood obtained from Washington at 04:43 a.m. on 03 Jan. 2004 contained 27 mg/dL of ethanol" and tested positive for PCP, containing "0.04 mg/L of phencyclidine as quantitated by gas chromatograph/spectrometry." *Cf. United States v. Washington,* 498 F.3d 225, 227–28 (4th Cir. 2007), *cert. denied,* 557 U.S. 934 (2009) (stating these facts, altered slightly here).

At trial the prosecutor offered this printout as an exhibit to prove the levels of alcohol and PCP in Washington's blood at 4:43 a.m. on January 3, 2004. Is the printout hearsay?

Problem 7.5
Boasts

Recall the defendant's testimony in *United States v. James* (page 29, above), a homicide case in which the defendant pled self-defense:

> [The defendant, Ernestine James, testified that the victim, David Ogden,] had boasted to her about once killing a man and getting away with it. He told her he had sold another man a fake watch, and when the man complained, had stabbed him in the neck with a ball point pen. Ogden told James that "it was pretty funny watching a guy with a pen dangling out of his neck." He also bragged that he had once "ripped a side view mirror off the car and beat a man unconscious with it," and that, in yet another incident, he had robbed an old man by holding him down with a knife in his face and threatening to cut his eyes out.

If the prosecutor had objected to this testimony as hearsay, should the trial judge have permitted it?

Problem 7.6
Horse Theft

In *State v. Getz*, 250 Kan. 560 (1992), Vicky Getz was charged with felony theft after selling two horses that belonged to William and Shirley Griffing. Testifying in her defense, Getz claimed she believed the horses belonged to Perry Patton, who had been living with her for about a month. According to the Kansas Supreme Court, "Getz sought permission [from the trial judge] to testify that Patton told her he had purchased the two paint horses and that he asked her help in selling the horses." *Id.* at 566.

Was the trial court correct in ruling that Getz's proposed testimony was hearsay?

Problem 7.7
Ineffective Assistance

On August 9, 1997, Abner Louima was brutally assaulted by two New York City police officers in a bathroom of the stationhouse. Louima's testimony and other evidence suggested his assailants were Officers Justin Volpe and Charles Schwarz. Both men initially denied any role, though Volpe later pled guilty.

After his conviction Schwarz moved for a new trial, alleging that his lawyer, Stephen Worth, had been ineffective. At a hearing on the motion Marvyn Kornberg, who had been Volpe's lawyer, testified that about a week before the end of Schwarz's trial, Kornberg told Worth that "my guy [Volpe] can take your guy [Schwarz] out of the bathroom." Although Volpe, who by then had pled guilty, was apparently prepared to testify that Schwarz was not in the bathroom during the assault on Louima, Worth never called Volpe to the stand. Schwarz alleged Worth's failure to call Volpe as one basis for a finding of ineffective assistance of counsel. *See United States v. Schwarz*, 283 F.3d 76, 93 (2d Cir. 2002).

Is evidence of Kornberg's statement to Worth hearsay if offered by Schwarz to support his claim of ineffective assistance?

Problem 7.8
Declarations

Consider the facts of *United States v. White*, 87 Fed. Appx. 566 (6th Cir.), *cert. denied*, 543 U.S. 818 (2004):

> On September 15, 1999, Defendant White and traveling companion, Tony Friese, arrived at the Cincinnati–Northern Kentucky Airport after two weeks of travel throughout Europe.... At the immigration booth, White and Friese provided declaration forms to United States Customs Officer Mary Fennell. White's form declared that he had acquired abroad beer, wine, and chocolate—totaling $102.00.... White denied having acquired other items abroad. Inspector [David] Smith searched White's bags and found forty-five high-capacity firearm magazines and a rifle stock.... At trial, Inspector Smith estimated the value of the firearm magazines to be in excess of $2000.00....
>
> A federal grand jury subsequently returned a two-count indictment against Defendant White, alleging one count ...

[of making] a false and fraudulent [customs] declaration in violation of 18 U.S.C. § 542. . . .

During the trial, White attempted to have Friese testify that White had, at one point during the customs inspection, stated that "I [Defendant White] have some more items to declare." The Government objected to this testimony as "classic hearsay."

(1) Assume the government offered evidence that White bought the firearm magazines while in Europe. Was the officers' testimony that White "denied having acquired other items abroad" hearsay if offered by the government to prove White lied to the officers?

(2) How should the trial court have ruled on the government's hearsay objection to Friese's proposed testimony?

---

2. DEFINING ASSERTIONS

Judson F. Falknor

The "Hear–Say" Rule as a "See–Do" Rule: Evidence of Conduct

33 U. COLO. L. REV. 133 (1961)

Reprinted by Permission.

It is time to go to lunch. When you left home for the office in the morning it was raining and you brought your umbrella. Will you need it at lunchtime? You consult your secretary, she looks out the window, and tells you that you had better take your umbrella. If, in some subsequent litigation, the question should arise whether it was raining when you went out to lunch, would the secretary be permitted to testify that when she looked out she saw a number of passers-by with their umbrellas up? More precisely, would her testimony as to what she saw these people do be equated to what she would have heard them say, had she called out, asked them whether it was raining, and they had replied that it was?

Or, take another one: You drive up to signal-controlled intersection and pull up behind a large truck and trailer which has stopped at the near side of the intersection. The truck and trailer block your view of the traffic light. In a moment or so the truck moves ahead and you follow it. If, in subsequent litigation, the question arises whether the light had changed to green when you started up, may you testify, as tending to show that the light had changed, that the truck driver had moved ahead before you did? More precisely, would your testimony as to what you saw the truck driver do, be equated to what you would have heard him say had he, before moving ahead, called back to tell you that the light had changed?

Of course, if, in either of these supposititious situations, the conduct proposed to be shown is to be treated as merely equivalent to an assertion of the fact the evidence is offered to establish, we are in trouble with the hearsay rule. And by many cases (probably in most of those where the hearsay question has been identified and raised) evidence of extra-judicial conduct, relevant only as an "implied assertion" of the fact the evidence is offered to prove, is within the hearsay ban. Put otherwise, where evidence of non-verbal conduct is relevant only as supporting inferences from the conduct to the belief of the actor and thence to the truth of his belief, prevailing doctrine stigmatizes the evidence as hearsay, inadmissible unless accommodated within one of the exceptions to the rule.* Thus, it seems quite correct to say that in situations of this sort, the "hearsay" rule actually operates as a "see-do" rule.

In the instances supposed, the conduct offered to be proven was completely "non-verbal"; but an identical problem arises where the conduct, although "verbal," is relevant, not as tending to prove the truth of what was said, but circumstantially, that is, as manifesting a belief in the existence of the fact the evidence is offered to prove. As a matter of fact the leading case[2] equating an "implied" to an "express" assertion—and thus stigmatizing the evidence as hearsay—concerned the admissibility, in a will contest, of evidence of the writing of a letter to the testator by the vicar of the parish about a matter of consequence, relevant not as evidence of the truth of anything in the letter, but as manifesting the vicar's apparent belief in the testator's mental competency as tending to prove competency....

The same problem arises with respect to evidence of "non-action" or "silence" when relevant as justifying inferences from the non-action of the individual to his apparent belief and thence to the truth of that belief. While there is a division of authority with respect to the applicability of the hearsay rule to evidence of this sort, it is undoubtedly correct to say that in most cases where the hearsay objection has been urged, it has been sustained. The typical case has to do with the admissibility, on an

* [The "prevailing doctrine" of Falknor's day, which "stigmatize[d]" as hearsay all evidence of conduct offered to show the belief of the actor, is no longer the law. Under the Federal Rules, only conduct "intended ... as an assertion" and offered to prove the matter asserted is hearsay. *See* FRE 801(a), (c). Falknor's critique of the old law (read on from here) helped persuade the Advisory Committee of the wisdom of the new approach. *See* FRE 801(a), Advisory Committee's Note (citing Falknor), at RB 196–97.—GF]

2. Wright v. Tatham, 5 Cl. & Fin. 670, 7 Eng. Rep. 559 (H.L. 1838).

issue of the quality of goods, of evidence of the failure of other purchasers to complain.

In any of these situations, the hearsay objection is likely to be overlooked. This is especially so when the evidence concerns "non-verbal" conduct because the hearsay rule is almost always, in the abstract, phrased in terms of "statements" or "utterances" and the possible application of the rule to "conduct" may not be immediately apparent. And the same is true, although perhaps to a lesser degree, when the evidence is of "verbal" conduct relevant only circumstantially. Cases are legion consequently where the hearsay objection, with strong supporting authority, might have been raised but was not.

But ought the hearsay rule be deemed applicable to evidence of conduct? As McCormick has observed, the problem "has only once received any adequate discussion in any decided case," in *Wright v. Tatham*, already referred to. And even in that case the court did not pursue its inquiry beyond the point of concluding that evidence of an "express" assertion would be inadmissible. But as has been pointed out more than once (although I find no judicial recognition of the difference), the "implied" assertion is, from the hearsay standpoint, not nearly as vulnerable as an express assertion of the fact which the evidence is offered to establish.

This is on the assumption that the conduct was "non-assertive"; that the passers-by had their umbrellas up for the sake of keeping dry, not for the purpose of telling anyone it was raining; that the truck driver started up for the sake of resuming his journey, not for the purpose of telling anyone that the light had changed; that the vicar wrote the letter to the testator for the purpose of settling the dispute with the latter, rather than with any idea of expressing his opinion of the testator's sanity. And in the typical "conduct as hearsay" case this assumption will be quite justifiable.[13]

On this assumption, it is clear that evidence of conduct must be taken as freed from at least one of the hearsay dangers, mendacity. A man does not lie to himself. Put otherwise, if in doing what he does a man has no intention of asserting the existence or non-existence of a fact, it would appear that the trustworthiness of evidence of this conduct is the same whether he is an egregious liar or a paragon of veracity. Accordingly, the lack of opportunity for cross-examination in relation to

13. Of course, if it appears that the individual did what he did in order to assert the fact the evidence is offered to prove, the hearsay rule must apply. There are a good many cases which hold inadmissible, for the accused in a criminal case, evidence that a third-party fled when suspected or accused of the crime, such conduct being characterized as an "implied" third-party confession. Ordinarily, such conduct may be presumed to have been "non-assertive." However, if it should appear in the particular case that the third party was deliberately attempting to exonerate someone else by casting suspicion upon himself, the conduct would be burdened with all the hearsay infirmities of an express confession.

his veracity or lack of it, would seem to be of no substantial importance. Accordingly, the usual judicial disposition to equate the "implied" to the "express" assertion is very questionable.

This is not to say that the "implied" assertion is completely free of hearsay infirmities or that cross-examination of the individual would not be helpful. His opportunity to observe the event or condition in question, the quality of the sense-impressions which he received, and of his recollection, are all matters which bear upon the trustworthiness of his conduct, and ideally, these ought to be subject to being probed by cross-examination. Nonetheless, the absence of the danger of misrepresentation does work strongly in favor of by-passing the hearsay objection....

The [better rule] would seem to be one which would eliminate completely the hearsay stigma from evidence of non-assertive conduct. Because such conduct is evidently more dependable than an assertion, there is rational basis for the differentiation. And there is a cogent practical argument for such a rule ... [as] experience has shown that very often, probably more often than not, and understandably, the hearsay objection to evidence of non-assertive conduct is overlooked in practice with the result that the present doctrine operates very unevenly.

Such is the solution proposed by the Uniform Rules of Evidence.... Non-assertive conduct is excluded from the definition of hearsay. Precisely, a statement (so as to be subject to the hearsay ban) would include ... "non-verbal conduct of a person [only when] intended by him as a substitute for words in expressing the matter stated." This, it seems clear, would operate to eliminate the hearsay stigma from evidence of conduct unless it appeared to the judge that what was done was done for the sake of asserting the fact the evidence is now offered to establish....

Problem 7.9

Ship Inspection

Judson Falknor mentioned the classic case of *Wright v. Tatham*, 7 Adolph. & E. 313, 388, 112 Eng. Rep. 488 (Exch. Ch. 1837), which concerned a challenge to a testator's competence. In framing the issue, the court posed a hypothetical almost as famous as the case: Would evidence of "the conduct of a deceased captain on a question of [the] seaworthiness" of a particular vessel be hearsay if the captain, "after examining every part of the vessel, embarked in it with his family"?

That is, suppose a ship sank and everyone on board, including the captain, perished. Assume too that the ship's owner filed a claim against the insurer, but the insurer refused payment, alleging the ship was unseaworthy and never should have left port. The owner sued for payment and at trial wishes to offer evidence that the ship was indeed seaworthy. If the ship's captain had lived, he could have testified as an expert that he believed the ship seaworthy. Instead the plaintiff calls as a witness a dockworker who watched the captain's actions immediately before leaving port. The dockworker is prepared to testify that after the captain made a careful inspection of the ship, he escorted his family on board and set sail.

If the plaintiff offers the dockworker's testimony as evidence that the captain believed the ship seaworthy, is the evidence hearsay?

Problem 7.10
Amchitka Holiday

In a well-known article exploring the definition of hearsay, Professor Laurence Tribe presented the following hypothetical:

> Suppose . . . that the issue in a lawsuit is whether the Government took adequate safety precautions in connection with the nuclear test at Amchitka in 1971. James Schlesinger, then Chairman of the Atomic Energy Commission, "told reporters at Elmendorf Air Force Base outside Anchorage that he was taking his wife . . . and daughters . . . with him [to the site of the Amchitka blast]. . . ."

Laurence Tribe, *Triangulating Hearsay*, 87 HARV. L. REV. 957, 957–61 (1974).

Suppose Schlesinger in fact traveled to Amchitka with his family. Would testimony of an observer describing Schlesinger's trip be hearsay if offered to show Schlesinger's expert opinion that the blast site was safe? Is this problem different from the last one, *Ship Inspection*?

THE NATURE OF ASSERTIONS

Until now, we have focused on the definitional problem presented by testimony such as, "Alice told me, 'Watch out for Joey. He's looking for you, and he has a gun.'" (See pages 380–81.) When confronted with such evidence, you can trace the distinction between hearsay and nonhearsay by asking whether the significance of the evidence depends on the truth of the out-of-court speaker's belief. In this example the important thing is not what the out-of-court speaker (Alice) believed, but what the out-of-court listener (the defendant) heard. The probative force of evidence of Alice's statement in showing the defendant's reasonable fear therefore does not depend on Alice's testimonial capacities. So the evidence is not hearsay.

Now we have to take up a somewhat trickier and thankfully rarer problem. Is there ever a time when the value of the evidence of an out-of-court statement or action *does* require us to rely on the declarant's beliefs and on some of her testimonial capacities, yet the evidence still is not hearsay? The answer is yes. To see why, we have to examine the significance of the word *assertion* in Rule 801.

Rule 801(c) defines hearsay as an out-of-court "statement" offered "to prove the truth of the matter *asserted*." Rule 801(a) defines a "statement" as an "oral *assertion*, written *assertion*, or nonverbal conduct, if . . . intended . . . as an *assertion*." (Emphasis added.) So hearsay is an out-of-court *assertion* offered to prove what it *asserts*. But what is an assertion?

Most evidence texts attack this question by examining nonverbal conduct. Casebooks focus on the problem of nonverbal conduct because almost all oral and written expressions assert *something* and so present little chance to trace the line between assertions and nonassertions. But not *all* oral and written expressions are assertions. Although this segment will follow the traditional route and begin with a focus on conduct, keep in mind that the distinction between assertions and nonassertions is the same, whether the evidence in question is verbal or nonverbal.

Conduct

Some conduct is clearly assertive. Problem 7.2 (*Gesture*), at page 384, presents a good example. In response to the question, "Why don't you replace that beat-up carcass of a bicycle?" the defendant rubbed his thumb and fingers together, making a gesture that means money. The defendant's gesture was equivalent to the verbal assertion, "The reason is money."

Other conduct is harder to classify. Problem 7.9 (*Ship Inspection*), at page 391, should be our starting point. At issue is whether the ship was seaworthy. The plaintiff wishes to prove it was seaworthy by showing that an experienced sea captain inspected the ship closely before setting sail with his family on board. If the captain's actions amounted to an assertion about the ship's seaworthiness, evidence of his conduct would be hearsay if offered to prove it seaworthy. But has the captain asserted anything?

Compare the Ship Inspection problem to Laurence Tribe's hypothetical about James Schlesinger (see Problem 7.10 (*Amchitka Holiday*), at page

392). Tribe reports that Schlesinger, as chair of the Atomic Energy Commission, responded to criticism of an atomic test by telling reporters he was taking his wife and daughters to the blast site. If Schlesinger indeed made the trip, did he assert anything by such conduct?

The essence of an assertion is found in the distinction between the sea captain's actions and Schlesinger's. The sea captain acted only for himself and his family. Schlesinger, in going to the blast site, acted for an audience. We know this because Schlesinger alerted reporters of his intention to go to the blast site. The sea captain wanted to *assure* that the vessel was safe. Schlesinger wanted to *assert* that the blast site was safe. Schlesinger, but not the sea captain, *intended* his actions to communicate something. That communicative intent is the essence of an assertion. As the advisory committee says in its Note to Rule 801(a), "nothing is an assertion unless intended to be one." (RB 196.)

Evidence of Schlesinger's actions, if offered to show that the blast site was safe, would be hearsay because that is exactly what he intended to assert. Evidence of the sea captain's actions, if offered to prove that the vessel was seaworthy, would not be hearsay because the sea captain had no audience and did not intend to assert anything. Nonassertive conduct is not hearsay.

So far, this distinction between assertions and nonassertions might seem formalistic. Yet there is a critical difference between the two, and that difference relates closely to the rationale behind the hearsay rule examined in the last section. Recall that hearsay is banned because opponents can't test the out-of-court declarant's perception, memory, narrative powers, and sincerity. Compare the sea captain problem and the Schlesinger scenario in these terms. On which testimonial capacities must we rely to conclude that the ship—or the blast site—was safe?

- In each case we must rely on the out-of-court actor's *perception*. The sea captain may have overlooked a leak in the hull. Schlesinger may have misread data about the proposed blast.
- In each case we must rely on the out-of-court actor's *memory*. The sea captain may have seen a leak in the hull, and Schlesinger may have spotted a flaw in the data, yet each may have forgotten it.
- In each case we must rely on the out-of-court actor's *narrative powers* (loosely construed). The sea captain may have judged ship A seaworthy, then mistakenly boarded ship B. Schlesinger may have judged Anchorage to be safe, then mistakenly journeyed to Amchitka.

The key difference between the two cases emerges when we focus on the out-of-court actor's *sincerity*. There is no question about the sea captain's sincerity. Since his actions had no audience—since he did not *intend* to assert anything—he could not have been lying. As Falknor said in the article excerpted earlier, "A man does not lie to himself." Schlesinger's case is different. Schlesinger was "apparently seeking to dispel fears of danger," Tribe writes, "so that his act may not bespeak an actual belief in the test's safety." By traveling to Amchitka with his family, Schlesinger intended to persuade observers that he believed the blast site was safe—though perhaps he thought it quite dangerous. That is, Schlesinger might have lied.

This exercise gives us an important insight into the rule against hearsay. By defining hearsay as an out-of-court *assertion*, the rule makes plain that sincerity is the testimonial capacity that most concerns us in this context. The sea captain's actions are admissible to prove that the ship was seaworthy. Hence the hearsay rule presents no bar to our reliance on the captain's apparent belief that the ship was safe—even though that belief rested on his capacities of perception, memory, and narration, *all of which must go untested.** Schlesinger's actions, on the other hand, similar in all respects except that any inference drawn from them depends on his sincerity, would be inadmissible hearsay. It appears the chief motivation behind the hearsay ban as expressed in Rule 801 is our unwillingness to rely on the out-of-court declarant's *sincerity.*

A Focus on Context

Note that the distinction between an assertion and a nonassertion often depends on context. At first glance Schlesinger's actions look much the same as the sea captain's. We recognize Schlesinger's actions as assertive only because we know that a controversy surrounded the atomic blast and that Schlesinger hoped to calm public fears. If there were reason to think the sea captain staged his inspection of the ship and took his family along for the benefit of nervous passengers watching from shore, his actions likewise would be assertive, and evidence of them would be barred as hearsay. In short, when trying to determine whether certain conduct is an assertion, ask yourself, "Could this conduct be a lie?" If the sea captain acted without an audience, the answer must be no because people do not (usually) lie to themselves.

This line between assertions and nonassertions cannot be drawn with mathematical precision. When deciding whether evidence of conduct should be excluded as hearsay, the trial judge must determine in light of all of the facts whether the conduct was intended as an assertion. The Advisory Committee's Note to Rule 801(a) says the burden of proof is on the party claiming an assertion was intended. Close cases should "be

* Although evidence of the sea captain's actions would not be hearsay if offered to prove the ship was seaworthy, the evidence might be inadmissible for other reasons. A judge might decide, for example, that the evidence is too time-consuming and too shaky to support any inference about the captain's judgment and thus exclude the evidence under Rule 403. Or a judge could rule that the evidence amounts to impermissible opinion testimony under Rule 701 or 702, studied in Chapter 9.

resolved ... in favor of admissibility"—and against deeming the evidence to be hearsay. (RB 197.)

A Glance Back at the Flowchart

Refer again to the hearsay flowchart on page 383. When assessing whether the actions of the sea captain and Schlesinger are hearsay, begin at the first branch at the top of the chart: Is the proponent offering evidence of the sea captain's or Schlesinger's actions to show each man's belief that the ship or blast site was safe? In each case the answer is yes. The litigant's purpose, whether proving the ship seaworthy or the blast site safe, depends on the truth of the captain's and Schlesinger's belief about those facts.

The distinction between these cases emerges at the second branch: Is the proponent offering evidence of the sea captain's or Schlesinger's actions to show what each man *intended to communicate*? In Schlesinger's case the answer is yes, as he meant to assert that the blast site was safe. Evidence that he took his family to Amchitka therefore is hearsay. In the sea captain's case the answer is no. Because he had no such communicative intent, evidence that he inspected the ship and set sail with his family is not hearsay.

Words

Most oral and written expressions are manifestly assertive. The declarative sentence, "This ship is safe," presumes an audience and relies for its meaning on the sincerity of the speaker. It is clearly an assertion. But assertions need not be declarative sentences. Commands also have assertive content. A person who warns, "Don't run that stop sign," intends to inform the listener there is a stop sign ahead. The statement is therefore an assertion. If offered to prove there indeed was a stop sign ahead, evidence of the statement would be hearsay. The command, "Close the door," is more ambiguous. If the person to whom the command is directed can see the door is open, the speaker probably does not intend to assert that fact. If offered to prove the door was open, the statement probably would not be hearsay. On the other hand, "Close the door" is clearly an assertion that the speaker would like the door to be closed—that is what the speaker means to convey. The statement would be hearsay if offered to prove that fact.

Questions too may be assertive. The questions, "Does Sarah sell drugs?? How do you think she affords that car?" would be hearsay if offered to prove Sarah sells drugs and bought her car from the proceeds. Even a simple, "What is your name?" probably would be hearsay if offered to prove the speaker did not know the other person's name. That is, by asking the question, the speaker asserts, "I do not know your name."

Implied Assertions

Such commands and questions are examples of *implied assertions*. The speaker does not expressly assert, "There is a stop sign ahead," or "I would like the door closed," or "I do not know your name." Yet the speaker *intends to communicate* those facts by implication. Each of these statements would be hearsay if offered to prove the truth of the implied assertion.

Declarative sentences likewise can carry implied assertions. If a friend says, "Laura ought to give that dog a bath," you naturally would conclude Laura's dog is dirty. That is what your friend *intends to communicate*. Your friend's statement asserts by implication that the dog needs a bath. Offered to prove that Laura's dog is dirty, the statement would be hearsay.

There is no reason to distinguish sharply between express and implied assertions. Both fit comfortably within Rule 801(c)'s definition of hearsay as an out-of-court "statement . . . offer[ed] . . . to prove the truth of the matter asserted." The important lesson is that implied assertions are intentionally communicative and therefore hearsay. Beware, though, that some courts and commentators, including Judson Falknor in the earlier excerpt, mistakenly use the phrase "implied assertions" even when the declarant had no intent to communicate the fact proved.

Indirect Assertions

Sometimes the matter asserted is just one link in a chain of inferences leading to the ultimate fact to be proved. We all can see that Angela's out-of-court statement, "I just spent all morning with the architect planning my retirement home," would be hearsay if offered to prove how Angela spent her morning. What if a prosecutor offered evidence of this statement to show that Angela, who died that afternoon of a drug overdose, was not contemplating suicide? In response to a hearsay objection, the prosecutor might argue that in speaking of her planned retirement home, Angela did not intend, expressly or impliedly, to communicate anything about suicide. The prosecutor might claim that because the government is offering Angela's statement to prove something *other* than what it asserts, the evidence is not hearsay.

You should recognize, however, that the immediate fact (Angela was planning her retirement home) is a necessary link in the chain of inferences leading to the intermediate fact (she was planning for the long term), which leads to the ultimate fact (she probably was not mulling suicide). The chain of inferences falls apart if it was *not* true that Angela spent the morning planning her retirement home. Hence her statement *is* being offered to prove what it asserts—and is hearsay.

Litigants often try to package hearsay as indirect evidence of the speaker's state of mind. Be wary of such arguments. For example, a litigant might offer the declarant's statement, "He is going to kill me," as evidence that the declarant was in fear. Because the statement is being offered to prove something other than what it asserts, the litigant argues, it is not hearsay. But "He is going to kill me" is best understood as, "I *think* he is going to kill me." To get from that statement to the conclusion that the speaker was in fear, we must assume the truth of the assertion. Hence the statement would be hearsay. (Note that the statement nonetheless might be admissible under one of the exceptions to the hearsay rule, which we take up shortly.)

Nonhearsay Uses of Out-of-Court Statements

Hearsay is an out-of-court statement offered by a litigant to prove what the declarant *intended to communicate*. This definition of hearsay helps us identify three more categories of nonhearsay, joining those discussed at pages 380 to 382. In each of these new categories the proponent aims to prove the declarant's belief, but does not rely on anything the declarant intended to communicate.

Nonassertive Words: The category of truly nonassertive words is quite small. Involuntary expressions are perhaps the only clear example. If you bang your knee and say, "Ouch!" you probably do not intend to communicate your pain to anyone. Evidence of your exclamation probably would not be hearsay if offered to prove you were in pain.

Words Offered to Prove Something Other Than What They Assert: Although almost all verbal conduct is assertive, not all out-of-court assertions are hearsay. Sometimes a lawyer offers the declarant's words to prove something *other* than what the declarant intended to communicate. Here the lawyer's claim does not depend on the truth of the declarant's assertion.

Wright v. Tatham, 7 Adolph. & E. 313, 386 (Exch. Ch. 1837), the source of the sea captain hypothetical, also supplied a famous real-life example of this category of nonhearsay. Wright was the beneficiary of a contested will. He sought to prove that the testator was competent by offering letters written to the testator by persons who had known him well. The letters concerned sundry business and political matters and made various assertions. But they said nothing—their authors *intended to communicate* nothing—about the testator's competence. Still, Wright argued that the tone and subject matter of the letters showed their authors, now dead, thought the testator was of sound mind.

Were these letters hearsay if offered to prove the testator's competence? The answer is almost certainly no. They contained no assertion that the testator was competent. There was no evidence that their authors intended to *imply* that the testator was competent. Rather, the letters proved only that their authors *believed* the testator was competent, a belief they felt no need to communicate.

Note that to use the letters as evidence of the testator's competence, we must rely on certain testimonial capacities of the letter writers. Most prominently, we rely on their perception. On what basis did they believe the testator was competent? How well did they know him? How recently had they seen him? No doubt the people challenging the will would have liked to cross-examine the letter writers about such things. And in fact the court excluded the letters as inadmissible hearsay.

But this case was decided long before the Federal Rules of Evidence—and in a jurisdiction not covered by the rules. By Rule 801(c)'s definition of hearsay, the letters would not be hearsay because they were not offered to prove the truth of what they asserted. The significance of this definition of hearsay, as we saw when discussing the sea captain, is that an out-of-court statement will not be hearsay unless its evidentiary force depends on the *sincerity* of the declarant. Here the question is whether the letter writers might have been lying about their belief that the testator was competent. Because they never asserted the testator's competence—they never intended to communicate that fact to anyone—they could not have been lying about it.

Note that *Wright v. Tatham* does not (as some authorities say) raise the problem of implied assertions. Implied assertions are intentionally communicative. The point here is that the letter writers did not *assert anything*, expressly or impliedly, about the testator's competence.

Assertions Offered as Circumstantial Proof of Knowledge: In *Bridges v. State*, 247 Wis. 350 (1945), a seven-year-old girl testified that a uniformed stranger took her to his room in a boarding house and sexually assaulted her. The defendant claimed he had never seen or had contact with the girl. To prove she had been in his room, the prosecutor offered testimony by the girl's mother and by police officers who interviewed the girl hours after the assault. They said she described where the defendant took her:*

> [The girl and the stranger] went up a wooden steps to a porch and entered the left one of two doors and went up a stairway and into the room. . . . [T]here were in the room a dresser, chest of drawers, bed, and by the latter a big shelf with some pictures and other little things like that on it, and also a chair with a clock and radio on it; that there was a table with a lamp on it and a lady's picture, which the soldier said was of his wife; and that there were two dolls, a boy

* The description that follows comes from the girl's testimony at trial. It is considerably more detailed than the out-of-court description of her assailant's quarters that the girl gave to her mother and police officers. I am changing the facts in this way to give the court's reasoning, which is sound as a matter of doctrine, a firmer factual footing. The girl's actual out-of-court description of the premises was, as the Wisconsin court admitted, "not distinctive enough." *Bridges*, 247 Wis. at 362.

> and a girl, with cloth faces and there were two little windows and a big one.

247 Wis. at 355. Police officers testified that the defendant's room matched the girl's detailed description.

Rejecting the defendant's claim that the girl's out-of-court description of his room was hearsay, the Wisconsin Supreme Court explained that her statements "constituted at least circumstantial evidence that she then had such knowledge [of his residence]; and that such state of mind on her part was acquired by reason of her having been in that room and house prior to making the statements." *Id.* at 364. That is, the girl's knowledge of the appearance of the man's residence proved circumstantially she had been there.

At first this case seems to present an *indirect assertion.* The prosecutor's intended conclusion—that the girl had been in the defendant's room—rested on the truth of her out-of-court assertions that she knew what his room looked like. That is, her description of his residence amounted to a series of claims about her knowledge: "*I know* there was a lady's picture; *I know* there were two dolls. . . ." At first it seems that the prosecution sought to prove the truth of these claims.

But if the girl's statement was offered to prove she had been in the defendant's room, we do not care about her testimonial capacities. *She could not possibly have been lying* about the appearance of the defendant's room—unless she was a clairvoyant liar—because she was exactly right about things that are hard to guess. Nor are we worried that she misperceived or misremembered or misstated the appearance of the defendant's room. The tight correlation between what she said and the room's actual appearance shows her statement was accurate—and proves she was in the room before.

In the terms of Rule 801(c), the prosecutor did not offer the girl's statement to prove the accuracy of her description of the defendant's room—any police officer who went to the room could describe it. Nor did the prosecutor offer the girl's statement to prove the truth of her *assertion* of knowledge. The prosecutor could prove her knowledge, while ignoring her *claim* of knowledge, simply by showing the close correspondence of her detailed description of the room with its actual appearance.

Defining Assertions: Problems

Here is a set of rather challenging problems that slowly build in difficulty. In each case the force of the evidence depends on the belief of the out-of-court speaker or actor. But is the evidence hearsay as defined in Rule 801(c)? You may find it useful to consult the cases or articles cited, but please don't assume they reach the right result (or even address the hearsay question).

1. On May 16, 1990, the British press reported that "Agriculture Minister John Gummer, facing calls for action over fears that 'mad cow' disease may spread to humans through British beef, tucked into a beefburger and said: 'This is delicious.' . . . His four-year-old daughter Cordelia also bit into the burger when it cooled down." *See Gummer Tucks into "Delicious" Beefburger*, PRESS ASS'N, May 16, 1990. As evidence that British beef was then safe to eat, a litigant offers the testimony of a reporter who witnessed these events.

2. At the 2004 trial of Scott Peterson for the murder of his pregnant wife, Laci, the prosecution alleged that Peterson dumped his wife's body at sea from a boat he had bought two weeks earlier and stored far from home. The prosecutor argued that Peterson's failure to tell his wife about the boat showed he bought it as part of his murder plan. To prove that Peterson never disclosed the purchase to his wife, the prosecutor offered the testimony of her only sister and of her facialist, both confidants of Laci Peterson. They testified that in the last weeks of her life, Laci Peterson never mentioned her husband's new boat. *See* Stacy Finz & Diana Walsh, *The Peterson Trial: Wife Never Spoke of Affair*, S.F. CHRON., June 4, 2004, at B1.

3. In a search of James Wicks's hotel room, agents found and opened two locked briefcases that held papers containing "a formula for making methamphetamine, a list of precursor chemicals, and a recipe to 'cook' crack cocaine." There was no evidence as to whether Wicks or someone else prepared the documents. Over Wicks's objection that the documents were hearsay, the government offered the documents, together with an expert's testimony that they contained a methamphetamine recipe, to show Wicks knew how to prepare the drug and therefore was more likely a member of a distribution ring. *United States v. Wicks*, 995 F.2d 964, 968, 974 (10th Cir.), *cert. denied*, 510 U.S. 982 (1993).

4. Police Officer Aaron Liberty was gunned down outside a pool hall in Woodville, Mississippi, in June 1969, as police tried to gain control of a hostile crowd. At the trial of Leon Chambers for Liberty's murder, Officer James Forman said he was looking in a different direction when the shooting started and did not see who shot Liberty. Forman turned to see Liberty down and bleeding. As proof that Chambers was the killer, the prosecutor offered Forman's testimony that "[b]efore Liberty died, he . . . fired both barrels of his riot gun into an alley in the area from which the shots appeared to have come." Seeming to take "deliberate aim," Liberty "hit one of the men in the crowd in the back of the head and neck as he ran down the alley. That man was Leon Chambers." *Chambers v. Mississippi*, 410 U.S. 284, 285–86 (1973) (excerpted more fully at pages 718 to 725).

5. As police officers searched the premises of a suspected gambling operation, the phone rang. When police answered, the anonymous speaker said, "I want to put two bills on Frankie's Favorite in the eighth."

At trial of the owners of the premises, the prosecutor offered evidence of this call to prove the premises were a gambling den. *See United States v. Zenni*, 492 F. Supp. 464, 465–69 (E.D. Ky. 1980); *Regina v. Kearley*, 2 App. Cas. 228 (1992).

6. Lemrick Nelson, Jr., was charged in the 1991 stabbing death of Yankel Rosenbaum in the Crown Heights area of Brooklyn. Nelson claimed he was wrongly identified. To prove Nelson's role in the attack, the prosecutor offered a detective's testimony that before Rosenbaum was taken to the hospital, the detective presented him with a lineup of four men. At the lineup, Rosenbaum "angrily asked [Nelson,] 'why did you stab me?' " *United States v. Nelson*, 277 F.3d 164, 170 (2d Cir.), *cert. denied*, 537 U.S. 835 (2002).

7. Postal inspectors arrested Reynolds as he left a bank after trying to cash a stolen check. While Reynolds stood handcuffed outside the bank, Parran walked past him along the sidewalk. When Parran was within earshot, Reynolds whispered to him, "I didn't tell them anything about you." Parran and Reynolds were charged with conspiring to cash checks stolen from the mail. To prove Parran's involvement in the scheme—and over Parran's hearsay objection—the prosecutor offered the testimony of a postal inspector who overheard Reynolds's statement to Parran outside the bank. *See United States v. Reynolds*, 715 F.2d 99, 100–04 (3d Cir. 1983); Roger C. Park, *"I Didn't Tell Them Anything About You": Implied Assertions as Hearsay Under the Federal Rules of Evidence*, 74 MINN. L. REV. 783 (1990).

8. At the sensational 1857 trial of Madeleine Smith, a well-born young Scotswoman, for poisoning her working-class ex-lover, Pierre Emile L'Angelier, a critical issue was whether L'Angelier visited Smith shortly before suffering ultimately fatal bouts of abdominal pain. Smith had bought arsenic, but claimed she took it for her complexion. Her counsel denied she had seen L'Angelier before his illnesses and suggested he had poisoned himself, perhaps hoping to frame his former mistress for his murder. A 1927 account of the case recalled:

> Amongst L'Angelier's effects was found a little pocket-book [or diary]. . . . There are various entries of no particular interest, then comes—"Thursday, 19th February. Saw Mimi [Madeleine] a few moments. Was very ill during the night. Friday, 20th February. Passed two pleasant hours with Mimi in the drawing-room. Saturday, 21st February. Did not feel well. Sunday, 22nd February. Saw Mimi in drawing-room. . . . Taken very ill." These dates cover, it will be observed, the dates of the first . . . illnesses. . . .
>
> The defence . . . fought hard to obtain the exclusion of this pocket-book from the evidence. . . .

TRIAL OF MADELEINE SMITH 35 (F. Tennyson Jesse ed., 1927).* Were the entries in L'Angelier's diary hearsay if offered to prove his visits with

* My thanks to Rick Underwood for pointing me to the Madeleine Smith case.

Smith shortly before his sick bouts? *Cf.* Lenora Ledwon, *Diaries and Hearsay: Gender, Selfhood, and the Trustworthiness of Narrative Structure*, 73 TEMP. L. REV. 1185, 1230 (2000).

HEARSAY QUIZ

On a warm and otherwise quiet Saturday night in Oakdale, the Quik–Stop convenience store was robbed. The resulting prosecution gave rise to many potential hearsay problems.

Each of the following bits of testimony either does or does not present hearsay as defined by Rule 801(c). For now your sole task is to determine whether the proposed evidence is or is not hearsay. Don't worry whether the evidence, if hearsay, still might be admissible—we will get to such questions soon. And don't worry that Rule 801(d) perhaps *excludes* this evidence from the realm of hearsay—for now please ignore Rule 801(d) altogether. The sole question is whether the evidence is hearsay as defined by Rule 801(c). You may find it useful when resolving these problems to refer to the hearsay flowchart on page 383.

Please consider each problem separately. That is, don't use facts supplied in one problem when resolving another.

---

1. The testimony of a witness that she immediately hailed a passing police cruiser, pointed to a fleeing car, and said, "That's the robber!"—if offered by the prosecutor to prove the driver of the fleeing car robbed the store.

2. The testimony of a police officer that she was hailed by the owner of the convenience store, who pointed frantically but speechlessly at a fleeing car—if offered by the prosecutor to prove the driver of the fleeing car robbed the store.

3. The testimony of a police officer that when she approached the vicinity of the Quik–Stop shortly after the robbery, she saw the owner of the store running after another man—if offered by the prosecutor to prove that the owner believed the other man robbed the store.

4. The testimony of the store-owner that the robber fled in a car with a license plate bearing the word "Wyoming" at the top—if offered by the prosecutor to prove the robber lived in Wyoming.

5. The prosecutor's display of a videotape of the robbery taken by an automatic surveillance camera—if offered by the prosecutor to prove the identity of the robber and his actions at the time.

6. The prosecutor's display of a videotape of a reenactment of the robbery made shortly before trial, in which the store-owner recreates his actions at the time of the robbery—if offered by the prosecutor to prove the store-owner's actions at the time of the robbery.

7. The store-owner's testimony that the defendant said, "I've got a gun, and I'm not afraid to use it"—if offered by the prosecutor to prove that the defendant threatened physical violence.

8. The store-owner's testimony that he called his wife about a minute after the robber fled the store and told her the store had been robbed, together with his wife's testimony that the store-owner called a few minutes after ten and told her the store had been robbed—if offered by the prosecutor to prove that the robber fled the store at about ten o'clock.

9. A police officer's testimony that the store-owner told her after the robbery, "I never rang up a single sale all night"—if offered by the prosecutor to prove that there probably were no customers in the store at the time of the robbery.

10. The testimony of an Oakdale Police switchboard operator that he received no other reports of robberies that night—if offered by the prosecutor to prove there were no other robberies in Oakdale that night.

11. The arresting officer's testimony that when she approached the defendant in downtown Oakdale several hours after the robbery, he began to stutter and hyperventilate—if offered by the prosecutor to prove that the officer's approach made the defendant nervous.

12. The testimony of a police officer that when she searched the defendant after his arrest, she found a plastic coffee stirrer in his pocket bearing the imprint, "Quik–Stop of Oakdale," and the store's logo—if offered by the prosecutor to prove the defendant recently had been in the Quik–Stop.

13. The arresting officer's testimony that at the time she arrested the defendant he told her his name was Jeffrey Small, when in fact his name is Kevin Martinson—if offered by the prosecutor to prove the defendant was conscious of his guilt of the robbery.

14. The arresting officer's testimony that at the time she arrested the defendant he told her his name was Jesse James, when in fact his name is Kevin Martinson—if offered by defense counsel to prove the defendant was insane.

15. The testimony of the defendant's neighbor that on the night before the robbery she overheard the defendant's sister say to the defendant, "My son borrowed my car without permission. How do you think I should discipline him?"—if offered by the prosecutor to prove the defendant's sister believed he was sane.

16. The testimony of the defendant's neighbor that on the night before the robbery she overheard the defendant's wife tell the defendant, "I wrecked our car today, and the insurance agent says they won't cover it"—if offered by the prosecutor to prove the defendant had a financial motive to rob the Quik–Stop.

17. The testimony of the defendant's neighbor that on the day after the robbery she overheard the defendant say to a friend, "Here's the ten grand I owe you"—if offered by the prosecutor to prove that the defendant had owed his friend $10,000.

18. The testimony of the defendant's neighbor that on the day after the robbery she overheard the defendant's friend say to the defendant, "I've got some extra forty-five shells if you need them"—if offered by the prosecutor to prove the defendant had a .45–caliber weapon.

19. The testimony of the defendant's neighbor that on the day after the robbery the defendant told her, "They have Guinness at the Quik–Stop, right between the Sam Adams and the Becks," together with evidence that the beer really was shelved in this manner—if offered by the prosecutor to prove the defendant had been in the Quik–Stop at some point.

20. The testimony of the defendant's neighbor that the defendant has a good reputation for peacefulness among his neighbors—if offered by defense counsel to prove the defendant is not a violent person.

21. An electronics store owner's testimony that on the day after the robbery the defendant's wife came into the store and said, "I'd like to buy your best wide-screen TV and four of your most expensive speakers, please"—if offered by the prosecutor to prove the defendant had substantial assets on the day after the robbery.

22. The testimony of the defendant's cellmate that the defendant, while sleeping, said the words, "Thomas Barrington O'Toole"—if offered by the prosecutor to prove the defendant knows the owner of the Quik–Stop, Thomas Barrington O'Toole.

23. At a later, civil proceeding, the arresting officer's testimony that the owner of the Quik–Stop told her that as the defendant left the store, he said, "I'll kill anyone who tries to stop me"—if offered by the officer's lawyer to prove that the officer reasonably believed she was in danger of serious physical violence at the time she arrested the defendant.

24. At a later, civil proceeding, the testimony of the manager of a real estate company, which rented space to the Quik–Stop, that she had warned the store-owner before the robbery that several robberies recently had taken place in the store's neighborhood—if offered by the real estate company's lawyer to prove the store-owner was on notice of the risk of being robbed.

25. The same manager's testimony that "my assistant told me before the robbery that he had warned the store-owner of several recent

robberies in the neighborhood"—if offered by the real estate company's lawyer to prove the store-owner was on notice of the risk of being robbed.

3. Exceptions to the Hearsay Rule: An Introduction

Rule 802 says that hearsay is not admissible unless the Federal Rules of Evidence or other federal statutes or Supreme Court rules provide otherwise. The rest of this chapter will focus on the many exceptions to the hearsay rule specified within the Federal Rules. When may an out-of-court statement be admitted to prove what it asserts?

Exceptions to the hearsay rule fall into five broad categories. The rules listed here are those we will study:

(1) **Rule 801(d)(1): Declarant–Witnesses' Prior Statements**

- (A) Prior Inconsistent Statements
- (B) Prior Consistent Statements
- (C) Statements of Identification

(2) **Rule 801(d)(2): Opposing Parties' Statements**

- (A) A Party's Own Statements
- (B) Adopted Statements
- (C) Statements by Spokespersons
- (D) Statements by Agents
- (E) Coconspirators' Statements

(3) **Rule 803: Exceptions Applicable Regardless of the Declarant's Availability**

- (1) Present Sense Impressions
- (2) Excited Utterances
- (3) Statements of Then–Existing Mental, Emotional, or Physical Condition
- (4) Statements for Medical Diagnosis or Treatment
- (5) Recorded Recollections
- (6 & 7) Business Records
- (8 & 10) Public Records and Reports

(4) **Rule 804: Exceptions Applicable Only When the Declarant Is Unavailable**

- (b)(1) Former Testimony
- (b)(2) Dying Declarations
- (b)(3) Statements Against Interest
- (b)(6) Forfeiture by Wrongdoing

(5) **Rule 807: Residual Exception**

Note that the Rules do not call all of these provisions "exceptions" to the hearsay ban. Rule 801(d) defines certain past statements of testifying witnesses and statements of opposing parties not as *exceptions* to the rule, but as "not hearsay." The Advisory Committee's Note acknowledges that these statements "would otherwise literally fall within the definition [of hearsay, but] are expressly excluded from it." (RB 198.) Do not struggle to find meaning in this Orwellian labeling. You are best off thinking of all of the rules listed above as exceptions to Rule 802's hearsay ban. *See* Roger Park, *The Rationale of Personal Admissions*, 21 IND. L. REV. 509, 509 n.3 (1988). You need not distinguish sharply between an exception to the hearsay rule and an exclusion from it except (perhaps) when advocating before a court.

When studying each exception, ponder its rationale. Most of the exceptions to the hearsay rule reflect two values: necessity and trustworthiness. There is said to be some special *need* for the hearsay evidence or some special reason to deem it more *reliable* than run-of-the-mill hearsay—or both. For example, a homicide victim's "dying declaration" about the cause of her impending death (admissible under Rule 804(b)(2)) may be necessary evidence in a murder case if the victim was the only eyewitness to the crime. Moreover (it is said), the victim was unlikely to lie with judgment day so near at hand, so her dying words are unusually reliable. *See Queen v. Osman*, 15 Cox Crim. Cas. 1, 3 (Eng. N. Wales Cir. 1881) (Lush, L.J.) ("No person, who is immediately going into the presence of his Maker, will do so with a lie upon his lips."). For each of the exceptions to the hearsay rule, consider carefully the soundness of such reasoning.

Necessity is perhaps clearest when the declarant is unavailable. Rule 804 establishes a separate list of exceptions that apply only when the declarant is unavailable. Be careful not to confuse unavailability, as defined in Rule 804(a), with the physical absence of the witness. A witness may be on the stand and yet "unavailable," because she asserts a privilege or simply refuses to testify or testifies to a loss of memory.

Some hearsay exceptions, on the other hand, apply only if the declarant is present and testifying. Rule 801(d)(1), which addresses a witness's own past statements, requires that the declarant be "subject to cross-examination about [the out-of-court] statement[s]." Rule 803(5) requires that the declarant testify that she is unable to "recall [a fact or event] well enough to testify fully and accurately" about it. Note that this rule requires that the declarant testify as a witness, but *not* that she be "available." A memory loss might render the witness "unavailable," though present.

The various exceptions to the hearsay rule, like the rule itself, are largely the product of slow, common-law evolution. It would be a mistake to look too hard for a single unifying theme or to seek deep meaning in the particular organization adopted by the Rules. We will take up the hearsay exceptions in a somewhat different order from that framed by the rule writers. After addressing opposing parties' statements, the topic of Rule 801(d)(2), we look at several exceptions to the hearsay rule that deal with a testifying witness's past statements or with past testimony. Then we consider Rule 804 and all those exceptions that require the declarant to be unavailable. Next is Rule 803 and the long list of exceptions that impose no special condition on the declarant's availability. Rule 807's residual exception closes the chapter.

C. Opposing Parties' Statements

Any casual moviegoer knows that if a suspect confesses her crime to a police officer, the officer usually may repeat the defendant's words to the jury. But if the prosecutor offers the defendant's words, "I robbed the bank," to prove the defendant robbed the bank, isn't the evidence hearsay?

Rule 801(d)(2)(A) declares otherwise. Though the Constitution protects against coerced confessions, the hearsay rule poses no obstacle to confessions made freely. Rule 801(d)(2)(A) states that a party's own words are "not hearsay" when offered against her at trial. It is clearer, as I've said, to think of this rule as providing that opposing parties' statements, *although hearsay*, are nonetheless admissible against their maker. But however the rule is formulated, we are left to search for a comprehensive and satisfying rationale. Consider three possible rationales:

Statements made against interest are unusually reliable: Most statements offered by a litigant against an opponent were against the opponent's interests when she made them. That is, when a prosecutor offers a defendant's words against her, usually it is because those words incriminate the defendant. Although people often lie to advance their interests, people rarely lie in ways that *hurt* themselves. As a general matter, then, a statement that harms the speaker's interests is more likely than ordinary hearsay to be truthful.

This explanation cannot fully account for Rule 801(d)(2), however, because the rule admits all "statement[s]" of opposing parties, whether or not those statements were against the speaker's interests when she made them. The rule requires only that there be a "statement" and that it be offered against its maker. There is no requirement that the opponent *admitted* anything, only that she *said* something. Still, most statements offered against opposing parties were against the party's interests when she made them. So the greater reliability of against-interest statements offers at least some justification for the rule. *See* Roger Park, *The Rationale of Personal Admissions*, 21 IND. L. REV. 509, 509, 516 (1988).

Parties cannot complain of their inability to cross-examine themselves: A second possible rationale deals with cross-examination. The usual inability to cross-examine hearsay declarants is a principal justification for the hearsay rule. It would seem odd, though, for a party to complain that she can't cross-examine the declarant when *she* is the declarant. If a party wishes to probe the circumstances under which her own statement was made, she can simply take the stand and say what she knows. *See* EDMUND M. MORGAN, BASIC PROBLEMS OF EVIDENCE 266 (1962). There is therefore no need to ban an opposing party's statement as hearsay.

This explanation has troubling consequences in criminal cases. Criminal defendants confront strong disincentives to testify at trial even when they have something useful to say. Those with criminal records face the risk that past offenses, otherwise hidden from the jury, may be admitted to impeach them under Rule 609. Moreover, in both civil and criminal actions, the exception for opposing parties' statements extends beyond the party's *own* statements to include those made by her spokespersons, agents, or coconspirators. If the actual maker of the statement is absent from trial, the party against whom it is offered may justly complain of her inability to cross-examine the declarant.

This is war: A third rationale offers a more complete explanation for the opposing-parties rule, but not a more satisfying one. The advisory committee tells us that "[a]dmissions by a party-opponent are excluded from the category of hearsay on the theory that their admissibility in evidence is the result of the adversary system...." (RB 206.) In other words, *this is war.* A party's own statement—or that of her spokesperson, agent, or coconspirator—is admissible against her *because she said it* or authorized it or associated herself with its maker. She cannot demand the statement's exclusion by complaining of its untrustworthiness.

Perhaps there is an explanation for this rule that comprehends the rule's full scope and satisfies a logically inquiring mind. *See, e.g.,* Park, *supra*, 21 IND. L. REV. at 513–21 (attempting such an explanation). But if so, it is an elusive one.

---

1. THE PARTY'S OWN WORDS

Focus on
FRE 801(d)(2)(A)

Problem 7.11
Billables

Louise Phillips, an associate at a large law firm, sued an airline after suffering injuries during an unusually rough landing. She claimed her injuries prevented her from working to her full capacity. At trial the defendant offers records signed by Phillips in which she billed clients an average of 104 hours per week during the six weeks after the flight. If offered to prove her capacity for work was not diminished, are the records admissible over Phillips's hearsay objection?

Problem 7.12
"Take My Blood"

Excerpt from the testimony of Los Angeles police detective Philip Vannatter at the trial of People v. Orenthal James Simpson, *March 21, 1995, concerning the defendant's willingness to submit to DNA testing soon after discovery of a bloody murder scene:*

Q *by Mr. Shapiro* [defense counsel]: Isn't it true, Sir, that when [you] asked about Mr. Simpson's blood he gave you the following response—

Mr. Darden [prosecutor]*:* Objection. Objection, Your Honor.

The Court: Sustained. Counsel, you need to share that [transcript page] with opposing counsel.

Mr. Darden: Before we do that, may we approach, Your Honor?

Mr. Shapiro: I will share it with him right now.

Mr. Darden: May we approach, Your Honor?

The Court: All right. With the court reporter, please.

(The following proceedings were held at the bench:)

The Court: We are over at the side bar. . . . What is the next question and answer?

Mr. Darden: Mr. Shapiro is about to read to the jury from the transcript of the defendant's statement.

Mr. Shapiro: . . . That is not what I'm going to do at all.

The Court: What are you going to do?

Mr. Shapiro: I'm going to ask Detective Vannatter, "Isn't it true that O.J. Simpson said, 'Well, take my blood test and we will—well, take my blood—

Mr. Darden: Keep your voice down.

Mr. Shapiro:—test.' " I'm sorry. ' "Well, take my blood test and we will see.' "

Mr. Darden: It is the defendant's statement. It is hearsay. I have been objecting.

The Court: All right. The objection will be—

Will it be sustained or overruled?

---

2. Adoptive Admissions

Focus on
FRE 801(d)(2)(B)

Problem 7.13
Buddies

Consider these facts from *United States v. Beckham*, 968 F.2d 47 (D.C. Cir. 1992):

> Several undercover police officers . . . noticed what appeared to be several persons engaged in drug transactions in the backyard of a house. . . . Officer Dunston saw two people in the yard: Robert Beckham was in a chair in the walkway leading up to the rear door of the house, and Monica Monroe sat on a bench approximately two feet away. As Officer Dunston approached the yard, Monroe inquired, "Are you looking?" Officer Dunston said that he was, and Monroe asked if he wanted "a fifty," which the officer took to mean a fifty dollar rock of crack.
>
> Officer Dunston replied yes, walked into the yard, and stood directly in front of Monroe, who reached into her pants pocket and produced a clear ziplock bag containing a single rock of crack. Beckham remained seated two feet away. Officer Dunston inspected the rock and asked Mon-

roe if he could purchase another fifty. Monroe replied, "I only had one, but you can get another from my buddy." At that moment, Beckham got up from his chair, walked past Dunston and Monroe to the far end of the bench on which Monroe was seated, and removed a large plastic bag, which contained numerous smaller ziplock bags, from underneath the bench. As Beckham began to open the bag, Officer Dunston identified himself as a police officer and arrested both Monroe and Beckham. The large plastic bag was found to contain slightly more than 13 grams of 89% pure crack, packaged in 34 smaller, $50 bags. . . .

. . . Beckham argues that the district court erred in denying a motion *in limine* and permitting the prosecution to introduce through Officer Dunston Monica Monroe's statement, "I only had one, but you can get another from my buddy." It is asserted that this statement was the most important evidence of Beckham's intent to distribute. Monroe failed to appear for trial and was therefore unavailable to testify and to be cross-examined. If he had cross-examined Monroe, Beckham tells us, she would have said, as she apparently did later at her own trial, that her statement had been "you can get another from anybody," not from "my buddy." . . .

In affirming Beckham's conviction, the appeals court held there was insufficient evidence of a conspiracy between him and Monroe to admit her statement against Beckham under the coconspirator exception to the hearsay rule, FRE 801(d)(2)(E). On what other theory was Monroe's statement (if she said "my buddy") admissible against Beckham?

Problem 7.14
Jailhouse Meeting

In 1990 George Franklin faced trial in California for the murder of eight-year-old Susan Nason twenty-one years earlier. The prosecution's chief witness was Franklin's daughter, Eileen Franklin–Lipsker, who had been a childhood playmate of Nason and who claimed she saw the murder. Shortly before trial Franklin–Lipsker visited her father at the county jail. At trial she testified about this visit. The prosecutor gave this summary of Franklin–Lipsker's testimony during closing argument:

> And when Eileen goes to visit him in the jail in January of this year, what happens?
>
> Well, imagine—just, if you can for a moment, think about it. Assume for the moment that Mr. Franklin is not guilty. He has not committed this murder; he knows it. He didn't do this. And he learns that his daughter, who is accusing him of this murder, who has caused him to be arrested, is there to see him at the jail.
>
> What is he going to say to her? What would any innocent person in a similar situation do?
>
> Eileen, why are you doing this? You know it's not true. Whatever it is, we'll talk about it. Don't do this to me. You know it's wrong. You're lying. Are you sick? Are you angry? What is going on? Why are you falsely accusing me?
>
> Does he say any one of those things?
>
> No.
>
> It's Eileen who says to the defendant: Dad, a lot of what I am is because of you. And you did some good things for me: You told me to always tell the truth—and that's what I'm doing—and you always said that the truth would set you free. Doesn't that apply to both of us?
>
> Those were Eileen's words to her father.
>
> And what was his response?
>
> Ladies and gentlemen, Mr. Franklin's response was to point to a sign that says: "Notice. This station may be monitored."
>
> Now, what does that tell you?
>
> That tells you law enforcement might be monitoring their conversation. . . .
>
> He believes the conversation is being monitored, and he does not deny a false accusation of murder?
>
> Well, why bother? Why bother to deny it when the only two people there are the two people that know? . . .

Assume the defendant objected to Franklin–Lipsker's testimony about this meeting on hearsay grounds. On what theory could the prosecutor argue for admission of Franklin–Lipsker's statement to her father? Was the judge right to allow the evidence? Does it affect your answer to know that at the time of his arrest in this case, authorities advised Franklin that he had the right to remain silent and that anything he said could be used against him? *See Franklin v. Duncan*, 70 F.3d 75 (9th Cir. 1995); *Franklin v. Duncan*, 884 F. Supp. 1435, 1445–48 (N.D. Cal. 1995).

---

3. STATEMENTS OF AGENTS

Focus on
FRE 801(d)(2)(C) & (D)

Pet Wolf Bites Boy in U. City

ST. LOUIS POST-DISPATCH, March 23, 1973, at 14A
Reprinted by Permission.

A wolf kept as a pet by a University City family attacked a 3-year-old boy this afternoon in the 6600 block of Pershing Avenue.

The child, identified as Daniel Mahlandt, was bitten on the face, chest and left leg. He was taken into surgery at St. Louis County Hospital at 1:30 p.m., about a half-hour after the attack.

The wolf, whose name was Sophie, has been used in recent exhibitions at schools to prove that wolves do not attack human beings.

Neighbors said the wolf that attacked Daniel . . . had attacked a beagle yesterday in the neighborhood.

University City police said that the wolf had been confined at home by its owner, Ken Poos. They said the County Health Department had been notified to check the wolf for rabies.

Spokesmen at St. Louis County Hospital said that Daniel was in serious condition when he was admitted to the hospital. . . .

Despite the reporter's apparent certainty about the cause of Daniel Mahlandt's injuries, the question whether Sophie bit the boy proved hotly contested . . . .

Mahlandt v. Wild Canid Survival & Research Center, Inc.

588 F.2d 626 (8th Cir. 1978).

■ Sickle, Circuit Judge. . . . On March 23, 1973, Daniel Mahlandt, then 3 years, 10 months, and 8 days old, was sent by his mother to a neighbor's home on an adjoining street to get his older brother, Donald. Daniel's mother watched him cross the street, and then turned into the house to get her car keys. Daniel's path took him along a walkway adjacent to the Poos' residence. Next to the walkway was a five foot chain link fence to which Sophie had been chained with a six foot chain. In other words, Sophie was free to move in a half circle having a six foot radius on the side of the fence opposite from Daniel.

Sophie . . . had been born at the St. Louis Zoo, and kept there until she reached 6 months of age, at which time she was given to the Wild Canid Survival and Research Center, Inc. . . . Kenneth Poos, as Director of Education for the [center], had been keeping her at his home because he was taking Sophie to schools and institutions where he showed films and gave programs with respect to the nature of wolves. Sophie was known as a very gentle wolf who had proved herself to be good natured and stable during her contacts with thousands of children while she was in the St. Louis Children's Zoo.

Sophie was chained because the evening before she had jumped the fence and attacked a beagle who was running along the fence and yapping at her. A neighbor who was ill in bed in the second floor of his home heard a child's screams and went to his window, where he saw a boy lying on his back within the enclosure, with a wolf straddling him. The wolf's face was near Daniel's face, but the distance was so great that he could not see what the wolf was doing, and did not see any biting. Within about 15 seconds the neighbor saw Clarke Poos, about seventeen, run around the house, get the wolf off of the boy, and disappear with the child in his arms to the back of the house. Clarke took the boy in and laid him on the kitchen floor.

Clarke had been returning from his friend's home immediately west when he heard a child's cries and ran around to the enclosure. He found Daniel lying within the enclosure, about three feet from the fence, and Sophie standing back from the boy the length of her chain, and wailing. An expert in the behavior of wolves stated that when a wolf licks a child's face . . . it is a sign of care and not a sign of attack; that a wolf's wail is a sign of compassion and an effort to get attention, not a sign of attack. No witness saw or knew how Daniel was injured. Clarke and his sister ran over to get Daniel's mother. She says that Clarke told her, "a wolf got Danny and he is dying." Clarke denies that statement.

The defendant, Mr. Poos, arrived home while Daniel and his mother were in the kitchen. After Daniel was taken in an ambulance, Mr. Poos talked to everyone present, including a neighbor who came in. Within an hour after he arrived home, Mr. Poos went to Washington University to inform Owen Sexton, President of Wild Canid Survival and Research Center, Inc., of the incident. Mr. Sexton was not in his office so Mr. Poos left the following note on his door:

> Owen, would [you] call me at home, 727–5080? Sophie bit a child that came in our back yard. All has been taken care of. I need to convey what happened to you.

Denial of admission of this note is one of the issues on appeal.

Later that day, Mr. Poos found Mr. Sexton at the Tyson Research Center and told him what had happened. Denial of plaintiff's offer to prove that Mr. Poos told Mr. Sexton that, "Sophie had bit a child that day," is the second issue on appeal.

A meeting of the Directors of the Wild Canid Survival and Research Center, Inc., was held on April 4, 1973. Mr. Poos was not present at that meeting. The minutes of that meeting reflect that there was a "great deal of discussion . . . about the legal aspects of the incident of Sophie biting the child." Plaintiff offered an abstract of the minutes containing that reference. Denial of the offer of that abstract is the third issue on appeal.

Daniel had lacerations of the face, left thigh, left calf, and right thigh, and abrasions and bruises of the abdomen and chest. Mr. Mahlandt was permitted to state that Daniel had indicated that he had gone under the fence. Mr. Mahlandt and Mr. Poos, about a month after the incident, examined the fence to determine what caused Daniel's lacerations. Mr. Mahlandt felt that they did not look like animal bites. The parallel scars on Daniel's thigh appeared to match the configuration of the barbs or tines on the fence. The expert as to the behavior of wolves opined that the lacerations were not wolf bites or wounds caused by wolf claws. Wolves have powerful jaws, and a wolf bite will result in massive crushing or severing of a limb. He stated that if Sophie had bitten Daniel there would have been clear apposition of teeth and massive crushing of Daniel's hands and arms, which were not injured. Also, if Sophie had pulled Daniel under the fence, tooth marks on the foot or leg would have been present, although Sophie possessed enough strength to pull the boy under the fence.

The jury brought in a verdict for the defense.

The trial judge's rationale for excluding the note, the statement, and the corporate minutes, was the same in each case. He reasoned that Mr. Poos did not have any personal knowledge of the facts, and accordingly, the first two admissions were based on hearsay; and the third admission contained in the minutes of the board meeting was subject to the same objection of hearsay, and unreliability because of lack of personal knowledge.* . . .

. . . [T]he statement in the note pinned on the door is not hearsay, and is admissible against Mr. Poos. It was his own statement, and as such was clearly different from the reported statement of another. . . . And the same observations may be made of the statement made later in the day to Mr. Sexton that, "Sophie had bit a child. . . ."

Are these statements admissible against Wild Canid Survival and Research Center, Inc.? They were made by Mr. Poos when he was an agent or servant of the Wild Canid Survival and Research Center, Inc., and they concerned a matter within the scope of his agency, or employment, i.e., his custody of Sophie, and were made during the existence of that relationship.

Defendant argues that Rule 801(d)(2) does not provide for the admission of "in house" statements; that is, it allows only admissions made to third parties. The notes of the Advisory Committee on the Proposed Rules discuss the problem of "in house" admissions with reference to Rule 801(d)(2)(C) situations. This is not a (C) situation because Mr. Poos was not authorized or directed to make a statement on the matter by anyone. But the rationale developed in that comment does apply to this (D) situation. Mr. Poos had actual physical custody of Sophie. His conclusions, his opinions, were obviously accepted as a basis for action by his principal. *See* minutes of corporate meeting. As the Advisory Committee points out in its note on (C) situations,

> . . . communication to an outsider has not generally been thought to be an essential characteristic of an admission. Thus a party's books or records are usable against him, without regard to any intent to disclose to third persons. [RB 207.]

* [Before ruling on the admissibility of Poos's note and statement, the trial judge quizzed him outside the jury's presence:

> THE COURT: Mr. Poos, did you at any time on the . . . day this incident occurred . . . see Danny inside the fence . . .?
>
> THE WITNESS: I did not see him inside the fence. I saw him only in the kitchen floor for a few brief minutes.
>
> THE COURT: Do you know—and I'm talking about eyeball knowledge or personal knowledge; do you know how he happened to get inside the fence?
>
> THE WITNESS: No, Your Honor, I do not.
>
> THE COURT: Do you know whether or not that child was bit, mauled, clawed or whatever by Sophie?
>
> THE WITNESS: I do not, no.
>
> THE COURT: Do you know whether he was bit or mauled or whatever by any other canine?
>
> THE WITNESS: No, sir. . . .
>
> THE COURT: [Your note says,] "I need to convey to you what happened." Now, do you know what happened?
>
> THE WITNESS: I do not know what caused it, no.

Professor Eleanor Swift recovered this very useful piece of the trial record. *See* Eleanor Swift, *The Story of* Mahlandt v. Wild Canid Survival & Research Center, Inc.*: Encounters of Three Different Kinds, in* EVIDENCE STORIES 239, 255 (Richard Lempert ed., 2006).—GF]

Weinstein's discussion of Rule 801(d)(2)(D) (WEINSTEIN'S EVIDENCE § 801(d)(2)(D)(01), p. 801–137), states that:

> Rule 801(d)(2)(D) adopts the approach ... which, as a general proposition, makes statements made by agents within the scope of their employment admissible.... Once agency, and the making of the statement while the relationship continues, are established, the statement is exempt from the hearsay rule so long as it relates to a matter within the scope of the agency.

After reciting a lengthy quotation which justifies the rule as necessary and suggests that such admissions are trustworthy and reliable, Weinstein states categorically that although an express requirement of personal knowledge on the part of the declarant of the facts underlying his statement is not written into the rule, it should be....

[In this case the trial judge] clearly found that the evidence was not reliable, pointing out that none of the [challenged] statements were based on the personal knowledge of the declarant.

Again, that problem was faced by the Advisory Committee on Proposed Rules. In its discussion of 801(d)(2) exceptions to the hearsay rule, the Committee said:

> The freedom which admissions have enjoyed from technical demands of searching for an assurance of trustworthiness in some against-interest circumstances, and from the restrictive influences of the opinion rule and the rule requiring firsthand knowledge, when taken with the apparently prevalent satisfaction with the results, calls for generous treatment of this avenue to admissibility. [RB 206.]

So here, ... applying the spirit of Rule 801(d)(2), we hold [the trial judge was wrong to exclude] the evidence of Mr. Poos' statements as against himself or Wild Canid Survival and Research Center, Inc....

As to the entry in the records of a corporate meeting, the directors as primary officers of the corporation had the authority to include their conclusions in the record of the meeting. So the evidence would fall within 801(d)(2)(C) as to Wild Canid Survival and Research Center, Inc., and be admissible. The "in house" aspect of this admission has already been discussed, Rule 801(d)(2)(D), *supra*.

But there was no servant, or agency, relationship which justified admitting the evidence of the board minutes as against Mr. Poos. None of the conditions of 801(d)(2) cover the claim that minutes of a corporate board meeting can be used against a non-attending, non-participating employee of that corporation. The evidence was not admissible as against Mr. Poos....*

* [I have moved the previous two paragraphs from their position slightly earlier in the opinion.—GF]

The judgment of the District Court is reversed and the matter remanded to the District Court for a new trial consistent with this opinion.

Problem 7.15

Shovel and Bucket

Consider the facts of *Pappas v. Middle Earth Condominium Ass'n*, 963 F.2d 534 (2d Cir. 1992):

> Immediately after arriving in Vermont after 10 p.m. on the evening of February 25, 1987, and while carrying his ski boots from the parking lot, the then 33–year-old Kevin Pappas slipped and fell on a dome of ice on a walkway that ran alongside a building leading into a condominium that he and a group of friends had rented for a five-day ski vacation. He suffered a severely broken ankle that required three operations, and which later was surgically fused. Plaintiff's suit sought damages [from the condominium management company].
>
> After Pappas fell, Sherry Cherris telephoned the management company, using a number she found pinned on the refrigerator, complaining of the walkway's icy condition. A man with a shovel and a bucket eventually appeared. At trial, plaintiff sought to introduce through Ms. Cherris the statements this [man] made regarding the performance of [other] employees in maintaining the walkway. . . .
>
> . . . The personnel manager . . . declared that one of two employees responsible for snow and ice removal would have been on duty on the night of the accident. . . .

The man with the shovel and bucket was never identified. Assume he told Ms. Cherris, "Those guys on the day shift were supposed to shovel and salt, but they bagged it and went home early." Should the court admit evidence of this statement against the condominium management company?

4. Coconspirators' Statements

Focus on
FRE 801(d)(2)(E) & 104(a)

A Note on the Next Case: When it appeared in 1987, *Bourjaily v. United States* settled several nagging evidentiary disputes and reserved another for future decision. Those disputes all concerned the coconspirator exception to the hearsay rule—and specifically how to decide if the preconditions of that exception have been met. There are three such preconditions:

- that a conspiracy existed at the time the out-of-court statement was made;
- that the conspiracy included both the declarant and the party against whom the statement is offered; and
- that the declarant spoke during the course of and in furtherance of the conspiracy.

The Supreme Court declared that a trial judge should decide these preliminary questions under Rule 104(a). The justices ruled that the proper standard of proof is preponderance of the evidence. And they ruled that the contested hearsay statement *itself* could be evidence of the existence of the conspiracy and other preliminary facts. They refrained from deciding whether the contested hearsay statement could serve as the *only* evidence of these preliminary facts.

Given the text of Rule 801(d)(2), the latter two issues might not strike you as controversial. After all, the last sentence of the rule resolves them explicitly: "The statement must be considered but does not by itself establish . . . the existence of the conspiracy or participation in it under (E)." But Congress added that sentence in 1997, a full decade after the Court's decision in *Bourjaily*. This late-coming amendment perhaps mooted the Court's holding that a contested coconspirator's statement may be evidence of its own admissibility. Still I've retained that part of the *Bourjaily* opinion because the more general question that underlies it—whether contested evidence *ever* may be evidence of its own admissibility—arguably remains a live issue in other contexts. The Court's resolution of this question in *Bourjaily* probably applies in most contexts in which the question arises.

BOURJAILY V. UNITED STATES

483 U.S. 171 (1987).

■ CHIEF JUSTICE REHNQUIST delivered the opinion of the Court.... In May 1984, Clarence Greathouse, an informant working for the Federal Bureau of Investigation (FBI), arranged to sell a kilogram of cocaine to Angelo Lonardo. Lonardo agreed that he would find individuals to distribute the drug. When the sale became imminent, Lonardo stated in a tape-recorded telephone conversation that he had a "gentleman friend" who had some questions to ask about the cocaine. In a subsequent telephone call, Greathouse spoke to the "friend" about the quality of the drug and the price. Greathouse then spoke again with Lonardo, and the two arranged the details of the purchase. They agreed that the sale would take place in a designated hotel parking lot, and Lonardo would transfer the drug from Greathouse's car to the "friend," who would be waiting in the parking lot in his own car. Greathouse proceeded with the transaction as planned, and FBI agents arrested Lonardo and petitioner immediately after Lonardo placed a kilogram of cocaine into petitioner's car in the hotel parking lot. In petitioner's car, the agents found over $20,000 in cash.

Petitioner was charged with conspiring to distribute cocaine ... and possession of cocaine with intent to distribute.... The Government introduced, over petitioner's objection, Angelo Lonardo's telephone statements regarding the participation of the "friend" in the transaction. The District Court found that, considering the events in the parking lot and Lonardo's statements over the telephone, the Government had established by a preponderance of the evidence that a conspiracy involving Lonardo and petitioner existed, and that Lonardo's statements over the telephone had been made in the course of and in furtherance of the conspiracy. Accordingly, the trial court held that Lonardo's out-of-court statements satisfied Rule 801(d)(2)(E) and were not hearsay. Petitioner was convicted on both counts and sentenced to 15 years. The United States Court of Appeals for the Sixth Circuit affirmed. 781 F.2d 539 (1986)....

Before admitting a co-conspirator's statement over an objection that it does not qualify under Rule 801(d)(2)(E), a court must be satisfied that the statement actually falls within the definition of the Rule. There must be evidence that there was a conspiracy involving the declarant and the nonoffering party, and that the statement was made "during the course and in furtherance of the conspiracy." [Unrestyled] Federal Rule of Evidence 104(a) provides: "Preliminary questions concerning ... the admissibility of evidence shall be determined by the court." Petitioner and the Government agree that the existence of a conspiracy and petitioner's involvement in it are preliminary questions of fact that, under Rule 104, must be resolved by the court. The Federal Rules, however, nowhere define the standard of proof the court must observe in resolving these questions.

We are therefore guided by our prior decisions regarding admissibility determinations that hinge on preliminary factual questions. We have traditionally required that these matters be established by a preponderance of proof. . . . The inquiry made by a court concerned with these matters is not whether the proponent of the evidence wins or loses his case on the merits, but whether the evidentiary Rules have been satisfied. Thus, the evidentiary standard is unrelated to the burden of proof on the substantive issues, be it a criminal case or a civil case. The preponderance standard ensures that before admitting evidence, the court will have found it more likely than not that the technical issues and policy concerns addressed by the Federal Rules of Evidence have been afforded due consideration. As in Lego v. Twomey, 404 U.S. 477, 488 (1972), we find "nothing to suggest that admissibility rulings have been unreliable or otherwise wanting in quality because not based on some higher standard." We think that our previous decisions in this area resolve the matter. Therefore, we hold that when the preliminary facts relevant to Rule 801(d)(2)(E) are disputed, the offering party must prove them by a preponderance of the evidence.[1]

Even though petitioner agrees that the courts below applied the proper standard of proof with regard to the preliminary facts relevant to Rule 801(d)(2)(E), he nevertheless challenges the admission of Lonardo's statements. Petitioner argues that in determining whether a conspiracy exists and whether the defendant was a member of it, the court must look only to independent evidence—that is, evidence other than the statements sought to be admitted. Petitioner relies on Glasser v. United States, 315 U.S. 60 (1942), in which this Court first mentioned the so-called "bootstrapping rule." . . . :

> "[Coconspirators' statements] are admissible over the objection of an alleged co-conspirator, who was not present when they were made, only if there is proof *aliunde** that he is connected with the conspiracy. . . . Otherwise, hearsay would lift itself by its own bootstraps to the level of competent evidence." *Id.* at 74–75.

. . . Read in the light most favorable to petitioner, *Glasser* could mean that a court should not consider hearsay statements at all in determining preliminary facts under Rule 801(d)(2)(E). Petitioner, of course, adopts this

1. We intimate no view on the proper standard of proof for questions falling under Federal Rule of Evidence 104(b) (conditional relevancy). [Note that *Huddleston v. United States*, excerpted earlier at page 201, which addressed the standard of proof under Rule 104(b), was not decided until 1988, a year after *Bourjaily.*—GF] . . . Finally, we do not express an opinion on the proper order of proof that trial courts should follow in concluding that the preponderance standard has been satisfied in an ongoing trial.

* [*Black's Law Dictionary* defines "aliunde" to mean "[f]rom another source; from elsewhere; from outside."—GF]

view of the bootstrapping rule. *Glasser*, however, could also mean that a court must have *some* proof *aliunde*, but may look at the hearsay statements themselves in light of this independent evidence to determine whether a conspiracy has been shown by a preponderance of the evidence. The Courts of Appeals have widely adopted the former view and held that in determining the preliminary facts relevant to co-conspirators' out-of-court statements, a court may not look at the hearsay statements themselves for their evidentiary value.

[But *Glasser* was] decided before Congress enacted the Federal Rules of Evidence in 1975. These Rules now govern the treatment of evidentiary questions in federal courts. [Unrestyled] Rule 104(a) provides: "Preliminary questions concerning ... the admissibility of evidence shall be determined by the court.... In making its determination it is not bound by the rules of evidence except those with respect to privileges." Similarly, [unrestyled] Rule 1101(d)(1) states that the Rules of Evidence (other than with respect to privileges) shall not apply to "the determination of questions of fact preliminary to admissibility of evidence when the issue is to be determined by the court under rule 104." The question thus presented is whether any aspect of *Glasser*'s bootstrapping rule remains viable after the enactment of the Federal Rules of Evidence.

Petitioner concedes that Rule 104, on its face, appears to allow the court to make the preliminary factual determinations relevant to Rule 801(d)(2)(E) by considering any evidence it wishes, unhindered by considerations of admissibility. That would seem to many to be the end of the matter. Congress has decided that courts may consider hearsay in making these factual determinations. Out-of-court statements made by anyone, including putative co-conspirators, are often hearsay. Even if they are, they may be considered, *Glasser* and the bootstrapping rule notwithstanding. But petitioner nevertheless argues that the bootstrapping rule, as most Courts of Appeals have construed it, survived this apparently unequivocal change in the law unscathed and that Rule 104, as applied to the admission of co-conspirator's statements, does not mean what it says. We disagree.

Petitioner claims that Congress evidenced no intent to disturb the bootstrapping rule, which was embedded in the previous approach, and we should not find that Congress altered the rule without affirmative evidence so indicating. It would be extraordinary to require legislative history to *confirm* the plain meaning of Rule 104. The Rule on its face allows the trial judge to consider any evidence whatsoever, bound only by the rules of privilege. We think that the Rule is sufficiently clear that to the extent that it is inconsistent with petitioner's interpretation of *Glasser* ..., the Rule prevails.[2]

2. The Advisory Committee Notes show that the Rule was not adopted in a fit of absentmindedness. The Note to Rule 104 specifically addresses the process by which

Nor do we agree with petitioner that this construction of Rule 104(a) will allow courts to admit hearsay statements without any credible proof of the conspiracy, thus fundamentally changing the nature of the co-conspirator exception. Petitioner starts with the proposition that co-conspirators' out-of-court statements are deemed unreliable and are inadmissible, at least until a conspiracy is shown. Since these statements are unreliable, petitioner contends that they should not form any part of the basis for establishing a conspiracy, the very antecedent that renders them admissible.

Petitioner's theory ignores two simple facts of evidentiary life. First, out-of-court statements are only *presumed* unreliable. The presumption may be rebutted by appropriate proof. Second, individual pieces of evidence, insufficient in themselves to prove a point, may in cumulation prove it. The sum of an evidentiary presentation may well be greater than its constituent parts. Taken together, these two propositions demonstrate that a piece of evidence, unreliable in isolation, may become quite probative when corroborated by other evidence. A *per se* rule barring consideration of these hearsay statements during preliminary factfinding is not therefore required. Even if out-of-court declarations by co-conspirators are presumptively unreliable, trial courts must be permitted to evaluate these statements for their evidentiary worth as revealed by the particular circumstances of the case.... If the opposing party is unsuccessful in keeping the evidence from the factfinder, he still has the opportunity to attack the probative value of the evidence as it relates to the substantive issue in the case. *See, e.g.,* FED. R. EVID. 806 (allowing attack on credibility of out-of-court declarant).

We think that there is little doubt that a co-conspirator's statements could themselves be probative of the existence of a conspiracy and the participation of both the defendant and the declarant in the conspiracy. Petitioner's case presents a paradigm. The out-of-court statements of Lonardo indicated that Lonardo was involved in a conspiracy with a

a federal court should make the factual determinations requisite to a finding of admissibility:

> "If the question is factual in nature, the judge will of necessity receive evidence pro and con on the issue. The rule provides that the rules of evidence in general do not apply to this process. MCCORMICK § 53, at 123 n.8, points out that the authorities are 'scattered and inconclusive,' and observes:
>
> > " 'Should the exclusionary law of evidence, "the child of the jury system" in Thayer's phrase, be applied to this hearing before the judge? Sound sense backs the view that it should not, and that the judge should be empowered to hear *any relevant evidence*, such as affidavits *or other reliable hearsay*.' "

28 U.S.C. App. at 681 (emphasis added). [RB 13.]

The Advisory Committee further noted: "An item, offered and objected to, *may itself be considered in ruling on admissibility*, though not yet admitted in evidence." *Id.* (emphasis added) [RB 13]. We think this language makes plain the drafters' intent to abolish any kind of bootstrapping rule. Silence is at best ambiguous, and we decline the invitation to rely on speculation to import ambiguity into what is otherwise a clear rule.

"friend." The statements indicated that the friend had agreed with Lonardo to buy a kilogram of cocaine and to distribute it. The statements also revealed that the friend would be at the hotel parking lot, in his car, and would accept the cocaine from Greathouse's car after Greathouse gave Lonardo the keys. Each one of Lonardo's statements may itself be unreliable, but taken as a whole, the entire conversation between Lonardo and Greathouse was corroborated by independent evidence. The friend, who turned out to be petitioner, showed up at the prearranged spot at the prearranged time. He picked up the cocaine, and a significant sum of money was found in his car. On these facts, the trial court concluded, in our view correctly, that the Government had established the existence of a conspiracy and petitioner's participation in it.

We need not decide in this case whether the courts below could have relied solely upon Lonardo's hearsay statements to determine that a conspiracy had been established by a preponderance of the evidence. To the extent that *Glasser* meant that courts could not look to the hearsay statements themselves for any purpose, it has clearly been superseded by Rule 104(a). It is sufficient for today to hold that a court, in making a preliminary factual determination under Rule 801(d)(2)(E), may examine the hearsay statements sought to be admitted. . . . The courts below properly considered the statements of Lonardo and the subsequent events in finding that the Government had established by a preponderance of the evidence that Lonardo was involved in a conspiracy with petitioner. We have no reason to believe that the District Court's factfinding of this point was clearly erroneous. We hold that Lonardo's out-of-court statements were properly admitted against petitioner. . . .

The judgment of the Court of Appeals is

Affirmed.

■ Justice Stevens, concurring. . . .

■ Justice Blackmun, with whom Justice Brennan and Justice Marshall join, dissenting. . . .

Bourjaily v. United States: *Afterthoughts*

The Theory of the Coconspirator Exception

In his dissenting opinion in *Bourjaily*, Justice Blackmun considered the rationale behind the coconspirator exception at common law:

> . . . By all accounts, the exemption was based upon agency principles, the underlying concept being that a conspiracy is a common undertaking where the conspirators are all agents of each other and where the acts and statements of one can be attributed to

all. As Judge Learned Hand explained this in a frequently quoted remark:

> "When men enter into an agreement for an unlawful end, they become ad hoc agents for one another, and have made a 'partnership in crime.' What one does pursuant to their common purpose, all do, and, as declarations may be such acts, they are competent against all." Van Riper v. United States, 13 F.2d 961, 967 (2d Cir.), *cert. denied sub nom.* Ackerson v. United States, 273 U.S. 702 (1926).
>
> Each of the components of this common-law exemption, in turn, had an agency justification. To fall within the exemption, the co-conspirator's statement had to be made "in furtherance of" the conspiracy, a requirement that arose from the agency rationale that an agent's acts or words could be attributed to his principal only so long as the agent was acting within the scope of his employment. The statement also had to be made "during the course of" the conspiracy. This feature necessarily accompanies the "in furtherance of" requirement, for there must be an employment or business relationship in effect between the agent and principal, in accordance with which the agent is acting, for the principal to be bound by his agent's deeds or words. . . .
>
> . . . As such, this exemption was considered to be a "vicarious admission." Although not an admission by a defendant himself, the vicarious admission was a statement imputed to the defendant from the co-conspirator on the basis of their agency relationship.

483 U.S. at 188–90 (Blackmun, J., dissenting).

In contrast, the Advisory Committee's Note to Rule 801(d)(2)(E) dismisses the agency theory of conspiracy as "at best a fiction." (RB 208.) But if we don't resort to the agency theory, what rationale is there for admitting statements of coconspirators?

The Existence of a "Conspiracy"

Application of the coconspirator exception does not depend on whether the government has formally charged conspiracy. Nor need you have mastered conspiracy law to know whether the exception applies. In its report on Rule 801(d)(2)(E), the Senate Judiciary Committee noted its "understanding that the rule is meant to carry forward the universally accepted doctrine that a joint venturer is considered as a coconspirator for the purposes of this rule even though no conspiracy has been charged." (RB 208.) A joint venturer is at minimum one who "knew of the venture and intended to associate with it. . . ." MUELLER & KIRKPATRICK, EVIDENCE § 8.33, at 841 (5th ed. 2012).

The coconspirator exception almost never applies to a confession made knowingly to the police and implicating one's associates. The rule requires that the statement be made "during the course and in furtherance of the conspiracy." Such a confession may well terminate the conspiracy. It almost never "further[s]" the conspiracy.

Distinguishing 104(a) Questions From 104(b) Questions

In *Bourjaily* the government had to meet several preconditions to qualify Lonardo's statements about his "friend" as coconspirator's statements under Rule 801(d)(2)(E). It had to show that a conspiracy existed, that the conspiracy included both Lonardo and Bourjaily, and that Lonardo made the statements during and in furtherance of the conspiracy. The Supreme Court said the trial judge must resolve these preliminary questions under Rule 104(a). Unfortunately, because Bourjaily and the government agreed on this point, the Court felt little need to explain this part of its decision. Yet the distinction between Rule 104(a) questions and Rule 104(b) questions is both important and perplexing.

Let's begin by reviewing what we already know. Rules 104(a) and 104(b) both address how we should resolve questions on which the admissibility of evidence turns. In *Bourjaily* the Court determined that Rule 104(a) requires that the trial judge decide whether the preliminary conditions of the coconspirator exception have been proved. The judge must resolve these questions, the Court ruled, by a preponderance of the evidence.

In footnote 1 at page 422 the Court reserved a different issue—"the proper standard of proof for questions falling under Federal Rule of Evidence 104(b)." The Court resolved that matter a year later in *Huddleston v. United States*, 485 U.S. 681, 688 (1988) (excerpted above at page 201). The justices held that "[i]n determining whether the Government has introduced sufficient evidence to meet Rule 104(b), the trial court . . . simply examines all the evidence in the case and decides whether the jury could reasonably find the conditional fact . . . by a preponderance of the evidence." (Page 205, above.)

We know two important facts about these dual standards of proof. The first is that the preponderance standard of Rule 104(a) is higher than the sufficient-evidence standard of Rule 104(b). Between the lines of the *Huddleston* opinion the Court acknowledged that Rule 104(a) imposes the more demanding standard of proof: "According to petitioner," the Court wrote, "the trial court must make this preliminary finding [about whether the television sets involved in that case were stolen] by at least a preponderance of the evidence. . . . We reject petitioner's position. . . ." (Page 204, above.) Hence the standard of proof imposed by Rule 104(b) and embraced in *Huddleston* is *lower* than a preponderance.

The second fact cuts somewhat in the opposite direction. Both Rule 104(a) and the Court's interpretation of that rule in *Bourjaily* make clear that the evidence used to prove facts under the rule need not itself be admissible. The coconspirator statements challenged in *Bourjaily*, therefore, were themselves proper evidence of the existence of a conspiracy. Under Rule 104(b), however, only *admissible* evidence may be used to prove contested preliminary facts. The rule requires that "proof . . . be *introduced* sufficient to support a finding that the [preliminary] fact does exist." (Emphasis added.) Only admissible evidence may be *introduced*.

But the most important question remains the most elusive: How can we distinguish Rule 104(a) questions from Rule 104(b) questions? How do we know which preliminary questions the judge should decide by a preponderance of the evidence under Rule 104(a) and which she should submit to the jury if the sufficient-evidence standard of Rule 104(b) is met? The clearest answer is the one given by Rule 104 itself: *All* preliminary questions are to be resolved by the court except "[w]hen the relevance of evidence depends on whether a fact exists," triggering application of Rule 104(b). That is, Rule 104(b) governs *only* matters of conditional relevance, and Rule 104(a) governs *everything else*.

Huddleston therefore presented a Rule 104(b) question. The Court assumed that Huddleston's sale of certain television sets was *relevant* to his knowledge that certain Memorex tapes were stolen only if the television sets also were stolen. So evidence of the TVs' sale was admissible only if the jury reasonably could find by a preponderance of the evidence that the TVs were stolen.

Bourjaily, in contrast, presented no question of conditional relevance. Lonardo's statements about his "friend" were *relevant* to Bourjaily's guilt whether or not those statements met the technical requirements of the coconspirator exception. Recall that the difficulty with hearsay is not that it is irrelevant. Rather hearsay is generally less *reliable* than live testimony because the speaker is not in court, under oath, and subject to cross-examination. Since the preliminary questions posed by the coconspirator exception therefore are not matters on which the relevance of Lonardo's statements turned, the judge had to resolve those questions under Rule 104(a).

Rationalizing the Distinction: Judge's and Jury's Separate Spheres?

Occasionally a judge will ask, "Is this a 104(a) question for the court or a 104(b) question for the jury?" The shorthand is misleading. *Both* 104(a) questions and 104(b) questions are in some sense for the court. In one case the judge must resolve the question herself by a preponderance of the evidence. In the other she must decide whether sufficient evidence has been introduced—or will be forthcoming—that the jury reasonably could find the conditional fact by a preponderance of the evidence. Under both rules admissibility is the court's to decide.

And both 104(a) questions and 104(b) questions are in some sense for the jury. Under Rule 104(b), of course, the jury either finds or does not find that the conditional fact has been established. If the *Huddleston* jury did not believe the television sets were stolen, it presumably ignored evidence of their sale. Likewise the jury may review the court's rulings under Rule 104(a). The jury is unlikely to do so when those rulings touched on technical matters of law. But Rule 104(a) questions often concern matters of obvious importance to the jury. Before a witness may offer an expert opinion, for example, the judge must find by a preponderance of the evidence that she is qualified in her field. Normally the lawyer who sponsors the witness will take care to lay out the expert's credentials for the jury. The jury is then free, regardless of the judge's view, to reject the expert as a charlatan.

The division of labor between judges and juries therefore is less distinct than the common shorthand—"a 104(a) question for the judge or a 104(b) question for the jury"—would suggest. As a consequence it may be hard to state a convincing rationale for the different tasks that Rule 104(a) and Rule 104(b) *seem* to impose on judge and jury. Take this as a challenge: As you work through the remainder of the book, consider how—if at all—we can justify the distinction the rule writers carved between 104(a) questions and 104(b) questions.

Problem 7.16

Translation

Consider these (somewhat simplified) facts of *United States v. Aboumoussallem*, 726 F.2d 906 (2d Cir. 1984):

> In April 1981, an undercover agent of the Rochester police department, posing as an organized crime figure, purchased fourteen ounces of heroin from N, who is the cousin of Y, the defendant. N identified Lebanon as the source of the heroin and told the agent that various family members based in Lebanon regularly transported drugs to the United States. Hoping to catch other participants in N's drug smuggling scheme [and still acting under cover], the agent subsequently arranged for a more substantial purchase of heroin.
>
> On August 17, 1981, the agent and N traveled to Kennedy Airport to await the arrival of N's Lebanese "courier." N informed the agent that his cousin Y would be transporting the heroin. Y was to deliver a black attaché case containing heroin to whoever handed him a passport-

size photograph of Y. The agent intercepted Y as soon as he left the aircraft. As arranged, Y exchanged the attaché case for his photograph. Inside the attaché case was a smuggler's vest that contained 1,823 grams of 53.8% pure heroin.

The three persons boarded a flight to Rochester, the planned destination. During the course of the flight the undercover agent posed a number of questions to Y. As Y spoke no English, and the agent no Arabic, N acted as interpreter. In response to the agent's inquiry as to the quality of the heroin, Y responded (according to N's translation) that it was so strong that when he packed the heroin into the vest, his nose bled.

At the Rochester airport, agents sought to arrest both Y and N. N resisted apprehension and was killed in a gun fight. . . .

At Y's trial, the Government calls the undercover agent as a witness and asks him to relate the conversation on the airplane. Y objects. Should the court admit the evidence of N's translation of Y's statement? What are the best arguments for and against admissibility?

D. Past Statements of Witnesses and Past Testimony

1. Introduction

Having dealt with opposing parties' statements, we now take up most of those exceptions to the hearsay rule that address either a witness's past statements or testimony from an earlier proceeding. The chart on the next page lays out the rules that fall under this heading and summarizes the conditions they impose for admission. There is no need to master all of these rules now. We examine each of them in time.

Notice that the chart addresses two rules that do not concern hearsay at all. Rule 613 governs the impeachment of witnesses with their past inconsistent statements. When used to impeach, past inconsistent statements are offered *not* for the truth of what they assert, but merely to show that the witness says different things at different times and therefore should not be believed on this question. The lawyer opposing a statement's admission may ask the judge for a limiting instruction to that effect. Of course the jury often may not grasp the distinction between

PAST STATEMENTS OF WITNESSES AND PAST TESTIMONY

Rule	*Topic*	*Conditions Regarding Declarant's Availability or Memory*	*Conditions Regarding Past Statement*
613	Past Inconsistent Statements Offered to Impeach	Declarant Must Testify at Current Proceeding	Questioning Lawyer Must Have Good–Faith Belief That Witness Made Past Statement
801(d)(1)(A)	Past Inconsistent Statements Offered Substantively	Declarant Must Testify at Current Proceeding and Be "Subject to Cross–Examination About [the] Prior Statement"	Past Statement Is Inconsistent and Was Given Under Oath at a "Proceeding" or Deposition
801(d)(1)(B)	Past Consistent Statements	Same	Past Statement Is Consistent, Is Offered to Rebut Charge of Recent Fabrication or Improper Motive, and Meets *Tome* Rule
801(d)(1)(C)	Statements of Identification	Same	Past Statement Identifies a Person Whom Declarant Perceived Earlier
804(b)(1)	Past Testimony	Declarant Must Be Unavailable as Defined by Rule 804(a)	Past Statement Was "Testimony" (i.e., Given Under Oath), and Was A. "[A]t a Trial, Hearing, or Lawful Deposition" and B. Subject to Examination by Party Against Whom Now Offered (or by Civil "Predecessor in Interest"), Who Then Had "Similar Motive"
612	Refreshing Witness's Memory	Witness Must Be on Stand; Memory Must Be Exhausted	None (Note That Memory May Be Refreshed with Many Things; If a Writing Is Used, Rule 612 Imposes Conditions)
803(5)	Recorded Recollection	Witness Must Be on Stand; Must Be Unable to "Recall Well Enough to Testify Fully and Accurately"	Record Was Made or Adopted When Witness's Memory Was Fresh and Accurately Reflects Witness's Knowledge

using an out-of-court statement *substantively*—that is, as proof of what it says—and using it only to impeach. (Consider *United States v. Ince*, 21 F.3d 576 (4th Cir. 1994), excerpted below at page 439, in this light.) This problem does not arise when a witness's past inconsistent statement is admitted under Rule 801(d)(1)(A). Such statements come in substantively, and the jury may consider them for their truth. Note that a litigant must satisfy far more stringent conditions to admit a past inconsistent statement for its truth under Rule 801(d)(1)(A) than to use it merely to impeach under Rule 613.

Rule 612 also does not concern hearsay. It deals instead with the mechanics of refreshing a witness's memory. Information used to refresh is not itself offered as evidence and need not be admissible. Rather, once the witness's memory has been refreshed, the witness simply testifies from memory in the ordinary way. We take up Rule 612 together with Rule 803(5), which governs admission of a record of past events when the witness's memory of those events has faded. Rule 803(5), unlike Rule 612, provides for the admission of hearsay statements for their truth. Again note that the conditions set out in Rule 803(5) are far more stringent than the rules for refreshing a witness's memory. Almost anything may be used to refresh a witness's memory—"a song, a scent, a photograph, an allusion," in the words of Learned Hand.* But Rule 803(5) is more restrictive.

Edmund M. Morgan

Hearsay Dangers and the Application of the Hearsay Concept

62 HARV. L. REV. 177, 192–96 (1948)

. . . *Prior Declarations of a Witness.*— . . . [T]here is one situation where the courts are prone to call hearsay what does not in fact involve in any substantial degree any of the hearsay risks. When the Declarant is also a witness, it is difficult to justify classifying as hearsay evidence of his own prior statements. This is especially true where Declarant as a witness is

* *United States v. Rappy*, 157 F.2d 964, 967 (2d Cir. 1946), *cert. denied*, 329 U.S. 806 (1947).

giving as part of his testimony his own prior statement.... The courts declare the prior statement to be hearsay because it was not made under oath, subject to the penalty for perjury or to the test of cross-examination. To which the answer might well be: "The declarant as a witness is now under oath and now purports to remember and narrate accurately. The adversary can now expose every element that may carry a danger of misleading the trier of fact both in the previous statement and in the present testimony, and the trier can judge whether both the previous declaration and the present testimony are reliable in whole or in part." To this Mr. Justice Stone of the Minnesota Supreme Court, speaking of evidence of prior contradictory statements, has framed this reply:

> The chief merit of cross-examination is not that at some future time it gives the party opponent the right to dissect adverse testimony. Its principal virtue is in its immediate application of the testing process. Its strokes fall while the iron is hot. False testimony is apt to harden and become unyielding to the blows of truth in proportion as the witness has opportunity for reconsideration and influence by the suggestion of others, whose interest may be, and often is, to maintain falsehood rather than truth.

State v. Saporen, 205 Minn. 358, 362 (1939).... Why does falsehood harden any more quickly or unyieldingly than truth? What has become of the idea that truth is eternal and, though crushed to earth, will rise again? Isn't the opportunity for reconsideration and for baneful influence by others even more likely to color the later testimony than the prior statement? Furthermore, it must be remembered that the trier of fact is often permitted to hear these prior statements to impeach ... the declarant-witness. In such event, of course, the trier will be told that he must not treat the statement as evidence of the truth of the matter stated. But to what practical effect? Wasn't Judge Swan right in saying, "Practically, men will often believe that if a witness has earlier sworn to the opposite of what he now swears to, he was speaking the truth when he first testified"? Do the judges deceive themselves or do they realize that they are indulging in a pious fraud?

Commentators and text writers are not alone in challenging the doctrine.... As early as 1925, in the *Di Carlo* case, referring to the admission of a prior inconsistent statement, made by the prosecution's witness who "surprised" the prosecutor by his testimony, Judge Learned Hand declared:

> If, from all that the jury see of the witness, they conclude that what he says now is not the truth, but what he said before, they are none the less deciding from what they see and hear of that person and in court. There is no mythical necessity that the case must be decided only in accordance with the truth of words uttered under oath in court.

Di Carlo v. United States, 6 F.2d 364, 368 (2d Cir. 1925). Unfortunately, Judge Hand in *United States v. Block*, 88 F.2d 618 (2d Cir. 1937), qualified this pronouncement as to prior contradictions, saying that they could be used only where the conduct of the witness in court, in spite of his express denial, could be rationally interpreted as an affirmation of the former statement. . . .

Perhaps [this] recantation[] reflected a presentiment of the negative attitude which the Supreme Court of the United States later took toward judicial reformation of this irrational rule of evidence. . . . In *Bridges v. Wixon*, 326 U.S. 135 (1945), the decision of the Attorney General in the deportation proceedings against Harry Bridges was under review. Before the trial examiner, one O'Neil testified that he had made statements to investigating officers some months before and that they were true, but he denied stating that he had seen Bridges pasting stamps in a Communist Party book or that Bridges had reminded him that he (O'Neil) had not been attending party meetings. Both the investigating officers and the stenographer who recorded the interview testified that O'Neil had made these statements. The trial examiner and the Attorney General found that O'Neil had made them, and the Court, assuming that both had used them as substantive evidence, held that such use was error. Mr. Justice Douglas, writing for the majority, said that the statements "certainly would not be admissible in any criminal case as substantive evidence. . . . So to hold would allow men to be convicted on unsworn testimony of witnesses—a practice which runs counter to the notions of fairness on which our legal system is founded." 326 U.S. at 153–54. No attempt to justify this speciously plausible conclusion was made. . . .

. . . [W]hether or not the declarant at the time of the utterance was subject to all the conditions usually imposed upon witnesses should be immaterial, for the declarant is now present as a witness. If his prior statement is consistent with his present testimony, he now affirms it under oath subject to all sanctions and to cross-examination in the presence of the trier who is to value it. Perhaps it ought not to be received because unnecessary, but surely the rejection should not be on the ground that the statement involves any danger inherent in hearsay. If the witness testifies that all the statements he made were true, as in the *Bridges* case, then the only debatable question is whether he made the statement; and as to that the trier has all the witnesses before him, and has also the benefit of thorough cross-examination as to the facts which are the subject matter of the statement. If the witness denies having made any statement at all, the situation is but little different, for he will usually swear that he tried to tell the truth in anything that he may have said. If he concedes that he made the statement but now swears that it wasn't true, the experience in human affairs which the average juror brings to a controversy will enable him to decide which story represents the truth in the light of all the facts, such as the demeanor of the witness, the matter brought out on direct and cross-examination, and the testimony of others.

In any of these situations Proponent is not asking Trier to rely upon the credibility of any one who is not present and subject to all the conditions imposed upon a witness. Adversary has all the protection which oath and cross-examination can give him. Trier is in a position to consider the evidence impartially and to give it no more than its reasonable persuasive effect. Consequently there is no real reason for classifying the evidence as hearsay. . . .

Afterthought on Morgan: Despite Professor Morgan's spirited arguments, the rule writers rejected his proposal that all past statements of testifying witnesses be exempt from the hearsay ban. As the chart on page 431 makes clear, the Rules admit only certain well-defined categories of past statements. The advisory committee frankly admitted that this "judgment [was] one more of experience than of logic." (ACN to FRE 801(d)(1), RB 198–99.) Much like Justice Jackson in *Michelson*, the rule writers apparently determined that though the scheme of common-law hearsay rules might be a "grotesque structure," it was unwise to pull out this one particular "misshapen stone."

---

2. Inconsistent Statements Offered to Impeach

Focus on
FRE 613

United States v. Barrett

539 F.2d 244 (1st Cir. 1976).

■ Campbell, Circuit Judge. Arthur ["Bucky"] Barrett appeals from his conviction after a jury trial for crimes arising from the theft and sale of a collection of postage stamps from the Cardinal Spellman Philatelic Museum in Weston, Massachusetts. Barrett and seven others were charged in a three-count indictment with the interstate transportation of stolen postage stamps. . . . Of the eight indicted, Barrett alone went to trial.

The Government called as its first witness the manager of the Cardinal Spellman Museum, who testified that on the morning of March 30, 1973, he arrived to find the Museum vault stripped and much of the stamp collection missing. There were virtually no clues. It was discovered that the burglars had bypassed the Museum's alarm system by attaching a jumper cable to the alarm wires at a juncture outside the Museum, thus neutralizing it. To do this, according to later expert testimony, the burglars would have had to measure the current in different wires in a sophisticated manner using a volt meter to assist in the process.

Three government witnesses implicated Barrett in the burglary and subsequent disposition of the stamps. . . . [One of these, Michael Bass,] identified Barrett, or "Bucky," as being present at [a house near Boston] when Bass examined the stamps. While looking at the stamps on his first visit to the house, Bass recollected Barrett's commenting . . . "that he had climbed the telephone pole, bypassed the alarm system . . . , and that there was a tremendous amount of work blowing—getting this big vault door off—and they were running around like mad pulling collections down, and they figured that this was the biggest score of their lives." . . .

["Buzzy"] Adams, an admitted and convicted burglar and thief, testified for the Government in exchange for protection for himself and his family. He testified that he was introduced to Barrett by Ben Tilley in early 1972 for the purpose of discussing alarms, and that Barrett displayed knowledge of the use of an ohmmeter to identify alarm wires. Adams also testified that right after being arrested Barrett described his involvement . . . in the Cardinal Spellman stamp theft. . . .

After the government rested, the defense unsuccessfully sought to introduce testimony from three witnesses under circumstances discussed below; otherwise it presented no testimony of consequence. The defense urged in closing argument . . . that Bass's identification of Barrett was . . . unreliable . . . and that "Buzzy" Adams was fingering "Bucky" Barrett to cover his own participation in the stamp theft. . . .

III

We turn next to the court's exclusion of the testimony of the defense's two remaining witnesses, Thomas J. Delaney and Jeanne Kelley. We hold such exclusion to have been error.

Delaney stated that he met with Buzzy Adams in or around November 1974 in a Boston area restaurant. He was then asked to relate their conversation. The Government objected and Barrett offered to prove that "Adams said that he had heard that Barrett had been indicted, or had gotten into trouble on this matter, and that it was too bad because he, Buzzy, knew that Barrett was not involved." Kelley, a waitress, was prepared to testify that, while waiting on Adams and Delaney at the same restaurant, she overheard Adams say "it was a shame that Bucky got arrested on this matter" because he (Adams) "knew that Bucky didn't have anything to do with it."

Conceding that this evidence was hearsay, FED. R. EVID. 801(d)(1), and so inadmissible to prove the truth of the matter asserted, Barrett argues that it was admissible as a prior inconsistent statement to impeach Adams' credibility. Adams had earlier testified that Barrett admitted to him shortly after his arrest that he had been involved in the stamp transaction.[9] Barrett contends that Adams' subsequent statement to Delaney in November 1974 that Barrett was not involved was contradictory and so admissible to impeach his credibility.

We believe the court erred in excluding this testimony. Counsel for Barrett advised the court, albeit rather succinctly, that the testimony went to the credibility of Adams who had testified. The court ruled it out on the ground that it was a "hearsay opinion by Mr. Adams, that this guy is innocent. That is all this amounts to." The Government now argues, in the same vein, that Adams' purported opinion was too vague and unsupported to be useful. However, the clear purport of Adams' direct testimony was that in late October 1974, after Barrett's arrest, Adams acquired first-hand knowledge of Barrett's involvement in the stamp affair, and the jury could have inferred from this and other testimony that at all times thereafter Adams remained of the impression that Barrett was involved. The statement to Delaney, therefore, made supposedly in November 1974, was clearly inconsistent. To be received as a prior inconsistent statement, the contradiction need not be "in plain terms. It is enough if the proffered testimony, taken as a whole, either by what it says or by what it omits to say, affords some indication that the fact was different from the testimony of the witness whom it is sought to contradict." Commonwealth v. West, 312 Mass. 438, 440 (1942), *cited in* McCORMICK ON EVIDENCE § 34, at 68 n.15. Furthermore, the fact that Adams' belief that Bucky was not involved might be called an "opinion" is immaterial. *Id.* § 35. The important point is the clear incompatibility between Adams' direct testimony and the alleged statement.

The Government also urges that Delaney's memory of the timing of the statement was uncertain, as well as his memory as to other details. And it may well be that Delaney's testimony would have turned out to be inadequate and thin in various respects. But this possibility is not a ground for keeping the evidence from the jury, which is the principal judge of the credibility of witnesses and the weight to be given to otherwise competent testimony.

A more serious argument pressed by the Government is that Barrett failed during cross-examination to lay a foundation for introducing extrinsic evidence of the statement by first directing Adams' attention to the occasion of the alleged contradictory statement and asking him if he made it. Such is the procedure laid down in Queen Caroline's Case, 2

9. Barrett was arrested and bailed in late October 1974. According to Adams they had a conversation a day or so later in which,

> "I asked him what was the story and how did they come down to his house and arrest him. He said that he didn't know too much about it. I said, 'How bad is it, how bad have they got you'? He said, 'Well, they got me. I bartered with the people that bought the stuff. They can identify me with no problem.' "

Brod. & Bing. 284, 313, 129 Eng. Rep. 976 (1820), and required in many jurisdictions (though not in Massachusetts). It is clear, however, that Fed. R. Evid. 613(b) has relaxed any absolute requirement that this practice be observed, only requiring instead that the witness be afforded at some time an opportunity to explain or deny, and for further interrogation.[10] . . .

A final question is whether the error was one which affected "substantial rights," requiring reversal. FED. R. CRIM. P. 52(a); *see* Kotteakos v. United States, 328 U.S. 750 (1946). The case against Barrett was strong, and we are tempted to say that the proffered testimony was unlikely to have affected the result. Barrett's defense rested, however, on the notion that [Bass was] lying in hope of reward and Adams was lying because he, not Bucky, was the real culprit. We cannot say, given Adams' criminal background, that if Delaney and Kelley had impressed the jury, the credibility of Adams would not have been substantially diminished, and, with this tangible achievement, the defense would not have achieved its goal of raising a reasonable doubt in the minds of the jury. This is not a result we would either look for or, on this record, applaud, but we cannot with certainty say that the error was harmless. . . .

Vacated and remanded.

Problem 7.17
Retraction

In the course of a murder investigation, a police detective interviewed Brenda Raymond, who said she saw Margaret Davis fire the fatal shot. At Davis's trial the prosecutor calls Raymond as a witness. She testifies that she was nowhere near the crime scene and has no idea who shot the deceased. When questioned by the prosecutor about her previous statement to the police, Raymond denies having made it.

The prosecutor then calls the police detective to the stand. The detective testifies that Raymond told him in an interview at her home that she saw Davis shoot the victim.

If the prosecutor now rests without producing any other evidence of the shooter's identity and if the defendant moves for

10. Clause (b) of [unrestyled] Fed. R. Evid. 613 provides, in part,

"Extrinsic evidence of a prior inconsistent statement by a witness is not admissible unless the witness is afforded an opportunity to explain or deny the same and the opposite party is afforded an opportunity to interrogate him thereon, or the interests of justice otherwise require."

a directed verdict of acquittal, how should the judge rule? (Assume the judge must grant the motion if no reasonable juror could find the defendant guilty beyond a reasonable doubt.)

UNITED STATES V. INCE

21 F.3d 576 (4th Cir. 1994).

■ MURNAGHAN, CIRCUIT JUDGE: Appellant Nigel D. Ince was convicted by a jury [of] assault with a dangerous weapon, with intent to do bodily harm. Because the United States' only apparent purpose for impeaching one of its own witnesses was to circumvent the hearsay rule and to expose the jury to otherwise inadmissible evidence of Ince's alleged confession, we reverse.

I

Late on the evening of September 4, 1992, a rap concert and dance at the Sosa Recreation Center at Fort Belvoir, Virginia, ended abruptly when members of two of the bands performing there got in a scuffle. Shortly thereafter, a [man] wearing an orange shirt or jacket fired a nine millimeter pistol twice at trucks leaving the Recreation Center's parking lot. Defendant-appellant Nigel Ince, Angela Neumann, and two of their friends hopped in their van and headed for Pence Gate, Fort Belvoir's nearest exit. The military police pulled the van, as well as other vehicles leaving the parking lot, over to the side of the road and asked the drivers and passengers to stand on the curb. Two men whose vehicles had also been pulled over identified Ince as the [one] who had fired the shots in the parking lot, although they noted that he was no longer wearing an orange shirt. As part of the investigation that followed, Military Policeman Roger D. Stevens interviewed and took a signed, unsworn statement from Neumann. She recounted that Ince had admitted to firing the shots, but said he no longer had the gun.

. . . At Ince's trial the Government called Neumann to the stand. When her memory supposedly failed her, the prosecution attempted to refresh her recollection with a copy of the signed statement that she had given Stevens on the night of the shooting. Even with her recollection refreshed, she testified that she could no longer recall the details of her conversation with Ince. Following Neumann's testimony, the Government excused her and called Stevens, who testified (over the objection of defense counsel) as to what Neumann had told him shortly after the shooting. The trial ended with a deadlocked jury.

At the second trial, the Government again called Neumann. She again acknowledged that she had given the military police a signed statement describing what Ince had told her immediately after the shooting. But she repeatedly testified that she could no longer recall the details of Ince's remarks, despite the prosecution's effort to refresh her recollection with a copy of the statement. The Government neither offered the statement into evidence as an exhibit nor read it into evidence under Rule 803(5) of the Federal Rules of Evidence. *See* FED. R. EVID. 803(5) (hearsay exception for past recorded recollections).

Over defense counsel's repeated objections, the Government again called MP Stevens to the stand, supposedly to impeach Neumann as to her memory loss. He testified that, within hours of the shooting, Neumann had told him that Ince had confessed to firing the gun. The Government also called two eyewitnesses who identified Ince as the gunman.

The defense's theory of the case was mistaken identity: Frank Kelly, not Nigel Ince, had fired the shots. Kelly . . . attended the dance, wore a long-sleeved orange jacket, was supposedly spotted by Neumann in the parking lot holding a handgun, and was found by the FBI five days later with a nine millimeter pistol hidden in his bedroom. In an attempt to undermine the defense's theory of the case, the prosecution, in its closing argument, reminded the jurors that they had "heard testimony that Ms. Neumann made a statement to an MP [immediately following the shooting]. And she told [him] at that time that the defendant said, 'Frank didn't shoot the gun; I shot the gun.' "

The second time around, the jury convicted Ince. The district judge sentenced him to forty-one months in prison, plus two years of supervised release. Ince now appeals, requesting a reversal of his conviction and a new trial.

II

Appellant Ince argues that the testimony of MP Stevens was inadmissible hearsay because the Government offered it to prove the truth of the matter asserted in Neumann's out-of-court statement (i.e., that Ince confessed to the crime). The United States counters that Stevens's testimony was admissible because the Government offered it only to impeach Neumann's credibility. Ince responds that the prosecution, having already seen Neumann's performance on the stand at the first trial, was fully aware that she would not testify as to Ince's alleged confession at the second trial either. Nevertheless, the prosecution put her on the stand a second time to elicit testimony inconsistent with her prior statement to Stevens, so as to provide a foundation to offer Stevens's so-called "impeaching" evidence and thereby to get Ince's confession before the jury. Thus, the sole question presented on appeal is whether the admission of Stevens's testimony constituted reversible error.

A

[Unrestyled] Rule 607 of the Federal Rules of Evidence provides that "the credibility of a witness may be attacked by any party, including the party calling the witness." One method of attacking the credibility of (*i.e.*, impeaching) a witness is to show that he has previously made a statement that is inconsistent with his present testimony. Even if that prior inconsistent statement would otherwise be inadmissible as hearsay, it may be admissible for the limited purpose of impeaching the witness. At a criminal trial, however, there are limits on the Government's power to impeach its own witness by presenting his prior inconsistent statements. *See* United States v. Morlang, 531 F.2d 183 (4th Cir. 1975). In *Morlang*, we reversed the defendant's conviction ... because the Government had employed impeachment by prior inconsistent statement "as a mere subterfuge to get before the jury evidence not otherwise admissible." *Id.* at 190.[2]

At Morlang's trial the Government had called Fred Wilmoth, an original codefendant who had subsequently pleaded guilty, as its first witness despite the fact that his previous statements to the Government suggested he would be hostile. The real purpose for calling Wilmoth was apparently to elicit a denial that he had ever had a conversation with a fellow prisoner in which he had implicated Morlang. Having obtained the expected denial, the Government then called Raymond Crist, another prisoner, to impeach Wilmoth with the alleged prior inconsistent statement. As expected, Crist testified that his fellow inmate Wilmoth had made a conclusory statement from which one could only infer Morlang's guilt. As expected, the jury delivered a guilty verdict.

In reversing Morlang's conviction, Judge Widener explained that courts must not "permit the government, in the name of impeachment, to present testimony to the jury by indirection which would not otherwise be admissible." *Id.* at 189.... "[D]espite proper instructions to the jury, it is often difficult for jurors to distinguish between impeachment and substantive evidence...." *Id.* at 190.

Federal evidence law does not ask the judge, either at trial or upon appellate review, to crawl inside the prosecutor's head to divine his or her true motivation. Rather, in determining whether a Government witness' testimony offered as impeachment is admissible, or on the contrary is a "mere subterfuge" to get before the jury substantive evidence which is otherwise inadmissible as hearsay, a trial court must apply Federal Rule of Evidence 403 and weigh the testimony's impeachment value against its tendency to prejudice the defendant unfairly or to confuse the jury.

2. ... [E]very circuit of the U.S. Court of Appeals has followed *Morlang*. *See* United States v. Peterman, 841 F.2d 1474, 1479 n. 3 (10th Cir. 1988) (citing cases), *cert. denied*, 488 U.S. 1004 (1989).

When the prosecution attempts to introduce a prior inconsistent statement to impeach its own witness, the statement's likely prejudicial impact often substantially outweighs its probative value for impeachment purposes because the jury may ignore the judge's limiting instructions and consider the "impeachment" testimony for substantive purposes. That risk is multiplied when the statement offered as impeachment testimony contains the defendant's alleged admission of guilt. Thus, a trial judge should rarely, if ever, permit the Government to "impeach" its own witness by presenting what would otherwise be inadmissible hearsay if that hearsay contains an alleged confession to the crime for which the defendant is being tried.

B

In the case at bar, MP Stevens testified that Ince had admitted to firing the gun—the critical element of the crime for which he was being tried. It is hard to imagine any piece of evidence that could have had a greater prejudicial impact than such a supposed naked confession of guilt. Even if the other evidence which was properly admitted at trial had provided overwhelming proof of Ince's guilt—which it did not—and even if the judge had given the jury a clear limiting instruction—which he did not, *see infra* Part IIIC—Stevens's presentation of additional unsworn hearsay testimony going directly to the issue of Ince's guilt was extremely prejudicial.

Given the likely prejudicial impact of Stevens's testimony, the trial judge should have excluded it absent some extraordinary probative value. Because evidence of Neumann's prior inconsistent statement was admitted solely for purposes of impeachment, its probative value must be assessed solely in terms of its impeaching effect upon Neumann's testimony or overall credibility. Our review of the record below, however, shows that the probative value of Stevens's testimony for impeachment purposes was nil. Unlike the classic "turncoat" witness, Neumann certainly had not shocked the Government with her "loss of memory" at the second trial, as she had made it plain during the first trial that she would not readily testify to the alleged confession of her friend, Nigel Ince.

Furthermore, Neumann's actual in-court testimony did not affirmatively damage the Government's case; she merely refused to give testimony that the Government had hoped she would give. Thus, the prosecution had no need to attack her credibility. *Cf.* 27 CHARLES ALAN WRIGHT & VICTOR JAMES GOLD, FEDERAL PRACTICE AND PROCEDURE: EVIDENCE § 6093, at 515 (1990) ("If testimony does no damage, impeachment evidence has no probative value."). She testified that, immediately after the shooting, as they left the scene of the crime but before the military police pulled them over, (1) Ince stated that Frank Kelly—the person whom Ince's lawyer identified at trial as the likely perpetrator of the crime—was *not* the person who had fired the gun, (2) Ince stated that "he didn't have [the gun] with him," and (3) Ince instructed Neumann to tell the military police that she knew nothing about the events of the evening. She presented no evidence affirming or denying Ince's alleged confession. Taken as a whole, then, Neumann's testimony probably *strengthened* the Government's case. Therefore, evidence attacking her credibility had no probative value *for impeachment purposes.*

Because Stevens's so-called "impeachment" testimony was both highly prejudicial and devoid of probative value as impeachment evidence, the trial judge should have recognized the Government's tactic for what it was—an attempt to circumvent the hearsay rule and to infect the jury with otherwise inadmissible evidence of Ince's alleged confession. Instead, the judge allowed Stevens's testimony to come before the jury in clear violation of *Morlang* and its progeny, notwithstanding defense counsel's proper and timely objections. . . .

III

* * *

C

. . . The United States points to two supposedly mitigating steps taken at Ince's trial, but they fall far short of purging the error committed here. First, the Government claims that it "clearly stated" at trial that MP Stevens's testimony was offered only for impeachment purposes. Our review of the transcript, however, shows that the prosecutor issued that "clear statement" during a sidebar. Therefore, it could not possibly have mitigated the effects that Stevens's erroneously admitted testimony might have had on the jurors, for they never heard the prosecutor's disclaimer. Second, the United States argues that the district judge instructed the jury to use prior inconsistent statements solely for the purpose of assessing a witness' credibility. Although we recognize the presumption of cure by a court's instruction, it seems probable here that the jury was unable to follow the instruction on impeachment by prior inconsistent statement, much less to realize that it pertained to Stevens's testimony.[10] *See* Krulewitch v. United States, 336 U.S. 440, 453 (1949) (Jackson, J., concurring) ("The naive assumption that prejudicial effects can be overcome by instructions to the jury, . . . all practicing lawyers know to be unmitigated fiction."). Moreover, the prosecutor, in her closing argument,

10. The jury instructions provided, in "relevant" part:

> . . . The testimony of a witness may be disregarded or impeached by showing that he previously made statements which are inconsistent with his present testimony. The earlier contradictory statements are admissible only to impeach the credibility of the witness, and not to establish the truth of these statements. It is the province of the jury to determine the credibility, if any, to be given to the testimony of a witness who has been impeached.
>
> If the witness is shown knowingly to have testified falsely concerning any material matter, you have the right to distrust such witness; . . . and you may reject all the testimony of that witness or give it such credibility as you may think it deserves.

argued the truth of Neumann's out-of-court statement recounting Ince's alleged confession, thus vitiating any possible curative function that the judge's limiting instruction might have otherwise served. . . .

D

. . . [W]e note that Ince was tried twice, the first time resulting in a mistrial. . . . [M]ore important, the tainted evidence here is a confession allegedly uttered by the defendant himself and the jury first heard of that confession through the testimony of a uniformed Military Police officer. . . . In combination, the closeness of the case, the centrality of the issue affected by the error, and the meager steps taken to mitigate the effects of that error leave us with but one possible conclusion. . . .

IV

Accordingly, we reverse the conviction of Nigel D. Ince and remand the case for a new trial.

Problem 7.18

Why Such Excitement?

After F and G were arrested on suspicion of involvement in a drug-running operation, a Customs Service agent overheard G say to F, "Why so much excitement? If they caught us with the goods, they caught us with the goods." F remained silent.

At F's trial, may the government offer evidence of G's statement, together with F's silence,

(1) as substantive evidence of F's guilt?

(2) to impeach F if he testifies and denies all knowledge of the drug operation?

Does your answer to either question depend on whether F already had been advised of his "right to remain silent" under *Miranda v. Arizona*, 384 U.S. 436 (1966)? *Cf. United States v. Flecha*, 539 F.2d 874 (2d Cir. 1976).

FLETCHER v. WEIR

455 U.S. 603 (1982).

■ PER CURIAM. In the course of a fight in a nightclub parking lot, Ronnie Buchanan pinned respondent Weir to the ground. Buchanan then jumped to his feet and shouted that he had been stabbed; he ultimately died from his stab wounds. Respondent immediately left the scene, and did not report the incident to the police.

At his trial for intentional murder, respondent took the stand in his own defense. He admitted stabbing Buchanan, but claimed that he acted in self-defense and that the stabbing was accidental. This in-court statement was the first occasion on which respondent offered an exculpatory version of the stabbing. The prosecutor cross-examined him as to why he had, when arrested, failed either to advance his exculpatory explanation to the arresting officers or to disclose the location of the knife he had used to stab Buchanan. Respondent was ultimately found guilty by a jury of first-degree manslaughter. The conviction was affirmed on appeal to the Supreme Court of Kentucky.

The United States District Court for the Western District of Kentucky then granted respondent a writ of habeas corpus, and the Court of Appeals for the Sixth Circuit affirmed. 658 F.2d 1126 (1981). The Court of Appeals concluded that respondent was denied due process of law guaranteed by the Fourteenth Amendment when the prosecutor used his postarrest silence for impeachment purposes.[1] Although it did not appear from the record that the arresting officers had immediately read respondent his *Miranda* warnings, the court concluded that a defendant cannot be impeached by use of his postarrest silence even if no *Miranda* warnings had been given. The court held that "it is inherently unfair to allow cross-examination concerning post-arrest silence," 658 F.2d at 1130, and rejected the contention that our decision in Doyle v. Ohio, 426 U.S. 610 (1976), applied only where the police had read *Miranda* warnings to a defendant. Because we think that the Court of Appeals gave an overly broad reading to our decision in *Doyle v. Ohio*, we reverse its judgment.

One year prior to our decision in *Doyle*, we held in the exercise of our supervisory power over the federal courts that silence following the giving of *Miranda* warnings was ordinarily so ambiguous as to have little probative value. United States v. Hale, 422 U.S. 171 (1975). There we said:

> "In light of the many alternative explanations for his pretrial silence, we do not think it sufficiently probative of an inconsistency with his in-court testimony to warrant admission of evidence thereof." *Id.* at 180.

. . . The year after our decision in *Hale*, we were called upon to decide an issue similar to that presented in *Hale* in the context of a state criminal proceeding. While recognizing the importance of cross-examination and of exposing fabricated defenses, we held in *Doyle v. Ohio*, *supra*,

1. During cross-examination, the prosecutor also questioned respondent concerning his failure *prior to his arrest* to report the incident to the police and offer his exculpatory story. Relying on our decision in Jenkins v. Anderson, 447 U.S. 231 (1980), the Court of Appeals correctly held that there was no constitutional impropriety in the prosecutor's use of respondent's pre-arrest silence for impeachment purposes.

that because of the nature of *Miranda* warnings it would be a violation of due process to allow comment on the silence which the warnings may well have encouraged:

> "[While] it is true that the *Miranda* warnings contain no express assurance that silence will carry no penalty, such assurance is implicit to any person who receives the warnings. In such circumstances, it would be fundamentally unfair and a deprivation of due process to allow the arrested person's silence to be used to impeach an explanation subsequently offered at trial." *Id.* at 618.

The significant difference between the present case and *Doyle* is that the record does not indicate that respondent Weir received any *Miranda* warnings during the period in which he remained silent immediately after his arrest. The majority of the Court of Appeals recognized the difference, but sought to extend *Doyle* to cover Weir's situation by stating that "[we] think an arrest, by itself, is governmental action which implicitly induces a defendant to remain silent." 658 F.2d at 1131. We think that this broadening of *Doyle* is unsupported by the reasoning of that case and contrary to our post-*Doyle* decisions.

In Jenkins v. Anderson, 447 U.S. 231, 239 (1980), a case dealing with pre-arrest silence, we said:

> "Common law traditionally has allowed witnesses to be impeached by their previous failure to state a fact in circumstances in which that fact naturally would have been asserted. Each jurisdiction may formulate its own rules of evidence to determine when prior silence is so inconsistent with present statements that impeachment by reference to such silence is probative."

In *Jenkins*, as in other post-*Doyle* cases, we have consistently explained *Doyle* as a case where the government had induced silence by implicitly assuring the defendant that his silence would not be used against him.... In *Jenkins*, we noted that the failure to speak involved in that case occurred before the defendant was taken into custody and was given his *Miranda* warnings, commenting that no governmental action induced the defendant to remain silent before his arrest....

In the absence of the sort of affirmative assurances embodied in the *Miranda* warnings, we do not believe that it violates due process of law for a State to permit cross-examination as to postarrest silence when a defendant chooses to take the stand. A State is entitled, in such situations, to leave to the judge and jury under its own rules of evidence the resolution of the extent to which postarrest silence may be deemed to impeach a criminal defendant's own testimony....

The ... judgment of the Court of Appeals is reversed....

■ JUSTICE BRENNAN would set the case for oral argument.

■ JUSTICE MARSHALL dissents from the summary reversal of this case.

MIRANDA AND SILENCE

If someone says, "I hear you robbed that bank," we normally would expect an innocent person to refute the implied accusation. A defendant's silence in the face of such a charge therefore may serve as an adoptive admission of guilt. And because silence may be inconsistent with a later claim of innocence, evidence of silence also may serve to impeach.

Adoptive admissions, governed by Rule 801(d)(2)(B), are substantive evidence of guilt, admissible to prove the truth of the adopted accusation. Caselaw and commentators have identified four preconditions to deeming silence an adoption: (1) the adopted statement was heard and understood by the party against whom it is offered; (2) the party was at liberty to respond; (3) the circumstances naturally called for a response; and (4) the party failed to respond. *See Jenkins v. Anderson*, 447 U.S. 231, 248–49 (1980) (Marshall, J., dissenting).

Silence may be used to *impeach* if a witness's past silence is inconsistent with his later testimony in court. Again one must ask "if it would have been natural, under the circumstances, to assert [or deny] the fact" at issue. *Id.*

Miranda warnings disrupt both lines of reasoning. If authorities have advised a suspect that she need not speak and that her words may be used against her, it no longer is natural to expect her to speak. Even in the face of a direct accusation, a person advised that she has "the right to remain silent" may choose to exercise that right rather than rebut the accusation. As the Supreme Court noted in *Doyle v. Ohio*, 426 U.S. 610, 617–18 (1976), her silence becomes "insolubly ambiguous." Moreover, because *Miranda* warnings contain an implicit assurance "that silence will carry no penalty," *id.* at 618, using her silence against her would be fundamentally unfair. Hence the *Doyle* Court held that post-*Miranda* silence may not be used to impeach a witness. *See id.*; *Wainwright v. Greenfield*, 474 U.S. 284, 291 (1986).

The diagram on the next page depicts the state of the law regarding the use of silence as an adoptive admission and to impeach. *Doyle* is noted in the box on the bottom right. Its holding, barring the use of post-*Miranda* silence to impeach, is probably the least controversial judgment in the diagram. Note that the top right box is almost blank. The Supreme Court has never ruled whether post-*Miranda* silence can serve as evidence of an adoptive admission. Still, both principle and precedent suggest the answer is no. As a matter of principle, post-*Miranda* silence is always "insolubly ambiguous," whether used to impeach or as evidence of an

adoption. And as for precedent, three Supreme Court rulings have hinted that prosecutors may not use post-*Miranda* silence for any purpose.

MIRANDA AND SILENCE

	Defendant Not in Custody	Defendant in Custody / Pre-*Miranda*	Defendant in Custody / Post-*Miranda*
May Silence Be an "Adoption" Under FRE 801(d)(2)(B)?	?? (Circuits are split.)	?? (YES: *US v. Frazier*, 408 F.3d 1102, 1111 (8th Cir. 2005) NO: *US v. Flecha*, 539 F.2d 874, 877 (2d Cir. 1976); *US v. Velarde-Gomez*, 269 F.3d 1023, 1027–33 (9th Cir. 2001) (en banc))	NO*
May Silence Be Used to Impeach?	YES: *Jenkins v. Anderson*, 447 U.S. 231, 240 (1980)	YES: *Fletcher v. Weir*, 455 U.S. 603, 607 (1982) (Page 444)	NO: *Doyle v. Ohio*, 426 U.S. 610, 617–18 (1976)

In the first of these cases, *Harris v. New York*, 401 U.S. 222, 226 (1971), the Court held that statements obtained in violation of *Miranda* during police interrogations, although not admissible substantively against the defendant, may be used to impeach the defendant's testimony. *Harris* suggests that the standards governing admission of impeachment evidence are more generous toward the prosecution than those governing evidence offered substantively. So if *Doyle* bars use of post-*Miranda* silence *even to impeach*, the Court very likely would bar such silence if offered substantively to establish an adoptive admission.

* *Cf. Harris v. New York*, 401 U.S. 222, 226 (1971) (holding that statements taken in violation of *Miranda*, although not admissible substantively against the defendant, may be used to impeach the defendant's testimony). *See also Kansas v. Ventris*, 556 U.S. 586, 593–94 (2009) (reaching a similar result on similar reasoning). The text offers a somewhat fuller treatment of these cases.

The second Supreme Court ruling, *Kansas v. Ventris*, 556 U.S. 586, 593–94 (2009), considered the related issue of a defendant's confession obtained in violation of his Sixth Amendment right to counsel. The Court quoted *Harris* and other authorities in reaching the analogous result: Although inadmissible in the prosecution's case-in-chief as substantive proof of his guilt, the defendant's statement could be used to impeach his claim of innocence on the stand.

And in *Wainwright v. Greenfield*, *supra*, the Court rejected the prosecutor's attempt to use the defendant's post-arrest, post-*Miranda* silence as substantive evidence of his sanity. The prosecutor had argued at trial that the defendant's good judgment in responding to *Miranda* warnings by saying he would not answer questions without a lawyer tended to prove his sanity. *Greenfield*, 474 U.S. at 286. The Supreme Court rejected this gambit and suggested that substantive use of post-*Miranda* silence did more violence to the Constitution than use of such silence to impeach. "The constitutional violation might thus be especially egregious," the justices wrote, "because, unlike *Doyle*, there was no risk 'that exclusion of the evidence [would] merely provide a shield for perjury.'" *Greenfield*, 474 U.S. at 292 n.8 (quoting *Doyle*, 426 U.S. at 626 (Stevens, J., dissenting)). That is, courts should be especially welcoming to evidence offered to impeach because barring impeachment evidence "merely provide[s] a shield for perjury." If evidence of post-arrest silence is not admissible *even to impeach*, it surely should not be admitted substantively.

Note that the Supreme Court has ruled against criminal defendants in the cases noted in the bottom middle and bottom left boxes in the diagram on page 448. In the absence of *Miranda* warnings a defendant's silence *may* be used to impeach his testimony, whether or not he was in custody at the time of the silence in question. The leading cases are *Jenkins v. Anderson*, 447 U.S. 231 (1980), and *Fletcher v. Weir*, 455 U.S. 603 (1982), excerpted above. *Jenkins* and *Weir* embraced much the same reasoning: *Doyle* held that *Miranda* warnings offered the implicit "'assurance that silence will carry no penalty.'" *Weir*, 455 U.S. at 605 (quoting *Doyle*, 426 U.S. at 618). But in the absence of such governmental action inducing the defendant's silence, courts should revert to the judgment of the common law, which "'traditionally has allowed witnesses to be impeached by their previous failure to state a fact in circumstances in which that fact naturally would have been asserted.'" *Weir*, 455 U.S. at 606 (quoting *Jenkins*, 447 U.S. at 239).

One can imagine at least two rejoinders to this reasoning. The first, and more powerful, is that "*Miranda* has become embedded in routine police practice to the point where the warnings have become part of our national culture." *Dickerson v. United States*, 530 U.S. 428, 443 (2000). Everyone with a television knows she has "the right to remain silent." The Supreme Court offered the implicit "'assurance that silence will carry no penalty' " to all Americans in 1966, when it decided *Miranda v. Arizona*, 384 U.S. 436 (1966). It's a legal fiction to say that an officer's failure to recite those words somehow erases common knowledge. And this common knowledge of *Miranda* warnings means that a defendant's silence always will be "insolubly ambiguous." It will be impossible to know whether a defendant's silence in the face of an accusation is an admission of guilt or an assertion of a broadly understood right to remain silent.

The second, less powerful rejoinder to the reasoning of *Jenkins* and *Weir* is that because defendants have a right to silence, any prosecutorial use of silence violates the Fifth Amendment. Cultural understandings aside, the Fifth Amendment does *not* create a right of silence. Rather it says, "No person . . . shall be compelled in any criminal case to be a witness against himself. . . ." As Justice Stevens emphasized in *Jenkins*, the amendment operates only in the face of *official compulsion* to speak. Absent such compulsion, there is no guarantee that a defendant's silence may not be used against her:

> The fact that a citizen has a constitutional right to remain silent when he is questioned has no bearing on the probative significance of his silence before he has any contact with the police. . . . When a citizen is under no official compulsion whatever, either to speak or to remain silent, I see no reason why his voluntary decision to do one or the other should raise any issue under the Fifth Amendment. For in determining whether the privilege is applicable, the question is whether petitioner was in a position to have his testimony compelled and then asserted his privilege, not simply whether he was silent. A different view ignores the clear words of the Fifth Amendment.

Jenkins, 447 U.S. at 243–44 (Stevens, J., concurring). This is not to say that *Miranda* warnings are false in stating that a suspect has "the right to remain silent." *Miranda* operates only in the context of custodial police interrogation, and the Court found that "in-custody interrogation . . . contains *inherently compelling* pressures." *Miranda*, 384 U.S. at 467 (emphasis added).

Rightly or wrongly, *Jenkins* and *Weir* have held that pre-*Miranda* silence, outside the context of custodial interrogation, is admissible to impeach a defendant's trial testimony. The Court has not considered whether a defendant's silence in the absence of *Miranda* warnings may be used as an adoptive admission. Hence the top middle and top left boxes of the diagram on page 448 bear question marks. The tenor and reasoning of *Jenkins* and *Weir* suggest that when they confront the question, the justices will permit the substantive use of pre-*Miranda* silence. Still, that result is not a foregone conclusion. As I noted above, *Harris v. New York* suggests that constitutional protections operate more effectively against evidence offered substantively than against evidence offered only to impeach. And faced with the questions posed by the top left and top middle boxes, lower courts stand divided.

Addressing *post-arrest,* pre-*Miranda* silence, the Second and Ninth Circuits have ruled that silence may not be used as an adoptive admission. In *United States v. Flecha,* 539 F.2d 874, 877 (2d Cir. 1976), the case on which Problem 7.18 (page 444) is based, several men were arrested on suspicion of smuggling drugs. After their arrest but before *Miranda* warnings were given, one of the men said, apparently to his codefendant, Flecha, "Why so much excitement? If we are caught we are caught." Flecha was standing near enough to have heard this statement, but said nothing to deny his involvement. In ruling that the statement should not have been admitted against Flecha as an adoptive admission, the Second Circuit reasoned that even in the absence of *Miranda* warnings, those under arrest might know that it's best to stay mum when the law is at hand. Likewise, the Ninth Circuit held in *United States v. Velarde–Gomez,* 269 F.3d 1023, 1027–33 (9th Cir. 2001) (en banc), that admission of the defendant's silence in the face of post-arrest, pre-*Miranda* accusations of criminal conduct violated the Fifth Amendment. But in *United States v. Frazier,* 408 F.3d 1102, 1109–11 (8th Cir. 2005), *cert. denied,* 546 U.S. 1151 (2006), the Eighth Circuit leaned on Justice Stevens's concurrence in *Jenkins* in approving substantive use of such silence. That case began with a roadside search of the defendant's rental truck. When officers told the defendant he was under arrest on drug charges, he said nothing. At trial the prosecutor argued that the defendant's silence betrayed his lack of surprise at the discovery of drugs hidden in the truck—and proved he knowingly possessed the drugs.*

Finally, can *pre-arrest,* pre-*Miranda* silence constitute an adoptive admission? The answer is very likely yes, as long as the accusation the defendant failed to rebut was made by a friend or private employer, rather than a police officer, and no police officer was nearby. Even the Second Circuit has distinguished *Flecha* in this context. *See United States v. Tocco,* 135 F.3d 116, 128–29 (2d Cir.), *cert. denied sub nom. Ferranti v. United States,* 523 U.S. 1096 (1998). Apparently, when the law is not close at hand, we can expect the innocent to speak out against false accusations. And absent involvement by the police, the Fifth Amendment, which protects only against the *government's compulsion of statements,* offers no protection. *See United States v. Oplinger,* 150 F.3d 1061, 1065–67 & n.6 (9th Cir. 1998), *overruled on other grounds by United States v. Contreras,* 593 F.3d 1135, 1136 (9th Cir. 2010).

* For a critique of *Frazier* see Frank R. Herrmann & Brownlow M. Speer, *Standing Mute at Arrest as Evidence of Guilt: The "Right to Silence" Under Attack,* 35 AM. J. CRIM L. 1, 16–21 (2007).

It is harder to find cases dealing with the rare situation in which a person who is not under arrest fails to rebut an accusation made by or in the presence of a police officer. At least one circuit court has ruled in this context that such pre-arrest silence can constitute an adoptive admission. *See United States v. Schaff*, 948 F.2d 501, 505 (9th Cir. 1991). Several circuit courts have addressed a closely related question—whether a suspect's silence in the face of pre-arrest, pre-*Miranda* questioning by police (or after incriminating discoveries by the police) may constitute substantive evidence of guilt. At least two courts have held that such use of pre-arrest silence does not violate a defendant's Fifth Amendment rights. *See United States v. Beckman*, 298 F.3d 788, 795 (9th Cir. 2002); *United States v. Rivera*, 944 F.2d 1563, 1567–68 (11th Cir. 1991). But four other circuit courts have held it does. *See Ouska v. Cahill–Masching*, 246 F.3d 1036, 1046–49 (7th Cir. 2001); *Combs v. Coyle*, 205 F.3d 269, 280–83 (6th Cir.), *cert. denied sub nom. Bagley v. Combs*, 531 U.S. 1035 (2000); *United States v. Burson*, 952 F.2d 1196, 1200–01 (10th Cir. 1991), *cert. denied*, 503 U.S. 997 (1992); *Coppola v. Powell*, 878 F.2d 1562, 1565–68 (1st Cir.), *cert. denied*, 493 U.S. 969 (1989). Courts that have rejected the use of pre-arrest silence for other substantive purposes probably would also reject its use as an adoptive admission.

---

3. INCONSISTENT STATEMENTS OFFERED SUBSTANTIVELY

452 - 69.

Focus on
FRE 801(d)(1)(A)

Problem 7.19

Domestic Violence I

At around 8:55 a.m. on April 12, 2003, F.T. checked into Abbott Northwestern Hospital for treatment of several injuries, the most serious of which was swelling of her left eye.... F.T. was diagnosed with a blowout fracture of her eye orbit....

[At a grand jury hearing the next day, where only the prosecutor, the jurors, and F.T. were present, F.T. testified under oath that her former boyfriend and the father of her children, Andre Robinson, had hit her in the eye with an open hand.] ... F.T. did not seek an order for protection and began living with Robinson again....

[At Robinson's trial on assault charges] the state called F.T. to testify. She stated that she was sleeping early in the morning on April 12, 2003, when Robinson started knocking loudly on her door. She let him in and they began arguing about a woman Robinson had been with. She eventually went into the bathroom and they began arguing through the closed door. After the argument deescalated, F.T. peeked out the door to see if Robinson was still there and Robinson pushed the door open, causing it to hit her [and inflicting the injuries to her eye]. She described it as an accident....

State v. Robinson, 718 N.W.2d 400, 402–03 (Minn. 2006) (modifications bracketed).

Assume that the prosecutor then offered a transcript of F.T.'s grand jury testimony and that the trial judge, over Robinson's hearsay objection, admitted the transcript as an exhibit. If the prosecutor rested without offering further evidence of the cause of F.T.'s injury, and if the defendant moved for a directed verdict of acquittal, how should the judge have ruled? In other words, could F.T.'s grand jury testimony serve as substantive evidence of Robinson's guilt? Assume that the Federal Rules of Evidence control.

Problem 7.20

Domestic Violence II

Assume the same facts as in the previous problem, with this exception: When F.T. took the stand at Robinson's trial, she did not claim she had been injured accidentally when Robinson pushed open the bathroom door. Rather she said she no longer remembered how she fractured her eye orbit because the injury damaged her memory.

If the prosecutor, over the defendant's hearsay objection, offered a transcript of F.T.'s grand jury testimony, how should the court have ruled? Again, assume that the Federal Rules of Evidence control the case.

4. PAST CONSISTENT STATEMENTS

Focus on

FRE 801(d)(1)(B)

TOME V. UNITED STATES

513 U.S. 150 (1995).

■ KENNEDY, J., announced the judgment of the Court and delivered the opinion of the Court with respect to Parts I, II–A, II–C, and III, in which STEVENS, SCALIA, SOUTER, and GINSBURG, JJ., joined, and an opinion with respect to Part II–B, in which STEVENS, SOUTER, and GINSBURG, JJ., joined. SCALIA, J., filed an opinion concurring in part and concurring in the judgment. BREYER, J., filed a dissenting opinion, in which REHNQUIST, C.J., and O'CONNOR and THOMAS, JJ., joined.

■ JUSTICE KENNEDY delivered the opinion of the Court, except as to Part II–B. Various federal Courts of Appeals are divided over the evidence question presented by this case. At issue is the interpretation of a provision in the Federal Rules of Evidence bearing upon the admissibility of statements, made by a declarant who testifies as a witness, that are consistent with the testimony and are offered to rebut a charge of a "recent fabrication or improper influence or motive." FED. R. EVID. 801(d)(1)(B) [unrestyled]. The question is whether out-of-court consistent statements made after the alleged fabrication, or after the alleged improper influence or motive arose, are admissible under the Rule.

I

Petitioner Tome was charged in a one-count indictment with the felony of sexual abuse of a child, his own daughter, aged four at the time of the alleged crime.... Tome was tried by a jury in the United States District Court for the District of New Mexico....

Tome and the child's mother had been divorced in 1988. A ... court awarded joint custody of the daughter, A.T., to both parents, but Tome had primary physical custody. In 1989 the mother was unsuccessful in petitioning the ... court for primary custody of A.T., but was awarded custody for the summer of 1990.... On August 27, 1990, the mother contacted Colorado authorities with allegations that Tome had committed sexual abuse against A.T.

The prosecution's theory was that Tome committed sexual assaults upon the child while she was in his custody and that the crime was disclosed when the child was spending vacation time with her mother. The defense argued that the allegations were concocted so the child would not be returned to her father. At trial A.T., then six and one-half years old, was the Government's first witness. For the most part, her direct testimony consisted of one-and two-word answers to a series of leading questions. Cross-examination took place over two trial days. The defense asked A.T. 348 questions. On the first day A.T. answered all the questions posed to her on general, background subjects.

The next day there was no testimony, and the prosecutor met with A.T. When cross-examination of A.T. resumed, she was questioned about those conversations but was reluctant to discuss them. Defense counsel then began questioning her about the allegations of abuse, and it appears she was reluctant at many points to answer. As the trial judge noted, however, some of the defense questions were imprecise or unclear. The judge expressed his concerns with the examination of A.T., observing there were lapses of as much as 40–55 seconds between some questions and the answers and that on the second day of examination the witness seemed to be losing concentration. The trial judge stated, "We have a very difficult situation here."

After A.T. testified, the Government produced six witnesses who testified about a total of seven statements made by A.T. describing the alleged sexual assaults: A.T.'s babysitter recited A.T.'s statement to her on August 22, 1990, that she did not want to return to her father because he "gets drunk and he thinks I'm his wife"; the babysitter related further details given by A.T. on August 27, 1990, while A.T.'s mother stood outside the room and listened after the mother had been unsuccessful in questioning A.T. herself; the mother recounted what she had heard A.T. tell the babysitter; a social worker recounted details A.T. told her on August 29, 1990, about the assaults; and three pediatricians, Drs. Kuper, Reich, and Spiegel, related A.T.'s statements to them describing how and where she had been touched by Tome. All but A.T.'s statement to Dr. Spiegel implicated Tome. . . .

A.T.'s out-of-court statements, recounted by the six witnesses, were offered by the Government under Rule 801(d)(1)(B). The trial court admitted all of the statements over defense counsel's objection, accepting the Government's argument that they rebutted the implicit charge that A.T.'s testimony was motivated by a desire to live with her mother. . . . Following trial, Tome was convicted and sentenced to 12 years imprisonment.

On appeal, the Court of Appeals for the Tenth Circuit affirmed, adopting the Government's argument that all of A.T.'s out-of-court statements were admissible under Rule 801(d)(1)(B) even though they had been made after A.T.'s alleged motive to fabricate arose. . . . 3 F.3d 342, 350 (10th Cir. 1993). . . . We granted certiorari, and now reverse.

II

The prevailing common-law rule for more than a century before adoption of the Federal Rules of Evidence was that a prior consistent statement introduced to rebut a charge of recent fabrication or improper influence or motive was admissible if the statement had been made before the alleged fabrication, influence, or motive came into being, but it was inadmissible if made afterwards. As Justice Story explained: "Where the testimony is assailed as a fabrication of a recent date, . . . in order to repel such imputation, proof of the *antecedent* declaration of the party may be admitted." Ellicott v. Pearl, 35 U.S. 412, 439 (1836) (emphasis added).

McCormick and Wigmore stated the rule in a more categorical manner: "The applicable principle is that the prior consistent statement has no relevancy to refute the charge unless the consistent statement was made before the source of the bias, interest, influence or incapacity originated." E. CLEARY, MCCORMICK ON EVIDENCE § 49, at 105 (2d ed. 1972) (hereafter MCCORMICK). *See also* 4 J. WIGMORE, EVIDENCE § 1128, at 268 (J. Chadbourn rev. 1972) (hereafter WIGMORE) ("A consistent statement, at a *time prior* to the existence of a fact said to indicate bias . . . , will effectively explain away the force of the impeaching evidence" (emphasis in original)). The question is whether Rule 801(d)(1)(B) embodies this temporal requirement. We hold that it does.

A

. . . Rule 801 defines prior consistent statements as nonhearsay only if they are offered to rebut a charge of "recent fabrication or improper influence or motive." FED. R. EVID. 801(d)(1)(B) [unrestyled]. Noting the "troublesome" logic of treating a witness' prior consistent statements as hearsay at all (because the declarant is present in court and subject to cross-examination), the Advisory Committee decided to treat those consistent statements, once the preconditions of the Rule were satisfied, as nonhearsay and admissible as substantive evidence, not just to rebut an attack on the witness's credibility. *See* Advisory Committee Notes on FED. R. EVID. 801(d)(1) [RB 198–99, 202]. A consistent statement meeting the requirements of the Rule is thus placed in the same category as a declarant's inconsistent statement made under oath in another proceeding, or prior identification testimony, or admissions by a party opponent. *See* FED. R. EVID. 801.

The Rules do not accord this weighty, nonhearsay status to all prior consistent statements. To the contrary, admissibility under the Rules is confined to those statements offered to rebut a charge of "recent fabrication or improper influence or motive," the same phrase used by the Advisory Committee in its description of the "traditional" common law of evidence, which was the background against which the Rules were drafted. *See* Advisory Committee Notes, *supra* [RB 202]. Prior consistent statements may not be admitted to counter all forms of impeachment* or to bolster the witness merely because she has been discredited. In the present context, the question is whether A.T.'s out-of-court statements rebutted the alleged link between her desire to be with her mother and her testimony, not whether they suggested that A.T.'s in-court testimony was true. The Rule speaks of a party rebutting an alleged motive, not bolstering the veracity of the story told.

This limitation is instructive, not only to establish the preconditions of admissibility but also to reinforce the significance of the requirement that the consistent statements must have been made before the alleged influence, or motive to fabricate arose. That is to say, the forms of impeachment within the Rule's coverage are the ones in which the temporal requirement makes the most sense. Impeachment by charging that the testimony is a recent fabrication or results from an improper influence or motive is, as a general matter, capable of direct and forceful refutation through introduction of out-of-court consistent statements that

* [But see the postscript at the conclusion of this case describing a proposed amendment to Rule 801(d)(1)(B) that is pending as this book goes to press.—GF]

predate the alleged fabrication, influence or motive. A consistent statement that predates the motive is a square rebuttal of the charge that the testimony was contrived as a consequence of that motive. By contrast, prior consistent statements carry little rebuttal force when most other types of impeachment are involved. MCCORMICK § 49, at 105 ("When the attack takes the form of impeachment of character, by showing misconduct, convictions or bad reputation, it is generally agreed that there is no color for sustaining by consistent statements. The defense does not meet the assault."); *see also* 4 WIGMORE § 1131, at 293 ("The broad rule obtains in a few courts that consistent statements may be admitted after impeachment of any sort—in particular after any impeachment by cross-examination. But there is no reason for such a loose rule").

There may arise instances when out-of-court statements that postdate the alleged fabrication have some probative force in rebutting a charge of fabrication or improper influence or motive, but those statements refute the charged fabrication in a less direct and forceful way. Evidence that a witness made consistent statements after the alleged motive to fabricate arose may suggest in some degree that the in-court testimony is truthful, and thus suggest in some degree that that testimony did not result from some improper influence; but if the drafters of Rule 801(d)(1)(B) intended to countenance rebuttal along that indirect inferential chain, the purpose of confining the types of impeachment that open the door to rebuttal by introducing consistent statements becomes unclear. If consistent statements are admissible without reference to the time frame we find imbedded in the Rule, there appears no sound reason not to admit consistent statements to rebut other forms of impeachment as well....

The underlying theory of the Government's position is that an out-of-court consistent statement, whenever it was made, tends to bolster the testimony of a witness and so tends also to rebut an express or implied charge that the testimony has been the product of an improper influence. Congress could have adopted that rule with ease, providing, for instance, that "a witness' prior consistent statements are admissible whenever relevant to assess the witness's truthfulness or accuracy." ... The narrow Rule enacted by Congress, however, cannot be understood to incorporate the Government's theory.

Our analysis is strengthened by the observation that the somewhat peculiar language of the Rule bears close similarity to the language used in many of the common law cases that describe the premotive requirement. "[Unrestyled] Rule 801(d)(1)(B) employs the precise language—'rebutting ... charges ... of recent fabrication or improper influence or motive'—consistently used in the panoply of pre-1975 decisions." E.O. Ohlbaum, *The Hobgoblin of the Federal Rules of Evidence: An Analysis of Rule 801(d)(1)(B), Prior Consistent Statements and a New Proposal*, 1987 B.Y.U. L. REV. 231, 245....

B*

Our conclusion that Rule 801(d)(1)(B) embodies the common-law premotive requirement is confirmed by an examination of the Advisory Committee Notes to the Federal Rules of Evidence. We have relied on those well-considered Notes as a useful guide in ascertaining the meaning of the Rules. *See, e.g.,* Huddleston v. United States, 485 U.S. 681, 688 (1988). Where, as with Rule 801(d)(1)(B), "Congress did not amend the Advisory Committee's draft in any way . . . the Committee's commentary is particularly relevant in determining the meaning of the document Congress enacted." Beech Aircraft Corp. v. Rainey, 488 U.S. 153, at 165–166 n.9 (1988). The Notes are also a respected source of scholarly commentary. Professor Cleary was a distinguished commentator on the law of evidence, and he and members of the Committee consulted and considered the views, criticisms, and suggestions of the academic community in preparing the Notes.

The Notes disclose a purpose to adhere to the common law in the application of evidentiary principles, absent express provisions to the contrary. Where the Rules did depart from their common-law antecedents, in general the Committee said so. The Notes give no indication, however, that Rule 801(d)(1)(B) abandoned the premotive requirement. The entire discussion of Rule 801(d)(1)(B) is limited to the following comment:

> "Prior consistent statements traditionally have been admissible to rebut charges of recent fabrication or improper influence or motive but not as substantive evidence. Under the rule they are substantive evidence. The prior statement is consistent with the testimony given on the stand, and, if the opposite party wishes to open the door for its admission in evidence, no sound reason is apparent why it should not be received generally." Notes on Rule 801(d)(1)(B) [RB 202].

Throughout their discussion of the Rules, the Advisory Committee Notes rely on Wigmore and McCormick as authority for the common-law approach. In light of the categorical manner in which those authors state the premotive requirement, it is difficult to imagine that the drafters, who noted the new substantive use of prior consistent statements, would have remained silent if they intended to modify the premotive requirement. As we observed with respect to another provision of the Rules, "with this state of unanimity confronting the drafters of the Federal Rules of Evidence, we think it unlikely that they intended to scuttle entirely [the common-law requirement]." United States v. Abel, 469 U.S. 45, 50 (1984). Here, we do not think the drafters of the Rule intended to scuttle the whole premotive requirement and rationale without so much as a whisper of explanation....

* [Only Justices Stevens, Souter, and Ginsburg joined Part II–B of Justice Kennedy's opinion.—GF]

Our conclusion is bolstered by the Advisory Committee's stated "unwillingness to countenance the general use of prior prepared statements as substantive evidence." *See* Notes on Rule 801(d)(1) [RB 198–99]. Rule 801(d), which "enumerates three situations in which the statement is excepted from the category of hearsay," *ibid.*, was expressly contrasted by the Committee with Uniform Rule of Evidence 63(1) (1953), "which allows *any* out-of-court statement of a declarant who is present at the trial and available for cross-examination." Notes on Rule 801(d)(1) (emphasis added) [RB 199]. . . .

C

The Government's final argument in favor of affirmance is that the common-law premotive rule advocated by petitioner is inconsistent with the Federal Rules' liberal approach to relevancy and with strong academic criticism, beginning in the 1940's, directed at the exclusion of out-of-court statements made by a declarant who is present in court and subject to cross-examination. This argument misconceives the design of the Rules' hearsay provisions.

Hearsay evidence is often relevant. "The only way in which the probative force of hearsay differs from the probative force of other testimony is in the absence of oath, demeanor, and cross-examination as aids in determining credibility." Advisory Committee's Introduction to Article VIII [RB 191]. That does not resolve the matter, however. Relevance is not the sole criterion of admissibility. Otherwise, it would be difficult to account for the Rules' general proscription of hearsay testimony (absent a specific exception), let alone the traditional analysis of hearsay that the Rules, for the most part, reflect. That certain out-of-court statements may be relevant does not dispose of the question whether they are admissible.

. . . To be sure, certain commentators in the years preceding the adoption of the Rules had been critical of the common-law approach to hearsay. . . . General criticism was directed to the exclusion of a declarant's out-of-court statements where the declarant testified at trial. *See, e.g.*, Morgan, *Hearsay Dangers and the Application of the Hearsay Concept*, 62 HARV. L. REV. 177, 192–96 (1948) [pages 432–35, above]. As an alternative, they suggested moving away from the categorical exclusion of hearsay and toward a case-by-case balancing of the probative value of particular statements against their likely prejudicial effect. The Advisory Committee, however, was explicit in rejecting this balancing approach to hearsay:

> "The Advisory Committee has rejected this approach to hearsay as involving too great a measure of judicial discretion, minimizing the predictability of rulings, [and] enhancing the difficulties of preparation for trial." Advisory Committee's Introduction, *supra* [RB 191].

Given the Advisory Committee's rejection of both the general balancing approach to hearsay and Uniform Rule 63(1), the Government's reliance on the views of those who advocated these positions is misplaced....

D

The case before us illustrates some of the important considerations supporting the Rule as we interpret it, especially in criminal cases. If the Rule were to permit the introduction of prior statements as substantive evidence to rebut every implicit charge that a witness' in-court testimony results from recent fabrication or improper influence or motive, the whole emphasis of the trial could shift to the out-of-court statements, not the in-court ones. The present case illustrates the point. In response to a rather weak charge that A.T.'s testimony was a fabrication created so the child could remain with her mother, the Government was permitted to present a parade of sympathetic and credible witnesses who did no more than recount A.T.'s detailed out-of-court statements to them. Although those statements might have been probative on the question whether the alleged conduct had occurred, they shed but minimal light on whether A.T. had the charged motive to fabricate. At closing argument before the jury, the Government placed great reliance on the prior statements for substantive purposes but did not once seek to use them to rebut the impact of the alleged motive....

III

... Rule 801(d)(1)(B) ... permits the introduction of a declarant's consistent out-of-court statements to rebut a charge of recent fabrication or improper influence or motive only when those statements were made before the charged recent fabrication or improper influence or motive. These conditions of admissibility were not established here.

The judgment of the Court of Appeals for the Tenth Circuit is reversed, and the case is remanded for further proceedings consistent with this opinion.

It is so ordered.

■ JUSTICE SCALIA, concurring in part and concurring in the judgment. I concur in the judgment of the Court, and join its opinion except for Part II–B. That Part, which is devoted entirely to a discussion of the Advisory Committee's Notes pertinent to Rule 801(d)(1)(B), gives effect to those Notes not only because they are "a respected source of scholarly commentary," but also because they display the "purpose" or "intent" of the draftsmen.

I have previously acquiesced in, and indeed myself engaged in, *see* United States v. Owens, 484 U.S. 554, 562 (1988), similar use of the Advisory Committee Notes. More mature consideration has persuaded me that is wrong. Having been prepared by a body of experts, the Notes are assuredly persuasive scholarly commentaries—ordinarily the most persuasive—concerning the meaning of the Rules. But they bear no special authoritativeness as the work of the draftsmen, any more than the views of Alexander Hamilton (a draftsman) bear more authority than the views of Thomas Jefferson (not a draftsman) with regard to the meaning of the Constitution. It is the words of the Rules that have been authoritatively adopted—by this Court, or by Congress if it makes a statutory change. In my view even the adopting Justices' thoughts, unpromulgated as Rules, have no authoritative (as opposed to persuasive) effect, any more than their thoughts regarding an opinion (reflected in exchanges of memoranda before the opinion issues) authoritatively demonstrate the meaning of that opinion. And the same for the thoughts of congressional draftsmen who prepare statutory amendments to the Rules. Like a judicial opinion and like a statute, the promulgated Rule says what it says, regardless of the intent of its drafters....

■ JUSTICE BREYER, with whom THE CHIEF JUSTICE, JUSTICE O'CONNOR and JUSTICE THOMAS join, dissenting. The basic issue in this case concerns not hearsay, but relevance. As the majority points out, the common law permitted a lawyer to rehabilitate a witness (after a charge of improper motive) by pointing to the fact that the witness had said the same thing earlier—but only if the witness made the earlier statement before the motive to lie arose. The reason for the time limitation was that, otherwise, the prior consistent statement had no relevance to rebut the charge that the in-court testimony was the product of the motive to lie. The ... majority believes that a hearsay-related rule ... codifies this absolute timing requirement. I do not. Rule 801(d)(1)(B) has nothing to do with relevance....

For one thing, one can find examples where the timing rule's claim of "no relevancy" is simply untrue. A postmotive statement is relevant to rebut, for example, a charge of recent fabrication based on improper motive, say, when the speaker made the prior statement while affected by a far more powerful motive to tell the truth. A speaker might be moved to lie to help an acquaintance. But, suppose the circumstances also make clear to the speaker that only the truth will save his child's life.... Hence, postmotive statements can ... directly refute the charge of fabrication based on improper motive ... because the circumstances indicate that the statements are not causally connected to the alleged motive to lie.

For another thing, the common law premotive rule was not as uniform as the majority suggests. A minority of courts recognized that postmotive statements could be relevant to rebut a charge of recent fabrication, improper influence or motive under the right circumstances. I concede that the majority of courts took the rule of thumb as absolute. But, I have searched the cases (and the commentators) in vain for an explanation of why that should be so.

One can imagine a possible explanation: Trial judges may find it easier to administer an absolute rule. Yet, there is no indication in any of the cases that trial judges would, or do, find it particularly difficult to administer a more flexible rule in this context. And there is something to be said for the greater authority that flexibility grants the trial judge to tie rulings on the admissibility of rehabilitative evidence more closely to the needs and circumstances of the particular case. 1 WEINSTEIN'S EVIDENCE ¶ 401[01], at 401–8 to 401–9 ("A flexible approach . . . is more apt to yield a sensible result than the application of a mechanical rule.") . . . .

Accordingly, I would hold that the Federal Rules authorize a district court to allow (where probative in respect to rehabilitation) the use of postmotive prior consistent statements to rebut a charge of recent fabrication or improper influence or motive (subject of course to, for example, Rule 403). . . . In most cases, this approach will not yield a different result from a strict adherence to the premotive rule for, in most cases, postmotive statements will not be significantly probative. . . .

In this case, the Court of Appeals, applying [a flexible] approach . . ., decided that A.T.'s prior consistent statements were probative on the question of whether her story as a witness reflected a motive to lie. There is no reason to reevaluate this factbound conclusion. Accordingly, I would affirm the judgment of the Court of Appeals.

Postscript to **Tome v. United States:** As this book goes to press in late 2012, a proposed amendment to Rule 801(d)(1)(B) is wending its way through the rulemaking process. Having been approved for publication and public comment in June 2012, the proposed amendment faces several more hurdles before possibly becoming law in December 2014. The amended rule would exempt from the hearsay ban a testifying witness's past statement if that statement:

> **(B)** is consistent with the declarant's testimony and
>
> **(i)** is offered to rebut an express or implied charge that the declarant recently fabricated it or acted from a recent improper influence or motive in so testifying; or
>
> **(ii)** otherwise rehabilitates the declarant's credibility as a witness. . . .

(RB 203–04.) The amendment aims to accommodate past consistent statements that rebut attacks *other* than a suggestion of recent fabrication or improper influence or motive. Two such attacks specified in the Advisory Committee's Note are an allegation of "inconsistency in the witness's testimony" and "a charge of faulty recollection." (RB 204.)

Even today trial judges may admit past consistent statements that rebut suggestions of inconsistency or faulty memory. Such statements do not come in to prove their truth, however, but only to corroborate the declarant's in-court testimony. Here the theory of *corroboration* is the mirror image of the theory of impeachment under Rule 613. Recall that past inconsistent statements offered only to impeach are not admitted for their truth. Rather the theory of impeachment is that the witness says different things at different times and therefore should not be believed on this point. Conversely, the theory of corroboration with past consistent statements is that the witness has said the same thing at a different time and therefore *should* be believed on this point.

When a consistent statement is admitted only to corroborate in-court testimony, the trial judge must on request instruct the jury under Rule 105 on the distinction between substantive use and corroborative use of the past statement. But as the advisory committee observes, " '[d]istinctions between the substantive and nonsubstantive use of prior consistent statements are normally distinctions without practical meaning,' because '[j]uries have a very difficult time understanding an instruction about the difference between substantive and nonsubstantive use.' " (ACN to Proposed Amendment to FRE 801(d)(1)(B) (quoting Frank W. Bullock, Jr. & Steven Gardner, *Prior Consistent Statements and the Premotive Rule,* 24 FLA. ST. U. L. REV. 509, 540 (1997)) (RB 204).) By making past consistent statements that are admissible to corroborate the declarant's present testimony admissible to prove their truth too, the proposed amendment would eliminate the need for such instructions.

Would the *Tome* rule survive this amendment? Note that Proposed Rule 801(d)(1)(B)(i), quoted above, preserves the present rule's hearsay exemption for those past consistent statements "offered to rebut an express or implied charge that the declarant recently fabricated [the declarant's trial testimony] or acted from a recent improper influence or motive in so testifying." As the *Tome* Court reasoned, a past consistent statement will rebut such a charge most effectively if the statement was made *before* the recent fabrication or improper influence or motive. The Court therefore limited the rule's hearsay exemption to "premotive" statements. But the breadth of Rule 801(d)(1)(B)(ii) may undermine the *Tome* rule by admitting for their truth past consistent statements that "rehabilitat[e] the declarant's credibility as a witness." Almost *any* consistent statement, by corroborating the declarant's present testimony, will tend to rehabilitate the credibility of a declarant whose version of events has faced challenge. Even a statement made after an alleged fabrication or improper influence or motive bears some corroborative force. It is true, as Justice Breyer wrote in dissent, that "in most cases, postmotive statements will not be significantly probative" and therefore may fail scrutiny under Rule 403. (Page 463, above.) But one suspects that some number of postmotive statements will survive Rule 403 weighing.

Hence it is a safe prediction that if the proposed amendment becomes law in its present form and without further guidance from the advisory committee, lower federal courts will struggle to discern whether the *Tome* rule still holds. But as the amendment will not take effect before December 2014, two years from this writing, there is yet time for clarification.*

The rulebook presents the current version of the proposed rule and of the Advisory Committee's Note at pages 203 to 205.

---

5. STATEMENTS OF IDENTIFICATION

Focus on FRE 801(d)(1)(C)

COMMONWEALTH V. WEICHELL

Supreme Judicial Court of Massachusetts.
390 Mass. 62 (1983), *cert. denied*, 465 U.S. 1032 (1984).

■ LYNCH, J. . . . Shortly before midnight on May 30, 1980, John Foley, . . . Frederick Laracy, and Lisa Krause went to Faxon Park, after attending a drive-in movie together. . . . At 12:15 a.m., Foley . . . heard four "bangs" and saw a man run out of the parking lot and turn up Faxon Street to a waiting car. Krause screamed. The man looked toward the group briefly but continued running. Foley testified that he had a full-face view of the man for approximately one second as the man passed under a street light. Foley and Laracy went across Faxon Street to the parking lot where they found the body of the victim on the ground. The police arrived shortly thereafter.

Foley described to the police the man he saw running as being five feet, nine inches tall, 175 pounds, wearing jeans and a pullover shirt. He said that the man had . . . bushy eyebrows, and sideburns. He also stated that the man had a slightly crooked nose, "as if it had been broken." At trial, he identified the defendant as the man he saw running that night.

Later that morning, Foley assisted Detective Wilson of the Braintree police department in making a composite drawing. After indicating that he could not draw a face by himself, Foley gave Wilson a general description. With the aid of an Identikit, Wilson and Foley assembled a

* I thank Professor Daniel Capra, reporter for the advisory committee, for his counsel on the proposed amendment's impact on the *Tome* rule.

composite [from hundreds of plastic overlays]. Foley examined the composite and asked for changes. Wilson then changed elements of the composite and put together a different face. Wilson used a pencil to alter the nose. After Foley altered the hair style, he declared that the composite "looks like him." A photostatic copy of the composite was introduced in evidence at trial.... [The defendant was convicted of first-degree murder and appealed.]

ADMISSION OF THE COMPOSITE DRAWING

The defendant argues that the composite sketch was inadmissible hearsay.... [I]f the composite was erroneously admitted, it is likely that the defendant would have been prejudiced. This is because of the emphasis placed upon the composite drawing in the Commonwealth's closing argument,[6] and because here the witness made his observations at night at a distance and for only a few seconds....

The defendant finds substantial support for his argument in Commonwealth v. McKenna, 355 Mass. 313, 326–27 (1969). There the court found error in the admission of a similarly made composite drawing. *See id.* at 327 (the drawing "could have been used to refresh [the maker's] recollection but it had no standing as evidence of the truth or accuracy of the matter contained in it").... [T]here is language in *McKenna* that can be read as a broad-based condemnation of such composites as inadmissible hearsay....

[In earlier cases, this court] frequently held that extrajudicial statements [offered merely] to corroborate a witness's in-court identification are not offered to prove the truth of the matter asserted and, therefore, are not hearsay. Those decisions are representative of an intermediate position between the orthodox banning of all out-of-court statements by the witness and the admission for all purposes suggested by some modern scholars. One authority has stated the rationale for [permitting past identifications to corroborate a witness's in-court identification] as follows:

6. The Commonwealth's closing argument on this point is as follows:

> *The prosecutor:* "He saw him that night. He did a picture of him, and I ask you to look at the picture of Fred Weichell that Mr. Foley did, and compare it with the camera's picture taken two months later. Now, I ask you to look at the hair in this picture.... And look at the eyebrows. Aren't they thick? Look, particularly, at the nose and see how good the match is between the nose in Mr. Foley's picture of Mr. Weichell, and the camera's picture of Mr. Weichell. Look at the mouth. Look, if you would, at the little marks under his lip here in the camera picture and see if that isn't here in Mr. Foley's picture. Look at the shape of the chin."
>
> *Defense counsel:* "Objection."
>
> *The judge:* "Your objection is overruled, sir."
>
> *The prosecutor:* "The shape of the chin here, ladies and gentlemen, in Mr. Foley's picture, and the shape of the chin in the camera's picture. John Foley told you he tried to match the plastic foils to the picture he had in his mind. I ask you to take some time to see how good that picture['s match is] with the camera's picture."

> "Ordinarily, when a witness is asked to identify the assailant or thief, . . . the witness' act of pointing out the accused . . . then and there in the courtroom, is of little testimonial force. After all that has intervened, it would seldom happen that the witness would not have come to believe in the [defendant's] identity. The failure to recognize would tell for the accused; but the affirmative recognition might mean little against him. The psychology of the situation is practically the same as when recent contrivance is alleged. To corroborate the witness, therefore, it is entirely proper . . . to prove that at a former time, when the suggestions of others could not have intervened to create a fancied recognition in the witness' mind, he recognized and declared the present accused to be the person. If, moreover (as sometimes is done), the [accused] was then so placed among others that all probability of suggestion (by seeing him handcuffed, for example) is still further removed, the evidence becomes stronger. . . ."

4 J. WIGMORE, EVIDENCE § 1130, at 277–79 (Chadbourn rev. 1972).

More recently, this court has held extrajudicial identification testimony to be admissible as substantive evidence of guilt even where there was no in-court identification by the person making the out-of-court identification. These decisions are based at least in part on the realization that "[a] pre-trial identification is regarded as having equal or greater testimonial value than one made in court because the circumstances of the earlier identification often were less suggestive and because that identification occurred closer to the time of the offense." Commonwealth v. Torres, 367 Mass. 737, 739 (1975). Since the admission of evidence of out-of-court identification is no longer dependent on an in-court identification, admissibility can no longer be supported by the theory that the hearsay rule does not bar the evidence because it merely corroborates the in-court identification. Since juries may have trouble making the distinction between corroboration evidence and substantive evidence, the elimination of this distinction is salutary.

Under the Federal Rules of Evidence and the Proposed Massachusetts Rules of Evidence (1980), a statement of prior identification is not hearsay if made by a witness who testifies at trial and is subject to cross-examination concerning it. FED. R. EVID. 801(d)(1)(C); PROPOSED MASS. R. EVID. 801(d)(1)(C) (1980). Paragraph C is consistent with Massachusetts law giving substantive effect to prior identification. The statements of the witness that form the basis for the composite drawing here would not be inadmissible under our more recent decisions since they are statements of an out-of-court identification ("his eyebrows, nose, and hair looked like that") by a witness who [testified at trial and was] available for cross-examination.

Since the statements of the witness that led to the creation of the composite are admissible, the composite which is prepared from the statements similarly ought to be admissible either because the composite retains the character of the statements that led to its creation or because the composite is not a statement within the meaning of the hearsay rule. *See* United States v. Moskowitz, 581 F.2d 14, 20 (2d Cir.), *cert. denied*, 439 U.S. 871 (1978). [In *Moskowitz*] a sketch made by a police artist from descriptions given him by two witnesses was held admissible under the Federal Rules of Evidence. Although the majority in that case concluded that the sketch was admissible because it was not a statement within the meaning of Fed. R. Evid. 801(a), the view expressed in the concurring opinion was that the sketch was a statement that was not hearsay by reason of Rule 801(d)(1)(C). Under either view the composite sketch would be admissible under Proposed Mass. R. Evid. 801(d)(1)(C) (1980).

There is no logical reason to permit the introduction of a witness's out-of-court identification and to exclude statements identifying the various physical characteristics of a person perceived by the witness, or the composite of all those physical characteristics, which is no more than the sum of the parts perceived. . . .

Judgment affirmed.

■ LIACOS, J. (dissenting). . . . This exception to the hearsay rule is premised on a practical assessment of the relative reliability of different methods of identification. The inherent suggestiveness of the courtroom setting and the passage of time serve to diminish the reliability of an in-court identification. A prior extrajudicial identification is therefore regarded as having testimonial value equal to or greater than one made in court.

Evidence of a pretrial composite identification is distinguishable from the other types of pretrial identification evidence. Unlike extrajudicial photographic or in-person identifications, composites have not as yet been shown to possess a fair degree of reliability, let alone greater reliability than in-court identification. It cannot be said that they are significantly more reliable than an in-court identification. "Translating a mental image to a composite drawing provides opportunities for communication failure, error in reproduction, and extraneous influence that are not present when a witness can compare his mental image directly with either a photographic image or a person." Commonwealth v. Blaney, 387 Mass. 628, 642 (1982) (O'Connor, J., dissenting). In the absence of evidence demonstrating their reliability, we should hold that composite drawings are inadmissible as probative evidence of guilt . . . and reverse the conviction.

■ O'CONNOR, J. (dissenting). . . .

Commonwealth v. Weichell—*Something To Ponder:* The *Weichell* court wrote that "the composite which is prepared from the [witness's] statements . . . ought to be admissible either because the composite retains the character of the statements that led to its creation or because the composite is not a statement within the meaning of the hearsay rule." The court ducked the hard question: Is a composite sketch a "statement" as defined by Rule 801(a)?

UNITED STATES V. OWENS

484 U.S. 554 (1988).

■ JUSTICE SCALIA delivered the opinion of the Court. This case requires us to determine whether . . . Rule 802 of the Federal Rules of Evidence bars testimony concerning a prior, out-of-court identification when the identifying witness is unable, because of memory loss, to explain the basis for the identification.

I

On April 12, 1982, John Foster, a correctional counselor at the federal prison in Lompoc, California, was attacked and brutally beaten with a metal pipe. His skull was fractured, and he remained hospitalized for almost a month. As a result of his injuries, Foster's memory was severely impaired. When Thomas Mansfield, an FBI agent investigating the assault, first attempted to interview Foster, on April 19, he found Foster lethargic and unable to remember his attacker's name. On May 5, Mansfield again spoke to Foster, who was much improved and able to describe the attack. Foster named respondent as his attacker and identified respondent from an array of photographs.

Respondent was tried in Federal District Court for assault with intent to commit murder. At trial, Foster recounted his activities just before the attack, and described feeling the blows to his head and seeing blood on the floor. He testified that he clearly remembered identifying respondent as his assailant during his May 5th interview with Mansfield. On cross-examination, he admitted that he could not remember seeing his assailant. He also admitted that, although there was evidence that he had received numerous visitors in the hospital, he was unable to remember any of them except Mansfield, and could not remember whether any of these visitors had suggested that respondent was the assailant. Defense counsel unsuccessfully sought to refresh his recollection with hospital records, including one indicating that Foster had attributed the assault to someone other than respondent. Respondent was convicted and sentenced to 20 years' imprisonment to be served consecutively to a previous sentence.

On appeal, the United States Court of Appeals for the Ninth Circuit . . . reversed the judgment of the District Court. 789 F. 2d 750 (1986). We granted certiorari to resolve the conflict with other Circuits on the significance of a hearsay declarant's memory loss . . . with respect to Rule 802.[1] . . .

II

The Confrontation Clause of the Sixth Amendment gives the accused the right "to be confronted with the witnesses against him." This has long been read as securing an adequate opportunity to cross-examine adverse witnesses. . . .

In Delaware v. Fensterer, 474 U.S. 15 (1985) (*per curiam*), we determined that there was no Confrontation Clause violation when an expert witness testified as to what opinion he had formed, but could not recollect the basis on which he had formed it. We said:

> "The Confrontation Clause includes no guarantee that every witness called by the prosecution will refrain from giving testimony that is marred by forgetfulness, confusion, or evasion. To the contrary, the Confrontation Clause is generally satisfied when the defense is given a full and fair opportunity to probe and expose these infirmities through cross-examination, thereby calling to the attention of the factfinder the reasons for giving scant weight to the witness' testimony." *Id.* at 21–22.

Our opinion noted that . . . the jury may be persuaded that "[the expert's] opinion is as unreliable as his memory." *Id.* at 19. . . .

[W]e agree with the [interpretation] suggested 18 years ago by Justice Harlan. "[T]he Confrontation Clause guarantees only 'an *opportunity* for effective cross-examination, not cross-examination that is effective in whatever way, and to whatever extent, the defense might wish.'" Kentucky v. Stincer, 482 U.S. 730, 739 (1987), quoting *Fensterer, supra,* at 20 (emphasis added). As *Fensterer* demonstrates, that opportunity is not denied when a witness testifies as to his current belief but is unable to recollect the reason for that belief. It is sufficient that the defendant has the opportunity to bring out such matters as the witness' bias, his lack of care and attentiveness, his poor eyesight, and even (what is often a prime objective of cross-examination) the very fact that he has a bad memory. . . . [T]he traditional protections of the oath, cross-examination, and opportunity for the jury to observe the witness' demeanor satisfy the constitutional requirements. . . .

III

. . . [Unrestyled] Rule 801(d)(1)(C) defines as not hearsay a prior statement "of identification of a person made after perceiving the per-

1. This case has been argued, both here and below, as though Federal Rule of Evidence 801(d)(1)(C) were the basis of the challenge. That is substantially but not technically correct. If respondent's arguments are accepted, it is Rule 802 that would render the out-of-court statement inadmissible as hearsay; but as explained in Part III, it is ultimately Rule 801(d)(1)(C) that determines whether Rule 802 is applicable.

son," if the declarant "testifies at the trial or hearing and is subject to cross-examination concerning the statement." The Court of Appeals found that Foster's identification statement did not come within this exclusion because his memory loss prevented his being "subject to cross-examination concerning the statement." . . .

It seems to us that the more natural reading of "subject to cross-examination concerning the statement" includes what was available here. Ordinarily a witness is regarded as "subject to cross-examination" when he is placed on the stand, under oath, and responds willingly to questions. . . . [L]imitations on the scope of examination by the trial court or assertions of privilege by the witness may undermine the process to such a degree that meaningful cross-examination within the intent of the Rule no longer exists. But that effect is not produced by the witness' assertion of memory loss—which . . . is often the very result sought to be produced by cross-examination, and can be effective in destroying the force of the prior statement. [Unrestyled] Rule 801(d)(1)(C), which specifies that the cross-examination need only "concer[n] the statement," does not on its face require more. . . .

The reasons for that choice are apparent from the Advisory Committee's Notes on Rule 801 and its legislative history. The premise for Rule 801(d)(1)(C) was that, given adequate safeguards against suggestiveness, out-of-court identifications were generally preferable to courtroom identifications. Thus, despite the traditional view that such statements were hearsay, the Advisory Committee believed that their use was to be fostered rather than discouraged. Similarly, the House Report on the Rule noted that since, "[a]s time goes by, a witness' memory will fade and his identification will become less reliable," minimizing the barriers to admission of more contemporaneous identification is fairer to defendants and prevents "cases falling through because the witness can no longer recall the identity of the person he saw commit the crime." H.R. REP. No. 94–355, at 3 (1975). *See also* S. REP. No. 94–199, at 2 (1975). To judge from the House and Senate Reports, Rule 801(d)(1)(C) was in part directed to the very problem here at issue: a memory loss that makes it impossible for the witness to provide an in-court identification or testify about details of the events underlying an earlier identification.

Respondent argues that this reading is impermissible because it creates an internal inconsistency in the Rules, since the forgetful witness who is deemed "subject to cross-examination" under 801(d)(1)(C) is simultaneously deemed "unavailable" under 804(a)(3). . . . It seems to us, however, that this is not a substantive inconsistency, but only a semantic oddity resulting from the fact that [unrestyled] Rule 804(a) has for convenience of reference in Rule 804(b) chosen to describe the circumstances necessary in order to admit certain categories of hearsay testimony under the rubric "Unavailability as a witness." These circumstances include not only absence from the hearing, but also claims of privilege, refusals to obey a court's order to testify, and inability to testify based on physical or mental illness or memory loss. Had the rubric instead been "unavailability as a witness, memory loss, and other special circumstances" there would be no apparent inconsistency with Rule 801. . . . The semantic inconsistency exists not only with respect to Rule 801(d)(1)(C), but also with respect to the other subparagraphs of Rule 801(d)(1). It would seem strange, for example, to assert that a witness can avoid introduction of testimony from a prior proceeding that is inconsistent with his trial testimony, *see* Rule 801(d)(1)(A), by simply asserting lack of memory of the facts to which the prior testimony related. But that situation, like this one, presents the verbal curiosity that the witness is "subject to cross-examination" under Rule 801 while at the same time "unavailable" under Rule 804(a)(3). Quite obviously, the two characterizations are made for two entirely different purposes and there is no requirement or expectation that they should coincide.

For the reasons stated, we hold that . . . Federal Rule of Evidence 802 is [not] violated by admission of an identification statement of a witness who is unable, because of a memory loss, to testify concerning the basis for the identification. The decision of the Court of Appeals is reversed, and the case is remanded for proceedings consistent with this opinion.

So ordered.

■ JUSTICE BRENNAN, with whom JUSTICE MARSHALL joins, dissenting.* In an interview during his month-long hospitalization, in what was apparently a singular moment of lucid recollection, John Foster selected respondent James Owens' photograph from an array of possible suspects and informed FBI Agent Thomas Mansfield that it was respondent who had attacked him with a metal pipe on the morning of April 12, 1982. Had Foster subsequently died from his injuries, there is no doubt that . . . the Federal Rules of Evidence would have barred Mansfield from repeating Foster's out-of-court identification at trial. Fortunately, Foster survived the beating; his memory, however, did not. . . .

The principal witness against respondent was not the John Foster who took the stand in December 1983—that witness could recall virtually nothing of the events of April 12, 1982, and candidly admitted that he had no idea whether respondent had assaulted him. Instead, respondent's sole accuser was the John Foster who, on May 5, 1982, identified respondent as his attacker. This John Foster, however, did not testify at respondent's trial: the profound memory loss he suffered during the approximately 18 months following his identification prevented him from affirming, explaining, or elaborating upon his out-of-court statement just as surely and completely as his assertion of a testimonial privilege, or his

* [Justice Brennan dissented on the grounds that admission of Foster's identification violated Owens's Sixth Amendment right to confront his accusers—a topic we take up a little later. Many of his arguments, however, apply equally well to application of Rule 801(d)(1)(C).—GF]

death, would have. Thus, while the Court asserts that defense counsel had "realistic weapons" with which to impugn Foster's prior statement, it does not and cannot claim that cross-examination could have elicited any information that would have enabled a jury to evaluate the trustworthiness or reliability of the identification. Indeed, although the Court suggests that defense counsel was able to explore Foster's "lack of care and attentiveness," his "bad memory," and the possibility that hospital visitors suggested respondent's name to him, Foster's memory loss precluded any such inquiries: he simply could not recall whether he had actually seen his assailant or even whether he had had an opportunity to see him, nor could he remember any of his visitors, let alone whether any of them had suggested that respondent had attacked him. Moreover, by the time of trial, Foster was unable to shed any light on the accuracy of his May 1982 recollection of the assault; the most he could state was that on the day of the interview he felt certain that his statements were true. As the court below found, "[c]learly, two of the three [hearsay] dangers surrounding Foster's out-of-court identifications—misperception and failure of memory—could not be mitigated in any way by the only cross-examination of Foster that was available to [respondent]." 789 F.2d 750, 759 (9th Cir. 1986). . . .

. . . [W]e have never before held that the Confrontation Clause protects nothing more than a defendant's right to question live witnesses, no matter how futile that questioning might be. On the contrary, . . . we have repeatedly affirmed that the right of confrontation ensures "an opportunity for *effective* cross-examination." While we have rejected the notion that effectiveness should be measured in terms of a defendant's ultimate success, we have never, until today, equated effectiveness with the mere opportunity to pose questions. Rather, . . . we have suggested that the touchstone of effectiveness is whether the cross-examination affords " 'the trier of fact . . . a satisfactory basis for evaluating the truth of the prior statement.' " . . .

. . . In the present case, respondent Owens was afforded no opportunity to probe and expose the infirmities of Foster's May 5, 1982, recollections, for here cross-examination, the "greatest legal engine ever invented for the discovery of truth," stood as helpless as current medical technology before Foster's profound memory loss. . . . I dissent.

Problem 7.21

Domestic Violence III

In *State v. Robinson*, 718 N.W.2d 400 (Minn. 2006), the subject of Problems 7.19 and 7.20 (pages 453–54), F.T. arrived at the hospital on April 12, 2003, with a "blowout fracture of her right orbit." At the assault trial of Andre Robinson, the father of F.T.'s children, she testified that her injury occurred when she peeked out of her bathroom door after an argument with Robinson, and he "pushed the door open, causing it to hit her" and inflicting the injuries to her eye. F.T. dismissed the incident as "an accident." The prosecutor also offered the testimony of a treating nurse who said F.T. told her on April 12, 2003, "[M]y kids' dad came over drunk; got to argue with me and then [with an] open hand slapped me really hard on the face." The trial court admitted the nurse's testimony over Robinson's hearsay objection, and he was convicted. On appeal the prosecution sought to justify admission of the nurse's account under the state's equivalent of Rule 801(d)(1)(C). *See id.* at 402–03, 407–08. How should the appeals court have ruled? Assume that F.T.'s trial testimony and her statement to the nurse were the only accounts of her injury offered at trial.

E. Hearsay Exceptions Under Rule 804: "Declarant Unavailable"

1. Past Testimony

Focus on

FRE 804(a) & 804(b)(1)

Problem 7.22

Domestic Violence IV

Consider one last variant of *State v. Robinson*, 718 N.W.2d 400 (Minn. 2006), in which F.T. arrived at the hospital on April 12, 2003, with a "blowout fracture of her right orbit." Assume that at a grand jury hearing the next day, where only the prosecutor, the jurors, and F.T. were present, F.T. testified under oath that Robinson hit her in the eye with an open hand. Also assume that at Robinson's assault trial, F.T. took the stand, but altogether refused to testify and persisted in her refusal even when the judge threatened to hold her in contempt. If the prosecutor, over the defendant's hearsay objection, offered a transcript of F.T.'s grand jury testimony, how should the trial court have ruled? Assume that the Federal Rules of Evidence control and that F.T.'s grand jury testimony is the only account of F.T.'s injury offered at trial.

Problem 7.23

Roadway Incident

Roger Crewing and Sarah Morgan collided in an intersection. A police officer who came to the scene charged Crewing with driving under the influence of alcohol. Later, Morgan sued Crewing for injuries resulting from the accident. At the trial of this civil suit Morgan testified about the accident and was cross-examined by Crewing's lawyer.

Four months later, Crewing's drunk driving prosecution came to trial. In the intervening months Morgan had suffered a serious head injury and was unable to attend the trial. The prosecutor sought to read into the record Morgan's testimony at the earlier trial. Crewing objected.

How should the judge have ruled? What additional facts might the judge have wanted to know?

UNITED STATES v. DUENAS

691 F.3d 1070 (9th Cir. 2012)

■ WARDLAW, CIRCUIT JUDGE: [This appeal arises] from the chaotic two-day execution of a search warrant [at the compound of Ray and Lou Duenas] by the Guam Police Department's ("GPD") SWAT team, in coordination with federal DEA and ATF agents. The search resulted in one of the largest "busts" of stolen items in Guam's history. . . .

Ray and Lou were arrested and separately gave statements to police officers. The district court denied their motions to suppress . . . their statements. A jury convicted each of the Duenases on multiple counts. [Ray appeals his conviction], contending that the . . . testimony of by-then-deceased Officer Frankie Smith should not have been admitted at trial . . . [We hold that t]he district court abused its discretion by admitting the former testimony of Officer Smith under Rule 804(b)(1) of the Federal Rules of Evidence, because it incorrectly concluded that defense counsel had a similar motive to cross-examine Officer Smith when it questioned him at the suppression hearing as it would have had at the trial. Because Ray's statement was admitted through Smith's former testimony, Ray's conviction must be reversed....

I. FACTUAL BACKGROUND

Ray and Lou lived on an isolated jungle property in Dededo, Guam.... A main house and a shipping container faced the dirt road leading up to the property. Behind the house and container, toward the rear of the property, was a make-shift four-room shack in which Ray and Lou lived.

At approximately 5:40 a.m. on April 19, 2007, GPD officers, along with DEA and ATF agents, executed a search warrant at the Duenases' residence for evidence of narcotics trafficking.... Officers seized approximately 82 grams of methamphetamine, including 74 grams found in a safe at the foot of the bed.... Officers also seized guns, drug paraphernalia, three ledgers, and several thousand pieces of stolen property. The ledgers, one of which Officer Frank Santos testified at trial "represented a typical drug ledger," identify dollar amounts in the hundreds and thousands....

Ray and Lou were arrested shortly after the search commenced and were taken to the Tamuning precinct. Thereafter, Ray and Lou each gave written and oral statements regarding the drugs and the stolen property. In his statement, Ray wrote that he had purchased numerous items, including firearms, plasma televisions, power tools, and jewelry, with either cash or methamphetamine. Ray added that he "received the drug 'ice' through a friend who needed help to find buyers." Officer Smith took Ray's statement, and later testified at a suppression hearing that Ray told him that he had been selling methamphetamine in exchange for stolen goods.

Ray, Officer Smith, and Special Agent Michelle Jong of the DEA gave contradictory testimony about how Ray came to give his statements to Officer Smith. After he was initially apprehended by the SWAT team, Ray complained of injury. He was eventually taken to the hospital by Officer Smith.... According to Smith, Ray called him over at the hospital and said, "Frank, the stuff at the house...." Smith testified that he interrupted Ray, telling him "Ray, this is not the time, let's get you treated first, talk about this at the precinct." Ray was examined at the hospital and returned to the Tamuning precinct that afternoon.

Once Ray returned to the precinct, Special Agents Jong and Than Churchin attempted to interview him, after advising him of his *Miranda* rights. Jong stated that Ray said that he wanted to talk with an attorney before making a statement. Jong testified that she then ended the interview and told Ray she would look into getting him a Federal Public Defender.... As she left the room, she encountered Officer Smith. Jong informed Smith that Ray had invoked his right to counsel. Smith then went into the conference room. . . .

At the suppression hearing, Smith offered a different story: he testified that Jong did not tell him that Ray had asked for an attorney, but instead "informed me that he didn't want to talk to her, but wanted to talk to one of us." . . . Smith went into the conference room and said: "How are you doing, Ray?" Ray responded that he did not want to talk to the federal agents, because they scared him, but that he would talk to Smith. Smith then re-advised Ray of his *Miranda* rights. Ray signed a form waiving those rights and indicating that he was willing to make a statement. Ray then gave oral and written statements admitting to selling methamphetamine out of his home in exchange for stolen items; he also named his source. . . .

A Superseding Indictment charged Ray [and Lou with] conspiracy to distribute more than 50 grams of methamphetamine [and a second drug offense and charged Ray with] . . . using and carrying a firearm during a drug trafficking crime . . . [and other gun offenses]. . . .

Ray . . . moved to suppress his statements, arguing that they were obtained in violation of *Miranda* because he had been questioned before his rights were read to him, and that, in any event, his statements were involuntary because his will "had been . . . overborne" by the police on the day of the search, as he had been injured, tired, frightened, and emotional when questioned. The district court denied Ray's motion, finding that despite his initial refusal to talk, Ray subsequently waived his right to counsel before speaking with Officer Smith and gave his statements voluntarily.

After the suppression hearing and before trial, Officer Smith was killed by a drunk driver. Over Ray's hearsay objection, the district court concluded that Smith's testimony was "former testimony" under Federal Rule of Evidence 804(b)(1), and allowed Special Agent Sedberry to read portions of Smith's suppression hearing testimony to the jury. . . .

On March 17, 2009, a jury convicted Ray of conspiracy and possession with intent to distribute, use of a firearm during a drug crime, and possession of stolen firearms. The jury convicted Lou of both conspiracy and possession with intent to distribute. . . . [The district court] sentenced Ray to 25 and Lou to 20 years of imprisonment, the statutory mandatory minimums for both. . . .

VI. Officer Smith's Former Testimony

[W]e are compelled to conclude that the district court should not have admitted Officer Smith's suppression hearing testimony following his unfortunate demise. The district court admitted the testimony as "former testimony" under Federal Rule of Evidence 804(b)(1), reasoning that Ray "had a meaningful opportunity to cross-examine Officer Smith" about the "context and details" of Officer Smith's testimony at the suppression hearing, but made "a tactical decision" not to do so. We disagree, because the district court failed to compare Ray's "fundamental objectives" at each hearing to find a similar motive under Rule 804(b)(1).

"Former testimony" is not hearsay if a declarant is unavailable. "Former testimony" is testimony that:

> (A) was given as a witness at a trial, hearing, or lawful deposition, whether given during the current proceeding or a different one; and
>
> (B) is now offered against a party who had—or, in a civil case, whose predecessor in interest had—an opportunity and similar motive to develop it by direct, cross-, or redirect examination.

Fed. R. Evid. 804(b)(1). Smith was "unavailable" because he was deceased, and his former testimony was given during the pre-trial suppression hearing. *See* Fed. R. Evid. 804(a)(4). Thus, the critical question is whether Ray had the "opportunity and similar motive" to develop Officer Smith's testimony by direct, cross-, or redirect examination at the suppression hearing as he would have had at trial. *See United States v. Salerno*, 505 U.S. 317, 321 (1992) (holding that former testimony may not be introduced under Rule 804(b)(1) without a showing of "similar motive").[10] Because Ray's motive at the suppression hearing was solely to demonstrate that his statements were involuntary and obtained in violation of *Miranda*, and thus inadmissible, his motive for cross-examining Officer Smith at trial, to challenge the substance of the statements as opposed to the circumstances in which they were given, was substantially dissimilar.

In *Salerno*, the only Supreme Court decision to address the "similar motive" requirement, the Court clarified that "similar motive" is a necessary element of Rule 804(b)(1). *Id.* at 321. However, it did not explain how courts should determine whether a party's motives are "similar." *Id.* at 325. Justice Blackmun, concurring, provided some guidance by noting that "similar motive" does not mean "identical motive," and that the "similar motive" analysis is "inherently a *factual* inquiry" based on "the similarity of the underlying issues and on the context of the . . . questioning." *Id.* at 326 (Blackmun, J., concurring) (emphasis in original).

We have twice addressed whether, under Rule 804(b)(1), suppression hearing testimony is admissible at a later proceeding. *See United States v. Geiger*, 263 F.3d 1034 (9th Cir. 2001); *United States v. Poland*, 659 F.2d 884 (9th Cir. 1981) (per curiam). The government argues that these cases dictate the outcome of our "similar motive" analysis. We find *Poland* and *Geiger* to be factually inapposite, however, and conclude that neither decision controls our "inherently . . . factual inquiry."

10. Ray does not argue that the admission of Smith's testimony violated his Sixth Amendment right to confrontation. Where the requirements of Rule 804(b)(1) are met, we generally conclude that the Confrontation Clause is not violated. *See United States v. Yida*, 498 F.3d 945, 950 (9th Cir. 2007) ("Rule 804(b)(1) implements the command of the Sixth Amendment's Confrontation Clause.").

In *Poland*, an eye-witness identified the defendant in a lineup. A suppression hearing, at which the defense cross-examined the witness, was held to determine whether the lineup was impermissibly suggestive. Denying the motion to suppress, the district court concluded that the lineup was "fair and not unjust." *Poland*, 659 F.2d at 895. The witness died before trial, and the district court granted the prosecution's motion to admit a transcript of the suppression hearing testimony at trial. On appeal, the defendant argued that he would have been motivated at trial to test the witness's reliability by cross-examining him about his eyesight, whether he was intoxicated, and the distance from which he observed the defendant, inquiries that he was not motivated to make at the suppression hearing. We rejected this argument and concluded that the "similar motive" requirement was satisfied, noting that pretrial identifications are admissible if they are reliable, even if the identification procedure is unduly suggestive. Thus the defendant's motive in cross-examining the witness at both the suppression hearing and trial was the same: to cast doubt on the witness's reliability with questions about his eyesight, intoxication, and the like.

In *Geiger*, the question was not whether suppression hearing testimony was admissible at trial, but rather whether an officer's testimony at a state suppression hearing was admissible at a subsequent federal suppression hearing. The defendant in *Geiger* admitted in a taped confession taken by Officer Churchill that he had placed a bomb in the victim's truck. Before Geiger was indicted in federal court, the state of Alaska charged him with first degree murder. Geiger successfully sought suppression of the recorded confession in state court, because the arresting officers, including Officer Churchill, had failed to comply with Alaska's custodial interrogation requirements. Officer Churchill, who testified at the state suppression hearing, died before the federal suppression hearing. The magistrate judge admitted his testimony at the federal hearing under Rule 804(b)(1). Geiger contended that the court erred in admitting the former testimony, because the state hearing focused on Alaska's custodial interrogation requirements, while the federal suppression hearing concerned the sufficiency of his *Miranda* warning, the voluntariness of his statement, and his request for counsel. We rejected Geiger's argument, reasoning that the similarity of his state and federal motions to suppress belied his claim of dissimilar motives: "Both motions to suppress presented virtually the same issues: whether Geiger's taped confession was coerced and involuntary; whether Geiger had been properly *Mirandized*; whether the arrest was pretextual; and whether Geiger had been unlawfully detained." *Geiger*, 263 F.3d at 1038.... Moreover, Churchill's testimony at the state hearing addressed issues pertinent to the federal hearing, such as ... whether Geiger asked for an attorney or refused to speak, whether [Churchill] coerced Geiger into confessing, and whether he threatened Geiger's family. Because the legal and factual issues in both hearings were "substantially similar," we concluded that Geiger had a "similar motive" at both hearings.

We have also addressed the "similar motive" prong in other contexts. In *United States v. McFall*, 558 F.3d 951 (9th Cir. 2009), we examined whether exculpatory grand jury testimony is admissible at trial against the prosecution, an issue on which the courts of appeals are split. The First and Second Circuits examine whether the government "t[ook] the same side on the same issue" and whether it had the same degree of interest to prevail at each proceeding. *Id.* at 962 (citing *United States v. DiNapoli*, 8 F.3d 909 (2d Cir. 1993) (en banc); *United States v. Omar*, 104 F.3d 519, 522–24 (1st Cir. 1997)). In *McFall*, we rejected this "fine-grained" method and followed the D.C. and Sixth Circuits in comparing motives at a "high level of generality." *Id.* (citing *United States v. Miller*, 904 F.2d 65, 68 (D.C. Cir. 1990)). We noted that the government need not have the same "intensity" of motivation at each proceeding, because the plain language of Rule 804(b)(1) requires similar, but not identical, motivation. *Id.* at 963.

McFall was charged with conspiracy to commit extortion. McFall's co-conspirator, Sawyer, at that point uncharged, appeared before a grand jury and offered a first-person account of key events that contradicted the testimony of the government's primary witness and corroborated McFall's version of the events. Sawyer died before trial, and McFall sought to introduce a transcript of the exculpatory grand jury testimony under Rule 804(b)(1). The district court did not admit the transcript, concluding that the government's motive at trial was "completely different" than its motive before the grand jury because Sawyer was not a suspect at the time of his testimony and because the grand jury was a fact-finding investigation, not an adversarial proceeding. We held that the district court "erred in concluding that the government's respective motives were 'completely different,' and the exclusion of Sawyer's grand jury testimony as hearsay amounted to an abuse of discretion." *Id.* at 963. Although we noted that the government's incentive to develop incriminating testimony before the grand jury was "likely not as intense as it would have been at trial," we nevertheless held that the government's "fundamental objective" was the same at each proceeding. *Id.* That "fundamental objective" was "to draw out testimony that would support its theory that McFall conspired with Sawyer to commit extortion—the same motive it possessed at trial." *Id.*

Finally, we recently had occasion to address the issue of "similar motive" in the context of an SEC investigation of a CFO involved in a stock option back-dating scandal. *See Sec. & Exch. Comm'n v. Jasper*, 678 F.3d 1116 (9th Cir. 2012). The SEC alleged that Jasper engaged in an illegal scheme to back-date stock options granted to employees and directors. The company's former treasurer, Ruehle, made exculpatory statements in sworn testimony taken in connection with the SEC's fact-gathering investigation. Because Ruehle was unavailable at the time of trial, Jasper attempted to introduce his testimony under Rule 804(b)(1). The district court found the testimony inadmissible, concluding that the SEC had a different motive at the accusatory stage of the proceedings than it did during the investigatory stage. We affirmed, because the district court did not abuse its discretion based on the inherently different motives involved in an early investigation, at which "open-ended questions are typically asked without expectation the witness will be needed at trial," and a cross-examination of an adverse witness. *Id.* at 1128–29.

As the foregoing cases demonstrate, we have not developed a bright-line test for determining similarity of motive. Nor should we. As Justice Blackmun instructed, the "similar motive" analysis is "inherently a factual inquiry" based on "the similarity of the underlying issues and on the context of the ... questioning." *Salerno*, 505 U.S. at 326 (BLACKMUN, J., concurring) (emphasis omitted). Here we are faced with a unique set of facts that does not fit squarely within the ambit of any of our aforementioned precedent.

The transcript of Ray's suppression hearing demonstrates that his counsel did not have a similar motive in questioning Officer Smith at the suppression hearing as at trial. Ray's "fundamental objective," *McFall*, 558 F.3d at 963, in questioning Officer Smith at the suppression hearing was to elicit testimony to prove that his statements to Smith were involuntary and obtained in violation of *Miranda*. This was Ray's sole purpose in examining Smith, a point Ray's counsel made emphatically when the prosecution veered into the substance of the statement and sought details about Ray's meetings with his drug source. Ray's counsel objected to this inquiry as "having no relevance or bearing on" the only question at issue—whether Ray voluntarily spoke with Smith. After the district court overruled Ray's objection, Ray's counsel offered to enter the written statement into evidence for purposes of the suppression hearing, rather than to permit the prosecutor to go into detail about the substance of the statement. The prosecutor acquiesced to the defense's limitation on its inquiry and simply asked Officer Smith to identify Ray's statement before introducing it into evidence.

During the cross-examination of Officer Smith at the suppression hearing, Ray's counsel inquired only about the circumstances under which Ray was arrested and made the statement. Counsel asked about the duration of Smith's interview with Ray, whether Ray was under the influence of any drugs or medication at the time of the statement, whether he had consumed alcohol the night before giving the statement, whether Smith offered leniency if Ray cooperated in finding an alleged associate, and whether Smith threatened Ray. The record of the suppression hearing plainly shows that Ray's motive at that proceeding was to question Officer Smith about circumstances bearing on the voluntariness of the statement and not to delve into the contents of the statement.

Ray's written motion to suppress confirms that his motive was confined to demonstrating involuntariness and a *Miranda* violation. The motion argues only that Ray was improperly *Mirandized* and that his statement was involuntary. The motion makes no reference to the substance of Ray's statement.

Ray's fundamental objective at the suppression hearing was not the same as his motive would have been had Smith testified at trial. The issue at trial was whether the evidence proved Ray's guilt beyond a reasonable doubt, not the circumstances of his confession. By the time of trial, neither voluntariness nor the alleged *Miranda* violation was even at issue. Rather, Ray's objective at trial would have been to vigorously challenge Officer Smith on the details of the oral and written statements, to cast doubt on his credibility and on the reliability and completeness of his version of Ray's statement. . . .

We therefore conclude that the district court's "similar motive" determination must be reversed. The district court failed to properly compare Ray's "fundamental objective" at the suppression hearing to his motive at trial, and instead focused on Ray's *opportunity* to cross-examine Officer Smith. . . .

The extent of the district court's comparison of Ray's motives is contained in its conclusory statement that "[a] purely tactical decision not to develop particular testimony despite the same issue and level of interest at each proceeding does not constitute a lack of opportunity or a dissimilar motive for purposes of Rule 804(b)(1)." This is of course circular, in that it predicates its conclusion that Ray's counsel's decision was tactical on the unfounded assumption that the same issue and level of interest existed at each proceeding. Because it failed to directly compare Ray's "fundamental objectives" at trial and at the suppression hearing, the district court abused its discretion by admitting Smith's testimony. . . .

[W]e have no difficulty concluding that the error was not harmless. As the government concedes, it would not have been able to introduce Ray's written statement at trial without Smith's testimony, because Smith was the only officer present when Ray executed the written statement. Aside from Ray's written and oral statements, both of which were admitted through Smith, there was no evidence directly tying him to the drugs, firearms, and stolen property in the compound. . . . Ray's confession was by far the most compelling and vital evidence. The government admitted as much at the hearing on the motion to introduce Smith's testimony, when it stated, "of course it's crucial to our case because it is a confession."

The prosecutor's closing argument amply illustrates just why its case against Ray would have unraveled without the confessions. After briefly explaining the nature of the charges against Ray and Lou, the prosecutor told the jury: "Go to the evidence in this case. *The crux of the case* against

Raymond Duenas is the confession. In fact, two confessions." (emphasis added). The prosecutor described the circumstances surrounding Ray's confession in some detail, and then argued to the jury, "Now you've got these confessions, both orally and in writing. Should you rely on them[?]. Absolutely." ... Because the government chose to make the confessions the centerpiece of its case, we are compelled to conclude that the erroneous admission of Officer Smith's testimony was not harmless....

VACATED and REVERSED.

LLOYD v. AMERICAN EXPORT LINES, INC.

580 F.2d 1179 (3d Cir.), *cert. denied*, 439 U.S. 969 (1978).

■ ALDISERT, CIRCUIT JUDGE.... This lawsuit emanates from a violent altercation between [Roland] Alvarez and a fellow crew member, electrician Frank Lloyd, that occurred on September 7, 1974, when their ship, the SS Export Commerce, was in the port of Yokohama, Japan. Lloyd filed an action against Export in the district court ... seeking redress for the injuries sustained in the fight. Export joined Alvarez as a third-party defendant and Alvarez, in turn, counterclaimed against Export, alleging, as did Lloyd, negligence and unseaworthiness. Lloyd did not proceed in his case as plaintiff, failing to appear on seven occasions for a pretrial deposition, and failing to appear when the case was called for trial on November 18, 1976. Accordingly, his complaint was dismissed by the district court for failure to prosecute, and thereafter trial was had on Alvarez' counterclaim. The jury found that [Export was] negligent, and its negligence contributed to Alvarez' injuries. The jury returned a verdict in favor of Alvarez against Export in the amount of $95,000.

It was Alvarez' theory that Export negligently failed to use reasonable precautions to safeguard him from Lloyd after Export had knowledge of Lloyd's dangerous propensities.... The jury was not permitted to hear any version of the fight other than that of Alvarez; it was denied the opportunity of hearing the account rendered by Lloyd, who was the other participant in the affray and its only other eyewitness. It is the refusal of the district court to admit a public record of a prior proceeding and excerpts of Lloyd's testimony therein that constitutes the major thrust of Export's appeal. Export contends that this evidence was admissible in the form of transcripts ... from a Coast Guard hearing conducted intermittently from January 20, 1975, through January 6, 1976, the purpose of which was to determine whether Lloyd's merchant mariner's document should have been suspended or revoked on the basis of charges of misconduct brought against him for the fight with Alvarez. At that hearing, both Lloyd and Alvarez were represented by counsel and testified under oath.

II.

The admissibility of ... excerpts from the transcript of [the Coast Guard proceeding is governed in part by Federal Rule] of Evidence 804(b)(1). Our examination of the record below compels the conclusion that [the Rule was] misinterpreted by the district court....

A.

The Coast Guard proceeding was a rather elaborate hearing conducted before a professional hearing examiner. In addition to documentary evidence, testimony was received under oath, subject to direct and cross examination, on two charges leveled against Lloyd: that he "did wrongfully assault and batter ROLANDO ALVAREZ, a fellow crew member, with his fists," and that he "did wrongfully fail to perform his duties due to intoxication." ...

B.

Our examination of the transcript of Frank Lloyd's testimony at the Coast Guard hearing convinces us that it is highly relevant to the negligence issue raised by Alvarez. Because Lloyd testified not only to the incident of September 1974, but to the history of his relationship with Alvarez as well, his testimony would have been most helpful to the jury in determining the ultimate issue of whether the officers and crew of the SS Export Commerce failed to take reasonable precautions to safeguard Alvarez against an attack by Lloyd. Indeed, Lloyd's testimony directly refuted the Alvarez theory.... Lloyd's description of the September 7, 1974, altercation is ... at variance with that of Alvarez:

Q: Now, did you ... punch or in any way strike Mr. Alvarez?

A: No sir....

C.

Alvarez objects to the admission of Lloyd's testimony on two grounds: first, there was insufficient proof that Lloyd was unavailable to testify at trial as contemplated in Rule 804(a)(5), and, second, the Coast Guard proceeding did not qualify under Rule 804(b)(1).

In order for the hearsay exceptions of Rule 804 to apply, it is required that the declarant be "unavailable"—in this case, that he be "absent from the hearing and the proponent of his statement [be] unable to procure his attendance ... by process or other reasonable means." Rule 804(a)(5) [unrestyled]. In preparation for trial, as has been noted, numerous attempts were made by Export to depose Lloyd, but he repeatedly failed to appear. Finally, on the day set for trial, Export learned that Lloyd would not appear to prosecute his case. Lloyd's counsel represented to the court that extensive efforts had been made to obtain his appearance, but they had failed, due at least in part to his seafaring occupation. We are satisfied that where Export and Lloyd's own counsel were unable to obtain his appearance in an action in which he had a formidable interest as a plaintiff, his unavailability status was sufficient to satisfy the requirement of Rule 804.

D.

We turn now to the more difficult question: did Alvarez or a "predecessor in interest" have the "opportunity and similar motive to develop the testimony by direct, cross or redirect examination" as required by [unrestyled] Rule 804(b)(1)? In rejecting the proffered evidence, the district court took a strict view of the new rule, one that we do not share.

We note at the outset that inasmuch as Congress did not define "predecessor in interest," that interpretive task is left to the courts. We find no definitive guidance in the reports accompanying language changes made as the Rules were considered, in turn, by the Supreme Court and the houses of Congress.... The House of Representatives adopted the present language, the Committee on the Judiciary offering this rationale:

> Rule 804(b)(1) as submitted by the Court allowed prior testimony of an unavailable witness to be admissible if the party against whom it is offered or a person "with motive and interest similar" to his had an opportunity to examine the witness. The Committee considered that it is generally unfair to impose upon the party against whom the hearsay evidence is being offered responsibility for the manner in which the witness was previously handled by another party. The sole exception to this, in the Committee's view, is when a party's predecessor in interest in a civil action or proceeding had an opportunity and similar motive to examine the witness. The Committee amended the Rule to reflect these policy determinations.[5]

The Senate Committee on the Judiciary viewed the import of this change as follows:

> ... Rule 804(b)(1) as submitted by the Court allowed prior testimony of an unavailable witness to be admissible if the party against whom it is offered or a person "with motive and interest similar" to his had an opportunity to examine the witness.
>
> The House amended the rule to apply only to a party's predecessor in interest. Although the committee recognizes considerable merit to the rule submitted by the Supreme Court, a position which has been advocated by many scholars and judges, we have concluded that the difference between the two versions is not great and we accept the House amendment.

We, too, fail to see a compelling difference between the two approaches.

5. ... We do not accept the view that this change in wording signaled a return to the common law approach to former testimony, requiring privity or a common property interest between the parties.

... [Rule 804(b)] was originally designed by the Advisory Committee ... to strike a proper balance between the recognized risk of introducing testimony of one not physically present on a witness stand and the equally recognized risk of denying to the factfinder important relevant evidence.... "The rule expresses preferences: testimony given on the stand in person is preferred over hearsay, and hearsay, if of the specified quality, is preferred over complete loss of the evidence of the declarant." [ACN to FRE 804(b) (RB 270).]

Although Congress did not furnish us with a definition of "predecessor in interest," our analysis of the concept of interests satisfies us that there was a sufficient community of interest shared by the Coast Guard in its hearing and Alvarez in the subsequent civil trial to satisfy Rule 804(b)(1).... Alvarez sought to vindicate his individual interest in recovering for his injuries; the Coast Guard sought to vindicate the public interest in safe and unimpeded merchant marine service.... [T]he nucleus of operative facts was the same—the conduct of Frank Lloyd and Roland Alvarez aboard the SS Export Commerce. And although the results sought in the two proceedings differed—the Coast Guard contemplated sanctions involving Lloyd's mariner's license, while Alvarez sought ... monetary damages—the basic interest advanced by both was that of determining culpability and, if appropriate, exacting a penalty for the same condemned behavior thought to have occurred.[12] The Coast Guard investigating officer not only preferred charges against Lloyd but functioned as a prosecutor at the subsequent proceeding as well. Thus, he attempted to establish at the Coast Guard hearing what Alvarez attempted to establish at the later trial: Lloyd's intoxication, his role as the aggressor, and his prior hostility toward Alvarez....

... We strive to ... favor those [interpretations of the Rules] that facilitate the presentation of a complete picture to the fact-finder. With this approach in mind, we are satisfied that there existed, in the language of Rule 804(b)(1), sufficient "opportunity and similar motive [for the Coast Guard investigating officer] to develop [Lloyd's] testimony" at the former hearing to justify its admission against Alvarez at the later trial.

While we do not endorse an extravagant interpretation of who or what constitutes a "predecessor in interest," we prefer one that is realistically generous over one that is formalistically grudging. We believe that what has been described as "the practical and expedient view"

12. In this regard, McCormick takes the position that "insistence upon precise identity of issues, which might have some appropriateness if the question were one of res judicata or estoppel by judgment, are out of place with respect to former testimony where the question is not of binding anyone, but merely of the salvaging, for what it may be worth, of the testimony of a witness not now available in person.... It follows that neither the form of the proceeding, the theory of the case, nor the nature of the relief sought needs be the same."

expresses the congressional intention: "if it appears that in the former suit a party having a like motive to cross-examine about the same matters as the present party would have, was accorded an adequate opportunity for such examination, the testimony may be received against the present party." McCORMICK, HANDBOOK OF THE LAW OF EVIDENCE § 256, at 619–20 (2d ed. 1972). Under these circumstances, the previous party having like motive to develop the testimony about the same material facts is, in the final analysis, a predecessor in interest to the present party. . . .

The judgment of the district court will be reversed and the cause remanded for a new trial. . . .

■ STERN, DISTRICT JUDGE, concurring. I join in the majority opinion, except insofar as it construes the "predecessor in interest" language of Rule 804(b)(1). The majority here holds that because the Coast Guard investigating officer shared a community of interest with Alvarez he was Alvarez's predecessor in interest. I believe that this analysis is contrary to the Rule's clear language and is foreclosed by its legislative history. . . .

As the majority points out, the rule enacted as 804(b)(1), as originally submitted by the Supreme Court, would have permitted the introduction of former testimony if the party against whom it was offered, or a person "with motive and interest similar" to the party, had an opportunity to examine the witness. But Congress rejected this approach [and specifically added the requirement that a party's "predecessor in interest . . . had an opportunity and similar motive" to examine the declarant]. . . .

It is true that Congress nowhere defined "predecessor in interest," but it seems clear that this phrase, a term of art, was used in its narrow, substantive law sense. Although the commentators have expressed disapproval of this traditional and restrictive rule, they recognize that a "predecessor in interest" is defined in terms of a privity relationship.

> " 'The term "privity" denotes mutual or successive relationships to the same rights of property. . . . Thus, there are privies in estate, as donor and donee, lessor and lessee, and joint tenants; privies in blood, as heir and ancestor . . .; privies in representation, as executor and testator, administrator and intestate. . . .' "

Metropolitan St. Ry. v. Gumby, 99 F. 192 (2d Cir. 1900).

The majority rejects the view that the Rule's wording signals a return to the common law approach requiring privity or a common property interest between the parties and finds it sufficient that the Coast Guard investigator shared a community of interest with Alvarez. But community of interest seems to mean only that the investigating officer sought to establish the same facts as Alvarez attempted to prove in the instant suit. Used in this sense, community of interest means nothing more than similarity of interest or similarity of motive. But similar motive is a separate prerequisite to admissibility under 804(b)(1), and thus the majority's analysis, which reads "predecessor in interest" to mean nothing more than person with "similar motive," eliminates the predecessor in interest requirement entirely.

Moreover, while I appreciate the fact that the Coast Guard investigator sought to establish Lloyd's wrongdoing and that Alvarez sought to do the same, I do not believe that this establishes the kind of "common motive" sufficient to satisfy 804(b)(1).

A prosecutor or an investigating officer represents no ordinary party. He shoulders a peculiar kind of duty, even to his very adversary, a duty which is foreign to the adversarial process among ordinary litigants. The prosecutor, it is true, must seek to vindicate the rights of the alleged victim, but his interests go far beyond that. His interest in a prosecution is not that he shall win a case, but that justice shall be done. *See* Berger v. United States, 295 U.S. 78, 79 (1935).

The interests of an attorney representing the government thus surely overlap those of the private litigant, but they do not coincide. The investigating officer was under no duty to advance every arguable issue against Lloyd in the vindication of Alvarez's interests, as Alvarez's own counsel would have been. He simply did not represent Alvarez.

Thus, even if I could agree that Congress intended to relax the common law requirement of actual privity between the parties before prior testimony could be admitted, I cannot endorse a rule which would automatically render admissible against a party evidence which was elicited in a different proceeding by an unrelated person merely because both shared an interest in establishing the same facts.... The net result would be charging the party against whom the hearsay evidence is being offered with all flaws in the manner in which the witness was previously handled by another, and all flaws in another's choice of witnesses, the very result characterized by the House Judiciary Committee as "generally unfair." ...*

---

2. Statements Against Interest

Focus on
FRE 804(b)(3)

---

* [Judge Stern nonetheless concurred with the majority in deeming Lloyd's testimony at the Coast Guard proceeding admissible at trial, but reached this judgment under the residual exception to the hearsay rule, addressed below at pages 574 to 584.—GF]

Problem 7.24
Ask Magnolia

A Brink's truck was robbed by a man and a woman acting as a team. Armed with substantial evidence, police charged Magnolia Sharp with taking part in the crime. Then, acting on a tip, a police detective went to the home of Robert Barton.

After the detective rang the bell, Barton's mother came to the door. The detective explained that she wished to speak to Robert in connection with an armored truck robbery. Barton's mother turned toward her son, who sat watching TV in the next room, and asked, "Bobby, did you rob that truck? Don't lie to me." Without looking up, Barton replied, "Ask Magnolia. It was her idea."

At the joint trial of Magnolia Sharp and Robert Barton, the prosecutor seeks to offer evidence of this conversation against both defendants. Sharp objects on hearsay grounds. What are the government's best arguments for admitting the evidence against Sharp? What are Sharp's best arguments against? How should the court rule?

(You should assume that Barton's Fifth Amendment privilege makes him unavailable as a witness for the government at trial. For now, please ignore any Confrontation Clause concerns, which we take up in the next chapter.)

WILLIAMSON V. UNITED STATES

512 U.S. 594 (1994).

■ O'CONNOR, J., announced the judgment of the Court and delivered the opinion of the Court with respect to Parts I, II–A, and II–B, in which BLACKMUN, STEVENS, SCALIA, SOUTER, and GINSBURG, JJ., joined, and an opinion with respect to Part II–C, in which SCALIA, J., joined. SCALIA, J., filed a concurring opinion. GINSBURG, J., filed an opinion concurring in part and concurring in the judgment, in which BLACKMUN, STEVENS, and SOUTER, JJ., joined. KENNEDY, J., filed an opinion concurring in the judgment, in which REHNQUIST, C.J., and THOMAS, J., joined.

■ JUSTICE O'CONNOR delivered the opinion of the Court, except as to Part II–C.... A deputy sheriff stopped the rental car driven by Reginald Harris for weaving on the highway. Harris consented to a search of the car, which revealed 19 kilograms of cocaine in two suitcases in the trunk. Harris was promptly arrested.

Shortly after Harris' arrest, Special Agent Donald Walton of the Drug Enforcement Administration (DEA) interviewed him by telephone. During that conversation, Harris said that he got the cocaine from an unidentified Cuban in Fort Lauderdale; that the cocaine belonged to petitioner Williamson; and that it was to be delivered that night to a particular dumpster. . . .

Several hours later, Agent Walton spoke to Harris in person. During that interview, Harris said he had rented the car a few days earlier and had driven it to Fort Lauderdale to meet Williamson. According to Harris, he had gotten the cocaine from a Cuban who was Williamson's acquaintance, and the Cuban had put the cocaine in the car with a note telling Harris how to deliver the drugs. Harris repeated that he had been instructed to leave the drugs in a certain dumpster, to return to his car, and to leave without waiting for anyone to pick up the drugs.

Agent Walton then took steps to arrange a controlled delivery of the cocaine. But as Walton was preparing to leave the interview room, Harris "got out of [his] chair . . . and . . . took a half step toward [Walton] . . . and . . . said, . . . 'I can't let you do that,' threw his hands up and said 'that's not true, I can't let you go up there for no reason.'" Harris told Walton he had lied about the Cuban, the note, and the dumpster. The real story, Harris said, was that he was transporting the cocaine to Atlanta for Williamson, and that Williamson was traveling in front of him in another rental car. Harris added that after his car was stopped, Williamson turned around and drove past the location of the stop, where he could see Harris' car with its trunk open. Because Williamson had apparently seen the police searching the car, Harris explained that it would be impossible to make a controlled delivery.

Harris told Walton that he had lied about the source of the drugs because he was afraid of Williamson. Though Harris freely implicated himself, he did not want his story to be recorded, and he refused to sign a written version of the statement. Walton testified that he had promised to report any cooperation by Harris to the Assistant United States Attorney. Walton said Harris was not promised any reward or other benefit for cooperating.

Williamson was eventually convicted of possessing cocaine with intent to distribute, conspiring to possess cocaine with intent to distribute, and traveling interstate to promote the distribution of cocaine. When called to testify at Williamson's trial, Harris refused, even though the prosecution gave him use immunity and the court ordered him to testify and eventually held him in contempt. The District Court then ruled that, under Rule 804(b)(3), Agent Walton could relate what Harris had said to him. . . .

Williamson appealed his conviction, claiming that the admission of Harris' statements violated Rule 804(b)(3) and the Confrontation Clause of the Sixth Amendment. The Court of Appeals for the Eleventh Circuit affirmed without opinion, 981 F.2d 1262 (1992), and we granted certiorari.

II

A

The hearsay rule is premised on the theory that out-of-court statements are subject to particular hazards. The declarant might be lying; he might have misperceived the events which he relates; he might have faulty memory; his words might be misunderstood or taken out of context by the listener....

Nonetheless, the Federal Rules of Evidence also recognize that some kinds of out-of-court statements are less subject to these hearsay dangers, and therefore except them from the general rule that hearsay is inadmissible. One such category covers statements that are against the declarant's interest:

> "statements which ... at the time of [their] making ... so far tended to subject the declarant to ... criminal liability ... that a reasonable person in the declarant's position would not have made the statements unless believing [them] to be true." FED. R. EVID. 804(b)(3) [unrestyled].

To decide whether Harris' confession is made admissible by Rule 804(b)(3), we must first determine what the Rule means by "statement," which [unrestyled] Federal Rule of Evidence [801(a)] defines as "an oral or written assertion." One possible meaning, "a report or narrative," WEBSTER'S THIRD NEW INTERNATIONAL DICTIONARY 2229, defn. 2(a) (1961), connotes an extended declaration. Under this reading, Harris' entire confession—even if it contains both self-inculpatory and non-self-inculpatory parts—would be admissible so long as in the aggregate the confession sufficiently inculpates him. Another meaning of "statement," "a single declaration or remark," *ibid.*, defn. 2(b), would make Rule 804(b)(3) cover only those declarations or remarks within the confession that are individually self-inculpatory.

Although the text of the Rule does not directly resolve the matter, the principle behind the Rule, so far as it is discernible from the text, points clearly to the narrower reading. Rule 804(b)(3) is founded on the commonsense notion that reasonable people, even reasonable people who are not especially honest, tend not to make self-inculpatory statements unless they believe them to be true. This notion simply does not extend to the broader definition of "statement." The fact that a person is making a broadly self-inculpatory confession does not make more credible the confession's non-self-inculpatory parts. One of the most effective ways to lie is to mix falsehood with truth, especially truth that seems particularly persuasive because of its self-inculpatory nature.

In this respect, it is telling that the non-self-inculpatory things Harris said in his first statement actually proved to be false, as Harris himself admitted during the second interrogation. And when part of the confession is actually self-exculpatory, the generalization on which Rule 804(b)(3) is founded becomes even less applicable. Self-exculpatory statements are exactly the ones which people are most likely to make even when they are false; and mere proximity to other, self-inculpatory, statements does not increase the plausibility of the self-exculpatory statements.

We therefore cannot agree with JUSTICE KENNEDY's suggestion that the Rule can be read as expressing a policy that collateral statements—even ones that are not in any way against the declarant's interest—are admissible. Nothing in the text of Rule 804(b)(3) or the general theory of the hearsay Rules suggests that admissibility should turn on whether a statement is collateral to a self-inculpatory statement. The fact that a statement is self-inculpatory does make it more reliable; but the fact that a statement is collateral to a self-inculpatory statement says nothing at all about the collateral statement's reliability. We see no reason why collateral statements, even ones that are neutral as to interest, should be treated any differently from other hearsay statements that are generally excluded.

Congress certainly could, subject to the constraints of the Confrontation Clause, make statements admissible based on their proximity to self-inculpatory statements. But we will not lightly assume that the ambiguous language means anything so inconsistent with the Rule's underlying theory. In our view, the most faithful reading of Rule 804(b)(3) is that it does not allow admission of non-self-inculpatory statements, even if they are made within a broader narrative that is generally self-inculpatory. . . . [T]his is especially true when the statement[s] implicate[] someone else. "The arrest statements of a codefendant have traditionally been viewed with special suspicion. Due to his strong motivation to implicate the defendant and to exonerate himself, a codefendant's statements about what the defendant said or did are less credible than ordinary hearsay evidence."* Lee v. Illinois, 476 U.S. 530, 541 (1986).

JUSTICE KENNEDY suggests that the Advisory Committee Notes to Rule 804(b)(3) should be read as endorsing the position we reject—that an entire narrative, including non-self-inculpatory parts (but excluding the clearly self-serving parts), may be admissible if it is in the aggregate self-inculpatory. The Notes read, in relevant part:

> "[T]he third-party confession . . . may include statements implicating [the accused], and under the general theory of declarations against interest they would be admissible as related statements. . . . Douglas v. Alabama, 380 U.S. 415 (1965), and Bruton v. United States, 391 U.S.

* [Recall Sir Walter Raleigh's argument at his trial that Cobham's accusation of Raleigh "may be a means to excuse himself." (Page 375, above.)—GF]

> 123 (1968), ... by no means require that all statements implicating another person be excluded from the category of declarations against interest. Whether a statement is in fact against interest must be determined from the circumstances of each case. Thus a statement admitting guilt and implicating another person, made while in custody, may well be motivated by a desire to curry favor with the authorities and hence fail to qualify as against interest.... On the other hand, the same words spoken under different circumstances, e.g., to an acquaintance, would have no difficulty in qualifying.... The balancing of self-serving against disserving aspects of a declaration is discussed in McCORMICK § 256." [RB 274–75.]

This language, however, is not particularly clear, and some of it—especially the Advisory Committee's endorsement of the position taken by Dean McCormick's treatise—points the other way:

> "A certain latitude as to contextual statements, neutral as to interest, giving meaning to the declaration against interest seems defensible, but bringing in self-serving statements contextually seems questionable.... Admitting the disserving parts of the declaration, and excluding the self-serving parts ... seems the most realistic method of adjusting admissibility to trustworthiness, where the serving and disserving parts can be severed." *See* C. McCORMICK, LAW OF EVIDENCE § 256, at 551–53 (1954).

Without deciding exactly how much weight to give the Notes in this particular situation, we conclude that the policy expressed in the statutory text points clearly enough in one direction that it outweighs whatever force the Notes may have. And though JUSTICE KENNEDY believes that the text can fairly be read as expressing a policy of admitting collateral statements, for the reasons given above we disagree.

B

We also do not share JUSTICE KENNEDY'S fears that our reading of the Rule "eviscerates the against penal interest exception" or makes it lack "meaningful effect." There are many circumstances in which Rule 804(b)(3) does allow the admission of statements that inculpate a criminal defendant....

For instance, ... by showing that the declarant knew something, a self-inculpatory statement can in some situations help the jury infer that his confederates knew it as well. And when seen with other evidence, an accomplice's self-inculpatory statement can inculpate the defendant directly: "I was robbing the bank on Friday morning," coupled with someone's testimony that the declarant and the defendant drove off together Friday morning, is evidence that the defendant also participated in the robbery.

Moreover, whether a statement is self-inculpatory or not can only be determined by viewing it in context. Even statements that are on their face neutral may actually be against the declarant's interest. "I hid the gun in Joe's apartment" may not be a confession of a crime; but if it is likely to help the police find the murder weapon, then it is certainly self-inculpatory. "Sam and I went to Joe's house" might be against the declarant's interest if a reasonable person in the declarant's shoes would realize that being linked to Joe and Sam would implicate the declarant in Joe and Sam's conspiracy. And other statements that give the police significant details about the crime may also, depending on the situation, be against the declarant's interest. The question under Rule 804(b)(3) is always whether the statement was sufficiently against the declarant's penal interest "that a reasonable person in the declarant's position would not have made the statement unless believing it to be true," and this question can only be answered in light of all the surrounding circumstances.

C*

In this case, however, we cannot conclude that all that Harris said was properly admitted. Some of Harris' confession would clearly have been [against interest] under Rule 804(b)(3); for instance, when he said he knew there was cocaine in the suitcase, he essentially forfeited his only possible defense to a charge of cocaine possession, lack of knowledge. But other parts of his confession, especially the parts that implicated Williamson, did little to subject Harris himself to criminal liability. A reasonable person in Harris' position might even think that implicating someone else would decrease his practical exposure to criminal liability, at least so far as sentencing goes. Small fish in a big conspiracy often get shorter sentences than people who are running the whole show, especially if the small fish are willing to help the authorities catch the big ones.

Nothing in the record shows that the District Court or the Court of Appeals inquired whether each of the statements in Harris' confession was truly self-inculpatory. As we explained above, this can be a fact-intensive inquiry, which would require careful examination of all the circumstances surrounding the criminal activity involved; we therefore remand to the Court of Appeals to conduct this inquiry in the first instance.

In light of this disposition, we need not address Williamson's claim that that the statements were also made inadmissible by the Confrontation Clause.... We also need not decide whether, as some Courts of Appeals have held, the second sentence of Rule 804(b)(3)—"A statement tending to expose the declarant to criminal liability *and offered to exculpate the accused* is not admissible unless corroborating circumstances clearly indicate the trustworthiness of the statement" (emphasis added)—also requires that statements inculpating the accused be supported by corrobo-

* [Only Justice Scalia joined in this part of Justice O'Connor's opinion.—GF]

rating circumstances.* The judgment of the Court of Appeals is vacated, and the case is remanded for further proceedings consistent with this opinion.

So ordered.

■ JUSTICE SCALIA, concurring. . . .

■ JUSTICE GINSBURG, with whom JUSTICE BLACKMUN, JUSTICE STEVENS, and JUSTICE SOUTER join, concurring in part and concurring in the judgment. . . .

■ JUSTICE KENNEDY, with whom THE CHIEF JUSTICE and JUSTICE THOMAS join, concurring in the judgment. . . .

Problem 7.25

Alice's Restaurant

Late on a February night, the Partridge Restaurant was gutted by fire. The restaurant, owned and run by Alice Ramsey, leased space in a building owned by Cityscape Properties.

After tracing the license plate number of a car seen fleeing from the scene, a police arson investigator drove to the home of Michael Akker. Akker made the following statement:

> "I owed Alice Ramsey a few favors, and she asked me to torch the Partridge for her so she could collect on the insurance. I drove to the restaurant with a can of gas the way she told me. But I lost my nerve when I remembered that a family with two little kids lived upstairs from the restaurant. So I just poured a little bit of gas into the window. Then I lit it and took off."

Cityscape Properties sued Alice Ramsey for willful destruction of property. Under the relevant law, Ramsey would be liable if she incited or participated in the burning of the building.

* [In 2010 Rule 804(b)(3) was amended to demand that the government as well as the defendant supply corroboration of third-party statements against penal interest when offered in a criminal case. This is the sort of statement at issue in *Williamson*. The former version of the rule had required special corroboration when a defendant offered a third person's statement against interest to exculpate the defendant. The rule did not, however, demand similar corroboration when the government offered a third person's—say, an accomplice's—statement against interest to *inculpate* the defendant. Explaining the amendment that ended this disparity, the advisory committee wrote, "A unitary approach to declarations against penal interest assures both the prosecution and the accused that the rule will not be abused and that only reliable hearsay statements will be admitted under the exception." (ACN to 2010 Amendment to FRE 804(b)(3), RB 278.)—GF]

At trial, Akker refused to testify, citing his Fifth Amendment privilege against self-incrimination. Cityscape's counsel called the investigator as a witness. When the lawyer asked the investigator what Akker had told her, Ramsey's counsel objected. After a conference with the lawyers out of the hearing of the jury—and despite the defendant's continuing objection—the judge permitted the investigator to testify as follows:

> "After Mr. Akker waived his *Miranda* rights and agreed to speak with me, he said: 'I drove to the restaurant with a can of gas. But I lost my nerve when I remembered that a family with two little kids lived upstairs from the restaurant. So I just poured a little bit of gas into the window. Then I lit it and took off.' "

Assume the plaintiff presented independent evidence linking Ramsey and Akker. If Ramsey is found liable after trial and appeals, how should the reviewing court rule on her claim that Akker's statement was inadmissible hearsay?

Problem 7.26

Accomplices

Consider the facts of *United States v. Barone*, 114 F.3d 1284 (1st Cir.), *cert. denied*, 522 U.S. 1021 (1997):

> . . . Barone was charged [with] the November 5, 1982, robbery of credit union teller Lucy LoPriore of a bag of cash belonging to the credit union as she and security guard Kenneth McPhee walked from the First National Bank on Hanover Street to the credit union at the corner of Parmenter and Salem Streets in [Boston's] North End. According to witnesses, the robbery occurred between 10:00 and 10:30 a.m. and was perpetrated by two masked men. In the course of the robbery, McPhee was shot in the calf and in the neck. . . .
>
> [Walter] Jordan testified that Barone told him that he and [James] Limoli were responsible for the robbery and that Barone had shot the security guard in the neck. . . .
>
> [Elizabeth] DiNunzio testified that, on the morning of the credit union robbery, [her brother, Limoli, who was murdered before trial,] came to her house carrying a box and asked her for lemon juice, saying that if you wash your hands with lemon juice, "they can't tell that you shot a gun." According to DiNunzio, after the robbery was reported on the noontime news, Limoli admitted to her that he and Barone had committed the robbery; that he had shot

security guard McPhee in the foot; and that Barone had shot McPhee in the neck. . . .

Should the trial court have admitted DiNunzio's testimony over Barone's hearsay objection? For now, please ignore any Confrontation Clause concerns.

Problem 7.27

"Bucky Wasn't Involved."

Recall the facts of *United States v. Barrett*, 539 F.2d 244 (1st Cir. 1976), excerpted above at page 435. "Bucky" Barrett and several others were charged with stealing a stamp collection from a philatelic museum in March 1973. The government's evidence suggested that Barrett's accomplices included "Buzzy" Adams and Ben Tilley. Consider these additional facts, arising during the defense case:

> . . . [James] Melvin testified that in February 1974, he was at a card game on Bowdoin Street, in Dorchester, Massachusetts, with Ben Tilley. When Melvin was asked to recount a conversation which he had there with Tilley, the Government objected. Barrett made an offer of proof that Melvin would testify that Tilley had told Melvin "that he, Tilley, and Buzzy [Adams] were going to have some trouble from the people from California" with respect to the "stamp theft or matter" and that "[Melvin] asked him did he mean Bucky or Buzzy, *and then [Tilley] said, 'No, Bucky [Barrett] wasn't involved. It was Buzzy.'* " [Emphasis added.]

Barrett argued on appeal that the trial court erred in refusing to admit Melvin's proposed testimony and claimed that Tilley's statement was admissible as a statement against interest. Was he right? (Assume Tilley was unavailable to testify.)

---

3. DYING DECLARATIONS

Focus on
FRE 804(b)(2)

William Shakespeare

On Truth and Dying

Exactly when the hearsay rule emerged is a matter of scholarly debate. Wigmore traced the rule to the late seventeenth or early eighteenth century, while John Langbein dates its origins almost a century later. *Compare* 5 JOHN HENRY WIGMORE, A TREATISE ON THE ANGLO-AMERICAN SYSTEM OF EVIDENCE IN TRIALS AT COMMON LAW § 1364, at 9 (3d ed. 1940), *with* John H. Langbein, *Historical Foundations of the Law of Evidence: A View from the Ryder Sources*, 96 COLUM. L. REV. 1168, 1172, 1174–76, 1186–90 (1996).

Long before the hearsay rule took form, William Shakespeare offered rationales for one of its best-known exceptions. Shakespeare's plays often left few survivors. With so many chances to comment on death and dying, he managed to offer more than one reason to trust the words of the dying more than ordinary hearsay. Compare the justifications for the exception for dying declarations found in *Richard II* and *King John*:

Richard II

Act II, i, 1–8

JOHN OF GAUNT

O, but they say the tongues of dying men
Enforce attention like deep harmony.
Where words are scarce they are seldom spent in vain,
For they breathe truth that breathe their words in pain.

King John

Act V, iv, 10–61

MELUN

What in the world should make me now deceive,
Since I must lose the use of all deceit?
Why should I then be false, since it is true
That I must die here and live hence by truth?

Problem 7.28

Clyde Mattox

Consider the facts of *Mattox v. United States*, 146 U.S. 140, 141–42 (1892), recounting Mattox's trial for John Mullen's murder:

> . . . The attending physician, who was called a little after nine o'clock and remained with the wounded man until about one o'clock in the morning, and visited him again between eight and nine o'clock, testified that Mrs. Hatch, the mother of Clyde Mattox, was present at that visit; that he regarded Mullen's recovery as hopeless; that Mullen, being "perfectly conscious" and "in a normal condition as regards his mind," asked his opinion, and the doctor said to him: "The chances are all against you; I do not think there is any show for you at all." . . . Counsel for defendant, after a colloquy with the court, propounded the following question: "Did or did not John Mullen, in your presence and at that time, say in reply to a question of Mrs. Hatch, 'I know your son, Clyde Mattox, and he did not shoot me; I saw the parties who shot me and Clyde was not one of them.' " This question was objected to [by the prosecutor] as incompetent [and] the objection sustained. . . .

Was the trial court's ruling correct?

SHEPARD v. UNITED STATES

290 U.S. 96 (1933).

■ MR. JUSTICE CARDOZO delivered the opinion of the Court. The petitioner, Charles A. Shepard, a major in the medical corps of the United States army, has been convicted of the murder of his wife, Zenana Shepard, at Fort Riley, Kansas, a United States military reservation. The jury having qualified their verdict by adding thereto the words "without capital punishment," the defendant was sentenced to imprisonment for life. The judgment of the United States District Court has been affirmed by the Circuit Court of Appeals for the Tenth Circuit, one of the judges of that court dissenting. A writ of certiorari brings the case here.

The crime is charged to have been committed by poisoning the victim with bichloride of mercury. The defendant was in love with another woman, and wished to make her his wife. There is circumstantial evidence to sustain a finding by the jury that to win himself his freedom he turned to poison and murder. Even so, guilt was contested and conflicting inferences are possible. The defendant asks us to hold that by the acceptance of incompetent evidence the scales were weighted to his prejudice and in the end to his undoing.

The evidence complained of was offered by the Government in rebuttal when the trial was nearly over. On May 22, 1929, there was a conversation in the absence of the defendant between Mrs. Shepard, then ill in bed, and Clara Brown, her nurse. The patient asked the nurse to go to the closet in the defendant's room and bring a bottle of whisky that would be found upon a shelf. When the bottle was produced, she said that this was the liquor she had taken just before collapsing. She asked whether enough was left to make a test for the presence of poison, insisting that the smell and taste were strange. And then she added the words "Dr. Shepard has poisoned me."

The conversation was proved twice. After the first proof of it, the Government asked to strike it out, being doubtful of its competence, and this request was granted. A little later, however, the offer was renewed, the nurse having then testified to statements by Mrs. Shepard as to the prospect of recovery. "She said she was not going to get well; she was going to die." With the aid of this new evidence, the conversation already summarized was proved a second time. There was a timely challenge of the ruling.

She said, "Dr. Shepard has poisoned me." The admission of this declaration, if erroneous, was more than unsubstantial error. As to that the parties are agreed. The voice of the dead wife was heard in accusation of her husband, and the accusation was accepted as evidence of guilt. If the evidence was incompetent, the verdict may not stand.

1. Upon the hearing in this court the Government finds its main prop in the position that what was said by Mrs. Shepard was admissible as a dying declaration. This is manifestly the theory upon which it was offered and received. The prop, however, is a broken reed. To make out a dying declaration the declarant must have spoken without hope of recovery and in the shadow of impending death. The record furnishes no proof of that indispensable condition. So, indeed, it was ruled by all the judges of the court below, though the majority held the view that the testimony was competent for quite another purpose, which will be considered later on [at page 520].

We have said that the declarant was not shown to have spoken without hope of recovery and in the shadow of impending death. Her illness began on May 20. She was found in a state of collapse, delirious, in pain, the pupils of her eyes dilated, and the retina suffused with blood. The conversation with the nurse occurred two days later. At that time her mind had cleared up, and her speech was rational and orderly. There was as yet no thought by any of her physicians that she was dangerously ill, still less that her case was hopeless. To all seeming she had greatly improved, and was moving forward to recovery. There had been no diagnosis of poison as the cause of her distress. Not till about a week afterwards was there a relapse, accompanied by an infection of the mouth, renewed congestion of the eyes, and later hemorrhages of the bowels. Death followed on June 15.

Nothing in the condition of the patient on May 22 gives fair support to the conclusion that hope had then been lost. She may have thought she was going to die and have said so to her nurse, but this was consistent with hope, which could not have been put aside without more to quench it. Indeed, a fortnight later, she said to one of her physicians, though her condition was then grave, "You will get me well, won't you?" Fear or even belief that illness will end in death will not avail of itself to make a dying declaration. There must be "a settled hopeless expectation" (Willes, J. in Reg. v. Peel, 2 F. & F. 21, 22) that death is near at hand, and what is said must have been spoken in the hush of its impending presence. Despair of recovery may indeed be gathered from the circumstances if the facts support the inference. There is no unyielding ritual of words to be spoken by the dying. Despair may even be gathered though the period of survival outruns the bounds of expectation. What is decisive is the state of mind. Even so, the state of mind must be exhibited in the evidence, and not left to conjecture. The patient must have spoken with the consciousness of a swift and certain doom.

What was said by this patient was not spoken in that mood. There was no warning to her in the circumstances that her words would be repeated and accepted as those of a dying wife, charging murder to her husband, and charging it deliberately and solemnly as a fact within her knowledge. To the focus of that responsibility her mind was never brought. She spoke as one ill, giving voice to the beliefs and perhaps the conjectures of the moment. The liquor was to be tested, to see whether her beliefs were sound. She did not speak as one dying, announcing to the survivors a definitive conviction, a legacy of knowledge on which the world might act when she had gone.

The petitioner insists that the form of the declaration exhibits other defects that call for its exclusion, apart from the objection that death was not imminent and that hope was still alive. Homicide may not be imputed to a defendant on the basis of mere suspicions, though they are the suspicions of the dying. To let the declaration in, the inference must be permissible that there was knowledge or the opportunity for knowledge as to the acts that are declared. The argument is pressed upon us that knowledge and opportunity are excluded when the declaration in question is read in the setting of the circumstances. The form is not decisive, though it be that of a conclusion, a statement of the result with the antecedent steps omitted. "He murdered me," does not cease to be competent as a dying declaration because in the statement of the act there is also an appraisal of the crime. One does not hold the dying to the observance of all the niceties of speech to which conformity is exacted from a witness on the stand. What is decisive is something deeper and more fundamental than any difference of form. The declaration is kept out if the setting of the occasion satisfies the judge, or in reason ought to satisfy him, that the speaker is giving expression to suspicion or conjecture, and not to known facts. The difficulty is not so much in respect of the governing principle as in its application to varying and equivocal conditions. In this case, the ruling that there was a failure to make out the imminence of death and the abandonment of hope relieves us of the duty of determining whether it is a legitimate inference that there was the opportunity for knowledge. We leave that question open. . . .

[Excerpts from the balance of this opinion appear in a different context at page 520.]

Focus on
FRE 806

SHEPARD V. UNITED STATES: *Afterthoughts*

Toward the end of this excerpt from *Shepard,* after laying out a few fundamentals of the exception for dying declarations, Justice Cardozo took up a matter that applies generally to most hearsay exceptions—the issue of the declarant's competency.

Testifying witnesses of course must be competent. The most basic competency rule is that non-expert witnesses must have "personal knowledge" of the facts they relate. *See* FRE 602. In its note to Rule 803, the advisory committee writes, "In a hearsay situation, the declarant is, of course, a witness, and neither this rule nor Rule 804 disposes with the requirement of firsthand knowledge." (RB 219.) It certainly would be odd if a hearsay declarant, already burdened by the suspicions of unreliability that confront out-of-court speakers, were permitted to stray beyond perceived facts and speculate in a way in which testifying witnesses may not.

By the same principle, hearsay declarants must abide by the opinion evidence rules that govern lay witnesses. *See* FRE 701 and Chapter 9A below. Testifying witnesses, if not qualified as experts, must confine their testimony to facts they have observed and to opinions drawn from those facts without the benefit of specialized knowledge. The same constraints apply to lay declarants.

Justice Cardozo worried that Mrs. Shepard's accusation, "Dr. Shepard has poisoned me," violated both of these principles. "Homicide may not be imputed to a defendant on the basis of mere suspicions," he wrote, "though they are the suspicions of the dying." There had to be evidence that Mrs. Shepard had "knowledge or the opportunity for knowledge as to the acts that are declared." Justice Cardozo seemed to think that Mrs. Shepard, in accusing her husband, was "giving voice to the beliefs and perhaps the conjectures of the moment."

Now we see the significance of the Eighth Circuit's ruling in *Mahlandt* (excerpted earlier at page 415). Kenneth Poos's conclusion that

"Sophie bit a child" was arguably no better informed than Mrs. Shepard's conclusion that "Dr. Shepard has poisoned me." Yet the court deemed his statement admissible against both him and the research institute that employed him. The distinction is that *Mahlandt* concerned statements of a party-opponent. And under the this-is-war rationale of Rule 801(d)(2), we all must live with our words—and with those of our agents and accomplices—even if those words are poorly informed or conjectural. As the advisory committee notes, party admissions have "enjoyed [freedom] from ... the restrictive influences of the opinion rule and the rule requiring firsthand knowledge." (RB 206.)

There is one way, however, in which Mrs. Shepard, Mr. Poos, and testifying witnesses are all alike. Rule 806 opens the credibility of each of them to attack (or support). The rule permits litigants to attack a hearsay declarant's credibility with most of the techniques available against testifying witnesses. These include proof of bias; contradiction by inconsistent statements; contradiction by other evidence; and evidence of untruthful character, whether in the form of opinion or reputation under Rule 608(a) or past convictions under Rule 609. One form of impeachment that is probably not available is evidence of the declarant's specific acts suggesting untruthful character, admissible on cross-examination of a testifying witness under Rule 608(b)(1). Those hearsay declarants who don't testify at trial can't be cross-examined, and Rule 608(b) explicitly bars extrinsic evidence of specific acts showing untruthful character.

By its terms Rule 806 extends to statements of spokespersons, agents, and coconspirators admitted under Rule 801(d)(2)(C), (D), or (E). And it applies to hearsay admitted under Rule 803 or 804. Only when a party's own statement or adoption comes in against her under Rule 801(d)(2)(A) or (B) and when a testifying witness's past words are admitted under Rule 801(d)(1) is there no provision for an attack on the declarant's credibility. With regard to Rules 801(d)(2)(A) and (B), Rule 806 apparently contemplates that parties can attack their own credibility by taking the witness stand. And with regard to Rule 801(d)(1), parties can attack the credibility of testifying witnesses in the normal fashion.

Bryan A. Liang

Shortcuts to "Truth": The Legal Mythology of Dying Declarations

35 AM. CRIM. L. REV. 229, 237–43 (1998)

... [H]ow does the scientific data inform the question of the reliability of dying declarations? ...

Epidemiologically, in the United States, penetrating trauma, such as [that] induced by gunshots and knives, is involved in greater than 80% of all homicides.... The primary cause of death when patients are injured by penetrating trauma is uncontrolled hemorrhage.... [U]ncontrolled hemorrhage results in a concomitant interruption of oxygen flow to neural tissues [and] will quickly lead to hypoxic or anoxic insult to the victim's brain....

One area that has been studied is the effect on cognition of experimentally induced hypoxia through acute simulated changes in altitude. In this context, there is overwhelming evidence that hypoxic changes significantly and negatively affect cognition. First, for healthy males aged twenty-three to thirty-one at simulated high altitudes ... and absent any other stresses ..., "mental functions ... degraded, particularly global functions [such as] ... intelligence, reasoning, and short-term memory." Others have reported that similarly induced hypoxia produces significant effects upon learning, vigilance, psychomotricity, and intellectual abilities....

In addition, hypoxic and anoxic states due to impaired blood flow or trauma can result in delirium.... Traditional features of delirium include significant global disorders of the patient's cognitive functions.... "Delusions, usually persecutory, are often, but not invariably, present.... *Memory* is impaired in all its key aspects." ... [A]n extremely wide range of misperceptions of reality and *de novo* hallucinatory perceptions, including mistaken identity, can occur when an individual is in a state of delirium secondary to hypoxia....

Answering Liang: Rejecting a homicide defendant's arguments challenging evidence of a victim's dying declaration, the Wisconsin Supreme Court recently wrote:

> The fairest way to resolve the tension between the State's interest in presenting a dying declaration and a defendant's concerns about its potential unreliability is not to prohibit such evidence, but to continue to freely permit, as the law does, the aggressive impeachment of a dying declaration on any grounds that may be relevant in a particular case. In other words, if there is evidence ... that the declarant was cognitively impaired and incapable of perceiving events accurately, introduce it. Such facts may, in particular cases, justifiably undermine the reliability of a dying declaration. The reliability of evidence is an issue for the trier of fact, and the assertion that some dying declarations may be unreliable cannot justify the per se exclusion of such potentially valuable evidence.

State v. Beauchamp, 333 Wis. 2d 1, 9–10, *cert. denied*, 132 S. Ct. 814 (2011).

4. Forfeiture by Wrongdoing

Focus on FRE 804(b)(6)

United States v. Gray

405 F.3d 227 (4th Cir.), *cert. denied*, 546 U.S. 912 (2005).

■ Shedd, Circuit Judge. A grand jury indicted Josephine Gray on five counts of mail fraud and three counts of wire fraud relating to her receipt of insurance proceeds following the deaths of her second husband and a former paramour. Gray was convicted on all counts, and the district court sentenced her to 40 years' imprisonment.... Gray now challenges her conviction, arguing that ... the district court improperly admitted ... hearsay evidence against Gray....

I.

Wilma Jean Wilson met Gray in the late summer of 2000, and the two became friends.... Wilson sometimes visited Gray's house. During one of those visits, ... [i]n an emotionless, matter-of-fact manner, Gray then told Wilson that "she had killed both her husbands and another gentleman."

Gray told Wilson that she had killed her first husband, Norman Stribbling, because she was tired of being abused by him. According to Wilson, "she told me that they had gone out for a ride and that she had shot him.... [I]t was set up to look like it was a robbery." Gray then confessed to Wilson that she had also killed her second husband, William "Robert" Gray. Although Gray said she was alone with Stribbling when she killed him, "she had help" killing Robert Gray ... from Clarence Goode, Gray's cousin and boyfriend. Gray explained to Wilson that Goode "had tried to blackmail her," demanding money in exchange for his silence about the murder of Robert Gray, so "she had to get rid of him too." ...

Gray's first husband, Stribbling, maintained a life insurance policy through John Hancock Mutual Life Insurance Company and named Gray as the beneficiary.... Shortly after Stribbling's death [in March 1974], Gray made a claim for insurance benefits and later received a check in the amount of $16,000....

Gray had been having an affair with Robert Gray while she was still married to Stribbling. In August 1975, the couple bought a house in Gaithersburg, Maryland, ... and three months later they married. Robert Gray maintained an insurance policy through Minnesota Mutual Life Insurance Company that provided for payment of the mortgage on the Grays' house in Gaithersburg in the event of his death, with any excess going to his spouse....

Robert Gray left the Gaithersburg house in August 1990, telling family members that his wife was trying to kill him and that she was having an affair with Goode, who had been living with the Grays. So convinced was Robert Gray that his wife intended him harm that he removed her as his beneficiary under two other insurance policies. He asked relatives and friends for help in avoiding a possible assault by Gray or Goode.

In late August 1990, Robert Gray brought criminal charges against Gray, alleging that Gray had assaulted him at his workplace by swinging at him with a club and lunging at him with a knife. Robert Gray also brought charges against Goode, alleging that Goode had threatened him with a 9–millimeter handgun. Robert Gray appeared in court on October 5, 1990, but the case against Gray and Goode was continued. Later that same day, Robert Gray was driving home when ... [Josephine Gray] drove her car alongside her husband's car. As Robert Gray turned to look toward his wife, Goode sat up (from a reclined position) in the front passenger seat and pointed a gun at him. Robert Gray reported this incident to police, and a warrant was issued for the arrests of Gray and Goode. One week before the November 16, 1990, trial date, Robert Gray was discovered dead in his new apartment, shot once in the chest and once in the neck with a .45–caliber handgun....

As a result of Robert Gray's death, Minnesota Mutual paid approximately $51,625 to Perpetual Savings Bank—the named beneficiary—to cover the mortgage on the Gaithersburg house. Once the mortgage was satisfied, Gray sold the house for a significant profit....

Gray told Wilson that she "had to get rid of" Goode because he was blackmailing her.... On June 21, 1996, Baltimore City Police officers found Goode's body in the trunk of his car.... Goode had told his sister that he was going to visit Gray at her house, where police later found ... a large blood stain on the floor of the garage.

Goode maintained a life insurance policy through Interstate Assurance Company and named Gray as his beneficiary.... Interstate Assurance advised Goode by letter in June 1996 that he had a 60–day grace period before the policy would be cancelled for non-payment. Goode's mail was sent to Gray's address, however, and Gray killed Goode shortly after learning that the policy might be cancelled. Gray filed a claim for benefits in September 1996, but Interstate Assurance refused to pay because it suspected that Gray was involved in Goode's death.... Because Gray's guilt could not be proved at that time, the parties settled the interpleader action and Interstate Assurance paid Gray $99,990 in benefits under Goode's policy....

Shortly after Goode's murder, Gray ... [made] inquiries about obtaining life insurance on [Andre Savoy, her new boyfriend]....

II.

... Gray seeks a new trial based upon the district court's admission of testimony concerning ... several out-of-court statements made by Robert Gray during the three months preceding his murder:

Robert Gray's criminal complaint alleging that Goode had tossed a 9–millimeter handgun on the table at his house to provoke an argument;

Robert Gray's criminal complaint alleging that Gray had tried to stab him with a knife and attack him with a club;

Statements made by Robert Gray to ... a police detective, claiming that Gray and Goode had assaulted him in October 1990; and

Statements made by Robert Gray to Rodney Gray claiming that Goode had pulled a gun on him outside a restaurant in September or October 1990.

... [T]he doctrine of forfeiture by wrongdoing allows such statements to be admitted where the defendant's own misconduct rendered the declarant unavailable as a witness at trial. The Supreme Court applied this doctrine in Reynolds v. United States, 98 U.S. 145, 158 (1878), stating that "... if a witness is absent by [the accused's] own wrongful procurement, he cannot complain if competent evidence is admitted to supply the place of that which he has kept away." By 1996, every circuit to address the issue had recognized this doctrine.

Fed. R. Evid. 804(b)(6), which took effect in 1997, codifies the common-law doctrine of forfeiture by wrongdoing as an exception to the general rule barring admission of hearsay evidence.... In order to apply the forfeiture-by-wrongdoing exception, the district court must find, by the preponderance of the evidence, that (1) the defendant engaged or acquiesced in wrongdoing (2) that was intended to render the declarant unavailable as a witness and (3) that did, in fact, render the declarant unavailable as a witness. The district court need not hold an independent evidentiary hearing if the requisite findings may be made based upon evidence presented in the course of the trial.

Gray contends that Rule 804(b)(6) should not apply in this case because she did not intend to procure Robert Gray's unavailability as a witness at *this* trial. "Because the Federal Rules of Evidence are a legislative enactment, we turn to the traditional tools of statutory construction in order to construe their provisions. We begin with the language itself." Beech Aircraft Corp. v. Rainey, 488 U.S. 153, 163 (1988). The text of Rule 804(b)(6) requires only that the defendant intend to render the declarant unavailable "as a witness." The text does not require that the declarant would otherwise be a witness at any *particular* trial, nor does it limit the subject matter of admissible statements to events distinct from the events at issue in the trial in which the statements are offered. Thus, we conclude that Rule 804(b)(6) applies *whenever* the defendant's wrongdoing was intended to, and did, render the declarant unavailable as a witness against the defendant, without regard to the nature of the charges at the trial in which the declarant's statements are offered. *Accord* C. MUELLER & L. KIRKPATRICK, FEDERAL EVIDENCE § 507.1, at 268 (2d ed. Supp. 2004) ("It seems that there is no limit on the subject matter of statements that can be admitted under this exception, which means that statements in which the declarant implicates a defendant in a plot to kill the declarant himself can fit the exception.").

Our interpretation of Rule 804(b)(6) advances the clear purpose of the forfeiture-by-wrongdoing exception. The advisory committee noted its specific goal to implement a "prophylactic rule to deal with abhorrent behavior which strikes at the heart of the system of justice itself." [RB 281.] More generally, federal courts have recognized that the forfeiture-by-wrongdoing exception is necessary to prevent wrongdoers from profiting by their misconduct. *See Reynolds*, 98 U.S. at 158–59.

Federal courts have sought to effect the purpose of the forfeiture-by-wrongdoing exception by construing broadly the elements required for its application. *See, e.g.*, United States v. Dhinsa, 243 F.3d 635, 652 (2d Cir.), *cert. denied*, 534 U.S. 897 (2001) (noting that the Rule may apply where the declarant was only a potential witness, *i.e.*, "there was no ongoing proceeding in which the declarant was scheduled to testify"); United States v. Cherry, 217 F.3d 811, 820 (10th Cir. 2000) (holding that the declarant's statements may be admitted against a person who participated in a conspiracy to silence the declarant even if that person did not himself engage in witness intimidation or other wrongdoing); Steele v. Taylor, 684 F.2d 1193, 1201 (6th Cir. 1982), *cert. denied sub nom. Kilbane v. Marshall*, 460 U.S. 1053 (1983) (stating that "any significant interference" with the declarant's appearance as a witness, including the exercise of "persuasion and control" or an instruction to invoke the Fifth Amendment privilege, amounts to wrongdoing that forfeits the defendant's right to confront the declarant). Although the Rule requires that the wrongdoing was *intended* to render the declarant unavailable as a witness, we have held that a defendant need only intend "in part" to procure the declarant's unavailability. United States v. Johnson, 219 F.3d 349, 356 (4th Cir.), *cert. denied*, 531 U.S. 1024 (2000).

Like these applications of the forfeiture-by-wrongdoing exception, our interpretation of Rule 804(b)(6) ensures that a defendant will not be permitted to avoid the evidentiary impact of statements made by his victim, whether or not he suspected that the victim would be a witness at the trial in which the evidence is offered against him. A defendant who wrongfully and intentionally renders a declarant unavailable as a witness in any proceeding forfeits the right to exclude, on hearsay grounds, the declarant's statements at that proceeding and any subsequent proceeding.[9]

Having rejected Gray's interpretation of Rule 804(b)(6), we need only determine whether the district court properly applied the Rule in admitting Robert Gray's out-of-court statements. Those statements were admissible only if the district court properly found, by a preponderance of the evidence, that (1) Gray engaged in some wrongdoing (2) that was intended to procure Robert Gray's unavailability as a witness and (3) that did, in fact, procure his unavailability as a witness. The district court in this case found that Robert Gray "was killed prior to the court date on November 15 and 16, and after the defendant was well aware of his status as a witness, justif[ying] the inference that . . . the killing was motivated . . . to prevent [Robert Gray] from being available . . . at court proceedings." These findings are supported by the evidence and are sufficient to warrant application of . . . Rule 804(b)(6). Accordingly, the district court did not abuse its discretion in admitting testimony concerning out-of-court statements made by Robert Gray. . . .

Rule 804(b)(6): Forfeiture by Wrongdoing

Public Comments

[In the course of vetting proposed Rule 804(b)(6) before its enactment in 1997, the Advisory Committee reviewed the following comments submitted by practitioners and academics. Note that the original title of the proposed rule was "Waiver by wrongdoing."—GF]

Robert F. Wise, Jr., Esq., on behalf of the Commercial and Federal Litigation Section of the New York State Bar Association, . . . states that the proposed amendment raises "two potential concerns." First, a higher clear and convincing standard would be more appropriate than the preponderance of the evidence standard because a penalty or punishment is at stake and because the consequences of admission may be severe. . . . Second, he finds that the words "wrongdoing" and "acquiesced" are somewhat nebulous and are likely to engender dispute. He asks whether the rule would apply to a corporation in civil litigation that refused to produce its employees in a foreign jurisdiction? . . .

9. We emphasize that the intent requirement in Rule 804(b)(6) continues to limit application of the forfeiture-by-wrongdoing exception to those cases in which the defendant intended, at least in part, to render the declarant unavailable as a witness against him. Absent such intent, Rule 804(b)(6) has no application.

Professor Myrna S. Raeder of Southwestern University School of Law, on behalf of ten professors of evidence and individuals interested in evidentiary policy, . . . made a number of suggestions. "Forfeiture" should be substituted for "waiver" because the concept of knowing waiver in this context is a fiction. The rule should be rewritten so that it would apply only when the defendant is aware that the victim is likely to be a witness in a proceeding. If the defendant is accused of murdering an individual, and there is no connection to witness tampering, a traditional hearsay exception should be required so as to ensure trustworthy evidence and to discourage persons from manufacturing inculpatory statements from victims in murder cases. . . .

William J. Genego and Peter Goldberger, co-chairs of the National Association of Criminal Defense Lawyers' Committee on Procedure, . . . write that "NACDL strongly opposes the addition of proposed subparagraph (b)(6)." "A rule necessarily allowing the admissibility of untrustworthy, immaterial, inferior-quality, and unjust evidence as a sanction for supposed misconduct is strong medicine, which should be more carefully formulated." . . . NACDL further objects to "a party who" instead of "a party that," which would more clearly be potentially applicable to the government. NACDL suggests that a more appropriate remedy is to admit evidence of the wrongdoing as tending to show "consciousness of guilt" by the defendant or "consciousness of doubt" by the government, accompanied by an "adverse inference" charge to the jury.

Professor Richard D. Friedman of the University of Michigan Law School . . . would apply the rule even when the conduct that rendered a potential witness unable to testify is the same conduct with which the defendant is charged, as in a child abuse case if the defendant's conduct prevented the victim from testifying fully. . . .

Report on Rule 804(b)(6) issued after public comment period: The title of the rule was changed to "Forfeiture by wrongdoing." The word "who" in line 33 was changed to "that" to indicate that the rule is potentially applicable against the government. Two sentences were added to the first paragraph of the committee note to clarify that the wrongdoing need not be criminal in nature, and to indicate the rule's potential applicability to the government. The word "forfeiture" was substituted for "waiver" in the note.

F. EXCEPTIONS UNDER RULE 803: DECLARANT'S AVAILABILITY IMMATERIAL

The rule writers apparently saw a clear distinction between those hearsay exceptions gathered under Rule 804 and those defined by Rule

803. Rule 804 allows hearsay only when the declarant cannot meaningfully testify and other conditions are met. Rule 803 operates "regardless of whether the declarant is available as a witness." What rationale justifies the distinction?

The Advisory Committee's Notes to the two rules supply some clues. In introducing Rule 804(b), the committee acknowledges that hearsay embraced by that rule "admittedly is not equal in quality to testimony of the declarant on the stand." Despite its inferiority to live testimony, such hearsay is admissible when the alternative is to do without the evidence altogether: "The rule expresses preferences: testimony given on the stand in person is preferred over hearsay, and hearsay, if of the specified quality, is preferred over complete loss of the evidence of the declarant." (RB 270.)

In contrast, the committee suggests that hearsay admitted under Rule 803 sometimes is *better* than the declarant's live testimony. Rule 803 "proceeds upon the theory that under appropriate circumstances a hearsay statement may possess circumstantial guarantees of trustworthiness sufficient to justify nonproduction of the declarant ... *even though he may be available*." (RB 219, emphasis added.)

As you work through the various exceptions that fall under Rule 803, consider critically the committee's judgment that such hearsay is so good it makes live testimony superfluous. In the case of business and public records, addressed by Rules 803(6) and 803(8), you may be readily convinced. The extreme difficulty of assembling in court every employee who took part in a routine transaction—and the unlikelihood that any employee would remember one transaction among thousands or had reason to falsify the records of that transaction—often amply justify admission of properly kept business or public records in place of live testimony. Likewise, in the case of recorded recollections admissible under Rule 803(5), it is easy to see how a forgetful witness's memorandum of something she once knew could be superior to her present hazy memory.

But we don't begin with these manifestly sensible exceptions to the hearsay rule. Instead we begin, as does Rule 803, with four categories of hearsay that stake far more contestable claims to superiority over live testimony. Examine closely the "circumstantial guarantees of trustworthiness" that justify the exceptions for present sense impressions, excited utterances, statements of then-existing condition, and statements for medical diagnosis or treatment. How persuaded are you that the theories behind these rules warrant the rule writers' readiness to give litigants the option to leave declarants at home?

---

1. Present Sense Impressions and Excited Utterances

Focus on
FRE 803(1) & (2)

Problem 7.29

Dog Mauling I

Dog–Mauling Judge OKs Testimony

Jaxon Van Derbeken

SAN FRANCISCO CHRONICLE, Jan. 30, 2002, at A13

The judge in the San Francisco dog-mauling trial gave prosecutors a major victory yesterday, ruling that Diane Whipple's domestic partner [Sharon Smith] can tell a jury about a warning the frightened woman [Whipple] delivered to one of the defendants the month before she was killed.

Whipple was bitten on the hand by one of Robert Noel's 120–pound Presa Canarios and bluntly told him to keep the animal under control, Sharon Smith testified yesterday. A few weeks later, one of the dogs mauled Whipple to death in her Pacific Heights apartment building.

The prosecution argued that the incident Smith described had put Noel and his wife, Marjorie Knoller, on notice of their dogs' dangerous behavior before the fatal attack [on] Jan. 26, 2001. The defense questioned whether the first incident had really happened.

Smith said she had learned of the incident in a lunchtime phone call in which an agitated Whipple exclaimed, "That dog just bit me!"

Whipple, said Smith, told her she had scolded Noel: "You need to control your dog!" . . .

When Smith came home, Whipple provided more details, saying . . . , "As I was walking by, the dog lunged at me. I put my hand out, and the dog bit me." . . .

Whipple had deep red marks on her hand and said she had been lucky to escape more serious injury, Smith said. She quoted Whipple as saying, "Thank God I had my sports watch on." . . .

Was the judge correct in admitting all of Smith's proposed testimony? Assume the Federal Rules of Evidence controlled the case.

Problem 7.30

Dog Mauling II

On January 26, 2001, an elderly woman who lived across the hall from Diane Whipple made the following 911 call to police:

Esther Birkmaier, Whipple's Neighbor: Yes, I'm just a wreck. Please send police to 2398 Pacific Avenue, corner of Fillmore. We have two dogs rampaging out in the hall up on the sixth floor, and I think they have their—you know even their owner cannot control them. They are huge.

911 Operator: OK, the owner knows that the dogs are in the hallway?

Birkmaier: Oh, I think they're attacking the owner too, I reckon. She's screaming right now, and I don't dare open the door because these dogs are huge.

911 Operator: What kind of dogs are they?

Birkmaier: Well I—you know I don't know. They're bigger than a police dog. Please hurry, I hear her screaming and I don't dare open the door. These dogs are ferocious.

911 Operator: Yes, ma'am. Don't open your door. We'll get somebody right over there, OK?

CNN DAYBREAK, Apr. 3, 2002 (Transcript #040310 CN.V73).

Defendant Marjorie Knoller, who had charge of the dogs at the time they killed Whipple, offered this tape in evidence at her trial on murder and manslaughter charges resulting from the incident. Knoller claimed the tape supported her account that she struggled in vain to gain control of the dogs as they attacked Whipple. The prosecutor objected on hearsay grounds to the tape's admission. How should the court have ruled?

Problem 7.31

Recantation

Consider the facts of *Impson v. State*, 721 N.E.2d 1275 (Ind. Ct. App. 2000):

> On July 4, 1998, Impson and his wife, Lori, engaged in a heated argument when Lori canceled a family outing. The argument ended with Impson leaving and Lori calling the police.
>
> When police officers arrived at the family residence, Lori was crying and upset. She told the officers that Impson had knocked her down and had pushed her head into a wall. Lori rubbed her head as she related the story of Impson's violence toward her. Officer Boyd Martin did not see any marks on Lori's head, but he did observe that her knees were scraped. When asked about her knees, Lori stated that they had been scraped when she hit the floor after Impson knocked her down. . . .
>
> [At Impson's trial, the] prosecutor called Lori as a witness, and although she did acknowledge that she had argued with Impson, she denied that he hit her or pushed her head into the wall. . . .
>
> During the State's case-in-chief, Officer Martin testified that immediately after the battery occurred, Lori told him that Impson had knocked her down and rammed her head into the wall. . . .

Assume defense counsel objected to Officer Martin's testimony about Lori Impson's statements to him. Was the trial judge right to admit the evidence? Assume the Federal Rules of Evidence controlled the case.

Problem 7.32

"Joe Puleio"

Jacqueline LaMothe testified for the prosecution at Joseph Puleio's trial for a 1980 shooting death outside an Amesbury, Massachusetts, bar. The Massachusetts Supreme Judicial Court summarized her account:

> Jacqueline LaMothe, the bartender, testified that while in the bar she heard a shot and then a scream, and that then someone ran into the bar and told her to telephone for an ambulance. She testified that after making the telephone call she went outside and "asked who had shot the gun once, and nobody answered me." Over the defendant's objection, LaMothe testified that Bonnie Eaton then "yelled out" a response to her inquiry. The defendant again objected, and counsel approached the bench. Defense counsel stated that

he based his objection on the rule against hearsay. . . . The judge allowed the prosecutor to ask LaMothe, "What did Bonnie Eaton say?" LaMothe responded, "Joe Puleio."

Commonwealth v. Puleio, 394 Mass. 101, 104, 474 N.E.2d 1078 (1985). Was the trial judge right to admit LaMothe's response? Assume the Federal Rules of Evidence controlled the case—and for now, please ignore any Confrontation Clause concerns.

2. STATEMENTS OF THEN-EXISTING CONDITION

Focus on **FRE 803(3)**

MUTUAL LIFE INSURANCE CO. V. HILLMON

145 U.S. 285 (1892).

On July 13, 1880, Sallie E. Hillmon, a citizen of Kansas, brought an action against the Mutual Life Insurance Company, a corporation of New York, on a policy of insurance, dated December 10, 1878, on the life of her husband, John W. Hillmon, in the sum of $10,000, payable to her within sixty days after notice and proof of his death. On the same day the plaintiff brought two other actions, the one against the New York Life Insurance Company, a corporation of New York, on two similar policies of life insurance, dated respectively November 30, 1878, and December 10, 1878, for the sum of $5000 each; and the other against the Connecticut Mutual Life Insurance Company, a corporation of Connecticut, on a similar policy, dated March 4, 1879, for the sum of $5000.

In each case, the declaration alleged that Hillmon died on March 17, 1879, during the continuance of the policy, but that the defendant, though duly notified of the fact, had refused to pay the amount of the policy, or any part thereof; and the answer denied the death of Hillmon, and alleged that he, together with John H. Brown and divers other persons, on or before November 30, 1878, conspiring to defraud the defendant, procured the issue of all the policies, and afterwards, in March and April 1879, falsely pretended and represented that Hillmon was dead, and that a dead body which they had procured was his, whereas in reality he was alive and in hiding. . . .

On February 29, 1888, after two trials at which the jury had disagreed, the three cases came on for trial.... At the trial the plaintiff introduced evidence tending to show that on or about March 5, 1879, Hillmon and Brown left Wichita in the State of Kansas, and travelled together through Southern Kansas in search of a site for a cattle ranch; that on the night of March 18, while they were in camp at a place called Crooked Creek, Hillmon was killed by the accidental discharge of a gun; that Brown at once notified persons living in the neighborhood; and that the body was thereupon taken to a neighboring town, where, after an inquest, it was buried. The defendants introduced evidence tending to show that the body found in the camp at Crooked Creek on the night of March 18 was not the body of Hillmon, but was the body of one Frederick Adolph Walters. Upon the question whose body this was, there was much conflicting evidence, including photographs and descriptions of the corpse, and of the marks and scars upon it, and testimony to its likeness to Hillmon and to Walters.

The defendants introduced testimony that Walters left his home at Fort Madison in the State of Iowa in March 1878, and was afterwards in Kansas in 1878, and in January and February 1879; that during that time his family frequently received letters from him, the last of which was written from Wichita; and that he had not been heard from since March 1879. The defendants also offered the following evidence:

Elizabeth Rieffenach testified that she was a sister of Frederick Adolph Walters, and lived at Fort Madison; and thereupon ... the following proceedings took place:

> "Witness further testified that she had received a letter written from Wichita, Kansas, about the 4th or 5th day of March, 1879, by her brother Frederick Adolph; that the letter was dated at Wichita, and was in the handwriting of her brother; that she had searched for the letter, but could not find the same, it being lost; that she remembered and could state the contents of the letter.
>
> "Thereupon the defendants' counsel asked the question: 'State the contents of that letter.' To which the plaintiff objected, on the ground that the same is incompetent, irrelevant, and hearsay. The objection was sustained, and the defendants duly excepted. The following is the letter as stated by witness:
>
>> 'March 4th or 5th or 3d or 4th—I don't know—1879.
>>
>> 'Dear sister and all: I now in my usual style drop you a few lines to let you know that I expect to leave Wichita on or about March the 5th, with a certain Mr. Hillmon, a sheeptrader, for Colorado or parts unknown to me. I expect to see the country now. News are of no interest to you, as you are not acquainted here. I will close with compliments to all inquiring friends. Love to all.

'I am truly your brother,

FRED. ADOLPH WALTERS.' "

Alvina D. Kasten testified that she was twenty-one years of age and resided in Fort Madison; that she was engaged to be married to Frederick Adolph Walters; that she last saw him on March 24, 1878, at Fort Madison; that he left there at that time, and had not returned; that she corresponded regularly with him, and received a letter about every two weeks until March 3, 1879, which was the last time she received a letter from him; that this letter was dated at Wichita, March 1, 1879, and was addressed to her at Fort Madison, and the envelope was postmarked "Wichita, Kansas, March 2, 1879"; and that she had never heard from or seen him since that time.

The defendants put in evidence the envelope with the postmark and address; and thereupon offered to read the letter in evidence. The plaintiff objected to the reading of the letter, the court sustained the objection, and the defendants excepted.

This letter was dated "Wichita, March 1, 1879," was signed by Walters, and began as follows:

> "Dearest Alvina: Your kind and ever welcome letter was received yesterday afternoon about an hour before I left Emporia. I will stay here until the fore part of next week, and then will leave here to see a part of the country that I never expected to see when I left home, as I am going with a man by the name of Hillmon, who intends to start a sheep ranch, and as he promised me more wages than I could make at anything else I concluded to take it, for a while at least, until I strike something better. There is so many folks in this country that have got the Leadville fever, and if I could not of got the situation that I have now I would have went there myself; but as it is at present I get to see the best portion of Kansas, Indian Territory, Colorado, and Mexico. The route that we intend to take would cost a man to travel from $150 to $200, but it will not cost me a cent; besides, I get good wages. I will drop you a letter occasionally until I get settled down; then I want you to answer it."

. . . The court, after recapitulating some of the testimony introduced, instructed the jury as follows: "You have perceived from the very beginning of the trial that the conclusion to be reached must practically turn upon one question of fact, and all the large volume of evidence, with its graphic and varied details, has no actual significance, save as the facts established thereby may throw light upon and aid you in answering the question, Whose body was it that on the evening of March 18, 1879, lay dead by the camp-fire on Crooked Creek? The decision of that question decides the verdict you should render."

The jury ... returned verdicts for the plaintiff against the three defendants respectively for the amounts of their policies, and interest.... The defendants sued out four writs of error....

■ MR. JUSTICE GRAY, after stating the case as above, delivered the opinion of the court.... The matter chiefly contested at the trial was the death of John W. Hillmon, the insured; and that depended upon the question whether the body found at Crooked Creek on the night of March 18, 1879, was his body, or the body of one Walters....

The evidence that Walters was at Wichita on or before March 5, and had not been heard from since, together with the evidence to identify as his the body found at Crooked Creek on March 18, tended to show that he went from Wichita to Crooked Creek between those dates. Evidence that just before March 5 he had the intention of leaving Wichita with Hillmon would tend to corroborate the evidence already admitted, and to show that he went from Wichita to Crooked Creek with Hillmon. Letters from him to his family and his betrothed were the natural, if not the only attainable, evidence of his intention.

The position, taken at the bar, that the letters were competent evidence ... as memoranda made in the ordinary course of business, cannot be maintained, for they were clearly not such.

But upon another ground suggested they should have been admitted.... The existence of a particular intention in a certain person at a certain time being a material fact to be proved, evidence that he expressed that intention at that time is as direct evidence of the fact, as his own testimony that he then had that intention would be. After his death there can hardly be any other way of proving it; and while he is still alive, his own memory of his state of mind at a former time is no more likely to be clear and true than a bystander's recollection of what he then said, and is less trustworthy than letters written by him at the very time and under circumstances precluding a suspicion of misrepresentation.

The letters in question were competent, not as narratives of facts communicated to the writer by others, nor yet as proof that he actually went away from Wichita, but as evidence that, shortly before the time when other evidence tended to show that he went away, he had the intention of going, and of going with Hillmon, which made it more probable both that he did go and that he went with Hillmon, than if there had been no proof of such intention. In view of the mass of conflicting testimony introduced upon the question whether it was the body of Walters that was found in Hillmon's camp, this evidence might properly influence the jury in determining that question...

[W]e are of opinion that the two letters were competent evidence of the intention of Walters at the time of writing them ... and that for the exclusion of these letters, ... the verdicts must be set aside, and a new trial had....

Problem 7.33
Kidnapper

Consider these facts from *United States v. Pheaster*, 544 F.2d 353 (9th Cir. 1976), *cert. denied*, 429 U.S. 1099 (1977):

> At approximately 9:30 p.m. on June 1, 1974, Larry Adell left a group of his high school friends in a Palm Springs restaurant ... [and] walked into the parking lot of the restaurant.... Larry never returned to his friends in the restaurant that evening, and his family never saw him thereafter....
>
> Appellant [Angelo] Inciso argues that the district court erred in admitting hearsay testimony by two teenaged friends of Larry Adell concerning statements made by Larry on June 1, 1974, the day that he disappeared.... Francine Gomes, Larry's date on the evening that he disappeared, testified that when Larry picked her up that evening, he told her that he was going to meet Angelo at [the restaurant] at 9:30 p.m. to "pick up a pound of marijuana which Angelo had promised him for free".... Miss Gomes stated that it was approximately 9:15 p.m. when Larry went into the parking lot. Doug Sendejas, one of Larry's friends who was with him at [the restaurant] just prior to his disappearance, testified that Larry had made similar statements to him in the afternoon and early evening of June 1st regarding a meeting that evening with Angelo. Mr. Sendejas also testified that when Larry left the table ... to go into the parking lot, Larry stated that "he was going to meet Angelo and he'd be right back."

(a) Should the trial judge have admitted the testimony of Gomes and Sendejas, over the defendant's objection, to prove that Larry Adell did not disappear voluntarily?

(b) Should the court have admitted their testimony to prove that Angelo Inciso was among those who kidnapped Larry from the parking lot? Do the Supreme Court's *Hillmon* doctrine and Rule 803(3) answer this question the same way?

SHEPARD v. UNITED STATES

290 U.S. 96 (1933).

■ MR. JUSTICE CARDOZO delivered the opinion of the Court.

[For the facts and the first part of the Court's analysis, see the earlier excerpt of this case at page 499.]

2. We pass to the question whether the statements to the nurse, though incompetent as dying declarations, were admissible on other grounds.

The Circuit Court of Appeals determined that they were. Witnesses for the defendant had testified to declarations by Mrs. Shepard which suggested a mind bent upon suicide, or at any rate were thought by the defendant to carry that suggestion. More than once before her illness she had stated in the hearing of these witnesses that she had no wish to live, and had nothing to live for, and on one occasion she added that she expected some day to make an end to her life. This testimony opened the door, so it is argued, to declarations in rebuttal that she had been poisoned by her husband. They were admissible, in that view, not as evidence of the truth of what was said, but as betokening a state of mind inconsistent with the presence of suicidal intent.

(a) The testimony was neither offered nor received for the strained and narrow purpose now suggested as legitimate. It was offered and received as proof of a dying declaration.... The course of the trial makes this an inescapable conclusion. The Government withdrew the testimony when it was unaccompanied by proof that the declarant expected to die. Only when proof of her expectation had been supplied was the offer renewed and the testimony received again. For the reasons already considered, the proof was inadequate to show a consciousness of impending death and the abandonment of hope; but inadequate though it was, there can be no doubt of the purpose that it was understood to serve. There is no disguise of that purpose by counsel for the Government. They concede in all candor that Mrs. Shepard's accusation of her husband, when it was finally let in, was received upon the footing of a dying declaration, and not merely as indicative of the persistence of a will to live. Beyond question the jury considered it for the broader purpose, as the court intended that they should. A different situation would be here if we could fairly say in the light of the whole record that the purpose had been left at large, without identifying token. There would then be room for argument that demand should have been made for an explanatory ruling. Here the course of the trial put the defendant off his guard.

The testimony was received by the trial judge and offered by the Government with the plain understanding that it was to be used for an illegitimate purpose, gravely prejudicial. A trial becomes unfair if testimony thus accepted may be used in an appellate court as though admitted for a different purpose, unavowed and unsuspected. Such at all events is the result when the purpose in reserve is so obscure and artificial that it would be unlikely to occur to the minds of uninstructed jurors, and even if it did, would be swallowed up and lost in the one that was disclosed.

(b) Aside, however, from this objection, the accusatory declaration must have been rejected as evidence of a state of mind, though the purpose thus to limit it had been brought to light upon the trial. The defendant had tried to show by Mrs. Shepard's declarations to her friends that she had exhibited a weariness of life and a readiness to end it, the testimony giving plausibility to the hypothesis of suicide. By the proof of these declarations evincing an unhappy state of mind the defendant opened the door to the offer by the Government of declarations evincing a different state of mind, declarations consistent with the persistence of a will to live. The defendant would have no grievance if the testimony in rebuttal had been narrowed to that point. What the Government put in evidence, however, was something very different. It did not use the declarations by Mrs. Shepard to prove her present thoughts and feelings, or even her thoughts and feelings in times past. It used the declarations as proof of an act committed by some one else, as evidence that she was dying of poison given by her husband. This fact, if fact it was, the Government was free to prove, but not by hearsay declarations. It will not do to say that the jury might accept the declarations for any light that they cast upon the existence of a vital urge, and reject them to the extent that they charged the death to some one else. Discrimination so subtle is a feat beyond the compass of ordinary minds. The reverberating clang of those accusatory words would drown all weaker sounds. It is for ordinary minds, and not for psychoanalysts, that our rules of evidence are framed.... When the risk of confusion is so great as to upset the balance of advantage, the evidence goes out.

... There are times when a state of mind, if relevant, may be proved by contemporaneous declarations of feeling or intent.... So ... in suits upon insurance policies, declarations by an insured that he intends to go upon a journey with another, may be evidence of a state of mind lending probability to the conclusion that the purpose was fulfilled. Mutual Life Ins. Co. v. Hillmon, 145 U.S. 285, 295. The ruling in that case marks the high water line beyond which courts have been unwilling to go. It has developed a substantial body of criticism and commentary. *See* Maguire, *The* Hillmon *Case—Thirty-three Years After*, 38 HARV. L. REV. 709, 721, 727 (1925). Declarations of intention, casting light upon the future, have been sharply distinguished from declarations of memory, pointing backwards to the past. There would be an end, or nearly that, to the rule against hearsay if the distinction were ignored.

The testimony now questioned faced backward and not forward. This at least it did in its most obvious implications. What is even more important, it spoke to a past act, and more than that, to an act by some one not the speaker. Other tendency, if it had any, was a filament too fine to be disentangled by a jury.

The judgment should be reversed and the cause remanded to the District Court for further proceedings in accordance with this opinion.

Reversed.

MUTUAL LIFE INSURANCE CO. V. HILLMON: *Historical Postscript*

The Hillmon *Doctrine's Rationale*

They say hard cases make bad law. And Justice Cardozo hinted strongly in *Shepard* that *Hillmon* was bad, or at least questionable, law: "The ruling in that case marks the high water line beyond which courts have been unwilling to go." For good measure he added that the case "has developed a substantial body of criticism and commentary."

Cardozo's "high water line" separated a statement "of intention, casting light upon the future," which he thought properly admissible, from a "declaration[] of memory, pointing backwards to the past," which he thought should stay out. Several years earlier, John MacArthur Maguire had explained the difference between these two uses of state-of-mind evidence in terms of the traditional concerns about hearsay:

> When a declaration of intention is used as tending to prove the performance or non-performance of a future act, we take one and only one of the risks inherent in [hearsay]. This is the risk of misstatement.* No question of memory is involved, and a man is usually capable of perceiving accurately his own state of mind....
>
> But when we employ a declaration of intention to do or not to do act A as evidence of the existence or non-existence of B, a past fact, our ... risks of inaccuracy correspondingly increase.... [S]ince we are to infer the past fact from the implied recollection of the declarant, we front the dangers of faulty perception and imperfect memory....

John MacArthur Maguire, *The* Hillmon *Case—Thirty–Three Years After*, 38 HARV. L. REV. 709, 721–22 (1925).

* [In a footnote Maguire explained that "[t]he term 'misstatement' is meant to include expressions either intentionally false, or false because of the declarant's inability to express himself accurately." He was speaking of the risks we call today faulty narration and insincerity.—GF]

That is, when a declarant's statement of intention is offered to prove her future act, we need not worry about two of the four sources of unreliability that normally infect hearsay: Faulty memory poses no concern because the declarant is speaking of her *present* intention to do some *future* act. Nor is faulty perception a risk because she is not relating an external event but merely the contents of her mind. Freed of these two concerns, statements of future intention arguably are somewhat more reliable than run-of-the-mill hearsay—and perhaps should be excused from the hearsay bar.

But when we rely on a declarant's description of her present state of mind—her present memory of a past event, for example—to prove the existence of that event, we depend on all four of her testimonial capacities: perception, memory, narration, and sincerity. As Justice Cardozo wrote, "[t]here would be an end, or nearly that, to the rule against hearsay" if such hearsay were admitted under the *Hillmon* doctrine. Such concerns underlie Rule 803(3)'s exclusion in most circumstances of "a statement of memory or belief to prove the fact remembered or believed." (*See* ACN to FRE 803(3), RB 221.)

The difficulty is that *Hillmon* itself admitted just such hearsay. The Court wrote that Walters's letters to his sister and Alvina Kasten were "evidence that, shortly before the time when other evidence tended to show that he went away, he had the intention of going, and of going with Hillmon, which made it more probable both that he did go and that he went with Hillmon." But how could Walters have known he would go *with Hillmon* unless he and Hillmon had planned in some past conversation to leave together? For Walters's letters to serve as evidence of what *Hillmon* did in the future, we must rely on Walters's memory of a *past* agreement with Hillmon. *See* Douglas D. McFarland, *Dead Men Tell Tales: Thirty Times Three Years of the Judicial Process After* Hillmon, 30 VILL. L. REV. 1, 24 (1985). This hidden inference, based on memory of a past event, presumably prompted the House Judiciary Committee to conclude that Rule 803(3) should "render statements of intent by a declarant admissible only to prove *his* future conduct, not the future conduct of another person." (RB 222 (emphasis added).) Reconsider Problem 7.33 (*Kidnapper*), at page 519, in this light.

Suspicions of Murder

So while part of the *Hillmon* doctrine lives on in the guise of Rule 803(3), *Hillmon* itself may have been bad law. But as I said at the outset, *Hillmon* was a hard case. By the time the matter reached the Supreme Court in 1892, Frederick Adolph Walters had been missing for thirteen years. Maguire cast the case nicely:

> [Years had passed since Walters] wrote letters to his sister and his sweetheart . . . declaring his intention to leave on an early date "with a certain Mr. Hillmon, a sheep-trader, for Colorado or parts un-

> known to me." The rest is silence. None of the persons who would naturally have heard from Walters if alive ever had any later communication of his existence or whereabouts. "Parts unknown" evidently included eternity.

Maguire, 38 HARV. L. REV. at 709. True, no one had heard from Hillmon either. Despite claimed sightings, reliable evidence of either man's survival was wanting. But as lawyers for the insurance companies argued at trial, Hillmon's motives for staying away (if he yet lived) were obvious—by returning, he would have condemned himself as a murderer and a fraud. Walters had no similar cause to desert his family and future bride. *See* JOHN HENRY WIGMORE, THE PRINCIPLES OF JUDICIAL PROOF 884, 886 (1913) (reprinting summaries of arguments of counsel).

Even before an absence of thirteen years hardened suspicions of Walters's demise, the facts had seemed quite suspicious enough. Hillmon had bought a lot of life insurance—over half a million dollars' worth in today's money—costing more in annual premiums than he earned. He promptly died in the middle of nowhere, far from those who knew him well, in the company of his old friend Brown. Brown's claim that he carelessly shot his friend through the skull and Brown's identification of the corpse as Hillmon seemed doubtful. A reasonable observer of the evidence could have concluded that the dead man was two inches taller and a decade younger than Hillmon and had better teeth, more hair, bigger feet, a larger nose, and a different arrangement of scars, marks, and moles. Though the corpse wore Hillmon's clothes, its hat and shoes—items typically expected to fit well—went missing. *See id.* at 857, 860, 862–69. Then there's the sworn and notarized confession that Brown made six months after the death (and later recanted). He told how Hillmon had shot a stranger and beat a hasty exit, leaving Brown with instructions to claim the body was Hillmon's and the death an accident. *See id.* at 871–72.

Things looked grim for Mrs. Hillmon. Yet her cause was hardly hopeless. She was after all a young "widow" and a Kansan, bringing suit in a Kansas court against three East Coast insurance companies. One of the trial judges laid the situation before the jury:

> [T]here comes to every man the thought that on the one side there is a poor woman, upon the other side wealthy corporations. You see also the thought . . . that these are foreign corporations, living and residing in the distant States, contesting with a citizen of your own State, and appealing to jurors of this State, whose sympathy may naturally be with their fellow citizens, for justice.

Id. at 891. The judge's admonition to set aside such sympathies perhaps fell on jurors unheard.

At the crux of it all lay Walters's letters home, expressing his intent to leave "with a certain Mr. Hillmon . . . for . . . parts unknown." All parties saw their significance. At the second trial of the case, at which the letters were admitted, the insurance companies' counsel "bore down with considerable stress" upon them. Mrs. Hillmon's lawyer contended that without the letter from Walters to Alvina Kasten, "nothing remains of" the theory that the dead body was Walters. Even one of the trial judges, reserving this topic of his charge for last, said of the letter to Kasten: "Whatsoever it tells, and whatsoever significance might fairly come from it, it is something which it seems to me no human mind can resist." As the judge explained, we are far more likely to trust things said "before the trouble" than those said afterward, when motives to lie have ripened. And this letter "tells its story from the fingers and mind of Walters, sixteen or seventeen days before this body was found." *Id.* at 879, 882, 896. The reasoning was not lost on the various juries that heard the evidence. Walters's letters were admitted at each of the first two Hillmon trials, and both ended in sharply divided juries. Only at the third trial did a jury finally reach a verdict for Mrs. Hillmon—and that jury never learned of Walters's letters home. *See id.* at 856, 876.

Nor was the significance of the letters lost on the Supreme Court, which set aside the results of the third trial. Justice Gray declared that even if Walters were "alive, his own memory of his state of mind at a former time [would be] . . . less trustworthy than letters written by him at the very time and under circumstances precluding a suspicion of misrepresentation." And the circumstances surely precluded suspicion of misrepresentation. For if Walters contrived his letters to frame Hillmon, he must have walked wittingly to his own murder. It seems the Court could not bear to affirm a Western jury's verdict in favor of the Western widow of an apparent murderer. Facing a hard case, the justices therefore made bad law.

Insurance Fraud—Or Insurers' Fraud?

But what if the letters were fakes? What if Brown really shot Hillmon in a mishap? What if insurance company lawyers contrived Walters's letters to defeat the widow's rightful claim?

In a series of studies published since 2005, Professor Marianne Wesson has argued just that. She says the man in Hillmon's grave is Hillmon after all. *See, e.g.,* Marianne Wesson, *"Remarkable Stratagems and Conspiracies": How Unscrupulous Lawyers and Credulous Judges Created an Exception to the Hearsay Rule*, 76 FORDHAM L. REV. 1675 (2007); Marianne Wesson, *"Particular Intentions": The* Hillmon *Case and the Supreme Court*, 18 LAW & LIT. 343 (2006).* Wesson has unearthed a trove of neglected evidence—trial transcripts, photographs, and contemporary press accounts. She even unearthed Hillmon's corpse—or is it Walters's?—hoping

* Professor Wesson has gathered her findings and analysis between two covers: A DEATH AT CROOKED CREEK: THE CASE OF THE COWBOY, THE CIGARMAKER, AND THE LOVE LETTER (forthcoming New York University Press 2013).

to settle the score with modern forensics. *See* Wesson, 76 FORDHAM L. REV. at 1697.

Though the grave's scattered bones yielded no DNA, Wesson has turned up other reasons to wonder if Hillmon was the villain history made him. First is the startling guile of the insurance lawyers. Take James W. Green, who was County Attorney in Lawrence, Kansas, Sallie Hillmon's hometown. After the corpse arrived from Crooked Creek, an inquest concluded the body was not Hillmon. Green and his assistant examined witnesses at the inquest, apparently in their official capacity, though both men later represented the insurance companies at trial. *See* Wesson, 18 LAW & LIT. at 357, 363; WIGMORE, JUDICIAL PROOF 863. Charles S. Gleed, also on the insurers' trial team, authored a slanted report on the case for the Kansas Superintendent of Insurance. That report informed Wigmore's view of the matter, which I've quoted above, and shaded the view of almost every historian since. *See* Wesson, 76 FORDHAM L. REV. at 1702–03. And State Senator W. J. Buchan, while acting as counsel to Hillmon's friend John Brown, coaxed Brown's sworn confession of a murderous plot even as the insurers paid his fees. At trial the companies' lawyers cheekily called Buchan Brown's "own attorney." WIGMORE, JUDICIAL PROOF 873, 883.

Buchan's duplicity drains Brown's confession of much of its force. Wesson argues that Walters's letters were likewise the work of the lawyers. Here her case is harder to make. She admits that the letter to Walters's sweetheart, Alvina Kasten—the only letter physically produced at trial—bore his handwriting. Its postmark read March 2, 1879, more than two weeks before the death at Crooked Creek and long before the first lawyer entered the scene. *See* Wesson, 76 FORDHAM L. REV. at 1693. Kasten swore she received the letter the next day. And both Walters's sister, Elizabeth Rieffenach, and his brother swore they too received letters in early March telling of Frederick's planned departure with "a certain Mr. Hillmon." *See* Wesson, 76 FORDHAM L. REV. at 1705. Yet Wesson alleges that Walters wrote his letter to Kasten long *after* the death—*Hillmon's* death—at Crooked Creek. And she says he did so at the bidding of the insurance lawyers.

Wesson surmises that the lawyers bribed Walters to write the famous Kasten letter and date it March 1, though months had passed. They forged the postmark, then persuaded Kasten and the Walters siblings to swear their letters came in early March 1879. Meanwhile, Frederick fled forever, playing along with the lawyers' scheme because he preferred a rake's life to one roped to Kasten. For him, a shammed trek to found a sheep ranch supplied a handy escape from a humdrum marriage. The Walters siblings, Wesson says, unaware of their brother's survival and believing Hillmon his killer, falsely claimed they got letters like Kasten's to help defeat the Hillmon "widow's" claim. And Kasten persuaded herself that Walters had sent his letter when dated. She preferred to think

Walters the victim of Hillmon's plot than a bored beau who got away. *See* Wesson, 18 LAW & LIT. at 377–83.

It is a colorful story brilliantly told. But doubts nag. Wesson's tale hangs on the unlikely claim that a bevy of savvy insurance lawyers chanced reputations and livelihood on the discretion of so many partners in fraud. Had Kasten or Rieffenach or Walters's brother loosed their tongues or had Walters grown tired of womanizing and come home to Kasten, the lawyers would have stood naked before the courts, exposed as forgers and cheats.

Even as Wesson tags the insurers' lawyers as daring villains, she paints Sallie Hillmon's lawyers as fools. Through fourteen years of litigation and five long trials, Hillmon's lawyers failed to claim the letters were frauds. *See* Wesson, 76 FORDHAM L. REV. at 1693, 1694, 1704. "Take the Kasten letter out of the Walters theory," a Hillmon lawyer said, "and nothing remains of it." Yet the Hillmon team watched in silence as company counsel claimed in closing that "[n]o one had questioned the genuineness of the letter." No one objected when a trial judge said in charging the jury, "That letter comes to us certainly before this dead body was found. It tells its story from the fingers and mind of Walters. . . ." Hillmon's lawyers were not naive—they properly "insisted that Buchan was not Brown's attorney, but attorney for the companies, and that he procured the statement from Brown against Brown's protest. . . ." WIGMORE, JUDICIAL PROOF 879, 882, 896. Had they harbored similar suspicions of the letters, they surely would have aired them. Yet not until the sixth trial in 1899 did Hillmon's lawyers allege the Kasten letter was forged. Even then they retreated when shown other letters from Walters in the same handwriting. *See Simmons' Testimony a Footless Fancy*, Leavenworth Times, Nov. 17, 1899, at 4.

And Wesson perhaps makes too much of Sallie Hillmon's remarriage, apparently in the 1880s, casting it as evidence that Sallie "always knew the truth of what she had claimed"—that John Hillmon was dead. Wesson, 18 LAW & LIT. at 388. Perhaps the Hillmon marriage was always a fraud, contrived to make the "widow" a lawful beneficiary of the insurance policies; perhaps Sallie never intended to await John's return. Indeed the marriage seemed halfhearted from the start. On the license to wed, issued in Lawrence on October 3, 1878, John listed New Mexico as his residence.* Barely ten weeks later, his life now heavily insured, he left his wife's home with John Brown, bound for treacherous territory. From Lawrence to Wichita, where Walters was staying, to the fatal campsite at Crooked Creek, Hillmon beelined southwest toward New Mexico. He and his companions stopped just one or two days' hike from the state line.

* Professor Wesson helpfully posted a copy of the marriage license on her Web site. It is available at: http://www.thehillmoncase.com/marriage.html. Her site is also my source for the photos on page 529. They are available at: http://www.thehillmoncase.com/photos.html.

Hillmon could have killed Walters, then slipped into Indian Territory and from there to New Mexico, never to see Sallie—or the law—again.

Wesson herself supplies the best evidence that the Hillmon marriage was shammed. She cites its possible inspiration—J. B. Lewis and C. C. Bombaugh's compendium of *Remarkable Stratagems and Conspiracies*, a thick volume with a subtitle that could have caught Hillmon's eye: *An Authentic Record of Surprising Attempts to Defraud Life Insurance Companies*. *See* Wesson, 76 FORDHAM L. REV. at 1677 n.9 (citing the first edition of *Remarkable Stratagems*, published in New York in 1878 by G. W. Carleton & Co.). Among many true-life plots recounted with blueprint precision was one laid in Wichita in 1873, a scant six years before Frederick Walters wrote home from that city. The plotters, McNutt and Winner, set their scheme in Wichita because they had heard it was "a city where we could execute our plans in daylight without being bothered with the law; a place where men were killed every day in the week, and . . . the offenders were allowed their liberty." *The Wichita Monsters, Winner and McNutt*, *in* LEWIS & BOMBAUGH, REMARKABLE STRATAGEMS 346, 349.

McNutt's role predicted Hillmon's almost turn for turn. Recently married "to legalize [a new insurance] policy," McNutt insured his life payable to his bride. His accomplice Winner then set out in search of a chump to fill McNutt's grave. Winner found his mark in a young painter and lured him to Wichita "on promise of a job of work." When a fire in McNutt and Winner's paint shop left a corpse charred past recognition, Winner said it was McNutt's and declared "they had been attacked in the night, McNutt killed, and the shop robbed and burned." McNutt's widowed bride promptly claimed her insurance proceeds. *Id.* at 346–47, 350. All this Hillmon could have copied from a volume published in New York in 1878. A review printed in San Francisco on September 14, 1878, confirms that Lewis and Bombaugh's how-to guide had spread cross-country in time to give Hillmon inspiration to wed on October 3. *See* *Stratagems Against Insurance Companies*, S.F. BULL. Sept. 14, 1878, at 1.

Of course we could solve the *Hillmon* mystery if only we knew who lies in Hillmon's grave. Here Wesson's trump card is the report of a forensic anthropologist who reexamined the photos presented more than a century ago at the *Hillmon* trials. Professor Dennis Van Gerven of the University of Colorado concluded the corpse cannot be Walters and very probably is Hillmon. You can judge for yourselves from the photos on page 529 and Van Gerven's report. *See* Dennis Van Gerven, *A Digital Photographic Solution to the Question of Who Lies Buried in Oak Hill Cemetery* (Feb. 13, 2007), available at: http://www.thehillmoncase.com/results.html.

JOHN W. HILLMON
(DATE UNCERTAIN)

FREDERICK ADOLPH WALTERS
(DATE UNCERTAIN)

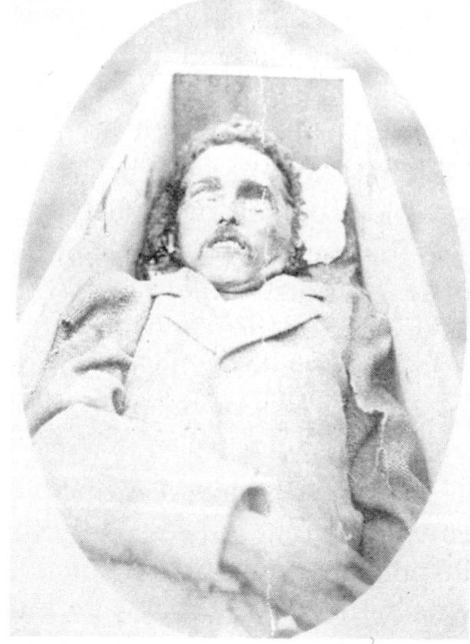

THE CORPSE
(APRIL 9, 1879, ABOUT THREE WEEKS AFTER DEATH)

Hillmon's *Legacy*

If the corpse at Crooked Creek was Hillmon's, as Wesson and Van Gerven believe, what would that mean for evidence law? Wesson argues that the Supreme Court's mistake of fact—if mistake it was—is reason to think *Hillmon* bad law. Bent on barring the "widow" from collecting on Walters's murdered corpse, the justices contrived a hearsay exception for statements of future intention that Wesson says defies common sense. Statements of intention, she writes, hardly claim unusual reliability. "On the contrary, it would seem to be easier to lie about one's intentions than about nearly anything else, since the likelihood of being caught out in a lie is small. . . . [A]llowing an expression of intention as evidence that the intention was accomplished disregards the folk wisdom that there is 'many a slip 'twixt cup and lip.' " Wesson, 18 LAW & LIT. at 348. After all, if the insurance lawyers did contrive the "Dearest Alvina" letter, the letter's falsehoods began with the very first line: "Today is March 1, 1879." *Id.* at 389.

But a hearsay exception for statements of future intention did not arise from scratch in the Supreme Court's 1892 *Hillmon* opinion. In an English case discussed by the *Hillmon* Court in some detail, justices of the Court of Appeal voiced a similar principle sixteen years earlier. To prove the contents of Lord St. Leonard's missing will, they allowed evidence of his intentions stated before executing the will. Amid a raft of muddy opinions, one justice expressed the controlling principle: "[I]t is more probable that the testator has than that he has not made a particular devise, or a particular bequest, when he has told a person previously that he intended to make it, inasmuch as it shews that he had it in his mind to make such a will at the time he made that declaration." *Hillmon*, 145 U.S. at 298; *Sugden v. Lord St. Leonards*, 1 P.D. 154, 251 (1876) (judgment of Mellish, L.J.). As Maguire argued decades later, statements of future intention are free at least from the usual hearsay risks of misperception and memory failure.

Still, Wesson seems right to doubt that such general principles moved the *Hillmon* Court. The justices seemed far more impressed by the case's singular facts, which they thought "preclud[ed] suspicion of misrepresentation." At all events the law seems settled: Rule 803(3) permits statements of intention to prove future acts of the declarant. Wesson's articles have roused historical interest and academic admiration, but no groundswell for change.

Though the law is settled, *Hillmon*'s factual controversy persists. Frederick Walters's journey to "parts unknown" evidently included eternity, "but not oblivion." Maguire, 38 HARV. L. REV. at 709. Tabloid-style stories of Hillmon's survival in the wilds of the far West surfaced as late as 1895 in such respectable places as the *New York Times*. In January 1894 the *Times* ran a front-page article under the headline *Hillmon Tells His Story: The Murderer Found in the Mountains of Utah.* A conscience-stricken old man claiming to be Hillmon played his part a bit too well: "I have not been afraid of the law," he said. "I have been afraid of myself." N.Y. TIMES, Jan. 2, 1894, at 2, col. 1. *See also Says He Can Produce Hillmon*, N.Y. TIMES, Apr. 5, 1895, at 5 (reporting railroad detective's insistence he knew Hillmon's hideout). Such accounts did not impress Kansas juries. Two more trials failed to yield a verdict before the sixth—and last—ended in a second judgment for Mrs. Hillmon. That verdict survived some three years before the Supreme Court again nullified it on grounds unrelated to the Walters letters. *See* WIGMORE, *supra*, at 856 n.2; *Conn. Mut. Life Ins. Co. v. Hillmon*, 188 U.S. 208 (1903).

With this last ruling of the Supreme Court, almost a quarter-century after the death at Crooked Creek, the *Hillmon* case closed. As for the Hillmon controversy, the confident prediction of the *New York Times* in 1893 that "[t]he mystery that has so long shrouded this remarkable case bids fair to be solved" proved both wishful and wrong. *Wanderings of a Murderer*, N.Y. TIMES, May 24, 1893, at 1. Wesson's work has stirred stilled waters—and left them swirling.

---

3. STATEMENTS FOR MEDICAL DIAGNOSIS OR TREATMENT

Focus on
FRE 803(4)

Problem 7.34
Elder Abuse

On January 12 Henry Browning, aged 80, called his lawyer. He reported that his caretaker, Deborah Maples, had pushed him during an argument on January 11 and that he had fallen and hit his head. Browning said he had decided to fire Maples and wanted to be sure that doing so would not expose him to a lawsuit.

Later that day Browning visited his doctor. He reported the same events he had told his lawyer and added that since his fall, he had suffered from severe headaches and bouts of nausea.

At Maples's trial on charges of battery and elder abuse, Browning took the witness stand, but gave confused and largely incoherent testimony. The prosecutor offered in addition the following evidence:

(1) The lawyer's testimony that Browning said he had fallen and hit his head;

(2) The doctor's testimony that Browning said he had fallen and hit his head;

(3) The doctor's testimony that Browning said Maples had pushed him.

On the defendant's objections to all this evidence, how should the judge have ruled? Suppose the doctor testified that she specifically asked Browning what caused his fall because her diagnosis depended on whether he fell during a dizzy spell or suffered some other sort of accident. Would this fact change any of your answers? (Please ignore any privilege Browning might have in the confidentiality of these conversations.)

UNITED STATES V. IRON SHELL

633 F.2d 77 (8th Cir. 1980), *cert. denied*, 450 U.S. 1001 (1981).

■ STEPHENSON, CIRCUIT JUDGE: Defendant, John Louis Iron Shell, appeals from a jury conviction of assault with intent to commit rape. . . .

The indictment in this case arose out of the defendant's acts on July 24, 1979, . . . near Mission, South Dakota. The defense conceded at trial that Iron Shell had assaulted Lucy, a nine-year-old . . . girl. The key questions at trial concerned the nature of the assault and the defendant's intent. . . .

Dr. Mark Hopkins, a physician . . ., examined Lucy at about 8:20 p.m. on the night of the assault. During his examination the doctor elicited a series of statements from Lucy concerning the cause of her injuries. Dr. Hopkins was only aware that Lucy was allegedly a rape victim and was not told of the details surrounding the assault. During the examination, in response to questions posed by the doctor, Lucy told Dr. Hopkins she had been [dragged] into the bushes, that her clothes, jeans and underwear, were removed and that the man had tried to [rape her]. She said she tried to scream but was unable because the man put his hand over her mouth and neck.[6] The doctor, over objection, repeated Lucy's statement at trial.

. . . [Dr. Hopkins] found superficial abrasions on both sides of Lucy's neck and testified that they were consistent with someone grabbing her

6. Out of the presence of the jury, the doctor testified that he first asked Lucy "what happened" and she didn't answer. He asked whether she was in any pain and

but qualified his statement by adding that he could not absolutely determine that they were so caused. Dr. Hopkins also testified that there was no physical evidence of penetration. . . .

. . . [Lucy] was able to answer a number of preliminary questions demonstrating her ability to understand and respond to counsel but was unable to detail what happened after she was assaulted by the defendant. She did testify that she remembered something happening near the bushes and that a man had pushed her down. Lucy also said at trial that the man told her if she "didn't shut up he would choke me." In response to a series of leading questions she confirmed that the man had put his hand over her neck, hit her on the side of the face, held her down, taken her clothes off and that [a neighbor] had scared the man, making him leave.[7] . . .

Defendant challenges the admission of statements made by Lucy to Dr. Hopkins during his examination. The prosecution offered this testimony admittedly as hearsay but within the exception expressed in [unrestyled] Rule 803(4). The rule states:

> The following are not excluded by the hearsay rule, even though the declarant is available as a witness:

she pointed to her vaginal area. He asked if she hurt anywhere else and she didn't answer. Dr. Hopkins again asked "what happened" and Lucy said she had been drug into the bushes. The doctor then asked if the man "had taken her clothes off." She said yes, and then related the facts set out above. Dr. Hopkins testified that he was not "badgering" the patient, nor "dragging information out," but was asking "simple questions."

7. The following is a representative sample of the prosecutor's direct examination of Lucy:

Q: What did the man do when he pushed you down, Lucy?

A: (Long hesitation)

Q: What did he do?

A: (Long hesitation)

Q: Did he hurt you any place?

A: (Long hesitation)

Q: Do you remember that?

A: (Long hesitation)

Q: Where did he put his hand, did he put his hand on your neck?

A: Yes.

Q: Did you get hit on the side of the face?

A: Yes.

Q: When he pushed you down, did he hold you down?

A: Yes.

Q: Did you start crying?

A: Yes.

THE COURT: As much as you can, phrase your questions in a way to avoid any unnecessary leading.

Q: What else happened when he had you down, Lucy; did he say anything to you, do you remember?

A: (Long hesitation)

Q: What did he say to you, can you tell me? Tell me what he said?

A: (Long hesitation)

Q: Could you do that for me?

A: Yes.

Q: Okay, tell me what he said?

A: If I didn't shut up he would choke me.

> (4) . . . Statements made for purposes of medical diagnosis or treatment and describing medical history, or past or present symptoms, pain, or sensations, or the inception or general character of the cause or external source thereof insofar as reasonably pertinent to diagnosis or treatment.

The defendant argues that the questions asked by Dr. Hopkins and the information received in response to those questions were not "reasonably pertinent" to diagnosis or treatment. The defense stresses Dr. Hopkins' question in which he asked Lucy whether the man had taken her clothes off and suggests that this was asked by one in the role of an investigator, seeking to solve the crime, rather than a doctor treating or diagnosing a patient. The defendant also asserts that the doctor's examination would have been the same whether or not this extra information had been received. The defense argues that this point supports his claim that the questions were not pertinent to treatment or diagnosis because they had no effect on the doctor's examination. Lastly, the defendant urges that the doctor was employed for the specific purpose of qualifying as an expert witness and as such his testimony should be more suspect.

It is clear that Rule 803(4) significantly liberalized prior practice concerning admissibility of statements made for purposes of medical diagnosis or treatment. *See* Notes of Advisory Committee on Proposed Rules, Rule 803. Rule 803(4) admits three types of statements: (1) medical history, (2) past or present sensations, and (3) inception or general cause of the disease or injury. All three types are admissible where they are "reasonably pertinent to diagnosis or treatment." The rule changed prior law in two main points. First, the rule adopted an expansive approach by allowing statements concerning past symptoms and those which related to the cause of the injury. Second, the rule abolished the distinction between the doctor who is consulted for the purpose of treatment and an examination for the purpose of diagnosis only; the latter usually refers to a doctor who is consulted only in order to testify as a witness.[8]

Lucy's statements fall primarily within the third category listed by 803(4).[9] The key question is whether these statements were reasonably

8. This is the first Eighth Circuit opinion to consider the effect of 803(4) on its pre-1975 case law. This circuit had followed the majority rule which prevented admission of testimony concerning the cause of the injury as not connected with treatment and excluded statements made to a physician who examined the patient solely for the purpose of testifying. These cases are no longer controlling but they may provide persuasive authority within the boundaries of 803(4) when analyzing whether statements are reasonably pertinent to diagnosis or treatment. Some courts had also held that a physician could repeat a patient's statement regarding medical history or past symptoms for the limited purpose of explaining the basis of an opinion and not in order to prove the truth of the out-of-court declarations. This distinction was likewise rejected by the federal rules. Notes of Advisory Committee on Proposed Rules, Rule 803.

9. Dr. Hopkins testified that Lucy said she was experiencing pain in her vaginal area. This expression of a present symptom

pertinent to diagnosis or treatment. The rationale behind the rule has often been stated. It focuses upon the patient and relies upon the patient's strong motive to tell the truth because diagnosis or treatment will depend in part upon what the patient says. It is thought that the declarant's motive guarantees trustworthiness sufficiently to allow an exception to the hearsay rule. Judge Weinstein, in his treatise, suggests another policy ground. He writes that "a fact reliable enough to serve as the basis for a diagnosis is also reliable enough to escape hearsay proscription." 4 WEINSTEIN & BERGER, WEINSTEIN'S EVIDENCE 803–129 (1979). This principle recognizes that life and death decisions are made by physicians in reliance on such facts and as such should have sufficient trustworthiness to be admissible in a court of law. This rationale closely parallels that underlying rule 703 and suggests a similar test should apply, namely—is this fact of a type reasonably relied upon by experts in a particular field in forming opinions. *See* FED. R. EVID. 703 (Basis of Opinion Testimony by Experts). Thus, two independent rationales support the rule and are helpful in its application. A two-part test flows naturally from this dual rationale: first, is the declarant's motive consistent with the purpose of the rule; and second, is it reasonable for the physician to rely on the information in diagnosis or treatment[?]

We find no facts in the record to indicate that Lucy's motive in making these statements was other than as a patient seeking treatment. Dr. Hopkins testified that the purpose of his examination was two-fold. He was to treat Lucy and to preserve any evidence that was available. There is nothing in the content of the statements to suggest that Lucy was responding to the doctor's questions for any reason other than promoting treatment. It is important to note that the statements concern what happened rather than who assaulted her. The former in most cases is pertinent to diagnosis and treatment while the latter would seldom, if ever, be sufficiently related.[10] All of Lucy's statements were within the scope of the rule because they were related to her physical condition and were consistent with a motive to promote treatment. The age of the patient also [militates] against a finding that Lucy's statements were not within the traditional rationale of the rule. The trial court placed special

falls within the second category of 803(4) and would also be excepted from the hearsay rule under rule 803(3) covering a then existing physical condition. FED. R. EVID. 803(3). The remainder of Lucy's statement concerns the general character and nature of the cause of the injury. Because of the result we reach in this case, it is not necessary to discuss this distinction at length.

10. The advisory committee notes on 803(4) provide that statements as to fault would not ordinarily qualify. The notes use this example: "a patient's statement that he was struck by an automobile would qualify but not his statement that the car was driven through a red light." [RB 222.] Another example concludes that a statement by a patient that he was shot would be admissible but a statement that he was shot by a white man would not. And the fact that a patient strained himself while operating a machine may be significant to treatment but the fact that the patient said the machine was defective may not.

emphasis on this factor and we likewise find that it is important to our holding.

During an extensive examination outside the presence of the jury, Dr. Hopkins explained in detail the relevancy of his questions to the task of diagnosis and treatment. He testified that a discussion of the cause of the injury was important to provide guidelines for his examination by pinpointing areas of the body to be examined more closely and by narrowing his examination by eliminating other areas. It is not dispositive that Dr. Hopkins' examination would have been identical to the one he performed if Lucy had been unable to utter a word. The doctor testified that his examination would have been more lengthy had he been unable to elicit a description of the general cause, although he stated the exam would have been basically the same. The fact that in this case the discussion of the cause of the injury did not lead to a fundamentally different exam does not mean that the discussion was not pertinent to diagnosis. It is enough that the information eliminated potential physical problems from the doctor's examination in order to meet the test of 803(4). Discovering what is not injured is equally as pertinent to treatment and diagnosis as finding what is injured. Dr. Hopkins also testified, in response to specific questions from the court, that most doctors would have sought such a history and that he relied upon Lucy's statements in deciding upon a course of treatment.[11]

In light of this analysis we hold that it was not an abuse of discretion to admit the doctor's testimony. . . .

Affirmed.

■ HEANEY, CIRCUIT JUDGE, concurring: . . . .

■ BRIGHT, CIRCUIT JUDGE, dissenting [on other grounds]: . . . .

---

11. Judge Weinstein approached the problem as follows:

> "Much depends on the doctor's analysis. The doctor may or may not need to know that his patient was struck by a train and what caused him to fall under the train since dizziness before the accident may bear on diagnosis. A doctor consulted after the patient was involved in an automobile accident may need to know that the accident was precipitated when the patient fainted while driving. Since doctors may be assumed not to want to waste their time with unnecessary history, the fact that a doctor took the information is prima facie evidence that it was pertinent. Courtroom practice has tended to let in medical records and statements to nurses and doctors fairly freely, leaving it to the jury to decide probative force."

WEINSTEIN & BERGER, *supra*, at 803–130 (footnotes omitted). It is not necessary to find, and we do not hold in this case, that the fact that the doctor took the information is prima facie evidence that it was pertinent. Rather, we conclude that a close examination of the facts and circumstances in each case is required.

Problem 7.35
Child Abuse I

Consider the facts of *State v. Reidhead*, 146 Ariz. 314, 315, 317, 705 P.2d 1365 (Ct. App. 1985):

> . . . On March 31, 1983, appellant brought his four-year-old son, Allen Jr., to the Northwest Medical Center, Urgent Care Center in Tucson for the treatment of a broken arm. The boy was examined by Dr. Margaret Buford, who also observed what appeared to be a slap mark on the child's face and a mark on his chest. Appellant told Dr. Buford that he had slapped his child and that the child had then fallen off the porch. . . .
>
> [At trial the prosecutor questioned Dr. Buford as follows:]
>
> *Q:* And can you tell us about your [first] conversation with the child?
>
> *A:* I initially approached the child and asked what had happened, and after initially not saying anything, the child told me that he had been playing with one of his father's record[s].
>
> *[Defense Counsel]:* Excuse me. I'll object as not being part of the basis for the treatment, Your Honor.
>
> *The Court:* Objection is overruled. She may answer.
>
> *Q:* (By [the prosecutor]) You may answer.
>
> *A: The child was playing with one of the father's records and got it dirty, and his father twisted his arm.*

The defendant was convicted of child abuse and appeals. Under Rule 803(4) and *Iron Shell*, what are his best arguments for reversal? How should the court rule?

Problem 7.36
Child Abuse II

In *Tome v. United States*, 513 U.S. 150 (1995) (excerpted at page 454 above), the Supreme Court rejected the prosecution's attempt to offer a five-year-old child's hearsay account of alleged sexual abuse under Rule 801(d)(1)(B). When the Tenth Circuit Court of Appeals heard the case on remand, the government argued that the statements the child made to Drs. Karen Kuper and Laura Reich were also admissible under Rule 803(4). Tome's counsel called the court's attention to these portions of the trial record:

Cross-examination of Dr. Karen Kuper:

Q [by defense counsel]: Do you let [patients] know that you're there to help kids?

A: I don't believe I use that term exactly, no.

Q: Do you ever talk with a child about truth telling?

A: No, I don't. . . .

Cross-examination of Dr. Laura Reich:

Q: Did you talk to her at all about the importance of truth telling with you?

A: No, I didn't talk to her about that.

Q: Did you get any sense that she—if anyone else had talked with her about that, that it was important to tell you the truth?

A: No, that particular issue didn't come up. I didn't get any sense of that.

Q: Did you talk with her at all about what might happen if she didn't—wasn't completely honest with you about things?

A: No, I didn't.

United States v. Tome, 61 F.3d 1446, 1459 (10th Cir. 1995) (*on remand*). How, if at all, should this testimony affect the admissibility of the child's statements under Rule 803(4)?

Melody R. Herbst, Margaret S. Steward, John E. B. Myers & Robin L. Hansen

Young Children's Understanding of the Physician's Role and the Medical Hearsay Exception

in CHILDREN'S UNDERSTANDING OF BIOLOGY AND HEALTH 235 (Michael Siegal & Candida C. Peterson eds., 1999)

The study described in this chapter was prompted by the report of a decision of the . . . Eighth Circuit Court of Appeals. . . . [A] child molestation conviction was overturned because the appellate court determined that the presiding trial judge had erred in allowing a 3–year-old child's hearsay statements to a physician to be admitted as testimony under the medical diagnosis and treatment exception. The Federal Court of Appeals ruled that the exception does not apply when the patient is too young to understand the importance of telling the truth to the physician.* ... This exception is based on the premise that patients have an incentive to be truthful with a health care professional, thus rendering the hearsay reliable....

The medical hearsay exception can be an important legal tool in cases of both sexual and physical abuse.... For example, in a review of 115 consecutive child sexual abuse felony cases, De Jong and Rose found that successful prosecution depended on the quality of verbal evidence as well as the effectiveness of the child victim's testimony, yet no difference was found in the rate of conviction between cases with and without physical evidence. *See* A. R. De Jong & M. Rose, *Legal Proof of Child Sexual Abuse in the Absence of Physical Evidence*, 88 PEDIATRICS 506 (1991). Frequently, in sexual abuse cases, ... neither medical [n]or laboratory findings exist, and there are no bystander witnesses. Thus the child's report to the physician is the only evidence to support a claim of sexual abuse....

... The assumption underlying the medical hearsay exception, that of young children's understanding of the physician's role, has not been empirically tested. We do know that by age 3 children are able to imitate some of the physician's activities using common medical equipment; by age 4 children know that truth-telling is expected in court.... However, there has been no direct assessment of children's understanding of the knowledge and social position of physicians or of what children expect in reciprocal doctor-patient relationships regarding telling the truth....

... We posed a series of questions to forty healthy children ranging in age from 3 years 6 months to 6 years 11 months. In order to assess developmental differences we decided to compare the responses of the younger group of children (mean age of 4 years 2 months) with the responses of the older group of children (mean age of 5 years 11 months). Each of the groups included ten boys and ten girls.... To begin, the interviewer introduced herself, noted parent and teacher consent, and stated, "I want to learn your ideas about the jobs grown-ups do." ...

* [The authors do not name the ruling and instead cite a news article that likewise describes but does not name the ruling. The case in question seems to be *Ring v. Erickson*, 968 F.2d 760, 762 (8th Cir. 1992). In reviewing a three-year-old's complaint of sexual abuse made to her doctor, the Eighth Circuit noted that Rule 803(4) rests on a "selfish-motive" theory—the patient wants accurate treatment and so tells her doctor the truth. "This underlying basis of reliability is not present in a case such as this one," the court wrote, "where ... there is no evidence that [the child] even knew she was talking to a doctor." The Eighth Circuit panel later reissued its opinion in amended form, but left this ruling undisturbed. *See Ring v. Erickson*, 983 F.2d 818, 820 (8th Cir. 1992).—GF]

Who is your doctor and what is the doctor's job?

Most of the children we interviewed were able to name their personal physician. In fact, 80 percent of the 5– and 6–year-olds and 68 percent of the 3– and 4–year-olds were able to do so. All of the children were able to tell us something about the doctor's job. . . . In response to structured multiple-choice questions beginning with the expression "Who knows best," we found that older children were significantly better able than younger children to select the appropriate role associated with specific knowledge areas. Most children mentioned the doctor's use of medical equipment or procedures such as use of stethoscopes and giving immunizations. . . . A significantly greater number of older subjects gave conceptual descriptors as well when describing what physicians do. They nearly always mentioned "help or helping people." At times treatment was implied, "to make them not sick so they won't die" (SH, 6 years 1 month) and more specifically, "[t]o help . . . when they're hurt or have an ear infection or cold or something like that. They tell you the right way to help the sickness . . ." (KN, 6 years 1 month). . . .

Do doctors already know what children know?

To tap the child's sense of whether or not doctors already know the answers to the questions they pose, we probed reports of the child's own injury with the question, "Does (physician's name) know what happened when you hurt yourself if you don't tell?" Only one subject, a 4–year-old, thought the physician knew this without being told by the child. . . .

Reporting body touch: What do you tell and to whom?

. . . [O]ur data indicate that young children are more likely to report painful than benign touch and that they understand the necessity to provide an accurate narrative to persons in authority. . . . The older children, in determining whether or not to tell a doctor, also made the discrimination between self-inflicted injury and injury caused by another—and were more likely to report the latter. These findings parallel research on children's highly accurate reports of painful medical procedures and suggest that even some very young children have the capacity to meet the medical hearsay exception. . . .

Truth and lies: "You're in big trouble now!"

Most older and younger children agreed that telling the truth is desirable (95 percent and 82 percent respectively) and that telling a lie is undesirable (95 percent and 75 percent respectively). As we had anticipated, older children were significantly better able to define and give appropriate examples of truth and lie concepts than younger children. . . . [I]t appears that younger subjects have little ability to define truth and lie, but were often able to recognize and label the words "telling the truth" positively and less often to label "telling a lie" negatively. . . .

. . . [We] asked our participants about the consequence of lying to a doctor. . . . Characteristic of the younger children were vague negative responses such as "You're in big trouble now" or punishments such as a time-out or a loud reprimand from the doctor. Older children often thought that the doctor would become angry; eight [of the nineteen older children who responded to this question] understood that the doctor would not be able to be helpful or would prescribe inappropriate treatment. . . .

Recommendations

. . . [Research] on conversational competence implies that a child may respond positively to physicians' stating their fact-finding role, the need for truth, and the child's self-interest in reporting truthfully. . . . Medical staff can increase the child's understanding of the need to be candid by . . . remarking "I'm going to do a checkup to see how strong you are, how healthy you are, and if there's anything that needs to be done." The professional can further emphasize the importance of being accurate and complete. . . .

Problem 7.37

Food Poisoning

Returning home from her accounting office for lunch, Monica found her husband sick in bed. "I think I ate some bad meat," he said and pointed toward an empty takeout food carton from the Downtown Deli that was on the bed table. "You'd better get me a doctor."

Monica's husband later died of arsenic poisoning. Monica sued the Downtown Deli, alleging negligence in supervising a disturbed employee who had poisoned some of the restaurant's food. At trial she offers the following evidence:

(1) Her own testimony about her husband's statements and gesture—offered to prove that he had eaten food from the Downtown Deli.

(2) A nurse's testimony that when Monica called the doctor's office that day, she said, "My husband told me he ate some bad meat from the Downtown Deli"—offered to prove that Monica's husband had eaten food from the Downtown Deli.

(3) Monica's own testimony that when the doctor arrived at their home, the doctor said, "This has all the signs of

> arsenic poisoning. We'll have to hospitalize immediately"—offered to prove that Monica's husband showed signs of arsenic poisoning.

If the Deli's counsel objects that each of these statements is inadmissible hearsay, how should the court rule?

---

4. REFRESHING MEMORY AND RECORDED RECOLLECTIONS

Focus on
FRE 803(5) & 612

Problem 7.38
License Plate

A speeding car killed Marietta Rathbun's husband as he crossed a street in Bayonne, New Jersey. The car didn't stop. At the trial of Rathbun's suit against Bruno Brancatella, Rathbun offered the testimony of a Mr. Menandier and a Miss Sullivan to prove the license plate number of the fleeing car. Each recounted his or her actions at the time:

> Menandier, a bystander, attracted by the noise of the impact, observing the character and color of the license plate upon the colliding [car], called out, in a loud voice, to Miss Sullivan, another observer, ... the number he had observed. She, for the purpose apparently of remembering the number, entered her home and wrote the number upon an envelope.
>
> For some time she retained the envelope, and used it as a reference for the purpose of enabling her to testify at various proceedings emanating from the accident.... [S]he imparted the number to a police official—Officer Grant—within ten or fifteen minutes after the accident....

Rathbun v. Brancatella, 93 N.J.L. 222, 223 (1919). Other evidence established that "the number thus transmitted [w]as the number of the defendant's car." Assume these facts:

(1) Sullivan testified first. She admitted she never saw the car's plate. She testified that although she was certain she wrote down the number Menandier called out, she no longer remembered it. When Rathbun's counsel handed her the envelope, Sullivan identified it as the memo she made of the plate number. But seeing the envelope, she said, did not refresh her memory of the plate number. Rathbun's counsel then offered the envelope as an exhibit to prove the car's license plate number. On Brancatella's objection, how should the judge have ruled? Assume the Federal Rules of Evidence controlled the case.

(2) Menandier then testified that he memorized the plate number on the speeding car by reciting it over and over. When Rathbun's counsel asked him the number, however, he said it had slipped his mind. Rathbun's counsel showed him the envelope and asked if it refreshed his memory. Menandier said it did and then recited the number without looking again at the envelope. If Brancatella objected to this procedure, how should the judge have ruled?

(3) After the events described in paragraph (1), the judge refused to admit the envelope as an exhibit. If Rathbun's counsel again offered the envelope at the conclusion of Menandier's testimony and Brancatella again objected, how should the judge have ruled?

JOHNSON V. STATE

Court of Criminal Appeals of Texas.
967 S.W.2d 410 (Tex. Crim. App. 1998).

■ MANSFIELD, J. A Bexar County jury found appellant, Arnold E. Johnson, guilty of the October 26, 1995, capital murder of Frank Johnson, Jr. At the punishment stage of trial, the jury answered the special issues in such a manner as to require the trial court to sentence appellant to death. Direct appeal to this Court is automatic. . . .

The State presented twenty-six witnesses and numerous exhibits. . . . The most incriminating evidence came from a statement made by the surviving victim, Reginald Taylor:

> My name is Reginald Taylor, I am 17 years old. . . .
>
> I have come to the Homicide Office at the San Antonio Police Department, to give Detective Hernandez a statement about how my friend Frank Johnson got killed.

At 2:30 p.m. on October 26th 1995 I ran into Frank Johnson at the Candle Stick Apartments off of Rigsby. I know Frank Johnson as Frank Jr. . . . [H]e said I'm gonna go drop some "dank" off "dank" being pot, marijuana. . . . I said lets go. . . . Frank parked near the Phillip 66 and frank went to Big Arnold's garage. He took the pound of weed in a towel. He wasn't coming back, about five minutes passed. . . .

[I] walked around and I saw this dude. . . . He pulled a Tech–9. . . . The guy with the Tech made me go in and sit down in the office. Frank was in the office behind the desk, Little Arnold was next to me on the couch. . . . Little Arnold was asking frank if he had any more money, and Frank said I give you all I had, the dude with the Tech said "all you had was a pound of weed and twenty-five Dollars". . . . Little Arnold drove the car from the back to the front and backed it into the garage near the office where we were. . . . [T]he guy with the Tech–9 pointed the gun at us and said get in the car. I got in the back seat first and FRANK got in the front passenger seat. Little Arnold had been sitting in the drivers seat since he had backed the car in. The guy with the Tech got in the back passenger seat right behind Frank . . . I don't know where we were going, we didn't drive more than ten minutes. . . . I remember we made a right turn. I heard a shot, I saw blood come off Franks neck the guy with the Tech–9 shot frank. Little Arnold said Shoot him in the head, and at the same time he say get out the car. so I bailed, I saw him raise the Tech–9 as I jumped out. the car never stopped rolling. I'm running down the street, I didn't know where I was I trying to get help. I never looked back. . . . After that [I] went to Frank's mother's house and waited for the Detectives to call so I could give my statement. . . . The Police brought me downtown where I spoke with you.

All I have told you is the truth, I really don't know little Arnold but can identify him if I see a picture of him, . . . and I don't know the guy with the Tech–9 but if I see a picture of him I can recognize him. I remember seeing a Tatoo on little Arnold that said "Pookie"

I have read this statement and it is the truth.

(All errors included are as they appear in the statement.)

During Taylor's cross-examination, Defense counsel had appellant strip down to his waist to demonstrate the absence of a tattoo which read "Pookie." Appellant did, however, have a tattoo on his right arm which read "Lil Arnold." . . .

. . . [A]ppellant argues that the trial judge violated Texas Rule of Criminal Evidence 803(5) by admitting Taylor's statement into evidence. Appellant contends that the State failed to lay the proper predicate in support of admission of this evidence. The State argues that the predicate requirements of Rule 803(5) were met and that the testimony was properly admitted.

During the guilt/innocence phase of trial, the State called Taylor to the stand to testify as an eyewitness to the offense. Unfortunately for the State, Taylor was not cooperative:

Q: Mr. Taylor, could you please state your name for the record, please.

A: You already know my name.

Q: Could you please state it for the record, sir?

A: For what? You already know it.

Q: Is your name Reginald Taylor?

A: It's right there in front of you man.

Q: All I'm asking you, sir, is that your name?

A: Yeah.

Q: Okay.

Prosecutor: May I approach the witness, Judge?

The Court: You may.

Prosecutor: Thank you.

Q: Mr. Taylor, I'm going to ask you, show you State's Exhibit Number 120. Is that your signature, sir?

A: Yeah.

Q: Excuse me?

A: Yeah.

Q: Okay. And did you give that statement on October 26th, 1995?

A: I don't remember.

Q: Okay. It says October 26th, 1995. Do you have any doubt on that or would you say that's correct, sir?

A: I don't remember. I don't even know the date.

Q: Okay. When you gave the statement to Detective Hernandez, was everything true and correct when you told him?

A: I don't even remember what I said.

Q: You don't remember what you said?

A: I don't.

Q: You don't remember what you said? But when you told the officer—why don't you just go look over State's Exhibit Number 120, just read it over, okay?

A: Are you trying to make me memorize what I said?

Q: No, sir. Just go ahead and read it over, okay. There's the next page behind it, sir. If you can read that one, the second one and the third one, please.

Mr. Taylor, the statement, 120, when you gave the statement to the police officers, was that more fresh in your mind at the time when you gave it, sir?

A: I really don't remember, just what I read. I don't remember what happened that day.

Q: Okay. You don't remember what happened that day?

A: No.

Q: Okay. But when you gave this statement to the police officers on October 26th, 1995, was it more fresh in your mind then as it is today?

A: I don't remember.

Q: Excuse me?

A: I don't remember.

Q: You don't remember what, sir?

A: About the statement, about what I just read.

Q: Okay. . . .

Q: But when you gave the statement to the police officers, was it more fresh in your mind when you gave it to them? I'm not talking about today. You said today you can't remember that well. But what I'm asking you, when you gave the statement to the police officers, was it more fresh in your mind then?

A: I guess so.

Q: Okay. So it was more fresh in your mind then. Is that what your are telling me?

A: Yeah.

Q: And that's your signature, October 26th, 1995. That's what it says there, correct?

A: Yeah.

Q: And you are telling us you can't remember anything today. Is that what you are saying?

A: Right.

Prosecutor: Your Honor, at this time I would like to offer into evidence State's Exhibit Number 120 and cite to the Court 803(5), Texas Rules of Criminal Evidence.

Defense Counsel: Defense would object on the grounds [that] . . . they have not met the requirements under 803(5). It is still hear-

> say.... It does not establish the circumstances that establish reliability of the statement whatsoever.

The Court: ... The objections are overruled....

The State was then allowed to read Taylor's statement in its entirety into evidence to the jury.

Texas Rule of Criminal Evidence 803(5) provides in relevant part:

> The following are not excluded by the hearsay rule, even though the declarant is available as a witness: ...
>
> (5) Recorded recollection. A memorandum or record concerning a matter about which a witness once had personal knowledge but now has insufficient recollection to enable him to testify fully and accurately, shown to have been made or adopted by the witness when the matter was fresh in his memory and to reflect that knowledge correctly, unless the circumstances of preparation cast doubt on the document's trustworthiness. If admitted, the memorandum or record may be read into evidence but may not itself be received as an exhibit unless offered by an adverse party.

The predicate for past recollection recorded is set forth in Rule 803(5) and requires that four elements be met: (1) the witness must have had firsthand knowledge of the event, (2) the written statement must be [a] ... memorandum made at or near the time of the event while the witness had a clear and accurate memory of it, (3) the witness must lack a present recollection of the event, and (4) the witness must vouch for the accuracy of the written memorandum. 2 J. STRONG, ET AL., MCCORMICK ON EVIDENCE §§ 279–83 (4th ed. 1992). In particular, to meet the fourth element, the witness may testify that she presently remembers recording the fact correctly or remembers recognizing the writing as accurate when she read it at an earlier time. *Id.* § 283. But if her present memory is less effective, it is sufficient if the witness testifies that she knows the memorandum is correct because of a habit or practice to record matters accurately or to check them for accuracy. At the extreme, it is even sufficient if the individual testifies to recognizing her signature on the statement and believes the statement is correct because she would not have signed it if she had not believed it true at the time. *Id.;* 3 WIGMORE, EVIDENCE § 747 (Chadbourn rev. 1970). However, the witness must acknowledge at trial the accuracy of the statement. 2 MCCORMICK ON EVIDENCE, *supra,* § 283. An assertion of the statement's accuracy in the acknowledgment line of a written memorandum or such an acknowledgment made previously under oath will not be sufficient. *Id.* No statement should be allowed to verify itself, especially by boilerplate language routinely added by police, lawyers, or others experienced in litigation. 4 LOUISELL & MUELLER, FEDERAL EVIDENCE §§ 445, 628–29 (1980).

We have addressed the past recollection recorded hearsay exception before. In Wood v. State, 511 S.W.2d 37 (Tex. Crim. App. 1974), a murder prosecution, the State attempted to prove that the defendant made a threat regarding the victim in the presence of a witness. In holding the witness' written statement admissible under the past recollection recorded hearsay exception, we explained:

> Although the original statement was exhibited to the witness on several occasions, she consistently contended she had no present recollection of the appellant having made the threat in question just prior to the alleged offense. She did testify that, while the written sworn statement made to the police did not refresh her present recollection as to appellant's threat . . ., she did give the statement on the "night" of the alleged offense, that she signed and swore to it and that if the statement reflected appellant made such threat it was true. It thus appears that rules of the use of a memorandum of past recollection were met. It was shown that the memorandum was made at or near the time of the event in question and that the witness guaranteed the correctness of the memorandum.

Wood, 511 S.W.2d at 44.

Given the record before us, it is apparent that the State did not lay a proper predicate for the admissibility of Taylor's statement under Rule 803(5). . . . Taylor never guaranteed that his memory was correctly transcribed or that the factual assertions contained in the statement were true. Consequently, the statement read into evidence was inadmissible hearsay. . . .

The judgment of the trial court is *reversed,* and the case *remanded* for a new trial.

■ BAIRD, MEYERS, and HOLLAND, JJ., concur in the result.

---

5. BUSINESS RECORDS

Focus on
FRE 803(6) & (7)

PALMER V. HOFFMAN: *Historical Prelude*

On Christmas Day, 1940, at about 3:15 p.m., newlyweds Howard Hoffman, a twenty-four-year-old graduate of Rensselaer Polytechnic Institute . . ., and his twenty-three-year-old wife, Inez T. Spraker Hoffman, a Vassar graduate, began their trip back home to Hartford,

Connecticut, from the home of Inez's parents in Cooperstown, New York. On Route 41 in West Stockbridge, Massachusetts, at about 6:10 p.m., ... [the Hoffmans' car] collided with a train of the New York, New Haven, and Hartford Railroad Company. Inez died, and Howard was "severely and permanently" injured.

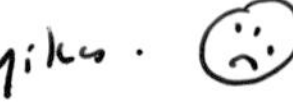

Howard Hoffman filed suit in the United States District Court for the Eastern District of New York, [where he claimed residence. At trial he] testified that he came to a stop fifteen to twenty feet from the Elkey–Buckley railroad crossing, looked both ways, and saw no light and heard no bell. He then started up in first gear, traveling between three and five miles per hour as he approached the grade crossing. As he was just about over the near rail, he saw a dark mass closely approaching from his left. He still saw no light. The next thing he knew, he was a patient at the Pittsfield, Massachusetts, hospital....

The Railroad claimed its agents acted with due care and asserted that Hoffman was contributorily negligent. To prove a whistle blew and a bell sounded, the defense offered the testimony of the conductor, a brakeman and a flagman ..., the sister and brother of the conductor, and five other witnesses....

... The jury evidently disagreed with the Railroad's theory of the case, finding for the plaintiff [and awarding substantial damages]. The Railroad appealed....

Michael Ariens, *A Short History of Hearsay Reform, with Particular Reference to* Hoffman v. Palmer, *Eddie Morgan and Jerry Frank*, 28 IND. L. REV. 183, 191–94 (1995).

On appeal the railroad complained that the trial judge wrongly excluded an interview of the train's engineer, Harold McDermott, who died before trial. The interview, conducted by the railroad's assistant superintendent, took place two days after the accident in the presence of the railroad's lawyer, a railroad police lieutenant, and a utilities official. Though the railroad raised other issues on appeal, the exclusion of McDermott's interview proved to be the crux of the matter.

Just five years earlier Congress had passed a statute to ease the admission of business records as an exception to the hearsay rule:

> In any court of the United States ..., any writing or record ... made as a memorandum or record of any act, transaction, occurrence, or event, shall be admissible as evidence of said act, transaction, occurrence, or event, if it shall appear that it was made in the regular course of any business, and that it was the regular course of such business to make such memorandum or record at the time of such act, transaction, occurrence, or event or within a reasonable time thereafter. All other circumstances of the making of such writing or record, including lack of personal knowledge by the entrant or

> maker, may be shown to affect its weight, but they shall not affect its admissibility. The term "business" shall include business, profession, occupation, and calling of every kind.

Act of June 20, 1936, 49 Stat. 1561, 28 U.S.C. § 695.

The rule's purpose, as the Attorney General had written to the Senate Judiciary Committee at the time of its adoption, was to avoid the difficulty of finding witnesses who could speak from firsthand knowledge about a business's routine and often nondescript activities. "[I]n a recent criminal case," the Attorney General complained, "the Government was prevented from making out a prima-facie case by a ruling that entries in the books of a bank made in the regular course of business were not admissible in evidence, unless the specific bookkeeper who made an entry could identify it. This was impossible [because] the bank employed 18 bookkeepers, and since the entries were made by bookkeeping machines, no one bookkeeper could recall which entries were made by him. . . ." *Hoffman v. Palmer*, 129 F.2d 976, 989 n.25b (2d Cir. 1942) (quoting Attorney General's memorandum).

The defendant railroad argued that its interview of the deceased engineer fell within the scope of the new rule. That interview, salvaged from the appellate record by Professor Michael Ariens, reads as follows:

Q: [By J.W. Cuineen, Assistant Superintendent of the Railroad]: How long employed by the New Haven Railroad?

A: 33 years.

Q: In what capacity?

A: Fireman and Engineer. . . .

Q: You were engineer on engine 438 with Conductor Johnson on December 25th?

A: Yes, Sir. . . .

Q: You were headed south?

A: Backing up. . . .

Q: You had a back-up headlight on the tender?

A: Yes, sir, a good one.

Q: Where did you light it?

A: Daly's [the previous station]. . . .

Q: Approaching Weststockbridge, the first highway crossing north of the station, what whistle signals were given for that crossing?

A: Regulation crossing whistle two long two short repeated. . . .

Q: You have an automatic bell ringer?

A: Yes.

Q: When did you start it?

A: It was going all the way from the whistling post at the first crossing until after the accident happened. . . .

Q: When did you last observe that the light on the tender was burning?

A: When I put it out at State Line.

Q: It was burning after the accident?

A: Yes. . . .

Q: In your experience in driving [in an automobile] over that crossing how far back on the highway could you see a headlight of an approaching train?

A: Why half a mile right near that house up there.

Q: There is a little bridge down there how far is that from the tracks?

A: 100 feet.

Q: You would be able to see a train from there and stop in time for it?

A: Yes, sir, if you had any brakes at all. . . .

I have read my statement consisting of 4 pages and it is true and correct.

Signed HAROLD D. McDERMOTT.

Ariens, *supra,* at 201 n.117 (quoting from Defendants' Exhibit J in appellate record).

On a split vote the Second Circuit Court of Appeals upheld the trial judge's decision to exclude McDermott's statement. *See Hoffman v. Palmer, supra.* Writing for the majority, Judge Jerome Frank began by justifying the business records exception in terms of the unusual trustworthiness of such records when made in the "regular course of business." These four words, he said, "came into the statute saturated with history":

> They connote—to recall Wigmore's comments—(1) a regularity serving "to counteract the possible temptation to misstatements"; (2) a situation which would lead to detection of falsification, so that misstatements "cannot safely be made"; (3) a relationship, when a writing is made by an employee under a duty to his employer, which includes the "risk of censure and disgrace" for misstatements.

129 F.2d at 984 (quoting Wigmore, Evidence § 1522 (3d ed. 1940)).

Frank argued that Congress had just such guarantees of trustworthiness in mind when it enacted the business records statute. Congress intended to relax the hearsay rule "in one respect only, i.e., that where there is a regular system of making entries, and the system is such as to be 'likely to ensure accuracy,' there is no necessity of introducing the [testimony] of the entrants." Frank said Congress was relying on earlier authorities that had held that "an essential condition of the admission of such hearsay is the 'circumstantial guaranty of trustworthiness' consisting of the accuracy ensured by the nature of the regular system of entries." *Id.* at 988–89.

Having established the "trustworthiness" of business records as an essential condition of their admissibility, Frank readily found that McDermott's statement did not qualify. It was, he said, "dripping with motivations to misrepresent":

> Accordingly, *we decide this and no more:*
>
> *The statute does not permit the introduction in evidence of a hearsay statement ... concerning an accident, if the statement was prepared after the accident has occurred, where the person who makes the memorandum or report knows at the time of making it that he is very likely, in a probable law suit relating to that accident, to be charged with wrongdoing as a participant in the accident, so that he is almost certain, when making the memorandum or report, to be sharply affected by a desire to exculpate himself and to relieve himself or his employer of liability.*

129 F.2d at 991 (emphasis in original).

Frank's opinion did not persuade dissenting Judge Charles Clark, who argued that if business records had to be free from the taint of possible litigation, few would qualify: "Since the first cave man made notches on a stick, I had supposed that both the purpose and the value of records were their use in future disputes...." *Id.* at 1000 (Clark, J., dissenting). Nor did Frank persuade legendary evidence scholar Edmund Morgan, a harsh critic of the traditional hearsay rules and author of an earlier version of the business records exception. Morgan excoriated Frank for what Morgan deemed a reactionary opinion: "I must say that you have done a fine job in statutory emasculation. If we should have a few more decisions like yours construing the business entry statute, we should get back almost to the common law rule.... [B]ut I do not want to argue the matter with you...." Ariens, *supra*, at 209 (quoting letter from Morgan to Frank, July 3, 1942).

In succeeding months Frank tried to placate Morgan by sending him copies of opinions in which Frank pursued more "liberal" results. Morgan was not to be placated: "You did not need to send me this opinion to convince me that you are not 100% reactionary. I know full well your liberal tendency, but I still can't get over the shock of your distorting the statute and excluding a statement made in the course of duty in the *Hoffman* case." *Id.* at 213 n.180 (quoting letter of Nov. 23, 1943).

"You have a hard heart," Frank replied. "Isn't it an extenuating fact that nine Supreme Court justices similarly 'distorted' the statute?" *Id.* (quoting letter of Nov. 27, 1943).

For indeed the Supreme Court had affirmed Frank's opinion unanimously . . . .

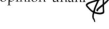

PALMER V. HOFFMAN

318 U.S. 109 (1943).

■ MR. JUSTICE DOUGLAS delivered the opinion of the Court. This case arose out of a grade crossing accident which occurred in Massachusetts. Diversity of citizenship brought it to the federal District Court in New York. . . . On the question of negligence the trial court submitted three issues to the jury—failure to ring a bell, to blow a whistle, to have a light burning in the front of the train. The jury returned a verdict in favor of respondent individually for some $25,000 and in favor of respondent as administrator for $9,000. . . .

I

The accident occurred on the night of December 25, 1940. On December 27, 1940, the engineer of the train, who died before the trial, made a statement at a freight office of petitioners where he was interviewed by an assistant superintendent of the road and by a representative of the Massachusetts Public Utilities Commission. This statement was offered in evidence by petitioners under the Act of June 20, 1936, 49 Stat. 1561, 28 U.S.C. § 695. They offered to prove (in the language of the Act) that the statement was signed in the regular course of business, it being the regular course of such business to make such a statement. Respondent's objection to its introduction was sustained.

We agree with the majority view below that it was properly excluded.

We may assume that if the statement was made "in the regular course" of business, it would satisfy the other provisions of the Act. But we do not think that it was made "in the regular course" of business within the meaning of the Act. The business of the petitioners is the railroad business. That business like other enterprises entails the keeping of numerous books and records essential to its conduct or useful in its efficient operation. Though such books and records were considered reliable and trustworthy for major decisions in the industrial and business world, their use in litigation was greatly circumscribed or hedged about by the hearsay rule—restrictions which greatly increased the time and cost of making the proof where those who made the records were numerous.[2] It was that problem which started the movement towards

2. The problem was well stated by Judge Learned Hand in Massachusetts Bonding & Ins. Co. v. Norwich Pharmacal Co., 18 F.2d 934, 937 (2d Cir. 1927): "The

adoption of legislation embodying the principles of the present Act. And the legislative history of the Act indicates the same purpose.

The engineer's statement which was held inadmissible in this case falls into quite a different category. It is not a record made for the systematic conduct of the business as a business. An accident report . . . [is not] typical of entries made systematically or as a matter of routine to record events or occurrences, to reflect transactions with others, or to provide internal controls. The conduct of a business commonly entails the payment of tort claims incurred by the negligence of its employees. But the fact that a company makes a business out of recording its employees' versions of their accidents does not put those statements in the class of records made "in the regular course" of the business within the meaning of the Act. If it did, then any law office in the land could follow the same course, since business as defined in the Act includes the professions. We would then have a real perversion of a rule designed to facilitate admission of records which experience has shown to be quite trustworthy. Any business by installing a regular system for recording and preserving its version of accidents for which it was potentially liable could qualify those reports under the Act. . . . The probability of trustworthiness of records because they were routine reflections of the day to day operations of a business would be forgotten as the basis of the rule. . . . We cannot so completely empty the words of the Act of their historic meaning. If the Act is to be extended to apply not only to a "regular course" of a business but also to any "regular course" of conduct which may have some relationship to business, Congress not this Court must extend it. Such a major change which opens wide the door to avoidance of cross-examination should not be left to implication. Nor is it any answer to say that Congress has provided in the Act that the various circumstances of the making of the record should affect its weight, not its admissibility. That provision comes into play only in case the other requirements of the Act are met.

In short, it is manifest that in this case those reports are not for the systematic conduct of the enterprise as a railroad business. Unlike payrolls, accounts receivable, accounts payable, bills of lading and the like, these reports are calculated for use essentially in the court, not in the business. Their primary utility is in litigating, not in railroading.

routine of modern affairs, mercantile, financial and industrial, is conducted with so extreme a division of labor that the transactions cannot be proved at first hand without the concurrence of persons, each of whom can contribute no more than a slight part, and that part not dependent on his memory of the event. Records, and records alone, are their adequate repository, and are in practice accepted as accurate upon the faith of the routine itself, and of the self-consistency of their contents. Unless they can be used in court without the task of calling those who at all stages had a part in the transactions recorded, nobody need ever pay a debt, if only his creditor does a large enough business."

It is, of course, not for us to take these reports out of the Act if Congress has put them in. But there is nothing in the background of the law on which this Act was built or in its legislative history which suggests for a moment that the business of preparing cases for trial should be included. In this connection it should be noted that the Act of May 6, 1910, 36 Stat. 350, 45 U.S.C. § 38, requires officers of common carriers by rail to make under oath monthly reports of railroad accidents to the Interstate Commerce Commission, setting forth the nature and causes of the accidents and the circumstances connected therewith. And the same Act (45 U.S.C. § 40) gives the Commission authority to investigate and to make reports upon such accidents. It is provided, however, that "Neither the report required by section 38 of this title nor any report of the investigation provided for in section 40 of this title nor any part thereof shall be admitted as evidence or used for any purpose in any suit or action for damages growing out of any matter mentioned in said report or investigation." 45 U.S.C. § 41. A similar provision bars the use in litigation of reports concerning accidents resulting from the failure of a locomotive boiler or its appurtenances. That legislation reveals an explicit Congressional policy to rule out reports of accidents which certainly have as great a claim to objectivity as the statement sought to be admitted in the present case. We can hardly suppose that Congress modified or qualified by implication these long standing statutes when it permitted records made "in the regular course" of business to be introduced. Nor can we assume that Congress having expressly prohibited the use of the company's reports on its accidents impliedly altered that policy when it came to reports by its employees to their superiors. The inference is wholly the other way....

Affirmed.

Problem 7.39
Lawn Mowers

Andrea Donohue bought her gas-powered lawn mower at Garden Depot, a large yard equipment store. Later she sued the mower's manufacturer for injuries she sustained when the pull cord came loose while she was trying to start the mower. Donohue claimed that the sudden release of the cord caused her to fall over backward and strike her head.

(1) At trial Donohue seeks to offer two merchandise-return records from the service counter at Garden Depot. The records reflect returns of other lawn mowers of the same make and model that Donohue had bought. Both records bear a clerk's

notation that the customer returned the mower because the cord had come loose. Called by Donohue as a witness, the manager of the service counter testifies that although he does not himself work at the counter, he is very familiar with the operations and record-keeping practices. He says counter employees routinely fill out a form for each merchandise return. Shown the two forms Donohue seeks to admit, he confirms they were kept in the regular course of Garden Depot's business. He adds that counter employees are required to ask each customer the reason for returning the item and to record the customer's answer. Employees do not routinely verify the customer's complaint or inspect the returned merchandise.

If defense counsel objects to admission of the forms on hearsay grounds, how should the court rule?

(2) Assume instead that the defendant manufacturer seeks to offer a form of the sort just mentioned against Donohue. This particular form reflects Donohue's own return of her mower following her injury. On this form, the clerk had written, "Customer Andrea Donohue states as reason for return that grass chute often clogs up."

If plaintiff's counsel objects to admission of this form, how should the court rule?

UNITED STATES v. VIGNEAU

187 F.3d 70 (1st Cir. 1999), *cert. denied*, 528 U.S. 1172 (2000).

■ BOUDIN, CIRCUIT JUDGE. . . . From around February 1995 to at least the end of that year, Patrick Vigneau and Richard Crandall conducted a venture to acquire marijuana and steroids in the Southwest and resell them in the Northeastern United States. Crandall obtained the marijuana and steroids from suppliers in El Paso, Texas, and in Mexico, and sent the drugs to Patrick Vigneau in Rhode Island and southeastern Massachusetts. . . .

Some of the proceeds from these Northeastern sales had to be sent to Crandall in Texas so that he could pay suppliers and share in the profits. Patrick Vigneau transmitted funds to Crandall primarily through Western Union money orders. The money orders were sent by Patrick Vigneau or others, sometimes in the sender's true name but often using false or borrowed names. Timothy Owens, who assisted Crandall in acquiring drugs, frequently picked up the checks from Western Union, cashed them, and gave the money to Crandall. . . .

At trial, the government relied on the testimony of over 20 witnesses, including Owens . . ., and on physical evidence, including . . . Western Union money transfer records. . . . The jury convicted Patrick Vigneau of . . . conspiracy to distribute marijuana and 21 counts of money laundering on specific occasions and conspiracy to launder money. . . . He now appeals. . . .

On this appeal, Patrick Vigneau's strongest claim is that the district court erred in allowing the government to introduce, without redaction and for all purposes, Western Union "To Send Money" forms, primarily in support of the money laundering charges. These forms, as a Western Union custodian testified, are handed by the sender of money to a Western Union agent after the sender completes the left side of the form by writing (1) the sender's name, address and telephone number; (2) the amount of the transfer; and (3) the intended recipient's name and location. The Western Union clerk then fills in the right side of the form with the clerk's signature, date, amount of the transfer and fee, and a computer-generated control number; but at least in 1995, Western Union clerks did not require independent proof of the sender's identity.*

WESTERN MONEY
UNION TRANSFER™

To send money

The fastest way to send money.®

To be completed by customer:	*To be completed by office:*
Cash amount delivered by sender: ______	Date: ______
Sender's name: ______	Amount received: ______
Sender's address: ______	Charge: ______
Sender's telephone: ______	Money Transfer control no.:
Name of authorized recipient: ______	______
Recipient's address: ______	Agent: ______

. . . The original forms are usually discarded after six months, but the information provided by the sender, as well as the information from all records associated with the money transfer, are recorded in a computer database. In this case, for some transfers the government had the forms completed by the sender, but for most it had only the computer records.

The government introduced over 70 records of Western Union money transfers. Patrick Vigneau's name, address and phone number appeared as that of the sender on 21 of the "To Send Money" forms (11

* [What follows is a simplified version of a Western Union "To Send Money" form. *See United States v. Arteaga*, 117 F.3d 388, 392 (9th Cir. 1997) (reprinting an actual form).—GF]

other names, including fictional names ..., appeared as those of the senders on the other forms), and those 21 forms corresponded to the 21 specific counts of money laundering on which Patrick Vigneau was ultimately convicted by the jury. Patrick Vigneau's most plausible objection, which was presented in the district court and is renewed on appeal, is that his name, address and telephone number on the "To Send Money" forms were inadmissible hearsay used to identify Patrick Vigneau as the sender.

... Whoever wrote the name "Patrick Vigneau" on the "To Send Money" forms was stating in substance: "I am Patrick Vigneau and this is my address and telephone number." Of course, if there were independent evidence that the writer was Patrick Vigneau, the statements would constitute party-opponent admissions and would fall within an exception to the rule against hearsay, FED. R. EVID. 801(d)(2) (the rule says admissions are "not hearsay," but that is an academic refinement). However, the government [lacked such independent evidence].

Instead, the government argues that the "To Send Money" forms and the computerized information reflecting those forms and the correlated material were admissible under the business records exception. FED. R. EVID. 803(6). [Unrestyled] Rule 803(6) provides that business records are admissible where shown to be business records by a qualified witness, "unless the source of information or the method and circumstances of preparation indicate lack of trustworthiness."* The district judge accepted the view that the Western Union records were trustworthy and admitted the "To Send Money" forms (or equivalent computer records) without redaction and for all purposes, advising the jury that "what weight you give to them will be your choice."

The district judge was correct that the "To Send Money" forms literally comply with the business records exception because each form is a business record, and in this case, the computer records appeared to be a trustworthy account of what was recorded on the original "To Send Money" forms. The difficulty is that despite its language, the business records exception does not embrace statements contained within a business record that were made by one who is not a part of the business if the embraced statements are offered for their truth. The classic case is Johnson v. Lutz, 253 N.Y. 124 (1930), which excluded an unredacted police report incorporating the statement of a bystander (even though the

* [As this book goes to press late in 2012, an amendment to Rule 803(6) is under review. If passed into law, the amendment would alter paragraph (E) of the rule to require that "the *opponent* ... *not* show that the source of information or the method or circumstances of preparation indicate a lack of trustworthiness." (RB 232–33 (emphasis added).) The advisory committee explains that "[i]t is appropriate to impose the burden of proving untrustworthiness on the opponent, as the basic admissibility requirements [set out in paragraphs (A) through (D)] are sufficient to establish a presumption that the record is reliable." (RB 234.) The amendment will not become law before December 1, 2014, and may be altered or abandoned in the rulemaking process.—GF]

police officer recorded it in the regular course of business) because the informant was not part of that business. The Advisory Committee Notes to Rule 803(6) cite *Johnson v. Lutz* and make clear that the rule is intended to incorporate its holding. [*See* RB 227.]

Johnson v. Lutz is not a technical formality but follows directly from the very rationale for the business records exception. When a clerk records the receipt of an order over the telephone, the regularity of the procedure, coupled with business incentives to keep accurate records, provide reasonable assurance that the record thus made reflects the clerk's original entry. Thus the business record, although an out-of-court statement and therefore hearsay, is admitted without calling the clerk to prove that the clerk received an order.

But no such safeguards of regularity or business checks automatically assure the truth of a statement to the business by a stranger to it, such as that made by the bystander to the police officer or that made by the money sender who gave the form containing his name, address, and telephone number to Western Union. Accordingly, the *Johnson v. Lutz* gloss excludes this "outsider" information, where offered for its truth, unless some other hearsay exception applies to the outsider's own statement. This gloss on the business records exception, which the Federal Rules elsewhere call the "hearsay within hearsay" problem, FED. R. EVID. 805, is well settled in this circuit. Other circuits are in accord....

Of course, in some situations, the statement by the "outsider" reflected in the business record may be admissible not for its truth but for some other purpose, but the disputed "To Send Money" forms here were admitted by the district court for all purposes, including as proof of the sender's identity....

No doubt, the "To Send Money" forms were relevant to the government's case regardless of whether Patrick Vigneau (or any other named sender) was the person who made an individual transfer: they showed transfers of money from Rhode Island directed to Crandall and others that tended to support the general description of the drug and money laundering activities described by the government's witnesses. Thus, the forms could have been offered in redacted form, omitting the information identifying Patrick Vigneau as the sender of 21 of the forms. But that is not what happened.

Some cases have admitted under the business records exception "outsider" statements contained in business records, like the sender's name on the Western Union form, where there is evidence that the business itself used a procedure for verifying identity (e.g., by requiring a credit card or driver's license). Probably the best analytical defense of this gloss is that in such a case, the verification procedure is circumstantial evidence of identity that goes beyond the mere bootstrap use of the name to establish identity. While this gloss may well represent a reasonable accommodation of conflicting values, verification was not Western Union's practice at the time. . . .

We thus conclude, in accord with the Tenth Circuit, United States v. Cestnik, 36 F.3d 904, 908 (10th Cir. 1994), *cert. denied*, 513 U.S. 1175 (1995), that the sender name, address and telephone number on the forms should not have been admitted for their truth. There is no plausible claim of harmless error as to 18 of the money laundering counts where, as here, the government might well have had difficulty in tying Patrick Vigneau to any of these 18 specific transactions except through the hearsay statements themselves.

The issue is much more difficult as to the three remaining transmissions. For two of them, it appears that the sender's cop[ies] of the "To Send Money" forms were among the papers seized from Patrick Vigneau's van, where they were in a suitcase together with other papers connected with Patrick Vigneau. This, we believe, was sufficient circumstantial evidence specific to these documents to allow [the inference] that the sender information was indeed an admission by Patrick Vigneau, curing the hearsay problem. . . .

The independent evidence as to the third transaction is somewhat thinner but still distinguishes it from the other 18. At trial, the government asked Owens about his memory of a transfer occurring on one of the dates charged as a money laundering count. Owens said not only that he remembered the transfer but that Crandall had told him that Patrick Vigneau was the sender. This double hearsay statement might well come in under the coconspirator exception, although the force of the proof is weakened because we have no idea of the basis for Crandall's statement that Patrick Vigneau was the sender.

Nevertheless, we cannot find the unqualified admission of the computer records harmless even as to these three transactions. While we are inclined to think that a jury would likely have accepted the slips in the van as reflecting transactions by Patrick Vigneau, the defense never had reason to argue the point—and argument was possible—since all of the Western Union records themselves were admitted for all purposes, including identification of the sender. In addition, given limited familiarity with the exhibits, we are somewhat uncomfortable with rescuing these three counts based on a line of argument never articulated by the government. . . .

Patrick Vigneau's . . . convictions for 21 counts of money laundering are vacated without prejudice to new trial on those counts. . . .

It is so ordered.

Problem 7.40
BALCO Logs

In 2001, Barry Bonds hit 73 home runs for the San Francisco Giants. Also in 2001, as well as in prior and succeeding years, BALCO Laboratories, Inc. in San Francisco recorded, under the name "Barry Bonds," positive results of urine and blood tests for performance enhancing drugs. In 2003, Bonds swore under oath he had not taken performance enhancing drugs, so the government is now prosecuting him for perjury. But to succeed it must prove the tested samples BALCO recorded actually came from Barry Bonds. . . .

The government tried to prove the source of the samples with the indisputably admissible testimony of a trainer, Greg Anderson, that Barry Bonds identified the samples as his own before giving them to Anderson, who took them to BALCO for testing. Anderson refused to testify, however, and has been jailed for contempt of court.

The government then went to Plan B, which was to offer the testimony of the BALCO employee, James Valente, to whom Anderson gave the samples. Valente would testify Anderson brought the samples to the lab and said they came from Barry Bonds. . . . [W]hen [Valente] received a . . . sample from [Anderson], he would assign the sample a code number in a log book, and then send the sample to Quest Diagnostics for analysis. Quest would send the result back to BALCO. BALCO would then record the result next to the code number [and Bonds's name] in the log book. . . .

Bonds testified that he had known Anderson since grade school. . . . [He] testified he took whatever supplements and creams Anderson gave him without question because he trusted Anderson as his friend. . . . Bonds stated that he did not believe anything Anderson provided him contained steroids. He specifically denied Anderson ever told him the cream was actually a steroid cream. . . . Anderson asked Bonds to provide blood samples on five or six occasions [and urine samples about four times], telling Bonds he would take the [samples] to BALCO to determine any nutritional deficiencies in his body. . . .

Bonds admitted to paying Anderson $15,000 a year for training. Bonds stated that this payment was not formally agreed to. . . . ("Greg has never asked me for a penny."). Bonds . . . considered Anderson a friend whom he paid for his help.

> On February 12, 2004, a grand jury indicted Anderson and other BALCO figures for their illegal steroid distribution. Anderson pled guilty to these charges and admitted to distributing performance enhancing drugs to professional athletes....
>
> *United States v. Bonds*, 608 F.3d 495, 497–99 (9th Cir. 2010). Was the trial judge correct in ruling that the "log sheets on which BALCO recorded the results of the testing under Bonds's name, were ... inadmissible to prove the samples" were Barry Bonds's? What were the best arguments for and against admissibility?

---

6. Public Records and Reports

Focus on **FRE 803(8) & (10)**

Beech Aircraft Corp. v. Rainey

488 U.S. 153 (1988).

■ BRENNAN, J., delivered the opinion of the Court, in which WHITE, MARSHALL, BLACKMUN, STEVENS, SCALIA, and KENNEDY, JJ., joined, and in Parts I and II of which REHNQUIST, C.J., and O'CONNOR, J., joined. REHNQUIST, C.J., filed an opinion concurring in part and dissenting in part, in which O'CONNOR, J., joined.

■ JUSTICE BRENNAN delivered the opinion of the Court. In this action we address a longstanding conflict among the Federal Courts of Appeals over whether Federal Rule of Evidence [803(8)(A)(iii)], which provides an exception to the hearsay rule for public investigatory reports containing "factual findings," extends to conclusions and opinions contained in such reports....

I

This litigation stems from the crash of a Navy training aircraft at Middleton Field, Alabama, on July 13, 1982, which took the lives of both pilots on board, Lieutenant Commander Barbara Ann Rainey and Ensign Donald Bruce Knowlton. The accident took place while Rainey, a Navy flight instructor, and Knowlton, her student, were flying "touch-and-go" exercises in a T–34C Turbo–Mentor aircraft, number 3E955. Their aircraft and several others flew in an oval pattern, each plane making successive landing/takeoff maneuvers on the runway. Following its fourth pass at the runway, 3E955 appeared to make a left turn prematurely, cutting out the aircraft ahead of it in the pattern and threatening a collision. After radio warnings from two other pilots, the plane banked sharply to the right in order to avoid the other aircraft. At that point it lost altitude rapidly, crashed, and burned.

Because of the damage to the plane and the lack of any survivors, the cause of the accident could not be determined with certainty. The two pilots' surviving spouses brought a product liability suit against petitioners Beech Aircraft Corporation, the plane's manufacturer, and Beech Aerospace Services, which serviced the plane under contract with the Navy. The plaintiffs alleged that the crash had been caused by a loss of engine power, known as "rollback," due to some defect in the aircraft's fuel control system. The defendants, on the other hand, advanced the theory of pilot error, suggesting that the plane had stalled during the abrupt avoidance maneuver.

. . . Both sides relied primarily on expert testimony. One piece of evidence presented by the defense was an investigative report prepared by Lieutenant Commander William Morgan on order of the training squadron's commanding officer and pursuant to authority granted in the Manual of the Judge Advocate General. This "JAG Report," completed during the six weeks following the accident, was organized into sections labeled "finding of fact," "opinions," and "recommendations," and was supported by some 60 attachments. The "finding[s] of fact" included statements like the following:

> "13. At approximately 1020, while turning crosswind without proper interval, 3E955 crashed, immediately caught fire and burned. . . .
>
> "27. At the time of impact, the engine of 3E955 was operating but was operating at reduced power."

Among his "opinions" Lieutenant Commander Morgan stated, in paragraph 5, that due to the deaths of the two pilots and the destruction of the aircraft "it is almost impossible to determine exactly what happened to Navy 3E955 from the time it left the runway on its last touch and go until it impacted the ground." He nonetheless continued with a detailed reconstruction of a possible set of events, based on pilot error, that could have caused the accident.[2] The next two paragraphs stated a caveat and a conclusion:

2. Paragraph 5 reads in its entirety as follows:

"Because both pilots were killed in the crash and because of the nearly total destruction of the aircraft by fire, it is almost impossible to determine exactly what happened to Navy 3E955 from the time it left the runway on its last touch and go until it impacted the ground. However, from evidence available and the information gained

"6. Although the above sequence of events is the most likely to have occurred, it does not change the possibility that a 'rollback' did occur.

"7. The most probable cause of the accident was the pilots [*sic*] failure to maintain proper interval."

The trial judge initially determined, at a pretrial conference, that the JAG Report was sufficiently trustworthy to be admissible, but that it "would be admissible only on its factual findings and would not be admissible insofar as any opinions or conclusions are concerned." The day before trial, however, the court reversed itself and ruled, over the plaintiffs' objection, that certain of the conclusions would be admitted. Accordingly, the court admitted most of the report's "opinions," including the first sentence of paragraph 5 about the impossibility of determining exactly what happened, and paragraph 7, which opined about failure to maintain proper interval as "[t]he most probable cause of the accident." On the other hand, the remainder of paragraph 5 was barred as "nothing but a possible scenario," and paragraph 6, in which investigator Morgan refused to rule out rollback, was deleted as well.[3] . . .

Following a 2–week trial, the jury returned a verdict for petitioners [the aircraft companies]. A panel of the Eleventh Circuit reversed and remanded for a new trial. . . . [T]he panel agreed with Rainey's argument that Federal Rule of Evidence [803(8)(A)(iii)], which excepts investigatory

from eyewitnesses, a possible scenario can be constructed as follows:

"a. 3E955 entered the Middleton pattern with ENS Knowlton at the controls attempting to make normal landings.

"b. After two unsuccessful attempts, LCDR Rainey took the aircraft and demonstrated two landings 'on the numbers.' After getting the aircraft safely airborne from the touch and go, LCDR Rainey transferred control to ENS Knowlton.

"c. Due to his physical strength, ENS Knowlton did not trim down elevator as the aircraft accelerated toward 100 knots; in fact, due to his inexperience, he may have trimmed incorrectly, putting in more up elevator.

"d. As ENS Knowlton was climbing to pattern altitude, he did not see the aircraft established on downwind so he began his crosswind turn. Due to ENS Knowlton's large size, LCDR Rainey was unable to see the conflicting traffic.

"e. Hearing the first call, LCDR Rainey probably cautioned ENS Knowlton to check for traffic. Hearing the second call, she took immediate action and told ENS Knowlton she had the aircraft as she initiated a turn toward an upwind heading.

"f. As the aircraft was rolling from a climbing left turn to a climbing right turn, ENS Knowlton released the stick letting the up elevator trim take effect causing the nose of the aircraft to pitch abruptly up.

"g. The large angle of bank used trying to maneuver for aircraft separation coupled with the abrupt pitch up caused the aircraft to stall. As the aircraft stalled and went into a nose low attitude, LCDR Rainey reduced the PCL (power control lever) toward idle. As she was rolling toward wings level, she advanced the PCL to maximum to stop the loss of altitude but due to the 2 to 4 second lag in engine response, the aircraft impacted the ground before power was available."

3. The record gives no indication why paragraph 6 was deleted. Neither at trial nor on appeal have respondents raised any objection to the deletion of paragraph 6.

reports from the hearsay rule, did not encompass evaluative conclusions or opinions. Therefore, it held, the "conclusions" contained in the JAG Report should have been excluded. . . .

II

. . . Because the Federal Rules of Evidence are a legislative enactment, we turn to the "traditional tools of statutory construction" in order to construe their provisions. We begin with the language of the Rule itself. Proponents of the narrow view have generally relied heavily on a perceived dichotomy between "fact" and "opinion" in arguing for the limited scope of the phrase "factual findings." Smith v. Ithaca Corp., 612 F.2d 215 (5th Cir. 1980), contrasted the term "factual findings" in Rule [803(8)(A)(iii)] with the language of Rule 803(6) (records of regularly conducted activity), which expressly refers to "opinions" and "diagnoses." "Factual findings," the court opined, must be something other than opinions. 612 F.2d at 221–22.[8]

For several reasons, we do not agree. In the first place, it is not apparent that the term "factual findings" should be read to mean simply "facts" (as opposed to "opinions" or "conclusions"). A common definition of "finding of fact" is, for example, "[a] conclusion by way of reasonable inference from the evidence." BLACK'S LAW DICTIONARY 569 (5th ed. 1979). To say the least, the language of the Rule does not compel us to reject the interpretation that "factual findings" includes conclusions or opinions that flow from a factual investigation. Second, we note that, contrary to what is often assumed, the language of the Rule does not state that "factual findings" are admissible, but that "*reports* . . . setting forth . . . factual findings" (emphasis added) are admissible. On this reading, the

8. The court in *Smith* found it significant that different language was used in Rules 803(6) and [803(8)(A)(iii)]: "Since these terms are used in similar context within the same Rule, it is logical to assume that Congress intended that the terms have different and distinct meanings." 612 F. 2d at 222. The Advisory Committee Notes to Rule 803(6) make clear, however, that the Committee was motivated by a particular concern in drafting the language of that Rule. While opinions were rarely found in traditional "business records," the expansion of that category to encompass documents such as medical diagnoses and test results brought with it some uncertainty in earlier versions of the Rule as to whether diagnoses and the like were admissible. "In order to make clear its adherence to the [position favoring admissibility]," the Committee stated, "the rule specifically includes both diagnoses and opinions, in addition to acts, events, and conditions, as proper subjects of admissible entries." Advisory Committee's Notes on FED. R. EVID. 803(6) [RB 228]. Since that specific concern was not present in the context of Rule [803(8)(A)(iii)], the absence of identical language should not be accorded much significance. What is more, the Committee's report on Rule [803(8)(A)(iii)] strongly suggests that that Rule has the same scope of admissibility as does Rule 803(6): "Hence the rule, *as in Exception [paragraph] (6)*, assumes admissibility in the first instance but with ample provision for escape if sufficient negative factors are present." Advisory Committee's Notes on FED. R. EVID. 803(8) [RB 238] (emphasis added).

language of the Rule does not create a distinction between "fact" and "opinion" contained in such reports.

Turning next to the legislative history of [803(8)(A)(iii)], we find no clear answer to the question of how the Rule's language should be interpreted. Indeed, in this litigation the legislative history may well be at the origin of the dispute. Rather than the more usual situation where a court must attempt to glean meaning from ambiguous comments of legislators who did not focus directly on the problem at hand, here the Committees in both Houses of Congress clearly recognized and expressed their opinions on the precise question at issue. Unfortunately, however, they took diametrically opposite positions. Moreover, the two Houses made no effort to reconcile their views, either through changes in the Rule's language or through a statement in the Report of the Conference Committee.

The House Judiciary Committee, which dealt first with the proposed rules after they had been transmitted to Congress by this Court, included in its Report but one brief paragraph on Rule [803(8)(A)(iii)]:

> "The Committee approved Rule 803(8) without substantive change from the form in which it was submitted by the Court. The Committee intends that the phrase 'factual findings' be strictly construed and that evaluations or opinions contained in public reports shall not be admissible under this Rule."

[RB 238.] The Senate Committee responded at somewhat greater length, but equally emphatically:

> "The House Judiciary Committee report contained a statement of intent that 'the phrase "factual findings" in subdivision [(A)(iii)] be strictly construed and that evaluations or opinions contained in public reports shall not be admissible under this rule.' The committee takes strong exception to this limiting understanding of the application of the rule. We do not think it reflects an understanding of the intended operation of the rule as explained in the Advisory Committee notes to this subsection.... We think the restrictive interpretation of the House overlooks the fact that while the Advisory Committee assumes admissibility in the first instance of evaluative reports, they are not admissible if, as the rule states, 'the sources of information or other circumstances indicate lack of trustworthiness.' ..."

[RB 246.] Clearly this legislative history reveals a difference of view between the Senate and the House that affords no definitive guide to the congressional understanding. It seems clear however that the Senate understanding is more in accord with the wording of the Rule and with the comments of the Advisory Committee.[9]

9. *See* Advisory Committee's Notes on FED. R. EVID. [803(8)(A)(iii)]. As Congress did not amend the Advisory Committee's draft in any way that touches on the question

The Advisory Committee's comments are notable, first, in that they contain no mention of any dichotomy between statements of "fact" and "opinions" or "conclusions." What was on the Committee's mind was simply whether what it called "evaluative reports" should be admissible. Illustrating the previous division among the courts on this subject, the Committee cited numerous cases in which the admissibility of such reports had been both sustained and denied. It also took note of various federal statutes that made certain kinds of evaluative reports admissible in evidence. What is striking about all of these examples is that these were *reports that stated conclusions. E.g.*, Moran v. Pittsburgh–Des Moines Steel Co., 183 F.2d 467, 472–73 (3d Cir. 1950) (report of Bureau of Mines concerning the cause of a gas tank explosion admissible). The Committee's concern was clearly whether reports of this kind should be admissible. Nowhere in its comments is there the slightest indication that it even considered the solution of admitting only "factual" statements from such reports. Rather, the Committee referred throughout to "reports," without any such differentiation regarding the statements they contained. What the Committee referred to in the Rule's language as "reports . . . setting forth . . . factual findings" is surely nothing more or less than what in its commentary it called "evaluative reports." Its solution as to their admissibility is clearly stated in the final paragraph of its report on this Rule. That solution consists of two principles: First, "the rule . . . assumes admissibility in the first instance. . . ." Second, it provides "ample provision for escape if sufficient negative factors are present." [RB 237–38.]

That "provision for escape" is contained in the final clause of the [unrestyled] Rule: evaluative reports are admissible "unless the sources of information or other circumstances indicate lack of trustworthiness."* This trustworthiness inquiry—and not an arbitrary distinction between "fact" and "opinion"—was the Committee's primary safeguard against the admission of unreliable evidence, and it is important to note that it applies to all elements of the report. Thus, a trial judge has the discretion, and indeed the obligation, to exclude an entire report or portions thereof—whether narrow "factual" statements or broader "conclu-

before us, the Committee's commentary is particularly relevant in determining the meaning of the document Congress enacted.

* [As this book goes to press late in 2012, an amendment to Rule 803(8) is under review. If passed into law, the amendment would alter paragraph (B) of the rule to require that "the *opponent* . . . *not* show that the source of information or other circumstances indicate a lack of trustworthiness." (RB 247–48 (emphasis added).) The proposed amendment is a counterpart to a pending amendment to Rule 803(6), mentioned earlier at page 558 n.* The advisory committee explains that "if the proponent has established that the record meets the stated requirements of the exception—prepared by a public office and setting out information as specified in the Rule—then the burden is on the opponent to show a lack of trustworthiness." (RB 248.) The amendment will not become law before December 1, 2014, and may be altered or dropped in the rulemaking process.—GF]

sions"—that she determines to be untrustworthy.[11] Moreover, safeguards built into other portions of the Federal Rules, such as those dealing with relevance and prejudice, provide the court with additional means of scrutinizing and, where appropriate, excluding evaluative reports or portions of them. And of course it goes without saying that the admission of a report containing "conclusions" is subject to the ultimate safeguard—the opponent's right to present evidence tending to contradict or diminish the weight of those conclusions.

Our conclusion that neither the language of the Rule nor the intent of its framers calls for a distinction between "fact" and "opinion" is strengthened by the analytical difficulty of drawing such a line. It has frequently been remarked that the distinction between statements of fact and opinion is, at best, one of degree:

> "All statements in language are statements of opinion, i.e., statements of mental processes or perceptions. So-called 'statements of fact' are only more specific statements of opinion. What the judge means to say, when he asks the witness to state the facts, is: 'The nature of this case requires that you be more specific, if you can, in your description of what you saw.' " W. KING & D. PILLINGER, OPINION EVIDENCE IN ILLINOIS 4 (1942).

See also E. CLEARY, MCCORMICK ON EVIDENCE 27 (3d ed. 1984) ("There is no conceivable statement however specific, detailed and 'factual,' that is not in some measure the product of inference and reflection as well as observation and memory"). . . .

In the present action, the trial court had no difficulty in admitting as a factual finding the statement in the JAG Report that "[a]t the time of impact, the engine of 3E955 was operating but was operating at reduced power." Surely this "factual finding" could also be characterized as an opinion, which the investigator presumably arrived at on the basis of clues contained in the airplane wreckage. Rather than requiring that we draw some inevitably arbitrary line between the various shades of fact/opinion that invariably will be present in investigatory reports, we believe the Rule instructs us—as its plain language states—to admit "reports . . . setting forth . . . factual findings." The Rule's limitations and safeguards lie elsewhere: First, the requirement that reports contain factual findings bars the admission of statements not based on factual investigation. Second, the trustworthiness provision requires the court to make a determination as to whether the report, or any portion thereof, is sufficiently trustworthy to be admitted.

11. The Advisory Committee proposed a nonexclusive list of four factors it thought would be helpful in passing on this question: (1) the timeliness of the investigation; (2) the investigator's skill or experience; (3) whether a hearing was held; and (4) possible bias when reports are prepared with a view to possible litigation (citing Palmer v. Hoffman, 318 U.S. 109 (1943)). Advisory Committee's Notes on FED. R. EVID. [803(8)(A)(iii)]. . . . [RB 238.]

A broad approach to admissibility under Rule [803(8)(A)(iii)] as we have outlined it, is also consistent with the Federal Rules' general approach of relaxing the traditional barriers to "opinion" testimony. Rules 702–705 permit experts to testify in the form of an opinion, and without any exclusion of opinions on "ultimate issues." And Rule 701 permits even a lay witness to testify in the form of opinions or inferences drawn from her observations when testimony in that form will be helpful to the trier of fact. We see no reason to strain to reach an interpretation of Rule [803(8)(A)(iii)] that is contrary to the liberal thrust of the Federal Rules.

We hold, therefore, that portions of investigatory reports otherwise admissible under Rule [803(8)(A)(iii)] are not inadmissible merely because they state a conclusion or opinion. As long as the conclusion is based on a factual investigation and satisfies the Rule's trustworthiness requirement, it should be admissible along with other portions of the report. As the trial judge in this action determined that certain of the JAG Report's conclusions were trustworthy, he rightly allowed them to be admitted into evidence. We therefore reverse the judgment of the Court of Appeals in respect of the Rule [803(8)(A)(iii)] issue. . . .

It is so ordered.

■ CHIEF JUSTICE REHNQUIST, with whom JUSTICE O'CONNOR joins, concurring in part and dissenting in part. . . .

POLICE REPORTS AND BUSINESS RECORDS

Rule 803(8) creates a hearsay exception for certain public records and reports. The rationales for the exception, according to the advisory committee, are "the assumption that a public official will perform his duty properly and the unlikelihood that he will remember details independently of the record." (RB 236.) By their clear terms, however, subsections 803(8)(A)(ii) and 803(8)(A)(iii) do not extend to the reports of law enforcement personnel or evaluative reports if offered against the defendant in a criminal case. The legislative history of the rule makes plain that Congress fully intended to exclude such reports against the accused. (*See* RB 238, 241–45.)

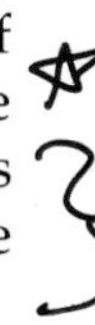

But what if a public record or report *also* satisfies the criteria of the business records exception, Rule 803(6)? May the trial court admit the report against a criminal defendant under that rule? Consider the divergent approaches of the Second and Tenth Circuits in the cases excerpted below. The Second Circuit addressed a government chemist's report in a drug case. *See United States v. Oates*, 560 F.2d 45 (2d Cir. 1977). The Tenth Circuit addressed IRS records in a tax-evasion case. *See United States v. Hayes*, 861 F.2d 1225 (10th Cir. 1988). The Ninth Circuit's more recent decision in *United States v. Weiland*, 420 F.3d 1062 (9th Cir. 2005), *cert.*

denied, *547 U.S. 1114 (2006), which dealt with certain prison records, suggests that courts see wisdom in both* Oates *and* Hayes *and are finding common ground between them.*

United States v. Oates

560 F.2d 45, 70–72 (2d Cir. 1977).

. . . Our conclusion that the chemist's report and worksheet do not satisfy the standards of FRE 803(8) comports perfectly with what we discern to be clear legislative intent not only to exclude such documents from the scope of FRE 803(8) but from the scope of FRE 803(6) as well. The reason why such a restrictive approach was adopted can be established by referring to the Advisory Committee's Notes and by examining the way in which Congress revised the draft legislation proposed by the Advisory Committee and which the Supreme Court submitted to Congress. . . . [A]n overriding concern of the Advisory Committee was that the rules be formulated so as to avoid impinging upon a criminal defendant's right to confront the witnesses against him. The Advisory Committee, in unequivocal language, offers the specter of collision with the confrontation clause as the explanation for the presence of FRE [803(8)(A)(iii)] in its proposed (and, since FRE [803(8)(A)(iii)] was unaltered during the legislative process, final) form:

> In one respect, however, the rule with respect to evaluative reports under [803(8)(A)(iii)] is very specific: they are admissible only in civil cases and against the government in criminal cases in view of the almost certain collision with confrontation rights which would result from their use against an accused in a criminal case.

Advisory Committee's Notes, Note to Paragraph (8) of Rule 803 [RB 238]. This preoccupation with preserving the confrontation rights of criminal defendants was shared by a Congress which established enhanced protection for those rights by substantially amending the proposed language of [803(8)(A)(ii)]. An amendment offered by Representative David Dennis added important qualifying language to item [(A)(ii)], which before the amendment deemed as "public records" under FRE 803(8) "matters observed pursuant to duty imposed by law as to which matters there was a duty to report." The amendment qualified the foregoing language by adding "excluding, however, in criminal cases matters observed by police officers and other law enforcement personnel." In the debate that followed the offer of this amendment, the accused's right to confront the witnesses against him was advanced as the impetus for the proposal. Speaking in support of the amendment, Representative Elizabeth Holtzman understood one of its purposes to be to "[reaffirm] the right of cross examination to the accused." In a similar vein, Representative Dennis, the sponsor of the proposal, confirmed that this was the intent of the amendment by emphasizing that the amendment pertained to "criminal cases, and in a criminal case the defendant should be confronted with the accuser to give him the chance to cross examine." . . .

The discussion in the preceding paragraphs describes why Congress decided to take the approach it did with regard to the use of "evaluative" reports under FRE [803(8)(A)(iii)] and reports of law enforcement personnel under [803(8)(A)(ii)]. The result Congress intended was the absolute inadmissibility of records of this nature, and that this was, indeed, the result which Congress believed it had achieved by Rules [803(8)(A)(ii)] and [(A)(iii)], could not have been articulated with any more clarity than it was by Representative William L. Hungate. . . . He informed the House that the Committee of Conference had rejected the Senate's attempt to create a new hearsay exception which would have permitted admission of police reports authored by officers unavailable to testify. He explained the meaning of the remaining related provisions:

> As the rules of evidence now stand, police and law enforcement reports are not admissible against defendants in criminal cases. This is made quite clear by the provisions of rule [803(8)(A)(ii)] and [(A)(iii)].

This unequivocal language shows that it was Representative Hungate's understanding that the language retained in FRE [803(8)(A)(ii)] and [(A)(iii)] meant that those provisions had the effect of rendering absolutely inadmissible against defendants in criminal cases the "police reports" of item [(A)(ii)] and the "evaluative reports" of item [(A)(iii)].

Representative Hungate's remarks would not be comprehensively all-encompassing, of course, if the police and evaluative reports denied the benefit of qualifying under FRE [803(8)(A)(ii)] and [(A)(iii)] were considered eligible for qualification under FRE 803(6), the so-called business records exception, or under any other exception to the hearsay rule. . . .

Indeed, this very question of whether so-called police reports disqualified under FRE 803(8) could nonetheless gain eventual admission by first satisfying the standards of some other hearsay exception was expressly raised by Representative Elizabeth Holtzman after Representative Hungate had presented to the House his explanation of the Committee of Conference's actions. Representative Holtzman was particularly concerned with the Committee of Conference's retention of what she termed the "open-ended" exceptions to the hearsay rule, the exceptions contained in FRE 803(24) and 804(b)(5) [now consolidated in Rule 807]. Speaking in opposition to the proposed legislation, Representative Holtzman suggested that the police reports which the Committee of Conference . . . had gone to such trouble to exclude, would now be able to qualify under another hearsay exception, specifically FRE 803(24) or 804(b)(5). She stated:

> The conference committee rejected a proposed rule from the Senate which would have allowed police reports to be admitted as substan-

> tive evidence. However, by simultaneously adopting this open-ended hearsay exception, the conference report opens a "back door" to these police reports and negates the conference committee's prior prohibition against admission of such evidence.

... Representative David Dennis, an active participant in the floor debate, the sponsor of the amendment excluding police reports, a floor manager of the legislation and a member of the Committee of Conference, responded, politely but bluntly:

> I would like to say in answer to my friend, the gentlewoman from New York, that this business of using a police report, if a policeman is unavailable, was not in the rules as they came to us. That was written in by the Senate, and we struck it out in the conference, I am very happy to say. It was a terrible idea. But since we did take it out in the conference, and since it is gone, and since we insisted that it go, I cannot see how anybody could suggest that introducing such a report is possible or a thing that could be done under these rules; because the Senators put it in and we took it out in conference, and that is the legislative history.

... We thus think it manifest that it was the clear intention of Congress to make ... law enforcement reports absolutely inadmissible against defendants in criminal cases....

United States v. Hayes

861 F.2d 1225, 1227–30 (10th Cir. 1988).

... Dorothy Vest, an I.R.S. tax examiner, was the custodian of the records and she testified that they were kept in the ordinary and regular course of business. During her search Vest obtained Certificates of Assessments and Payments for the 1978, 1979, 1980, and 1981 tax years.... Hayes strenuously objected to the admission of the certificates (the computer data evidence) both prior to and during trial. They show that he failed to file a return for the 1981 tax year....

The trial court admitted the computer data evidence under Fed. R. Evid. 803(6).... The [question] is whether it should have been excluded under the rationale of *United States v. Oates*.... *Oates* has been criticized by both courts and commentators as an unduly broad interpretation of Rule 803(8). The Fifth [Circuit has] rejected the breadth of *Oates*, and reason[s] that the exclusionary provision of [803(8)(A)(ii)] was only intended to apply to observations made by law enforcement officials at the scene of a crime or in investigating a crime, and not to reports of routine matters made in nonadversarial settings. United States v. Quezada, 754 F.2d 1190, 1193–94 (5th Cir. 1985). And the Second Circuit itself confined *Oates* in United States v. Yakobov, 712 F.2d 20, 24–27 (2d Cir. 1983), where it held that "*Oates* should not be extended to [exclude materials admissible under] Rule 803(10)." ...

Rule [803(8)(A)(iii)] does not compel the exclusion of documents properly admitted under Rule 803(6) where the authoring officer or investigator testifies. This is because such testimony protects against the loss of an accused's confrontation rights, the underlying rationale for Rule 803(8) and the basis of the court's concern in *Oates*.

In *Oates*, the Custom Service Chemist who analyzed the heroin and prepared the report did not testify (although another chemist did) and could not, therefore, be questioned about the source of information or the specific circumstances of preparation. Here, Vest testified and was cross examined at some length . . . , and there was no loss of confrontation rights. . . .

United States v. Weiland

420 F.3d 1062, 1074–75 (9th Cir. 2005), *cert. denied*, 547 U.S. 1114 (2006).

[*Weiland* concerned the admission against a criminal defendant of items contained in his "penitentiary packet"—the cluster of documents concerning an inmate kept by a corrections department's records office. The defendant challenged in particular the admission of records reflecting his criminal convictions, a booking-style identification photo, and a booking-style fingerprint card. The government used these documents at trial to prove Weiland's status as a convicted felon. As you read this excerpt, note that the Ninth Circuit respects the principles of both *Oates* and *Hayes*. On the one hand, the judges declare that Rule 803(6) cannot trump the specific restrictions of Rule 803(8) concerning admission of law enforcement reports against criminal defendants. On the other hand, they borrow from the language of *Hayes* in holding that neither Rule 803(6) nor Rule 803(8) bars such reports when they concern "routine and nonadversarial matters."—GF]

. . . We begin by rejecting the argument that the convictions, fingerprints and photograph were properly admitted pursuant to the business records hearsay exception in Rule 803(6). The law of this circuit has long established that public records, including records of conviction, must be admitted, if at all, under Rule 803(8), or, in some cases, under a specific hearsay rule, such as Rule 803(22), governing the admission of prior convictions. The government may not circumvent the specific requirements of Rule 803(8) by seeking to admit public records as business records under Rule 803(6). Nor may the government attempt to combine Rules 803(6) and 803(8) into a hybrid rule to excuse its failure to comply with either. . . .

Because the district court erred in holding that the documents in the "penitentiary packet" and the certified convictions were admissible as records of regularly conducted activity under Rule 803(6), we next turn to the question of whether the convictions, photograph and fingerprints are admissible under any other hearsay exception. First, with respect to the documents titled "Judgment and Sentence on Plea of Guilty" only, we hold that these records are evidence of previous convictions that are independently admissible under Rule 803(22). Second, with respect to the fingerprints and photograph contained in the "penitentiary packet," we conclude that these documents are public records of routine and nonadversarial matters that fall within [803(8)(A)(ii)], and were admissible thereunder. The fingerprints and photograph do not contain information akin to "police officers' reports of their contemporaneous observations of crime" that might be biased by the adversarial nature of the report. To the contrary, fingerprinting and photographing a suspect, and cataloguing a judgment and sentence are the types of routine and unambiguous matters to which the public records hearsay exception in Rule [803(8)(A)(ii)] is designed to apply. In addition, we hold that "the sources of the information or other circumstances" in this case do not "indicate lack of trustworthiness." FED. R. EVID. 803(8) [unrestyled]. There is no allegation here that any document in the "penitentiary packet" is factually inaccurate, and, further, there is no reason to think that persons making routine court and prison records in Oklahoma have either motive or opportunity to fabricate or falsify these documents. We hold that the relevant contents of the "penitentiary packet," including the documents titled "Judgment and Sentence on Plea of Guilty," the fingerprints, and the photograph, were properly admitted pursuant to the public records hearsay exception in Rule 803(8)....

G. RESIDUAL EXCEPTION

Focus on FRE 807

(Most of the legislative materials for Rule 807 are printed under the heading 803(24) in the Rulebook. See RB 260–63.)

NEW COURTHOUSE

Badly Damaged by Fire This Morning—Dome Burned Off

Incendiary Origin

SELMA MORNING TIMES, June 9, 1901

At a few minutes past two o'clock this morning the alarm was sent in from box 21, calling the firemen to the corner of Lauderdale and Alabama streets. The unfinished dome of Dallas county's new courthouse was in flames near the top, and before a stream could be brought to bear upon it the structure was a mass of flames and soon fell in. The fire was soon under control and the main building was saved. The fire was evidently the work of an incendiary. When first seen the fire was in the top of the dome. We could not learn whether there was any insurance on the building, but presume that the county is protected against loss.

Many years later, this brief report inspired a landmark in the development of hearsay law. . . .

DALLAS COUNTY V. COMMERCIAL UNION ASSURANCE CO.

286 F.2d 388 (5th Cir. 1961).

■ WISDOM, J. This appeal presents a single question—the admissibility in evidence of a newspaper to show that the Dallas County Courthouse in Selma, Alabama, was damaged by fire in 1901. We hold that the newspaper was admissible, and affirm the judgment below.

On a bright, sunny morning, July 7, 1957, the clock tower of the Dallas County Courthouse at Selma, Alabama, commenced to lean, made loud cracking and popping noises, then fell, and telescoped into the courtroom. Fortunately, the collapse of the tower took place on a Sunday morning; no one was injured, but damage to the courthouse exceeded $100,000. An examination of the tower debris showed the presence of charcoal and charred timbers. The State Toxicologist, called in by Dallas County, reported the char was evidence that lightning struck the courthouse. Later, several residents of Selma reported that a bolt of lightning struck the courthouse July 2, 1957. On this information, Dallas County concluded that a lightning bolt had hit the building causing the collapse of the clock tower five days later. Dallas County carried insurance for loss to its courthouse caused by fire or lightning. The insurers' engineers and investigators found that the courthouse collapsed of its own weight. They reported that the courthouse had not been struck by lightning; that lightning could not have caused the collapse of the tower; that the collapse of the tower was caused by structural weaknesses attributable to a faulty design, poor construction, gradual deterioration of the structure, and overloading brought about by remodeling and the recent installation of an air-conditioning system, part of which was constructed over the courtroom trusses. In their opinion, the char was the result of a fire in the courthouse tower and roof that must have occurred many, many years before July 2, 1957. The insurers denied liability.

The County sued its insurers in the Circuit Court of Dallas County. As many of the suits as could be removed, seven, were removed to the United States District Court for the Southern District of Alabama, and were consolidated for trial. The case went to the jury on one issue: did lightning cause the collapse of the clock tower?

The record contains ample evidence to support a jury verdict either way. The County produced witnesses who testified they saw lighting strike the clock tower; the insurers produced witnesses who testified an examination of the debris showed that lightning did not strike the clock tower. Some witnesses said the char was fresh and smelled smoky; other witnesses said it was obviously old and had no fresh smoky smell at all. Both sides presented a great mass of engineering testimony bearing on the design, construction, overload or lack of overload. All of this was for the jury to evaluate. The jury chose to believe the insurers' witnesses and brought in a verdict for the defendants.

During the trial the defendants introduced a copy of the *Morning Times* of Selma for June 9, 1901. This issue carried an unsigned article describing a fire that occurred at two in the morning of June 9, 1901, while the courthouse was still under construction. The article stated, in part: "The unfinished dome of the County's new courthouse was in flames at the top, and . . . soon fell in. The fire was soon under control and the main building was saved." The insurers do not contend that the collapse of the tower resulted from unsound charred timbers used in the repair of the building after the fire; they offered the newspaper account to show there had been a fire long before 1957 that would account for charred timber in the clock tower.

As a predicate for introducing the newspaper in evidence, the defendants called to the stand the editor of the *Selma Times–Journal* who testified that his publishing company maintains archives of the published issues of the *Times–Journal* and of the *Morning Times*, its predecessor, and that the archives contain the issue of the *Morning Times* of Selma for June 9, 1901, offered in evidence. The plaintiff objected that the newspaper article was hearsay; that it was not a business record nor an ancient document, nor was it admissible under any recognized exception to the hearsay doctrine. The trial judge admitted the newspaper as part of the records of the *Selma Times–Journal*. The sole error Dallas County specifies on appeal is the admission of the newspaper in evidence.

In the Anglo–American adversary system of law, courts usually will not admit evidence unless its accuracy and trustworthiness may be tested by cross-examination. Here, therefore, the plaintiff argues that the newspaper should not be admitted: "You cannot cross-examine a newspaper."[1]

1. . . . Wigmore [is] often quoted for the statement that "cross-examination is beyond any doubt the greatest legal engine ever invented for the discovery of the

Of course, a newspaper article is hearsay, and in almost all circumstances is inadmissible. However, the law governing hearsay is somewhat less than pellucid. And, as with most rules, the hearsay rule is not absolute; it is replete with exceptions. Witnesses die, documents are lost, deeds are destroyed, memories fade. All too often, primary evidence is not available and courts and lawyers must rely on secondary evidence....

We turn now to a case ... in which the court used an approach we consider appropriate for the solution of the problem before us. G. & C. Merriam Co. v. Syndicate Pub. Co., 207 F. 515, 518 (2d Cir. 1913), concerned a controversy between dictionary publishers over the use of the title 'Webster's Dictionary' when the defendant's dictionary allegedly was not based upon Webster's dictionary at all. The bone of contention was whether a statement in the preface to the dictionary was admissible as evidence of the facts it recited. Ogilvie, the compiler of the dictionary, stated in his preface that he used *Webster's Dictionary* as the basis for his own publication. The dictionary, with its preface, was published in 1850, sixty-three years before the trial of the case. Ogilvie's published statement was challenged as hearsay. Judge Learned Hand, then a district judge, unable, as we are here, to find a case in point, for authority relied solely on *Wigmore on Evidence* (then a recent publication), particularly on Wigmore's analysis that "the requisites of an exception to the hearsay rule are necessity and circumstantial guaranty of trustworthiness." WIGMORE ON truth." 5 WIGMORE § 1367 (3rd ed.). In over 1200 pages devoted to the hearsay rule, however, he makes it very clear that:

> "The rule aims to insist on testing all statements by cross-examination, if they can be.... No one could defend a rule which pronounced that all statements thus untested are worthless; for all historical truth is based on uncross-examined assertions; and every day's experience of life gives denial to such an exaggeration. What the Hearsay Rule implies—and with profound verity—is that all testimonial assertions ought to be tested by cross-examination, as the best attainable measure; and it should not be burdened with the pedantic implication that they must be rejected as worthless if the test is unavailable."

1 WIGMORE § 8c.

In The Introductory Note to Chapter VI, Hearsay Evidence, American Law Institute, Model Code of Evidence (1942), Edmund M. Morgan, Reporter, it is pointed out that common law "judges discovered a special sort of necessity in ... exceptional cases ... (making) the admissible hearsay less unreliable than hearsay in general.... Modern textwriters and judges have purported to find for each exception some sort of necessity for resort to hearsay and some condition attending the making of the excepted statement which will enable the jury to put a fair value upon it and will thus serve as a substitute for cross-examination. A careful examination of the eighteen or nineteen classes of utterances, each of which is now recognized as an exception to the hearsay rule by some respectable authority, will reveal that in many of them the necessity resolves itself into mere convenience and the substitute for cross-examination is imperceptible.... In most of the exceptions, ... [t]here is nothing ... to warrant depriving the adversary of an opportunity to cross-examine.... In most instances one will look in vain for anything more than a situation in which an ordinary man making such a statement would positively desire to tell the truth; and in some the most that can be claimed is the absence of a motive to falsify." ...

EVIDENCE §§ 1421, 1422, 1690 (1st ed. 1913). Applying these criteria, Judge Hand held that the statement was admissible as an exception to the hearsay rule:

> "Ogilvie's preface is of course . . . hearsay testimony, which may be admitted only as an exception to the general rule. The question is whether there is such an exception. I have been unable to find any express authority in point and must decide the question upon principle. In the first place, I think it fair to insist that to reject such a statement is to refuse evidence about the truth of which no reasonable person should have any doubt whatever, because it fulfills both the requisites of an exception to the hearsay rule, necessity and circumstantial guaranty of trustworthiness. WIGMORE §§ 1421, 1422, 1690. . . . Besides Ogilvie, everyone else is dead who ever knew anything about the matter and could intelligently tell us what the fact is. . . . As to the trustworthiness of the testimony, it has the guaranty of the occasion, at which there was no motive for fabrication." 207 F. 515, 518.

The Court of Appeals adopted the district court's opinion in its entirety.

The first of the two requisites is necessity. As to necessity, Wigmore points out this requisite means that unless the hearsay statement is admitted, the facts it brings out may otherwise be lost, either because the person whose assertion is offered may be dead or unavailable, or because the assertion is of such a nature that one could not expect to obtain evidence of the same value from the same person or from other sources. WIGMORE § 1421 (3d ed.). "In effect, Wigmore says that, as the word necessity is here used, it is not to be interpreted as uniformly demanding a showing of total inaccessibility of firsthand evidence as a condition precedent to the acceptance of a particular piece of hearsay, but that necessity exists where otherwise great practical inconvenience would be experienced in making the desired proof. (5 WIGMORE § 1421 (3d. ed.); 6 *id.* § 1702). . . ." United States v. Aluminum Co. of America, 35 F. Supp. 820, 823 (S.D.N.Y. 1940).

The fire referred to in the newspaper account occurred fifty-eight years before the trial of this case. Any witness who saw that fire with sufficient understanding to observe it and describe it accurately, would have been older than a young child at the time of the fire. We may reasonably assume that at the time of the trial he was either dead or his faculties were dimmed by the passage of fifty-eight years. It would have been burdensome, but not impossible, for the defendant to have discovered the name of the author of the article (although it had no by-line) and, perhaps, to have found an eye-witness to the fire. But it is improbable—so it seems to us—that any witness could have been found whose recollection would have been accurate at the time of the trial of this case. And it seems impossible that the testimony of any witness would have been as accurate and as reliable as the statement of facts in the contemporary newspaper article.

The rationale behind the "ancient documents" exception is applicable here: after a long lapse of time, ordinary evidence regarding signatures or handwriting is virtually unavailable, and it is therefore permissible to resort to circumstantial evidence. Thus, in Trustees of German Township, Montgomery County v. Farmers & Citizens Savings Bank Co., 113 N.E.2d 409, 412, *affirmed* Ohio App., 115 N.E.2d 690 (Ohio Com. Pl. 1953), the court admitted as ancient documents newspapers eighty years old containing notices of advertisements for bids relating to the town hall: "Such exhibits, by reason of age, alone, and unquestioned authenticity, qualify as ancient documents."[16] The ancient documents rule applies to documents a generation or more in age. Here, the *Selma Times–Journal* article is almost two generations old. The principle of necessity, not requiring absolute impossibility or total inaccessibility of first-hand knowledge, is satisfied by the practicalities of the situation before us.

The second requisite for admission of hearsay evidence is trustworthiness. According to Wigmore, there are three sets of circumstances when hearsay is trustworthy enough to serve as a practicable substitute for the ordinary test of cross-examination: "Where the circumstances are such that a sincere and accurate statement would naturally be uttered, and no plan of falsification be formed; where, even though a desire to falsify might present itself, other considerations, such as the danger of easy detection or the fear of punishment, would probably counteract its force; where the statement was made under such conditions of publicity that an error, if it had occurred, would probably have been detected and corrected." 5 WIGMORE, EVIDENCE § 1422 (3d ed.) These circumstances fit the instant case.

There is no procedural canon against the exercise of common sense in deciding the admissibility of hearsay evidence. In 1901 Selma, Alabama, was a small town. Taking a common sense view of this case, it is inconceivable to us that a newspaper reporter in a small town would report there was a fire in the dome of the new courthouse—if there had been no fire. He is without motive to falsify, and a false report would have subjected the newspaper and him to embarrassment in the community. The usual dangers inherent in hearsay evidence, such as lack of memory, faulty narration, intent to influence the court proceedings, and plain lack of truthfulness are not present here. To our minds, the article published in the *Selma Morning–Times* on the day of the fire is more reliable, more trustworthy, more competent evidence than the testimony of a witness called to the stand fifty-eight years later.

16. *See also* Wickes, *Ancient Documents and Hearsay*, 8 TEX. L. REV. 451 (1930); 7 WIGMORE, EVIDENCE § 2137 (3d ed.); MCCORMICK, EVIDENCE §§ 190, 298 (1954 ed.).

We hold, that in matters of local interest, when the fact in question is of such a public nature it would be generally known throughout the community, and when the questioned fact occurred so long ago that the testimony of an eye-witness would probably be less trustworthy than a contemporary newspaper account, a federal court ... may relax the exclusionary rules to the extent of admitting the newspaper article in evidence. We do not characterize this newspaper as a "business record," nor as an "ancient document," nor as any other readily identifiable and happily tagged species of hearsay exception. It is admissible because it is necessary and trustworthy, relevant and material, and its admission is within the trial judge's exercise of discretion in holding the hearing within reasonable bounds.

Judgment is affirmed.

DALLAS COUNTY V. COMMERCIAL UNION ASSURANCE CO.: *Afterthoughts*

Dallas County is "universally acknowledged to be the direct antecedent of the catch-all philosophy" that lies behind the residual exception to the hearsay rule. John Norman Scott, *Michigan Catches Up to the "Catch–Alls": How Much Hearsay Will They Catch?*, 14 T.M. COOLEY L. REV. 1, 5 (1997). And indeed *Dallas County* is the only case the advisory committee thought worth citing in its note to Rule 803(24), the precursor to Rule 807, which now governs the residual exception. (*See* ACN to 803(24), RB 261.)

Yet at least one commentator has dismissed the case as "a poor justification for the federal residual exceptions." Alfred H. Knight, III, *The Federal Influence on the Tennessee Hearsay Rule*, 57 TENN. L. REV. 117, 141 n.127 (1989). After all, the whole point of having a "residual" exception is that it may serve to admit hearsay when no other exception suits the purpose. And as many authorities have noted, the *Selma Morning Times* article at issue in *Dallas County* seems to have been admissible via the "ancient documents" exception to the hearsay rule.

Today the ancient documents exception, as embodied by Rule 803(16), applies to "[s]tatements in a document in existence twenty years or more the authenticity of which is established." FRE 803(16). At the time of *Dallas County* the ancient documents exception usually required the document to be at least thirty years old. Either way the *Selma Morning Times* article, aged fifty-eight at the time of trial, surely qualified. As no one challenged the article's authenticity, it seems to have passed muster as an ancient document under the rule. Judge Wisdom himself acknowledged that "[t]he rationale behind the 'ancient documents' exception is applicable here...." Perhaps most remarkably, the only case the advisory committee chose to cite in support of Rule 803(16) was *Dallas County*. (*See* RB 254.)

How then to explain Judge Wisdom's "apparent delight," Scott, *supra*, at 8, in declaring at the end of his opinion that "[w]e do not characterize this newspaper as a 'business record,' nor as an 'ancient document,' nor as any other readily identifiable and happily tagged species of hearsay exception"? In Joseph Rand's view, Wisdom's motives were cynical: "Certainly," he writes, Judge Wisdom "could have found the basis for admission under the [ancient documents] exception. That he chose to ignore a traditional exception to affirm the admission of the article on the basis of its necessity and trustworthiness alone is inexplicable, unless he was intentionally establishing a precedent for expanding the discretion and authority of the trial judge to admit hearsay regardless of the class exemptions." Joseph W. Rand, *The Residual Exceptions to the Federal Hearsay Rule: The Futile and Misguided Attempt to Restrain Judicial Discretion*, 80 Geo. L.J. 873, 875 n.9 (1992).

Perhaps Rand is right that Wisdom's opinion was a brash grab for judicial power. More charitably, Professor Dale Nance reads the opinion as a product of "reformist zeal" from one of the most progressive judges on the Fifth Circuit Court of Appeals, "a veritable nest of progressive judges" known for vigorous enforcement of *Brown v. Board of Education*, 347 U.S. 483 (1954). Loosing the bonds of the hearsay rule may have been Wisdom's way of achieving justice in each individual case. *See* Dale A. Nance, *The Wisdom of* Dallas County, *in* Evidence Stories 307, 310–12 (Richard Lempert ed., 2006).

But perhaps Judge Wisdom saw a simple evidentiary obstacle to admitting the *Morning Times* account as an ancient document. Look again at the article reproduced at pages 574 to 575. "When first seen," the reporter wrote, "the fire was in the top of the dome." Did the reporter see the fire? If the reporter was merely repeating someone else's account, the article is an example of hearsay within hearsay: one out-of-court statement (the reporter's article) repeats another out-of-court statement (the account of the person who saw the fire).

At least two authorities cited by Judge Wisdom in footnote 16 of his opinion had declared that the ancient documents exception applied only when the declarant had first-hand knowledge of the events. *See* Charles T. McCormick, Handbook of the Law of Evidence § 298, at 623 (1954) ("[The writing] would be excluded [under the ancient documents exception] if it appeared that the writer did not have an opportunity to know the facts at first hand."); Joseph A. Wickes, *Ancient Documents and Hearsay*, 8 Tex. L. Rev. 451, 469–70 (1930) ("[T]he recital must have been made on the personal knowledge of the person making it."); *id.* at 472–74, 479 ("This limitation . . . should be insisted on by the courts."). It seems likely, then, that Wisdom rejected the ancient documents exception because it could not overcome the double-hearsay nature of the *Morning*

Times article. His rejection of the business records exception perhaps rested on the same ground. That exception, as construed by *Johnson v. Lutz*, 253 N.Y. 124, 127–29, 170 N.E. 517 (1930), does not apply to an outsider's statement couched within a business record. *See Vigneau, supra*, pages 558–59 (discussing *Johnson v. Lutz*); ACN to FRE 803(6), RB 227 (same).

Under Rule 805 hearsay within hearsay is admissible "if each part of the combined statements conforms with an exception to the hearsay rule"—either the same exception or two or more different exceptions. Perhaps the reporter's own words—the top layer of hearsay—would have been admissible through the ancient documents exception because the reporter wrote the document. But what exception could admit the words of the unnamed reporter's unnamed source? This bottom layer of hearsay was the nub of the problem. Perhaps the source spoke excitedly, in the fire's immediate aftermath (*see* Rule 803(2)), but we don't know that. Perhaps the source admitted his own complicity in the blaze (*see* Rule 804(b)(3)), but there is nothing to suggest it. Knowing so little of the story's provenance, Judge Wisdom quite properly reached an impasse at this point in the analysis—an impasse he overcame by boldly announcing a new and potentially cavernous exception to the hearsay rule.

Arguably, then, *Dallas County* set a precedent for invoking the residual exception when necessary and reliable hearsay almost fits—but does not quite fit—within an established exception to the rule. If so, the case that most directly gave rise to the residual exception also introduced its use in cases of *near misses*—hearsay that narrowly fails to qualify under one of the traditional exceptions. Today near misses stand at the center an evidence-law controversy—but one perhaps fading from the scene.

RULE 807 AND DEMISE OF THE "NEAR-MISS" THEORY

Before the 2011 restyling of the Federal Rules of Evidence, Rule 807 opened with the words, "A statement not specifically covered by Rule 803 or 804, but having equivalent circumstantial guarantees of trustworthiness, is not excluded by the hearsay rule if. . . ." (RB 472.) The seemingly harmless phrase "not specifically covered" engendered much controversy.

United States v. Laster, 258 F.3d 525 (6th Cir. 2001), *cert. denied*, 534 U.S. 1151 (2002), presented both sides of the debate. At issue were shipments to defendant James Laster of several bottles of hydriodic acid, a component of methamphetamine. Sales records of Wilson Oil Company could have established Laster's role in purchasing the hydriodic acid. But the apparent sole owner and operator of Wilson Oil died before trial. *See id.* at 529 n.2. Undaunted, the prosecutor persuaded the trial judge that Wilson Oil's records qualified as business records under Rule 803(6). To act as "the custodian or another qualified witness" required by paragraph (E) of that rule, the prosecutor substituted James Acquisto, a detective for a state drug task force, who had investigated the case. As the Sixth Circuit wrote on review, however, "Acquisto did not examine the books or ledger sheets of Wilson Oil Company, nor did he know whether Wilson had an accountant or bookkeeper. Neither did Acquisto ask Wilson whether these documents were prepared simultaneously with the transactions reflected thereon." In short, "[o]ther than a few conversations between Acquisto and Wilson, there is no evidence that Acquisto was familiar with the record-keeping system of Wilson Oil Company." Hence the appeals court deemed the sales records inadmissible under Rule 803(6). *Id.* at 529.

Instead the court turned to Rule 807 and the residual exception. A majority of the three-judge panel deemed the records admissible under this rule, as they were "equally trustworthy . . . , 'material,' 'more probative on the point for which [they were] offered than any other evidence . . . the proponent can [obtain] through reasonable efforts,' and [their] admission best serve[d] the interests of justice." *Id.* at 529–30 (quoting FRE 807). These conclusions, seemingly at the heart of Rule 807, stirred no dissent. Instead controversy turned on the appeals court's determination that Wilson Oil's records were "not specifically covered" by any exception in Rule 803 or 804—a precondition to admission in unrestyled Rule 807. (RB 472.) Here the appeals court endorsed the Eighth Circuit's view that " 'the phrase "specifically covered" [by a hearsay exception] means only that if a statement is *admissible* under one of the [803 or 804] exceptions, such [] subsection should be relied upon' instead of the residual exception." *Id.* at 530 (quoting *United States v. Earles*, 113 F.3d 796, 800 (8th Cir. 1997), *cert. denied*, 522 U.S. 1075 (1998) (emphasis supplied by *Earles* court)). As the Sixth Circuit had determined that Wilson Oil's records were not admissible under any standard hearsay exception, application of Rule 807 was proper.

Judge Karen Nelson Moore disputed this construction of the phrase "not specifically covered." She argued in dissent "that the residual exception means what it says—i.e., that it applies to those exceptional cases in which an established exception to the hearsay rule does not apply but in which circumstantial guarantees of trustworthiness, equivalent to those existing for the established hearsay exceptions, are present." The rule does not, she said, apply to "near misses"—statements that *almost* fit under one of the recognized hearsay exceptions, but narrowly fail to meet the exception's preconditions. Under her "near-miss" theory of the residual exception, Wilson Oil's records would have failed scrutiny, for they *almost* satisfied the preconditions of the business records exception, but lacked a qualified witness to say how they were made and kept. "[A]n established hearsay exception clearly *applied*," Judge Moore concluded, "but rendered the documents inadmissible." *Laster*, 258 F.3d at 533, 535 (Moore, J., dissenting) (emphasis added). As the records were "specifically covered"—though excluded—by the business-records exception, Rule 807 would not save them.

Judge Moore readily acknowledged that hers was the minority view among federal courts. She cited in her defense only one opinion of the Federal Circuit Court of Appeals and dicta in a concurring opinion signed by two judges of the Seventh Circuit. *See id.* at 533. The majority in contrast claimed the support of the Courts of Appeals for the Fourth, Fifth, Seventh, Eighth, Ninth, and Eleventh Circuits. *See Laster*, 258 F.3d at 530 & n.3. Rejecting the near-miss theory, the Fourth Circuit had written that "[b]oth litigants and courts spend their time more productively in analyzing the trustworthiness of the particular statement, rather than debating the abstract question of 'How close is too close?' to a specified hearsay exception." *United States v. Clarke*, 2 F.3d 81, 84 (4th Cir. 1993), *cert. denied*, 510 U.S. 1166 (1994).

In deference perhaps to this precedential tide, the drafters of the restyled Federal Rules of Evidence mooted the near-miss controversy with a subtle change of syntax. They dropped unrestyled Rule 807's opening words: "A statement not specifically covered by Rule 803 or 804. . . ." (RB 472.) Instead the rule now begins: "Under the following circumstances, a hearsay statement is not excluded by the rule against hearsay *even if the statement is not specifically covered* by a hearsay exception in Rule 803 or 804. . . ." (RB 473 (emphasis added).) Suddenly it no longer matters whether a contested statement is or isn't "specifically covered" by a traditional hearsay exception. Admissibility hangs only on meeting Rule 807's other preconditions.

This is now the third time we've seen the rule writers engage in stylistic arbitration. The first instance dealt with the phrase "if disputed" (formerly "if controverted") in Rule 407, which generally bars evidence of later remedies. The restyling eliminated an old ambiguity about whether evidence of later repair could be offered to prove ownership or control before one's opponent had disputed ownership or control. As restyled, the rule makes clear that ownership and control, like feasibility, must be disputed before a litigant may prove them with evidence of later repair. (*See* RB 398–99; page 113 above.)

The second case of stylistic problem solving addressed an uncertainty that once troubled Rules 413, 414, and 415. As enacted, these rules had provided that evidence of past sexual assaults committed by criminal defendants or civil parties "is admissible" if the rules' other terms were met. (RB 408, 410, 412.) Some commentators feared this language made the rules mandatory, requiring admission of evidence of past assaults without regard to Rule 403 or any other evidence rule. As restyled, Rules 413 through 415 now provide that if the other conditions of the rules are met, "the court *may admit* evidence that the defendant [or civil party] committed any other" sexual assault. (RB 409, 411, 413 (emphasis added).)

The change took arguably mandatory rules and rendered them discretionary. (*See* pages 231–232 above.)

In all three cases of syntactical dispute resolution, the restyling project settled a controversy in accord with overwhelming judicial and scholarly authority. Even so, these bits of stylistic housekeeping worked substantive changes in the rules. They reached beyond the rule writers' avowed purpose throughout the restyling project to make "*No Substantive Change.*" (RB 4, 376.)

CHAPTER 8

CONFRONTATION AND COMPULSORY PROCESS

A. THE CONFRONTATION CLAUSE AND HEARSAY

MATTOX V. UNITED STATES

156 U.S. 237 (1895).

PLAINTIFF in error was convicted on January 16, 1894, ... of the murder of one John Mullen, which was alleged to have been committed on December 12, 1889.... The indictment was returned to the September term, 1891, of the District Court at Wichita, at which term defendant was first tried and convicted. From this conviction he sued out a writ of error from this court, which reversed the judgment of the District Court and remanded the case for a new trial. 146 U.S. 140.* The case was continued until the December term, 1893, at which term plaintiff was again put upon his trial, and again convicted, whereupon he sued out this writ of error....

■ MR. JUSTICE BROWN delivered the opinion of the court.... Upon the trial it was shown by the government that two of its witnesses on the former trial, namely, Thomas Whitman and George Thornton, had since died, whereupon a transcribed copy of the reporter's stenographic notes of their testimony upon such trial, supported by his testimony that it was correct, was admitted to be read in evidence, and constituted the strongest proof against the accused. Both these witnesses were present and were fully examined and cross-examined on the former trial. It is claimed, however, that the constitutional provision that the accused shall "be confronted with the witnesses against him" was infringed, by permitting the testimony of witnesses sworn upon the former trial to be read against him. No question is made that this may not be done in a civil case, but it is insisted that the reasons of convenience and necessity which excuse a

* [The Supreme Court's first ruling in this case gave rise to Problem 7.28 at page 498—GF.]

departure from the ordinary course of procedure in civil cases cannot override the constitutional provision in question....

The primary object of the constitutional provision in question was to prevent depositions or ex parte affidavits, such as were sometimes admitted in civil cases, being used against the prisoner in lieu of a personal examination and cross-examination of the witness in which the accused has an opportunity, not only of testing the recollection and sifting the conscience of the witness, but of compelling him to stand face to face with the jury in order that they may look at him, and judge by his demeanor upon the stand and the manner in which he gives his testimony whether he is worthy of belief. There is doubtless reason for saying that the accused should never lose the benefit of any of these safeguards even by the death of the witness; and that, if notes of his testimony are permitted to be read, he is deprived of the advantage of that personal presence of the witness before the jury which the law has designed for his protection. But general rules of law of this kind, however beneficent in their operation and valuable to the accused, must occasionally give way to considerations of public policy and the necessities of the case. To say that a criminal, after having once been convicted by the testimony of a certain witness, should go scot free simply because death has closed the mouth of that witness, would be carrying his constitutional protection to an unwarrantable extent. The law in its wisdom declares that the rights of the public shall not be wholly sacrificed in order that an incidental benefit may be preserved to the accused.

... Many of [the Constitution's] provisions in the nature of a Bill of Rights are subject to exceptions, recognized long before the adoption of the Constitution, and not interfering at all with its spirit. Such exceptions were obviously intended to be respected. A technical adherence to the letter of a constitutional provision may occasionally be carried farther than is necessary to the just protection of the accused, and farther than the safety of the public will warrant. For instance, there could be nothing more directly contrary to the letter of the provision in question than the admission of dying declarations. They are rarely made in the presence of the accused; they are made without any opportunity for examination or cross-examination; nor is the witness brought face to face with the jury; yet from time immemorial they have been treated as competent testimony, and no one would have the hardihood at this day to question their admissibility. They are admitted not in conformity with any general rule regarding the admission of testimony, but as an exception to such rules, simply from the necessities of the case, and to prevent a manifest failure of justice. As was said by the Chief Justice when this case was here upon the first writ of error, the sense of impending death is presumed to remove all temptation to falsehood, and to enforce as strict an adherence to the truth as would the obligation of an oath. If such declarations are admitted, because made by a person then dead, under circumstances which give his statements the same weight as if made under oath, there is equal if not greater reason for admitting testimony of his statements which were made under oath.

The substance of the constitutional protection is preserved to the prisoner in the advantage he has once had of seeing the witness face to face, and of subjecting him to the ordeal of a cross-examination. This, the law says, he shall under no circumstances be deprived of. . . .

There was no error in the action of the court below and its judgment is, therefore,

Affirmed.

CONFRONTATION CLAUSE AND HEARSAY: *Case Notes*

The Sixth Amendment provides that "in all criminal prosecutions, the accused shall enjoy the right ... to be confronted with the witnesses against him. . . ." We saw in *Olden v. Kentucky* that when the defendant's accuser testifies against him at trial, the Confrontation Clause protects his right to test her accusation through cross-examination. (Pages 340–41, above.) Even a state's rape shield law must sometimes give way when a rape defendant wishes to expose a bias that might have prompted his accuser to charge him falsely.

But what if the defendant's accuser speaks outside rather than inside court? Do "the witnesses against" the defendant include hearsay declarants? If so, the Confrontation Clause might forbid the prosecution's use of hearsay evidence whenever the defendant cannot cross-examine the declarant. A great deal of hearsay that fits cleanly within established exceptions to the hearsay rule would be barred.

The Supreme Court has never read the Confrontation Clause so broadly. For well over a century the Court has recognized that some hearsay may be admitted against criminal defendants even if the declarant never submits to cross-examination. At the same time the Court has insisted that the Confrontation Clause bars at least some out-of-court statements by absent declarants even when those statements satisfy an exception to the hearsay rule.

As the cases summarized below make clear, the Court's many attempts to reconcile the hearsay rule's exceptions with the Confrontation Clause's command have been halting and nonlinear. These cases arose in three eras. In the *Mattox* era the Supreme Court issued a number of ad hoc judgments to resolve particular controversies, but made little attempt to systematize the Confrontation Clause's impact on admission of hearsay. The Court first undertook this task in earnest in *Ohio v. Roberts*, 448 U.S. 56 (1980). There the Court launched an ultimately aborted attempt to crystallize confrontation doctrine around the familiar hearsay principles of necessity and reliability. Early in 2004, after tinkering with the *Roberts* framework for nearly a quarter-century, the Court finally abandoned the task. In *Crawford v. Washington*, 541 U.S. 36 (2004), it set Confrontation doctrine on an entirely new footing, centered on the "testimonial" nature of the out-of-court statement. After *Crawford, Roberts* and its reliability-based analysis are dead.

As you read this material, bear in mind that the Constitution is a *higher law* than the Federal Rules of Evidence, but not always a *stricter* law. And the stricter rule trumps. Hence evidence permitted by the rules of evidence but forbidden by the Confrontation Clause must stay out. Evidence permitted by the Confrontation Clause but excluded by the rules of evidence also must stay out. Bear in mind, too, that while the Confrontation Clause applies in both federal and state trials, the Federal Rules of Evidence have no force in state courts unless adopted by state law. State hearsay rules often differ, if not greatly, from federal hearsay rules. The interplay between the Confrontation Clause and hearsay rules therefore may differ according to the jurisdiction's hearsay rules.

I. *The* Mattox *Era*

Pointer v. Texas, 380 U.S. 400 (1965)

The Supreme Court held that the Sixth Amendment's Confrontation Clause was incorporated by the Due Process Clause of the Fourteenth Amendment and therefore is binding on the states.

California v. Green, 399 U.S. 149 (1970)

A juvenile arrested for selling marijuana said Green was his supplier. At a preliminary hearing the juvenile repeated this claim under oath and was cross-examined by Green's lawyer. But at trial the juvenile testified differently. The state then read excerpts of his earlier testimony, which were admitted under a section of the California Evidence Code that allows past inconsistent statements of testifying witnesses to prove the truth of those statements. *Cf.* FRE 801(d)(1)(A).

The Supreme Court rejected the notion "that the Confrontation Clause is nothing more or less than a codification of the rules of hearsay and their exceptions as they existed historically at common law." The Court then made two broad holdings, both of which remain good law today:

(1) If the declarant is present, testifies at trial, and responds to questions about the earlier hearsay statement, "the out-of-court statement for all practical purposes regains most of the lost protections" of in-court testimony. The Confrontation Clause therefore does not bar admission of

the out-of-court statement. This is true whether or not the out-of-court statement was made under oath and subject to cross-examination.

(2) If the prosecutor has made "every effort" to produce the declarant, but the declarant proves unavailable, and if the out-of-court statement was made under oath and subject to cross-examination by the accused, the Confrontation Clause does not bar its admission.

II. The **Roberts** *Era*

Ohio v. Roberts, 448 U.S. 56 (1980)

Like *Mattox* and *Green, Ohio v. Roberts* concerned the use of a witness's past testimony against the defendant at a later trial. Here the prosecutor failed to produce the declarant, whom Ohio courts found to be unavailable. The U.S. Supreme Court set out a two-part interpretation of the Confrontation Clause as it applies to admission of hearsay:

(1) **The rule of "necessity":** Whether or not the out-of-court statement was subject to cross-examination, the "prosecution must either produce, or demonstrate the unavailability of, the declarant whose statement it wishes to use against the defendant."

(2) **The rule of "reliability":** If the declarant is unavailable, the hearsay statement "is admissible only if it bears adequate 'indicia of reliability.' Reliability can be inferred without more in a case where the evidence falls within a firmly rooted hearsay exception [or where the defendant had an earlier, adequate chance to cross-examine the declarant about the statement]. In other cases, the evidence must be excluded, at least absent a showing of particularized guarantees of trustworthiness."

Roberts gave rise to a stream of caselaw that lasted nearly a quarter-century. As we will see, neither *Roberts* nor any of its hearsay-related progeny survived *Crawford v. Washington.*

Idaho v. Wright, 497 U.S. 805 (1990)

Here the Court applied the *Roberts* rule of reliability to admission of statements by the defendants' daughter, aged two and a half, to a pediatrician in the course of a police investigation. The trial judge had deemed the girl to be incapable of testifying at trial and admitted her hearsay statements under Idaho's residual exception to the hearsay rule.

The justices ruled that the residual exception, by its nature, is not a "firmly rooted" exception to the hearsay rule. Hence the girl's statements to the pediatrician were "'presumptively unreliable and inadmissible for Confrontation Clause purposes'" unless the state showed that the challenged hearsay statements bore "particularized guarantees of trustworthiness."

In what proved to be the most controversial part of its ruling, the Court held that evidence *corroborating* the truth of a hearsay statement could not support a finding that the statement bore "particularized guarantees of trustworthiness." So the Court disregarded the doctor's description of physical evidence of sexual abuse. It likewise ignored testimony of the girl's older half sister that the younger girl's father had abused her.

The Court ruled that the state instead must show particularized guarantees of trustworthiness based "only [on] those [circumstances] that surround the making of the statement and that render the declarant particularly worthy of belief." These circumstances might include the apparent spontaneity of the statement and the declarant's motivation to speak truthfully. Here the young girl's allegations came up wanting, as she spoke mainly in response to the pediatrician's blatantly leading questions ("Does daddy touch you with his pee-pee? Do you touch his pee-pee?"). Hence the state failed to show "particularized guarantees of trustworthiness," and admission of the younger girl's statements violated the Confrontation Clause.

Maryland v. Craig, 497 U.S. 836 (1990)

This case does not concern the admissibility of hearsay under the Confrontation Clause, but addresses a different Confrontation Clause concern. I include it here to shed light on Justice Scalia's vision of the Confrontation Clause. As the author of four foundational *Crawford*-era cases—*Crawford, Davis, Giles,* and *Melendez-Diaz,* all addressed below—Justice Scalia played a critical role in shaping this area of law.

Before trial of a daycare center owner charged with sexually abusing a child, the state asked the judge to permit the child to testify by one-way closed-circuit television. Maryland law permitted this procedure if the trial judge found that the child would suffer "serious emotional distress such that [she could not] reasonably communicate" if required to testify in the courtroom while face-to-face with the defendant. Based on expert testimony, the trial judge made the requisite finding and granted the state's motion. The child testified in a separate room with only the prosecutor and defense lawyer present. The child was under oath and subject to cross-examination. The judge, jury, and defendant remained in the courtroom, where they could observe the child's testimony by closed-circuit television. The child could not, however, see the defendant.

Two years earlier, in *Coy v. Iowa,* 487 U.S. 1012 (1988), the Court had ruled that "the Confrontation Clause guarantees the defendant a face-to-face meeting with witnesses appearing before the trier of fact." In that case two children were permitted to testify behind a screen that shielded the defendant from their view. Writing for the Court, Justice Scalia reasoned that the visual obstruction invaded the defendant's confrontation right because witnesses might be less willing to lie while looking the accused in the eye. The Court rejected the notion that a "legislatively imposed presumption of trauma" could defeat the right to a face-to-face confrontation and noted that "there have been no individualized findings that these particular witnesses needed special protection."

In *Craig*, in contrast, the trial court made such an individualized finding that the child would suffer serious emotional distress and be unable to communicate. This difference between *Coy* and *Craig* tipped the balance. Given the minimal intrusion on the defendant's confrontation right—after all, the child was under oath and subject to contemporaneous cross-examination, and the jury could observe her demeanor by video monitor—the Court held that "the state interest in protecting child witnesses from the trauma of testifying in a child abuse case is sufficiently important to justify the use of a special procedure":

> [W]here necessary to protect a child witness from trauma that would be caused by testifying in the physical presence of the defendant, at least where such trauma would impair the child's ability to communicate, the Confrontation Clause does not prohibit the use of a procedure that, despite the absence of face-to-face confrontation, ensures the reliability of the evidence by subjecting it to rigorous adversarial testing and thereby preserves the essence of effective confrontation.

Justice Scalia dissented, arguing that a barrier between the defendant and a testifying witness "is explicitly forbidden by the constitutional text; there is simply no room for interpretation with regard to 'the irreducible literal meaning of the Clause.'" (Quoting *Coy*.) He then elaborated:

> The [Court's] reasoning is as follows: The Confrontation Clause guarantees not only what it explicitly provides for—"face-to-face" confrontation—but also implied and collateral rights such as cross-examination, oath, and observation of demeanor (TRUE); the purpose of this entire cluster of rights is to ensure the reliability of evidence (TRUE); the Maryland procedure preserves the implied and collateral rights (TRUE), which adequately ensure the reliability of evidence (perhaps TRUE); therefore the Confrontation Clause is not violated by denying what it explicitly provides for—"face-to-face" confrontation (unquestionably FALSE). This reasoning abstracts from the right to its purposes, and then eliminates the right. It is wrong because the Confrontation Clause does not guarantee reliable evidence; it guarantees specific trial procedures that were thought to assure reliable evidence, undeniably among which was "face-to-face" confrontation.

Bear in mind Justice Scalia's approach here, exalting the "trial procedures that were thought to assure reliable evidence," when we reach *Crawford v. Washington*.

Maryland v. Craig appears to remain good law. *See* Myrna S. Raeder, *Comments on Child Abuse Litigation in a "Testimonial" World: The Intersection of Competency, Hearsay, and Confrontation*, 82 IND. L.J. 1009, 1015–17 (2007).

White v. Illinois, 502 U.S. 346 (1992)

Elaborating on the *Roberts* rule of necessity, the Supreme Court addressed the admissibility of a four-year-old girl's complaints of sexual abuse, made in the minutes and hours after the crime to her babysitter, her mother, a police officer, an emergency room nurse, and a doctor. The state trial judge had admitted all these statements as either spontaneous declarations or statements made for purposes of medical treatment or diagnosis. The trial court never found that the girl, who did not testify, was unavailable to do so.

The Court reasoned that excited utterances and medical statements are made in circumstances that "cannot be recaptured even by later in-court testimony." Because such statements bore circumstantial guarantees of reliability that even trial testimony lacked, it made little sense to insist that the child testify or be shown to be unavailable before admitting her hearsay complaints. The Court held, therefore, that the *Roberts* rule of necessity would not apply to excited utterances and medical statements.

In a concurring opinion joined by Justice Scalia, Justice Thomas argued that "a narrower reading of the Confrontation Clause than the one given to it since 1980 [in *Roberts*] may well be correct." The original purpose of the Clause, he said, was to prevent the abusive practice of securing convictions based on ex parte affidavits of absent declarants. Hence "the Confrontation Clause is implicated by [out-of-court] statements only insofar as they are contained in formalized testimonial materials, such as affidavits, depositions, prior testimony, or confessions."* The Clause therefore has no application to a four-year-old girl's complaints of sexual abuse made to her babysitter, mother, nurse, and doctor. Nor would it apply to statements the girl made to a police officer shortly after the crime. True, "statements to the investigating police officer might be considered the functional equivalent of in-court testimony because the statements arguably were made in contemplation of legal proceedings." But Justice Thomas rejected that approach because focusing on the intent of the declarant would "entangle the courts in a multitude of difficulties."

Lilly v. Virginia, 527 U.S. 116 (1999)

In what would prove to be the last gasp of the *Roberts* rule of reliability, the Court considered the admissibility of an accomplice's

* As Professor Jeffrey Bellin recently noted, this formula for defining the Confrontation Clause's reach may have found first expression in an amicus brief filed in *White* by the U.S. Solicitor General. Jeffrey Bellin, *The Incredible Shrinking Confrontation Clause*, 92 B.U. L. REV. ___ (forthcoming Dec. 2012).

custodial confession to the police that also implicated the defendant. Writing for four members of the Court, Justice Stevens reasoned that such statements, as a class, could not survive Confrontation Clause scrutiny: They do not fall within a firmly rooted exception to the hearsay rule; and far from having "particularized guarantees of trustworthiness," they "are inherently unreliable . . . because an accomplice often has a considerable interest in 'confessing and betraying his cocriminals.'" These statements "are given under conditions that implicate the core concerns of the old ex parte affidavit practice—that is, when the government is involved in the statements' production, and when the statements describe past events and have not been subjected to adversarial testing."

Concurring separately, Justices Breyer, Scalia, and Thomas indicated their readiness to move beyond the *Roberts* framework and to consider an approach that focuses on whether the challenged hearsay resembles the old ex parte affidavits against which the Confrontation Clause originally guarded.

III. The Crawford *Era*

The Court's inability to assemble a majority in *Lilly* and the willingness of three justices to abandon the *Roberts* approach proved to be straws in the wind. When next given the chance to recast Confrontation Clause doctrine, Justice Scalia assembled a majority of seven and set the Court on an entirely new course. . . .

CRAWFORD V. WASHINGTON

541 U.S. 36 (2004)

■ JUSTICE SCALIA delivered the opinion of the Court. Petitioner Michael Crawford stabbed a man who allegedly tried to rape his wife, Sylvia. At his trial, the State played for the jury Sylvia's tape-recorded statement to the police describing the stabbing, even though he had no opportunity for cross-examination. The Washington Supreme Court upheld petitioner's conviction after determining that Sylvia's statement was reliable. The question presented is whether this procedure complied with the Sixth Amendment's guarantee that, "in all criminal prosecutions, the accused shall enjoy the right . . . to be confronted with the witnesses against him."

I

On August 5, 1999, Kenneth Lee was stabbed at his apartment. Police arrested petitioner later that night. After giving petitioner and his wife *Miranda* warnings, detectives interrogated each of them twice. Petitioner eventually confessed that he and Sylvia had gone in search of Lee because he was upset over an earlier incident in which Lee had tried to rape her. The two had found Lee at his apartment, and a fight ensued in which Lee was stabbed in the torso and petitioner's hand was cut.

Petitioner gave the following account of the fight:

> "*Q:* Okay. Did you ever see anything in [Lee's] hands?
>
> "*A:* I think so, but I'm not positive.
>
> "*Q:* Okay, when you think so, what do you mean by that?
>
> "*A:* I coulda swore I seen him goin' for somethin' before, right before everything happened. He was like reachin', fiddlin' around down here and stuff . . . and I just . . . I don't know, I think, this is just a possibility, but I think, I think that he pulled somethin' out and I grabbed for it and that's how I got cut. . . ."

Sylvia generally corroborated petitioner's story about the events leading up to the fight, but her account of the fight itself was arguably different—particularly with respect to whether Lee had drawn a weapon before petitioner assaulted him:

> "*Q:* Did Kenny do anything to fight back from this assault?
>
> "*A*: (pausing) I know he reached into his pocket . . . or somethin' . . . I don't know what.
>
> "*Q:* After he was stabbed?
>
> "*A:* He saw Michael coming up. He lifted his hand . . . his chest open, he might [have] went to go strike his hand out or something and then (inaudible).
>
> "*Q:* Okay, you, you gotta speak up.
>
> "*A:* Okay, he lifted his hand over his head maybe to strike Michael's hand down or something and then he put his hands in his . . . put his right hand in his right pocket . . . took a step back . . . Michael proceeded to stab him . . . then his hands were like . . . how do you explain this . . . open arms . . . with his hands open and he fell down . . . and we ran (describing subject holding hands open, palms toward assailant).
>
> "*Q:* Okay, when he's standing there with his open hands, you're talking about Kenny, correct?
>
> "*A:* Yeah, after, after the fact, yes.
>
> "*Q:* Did you see anything in his hands at that point?
>
> "*A:* (pausing) um um (no)."

The State charged petitioner with assault and attempted murder. At trial, he claimed self-defense. Sylvia did not testify because of the state marital privilege, which generally bars a spouse from testifying without the other spouse's consent. In Washington, this privilege does not extend

to a spouse's out-of-court statements admissible under a hearsay exception, so the State sought to introduce Sylvia's tape-recorded statements to the police as evidence that the stabbing was not in self-defense. Noting that Sylvia had admitted she led petitioner to Lee's apartment and thus had facilitated the assault, the State invoked the hearsay exception for statements against penal interest, Wash. Rule Evid. 804(b)(3) (2003).

Petitioner countered that, state law notwithstanding, admitting the evidence would violate his federal constitutional right to be "confronted with the witnesses against him." AMDT. 6. According to our description of that right in *Ohio v. Roberts,* 448 U.S. 56 (1980), it does not bar admission of an unavailable witness's statement against a criminal defendant if the statement bears "adequate 'indicia of reliability.'" To meet that test, evidence must either fall within a "firmly rooted hearsay exception" or bear "particularized guarantees of trustworthiness." The trial court here admitted the statement on the latter ground, offering several reasons why it was trustworthy: Sylvia was not shifting blame but rather corroborating her husband's story that he acted in self-defense or "justified reprisal"; she had direct knowledge as an eyewitness; she was describing recent events; and she was being questioned by a "neutral" law enforcement officer. The prosecution played the tape for the jury and relied on it in closing, arguing that it was "damning evidence" that "completely refutes [petitioner's] claim of self-defense." The jury convicted petitioner of assault.

The Washington Court of Appeals reversed. It applied a nine-factor test to determine whether Sylvia's statement bore particularized guarantees of trustworthiness, and noted several reasons why it did not: The statement contradicted one she had previously given; it was made in response to specific questions; and at one point she admitted she had shut her eyes during the stabbing. The court considered and rejected the State's argument that Sylvia's statement was reliable because it coincided with petitioner's to such a degree that the two "interlocked." The court determined that, although the two statements agreed about the events leading up to the stabbing, they differed on the issue crucial to petitioner's self-defense claim: "[Petitioner's] version asserts that Lee may have had something in his hand when he stabbed him; but Sylvia's version has Lee grabbing for something only after he has been stabbed."

The Washington Supreme Court reinstated the conviction, unanimously concluding that, although Sylvia's statement did not fall under a firmly rooted hearsay exception, it bore guarantees of trustworthiness: " 'When a codefendant's confession is virtually identical [to, *i.e.*, interlocks with,] that of a defendant, it may be deemed reliable.' " The court explained:

> "Although the Court of Appeals concluded that the statements were contradictory, upon closer inspection they appear to overlap. . . .

"Both of the Crawfords' statements indicate that Lee was possibly grabbing for a weapon, but they are equally unsure when this event may have taken place. They are also equally unsure how Michael received the cut on his hand, leading the court to question when, if ever, Lee possessed a weapon. In this respect they overlap.

"Neither Michael nor Sylvia clearly stated that Lee had a weapon in hand from which Michael was simply defending himself. And it is this omission by both that interlocks the statements and makes Sylvia's statement reliable."[1]

We granted certiorari to determine whether the State's use of Sylvia's statement violated the Confrontation Clause.

II

The Sixth Amendment's Confrontation Clause provides that, "in all criminal prosecutions, the accused shall enjoy the right . . . to be confronted with the witnesses against him." . . . Petitioner argues that [the *Roberts*] test strays from the original meaning of the Confrontation Clause and urges us to reconsider it.

A

The Constitution's text does not alone resolve this case. One could plausibly read "witnesses against" a defendant to mean those who actually testify at trial, those whose statements are offered at trial, or something in-between. We must therefore turn to the historical background of the Clause to understand its meaning.

The right to confront one's accusers is a concept that dates back to Roman times. *See* Herrmann & Speer, *Facing the Accuser: Ancient and Medieval Precursors of the Confrontation Clause*, 34 VA. J. INT'L L. 481 (1994). The founding generation's immediate source of the concept, however, was the common law. English common law has long differed from continental civil law in regard to the manner in which witnesses give testimony in criminal trials. The common-law tradition is one of live testimony in court subject to adversarial testing, while the civil law condones examination in private by judicial officers.

Nonetheless, England at times adopted elements of the civil-law practice. Justices of the peace or other officials examined suspects and witnesses before trial. These examinations were sometimes read in court

1. The court rejected the State's argument that guarantees of trustworthiness were unnecessary since petitioner waived his confrontation rights by invoking the marital privilege. It reasoned that "forcing the defendant to choose between the marital privilege and confronting his spouse presents an untenable Hobson's choice." The State has not challenged this holding here. The State also has not challenged the Court of Appeals' conclusion (not reached by the State Supreme Court) that the confrontation violation, if it occurred, was not harmless. We express no opinion on these matters.

in lieu of live testimony, a practice that "occasioned frequent demands by the prisoner to have his 'accusers,' *i.e.* the witnesses against him, brought before him face to face." 1 J. STEPHEN, HISTORY OF THE CRIMINAL LAW OF ENGLAND 326 (1883). In some cases, these demands were refused. *See, e.g., Raleigh's Case*, 2 HOW. ST. TR. 1, 15–16, 24 (1603).

Pretrial examinations became routine under two statutes passed during the reign of Queen Mary in the 16th century, 1 & 2 Phil. & M., c. 13 (1554), and 2 & 3 *id.*, c. 10 (1555). These Marian bail and committal statutes required justices of the peace to examine suspects and witnesses in felony cases and to certify the results to the court. It is doubtful that the original purpose of the examinations was to produce evidence admissible at trial. Whatever the original purpose, however, they came to be used as evidence in some cases, resulting in an adoption of continental procedure.

The most notorious instances of civil-law examination occurred in the great political trials of the 16th and 17th centuries. One such was the 1603 trial of Sir Walter Raleigh for treason. Lord Cobham, Raleigh's alleged accomplice, had implicated him in an examination before the Privy Council and in a letter. At Raleigh's trial, these were read to the jury. Raleigh argued that Cobham had lied to save himself: "Cobham is absolutely in the King's mercy; to excuse me cannot avail him; by accusing me he may hope for favour." 1 D. JARDINE, CRIMINAL TRIALS 435 (1832). Suspecting that Cobham would recant, Raleigh demanded that the judges call him to appear, arguing that "the Proof of the Common Law is by witness and jury: let Cobham be here, let him speak it. Call my accuser before my face. . . ." 2 HOW. ST. TR., at 15–16. The judges refused, and, despite Raleigh's protestations that he was being tried "by the Spanish Inquisition," the jury convicted, and Raleigh was sentenced to death.

One of Raleigh's trial judges later lamented that "'the justice of England has never been so degraded and injured as by the condemnation of Sir Walter Raleigh.'" 1 JARDINE, *supra*, at 520. Through a series of statutory and judicial reforms, English law developed a right of confrontation that limited these abuses. For example, treason statutes required witnesses to confront the accused "face to face" at his arraignment. *E.g.*, 13 Car. 2, c. 1, § 5 (1661). Courts, meanwhile, developed relatively strict rules of unavailability, admitting examinations only if the witness was demonstrably unable to testify in person. Several authorities also stated that a suspect's confession could be admitted only against himself, and not against others he implicated.

One recurring question was whether the admissibility of an unavailable witness's pretrial examination depended on whether the defendant had had an opportunity to cross-examine him. In 1696, the Court of King's Bench answered this question in the affirmative, in the widely reported misdemeanor libel case of *King v. Paine*, 5 Mod. 163, 87 Eng. Rep.

584. The court ruled that, even though a witness was dead, his examination was not admissible where "the defendant not being present when [it was] taken before the mayor . . . had lost the benefit of a cross-examination." The question was also debated at length during the infamous proceedings against Sir John Fenwick on a bill of attainder. Fenwick's counsel objected to admitting the examination of a witness who had been spirited away, on the ground that Fenwick had had no opportunity to cross-examine. *See Fenwick's Case*, 13 HOW. ST. TR. 537, 591–92 (H. C. 1696). The examination was nonetheless admitted on a closely divided vote after several of those present opined that the common-law rules of procedure did not apply to parliamentary attainder proceedings—one speaker even admitting that the evidence would normally be inadmissible. . . .

Paine had settled the rule requiring a prior opportunity for cross-examination as a matter of common law, but some doubts remained over whether the Marian statutes prescribed an exception to it in felony cases. The statutes did not identify the circumstances under which examinations were admissible, and some inferred that no prior opportunity for cross-examination was required. Many who expressed this view acknowledged that it meant the statutes were in derogation of the common law. Nevertheless, by 1791 (the year the Sixth Amendment was ratified), courts were applying the cross-examination rule even to examinations by justices of the peace in felony cases. *See King v. Dingler*, 2 Leach 561, 562–63 (1791); *King v. Woodcock*, 1 Leach 500, 502–04 (1789); *cf. King v. Radbourne*, 1 Leach 457, 459–61 (1787). Early 19th-century treatises confirm that requirement.

B

. . . Many declarations of rights adopted [by the former Colonies] around the time of the Revolution guaranteed a right of confrontation. The proposed Federal Constitution, however, did not. At the Massachusetts ratifying convention, Abraham Holmes objected to this omission precisely on the ground that it would lead to civil-law practices: "The mode of trial is altogether indetermined; . . . whether [the defendant] is to be allowed to confront the witnesses, and have the advantage of cross-examination, we are not yet told. . . . We shall find Congress possessed of powers enabling them to institute judicatories little less inauspicious than a certain tribunal in Spain, . . . the *Inquisition.*" 2 DEBATES ON THE FEDERAL CONSTITUTION 110–11 (J. Elliot 2d ed. 1863). Similarly, a prominent Antifederalist writing under the pseudonym Federal Farmer criticized the use of "written evidence" . . .: "Nothing can be more essential than the cross examining [of] witnesses, and generally before the triers of the facts in question. . . . Written evidence . . . [is] almost useless; it must be frequently taken *ex parte*, and but very seldom leads to the proper discovery of truth." R. Lee, *Letter IV by the Federal Farmer* (Oct. 15, 1787). The First Congress responded by including the Confrontation Clause in the proposal that became the Sixth Amendment. . . .

III

This history supports two inferences about the meaning of the Sixth Amendment.

A

First, the principal evil at which the Confrontation Clause was directed was the civil-law mode of criminal procedure, and particularly its use of *ex parte* examinations as evidence against the accused. It was these practices that the Crown deployed in notorious treason cases like Raleigh's; that the Marian statutes invited; that English law's assertion of a right to confrontation was meant to prohibit; and that the founding-era rhetoric decried. The Sixth Amendment must be interpreted with this focus in mind. . . .

This focus also suggests that not all hearsay implicates the Sixth Amendment's core concerns. An off-hand, overheard remark might be unreliable evidence and thus a good candidate for exclusion under hearsay rules, but it bears little resemblance to the civil-law abuses the Confrontation Clause targeted. On the other hand, *ex parte* examinations might sometimes be admissible under modern hearsay rules, but the Framers certainly would not have condoned them.

The text of the Confrontation Clause reflects this focus. It applies to "witnesses" against the accused—in other words, those who "bear testimony." 1 N. WEBSTER, AN AMERICAN DICTIONARY OF THE ENGLISH LANGUAGE (1828). "Testimony," in turn, is typically "[a] solemn declaration or affirmation made for the purpose of establishing or proving some fact." *Ibid.* An accuser who makes a formal statement to government officers bears testimony in a sense that a person who makes a casual remark to an acquaintance does not. The constitutional text, like the history underlying the common-law right of confrontation, thus reflects an especially acute concern with a specific type of out-of-court statement.

Various formulations of this core class of "testimonial" statements exist: "*ex parte* in-court testimony or its functional equivalent—that is, material such as affidavits, custodial examinations, prior testimony that the defendant was unable to cross-examine, or similar pretrial statements that declarants would reasonably expect to be used prosecutorially," Brief for Petitioner 23; "extrajudicial statements . . . contained in formalized testimonial materials, such as affidavits, depositions, prior testimony, or confessions," *White v. Illinois,* 502 U.S. 346, 365 (1992) (THOMAS, J., joined by SCALIA, J., concurring in part and concurring in judgment); "statements that were made under circumstances which would lead an objective witness reasonably to believe that the statement would be available for use at a later trial," Brief for National Association of Criminal Defense Lawyers et al. as *Amici Curiae* 3. These formulations all share a common nucleus and then define the Clause's coverage at various levels of abstraction around it. Regardless of the precise articulation, some statements qualify under any definition—for example, *ex parte* testimony at a preliminary hearing.

Statements taken by police officers in the course of interrogations are also testimonial under even a narrow standard. Police interrogations bear a striking resemblance to examinations by justices of the peace in England. The statements are not *sworn* testimony, but the absence of oath was not dispositive. Cobham's examination was unsworn, yet Raleigh's trial has long been thought a paradigmatic confrontation violation....

That interrogators are police officers rather than magistrates does not change the picture either. Justices of the peace conducting examinations under the Marian statutes were not magistrates as we understand that office today, but had an essentially investigative and prosecutorial function. England did not have a professional police force until the 19th century, so it is not surprising that other government officers performed the investigative functions now associated primarily with the police. The involvement of government officers in the production of testimonial evidence presents the same risk, whether the officers are police or justices of the peace.

In sum, even if the Sixth Amendment is not solely concerned with testimonial hearsay, that is its primary object, and interrogations by law enforcement officers fall squarely within that class.[4]

B

The historical record also supports a second proposition: that the Framers would not have allowed admission of testimonial statements of a witness who did not appear at trial unless he was unavailable to testify, and the defendant had had a prior opportunity for cross-examination. The text of the Sixth Amendment does not suggest any open-ended exceptions from the confrontation requirement to be developed by the courts. Rather, the "right ... to be confronted with the witnesses against him," AMDT. 6, is most naturally read as a reference to the right of confrontation at common law, admitting only those exceptions established at the time of the founding. *See Mattox v. United States,* 156 U.S. 237, 243 (1895). As the English authorities above reveal, the common law in 1791 conditioned admissibility of an absent witness's examination on unavailability and a prior opportunity to cross-examine. The Sixth Amendment therefore incorporates those limitations. The numerous early state decisions applying the same test confirm that these principles were received as part of the common law in this country.

4. We use the term "interrogation" in its colloquial, rather than any technical legal, sense. *Cf. Rhode Island* v. *Innis,* 446 U.S. 291, 300–01 (1980). Just as various definitions of "testimonial" exist, one can imagine various definitions of "interrogation," and we need not select among them in this case. Sylvia's recorded statement, knowingly given in response to structured police questioning, qualifies under any conceivable definition.

. . . This is not to deny, as THE CHIEF JUSTICE notes, that "there were always exceptions to the general rule of exclusion" of hearsay evidence. Several had become well established by 1791. *See* 3 WIGMORE § 1397, at 101. But there is scant evidence that exceptions were invoked to admit *testimonial* statements against the accused in a *criminal* case.[6] Most of the hearsay exceptions covered statements that by their nature were not testimonial—for example, business records or statements in furtherance of a conspiracy. We do not infer from these that the Framers thought exceptions would apply even to prior testimony.[7]

IV

Our case law has been largely consistent with these two principles. Our leading early decision, for example, involved a deceased witness's prior trial testimony. *Mattox v. United States,* 156 U.S. 237 (1895). In allowing the statement to be admitted, we relied on the fact that the defendant had had, at the first trial, an adequate opportunity to confront the witness: "The substance of the constitutional protection is preserved to the prisoner in the advantage he has once had of seeing the witness face to face, and of subjecting him to the ordeal of a cross-examination. This, the law says, he shall under no circumstances be deprived of. . . ." *Id.* at 244.

Our later cases conform to *Mattox*'s holding that prior trial or preliminary hearing testimony is admissible only if the defendant had an adequate opportunity to cross-examine. *See California v. Green,* 399 U.S. 149, 165–68 (1970); *Pointer v. Texas,* 380 U.S. at 406–08. Even where the defendant had such an opportunity, we excluded the testimony where the government had not established unavailability of the witness. We similarly excluded accomplice confessions where the defendant had no opportunity to cross-examine. *See Bruton v. United States,* 391 U.S. 123, 126–28 (1968). In contrast, we considered reliability factors beyond prior opportunity for cross-examination when the hearsay statement at issue was not testimonial.

6. The one deviation we have found involves dying declarations. The existence of that exception as a general rule of criminal hearsay law cannot be disputed. *See, e.g., Mattox* v. *United States,* 156 U.S. 237, 243–44 (1895). Although many dying declarations may not be testimonial, there is authority for admitting even those that clearly are. We need not decide in this case whether the Sixth Amendment incorporates an exception for testimonial dying declarations. If this exception must be accepted on historical grounds, it is *sui generis.*

7. We cannot agree with THE CHIEF JUSTICE that the fact "that a statement might be testimonial does nothing to undermine the wisdom of one of these [hearsay] exceptions." Involvement of government officers in the production of testimony with an eye toward trial presents unique potential for prosecutorial abuse—a fact borne out time and again throughout a history with which the Framers were keenly familiar. This consideration does not evaporate when testimony happens to fall within some broad, modern hearsay exception, even if that exception might be justifiable in other circumstances.

Even our recent cases, in their outcomes, hew closely to the traditional line. *Ohio v. Roberts,* 448 U.S. at 67–70, admitted testimony from a preliminary hearing at which the defendant had examined the witness. *Lilly v. Virginia, supra,* 527 U.S. 116, excluded testimonial statements that the defendant had had no opportunity to test by cross-examination. And *Bourjaily v. United States,* 483 U.S. 171, 181–84 (1987), admitted statements made unwittingly to an FBI informant after applying a more general test that did *not* make prior cross-examination an indispensable requirement.[8] . . .

Our cases have thus remained faithful to the Framers' understanding: Testimonial statements of witnesses absent from trial have been admitted only where the declarant is unavailable, and only where the defendant has had a prior opportunity to cross-examine.[9]

V

Although the results of our decisions have generally been faithful to the original meaning of the Confrontation Clause, the same cannot be said of our rationales. *Roberts* conditions the admissibility of all hearsay evidence on whether it falls under a "firmly rooted hearsay exception" or bears "particularized guarantees of trustworthiness." This test departs from the historical principles identified above in two respects. First, it is too broad: It applies the same mode of analysis whether or not the hearsay consists of *ex parte* testimony. This often results in close constitutional scrutiny in cases that are far removed from the core concerns of the

8. One case arguably in tension with the rule requiring a prior opportunity for cross-examination when the proffered statement is testimonial is *White* v. *Illinois,* 502 U.S. 346 (1992), which involved, *inter alia,* statements of a child victim to an investigating police officer admitted as spontaneous declarations. It is questionable whether testimonial statements would ever have been admissible on that ground in 1791; to the extent the hearsay exception for spontaneous declarations existed at all, it required that the statements be made "immediately upon the hurt received, and before [the declarant] had time to devise or contrive any thing for her own advantage." *Thompson* v. *Trevanion,* Skin. 402, 90 Eng. Rep. 179 (K. B. 1694). In any case, the only question presented in *White* was whether the Confrontation Clause imposed an unavailability requirement on the types of hearsay at issue. The holding did not address the question whether certain of the statements, because they were testimonial, had to be excluded *even if* the witness was unavailable. We "[took] as a given . . . that the testimony properly falls within the relevant hearsay exceptions."

9. . . . THE CHIEF JUSTICE fails to identify a single case (aside from one minor, arguable exception, *see supra,* n. 8), where we have admitted testimonial statements based on indicia of reliability other than a prior opportunity for cross-examination. If nothing else, the test we announce is an empirically accurate explanation of the results our cases have reached.

. . . [W]e reiterate that, when the declarant appears for cross-examination at trial, the Confrontation Clause places no constraints at all on the use of his prior testimonial statements. *See California* v. *Green,* 399 U.S. 149, 162 (1970). . . . (The Clause also does not bar the use of testimonial statements for purposes other than establishing the truth of the matter asserted. *See Tennessee v. Street,* 471 U.S. 409, 414 (1985).)

Clause. At the same time, however, the test is too narrow: It admits statements that *do* consist of *ex parte* testimony upon a mere finding of reliability. This malleable standard often fails to protect against paradigmatic confrontation violations.

Members of this Court and academics have suggested that we revise our doctrine to reflect more accurately the original understanding of the Clause. They offer two proposals: First, that we apply the Confrontation Clause only to testimonial statements, leaving the remainder to regulation by hearsay law—thus eliminating the overbreadth referred to above. Second, that we impose an absolute bar to statements that are testimonial, absent a prior opportunity to cross-examine—thus eliminating the excessive narrowness referred to above.

In *White*, we considered the first proposal and rejected it. Although our analysis in this case casts doubt on that holding, we need not definitively resolve whether it survives our decision today, because Sylvia Crawford's statement is testimonial under any definition. This case does, however, squarely implicate the second proposal.

A

Where testimonial statements are involved, we do not think the Framers meant to leave the Sixth Amendment's protection to the vagaries of the rules of evidence, much less to amorphous notions of "reliability." Certainly none of the authorities discussed above acknowledges any general reliability exception to the common-law rule. Admitting statements deemed reliable by a judge is fundamentally at odds with the right of confrontation. To be sure, the Clause's ultimate goal is to ensure reliability of evidence, but it is a procedural rather than a substantive guarantee. It commands, not that evidence be reliable, but that reliability be assessed in a particular manner: by testing in the crucible of cross-examination. The Clause thus reflects a judgment, not only about the desirability of reliable evidence (a point on which there could be little dissent), but about how reliability can best be determined. *Cf.* 3 BLACKSTONE, COMMENTARIES, at 373 ("This open examination of witnesses . . . is much more conducive to the clearing up of truth"); M. HALE, HISTORY AND ANALYSIS OF THE COMMON LAW OF ENGLAND 258 (1713) (adversarial testing "beats and bolts out the Truth much better").

The *Roberts* test allows a jury to hear evidence, untested by the adversary process, based on a mere judicial determination of reliability. It thus replaces the constitutionally prescribed method of assessing reliability with a wholly foreign one. In this respect, it is very different from exceptions to the Confrontation Clause that make no claim to be a surrogate means of assessing reliability. For example, the rule of forfeiture by wrongdoing (which we accept) extinguishes confrontation claims on essentially equitable grounds; it does not purport to be an alternative means of determining reliability. *See Reynolds v. United States*, 98 U.S. 145, 158–59 (1879). . . .

Dispensing with confrontation because testimony is obviously reliable is akin to dispensing with jury trial because a defendant is obviously guilty. This is not what the Sixth Amendment prescribes.

B

. . . Reliability is an amorphous, if not entirely subjective, concept. There are countless factors bearing on whether a statement is reliable; the nine-factor balancing test applied by the Court of Appeals below is representative. Whether a statement is deemed reliable depends heavily on which factors the judge considers and how much weight he accords each of them. . . .

The unpardonable vice of the *Roberts* test, however, is not its unpredictability, but its demonstrated capacity to admit core testimonial statements that the Confrontation Clause plainly meant to exclude. Despite the plurality's speculation in *Lilly*, 527 U.S. at 137, that it was "highly unlikely" that accomplice confessions implicating the accused could survive *Roberts*, courts continue routinely to admit them. One recent study found that, after *Lilly*, appellate courts admitted accomplice statements to the authorities in 25 out of 70 cases—more than one-third of the time. Kirst, *Appellate Court Answers to the Confrontation Questions in* Lilly v. Virginia, 53 SYRACUSE L. REV. 87, 105 (2003). . . .

C

Roberts' failings were on full display in the proceedings below. Sylvia Crawford made her statement while in police custody, herself a potential suspect in the case. . . . In response to often leading questions from police detectives, she implicated her husband in Lee's stabbing and at least arguably undermined his self-defense claim. Despite all this, the trial court admitted her statement, listing several reasons why it was reliable. In its opinion reversing, the Court of Appeals listed several *other* reasons why the statement was *not* reliable. Finally, the State Supreme Court relied exclusively on the interlocking character of the statement and disregarded every other factor the lower courts had considered. The case is thus a self-contained demonstration of *Roberts'* unpredictable and inconsistent application.

. . . The trial court . . . buttressed its reliability finding by claiming that Sylvia was "being questioned by law enforcement, and, thus, the [questioner] is . . . neutral to her and not someone who would be inclined to advance her interests and shade her version of the truth unfavorably toward the defendant." The Framers would be astounded to learn that *ex parte* testimony could be admitted against a criminal defendant because it was elicited by "neutral" government officers. . . .

We readily concede that we could resolve this case by simply reweighing the "reliability factors" under *Roberts* and finding that Sylvia Crawford's statement falls short. But we view this as one of those rare cases in which the result below is so improbable that it reveals a fundamental failure on our part to interpret the Constitution in a way that secures its intended constraint on judicial discretion. Moreover, to reverse the Washington Supreme Court's decision after conducting our own reliability analysis would perpetuate, not avoid, what the Sixth Amendment condemns. The Constitution prescribes a procedure for determining the reliability of testimony in criminal trials, and we, no less than the state courts, lack authority to replace it with one of our own devising....

* * *

Where nontestimonial hearsay is at issue, it is wholly consistent with the Framers' design to afford the States flexibility in their development of hearsay law—as does *Roberts*, and as would an approach that exempted such statements from Confrontation Clause scrutiny altogether. Where testimonial evidence is at issue, however, the Sixth Amendment demands what the common law required: unavailability and a prior opportunity for cross-examination. We leave for another day any effort to spell out a comprehensive definition of "testimonial."[10] Whatever else the term covers, it applies at a minimum to prior testimony at a preliminary hearing, before a grand jury, or at a former trial; and to police interrogations. These are the modern practices with closest kinship to the abuses at which the Confrontation Clause was directed.

In this case, the State admitted Sylvia's testimonial statement against petitioner, despite the fact that he had no opportunity to cross-examine her. That alone is sufficient to make out a violation of the Sixth Amendment. *Roberts* notwithstanding, we decline to mine the record in search of indicia of reliability. Where testimonial statements are at issue, the only indicium of reliability sufficient to satisfy constitutional demands is the one the Constitution actually prescribes: confrontation.

The judgment of the Washington Supreme Court is reversed, and the case is remanded for further proceedings not inconsistent with this opinion....

■ CHIEF JUSTICE REHNQUIST, with whom JUSTICE O'CONNOR joins, concurring in the judgment. I dissent from the Court's decision to overrule *Ohio v. Roberts*, 448 U.S. 56 (1980). I believe that the Court's adoption of a new interpretation of the Confrontation Clause is not backed by sufficiently persuasive reasoning to overrule long-established precedent. Its decision

10. We acknowledge THE CHIEF JUSTICE's objection that our refusal to articulate a comprehensive definition in this case will cause interim uncertainty. But it can hardly be any worse than the status quo. The difference is that the *Roberts* test is *inherently*, and therefore *permanently*, unpredictable.

casts a mantle of uncertainty over future criminal trials in both federal and state courts, and is by no means necessary to decide the present case.

The Court's distinction between testimonial and nontestimonial statements, contrary to its claim, is no better rooted in history than our current doctrine.... [W]hile I agree that the Framers were mainly concerned about sworn affidavits and depositions, it does not follow that they were similarly concerned about the Court's broader category of testimonial statements.... [A]nd it seems to me any classification of statements as testimonial beyond that of sworn affidavits and depositions will be somewhat arbitrary....

I therefore see no reason why the distinction the Court draws is preferable to our precedent. Starting with Chief Justice Marshall's interpretation as a Circuit Justice in 1807, 16 years after the ratification of the Sixth Amendment, *United States v. Burr*, 25 F. Cas. 187, 193, F. Cas. No. 14694 (CC Va. 1807), continuing with our cases in the late 19th century, *Mattox v. United States,* 156 U.S. 237, 243–44 (1895), and through today, *e.g., White v. Illinois,* 502 U.S. 346, 352–53 (1992), we have never drawn a distinction between testimonial and nontestimonial statements. And for that matter, neither has any other court of which I am aware. I see little value in trading our precedent for an imprecise approximation at this late date.

I am also not convinced that the Confrontation Clause categorically requires the exclusion of testimonial statements.... With respect to unsworn testimonial statements, there is no indication that once the hearsay rule was developed courts ever excluded these statements if they otherwise fell within a firmly rooted exception. Dying declarations are one example.

Between 1700 and 1800 the rules regarding the admissibility of out-of-court statements were still being developed. There were always exceptions to the general rule of exclusion, and it is not clear to me that the Framers categorically wanted to eliminate further ones.... It is an odd conclusion indeed to think that the Framers created a cut-and-dried rule with respect to the admissibility of testimonial statements when the law during their own time was not fully settled....

Exceptions to confrontation have always been derived from the experience that some out-of-court statements are just as reliable as cross-examined in-court testimony due to the circumstances under which they were made. We have recognized, for example, that co-conspirator statements simply "cannot be replicated, even if the declarant testifies to the same matters in court." *United States v. Inadi,* 475 U.S. 387, 395 (1986). Because the statements are made while the declarant and the accused are partners in an illegal enterprise, the statements are unlikely to be false and their admission "actually furthers the 'Confrontation Clause's very mission' which is to 'advance the accuracy of the truth-determining process in criminal trials.'" Similar reasons justify the introduction of spontaneous declarations, *see White*, 502 U.S. at 356, statements made in the course of procuring medical services, *see ibid.*, dying declarations, and countless other hearsay exceptions. That a statement might be testimonial does nothing to undermine the wisdom of one of these exceptions.

Indeed, cross-examination is a tool used to flesh out the truth, not an empty procedure. "In a given instance [cross-examination may] be superfluous; it may be sufficiently clear, in that instance, that the statement offered is free enough from the risk of inaccuracy and untrustworthiness, so that the test of cross-examination would be a work of supererogation." 5 WIGMORE § 1420, at 251. . . . By creating an immutable category of excluded evidence, the Court adds little to a trial's truth-finding function and ignores this longstanding guidance.

In choosing the path it does, the Court of course overrules *Ohio v. Roberts*, 448 U.S. 56 (1980), a case decided nearly a quarter of a century ago. . . . [U]nresolved questions for the future of everyday criminal trials throughout the country surely counsel . . . caution. The Court grandly declares that "we leave for another day any effort to spell out a comprehensive definition of 'testimonial.'" But the thousands of federal prosecutors and the tens of thousands of state prosecutors need answers as to what beyond the specific kinds of "testimony" the Court lists is covered by the new rule. They need them now, not months or years from now. Rules of criminal evidence are applied every day in courts throughout the country, and parties should not be left in the dark in this manner.

To its credit, the Court's analysis of "testimony" excludes at least some hearsay exceptions, such as business records and official records. To hold otherwise would require numerous additional witnesses without any apparent gain in the truth-seeking process. Likewise to the Court's credit is its implicit recognition that the mistaken application of its new rule by courts which guess wrong as to the scope of the rule is subject to harmless-error analysis. *See ante*, n.1.

But these are palliatives to what I believe is a mistaken change of course. It is a change of course not in the least necessary to reverse the judgment of the Supreme Court of Washington in this case. The result the Court reaches follows inexorably from *Roberts* and its progeny without any need for overruling that line of cases. In *Idaho v. Wright*, 497 U.S. 805, 820–24 (1990), we held that an out-of-court statement was not admissible simply because the truthfulness of that statement was corroborated by other evidence at trial. As the Court notes, the Supreme Court of Washington gave decisive weight to the "interlocking nature of the two statements." No re-weighing of the "reliability factors," which is hypothesized by the Court, is required to reverse the judgment here. A citation to *Idaho v. Wright* would suffice. For the reasons stated, I believe that this would be a far preferable course for the Court to take here.

CRAWFORD V. WASHINGTON: *The Court's Contested Originalism*

Even as judges and trial lawyers around the country scrambled to adjust courtroom practice to *Crawford*'s new ground rules, legal historians turned a critical eye on the *Crawford* Court's originalist methods. A stream of essays and articles took issue with the twin pillars of Justice Scalia's historical analysis. First was his claim that the Framers distinguished between "testimonial" and "nontestimonial" hearsay statements and imposed little or no restraint on the latter: "[N]ot all hearsay implicates the Sixth Amendment's core concerns," he wrote. Second was his claim of a cross-examination rule that was known and established at the time of the framing: "[T]he Framers would not have allowed admission of testimonial statements of a witness who did not appear at trial unless he was unavailable to testify, and the defendant had had a prior opportunity for cross-examination." (Pages 601, 606, above.)

Were the Framers Open Toward Nontestimonial Hearsay?

In challenging the Framers' alleged unconcern about nontestimonial hearsay, scholars began where Justice Scalia began—with the word *witnesses* as used in the Confrontation Clause: "in all criminal prosecutions, the accused shall enjoy the right ... to be confronted with the *witnesses* against him. . . ." To unlock the Framers' meaning, Justice Scalia had consulted a (roughly) contemporaneous dictionary—the 1828 edition of Noah Webster's *American Dictionary of the English Language*, which arguably can help decode a clause framed in 1789. The dictionary, Justice Scalia reported, defined *witnesses* as those who "bear testimony" and *testimony* as "[a] solemn declaration or affirmation made for the purpose of establishing or proving some fact." Hence a witness against the defendant, he said, can be "[a]n accuser who makes a formal statement to government officers," but not "a person who makes a casual remark to an acquaintance." (Page 600.) The former's out-of-court statement would be testimonial hearsay, while the latter's would not.

As several historical fact checkers soon saw, Webster was not so clear. His dictionary supplied five definitions of *witness*, of which Justice Scalia chose the fifth—"One who gives testimony; as, the witnesses in court agreed in all essential facts." Webster's first and fourth entries clearly did not apply to *witness* as used in the Confrontation Clause. His second definition—"That which furnishes evidence or proof"—possibly applied not to persons, but to documents or physical artifacts such as blood stains. But what was wrong with the third definition? It defined a witness as "[a] person who knows or sees any thing; one personally present; as, he was *witness*; he was an *eye-witness*." As Professor Randolph Jonakait and others note, this definition of witness would suggest that nearly all hearsay—not merely Justice Scalia's narrow class of "testimonial" hearsay—falls under the Confrontation Clause's command. Because almost all hearsay declarants knew or saw something, the Sixth Amendment could bar almost all hearsay offered against criminal defendants unless they can cross-examine the declarant. *See* Randolph N. Jonakait, *"Witnesses" in the Confrontation Clause:* Crawford v. Washington, *Noah Webster, and Compulsory Process*, 79 TEMP. L. REV. 155, 159–61 & nn.26–27 (2006).

Justice Scalia acknowledged this uncertainty in Webster's treatment of *witness*—but not in *Crawford*. Dissenting in *Maryland v. Craig*, he argued that Webster's broader definition of *witness* could not be the one the Framers had in mind. It "is excluded in the Sixth Amendment by the words following the noun: 'witnesses *against him*.' The phrase obviously refers to those who give testimony against the defendant at trial." *Maryland v. Craig*, 497 U.S. 836, 864–65 (1990) (Scalia, J., dissenting). But as Professor Daniel Shaviro has asked, "Why cannot the term 'witnesses against him' refer to all persons having knowledge about the case and whose statements reporting such knowledge the prosecution uses as evidence against the defendant?" Daniel Shaviro, *The Confrontation Clause Today in Light of Its Common Law Background*, 26 VAL. U. L. REV. 337, 365 (1991).

Moving past semantics to procedural history, scholars have challenged Justice Scalia's suggestion that the Framers and lawyers of their time viewed admission of nontestimonial hearsay against criminal defendants with complacency. On the contrary, Professor Thomas Davies argues, the Framers never contemplated the matter "because they never anticipated that informal hearsay statements could come to be viewed as valid evidence in criminal trials." Davies notes that hearsay law was just taking form and had not yet generated the modern jumble of hearsay exceptions. In the jargon of the day, all unsworn statements—and hence virtually all hearsay—was simply "no evidence." Thomas Y. Davies, *What Did the Framers Know, and When Did They Know It? Fictional Originalism in* Crawford v. Washington, 71 BROOK. L. REV. 105, 107, 119 (2005).

Indeed he says only four sorts of hearsay typically found their way into criminal trials. The Marian statutes of the mid-sixteenth century required justices of the peace to record sworn examinations of witnesses soon after any felony arrest. These depositions were deemed admissible at trial against the accused if the witness was dead or too sick to travel or was kept away by the accused, even if the defendant never had the chance to cross-examine him. The Marian statutes likewise provided for sworn examinations at coroners' inquests. Treatise authors wrote that these examinations were admissible against the accused at trial if the witnesses became unavailable. Third, dying declarations were admissible, even if testimonial, on the theory that impending death enforced truth-telling about as well as an oath. *See* Davies, *supra*, at 107–08; Thomas Y. Davies, *Revisiting the Fictional Originalism in* Crawford's *"Cross-Examination Rule": A Reply to Mr. Kry*, 72 BROOK. L. REV. 557, 578 & n.73, 604 n.172,

622, 636 & n.318 (2007); *Crawford*, page 602 n.6. Finally, coconspirators' statements were admitted to prove the existence of a conspiracy but not the defendant's role in that conspiracy. *See* Thomas Y. Davies, *Not "The Framers' Design": How the Framing–Era Ban Against Hearsay Evidence Refutes the* Crawford–Davis *"Testimonial" Formulation of the Scope of the Original Confrontation Clause*, 15 J. L. & POL'Y 349, 401–06 (2007).

Far from viewing admission of *other*, less formal hearsay with indifference, Davies writes, the Framers would have viewed the prospect with alarm. In any event, Justice Scalia "did not identify any framing-era source that distinguished between testimonial and nontestimonial hearsay. So far as I can tell, none did." Davies, *supra*, 71 BROOK. L. REV. at 191. Hence "*Crawford*'s categorization of some out-of-court statements as 'nontestimonial' permits the admission of *unsworn* hearsay statements that would have been inadmissible under framing-era law." Davies, *supra*, 72 BROOK. L. REV. at 562.

Joining forces against Justice Scalia on the matter of nontestimonial hearsay, Professor Jonakait points to an early American reading of *witnesses* as used in the Confrontation Clause. The 1807 trial of Aaron Burr produced "the first interpretation of confrontation by a Supreme Court Justice." Presiding at trial, Chief Justice John Marshall excluded evidence of a coconspirator's statement, a form of hearsay the *Crawford* Court deems nontestimonial. (*See* page 602.) "I know not why . . . a man should have a constitutional claim to be confronted with the witnesses against him," Marshall wrote, "if mere verbal declarations, made in his absence, may be evidence against him." *United States v. Burr*, 25 F. Cas. 187, 193 (C.C. D. Va. 1807) (No. 14,694), *quoted in* Randolph N. Jonakait, *The Too-Easy Historical Assumptions of* Crawford v. Washington, 71 BROOK. L. REV. 219, 228–29 (2005). A "mere verbal declaration" sounds like what the *Crawford* Court calls nontestimonial hearsay. Unlike the *Crawford* Court, Chief Justice Marshall apparently believed that admission of such hearsay could offend the Confrontation Clause.

Indeed Justice Scalia once endorsed a reading of Marshall's opinion distinctly at odds with his analysis in *Crawford*. In *United States v. Hubbell*, 530 U.S. 27 (2000), he joined Justice Thomas's effort in a concurring opinion to expand the bounds of the Fifth Amendment's guarantee that "[n]o person . . . shall be compelled in any criminal case to be a *witness* against himself." Referring to a different part of Marshall's opinion in *Burr*, Justice Thomas argued that "a narrow definition of the term 'witness' as a person who testifies seems incompatible with *Burr*'s holding." *Hubbell*, 530 U.S. at 55 (Thomas, J., concurring), *quoted in* Jonakait, 79 TEMP. L. REV. at 179. Instead Justice Thomas used the same 1828 edition of Webster's dictionary that figured prominently in *Crawford* to define *witness* as "[t]hat which furnishes evidence or proof"—the second of Webster's five definitions of witness and one that arguably would not confine the scope of the Confrontation Clause to testimonial hearsay. *Hubbell*, 530 U.S. at 50 (Thomas, J., concurring); Jonakait, *supra*, at 178.

Did the Framers Demand Past Cross–Examination?

Justice Scalia's second originalist thesis has faced similar historical assault. In *Crawford* Scalia argued that by the time of the Confrontation Clause's framing, testimonial hearsay statements were admitted against an accused only if the declarant was unavailable and the defendant had an earlier chance to cross-examine him. On this front Professor Davies lists—and dismisses—five cases on which Justice Scalia staked his claim of a settled cross-examination rule. Davies argues that *King v. Paine* (1696) concerned a misdemeanor, whereas the Marian procedure applied only to felonies; *Fenwick's Case* (1696) was too obscurely reported to have guided the Framers; and *King v. Radbourne* (1787), *King v. Woodcock* (1789), and *King v. Dingler* (1791), among other shortcomings, remained unpublished in the United States until after the Confrontation Clause's framing and probably were not known to its authors. *See* pages 598–99, above; Davies, *supra*, 72 BROOK. L. REV. at 563–64, 569, 590–602, 605–13 (2007). At bottom, he says, "the legal authorities that framing-era Americans could have consulted regarding the arrestee's presence or opportunity to cross-examine during a Marian witness examination did not indicate any such legal requirements." Davies, *supra*, 72 BROOK. L. REV. at 569.

Amid this hailstorm of historical criticism, Justice Scalia's originalist arguments have found few prominent defenders. Among the first to rise in the Justice's defense was Robert Kry, one of his law clerks when *Crawford* was decided. Kry's extensive rebuttal to Professor Davies offers no defense of the Court's first originalist claim—that the Framers and lawyers of their era focused little concern on nontestimonial hearsay statements. And Kry's defense of the Court's second originalist claim is less than full throated. Kry allows that the Marian statutes did not condition the admission of an absent declarant's out-of-court statement on the defendant's earlier chance to cross-examine. Still, he says, a requirement of cross-examination took hold in England over the course of the eighteenth century. And he insists that such cases as *Radbourne*, *Woodcock*, and *Dingler*, even if not known to the Framers, supply valid evidence of an evolutionary spirit that the Framers would have sensed. At bottom Kry claims only that his evidence "suggests that, at the time of the framing, the right to cross-examine at a committal hearing was not firmly established, but nor was the absence of such a right firmly established. Rather, there was disagreement over the point. Most criminal lawyers probably thought the right existed; most magistrates probably thought it did not; other opinion was divided. . . . Opinion was clearly shifting in favor of the right to cross-examine over time." Robert Kry, *Confrontation Under the Marian Statutes: A Response to Professor Davies*, 72 BROOK. L. REV. 493, 521–24, 541 (2007).

Scattered Errata

Other scholars allege other flaws in Justice Scalia's originalist account. Professor Robert Mosteller shows that at least some English judges subscribed to a reliability-based exception to the usual hearsay ban, admitting even an accusatory hearsay statement if uttered " 'recently after the fact, so that it excluded a possibility of practising on' " (or influencing) the declarant. Robert P. Mosteller, *Testing the Testimonial Concept and Exceptions to Confrontation: "A Little Child Shall Lead Them,"* 82 IND. L.J. 917, 930 & n.30 (2007) (quoting an 1806 report of the 1779 case, *King v. Brasier*). And Professor Frank Herrmann asks why Justice Scalia (and Chief Justice Rehnquist, for that matter) ignored *Craig v. Anglesea*, 17 HOW. ST. TR. 1139 (Ex. Ir. 1743), a civil case that nonetheless bears on the historical dispute that divided the justices. The case turned on whether Lord Altham had a son. Professor Herrmann quotes from the case report:

> [Counsel for the plaintiff's lessor] were going to ask [the witness] Mr. Pigott, what he heard his stepmother [Mrs. Pigott] say about her being godmother to [a child of Lord Altham's]; but this was objected to by defendant's counsel, who insisted that hearsay was not evidence, and that the witness, Mr. Pigott, ought not to be suffered to give any account thereof.
>
> In answer to [the defendant's objection] counsel for the lessor of the plaintiff insisted, that matter of hearsay, which could not be supposed originally intended to be made use of in the cause ... ought to be admitted ... for Mrs. Pigott [the declarant] could not foresee that what she said on that occasion was ever to be given in evidence, and therefore her declaration could not be supposed calculated for any particular purpose.

The court barred the hearsay, according to the case reporter, "on the principal reason, that hearsay evidence ought not to be admitted, because of the adverse party's having no opportunity of cross-examining." *Id.* at 1160–61, *quoted in* Frank R. Herrmann, *The Uses of History in* Crawford v. Washington, 2 INT'L COMMENTARY ON EVID., No. 1, Art. 5, at 18–19 (2004).

As a civil case, *Anglesea* does not bear directly on the admissibility of hearsay against criminal defendants. English courts recognized a right to cross-examine hearsay declarants in civil trials before they did so in felony proceedings. *See* Davies, *supra*, 72 BROOK. L. REV. at 590–94. Still, Justice Scalia could have spotlighted the plaintiff's counsel's insistence on a distinction between testimonial and nontestimonial hearsay. Counsel's argument that "Mrs. Pigott could not foresee that what she said on that occasion was ever to be given in evidence" elegantly evokes two of the three "formulations" of testimonial hearsay quoted by the *Crawford* Court: " 'statements that declarants would reasonably expect to be used prosecutorially' " and statements " 'made under circumstances which would lead an objective witness reasonably to believe that the statement[s] would be available for use at a later trial.' " (Page 600.)

Yet one can imagine why Justice Scalia never mentioned *Anglesea*. Although plaintiff's counsel neatly expressed the distinction between testimonial and nontestimonial hearsay, counsel rooted that distinction in concerns about *reliability*: "Mrs. Pigott could not foresee that what she said on that occasion was ever to be given in evidence, *and therefore her declaration could not be supposed calculated for any particular purpose*." Justice Scalia hardly wished to suggest that *Crawford*'s new emphasis on testimonial hearsay embraces in different terms the *Roberts* Court's old emphasis on the "amorphous, if not entirely subjective, concept" of reliability. (Page 605 (emphasis added).)

Professor Herrmann argues that justices use history selectively—that their "real project is not history, as an historian would write it, but the search for a usable past." *Anglesea* was not particularly "usable" for Justice Scalia because it offered him a two-edged historical weapon. And judicial opinions, Herrmann writes, "do not happily tolerate historical ambiguity." Herrmann, *supra*, at 16, 21.

This real-world jurisprudential lesson finds a parallel in the nitty-gritty realm of criminal practice. For *Crawford* left unanswered many questions about its scope and meaning. And criminal practice does not happily tolerate judicial ambiguity. . . .

Domestic Violence Cases Face New Test

Ruling That Suspects Can Confront Accusers Scares Some Victims from Court

Robert Tharp

THE DALLAS MORNING NEWS, July 6, 2004, at 1A

Each day, up to one-half of all domestic-violence cases set for trial in Dallas County are thrown out because of a recent U.S. Supreme Court ruling reasserting a suspect's right to confront his accuser in court.

The ruling applies to all criminal trials, but the county's two bustling courts devoted to domestic-violence offenses are affected the most. The reason: Domestic-violence victims, usually wives or partners, often refuse to cooperate with prosecutors out of fear for their safety or because they reconcile with their alleged attackers.

"Women are terrified sometimes to testify because they're scared he might kill them," said Paige Flink, executive director of The Family Place, a Dallas domestic-violence shelter. "If it's the first offense, it's not likely going to be jail time. If she sits up and tells the truth on the stand, it can really put her in jeopardy."

In the past, prosecutors rarely flinched when a battered woman changed her mind about prosecuting her mate. The widely accepted practice was to hold a trial anyway, often winning a conviction by having a police officer recount what a victim said happened at the scene of an assault.

But since the Supreme Court handed down its ruling in the case of *Crawford vs. Washington* in March, courts across the country have found it much harder to use those statements in trial unless the victim is available to be cross-examined by the defense.

In Dallas County's two domestic-violence courts:

- As many as a dozen cases or more are being dismissed each day.
- Prosecutors are now reviewing more than 3,000 active cases to determine those affected by the ruling as each case's trial date approaches.
- Longstanding prosecutorial practices of treating domestic-violence victims with a light hand are coming to an end as subpoenas are being used to compel victims to testify.
- And when a victim ignores a court order, prosecutors in a handful of cases have threatened battered women with arrest unless they appear for their mate's trial....

Convictions on Hearsay

Defense attorneys, such as public defender Susan Anderson, praise the ruling, saying it levels the playing field. The reliance on the use of police officers' hearsay statements to win convictions had become an "epidemic" across the country, she said.

"... What it's saying is: We're not willing to convict ... on the word of someone else. We want to look [you] in the face and determine whether or not you're lying to me."

...

Battered women are now increasingly receiving subpoenas to appear in court.... "We're having to choose between [failing to hold] defendants accountable and doing something that could revictimize the victims," said assistant district attorney Cindy Dyer, a supervisor over family violence cases.

As a result, advocates for domestic-violence victims fear that fewer cases will be prosecuted, meaning fewer abusers will get help. That will only extend the cycle of violence and reconciliation in troubled relationships, Ms. Flink said....

Ms. Dyer said her office is still working out a uniform response to the ruling and waiting for guidance as appellate courts begin reviewing trial outcomes....

Crawford v. Washington: *Afterthoughts*

In the days and weeks after the Supreme Court handed down its ruling in *Crawford*, state and lower federal courts began the long slog of defining the borders of the new doctrine. Making the task harder, the

Supreme Court pointedly left certain crucial questions unanswered. The justices confined their newly rigid protection of the confrontation right to cases "[w]here testimonial statements are at issue." Yet they left "for another day any effort to spell out a comprehensive definition of 'testimonial.'" (Page 606.) Helpfully the justices hinted that "[s]tatements taken by police officers in the course of interrogations are also testimonial under even a narrow standard." But coyly they wrote that "one can imagine various definitions of 'interrogation,' and we need not select among them in this case." (Page 601 & n.4.)

As Robert Tharp reported in the *Dallas Morning News*, the justices' reticence especially vexed trial judges who faced domestic-violence cases staked on the hearsay statements of absent victims. Hungry for guidance, courts around the country looked to one another for insights. When a Bronx criminal court judge issued a detailed application of *Crawford* within weeks of the high Court's ruling, his opinion drew throngs of imitators. Braving the uncertainties of the new legal terrain, Judge Ethan Greenberg addressed a suddenly urgent question—whether 911 calls in domestic-violence prosecutions constitute "testimonial" hearsay under *Crawford*. Much turned on the answer. As Judge Greenberg wrote in *People v. Moscat*, "There are thousands of homicide and assault cases every year where a 911 call for help made by the victim to the police is an important piece of evidence." *People v. Moscat*, 3 Misc. 3d 739, 743 (N.Y. Crim. Ct. 2004).

Judge Greenberg's analysis was both sensible and memorable: "Typically, a woman who calls 911 for help because she has just been stabbed or shot is not contemplating being a 'witness' in future legal proceedings; she is usually trying simply to save her own life." He elaborated in striking language:

> The 911 call—usually, a hurried and panicked conversation between an injured victim and a police telephone operator—is simply not equivalent to a formal pretrial examination by a Justice of the Peace in Reformation England. If anything, it is the electronically augmented equivalent of a loud cry for help.

Moscat, 3 Misc. 3d at 746.

Eight months later the *New York Times* revealed that Judge Greenberg's decision stood on false facts: The 911 call in his case was placed not by a woman in the throes of a domestic assault, but by an anxious (or meddlesome) neighbor some nine hours later. *See* Sabrina Tavernise, *Legal Precedent Doesn't Let Facts Stand in the Way*, N.Y. TIMES, Nov. 26, 2004, at A1. The mistake was critical: Unlike a frightened woman calling for help, a neighbor who reports an alleged attack hours later probably is "contemplating being a 'witness' in future legal proceedings." But the *Times*'s disclosure came too late. Judge Greenberg's "decision had already taken flight," as the *Times* wrote, and had become the most influential post-*Crawford* ruling in the land. And his distinction between a declarant who is "contemplating being a 'witness' in future legal proceedings" and one who is simply "cry[ing] for help" became a dominant statement of the line dividing "testimonial" from "nontestimonial" hearsay statements.

POST-*CRAWFORD* CONFRONTATION CASELAW

In the years since *Crawford* declared a new day in Confrontation Clause interpretation, Supreme Court caselaw elaborating on the nature of testimonial hearsay and examining possible exceptions to the *Crawford* rule has swollen both case reporters and evidence texts. In eight major cases decided during the first eight years of the *Crawford* era, the justices strived to resolve the questions *Crawford* left open. At the same time they seemingly lost hope of achieving consensus concerning *Crawford*'s lessons or the Confrontation Clause's scope.

• ***Davis* v. *Washington/Hammon* v. *Indiana*,** 547 U.S. 813 (2006): To assess whether statements made during police interrogation are testimonial, trial courts should apply a "primary-purpose" test distinguishing between statements aimed primarily to assist a criminal investigation and those aimed primarily to resolve an ongoing emergency.

• ***Whorton v. Bockting*,** 549 U.S. 406 (2007): The Confrontation Clause offers no protection against admission of *non*testimonial statements, even if unreliable.

• ***Giles v. California*,** 554 U.S. 353 (2008): A defendant's wrongful conduct forfeits his confrontation right only if that conduct made a witness unavailable *and* the accused intended to prevent the witness's trial testimony.

• ***Melendez-Diaz v. Massachusetts*,** 557 U.S. 305 (2009): A state lab technician's sworn statement declaring a substance the defendant possessed to be cocaine is testimonial and therefore inadmissible absent testimony by the certifying chemist.

• ***Michigan v. Bryant*,** 131 S. Ct. 1143 (2011): A dying gunshot victim's answers to police questions about who shot him were not testimonial because the gunman's unknown motives, intentions, and location created an ongoing emergency.

• ***Bullcoming v. New Mexico*,** 131 S. Ct. 2705 (2011): An analysis of the defendant's blood alcohol content certified by an absent state lab technician is testimonial and inadmissible even though another technician testified about the procedures followed and equipment used in such analyses.

• ***Williams v. Illinois*,** 132 S. Ct. 2221 (2012): Testimony by an expert witness who relies heavily on the lab report of an absent technician does not violate the Confrontation Clause at least when the author of the underlying report did not know if the reported results would aid the prosecution.

The pages ahead explore all eight cases. Because the Court's recent opinions in *Bryant* and *Bullcoming* review at length *Davis* and *Melendez-Diaz*, the latter cases don't appear separately. We'll return to *Bryant* and *Bullcoming* after summaries of *Bockting* and *Giles*.

WHORTON V. BOCKTING: *Case Note*

Where testimonial hearsay is at issue, *Crawford* displaced *Roberts*-style reliability analysis. But the *Crawford* Court said almost nothing about constitutional safeguards against admission of *non*testimonial hearsay. Because Sylvia Crawford's interrogation yielded clearly testimonial statements, the Court refused to rule out application of *Ohio v. Roberts* to nontestimonial statements. True, much of *Crawford*'s reasoning was starkly at odds with *Roberts*. But absent the Court's explicit permission to abandon *Roberts*, virtually no state or lower federal court dared take that course.

Two years later, in *Davis v. Washington*, 547 U.S. 813 (2006), the Justices ruled that the Confrontation Clause imposes no limit on admission of nontestimonial statements. But they cast this holding in language so cagily coded that many post-*Davis* courts continued to apply *Roberts* and its reliability-based analysis to nontestimonial statements. As if aware of the confusion they had sown, the Justices spoke again a year later, this time with startling clarity. In *Whorton v. Bockting*, 549 U.S. 406 (2007), the Court ruled unanimously that *Crawford* "is flatly inconsistent with the prior governing precedent, *Roberts*, which *Crawford* overruled." Assessing *Crawford*'s impact on trial accuracy, the Court said *Crawford* might avoid some inaccurate trial outcomes by excluding unreliable testimonial statements that had slipped past trial judges under *Roberts*. But the Court allowed that *Crawford*'s overall impact on trial accuracy may prove negative:

> [W]hatever improvement in reliability *Crawford* produced in this respect must be considered together with *Crawford*'s *elimination of Confrontation Clause protection against the admission of unreliable out-of-court nontestimonial statements.* Under *Roberts*, an out-of-court nontestimonial statement not subject to prior cross-examination could not be admitted without a judicial determination regarding reliability. Under *Crawford*, in contrast, the Confrontation Clause has no application to such statements *and therefore permits their admission even if they lack indicia of reliability.*

(Emphasis added). Remarkably, the Court did not merely admit but trumpeted that *Crawford* perhaps made trials less accurate.

Although it is now clear that the Confrontation Clause offers no protection against unreliable nontestimonial hearsay, can criminal defendants find cover elsewhere in the Constitution? Some defense counsel and legal scholars argue that the Due Process Clauses of the Fifth and Fourteenth Amendments bar unreliable hearsay whenever its admission would render a trial fundamentally unfair. The difficulty of this approach is that it mimics *Roberts* in conditioning a constitutional right on "a mere judicial determination of [the] reliability" of prosecution hearsay evidence. The *Crawford* Court went out of its way to reject reliability—"an amorphous, if not entirely subjective, concept"—as a constitutional rubric. (Page 605 above.) Still, the Court recently hinted its readiness to weigh these arguments. Writing for the Court in *Michigan v. Bryant*, Justice Sotomayor footnoted a musing suggestion that "the Due Process Clauses of the Fifth and Fourteenth Amendments may constitute a further bar to admission of, for example, unreliable evidence." (Page 635 n.13 below.) And Justice Thomas wrote decades ago that "[r]eliability is more properly a due process concern." *White v. Illinois*, 502 U.S. 346, 363–64 (1992).

GILES V. CALIFORNIA: *Case Note*

Almost offhandedly the *Crawford* Court wrote that "the rule of forfeiture by wrongdoing . . . extinguishes confrontation claims on essentially equitable grounds. . . ." (Page 604.) The Court did not say whether this forfeiture principle follows Rule 804(b)(6) in applying only if the defendant's wrongdoing was intended to cause "the declarant's unavailability *as a witness*." (Emphasis added.) The Justices left lower courts and commentators wondering if defendants perhaps forfeit their right to confront accusers whenever their wrongful acts render those accusers unavailable to testify at trial.

The question was consequential. The category of cases in which a defendant's wrongdoing makes his accuser unavailable is potentially huge. Every homicide of course qualifies, as do many assaults and threats that scare victims into staying scarce. So do many crimes against children. Even absent an abuser's explicit threat to harm a child or her family should she disclose the abuse, a child victim may prove too intimidated or emotionally conflicted to testify. An adult victim of domestic violence likewise may prove reluctant to testify because of the very crime for which the defendant stands trial.

In contrast a requirement that prosecutors prove that the defendant's *purpose* was to make the declarant unavailable as a witness could vastly shrink the forfeiture doctrine's scope. Even if many murderers, assailants, and abusers harbor such an intent and act on it, prosecutors typically have no ready means of proving such unspoken motives.

Having prompted much scholarly speculation and many conflicting court opinions, the Justices at last addressed the question of intent in *Giles v. California*, 554 U.S. 353 (2008). The California Supreme Court had held that in killing his former girlfriend, Dwayne Giles forfeited his right to cross-examine her about a claim that he had beaten her, which she had made to a police officer who responded to a domestic-violence complaint about three weeks before her death, and which now was offered as evidence against him. The prosecution need not show Giles's purpose in killing her, the California court ruled. Because *Crawford* had framed the forfeiture rule in equitable terms, Giles's wrongful agency in keeping his victim from testifying was enough to trigger forfeiture. The fundamental equitable maxim that no one should profit from his own wrongs applies whether or not those wrongs aimed to eliminate a trial witness. *See People v. Giles*, 40 Cal. 4th 833, 842, 848–49 & n.5, 152 P.3d 433 (2007).

The Supreme Court's 2008 ruling made it clear why the Justices had waited so long to clarify the contours of the forfeiture doctrine: There was no consensus among them. They had agreed to address the issue in a painfully common sort of case—a defendant's murder of a former girlfriend. Still they proved unable to agree on a rationale.

The Votes

Six Justices joined almost all of Justice Scalia's opinion for the Court, holding that the constitutional doctrine of forfeiture by wrongdoing, like Rule 804(b)(6), requires a showing that the defendant acted with the purpose of preventing the declarant from testifying. From this holding only Justice Breyer, joined by Justices Stevens and Kennedy, dissented.

This six-to-three result concealed deeper divisions in the Court that cast doubt on the Justices' continuing fidelity to the originalist principles that animated *Crawford*. Only Chief Justice Roberts joined Justice Scalia in full and without qualification. Justices Thomas and Alito, while joining the Court's opinion in full, also concurred separately. They agreed with Justice Scalia's statement of the forfeiture rule, but emphasized a much narrower understanding of the category of testimonial statements than the one embraced by the Court in *Crawford*. Justice Thomas restated his view, familiar since *White v. Illinois*, 502 U.S. 346 (1992) (page 593) that the Confrontation Clause applies only to such "formalized" hearsay as past testimony and custodial, Mirandized police interrogations. Justice Alito, newer to this realm of lawmaking, wrote more tentatively "to make clear that, like Justice Thomas, [he was] not convinced that the out-of-court statement at issue here fell within the Confrontation Clause in the first place."

Justice Souter, joined by Justice Ginsburg, also wrote separately. Though he endorsed the Court's interpretation of the forfeiture doctrine, he explained his position in terms of modern procedure and made little mention of the common-law history that undergirded Justice Scalia's reasoning:

> If the victim's prior statement were admissible solely because the defendant kept the witness out of court by committing homicide, admissibility of the victim's statement to prove guilt would turn on finding the defendant guilty of the homicidal act causing the absence; evidence that the defendant killed would come in because the defendant probably killed. The only thing saving admissibility and liability determinations from question begging would be (in a jury case) the distinct functions of judge and jury: judges would find by a preponderance of evidence that the defendant killed (and so would admit the testimonial statement), while the jury could so find only on proof beyond a reasonable doubt.

"Equity demands something more," Justice Souter concluded, "than this near circularity before the right to confrontation is forfeited, and more is supplied by showing intent to prevent the witness from testifying."

Originalism's Limits

Justice Scalia's opinion for the Court in *Giles* was of a piece with his approach in *Crawford*. He dwelt on many of the same common-law cases and used some of the same dictionaries to define their terms. Here his starting point was *Lord Morley's Case*, (1666) 6 HOW. ST. TR. 769 (H.L.) 771, where he said the doctrine of forfeiture by wrongdoing "has its roots." There "judges concluded that a witness's having been 'detained by the means or procurement of the prisoner,' provided a basis to read testimony previously given at a coroner's inquest." Although both Justice Scalia in writing for the Court and Justice Breyer in dissent looked to many other common-law authorities, their word-by-word dispute about the three key words of *Lord Morley's Case*, "means or procurement," conveys both the tone and much of the substance of their debate.

For Justice Scalia these words stated a requirement that "the defendant engaged in conduct *designed* to prevent the witness from testifying." Some if not all dictionary definitions of *procure*, he wrote, limited its meaning to action "*designed* to bring about the result 'procured.' " True, the pesky word "or," as in "means *or* procurement," might suggest that a defendant's wrongdoing could trigger forfeiture of his confrontation right without regard to his design if he merely *caused* the declarant's absence. To this argument, made with force by Justice Breyer, Justice Scalia offered two rebuttals. The word *means* can connote intent, he wrote, citing the *Oxford English Dictionary*. Moreover, many contemporary sources replaced *Morley*'s "or" with "and" or otherwise made clear that proof of causation wasn't enough.

If mere causation had been enough to trigger forfeiture, Justice Scalia reasoned, there would have been little need for an exception for dying declarations. In most homicide cases in which the victim made a deathbed accusation, the prosecutor could readily show that the defendant wrongfully *caused* the victim's death. But absent evidence of the defendant's purpose to eliminate a witness, proof of the defendant's agency in the death was never enough. Instead prosecutors in such cases took pains to prove the declarant's belief in impending death and the other facts needed to admit dying declarations.

At extraordinary length, Justice Breyer mined much the same historical record to contest each of these points. He emphasized that the most natural reading of "means or procurement" would construe "means" as "cause" and "or" as "or." Hence a prosecutor could satisfy this condition simply by showing that the defendant wrongfully caused the declarant's absence. And he dismissed Justice Scalia's argument about dying declarations, saying that at common law the forfeiture doctrine played little role in murder cases. That's because the law permitted use of a witness's testimony at a proper Marian deposition any time the declarant died before trial without regard to the defendant's agency in the death. If a murder victim testified at such a deposition before her death, there was no need to invoke the forfeiture doctrine to use her testimony at trial.

Coming at last to historical loggerheads, Justices Scalia and Breyer summarized their findings in contradictory terms. Justice Scalia wrote that he could find *no* common-law or founding-era case in which a defendant was deemed to have forfeited his confrontation right absent proof that his purpose was to render the declarant unavailable *as a witness*. Indeed, he said, there is no evidence that any prosecutor even *argued* for forfeiture on a lesser showing before 1985. He deemed "conclusive" the "common law's uniform exclusion of unconfronted inculpatory testimony by murder victims (except testimony given with awareness of impending death) in the innumerable cases in which the defendant was on trial for killing the victim, but was not shown to have done so for the purpose of preventing testimony."

Justice Breyer countered that *he* could find no common-law or founding-era case that stated the forfeiture rule in terms requiring proof that the defendant's purpose was to keep the declarant from the witness stand. Nor was such a rule supported by the equitable principle usually thought to justify the forfeiture doctrine—"the maxim that no one shall be permitted to take advantage of his own wrong," expressed by the Supreme Court in *Reynolds v. United States*, 98 U.S. 145, 158–59 (1879), and endorsed in both *Crawford* and *Davis*. Even a defendant who killed in anger and not with the purpose of eliminating a witness has committed a wrong from which he should not profit.

In wrestling Justice Scalia to a historical draw, Justice Breyer seemed less concerned to win the originalist dispute than to show the futility of gleaning an original understanding of the forfeiture rule: "While I have set forth what I believe is the better reading of the common-law cases, I recognize that different modern judges might read that handful of cases differently. All the more reason then *not* to reach firm conclusions about the precise metes and bounds of a contemporary forfeiture exception by trying to guess the state of mind of 18th century lawyers when they decided *not* to make a particular argument, i.e., forfeiture, in a reported case."

On this score Justice Breyer, who wrote for himself and Justices Stevens and Kennedy, found eager allies in Justices Souter and Ginsburg. Whereas Justice Breyer devoted thousands of words to refuting the Court's historical evidence, Justice Souter dispatched the originalist dispute in a sentence. After opening his concurrence with a declaration that "the Court's historical analysis is sound," he later declared the historical dispute a stalemate: "The contrast between the Court's and JUSTICE BREYER'S careful examinations of the historical record tells me that the early cases on the exception were not calibrated finely enough to answer the narrow question here."

Liberality in Domestic–Violence Cases

Between the lines of these several opinions all nine Justices announced their readiness in many domestic-violence cases to glean from the defendant's history of abuse and ultimate murder of his partner the *purpose* of ridding her as a witness against him. Hence Justice Souter wrote:

> [There is no] reason to doubt that the element of intention would normally be satisfied by the intent inferred on the part of the domestic abuser in the classic abusive relationship, which is meant to isolate the victim from outside help, including the aid of law enforcement and the judicial process. If the evidence for admissibility shows a continuing relationship of this sort, it would make no sense to suggest that the oppressing defendant miraculously abandoned the dynamics of abuse the instant before he killed his victim....

To this suggestion Justice Breyer readily assented even as he spun Justice Souter's words to his own advantage:

> This seems to say that a showing of domestic abuse is sufficient to call into play the protection of the forfeiture rule in a trial for murder of the domestic abuse victim. Doing so when, in fact, the abuser may have had other matters in mind apart from preventing the witness from testifying, is in effect not to insist upon a showing of "purpose." Consequently, I agree with this formulation....

Justice Scalia announced an understanding of abusive domestic relationships similar to Justice Souter's, though he continued to insist on "conduct designed to prevent testimony ... or cooperation in criminal prosecutions":

> Acts of domestic violence often are intended to dissuade a victim from resorting to outside help and include conduct designed to prevent testimony to police officers or cooperation in criminal prosecutions. Where such an abusive relationship culminates in murder, the evidence may support a finding that the crime expressed the intent to isolate the victim and to stop her from reporting abuse to the authorities or cooperating with a criminal prosecution—rendering her prior statements admissible under the forfeiture doctrine. Earlier abuse, or threats of abuse, intended to dissuade the victim from resorting to outside help would be highly relevant to this inquiry. . . .

At least in the context of *Giles*, then, the Justices' long originalist debate was neither here nor there. In the modern realm of domestic-violence prosecutions, the Justices seem prepared in many cases to infer from the course of abuse the defendant's purpose to keep his victim from the witness stand.

Apparent unanimity on this point, however, should not distract us from other divisions among the Justices.

Cracks in the Crawford Coalition

Oral argument in *Giles* was as scattered as the Justices' five opinions. But amid many unfinished thoughts was a telling exchange between Justices Scalia and Breyer. After counsel for Giles had invoked the authority of the common law several times, Justice Breyer broke in impatiently: "How much are we supposed to follow the common law, in your opinion, as it was in the 18th century or 12th century, or something?" Should we, he asked, ban from the witness stand atheists, felons, and parties' spouses because the common law did so? "Which [common-law rules] do we ignore, and which don't—?" he asked, before being cut off.

Moments later Justice Scalia responded to Justice Breyer in remarks to Giles's counsel: "And besides which, the question that Justice Breyer was asking was already answered in *Crawford*; wasn't it?" Then he added, "A case from which he dissented." Justice Breyer attempted to correct the historical record. "I don't think I did—" he said, but was cut off before he could say "dissent."

Later Justice Breyer returned to the topic and, in clarifying the record, made a telling disclosure: "I joined *Crawford*, and Justice Scalia would like to kick me off the boat, which I'm rapidly leaving in any event. . . ."

It was of course a joke, and the Court's transcript duly notes laughter. Later, however, Justice Breyer returned in earnest to his original inquiry: "That's where I'm having the trouble. What precisely are the principles I should follow to prevent my going back to look at [how common-law authorities] dunked witches [to determine guilt or innocence], but allowing the heart of *Crawford* to be maintained[?] How do I do it?" How can we distinguish, he wondered, between those common-law rules the Constitution has frozen in place and those history has cast aside?

Frustrated with the inconclusive guidance of the common law, Justice Breyer looked to other principles to resolve this case. Among these were the "essentially equitable roots" of the forfeiture doctrine and the broad reach of "'the maxim that no one shall be permitted to take advantage of his own wrong.'" To such reasoning Justice Scalia responded in his opinion for the Court with a bitter accusation: "[T]he dissent issues a thinly veiled invitation to overrule *Crawford* and adopt an approach not much different from the regime of *Ohio v. Roberts*, 448 U.S. 56 (1980), under which the Court would create the exceptions that it thinks consistent with the policies underlying the confrontation guarantee, regardless of how that guarantee was historically understood."

That Justice Breyer sought to topple a four-year-old precedent of historical dimensions endorsed by all nine sitting Justices either originally or in deciding *Davis v. Washington*, 547 U.S. 813 (2006), was a stunning accusation. It was not, however, entirely without basis. In an oddly nostalgic passage, Justice Breyer wrote in *Giles* of those traditional hearsay exceptions, rooted in reliability, that defined the bulk of admissible hearsay under *Roberts*: "[T]he hearsay rule has always contained exceptions that permit the admission of evidence where the need is significant, often in a direction that permits admission of hearsay only where adequate alternative assurance of reliability exists."

Though Justice Scalia's accusation was perhaps premature, it proved prescient. . . .

Problem 8.1

Forfeiture Motion

In *People v. Santiago*, 2003 N.Y. Slip Op. 51034(U) (Sup. Ct. 2003), the defendant faced charges of violating a domestic protective order issued to protect his longtime domestic partner, Angela R. As trial approached, Angela R. informed the prosecutor "that she no longer wished to press charges, that she would decline to testify at trial, and that if she were made to testify she would declare that all the allegations she previously made to the police, prosecutor, and Grand Jury were fabricated by the police and the District Attorney." At a pretrial hearing held in late 2002 to address the prosecution's in limine motion, the prosecutor argued that a transcript of Angela R.'s grand jury testimony against the defendant should be admitted at trial on the theory that "the defendant's longstanding pattern of physical and emotional abuse toward Angela R. effectively forced her to become unavailable as a witness for the People at trial."

Prosecution evidence admitted at the hearing showed that between January 1996 and May 2002, Angela R. had complained of physical attacks by the defendant at least six times. At least four of these incidents resulted in charges against the defendant, later dismissed when Angela R. failed to appear for trial or refused to testify. Other evidence revealed that in the months before the hearing, Angela R. visited the defendant at the Rikers Island jail ten times, and he phoned her from jail at least 100 times. The court also heard a taped message that Angela R. left for the prosecutor before the hearing: "[T]hings are very hard for me as a single parent right now.... I know you're just doing your job, and you protected me and I appreciate the fact that you did help me when I needed you.... [But] I cannot work full time because I have no one to take care of [our daughter].... I'm sure [the defendant] learned his lesson, so let's try to work something out...."

Dr. Ann Wolbert Burgess, an expert in the field of relationship violence, testified at the hearing for the prosecution. "Domestic violence," she said, "is characterized by the three phases of behavior which are commonly referred to as the 'cycle of violence.' These are (1) the tension-building phase, (2) the violent phase, and (3) the honeymoon phase.... [T]he honeymoon phase ... is characterized by acts of contrition by the abuser, his requests for forgiveness and his declarations of love."

Angela R. also testified at the hearing, as summarized by the trial judge:

> [She] testified that she and the defendant are married by common-law and by love, and have been living together, as she put it, for "ten beautiful years." ... Angela R. answered the prosecutor's questions: "I don't remember," "I don't recall," "No, I did not," "I do not understand," and "I do not know" over 100 times ..., all the while nervously watching the defendant for his approval, as he blew kisses to her from his seat at counsel table.... Angela R. testified that she has been jealous and becomes violent with the defendant when he wants to leave her.... [She] claim[ed] that she fabricates stories of abuse to get Orders of Protection....

Finally, the defendant testified "that he and Angela R. are husband and wife, lovers and the best of friends, who celebrate every day they are together like a 'special holiday,'" but that sometimes Angela R. "would 'snap,' hit and abuse him, and then go to the police and lie to them." The defendant testified that "she's a physical person," but he is "a forgiving kind of guy." He also testified that in one of his phone calls to Angela R. from jail, he said, "[Y]ou know, I can't get myself out of this, you put me in here so if anything, it's either you can take me out or, I don't know what, you know, I don't know the law."

Assume that this pretrial hearing takes place after *Giles*, rather than in 2002. What are the prosecution's best arguments in support of its forfeiture motion? What are the defense's best arguments against? How should the court rule? *See* Deborah Tuerkheimer, Crawford*'s Triangle: Domestic Violence and the Right of Confrontation*, 85 N.C. L. Rev. 1 (2006).

MICHIGAN v. BRYANT

131 S. Ct. 1143 (2011).

■ SOTOMAYOR, J., delivered the opinion of the Court, in which ROBERTS, C. J., and KENNEDY, BREYER, and ALITO, JJ., joined. THOMAS, J., filed an opinion concurring in the judgment. SCALIA, J., and GINSBURG, JJ., filed dissenting opinions. KAGAN, J., took no part in the consideration or decision of the case.

■ JUSTICE SOTOMAYOR delivered the opinion of the Court. . . .

I

Around 3:25 a.m. on April 29, 2001, Detroit, Michigan police officers responded to a radio dispatch indicating that a man had been shot. At the scene, they found the victim, Anthony Covington, lying on the ground next to his car in a gas station parking lot. Covington had a gunshot wound to his abdomen, appeared to be in great pain, and spoke with difficulty.

The police asked him "what had happened, who had shot him, and where the shooting had occurred." Covington stated that "Rick" shot him at around 3 a.m. He also indicated that he had a conversation with [Richard] Bryant, whom he recognized based on his voice, through the back door of Bryant's house. Covington explained that when he turned to leave, he was shot through the door and then drove to the gas station, where police found him.

Covington's conversation with the police ended within 5 to 10 minutes when emergency medical services arrived. Covington was transported to a hospital and died within hours. The police left the gas station after speaking with Covington, called for backup, and traveled to Bryant's house. They did not find Bryant there but did find blood and a bullet on the back porch and an apparent bullet hole in the back door. Police also found Covington's wallet and identification outside the house.

At [Bryant's] trial, which occurred prior to our decisions in *Crawford* [*v. Washington*, 541 U.S. 36 (2004)], and *Davis* [*v. Washington*, 547 U.S. 813 (2006)], the police officers who spoke with Covington at the gas station testified about what Covington had told them. The jury returned a guilty verdict on charges of second-degree murder [and firearms offenses].

Bryant appealed ... to the Supreme Court of Michigan, which reversed his conviction.... The court concluded that the circumstances "clearly indicate that the 'primary purpose' of the questioning was to establish the facts of an event that had *already* occurred; the 'primary purpose' was not to enable police assistance to meet an ongoing emergency." ... The court did not address whether, absent a Confrontation Clause bar, the statements' admission would have been otherwise consistent with Michigan's hearsay rules or due process.[1] ...

We granted certiorari to determine whether the Confrontation Clause barred admission of Covington's statements.

II

... [I]n *Davis* v. *Washington* and *Hammon* v. *Indiana,* 547 U.S. 813 (2006), [this Court sought] to "determine more precisely which police interrogations produce testimony" and therefore implicate a Confrontation Clause bar. We explained that when *Crawford* said that

> "'interrogations by law enforcement officers fall squarely within [the] class' of testimonial hearsay, we had immediately in mind (for that was the case before us) interrogations solely directed at establishing the facts of a past crime, in order to identify (or provide evidence to convict) the perpetrator. The product of such interrogation, whether reduced to a writing signed by the declarant or embedded in the memory (and perhaps notes) of the interrogating officer, is testimonial." *Davis* 547 U.S. at 826.

We thus made clear in *Davis* that not all those questioned by the police are witnesses and not all "interrogations by law enforcement officers," are subject to the Confrontation Clause.

Davis and *Hammon* were both domestic violence cases. In *Davis,* Michelle McCottry made the statements at issue to a 911 operator during

1. The Supreme Court of Michigan held that the question whether the victim's statements would have been admissible as "dying declarations" was not properly before it because at the preliminary examination, the prosecution, after first invoking both the dying declaration and excited utterance hearsay exceptions, established the factual foundation only for admission of the statements as excited utterances. The trial court ruled that the statements were admissible as excited utterances and did not address their admissibility as dying declarations.... Because of the State's failure to preserve its argument with regard to dying declarations, we similarly need not decide that question here.

a domestic disturbance with Adrian Davis, her former boyfriend. McCottry told the operator, "'He's here jumpin' on me again,'" and, "'He's usin' his fists.'" 547 U.S. at 817. The operator then asked McCottry for Davis' first and last names and middle initial, and at that point in the conversation McCottry reported that Davis had fled in a car. McCottry did not appear at Davis' trial, and the State introduced the recording of her conversation with the 911 operator.

In *Hammon*, decided along with *Davis*, police responded to a domestic disturbance call at the home of Amy and Hershel Hammon, where they found Amy alone on the front porch. She appeared "'somewhat frightened,'" but told them "'nothing was the matter.'" 547 U.S. at 819. She gave the police permission to enter the house, where they saw a gas heating unit with the glass front shattered on the floor. One officer remained in the kitchen with Hershel, while another officer talked to Amy in the living room about what had happened. . . . The police asked Amy to fill out and sign a battery affidavit. She wrote: "'Broke our Furnace & shoved me down on the floor into the broken glass. Hit me in the chest and threw me down. Broke our lamps & phone. Tore up my van where I couldn't leave the house. Attacked my daughter.'" *Id.* at 820. Amy did not appear at Hershel's trial, so the police officers who spoke with her testified as to her statements and authenticated the affidavit. The trial court admitted the affidavit as a present sense impression and admitted the oral statements as excited utterances under state hearsay rules. The Indiana Supreme Court affirmed Hammon's conviction, holding that Amy's oral statements were not testimonial and that the admission of the affidavit, although erroneous because the affidavit was testimonial, was harmless.

To address the facts of both cases, we expanded upon the meaning of "testimonial" that we first employed in *Crawford* and discussed the concept of an ongoing emergency. We explained:

> "Statements are nontestimonial when made in the course of police interrogation under circumstances objectively indicating that the primary purpose of the interrogation is to enable police assistance to meet an ongoing emergency. They are testimonial when the circumstances objectively indicate that there is no such ongoing emergency, and that the primary purpose of the interrogation is to establish or prove past events potentially relevant to later criminal prosecution." *Davis*, 547 U.S. at 822.

Examining the *Davis* and *Hammon* statements in light of those definitions, we held that the statements at issue in *Davis* were nontestimonial and the statements in *Hammon* were testimonial. We distinguished the statements in *Davis* from the testimonial statements in *Crawford* on several grounds, including that the victim in *Davis* was "speaking about events *as they were actually happening*, rather than 'describ[ing] past events,'" that there was an ongoing emergency, that the "elicited statements were necessary to be able to *resolve* the present emergency," and that the statements were not formal. 547 U.S. at 827. In *Hammon*, on the other hand, we held that, "[i]t is entirely clear from the circumstances that the interrogation was part of an investigation into possibly criminal past conduct." There was "no emergency in progress." The officer questioning Amy "was not seeking to determine . . . 'what is happening,' but rather 'what happened.' " It was "formal enough" that the police interrogated Amy in a room separate from her husband where, "some time after the events described were over," she "deliberately recounted, in response to police questioning, how potentially criminal past events began and progressed." Because her statements "were neither a cry for help nor the provision of information enabling officers immediately to end a threatening situation," we held that they were testimonial. *Id.* at 829–30, 832.

Davis did not "attemp[t] to produce an exhaustive classification of all conceivable statements—or even all conceivable statements in response to police interrogation—as either testimonial or nontestimonial." *Id.* at 822. The . . . most important instances in which the Clause restricts the introduction of out-of-court statements are those in which state actors are involved in a formal, out-of-court interrogation of a witness to obtain evidence for trial. . . . Whether formal or informal, out-of-court statements can evade the basic objective of the Confrontation Clause, which is to prevent the accused from being deprived of the opportunity to cross-examine the declarant about statements taken for use at trial. When, as in *Davis*, the primary purpose of an interrogation is to respond to an "ongoing emergency," its purpose is not to create a record for trial and thus is not within the scope of the Clause. But there may be *other* circumstances, aside from ongoing emergencies, when a statement is not procured with a primary purpose of creating an out-of-court substitute for trial testimony. In making the primary purpose determination, standard rules of hearsay, designed to identify some statements as reliable, will be relevant. Where no such primary purpose exists, the admissibility of a statement is the concern of state and federal rules of evidence, not the Confrontation Clause. . . .

III

To determine whether the "primary purpose" of an interrogation is "to enable police assistance to meet an ongoing emergency," which would render the resulting statements nontestimonial, we objectively evaluate the circumstances in which the encounter occurs and the statements and actions of the parties.

A

The Michigan Supreme Court correctly understood that this inquiry is objective. *Davis* uses the word "objective" or "objectively" no fewer than eight times in describing the relevant inquiry. "Objectively" also appears in the definitions of both testimonial and nontestimonial statements that *Davis* established.

An objective analysis of the circumstances of an encounter and the statements and actions of the parties to it provides the most accurate assessment of the "primary purpose of the interrogation." The circumstances in which an encounter occurs—*e.g.*, at or near the scene of the crime versus at a police station, during an ongoing emergency or afterwards—are clearly matters of objective fact. The statements and actions of the parties must also be objectively evaluated. That is, the relevant inquiry is not the subjective or actual purpose of the individuals involved in a particular encounter, but rather the purpose that reasonable participants would have had, as ascertained from the individuals' statements and actions and the circumstances in which the encounter occurred.

B

. . . [T]he existence of an "ongoing emergency" at the time of an encounter between an individual and the police is among the most important circumstances informing the "primary purpose" of an interrogation. . . . [A]n emergency focuses the participants on something other than "prov[ing] past events potentially relevant to later criminal prosecution."[8] Rather, it focuses them on "end[ing] a threatening situation." Implicit in *Davis* is the idea that because the prospect of fabrication in statements given for the primary purpose of resolving that emergency is presumably significantly diminished, the Confrontation Clause does not require such statements to be subject to the crucible of cross-examination.

This logic is not unlike that justifying the excited utterance exception in hearsay law. Statements "relating to a startling event or condition made while the declarant was under the stress of excitement caused by the event or condition," FED. R. EVID. 803(2), are considered reliable because the declarant, in the excitement, presumably cannot form a falsehood. *See Idaho v. Wright*, 497 U.S. 805, 820 (1990) ("The basis for the 'excited utterance' exception . . . is that such statements are given under circumstances that eliminate the possibility of fabrication, coaching, or confabulation. . . . "); Advisory Committee's Notes on FED. R. EVID. 803(2) (same). An ongoing emergency has a similar effect of focusing an individual's attention on responding to the emergency.[9]

8. The existence of an ongoing emergency must be objectively assessed from the perspective of the parties to the interrogation at the time, not with the benefit of hindsight. If the information the parties knew at the time of the encounter would lead a reasonable person to believe that there was an emergency, even if that belief was later proved incorrect, that is sufficient for purposes of the Confrontation Clause. The emergency is relevant to the "primary purpose of the interrogation" because of the effect it has on the parties' purpose, not because of its actual existence.

9. Many other exceptions to the hearsay rules similarly rest on the belief that certain statements are, by their nature, made for a purpose other than use in a prosecution and therefore should not be

Following our precedents, the court below correctly began its analysis with the circumstances in which Covington interacted with the police. But in doing so, the court construed *Davis* to have decided more than it did and thus employed an unduly narrow understanding of "ongoing emergency" that *Davis* does not require.

. . . The Michigan Supreme Court erroneously read *Davis* as deciding that "the statements made after the defendant stopped assaulting the victim and left the premises did *not* occur during an 'ongoing emergency.'" . . . [T]he Michigan Supreme Court failed to appreciate that whether an emergency exists and is ongoing is a highly context-dependent inquiry. *Davis* and *Hammon* involved domestic violence, a known and identified perpetrator, and, in *Hammon*, a neutralized threat. Because *Davis* and *Hammon* were domestic violence cases, we focused only on the threat to the victims and assessed the ongoing emergency from the perspective of whether there was a continuing threat *to them*.

Domestic violence cases like *Davis* and *Hammon* often have a narrower zone of potential victims than cases involving threats to public safety. An assessment of whether an emergency that threatens the police and public is ongoing cannot narrowly focus on whether the threat solely to the first victim has been neutralized because the threat to the first responders and public may continue. Brief for United States as *Amicus Curiae* 19–20 ("An emergency posed by an unknown shooter who remains at large does not automatically abate just because the police can provide security to his first victim.").

The Michigan Supreme Court also did not appreciate that the duration and scope of an emergency may depend in part on the type of weapon employed. The court relied on *Davis* and *Hammon*, in which the assailants used their fists, as controlling the scope of the emergency here, which involved the use of a gun. The problem with that reasoning is clear when considered in light of the assault on Amy Hammon. Hershel Hammon was armed only with his fists when he attacked his wife, so

barred by hearsay prohibitions. *See, e.g.*, FED. R. EVID. 801(d)(2)(E) (statement by a co-conspirator during and in furtherance of the conspiracy); 803(4) (Statements for Purposes of Medical Diagnosis or Treatment); 803(6) (Records of Regularly Conducted Activity); 803(8) (Public Records and Reports); 803(9) (Records of Vital Statistics); 803(11) (Records of Religious Organizations); 803(12) (Marriage, Baptismal, and Similar Certificates); 803(13) (Family Records); 804(b)(3) (Statement Against Interest); *see also Melendez-Diaz v. Massachusetts*, 129 S. Ct. 2527, 2539–40 (2009) ("Business and public records are generally admissible absent confrontation not because they qualify under an exception to the hearsay rules, but because—having been created for the administration of an entity's affairs and not for the purpose of establishing or proving some fact at trial—they are not testimonial."); *Giles v. California*, 554 U.S. 353, 376 (2008) (noting in the context of domestic violence that "[s]tatements to friends and neighbors about abuse and intimidation and statements to physicians in the course of receiving treatment would be excluded, if at all, only by hearsay rules"); *Crawford*, 541 U.S. at 56 ("Most of the hearsay exceptions covered statements that by their nature were not testimonial—for example, business records or statements in furtherance of a conspiracy.").

removing Amy to a separate room was sufficient to end the emergency. . . .

The Michigan Supreme Court's failure to focus on the context-dependent nature of our *Davis* decision also led it to conclude that the medical condition of a declarant is irrelevant. . . . The medical condition of the victim is important to the primary purpose inquiry to the extent that it sheds light on the ability of the victim to have any purpose at all in responding to police questions and on the likelihood that any purpose formed would necessarily be a testimonial one. The victim's medical state also provides important context for first responders to judge the existence and magnitude of a continuing threat to the victim, themselves, and the public.

. . . [N]one of this suggests that an emergency is ongoing in every place . . . for the entire time that the perpetrator of a violent crime is on the loose. As we recognized in *Davis*, "a conversation which begins as an interrogation to determine the need for emergency assistance" can "evolve into testimonial statements." This evolution may occur if, for example, . . . a perpetrator is disarmed, surrenders, is apprehended, or, as in *Davis*, flees with little prospect of posing a threat to the public. Trial courts can determine in the first instance when any transition from nontestimonial to testimonial occurs, and exclude "the portions of any statement that have become testimonial. . . ." *Davis*, 547 U.S. at 829.

. . . As *Davis* made clear, whether an ongoing emergency exists is simply one factor—albeit an important factor—that informs the ultimate inquiry regarding the "primary purpose" of an interrogation. Another factor . . . is the importance of *informality* in an encounter between a victim and police. Formality is not the sole touchstone of our primary purpose inquiry because, although formality suggests the absence of an emergency and therefore an increased likelihood that the purpose of the interrogation is to "establish or prove past events potentially relevant to later criminal prosecution," informality does not necessarily indicate the presence of an emergency or the lack of testimonial intent. The . . . questioning in this case occurred in an exposed, public area, prior to the arrival of emergency medical services, and in a disorganized fashion. All of those facts make this case distinguishable from the formal station-house interrogation in *Crawford*.

C

In addition to the circumstances in which an encounter occurs, the statements and actions of both the declarant and interrogators provide objective evidence of the primary purpose of the interrogation. . . . In many instances, the primary purpose of the interrogation will be most accurately ascertained by looking to the contents of both the questions and the answers. . . .

The combined approach . . . ameliorates problems that could arise from looking solely to one participant. Predominant among these is the problem of mixed motives on the part of both interrogators and declarants. Police officers in our society function as both first responders and criminal investigators. Their dual responsibilities may mean that they act with different motives simultaneously or in quick succession. *See Davis*, 547 U.S. at 839 (THOMAS, J., concurring in judgment in part and dissenting in part) ("In many, if not most, cases where police respond to a report of a crime, whether pursuant to a 911 call from the victim or otherwise, the purposes of an interrogation, viewed from the perspective of the police, are *both* to respond to the emergency situation *and* to gather evidence.").

Victims are also likely to have mixed motives when they make statements to the police. During an ongoing emergency, a victim is most likely to want the threat to her and to other potential victims to end, but that does not necessarily mean that the victim wants or envisions prosecution of the assailant. A victim may want the attacker to be incapacitated temporarily or rehabilitated. Alternatively, a severely injured victim may have no purpose at all in answering questions posed; the answers may be simply reflexive. The victim's injuries could be so debilitating as to prevent her from thinking sufficiently clearly to understand whether her statements are for the purpose of addressing an ongoing emergency or for the purpose of future prosecution.[12] Taking into account a victim's injuries does not transform this objective inquiry into a subjective one. The inquiry is still objective because it focuses on the understanding and purpose of a reasonable victim in the circumstances of the actual victim—circumstances that prominently include the victim's physical state. . . .

The dissent suggests that we intend to give controlling weight to the "intentions of the police." That is a misreading of our opinion. At trial, the declarant's statements, not the interrogator's questions, will be introduced to "establis[h] the truth of the matter asserted," *Crawford*, 541 U.S. at 60 n.9, and must therefore pass the Sixth Amendment test. In determining whether a declarant's statements are testimonial, courts should look to all of the relevant circumstances. Even Justice Scalia concedes that the interrogator is relevant to this evaluation, and we agree that "[t]he identity of an interrogator, and the content and tenor of his questions," can illuminate the "primary purpose of the interrogation." (*Post*, at [page 639.]) . . .

12. In such a situation, the severe injuries of the victim would undoubtedly also weigh on the credibility and reliability that the trier of fact would afford to the statements. *Cf.* Advisory Committee's Notes on FED. R. EVID. 803(2) (noting that although the "theory" of the excited utterance exception "has been criticized on the ground that excitement impairs [the] accuracy of observation as well as eliminating conscious fabrication," it "finds support in cases without number").

IV

. . . [S]tatements made to assist police in addressing an ongoing emergency presumably lack the testimonial purpose that would subject them to the requirement of confrontation.[13] As the context of this case brings into sharp relief, the existence and duration of an emergency depend on the type and scope of danger posed to the victim, the police, and the public. . . .

We first examine the circumstances in which the interrogation occurred. The parties disagree over whether there was an emergency when the police arrived at the gas station. Bryant argues, and the Michigan Supreme Court accepted, that there was no ongoing emergency because "there . . . was no criminal conduct occurring. No shots were being fired, no one was seen in possession of a firearm, nor were any witnesses seen cowering in fear or running from the scene." Bryant, while conceding that "a serious or life-threatening injury creates a medical emergency for a victim," further argues that a declarant's medical emergency is not relevant to the ongoing emergency determination.

In contrast, Michigan and the Solicitor General explain that when the police responded to the call that a man had been shot and found Covington bleeding on the gas station parking lot, "they did not know who Covington was, whether the shooting had occurred at the gas station or at a different location, who the assailant was, or whether the assailant posed a continuing threat to Covington or others."

The Michigan Supreme Court stated that the police asked Covington, "what had happened, who had shot him, and where the shooting had occurred." . . . The officers basically agree on what information they learned from Covington, but not on the order in which they learned it or on whether Covington's statements were in response to general or detailed questions. They all agree that the first question was "what happened?" The answer was either "I was shot" or "Rick shot me."

As explained above, the scope of an emergency in terms of its threat to individuals other than the initial assailant and victim will often depend on the type of dispute involved. Nothing Covington said to the police indicated that the cause of the shooting was a purely private dispute or that the threat from the shooter had ended. The record reveals little about the motive for the shooting. The police officers who spoke with Covington at the gas station testified that Covington . . . [told] the officers . . . that he fled Bryant's back porch, indicating that he perceived an ongoing threat. The police did not know, and Covington did not tell them, whether the threat was limited to him. The potential scope of the dispute

13. Of course the Confrontation Clause is not the only bar to admissibility of hearsay statements at trial. State and federal rules of evidence prohibit the introduction of hearsay, subject to exceptions. Consistent with those rules, the Due Process Clauses of the Fifth and Fourteenth Amendments may constitute a further bar to admission of, for example, unreliable evidence.

and therefore the emergency in this case thus stretches more broadly than those at issue in *Davis* and *Hammon* and encompasses a threat potentially to the police and the public.

This is . . . the first of our post-*Crawford* Confrontation Clause cases to involve a gun. . . . Bryant's argument that there was no ongoing emergency because "[n]o shots were being fired," surely construes ongoing emergency too narrowly. An emergency does not last only for the time between when the assailant pulls the trigger and the bullet hits the victim. If an out-of-sight sniper pauses between shots, no one would say that the emergency ceases during the pause. . . .

At no point during the questioning did either Covington or the police know the location of the shooter. In fact, Bryant was not at home by the time the police searched his house at approximately 5:30 a.m. . . . At bottom, there was an ongoing emergency here where an armed shooter, whose motive for and location after the shooting were unknown, had mortally wounded Covington within a few blocks and a few minutes of the location where the police found Covington.

This is not to suggest that the emergency continued until Bryant was arrested in California a year after the shooting. We need not decide precisely when the emergency ended because Covington's encounter with the police and all of the statements he made during that interaction occurred within the first few minutes of the police officers' arrival and well before they secured the scene of the shooting—the shooter's last known location.

We reiterate, moreover, that the existence *vel non* of an ongoing emergency is not the touchstone of the testimonial inquiry. . . . We turn now to that inquiry, as informed by the circumstances of the ongoing emergency just described. . . . When the police arrived at Covington's side, their first question to him was "What happened?" Covington's response was either "Rick shot me" or "I was shot," followed very quickly by an identification of "Rick" as the shooter. In response to further questions, Covington explained that the shooting occurred through the back door of Bryant's house and provided a physical description of the shooter. When he made the statements, Covington was lying in a gas station parking lot bleeding from a mortal gunshot wound to his abdomen. His answers to the police officers' questions were punctuated with questions about when emergency medical services would arrive. He was obviously in considerable pain and had difficulty breathing and talking. From this description of his condition and report of his statements, we cannot say that a person in Covington's situation would have had a "primary purpose" "to establish or prove past events potentially relevant to later criminal prosecution."

For their part, the police responded to a call that a man had been shot. . . . [T]hey did not know why, where, or when the shooting had occurred. Nor did they know the location of the shooter or anything else about the circumstances in which the crime occurred.[19] The questions they asked—"what had happened, who had shot him, and where the shooting occurred"—were the exact type of questions necessary to allow the police to " 'assess the situation, the threat to their own safety, and possible danger to the potential victim' " and to the public, *Davis*, 547 U.S. at 832, including to allow them to ascertain "whether they would be encountering a violent felon." *Id.* at 827. In other words, they solicited the information necessary to enable them "to meet an ongoing emergency."

Nothing in Covington's responses indicated to the police that, contrary to their expectation upon responding to a call reporting a shooting, there was no emergency or that a prior emergency had ended. Covington did indicate that he had been shot at another location about 25 minutes earlier, but he did not know the location of the shooter at the time the police arrived and, as far as we can tell from the record, he gave no indication that the shooter, having shot at him twice, would be satisfied that Covington was only wounded. In fact, Covington did not indicate any possible motive for the shooting, and thereby gave no reason to think that the shooter would not shoot again if he arrived on the scene. As we noted in *Davis*, "initial inquiries" may "*often* . . . produce nontestimonial statements." The initial inquiries in this case resulted in the type of nontestimonial statements we contemplated in *Davis*.

Finally, we consider the informality of the situation and the interrogation. This situation is more similar, though not identical, to the informal, harried 911 call in *Davis* than to the structured, station-house interview in *Crawford*. As the officers' trial testimony reflects, the situation was fluid and somewhat confused: the officers arrived at different times; apparently each, upon arrival, asked Covington "what happened?"; and, contrary to the dissent's portrayal, they did not conduct a structured interrogation. The informality suggests that the interrogators' primary purpose was simply to address what they perceived to be an ongoing emergency, and the circumstances lacked any formality that would have alerted Covington to or focused him on the possible future prosecutorial use of his statements.

Because the circumstances of the encounter as well as the statements and actions of Covington and the police objectively indicate that the "primary purpose of the interrogation" was "to enable police assistance to meet an ongoing emergency," Covington's identification and description of the shooter and the location of the shooting were not testimonial

19. Contrary to the dissent's suggestion and despite the fact that the record was developed prior to *Davis'* focus on the existence of an "ongoing emergency," the record contains some testimony to support the idea that the police officers were concerned about the location of the shooter when they arrived on the scene and thus to suggest that the purpose of the questioning of Covington was to determine the shooter's location. *See* App. 136 (testimony of Officer Stuglin) (stating that upon arrival officers questioned the gas station clerk about whether the shooting occurred in the gas station parking lot and about concern for safety).

hearsay. The Confrontation Clause did not bar their admission at Bryant's trial.

* * *

. . . We leave for the Michigan courts to decide on remand whether the statements' admission was otherwise permitted by state hearsay rules. The judgment of the Supreme Court of Michigan is vacated, and the case is remanded for further proceedings not inconsistent with this opinion.

It is so ordered.

■ JUSTICE KAGAN took no part in the consideration or decision of this case.

■ JUSTICE THOMAS, concurring in the judgment. I agree with the Court that the admission of Covington's out-of-court statements did not violate the Confrontation Clause, but I reach this conclusion because Covington's questioning by police lacked sufficient formality and solemnity for his statements to be considered "testimonial."

In determining whether Covington's statements to police implicate the Confrontation Clause, the Court evaluates the " 'primary purpose' " of the interrogation. The majority's analysis, which relies on, *inter alia,* what the police knew when they arrived at the scene, the specific questions they asked, the particular information Covington conveyed, the weapon involved, and Covington's medical condition illustrates the uncertainty that this test creates for law enforcement and the lower courts. . . .

Rather than attempting to reconstruct the "primary purpose" of the participants, I would consider the extent to which the interrogation resembles those historical practices that the Confrontation Clause addressed. As the majority notes, Covington interacted with the police under highly informal circumstances, while he bled from a fatal gunshot wound. The police questioning was not "a formalized dialogue," did not result in "formalized testimonial materials" such as a deposition or affidavit, and bore no "indicia of solemnity." Nor is there any indication that the statements were offered at trial "in order to evade confrontation." This interrogation bears little if any resemblance to the historical practices that the Confrontation Clause aimed to eliminate. Covington thus did not "bea[r] testimony" against Bryant, and the introduction of his statements at trial did not implicate the Confrontation Clause. . . .

■ JUSTICE SCALIA, dissenting. Today's tale—a story of five officers conducting successive examinations of a dying man with the primary purpose, not of obtaining and preserving his testimony regarding his killer, but of protecting him, them, and others from a murderer somewhere on the loose—is so transparently false that professing to believe it demeans this institution. But reaching a patently incorrect conclusion on the facts is a relatively benign judicial mischief; it affects, after all, only the case at hand. In its vain attempt to make the incredible plausible, however—or perhaps as an intended second goal—today's opinion distorts our Confrontation Clause jurisprudence and leaves it in a shambles. Instead of clarifying the law, the Court makes itself the obfuscator of last resort....

I

A

... *Crawford* and *Davis* did not address whose perspective matters—the declarant's, the interrogator's, or both—when assessing "the primary purpose of [an] interrogation." In those cases the statements were testimonial from any perspective. I think the same is true here, but because the Court picks a perspective so will I: The declarant's intent is what counts. In-court testimony is more than a narrative of past events; it is a solemn declaration made in the course of a criminal trial. For an out-of-court statement to qualify as testimonial, the declarant must intend the statement to be a solemn declaration rather than an unconsidered or offhand remark; and he must make the statement with the understanding that it may be used to invoke the coercive machinery of the State against the accused.... The hidden purpose of an interrogator cannot substitute for the declarant's intentional solemnity or his understanding of how his words may be used.

A declarant-focused inquiry is also the only inquiry that would work in every fact pattern implicating the Confrontation Clause. The Clause applies to volunteered testimony as well as statements solicited through police interrogation. *See Davis*, 547 U.S. at 822 n.1. An inquiry into an officer's purposes would make no sense when a declarant blurts out "Rick shot me" as soon as the officer arrives on the scene. I see no reason to adopt a different test—one that accounts for an officer's intent—when the officer asks "what happened" before the declarant makes his accusation. (This does not mean the interrogator is irrelevant. The identity of an interrogator, and the content and tenor of his questions, can bear upon whether a declarant intends to make a solemn statement, and envisions its use at a criminal trial. But none of this means that the interrogator's purpose matters.) ...

B

Looking to the declarant's purpose (as we should), this is an absurdly easy case. Roughly 25 minutes after Anthony Covington had been shot, Detroit police responded to a 911 call reporting that a gunshot victim had appeared at a neighborhood gas station. They quickly arrived at the scene, and in less than 10 minutes five different Detroit police officers questioned Covington about the shooting. Each asked him a similar battery of questions: "what happened" and when, who shot "the victim," and "where" did the shooting take place. After Covington would answer, they would ask follow-up questions, such as "how tall is" the shooter, "[h]ow much does he weigh," what is the exact address or physical description of the house where the shooting took place, and what chain of events led to the shooting. The battery relented when the paramedics arrived and began tending to Covington's wounds.

From Covington's perspective, his statements had little value except to ensure the arrest and eventual prosecution of Richard Bryant. He knew the "threatening situation," *Davis*, 547 U.S. at 832, had ended six blocks away and 25 minutes earlier when he fled from Bryant's back porch.... Even if Bryant had pursued him (unlikely), ... it was entirely beyond imagination that Bryant would again open fire while Covington was surrounded by five armed police officers. And Covington knew the shooting was the work of a drug dealer, not a spree killer who might randomly threaten others.

Covington's knowledge that he had nothing to fear differs significantly from Michelle McCottry's state of mind during her "frantic" statements to a 911 operator at issue in *Davis*. Her "call was plainly a call for help against a bona fide physical threat" describing "events *as they were actually happening*." She did not have the luxuries of police protection and of time and space separating her from immediate danger that Covington enjoyed when he made his statements.

Covington's pressing medical needs do not suggest that he was responding to an emergency, but to the contrary reinforce the testimonial character of his statements. He understood the police were focused on investigating a past crime, not his medical needs. None of the officers asked Covington how he was doing, attempted more than superficially to assess the severity of his wounds, or attempted to administer first aid.... Underscoring that Covington understood the officers' investigative role, he interrupted their interrogation to ask "when is EMS coming?" When, in other words, would the focus shift to his medical needs rather than Bryant's crime?

Neither Covington's statements nor the colloquy between him and the officers would have been out of place at a trial; it would have been a routine direct examination.... Preventing the admission of "weaker substitute[s] for live testimony at trial" such as this is precisely what motivated the Framers to adopt the Confrontation Clause....

C

Worse still for the repute of today's opinion, this is an absurdly easy case even if one (erroneously) takes the interrogating officers' purpose into account. The five officers interrogated Covington primarily to investigate past criminal events. None—absolutely none—of their actions indicated that they perceived an imminent threat. They did not draw their weapons, and indeed did not immediately search the gas station for potential shooters. To the contrary, all five testified that they questioned Covington *before conducting any investigation at the scene*. Would this have made any sense if they feared the presence of a shooter? Most tellingly, none of the officers started his interrogation by asking what would have been the obvious first question if any hint of such a fear existed: Where is the shooter?

But do not rely solely on my word about the officers' primary purpose. Listen to Sergeant Wenturine, who candidly admitted that he interrogated Covington because he "ha[d] a man here that [he] believe[d] [was] dying [so he was] gonna find out who did this, period." In short, he needed to interrogate Covington to solve a crime. Wenturine never mentioned an interest in ending an ongoing emergency....

II

A

But today's decision is not only a gross distortion of the facts. It is a gross distortion of the law—a revisionist narrative in which reliability continues to guide our Confrontation Clause jurisprudence, at least where emergencies and faux emergencies are concerned.

According to today's opinion, the *Davis* inquiry into whether a declarant spoke to end an ongoing emergency or rather to "prove past events potentially relevant to later criminal prosecution," is *not* aimed at answering whether the declarant acted as a witness. Instead, the *Davis* inquiry probes the *reliability* of a declarant's statements, "[i]mplicit[ly]" importing the excited-utterances hearsay exception into the Constitution. A statement during an ongoing emergency is sufficiently reliable, the Court says, "because the prospect of fabrication ... is presumably significantly diminished," so it "does not [need] to be subject to the crucible of cross-examination."

Compare that with the holding of *Crawford:* "Where testimonial statements are at issue, the only indicium of reliability sufficient to satisfy constitutional demands is the one the Constitution actually prescribes: confrontation." ... (This is not to say that that "reliability" logic can actually justify today's result: Twenty-five minutes is plenty of time for a shooting victim to reflect and fabricate a false story.)

The Court announces that in future cases it will look to "standard rules of hearsay, designed to identify some statements as reliable," when deciding whether a statement is testimonial. *Ohio v. Roberts* said something remarkably similar: An out-of-court statement is admissible if it "falls within a firmly rooted hearsay exception" or otherwise "bears adequate 'indicia of reliability.'" We tried that approach to the Confrontation Clause for nearly 25 years before *Crawford rejected* it as an unworkable standard unmoored from the text and the historical roots of the Confrontation Clause....

... Reliability, the Court tells us, is a good indicator of whether "a statement is ... an out-of-court substitute for trial testimony." That is patently false. Reliability tells us *nothing* about whether a statement is testimonial. Testimonial and nontestimonial statements alike come in varying degrees of reliability. An eyewitness's statements to the police after a fender-bender, for example, are both reliable and testimonial. Statements to the police from one driver attempting to blame the other would be similarly testimonial but rarely reliable.

The Court suggests otherwise because it "misunderstands the relationship" between qualification for one of the standard hearsay exceptions and exemption from the confrontation requirement. That relationship is not a causal one. Hearsay law exempts business records, for example, because businesses have a financial incentive to keep reliable records. The Sixth Amendment also generally admits business records into evidence, but not because the records are reliable or because hearsay law says so. It admits them "because—having been created for the administration of an entity's affairs and not for the purpose of establishing or proving some fact at trial—they are not" weaker substitutes for live testimony. Moreover, the scope of the exemption from confrontation and that of the hearsay exceptions also are not always coextensive. The reliability logic of the business-record exception would extend to records maintained by neutral parties providing litigation-support services, such as evidence testing. The Confrontation Clause is not so forgiving. Business records prepared specifically for use at a criminal trial are testimonial and require confrontation.

. . . Does [the Court] . . . intend, by following today's illogical roadmap, to resurrect *Roberts* by a thousand unprincipled distinctions without ever explicitly overruling *Crawford?* . . .

■ JUSTICE GINSBURG, dissenting. I agree with Justice Scalia that Covington's statements were testimonial and that "[t]he declarant's intent is what counts." Even if the interrogators' intent were what counts, I further agree, Covington's statements would still be testimonial. It is most likely that "the officers viewed their encounter with Covington [as] an investigation into a past crime with no ongoing or immediate consequences." Today's decision, Justice Scalia rightly notes, . . . confounds our recent Confrontation Clause jurisprudence, which made it plain that "[r]eliability tells us nothing about whether a statement is testimonial."

. . . I would add, however, this observation. In *Crawford v. Washington* this Court noted that, in the law we inherited from England, there was a well-established exception to the confrontation requirement: The cloak protecting the accused against admission of out-of-court testimonial statements was removed for dying declarations. This historic exception, we recalled in *Giles v. California*, applied to statements made by a person about to die and aware that death was imminent. Were the issue properly tendered here, I would take up the question whether the exception for dying declarations survives our recent Confrontation Clause decisions. The Michigan Supreme Court, however, held, as a matter of state law, that the prosecutor had abandoned the issue. The matter, therefore, is not one the Court can address in this case.

Problem 8.2

"Ralph Nesbitt"

Minutes before midnight on a fall evening, Dawne Brault made a desperate 911 call from her home:

The dispatcher: "Attleboro police, recorded line."

Brault: "Oh, God. Hurry up and help me."

The dispatcher: "What's the problem, ma'am?"

Brault: "(Inaudible) just came in my house and tried to kill me."

The dispatcher: "Who came in? Hello?"

Brault: "Hello. Help me."

The dispatcher: "Are you going to answer my questions so we can? What's your address?"

Brault: "147 Wilmarth Street."

The dispatcher: "And who came in?"

Brault: "Ralph Nesbitt." . . .

The dispatcher: "Do you need a rescue?"

Brault: "I need it now."

The dispatcher: "Okay."

Brault: "Please hurry."

The dispatcher: "Is he still there?"

Brault: "No. Hurry. Hurry up."

The dispatcher: "887 to 3A and 7A."

Brault: "Hurry up. (Inaudible)"

The dispatcher: "Start heading to 127 [*sic*] Wilmarth Street, 1–2–7 Wilmarth Street . . . Ma'am, do you need a rescue?"

Brault: "Yes. I need it now. . . . Oh, he beat the [expletive] out of me."

The dispatcher: "127 Wilmarth Street, I need a rescue. It sounds like it might be a domestic. . . . Okay. Where did he go, ma'am?"

Brault: "I don't know."

The dispatcher: "What's your name?"

Brault: "Dawne."

The dispatcher: "What's your last name?"

Brault: "Brault. Hurry. Hurry."

The dispatcher: "What is your last name?"

Brault: "Brault."

The dispatcher: "Spell it for me."

Brault: "I can't."

The dispatcher: "Okay. Try to say it a little slower and a little calmer, then."

Brault: "I can't talk (inaudible). Oh. Hurry up. I don't want to die. . . . Please hurry." . . .

The dispatcher: "Is he still there?"

Brault: "No. Oh."

The dispatcher: "Okay. What kind of injury do you have?"

Brault: "I don't know. I don't—I can't—oh."

Commonwealth v. Nesbitt, 452 Mass. 236, 236–37, 244 n.13 (2008). Paramedics responding to the scene took Brault to a hospital where she died ten minutes later of twenty-three stab wounds.

Ralph Nesbitt, an acquaintance of Brault but not a house-mate or romantic partner, was charged with her murder. At trial the prosecutor sought to admit and play for the jury a recording of Brault's call. On Nesbitt's objection that admission of the tape would violate his right to confront Brault, how should the trial judge have ruled? Assume all these events took place after the Supreme Court's ruling in *Bryant*.

Problem 8.3
Dealing in Progress

Shortly after midnight a 911 police dispatch operator received two back-to-back calls:

First call, 12:15 a.m.:

Operator: 911, where is your emergency? . . .

Caller: All of this drug activity over off Sweetgum[.]

Operator: What address on Sweetgum?

Caller: . . . Why would I tell you? I'm trying to be anonymous. . . .

Operator: . . . I [need to] send the officers to the right place, where you're at.

Caller: It's a red PT Cruiser. This guy is selling—

Operator: Sir, give me the address.

Caller: 2505 Sweetgum. . . .

Operator: Okay, do you know his name?

Caller: Kennedy Polidore.

Operator: Do you know what kind of drugs he's selling?

Caller: He's selling crack. . . . He's just sitting on the steps. He's running in and out, in and out. People coming—

Operator: What's he wearing tonight? . . .

Caller: He's got some green shorts on and a white t-shirt. The car is sitting off of—uh—11th, yeah that's 11th, and—uh—Sweetgum. . . .

Second 911 call, 12:24 a.m.:

Operator: Phone line 911, where is your emergency?

Caller: Hey, I was the one just called about the drug deal that's going down over here on Sweetgum. . . . He's got the dope in the side door panel. . . .

Operator: The right or the left side?

Caller: Uh—of the driver's side. . . . I seen him put it in there. I can see it right now.

Operator: Okay, I'm adding the information to the call. Thank you, sir.

Caller: Okay. But would you tell [the officers] not to do it here? Cause I don't want him to think that I was the one told. . . .

United States v. Polidore, 690 F.3d 705 (5th Cir. 2012).

Two police officers, alerted to this information, drove to the Sweetgum address. A man who identified himself as the 911 caller pointed out the red PT Cruiser, then parked and unoccupied. Some time later the defendant, Kennedy Polidore, dressed in dark shorts and a white t-shirt, emerged from a nearby building, got behind the wheel, and drove off. One of the officers followed and stopped the defendant, who tossed something under his car. The officer later found a bag of crack cocaine under the car and a bag of powder cocaine on the floor near the driver's seat. No drugs were found in the door panels.

At the defendant's trial for possession of crack cocaine with intent to distribute, the officers described their encounter with the anonymous caller, the defendant's actions, and the discovery of the drugs. The prosecutor then sought to admit a recording of the two 911 calls and play them for the jury. The defendant objected that evidence of the calls would violate his right to confront the 911 caller, who never gave his name, was not identified, and did not appear at trial. If trial took place after the Supreme Court's ruling in *Michigan v. Bryant*, how should the judge have ruled?

BULLCOMING V. NEW MEXICO

131 S. Ct. 2705 (2011).

■ GINSBURG, J., delivered the opinion of the Court, except as to Part IV and footnote 6. SCALIA, J., joined that opinion in full, SOTOMAYOR and KAGAN, JJ., joined as to all but Part IV, and THOMAS, J., joined as to all but Part IV and footnote 6. SOTOMAYOR, J., filed an opinion concurring in part. KENNEDY, J., filed a dissenting opinion, in which ROBERTS, C. J., and BREYER and ALITO, JJ., joined.

■ JUSTICE GINSBURG delivered the opinion of the Court, except as to Part IV and footnote 6.... In *Melendez-Diaz v. Massachusetts*, 129 S. Ct. 2527 (2009), this Court held that a forensic laboratory report stating that a suspect substance was cocaine ranked as testimonial for purposes of the Sixth Amendment's Confrontation Clause. The report had been created specifically to serve as evidence in a criminal proceeding. Absent stipulation, the Court ruled, the prosecution may not introduce such a report without offering a live witness competent to testify to the truth of the statements made in the report.

In the case before us, petitioner Donald Bullcoming was arrested on charges of driving while intoxicated (DWI). Principal evidence against Bullcoming was a forensic laboratory report certifying that Bullcoming's blood-alcohol concentration was well above the threshold for aggravated DWI. At trial, the prosecution did not call as a witness the analyst who signed the certification. Instead, the State called another analyst who was familiar with the laboratory's testing procedures, but had neither participated in nor observed the test on Bullcoming's blood sample. The New Mexico Supreme Court determined that, although the blood-alcohol analysis was "testimonial," the Confrontation Clause did not require the certifying analyst's in-court testimony. Instead, New Mexico's high court held, live testimony of another analyst satisfied the constitutional requirements.

The question presented is whether the Confrontation Clause permits the prosecution to introduce a forensic laboratory report containing a testimonial certification—made for the purpose of proving a particular fact—through the in-court testimony of a scientist who did not sign the certification or perform or observe the test reported in the certification. We hold that surrogate testimony of that order does not meet the constitutional requirement. The accused's right is to be confronted with the analyst who made the certification, unless that analyst is unavailable at trial, and the accused had an opportunity, pretrial, to cross-examine that particular scientist.

I

A

In August 2005, a vehicle driven by petitioner Donald Bullcoming rear-ended a pick-up truck at an intersection in Farmington, New Mexico. When the truck driver exited his vehicle and approached Bullcoming to exchange insurance information, he . . . Smell[ed] alcohol on Bullcoming's breath. . . .

Because Bullcoming refused to take a breath test, the police obtained a warrant authorizing a blood-alcohol analysis. Pursuant to the warrant, a sample of Bullcoming's blood was drawn at a local hospital. To determine Bullcoming's blood-alcohol concentration (BAC), the police sent the sample to the New Mexico Department of Health, Scientific Laboratory Division (SLD). In a standard SLD form titled "Report of Blood Alcohol Analysis," participants in the testing were identified, and the forensic analyst certified his finding.

SLD's report contained . . . the "certificate of analyst," completed and signed by Curtis Caylor, the SLD forensic analyst assigned to test Bullcoming's blood sample. Caylor recorded that the BAC in Bullcoming's sample was 0.21 grams per hundred milliliters, an inordinately high level. Caylor also affirmed that "[t]he seal of th[e] sample was received intact . . . ," and that he had "followed the procedures set out on the reverse of th[e] report." Those "procedures" instructed analysts . . . to "not[e] any circumstance or condition which might affect the integrity of the sample or otherwise affect the validity of the analysis." . . .

SLD analysts use gas chromatograph machines to determine BAC levels. Operation of the machines requires specialized knowledge and training. Several steps are involved in the gas chromatograph process, and human error can occur at each step.[1]

Caylor's report that Bullcoming's BAC was 0.21 supported a prosecution for aggravated DWI, the threshold for which is a BAC of 0.16 grams per hundred milliliters. The State accordingly charged Bullcoming with this more serious crime.

1. Gas chromatography is a widely used scientific method of quantitatively analyzing the constituents of a mixture. Under SLD's standard testing protocol, the analyst extracts two blood samples and inserts them into vials containing an "internal standard"—a chemical additive. The analyst then "cap[s] the [two] sample[s]," "crimp[s] them with an aluminum top," and places the vials into the gas chromatograph ma-

B

The case was tried to a jury in November 2005, after our decision in *Crawford v. Washington*, but before *Melendez-Diaz*. On the day of trial, the State announced that it would not be calling SLD analyst Curtis Caylor as a witness because he had "very recently [been] put on unpaid leave" for a reason not revealed.... The State ... proposed to introduce Caylor's finding as a "business record" during the testimony of Gerasimos Razatos, an SLD scientist who had neither observed nor reviewed Caylor's analysis.

Bullcoming's counsel opposed the State's proposal. Without Caylor's testimony, defense counsel maintained, introduction of the analyst's finding would violate Bullcoming's Sixth Amendment right "to be confronted with the witnesses against him." The trial court overruled the objection, and admitted the SLD report as a business record. The jury convicted Bullcoming of aggravated DWI, and the New Mexico Court of Appeals upheld the conviction, concluding that "the blood alcohol report in the present case was non-testimonial and prepared routinely with guarantees of trustworthiness." *State v. Bullcoming*, 147 N.M. 487, 494 (2010).

C

While Bullcoming's appeal was pending before the New Mexico Supreme Court, this Court decided *Melendez-Diaz*. In that case, "[t]he Massachusetts courts [had] admitted into evidence affidavits reporting the results of forensic analysis which showed that material seized by the police and connected to the defendant was cocaine." Those affidavits, the Court held, were " 'testimonial,' rendering the affiants 'witnesses' subject to the defendant's right of confrontation under the Sixth Amendment."

chine. Within a few hours, this device produces a printed graph—a chromatogram—along with calculations representing a software-generated interpretation of the data.

Although the State presented testimony that obtaining an accurate BAC measurement merely entails "look[ing] at the [gas chromatograph] machine and record[ing] the results," authoritative sources reveal that the matter is not so simple or certain.... *See* H. McNair & J. Miller, Basic Gas Chromatography 137 (2d ed. 2009) ("Errors that occur in any step can invalidate the best chromatographic analysis, so attention must be paid to all steps."); D. Bartell, M. McMurray & A. ImObersteg, Attacking and Defending Drunk Driving Tests § 16:80 (2d rev. 2010) (stating that 93% of errors in laboratory tests for BAC levels are human errors that occur either before or after machines analyze samples)....

Nor is the risk of human error so remote as to be negligible. *Amici* inform us, for example, that in neighboring Colorado, a single forensic laboratory produced at least 206 flawed blood-alcohol readings over a three-year span, prompting the dismissal of several criminal prosecutions. *See* Brief for National Association of Criminal Defense Lawyers et al. as Amici Curiae Supporting Petitioner, at 32–33. An analyst had used improper amounts of the internal standard, causing the chromatograph machine systematically to inflate BAC measurements. The analyst's error, a supervisor said, was "fairly complex."

In light of *Melendez-Diaz*, the New Mexico Supreme Court acknowledged that the blood-alcohol report introduced at Bullcoming's trial qualified as testimonial evidence. Like the affidavits in *Melendez-Diaz*, the court observed, the report was " 'functionally identical to live, in-court testimony, doing precisely what a witness does on direct examination.' " *State v. Bullcoming*, 147 N.M. 487, 494 (2010) (quoting *Melendez-Diaz*, 129 S. Ct. at 2532). Nevertheless, for two reasons, the court held that admission of the report did not violate the Confrontation Clause.

First, the court said certifying analyst Caylor "was a mere scrivener," who "simply transcribed the results generated by the gas chromatograph machine." Second, SLD analyst Razatos, although he did not participate in testing Bullcoming's blood, "qualified as an expert witness with respect to the gas chromatograph machine.... Razatos provided live, in-court testimony," the court stated, "and, thus, was available for cross-examination regarding the operation of the ... machine, the results of [Bullcoming's] BAC test, and the SLD's established laboratory procedures." Razatos' testimony was crucial, the court explained, because Bullcoming could not cross-examine the machine or the written report. But "[Bullcoming's] right of confrontation was preserved," the court concluded, because Razatos was a qualified analyst, able to serve as a surrogate for Caylor. 147 N.M. at 494–96.

We granted certiorari to address this question: Does the Confrontation Clause permit the prosecution to introduce a forensic laboratory report containing a testimonial certification, made in order to prove a fact at a criminal trial, through the in-court testimony of an analyst who did not sign the certification or personally perform or observe the performance of the test reported in the certification[?] ...[5].... [6]

[II]

A

The New Mexico Supreme Court held surrogate testimony adequate to satisfy the Confrontation Clause in this case because analyst Caylor

5. The dissent makes plain that its objection is less to the application of the Court's decisions in *Crawford* and *Melendez-Diaz* to this case than to those pathmarking decisions themselves. *See post*, at [page 655] (criticizing the "*Crawford* line of cases" for rejecting "reliable evidence"); *post*, at [pages 655–57] (deploring "*Crawford*'s rejection of the [reliability-centered] regime of *Ohio* v. *Roberts*").

6. To rank as "testimonial," a statement must have a "primary purpose" of "establish[ing] or prov[ing] past events potentially relevant to later criminal prosecution." *Davis v. Washington*, 547 U.S. 813, 822 (2006). *See also Michigan v. Bryant*, at [page 629]. Elaborating on the purpose for which a "testimonial report" is created, we observed in *Melendez-Diaz* that business and public records "are generally admissible absent confrontation ... because—having been created for the administration of an entity's affairs and not for the purpose of establishing or proving some fact at trial—they are not testimonial." 129 S. Ct. at 2539. [Only Justices Scalia, Sotomayor, and Kagan joined Justice Ginsburg in endorsing this footnote.—GF]

"simply transcribed the resul[t] generated by the gas chromatograph machine," presenting no interpretation and exercising no independent judgment. Bullcoming's "true 'accuser,' " the court said, was the machine, while testing analyst Caylor's role was that of "mere scrivener." 147 N.M. at 494–95. Caylor's certification, however, reported more than a machine-generated number.

Caylor certified that he received Bullcoming's blood sample intact with the seal unbroken, that he checked to make sure that the forensic report number and the sample number "correspond[ed]," and that he performed on Bullcoming's sample a particular test, adhering to a precise protocol. He further represented, by leaving the "[r]emarks" section of the report blank, that no "circumstance or condition . . . affect[ed] the integrity of the sample or . . . the validity of the analysis." These representations, relating to past events and human actions not revealed in raw, machine-produced data, are meet for cross-examination. . . .

B

Recognizing that admission of the blood-alcohol analysis depended on "live, in-court testimony [by] a qualified analyst," the New Mexico Supreme Court believed that Razatos could substitute for Caylor because Razatos "qualified as an expert witness with respect to the gas chromatograph machine and the SLD's laboratory procedures." But surrogate testimony of the kind Razatos was equipped to give could not convey what Caylor knew or observed about the events his certification concerned, *i.e.*, the particular test and testing process he employed.[7] Nor could such surrogate testimony expose any lapses or lies on the certifying analyst's part. Significant here, Razatos had no knowledge of the reason why Caylor had been placed on unpaid leave. With Caylor on the stand, Bullcoming's counsel could have asked questions designed to reveal whether incompetence, evasiveness, or dishonesty accounted for Caylor's removal from his work station. Notable in this regard, the State never asserted that Caylor was "unavailable"; the prosecution conveyed only that Caylor was on uncompensated leave. Nor did the State assert that Razatos had any "independent opinion" concerning Bullcoming's BAC. In this light, Caylor's live testimony could hardly be typed "a hollow formality." . . .

In short, when the State elected to introduce Caylor's certification, Caylor became a witness Bullcoming had the right to confront. Our precedent cannot sensibly be read any other way. *See Melendez-Diaz*, 129

7. We do not question that analyst Caylor, in common with other analysts employed by SLD, likely would not recall a particular test, given the number of tests each analyst conducts and the standard procedure followed in testing. Even so, Caylor's testimony under oath would have enabled Bullcoming's counsel to raise before a jury questions concerning Caylor's proficiency, the care he took in performing his work, and his veracity. . . .

S. Ct. at 2545 (Kennedy, J., dissenting) (Court's holding means "the . . . analyst who must testify is the person who signed the certificate").

III

We turn, finally, to the State's contention that the SLD's blood-alcohol analysis reports are nontestimonial in character, therefore no Confrontation Clause question even arises in this case. *Melendez-Diaz* left no room for that argument, the New Mexico Supreme Court concluded, a conclusion we find inescapable.

In *Melendez-Diaz*, a state forensic laboratory, on police request, analyzed seized evidence (plastic bags) and reported the laboratory's analysis to the police (the substance found in the bags contained cocaine). The "certificates of analysis" prepared by the analysts who tested the evidence in *Melendez-Diaz*, this Court held, were "incontrovertibly . . . affirmation[s] made for the purpose of establishing or proving some fact" in a criminal proceeding. 129 S. Ct. at 2540. The same purpose was served by the certificate in question here.

The State maintains that the affirmations made by analyst Caylor were not "adversarial" or "inquisitorial"; instead, they were simply observations of an "independent scientis[t]" made "according to a non-adversarial public duty." That argument fares no better here than it did in *Melendez-Diaz*. A document created solely for an "evidentiary purpose," *Melendez-Diaz* clarified, made in aid of a police investigation, ranks as testimonial. . . .

In all material respects, the laboratory report in this case resembles those in *Melendez-Diaz*. Here, as in *Melendez-Diaz*, a law-enforcement officer provided seized evidence to a state laboratory required by law to assist in police investigations. Like the analysts in *Melendez-Diaz*, analyst Caylor tested the evidence and prepared a certificate concerning the result of his analysis. Like the *Melendez-Diaz* certificates, Caylor's certificate is "formalized" in a signed document. . . . Noteworthy as well, the SLD report form contains a legend referring to municipal and magistrate courts' rules that provide for the admission of certified blood-alcohol analyses.

In sum, the formalities attending the "report of blood alcohol analysis" are more than adequate to qualify Caylor's assertions as testimonial. . . . The New Mexico Supreme Court, guided by *Melendez-Diaz*, correctly recognized that Caylor's report "fell within the core class of testimonial statements," 147 N.M. at 493, described in this Court's leading Confrontation Clause decisions.

IV*

The State and its *amici* urge that unbending application of the Confrontation Clause to forensic evidence would impose an undue

* [Only Justice Scalia joined Justice Ginsburg in Part IV of this opinion.—GF]

burden on the prosecution. This argument, also advanced in the dissent, largely repeats a refrain rehearsed and rejected in *Melendez-Diaz.* The constitutional requirement, we reiterate, "may not [be] disregard[ed] . . . at our convenience," 129 S. Ct. at 2540, and the predictions of dire consequences, we again observe, are dubious.

New Mexico law, it bears emphasis, requires the laboratory to preserve samples, which can be retested by other analysts, and neither party questions SLD's compliance with that requirement. Retesting "is almost always an option . . . in [DWI] cases," Brief for Public Defender Service for District of Columbia et al. as Amici Curiae Supporting Petitioner at 25 [hereinafter PDS Brief], and the State had that option here: New Mexico could have avoided any Confrontation Clause problem by asking Razatos to retest the sample, and then testify to the results of his retest rather than to the results of a test he did not conduct or observe.

Notably, New Mexico advocates retesting as an effective means to preserve a defendant's confrontation right. . . . But the State would require the defendant to initiate retesting. The prosecution, however, bears the burden of proof. *Melendez-Diaz,* 129 S. Ct. at 2540 ("[T]he Confrontation Clause imposes a burden on the prosecution to present its witnesses, not on the defendant to bring those adverse witnesses into court."). Hence the obligation to propel retesting when the original analyst is unavailable is the State's, not the defendant's.

Furthermore, notice-and-demand procedures, long in effect in many jurisdictions, can reduce burdens on forensic laboratories. Statutes governing these procedures typically "render . . . otherwise hearsay forensic reports admissible[,] while specifically preserving a defendant's right to demand that the prosecution call the author/analyst of [the] report." PDS Brief 9; *see Melendez-Diaz,* 129 S. Ct. at 2540–41 (observing that notice-and-demand statutes "permit the defendant to assert (or forfeit by silence) his Confrontation Clause right after receiving notice of the prosecution's intent to use a forensic analyst's report")* . . . .

We note also the "small fraction of . . . cases" that "actually proceed to trial." *Melendez-Diaz,* 129 S. Ct. at 2540 (citing estimate that "nearly 95% of convictions in state and federal courts are obtained via guilty plea"). And, "when cases in which forensic analysis has been conducted [do] go to trial," defendants "regularly . . . [stipulate] to the admission of [the] analysis." PDS Brief 20. "[A]s a result, analysts testify in only a very small percentage of cases," *id.* at 21, for "[i]t is unlikely that defense counsel will insist on live testimony whose effect will be merely to highlight

* [As this casebook goes to press in late 2012, a pending amendment to Rule 803(10) proposes to build into the Federal Rules a notice-and-demand procedure of the sort that Justice Ginsburg suggests here and that the *Melendez-Diaz* Court endorsed in 2009. The proposed amendment will not become law before December 1, 2013. The amendment's text and accompanying editor's and advisory committee's notes appear in the rulebook at pages 251 to 252.—GF]

rather than cast doubt upon the forensic analysis." *Melendez-Diaz*, 129 S. Ct. at 2542. . . .

For the reasons stated, the judgment of the New Mexico Supreme Court is reversed, and the case is remanded for further proceedings not inconsistent with this opinion.

It is so ordered.

■ JUSTICE SOTOMAYOR, concurring in part. I agree with the Court that the trial court erred by admitting the blood alcohol concentration report. I write separately first to highlight why I view the report at issue to be testimonial—specifically because its "primary purpose" is evidentiary—and second to emphasize the limited reach of the Court's opinion.

I

A

Under our precedents, the New Mexico Supreme Court was correct to hold that the certified BAC report in this case is testimonial.

To determine if a statement is testimonial, we must decide whether it has "a primary purpose of creating an out-of-court substitute for trial testimony." *Michigan v. Bryant*, 131 S. Ct. 1143, 1155 (2011) [page 630]. When the "primary purpose" of a statement is "not to create a record for trial," *id.*, "the admissibility of [the] statement is the concern of state and federal rules of evidence, not the Confrontation Clause." *Id.* . . .

As we explained earlier this Term in *Michigan v. Bryant*, "[i]n making the primary purpose determination, standard rules of hearsay . . . will be relevant."[1] [Page 630.] As applied to a scientific report, *Melendez-Diaz* explained that pursuant to Federal Rule of Evidence 803, "[d]ocuments kept in the regular course of business may ordinarily be admitted at trial despite their hearsay status," except "if the regularly conducted business activity is the production of evidence for use at trial." 129 S. Ct. at 2538. In that circumstance, the hearsay rules bar admission of even business records. Relatedly, in the Confrontation Clause context, business and public records "are generally admissible absent confrontation . . . because—having been created for the administration of an entity's affairs and not for the purpose of establishing or proving some fact at trial—they are not testimonial." 129 S. Ct. at 2539–40. We concluded, therefore, that because the purpose of the certificates of analysis was use at trial, they were not properly admissible as business or public records under the hearsay rules, nor were they admissible under the Confrontation Clause. The hearsay rule's recognition of the certificates' evidentiary purpose thus

1. Contrary to the dissent's characterization, *Bryant* deemed reliability, as reflected in the hearsay rules, to be "relevant" [page 630], not "essential" [page 655] (opinion of KENNEDY, J.). The rules of evidence, not the Confrontation Clause, are designed primarily to police reliability; the purpose of the Confrontation Clause is to determine whether statements are testimonial and therefore require confrontation.

confirmed our decision that the certificates were testimonial under the primary purpose analysis required by the Confrontation Clause. . . .

In sum, I am compelled to conclude that the report has a "primary purpose of creating an out-of-court substitute for trial testimony," *Bryant*, [page 630], which renders it testimonial. . . .

II

Although this case is materially indistinguishable from the facts we considered in *Melendez-Diaz*, I highlight some of the factual circumstances that this case does *not* present.

First, this is not a case in which the State suggested an alternate purpose, much less an alternate *primary* purpose, for the BAC report. For example, the State has not claimed that the report was necessary to provide Bullcoming with medical treatment. *See Bryant*, at [pages 631–32] n.9 (listing "Statements for Purposes of Medical Diagnosis or Treatment" under Federal Rule of Evidence 803(4) as an example of statements that are "by their nature, made for a purpose other than use in a prosecution"); *Melendez-Diaz*, 129 S. Ct. at 2533 n.2 ("[M]edical reports created for treatment purposes . . . would not be testimonial under our decision today."); *Giles v. California*, 554 U.S. 353, 376 (2008) ("[S]tatements to physicians in the course of receiving treatment would be excluded, if at all, only by hearsay rules.").

Second, this is not a case in which the person testifying is a supervisor, reviewer, or someone else with a personal, albeit limited, connection to the scientific test at issue. Razatos conceded on cross-examination that he played no role in producing the BAC report and did not observe any portion of Curtis Caylor's conduct of the testing. . . . It would be a different case if, for example, a supervisor who observed an analyst conducting a test testified about the results or a report about such results. We need not address what degree of involvement is sufficient because here Razatos had no involvement whatsoever in the relevant test and report. . . .

Finally, this is not a case in which the State introduced only machine-generated results, such as a printout from a gas chromatograph. The State here introduced Caylor's statements, which included his transcription of a blood alcohol concentration, apparently copied from a gas chromatograph printout, along with other statements about the procedures used in handling the blood sample. Thus, we do not decide whether, as the New Mexico Supreme Court suggests, a State could introduce (assuming an adequate chain of custody foundation) raw data generated by a machine in conjunction with the testimony of an expert witness.

This case does not present, and thus the Court's opinion does not address, any of these factual scenarios. . . .

■ JUSTICE KENNEDY, with whom THE CHIEF JUSTICE, JUSTICE BREYER, and JUSTICE ALITO join, dissenting. . . .

Whether or not one agrees with the reasoning and the result in *Melendez-Diaz,* the Court today takes the new and serious misstep of extending that holding to instances like this one. Here a knowledgeable representative of the laboratory was present to testify and to explain the lab's processes and the details of the report; but because he was not the analyst who filled out part of the form and transcribed onto it the test result from a machine printout, the Court finds a confrontation violation. . . .

I

Before today, the Court had not held that the Confrontation Clause bars admission of scientific findings when an employee of the testing laboratory authenticates the findings, testifies to the laboratory's methods and practices, and is cross-examined at trial. Far from replacing live testimony with "systematic" and "extrajudicial" examinations, *Davis v. Washington,* 547 U.S. 813, 835, 836 (2006) (THOMAS, J., concurring in judgment in part and dissenting in part), these procedures are fully consistent with the Confrontation Clause and with well-established principles for ensuring that criminal trials are conducted in full accord with requirements of fairness and reliability and with the confrontation guarantee. . . .

In these circumstances, requiring the State to call the technician who filled out a form and recorded the results of a test is a hollow formality. The defense remains free to challenge any and all forensic evidence. It may call and examine the technician who performed a test. And it may call other expert witnesses to explain that tests are not always reliable or that the technician might have made a mistake. The jury can then decide whether to credit the test, as it did here. The States, furthermore, can assess the progress of scientific testing and enact or adopt statutes and rules to ensure that only reliable evidence is admitted. Rejecting these commonsense arguments and the concept that reliability is a legitimate concern, the Court today takes a different course. It once more assumes for itself a central role in mandating detailed evidentiary rules, thereby extending and confirming *Melendez-Diaz*'s "vast potential to disrupt criminal procedures." 129 S. Ct. at 2544 (KENNEDY, J., dissenting).

II

The protections in the Confrontation Clause, and indeed the Sixth Amendment in general, are designed to ensure a fair trial with reliable evidence. But . . . the Court insists [that] reliability does not animate the Confrontation Clause. *Crawford v. Washington,* 541 U.S. 36, 62–62 (2004). Yet just this Term the Court ruled that, in another confrontation context, reliability was an essential part of the constitutional inquiry. *See Michigan v. Bryant* [page 630 above].

Like reliability, other principles have weaved in and out of the *Crawford* jurisprudence. Solemnity has sometimes been dispositive, *see*

Melendez-Diaz, 129 S. Ct. at 2543 (THOMAS, J., concurring), and sometimes not, *see Davis*, 547 U.S. at 834–37 (THOMAS, J., concurring in judgment in part and dissenting in part). So, too, with the elusive distinction between utterances aimed at proving past events, and those calculated to help police keep the peace. *Compare Bryant, supra*, at [pages 631–33, 635–38], *with Bryant, supra*, at [pages 639–41] (SCALIA, J., dissenting). . . .

Today's majority is not committed in equal shares to a common set of principles in applying the holding of *Crawford*. *Compare ante* (opinion of the Court), *with ante* (SOTOMAYOR, J., concurring). That the Court in the wake of *Crawford* has had such trouble fashioning a clear vision of that case's meaning is unsettling; for *Crawford* binds every judge in every criminal trial in every local, state, and federal court in the Nation. This Court's prior decisions leave trial judges to "guess what future rules this Court will distill from the sparse constitutional text," *Melendez-Diaz*, 129 S. Ct. at 2544 (KENNEDY, J., dissenting), or to struggle to apply an "amorphous, if not entirely subjective," "highly context-dependent inquiry" involving "open-ended balancing." *Bryant, supra* (SCALIA, J., dissenting) (internal quotation marks omitted) (listing 11 factors relevant under the majority's approach).

The persistent ambiguities in the Court's approach are symptomatic of a rule not amenable to sensible applications. . . .

III

Crawford itself does not compel today's conclusion. It is true, as *Crawford* confirmed, that the Confrontation Clause seeks in part to bar the government from replicating trial procedures outside of public view. . . . On this view the Clause operates to bar admission of out-of-court statements obtained through formal interrogation in preparation for trial. The danger is that innocent defendants may be convicted on the basis of unreliable, untested statements by those who observed—or claimed to have observed—preparation for or commission of the crime. . . .

A rule that bars testimony of that sort, however, provides neither cause nor necessity to impose a constitutional bar on the admission of impartial lab reports like the instant one, reports prepared by experienced technicians in laboratories that follow professional norms and scientific protocols. In addition to the constitutional right to call witnesses in his own defense, the defendant in this case was already protected by checks on potential prosecutorial abuse such as free retesting for defendants; result-blind issuance of reports; testing by an independent agency; routine processes performed en masse, which reduce opportunities for targeted bias; and labs operating pursuant to scientific and professional norms and oversight . . . .

[Under *Melendez-Diaz* and today's ruling], the States are not just at risk of having some of their hearsay rules reviewed by this Court. They often are foreclosed now from contributing to the formulation and enactment of rules that make trials fairer and more reliable. For instance, recent state laws allowing admission of well-documented and supported reports of abuse by women whose abusers later murdered them must give way, unless that abuser murdered with the specific purpose of foreclosing the testimony. *Giles v. California*, 554 U.S. 353 (2008). Whether those statutes could provide sufficient indicia of reliability and other safeguards to comply with the Confrontation Clause as it should be understood is, to be sure, an open question. The point is that the States cannot now participate in the development of this difficult part of the law.

. . . If this Court persists in applying wooden formalism in order to bar reliable testimony offered by the prosecution—testimony thought proper for many decades in state and federal courts committed to devising fair trial processes—then the States might find it necessary and appropriate to enact statutes to accommodate this new, intrusive federal regime. If they do, those rules could remain on State statute books for decades, even if subsequent decisions of this Court were to better implement the objectives of *Crawford*. This underscores the disruptive, long-term structural consequences of decisions like the one the Court announces today.

States also may decide it is proper and appropriate to enact statutes that require defense counsel to give advance notice if they are going to object to introduction of a report without the presence in court of the technician who prepared it. Indeed, today's opinion relies upon laws of that sort as a palliative to the disruption it is causing. *Ante*, at [page 652] (plurality opinion). It is quite unrealistic, however, to think that this will take away from the defense the incentives to insist on having the certifying analyst present. There is in the ordinary case that proceeds to trial no good reason for defense counsel to waive the right of confrontation as the Court now interprets it.

Today's opinion repeats an assertion from *Melendez-Diaz* that its decision will not "impose an undue burden on the prosecution." *Ante*, at [pages 651–52] (plurality opinion). But evidence to the contrary already has begun to mount. *See, e.g.*, Brief for State of California et al. as Amici Curiae Supporting Respondent, at 7 (explaining that the 10 toxicologists for the Los Angeles Police Department spent 782 hours at 261 court appearances during a 1–year period); Brief for National District Attorneys Association et al. as Amici Curiae Supporting Respondent, at 23 (observing that each blood-alcohol analyst in California processes 3,220 cases per year on average). . . .

In the meantime, New Mexico's experience exemplifies the problems ahead. From 2008 to 2010, subpoenas requiring New Mexico analysts to testify in impaired-driving cases rose 71%, to 1,600—or 8 or 9 every workday. New Mexico Scientific Laboratory Brief 2. In a State that is the Nation's fifth largest by area and that employs just 10 total analysts, each analyst in blood alcohol cases recently received 200 subpoenas per year, *id.* at 33. The analysts now must travel great distances on most working days. The result has been, in the laboratory's words, "chaotic." And if the defense raises an objection and the analyst is tied up in another court proceeding; or on leave; or absent; or delayed in transit; or no longer employed; or ill; or no longer living, the defense gets a windfall. As a result, good defense attorneys will object in ever-greater numbers to a prosecution failure or inability to produce laboratory analysts at trial. The concomitant increases in subpoenas will further impede the state laboratory's ability to keep pace with its obligations. Scarce state resources could be committed to other urgent needs in the criminal justice system.

* * *

Seven years after its initiation, it bears remembering that the *Crawford* approach was not preordained. This Court's missteps have produced an interpretation of the word "witness" at odds with its meaning elsewhere in the Constitution, . . . and at odds with the sound administration of justice. It is time to return to solid ground. A proper place to begin that return is to decline to extend *Melendez-Diaz* to bar the reliable, commonsense evidentiary framework the State sought to follow in this case.

***Postscript to* Bullcoming v. New Mexico:** "[S]urrogate testimony of the kind Razatos was equipped to give," Justice Ginsburg wrote for the Court in *Bullcoming*, "could not . . . expose any lapses or lies on the certifying analyst's part. Significant here, Razatos had no knowledge of the reason why Caylor had been placed on unpaid leave. With Caylor on the stand, Bullcoming's counsel could have asked questions designed to reveal whether incompetence, evasiveness, or dishonesty accounted for Caylor's removal from his work station. . . . In this light, Caylor's live testimony could hardly be typed 'a hollow formality.'" (Page 650.)

As if in confirmation of Justice Ginsburg's suspicions of rogue analysts in state drug labs, the Boston Globe recently reported on a former analyst at the lab that produced the test results at issue in *Melendez-Diaz*:*

'I Messed Up Bad. It's My Fault,' Chemist Says

Brian Ballou & Andrea Estes

BOSTON GLOBE, Sept. 27, 2012, at A1

The former chemist at the heart of the state drug lab scandal admitted that she altered test results, forged colleagues' initials, and did

* I thank Professors Ann Murphy and Tom Workman for pointing me to this article.

not perform proper tests on drugs "for about two to three years," according to a State Police report. . . .

The 100–page . . . report, obtained by the GLOBE Wednesday morning, makes it clear that Annie Dookhan's colleagues were deeply suspicious of her shoddy work habits and extremely high output for years. But supervisors took little action for more than a year, even when confronted with evidence that she had lied on her resume and removed drug evidence without authorization.

When police finally questioned her in August, Dookhan said she alone was to blame for the rampant breaches of protocol that have jeopardized the reliability of drug evidence used in 34,000 cases during her nine-year career at the lab. . . .

. . . [The] crisis . . . has prompted closure of the state Department of Public Health drug lab, the resignation of the public health commissioner, and the disciplining or firing of several lab supervisors.

. . . [The] drug lab scandal has raised profound doubts about thousands of drug cases, including those of 1,141 inmates of state prisons and county jails who were convicted based on evidence analyzed by Dookhan. Already, judges have freed, reduced bail for, or suspended the sentences of at least 20 drug defendants in the scandal. . . .

[C]o-workers . . . described Dookhan as driven to do more. She would work overtime without extra pay, and she tested several times more drug samples per month than the average chemist.

At the same time, Dookhan apparently padded her resume to make herself look more impressive, falsely claiming to have a master's degree in chemistry, to have graduated magna cum laude from Latin Academy in Boston, and to have taken additional courses. . . .

[During] the police interrogation . . . she confessed to at least seven different major breaches of lab protocol, including deliberately claiming that negative drug tests were positive. . . . [S]he confessed that she had assessed numerous drug samples for two or three years without actually doing the required tests. . . .

By the time police talked to Dookhan in late August, problems at the drug lab in Jamaica Plain had been festering for more than a year. Dookhan had been barred from doing lab analysis in June 2011 after she was caught removing 90 drug samples from the evidence room without authorization. But, even after a confrontation with three lab supervisors, . . . over the mishandled evidence, Dookhan stayed on the payroll and appeared as an expert witness in drug trials. . . .

[C]hemist Michael Lawler told police that the warning signs were obvious: Dookhan's production numbers were "inconsistent with the amount of samples she could test properly." He said the average chemist could analyze 50 to 150 samples a month, but Dookhan was doing more than 500. . . .

Co-workers were also concerned about Dookhan's close relationship with prosecutors, some of whom called her on her cellphone. Piro said she would sometimes do favors for certain prosecutors and police, such as pulling samples out of order for them. . . .

Despite the problems, Piro said the Department of Public Health did not begin an internal investigation of Dookhan until December 2011, six months after she was caught improperly removing samples from the evidence room. "The chemists were all wondering why Annie Dookhan was able to stay in the lab," Piro told investigators. . . .

WILLIAMS V. ILLINOIS: *Case Note*

Melendez-Diaz and *Bullcoming* addressed lab reports of little complexity—reflecting that a white powder contained cocaine in *Melendez-Diaz* and that a blood sample had a high alcohol concentration in *Bullcoming*. The chief difference was that in *Melendez-Diaz* no one from the lab testified about the lab's procedures or the test at issue, whereas in *Bullcoming* a lab technician did testify, but not one who tested Bullcoming's blood or observed that test or confirmed its results.

Deeming the two cases constitutional equivalents, the Justices fractured along similar four-one-four fault lines. Justices Scalia and Ginsburg, joined in *Melendez-Diaz* by Justices Stevens and Souter and in *Bullcoming* by their successors, Justices Sotomayor and Kagan, condemned admission of both lab reports as confrontation violations. Justice Kennedy, joined by Chief Justice Roberts and Justices Breyer and Alito, saw no constitutional offense. And Justice Thomas brokered power in the middle, joining the first cohort in both cases, but stating narrower grounds in each.

Tackling the topic of lab reports a third time in *Williams v. Illinois*, 132 S. Ct. 2221 (2012), the Justices considered a more complex report in a more complex procedural setting. The report detailed a DNA analysis linking the defendant, Sandy Williams, with semen recovered from a rape victim. Again a critical lab technician was missing at trial. Again, as in *Bullcoming*, a different technician testified about the missing technician's results. But this time the technician on the stand testified as an expert *who based her opinion in part on the missing technician's report*. And under an Illinois evidence doctrine modeled after Federal Rule 703, which we take up in Chapter 9 (pages 783–91), experts sometimes may offer an opinion based in part on inadmissible hearsay evidence. The timeworn theory of this rule is that the underlying evidence, if disclosed to the jury, is not admissible for its truth, but only to assist the jury in assessing the reliability of the testifying expert's methods and opinions.

Hence the Justices faced this question: If the prosecutor's expert witness relied on out-of-court statements by an absent technician not offered (in theory) for their truth, did admission of the expert's opinion against Sandy Williams violate his right to confront his accusers? Again the Justices fractured along familiar lines, with the usual foursomes mediated by their usual fulcrum, Justice Thomas. This time, however, Justice Thomas voted with the *other* foursome, if only grudgingly.

The Facts

On February 10, 2000, 22–year-old L.J. was abducted from a Chicago street, robbed, and raped. Soon after, a doctor took a blood sample and vaginal swabs, later collected by a Chicago Police detective who in turn sent them to the Illinois State Police (ISP) laboratory. Lab scientist Brian Hapack detected semen on the vaginal swabs on February 15 and put them in a freezer, where they remained until November 28, 2000. The lab then sent the swabs to Cellmark Diagnostics Laboratory in Germantown, Maryland, which often supplied testing services for the state. On April 3, 2001, after Cellmark tested the swabs, it returned them together with Cellmark's report.

The report contained male DNA data ostensibly derived from the semen on L.J.'s vaginal swabs. ISP forensic biologist Sandra Lambatos constructed a male profile from the Cellmark data, searched a computerized Illinois DNA database, and found a matching profile attributed to Sandy Williams, produced after his arrest on unrelated charges in August 2000. Williams, never till then a suspect in L.J.'s attack, took part in a police lineup held April 17, 2001. After L.J. identified him as her attacker, the state sought his indictment on sexual assault, robbery, and kidnapping charges.

Williams elected to stand trial before a judge, forgoing his jury trial right. The state's case rested heavily on five items of proof:

- L.J.'s identification of Williams as her attacker, first in a lineup, later in court;

- Lab scientist Brian Hapack's testimony that a test he ran detected semen on L.J.'s vaginal swabs;

- State forensic analyst Karen Abbinanti's testimony that she tested a sample of Williams's blood after his unrelated August 2000 arrest and entered the resulting DNA profile into the state's database;

- Testimony and documents tending to show that the ISP lab properly secured and preserved L.J.'s vaginal swabs, sent them to Cellmark, and received back both the swabs and Cellmark's report; and

- Lambatos's expert testimony for the state as follows:

  Q: Was there a computer match generated of the male DNA profile found in semen from the vaginal swabs of [L.J.] to a male DNA profile that had been identified [by Karen Abbinanti] as having originated from Sandy Williams?

  A: Yes, there was.

  Q: Did you compare the semen . . . from the vaginal swabs of [L.J.] to the male DNA profile . . . from the blood of Sandy Williams?

  A: Yes, I did. . . .

  Q: [I]s the semen identified in the vaginal swabs of [L.J.] consistent with having originated from Sandy Williams?

  A: Yes.

  The tests showed a "match," Lambatos said, between the profile generated from the vaginal swabs and that derived from Williams's blood. She said the probability of the profile's appearing in the general population was "1 in 8.7 quadrillion black, 1 in 390 quadrillion white, or 1 in 109 quadrillion Hispanic unrelated individuals."

Williams was convicted and sentenced. Although the prosecutor never entered Cellmark's report in evidence or showed or read it to the judge, Williams claimed on appeal that Lambatos's testimony about Cellmark's tests violated his confrontation right. Lambatos had said she examined a "male DNA profile found in semen from the vaginal swabs of [L.J.]." Indeed, as quoted above, she affirmed three times that Cellmark derived the male DNA data from L.J.'s swabs. Yet Lambatos did not observe Cellmark's tests and had no firsthand knowledge of them. No one from Cellmark testified at trial, nor did Williams have a chance to cross-examine anyone from Cellmark before trial.

After the Illinois Appellate Court and Supreme Court both affirmed Williams's conviction, the United States Supreme Court granted certiorari.

The Plurality

Justice Alito, joined by Chief Justice Roberts and Justices Kennedy and Breyer, delivered the Court's judgment rejecting Williams's Confrontation Clause claim. As in *Bullcoming*, in which only four Justices endorsed Justice Ginsburg's usefully concise definition of a testimonial statement in footnote 6 (page 649), no opinion spoke for the Court.

Justice Alito rooted his reasoning in two technical and initially implausible claims:

The Statements in Cellmark's Report Were Not Offered for Their Truth: Here Justice Alito turned to Illinois' counterpart to Federal Rule of Evidence 703. That rule permits experts to testify on the basis of otherwise inadmissible evidence if experts in the same field "would reasonably rely on those kinds of facts or data in forming an opinion on the subject."

Typically the underlying, inadmissible evidence may not be revealed to the jury, which hears only the conclusions the expert reached based on that evidence. If the underlying evidence is disclosed at trial, the factfinder may not consider that evidence for its truth, and the judge typically must instruct the jury to consider the evidence only in assessing the reliability of the testifying expert's methods and conclusions.

In essence that's what happened at Williams's non-jury trial, Justice Alito said. Lambatos testified that it is a "commonly accepted" practice within the scientific community for "one DNA expert to rely on the records of another DNA expert." And the judge, sitting alone as factfinder and governed by Rule 703, presumably limited his consideration of Lambatos's testimony about statements in Cellmark's report to its permitted purpose—assisting him in assessing the reliability of Lambatos's methods and conclusions.

So limited, Justice Alito argued, Lambatos's references to Cellmark's reported findings could not violate Williams's confrontation right. As the *Crawford* Court acknowledged in citing an earlier Supreme Court ruling, the Confrontation Clause "does not bar the use of testimonial statements for purposes other than establishing the truth of the matter asserted." *Crawford*, page 603 n.9 (citing *Tennessee v. Street*, 471 U.S. 409, 414 (1985)).

Though the three other Justices in Alito's cohort apparently deemed this reasoning sound, Justice Thomas and the four dissenters slapped it down. "There is no meaningful distinction," Thomas wrote, "between disclosing an out-of-court statement so that the factfinder may evaluate the expert's opinion and disclosing that statement for its truth. 'To use the inadmissible information in evaluating the expert's testimony, the jury must make a preliminary judgment about whether this information is true.' " (Quoting D. KAYE, D. BERNSTEIN, & J. MNOOKIN, THE NEW WIGMORE: A TREATISE ON EVIDENCE: EXPERT EVIDENCE § 4.10.1, at 196 (2d ed. 2011).) Writing for the dissenters, Justice Kagan dismissed "the purportedly 'limited reason' " as a "prosecutorial dodge": "If the statement is true, then the conclusion based on it is probably true; if not, not. So to determine the validity of the witness's conclusion, the factfinder must assess the truth of the out-of-court statement on which it relies."

Justice Alito pressed his point: If *other* evidence established the truth of the facts related in Cellmark's report, the factfinder could limit Lambatos's testimony about the report's contents to its intended purpose—evaluating the reliability of her reasoning and hence of her results. Here Justice Alito was arguably sound in theory but wobbly on facts.

His theory was sound because a factfinder often would need to know the facts on which an expert relied and how she deployed them to assess the good sense and rigor of her analysis. In science as in law, true facts do not assure sound reasoning or correct conclusions. But if the expert's conclusions depend on the truth of the facts on which she relied, there must be proof of those facts independent of her hearsay rendition of them on the stand. Here Justice Alito's argument showed strain. For the *other* evidence that he claimed proved the contested fact—that the semen on L.J.'s vaginal swabs yielded the DNA data contained in Cellmark's report—was less than convincing:*

• First he pointed to testimony and documents tracing L.J.'s blood and vaginal swabs from the doctor who took them to the Chicago Police to the ISP lab to Cellmark and back again. Such chain-of-custody evidence, which we examine in Chapter 10 (pages 895–97), often suffices to show, for example, that a gun police found at a crime scene is the same gun that proved on later testing to bear the defendant's fingerprints. But in Williams's case several critical steps in the chain of custody took place while Cellmark clerks and analysts were handling the swabs and preparing them for testing. No one from Cellmark testified about the care Cellmark employees took to avoid confusing one rape kit with another when labeling and testing those kits.

• Justice Alito pointed next to the DNA data included in Cellmark's report, which yielded a one-in-quadrillions match of Williams's profile. *How else*, Justice Alito asked, could Cellmark have generated Williams's DNA data except by testing L.J.'s vaginal swabs? Lambatos testified that random contamination or degradation of a semen sample could not transform another person's DNA profile into Williams's. *Somehow* his DNA got into Cellmark's lab, and no other evidence except L.J.'s swabs suggested how. But this "striking confirmation" that Cellmark extracted Williams's DNA data from L.J.'s swabs falls short. After all, Lambatos testified that the ISP lab regularly sent forensic samples to Cellmark to ease the ISP's backlog. Among those samples must have been many rape kits arising from Chicago-area offenses. Perhaps Williams did not rape L.J., but had sex with another woman whose rape kit was shipped to Cellmark at about the same time. Had a Cellmark clerk or technician carelessly switched one kit for another, Cellmark could have generated the right DNA profile but for the wrong case. Cross-examination of Cellmark employees could help expose—or rule out—such negligence.

• Justice Alito rested finally on L.J.'s identifications of Williams as her attacker, first at a lineup and later in court. Again he stressed the unlikelihood that Cellmark's DNA data would lead to a man whom L.J., on viewing, twice declared her attacker unless Cellmark derived its data from L.J.'s swabs. But the flaws of such eyewitness identification procedures are notorious. Williams was one of perhaps six or eight men in the lineup L.J. viewed (none of the reported opinions or available materials bearing on this case says how many men took part). By sheer chance L.J. could have picked the man with the DNA-databank match. After a lapse of some fourteen months since the attack, L.J.'s memory of her attacker could have dimmed, and his appearance could have changed, increasing

* I thank Professors Michael Avery, David Kaye, and Deborah Merritt, whose blog posts and e-mails helped clarify these factual issues.

the likelihood her choice was happenstance. As for the in-court identification, presumably made while Williams sat alongside trial counsel, the Supreme Court recently said that all such identifications "involve some element of suggestion." *Perry v. New Hampshire*, 132 S. Ct. 716, 727 (2012). Moreover, "there was conflicting evidence presented as to whether L.J. positively identified" *another* suspect shown to her by police shortly after her attack. Although she retracted this identification on viewing the man again, the episode undermines confidence in her identification of Williams fourteen months later. *People v. Williams*, 385 Ill. App. 3d 359, 361 (2008).

Clever as they are, these factual arguments seem shaky—or at all events obscure. Any factfinder might have overlooked or ignored them and trusted instead Lambatos's hearsay claim that Cellmark generated Williams's DNA data from the semen on L.J.'s swabs. Justice Alito allowed that a *jury* might fail to limit Lambatos's references to Cellmark's report to their permitted purpose of assessing Lambatos's opinion. Over and over, however, he noted that the trial judge sat alone. Yet even a trial judge who understood Rule 703, if unaided by clear argument detailing the circumstantial proof outlined above, could have succumbed to the alluring ease of taking Lambatos's description of Cellmark's report as truth.

The Statements in Cellmark's Report Were Not Testimonial: The plurality's conclusion that Williams suffered no confrontation violation rested as well on a second rationale. Assume that the trial judge improperly took as true the statements in Cellmark's report relayed by Lambatos. Still there was no Confrontation Clause violation, Justice Alito argued, because those statements were not testimonial. Here he fronted two theories—that Cellmark's statements aimed to resolve an ongoing emergency and that they had no inculpatory, prosecutorial purpose.

Though Alito strived to squeeze this case, involving "a dangerous rapist who was still at large," into the *Davis/Bryant* paradigm of an ongoing emergency, Justices Thomas and Kagan flayed his reasoning. They highlighted the investigation's languorous pace, which betrayed no exigency. Between February 15, 2000, when Brian Hapack detected semen on L.J.'s vaginal swabs, and November 28, 2000, when the ISP lab sent the swabs to Cellmark, they sat in a freezer. Cellmark's report followed four full months later. "Given this timeline," Justice Thomas wrote, "it strains credulity to assert that the police and Cellmark were primarily concerned with the exigencies of an ongoing emergency. . . ." Likewise, Justice Kagan contrasted the unhurried methods of "laboratory analysts conducting routine tests far away from a crime scene" with Michelle McCottry's "frantic" and "harried" pleas for help as her attack was "actually happening" and with police officers' urgent efforts in the aftermath of a shooting to determine what happened and what threats remained. *Michigan v. Bryant*, pages 628–30, 635–37 (reviewing facts of *Davis* and *Bryant*).

Justice Alito's second argument had more tread but suffered attack just the same. There is nothing inherently inculpatory, he said, about the results of a DNA analysis of a rapist's semen when no suspect is in view. "On the contrary, a DNA profile is evidence that tends to exculpate all but one of the more than 7 billion people in the world today. The use of DNA evidence to exonerate persons who have been wrongfully accused or convicted is well known." The subtext of this argument is that *exculpatory* evidence, suited for use by defendants *against* the government, cannot offend the Confrontation Clause, which protects only "the accused." Justice Kagan dismissed this attempted distinction between DNA analyses and other testimonial evidence generated by the prosecution with an eye toward trial: "*All* evidence shares this feature," she wrote—"the more inculpatory it is of a single person, the more exculpatory it is of the rest of the world."

But there is a difference between the forensic tests at issue in *Melendez-Diaz* and *Bullcoming* and the DNA analysis at issue here. Every lab chemist, if presented with a baggie of white powder of the sort tested in *Melendez-Diaz*, knows the result the prosecution wants—a positive test for narcotics. And every lab chemist, if presented with a blood sample of the sort analyzed in *Bullcoming*, together with an inquiry about alcohol concentration, knows the prosecution's desired result—a high blood alcohol concentration. Cellmark's analysts in contrast apparently had no idea what result Chicago prosecutors hoped to see. True, a report that *no* male DNA was present would have disappointed, but that result was unlikely in light of Brian Hapack's detection of semen on L.J.'s vaginal swabs. In the apparent absence of a known suspect, *any* positive result would have assisted the prosecution as long as the resulting suspect was in or near Chicago on the day of L.J.'s attack and had no clear alibi at the relevant hour. Hence Cellmark's analysts, even if bent on pleasing the authorities who hired them, had no motive to falsify their results.

Moreover, even if police already have a suspect in view, there often is no need to disclose that suspect's identity to an analyst whose task is simply to generate a DNA profile from a biological sample. That is, Cellmark can operate "behind a veil of ignorance," as Justice Breyer put it in his concurrence, unsure whether its findings will aid the prosecution or the defense. And amended lab procedures could darken that veil by concealing even the client's identity. Uncertain whether a district attorney's office or an innocence project paid their fees, analysts could not operate with meaningful intent to aid the prosecution. So their findings could not be testimonial.

Justice Thomas's Concurrence

Justice Thomas concurred only in the judgment. Though he agreed that disclosure of Cellmark's out-of-court statements through Lambatos's testimony triggered no Confrontation Clause violation, he did so "solely because Cellmark's statements lacked the requisite 'formality and solemnity' to be considered 'testimonial' for purposes of the Confrontation Clause." Then he devoted the balance of his long opinion to a frontal rebuttal of Justice Alito's reasoning.

Till now Justice Thomas has constrained the Confrontation Clause's reach in clear and consistent terms, first stated in *White v. Illinois* in 1992 and often repeated: "the Confrontation Clause is implicated by [out-of-court] statements only insofar as they are contained in formalized testimonial materials, such as affidavits, depositions, prior testimony, or confessions." *White* (page 593) (Thomas, J., concurring in part and concurring in the judgment); *Davis v. Washington*, 547 U.S. 813, 836 (2006) (Thomas, J., concurring in the judgment in part and dissenting in part); *Melendez-Diaz v. Massachusetts*, 557 U.S. 305, 329 (2009) (Thomas, J., concurring); *Michigan v. Bryant* (page 638) (Thomas, J., concurring in the judgment).

In *Williams* Thomas shifted emphasis, though only slightly, stressing solemnity more than formality. Quoting *Crawford*'s discussion of Webster's 1828 dictionary, he said "testimony" is " '[a] solemn declaration or affirmation made for the purpose of establishing or proving some fact.' " Evidence bearing such "indicia of solemnity" includes the familiar litany of " 'formalized testimonial materials,' such as depositions, affidavits, and prior testimony, or statements resulting from 'formalized dialogue,' such as custodial interrogation."

But the complex facts of *Williams* blurred Justice Thomas's once bright line. He strained to distinguish Cellmark's report from the cocaine analysis in *Melendez-Diaz* and the blood alcohol analysis in *Bullcoming*, both of which he had deemed testimonial. The *Melendez-Diaz* analysis was sworn before a notary, he said, whereas Cellmark's report was unsworn. The *Bullcoming* analysis was unsworn, he allowed, but contained a "Certificate of Analyst" affirming that the technician followed proper protocol. Cellmark's report bore no such certificate.

Justice Kagan poked fun at such hairsplitting, which no other justice endorsed. Justice Thomas's distinctions among the lab reports in *Melendez-Diaz*, *Bullcoming*, and *Williams*, she said, "amount[] to (maybe) a nickel's worth of difference. . . ." All are official, signed records of lab test results prepared for law-enforcement officers and intended for use in criminal proceedings. "Neither looks any more 'formal' than the other. . . ." If an oath and the label "certificate" are constitutional touchstones, she warned, prosecutors can evade the Confrontation Clause's command simply by offering unsworn documents called "reports."

The Dissent

Though acerbic in her attacks on Justices Alito's and Thomas's reasoning, Justice Kagan framed her own approach, joined by Justices

Scalia, Ginsburg, and Sotomayor, in modest terms: "I would . . . adhere to the simple rule established in our decisions, for the good reasons we have previously given." Analyst Sandra Lambatos played the same role in this case that analyst Gerasimos Razatos played in *Bullcoming*, she said. Neither took part in the tests described to the factfinder, and neither authored the contested scientific reports. Hence the result in both cases must be the same: the testimony of the surrogate analyst and the surrogate's availability for cross-examination cannot satisfy the defendant's right to confront the analyst who performed the tests and wrote the reports.

"Have we not already decided this case?" Justice Kagan asked. "Been there, done that."

Yet the most striking part of Justice Kagan's opinion was not her restrained deference to precedent, but her account of an entirely different rape case—the San Diego prosecution of John Kocak in 1995. Like Williams, Kocak faced a Cellmark DNA report that presented seemingly conclusive evidence of guilt. A Cellmark analyst had tested a bloodstain on a sweatshirt found at the crime scene and compared the blood with samples drawn from the defendant and victim. There was a single match, she testified, between the bloodstain from the sweatshirt and Kocak. "But after undergoing cross-examination, the analyst realized she had made a mortifying error. She took the stand again, but this time to admit that the report listed the victim's control sample as coming from Kocak, and Kocak's as coming from the victim." Hence the bloodstain traced not to Kocak, but to the victim herself.

Kocak's plight, Justice Kagan argued, shows that devastating evidence of a one-in-quadrillions match may trace to a human error that renders it worthless. Because scientific testing "is only as reliable as the people who perform it," the accused "may wish to ask the analyst a variety of questions: How much experience do you have? Have you ever made mistakes in the past? Did you test the right sample? Use the right procedures? Contaminate the sample in any way?"

"Our Constitution contains a mechanism for catching such errors," Justice Kagan wrote—"the Sixth Amendment's Confrontation Clause."

There was yet another opinion in this vexed case. I will take up Justice Breyer's concurrence shortly.

BRYANT, BULLCOMING, & WILLIAMS: *Afterthoughts*

The Crumbled **Crawford** *Coalition*

Hardly a decade after seven Justices joined in proclaiming a new day in Confrontation Clause lawmaking, a seemingly sturdy *Crawford* coalition lies in ruins. Today, while every justice claims fealty to *Crawford,* only four approach a common definition of *testimonial* hearsay. Four others have flirted with scrapping testimonial hearsay as a useful constitutional category. In the balance stands Justice Thomas, whose anemic conception of testimonial hearsay is the broadest that could claim five votes.

Justice Thomas: Despite his shifting emphasis in *Williams,* Justice Thomas has wavered least over time. Over and over since 1992 he has repeated his view that "the Confrontation Clause is implicated by [out-of-court] statements only insofar as they are contained in formalized testimonial materials, such as affidavits, depositions, prior testimony, or confessions." *White v. Illinois* (page 593). Even in *Bullcoming v. New Mexico,* while joining much of the majority opinion, he carefully abstained from footnote 6, where Justice Ginsburg offered a broader conception of testimonial hearsay than his familiar formula. (*See* pages 646, 649 n.6.) And even in stressing solemnity over formality in *Williams,* as we saw a few pages back, he wrote that evidence bearing "indicia of solemnity" includes " 'formalized testimonial materials,' such as depositions, affidavits, and prior testimony, or statements resulting from 'formalized dialogue,' such as custodial interrogation."

Justices Scalia, Ginsburg, Sotomayor, and Kagan: In refusing to join Justice Kagan's dissent in *Williams,* Justice Thomas exposed the gap between his tight-waisted conception of testimonial hearsay and the more expansive category embraced by Justices Scalia, Ginsburg, Sotomayor, and Kagan. All four endorsed Justice Ginsburg's definition of a testimonial statement in note 6 of *Bullcoming*: "To rank as 'testimonial,' a statement must have a 'primary purpose' of 'establish[ing] or prov[ing] past events potentially relevant to later criminal prosecution.' " *Bullcoming* (page 649 n.6) (quoting *Davis v. Washington,* 547 U.S. 813, 822 (2006)). Although arguably the clearest general definition of testimonial hearsay we have seen in the Supreme Court's post-*Crawford* lawmaking, this formula is not law. Because Justice Thomas disavowed footnote 6, Justice Ginsburg's definition claimed only four votes.

Borrowing heavily from the primary-purpose test of *Davis v. Washington* (*see* page 629), Justice Ginsburg's formula differs in two ways. The *Davis* test applied by its terms only to statements made during police interrogation. Justice Ginsburg's test labors under no similar limit. And Justice Ginsburg's formula omits the second half of the *Davis* test and its reference to "ongoing emergency." That omission was deliberate. Just a few months before, the *Bryant* court had hinted that the significance of an ongoing emergency lies only in clarifying whether a statement's primary purpose was to generate prosecutorial evidence: "When, as in *Davis,* the primary purpose of an interrogation is to respond to an 'ongoing emergency,' its purpose is not to create a record for trial and thus is not within the scope of the Clause. But there may be *other* circumstances, aside from ongoing emergencies, when a statement is not procured with a primary purpose of creating an out-of-court substitute for trial testimony." *Bryant* (page 630).

In one frustrating way Justice Ginsburg's definition resembles the *Davis* primary-purpose test: neither says *whose* purpose controls. Justice Ginsburg deftly ducked the question by assigning motive force to the statement itself. "To rank as 'testimonial,' a *statement* must have a 'primary purpose' of. . . ." (Emphasis added.) Again, she chose her words deliberately and with an eye cast backward on *Bryant*. Justice Scalia's dissent in *Bryant* had dismissed Justice Sotomayor's view, stated in her opinion for the Court, that trial judges should assess *both* the declarant's purpose in speaking and the interrogator's purpose in asking questions. More precisely, the *Bryant* Court held that trial judges should look to the purpose of reasonable persons in the declarant's and interrogator's shoes when assessing the primary purpose *of the interrogation*: "[T]he statements and actions of both the declarant and interrogators provide objective evidence of the primary purpose of the interrogation. . . . In many instances, the primary purpose of the interrogation will be most accurately ascertained by looking to the contents of both the questions and the answers." (Page 633.) Although Justice Sotomayor then scripted two paragraphs to defend this view, Justice Scalia was dyspeptic in reply. "[B]ecause the Court picks a perspective so will I: The declarant's intent is what counts. . . . For an out-of-court statement to qualify as testimonial, the declarant must intend the statement to be a solemn declaration rather than an unconsidered or offhand remark. . . ." (Page 639.)

In *Bryant* Justice Ginsburg linked arms with Justice Scalia on this point: "I agree with Justice Scalia that . . . '[t]he declarant's intent is what counts.' " (Page 642.) But in *Bullcoming*, anxious to crib together a five-person majority, she walked nimbly between her two sparring colleagues and wrote of the primary purpose of the *statement*. Her diplomacy could not, however, claim Justice Thomas's fifth vote in endorsing footnote 6 and its definition of testimonial hearsay.

The Chief Justice and Justices Kennedy, Breyer, and Alito: Meanwhile, their Chief and three remaining colleagues at times abandoned the term *testimonial* altogether when measuring the Confrontation Clause's reach. Justice Kennedy's dissent for the group in *Melendez-Diaz* declared, "The Court's fundamental mistake is to read the Confrontation Clause as referring to a kind of out-of-court statement—namely, a testimonial statement—that must be excluded from evidence." After all, the term *testimonial* "does not appear in the text of the Clause." *Melendez-Diaz*, 129 S. Ct. at 2544, 2550 (Kennedy, J., dissenting). Two years later in *Bullcoming*, Justice Kennedy's dissent for the same foursome employed the word *testimonial* only once—when referring dismissively to the "inflexible rule" of *Melendez-Diaz*: "Where 'analysts' affidavits' included 'testimonial statements,' defendants were 'entitled to be confronted with the analysts' themselves." *Bullcoming*, 131 S. Ct. at 2725 (Kennedy, J., dissenting).

It is true that in *Bryant* and *Williams* these four Justices either joined or authored opinions that liberally deployed the term *testimonial*. In both cases, however, their words seemed to diverge from their core beliefs. In *Bryant* they formed a likely partnership of convenience with Justice Sotomayor, whose opinion for the Court reached their desired outcome while respecting the Court's *Crawford* caselaw, still governing precedent. And even as Justice Alito's opinion for the group in *Williams* dutifully recited post-*Crawford* caselaw, Alito reserved the option to retreat from this precedent at some point to come: "Experience might yet show that the holdings in [*Crawford, Melendez-Diaz*, and *Bullcoming*] should be reconsidered for the reasons, among others, expressed in the dissents the decisions produced. Those decisions are not challenged in this case. . . ." *Williams*, 132 S. Ct. at 2242 n.13. Should these three cases one day be challenged and fall, the constitutional category of testimonial hearsay will go down with them.

How then would these four Justices measure the reach of the Confrontation Clause?

Reliability Analysis Resurgent

Writing for the four in *Bullcoming*, Justice Kennedy despaired that the Court's rigid rejection of testimonial hearsay would discourage states from revising hearsay rules to "make trials fairer and more reliable." He highlighted recent state laws admitting "well-documented and supported reports of abuse by women whose abusers later murdered them." The Court's "wooden formalism" would bar such reports as testimonial hearsay if the victims intended their complaints to reach authorities. Disdaining this approach, Justice Kennedy revived the *Roberts* Court's reference to "indicia of reliability": "Whether those [state] statutes could provide sufficient indicia of reliability and other safeguards to comply with the Confrontation Clause as it should be understood is, to be sure, an open question." (Page 657.)

As it should be understood. Surely Justice Kennedy did not utter those five words thoughtlessly. For *Crawford* had put such reliability-based reasoning to bed. The Court had condemned the rule of *Ohio v. Roberts*, which generally deemed the Confrontation Clause satisfied if hearsay statements bore "adequate 'indicia of reliability.'" (Page 590.) Reliability, the *Crawford* Court said, was "an amorphous, if not entirely subjective, concept." (Page 605.) Three years later a unanimous Court in *Whorton v. Bockting* declared that *Crawford* had "eliminat[ed] . . . Confrontation Clause protection against the admission of unreliable out-of-court nontestimonial statements." (Page 618.) Undaunted by such scorn, Justice Kennedy announced that four Justices now stand ready to restore reliability to Confrontation Clause caselaw.

Indeed it seems five Justices stand ready. In *Bryant* Justice Sotomayor, joined by the same four, deployed the rhetoric of reliability to explain the primary-purpose test of *Davis v. Washington*: "Implicit in *Davis* is the idea that because the prospect of fabrication in statements given for the primary purpose of resolving that emergency is presumably significantly diminished, the Confrontation Clause does not require such statements to be subject to the crucible of cross-examination." She continued:

> This logic is not unlike that justifying the excited utterance exception in hearsay law. Statements "relating to a startling event or condition made while the declarant was under the stress of excitement caused by the event or condition," FED. R. EVID. 803(2), are considered reliable because the declarant, in the excitement, presumably cannot form a falsehood. *See Idaho v. Wright*, 497 U.S. 805, 820 (1990) ("The basis for the 'excited utterance' exception . . . is that such statements are given under circumstances that eliminate the possibility of fabrication, coaching, or confabulation. . . . "); Advisory Committee's Notes on FED. R. EVID. 803(2) (same). An ongoing emergency has a similar effect of focusing an individual's attention on responding to the emergency.

Hence "[i]n making the primary purpose determination, standard rules of hearsay, designed to identify some statements as reliable, will be relevant." (Pages 630, 631.) Then in a long footnote Justice Sotomayor listed nine hearsay exceptions that "rest on the belief that certain statements are, by their nature, made for a purpose other than use in a prosecution and therefore should not be barred by hearsay prohibitions." (Pages 631–32, n.9.) Here these five Justices came daringly close to reviving that part of the old *Roberts* analysis, perhaps its most reviled component, that deemed reliable any statement that fell within a "firmly rooted" hearsay exception. (Page 590.)

Justice Alito's plurality opinion in *Williams* built on such statements and used them to justify admission of Cellmark's report. The *Bryant* Court, he said, "noted that . . . reliability is a salient characteristic of a statement that falls outside the reach of the Confrontation Clause." Because "no one at Cellmark could have possibly known that the profile that it produced would turn out to inculpate petitioner" or anyone else in the DNA database, "there was no 'prospect of fabrication' and no incentive to produce anything other than a scientifically sound and reliable profile."

Justice Breyer's concurring opinion in *Williams* likewise displayed the persistent allure of reliability reasoning. He staked out the broadest proposal yet seen in post-*Crawford* caselaw for reviving reliability—or more particularly, the risk of *un*reliability—in defining the scope of Confrontation Clause protection. He did so not by jettisoning *Crawford*, but by infusing the still-unsettled meaning of a *testimonial* statement with a concern that the statement carry a real risk of unreliability.

Here he built on *Crawford*'s concession that business records are not testimonial hearsay. "Cellmark's DNA report embodies technical or professional data, observations, and judgments; the employees who contributed to the report's findings were professional analysts working on technical matters at a certified laboratory" and "at a remove from the investigation in the ordinary course of professional work." Hence the report was a business record, he said, and "presumptively fall[s] outside the category of 'testimonial' statements that the Confrontation Clause makes inadmissible." And "as the hearsay exception itself reflects, alternative features of such situations help to guarantee its accuracy."

One such feature is Cellmark's accreditation, which requires it to "satisfy well-established professional guidelines that seek to ensure the scientific reliability of the laboratory's results." Another is the "veil of ignorance" behind which the lab testing takes place, concealing from technicians whether their results will incriminate anyone and "mak[ing] it unlikely that a particular researcher has a defendant-related motive to behave dishonestly, say, to misrepresent a step in an analysis or otherwise to misreport testing results."

Justice Breyer allowed that the presumption of reliability attaching to business records must yield if facts cast doubt on the records' trustworthiness:

> [S]hould the defendant provide good reason to doubt the laboratory's competence or the validity of its accreditation, then the alternative safeguard of reliability would no longer exist and the Constitution would entitle defendant to Confrontation Clause protection. Similarly, should the defendant demonstrate the existence of a motive to falsify, then the alternative safeguard of honesty would no longer exist and the Constitution would entitle the defendant to Confrontation Clause protection.

Typically, though, the records of a competent, accredited lab made in the ordinary course of business at a remove from the criminal investigation would be deemed nontestimonial and admissible.

Far from regarding cross-examination as the best guarantor of truth, Justice Breyer worried that assuring defendants the right to confront lab technicians could *undermine* the accuracy of trial evidence:

> [T]he additional cost and complexity involved in requiring live testimony from perhaps dozens of ordinary laboratory technicians who participate in the preparation of a DNA profile may well force a laboratory to reduce the amount of DNA testing it conducts, and force prosecutors to forgo forensic DNA analysis in cases where it might be highly probative. In the absence of DNA testing, defendants might well be prosecuted solely on the basis of eyewitness testimony, the reliability of which is often questioned.

(Internal quote marks deleted.) Justice Kagan, confident that no prosecutor would forgo one-in-quadrillions proof of guilt simply because of the inconvenience of calling analysts to the stand, dismissed this concern. But whether Breyer or Kagan is right in this regard, the broader question is whether resurgent reliability reasoning can claim a stable Court majority.

For now stability on any score seems very far from view. No other justice joined Justice Breyer in *Williams*. Amid a clamorous exchange of rebuttals and unvarnished putdowns, the other Justices largely ignored his opinion. Meanwhile, an atmosphere of open and mutual disdain among the fractured factions threatens congressional gridlock on the High Court.

Firm Footholds and the Confrontation Flowchart

With the Court badly splintered, with coalitions in flux, and with so little certainty about the role of reliability in confrontation caselaw, it is useful to plot patches of firm ground. The flowchart on the next page attempts to capture these points of certainty.

Statements Not Offered for Their Truth: Note first that we never need address the Confrontation Clause except when facing hearsay as defined by FRE 801(c). *Crawford* says plainly, "The Clause does not bar the use of testimonial statements for purposes other than establishing the truth of the matter asserted." (Page 603 n.9.) Out-of-court statements offered for a nonhearsay purpose, such as to show their impact on listeners, evade Confrontation Clause scrutiny. After all, if the significance of a statement does not derive from its truth, why would the defendant need to cross-examine the declarant? Any testifying witness who heard the statement could say when and where it was made, how loudly, and in what tone. Because the truthfulness or accuracy of the statement typically would not affect its impact on someone who heard it, the defendant has no need to probe those matters.

Statements Offered in Civil Cases or against the Prosecution: We also avoid Confrontation Clause analysis if hearsay is offered in a civil

HEARSAY AND CONFRONTATION

ROUTES OF ADMISSIBILITY

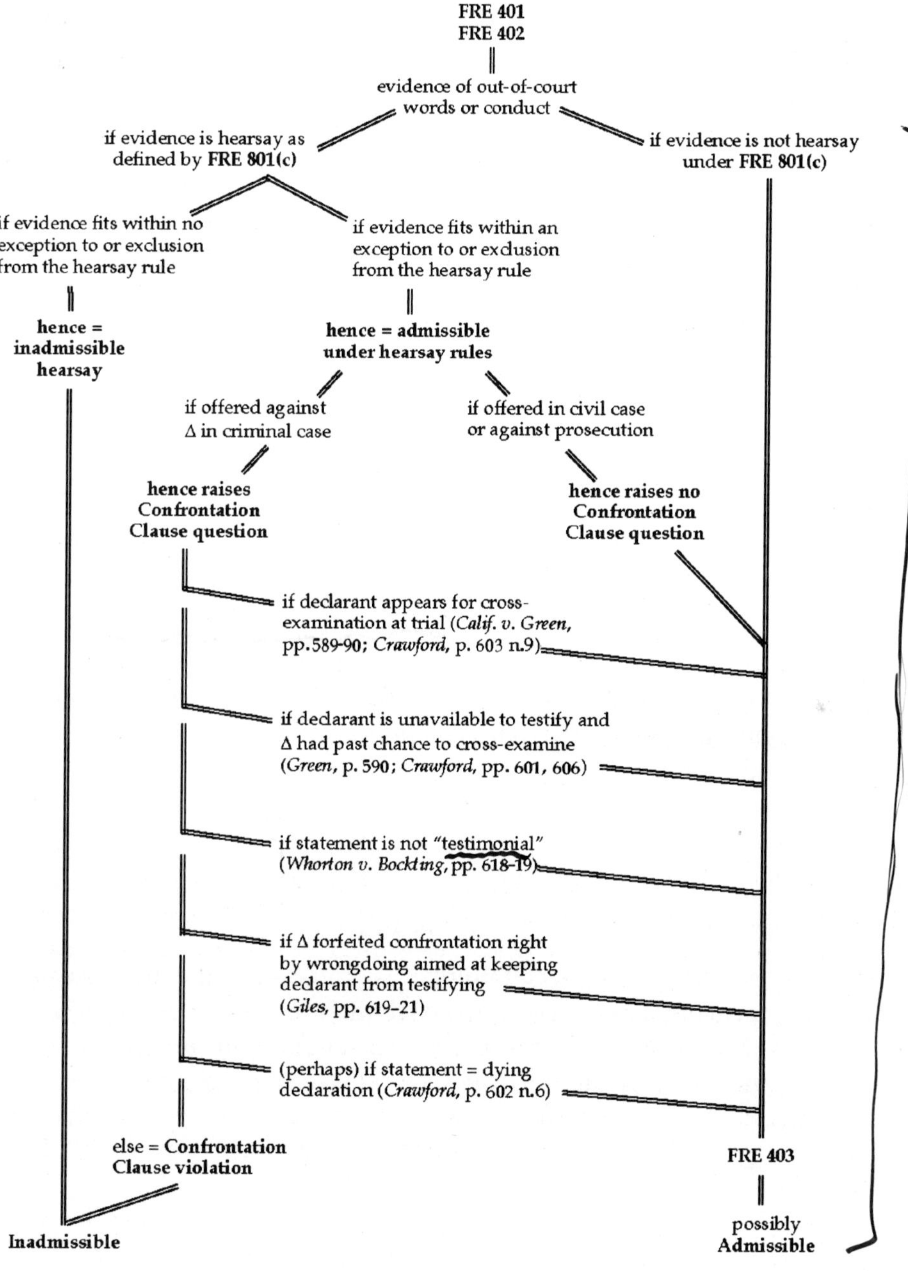
FRE 401
FRE 402
evidence of out-of-court words or conduct
if evidence is hearsay as defined by FRE 801(c)
if evidence is not hearsay under FRE 801(c)
if evidence fits within no exception to or exclusion from the hearsay rule
if evidence fits within an exception to or exclusion from the hearsay rule
hence = inadmissible hearsay
hence = admissible under hearsay rules
if offered against Δ in criminal case
if offered in civil case or against prosecution
hence raises Confrontation Clause question
hence raises no Confrontation Clause question
if declarant appears for cross-examination at trial (Calif. v. Green, pp.589-90; Crawford, p. 603 n.9)
if declarant is unavailable to testify and Δ had past chance to cross-examine (Green, p. 590; Crawford, pp. 601, 606)
if statement is not "testimonial" (Whorton v. Bockting, pp. 618-19)
if Δ forfeited confrontation right by wrongdoing aimed at keeping declarant from testifying (Giles, pp. 619-21)
(perhaps) if statement = dying declaration (Crawford, p. 602 n.6)
else = Confrontation Clause violation
FRE 403
Inadmissible
possibly Admissible

case or against the government in a criminal case. The Sixth Amendment protects only criminal defendants: "In all *criminal* prosecutions, the *accused* shall enjoy the right . . . to be confronted with the witnesses against him. . . ." (Emphasis added.) Hence we encounter the Confrontation Clause, explored in the lower two-thirds of the flowchart, only if the government offers hearsay evidence against a criminal defendant.

Past Statements of Trial Witnesses: The law of *California v. Green* (pages 589–90), restated in *Crawford*, remains sound. So "when the declarant appears for cross-examination at trial, the Confrontation Clause places no constraints at all on the use of his prior testimonial statements." (*Crawford*, page 603 n.9.)

Statements by Unavailable Declarants Once Subject to Cross-Examination by the Defendant: The holding of *Mattox*, reaffirmed in *Green* and restated in *Crawford*, likewise retains force: A defendant's past chance to cross-examine a declarant who proves unavailable at trial typically satisfies the Confrontation Clause. (*Mattox*, page 588; *Green*, page 590; *Crawford*, pages 601, 606.)

Statements Admitted by Forfeiture: A defendant who intends by his wrongdoing to keep the declarant from testifying at trial and thereby renders the declarant unavailable forfeits his confrontation right. (*Giles v. California*, pages 619–21.)

Nontestimonial Statements: *Whorton v. Bockting* declared flatly that "the Confrontation Clause has no application to [nontestimonial] statements and therefore permits their admission. . . ." (Page 618.) As clear as this ruling may be, it supplies no guidance on distinguishing testimonial from nontestimonial statements. Again *Crawford* and related caselaw stake out a few plots of firm ground:

Clearly testimonial statements include—

- **" '[S]olemn declaration[s] . . . made for the purpose of . . . proving some fact' ":** Justice Scalia's opinion in *Crawford* derived this formulation of a testimonial statement from the definition of *testimony* in the 1828 edition of Webster's *American Dictionary*. (*Crawford*, page 600).

- ***"Formalized Testimonial Materials":*** Even Justice Thomas, who long has held the stingiest view of Confrontation Clause protections, extends them to reach "formalized testimonial materials, such as affidavits, depositions, prior testimony, or confessions." (Page 593.) The holding of *Crawford* itself, which concerned Sylvia Crawford's tape-recorded statement made while in custody and under formal interrogation, therefore remains secure.

Clearly nontestimonial statements include—

- ***Casual and Offhand Remarks:*** "[A] person who makes a casual remark to an acquaintance" does not bear testimony, Justice Scalia wrote in *Crawford*. And "[a]n off-hand, overheard remark . . . bears little resemblance to the civil-law abuses the Confrontation Clause targeted." (Page 600.)

- ***Coconspirators' Statements:*** Statements made during and in furtherance of a conspiracy "by their nature [are] not testimonial." (*Crawford*, page 602.) They do *not* "have a 'primary purpose' of 'establish[ing] or prov[ing] past events potentially relevant to later criminal prosecution.'" (*Bullcoming*, page 649 n.6 (plurality opinion).)

- ***(Some) Business Records:*** In *Crawford* Justice Scalia lumped business records together with coconspirator statements, deeming both "by their nature . . . not testimonial." The facts of *Melendez-Diaz*, however, prompted him to qualify his words. Writing for the Court, he declared that certificates of analysis, sworn to before a notary by state drug lab analysts, were not the sort of business records the *Crawford* Court had in mind. These certificates were affidavits, "'solemn declaration[s] . . . made for the purpose of establishing or proving some fact.'" By law in Massachusetts they were "prima facie evidence of the composition, quality, and the net weight" of the analyzed substance, "prepared specifically for use at petitioner's trial." Therefore they fell within the "'core class of testimonial statements.'" The sort of business records readily deemed nontestimonial, by contrast, are those "created for the administration of an entity's affairs and not for the purpose of establishing or proving some fact at trial." *Melendez-Diaz*, 557 U.S. at 310, 324.

Beyond these (fairly) firm categories of testimonial and nontestimonial evidence are several other categories defined by fuzzier boundaries. Statements that involved "government officers in the production of testimony with an eye toward trial," for example, are testimonial (*Crawford*, page 602 n.7), as are statements that do "precisely what a witness does on direct examination" (*Bullcoming*, page 649 (quoting *Melendez-Diaz*)). Although these and other definitional hints are useful when arguing before a court, they permit too much play at the edges to qualify as "firm footholds." Classifying them as testimonial or nontestimonial will demand longer and less certain analysis.

Problem 8.4

Deliver After Death

Court Considers Letter Predicting Death

Woman Expressed Worries That Husband Was Going to Poison Her

Carrie Antlfinger

Charleston (W.V.) Daily Mail, Apr. 17, 2006, at 3A

MILWAUKEE (AP)—About two weeks before her death, Julie Jensen went to a neighbor, shaking and crying, and handed over a sealed envelope. If anything happened to her, she said, he should give it to police.

She wrote that she felt her husband never forgave her for a brief affair she had seven years earlier, and that she had seen him visit Internet sites about poisoning.

"I pray I'm wrong + nothing happens . . . but I am suspicious of Mark's suspicious behaviors + fear for my demise," the 40-year-old woman allegedly wrote in the letter dated Nov. 21, 1998.

More than seven years after the southern Wisconsin woman died from poisoning, the state Supreme Court is considering whether to allow her statements as evidence in her husband's murder trial.

Jensen was found dead Dec. 3, 1998, in her bed in her Pleasant Prairie home about 40 miles south of Milwaukee. An autopsy revealed she died from at least two doses of ethylene glycol, commonly used as antifreeze.

Toxicology tests led to a first-degree intentional homicide charge against her 46-year-old husband, Mark, in 2002. His defense lawyer has claimed she committed suicide. . . .

After her death, the neighbor gave the envelope to police. Julie Jensen . . . wrote she would never take her own life because of her love for her children. . . .

Mark Jensen was later ordered to stand trial.

But in March 2004, the U.S. Supreme Court overruled a 1980 case that laid out complex rules for when statements can be used without the opportunity for cross-examination. . . .

Assume that admission of Julie Jensen's letter against Mark Jensen at his forthcoming murder trial would not violate Wisconsin hearsay law. If Mark Jensen claims instead that the letter's admission would violate his confrontation right, how should the Wisconsin Supreme Court rule? Assume today's caselaw applies. *See State v. Jensen*, 299 Wis. 2d 267 (2007).

Problem 8.5

Confession in Blood

On October 17, 1996, Audrey Lover's strangled and burned body was found in her Connecticut home. In May 1998 Anthony Rivera was charged with her murder. At his trial the prosecution's evidence included the testimony of Julio Caraballo, a nephew of Michael Glanville, who was an acquaintance of Rivera. Caraballo described a conversation between him and Glanville while driving to a nearby lake in March 1997:

> ... Caraballo testified that Glanville had told him ... that he and the defendant had broken into the victim's house in search of jewelry, and that Glanville had remained in the kitchen as a lookout as the defendant went through the house. The victim came into the kitchen and noticed Glanville, who covered his face. The defendant then emerged from a bedroom and entered the kitchen where he started choking the victim, who fell to the floor. At that point, the defendant picked up a lamp and Glanville ran out of the house....
>
> Over the defendant's objection, the trial court admitted Glanville's statement to Caraballo as a declaration against penal interest.... Specifically, the court determined that Glanville was unavailable to testify, by virtue of his having invoked the Fifth Amendment privilege against self-incrimination, and thereafter concluded that there were "clearly corroborated circumstances that indicate the trustworthiness of this statement." The court stated: "This statement was made to [Glanville's nephew] in a milieu of trust.... The declarant admitted to and incriminated himself to at least the crime of felony murder. If there's any minimizing here, it's one type of murder versus another type of murder.... And so I'm going to find that ... the circumstances under which the statement was made were trustworthy, particularly in view of the blood relationship between the declarant [Glanville] and the third party [Caraballo]."

State v. Rivera, 268 Conn. 351, 359–60 (2004). As the law stands today, would admission of Caraballo's testimony violate Rivera's confrontation right?

Problem 8.6
DOVE Interview

Consider the facts of *State v. Stahl*, 111 Ohio St. 3d 186 (2006), as summarized by the lower court in *State v. Stahl*, 2005–Ohio–1137 (Ct. App. 2005):

On December 23, 2003, an adult woman presented to the Richfield Police Department, claiming that she had been the victim of rape. Officer Amy Ellis recorded a statement for the purpose of filing charges and then drove the alleged victim to St. Thomas Hospital for treatment in the Developing Options for Violent Emergencies (DOVE) unit. DOVE is a specialized healthcare facility designed to provide expert care to victims of violent sexual assault.

[On arriving at the unit, the complainant signed a form entitled, "CONSENT FOR FORENSIC EXAM AND RELEASE OF EVIDENCE." It provided in part: "I voluntarily consent to this forensic examination and collection of evidence.... I authorize the release of evidence, ... clothing, ... and photography documentation of injuries to a law enforcement agency for use only in the investigation and prosecution of this crime."]

... [T]he victim met with [Nurse Practitioner] Jenifer Markowitz, ... who offered immediate care and began a dialogue about the assault.... The victim ... described the assault and her resulting trauma, and explained the surrounding circumstances.... Although Officer Ellis was present, she did not ask questions or participate in the exam. According to DOVE policy, officers are permitted to be present, upon the victim's permission or request, but are forbidden from intervening or asking questions until the exam is complete....

Nurse Markowitz conducted the exam, which included collection of physical evidence and testing for sexually transmitted diseases, and prepared a discharge plan. A typical DOVE discharge plan would include medical prescriptions, follow-up treatment, and enhanced personal or family counseling to account for possible pregnancy, sexually transmitted disease, emotional distress, or contemplation of suicide. There is a special concern that the victim be discharged to a safe environment....

The victim relayed to Nurse Markowitz that Mr. Stahl had been her boyfriend's boss, and that she had gone to his office to ask him to give her boyfriend his job back. According to the victim, Mr. Stahl greeted her warmly and led her to a vacant office where he offered that he would help her if she would do something for him. He then . . . forced her . . . to perform oral sex. . . .

Nurse Markowitz indicated a number of reasons why this information is crucial to the exam: it creates a comfort level between the victim and herself . . .; it defines the preliminary scope of the physical exam, allowing her to concentrate on certain probable injuries or concerns, or postpone secondary or minor concerns . . .; it alerts her to any actions that the victim may have taken in response to the assault, such as washing or self medicating . . .; and it provides the information necessary to prepare a practical and beneficial discharge plan.

Nurse Markowitz explained that a full knowledge of the sexual assault also allows DOVE to collect physical evidence during the examination in a thorough, timely and legally defensible manner, while minimizing the intrusion to the victim. Therefore, the exam includes aspects that are not specifically intended to treat the victim's physical condition, such as collection of clothing, DNA samples [from oral swabs, dental floss, and fingernail scrapings] for the rape kit, and photos using ultraviolet light. . . . Finally, she testified that the identity of the assailant allows for appropriate prescriptions in the complex treatment of certain diseases, such as HIV, and further ensures that DOVE will not unknowingly discharge the victim back into a dangerous situation.

Eventually, the police charged Mr. Stahl with rape . . . and kidnapping. . . . [T]he victim unexpectedly died prior to trial, as the result of an epileptic seizure unrelated to the alleged sexual assault. Thereafter, Mr. Stahl filed a motion to prohibit the State from introducing the statements the victim had made to Nurse Markowitz, arguing that introduction of such testimony would violate his Sixth Amendment right to confront his accuser under *Crawford v. Washington*.

Assume today's confrontation caselaw applies. What are the defendant's best arguments in support of his motion? What are the prosecutor's best arguments against?

THE CONFRONTATION FRONTIER: *Remaining Battles in the* Crawford *Revolution*

Despite the Supreme Court's recent spate of Confrontation Clause lawmaking, several issues stand unresolved. Two of the most vexing have awaited a definitive ruling since the dawn of the *Crawford* era.

Statements of Child Victims

It is no easy task to classify a young child's claim of physical or sexual abuse as testimonial or nontestimonial. The primary-purpose test, conceived in *Davis* and refined in *Bryant* and *Bullcoming*, seems poorly suited to the task. Does it make sense to ask whether a reasonable person in the shoes of a four-year-old who complained of abuse had "a 'primary purpose' of 'establish[ing] or prov[ing] past events potentially relevant to later criminal prosecution' "? (*Bullcoming*, page 649 n.6.) And if that child's mother quizzed her about an odd rash or an odd remark about the daddy next door, can we assess whether the mother—or a reasonable person in her shoes—sought primarily to protect the child from infection and further abuse or instead to gather facts for the police? Even if we asked the mother, would she be able to disentangle her motives?

Still, there will be clear cases. If the child simply wept and said nothing until a parent prompted her to speak, the child hardly could be called an accuser. And if the parent asked about times, dates, and witnesses present, took careful notes, and called police without delay, the parent's motives too would be clear. If questions were posed not by a parent but by a police officer or a social worker employed by the police, motives would grow even clearer.

Recent rulings by prominent state and lower federal courts reflect the struggle trial judges face. Given the intricate interplay of facts and law, systemizing their rulings is difficult. But a brief survey of the judgments of prominent state courts allows us to distill a few guiding principles.

In *People v. Loy*, 52 Cal. 4th 46 (2011), the California Supreme Court reviewed Eloy Loy's conviction of sexually assaulting and killing his twelve-year-old niece. A friend of the victim testified for the prosecution that about a week before her murder, the victim "said she was afraid of her uncle Eloy because he would 'make weird looks at her and sneak up to her room and touch her . . . chest and . . . grab her crotch.' " As the victim spoke, she "was crying, but not heavily," her friend said. "You could just hear her holding back tears." The victim told her friend "not to tell anyone."

In rejecting Loy's claim that the friend's testimony violated his confrontation right, the court cited *Bryant* and *Bullcoming* only in passing and said nothing at all of *Davis v. Washington* or its primary-purpose test. Instead, relying almost entirely on *Crawford*, the court held that the victim's statement to her friend, made in private with an admonition to tell no one, hardly resembled " 'a formal statement to government officers.' " It appeared instead to be " 'a casual remark to an acquaintance.' " (*Crawford*, page 600.) The court drew support from its 2009 opinion in *People v. Gutierrez*, 45 Cal. 4th 789, 812–13, *cert. denied*, 130 S. Ct. 490 (2009), where it had held in a domestic murder case that "[t]he statement of a three-year-old declarant made to his aunt is more like a 'casual remark to an acquaintance' and is therefore not a testimonial statement under *Crawford*." The *Loy* court concluded simply, "The same is true here."

In general, the younger the declarant and the more private her disclosure, the more readily a court will follow *Loy* and deem the statement nontestimonial. As the child ages and the setting loses intimacy, a primary-purpose inquiry grows fuzzier. A fourth-grader's disclosure of parental abuse to a teacher is no "casual remark to an acquaintance." But did that disclosure have "a 'primary purpose' of 'establish[ing] or prov[ing] past events potentially relevant to later criminal prosecution' "? How could a court know?

In *People v. Cage*, 40 Cal. 4th 965, *cert. denied*, 552 U.S. 1023 (2007), the California Supreme Court eluded this quandary by shifting focus from the child's motives to the questioner's. A surgeon asked a bloodied fifteen-year-old what happened to him. The young man reported that his mother cut him in the face with a shard of glass. Largely ignoring the victim's motives in speaking, the court instead assessed the doctor's "primary purpose" in questioning. It quoted his testimony that " 'the specific reason why I asked him about how it happened' was to determine whether the cut might contain ground-in debris that must be cleaned out to prevent infection." The court concluded that "[o]bjectively viewed, the primary purpose of the question, and the answer, was not to establish or prove past facts for possible criminal use, but to help [the doctor] deal with the immediate medical situation he faced. It was thus akin to the 911 operator's emergency questioning of Michelle McCottry in *Davis*." The doctor's status as a "mandated reporter," required by state law to file a report whenever he "knows or reasonably suspects" that a child in his care has been abused, did not alter the court's judgment, for the statute did not oblige doctors to question patients about possible abuse.

These California cases permit the glib but arguably accurate conclusion that reviewing courts will focus on whichever person—questioner or child victim—had the clearest motives in speaking. Hence in *Bobadilla v. Carlson*, 575 F.3d 785 (8th Cir. 2009), *cert. denied*, 130 S. Ct. 1081 (2010), the Eighth Circuit Court of Appeals evaded the question whether a three-year-old boy who accused his uncle of sexual molestation intended his words for prosecutorial use. That question, normally so simple with so young a victim, proved harder here because the boy spoke to a county social worker inside the police department while in the company of a police detective who sat a few feet away and who had solicited the social worker's participation. As the boy already had reported the abuse to his mother and as she had told his father, he may have grasped that this very official interview could get his uncle in trouble.

Avoiding the thorny question of the three-year-old's motives, the *Bobadilla* court focused instead on the transparent motives of the social worker. She spoke with the boy at the behest of and in the company of a police detective while in the department in a room specifically designed for interviews of child victims in sexual abuse investigations. She "utilized a 'forensic' technique known as the 'CornerHouse technique,' which consists of asking questions in a structured manner to ascertain the nature of any sexual abuse." And her interview was videotaped for future use. The court concluded simply, "[T]he interview was conducted for the purpose of the criminal investigation."

In the aftermath of *Michigan v. Bryant*, decided early in 2011, most courts have heeded the Supreme Court's counsel that a trial judge should examine "the statements and actions of *both* the declarant and interrogators" in light of "all of the relevant circumstances" of their encounter. The Court emphasized that "the relevant inquiry is not the subjective or actual purpose of the individuals involved . . . , but rather the purpose that reasonable participants would have had, as ascertained from the individuals' statements and actions and the circumstances in which the encounter occurred." (*Bryant*, pages 631, 633–34 (emphasis added).)

Evidence of the questioner's purpose may include her job or relationship to the victim, her formal duties, the timing of the interview, the formality or official nature of the setting, the questions she poses, and the actions she takes after the victim's disclosures. Notably, the questioner can *explain* at trial her motives in questioning. Because the child in contrast does not testify at trial—for if she did, no confrontation issue would arise—proof of her motives in speaking typically must be circumstantial. Among the most important circumstances to assess are her age and likely grasp of the criminal consequences of her report.

The analysis of the Pennsylvania Supreme Court in *Commonwealth v. Allshouse*, 36 A.3d 163 (Pa. 2012), is of a piece with other recent decisions. The child witness at the center of *Allshouse* was not the victim, seven-month-old J.A., but his four-year-old sister, A.A. She was present the day J.A. suffered a broken arm while in their father's care, and she later reported the father's role in the crime to a caseworker for the county Children and Youth Services.

The caseworker had begun his investigation after an emergency-room doctor advised him that the infant's spiral humerus fracture indicated abuse. The Pennsylvania high court looked to a number of factors in concluding that A.A.'s report to the caseworker of her father's role in the crime was not testimonial. The caseworker, first of all, did not seek to speak with A.A. until a week after the crime—and even then did so only because the defendant suggested that A.A. may have broken her brother's arm. The caseworker spoke with A.A. on the front porch of her grandparents' home, the most informal of settings, where nearby family members could interrupt them at any moment. The caseworker wore blue jeans and never told A.A. of his role, his suspicions about the crime, or the child's possible testimony at trial. And after hearing her accusation of her father, he did not call the police, but rather reported the information to his supervisor. "[T]here is little question," the court concluded, that the caseworker's "primary purpose in interviewing A.A. was not to establish past events which would be potentially relevant in a criminal trial, but to ensure both A.A. and her siblings' welfare was secure while they remained in the custody of her grandparents." *Id.* at 167, 176–77.

As for four-year-old A.A.'s purpose in reporting her father's wrongdoing, the court declared "it would be absurd to assume A.A. had intended to give statements for use in a legal proceeding." *Id.* at 177. Nothing in the front-porch setting of the conversation or the caseworker's clothing or his statements to her gave the child reason to suspect the penal consequences of her report. And although the child's *own* intentions were not at issue, but rather the intentions of a reasonable person in her circumstances, those circumstances included her tender age of four.

Recent decisions of other prominent courts resemble *Allshouse* in examining "the statements and actions of *both* the declarant and interrogators" in light of "all of the relevant circumstances" of their encounter. As in *Allshouse,* evidence of the adult interrogator's purposes generally proves richer than evidence of the child's. "Evaluating the primary purpose of a child declarant," the Fourth Circuit confessed, "is a bit more difficult." *United States v. DeLeon,* 678 F.3d 317, 325 (4th Cir. 2012). The Kansas Supreme Court similarly conceded it could look to the intent of a four-year-old victim only "to the extent she would have developed an intent." *State v. Miller,* 293 Kan. 535, 580, 264 P.3d 461 (2011).

Most courts have deemed children's statements to doctors and nurses to be nontestimonial. Supreme Court dicta in *Giles v. California,* 554 U.S. 353 (2008) (page 619), helped fuel this trend. Writing for six members of the Court, Justice Scalia noted that "statements to physicians in the course of receiving treatment would be excluded, if at all, only by hearsay rules. . . . " *Id.* at 376. The three dissenting Justices, likewise in dictum, agreed that a victim's complaint would not be testimonial if "she made it to a nurse." *Id.* at 389 (Breyer, J., dissenting). It would be surprising if these remarks, though uttered in a case concerning an adult victim of domestic violence, lack force when those who complain of abuse to doctors and nurses are children.

Despite helpful hints in *Giles,* it's hard to predict how the Supreme Court would analyze a child victim's hearsay statement today. True, Justice Thomas's position seems clear. In *White v. Illinois* 502 U.S. 346 (1992) (page 593), Thomas first stated his view that "the Confrontation

Clause is implicated by [out-of-court] statements only insofar as they are contained in formalized testimonial materials, such as affidavits, depositions, prior testimony, or confessions." This formula readily placed a four-year-old victim's complaints of sexual abuse, at issue in *White*, outside the Clause's realm of protection, even when the child spoke to a police officer in her home.

The approach of Justices Scalia, Ginsburg, and Kagan also seems clear. They likely will hold to the formula of testimonial statements they embraced in footnote 6 of *Bullcoming*. Hence they will ask if the child's complaint had "a 'primary purpose' of 'establish[ing] or prov[ing] past events potentially relevant to later criminal prosecution.' " (Page 649 n.6.)

Real questions remain about the commitment of the four *Bullcoming* dissenters to their stated view that the Confrontation Clause "should be understood" to require "sufficient indicia of reliability and other safeguards." (*Bullcoming*, page 657 (Kennedy, J., dissenting).) It's likewise unclear how much weight Justice Sotomayor meant to put on the reliability inquiry. She wrote for the Court in *Bryant* that when a court "mak[es] the primary purpose determination, standard rules of hearsay, designed to identify some statements as reliable, will be relevant"—a view she restated in *Bullcoming*. (Pages 630, 653 n.1.) As the Court long ago made clear in *Idaho v. Wright*, 497 U.S. 805 (1990) (pages 590–91), the reliability inquiry is not wholly toothless when assessing statements of child victims of sexual abuse.

Dying Declarations

A dying person who tells police or other witnesses her killer's name arguably speaks with the " 'primary purpose' of 'establish[ing] or prov[ing] past events potentially relevant to later criminal prosecution.' " (*Bullcoming*, page 649 n.6.) Absent proof under *Giles* that the defendant killed to mute his victim's trial testimony, many dying declarations, deemed testimonial by this definition, could fail Confrontation Clause scrutiny.

The *Crawford* Court hinted, however, that dying declarations might evade the usual exclusion of unconfronted testimonial hearsay. The Court set aside as "*sui generis*" the founding-era practice of admitting testimonial dying declarations against criminal defendants. (Page 602 n.6.) In *Giles* the Court again acknowledged this common-law practice. (Pages 621–22.) Yet the Justices have not addressed whether this exceptional treatment of dying declarations survived *Crawford* and its progeny. In *Bryant* Justice Ginsburg stated her readiness to take up the question whenever it is "properly tendered." (Page 642 (Ginsburg, J., dissenting).)

The *outcome* of that future case seems hardly in doubt. The four *Bullcoming* dissenters—the Chief Justice and Justices Kennedy, Breyer, and Alito—almost surely will rule that the common-law practice survived

Crawford, at least if the contested statement appears reliable and necessary to prove the crime, for such pragmatic concerns undergirded their *Bullcoming* dissent. Justice Thomas as surely will join them unless the victim somehow made her accusation by affidavit or during a structured, formalized police interrogation—the conditions he has imposed before giving force to the Confrontation Clause.

The four Justices most loyal to *Crawford* would face a choice between *Crawford*'s general rejection of unconfronted testimonial statements and its originalist fealty to founding-era practice. Justice Scalia's colicky dissent in *Bryant*, a case that arguably presented a classic dying declaration deemed nontestimonial by the Court, suggests he would hew to principle rather than historical practice. True, the state did not seek to introduce Anthony Covington's accusation of Bryant as a dying declaration, nor did the Court analyze his statements in that guise. Still, Justice Scalia's bitter tone suggests he thought exclusion the right result by any analysis. Should he indeed reject an exception for dying declarations, he would lend support to two of the very few federal courts that have ruled in this realm since *Crawford*. *See United States v. Mayhew*, 380 F. Supp. 2d 961, 965 (S.D. Ohio 2005); *United States v. Jordan*, 66 Fed. R. Evid. Serv. 790 (D. Colo. 2005) (unpublished).

Justice Sotomayor's majority opinion in *Bryant* aligned her in contrast with the pragmatic, reliability-focused concerns that motivated the *Bullcoming* dissenters. Should she therefore recognize a dying-declaration exception, she would join at least seven state supreme courts that have chosen historical practice over the constitutional principles *Crawford* claimed to embody. *See, e.g., State v. Beauchamp*, 333 Wis. 2d 1, 29–31, *cert. denied*, ___ U.S. ___ (2011) (collecting cases); *Commonwealth v. Nesbitt*, 452 Mass. 236, 251 (2008); *People v. Monterroso*, 34 Cal. 4th 743, 764–65 (2004), *cert. denied*, 546 U.S. 834 (2005).

Justices Ginsburg and Kagan would cast the most interesting votes. For if they join Justice Sotomayor and the four *Bullcoming* dissenters in prizing pragmatism and apparent reliability over *Crawford*'s rigid first principles, Justice Scalia could remain the last sailor standing on *Crawford*'s deck.

Problem 8.7

Child's Statements

Consider the facts of *White v. Illinois*, 502 U.S. 346 (1992):

> . . . The events giving rise to the charges related to the sexual assault of S.G., then four years old. Testimony at the trial established that in the early morning hours of April 16, 1988, S.G.'s babysitter, Tony DeVore, was awakened by

S.G.'s scream. DeVore went to S.G.'s bedroom and witnessed petitioner leaving the room, and petitioner then left the house. DeVore knew petitioner because petitioner was a friend of S.G.'s mother, Tammy Grigsby. DeVore asked S.G. what had happened. According to DeVore's trial testimony, S.G. stated that petitioner had put his hand over her mouth, choked her, threatened to whip her if she screamed and had "touched her in the wrong places." Asked by DeVore to point to where she had been touched, S.G. identified the vaginal area.

Tammy Grigsby, S.G.'s mother, returned home about 30 minutes later. Grigsby testified that her daughter appeared "scared" and a "little hyper." Grigsby proceeded to question her daughter about what had happened. At trial, Grigsby testified that S.G. repeated her claims that petitioner had choked and threatened her. Grigsby also testified that S.G. stated that petitioner had "put his mouth on her front part." Grigsby also noticed that S.G. had bruises and red marks on her neck that had not been there previously. Grigsby called the police.

Officer Terry Lewis arrived a few minutes later, roughly 45 minutes after S.G.'s scream had first awakened DeVore. Lewis questioned S.G. alone in the kitchen. At trial, Lewis' summary of S.G.'s statement indicated that she had offered essentially the same story as she had first reported to DeVore and to Grigsby, including a statement that petitioner had "used his tongue on her in her private parts."

After Lewis concluded his investigation, and approximately four hours after DeVore first heard S.G.'s scream, S.G. was taken to the hospital. She was examined first by Cheryl Reents, an emergency room nurse, and then by Dr. Michael Meinzen. Each testified at trial, and their testimony indicated that, in response to questioning, S.G. again provided an account of events that was essentially identical to the one she had given to DeVore, Grigsby, and Lewis.

S.G. never testified at petitioner's trial. The State attempted on two occasions to call her as a witness, but she apparently experienced emotional difficulty on being brought to the courtroom and in each instance left without testifying. The defense made no attempt to call S.G. as a witness, and the trial court neither made, nor was asked to make, a finding that S.G. was unavailable to testify.

Assume that these events took place after *Bullcoming* was decided. Assume as well that White objects to admission of each of S.G.'s statements—to DeVore, Grigsby, Lewis, Reents, and

Meinzen—claiming each would violate his confrontation right. Which of these statements should the trial court deem testimonial? Would you need to know other facts to resolve this question?

CRAWFORD AND ITS PROGENY: *Have They Helped or Hurt Criminal Defendants?*

The day after the Supreme Court announced its ruling in *Crawford,* the *New York Times* predicted the decision "could prove highly favorable for many criminal defendants." Linda Greenhouse, *Court Alters Rule on Statements of Unavailable Witnesses,* N.Y. TIMES, Mar. 9, 2004, at A21. On first reading, *Crawford* seems to have been a triumph for the defense bar. The *Times* quoted Justice Scalia's very quotable condemnation of *Roberts*—"Dispensing with confrontation because testimony is obviously reliable is akin to dispensing with jury trial because a defendant is obviously guilty." (Page 605.) And of course the Court had reversed Crawford's conviction, a strong signal that criminal defendants had cause to celebrate.

But did they? During *Crawford*'s first two years in force, the answer surely was yes. Because courts overwhelmingly continued to apply *Ohio v. Roberts* (page 590) to nontestimonial statements, *Crawford* had almost no downside for defendants. They gained the extra protections of *Crawford* in cases concerning testimonial statements while retaining the old, less complete protection of *Roberts* in most other cases.

And with regard to two sorts of hearsay often offered by prosecutors against criminal defendants, *Crawford* resulted in almost wholesale exclusion. One is the kind of hearsay considered in *Crawford* itself—a statement by an accomplice or former accomplice to police investigators during a stationhouse interrogation. Virtually unanimously courts found such statements to be testimonial. They are after all the modern analogues of Lord Cobham's ex parte accusation of Sir Walter Raleigh. (*See* pages 374–76.) Even during the *Roberts* era, a plurality of the Court wrote in *Lilly v. Virginia* that custodial confessions "are inherently unreliable . . . because an accomplice often has a considerable interest in 'confessing and betraying his cocriminals.'" But this reasoning attracted only four votes. (Page 594.) And as Justice Scalia noted in *Crawford,* many lower courts still admitted such statements, even if they did so wrongly. (*See* page 605.)

Post-*Crawford* courts also proved vigilant against statements made in past court proceedings or grand jury hearings. Lower courts in the *Roberts* era often had admitted grand jury testimony of absent declarants, though they probably did so wrongly. After *Crawford* such evidence met a solid wall of exclusion. *See, e.g., People v. Patterson,* 217 Ill.2d 407, 423, 841 N.E.2d 889 (2005) (holding that the trial court erred in admitting grand jury testimony that fit within a hearsay exception defined by state law).

The *Davis* Court's application of *Crawford* to the facts of *Hammon v. Indiana* gave defense counsel more confirmation of *Crawford*'s promise. (See pages 629–30.) The affidavit that Amy Hammon wrote in the presence of police officers probably never should have been admitted, even under *Roberts*. Indiana appeals courts excused the likely error of its admission as harmless, in part because the trial judge, who sat without a jury, also heard evidence of Amy Hammon's oral complaint to the officers. *See Hammon v. State*, 829 N.E.2d 444, 459 (Ind. 2005); *Hammon v. State*, 809 N.E.2d 945, 948 n.1 (Ind. App. 2004). Admission of that oral complaint as an excited utterance survived two layers of review in state courts and probably would have survived federal scrutiny under *Roberts*. As the exception for excited utterances is "firmly rooted," Hershel Hammon likely could have raised no viable constitutional objection to admission of his wife's oral statements. (*See Roberts*, page 590.) His victory before the Supreme Court therefore represented a clear advance for criminal defendants.

The result in *Giles*, too, was strongly pro-defendant. In marking the boundaries of constitutional forfeiture, the Court could have stood on the familiar equitable slogan that a defendant should not profit from his wrongdoing. Surely a killer can't demand a chance to cross-examine the ex-girlfriend he sent to her grave. Had the Court ruled in a homicide case that the defendant's wrongdoing in killing his victim always forfeits his confrontation right, the accused also could have lost that right whenever a prosecutor could show that his abusive or assaultive acts scared a witness away. By triggering forfeiture only when the defendant intended to eliminate the declarant *as a witness*, *Giles* avoided this result.

Lastly there are *Melendez-Diaz* and *Bullcoming*, arguably the most stunning displays of the *Crawford* doctrine's force. The pro-defendant result in *Crawford*, as Chief Justice Rehnquist noted in his concurrence, delivered no more than Michael Crawford could have secured under *Roberts* and *Idaho v. Wright*. (*See* pages 590–91.) And *Giles* merely gave constitutional force to the forfeiture doctrine embodied in Rule 804(b)(6), which took effect seven years before the *Crawford* revolution's dawn. *Melendez-Diaz* and *Bullcoming*, in contrast, forced many states to scuttle hearsay exceptions that had exempted certificates of analysis signed or sworn by lab technicians. The Court spurned a widely held view that lab technicians, employed or contracted by the state to perform numberless identical tests on faceless baggies of white powder or vials of blood and laboring under a duty of accuracy, would have no incentive to lie. And it acted in the face of dire warnings of the chaos caused by defense demands that technicians crisscross the state to testify about long-forgotten chromatograms.

Yet the caselaw has begun to break prosecutors' way—and in a fashion that may rattle the defense bar. Had *Michigan v. Bryant* concerned merely dying declarations, admitted as a *sui generis* exception to the

Confrontation Clause, or had the Court ruled narrowly to address gun-toting killers with unknown motives on the loose, the case would pose little threat to most defendants. But as Justice Scalia complained in dissent after ticking off ten factors cited in the majority's totality-of-the-circumstances approach, the Court's "highly context-dependent inquiry" too greatly resembles the "amorphous, if not entirely subjective" analysis of reliability that *Crawford* had condemned. "[U]nder this malleable approach," Scalia warned, " 'the guarantee of confrontation is no guarantee at all.' " *Bryant*, 131 S. Ct. at 1170, 1175–76 (Scalia, J., dissenting).

Williams v. Illinois presents the same risk of malleable decisionmaking but in a different guise. With four Justices allowing Sandra Lambatos's testimony about the contents of Cellmark's report and four deeming her testimony a confrontation violation, Justice Thomas controlled the result. His vote turned on whether Cellmark's report bore too close a resemblance to "the *ex parte* examination of witnesses under the English bail and committal statutes passed during the reign of Queen Mary." He concluded it did not because unlike the lab report at issue in *Melendez-Diaz*, Cellmark's report was not sworn, and unlike the report at issue in *Bullcoming*, Cellmark's was not certified. Perhaps these distinctions "amount[] to (maybe) a nickel's worth of difference," as Justice Kagan alleged, but they controlled Williams's fate.

The seeming serendipity of these results would set any rights holder on edge. Amorphous multifactor analyses and unpredictable line drawing permit those judges so inclined to achieve the result their gut deems right. With the Court so delicately balanced between two wings adhering to competing visions of the confrontation right, the result of each new case may supply little guidance to advocates hoping to sway the outcome in the next.

If the next case concerns a child's hearsay complaint of physical or sexual abuse, defense counsel have more reason to worry. Long ago, in *White v. Illinois*, Justice Thomas hinted that a small child's unrehearsed oral complaint could not amount to the sort of "formalized testimonial material[]" covered by the Confrontation Clause. (Page 593.) Far more recently, in *Michigan v. Bryant*, Justices Scalia and Ginsburg both insisted that "[t]he declarant's intent is what counts." That is, as Justice Scalia explained, "the *declarant* must intend the statement to be a solemn declaration . . . with the understanding that it may be used to invoke the coercive machinery of the State against the accused." (Pages 639, 642 (emphasis added).) A young child's complaint to parent or teacher or pastor or friend rarely could be judged testimonial on this standard. What is more, dicta of both the majority and dissent in *Giles v. California* suggested that statements to doctors and nurses typically are not testimonial, and the majority said the same about statements to neighbors and friends. *See Giles v. California*, 554 U.S. 353, 376 (2008); *id.* at 389 (Breyer, J., dissenting).

A ruling that a child's complaint is nontestimonial likely will leave the defendant with no constitutional protection against its admission, however unreliable that complaint may seem. That is the lesson of *Whorton v. Bockting*: "the Confrontation Clause has no application to [nontestimonial] statements and therefore permits their admission *even if they lack indicia of reliability.*" (Page 618 (emphasis added).) *Roberts* at least had offered some shield. *Idaho v. Wright*, which held a child's complaint unreliable and wrongly admitted, stands as evidence that *Roberts* was not spineless against children's statements resulting from suggestive or manipulative questioning. (*See* pages 590–91.) That residuum of protection now is lost.

There is an irony in Justice Scalia's role in stripping nontestimonial hearsay of constitutional scrutiny. Scalia dissented in *Maryland v. Craig*. (*See* pages 591–92.) He assailed the *Craig* majority for permitting procedures that spare child victims the trauma of testifying face-to-face with their alleged abusers. What the Court saw as a minimal intrusion on the defendant's confrontation right—the child faced defense counsel but not the defendant, and the jury viewed cross-examination by video monitor—Justice Scalia saw as an intolerable variance from the " 'face-to-face' confrontation" guaranteed by the Sixth Amendment. But after *Bockting*, as Professor Laird Kirkpatrick has noted, "Justice Scalia's concern about the need for confrontation in *Craig* can be completely circumvented under a regime that simply eliminates the requirement of in-court testimony by an available child when the child's out-of-court statement is found to be nontestimonial." Laird C. Kirkpatrick, *Nontestimonial Hearsay After* Crawford, Davis, *and* Bockting, 19 REGENT U. L. REV. 367, 377–78 (2007).

Then there is the irony of Justice Scalia's handwringing over the fate of Sir Walter Raleigh, convicted of treason by the out-of-court words of the turncoat Lord Cobham. Scalia's opinion in *Crawford* lamented Cobham's role in " 'degrad[ing] and injur[ing]' " the justice of England. But what of the *other* notoriously rank hearsay used to condemn Sir Walter—the words of a certain Portuguese gentleman relayed in court by a boat pilot named Dyer? After the death of *Roberts*, how could a post-*Crawford* court protect Sir Walter against *this*?

THE TRIAL OF SIR WALTER RALEIGH: *Historical Postscript*

For all the attention the *Crawford* Court lavished on Raleigh's complaints about his absent accuser Cobham—" 'let Cobham be here, let him speak it. Call my accuser before my face' "—it paid none at all to Raleigh's *second* absent accuser. Justice Scalia said nothing of the unnamed "gentleman" whom the witness Dyer encountered in Lisbon:

> *Attorney General.* I shall now produce a witness *viva voce.* [He then produced one Dyer, a boat pilot:]
>
> *Dyer.* I came to a merchant's house in Lisbon . . .; there came a gentleman into the house, and enquiring what countryman I was, I said, an Englishman. Whereupon he asked me, if the king was crowned? And I answered, No, but that I hoped he should be so shortly. Nay, saith he, he shall never be crowned; for Don Raleigh and Don Cobham will cut his throat ere that day come.

(Pages 375–76.) Here followed perhaps the most memorable moment of this memorable trial—Raleigh's outraged cry that "[t]his is the saying of some wild Jesuit or beggarly Priest; but what proof is it against me?" The Attorney General rejoined coldly, "It . . . shows that your treason had wings."

Memorable as this scene was, it would have muddled Justice Scalia's carefully wrought historical argument. The *Crawford* Court focused on Raleigh's trial to make a point—that the historical concern underlying the Confrontation Clause was the admission of accusations made in formalized ex parte affidavits. Dyer's account decidedly did not fit that mold.

No doubt Sir Walter would be chagrined to learn that the Supreme Court's recent efforts to right the injustice done him in 1603 in fact have stripped him of the constitutional protection he once would have enjoyed against the accusation of the unnamed gentleman. For while both *Roberts,* as applied by the plurality in *Lilly v. Virginia,* and *Crawford* would protect Raleigh against Cobham's accusation, only *Roberts* protected him as well against the Portuguese stranger's claim. Had Cobham's words been offered against Raleigh in pre-*Crawford* days, the reasoning of *Lilly* would have supplied a conclusive rebuttal: Such custodial confessions by an accomplice, which also implicate the defendant, "are inherently unreliable . . . because an accomplice often has a considerable interest in 'confessing and betraying his cocriminals.' " (*Lilly,* page 594.)

But *Roberts*—unlike *Crawford*—also would have barred the words of the Portuguese stranger. Because that accusation fit within no firmly rooted hearsay exception and bore no particularized guarantees of trustworthiness, it would have failed Confrontation Clause analysis under *Roberts.* (*See* page 590.) *Crawford* stripped Raleigh of any such protection, for the distant gentleman made no "solemn declaration or affirmation for the purpose of establishing or proving some fact"—the 1828 definition of "testimony" embraced by the *Crawford* Court. Nor did he speak with any purpose of generating evidence for trial. Rather he made his accusation to a boat pilot in a private, unrecorded conversation hundreds of miles from the nearest English court. It was "a casual remark to an acquaintance," the clearest kind of nontestimonial evidence. And now, after *Bockting* and the death of *Roberts,* nontestimonial evidence likely evades all constitutional scrutiny.

Though perhaps chagrined by this result, Raleigh hardly would be surprised at the wanton ways of justice. Convicted of treason under a procedure he likened to the Spanish Inquisition, he was packed off to prison to await execution. There he languished long enough to write his *History of the World.* At last, having found again the Crown's favor, he was released in 1616 to lead an expedition to the New World. In Guiana, on the northeast coast of South America, he committed the diplomatic indiscretion that ultimately proved his undoing. On encountering a Spanish settlement, Raleigh attacked. His actions enraged not only the Spanish, who demanded his death, but his own sovereign, James I, who wanted good relations with Spain and had forbidden Raleigh to accost Spanish settlers. To appease Spain—and perhaps to vindicate his own authority—the King ordered Raleigh's death.

Here diplomacy and law converged, for while international controversy prompted the execution, Raleigh's fifteen-year-old treason conviction supplied the legal justification. In the words of one contemporary, "Sir Walter Raleigh shall pay this new reckoning upon the old score. . . ."*

B. THE *BRUTON* DOCTRINE

Till now, our investigation of hearsay has fixed on one question: Is this out-of-court statement admissible? That question has two parts: Would admission of this statement violate the hearsay rule? And would it offend the Confrontation Clause?

The *Bruton* doctrine presents an altogether different question. Here we begin with the proposition that the out-of-court statement is *not* admissible. To be precise, the *Bruton* doctrine concerns an out-of-court admission made by an accomplice tried jointly with the defendant. The confessing accomplice's words are admissible against *her* as an opposing party's statement. If offered against the defendant, however, they most likely will fail Confrontation Clause scrutiny.

Crawford explains why the accomplice's confession very often will offend the Confrontation Clause if offered against the defendant. That was exactly the scenario of *Crawford.* Imagine now that Sylvia and Michael Crawford were tried jointly before a single jury. Sylvia's statements to the police surely would have been admissible against her. Just as surely—for this was the holding of *Crawford*—her words would have violated Michael's confrontation right if offered against him.

* *See* RALEIGH TREVELYAN, SIR WALTER RALEIGH 538 (2002) (quoting John Chamberlain); *see generally id.* at 465–553 (narrating Raleigh's post-trial rehabilitation and ultimate fall from grace). I thank David Kaye and Michael Saks for pointing me to the story of Raleigh's undoing.—GF

A prosecutor who wishes to try both Sylvia and Michael for the attack on Kenneth Lee has several ways to avoid this confrontation violation:

• ***Severed Trials:*** Most obvious, perhaps, is the option of trying Sylvia and Michael separately. At Sylvia's trial, the prosecution could offer her police statements against her. At Michael's trial, the prosecutor would make no mention of Sylvia's statements. Severed trials are, however, both expensive and difficult for the prosecution. Witnesses, including vulnerable victims, must endure the ordeal of testifying twice.

• ***Separate Juries:*** Creative judges sometimes empanel two juries, sitting on opposite sides of the courtroom, each weighing a single defendant's guilt and hearing only the evidence admissible against her. In the Crawfords' case, one jury would decide Sylvia's guilt or innocence, the other would decide Michael's. Only the first jury would hear of Sylvia's statements to the police. Michael's jury would not be present when that evidence was offered or discussed. Empaneling two juries at one trial can secure the benefits of severed trials while avoiding the ills. But managing two juries that hear different evidence poses weighty logistical challenges. And many courtrooms simply aren't big enough for two juries.

• ***Testimony by the Confessing Accomplice:*** If Sylvia takes the witness stand and submits to cross-examination, Michael's Confrontation Clause objection melts away. This is the first holding of *California v. Green*, 399 U.S. 149 (1970), as reaffirmed in *Crawford*. (Pages 589–90, 603 n.9.) But as a practical matter, prosecutors typically present their evidence before defendants face the choice of taking or not taking the witness stand. Because Sylvia would have a right under the Fifth Amendment to stay silent at trial, a wise prosecutor would not offer her statements implicating Michael against her at a joint trial unless she already has taken the stand.

• ***Redaction:*** We will see that if Sylvia's statements are redacted by the court or prosecutor or by stipulation of the parties so that they avoid all mention of Michael's alleged involvement in the crime, and if those statements are admitted only against Sylvia, Michael likely can claim no confrontation violation. *See Richardson v. Marsh*, 481 U.S. 200 (1987) (discussed below at page 710). Note that while redacting references to Michael's role in the assault on Kenneth Lee might erase any basis for a constitutional complaint by Michael, *Sylvia* could object that altering her statements to focus more blame on her violates her due-process right to a fair trial. Hence the prosecutor could not simply redact a statement that reads, "Michael and I attacked Kenny Lee," by rendering it, "I attacked Kenny Lee."

• ***Bench Trial:*** The law presumes judges more able than jurors to segregate evidence in their minds. Judges presiding as factfinders over joint trials are trusted to consider an accomplice's statement only against its maker while disregarding it against codefendants. All defendants facing non-petty charges, however, have a Sixth Amendment right to trial by jury and must waive that right voluntarily before a bench trial may take place.

• ***Admissibility of Statement Against Non–Maker:*** The *Bruton* doctrine concerns statements admitted against the confessing accomplice that could *not* be admitted against the nonconfessing defendant without violating his confrontation right. If Sylvia's confessions were directly admissible against Michael—say, if they constituted coconspirator's statements and hence not testimonial hearsay—Michael could raise no objection under the Confrontation Clause to their admission against Sylvia at their joint trial. The difficulty is that an accomplice's confession to law-enforcement authorities almost *never* will qualify as a coconspirator's statement. After all, such confessions rarely occur during the course of the conspiracy, and they never (in the normal pattern of events) further the conspiracy.

• ***When None of These Options Applies:*** The *Bruton* problem arises when none of these tactics proves possible or attractive for the prosecution. Assume therefore that an accomplice has confessed, implicating both herself and her confederate. Assume that they are tried jointly before a single jury. Assume that the confessing accomplice does not testify. And assume finally that the accomplice's confession, though admissible against her, would fail Confrontation Clause scrutiny if offered against the nonconfessing defendant.

Bruton presents this question: May the trial court permit the jury to hear the accomplice's out-of-court confession so long as the court carefully instructs the jury to consider the statement only against its maker?

BRUTON v. UNITED STATES

391 U.S. 123 (1968).

■ MR. JUSTICE BRENNAN delivered the opinion of the Court. This case presents the question, last considered in Delli Paoli v. United States, 352 U.S. 232 (1957), whether the conviction of a defendant at a joint trial should be set aside although the jury was instructed that a codefendant's confession inculpating the defendant had to be disregarded in determining his guilt or innocence.

A joint trial of petitioner and one Evans in the District Court for the Eastern District of Missouri resulted in the conviction of both by a jury on a federal charge of armed postal robbery. A postal inspector testified that Evans orally confessed to him that Evans and petitioner committed the armed robbery. The postal inspector obtained the oral confession, and another in which Evans admitted he had an accomplice whom he would not name, in the course of two interrogations of Evans at the city jail in St. Louis, Missouri, where Evans was held in custody on state criminal charges. Both petitioner and Evans appealed their convictions to the Court of Appeals for the Eighth Circuit. That court set aside Evans' conviction on the ground that his oral confessions to the postal inspector should not have been received in evidence against him. However, the court, relying upon *Delli Paoli*, affirmed petitioner's conviction because the trial judge instructed the jury that although Evans' confession was competent evidence against Evans it was inadmissible hearsay against petitioner and therefore had to be disregarded in determining petitioner's guilt or innocence.[2] We granted certiorari to reconsider *Delli Paoli*. The Solicitor General has since submitted a memorandum stating that "in the light of the record in this particular case and in the interests of justice, the judgment below should be reversed and the cause remanded for a new trial." The Solicitor General states that this disposition is urged in part because "here it has been determined that the confession was wrongly admitted against [Evans] and his conviction has been reversed, leading to a new trial at which he was acquitted. To argue, in this situation, that [petitioner's] conviction should nevertheless stand may be to place too great a strain upon the [*Delli Paoli*] rule—at least, where, as here, the other evidence against [petitioner] is not strong." We have concluded, however, that *Delli Paoli* should be overruled. We hold that, because of the substantial risk that the jury, despite instructions to the contrary, looked to the incriminating extrajudicial statements in determining petitioner's guilt, admission of Evans' confession in this joint trial violated petitioner's right of cross-examination secured by the Confrontation Clause of the Sixth Amendment. We therefore overrule *Delli Paoli* and reverse.

2. At the close of the Government's direct case, the trial judge cautioned the jury that Evans' admission implicating petitioner "if used, can only be used against the defendant Evans. It is hearsay insofar as the defendant George William Bruton is concerned, and you are not to consider it in any respect to the defendant Bruton, because insofar as he is concerned it is hearsay."

The instructions to the jury included the following:

> "A confession made outside of court by one defendant may not be considered as evidence against the other defendant, who was not present and in no way a party to the confession. Therefore, if you find that a confession was in fact voluntarily and intentionally made by the defendant Evans, you should consider it as evidence in the case against Evans, but you must not consider it, and should disregard it, in considering the evidence in the case against the defendant Bruton....
>
> "It is your duty to give separate, personal consideration to the cause of each individual defendant. When you do so, you should analyze what the evidence shows with respect to that individual, leaving out of consideration entirely any evidence admitted solely against some other defendant. Each defendant is entitled to have his case determined from his own acts and statements and the other evidence in the case which may be applicable to him."

The basic premise of *Delli Paoli* was that it is "reasonably possible for the jury to follow" sufficiently clear instructions to disregard the confessor's extrajudicial statement that his codefendant participated with him in committing the crime. If it were true that the jury disregarded the reference to the codefendant, no question would arise under the Confrontation Clause, because by hypothesis the case is treated as if the confessor made no statement inculpating the nonconfessor. . . .

Here Evans' oral confessions were in fact testified to, and were therefore actually in evidence. That testimony was legitimate evidence against Evans and to that extent was properly before the jury during its deliberations. Even greater, then, was the likelihood that the jury would believe Evans made the statements and that they were true—not just the self-incriminating portions but those implicating petitioner as well. Plainly, the introduction of Evans' confession added substantial, perhaps even critical, weight to the Government's case in a form not subject to cross-examination, since Evans did not take the stand. Petitioner thus was denied his constitutional right of confrontation.

Delli Paoli assumed that this encroachment on the right to confrontation could be avoided by the instruction to the jury to disregard the inadmissible hearsay evidence.[3] But . . . that assumption has since been effectively repudiated. True, the repudiation was not in the context of the admission of a confession inculpating a codefendant but in the context of a New York rule which submitted to the jury the question of the voluntariness of the confession itself. Jackson v. Denno, 378 U.S. 368 (1964). Nonetheless the message of *Jackson* for *Delli Paoli* was clear. We there held that a defendant is constitutionally entitled at least to have the trial judge first determine whether a confession was made voluntarily before submitting it to the jury for an assessment of its credibility. More specifically, we expressly rejected the proposition that a jury, when determining the confessor's guilt, could be relied on to ignore his confession of guilt should it find the confession involuntary. Significantly, we supported that conclusion in part by reliance upon the dissenting opinion of Mr. Justice Frankfurter for the four Justices who dissented in *Delli Paoli. Id.* at 388 n.15.

That dissent challenged the basic premise of *Delli Paoli* that a properly instructed jury would ignore the confessor's inculpation of the nonconfessor in determining the latter's guilt. "The fact of the matter is that too often such admonition against misuse is intrinsically ineffective in that the effect of such a nonadmissible declaration cannot be wiped from the brains of the jurors. The admonition therefore becomes a futile

3. We emphasize that the hearsay statement inculpating petitioner was clearly inadmissible against him under traditional rules of evidence. . . . There is not before us, therefore, any recognized exception to the hearsay rule insofar as petitioner is concerned and we intimate no view whatever that such exceptions necessarily raise questions under the Confrontation Clause.

collocation of words and fails of its purpose as a legal protection to defendants against whom such a declaration should not tell." The dissent went on to say, as quoted in the cited note in *Jackson*, "The government should not have the windfall of having the jury be influenced by evidence against a defendant which, as a matter of law, they should not consider but which they cannot put out of their minds." To the same effect, and also cited in the *Jackson* note, is the statement of Mr. Justice Jackson in his concurring opinion in Krulewitch v. United States, 336 U.S. 440, 453 (1949): "The naive assumption that prejudicial effects can be overcome by instructions to the jury . . . all practicing lawyers know to be unmitigated fiction. . . ."

The significance of *Jackson* for *Delli Paoli* was suggested by Chief Justice Traynor in People v. Aranda, 63 Cal. 2d 518, 528–29 (1965):

> "Although *Jackson* was directly concerned with obviating any risk that a jury might rely on an unconstitutionally obtained confession in determining the defendant's guilt, its logic extends to obviating the risks that the jury may rely on any inadmissible statements. If it is a denial of due process to rely on a jury's presumed ability to disregard an involuntary confession, it may also be a denial of due process to rely on a jury's presumed ability to disregard a codefendant's confession implicating another defendant when it is determining that defendant's guilt or innocence.
>
> "Indeed, the latter task may be an even more difficult one for the jury to perform than the former. Under the New York procedure, which *Jackson* held violated due process, the jury was only required to disregard a confession it found to be involuntary. If it made such a finding, then the confession was presumably out of the case. In joint trials, however, when the admissible confession of one defendant inculpates another defendant, the confession is never deleted from the case and the jury is expected to perform the overwhelming task of considering it in determining the guilt or innocence of the declarant and then of ignoring it in determining the guilt or innocence of any codefendants of the declarant. A jury cannot 'segregate evidence into separate intellectual boxes.' . . . It cannot determine that a confession is true insofar as it admits that A has committed criminal acts with B and at the same time effectively ignore the inevitable conclusion that B has committed those same criminal acts with A."

. . . [A] reason cited in defense of *Delli Paoli* is the justification for joint trials in general, the argument being that the benefits of joint proceedings should not have to be sacrificed by requiring separate trials in order to use the confession against the declarant. Joint trials do conserve state funds, diminish inconvenience to witnesses and public authorities, and avoid delays in bringing those accused of crime to trial. But the answer to this argument was cogently stated by Judge Lehman of the New York Court of Appeals, dissenting in People v. Fisher, 249 N.Y. 419, 432 (1928): "We . . . secure greater speed, economy and convenience in the administration of the law at the price of fundamental principles of constitutional liberty. That price is too high."

. . . [T]he reason advanced by the majority in *Delli Paoli* was to tie the result to maintenance of the jury system. "Unless we proceed on the basis that the jury will follow the court's instructions where those instructions are clear and the circumstances are such that the jury can reasonably be expected to follow them, the jury system makes little sense." We agree that there are many circumstances in which this reliance is justified. Not every admission of inadmissible hearsay or other evidence can be considered to be reversible error unavoidable through limiting instructions; instances occur in almost every trial where inadmissible evidence creeps in, usually inadvertently. "A defendant is entitled to a fair trial but not a perfect one." Lutwak v. United States, 344 U.S. 604, 619 (1953). It is not unreasonable to conclude that in many such cases the jury can and will follow the trial judge's instructions to disregard such information. Nevertheless, as was recognized in *Jackson v. Denno, supra,* there are some contexts in which the risk that the jury will not, or cannot, follow instructions is so great, and the consequences of failure so vital to the defendant, that the practical and human limitations of the jury system cannot be ignored. Such a context is presented here, where the powerfully incriminating extrajudicial statements of a codefendant, who stands accused side-by-side with the defendant, are deliberately spread before the jury in a joint trial. Not only are the incriminations devastating to the defendant but their credibility is inevitably suspect, a fact recognized when accomplices do take the stand and the jury is instructed to weigh their testimony carefully given the recognized motivation to shift blame onto others. The unreliability of such evidence is intolerably compounded when the alleged accomplice, as here, does not testify and cannot be tested by cross-examination. It was against such threats to a fair trial that the Confrontation Clause was directed.

We, of course, acknowledge the impossibility of determining whether in fact the jury did or did not ignore Evans' statement inculpating petitioner in determining petitioner's guilt. But that was also true in the analogous situation in *Jackson* v. *Denno,* and was not regarded as militating against striking down the New York procedure there involved. It was enough that that procedure posed "substantial threats to a defendant's constitutional rights to have an involuntary confession entirely disregarded and to have the coercion issue fairly and reliably determined. These hazards we cannot ignore." Here the introduction of Evans' confession posed a substantial threat to petitioner's right to confront the witnesses against him, and this is a hazard we cannot ignore. Despite the concededly clear instructions to the jury to disregard Evans' inadmissible hearsay evidence inculpating petitioner, in the context of a joint trial we cannot accept limiting instructions as an adequate substitute for petitioner's constitutional right of cross-examination. The effect is the same as if there had been no instruction at all.

Reversed.

■ MR. JUSTICE BLACK concurs in the result for the reasons stated in the dissent in Delli Paoli v. United States, 352 U.S. 232, 246 (1957).

■ MR. JUSTICE MARSHALL took no part in the consideration or decision of this case.

■ MR. JUSTICE STEWART, concurring. . . .

■ MR. JUSTICE WHITE, dissenting. Whether or not Evans' confession was inadmissible against him, nothing in that confession which was relevant and material to Bruton's case was admissible against Bruton. As to him it was inadmissible hearsay, a presumptively unreliable out-of-court statement of a nonparty who was not a witness subject to cross-examination. Admitting Evans' confession against Bruton would require a new trial unless the error was harmless.

The trial judge in this case had no different view. He admitted Evans' confession only against Evans, not against Bruton, and carefully instructed the jury to disregard it in determining Bruton's guilt or innocence.* Contrary to its ruling just a decade ago in Delli Paoli v. United States, 352 U.S. 232 (1957), the Court now holds this instruction insufficient and reverses Bruton's conviction. It would apparently also reverse every other case where a court admits a codefendant's confession implicating a defendant, regardless of cautionary instructions and regardless of the circumstances. I dissent from this excessively rigid rule. There is nothing in this record to suggest that the jury did not follow the trial judge's instructions. There has been no new learning since *Delli Paoli* indicating that juries are less reliable than they were considered in that case to be. There is nothing in the prior decisions of this Court which supports this new constitutional rule.

The Court concedes that there are many instances in which reliance on limiting instructions is justified . . . The Court asserts, however, that the hazards to the defendant of permitting the jury to hear a codefendant's confession implicating him are so severe that we must assume the jury's inability to heed a limiting instruction. This was the holding of the Court with respect to a confession of the defendant himself in Jackson v. Denno, 378 U.S. 368 (1964). There are good reasons, however, for distinguishing the codefendant's confession from that of the defendant himself

* As the Court observes, "if . . . the jury disregarded the reference to the codefendant, no question would arise under the Confrontation Clause. . . ." Because in my view juries can reasonably be relied upon to disregard the codefendant's references to the defendant, there is no need to explore the special considerations involved in the Confrontation Clause.

and for trusting in the jury's ability to disregard the former when instructed to do so.

First, the defendant's own confession is probably the most probative and damaging evidence that can be admitted against him. Though itself an out-of-court statement, it is admitted as reliable evidence because it is an admission of guilt by the defendant and constitutes direct evidence of the facts to which it relates. Even the testimony of an eyewitness may be less reliable than the defendant's own confession. An observer may not correctly perceive, understand, or remember the acts of another, but the admissions of a defendant come from the actor himself, the most knowledgeable and unimpeachable source of information about his past conduct. Certainly, confessions have profound impact on the jury, so much so that we may justifiably doubt its ability to put them out of mind even if told to do so. This was the conclusion of the Court in *Jackson*, and I continue to believe that case to be sound law.

Second, it must be remembered that a coerced confession is not excluded because it is thought to be unreliable. Regardless of how true it may be, it is excluded because specific provisions of the Constitution demand it, whatever the consequences for the criminal trial. In *Jackson* itself it was stated that "it is now axiomatic that a defendant in a criminal case is deprived of due process of law if his conviction is founded, in whole or in part, upon an involuntary confession, without regard for the truth or falsity of the confession. . . ." . . .

The situation in this case is very different. Here we deal with a codefendant's confession which is admitted only against the codefendant and with a firm instruction to the jury to disregard it in determining the defendant's guilt or innocence. That confession cannot compare with the defendant's own confession in evidentiary value. As to the defendant, the confession of the codefendant is wholly inadmissible. It is hearsay, subject to all the dangers of inaccuracy which characterize hearsay generally. Furthermore, the codefendant is no more than an eyewitness, the accuracy of whose testimony about the defendant's conduct is open to more doubt than would be the defendant's own account of his actions. More than this, however, the statements of a codefendant have traditionally been viewed with special suspicion. Due to his strong motivation to implicate the defendant and to exonerate himself, a codefendant's statements about what the defendant said or did are less credible than ordinary hearsay evidence. Whereas the defendant's own confession possesses greater reliability and evidentiary value than ordinary hearsay, the codefendant's confession implicating the defendant is intrinsically much less reliable.

The defendant's own confession may not be used against him if coerced, not because it is untrue but to protect other constitutional values. The jury may have great difficulty understanding such a rule and following an instruction to disregard the confession. In contrast, the codefendant's admissions cannot enter into the determination of the defendant's guilt or innocence because they are unreliable. This the jury can be told and can understand. Just as the Court believes that juries can reasonably be expected to disregard ordinary hearsay or other inadmissible evidence when instructed to do so, I believe juries will disregard the portions of a codefendant's confession implicating the defendant when so instructed. Indeed, if we must pick and choose between hearsay as to which limiting instructions will be deemed effective and hearsay the admission of which cannot be cured by instructions, codefendants' admissions belong in the former category rather than the latter, for they are not only hearsay but hearsay which is doubly suspect. . . .

The rule which the Court announces today will severely limit the circumstances in which defendants may be tried together for a crime which they are both charged with committing. Unquestionably, joint trials are more economical and minimize the burden on witnesses, prosecutors, and courts. They also avoid delays in bringing those accused of crime to trial. This much the Court concedes. . . .

In view of the practical difficulties of separate trials and their potential unfairness, I am disappointed that the Court has not spelled out how the federal courts might conduct their business consistent with today's opinion. I would suppose that it will be necessary to exclude all extrajudicial confessions unless all portions of them which implicate defendants other than the declarant are effectively deleted. Effective deletion will probably require not only omission of all direct and indirect inculpations of codefendants but also of any statement that could be employed against those defendants once their identity is otherwise established. Of course, the deletion must not be such that it will distort the statements to the substantial prejudice of either the declarant or the Government. If deletion is not feasible, then the Government will have to choose either not to use the confession at all or to try the defendants separately. To save time, money, and effort, the Government might best seek a ruling at the earliest possible stage of the trial proceedings as to whether the confession is admissible once offending portions are deleted. . . . Oral statements, such as that involved in the present case, will present special problems, for there is a risk that the witness in testifying will inadvertently exceed permissible limits. . . .

. . . [T]he reversal of *Delli Paoli* unnecessarily burdens the already difficult task of conducting criminal trials, and therefore I dissent in this case.

MR. JUSTICE HARLAN joins this opinion without abandoning his original disagreement with Jackson v. Denno, 378 U.S. 368, 427 (1964), expressed in his dissenting opinion in that case.

Problem 8.8
"Dog O' War"

Witness Links Attorneys to Prison Gang Testimony in Dog–Mauling Trial

Jaxon Van Derbeken

SAN FRANCISCO CHRONICLE, Feb. 22, 2002, at A21

The two lawyers on trial in the dog-mauling death of Diane Whipple were "associates" of the Aryan Brotherhood prison gang, . . . a state prison investigator testified yesterday.

Prosecutors called Devan Hawkes, a special agent with the state Department of Corrections who investigates prison gangs, to demonstrate the link between the white supremacist Aryan Brotherhood, defendants Marjorie Knoller and Robert Noel and the dogs that killed Whipple on Jan. 26, 2001.

Convincing the jury of that link would help prosecutors in their efforts to convict . . . Knoller of second-degree murder and both her and Noel . . . of involuntary manslaughter. Prosecutors need to show the husband-and-wife attorneys knew the two dogs they were keeping in their Pacific Heights apartment were dangerous to make their case.

"It is my opinion that Mr. Noel and Ms. Knoller were actively involved in raising, breeding and training dogs with these members of the Aryan Brotherhood," Hawkes said.

He said Noel and Knoller . . . had helped the inmates by making contacts to arrange the movement of the dogs around the state. . . .

As for the dogs, it was plain that the Pelican Bay inmates and Knoller and Noel knew they were raising dangerous animals, Hawkes said. . . .

In one letter to the inmates, Noel said Knoller liked to refer to the scheme to raise aggressive Presa Canarios as the "Dog O' War" operation. . . .

Noel and Knoller were tried jointly before a single jury, and Noel did not testify. If Knoller cited *Bruton* in objecting to admission against Noel of Noel's statement about the "Dog O' War" operation, on what theory might the trial judge have admitted the statement?

CRUZ V. NEW YORK

481 U.S. 186 (1987).

■ SCALIA, J., delivered the opinion of the Court, in which BRENNAN, MARSHALL, BLACKMUN, and STEVENS, JJ., joined. WHITE, J., filed a dissenting opinion, in which REHNQUIST, C.J., and POWELL and O'CONNOR, JJ., joined.

■ JUSTICE SCALIA delivered the opinion of the Court. In Bruton v. United States, 391 U.S. 123 (1968), we held that a defendant is deprived of his rights under the Confrontation Clause when his codefendant's incriminating confession is introduced at their joint trial, even if the jury is instructed to consider that confession only against the codefendant. In Parker v. Randolph, 442 U.S. 62 (1979), we considered, but were unable authoritatively to resolve, the question whether *Bruton* applies where the defendant's own confession, corroborating that of his codefendant, is introduced against him. We resolve that question today.

I

Jerry Cruz was murdered on March 15, 1982. That is not the murder for which petitioner was tried and convicted, but the investigation of the one led to the solving of the other. On the day following Jerry Cruz's murder, and on several later occasions, the police talked to Jerry's brother Norberto about the killing. On April 27, Norberto for the first time informed the police of a November 29, 1981, visit by petitioner Eulogio Cruz and his brother Benjamin to the apartment Norberto shared with Jerry. (Eulogio and Benjamin Cruz were longtime friends of Norberto and Jerry Cruz, but the two sets of brothers were not related.) Norberto said that at the time of the visit Eulogio was nervous and was wearing a bloodstained bandage around his arm. According to Norberto, Eulogio confided that he and Benjamin had gone to a Bronx gas station the night before, intending to rob it; that Eulogio and the attendant had struggled; and that, after the attendant had grabbed a gun from behind a counter and shot Eulogio in the arm, Benjamin had killed him. Norberto claimed that Benjamin gave a similar account of the incident.

On May 3, 1982, the police questioned Benjamin about the murder of Jerry Cruz. He strongly denied any connection with that homicide and became frustrated when the police seemed unwilling to believe him. Suddenly, to prove that he would tell the truth about killing someone if he were guilty, Benjamin spontaneously confessed to the murder of the gas station attendant. Later that evening, he gave a detailed videotaped confession to an Assistant District Attorney, in which he admitted that he, Eulogio, Jerry Cruz, and a fourth man had robbed the gas station, and that he had killed the attendant after the attendant shot Eulogio. Benjamin and Eulogio were indicted for felony murder of the station attendant.

The brothers were tried jointly, over Eulogio's objection. Likewise over Eulogio's objection, the trial judge allowed the prosecutor to introduce Benjamin's videotaped confession, warning the jury that the confession was not to be used against Eulogio. The government also called Norberto, who testified about his November 29 conversation with Eulogio and Benjamin.... At the trial's end, ... Norberto's testimony stood as the only evidence admissible against Eulogio that directly linked him to the crime. Eulogio's attorney tried to persuade the jury that Norberto had suspected Eulogio and Benjamin of killing his brother Jerry and had fabricated his testimony to gain revenge. Unconvinced, the jury convicted both defendants.

The New York Court of Appeals affirmed Eulogio's conviction, 66 N.Y.2d 61 (1985), adopting the reasoning of the plurality opinion in *Parker* that *Bruton* did not require the codefendant's confession to be excluded because Eulogio had himself confessed [in his conversation with Norberto Cruz] and his confession "interlocked" with Benjamin's. We granted certiorari.

II

. . . *Parker* . . . resembled *Bruton* in all major respects save one: Each of the jointly tried defendants had himself confessed, his own confession was introduced against him, and his confession recited essentially the same facts as those of his nontestifying codefendants. The plurality of four Justices found no Sixth Amendment violation. It understood *Bruton* to hold that the Confrontation Clause is violated only when introduction of a codefendant's confession is "devastating" to the defendant's case. When the defendant has himself confessed, the plurality reasoned, "[his] case has already been devastated," 442 U.S. at 75 n.7, so that the codefendant's confession "will seldom, if ever, be of the 'devastating' character referred to in *Bruton*," and impeaching that confession on cross-examination "would likely yield small advantage," *id.* at 73. Thus, the plurality would have held *Bruton* inapplicable to cases involving interlocking confessions. The four remaining Justices participating in the case disagreed, subscribing to the view expressed by JUSTICE BLACKMUN that introduction of the defendant's own interlocking confession might, in some cases, render the violation of the Confrontation Clause harmless, but could not cause introduction of the nontestifying codefendant's confession not to constitute a violation. . . . We face again today the issue on which the Court was evenly divided in *Parker*.

We adopt the approach espoused by JUSTICE BLACKMUN. While "devastating" practical effect was one of the factors that *Bruton* considered in assessing whether the Confrontation Clause might sometimes require departure from the general rule that jury instructions suffice to exclude improper testimony, it did not suggest that the existence of such an effect should be assessed on a case-by-case basis. Rather, that factor was one of the justifications for excepting from the general rule the entire category of codefendant confessions that implicate the defendant in the crime. It is impossible to imagine why there should be excluded from that category, as generally not "devastating," codefendant confessions that "interlock" with the defendant's own confession. "The infinite variability of inculpatory statements (whether made by defendants or codefendants), and of their likely effect on juries, makes [the assumption that an interlocking confession will preclude devastation] untenable." *Parker,* 442 U.S. at 84 (STEVENS, J., dissenting). In this case, for example, the precise content and even the existence of petitioner's own confession were open to question, since they depended upon acceptance of Norberto's testimony, whereas the incriminating confession of codefendant Benjamin was on videotape.

In fact, it seems to us that "interlocking" bears a positively inverse [*sic*] relationship to devastation. A codefendant's confession will be relatively harmless if the incriminating story it tells is different from that which the defendant himself is alleged to have told, but enormously damaging if it confirms, in all essential respects, the defendant's alleged confession. It might be otherwise if the defendant were *standing by* his confession, in which case it could be said that the codefendant's confession does no more than support the defendant's very own case. But in the real world of criminal litigation, the defendant is seeking to *avoid* his confession—on the ground that it was not accurately reported, or that it was not really true when made. In the present case, for example, petitioner sought to establish that Norberto had a motive for falsely reporting a confession that never in fact occurred. In such circumstances a codefendant's confession that corroborates the defendant's confession significantly harms the defendant's case, whereas one that is positively incompatible gives credence to the defendant's assertion that his own alleged confession was nonexistent or false. . . .

The dissent makes no effort to respond to these points, urging instead a rejection of our "remorseless logic" in favor of "common sense and judgment." But those qualities, even in their most remorseless form, are not separable. It seems to us illogical, and therefore contrary to common sense and good judgment, to believe that codefendant confessions are less likely to be taken into account by the jury the more they are corroborated by the defendant's own admissions; or that they are less likely to be harmful when they confirm the validity of the defendant's alleged confession. Far from carrying *Bruton* "to the outer limits of its logic," our holding here does no more than reaffirm its central proposition. This case is indistinguishable from *Bruton* with respect to those factors the Court has deemed relevant in this area: the likelihood that the instruction [to consider the confession only against its maker] will be disregarded; the probability that such disregard will have a devastating effect; and the determinability of these facts in advance of trial.

We hold that, where a nontestifying codefendant's confession incriminating the defendant is not directly admissible against the defendant, the Confrontation Clause bars its admission at their joint trial, even if the jury is instructed not to consider it against the defendant, and even if the defendant's own confession is admitted against him. Of course, the defendant's confession may be considered . . . on appeal in assessing whether any Confrontation Clause violation was harmless.

. . . [W]e reverse and remand for further proceedings not inconsistent with this opinion.

So ordered.

■ Justice White, with whom The Chief Justice, Justice Powell, and Justice O'Connor join, dissenting. . . . *Bruton* held that where the defendant has not himself confessed, there is too great a chance that the jury would rely on the codefendant's confession. But here, Cruz had admitted the crime and this fact was before the jury. I disagree with the Court's proposition that in every interlocking confession case, the jury, with the defendant's confession properly before it, would be tempted to disobey its instructions and fail to understand that presumptively unreliable evidence must not be used against the defendant. Nor is it remotely possible that in every case the admission of an interlocking confession by a codefendant will have the devastating effect referred to in *Bruton*.[2]

The Court finds it "impossible to imagine" why the defendant's interlocking confession could ever make the *Bruton* rule inapplicable; any such conclusion would be "illogical." But many Court of Appeals Judges ... are not so unimaginative; they see nothing illogical, in interlocking confession cases, in adhering to the traditional presumption that juries follow their instructions. Of course, the decision here is not a matter of imagination or logic, but one of common sense and judgment in interpreting the Constitution.... Even where remorseless logic may seem to justify the extension of what otherwise might be a sound constitutional rule, common sense should prevail. Otherwise, especially in applying prophylactic rules, we may trivialize the principles of prior cases by applying them to situations that in general do not really pose the dangers that the rules were intended to obviate....

That the error the Court finds may be harmless and the conviction saved will not comfort prosecutors and judges. I doubt that the former will seek joint trials in interlocking confession cases, and if that occurs, the judge is not likely to commit error by admitting the codefendant's confession....

... [A] codefendant's interlocking confession [may] be admissible against the defendant, in which event there would not be the Confrontation Clause issue *Bruton* identified.[4] ... [A]nd I gather that the Court's

2. The Court is of the view that " 'interlocking' bears a positively inverse relationship to devastation." In so reasoning, the Court gives no weight whatsoever to the devastating effect that the defendant's own confession is likely to have upon his case. The majority's excuse for ignoring this consideration apparently is that the damaging effect of the defendant's confession may vary somewhat from case to case. But the *Bruton* rule is prophylactic in nature, and, in view of the fact that it imposes significant burdens on the prosecution, the rule should be confined to those cases where the jury's ignoring of limiting instructions is most likely to change the verdict, which is to say, those cases where there is the greatest risk that jury misconduct will lead to the conviction of an innocent defendant. It is self-evident that, as a class, cases where the defendant has not confessed fit that description far better than cases where the defendant has confessed.

4. As JUSTICE BLACKMUN commented in dissent in Lee v. Illinois, 476 U.S. 530 (1986):

> "In Bruton v. United States, 391 U.S. 123 (1968), the inadmissibility of the codefendant's out-of-court statements against the defendant was not contested.... The *Bruton* rule thus necessarily applies only to situations in which the out-of-court statements are constitutionally inadmissible against the defendant." 476 U.S. at 552 n.5.

disposition does not deny the state courts, on remand, the opportunity to deal with the admissibility of that confession against Cruz.

GRAY V. MARYLAND

523 U.S. 185 (1998).

■ BREYER, J., delivered the opinion of the Court, in which STEVENS, O'CONNOR, SOUTER, and GINSBURG, JJ., joined. SCALIA, J., filed a dissenting opinion, in which REHNQUIST, C.J., and KENNEDY and THOMAS, JJ., joined.

■ JUSTICE BREYER delivered the opinion of the Court.... The case before us differs from *Bruton* in that the prosecution here redacted the codefendant's confession by substituting for the defendant's name in the confession a blank space or the word "deleted." We must decide whether these substitutions make a significant legal difference. We hold that they do not and that *Bruton*'s protective rule applies.

I

In 1993, Stacy Williams died after a severe beating. Anthony Bell gave a confession, to the Baltimore City police, in which he said that he (Bell), Kevin Gray, and Jacquin "Tank" Vanlandingham had participated in the beating that resulted in Williams' death. Vanlandingham later died. A Maryland grand jury indicted Bell and Gray for murder. The State of Maryland tried them jointly.

The trial judge, after denying Gray's motion for a separate trial, permitted the State to introduce Bell's confession into evidence at trial. But the judge ordered the confession redacted. Consequently, the police detective who read the confession into evidence said the word "deleted" or "deletion" whenever Gray's name or Vanlandingham's name appeared. Immediately after the police detective read the redacted confession to the jury, the prosecutor asked, "after [Bell] gave you that information, you subsequently were able to arrest Mr. Kevin Gray; is that correct?" The officer responded, "That's correct." The State also introduced into evidence a written copy of the confession with those two names omitted, leaving in their place blank white spaces separated by commas. The State produced other witnesses, who said that six persons (including Bell, Gray, and Vanlandingham) participated in the beating. Gray testified and denied his participation. Bell did not testify.

When instructing the jury, the trial judge specified that the confession was evidence only against Bell; the instructions said that the jury should not use the confession as evidence against Gray. The jury convicted both Bell and Gray. Gray appealed....

II

... Richardson v. Marsh, 481 U.S. 200 (1987), ... involved a joint murder trial of Marsh and Williams. The State had redacted the confession of one defendant, Williams, so as to "omit all reference" to his codefendant, Marsh—"indeed, to omit all indication that anyone other than ... Williams" and a third person had "participated in the crime." The trial court also instructed the jury not to consider the confession against Marsh. As redacted, the confession indicated that Williams and the third person had discussed the murder in the front seat of a car while they traveled to the victim's house. The redacted confession contained no indication that Marsh—or any other person—was in the car. Later in the trial, however, Marsh testified that she was in the back seat of the car. For that reason, in context, the confession still could have helped convince the jury that Marsh knew about the murder in advance and therefore had participated knowingly in the crime.

The Court held that this redacted confession fell outside *Bruton*'s scope and was admissible (with appropriate limiting instructions) at the joint trial. The Court distinguished Evans' confession in *Bruton* as a confession that was "incriminating on its face," and which had "expressly implicated" *Bruton*. By contrast, Williams' confession amounted to "evidence requiring linkage" in that it "became" incriminating in respect to Marsh "only when linked with evidence introduced later at trial." The Court held

> "that the Confrontation Clause is not violated by the admission of a nontestifying codefendant's confession with a proper limiting instruction when, as here, the confession is redacted to eliminate not only the defendant's name, but any reference to his or her existence."

The Court added: "We express no opinion on the admissibility of a confession in which the defendant's name has been replaced with a symbol or neutral pronoun."

III

Originally, the codefendant's confession in the case before us, like that in *Bruton*, referred to, and directly implicated another defendant. The State, however, redacted that confession by removing the nonconfessing defendant's name. Nonetheless, unlike *Richardson*'s redacted confession, this confession refers directly to the "existence" of the nonconfessing defendant. The State has simply replaced the nonconfessing defendant's name with a kind of symbol, namely the word "deleted" or a blank space set off by commas. The redacted confession, for example, responded to the question "Who was in the group that beat Stacey," with the phrase, "Me, ________, ________ and a few other guys." And when the police witness read the confession in court, he said the word "deleted" or "deletion" where the blank spaces appear. We therefore must decide a question that *Richardson* left open, namely whether redaction that replaces a defendant's name with an obvious indication of deletion, such as a blank space, the word "deleted," or a similar symbol, still falls within *Bruton*'s protective rule. We hold that it does.

Bruton, as interpreted by *Richardson*, holds that certain "powerfully incriminating extrajudicial statements of a codefendant"—those naming another defendant—considered as a class, are so prejudicial that limiting instructions cannot work. *Richardson*, 481 U.S. at 207; *Bruton*, 391 U.S. at 135. Unless the prosecutor wishes to hold separate trials or to use separate juries or to abandon use of the confession, he must redact the confession to reduce significantly or to eliminate the special prejudice that the *Bruton* Court found. Redactions that simply replace a name with an obvious blank space or a word such as "deleted" or a symbol or other similarly obvious indications of alteration, however, leave statements that, considered as a class, so closely resemble *Bruton*'s unredacted statements that, in our view, the law must require the same result.

For one thing, a jury will often react similarly to an unredacted confession and a confession redacted in this way, for the jury will often realize that the confession refers specifically to the defendant. This is true even when the State does not blatantly link the defendant to the deleted name, as it did in this case by asking whether Gray was arrested on the basis of information in Bell's confession as soon as the officer had finished reading the redacted statement. Consider a simplified but typical example, a confession that reads "I, Bob Smith, along with Sam Jones, robbed the bank." To replace the words "Sam Jones" with an obvious blank will not likely fool anyone. A juror somewhat familiar with criminal law would know immediately that the blank, in the phrase "I, Bob Smith, along with   , robbed the bank," refers to defendant Jones. A juror who does not know the law and who therefore wonders to whom the blank might refer need only lift his eyes to Jones, sitting at counsel table, to find what will seem the obvious answer, at least if the juror hears the judge's instruction not to consider the confession as evidence against Jones, for that instruction will provide an obvious reason for the blank. A more sophisticated juror, wondering if the blank refers to someone else, might also wonder how, if it did, the prosecutor could argue the confession is reliable, for the prosecutor, after all, has been arguing that Jones, not someone else, helped Smith commit the crime.

For another thing, the obvious deletion may well call the jurors' attention specially to the removed name. By encouraging the jury to speculate about the reference, the redaction may overemphasize the importance of the confession's accusation—once the jurors work out the reference. That is why Judge Learned Hand, many years ago, wrote in a similar instance that blacking out the name of a codefendant not only "would have been futile.... There could not have been the slightest doubt as to whose names had been blacked out," but "even if there had been, that blacking out itself would have not only laid the doubt, but underscored the answer.'' United States v. Delli Paoli, 229 F.2d 319, 321 (2d Cir. 1956). *See also* Malinski v. New York, 324 U.S. 401, 430 (1945) (Rutledge, J., dissenting) (describing substitution of names in confession with ''X'' or ''Y'' and other similar redactions as ''devices . . . so obvious as perhaps to emphasize the identity of those they purported to conceal'').

Finally, *Bruton*'s protected statements and statements redacted to leave a blank or some other similarly obvious alteration function the same way grammatically. They are directly accusatory. Evans' statement in *Bruton* used a proper name to point explicitly to an accused defendant. . . . The blank space in an obviously redacted confession also points directly to the defendant. . . . By way of contrast, the factual statement at issue in *Richardson*—a statement about what others said in the front seat of a car—differs from directly accusatory evidence in this respect, for it does not point directly to a defendant at all.

We concede certain differences between *Bruton* and this case. A confession that uses a blank or the word ''delete'' (or, for that matter, a first name or a nickname) less obviously refers to the defendant than a confession that uses the defendant's full and proper name. Moreover, in some instances the person to whom the blank refers may not be clear: Although the follow-up question asked by the State in this case eliminated all doubt, the reference might not be transparent in other cases in which a confession, like the present confession, uses two (or more) blanks, even though only one other defendant appears at trial, and in which the trial indicates that there are more participants than the confession has named. Nonetheless, . . . we believe that, considered as a class, redactions that replace a proper name with an obvious blank, the word ''delete,'' a symbol, or similarly notify the jury that a name has been deleted are similar enough to *Bruton*'s unredacted confessions as to warrant the same legal results.

IV

. . . We concede that *Richardson* placed outside the scope of *Bruton*'s rule those statements that incriminate inferentially. We also concede that the jury must use inference to connect the statement in this redacted confession with the defendant. But inference pure and simple cannot make the critical difference, for if it did, then *Richardson* would also place outside *Bruton*'s scope confessions that use shortened first names, nicknames, descriptions as unique as the ''red-haired, bearded, one-eyed man-with-a-limp,'' and perhaps even full names of defendants who are always known by a nickname. This Court has assumed, however, that nicknames and specific descriptions fall inside, not outside, *Bruton*'s protection. *See* Harrington v. California, 395 U.S. 250 (1969) (assuming *Bruton* violation where confessions describe codefendant as the ''white guy" and gives a description of his age, height, weight, and hair color). . . .

That being so, *Richardson* must depend in significant part upon the kind of, not the simple fact of, inference. *Richardson*'s inferences involved statements that did not refer directly to the defendant [herself] and which became incriminating "only when linked with evidence introduced later at trial." The inferences at issue here involve statements that, despite redaction, obviously refer directly to someone, often obviously the defendant, and which involve inferences that a jury ordinarily could make immediately, even were the confession the very first item introduced at trial. Moreover, the redacted confession with the blank prominent on its face, in *Richardson*'s words, "facially incriminates" the codefendant. Like the confession in *Bruton* itself, the accusation that the redacted confession makes "is more vivid than inferential incrimination, and hence more difficult to thrust out of mind." *Richardson*, 481 U.S. at 208.

Nor are the policy reasons that *Richardson* provided in support of its conclusion applicable here. *Richardson* expressed concern lest application of *Bruton*'s rule apply where "redaction" of confessions, particularly "confessions incriminating by connection," would often "not [be] possible," thereby forcing prosecutors too often to abandon use either of the confession or of a joint trial. Additional redaction of a confession that uses a blank space, the word "delete," or a symbol, however, normally is possible. Consider as an example a portion of the confession before us: The witness who read the confession told the jury that the confession (among other things) said,

"*Question:* Who was in the group that beat Stacey?

"*Answer:* Me, deleted, deleted, and a few other guys."

Why could the witness not, instead, have said:

"*Question:* Who was in the group that beat Stacey?

"*Answer:* Me and a few other guys."

Richardson itself provides a similar example of this kind of redaction. The confession there at issue had been "redacted to omit all reference to respondent—indeed, to omit all indication that anyone other than Martin and Williams participated in the crime," and it did not indicate that it had been redacted. *But cf. post* (SCALIA, J., dissenting) (suggesting that the Court has "never before endorsed . . . the redaction of a statement by some means other than the deletion of certain words, with the fact of the deletion shown").

The *Richardson* Court also feared that the inclusion, within *Bruton*'s protective rule, of confessions that incriminated "by connection" too often would provoke mistrials, or would unnecessarily lead prosecutors to abandon the confession or joint trial, because neither the prosecutors nor the judge could easily predict, until after the introduction of all the evidence, whether or not *Bruton* had barred use of the confession. To include the use of blanks, the word "delete," symbols, or other indications of redaction, within *Bruton*'s protections, however, runs no such risk. Their use is easily identified prior to trial and does not depend, in any special way, upon the other evidence introduced in the case. We also note that several Circuits have interpreted *Bruton* similarly for many years, yet no one has told us of any significant practical difficulties arising out of their administration of that rule.

For these reasons, we hold that the confession here at issue, which substituted blanks and the word "delete" for the respondent's proper name, falls within the class of statements to which *Bruton*'s protections apply. . . .

■ JUSTICE SCALIA, with whom the CHIEF JUSTICE, JUSTICE KENNEDY, and JUSTICE THOMAS join, dissenting. In Richardson v. Marsh, 481 U.S. 200 (1987), we declined to extend the "narrow exception" of *Bruton v. United States* beyond confessions that facially incriminate a defendant. Today the Court "concedes that *Richardson* placed outside the scope of *Bruton's* rule those statements that incriminate inferentially," "concedes that the jury must use inference to connect the statement in this redacted confession with the defendant," but nonetheless extends *Bruton* to confessions that have been redacted to delete the defendant's name. Because I believe the line drawn in *Richardson* should not be changed, I respectfully dissent.

The almost invariable assumption of the law is that jurors follow their instructions. This rule "is a pragmatic one, rooted less in the absolute certitude that the presumption is true than in the belief that it represents a reasonable practical accommodation of the interests of the state and the defendant in the criminal justice process." *Richardson*, 481 U.S. at 211. . . . In *Bruton*, we recognized a "narrow exception" to this rule: "We held that a defendant is deprived of his Sixth Amendment right of confrontation when the facially incriminating confession of a nontestifying codefendant is introduced at their joint trial, even if the jury is instructed to consider the confession only against the codefendant." *Richardson*, 481 U.S. at 207.

We declined in *Richardson*, however, to extend *Bruton* to confessions that incriminate only by inference from other evidence. When incrimination is inferential, "it is a less valid generalization that the jury will not likely obey the instruction to disregard the evidence." 481 U.S. at 208. Today the Court struggles to decide whether a confession redacted to omit the defendant's name is incriminating on its face or by inference. . . . [T]he statement "Me, deleted, deleted, and a few other guys" does not facially incriminate anyone but the speaker. . . . [T]he person to whom "deleted" refers in "Me, deleted, deleted, and a few other guys" is not apparent from anything the jury knows independent of the evidence at trial. . . .

Of course the Court is correct that confessions redacted to omit the defendant's name are more likely to incriminate than confessions redacted to omit any reference to his existence. But it is also true—and more relevant here—that confessions redacted to omit the defendant's name are less likely to incriminate than confessions that expressly state it. The latter are "powerfully incriminating" as a class, *Bruton, supra,* at 124, n. 1, 135; the former are not so. Here, for instance, there were two names deleted, five or more participants in the crime, and only one other defendant on trial. The jury no doubt may "speculate about the reference" as it speculates when evidence connects a defendant to a confession that does not refer to his existence. The issue, however, is not whether the confession incriminated petitioner, but whether the incrimination is so "powerful" that we must depart from the normal presumption that the jury follows its instructions. I think it is not—and I am certain that drawing the line for departing from the ordinary rule at the facial identification of the defendant makes more sense than drawing it anywhere else. . . .

The Court minimizes the damage that it does by suggesting that "additional redaction of a confession that uses a blank space, the word 'delete,' or a symbol . . . normally is possible." In the present case, it asks, why could the police officer not have testified that Bell's answer was "Me and a few other guys"? The answer, it seems obvious to me, is because that is not what Bell said. Bell's answer was "Me, Tank, Kevin and a few other guys." Introducing the statement with full disclosure of deletions is one thing; introducing as the complete statement what was in fact only a part is something else. And of course even concealed deletions from the text will often not do the job that the Court demands. For inchoate offenses—conspiracy in particular—redaction to delete all reference to a confederate would often render the confession nonsensical. If the question was "Who agreed to beat Stacey?", and the answer was "Me and Kevin," we might redact the answer to "Me and [deleted]," or perhaps to "Me and somebody else," but surely not to just "Me"—for that would no longer be a confession to the conspiracy charge, but rather the foundation for an insanity defense. To my knowledge we have never before endorsed—and to my strong belief we ought not endorse—the redaction of a statement by some means other than the deletion of certain words, with the fact of the deletion shown.[1] The risk to the integrity of our system (not to mention the increase in its complexity) posed by the approval of such free-lance editing seems to me infinitely greater than the risk posed by the entirely honest reproduction that the Court disapproves.

. . . Here, petitioner moved for a severance on the ground that the admission of Bell's confession would be unfairly prejudicial. The trial court denied the motion, explaining that where a confession names two

1. The Court is mistaken to suggest that in *Richardson* we endorsed rewriting confessions as a proper method of redaction. There the parties agreed to the method of redaction, and we had no occasion to address the propriety of editing confessions without showing the nature of the editing.

others, and the evidence is that five or six others participated, redaction of petitioner's name would not leave the jury with the "unavoidable inference" that Bell implicated Gray.

I do not understand the Court to disagree that the redaction itself left unclear to whom the blank referred.[2] That being so, the rule set forth in *Richardson* applies, and the statement could constitutionally be admitted with limiting instruction. This remains, insofar as the Sixth Amendment is concerned, the most "reasonable practical accommodation of the interests of the state and the defendant in the criminal justice process." *Richardson*, 481 U.S. at 211....

Problem 8.9

"He, She, or They"

On November 29, 1988, a fire at a highway construction site in Kansas City killed six firefighters. Several years later the government charged Darlene Edwards, Bryan Sheppard, Richard Brown, and two others with setting the fire. Consider these facts:

> The government's evidence at trial included Darlene Edwards's 1995 tape-recorded statement. Edwards told investigators that sometime between 1:30 and 2:30 a.m. Bryan Sheppard came to her house and asked if she would take Bryan and Richard Brown to get gas because their car had run out. Leaving Frank Sheppard [Bryan's uncle] asleep, Edwards drove Bryan and Brown to the nearby Quik Trip where they filled a gas can. They told Edwards their car was

2. The Court does believe, however, that the answer to a "follow-up question"—"All right, now, officer, after he gave you that information, you subsequently were able to arrest Mr. Kevin Gray; is that correct?" ("That's correct")—"eliminated all doubt" as to the subject of the redaction. That is probably not so, and is certainly far from clear. Testimony that preceded the introduction of Bell's confession had already established that Gray had become a suspect in the case, and that a warrant had been issued for his arrest, before Bell confessed. Respondent contends that, given this trial background, and in its context, the prosecutor's question did not imply any connection between Bell's confession and Gray's arrest, and was simply a means of making the transition from Bell's statement to the next piece of evidence, Gray's statement. That is at least arguable, and an appellate court is in a poor position to resolve such a contextual question de novo. That is why objections to trial testimony are supposed to be made at the time—so that trial judges, who hear the testimony in full, live context, can make such determinations in the first instance. But if the question did bring the redaction home to the defendant, surely that shows the impropriety of the question rather than of the redaction—and the question was not objected to.... Of course the Court's reliance upon this testimony belies its contention that name-redacted confessions are powerfully incriminating "as a class."

near the construction site, but when she neared the site her companions explained they planned to set a fire with the gasoline to divert security guards while they stole from the site. Edwards refused to go with them but agreed to drop them off. . . .

Prior to trial, the district court denied defendants' motions to sever the joint trial. . . . Instead, the court ordered Darlene Edwards's statement redacted to replace inculpatory references to her codefendants with neutral pronouns such as "we," "they," "someone," and "others." The court also approved the government's plan to instruct its witnesses not to mention the names of codefendants when testifying to each defendant's out-of-court admissions. During the trial, the court repeatedly instructed the jury to consider each admission only against the declarant. . . . No defendant testified at the trial. . . .

[Edwards's statement was] the only transcribed statement to authorities introduced at trial and therefore potentially the most incriminating of the many out-of-court declarations. [In its redacted form, it read as follows:]

> Frank and I had come home. . . . Someone come up and said they'd run out of gas. Wanted to know, could I take them down to get some gas, right? . . . Okay, and I took them down to Quik Trip. . . . The Quik Trip at 85th and 71 Highway. Yeah, they went around. They got some gas. They got in the car. They said the car was up the road. I said, what are you doing up there? They said, well, we're just doing 4–wheeling up in the hills, right? So, we get up there. Like, we're going to go over here and over there, and I said, what are you doing? Well, we're going to steal something. We're going, we're gonna take care of something. I said, well, look, I'm not staying here and playing if you are playing with gasoline. I'm not getting my . . . ass blown up . . . and I left them there, period! And then after I had gotten home and gotten in bed . . . is probably what must have woke Frank up, you know, when I'd gotten undressed and got back in bed.

United States v. Edwards, 159 F.3d 1117, 1126 (8th Cir. 1998), *cert. denied*, 528 U.S. 825 (1999). On appeal Edwards's codefendants argue that admission of her statement against Edwards violated their confrontation rights. How should the court rule?

C. COMPULSORY PROCESS

CHAMBERS v. MISSISSIPPI

410 U.S. 284 (1973).

■ POWELL, J., delivered the opinion of the Court, in which BURGER, C.J., and DOUGLAS, BRENNAN, STEWART, WHITE, MARSHALL, and BLACKMUN, JJ., joined. WHITE, J., filed a concurring opinion. REHNQUIST, J., filed a dissenting opinion.

■ MR. JUSTICE POWELL delivered the opinion of the Court. Petitioner, Leon Chambers, was tried by a jury in a Mississippi trial court and convicted of murdering a policeman. The jury assessed punishment at life imprisonment, and the Mississippi Supreme Court affirmed, one justice dissenting. Pending disposition of his application for certiorari to this Court, petitioner was granted bail by order of the Circuit Justice, dated February 1, 1972. Two weeks later, on the State's request for reconsideration, that order was reaffirmed. 405 U.S. 1205 (1972). Subsequently, the petition for certiorari was granted, 405 U.S. 987 (1972), to consider whether petitioner's trial was conducted in accord with principles of due process under the Fourteenth Amendment. We conclude that it was not.

I

The events that led to petitioner's prosecution for murder occurred in the small town of Woodville in southern Mississippi. On Saturday evening, June 14, 1969, two Woodville policemen, James Forman and Aaron "Sonny" Liberty, entered a local bar and pool hall to execute a warrant for the arrest of a youth named C.C. Jackson. Jackson resisted and a hostile crowd of some 50 or 60 persons gathered. The officers' first attempt to handcuff Jackson was frustrated when 20 or 25 men in the crowd intervened and wrestled him free. Forman then radioed for assistance and Liberty removed his riot gun, a 12–gauge sawed-off shotgun, from the car. Three deputy sheriffs arrived shortly thereafter and the officers again attempted to make their arrest. Once more, the officers were attacked by the onlookers, and during the commotion five or six pistol shots were fired. Forman was looking in a different direction when the shooting began, but immediately saw that Liberty had been shot several times in the back. Before Liberty died, he turned around and fired both barrels of his riot gun into an alley in the area from which the shots appeared to have come. The first shot was wild and high and scattered the crowd standing at the face of the alley. Liberty appeared, however, to take more deliberate aim before the second shot and hit one of the men in the crowd in the back of the head and neck as he ran down the alley. That man was Leon Chambers.

Officer Forman could not see from his vantage point who shot Liberty or whether Liberty's shots hit anyone. One of the deputy sheriffs testified at trial that he was standing several feet from Liberty and that he saw Chambers shoot him. Another deputy sheriff stated that, although he could not see whether Chambers had a gun in his hand, he did see Chambers "break his arm down" shortly before the shots were fired. The officers who saw Chambers fall testified that they thought he was dead, but they made no effort at that time either to examine him or to search for the murder weapon. Instead, they attended to Liberty, who was placed in the police car and taken to a hospital where he was declared dead on arrival. A subsequent autopsy showed that he had been hit with four bullets from a .22–caliber revolver.

Shortly after the shooting, three of Chambers' friends discovered that he was not yet dead. James Williams, Berkley Turner, and Gable McDonald loaded him into a car and transported him to the same hospital. Later that night, when the county sheriff discovered that Chambers was still alive, a guard was placed outside his room. Chambers was subsequently charged with Liberty's murder. He pleaded not guilty and has asserted his innocence throughout.

The story of Leon Chambers is intertwined with the story of another man, Gable McDonald. McDonald, a lifelong resident of Woodville, was in the crowd on the evening of Liberty's death. Sometime shortly after that day, he left his wife in Woodville and moved to Louisiana and found a job at a sugar mill. In November of that same year, he returned to Woodville when his wife informed him that an acquaintance of his, known as Reverend Stokes, wanted to see him. Stokes owned a gas station in Natchez, Mississippi, several miles north of Woodville, and upon his return McDonald went to see him. After talking to Stokes, McDonald agreed to make a statement to Chambers' attorneys, who maintained offices in Natchez. Two days later, he appeared at the attorneys' offices and gave a sworn confession that he shot Officer Liberty. He also stated that he had already told a friend of his, James Williams, that he shot Liberty. He said that he used his own pistol, a nine-shot .22–caliber revolver, which he had discarded shortly after the shooting. In response to questions from Chambers' attorneys, McDonald affirmed that his confession was voluntary and that no one had compelled him to come to them. Once the confession had been transcribed, signed, and witnessed, McDonald was turned over to the local police authorities and was placed in jail.

One month later, at a preliminary hearing, McDonald repudiated his prior sworn confession. He testified that Stokes had persuaded him to confess that he shot Liberty. He claimed that Stokes had promised that he would not go to jail and that he would share in the proceeds of a lawsuit that Chambers would bring against the town of Woodville. On examination by his own attorney and on cross-examination by the State, McDonald swore that he had not been at the scene when Liberty was shot but had been down the street drinking beer in a cafe with a friend, Berkley Turner. When he and Turner heard the shooting, he testified, they walked up the street and found Chambers lying in the alley. He, Turner, and Williams took Chambers to the hospital. McDonald further testified at the preliminary hearing that . . . while he once owned a .22–caliber pistol he had lost it many months before the shooting and did not own or possess a weapon at that time. The local justice of the peace accepted McDonald's repudiation and released him from custody. The local authorities undertook no further investigation of his possible involvement.

Chambers' case came on for trial in October of the next year. At trial, he endeavored to develop two grounds of defense. He first attempted to show that he did not shoot Liberty. Only one officer testified that he actually saw Chambers fire the shots. Although three officers saw Liberty shoot Chambers and testified that they assumed he was shooting his attacker, none of them examined Chambers to see whether he was still alive or whether he possessed a gun. Indeed, no weapon was ever recovered from the scene and there was no proof that Chambers had ever owned a .22–caliber pistol. One witness testified that he was standing in the street near where Liberty was shot, that he was looking at Chambers when the shooting began, and that he was sure that Chambers did not fire the shots.

Petitioner's second defense was that Gable McDonald had shot Officer Liberty. He was only partially successful, however, in his efforts to bring before the jury the testimony supporting this defense. Sam Hardin, a lifelong friend of McDonald's, testified that he saw McDonald shoot Liberty. A second witness, one of Liberty's cousins, testified that he saw McDonald immediately after the shooting with a pistol in his hand. In addition to the testimony of these two witnesses, Chambers endeavored to show the jury that McDonald had repeatedly confessed to the crime. Chambers attempted to prove that McDonald had admitted responsibility for the murder on four separate occasions, once when he gave the sworn statement to Chambers' counsel and three other times prior to that occasion in private conversations with friends.

In large measure, he was thwarted in his attempt to present this portion of his defense by the strict application of certain Mississippi rules of evidence. Chambers asserts in this Court, as he did unsuccessfully in his motion for new trial and on appeal to the State Supreme Court, that the application of these evidentiary rules rendered his trial fundamentally unfair and deprived him of due process of law. It is necessary, therefore, to examine carefully the rulings made during the trial.

II

Chambers filed a pretrial motion requesting the court to order McDonald to appear. Chambers also sought a ruling at that time that, if the State itself chose not to call McDonald, he be allowed to call him as an adverse witness.... The trial court granted the motion requiring McDonald to appear but reserved ruling on the adverse-witness motion. At trial, after the State failed to put McDonald on the stand, Chambers called McDonald, laid a predicate for the introduction of his sworn out-of-court confession, had it admitted into evidence, and read it to the jury. The State, upon cross-examination, elicited from McDonald the fact that he had repudiated his prior confession. McDonald further testified, as he had at the preliminary hearing, that he did not shoot Liberty, and that he confessed to the crime only on the promise of Reverend Stokes that he would not go to jail and would share in a sizable tort recovery from the town. He also retold his own story of his actions on the evening of the shooting, including his visit to the cafe down the street, his absence from the scene during the critical period, and his subsequent trip to the hospital with Chambers....

At the conclusion of the State's cross-examination, Chambers renewed his motion to examine McDonald as an adverse witness. The trial court denied the motion, stating: "He may be hostile, but he is not adverse in the sense of the word, so your request will be overruled." On appeal, the State Supreme Court upheld the trial court's ruling, finding that "McDonald's testimony was not adverse to appellant" because "nowhere did he point the finger at Chambers."

Defeated in his attempt to challenge directly McDonald's renunciation of his prior confession, Chambers sought to introduce the testimony of the three witnesses to whom McDonald had admitted that he shot the officer. The first of these, Sam Hardin, would have testified that, on the night of the shooting, he spent the late evening hours with McDonald at a friend's house after their return from the hospital and that, while driving McDonald home later that night, McDonald stated that he shot Liberty. The State objected to the admission of this testimony on the ground that it was hearsay. The trial court sustained the objection.[4]

Berkley Turner, the friend with whom McDonald said he was drinking beer when the shooting occurred, was then called to testify. In the jury's presence, and without objection, he testified that he had not been in the cafe that Saturday and had not had any beers with McDonald. The jury was then excused. In the absence of the jury, Turner recounted his conversations with McDonald while they were riding with James Williams to take Chambers to the hospital. When asked whether

4. Hardin's testimony, unlike the testimony of the other two men who stated that McDonald had confessed to them, was actually given in the jury's presence. After the State's objection to Hardin's account of McDonald's statement was sustained, the trial court ordered the jury to disregard it.

McDonald said anything regarding the shooting of Liberty, Turner testified that McDonald told him that he "shot him." Turner further stated that one week later, when he met McDonald at a friend's house, McDonald reminded him of their prior conversation and urged Turner not to "mess him up." Petitioner argued to the court that, especially where there was other proof in the case that was corroborative of these out-of-court statements, Turner's testimony as to McDonald's self-incriminating remarks should have been admitted as an exception to the hearsay rule. Again, the trial court sustained the State's objection.

The third witness, Albert Carter, was McDonald's neighbor. They had been friends for about 25 years. Although Carter had not been in Woodville on the evening of the shooting, he stated that he learned about it the next morning from McDonald. That same day, he and McDonald walked out to a well near McDonald's house, and there McDonald told him that he was the one who shot Officer Liberty. Carter testified that McDonald also told him that he had disposed of the .22–caliber revolver later that night. He further testified that several weeks after the shooting, he accompanied McDonald to Natchez where McDonald purchased another .22 pistol to replace the one he had discarded.[5] The jury was not allowed to hear Carter's testimony. Chambers urged that these statements were admissible, the State objected, and the court sustained the objection. On appeal, the State Supreme Court approved the lower court's exclusion of these witnesses' testimony on hearsay grounds.

In sum, then, this was Chambers' predicament. As a consequence of the combination of Mississippi's "party witness" or "voucher" rule and its hearsay rule, he was unable either to cross-examine McDonald or to present witnesses in his own behalf who would have discredited McDonald's repudiation and demonstrated his complicity. Chambers had, however, chipped away at the fringes of McDonald's story by introducing admissible testimony from other sources indicating that he had not been seen in the cafe where he said he was when the shooting started, that he had not been having beer with Turner, and that he possessed a .22 pistol at the time of the crime. But all that remained from McDonald's own testimony was a single written confession countered by an arguably acceptable renunciation. Chambers' defense was far less persuasive than it might have been had he been given an opportunity to subject McDonald's statements to cross-examination or had the other confessions been admitted.

III

The right of an accused in a criminal trial to due process is, in essence, the right to a fair opportunity to defend against the State's

5. A gun dealer from Natchez testified that McDonald had made two purchases. The witness' business records indicated that McDonald purchased a nine-shot .22–caliber revolver about a year prior to the murder. He purchased a different style .22 three weeks after Liberty's death.

accusations. The rights to confront and cross-examine witnesses and to call witnesses in one's own behalf have long been recognized as essential to due process. . . . Both of these elements of a fair trial are implicated in the present case. . . .

B

. . . The trial court refused to allow [Chambers] to introduce the testimony of Hardin, Turner, and Carter. Each would have testified to the statements purportedly made by McDonald, on three separate occasions shortly after the crime, naming himself as the murderer. The State Supreme Court approved the exclusion of this evidence on the ground that it was hearsay.

The hearsay rule, which has long been recognized and respected by virtually every State, is based on experience and grounded in the notion that untrustworthy evidence should not be presented to the triers of fact. . . . A number of exceptions have developed over the years to allow admission of hearsay statements made under circumstances that tend to assure reliability and thereby compensate for the absence of the oath and opportunity for cross-examination. Among the most prevalent of these exceptions is the one applicable to declarations against interest—an exception founded on the assumption that a person is unlikely to fabricate a statement against his own interest at the time it is made. Mississippi recognizes this exception but applies it only to declarations against pecuniary interest. It recognizes no such exception for declarations, like McDonald's in this case, that are against the penal interest of the declarant.

This materialistic limitation on the declaration-against-interest hearsay exception appears to be accepted by most States in their criminal trial processes, although a number of States have discarded it. Declarations against penal interest have also been excluded in federal courts under the authority of Donnelly v. United States, 228 U.S. 243, 272–273 (1913), although exclusion would not be required under the newly proposed Federal Rules of Evidence.[18] Exclusion, where the limitation prevails, is usually premised on the view that admission would lead to the frequent presentation of perjured testimony to the jury. It is believed that confessions of criminal activity are often motivated by extraneous considerations and, therefore, are not as inherently reliable as statements against pecuniary or proprietary interest. While that rationale has been the subject of considerable scholarly criticism, we need not decide in this case whether, under other circumstances, it might serve some valid state purpose by excluding untrustworthy testimony.

18. Rule 804, Rules of Evidence for United States Courts and Magistrates (approved Nov. 20, 1972, and transmitted to Congress to become effective July 1, 1973, unless the Congress otherwise determines).

The hearsay statements involved in this case were originally made and subsequently offered at trial under circumstances that provided considerable assurance of their reliability. First, each of McDonald's confessions was made spontaneously to a close acquaintance shortly after the murder had occurred. Second, each one was corroborated by some other evidence in the case—McDonald's sworn confession, the testimony of an eyewitness to the shooting, the testimony that McDonald was seen with a gun immediately after the shooting, and proof of his prior ownership of a .22–caliber revolver and subsequent purchase of a new weapon. The sheer number of independent confessions provided additional corroboration for each. Third, whatever may be the parameters of the penal-interest rationale,[20] each confession here was in a very real sense self-incriminatory and unquestionably against interest. McDonald stood to benefit nothing by disclosing his role in the shooting to any of his three friends, and he must have been aware of the possibility that disclosure would lead to criminal prosecution. Indeed, after telling Turner of his involvement, he subsequently urged Turner not to "mess him up." Finally, if there was any question about the truthfulness of the extrajudicial statements, McDonald was present in the courtroom and was under oath. He could have been cross-examined by the State, and his demeanor and responses weighed by the jury. The availability of McDonald significantly distinguishes this case from the prior Mississippi precedent, *Brown v. State, supra* n. 20, and from the *Donnelly*-type situation, since in both cases the declarant was unavailable at the time of trial.

Few rights are more fundamental than that of an accused to present witnesses in his own defense. *E.g.*, Washington v. Texas, 388 U.S. 14, 19 (1967). In the exercise of this right, the accused, as is required of the State, must comply with established rules of procedure and evidence designed to assure both fairness and reliability in the ascertainment of guilt and innocence. Although perhaps no rule of evidence has been more respected or more frequently applied in jury trials than that applicable to the exclusion of hearsay, exceptions tailored to allow the introduction of evidence which in fact is likely to be trustworthy have long existed. The testimony rejected by the trial court here bore persuasive assurances of trustworthiness and thus was well within the basic rationale of the exception for declarations against interest. That testimony also was critical to Chambers' defense. In these circumstances, where constitutional rights

20. The Mississippi case which refused to adopt a hearsay exception for declarations against penal interest concerned an out-of-court declarant who purportedly stated that he had committed the murder with which his brother had been charged. The Mississippi Supreme Court believed that the declarant might have been motivated by a desire to free his brother rather than by any compulsion of guilt. The Court also noted that the declarant had fled, was unavailable for cross-examination, and might well have known at the time he made the statement that he would not suffer for it. Brown v. State, 99 Miss. 719 (1911). There is, in the present case, no such basis for doubting McDonald's statements.

directly affecting the ascertainment of guilt are implicated, the hearsay rule may not be applied mechanistically to defeat the ends of justice.

We conclude that the exclusion of this critical evidence, coupled with the State's refusal to permit Chambers to cross-examine McDonald, denied him a trial in accord with traditional and fundamental standards of due process. In reaching this judgment, we establish no new principles of constitutional law. Nor does our holding signal any diminution in the respect traditionally accorded to the States in the establishment and implementation of their own criminal trial rules and procedures. Rather, we hold quite simply that under the facts and circumstances of this case the rulings of the trial court deprived Chambers of a fair trial.

The judgment is reversed, and the case is remanded to the Supreme Court of Mississippi for further proceedings not inconsistent with this opinion.

It is so ordered.

■ MR. JUSTICE WHITE, concurring....

■ MR. JUSTICE REHNQUIST, dissenting....

CHAMBERS V. MISSISSIPPI: *Historical Postscript*

Chambers v. Mississippi catches one a little by surprise. Convicted of murdering a police officer, Leon Chambers won a new trial from a nearly unanimous and none-too-liberal Supreme Court. Three out of four recent Republican appointees voted with the majority. And Lewis F. Powell, the Court's first Southern conservative in a generation, wrote the opinion.

The portion of the opinion reproduced above is particularly surprising. Chambers had complained that Mississippi's hearsay law, which did not recognize an exception for statements against penal interest, prevented him from introducing certain critical evidence at trial. That evidence would have shown that another man, Gable McDonald, had confessed to shooting Officer Aaron Liberty. In particular, Chambers had been unable to offer evidence of three separate oral confessions that McDonald made to different friends.

Yet Chambers's plight at trial was not quite as dire as these facts make it seem. After all, he succeeded in offering evidence of McDonald's *written* confession, made under oath in the office of Chambers's lawyers. (Page 721, above.) And though McDonald's three oral confessions stayed out, the jurors at least *heard* about one of them before the judge instructed them to disregard it. (Page 721 n.4.) Moreover, there was no suggestion that the state applied its hearsay law other than evenhandedly. Chambers was barred from offering statements against penal interest, but so were all other litigants.

Nor was Mississippi law backward or even out of the mainstream in this regard. The Court acknowledged that "most States" had no hearsay exception for statements against penal interest and that even in federal court, under the doctrine of *Donnelly v. United States*, 228 U.S. 243, 272–73 (1913), declarations against penal interest were kept out.* Justice Powell's claim that "exclusion would not be required under the newly proposed Federal Rules of Evidence" left the impression that Chambers would have fared better in federal court once the new evidence rules took effect. But while Rule 804(b)(3) generally admits statements against penal interest, it does so only if the declarant is unavailable. Far from being unavailable, McDonald was present and testified at trial. In fact, had Chambers been tried under the Federal Rules, he might have fared *worse* than under Mississippi law because he might not have succeeded in admitting McDonald's signed and sworn confession. It is at least uncertain whether McDonald's encounter with Chambers's lawyers, during which he made the confession, would have qualified as a "proceeding" or "deposition" for purposes of Rule 801(d)(1)(A).

In a part of the opinion I have omitted above, the Court was properly more dismissive of Mississippi's trial practice. The Court considered the state's "voucher" rule, which held that a party may not impeach his own witness and "is bound by anything [the witness] might say." The rule prevented Chambers from cross-examining McDonald, whom Chambers himself had called to the stand, even though McDonald had contradicted Chambers's claim that McDonald shot Officer Liberty. *Chambers*, 410 U.S. at 296–97. The Supreme Court dismissed the voucher rule as "archaic" and "irrational" and noted that it "has been rejected altogether by the newly proposed Federal Rules of Evidence, Rule 607." *Id.* at 296 nn.8, 9.

In light of this second evidentiary difficulty, the claim that Chambers had received a constitutionally deficient trial seems a good deal stronger. Notably, the Court staked its reversal of his conviction on both issues: "We conclude that the exclusion of this critical [hearsay] evidence, *coupled with* the State's refusal to permit Chambers to cross-examine McDonald, denied him a trial in accord with traditional and fundamental standards of due process." (Page 725, above (emphasis added).) But the Supreme Court normally does not sit to correct every failing of state procedure. The particular "facts and circumstances of this case," to which the Court limited its holding, were not likely to recur. A case that finds fault with a particular concatenation of two separate issues is unlikely to have much value as precedent.

So why did the Court agree to hear Chambers's case? An unobtrusive sentence from the first paragraph of Justice Powell's opinion suggests a possible explanation: "Pending disposition of his application for certiorari

* *See* Richard A. Nagareda, *Reconceiving the Right to Present Witnesses*, 97 MICH. L. REV. 1063, 1081 (1999) ("[T]he position of the Mississippi courts was hardly anomalous.").

to this Court, petitioner was granted bail by order of the Circuit Justice." (Page 718.) This is a remarkable disclosure. Leon Chambers, convicted of murdering a Mississippi police officer, had been set free. He had not been freed by the Supreme Court. Rather a single Justice of the Court—the "Circuit Justice" responsible for the Fifth Circuit, which includes Mississippi—had let Chambers go. And he had done so *pending disposition* of Chambers's application for certiorari. That year the Court granted 299 out of 4515 petitions for certiorari. *See* SUPREME COURT COMPENDIUM: DATA, DECISIONS, AND DEVELOPMENTS 82, tbls.2–6 (2d ed. 1996). The Court had not even agreed to hear Chambers's case, and he was free.

The Circuit Justice for the Fifth Circuit was of course Lewis Powell. As a Southerner, he had inherited the post from Justice Hugo Black of Alabama, whom he succeeded on the Court. At the time Powell made the rather grave decision to free a man convicted of murdering a police officer, he had very little experience in such matters. Never having been a judge or even a criminal practitioner, Powell was sworn in as an Associate Justice of the Supreme Court on January 7, 1972. Chambers's counsel presented him with their application for bail on January 31. Powell granted it the next day. *See Chambers v. Mississippi*, 405 U.S. 1205, 1205 (1972) (denying application for reconsideration of order granting Chambers bail).

One of Powell's law clerks, Lawrence Hammond, has reported that this was almost certainly Powell's first bail application. (Conversation with the author, Aug. 14, 2001.) Hammond recalled that an important factor in the decision to grant bail was the Mississippi attorney general's failure to file an objection despite an invitation to do so. The state first objected ten days after Chambers's release, claiming that his return to Woodville "will create a tense and explosive situation in the community, which might result in bloodshed." 405 U.S. at 1206 (paraphrasing affidavits submitted by the state). Powell dismissed such alarmist predictions as "conclusory" and rejected the state's application for reconsideration, leaving his original bail order in effect. He reasoned that as a church deacon and the father of nine, with a home, a mortgage, and no previous criminal record, Chambers presented little risk of flight. *See id.*

Not taking any chances, however, and concerned for their client's safety at Mississippi's Parchman Prison, Chambers's lawyers had set about securing his release before Powell could change his mind. One of Chambers's lawyers in the proceedings before the Supreme Court, former Attorney General Ramsey Clark, described the scene:

> [T]he day Justice Powell granted the motion for release, we called immediately to make arrangement for Mr. Chambers to be picked up at the prison by family, or [by] friends of mine in the area. We learned from the prison that he had already been released. His family had not heard from him. His home was far to the south of the prison and he was apparently alone, without money in prison

> clothes. We were desperately concerned for his safety and uncertain about state and local law enforcement assistance.
>
> When his children got home from school that same afternoon, they found their father asleep in his bed. He had hitchhiked home in the course of the day. . . .

(Correspondence with the author, Aug. 28, 2001.)

Back at the Court, one can only imagine that Justice Powell felt somewhat overextended. Chambers was free, and the Justices had not even resolved to hear his case. Worse, the vote on his application for certiorari was close. Only five Justices—one more than necessary—wanted to hear the case.*

After oral argument, however, every Justice except William H. Rehnquist stood ready to reverse Chambers's conviction. Still, Powell's instructions from his colleagues were to craft the holding narrowly. In a memo assigning Powell the task of writing the opinion, Chief Justice Burger offered this advice:

> Dear Lewis:
>
> I am assigning [*Chambers v. Mississippi*] to you and I agree with you that it must be written very narrowly.
>
> . . . [T]here is much in what Bill Rehnquist said about intruding in state procedures and "constitutionalizing everything." Nonetheless, this can be reversed on no grounds except the Federal Constitution, and were I doing it, I would rest it on the unique factors of this case and even call them unique. . . .

Before closing his brief note, the Chief Justice referred once again to the "peculiar and unique circumstances" of the case. Then he made one last appeal: "If this is narrowly done, there is a good chance to pick up Rehnquist and I would try to do that."

Powell did not in the end win Justice Rehnquist's ninth vote. But he did manage to keep the support of each of the other Justices. The cost of their consent was to cast the ruling narrowly. Advising Powell that he would join the Court's opinion, Justice Blackmun wrote: "You have prepared an appropriately narrow opinion which meets the issues, and I am glad to join."

The Legacy of Chambers

It was not long before the Court restated the *Chambers* doctrine in slightly broader terms. In *Green v. Georgia*, 442 U.S. 95, 97 (1979), the

* The five were Justices Powell, Douglas, Brennan, Stewart, and Marshall. Chief Justice Burger and Justices White, Blackmun, and Rehnquist voted no. This information—as well as the results of the conference vote and other references to internal Court memoranda—is drawn from Justice Powell's papers, housed at the law library of Washington and Lee University.

Justices made it clear that a state's unreasonable application of its hearsay rule against a criminal defendant, even absent a procedural flaw such as Mississippi's voucher rule, can violate the Fourteenth Amendment's Due Process Clause. Like Mississippi, Georgia did not recognize a hearsay exception for statements against penal interest. During the penalty phase of Green's capital murder trial, the trial court had prevented the defendant from offering his accomplice's confession that he (and not Green) was the triggerman. Making matters worse, the prosecutor had argued before the jury at Green's penalty proceeding "that you Ladies and Gentlemen can believe that each one of them fired the shots so that they would be as equally involved and one did not exceed the other's part in the commission of this crime." *Id.* at 96 n.2.

Repeating many of Justice Powell's arguments in *Chambers,* the Court emphasized in per curiam opinion that the excluded hearsay was both critical to the defendant's case and unusually reliable:

> The excluded testimony was highly relevant to a critical issue in the punishment phase of the trial, and substantial reasons existed to assume its reliability. Moore [the accomplice] made his statement spontaneously to a close friend. The evidence corroborating the confession was ample, and indeed sufficient to procure a conviction of Moore and a capital sentence. The statement was against interest, and there was no reason to believe that Moore had any ulterior motive in making it. Perhaps most important, the State considered the testimony sufficiently reliable to use it against Moore, and to base a sentence of death upon it.

"In these unique circumstances," the Court concluded, " 'the hearsay rule may not be applied mechanistically to defeat the ends of justice.' " *Id.* at 97 (quoting *Chambers*).

Despite their reference to the "unique circumstances" of the case, the Justices reached further in *Green* than in *Chambers.* For they grounded reversal in a single evidentiary issue—the exclusion of proffered hearsay evidence. And less than a decade later, in *Crane v. Kentucky,* 476 U.S. 683 (1986), they stated the principle of *Chambers* and *Green* yet more broadly: "Whether rooted directly in the Due Process Clause of the Fourteenth Amendment, *Chambers v. Mississippi,* or in the Compulsory Process or Confrontation clauses of the Sixth Amendment, *Washington v. Texas,* 388 U.S. 14, 23 (1967); *Davis v. Alaska,* 415 U.S. 308 (1974), the Constitution guarantees criminal defendants 'a meaningful opportunity to present a complete defense.' " 476 U.S. at 690. The much later case of *Holmes v. South Carolina,* 547 U.S. 319 (2006), which I discuss in detail shortly, assures the continued force of this principle. (*See* pages 731–34.)

The progeny of the Court's tentative holding in *Chambers,* the right of "a meaningful opportunity to present a complete defense" now serves as a potentially powerful tool in the hands of criminal defendants. It does not operate as a general release from the strictures of the evidence rules.

As *Chambers* itself stated, the defendant, like the prosecution, "must comply with established rules of procedure and evidence designed to assure both fairness and reliability in the ascertainment of guilt and innocence." (Page 724.) But when the evidence offered is "critical" to the defendant's case and bears "persuasive assurances of trustworthiness" (page 724, above), the principle that the Constitution guarantees "a meaningful opportunity to present a complete defense" often will defeat a rule of evidence that otherwise would keep the information out.

The Compulsory Process Clause

Although I have presented *Chambers* under the heading of the Compulsory Process Clause, the Court in fact decided the case under the Fourteenth Amendment's Due Process Clause. Application of Mississippi's hearsay and voucher rules, the Court held, had "denied [Chambers] a trial in accord with traditional and fundamental standards of due process." In the Court's view, the Due Process Clause embraced "[t]he rights to confront and cross-examine witnesses and to call witnesses in one's own behalf. . . ." (Page 723, above.) The latter right—"to call witnesses in one's own behalf"—is of course the guarantee of the Sixth Amendment's Compulsory Process Clause, which secures criminal defendants "the right . . . to have compulsory process for obtaining witnesses in [their] favor." Loosely construed, this right to demand appearance of defense witnesses arguably entitled Chambers to put on evidence of McDonald's excluded hearsay confessions.

So it is something of a mystery why the Court did not resolve the matter of McDonald's confessions under the Compulsory Process Clause. After all, a precedent was readily at hand. Six years earlier, in *Washington v. Texas*, 388 U.S. 14 (1967), the Court for the first time had invoked the Compulsory Process Clause to strike down application of a state evidence rule. Confronting a Texas competency rule that barred accomplices from testifying on one another's behalf, the Court ruled that the Compulsory Process Clause encompassed "in plain terms the right to present a defense." *Id.* at 19. Texas courts had violated this guarantee by "arbitrarily den[ying the defendant] the right to put on the stand a witness . . . whose testimony would have been relevant and material to the defense." *Id.* at 23. Justice Powell in fact cited *Washington* in his opinion in *Chambers*. (See page 724, above.) He did not say, however, that *Washington* had been decided under the Compulsory Process Clause, nor did he apply *Washington*'s "arbitrari[ness]" standard.

Professor Peter Westen, who argued Chambers's cause before the Supreme Court, has suggested two possible explanations for Justice Powell's reliance on the Due Process Clause rather than the Compulsory Process Clause. First, Westen notes, Powell "oppose[d] incorporating the specifics of the Bill of Rights into the due process clause of the fourteenth amendment." Moreover, Chambers "had not mentioned the compulsory process clause as the basis of [his appeal] in the court below." Peter Westen, *The Compulsory Process Clause*, 73 MICH. L. REV. 71, 151 n.384 (1974).

A third explanation might be the difficulty of applying *Washington*'s arbitrariness standard in the context of *Chambers*. An arbitrariness standard seems well suited to the question the Court faced in *Washington*. That case dealt with a witness competency rule—and as a class, competency rules had slipped from favor and were vulnerable to general attack. (See pages 364–73.) The Texas rule at issue in *Washington* was the only one like it in the country, and even Texas had repealed it by the time the Court issued its ruling. *See Washington*, 388 U.S. at 17 n.4. Likewise, when the Court addressed a state competency rule that operated to exclude a defendant's hypnotically refreshed testimony in *Rock v. Arkansas*, 483 U.S. 44 (1987), it applied—and expanded on—*Washington*'s arbitrariness standard. The Court held that "restrictions of a defendant's right to testify"—a right the Court traced to the Compulsory Process Clause and other constitutional provisions—"may not be arbitrary or disproportionate to the purposes they are designed to serve." *Id.* at 55–56.

In contrast to *Washington* and *Rock*, *Chambers* did not present the Court with an outmoded rule it could declare to be generally "arbitrary" or "disproportionate." Both the hearsay rule and the exception for statements against interest fell well within the mainstream of traditional American evidence law. An "arbitrary or disproportionate" test is a clumsy tool for resolving a defendant's claim that a generally valid rule, when applied to the specific facts of his case, unfairly constrained his defense. Justice Powell therefore adopted a test better suited to Chambers's fact-specific challenge. He reasoned that because the hearsay rule is "grounded in the notion that untrustworthy evidence should not be presented to the triers of fact," the rule should not be applied to exclude evidence supported by "persuasive assurances of trustworthiness"—at least where such evidence is "critical" to the defense of an accused. (Pages 723, 724–25, above.)

HOLMES V. SOUTH CAROLINA: *Case Note*

In *Holmes v. South Carolina*, 547 U.S. 319 (2006), the Supreme Court reviewed the conviction of Bobby Lee Holmes, condemned by a jury for sodomizing and murdering 86–year-old Mary Stewart in her small-town York home. At trial prosecution eyewitnesses testified they saw Holmes near Stewart's apartment at about the time of the crime. Various forensic experts testified for the state that:

- DNA analysis showed Stewart's blood on Holmes's shirt and Stewart's DNA on Holmes's underwear;

- fiber analysis showed strands consistent with Holmes's sweatshirt on Stewart's bed sheets and detected matching fibers on Holmes's jeans and underwear and Stewart's nightgown; and
- fingerprint analysis revealed Holmes's palm print on the inside of Stewart's front door.

Holmes claimed at trial that all this forensic evidence resulted from police contamination or contrivance. And he sought to offer evidence of "third-party guilt." At a pretrial hearing he presented several witnesses who said they had seen another man, Jimmy McCaw White, in the victim's neighborhood around the time of the crime. Others testified that White confessed the crime to them or made statements implying his guilt.

The trial judge excluded all evidence of White's guilt under South Carolina's third-party guilt rule. As formulated in *State v. Gregory*, 198 S.C. 98 (1941), that rule permitted criminal defendants to offer evidence of another person's guilt if the evidence "raise[d] a reasonable inference or presumption as to [the defendant's] own innocence"—but not if it merely "cast a bare suspicion upon another" or "raise[d] a conjectural inference as to the commission of the crime by another." *Gregory*, 198 S.C. at 104.

In affirming the trial judge's ruling, the South Carolina Supreme Court held that "where there is strong evidence of an appellant's guilt, especially where there is strong forensic evidence, the proffered evidence about a third party's alleged guilt does not raise a reasonable inference as to the appellant's own innocence." The court ruled that Holmes could not "overcome the forensic evidence against him to raise a reasonable inference of his own innocence." *State v. Holmes*, 361 S.C. 333, 342–43 (2004).

In a unanimous opinion by Justice Alito, the Supreme Court held that South Carolina's third-party guilt rule, as interpreted by the state's high court in this case, arbitrarily and unconstitutionally limited a defendant's ability to present evidence in his defense. Justice Alito emphasized that criminal defendants are not entitled to present any evidence they choose—and that "state and federal rulemakers have broad latitude under the Constitution to establish rules excluding evidence from criminal trials." *Holmes*, 547 U.S. at 324. In particular, states may enforce rules similar to FRE 403, excluding evidence, even if offered by a criminal defendant, if its probative force is substantially outweighed by the risk of unfair prejudice, juror confusion, or other concerns. The Court suggested that South Carolina's original third-party guilt rule, as formulated in *Gregory*, simply expressed this principle and did not offend the Constitution. "Such [third-party guilt] rules are widely accepted" across the country, the Court said—and it showed no inclination to brand them unconstitutional. *Id.* at 327.

But the Justices held that the South Carolina court's restatement of the third-party guilt rule in this case confronted Holmes with an impermissible hurdle to admission. It is one thing, Justice Alito wrote, to exclude a defendant's evidence if, examined on its own merits, it has little probative value and risks unfair prejudice or confusion. It is another thing entirely for a trial judge to examine the *prosecution's* evidence and deem it so compelling that the defendant cannot present evidence that someone else committed the crime.

Such a practice is especially troubling, the Court said, if the strength of the prosecution's evidence depends on the truthfulness of the prosecution's witnesses: "Just because the prosecution's evidence, *if credited*, would provide strong support for a guilty verdict, it does not follow that evidence of third-party guilt has only a weak logical connection to the central issues in the case." *Holmes*, 547 U.S. at 330 (emphasis in original). Consider the converse, Justice Alito suggested. What if the *defendant* came forward with "evidence that, if believed, strongly supports a verdict of not guilty"? Would the prosecution then be foreclosed from "introducing its evidence, including the forensic evidence that, if credited, provided strong proof of the petitioner's guilt"? *Id.*

The Court held that South Carolina's third-party guilt rule, as interpreted and applied by the state court in *Holmes*, "is 'arbitrary' in the sense that it does not rationally serve the end that the *Gregory* rule and other similar third-party guilt rules were designed to further." That is, the *Holmes* rule goes far beyond excluding evidence that has little probative value and that risks substantial unfair prejudice or juror confusion. "It follows that the rule applied in this case by the State Supreme Court violates a criminal defendant's right to have 'a meaningful opportunity to present a complete defense.'" *Id.* at 331.

There are several points of note in the Court's ruling:

- Although the Court ultimately ruled narrowly (see below), it twice restated with approval the very broad formulation of the defendant's right to present a defense expressed in *Crane v. Kentucky*, 476 U.S. 683, 690 (1986): "Whether rooted directly in the Due Process Clause of the Fourteenth Amendment or in the Compulsory Process or Confrontation Clauses of the Sixth Amendment, the Constitution guarantees criminal defendants 'a meaningful opportunity to present a complete defense.'" *Holmes*, 547 U.S. at 324, 331.

- Although the Court did not rest its ruling on *Chambers v. Mississippi*, it cited and discussed *Chambers* with approval. *Id.* at 325–26.

- Instead the Court relied on *Washington v. Texas*, 388 U.S. 14 (1967), and later cases deeming state evidence rules unconstitutional if they "arbitrarily" constrain a defendant's ability to put on a defense. It is arbitrary, the Court wrote, to assess the probative value of the defendant's evidence by examining exclusively the prosecution's evidence:

> The point is that, by evaluating the strength of only one party's evidence, no logical conclusion can be reached regarding the strength of contrary evidence offered by the other side to rebut or cast doubt. Because the rule applied by the State Supreme Court in this case did not heed this point, the rule is "arbitrary" in the sense that it does not rationally serve the end that the *Gregory* rule and other similar third-party guilt rules were designed to further.

Holmes, 547 U.S. at 331.

• As this last quote makes clear, the Court ruled narrowly on the specific construction given the state's third-party guilt rule by the South Carolina Supreme Court in *Holmes*. The Justices did not broadly condemn third-party guilt rules, which exist in one form or other in many states. The Justices cast such rules as expressions of the principle of Rule 403.

• The Court did not specify which constitutional provisions the South Carolina court's "arbitrary" rule violated. Presumably the Justices preferred the ambiguity of *Crane*: "Whether rooted directly in the Due Process Clause of the Fourteenth Amendment or in the Compulsory Process or Confrontation Clauses of the Sixth Amendment, the Constitution guarantees criminal defendants 'a meaningful opportunity to present a complete defense.'" *Crane*, 476 U.S. at 690. After quoting this principle, Justice Alito wrote, "This right is abridged by evidence rules that infr-ing[e] upon a weighty interest of the accused and are arbitrary or disproportionate to the purposes they are designed to serve." *Holmes*, 547 U.S. at 324 (internal quote marks deleted). A few paragraphs later, after reviewing *Washington*, *Chambers*, *Crane*, and related cases, Alito wrote somewhat more vaguely that "the Constitution thus prohibits exclusion of defense evidence under rules that serve no legitimate purpose or that are disproportionate to the ends that they are designed to promote. . . ." *Id.* at 326.

• The Supreme Court said nothing that calls in question any part of the Federal Rules of Evidence and did not disturb *Washington*, *Chambers*, *Crane*, or any other Supreme Court precedent.

CHAPTER 9

Lay Opinions and Expert Testimony

A. Lay Opinions

Focus on FRE 701

Problem 9.1

Despondently

An insurance claims investigator, testifying at trial as a prosecution witness, describes a conversation he had with the defendant about the defendant's claim on a truck destroyed by fire:

Q: What did you say to the defendant?

A: I told him that our investigator had gone to the scene of the fire and that she had found a pile of kerosene-soaked shavings under the defendant's truck. And I accused the defendant of setting fire to his own truck.

Q: How did the defendant respond?

A: He said, "Look Mister, I'm just a poor man."

Q: In what tone of voice did he say that?

A: He sounded depressed.

If defense counsel objects to the last answer as improper opinion testimony, how should the court rule?

Problem 9.2
How Old?

Yazzie is charged with selling cigarettes to a minor, defined as a person under age seventeen. The statute permits the defendant to raise the affirmative defense that he reasonably believed the buyer to be of age. Yazzie seeks to offer the testimony of witnesses who were familiar with the buyer and would testify that at about the time of the charged cigarette sale, she appeared to them to be twenty or twenty-one years old.

Admissible? *Cf. United States v. Yazzie*, 976 F.2d 1252 (9th Cir. 1992).

LAY OPINIONS: AN INTRODUCTION

It is sometimes said that lay witnesses may state only facts, while opinion testimony is the realm of experts. In its most rigid interpretation, this supposed rule against lay opinion testimony would confine lay witnesses to telling what they have seen, heard, felt, smelled, or tasted—without characterizing or drawing inferences from the raw perceptions of their senses. The theory behind the rule is that a lay witness's opinions wouldn't help the jury. Since lay jurors presumably come equipped with all the inferential skills of the average lay witness, they would do just fine if the witness presented "just the facts," leaving jurors to draw their own inferences. Permitting the witness to state opinions would give voice simply to her views of the case.

But judges never have demanded that lay witnesses purge all inferences from their testimony—nor could a witness comply with any such demand. There simply is no clear line carving the realm of inference from that of cold facts. Something as plain as a witness's declaration that "the man was tall" or "the weather was hot" incorporates a collection of inferences about what constitutes tallness in a man or hotness in a day. A judge's directive that the witness confine herself to the facts would leave the witness either struggling for a precision past her powers—"he was six feet, two inches tall," "it was eighty-seven degrees"—or altogether tongue-tied.

So even before the Federal Rules established a newly liberal evidence regime, common-law judges typically gave lay witnesses leeway to state two broad sorts of opinions. As we will see, the present language of Rule

701 is generous enough to permit these two categories of traditional lay opinions—and a fair deal more.

Inferences That Resist Reduction to Fundamental "Facts"

The first, most basic, and least controversial kind of permissible lay opinions are those inferences that can hardly be stated in the form of sensory perceptions alone. In its note to the 2000 amendment to Rule 701, the advisory committee lists "'prototypical example[s]'" of this sort of opinion evidence: "'the appearance of persons or things,' . . . the manner of conduct, . . . degrees of light or darkness, sound, size, weight, distance, and an endless number of items that cannot be described factually in words apart from inferences." RB 165 (quoting *Asplundh Mfg. Div. v. Benton Harbor Eng'g*, 57 F.3d 1190, 1196 (3d Cir. 1995).)

Assume the prosecutor's theory of a case is that the defendant fired a shot in anger. The prosecutor might offer the testimony of a neighbor who saw the defendant moments before the crime and is prepared to say the defendant "looked furious." Most of us recognize fury when we see it, especially when we see it in someone we know. But if asked to say what fury looks like, most of us will fail for words. Through a cartoonist's eyes, fury looks like steam rising from the head. But to the rest of us, fury looks like, well, *fury*. And while some people turn red and some flex their jaws and others bulge at the neck, many people appear decidedly furious without any of these signs. Common-law judges therefore permitted laypersons to offer an opinion that someone looked furious—or sad or scared or shocked—without demanding that the witness detail the sensory observations that underlay this opinion. Courts generally left lay witnesses "free to speak in ordinary language unbewildered by admonition from the judge to testify to *facts*. . . ." *Stone v. United States*, 385 F.2d 713, 716 (10th Cir. 1967), *cert. denied*, 391 U.S. 966 (1968) (emphasis added).

Consider the advisory committee's other "'prototypical example[s]'" of permissible lay opinions, such as manner of conduct, sound, and weight. Testimony that a person "walked unsteadily" or "spoke loudly" or that a package "weighed about 40 pounds" cannot readily be reduced to more fundamental factual units. Nor could the opinion that a light was "very bright" or that a voice "sounded as though it came from the next room." Common law judges readily admitted these opinions too.

Opinions That Can Be Reduced to More Fundamental Facts but Still Gain from the Inference

At a somewhat more complex level, most common-law judges also permitted laypersons to opine on such matters as intoxication. Of course we all know what drunkenness looks like. But it is also true that we normally can break down our opinion that someone seemed drunk into several more basic sensory facts. Drunken people often have bloodshot eyes, sway when standing, walk unsteadily, speak thickly, and smell of alcohol. Many judges and opposing counsel therefore insist that a litigant "lay a foundation" by drawing these perceptions from a lay witness before permitting the witness to opine that someone was drunk. Foundational facts may be especially critical if intoxication goes to the heart of the case. Still, few judges will confine lay witnesses to such raw facts. Once a lawyer has elicited the various data points on which the witness bases her opinion, the witness generally may conclude that she "thought the man was drunk." Courts see that the witness's opinion adds something useful to the foundational facts—something that will help the jury decide whether the man really was drunk.

Likewise, a lay witness's opinion that the defendant is the same man she saw fleeing the crime scene depends on—and adds to—many foundational facts. When the witness and defendant are strangers, the prosecutor normally lays a foundation by asking the witness to describe the man who fled—his height, build, approximate age, hair color, skin tone, scars, tattoos. Once these facts are in evidence, the prosecutor will ask the familiar question: "Do you see in the courtroom today the man you saw fleeing the bank that afternoon?" The witness's answer to this question surely adds something beyond what she can convey with a list of identifying features.

Rule 701

Rule 701, which governs admission of lay testimony under the Federal Rules, plainly permits the sorts of lay opinions I've just described, as well as many lay opinions that arguably fall outside the traditional categories. The rule imposes only three constraints. Rule 701(a) demands, first, that a lay witness's opinions be "rationally based on [her] perception"—hence reaffirming the firsthand knowledge requirement of Rule 602. Rule 701(b) requires that lay opinions be helpful to the jury's fact finding. Most lay opinions that convey reliable and material information (beyond what jurors already know) clear this second hurdle.

The remainder of this brief unit focuses on the third, far trickier constraint—Rule 701(c)'s command that a lay witness not invade the experts' realm. At what point does a lay witness cross the nearly evanescent line that separates an opinion rooted in common knowledge from one "based on scientific, technical, or other specialized knowledge" of the sort only experts may deploy? Although *United States v. Ganier*, 468 F.3d 920 (6th Cir. 2006), which appears on the next page, offers a good deal of

guidance on this question, the line remains blurry in many contexts.

Problem 9.3
White Powder

... Paiva asserts that the district court abused its discretion in admitting the testimony of a lay witness, Christina Christo, who expressed her opinion as to the identity of a substance. During the trial, Christina Christo, the 21–year-old daughter of Paiva's ex-wife, ... testified for the government. Ms. Christo testified that in 1983, while she resided with her mother and Paiva in a condominium in Florida, she discovered inside one of Paiva's shoes a plastic bag containing a white powder. Ms. Christo testified that prior to 1983 she had used and tasted cocaine on many occasions and had developed a cocaine problem at age fourteen. Ms. Christo described the substance she found inside Paiva's shoe as a white powder with little bits of rocks in it. She stated that she tasted this white powder and that it tasted like cocaine. Ms. Christo testified that based upon looking at the substance and tasting it, the substance, in her opinion, was cocaine.

Should the trial court have admitted this testimony over the defendant's objection? *See United States v. Paiva*, 892 F.2d 148, 155–57 (1st Cir. 1989).

United States v. Ganier

468 F.3d 920 (6th Cir. 2006).

■ Karen Nelson Moore, *Circuit Judge*. The United States appeals the district court's decision excluding certain evidence from the criminal trial of Defendant–Appellee Albert Ganier, III ("Ganier").... On the morning on which Ganier's trial was to begin, Ganier filed a motion to exclude the proposed testimony of a government computer specialist, arguing that it was expert testimony for which the government had not provided a written summary as required by Federal Rule of Criminal Procedure 16(a)(1)(G). The district court granted the motion, bringing the proceedings to a halt while the government filed this interlocutory appeal....

I. Background

... Ganier was Chief Executive Officer, Chairman of the Board, a shareholder, and a founder of Education Networks of America, Inc. ("ENA") and its predecessor companies. In July 2002, a television station broadcast news stories discussing alleged relationships between Ganier, certain high-ranking Tennessee officials, and John Stamps, a lobbyist for ENA. The news stories included allegations of improprieties and favoritism in connection with contracts awarded to ENA by the State of Tennessee and solicitations of Tennessee and Texas officials for additional contracts.

In August 2002, a federal task force . . . began a criminal investigation of the contracts and solicitations as well as various companies associated with John Stamps. Assisted by the federal task force, a federal grand jury began an investigation in September 2002. . . . In December 2002, after the grand jury issued subpoenas on various companies and state agencies, Ganier allegedly attempted to implement an email "retention" policy at ENA in which employees' emails would be set to delete after six months, deleted files relevant to the ongoing investigation from his laptop computer, deleted relevant files from his desktop computer, and deleted relevant files from an ENA employee's computer.

Ganier was ultimately indicted on one count of endeavoring to obstruct justice and three counts of altering, destroying, or concealing documents with intent to impede a federal investigation, and the case proceeded towards trial. As ordered by the district court, Ganier filed a summary of expected expert testimony on June 17, 2005, in which he indicated that he would offer evidence that the files in question were transferred to the recycle bin rather than deleted, and that approximately 225 duplicates and similar drafts of the allegedly deleted documents remained on the computers. He also indicated that he would offer evidence showing the following:

> The computers in question each possessed "search" functions that, if utilized, would have located all or substantially all of the duplicates and similar drafts or versions of the allegedly "deleted" documents, thereby permitting a user intent on concealment to delete all or substantially all copies of particular documents on those computers.

According to the government, its forensic computer specialist, Special Agent Wallace Drueck of the IRS, decided to use forensic software to determine what searches were run on the three computers. On August 1, 2005, the day before the date set for trial, Drueck determined from reports generated by the forensic software that searches had been run in December 2002 using search terms relevant to the grand jury investigation and the allegedly deleted files. The next morning, before the jury was impaneled, Ganier filed a motion to exclude the reports and related testimony, which the district court granted. The government timely appealed, and the district court stayed the trial pending the appeal.

II. ANALYSIS

* * *

B. Exclusion of Evidence

* * *

2. *Violation of Federal Rule of Criminal Procedure 16(a)(1)(G)*

We must first determine whether the district court erred by concluding that Drueck's proposed testimony fell within the scope of Federal Rule of Criminal Procedure 16(a)(1)(G). Rule 16(a)(1)(G) requires, in part, that "[a]t the defendant's request, the government must give to the defendant a written summary of any testimony that the government intends to use under Rules 702, 703, or 705 of the Federal Rules of Evidence during its case-in-chief at trial." Testimony falls under Federal Rule of Evidence 702 if it is based on "scientific, technical, or other specialized knowledge."

The government argues that Drueck's proposed testimony is not based on scientific, technical, or other specialized knowledge, but is simply lay testimony available by "running commercially available software, obtaining results, and reciting them." The government contends that this testimony is of the same type as "facts ... that could be observed by any person reasonably proficient in the use of commonly used computer software, such as Microsoft Word and Microsoft Outlook (such as the existence and location of multiple copies of documents that are identical or virtually identical to the allegedly 'deleted' documents)," which Ganier previously indicated he did not consider to be expert testimony.

The reports generated by the forensic software display a heading, a string of words and symbols, a date and time, and a list of words.[4] The government asserts that these reports reveal three different types of searches performed with particular search terms at particular times, but such an interpretation would require Drueck to apply knowledge and familiarity with computers and the particular forensic software well

4. For example, a portion of one report reads as follows:

Registry—Al Ganier Desktop
Software Microsoft Internet Explorer Bars C4EE31F3-4768-11D2-BE5C-00A0C9A83DA1 FilesNamedMRU
Last Written Time 12/09/02 08:34:57

Name	Type	Data
000	REG_SZ	al ...
001	REG_SZ	sony ...
002	REG_SZ	RFP ...
003	REG_SZ	sundquist ...
004	REG_SZ	ARC ...
005	REG_SZ	roadmap to
		revenue ...
006	REG_SZ	road ...
007	REG_SZ	roadmap ...

beyond that of the average layperson. This constitutes "scientific, technical, or other specialized knowledge" within the scope of Rule 702.

Because the categorization of computer-related testimony is a relatively new question, comparisons with other areas of expert testimony are instructive. Software programs such as Microsoft Word and Outlook may be as commonly used as home medical thermometers, but the forensic tests Drueck ran are more akin to specialized medical tests run by physicians. *Cf.* Lyons v. Stovall, 188 F.3d 327, 330 (6th Cir. 1999) (describing as "expert witnesses" two doctors who performed blood paternity tests and testified as to the results), *cert. denied*, 530 U.S. 1203 (2000). The average layperson today may be able to interpret the outputs of popular software programs as easily as he or she interprets everyday vernacular, but the interpretation Drueck needed to apply to make sense of the software reports is more similar to the specialized knowledge police officers use to interpret slang and code words used by drug dealers. *Cf.* United States v. Garcia, No. 95–1224, 1995 WL 712757, at *4–*5 (6th Cir. Dec. 4, 1995) (unpublished) (affirming a decision to allow a police officer to give expert testimony as to the meaning of certain code words); United States v. Peoples, 250 F.3d 630, 640–41 (8th Cir. 2001) (concluding that a police officer should not have been allowed to testify as to the meaning of code words [i]n recorded conversations because she had not been qualified as an expert).

. . . [T]he 2000 amendment to Federal Rule of Evidence 701 clarified that lay opinions or inferences cannot be based on "scientific, technical, or other specialized knowledge within the scope of Rule 702." Even before the amendment, witnesses who performed after-the-fact investigations were generally not allowed to apply specialized knowledge in giving lay testimony. *See Peoples*, 250 F.3d at 641 ("When a law enforcement officer is not qualified as an expert by the court, her testimony is admissible as lay opinion only when the law enforcement officer is a participant in the conversation, has personal knowledge of the facts being related in the conversation, or observed the conversations as they occurred."). Thus, the district court did not err by concluding that Drueck's proposed testimony could be offered only pursuant to Rule 702. Accordingly, the government violated Federal Rule of Criminal Procedure 16(a)(1)(G) by not providing a written summary of the testimony to Ganier.

3. *Remedy*

We still must determine whether the district court imposed an appropriate remedy. Federal Rule of Criminal Procedure 16(d)(2) states:

> If a party fails to comply with [Rule 16], the court may:
>
> (A) order that party to permit the discovery or inspection; specify its time, place, and manner; and prescribe other just terms and conditions;
>
> (B) grant a continuance;

(C) prohibit that party from introducing the undisclosed evidence; or

(D) enter any other order that is just under the circumstances.

In deciding whether suppression of evidence is an appropriate remedy, a district court should consider:

(1) the reasons for the government's delay in producing the materials, including whether it acted intentionally or in bad faith;

(2) the degree of prejudice, if any, to the defendant; and

(3) whether the prejudice to the defendant can be cured with a less severe course of action, such as granting a continuance or a recess.

United States v. Maples, 60 F.3d 244, 247 (6th Cir. 1995). "District courts should embrace the 'least severe sanction necessary' doctrine, and hold that suppression of relevant evidence as a remedial device should be limited to circumstances in which it is necessary to serve remedial objectives." *Id.* at 247–48. . . .

. . . [T]he record does not reflect bad-faith conduct by the government. The government disclosed the reports that Drueck generated with forensic software almost immediately after it received them. Ganier argues that the government's failure to give a written summary of proposed testimony was an intentional violation of Rule 16(a)(1)(G) once it became clear that Drueck would offer expert testimony. However, there is no evidence that the government argued in bad faith that Drueck would be giving only fact testimony, and this appeal immediately followed the district court's decision to the contrary. The government may have been negligent in waiting until the day before trial to investigate search terms, but negligence does not, by itself, warrant suppression.

Finally, the record does not reflect any prejudice to Ganier that could not have been cured with a less severe sanction, such as a continuance or a limitation in the scope of Drueck's testimony. Ganier raised the issue of computer searches himself and had an expert prepared to testify about searches and search functions. Ganier was thus well aware that the issue could be raised at trial, reducing any potential prejudice. . . .

III. Conclusion

Because remedies less severe than exclusion were not given adequate consideration, we VACATE the decision of the district court and REMAND the case for further proceedings consistent with this opinion.

United States v. Ganier: *Afterthoughts*

In examining whether Drueck's testimony amounted to an expert opinion that the government was required—but failed—to disclose in advance, the Sixth Circuit panel never paused to consider whether his testimony might slip through a seeming loophole opened by the advisory committee. In its note to the 2000 amendment to Rule 701, the committee suggested that while a lay witness may not offer an opinion based on "specialized knowledge," the witness occasionally may offer an opinion based on the witness's "particularized knowledge," gained "by virtue of his or her position in [a] business." (ACN to 2000 amendment to FRE 701, RB 165.)

The Sixth Circuit apparently has never sought to define the bounds of the "particularized knowledge" that may inform lay opinions. It has invoked the concept only once—and then only in passing in an unpublished opinion. *See Lativafter Liquidating Trust v. Clear Channel Commc'ns, Inc.*, 345 Fed. Appx. 46, 51 (6th Cir. 2009). Two of the rather few courts to measure the breadth of particularized knowledge have reached very different conclusions. Both took as their natural starting point the advisory committee's announcement of the category of particularized knowledge and the examples it offered. The committee began with an instance from the business world:

> For example, most courts have permitted the owner or officer of a business to testify to the value or projected profits of the business, without the necessity of qualifying the witness as an accountant, appraiser, or similar expert. *See, e.g.*, Lightning Lube, Inc. v. Witco Corp. 4 F.3d 1153 (3d Cir. 1993) (no abuse of discretion in permitting the plaintiff's owner to give lay opinion testimony as to damages, as it was based on his knowledge and participation in the day-to-day affairs of the business). Such opinion testimony is admitted not because of experience, training or specialized knowledge within the realm of an expert, but because of the *particularized knowledge* that the witness has by virtue of his or her position in the business.

After stating this example of particularized knowledge, the committee wrote that the 2000 amendment, in adding the requirement that lay opinions "not [be] based on scientific, technical, or other specialized knowledge within the scope of Rule 702," "does not purport to change this analysis." (FRE 701(c); ACN to 2000 amendment to FRE 701, RB 165 (emphasis added).)

In another case arising in the business world, the Eleventh Circuit read broadly the committee's apparent sanction of lay opinions based on "knowledge that the witness has by virtue of his or her position in the business." That case—*Tampa Bay Shipbuilding & Repair Co. v. Cedar Shipping Co.*, 320 F.3d 1213 (11th Cir. 2003)—concerned a dispute arising out of alleged over-charges on a ship-repair contract. At trial the defendant ship owner objected to testimony by plaintiffs' officers, employees, and consultants that charges billed for repairs were "fair" and "reasonable" and "in line with similar services provided by other similar operations" in the industry. Although none of the challenged witnesses had been qualified as an expert, the appeals court approved their testimony. The court acknowledged that Rule 701 as amended in 2000 barred lay opinion testimony based on "specialized knowledge." But after reviewing the advisory committee's permission of lay opinions based on particularized knowledge, the court concluded: "it would appear that opinion testimony by business owners and officers is one of the prototypical areas [of permitted lay opinions] intended to remain undisturbed" by the 2000 amendment. 320 F.3d at 1222.

A federal district court in San Jose declined to follow the Eleventh Circuit in reading the advisory committee's sanction of opinions based on particularized knowledge to extend to all "opinion testimony by business owners and operators." In *Hynix Semiconductor, Inc. v. Rambus, Inc.*, 75 Fed. R. Evid. Serv. (Callaghan) 1009 (N.D. Cal. 2008), Judge Ronald Whyte noted that "[w]hile the text of Rule 701 appears unflinching in separating lay opinions from expert opinions, the advisory committee note regarding the amendment blinks"—and arguably opens the way for many lay opinions based on particularized knowledge to drift into the realm of expert opinions based on specialized knowledge.

Judge Whyte sought to stop that drift by focusing on the advisory committee's use of the words "a" and "the." The committee's note reports that courts have permitted the "owner or officer of *a* business to testify to the value or projected profits of *the* business" because of the witness's "particularized knowledge . . . [gained by] his or her position in *the* business." (Emphasis added.) After reviewing opinions of courts that, like the Eleventh Circuit, have read the committee's note broadly, Judge Whyte sought to narrow the note to its literal limits:

> The court finds these cases persuasive only in the limited context described in the advisory committee note regarding testimony about *one's* business, and it does not believe they can be read to support a broader "particularized knowledge" exception to the expert disclosure rules. As a general matter, " '[l]ay opinion testimony is admissible only to help the jury or the court to understand the facts about which the witness is testifying and not to provide specialized explanations or interpretations that an untrained layman could not make if perceiving the same acts or events.' " United States v. Conn, 297 F.3d 548, 554 (7th Cir. 2002) (quoting United States v. Peoples, 250 F.3d 630, 641 (8th Cir. 2001)). . . . Nonetheless, the rules of evidence have long permitted [persons] to testify to opinions about *their own* businesses based on their personal knowledge of *their* business, . . . and the court does not believe that the revised Rule 701 was meant to work a sea change with respect to that form of personal testimony.

Hynix, 75 Fed. R. Evid. Serv. (Callaghan) 1009 (emphasis added). Interestingly, the Eleventh Circuit recently recharacterized its opinion in *Tampa Bay* to narrow its holding along the lines Judge Whyte suggested: "we held in *Tampa Bay* that the opinion testimony of a business owner or officer about the manner in which *that company* conducts *its* business, which is based on particularized knowledge she gained in her position, is properly treated as lay testimony." *United States v. Hill*, 643 F.3d 807, 842 (11th Cir. 2011), *cert. denied*, 132 S. Ct. 1988 (2012) (emphasis added).

The significance of the advisory committee's reference to testimony about *one's own* business may become clearer if we step outside the realm of business and focus on the kindred matter of home ownership. Most lay homeowners have a well-informed opinion of the value of their own homes. They know how much they paid for their homes, what improvements they've made, what repairs are needed. They probably have followed the general trend of home prices in their neighborhoods and especially the selling prices of similar homes. Their knowledge of their homes' value is arguably "specialized," but only in the sense that no other layperson is likely to know as much about a home's value as its owner. Their knowledge is not, in the words of Rule 701(c), "specialized knowledge within the scope of Rule 702" requiring expert testimony. Instead, a homeowner's knowledge of her own home's value is, in words Judge Whyte quotes above, knowledge "that an untrained layman could [achieve] if perceiving the same acts or events."

Judge Whyte's reading of the committee's note tends to support the Sixth Circuit's ruling in *Ganier*. In rejecting the government's attempt to classify Drueck's testimony as a permitted lay opinion, the court implicitly rejected the broad meaning assigned "particularized knowledge" by the Eleventh Circuit in *Tampa Bay*. More explicitly, the court rejected the government's suggestion that "any person reasonably proficient in the use of commonly used computer software" could have decoded the search history recorded on Ganier's computer. On the contrary, the court wrote, "such an interpretation would require Drueck to apply knowledge and familiarity with computers and the particular forensic software well beyond that of the average layperson. This constitutes 'scientific, technical, or other specialized knowledge' within the scope of Rule 702." (Pages 741–42.)

Hence the *Ganier* court aimed, in the advisory committee's words, "to eliminate the risk that the reliability requirements set forth in Rule 702 will be evaded through the simple expedient of proffering an expert in lay witness clothing." (ACN to 2000 amendment to FRE 701, RB 164.) Drueck's testimony went beyond that of a home owner commenting on the value of her own home. Instead his knowledge was more like that of an expert home appraiser, aware of general market conditions and prevailing mortgage terms and able to evaluate homes across the community based on an array of facts from location to number of bathrooms to "curb appeal," even if lacking the intimate knowledge homeowners have of their homes.

Seen this way, a witness's "particularized knowledge" may be *exclusive* to that witness and yet not be the sort of "specialized knowledge" that falls "within the scope of Rule 702." FED. R. EVID. 701(c). Does this concept of particularized knowledge play a role outside business and related matters? "Similarly," the advisory committee wrote, "courts have permitted lay witnesses to testify that a substance appeared to be a narcotic, so long as a foundation of familiarity with the substance is established." (RB 165.) That is, a witness's knowledge of her body's reactions to various drugs could be exclusive to her and yet be the sort of knowledge "that an untrained layman could [achieve] if perceiving" comparable reactions in his own body. The witness's knowledge would be particularized, but not the sort of specialized knowledge that characterizes experts. And her lay testimony about her body's drug reactions, if relevant to the case, likely would be allowed. In all aspects of our lives, similar examples abound.

Problem 9.4

Hieroglyphics

In *United States v. Cano*, 289 F.3d 1354 (11th Cir. 2002), *cert. denied*, 540 U.S. 985 (2003), the government sought to introduce evidence of what it alleged was a phone book found in a lawful search of a "stash" house used by members of an alleged drug-trafficking conspiracy. The phone book contained a list of names, each followed by a series of ten symbols described by police detective Eugene Donnelly as "hieroglyphics." The government wished to present Donnelly's testimony about how he deciphered the hieroglyphic code and determined the phone numbers of persons listed in the book. Over the defendant's objection that Donnelly was not qualified as an expert cryptographer, the trial judge "conclud[ed] Donnelly would not be testifying as an expert witness" and permitted him to testify as follows:

> . . . First, [Donnelly] explained how he deciphered the hieroglyphics. Using wiretap information, he selected the telephone numbers associated with two of the members of the conspiracy, Homey and MiLagro, whose names appeared in the phone book. Their telephone numbers had ten digits. Looking at the phone book, he found the conspirator's name and aligned the ten digits (contained in the conspirator's phone number) with the hieroglyphic symbols appearing opposite the name; then, going from left to right, he assigned an Arabic number to each symbol. When he compared the symbols and phone numbers for these conspirators, he discovered that each symbol represented a specific Arabic numeral. In demonstrating how he deciphered the hieroglyphics, Donnelly used a poster board the prosecutor's office had prepared. The board had a line of

> ten numbers, zero to nine, going left to right. A hieroglyphic symbol, representing a specific Arabic numeral, appeared above each numeral.
>
> *Cano*, 289 F.3d at 1361. Should the trial court have permitted Donnelly to offer this testimony as a lay witness?

B. Expert Testimony

In the realm of evidence law the 1990s were the *Daubert* decade. Responding to the Supreme Court's ruling in *Daubert v. Merrell Dow Pharmaceuticals, Inc.*, 509 U.S. 579 (1993) (excerpted below at page 794), scholars and practitioners flooded law journals and judges crowded court reporters with complex analyses of different aspects of the law governing expert opinions. Although the Supreme Court's decision a decade later in *Crawford v. Washington*, 541 U.S. 36 (2004) (studied in Chapter 8), diverted scholarly interest elsewhere, courts continue to wrestle with issues presented by expert testimony. Those issues fall under five headings, which lay out the five demands the law places on expert opinion testimony:

1. ***Proper Qualifications:*** The witness must be "qualified as an expert by knowledge, skill, experience, training, or education." (Rule 702.)

2. ***Proper Topic:*** The expert's testimony typically must concern a topic that is beyond the ken of jurors. Moreover, the expert may not simply tell the jurors what result to reach in the case and may not intrude on the judge's role as legal expert. That is, the expert's opinion must "help" the jurors by supplying information or insights they otherwise would lack. (Rules 702(a) and 704.)

3. ***Sufficient Basis:*** The expert must have an adequate factual basis for her opinions. (Rules 702(b) and 703.)

4. ***Relevant and Reliable Methods:*** The expert's testimony must be "the product of reliable principles and methods . . . reliably applied . . . to the facts of the case." (Rule 702(c), (d); *cf. Daubert; Kumho Tire*).

5. ***Rule 403 Challenge:*** The evidence, if challenged, must survive a Rule 403 weighing test.

You already are familiar with the last of these demands. We now take up the first four.

1. WHO QUALIFIES AS AN EXPERT?

Focus on **FRE 702**

Problem 9.5
Horticulturist

Man Says He Helped Bring Drugs to State

Brian Richardson

TALLAHASSEE DEMOCRAT, Apr. 20, 1977, at 33

A 34–year-old California man said Tuesday he helped the alleged leader of a drug smuggling ring . . . ship[] nearly eight tons of marijuana, estimated to be worth $4.8 million, into the United States. . . .

[John] DePianelli testified Tuesday he . . . smoked the marijuana each time he helped unload it to make sure it was Colombian.

Defense attorneys claimed the only way DePianelli knew the marijuana was Colombian and not American-grown was that someone told him it was Colombian.

He [testified], however, that he could tell by its appearance, the smell of the smoke and the "high" he got that it was Colombian marijuana.

DePianelli said he had smoked marijuana more than 1,000 times. He said he has been called on to identify it more than 100 times, and has sold it more than 20 times. . . .

Assume the government must prove that the marijuana in question, which was never seized, came from outside the customs territory of the United States. As mentioned earlier, the Advisory Committee's Note to the 2000 amendment to Rule 701 suggests a lay witness may "testify that a substance appeared to be a narcotic, so long as a foundation of familiarity with the substance is established." (RB 165.) Is this language broad enough to permit de Pianelli (his actual name) to testify as a lay witness that the marijuana he smoked was imported from Colombia? If not, should the court deem de Pianelli qualified as an expert in identifying the source of marijuana shipments?

UNITED STATES V. JOHNSON

575 F.2d 1347 (5th Cir. 1978), *cert. denied*, 440 U.S. 907 (1979).

■ CHARLES CLARK, CIRCUIT JUDGE. The six appellants in this case ... [claim] it was improper to permit de Pianelli to testify as an expert concerning the origin of the marijuana. Appellants concede that the substance with which they were dealing was marijuana. They contend, however, that there was no objective evidence showing that the marijuana was imported from outside the customs territory of the United States. Since no marijuana was ever seized, the only non-hearsay evidence concerning the origin of this marijuana came from de Pianelli. When de Pianelli was first asked to state whether the marijuana had come from Colombia, counsel for defendants objected. The jury was then excused and de Pianelli was examined on voir dire and cross-examined by defense counsel. During voir dire, he admitted that he had smoked marijuana over a thousand times and that he had dealt in marijuana as many as twenty times. He also said that he had been asked to identify marijuana over a hundred times and had done so without making a mistake. He based his identification upon the plant's appearance, its leaf, buds, stems, and other physical characteristics, as well as upon the smell and the effect of smoking it.... It was stipulated that he had no special training or education for such identification. Instead, his qualifications came entirely from "the experience of being around a great deal and smoking it." He also said that he had compared Colombian marijuana with marijuana from other places as many as twenty times. Moreover, he had seen Colombian marijuana that had been grown in the United States and had found that it was different from marijuana grown in Colombia.

After the voir dire examination, the defendants objected to de Pianelli's expertise.... Despite the objection, the trial court permitted de Pianelli to give opinion evidence. Before the jury he related his experiences with marijuana and explained that he had tested a sample of marijuana from each importation and had verified that it came from Colombia....

The Ninth Circuit has [held]:

> To warrant the use of expert testimony, two elements are required. First, the subject of the inference must be so distinctly related to some science, profession, business or occupation as to be beyond the knowledge of the average layman, and second, the witness must

have such knowledge or experience in that field or calling as to make it appear that his opinion or inference will probably aid the trier in his search for truth.

Fineberg v. United States, 393 F.2d 417, 421 (9th Cir. 1968).

Here the subject of the inference, the source of the marijuana, is related to the occupation of selling illegal drugs and to the science of botany, neither of which is likely to be within the knowledge of an average juror. For the government to obtain a conviction it was necessary that it prove that the marijuana came from outside the customs territory of the United States. Testimony which would identify the source of the marijuana would be of obvious assistance to the jury. It was therefore proper for the trial court to consider whether de Pianelli was qualified to provide such testimony.

Rule 702 of the Federal Rules of Evidence provides that expertise may be obtained by experience as well as from formal training or education. de Pianelli's testimony during voir dire revealed that his substantial experience in dealing with marijuana included identification of Colombian marijuana. In light of that testimony, the trial court was within its discretion in deciding to admit the testimony for the jury's consideration.

The introduction of testimony from an expert witness does not foreclose the issue from consideration by the jury, which need not accept the expert's testimony. A defendant is free to introduce his own expert to challenge the prosecution's witness. Here the defense introduced the testimony of [an associate professor of biological science at Florida State University, Loren C.] Anderson, who said that it was impossible to determine the origin of a particular sample of marijuana by examining its physical characteristics. The trial court instructed the jury in general terms concerning the weight it should give to testimony. In addition, it specifically instructed the jury regarding expert witnesses and concluded with this admonition: "You should consider such expert opinion received in this case and give it such weight as you think it deserves." Thus the conflict between the experts was correctly presented to the jury for resolution....

... de Pianelli claimed that he could identify Colombian marijuana. Professor Anderson disputed that claim. But Professor Anderson admitted that climatological differences could produce differences in the marijuana plants. Professor Anderson's testimony was based upon the lack of scientific tests which would demonstrate that marijuana grown in Colombia differed from that grown elsewhere. Tests had shown, however, that marijuana grown in Canada differed from marijuana grown in other locations. Thus, there was some ambiguity in Professor Anderson's testimony. The issue was one that could have been resolved by the jury. In allowing the jury to consider the question and to hear the same arguments counsel now make to us, the trial court did not err. . . .

Historical Postscript to **United States v. Johnson***:* Novel as the government's gambit may seem, taking testimony from expert dope smokers is a timeworn tradition. . . .

The Proof of the Pudding

A Novel Proceeding in the United States District Court

SAN FRANCISCO CHRONICLE, Jan. 26, 1880, at 3

A novel proceeding took place in the United States District Court a few days ago. Some [men] were arrested and charged with attempting to sell opium so much below the market price as to create the suspicion that the drug was smuggled. In defense, they set up that the opium was a second-class article, and, therefore, worth no more than they asked for it. An expert being called to the stand said that the only way to determine the quality was to smoke the opium. The [prosecutor] . . . found the keeper of an opium den, who appeared with all the implements for the trial, and deftly molding the drug into a ball on a skewer, placed it on his pipe and whiffed away in court with great deliberation and apparent satisfaction, while Judge, jury, lawyers and spectators looked on. He pronounced the opium of the best quality, and being attacked by the attorney for the defense to reveal the location of his den, the expert would only say that he had been in the business for 35 years. . . .

JINRO AMERICA, INC. V. SECURE INVESTMENTS, INC.

266 F.3d 993 (9th Cir. 2001).

■ FISHER, CIRCUIT JUDGE: . . . This case arises out of a business deal ostensibly for the international trade of frozen chicken. . . . When the parties' deal unraveled, Jinro sued the defendants to recover millions of dollars for breach of contract, fraud and racketeering, but were met with the defendants' claim that the transaction was a sham. . . . [A] jury agreed with defendants' characterization of the transaction, whereupon the district court sua sponte entered summary judgment against Jinro on all its claims. . . .

DISCUSSION

. . . [W]e address the district court's admission of expert testimony, which we review for an abuse of discretion. As a key component of their defense, defendants relied on David Herbert Pelham as an expert witness to testify about Korean law and the business practices of Korean companies—particularly their alleged propensity to engage in fraudulent activity, including the avoidance of Korean currency laws. Since 1994, Pelham had been the general manager of the Pinkerton Detective Agency's office in Korea. Although he claimed to have familiarized himself with Korean business practices as part of his job duties and as "a hobby of his," Pelham had no formal education or training in business or as a cultural expert. He was not a lawyer. Rather, he was a private investigator who had been providing "commercial security" for over four years for various non-Korean corporations doing business in Korea. Prior to his employment by Pinkerton, Pelham had been trained as an investigator with the United States Air Force Office of Special Investigations, and had commanded the office that investigated Korean companies doing business with the Air Force. Pelham's other purported qualifications were that he had "served five tours of duty in Korea," lived there for about 12 years and was married to a Korean woman.

Although Pelham had not investigated Jinro itself, defendants offered his testimony ostensibly to educate the jury about the "modus operandi" of Korean businesses.... At trial, Pelham testified about how, in his experience, "Korean businessmen" behave in general. Little of this testimony was directly connected to Jinro itself, and none was based on Pelham's personal knowledge of Jinro or its affiliates. Rather, Pelham addressed himself to generalizations about Korean business attitudes and behavior.

Thus, Pelham was asked ... to opine on the merits of entering into oral contracts "with Koreans." ...

> *Q:* Would you recommend to your clients that they enter into oral agreements with Koreans?
>
> *A:* I would never recommend anybody rely on oral agreements.
>
> *Q:* Why is that?
>
> *A:* Well, I don't think oral agreements are a very safe way to do business anyplace, but particularly in Asia and probably more particularly in Korea.
>
> *Q:* Why is that?
>
> *A:* Well, because of the culture, dealing with Korean businessmen can end up with some pretty sorry results if you haven't safeguarded yourself....

When asked to explain the basis for this conclusion, Pelham stated that "newspaper articles" were one indicator. Indeed, his declaration revealed newspaper articles to be a principal source for his opinion on the alleged prevalence of corruption in the Korean business community. There he referred specifically, for instance, to a *Wall Street Journal* article and a public opinion poll in the *Korean Herald* as sources. He also based his opinion on unspecified information from his office staff. By the end of his testimony, Pelham had cited no research or study, [or] any empirical data, and had made only generalized, anecdotal references to his personal experience....

Pelham came before the jury cloaked with the mantle of an expert. This is significant for two reasons: First, it allowed him to testify based on hearsay information, and to couch his observations as generalized "opinions" rather than as first-hand knowledge about Jinro and its activities in particular. Second, as the opinion of a purported "expert" on Korean business practices and culture, his statements were likely to carry special weight with the jury. For these reasons, care must be taken to assure that a proffered witness truly qualifies as an expert [under] the requirements of Rule 702....

... In actuality, [Pelham's] qualifications to render such opinion testimony were glaringly inadequate, amounting to little more than the limited perspective of a professional investigator whose work experience had exposed him to instances of corrupt business behavior. He did not have the legal, business or financial expertise to evaluate the substance of the Jinro transaction. He had no education or training as a cultural expert generally, or as an expert on Korean culture specifically. He was not a trained sociologist or anthropologist, academic disciplines that might qualify one to provide reliable information about the cultural traits and behavior patterns of a particular group of people of a given ethnicity or nationality.

Rather, Pelham offered his impressionistic generalizations about Korean businesses based on his personal investigative experiences, his "hobby" of studying Korean business practices, unspecified input from his office staff and his marriage to a Korean woman—hardly an adequate foundation for the type of expert opinion he offered the jury. Moreover, he provided no empirical evidence or studies to support his sweeping indictment of the Korean business community—other than to cite newspaper articles and a few anecdotal examples, some of them clearly hearsay. We recognize that persons experienced in a particular field may have a "practical" expertise or specialized knowledge that might qualify them to provide relevant and reliable information to a lay jury. For example, Pelham perhaps might have been qualified to testify based on his experience as a professional commercial investigator (his "discipline") about the structure of the Korean governmental and banking systems—to illuminate for the jury how that country's regulatory system worked. This might have helped jurors understand and contextualize Jinro's interaction (or lack thereof) with that system.[8]

8. Experts routinely provide technical information or explain how certain processes work. United States v. Mohrbacher, 182 F.3d 1041 (9th Cir. 1999), for instance, involved a prosecution for transporting and receiving child pornography that had been

2. (IM)PROPER TOPICS OF EXPERT TESTIMONY

Focus on FRE 702 & 704

a. MATTERS OF COMMON KNOWLEDGE

Problem 9.7
Confusion?

... In February 1975, [Chesebrough–Pond's, Inc.,] filed an application to register its trademark, "Match," for a line of men's toiletries and cosmetics.... In June 1975, Fabergé acquired the "Macho" trademark, which had been registered by its prior owner in February 1973. This mark also covered a line of men's toiletries and cosmetics....

After receiving notice of the pending registration of "Match," Fabergé sent Chesebrough a letter on August 25, 1975, stating that it believed the two marks to be "confusingly similar," and that unless Chesebrough withdrew its application, Fabergé would file opposition thereto. When Chesebrough refused, Fabergé did file an opposition proceeding ... alleg[ing] that the " 'Match' mark so resembles opposer's mark 'Macho' as to be likely ... to cause confusion, mistake and deception." ...

In October 1978, Chesebrough filed this action in the district court seeking a declaratory judgment that use of "Match" would not infringe upon Fabergé's rights in "Macho." ...

Chesebrough–Pond's, Inc. v. Fabergé, Inc., 666 F.2d 393 (9th Cir.), *cert. denied*, 459 U.S. 967 (1982). Fabergé sought to offer the testimony of Dr. Bernard Einbond, an associate professor of English, who was expected to testify that the "sounds and spellings" of Match and Macho rendered the two words confusingly similar. Would such testimony satisfy Rule 702's requirement that expert testimony involve "scientific, technical, or other specialized knowledge [that] will help the trier of fact to understand the evidence or to determine a fact in issue"?

The factfinder in this declaratory judgment action was the judge. Would your answer to the last question differ if a jury had been deciding the critical question—whether the similarity between the trademarks creates a "likelihood of confusion"?

Problem 9.8

Housing Ads

Consider the facts of *Tyus v. Urban Search Management*, 102 F.3d 256 (7th Cir. 1996), *cert. denied*, 520 U.S. 1251 (1997):

> The New York is an upscale apartment house located on North Lake Shore Drive in Chicago [and owned and managed by the defendants].... Plaintiffs Thomas Walker and Anthony Tyus, both African Americans, noticed in the course of their own private efforts to find housing in the Chicago area that the advertisements for The New York, whether in the form of billboards, newspaper ads, or brochures, featured only White human models.... [F]rom 1989 through [1992, the] New York continued its exclusive use of White human models in its billboard and newspaper advertisements. Radio advertisements were aired that made no reference to The New York's commitment to being an equal housing opportunity provider, and many of the print advertisements omitted the Equal Opportunity Logo.... Only after the plaintiffs filed the present lawsuit [alleging discrimination in violation of the Fair Housing Act] did The New York's advertising consultant prepare any advertisement depicting a racially diverse group of people, and the one ad the consultant prepared did not appear in the publications normally used by The New York, such as the *Chicago Tribune* and *The Chicago Reader*. ...
>
> Dr. John Tarini, a psychologist, statistician, and chair of the Department of Marketing Communication at Columbia College (Chicago), [was prepared to testify] about how advertising sends a message to its target market and how an all-White advertising campaign affects African–Americans.... Dr. Tarini looked at The New York's ads in particular, using the well known "focus group" method, to see how they came across to African–American viewers.

Did Dr. Tarini's proposed testimony satisfy Rule 702's requirement that expert testimony involve "scientific, technical, or other specialized knowledge [that] will help the trier of fact"?

Problem 9.9

Slip and Fall

While a passenger aboard the *M/V Nautica*, Lydia Rosenfeld slipped and fell on a ceramic tile floor near the buffet bar of the vessel's Terrace Café. She suffered a shoulder fracture and incurred medical expenses as a result of her fall. Rosenfeld brought this diversity action against the operator of the *M/V Nautica*, Oceania Cruises, Inc. ("Oceania"), to recover damages for her injuries. She claimed . . . that Oceania negligently caused the accident by failing to provide an adequate flooring surface for the buffet area of the Terrace Café.

To prove her case, Rosenfeld offered the expert testimony of Peter Vournechis, an Australian floor-safety specialist who performed various coefficient-of-friction tests to determine the slip resistance of the *M/V Nautica*'s flooring surfaces. Vournechis found that, under wet conditions, the ceramic-tile surface surrounding the Terrace Café had an inadequately low coefficient of friction. Thus, he proposed to testify at trial that the flooring surface was not reasonably safe for a self-serve or bistro area, because it posed a high risk for those passing through the Café to slip and fall.

Following briefing, the district court entered a pretrial order precluding Vournechis's testimony. The court stated only one ground for its decision:

> [Rosenfeld] . . . has not established that the proposed liability expert will provide helpful analysis to the Court in understanding a matter of scientific, technical or specialized expertise. Instead, the liability expert intends to testify that the floor where plaintiff fell is unreasonably safe for its intended use. Such conclusions are properly left for the Court or jury to decide.

At the close of the evidence, the court instructed the jury, in relevant part, as follows:

> In this case the plaintiff claims that the defendant was negligent and that such negligence was the legal cause of damage sustained by the plaintiff. Specifically, the plaintiff alleges that the injury was caused by Defendant's failure to choose an adequate flooring surface for the area where the accident occurred. . . .
>
> In order to prevail on this claim the Plaintiff must prove both of the following facts by a preponderance of the evidence:

First: That the defendant was "negligent;" and

Second: That such negligence was a "legal cause" of damage sustained by the plaintiff.

Rosenfeld v. Oceania Cruises, Inc., 654 F.3d 1190, 1191–92 (11th Cir. 2011). In light of these closing instructions, was the trial judge right to exclude Vournechis's proposed testimony as unhelpful? What are the best arguments for both sides?

---

b. OPINIONS ON LAW AND OPINIONS ON ULTIMATE ISSUES

Problem 9.10
Defendant's Intent

Virgil Montgomery, a 60–year-old retired minister, challenged his conviction of possessing pseudoephedrine with intent to manufacture methamphetamine. Prosecution witnesses testified at trial that on June 23, 2004, Montgomery and Joyce Biby, age 63, left their small-town homes on the Washington–Idaho border and drove to Spokane. Over the course of the day they shopped at several Spokane-area stores:

- At a large grocery, Montgomery bought five boxes of matches.
- At a Target store, Montgomery and Biby each bought two boxes of Target-brand cold medicine containing the decongestant pseudoephedrine.
- At a Rosauers grocery Montgomery bought one box of Sudafed-brand cold medicine, and Biby bought three boxes of matches, paying separately.
- At a Wal–Mart store Montgomery bought a gallon of acetone while Biby, shopping separately, bought two cans of denatured alcohol.
- At a second Target on the north side of Spokane, Biby bought two boxes of Target-brand cold medicine, and Montgomery bought a large bottle of hydrogen peroxide.

Unchallenged evidence showed that making methamphetamine requires ephedrine or pseudoephedrine (found in common cold medications such as Sudafed), red phosphorus (found in the striking surfaces on matchbooks and extracted using acetone), a solvent such as denatured or isopropyl alcohol, iodine (which can be extracted from commonly sold tinctures of iodine using hydrogen peroxide), lye, and hydrochloric or muriatic acid.

Montgomery claimed he was unaware of Biby's purchases and offered explanations for each of his own. He said, for example, that the Sudafed was for his son, whose other medications react badly with Target-brand cold medicine, and that Montgomery needed the acetone to remove loose floor tiles in his trailer.

Over Montgomery's objection a forensic chemist testified in response to the prosecutor's questions that the combined purchases of Biby and Montgomery "are all what lead me toward [the opinion that] this pseudoephedrine is possessed with intent [to manufacture methamphetamine]." He conceded on cross-examination that he would not be able to come to this conclusion based on Montgomery's purchases alone.

Assume the Federal Rules of Evidence govern. Was the trial judge right to admit the forensic chemist's opinion? What are the strongest arguments for and against admission? *See State v. Montgomery*, 183 P.3d 267 (Wash. 2008).

Hygh v. Jacobs

961 F.2d 359 (2d Cir. 1992).

■ Mahoney, Circuit Judge: Invoking 42 U.S.C. § 1983 (1988), . . . William C. Hygh sued a number of defendants for alleged constitutional violations [including excessive use of force] stemming from his arrest by . . . William Jacobs, a police officer of the Village of Catskill, New York, on May 21, 1987. Hygh attained judgments [and attorney's fees in various amounts]. . . . Jacobs appeals. . . .

Background

On the evening of May 21, 1987, Hygh visited his friend Deborah Moore at her Catskill home, during which visit he consumed two beers. The couple had a disagreement, and Hygh departed. Once outside, he removed a propane tank attached to the house and placed it on the ground. Moore then became alarmed, and instructed her daughter to telephone the police.

Jacobs arrived shortly thereafter, and a heated exchange between Hygh and Jacobs took place. Hygh volunteered that if Jacobs had any charges, Jacobs should arrest him. After further conversation, a shoving match ensued, during which Jacobs informed Hygh that he was under arrest. At this juncture, Jacobs struck Hygh in the cheek. Hygh claims that Jacobs struck him in the face from behind while Hygh was bending over to pick up his jacket after being informed that he was under arrest. Jacobs asserts that he hit Hygh with his fist in self-defense, while they were erect and facing each other, after being shoved by Hygh.

In any event, the blow to Hygh's cheek fractured his cheekbones, and plastic surgery under general anesthesia was subsequently required to deal with the injury. The plastic surgeon who performed the operation testified that the infliction of the injuries suffered by Hygh "would take ... an extremely strong blow. And classically it's a blunt instrument of some sort that we would see it." He also testified that Hygh suffered permanent nerve damage as a result of the blow. Jacobs testified that because the confrontation with Hygh occurred at night, he had a flashlight in one hand throughout the encounter....

At trial, Hygh called Terry C. Cox, a professor at Eastern Kentucky University, as an expert witness concerning law enforcement. Citing the results of a study in which he had participated, Cox testified that the use of a flashlight as an offensive or defensive weapon greatly increased the risk of physical injury posed by the use of a baton or nightstick. Cox also testified that in his opinion, the use of a baton or flashlight to strike a person in the head would constitute "deadly physical force" that would not be "justified under the circumstances." He further testified that, accepting Hygh's version of his encounter with Jacobs, there was no "real legitimate reason" for the use of "any force" by Jacobs.

In answer to a question whether, accepting Jacobs' version of the incident (including the dubious premise that Jacobs conceded that he hit Hygh with his flashlight rather than his fist), "Jacobs acted in an objectively reasonable manner for a police officer under the circumstances as he described them," Cox responded that Jacobs had employed "deadly physical force" whose use was not "warranted under the circumstances." He further testified that Jacobs' conduct in these circumstances was "totally improper." Cox subsequently described "deadly physical force" as "using force in such a way that it has the potential to kill someone." ...

DISCUSSION

Jacobs contends on appeal that [the] expert testimony by Professor Cox invaded the province of the jury....

The standard for evaluation of Cox's expert testimony regarding Jacobs' conduct is provided by [unrestyled] Fed. R. Evid. 704(a), which provides in pertinent part: "Testimony in the form of an opinion or inference otherwise admissible is not objectionable because it embraces an ultimate issue to be decided by the trier of fact." While Rule 704 has abolished the common law "ultimate issue" rule, however, it has not "lowered the bars so as to admit all opinions." FED. R. EVID. 704 advisory committee's note.

This circuit is in accord with other circuits in requiring exclusion of expert testimony that expresses a legal conclusion. As several courts have already done, we invoke the advisory committee note's illuminating distinction between admissible and excludable versions of an expert's opinion testimony:

> Under Rules 701 and 702, opinions must be helpful to the trier of fact, and Rule 403 provides for exclusion of evidence which wastes time. These provisions afford ample assurances *against the admission of opinions which would merely tell the jury what result to reach,* somewhat in manner of the oath-helpers of an earlier day. They also stand ready to exclude opinions phrased in terms of inadequately explored legal criteria....

FED. R. EVID. 704 advisory committee's note (emphasis added) [RB 180]; *see also* United States v. Scop, 846 F.2d 135, 142 (2d Cir. 1988) (opinion that defendant acted as a "steerer" would be legitimate under Rule 704, but testimony that defendant "possessed narcotics ... with the intent to sell" would not).

Even if a jury were not misled into adopting outright a legal conclusion proffered by an expert witness, the testimony would remain objectionable by communicating a legal standard—explicit or implicit—to the jury. Whereas an expert may be uniquely qualified by experience to assist the trier of fact, he is not qualified to compete with the judge in the function of instructing the jury. As we stated in Marx & Co., Inc. v. Diners' Club, Inc., 550 F.2d 505 (2d Cir. 1977):

> The basis of expert capacity, according to Wigmore, may "be summed up in the term 'experience.'" But experience is hardly a qualification for construing a document for its legal effect when there is a knowledgeable gentleman in a robe whose exclusive province it is to instruct the jury on the law. The danger is that the jury may think that the "expert" in the particular branch of the law knows more than the judge—surely an inadmissible inference in our system of law.

In this case, Professor Cox was questioned extensively concerning Jacobs' use of force. In the course of that testimony, he tendered some conclusions that we deem to have crossed the line provided by Rule 704. He provided a definition of deadly physical force as "using force in such a way that it has the potential to kill someone." [But] § 1983 actions that are premised upon traditional torts generally incorporate the law of the pertinent state jurisdiction, and New York provides a statutory definition of deadly physical force that is pertinent here. *See* N.Y. PENAL LAW § 10.00(11) (McKinney 1987) ("'Deadly physical force' means physical force which, under the circumstances in which it is used, is readily capable of causing death or other serious physical injury."). The difference between the Cox and statutory formulations is not substantial, however, and the court later charged the jury comprehensively regarding the standards by which Jacobs' use of force against Hygh was to be measured.

Far more troubling, Cox testified that Jacobs' conduct was not "justified under the circumstances," not "warranted under the circumstances," and "totally improper." We have held that an expert's testimony that a defendant was "negligent" should not have been allowed. We see no significant distinction in Cox's conclusory condemnations of Jacobs' actions here, which, in the language of the advisory committee, "merely [told] the jury what result to reach." FED. R. [EVID.] 704 advisory committee's note.

... [W]e conclude that Cox's testimony regarding the ultimate legal conclusion entrusted to the jury crossed the line and should have been excluded.... We conclude, however, that the error was harmless and therefore does not call for reversal.

... Cox's impermissible testimony was expressed within a larger body of otherwise unobjectionable testimony concerning police procedures involving violent arrestees from which the jury could easily have drawn the same conclusions that Cox did.

Further, the evidence that Jacobs did in fact use excessive force against Hygh was strong. The trial judge instructed the jury that it could reject expert testimony "if, after careful consideration of the evidence, you simply disagree with it." The trial judge also instructed the jury extensively concerning Jacobs' use of force.... Although the question is close, we conclude that the standard of "substantial justice," FED. R. CIV. P. 61, does not call for a new trial because of the erroneous admission of Cox's impermissibly conclusory testimony....

---

c. OPINIONS ON CREDIBILITY

Problem 9.11

Officers' Truthfulness

Thomas Nimely was shot and paralyzed by New York City Police Officer John Muirhead. Later he brought a federal civil rights action against the officer, the department, and the city. The central dispute at trial was whether the officer, as Nimely alleged, shot Nimely in the back as he fled empty-handed or, as Officer Muirhead claimed, shot Nimely as he turned toward Muirhead and aimed a gun at him. Muirhead and his partner testified that they saw Nimely face Muirhead and raise his gun toward him, prompting Muirhead to shoot Nimely in the chest.

Medical evidence contradicted the officers' accounts. Plaintiff's and defendants' experts agreed that the bullet entered the left side of Nimely's back, hit his spinal cord, and lodged in the right side of his body. They agreed Nimely could not have been facing Muirhead when shot. But the defense's medical expert, Dr. Stuart Dawson, sought to reconcile the medical evidence with Muirhead's and his partner's perception that Muirhead shot Nimely in the chest: "Dawson explained that if Nimely had been turning with a gun in the split second before being shot by Muirhead, Nimely would have still completed his turn as he fell to the ground." Dawson added that the speed of these events, together with the limited powers of human perception, could have caused Muirhead and his partner to "perceive[] Nimely to have been fully turned when Muirhead pulled the trigger, notwithstanding that, in reality, Nimely could not have been facing Muirhead until after the bullet had already entered Nimely's body."

Defense counsel pressed Dawson to explain why he did not conclude that Muirhead simply lied in claiming he shot Nimely in the chest:

> *Q:* In doing your analysis, ... did you consider that the police officer who said that he shot him straight in the chest wasn't telling the truth?
>
> *A:* ... I considered that possibility and—but fairly quickly rejected it as being the less likely of the things that happened.
>
> *Q:* Why did you reject it?
>
> MR. KELTON [PLAINTIFF'S COUNSEL]: Objection, your Honor.
>
> THE COURT: Overruled. You may answer....
>
> *A:* ... [I]t's reasonable to infer that a police officer is going to know that whenever a discharge [of his weapon] does occur, there is going to be a big investigation and that will include forensic examination of wounds, so it didn't make much sense to me that the police officer would say that the person was shot in the front if it would be obvious to the police officer that an investigation would be done and that would show the person was shot in the back.

Later Dawson added, "I rejected the idea that they were lying because it would be such an easily disproved lie."

Should the trial judge have overruled plaintiff's objections to this testimony? *See Nimely v. City of New York*, 414 F.3d 381 (2d Cir. 2005).

STATE v. BATANGAN

Supreme Court of Hawaii.
71 Haw. 552 (1990).

■ WAKATSUKI, J. Felomino Batangan (Defendant) was accused of having sexual contact with his daughter (Complainant). Complainant alleged that when she was 6 or 7 years old, on four or five occasions, Defendant performed sexual acts on her. Complainant could not provide any specific dates or reference points in time. Nor were the acts described specific as to one incident or another. There was no evidence of physical injury and no third-party witnesses to these incidents.

Complainant did not report these incidents until several months after the occurrences. She first reported to school authorities that Defendant had physically abused her. When no injuries were found, she admitted that she had lied about the physical abuse, but instead accused Defendant of sexually abusing her. Complainant subsequently recanted her allegations of sexual abuse. At trial, however, Complainant testified that she had been sexually abused by Defendant.

Defendant was indicted on one count of second-degree rape and one count of first-degree sexual abuse. At the first trial, Defendant was acquitted of the rape charge, and a mistrial (due to a hung jury) was declared on the sexual abuse charge. The State proceeded to retry Defendant on the sex abuse count.

At the second trial, the State presented Dr. John Bond as an expert witness in the field of clinical psychology with a subspecialty in the treatment of sexually abused children. Dr. Bond had evaluated Complainant on one occasion three weeks prior to the second trial.

Dr. Bond testified regarding his evaluation of Complainant (her personality, intelligence, behavior) and what Complainant had related to him regarding the incidents of sexual abuse. There was also some testimony about behavior of child sex abuse victims in general. Finally, Dr. Bond testified as to how he evaluates whether a child is telling the truth about being sexually abused. He then implicitly testified that Complainant was believable and that she had been abused by Defendant.

Defendant objected to the admission of Dr. Bond's testimony. The trial court, however, determined that such testimony was admissible under State v. Kim, 64 Haw. 598 (1982).

Defendant was convicted of first-degree sexual abuse. He appeals on the ground that the trial court committed error in admitting Dr. Bond's testimony. We agree.

I.

. . . Rule 702, Hawaii Rules of Evidence (HRE) governs the admission of expert testimony at a trial:

> *Testimony by experts.* If scientific, technical, or other specialized knowledge will assist the trier of fact to understand the evidence or to determine a fact in issue, a witness qualified as an expert by knowledge, skill, experience, training, or education may testify thereto in the form of an opinion or otherwise.*

Expert testimony assists the trier of fact by providing "a resource for ascertaining truth in relevant areas outside the ken of ordinary laity." Specialized knowledge which is the proper subject of expert testimony is knowledge not possessed by the average trier of fact who lacks the expert's skill, experience, training, or education. Although an expert's testimony on matters within the competence of the jurors may be relevant and helpful, "the possibility that the jury may be unduly influenced by the expert's opinion would [militate] against admission." *Kim*, 64 Haw. at 607. Scientific and expert testimony, with [its] "aura of special reliability and trustworthiness," courts the danger that the triers of fact will "abdicate [their] role of critical assessment," and "surrender [] their own common sense in weighing testimony." United States v. Azure, 801 F.2d 336, 341 (8th Cir. 1986).

The common experience of a jury, in most cases, provides a sufficient basis for assessment of a witness' credibility. Thus, expert testimony on a witness' credibility is inappropriate. *Kim*, 64 Haw. at 607. However, sexual abuse of children "is a particularly mysterious phenomenon," State v. Castro, 69 Haw. 633, 648 (1988), "and the common experience of the jury may represent a less than adequate foundation for assessing the credibility of a young child who complains of sexual abuse." State v. Myers, 359 N.W.2d 604, 610 (Minn. 1984).

> While jurors may be capable of personalizing the emotions of victims of physical assault generally, and of assessing witness credibility accordingly, tensions unique to trauma experienced by a child sexually abused by a family member have remained largely unknown to the public. . . . [T]he routine indicia of witness credibility—consistency, willingness to aid the prosecution, straightforward rendition of the facts—may, for good reason be lacking. As a result jurors may

* [At the time *Batangan* was decided, a decade before the 2000 amendment to FRE 702 and the addition of what are now parts (b), (c), and (d), Hawaii's Rule 702 matched the federal rule word for word.—GF]

> impose standards of normalcy on child victim/witnesses who consistently respond in distinctly abnormal fashion.

State v. Moran, 151 Ariz. 378, 381 (1986).

Child victims of sexual abuse have exhibited some patterns of behavior which are seemingly inconsistent with behavioral norms of other victims of assault. Two such types of behavior are delayed reporting of the offenses and recantation of allegations of abuse. Normally, such behavior would be attributed to inaccuracy or prevarication. In these situations it is helpful for the jury to know that many child victims of sexual abuse behave in the same manner. Expert testimony "[e]xposing jurors to the unique interpersonal dynamics involved in prosecutions for intrafamily child sexual abuse," Wheat v. State, 527 A.2d 269, 273 (Del. Supr. Ct. 1987), "may play a particularly useful role by disabusing the jury of some widely held misconceptions . . . so that it may evaluate the evidence free of the constraints of popular myths." People v. Gray, 187 Cal. App. 3d 213, 218 (1986).

We recognize that even this type of expert testimony carries the potential of bolstering the credibility of one witness and conversely refuting the credibility of another. Much expert testimony on any subject will tend to do this. Such testimony, by itself, does not render the evidence inadmissible. . . .

Thus, while expert testimony explaining "seemingly bizarre" behavior of child sex abuse victims is helpful to the jury and should be admitted, conclusory opinions that abuse did occur and that the child victim's report of abuse is truthful and believable is of no assistance to the jury, and therefore, should not be admitted. Such testimony is precluded by HRE Rule 702. "Once the jury has learned the victim's behavior from the evidence and has heard experts explain why sexual abuse may cause delayed reporting, inconsistency, or recantation, we do not believe the jury needs an expert to explain that the victim's behavior is consistent or inconsistent with the crime having occurred." *Moran*, 151 Ariz. at 385. The jury is fully capable, on its own, of making the connections to the facts of the particular case before them and drawing inferences and conclusions therefrom.

II.

We are cognizant that HRE Rule 704 permits "[t]estimony in the form of opinion or inference" even though "it embraces an ultimate issue to be decided by the trier of fact." But Rule 704 does not allow "the admission of opinions which would merely tell the jury what result to reach[.]" Commentary to HRE Rule 704. [*Cf.* RB 180.]

As in most child sexual abuse cases, where "the only evidence consists of the victim's accusation and the defendant's denial, expert testimony on the question of who to believe is nothing more than advice to jurors on how to decide the case." *Moran*, 151 Ariz. at 383. The expert's use of words such as "truthful" and "believable" is not talismanic. But where the effect of the expert's opinion is "the same as directly opining on the truthfulness of the complaining witness," State v. Myers, 382 N.W.2d 91, 97 (Iowa 1986), such testimony invades the province of the jury.

> Unless the function of a jury is to find the truth, its role is devoid of substance. Often the jury can meet this obligation only by determining the credibility of witnesses.... It has not been demonstrated that the art of psychiatry has yet developed into a science so exact as to warrant such a basic intrusion into the jury process.

State v. Walgraeve, 243 Or. 328, 333 (1966)....

V.

In this case, although Dr. Bond's qualification as an expert was not objected to, his testimony regarding general principles of social or behavioral science of a child victim in a sexual abuse case was so minuscule, we are convinced that his testimony could not have assisted the jury in understanding an otherwise bizarre behavior. In fact, Dr. Bond several times asked the jury to recall their own childhood days and suggested that Complainant's actions were actions of normal children under similar circumstances. When queried about retractions of accusations—a common behavior recognized as unique to intrafamily sex abuse—Dr. Bond admitted that he lacked data on the subject. Finally, when Dr. Bond was asked to evaluate Complainant's credibility in her accusation of sexual abuse by Defendant, he did not explicitly say that Complainant was "truthful" or "believable," but there is no doubt in our minds that the jury was left with a clear indication of his conclusion that Complainant was truthful and believable.

We hold that Dr. Bond's testimony was impermissible under HRE Rule 702 and therefore clearly prejudicial to Defendant. To the extent that any holding in *Kim* is inconsistent with our holding herein, such holding in *Kim* is overruled.

Defendant's conviction is vacated. Case is remanded for a new trial.

STATE V. BATANGAN: *Afterthoughts**

Courts say that lie detecting is something the jury does best. In the liturgy of the trial, judges tell jurors that they "are the sole judges of the credibility or 'believability' of each witness...." FIFTH CIRCUIT CRIMINAL JURY INSTRUCTIONS § 1.08 (2001). The Ninth Circuit has said simply that

* Much of the material for this section appeared in a somewhat different form in George Fisher, *The Jury's Rise as Lie Detector,* 107 YALE L.J. 575, 577–79, 707 (1997).

"the jury is the lie detector in the courtroom." United States v. Barnard, 490 F.2d 907, 912 (9th Cir. 1973), *cert. denied*, 416 U.S. 959 (1974).

What tools do jurors have for this task of lie detection? They come to court, as we so often tell them, with their common sense and may reject any evidence that defies it. In court we give them three more lie-detecting tools—the oath, demeanor evidence, and cross-examination. If these tools are lacking, we generally do not put jurors to the task of detecting lies. Hence we usually do not ask jurors to judge the truthfulness of hearsay.

Still, with some regularity, we present jurors with two witnesses who tell irreconcilable stories about the same event. In many criminal cases we supply little evidence other than the oath of the accuser and the oath of the accused and the demeanor of each under cross-examination. Jurors therefore confront the intractable task of searching the faces and gestures of strangers for the signs of deceit.

Our unguarded confidence that jurors are up to this task is both remarkable and probably wrong. Most evidence suggests jurors have no particular talent for spotting lies. Not only do experimental subjects rarely perform much better than chance at distinguishing truth from falsehood, but they *think* they are better lie detectors than they are. *See* ALDERT VRIJ, DETECTING LIES AND DECEIT 68–69, 76, 98–99 (2000) (collecting studies); Mark Gregory Frank, Human Lie Detection Ability as a Function of the Liar's Motivation 1 (unpublished Ph.D. dissertation, Cornell University 1989); Olin Guy Wellborn III, *Demeanor*, 76 CORNELL L. REV. 1075, 1082–88 (1991) (summarizing studies).

Of course, lie-detecting talent is not an easy thing to measure. In the context of real trials we almost never can know if jurors have judged the truth right. To measure their accuracy as lie detectors, we normally must resort to experimental techniques. Many attempts by social scientists to test lie-detecting skill have two shortcomings. The first, and less damning, is that many studies measure the capacity of *persons* but not of *jurors* to detect lies. They teach us little about whether the collective, deliberative process improves the accuracy of lie detection.

The second, far greater flaw of these studies is that they fail to replicate with any realism the trial witness's intense interest in being believed. *See* VRIJ, *supra*, at 43–44, 195. Sometimes the attempts of social scientists to create a real incentive to lie seem silly. In one experiment, subjects were asked to make statements about whether they had cheated on an exam. The experimenters asked half of the subjects to *pretend* they really had cheated on the exam and the other half to pretend they had not. The researchers then tested to see if experimental jurors could tell who was "lying." *See* Wellborn, *supra*, at 1082.

Another study employed nursing students as experimental liars. Researchers told the students that their capacity to lie persuasively was an important part of being a good nurse. The researchers then asked the would-be nurses to watch a video screen and describe what they saw on the video as pleasant ocean scenes. At some point the image on the screen switched to one of horrible carnage, but the nurses were told to describe it as a flowery park. Later the researchers showed videotapes of the nursing students to experimental jurors to test whether they could tell when the students were telling the truth and when they were lying about the images on the screen. The study found that very few viewers of the videotapes "did better than chance" at this task. *See* PAUL EKMAN, TELLING LIES: CLUES TO DECEIT IN THE MARKETPLACE, POLITICS, AND MARRIAGE 54–56, 85–87 (1992).

Studies that show jurors to be poor lie detectors perhaps undermine only the rhetoric and not the rationale of cases such as *Batangan*. Even if jurors are bad judges of credibility, it is still possible that an expert opinion about the truthfulness of a witness would not help the jury. After all, how do we know that one or another expert is any better than the average juror at assessing the credibility of strangers?

---

d. OPINIONS ON EYEWITNESS IDENTIFICATION

STATE v. GUILBERT

Supreme Court of Connecticut.
306 Conn. 218 (2012).

■ PALMER, J. A jury found the defendant, Brady Guilbert, guilty of . . . two counts of murder . . . and assault in the first degree. . . . The trial court . . . sentenced the defendant to a term of life imprisonment without the possibility of release, plus twenty years. On appeal, the defendant . . . contends that the trial court improperly precluded him from presenting expert testimony on the fallibility of eyewitness identification testimony. The defendant maintains that this court should overrule State v. Kemp, 199 Conn. 473, 477 (1986), and State v. McClendon, 248 Conn. 572, 586 (1999), in which we concluded that the average juror knows about the factors affecting the reliability of eyewitness identification and that expert testimony on the issue is disfavored because it invades the province of the jury to determine what weight to give the evidence. We agree that the time has come to overrule *Kemp* and *McClendon* and, further, that testimony by a qualified expert on the fallibility of eyewitness identification is admissible . . . when that testimony would aid the jury in evaluating the state's identification evidence. . . .

The jury reasonably could have found the following facts. At approximately 11:30 p.m. on October 8, 2004, Cedric Williams and Terry Ross arrived at a bar in New London.... At approximately 11:45 p.m., William Robinson arrived at the bar. About one hour later, as Robinson walked to the restroom, he was shot in the face and suffered a life-threatening wound....

At approximately 12:40 a.m. on October 9, 2004, Officer Jose Olivero of the New London police department received a radio transmission about a disturbance at the bar. As he responded to the call, he saw the defendant running away from the bar, clutching something in both hands. At trial, Olivero testified that the defendant had been wearing light blue sweatpants, a white tee shirt, and a black or dark blue bomber jacket.

At approximately 12:51 a.m., the New London police department received a 911 call about a shooting at the intersection of Hope and Hempstead Streets in New London. Police officers responding to the call found Ross' Volvo station wagon crashed into a tree. Ross and Williams were inside the vehicle, and both had been shot in the head. Williams was pronounced dead at the scene and Ross was taken to Lawrence Memorial Hospital in New London, where he was pronounced dead. An examiner with the state forensic science laboratory ultimately determined that Ross and Williams had been shot with the gun that had been used to shoot Robinson.

Later that day, the defendant's friend, Gary Holland, drove the defendant to Bronx County, New York. Holland returned to Connecticut at about 5:00 p.m. and learned from watching television that three people had been shot in New London and that the police were looking for the defendant. Holland called the defendant and informed him of what he had learned. The defendant neither admitted nor denied involvement in the shootings.

On the evening of October 9, 2004, Detective Keith Crandall and Officer George Potts of the New London police department visited Robinson at Rhode Island Hospital. When Potts asked Robinson who had shot him, Robinson responded, ... "Fats did it." Potts and Crandall then showed Robinson several photographic arrays, and Robinson identified the defendant as the person who had shot him. Robinson gave a statement to Crandall indicating that he had known the defendant "for a while" and had "had words" with him "a couple of months" earlier....

Nine days after the shooting, Lashon Baldwin saw the defendant's photograph in a newspaper and gave a statement to the New London police about the incident at the intersection of Hope and Hempstead Streets. At trial, Baldwin testified ... [that at] the time of the shooting, Baldwin and her cousin, Jackie Gomez, were seated in a car parked on Hempstead Street. Baldwin saw a car traveling down Hempstead Street and, as the car reached Hope Street, she heard three "loud pops." The car then came to a stop after hitting another parked car, and the defendant exited through the back door on the driver's side. The defendant was wearing "a black flight [jacket]. . . ." Baldwin recognized the defendant and knew him as "Fats" because she had seen him as a "regular customer" in a donut shop where she had worked for more than one and one-half years. . . .

At trial, [Gomez] testified . . . [that he] was with Baldwin in the car on Hempstead Street when he heard three gunshots. He . . . saw a car drive up Hope Street and hit another car. A person wearing a "black hoodie" and "blue jeans" exited from the car and wiped the door handle with his sleeve. The person came toward the car that Gomez and Baldwin were in, and Gomez recognized him as the defendant. Gomez knew the defendant because they previously had lived together for "quite some time." . . .

Ten days after the shootings, Scott Lang, who had been at the bar when Robinson was shot, saw the defendant's photograph in a newspaper and recognized him as the person who had shot Robinson. . . . At trial, he testified . . . [that on] the night of the shooting, Lang was waiting in line to use the restroom at the bar when he was shoved against a door and a shot was fired. Lang was "shoulder to shoulder" with the shooter and observed that he was wearing "a black quilted jacket, possibly North Face." At trial, Lang identified the defendant as the shooter.

On October 14, 2004, police apprehended the defendant in New York. . . .

Before trial, defense counsel indicated that he intended to call Charles A. Morgan III as an expert on eyewitness identifications. The state filed a motion to preclude Morgan's testimony on the ground that the reliability of eyewitness identifications is within the knowledge of the average juror. The trial court then conducted an evidentiary hearing on the state's motion at which Morgan proffered testimony that he is a medical doctor with "specialty training" in psychiatry and that, for the last seventeen years, he has spent 50 percent of his time researching how stress affects thought processes and memory. . . .

Morgan explained that there are three phases of memory formation—encoding, storage and retrieval—and that stress can disrupt both encoding and storage. When a subject is exposed to information about the remembered event during the storage phase—for example, when, following the event, the subject . . . sees a photograph of the person in the newspaper—the subject may incorporate the information into his or her memory and come to believe that the information actually was obtained at an earlier time. This process is known as retrofitting. Furthermore, Morgan testified that the majority of eyewitness identification researchers agree that there is little or no correlation between confidence and accuracy; in other words, an eyewitness' confidence in the accuracy of an identification is not a reliable indicator of the identification's true accuracy. Although Morgan observed that, if an eyewitness is familiar with a person, the eyewitness' identification of that person is likely to be more accurate, he explained that an identification's accuracy may be adversely affected by such factors as the length of time during which the eyewitness was able to observe the person, lighting, distance, and whether the eyewitness was paying attention....

At the conclusion of the hearing, the trial court granted the state's motion to preclude Morgan's testimony.... The court ... appeared to conclude that Morgan's general opinions about the effects of stress on memory, the lack of a correlation between confidence and accuracy of identifications, and the risk of retrofitting were all inadmissible because these matters generally were within the common knowledge of jurors.

Although the trial court granted the motion to preclude Morgan's testimony, the court indicated that it had prepared jury instructions on the reliability of eyewitness identifications.... Ultimately, the trial court instructed the jury that stress and the receipt of postevent information can reduce the accuracy of an eyewitness identification and that confidence often is not a reliable indicator of accuracy.[5] ...

"It is well settled that [t]he true test of the admissibility of [expert] testimony is ... whether the witnesses offered as experts have any peculiar knowledge or experience, not common to the world, which renders their opinions founded on such knowledge or experience any aid to the court or the jury in determining the questions at issue...." Sullivan v. Metro–North Commuter Railroad Co., 292 Conn. 150, 157–59 (2009)....

5. The trial court instructed the jury that "[i]dentification is ... a question of fact for you to decide, taking into consideration all of the evidence. The identification of the defendant by a single witness as the one involved in the commission of a crime is, in and of itself, sufficient to justify a conviction, provided that you are satisfied beyond a reasonable doubt of the identity of the defendant as the one who committed the crime in question as well as all of the other essential elements of that alleged crime....

"In appraising identification testimony, you should take into account whether the witness had adequate opportunity to observe the perpetrator. This may be affected by such matters as the length of time available to make the observation, the distance between the witness and the perpetrator, the lighting conditions at the time of the offense, whether the witness had known or seen the person in the past, and whether anything distracted the attention of the witness.

"You should also consider a witness' physical and emotional condition, such as stress during an incident where a weapon was used, since that may impact on the reliability of an identification. That identification may be affected by postevent information such as media coverage ... or listening to others about who was the perpetrator.... [M]emory can change over time, and ... the level of certainty indicated by a person [in his or her identification] may not always reflect a corresponding level of accuracy of [the] identification.

"In short, you must consider the totality of the circumstances affecting the identification of the defendant as the perpetrator of the alleged crime that you are considering. Remember, you must be satisfied beyond a reasonable doubt of the identity of the defendant as the one who committed the alleged crime ... as well as all other essential elements of that alleged crime."

We now conclude that *Kemp* and *McClendon* are out of step with the widespread judicial recognition that eyewitness identifications are potentially unreliable in a variety of ways unknown to the average juror.[8] This broad-based judicial recognition tracks a near perfect scientific consensus.[9] The extensive and comprehensive scientific research, as reflected in hundreds of peer-reviewed studies and meta-analyses, convincingly demonstrates the fallibility of eyewitness identification testimony and pinpoints an array of variables that are most likely to lead to a mistaken identification. "[T]he scientific evidence . . . is both reliable and useful." State v. Henderson, 208 N.J. 208, 283 (2011). "Experimental methods and findings have been tested and retested, subjected to scientific scrutiny through peer-reviewed journals, evaluated through the lens of meta-analyses, and replicated at times in real-world settings. . . . [C]onsensus exists among the experts . . . within the . . . research community." *Id.* "[T]he science abundantly demonstrates the many vagaries of memory encoding, storage and retrieval; the malleability of memory; the contaminating effects of extrinsic information; the influence of police interview techniques and identification procedures; and the many other factors that bear on the reliability of eyewitness identifications." *Id.*

Courts across the country now accept that (1) there is at best a weak correlation between a witness' confidence in his or her identification and its accuracy, (2) the reliability of an identification can be diminished by a witness' focus on a weapon, (3) high stress at the time of observation may render a witness less able to retain an accurate perception and memory of the observed events, (4) cross-racial identifications are considerably less accurate than same-race identifications, (5) a person's memory diminishes rapidly over a period of hours rather than days or weeks, (6) identifications are likely to be less reliable in the absence of a double-blind, sequential identification procedure, (7) witnesses are prone to develop unwarranted confidence in their identifications if they are privy to postevent or postidentification information about the event or the identification, and (8) the accuracy of an eyewitness identification may be undermined by unconscious transference, which occurs when a person seen in one context is confused with a person seen in another. This list is not exhaustive; courts have permitted expert testimony on other factors deemed to affect the accuracy of eyewitness identification testimony.

Although these findings are widely accepted by scientists, they are largely unfamiliar to the average person, and, in fact, many of the findings are counterintuitive. For example, people often believe that the

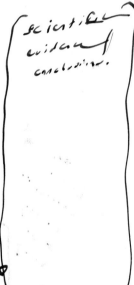

8. [Here the court cites rulings of three federal circuit courts of appeals, one federal district court, and eight state high courts acknowledging the scientific validity and persuasiveness of studies demonstrating the risk of mistaken eyewitness IDs.—GF]

9. [As examples reflecting this "near perfect scientific consensus," the court cites eleven studies, surveys, and meta-analyses, all showing flaws in eyewitness accounts.—GF]

more confident an eyewitness is in an identification, the more likely the identification is to be accurate. Similarly, the average person is likely to believe that eyewitnesses held at gunpoint or otherwise placed in fear are likely to have been acutely observant and therefore more accurate in their identifications. Most people also tend to think that cross-racial identifications are no less likely to be accurate than same-race identifications. Yet none of these beliefs is true. Indeed, laypersons commonly are unaware of the effect of the other aforementioned factors, including the rate at which memory fades, the influence of postevent or postidentification information, the phenomenon of unconscious transference, and the risks inherent in the use by police of identification procedures that are not double-blind and sequential. Moreover, although there is little if any correlation between confidence and accuracy, an eyewitness' confidence "is the most powerful single determinant of whether . . . observers . . . will believe that the eyewitness made an accurate identification. . . ." G. Wells et al., *Eyewitness Identification Procedures: Recommendations for Lineups and Photospreads*, 22 LAW & HUM. BEHAV. 603, 620 (1998).

As a result of this strong scientific consensus, federal and state courts around the country have recognized that the methods traditionally employed for alerting juries to the fallibility of eyewitness identifications—cross-examination, closing argument and generalized jury instructions on the subject—frequently are not adequate to inform them of the factors affecting the reliability of such identifications.

Cross-examination, the most common method, often is not as effective as expert testimony at identifying the weaknesses of eyewitness identification testimony because cross-examination is far better at exposing lies than at countering sincere but mistaken beliefs.[25] An eyewitness who expresses confidence in the accuracy of his or her identification may of course believe sincerely that the identification is accurate. Furthermore, although cross-examination may expose the *existence* of factors that undermine the accuracy of eyewitness identifications, it cannot effectively educate the jury about the *import* of these factors. "Thus, while skillful cross-examination may succeed in exposing obvious inconsistencies in an [eyewitness'] account, because nothing is obvious about the psychology of eyewitness identification and most people's intuitions on the subject of identification are wrong, . . . some circumstances undoubtedly call for more than mere cross-examination of the eyewitness." Moore v. Keller, No. 5:11–HC–2148–F (E.D.N.C. March 30, 2012).

25. State v. Clopten, 223 P.3d 1103, 1110 (Utah 2009) ("[B]ecause eyewitnesses may express almost absolute certainty about identifications that are inaccurate, research shows the effectiveness of cross-examination is badly hampered. . . . [E]yewitnesses are likely to use their expectations, personal experience, biases, and prejudices to fill in the gaps created by imperfect memory. . . . Because it is unlikely that witnesses will be aware that this process has occurred, they may express far more confidence in the identification than is warranted.").

Defense counsel's closing argument to the jury that an eyewitness identification is unreliable also is an inadequate substitute for expert testimony. In the absence of evidentiary support, such an argument is likely to be viewed as little more than partisan rhetoric. This is especially true if the argument relates to a factor that is counterintuitive.

Finally, research has revealed that jury instructions that direct jurors in broad terms to exercise caution in evaluating eyewitness identifications are less effective than expert testimony in apprising the jury of the potential unreliability of eyewitness identification testimony. "[Generalized] instructions given at the end of what might be a long and fatiguing trial, and buried in an overall charge by the court, are unlikely to have much effect on the minds of [the jurors]. . . . [Moreover], instructions may come too late to alter [a juror's] opinion of a witness whose testimony might have been heard days before. [Perhaps most important], even the best cautionary instructions tend to touch only generally on the empirical evidence. The judge may explain that certain factors are known to influence perception and memory . . . but will not explain how this occurs or to what extent." State v. Clopten, 223 P.3d 1103, 1110–11 (Utah 2009).[27]

27. Recently, the New Jersey Supreme Court undertook a comprehensive review of the various issues pertaining to eyewitness identification testimony. *See generally State v. Henderson, supra*. This review followed the New Jersey Supreme Court's remand of the case and appointment of a special master to evaluate scientific and other evidence concerning eyewitness identifications. The special master conducted a hearing that included testimony from numerous expert witnesses and consideration of "hundreds of scientific studies" and reports. *Id.* at 217–18. Following the hearing, the special master issued a detailed report in which he concluded that scientific studies demonstrate convincingly that eyewitness testimony frequently is unreliable and that jurors generally are unaware of the problems associated with such testimony. *See* G. Gaulkin, Report of the Special Master, *State v. Henderson*, 208 N.J. 208 (2011), at 48–49, available at http://www.judiciary.state.nj.us/pressrel/HENDERSON% 20FINAL% 20BRIEF% 20.PDF% 20 (00621142).PDF (last visited August 14, 2012). The court in *Henderson* adopted much of the report and, in particular, agreed with the special master that the evidence adduced at the remand hearing establishes that the traditional means of evaluating the trustworthiness of eyewitness identification testimony, including cross-examination and generalized jury instructions, do "not offer an adequate measure for reliability" of eyewitness identification evidence and "[overstate] the jury's inherent ability to evaluate evidence offered by eyewitnesses who honestly believe their testimony is accurate." *State v. Henderson, supra*, 218. . . .

Contrary to our prior holdings, and consistent with the recent scientific findings on the subject, we agree with the New Jersey Supreme Court that . . . generalized jury instructions are inadequate to apprise the jury of the various ways in which eyewitness identification testimony may be unreliable. We also agree with the New Jersey Supreme Court that revised, enhanced jury instructions reflecting the substance of those scientific findings—instructions that would go well beyond the instructions that ordinarily have been given on eyewitness identifications, and which may be given immediately following the eyewitness identification testimony at issue—ultimately may render proffered expert testimony redundant or otherwise unnecessary in some cases. In the present case, however, the defendant did not seek such enhanced or focused jury instructions. We believe, more-

We now recognize that, contrary to our reasoning in *Kemp* and *McClendon*, expert testimony on the reliability of eyewitness identifications does not "[invade] the province of the jury to determine what weight or effect it wishes to give to eyewitness testimony." *Kemp, supra*, 199 Conn. at 477. An expert should not be permitted to give an opinion about the credibility or accuracy of the eyewitness testimony itself; that determination is solely within the province of the jury. Rather, the expert should be permitted to testify only about factors that generally have an adverse effect on the reliability of eyewitness identifications and are relevant to the specific eyewitness identification at issue.[28]

We depart from *Kemp* and *McClendon* mindful of recent studies confirming what courts have long suspected,[29] namely, that mistaken eyewitness identification testimony is by far the leading cause of wrongful convictions.[30] A highly effective safeguard against this serious and

over, that the proper approach to this issue is to leave the development of any such jury instructions to the sound discretion of our trial courts on a case-by-case basis, subject to appellate review.

28. ... [In cases concerning child sex abuse or domestic abuse, courts likewise distinguish between expert testimony describing common behaviors of victims and expert testimony opining on a particular victim's credibility.] *Cf.* State v. Iban C., 275 Conn. 624, 635 (2005) ("[E]xpert testimony of reactions and behaviors common to victims of sexual abuse is admissible.... Such evidence assists a jury in its determination of the victim's credibility by explaining the typical consequences of the trauma of sexual abuse on a child.... It is not permissible, however, for an expert to testify as to his opinion of whether a victim in a particular case is credible or whether a particular victim's claims are truthful."); State v. Borrelli, 227 Conn. 153, 174 (1993) ("[The] expert testimony was properly admitted to assist the jury in understanding, not whether [the victim] was a credible witness on the witness stand, but whether her conduct ... was consistent with the pattern and profile of a battered woman.... [Such] expert testimony [does] not invade the province of the jury in [the determination of] the credibility of witnesses."

29. *See, e.g.,* United States v. Wade, 388 U.S. 218, 228 (1967) ("The vagaries of eyewitness identification are well known; the annals of criminal law are rife with instances of mistaken identification. Justice Frankfurter once said: 'What is the worth of identification testimony even when uncontradicted? The identification of strangers is proverbially untrustworthy....' "); *see also* Perry v. New Hampshire, 132 S. Ct. 716, 730–31 (2012) (Sotomayor, J., dissenting) ("[The United States Supreme] Court has long recognized that eyewitness identifications' unique confluence of features—their unreliability, susceptibility to suggestion, powerful impact on the jury, and resistance to the ordinary tests of the adversarial process—can undermine the fairness of a trial"); Watkins v. Sowders, 449 U.S. 341, 352 (1981) (Brennan, J., dissenting) ("[Eyewitness] testimony is likely to be believed by jurors, especially when it is offered with a high level of confidence, even though the accuracy of an eyewitness and the confidence of that witness may not be related to one another at all. All the evidence points rather strikingly to the conclusion that there is almost nothing more convincing than a live human being who takes the stand, points a finger at the defendant, and says 'That's the one!' ").

30. *See, e.g.,* EYEWITNESS IDENTIFICATION TASK FORCE, REPORT TO THE JUDICIARY COMMITTEE OF THE CONNECTICUT GENERAL ASSEMBLY (February 8, 2012) p. 4 ("Mistaken eyewitness identification is the leading cause of wrongful convictions in the United States. It is now undisputed that nationwide, within

well-documented risk is the admission of expert testimony on the reliability of eyewitness identification. *See, e.g.*, J. McMurtrie, *The Role of the Social Sciences in Preventing Wrongful Convictions*, 42 Am. Crim. L. Rev. 1271, 1276 (2005) ("Research . . . has shown that expert testimony on memory and eyewitness identification is the only legal safeguard that is effective in sensitizing jurors to eyewitness errors. . . .") . . .

Of course, a trial court retains broad discretion in ruling on the qualifications of expert witnesses and determining whether their opinions are relevant. Consequently, whether to permit expert testimony concerning the reliability of eyewitness identification evidence in any individual case ultimately is a matter within the sound discretion of the trial court. . . . [T]he trial court may preclude such testimony if the court reasonably determines . . . that the particular issue presented is not beyond the ken of the average juror or that the proffered testimony would not aid the jury in resolving the issues presented. In other words, although we overrule our prior case law holding that expert testimony on eyewitness identifications is generally inadmissible, such evidence is subject to the same threshold reliability and relevance requirements as any other expert testimony. . . .

The state contends that Morgan's testimony was not applicable to the specific facts of this case and would not have been helpful to the jury because most of the eyewitnesses knew the defendant and were therefore much less likely to render a mistaken identification. We agree with the state that, although there are exceptions, identification of a person who is well-known to the eyewitness generally does not give rise to the same risk of misidentification as does the identification of a person who is not well-known to the eyewitness. We also agree that four of the five eyewitnesses in the present case—Robinson, Olivero, Baldwin, and Gomez—were familiar enough with the defendant that the risk of misidentification was small.[40] Accordingly, we conclude that the trial court did not abuse its discretion in precluding Morgan from testifying on the reliability of the identification testimony of these four witnesses.[41] Because the

the past [fifteen] years, 289 persons convicted of serious crimes—mainly murder and sexual assault—have been exonerated of those crimes by DNA evidence. More than 75 percent of those convictions rested, in significant part, on positive, but false, eyewitness identification evidence. These figures do not include, of course, the many convictions for crimes that did not involve DNA evidence; e.g., the drive-by shootings, the street muggings, the convenience store robberies, and the homicides and sexual assaults for which no DNA evidence may be available."); *see also* S. Gross et al., *Exonerations in the United States, 1989 Through 2003*, 95 J. Crim. L. & Criminology 523, 542 (2005) (citing study demonstrating that 64 percent of wrongful convictions involved at least one erroneous eyewitness identification).

40. . . . Olivero had known the defendant for approximately ten years and knew him by name. . . .

41. The defendant argues that "[f]amiliarity is merely one factor to be considered along with negative factors such as distance, lighting, and duration, which all degrade perception and memory." These factors, however, are within the knowledge

state's case concerning the murders of Ross and Williams was predicated on the testimony of three of those eyewitnesses, Olivero, Baldwin and Gomez, the defendant's claim must fail with respect to the two murder charges. . . .

Unlike the other eyewitnesses, however, Lang, who testified that he had observed the defendant shoot Robinson, . . . did not know the defendant at all. Moreover, according to Lang, he had been standing next to the shooter at the time of the shooting and saw the defendant's photograph in the newspaper before identifying him as the shooter. We conclude that, with respect to Lang, Morgan's proposed testimony on the effect of stress on memory, the risk of retrofitting based on postevent information, and the relationship, or lack thereof, between confidence and accuracy, was relevant and would have been helpful to the jury. The trial court therefore abused its discretion in precluding Morgan's expert testimony insofar as it pertained to Lang's identification of the defendant as Robinson's assailant. . . .

Although some courts have concluded that it is not an abuse of discretion for a trial court to exclude otherwise admissible expert testimony on the reliability of eyewitness identifications when the eyewitness' testimony is corroborated by other evidence of the defendant's guilt, we do not believe that a defendant should be precluded from presenting such testimony merely because the state has presented other evidence of guilt that the jury reasonably could credit. Broadly speaking, when the identity of the perpetrator is disputed and the state seeks to use eyewitness testimony to identify the defendant as the perpetrator, the defendant should be permitted to adduce relevant expert testimony on the fallibility of the eyewitness' identification. . . . A contrary rule would unfairly restrict the defendant's opportunity to mount a defense.[44] . . .

[Corroborative evidence of the defendant's guilt, however, may render harmless the trial judge's error in excluding Morgan's proposed testimony. Here the corroborative evidence was substantial.] First, several witnesses who knew the defendant well placed him at the bar a short time before the shooting. Second, Robinson provided the police with a

of an average juror and can be explored on cross-examination. As we have indicated, factors such as stress and exposure to postevent information about the perpetrator are, for obvious reasons, far less likely to affect the reliability of an identification when the eyewitness identifies someone whom he or she knows. . . .

44. Indeed, it [could be] argued that a contrary rule would impermissibly infringe on a defendant's constitutionally protected right to present a defense. *Cf.* Holmes v. South Carolina, 547 U.S. 319, 321, 330–31 (2006) [page 731, above] (rejecting as unconstitutional "an evidence rule under which the defendant may not introduce proof of third-party guilt if the prosecution has introduced forensic evidence that, if believed, strongly supports a guilty verdict," explaining that, "[j]ust because the prosecution's evidence, *if credited*, would provide strong support for a guilty verdict, it does not follow that evidence of third-party guilt has only a weak logical connection to the central issues in the case" . . . [emphasis in original]). . . .

written statement describing the shooting and identifying the defendant as the shooter.... Third, the state presented evidence that the same gun had been used in the shooting of Robinson and in the shootings of Williams and Ross, that the defendant had fled to New York on the day of the shootings, and that the defendant, when informed that the police were looking for him in connection with the shootings, had not denied his involvement.... [This] convincing evidence of the defendant's guilt, ensured that the trial court's erroneous exclusion of Morgan's testimony on the reliability of Lang's identification testimony did not substantially affect the verdict....

The judgments are *affirmed.*

■ In this opinion ROGERS, C.J., and NORCOTT, EVELEIGH, and VERTEFEUILLE, Js., concurred.

■ ZARELLA, J., with whom MCLACHLAN, J., joins, concurring in the judgment. I agree with the majority that expert testimony may assist the jury in understanding certain factors that may affect the reliability of eyewitness identifications. I further agree that, to the extent this court concluded in *State v. Kemp* and *State v. McClendon* that expert testimony regarding such factors is "disfavored" because they are within the common knowledge of the average juror, *Kemp* and *McClendon* should be overruled....

I ... disagree with the majority that a defendant should be allowed to present expert testimony on eyewitness identifications even when there is strong corroborating evidence of the defendant's guilt.... I believe that trial courts should be allowed to consider substantial corroborating evidence when determining whether to admit expert testimony because, in cases in which the record contains such evidence, the importance of expert testimony is correspondingly diminished and would be an unnecessary distraction to the jury. *See, e.g.,* United States v. Crotteau, 218 F.3d 826, 833 (7th Cir. 2000) ("[W]hen there is corroborating evidence, expert testimony regarding the reliability of eyewitness identification is not necessary"); Commonwealth v. Watson, 455 Mass. 246, 258 (2009) ("[when] there is additional evidence to corroborate an [eyewitness'] identification, a judge does not overstep the bounds of discretion in excluding expert testimony"); People v. Young, 7 N.Y.3d 40, 45 (2006) (corroborating evidence "was strong enough for the trial court reasonably to conclude that the expert's testimony would be of minor importance"). Thus, for example, when the state introduces uncontested DNA evidence as well as an eyewitness identification linking the defendant to the crime, there generally is no need for expert testimony on the reliability of the identification.... The majority, however, fails to recognize that when strong corroborating evidence is consistent with an eyewitness identification, expert testimony would be not only time consuming and costly, but potentially confusing rather than helpful to the jury....

Accordingly, I do not agree that the trial court in the present case abused its discretion in precluding Morgan's testimony.

... I respectfully concur in the judgment.

Problem 9.12
Street Corner Stickup

At approximately 6:30 p.m. on April 11, 2007, near 31st Street and Avon Lane [in Washington, D.C.], a man, whose face was unobstructed, approached the victim, Mira Kuczynska, within three to four feet. The man mumbled what sounded like "this is a robbery," and he displayed a "western-style" revolver with a brown and dark yellow handle in his waistband. After approximately ten seconds, the man grabbed her purse and then ran off. Her purse contained, among other things, her wallet, credit cards, identification, a checkbook, and mobile phones.

After the incident, Ms. Kuczynska described the man to police as [a] male in his late twenties or thirties who was about six feet tall, thin-figured, with a medium skin complexion, and short hair with some facial hair. [This description roughly matches appellant Marcus Patterson, who stands 6′3″ tall.] . . .

Approximately twenty minutes after the robbery, Monica Barnes, [whom Patterson later] . . . characterized as his girlfriend, placed a phone call using Ms. Kuczynska's cellular telephone. A Giant store video surveillance revealed that on April 14th, 2007, Monica Barnes alighted from a silver minivan in a Giant food store parking lot in Laurel, Maryland, entered the store, and used an altered check belonging to Ms. Kuczynska to purchase gift cards. Approximately twenty minutes later, appellant, wearing a multi-colored sweater-jacket, returned to the same cashier to purchase a large amount of gift cards with another one of Ms. Kuczynska's altered checks, but the store detective refused to accept the check and escorted appellant out of the store. Appellant entered a silver minivan in the parking lot and drove off with Monica Barnes. . . .

[After investigation] Police obtained a search warrant to search [a] Motel 6 room [in Laurel, Maryland. After detectives knocked,] Monica Barnes opened the door. . . . In the room police recovered a multi-colored jacket appearing to be the same jacket worn by appellant in the surveillance tape from the Giant food store. . . . Police seized a cell phone, personal check, and a credit or debit card—all Ms. Kuczynska's stolen property. A black .38-caliber revolver

> with a brown handle—similar to the description provided by Ms. Kuczynska—was hidden under the mattress. . . .
>
> Nine days after the robbery, Ms. Kuczynska identified appellant in a photo array and stated she was positive that appellant was the robber. She also identified appellant at trial. . . .
>
> [Before trial] appellant filed a motion seeking leave to introduce expert testimony of Dr. Henry Shulman, a professor of psychology at Ohio State University, "on psychological factors of memory and perception that may affect the accuracy of eyewitness identifications." The government filed a "motion in opposition" to the expert testimony. . . .

Patterson v. United States, 37 A.3d 230 (D.C. App.), *as amended*, ___ A.3d ___ (D.C. App. Oct. 11, 2012). Assume that Shulman's testimony would mirror Morgan's proposed testimony in *Guilbert* and that the present Federal Rules of Evidence govern this case. Should the trial judge permit Shulman to testify? What are the best arguments for both sides?

3. PROPER BASES OF OPINION TESTIMONY

Focus on
FRE 703 & FRE 705

RULE 703: AN INTRODUCTION

Two things distinguish expert opinions from lay opinions—the background knowledge that informs them and the specific facts on which they rest. Only expert opinions may draw on the witness's "scientific, technical, or other specialized knowledge." This is the command of Rule 701(c), which bars lay witnesses from straying into these higher realms. And only lay opinions *must* be "based on [facts within] the witness's perception." This is the command of Rule 701(a), which imposes the usual personal knowledge rule on lay witnesses. Expert witnesses need not testify from personal knowledge. In fact Rule 602, the source of the personal knowledge requirement, explicitly states, "This rule is subject to the provisions of rule 703, relating to opinion testimony by expert witnesses." So our next step is to look more closely at Rule 703, which generally governs the proper bases of expert testimony.

The first sentence of Rule 703 is deceptively simple: "An expert may base an opinion on facts or data in the case that the expert has been made aware of or personally observed." When carefully taken apart, this sentence permits an expert to base her opinion on three sorts of facts (*see* ACN to FRE 703, RB 176):

First, she may rely "on facts or data ... that the expert ... personally observed": An expert, like a lay witness, may testify based on facts she observed. Therefore a fiber analyst who examined a piece of torn clothing under a microscope may rely on what she saw when forming an opinion about whether the cloth tore from wear or was forcibly ripped.

Second, she may rely "on facts or data ... that the expert has been made aware of" *at the hearing*: An expert who attends trial and watches the proceedings may rely on trial testimony and exhibits when forming her opinions. If the pertinent facts are in dispute, the lawyers may need to tell the expert which facts to accept as true. Here lawyers often deploy hypothetical questions: "Doctor, assume that Dorothy James was accurate when she estimated the defendant's speed at forty-five miles per hour and that Michael Alexon was accurate when he said the roadway was icy. Based on these facts and on your training and experience, do you have an opinion as to the cause of this crash?"

Such hypothetical questions hold a more central role when the expert has *not* viewed the trial testimony. Because few litigants can pay an expert to watch other witnesses testify, lawyers often use hypothetical questions to inform the expert about facts already in evidence: "Doctor, assume the following facts to be true: That a car was proceeding northbound on Wellfleet Avenue and approaching the intersection of Spark Street at about forty-five miles per hour and that the surface of the road was icy. Based on these facts...." The lawyer may not of course simply make up the facts. Rather there must be "enough evidence to support a finding that the necessary facts exist." CHRISTOPHER B. MUELLER & LAIRD C. KIRKPATRICK, EVIDENCE § 7.9, at 666 (5th ed. 2012). This standard is similar to that governing questions of conditional relevance under Rule 104(b). The similarity is no coincidence. An expert's opinion, based on certain assumptions, has no relevance if those assumptions are false.

Note that Rule 104(b)'s low standard permits opposing lawyers to pose competing hypotheses. On cross-examination, you can expect opposing counsel to ask, "Doctor, assume instead that the surface of the road where the collision took place was dry and ice-free...." As long as there is enough evidence in the record to support each lawyer's factual assumptions, both questions are proper.

Third, the expert may rely "on facts or data ... that the expert has been made aware of" *before* the hearing: Here we enter the realm of hearsay. Consider, for example, an aeronautical expert who is to testify about why a jet crashed on its approach to a runway. During her investigation she may speak with ground controllers who witnessed the crash and who tell her the jet was spewing smoke and approaching the runway erratically. Unless the ground controllers testify at trial, their accounts are hearsay. If they speak with the expert shortly after the crash, while still agitated by the event, their words perhaps are admissible as excited utterances under Rule 803(2). More likely, however, their out-of-court statements are not admissible.

Nonetheless, as the second sentence of Rule 703 makes clear, the expert still may rely on the ground controllers' reports "[i]f experts in the particular field would reasonably rely on those kinds of facts or data in forming an opinion on the subject." Hence if aeronautical experts "reasonably" rely on ground controllers' accounts about how an aircraft approached the runway when determining the cause of a crash, the expert's opinion may be admissible even though it relies in part on such accounts and even though the accounts themselves are not admissible. The expert may not, however, merely act as a conduit, transmitting otherwise inadmissible secondhand reports to the jury. Rather, she may *reasonably* rely upon such reports in reaching an opinion that is otherwise informed by the tools of her discipline.

Congress amended Rule 703 in 2000 to "emphasize" that the expert's reliance on otherwise inadmissible facts *does not make those facts admissible.* (ACN to FRE 703, RB 177.) Only the expert's *opinion*, based in part on those facts, is admissible. On cross-examination, opposing counsel may, if he chooses, seek to undermine the expert's opinion by asking her about the underlying facts. (*See* FRE 705.) But the lawyer who sponsors the witness may *not* disclose the otherwise inadmissible facts to the jury unless the court determines that "their probative value in helping the jury evaluate the opinion substantially outweighs their prejudicial effect." (FRE 703.) As the advisory committee observes, this reverse–Rule 403 weighing test creates "a presumption against disclosure to the jury of [the underlying hearsay] . . . by the proponent of the expert." (RB 178.) Even if the underlying hearsay is disclosed to the jury, it is not admissible substantively—for its truth—but only to help the jury assess the reliability of the expert's opinion. Consequently, if the hearsay account is admitted under the balancing test set out by the rule, "the trial judge must give a limiting instruction upon request, informing the jury that the underlying information must not be used for substantive purposes." (RB 177.)

Rule 703 therefore completely disengages the admissibility of the expert's opinion from the admissibility of the facts supporting it, as long as other "experts in the particular field would reasonably rely on" such facts. To make this disengagement more explicit, Rule 705 permits "an expert [to] state an opinion—and give the reasons for it—without first testifying to the underlying facts or data" unless the court orders otherwise.

Learned Treatises and Medical Statements

There is one context in which an expert's reliance on inadmissible hearsay actually *makes* that hearsay admissible as substantive evidence. Under Rule 803(18), an expert's reliance on a learned treatise during direct examination or her acknowledgment of its authority on cross-examination dissolves any hearsay objection to pertinent parts of the document. The rule extends broadly to "treatise[s], periodical[s], or pamphlet[s]." The proponent must establish the document's authority either through the expert's testimony or through another expert's testimony or by judicial notice.

Recall, too, that Rule 803(4) renders statements made for purposes of medical diagnosis or treatment substantively admissible. This rule applies even if the patient speaks with her doctor not to obtain medical treatment, but merely to enable the doctor to form a diagnosis and testify about that diagnosis at an upcoming trial. (*See* ACN to FRE 803(4), RB 222.) Unlike Rule 803(18) governing learned treatises, Rule 803(4) does not specifically require that the expert in some way rely upon the out-of-court statements. Still, as you know from *United States v. Iron Shell*, 633 F.2d 77 (8th Cir. 1980), the doctor's reliance on the hearsay supplies one rationale for the rule: "[L]ife and death decisions are made by physicians in reliance on [their patients' statements] and as such [those statements] should have sufficient trustworthiness to be admissible in a court of law." (Page 535, above.)

Williams v. Illinois *Revisited*

Discussion of Rule 703 may call to mind the Supreme Court's recent ruling in *Williams v. Illinois*, 132 S.Ct. 2221 (2012), presented in the last chapter at pages 660 to 668. Recall that forensic biologist Sandra Lambatos testified as an expert against Sandy Williams at his Illinois trial on charges of sexual assault, robbery, and kidnapping. Lambatos said she had determined that the defendant's DNA profile "match[ed]" the male DNA profile isolated from vaginal swabs taken from the victim L.J. She based this opinion in part on a report issued by Cellmark Diagnostics Laboratory, where L.J.'s vaginal swabs had been sent for testing. That report included male DNA data that Cellmark technicians said they had detected in L.J.'s swabs. As no one from Cellmark testified at his trial, Williams complained he was unable to confront the technicians whose testimonial report was used against him.

The state responded that it offered Cellmark's findings not for their truth, but only to show the basis of Lambatos's opinion. It argued that the trial judge, who sat alone as factfinder, could not intelligently assess the soundness of Lambatos's analysis and opinion absent evidence of the data on which she relied. With an eye toward the Illinois equivalent of Rule 703, which allows experts to base an opinion on inadmissible facts if those facts are "of a type reasonably relied upon by experts in the particular field," Lambatos testified that it is a "commonly accepted" practice within the scientific community for "one DNA expert to rely on the records of another DNA expert." And the judge, likewise governed by Rule 703, presumably limited his consideration of the contents of Cellmark's report, which Lambatos revealed when testifying, to their permitted purpose—assisting him in assessing the reliability of Lambatos's methods and conclusions.

Much of the dispute among the Justices focused on whether there is a sensible distinction between the state's use of Cellmark's DNA findings to support Lambatos's opinion and its disavowed use of those findings for their truth. Justice Kagan, for herself and three dissenting colleagues, scoffed at this sketchy line drawing: "when a witness, expert or otherwise, repeats an out-of-court statement as the basis for a conclusion, . . . the statement's utility is then dependent on its truth. If the statement is true, then the conclusion based on it is probably true; if not, not." *Id.* at 2268 (Kagan, J., dissenting). Justice Thomas agreed: " 'If the jury believes that the basis evidence is true, it will likely also believe that the expert's reliance is justified; inversely, if the jury doubts the accuracy or validity of the basis evidence, it will be skeptical of the expert's conclusions.' " *Williams*, 132 S. Ct. at 2257 (Thomas, J., concurring in the judgment) (quoting D. Kaye, D. Bernstein, & J. Mnookin, The New Wigmore: A Treatise on Evidence: Expert Evidence § 4.10.1, at 196 (2d ed. 2011)). For the dissenters the constitutional consequence of this conclusion was substantial: If Cellmark's findings, which the dissenters deemed testimonial, were admitted against Williams for their truth, his inability to confront the technicians who generated those findings frustrated his confrontation right.

Justice Alito, who wrote for a plurality of four Justices, disagreed. He insisted that the trial judge logically could have used the DNA findings in Cellmark's report to support Lambatos's opinion *without* relying on the report to prove the truth of those findings. That's because *other* evidence and circumstances demonstrated their truth, an argument I reviewed at length at pages 663 to 665. Rather than return to that complex reasoning, we should examine instead Rule 703 in a simpler factual and legal context, one lacking the circumstantial evidence that arguably supported Justice Alito's bold claim and lacking the complicating overlay of Confrontation Clause doctrine. And we should view the rule's operation at a jury trial, where the distinction between out-of-court words offered substantively and such words offered only to support an expert's opinion poses a weightier conceptual challenge.

In re Melton: *Case Note*

In re Melton, 597 A.2d 892 (D.C. 1991), concerned a civil commitment proceeding mounted by the District of Columbia against 44-year-old

Tommie Lee Melton. The jury's verdict that Melton was "likely to injure himself or others" depended completely on the testimony of two psychiatric experts, Dr. James Byrd and Dr. Antoine Cornet, who offered their opinion that Melton was suffering from schizophrenia and, "if released, ... would be likely to injure himself or others." Although the doctors had a good deal of firsthand information that Melton posed a danger to himself, their opinion that he posed a danger to others rested almost entirely on hearsay and in particular on Melton's mother's report that he had punched her in the face.

Because Melton's mother did not testify at trial, the court assumed her account of the punch was not admissible. Melton's complaints—that Drs. Byrd and Cornet wrongly relied on his mother's inadmissible accusation and that the jury heard about that accusation though he had no chance to cross-examine its maker—prompted the appellate court to examine the principles underlying Rule 703's "reasonable reliance" standard:

> ... [T]he precise issue on appeal is whether, ... in assessing Melton's dangerousness, a psychiatrist would reasonably rely on the reports and observations of family members....
>
> We do not find this issue to be an especially troublesome one. The Advisory Committee's Notes to Rule 703 recognize that
>
> > a physician in his [or her] own practice bases his [or her] diagnosis on information from numerous sources and of considerable variety, *including statements by patients and relatives,* reports and opinions from nurses, technicians, and other doctors, *hospital records,* and X rays. Most of them are admissible in evidence, but only with the expenditure of substantial time in producing and examining various authenticating witnesses. The physician makes life-and-death decisions in reliance upon them. His [or her] validation, expertly performed and subject to cross-examination, ought to suffice for judicial purposes.
>
> [RB 176 (emphasis added by *Melton* court).] The conclusion that a competent psychiatrist charged with assessing dangerousness would obtain information from the patient's relatives ... is also dictated by what Justice Frankfurter has described as "the saving grace of common sense." Bell v. United States, 349 U.S. 81, 83 (1955). Where else would the doctor go for such information? Indeed, as the United States points out in its brief as amicus curiae, a psychiatrist could be roundly criticized within and without the profession for not interviewing family members; by ignoring information which the profession views as vital, the psychiatrist would, at least, undercut the reliability of his or her opinion....
>
> This is not to say that everything a family member tells a psychiatrist is necessarily reliable or true.... [A] properly qualified

expert is assumed to have the necessary skill to evaluate any second-hand information and to give it only such probative force as the circumstances warrant. Accordingly, the court should accord an expert wide latitude in choosing the sources on which to base his or her opinions. But

> the court may not abdicate its independent responsibilities to decide if the bases meet minimum standards of reliability as a condition of admissibility. *See* FED. R. EVID. 104(a). If the underlying data are so lacking in probative force and reliability that no reasonable expert could base an opinion on them, an opinion which rests entirely upon them must be excluded. The jury will not be permitted to be misled by the glitter of an expert's accomplishments outside the courtroom.

In re "Agent Orange" Prod. Liab. Litig., 611 F. Supp. 1223, 1245 (E.D.N.Y. 1985) (Weinstein, J.), *aff'd,* 818 F.2d 187 (2d Cir. 1987), *cert. denied,* 487 U.S. 1234 (1988).

Because Rule 703 was intended to bring judicial practice into line with the practice of experts when they are not in court, *see* Advisory Committee's Note quoted *supra* [RB 176], the judge may not substitute his or her judgment for the expert's as to what data are sufficiently reliable, provided that such reliance falls within the broad bounds of reasonableness. "The proper inquiry is not what the court deems reliable, but what experts in the relevant discipline [reasonably] deem it to be." In re Japanese Elec. Prods. Antitrust Litig., 723 F.2d 238, 276 (3d Cir. 1983), *rev'd on other grounds sub nom.* Matsushita Elec. Indus. Co. v. Zenith Radio Corp., 475 U.S. 574 (1986) (bracketed word added). . . .

"The authorities cited in this opinion," the *Melton* court concluded, "and especially the Advisory Committee's Note to Rule 703, persuade us that the drafters of that Rule viewed psychiatric reliance on information provided by family members and hospital records as reliable in principle."

But did that mean the doctors could tell the jury about the mother's hearsay accusation that her son punched her? In permitting the experts to rely on the mother's report, Rule 703 did not somehow transform her hearsay into admissible evidence. It is true, the *Melton* court said, that "when the expert witness has consulted numerous sources, and uses that information, together with his own professional knowledge and experience, to arrive at his opinion, *that opinion is regarded as evidence in its own right and not as hearsay in disguise.*" *Melton*, 597 A.2d at 901 (quoting *United States v. Williams*, 447 F.2d 1285, 1290 (5th Cir. 1971), *cert. denied*, 405 U.S. 954 (1972)) (emphasis added by the *Melton* court). But it is also true, the court added, that "[t]he problem raised by Melton cannot . . . be avoided simply by calling the evidence expert testimony rather than hearsay. Labels cannot perform juridical alchemy." *Melton*, 597 A.2d at 901.

Under Rule 703 in its present guise, the government could disclose the mother's hearsay accusation to the jury "only if [its] probative value in helping the jury evaluate the [doctors'] opinion substantially outweighs [its] prejudicial effect." According to the advisory committee, "[i]f the otherwise inadmissible information is admitted under this balancing test, the trial judge must give a limiting instruction upon request, informing the jury that the underlying information must not be used for substantive purposes." (ACN to 2000 Amendment to FRE 703, RB 177.) In *Melton* the trial judge indeed permitted the doctors to testify about what Melton's mother had told them. The judge therefore delivered a limiting instruction of the sort the advisory committee had in mind. He told the jury that the mother's statement and a second, similar hearsay accusation

> are admitted only to demonstrate the information relied upon by the doctors in forming their conclusion. They are to be considered by you only for the purpose of evaluating the reasonableness and correctness of the doctors' conclusions. They are not to be considered by you as actual proof of the incidents described. They are hearsay and as such are not admissible to establish the truth of the matters asserted by them.

The advisory committee notes that "the trial court should consider the probable effectiveness or lack of effectiveness of [such] a limiting instruction" when evaluating the unfair prejudice caused by the hearsay statement. (RB 177.) The trial judge in *Melton*, who was operating under an earlier version of Rule 703, said nothing about the probable effectiveness of his limiting instruction. The appellate court, however, had a good deal to say on this question:

> This court has recently noted that some students of the law of evidence consider the distinction sought to be articulated in such a "limiting" instruction as "most unlikely to be made by juries." *In re Samuels*, 507 A.2d 150, 153 n.5 (D.C. App. 1986). . . . With his customary eloquence, Justice Cardozo made a similar point for the Court in a somewhat different context in *Shepard v. United States*, 290 U.S. 96, 104 (1933):
>
> > Discrimination so subtle is a feat beyond the compass of ordinary minds. The reverberating clang of those accusatory words would drown all weaker sounds. It is for ordinary minds, and not for psychoanalysts, that our rules of evidence are framed.
>
> [Such] problems . . . are especially serious with respect to a discrete dramatic act like punching one's mother on the nose. To tell the jurors that they are to consider the testimony about the punch as a basis for the expert's finding of dangerousness, but not with respect to whether Mr. Melton punched his mother, may call for mental gymnastics which only the most pristine theoretician could perform. We suspect that the reaction of that elusive individual, the reasonable

> person, would be that you cannot believe that the testimony about the punch tends to show that Melton is dangerous unless you first believe that he actually punched his mother. . . .

"The problem is a perplexing one," the court continued, "because it is difficult to articulate reasonable or workable limits on any rule which would exclude testimony of the kind here at issue and still vindicate the policies underlying Rule 703."

The court's concern about "vindicat[ing] the policies" of Rule 703 is telling. How could the jury begin to evaluate the psychiatrists' opinion that Melton posed a danger to others without some idea of the facts on which that opinion rested? The government's interest in disclosing the mother's accusation, which strongly supported the doctors' opinion, was substantial. But at the same time Melton quite reasonably complained that his mother's accusation threatened him with a clear risk of unfair prejudice—a risk her absence left him powerless to confront.

In most such cases, Rule 703's weighing test favors the party opposing the expert testimony: Only if the probative value of the inadmissible hearsay "*substantially* outweighs [its] prejudicial effect" may the proponent disclose the hearsay to the jury. (Emphasis added.) The rule therefore protects litigants in Melton's shoes from the "juridical alchemy" against which the *Melton* court warned. By relying on out-of-court statements, an expert does not somehow convert base hearsay into precious (and admissible) evidence. But by siding with the opponent to the expert testimony, Rule 703 generally forces the proponent to present expert opinions shorn from the factual foundation that supports them.

Problem 9.13

Stashing Guns

In *United States v. Webb,* 115 F.3d 711 (9th Cir. 1997), police discovered a gun concealed in the engine compartment of the defendant's car. The main issue at trial was whether the defendant knew the gun was there. A Los Angeles police officer testified that "it is typical for people to conceal weapons in the engine compartments of their cars; . . . people typically store weapons in the engine compartments rather than the passenger compartments because, if discovered, it is easier to claim that they did not know about the weapon." On review, the Ninth Circuit wrote:

> Significantly, the expert was particularly qualified to give such an opinion. He testified that, in his nineteen years as a

police officer, he had training and experience in the way that guns are concealed in cars. While working in the county jail for a period of one year, the officer talked to 50 to 60 inmates per day about how and why criminals conceal weapons. Thus, the officer's experience qualified him to render an opinion regarding one of the most important concerns faced by police officers—where, how, and why criminals conceal their weapons.

Assume the court is correct that the officer was properly qualified as an expert. Did he have a proper basis for the testimony he gave? How would you persuade a court that experts in gun concealment reasonably rely on inmates' accounts "about how and why criminals conceal weapons"?

Problem 9.14

Doctor's Note

Consider the facts of *Ricciardi v. Children's Hospital Medical Center*, 811 F.2d 18 (1st Cir. 1987):

> . . . On July 11, 1979, [Peter] Ricciardi underwent surgery at the Children's Hospital Medical Center in Boston, for the replacement of his aortic valve. He suffered neurological difficulties after the operation because, according to him, someone was negligent during his operation. . . .
>
> Ricciardi's only proof of negligence was a note dated July 13, 1979, two days after the operation, entered into his medical chart by Dr. Krishna Nirmel, a neurology resident at the Hospital. The note, contained in a three-page handwritten consultant's report, said: "during surg. episode of aortic cannula accidently out x 40–60 secs." An aortic cannula provides a means of circulating blood from the heart-lung machine back into the body when the heart is being bypassed for surgery. The note was the basis for Ricciardi's theory that a cannula being used during his operation came out because of someone's negligence and an air embolus was introduced into his blood stream. Dr. Nirmel, however, did not have personal knowledge of the alleged event and did not know where he obtained the information he recorded in the note. He said he usually spoke with the nurses and staff attending to the patient before, during, and after surgery, but in this instance he could not recall speaking

> with any members of the surgical team. He assumed that he obtained the information from "professional people." ...
>
> ... [T]o prove that the cannula came out during surgery, Ricciardi sought to have an expert witness, Dr. [Harold] Kay, rely on the statement to form an opinion that this occurred.... Dr. Kay told the court that if he could rely on Dr. Nirmel's note, it would be his opinion that the cause of the embolus was that the cannula came out....
>
> ... Dr. Kay said that never before had he seen such a statement in a hospital chart.... [He] characteriz[ed] the note as "bizarre".... Dr. Michael Bresnan, a pediatric neurologist at the Hospital, ... said he did not have any doubt about what was written in the chart and that he accepted what Dr. Nirmel wrote "to be the truth as he has reported it to be." ...

Should the trial judge have permitted Dr. Kay to offer his opinion that the cause of the embolus was that the cannula came out during surgery?

4. Assessing the Reliability of Expert Scientific Testimony

a. THE DOCTRINE

Frye v. United States

293 Fed. 1013 (D.C. Cir. 1923).

■ Van Orsdel, Associate Justice. Appellant, defendant below, was convicted of the crime of murder in the second degree, and from the judgment prosecutes this appeal.

A single assignment of error is presented for our consideration. In the course of the trial counsel for defendant offered an expert witness to testify to the result of a deception test made upon defendant. The test is described as the systolic blood pressure deception test. It is asserted that blood pressure is influenced by change in the emotions of the witness, and that the systolic blood pressure rises are brought about by nervous impulses sent to the sympathetic branch of the autonomic nervous system. Scientific experiments, it is claimed, have demonstrated that ...

conscious deception or falsehood, concealment of facts, or guilt of crime, accompanied by fear of detection when the person is under examination, raises the systolic blood pressure in a curve, which corresponds exactly to the struggle going on in the subject's mind, between fear and attempted control of that fear, as the examination touches the vital points in respect of which he is attempting to deceive the examiner.

In other words, the theory seems to be that truth is spontaneous, and comes without conscious effort, while the utterance of a falsehood requires a conscious effort, which is reflected in the blood pressure....

Prior to the trial defendant was subjected to this deception test, and counsel offered the scientist who conducted the test as an expert to testify to the results obtained. The offer was objected to by counsel for the government, and the court sustained the objection. Counsel for defendant then offered to have the proffered witness conduct a test in the presence of the jury. This also was denied.

Counsel for defendant, in their able presentation of the novel question involved, correctly state in their brief that no cases directly in point have been found....

Just when a scientific principle or discovery crosses the line between the experimental and demonstrable stages is difficult to define. Somewhere in this twilight zone the evidential force of the principle must be recognized, and while courts will go a long way in admitting expert testimony deduced from a well-recognized scientific principle or discovery, the thing from which the deduction is made must be sufficiently established to have gained general acceptance in the particular field in which it belongs.

We think the systolic blood pressure deception test has not yet gained such standing and scientific recognition among physiological and psychological authorities as would justify the courts in admitting expert testimony deduced from the discovery, development, and experiments thus far made.

The judgment is *affirmed*.

DAUBERT V. MERRELL DOW PHARMACEUTICALS, INC.

509 U.S. 579 (1993).

■ JUSTICE BLACKMUN delivered the opinion of the Court. In this case we are called upon to determine the standard for admitting expert scientific testimony in a federal trial.

I

Petitioners Jason Daubert and Eric Schuller are minor children born with serious birth defects. They and their parents sued respondent in California state court, alleging that the birth defects had been caused by the mothers' ingestion of Bendectin, a prescription antinausea drug marketed by respondent. Respondent removed the suits to federal court on diversity grounds.

After extensive discovery, respondent moved for summary judgment, contending that Bendectin does not cause birth defects in humans and that petitioners would be unable to come forward with any admissible evidence that it does. In support of its motion, respondent submitted an affidavit of Steven H. Lamm, physician and epidemiologist, who is a well-credentialed expert on the risks from exposure to various chemical substances. Doctor Lamm stated that he had reviewed all the literature on Bendectin and human birth defects—more than 30 published studies involving over 130,000 patients. No study had found Bendectin to be a human teratogen (*i.e.*, a substance capable of causing malformations in fetuses). On the basis of this review, Doctor Lamm concluded that maternal use of Bendectin during the first trimester of pregnancy has not been shown to be a risk factor for human birth defects.

Petitioners did not (and do not) contest this characterization of the published record regarding Bendectin. Instead, they responded to respondent's motion with the testimony of eight experts of their own, each of whom also possessed impressive credentials. These experts had concluded that Bendectin can cause birth defects. Their conclusions were based upon "in vitro" (test tube) and "in vivo" (live) animal studies that found a link between Bendectin and malformations; pharmacological studies of the chemical structure of Bendectin that purported to show similarities between the structure of the drug and that of other substances known to cause birth defects; and the "reanalysis" of previously published epidemiological (human statistical) studies.

The District Court granted respondent's motion for summary judgment.... The United States Court of Appeals for the Ninth Circuit affirmed. 951 F.2d 1128 (1991). Citing Frye v. United States, 293 F. 1013, 1014 (1923), the court stated that expert opinion based on a scientific technique is inadmissible unless the technique is "generally accepted" as reliable in the relevant scientific community. The court declared that expert opinion based on a methodology that diverges "significantly from the procedures accepted by recognized authorities in the field ... cannot be shown to be 'generally accepted as a reliable technique.'"

The ... Court of Appeals rejected petitioners' reanalyses as "unpublished, not subjected to the normal peer-review process and generated solely for use in litigation." The court concluded that petitioners' evidence provided an insufficient foundation to allow admission of expert testimony that Bendectin caused their injuries and, accordingly, that petitioners could not satisfy their burden of proving causation at trial.

II

A

In the 70 years since its formulation in the *Frye* case, the "general acceptance" test has been the dominant standard for determining the admissibility of novel scientific evidence at trial. Although under increasing attack of late, the rule continues to be followed by a majority of courts, including the Ninth Circuit.

The *Frye* test has its origin in a short and citation-free 1923 decision concerning the admissibility of evidence derived from a systolic blood pressure deception test, a crude precursor to the polygraph machine. In what has become a famous (perhaps infamous) passage, the then Court of Appeals for the District of Columbia described the device and its operation and declared:

> "[W]hile courts will go a long way in admitting expert testimony deduced from a well-recognized scientific principle or discovery, *the thing from which the deduction is made must be sufficiently established to have gained general acceptance in the particular field in which it belongs.*" 293 F. at 1014 (emphasis added).

. . . Petitioners . . . contend that the *Frye* test was superseded by the adoption of the Federal Rules of Evidence. We agree. . . . Rule 702, governing expert testimony, provides:

> "If scientific, technical, or other specialized knowledge will assist the trier of fact to understand the evidence or to determine a fact in issue, a witness qualified as an expert by knowledge, skill, experience, training, or education, may testify thereto in the form of an opinion or otherwise."*

Nothing in the text of this Rule establishes "general acceptance" as an absolute prerequisite to admissibility. Nor does respondent present any clear indication that Rule 702 or the Rules as a whole were intended to incorporate a "general acceptance" standard. The drafting history makes no mention of *Frye*, and a rigid "general acceptance" requirement would be at odds with the "liberal thrust" of the Federal Rules and their "general approach of relaxing the traditional barriers to 'opinion' testimony." Beech Aircraft Corp. v. Rainey, 488 U.S. 153, 169 (1988). Given the Rules' permissive backdrop and their inclusion of a specific rule on expert testimony that does not mention "general acceptance," the assertion that the Rules somehow assimilated *Frye* is unconvincing. *Frye* made "general acceptance" the exclusive test for admitting expert scientific testimony.

* [Rule 702 was amended in 2000 and restyled in 2011. Today the rule is bulkier and more detailed.—GF]

That austere standard, absent from, and incompatible with, the Federal Rules of Evidence, should not be applied in federal trials.

B

That the *Frye* test was displaced by the Rules of Evidence does not mean, however, that the Rules themselves place no limits on the admissibility of purportedly scientific evidence. Nor is the trial judge disabled from screening such evidence. To the contrary, under the Rules the trial judge must ensure that any and all scientific testimony or evidence admitted is not only relevant, but reliable.

The primary locus of this obligation is Rule 702, which clearly contemplates some degree of regulation of the subjects and theories about which an expert may testify. "*If scientific*, technical, or other specialized *knowledge will assist the trier of fact* to understand the evidence or to determine a fact in issue" an expert "may testify *thereto*." (FRE 702 [unrestyled] (emphasis added).) The subject of an expert's testimony must be "scientific . . . knowledge."[8] The adjective "scientific" implies a grounding in the methods and procedures of science. Similarly, the word "knowledge" connotes more than subjective belief or unsupported speculation. The term "applies to any body of known facts or to any body of ideas inferred from such facts or accepted as truths on good grounds." WEBSTER'S THIRD NEW INTERNATIONAL DICTIONARY 1252 (1986). Of course, it would be unreasonable to conclude that the subject of scientific testimony must be "known" to a certainty; arguably, there are no certainties in science. *See, e.g.*, Brief for Nicolaas Bloembergen et al. as *Amici Curiae* 9 ("Indeed, scientists do not assert that they know what is immutably 'true'—they are committed to searching for new, temporary, theories to explain, as best they can, phenomena"); Brief for American Association for the Advancement of Science et al. as *Amici Curiae* 7–8 ("Science is not an encyclopedic body of knowledge about the universe. Instead, it represents a *process* for proposing and refining theoretical explanations about the world that are subject to further testing and refinement" (emphasis in original)). But, in order to qualify as "scientific knowledge," an inference or assertion must be derived by the scientific method. Proposed testimony must be supported by appropriate validation—*i.e.*, "good grounds," based on what is known. In short, the requirement that an expert's testimony pertain to "scientific knowledge" establishes a standard of evidentiary reliability.[9]

8. Rule 702 also applies to "technical, or other specialized knowledge." Our discussion is limited to the scientific context because that is the nature of the expertise offered here.

9. We note that scientists typically distinguish between "validity" (does the principle support what it purports to show?) and "reliability" (does application of the principle produce consistent results?). Although "the difference between accuracy, validity, and reliability may be such that each is distinct from the other by no more than a hen's kick," Starrs, Frye v. United States *Restructured and Revitalized: A Proposal To Amend Federal Evidence Rule 702*, 26 JURI-

[Unrestyled] Rule 702 further requires that the evidence or testimony "assist the trier of fact to understand the evidence or to determine a fact in issue." This condition goes primarily to relevance. "Expert testimony which does not relate to any issue in the case is not relevant and, ergo, non-helpful." 3 WEINSTEIN & BERGER, EVIDENCE ¶ 702[02], p. 702–18. The consideration has been aptly described by Judge Becker as one of "fit." United States v. Downing, 753 F.2d 1224, 1242 (3d Cir. 1985). "Fit" is not always obvious, and scientific validity for one purpose is not necessarily scientific validity for other, unrelated purposes. The study of the phases of the moon, for example, may provide valid scientific "knowledge" about whether a certain night was dark, and if darkness is a fact in issue, the knowledge will assist the trier of fact. However (absent creditable grounds supporting such a link), evidence that the moon was full on a certain night will not assist the trier of fact in determining whether an individual was unusually likely to have behaved irrationally on that night. Rule 702's "helpfulness" standard requires a valid scientific connection to the pertinent inquiry as a precondition to admissibility.

That these requirements are embodied in Rule 702 is not surprising. Unlike an ordinary witness, *see* Rule 701, an expert is permitted wide latitude to offer opinions, including those that are not based on firsthand knowledge or observation. See Rules 702 and 703. Presumably, this relaxation of the usual requirement of firsthand knowledge—a rule which represents "a 'most pervasive manifestation' of the common law insistence upon 'the most reliable sources of information,' " Advisory Committee's Notes on Fed. Rule Evid. 602—is premised on an assumption that the expert's opinion will have a reliable basis in the knowledge and experience of his discipline.

C

Faced with a proffer of expert scientific testimony, then, the trial judge must determine at the outset, pursuant to Rule 104(a), whether the expert is proposing to testify to (1) scientific knowledge that (2) will assist the trier of fact to understand or determine a fact in issue.[11] This entails a preliminary assessment of whether the reasoning or methodology underlying the testimony is scientifically valid and of whether that reasoning or methodology properly can be applied to the facts in issue. We are confident that federal judges possess the capacity to undertake this

METRICS J. 249, 256 (1986), our reference here is to *evidentiary* reliability—that is, trustworthiness. In a case involving scientific evidence, *evidentiary reliability* will be based upon *scientific validity*.

11. Although the *Frye* decision itself focused exclusively on "novel" scientific techniques, we do not read the requirements of Rule 702 to apply specially or exclusively to unconventional evidence. Of course, well-established propositions are less likely to be challenged than those that are novel, and they are more handily defended. Indeed, theories that are so firmly established as to have attained the status of scientific law, such as the laws of thermodynamics, properly are subject to judicial notice under Federal Rule of Evidence 201.

review. Many factors will bear on the inquiry, and we do not presume to set out a definitive checklist or test. But some general observations are appropriate.

Ordinarily, a key question to be answered in determining whether a theory or technique is scientific knowledge that will assist the trier of fact will be whether it can be (and has been) tested. "Scientific methodology today is based on generating hypotheses and testing them to see if they can be falsified; indeed, this methodology is what distinguishes science from other fields of human inquiry." Green, *Expert Witnesses and Sufficiency of Evidence in Toxic Substances Litigation: The Legacy of* Agent Orange *and Bendectin Litigation*, 86 NW. U. L. REV. 643, 645 (1992). *See also* C. HEMPEL, PHILOSOPHY OF NATURAL SCIENCE 49 (1966) ("The statements constituting a scientific explanation must be capable of empirical test. . . ."); K. POPPER, CONJECTURES AND REFUTATIONS: THE GROWTH OF SCIENTIFIC KNOWLEDGE 37 (5th ed. 1989) ("The criterion of the scientific status of a theory is its falsifiability, or refutability, or testability. . . .") (emphasis deleted).

Another pertinent consideration is whether the theory or technique has been subjected to peer review and publication. Publication (which is but one element of peer review) is not a *sine qua non* of admissibility; it does not necessarily correlate with reliability, and in some instances well-grounded but innovative theories will not have been published. Some propositions, moreover, are too particular, too new, or of too limited interest to be published. But submission to the scrutiny of the scientific community is a component of "good science," in part because it increases the likelihood that substantive flaws in methodology will be detected. The fact of publication (or lack thereof) in a peer-reviewed journal thus will be a relevant, though not dispositive, consideration in assessing the scientific validity of a particular technique or methodology on which an opinion is premised.

Additionally, in the case of a particular scientific technique, the court ordinarily should consider the known or potential rate of error and the existence and maintenance of standards controlling the technique's operation.

Finally, "general acceptance" can yet have a bearing on the inquiry. A "reliability assessment does not require, although it does permit, explicit identification of a relevant scientific community and an express determination of a particular degree of acceptance within that community." *United States v. Downing*, 753 F.2d at 1238. Widespread acceptance can be an important factor in ruling particular evidence admissible, and "a known technique which has been able to attract only minimal support within the community," *Downing*, 753 F.2d at 1238, may properly be viewed with skepticism.

The inquiry envisioned by Rule 702 is, we emphasize, a flexible one. Its overarching subject is the scientific validity—and thus the evidentiary relevance and reliability—of the principles that underlie a proposed submission. The focus, of course, must be solely on principles and methodology, not on the conclusions that they generate.

Throughout, a judge assessing a proffer of expert scientific testimony under Rule 702 should also be mindful of other applicable rules. [Unrestyled] Rule 703 provides that expert opinions based on otherwise inadmissible hearsay are to be admitted only if the facts or data are "of a type reasonably relied upon by experts in the particular field in forming opinions or inferences upon the subject." Rule 706 allows the court at its discretion to procure the assistance of an expert of its own choosing. Finally, [unrestyled] Rule 403 permits the exclusion of relevant evidence "if its probative value is substantially outweighed by the danger of unfair prejudice, confusion of the issues, or misleading the jury. . . ." Judge Weinstein has explained: "Expert evidence can be both powerful and quite misleading because of the difficulty in evaluating it. Because of this risk, the judge in weighing possible prejudice against probative force under Rule 403 of the present rules exercises more control over experts than over lay witnesses." Weinstein, 138 F.R.D. at 632.

III

We conclude by briefly addressing what appear to be two underlying concerns of the parties and *amici* in this case. Respondent expresses apprehension that abandonment of "general acceptance" as the exclusive requirement for admission will result in a "free-for-all" in which befuddled juries are confounded by absurd and irrational pseudoscientific assertions. In this regard respondent seems to us to be overly pessimistic about the capabilities of the jury and of the adversary system generally. Vigorous cross-examination, presentation of contrary evidence, and careful instruction on the burden of proof are the traditional and appropriate means of attacking shaky but admissible evidence. . . . These conventional devices, rather than wholesale exclusion under an uncompromising "general acceptance" test, are the appropriate safeguards where the basis of scientific testimony meets the standards of Rule 702.

Petitioners and, to a greater extent, their *amici* exhibit a different concern. They suggest that recognition of a screening role for the judge that allows for the exclusion of "invalid" evidence will sanction a stifling and repressive scientific orthodoxy and will be inimical to the search for truth. It is true that open debate is an essential part of both legal and scientific analyses. Yet there are important differences between the quest for truth in the courtroom and the quest for truth in the laboratory. Scientific conclusions are subject to perpetual revision. Law, on the other hand, must resolve disputes finally and quickly. The scientific project is advanced by broad and wide-ranging consideration of a multitude of hypotheses, for those that are incorrect will eventually be shown to be so, and that in itself is an advance. Conjectures that are probably wrong are of little use, however, in the project of reaching a quick, final, and binding legal judgment—often of great consequence—about a particular set of events in the past. We recognize that, in practice, a gatekeeping role for the judge, no matter how flexible, inevitably on occasion will prevent the jury from learning of authentic insights and innovations. That, nevertheless, is the balance that is struck by Rules of Evidence designed not for the exhaustive search for cosmic understanding but for the particularized resolution of legal disputes.[13]

IV

To summarize: "General acceptance" is not a necessary precondition to the admissibility of scientific evidence under the Federal Rules of Evidence, but the Rules of Evidence—especially Rule 702—do assign to the trial judge the task of ensuring that an expert's testimony both rests on a reliable foundation and is relevant to the task at hand. Pertinent evidence based on scientifically valid principles will satisfy those demands.

The inquiries of the District Court and the Court of Appeals focused almost exclusively on "general acceptance," as gauged by publication and the decisions of other courts. Accordingly, the judgment of the Court of Appeals is vacated, and the case is remanded for further proceedings consistent with this opinion.

It is so ordered.

■ CHIEF JUSTICE REHNQUIST, with whom JUSTICE STEVENS joins, concurring in part and dissenting in part.... The Court concludes, correctly in my view, that the *Frye* rule did not survive the enactment of the Federal Rules of Evidence, and I therefore join Parts I and II–A of its opinion. The ... Court ... proceeds to construe Rules 702 and 703 very much in the abstract, and then offers some "general observations."

"General observations" by this Court customarily carry great weight with lower federal courts, but the ones offered here suffer from the flaw common to most such observations—they are not applied to deciding whether particular testimony was or was not admissible, and therefore they tend to be not only general, but vague and abstract. This is particularly unfortunate in a case such as this, where the ultimate legal question depends on an appreciation of one or more bodies of knowledge not judicially noticeable, and subject to different interpretations in the briefs of the parties and their *amici*....

The various briefs filed in this case are markedly different from typical briefs, in that large parts of them do not deal with decided cases or statutory language—the sort of material we customarily interpret.

13. This is not to say that judicial interpretation, as opposed to adjudicative factfinding, does not share basic characteristics of the scientific endeavor: "The work of a judge is in one sense enduring and in another ephemeral.... In the endless process of testing and retesting, there is a constant rejection of the dross and a constant retention of whatever is pure and sound and fine." B. CARDOZO, THE NATURE OF THE JUDICIAL PROCESS 178–79 (1921).

Instead, they deal with definitions of scientific knowledge, scientific method, scientific validity, and peer review—in short, matters far afield from the expertise of judges. This is not to say that such materials are not useful or even necessary in deciding how Rule 702 should be applied; but it is to say that the unusual subject matter should cause us to proceed with great caution in deciding more than we have to, because our reach can so easily exceed our grasp.

But even if it were desirable to make "general observations" not necessary to decide the questions presented, I cannot subscribe to some of the observations made by the Court.... Questions arise simply from reading this part of the Court's opinion, and countless more questions will surely arise when hundreds of district judges try to apply its teaching to particular offers of expert testimony. Does all of this *dicta* apply to an expert seeking to testify on the basis of "technical or other specialized knowledge"—the other types of expert knowledge to which Rule 702 applies—or are the "general observations" limited only to "scientific knowledge"? What is the difference between scientific knowledge and technical knowledge; does Rule 702 actually contemplate that the phrase "scientific, technical, or other specialized knowledge" be broken down into numerous subspecies of expertise, or did its authors simply pick general descriptive language covering the sort of expert testimony which courts have customarily received? The Court speaks of its confidence that federal judges can make a "preliminary assessment of whether the reasoning or methodology underlying the testimony is scientifically valid and of whether that reasoning or methodology properly can be applied to the facts in issue." The Court then states that a "key question" to be answered in deciding whether something is "scientific knowledge" "will be whether it can be (and has been) tested." Following this sentence are three quotations from treatises, which not only speak of empirical testing, but one of which states that the " 'criterion of the scientific status of a theory is its falsifiability, or refutability, or testability.' "

I defer to no one in my confidence in federal judges; but I am at a loss to know what is meant when it is said that the scientific status of a theory depends on its "falsifiability," and I suspect some of them will be, too.

I do not doubt that Rule 702 confides to the judge some gatekeeping responsibility in deciding questions of the admissibility of proffered expert testimony. But I do not think it imposes on them either the obligation or the authority to become amateur scientists in order to perform that role. I think the Court would be far better advised in this case to decide only the questions presented, and to leave the further development of this important area of the law to future cases.

DAUBERT V. MERRELL DOW: *Afterthoughts*

Five Easy Words

If you happened to read Rule 702 before you turned to *Daubert*, the case's outcome might have seemed preordained. After all, subsections (c) and (d) of Rule 702 essentially state the Court's holding. But Congress added those parts of the rule by amendment in 2000. In crafting the Court's opinion, Justice Blackmun had only the scant raw material of the original rule:

> **Rule 702. Testimony by Experts.** If scientific, technical, or otherwise specialized knowledge will assist the trier of fact to understand the evidence or to determine a fact in issue, a witness qualified as an expert by knowledge, skill, experience, training, or education, may testify thereto in the form of an opinion or otherwise.

Making the most of what he had, Blackmun managed to spin out the bulk of his analysis from just five words—"scientific knowledge" and "assist the trier":

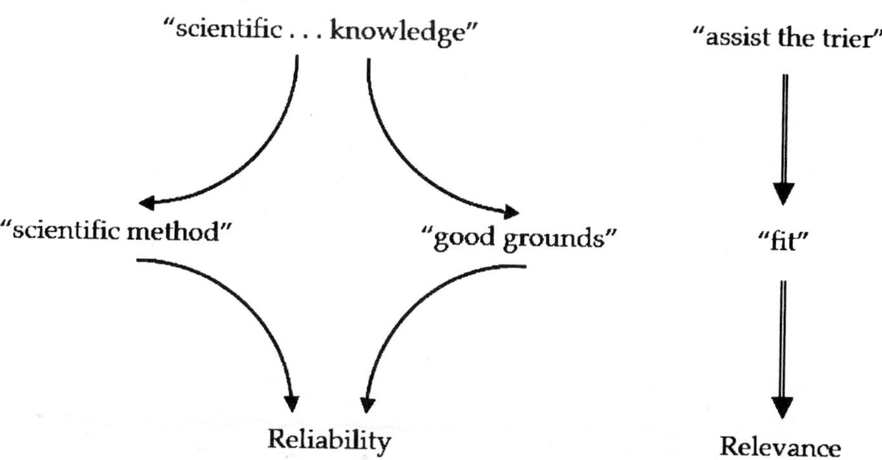

From the adjective "scientific" Justice Blackmun concluded that Rule 702 requires that an expert's methodology rest on "inference[s] or assertion[s] . . . derived by the scientific method." In the word "knowledge" he found a requirement that the methodology draw from a " 'body of known facts or [from] any body of ideas inferred from such facts or accepted as truths on good grounds.' " Uniting these two ideas, he concluded that "the requirement that an expert's testimony pertain to 'scientific knowledge' establishes a standard of evidentiary *reliability*."

(Emphasis added.) Later he elaborated on the notion of "reliability" by offering five "general observations" to trial judges faced with the task of assessing the reliability of a scientific theory or technique. These have become known as the *Daubert* "factors":

(1) whether the technique "can be (and has been) tested";

(2) whether it has been "subjected to peer review and publication";

(3) "the known or potential rate of error";

(4) "the existence and maintenance of standards controlling the technique's operation"; and

(5) " 'general acceptance' " in the relevant scientific community.

Justice Blackmun emphasized that these factors do not constitute "a definitive checklist or test"—and that the inquiry is "a flexible one."

Turning next to Rule 702's requirement that an expert's testimony "assist the trier" of fact, Justice Blackmun wrote that this condition "goes primarily to relevance"—and that relevance, in this context, is a matter of *fit*: " 'Expert testimony which does not relate to any issue in the case is not relevant and, ergo, non-helpful.' The consideration has been aptly described by Judge Becker as one of 'fit.' " (Citations omitted.)

To be admissible, expert scientific testimony must be both reliable and relevant as the *Daubert* Court defines those terms. But what about the other sorts of expert testimony contemplated by Rule 702—those based on "technical" or "other specialized knowledge"? As Chief Justice Rehnquist noted in his separate opinion, *Daubert* left this question unexplored. We will see in the next section that the Court later extended *Daubert*-style analysis to these other realms of knowledge. The balance of this section, however, explores *Daubert*'s consequences largely in the realm in which the case arose—scientific expertise.

The Daubert *Trilogy*

Daubert was the first of three cases composing the "*Daubert* trilogy." The third, *Kumho Tire Company v. Carmichael*, 526 U.S. 137 (1999), which lies ahead, extended *Daubert*'s holding to all expert testimony, not merely "scientific" expertise. (*See* page 847 below.) In between and sometimes forgotten stands *General Electric Co. v. Joiner*, 522 U.S. 136 (1997). *Joiner* subtly but significantly eased the impact of *Daubert* on district court judges even as it raised the barrier against admission of proposed scientific expertise. The Justices held that appellate courts are to review lower-court rulings on the admissibility of expert testimony under *Daubert* only for abuse of discretion. *See id.* at 138–39. While easing review of district judges' rulings, *Joiner* heightened scrutiny of proposed scientific expertise. *Daubert* had deemed "[t]he inquiry envisioned by Rule 702 [to be] . . . a flexible one. . . . The focus, of course, must be solely on principles and methodology, not on the conclusions that they generate."

(Pages 799–800, above.) But the *Joiner* Court insisted that an expert's conclusions must withstand the trial judge's scrutiny:

> [C]onclusions and methodology are not entirely distinct from one another.... [N]othing in either *Daubert* or the Federal Rules of Evidence requires a district court to admit opinion evidence which is connected to existing data only by the *ipse dixit* of the expert. A court may conclude that there is simply too great an analytical gap between the data and the opinion proffered.

Joiner, 522 U.S. at 146.*

Daubert's *Aftermath: Is the Hurdle Higher or Lower?*

Do *Daubert*'s rise and *Frye*'s fall make it easier or harder for litigants to present expert scientific evidence at trial? The Justices who decided *Daubert* surely thought they were easing the standards for admission. After all, they vacated a lower-court judgment that had excluded testimony of the plaintiffs' Bendectin experts and remanded the case for reconsideration. Moreover, the Court noted that the "rigid 'general acceptance' requirement" of *Frye* was "at odds with the 'liberal thrust' of the Federal Rules"—implying that the Court was ushering in a newly liberal regime. Under the new order, in Justice Blackmun's words, expert scientific evidence could be "shaky but admissible."

Initial reports in the nation's business press agreed that *Daubert* had lowered the bar for scientific expertise. "Justices Rule Against Business in Evidence Case," the *Wall Street Journal* headlined the day after *Daubert* came down. Reporter Paul Barrett declared the decision "a defeat for business and the medical profession." Despite industry complaints about "countless consumer lawsuits based on dubious scientific evidence," the Court had "rejected a strict standard"—the old *Frye* standard—"widely used by federal judges to keep scientific evidence out of personal-injury lawsuits and other trials." Paul M. Barrett, *Justices Rule Against Business in Evidence Case*, WALL ST. J., June 29, 1993, at A3.**

And when the Supreme Court next took up the matter of expert scientific evidence—in *Joiner*—it restated its view that "the Federal Rules of Evidence [and hence presumably *Daubert*] allow district courts to admit a somewhat broader range of scientific testimony than would have been admissible under *Frye*." *Joiner*, 522 U.S. at 142. The Advisory Committee's Note to the 2000 amendment to Rule 702, which embraced the Court's analysis in *Daubert*, agreed that the new regime has been friendly to expert evidence: "A review of the caselaw after *Daubert* shows that the rejection of expert testimony is the exception rather than the rule." (RB 170.)

* I thank Professor Michael Gottesman for prompting me to add this segment.

** Professors Edward Cheng and Albert Yoon helpfully pointed me to this article

Yet for many observers (and perhaps for many lower-court judges), the most striking and memorable passage in Justice Blackmun's opinion was his reference to the "gatekeeping role" of the trial judge. In the legal lore *Daubert* stands today as the Court's counterstrike against the invasion of "junk science" into the nation's courtrooms—a "response to … the perceived problem of the hired-gun expert witness." 1 DAVID L. FAIGMAN, ET AL., MODERN SCIENTIFIC EVIDENCE § 1.3–4.1 (1997). Under *Frye*, some said, standards governing admission of expert scientific evidence had grown "decidedly lax." D. Michael Risinger, *Navigating Expert Reliability: Are Criminal Standards of Certainty Being Left on the Dock?* 64 ALB. L. REV. 99, 101 (2000).

Indeed the most rigorous study of *Daubert*'s early impact suggested that *Daubert* generally raised the bar against admission of expert testimony. A Rand Institute report released early in 2002 concluded that for several years after *Daubert*, challenges to expert evidence in federal civil actions prevailed more often than before. Focusing on cases from the Third Circuit, the authors found that among those cases in which expert evidence was challenged, "the exclusion rate … for evidence based on physical science in a product liability case jumped from 53 percent during the two years before *Daubert* to 70 percent between mid–1995 and mid–1996"—though the rate subsided after that. LLOYD DIXON & BRIAN GILL, CHANGES IN THE STANDARDS FOR ADMITTING EXPERT EVIDENCE IN FEDERAL CIVIL CASES SINCE THE *DAUBERT* DECISION, at xvi (2001).

One tangible result of this increasing scrutiny of expert evidence was an apparent increase in both summary judgment motions and their success rate. "[S]ummary judgments were granted in 21 percent of challenges during the four years preceding *Daubert*, compared to 48 percent between July 1995 and June 1997." *Id.* at xvi, 56. Noting that the success rate of *Daubert* challenges declined after 1997, the authors speculate that litigants "either did not propose … [expert] evidence not meeting the new standards, or better tailored the evidence they did propose to fit the new standards." *Id.* at xvii.

The Rand study's most surprising discovery is how little *Daubert* seems to have changed the significance of *Frye*'s "general acceptance" test. Before *Daubert* a judge's finding that an expert's methods were generally accepted always or almost always assured a judgment that the evidence was reliable. After *Daubert* a favorable finding on general acceptance secured such a judgment ninety percent of the time. Conversely, an *unfavorable* finding on general acceptance resulted in a finding of unreliability in an overwhelming majority of cases before *Daubert*—and if anything made exclusion of the evidence even more certain afterward. *See id.* at 44. Despite the *Daubert* Court's disdain for *Frye*'s "rigid 'general acceptance' requirement," the old standard stood before the courthouse doors with much the same vigilance as before.

Comparing Daubert *and* Frye *States*

Another way to measure *Daubert*'s impact is to compare those states that have stuck with the *Frye* standard and those that have followed the Supreme Court's lead in *Daubert*. Because *Daubert* merely interpreted Rule 702 and did not announce a constitutional rule binding on the states, state courts and legislatures remain free to retain *Frye* or embrace *Daubert* or take a different tack altogether. In 2005, when Professors Edward Cheng and Albert Yoon canvassed the rules and caselaw of the fifty states, they identified twenty-five *Daubert* states, thirteen *Frye* states, and twelve states that fell cleanly into neither camp. *See* Edward K. Cheng & Albert H. Yoon, *Does* Frye *or* Daubert *Matter? A Study of Scientific Admissibility Standards*, 91 VA. L. REV. 471, 473 (2005). Today the tally and pattern of the states stands somewhat different, with twenty-two *Daubert* states, nine *Frye* states, and nineteen states with diverging standards.* The map on page 808 updates a similar map that Professors Cheng and Yoon presented in their study. *See id.* at 473.

Cheng and Yoon examined the impact in tort cases of a state's choice to adhere to the *Frye* standard or instead adopt *Daubert*. Their deft analytical technique counted on defense counsel to know which standard would prove better for tort defendants. Hence the authors examined how commonly defense counsel sought to remove tort cases originally filed in state court to federal court. If *Daubert* had proved substantially

* Identifying states as adherents of *Frye*, *Daubert*, or some other standard requires a number of judgment calls, some of them close. In Washington, for example, *Frye* controls in criminal cases, but is merely assumed to control in civil cases. *See Anderson v. Akzo Nobel Coatings, Inc.*, 172 Wash. 2d 593, 602–03 (2011). All in all, labeling Washington a *Frye* state seems most accurate. Similarly, Oregon's standard for admission of expert evidence does not quite match *Daubert*'s, but mimics it closely enough to put the state in the *Daubert* camp. *See State v. Southard*, 347 Ore. 127, 132–35 (2009).

Several states reside awkwardly in the "Other" column. The standards in Indiana and Tennessee tread very near *Daubert*, but diverge enough to merit an "Other" label. *See Turner v. State*, 953 N.E.2d 1039, 1050 & n.6 (Ind. 2011); *McDaniel v. CSX Transp., Inc.*, 955 S.W.2d 257, 265 (Tenn. 1997). A slight variant of *Frye* holds sway in New Jersey. *See State v. Henderson*, 208 N.J. 208, 247–48 (2011); *Hisenaj v. Kuehner*, 194 N.J. 6, 17 (2008). In Georgia *Daubert* reigns in civil but not criminal cases. *See* GA. CODE ANN. §§ 24–9–67, 24–9–67.1(f); *Butler v. Union Carbide Corp.*, 310 Ga. App. 21, 25–26, 32–33 & n.3 (2011); *Vaughn v. State*, 282 Ga. 99, 101 (2007). And in Alabama *Daubert* governs only in cases involving DNA evidence. *See* ALA. CODE § 36–18–30 (2012); *ArvinMeritor, Inc. v. Curtis Dale Johnson*, 1 So. 3d 77, 87 n.1 (2008).

Faced with so many close calls, different researchers will arrive at different tallies even absent intervening law changes. The variance between Cheng and Yoon's count and the results I present here reflects both law changes and differing judgment calls.

My thanks to Gabriel Schlabach for his voluminous collection and review of state codes and caselaw—and for producing, on Cheng and Yoon's model, the map presented on the next page.

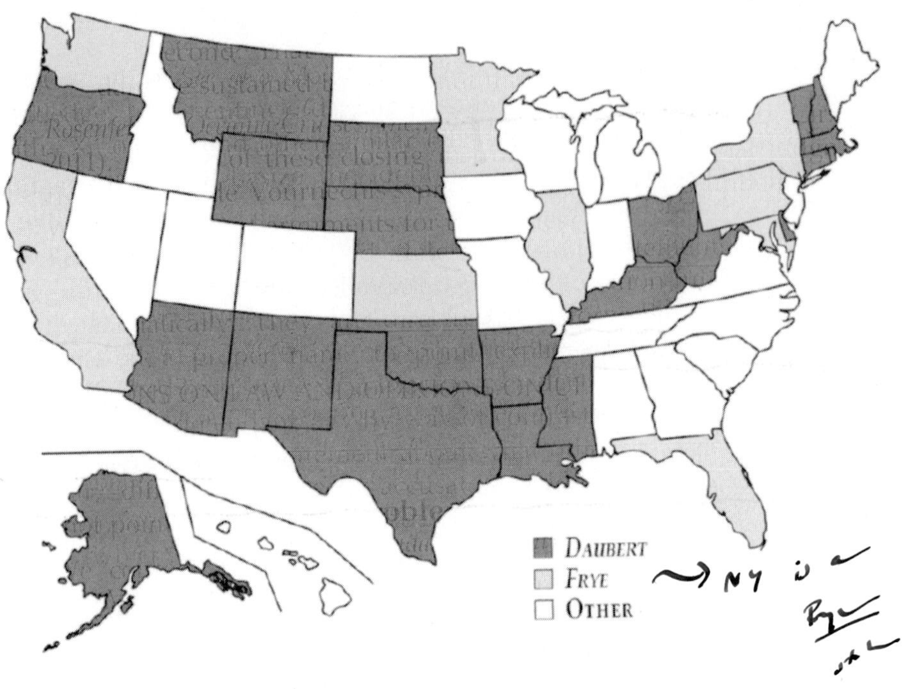

DAUBERT AND FRYE STATES, 2012

stricter than *Frye*, erecting a higher barrier to admission of scientific expertise, defense counsel likely would have sought to remove cases to federal court especially in those states that abided by *Frye*. That's because most tort defendants, as in *Daubert* itself, hope to exclude the expert scientific evidence on which plaintiffs' claims often rely. Conversely, if *Daubert* had proved the *laxer* standard, removal to federal court might have been *less* likely in *Frye* states.

Cheng and Yoon first compared two geographically close and demographically similar federal districts, the Eastern District of New York and the District of Connecticut. After federal courts abandoned *Frye* and embraced *Daubert* in 1993, New York courts continued to apply *Frye*, whereas Connecticut courts followed the federal lead and adopted *Daubert* in 1997. Had Connecticut's switch mattered, Cheng and Yoon surmised, removal rates in tort actions should have changed in Connecticut relative to the Eastern District of New York after 1997. Between 1997 and 1998, however, removal rates in the two jurisdictions "appear[ed] to move in lockstep." Cheng & Yoon, *supra*, 91 VA. L. REV. at 488. A broader comparison of cases filed during Connecticut's pre-*Daubert* period (1994–1996) and post-*Daubert* period (1998–2000) showed "a slight upward trend" in removal rates in New York, but no statistically significant difference between the two jurisdictions. *Id.* at 489.

Cheng and Yoon then extended their study to many *Frye* and *Daubert* states nationwide and to the entire decade spanning 1990 and 2000. Even then a state's choice between *Frye* and *Daubert* "ha[d] a vanishingly small effect on removal rate," suggesting that "a state's adoption of *Frye* or *Daubert* makes no difference in practice." *Id.* at 498, 503. "Perhaps it is time," the authors concluded, "to move away from debating the merits of *Frye* versus *Daubert* and toward a broader focus on how judges actually make decisions about science." *Id.* at 511.

More recently Professors Eric Helland and Jonathan Klick have assessed state-to-state variance by measuring litigants' likelihood to offer different types of expert witnesses. Helland and Klick's sample of 9125 cases spanned fifty states from 1990 to 2003. *See* Eric Helland & Jonathan Klick, *Does Anyone Get Stopped at the Gate? An Empirical Assessment of the* Daubert *Trilogy in the States* (University of Pennsylvania Law School, Institute for Law and Economics, Research Paper 09–12 (March 2009)), at 13. This large dataset allowed the authors to examine eighteen sorts of expert witnesses, such as epidemiologists, toxicologists, and chiropractors, and permitted the authors to distinguish experts according to the degrees they held. An expert's degree was valuable evidence, the authors reasoned. Because *Daubert* prizes methodological rigor, litigants in *Daubert* states might seek out experts who hold Ph.D.s and who therefore gained the methodological training doctoral programs often entail.

Yet across virtually every category of expertise, the impact of a state's adoption of *Daubert, Joiner*, or *Kumho Tire* on the likelihood that a litigant would offer expert testimony proved "not distinguishable from zero." *Id.* at 23 & tbl 10. Moreover the adoption of these cases had "no systematic effect" on the likelihood that a proposed expert would hold a Ph.D. or any other academic or professional degree. *Id.* at 24. Even when the authors isolated a dataset of products-liability cases, in which *Daubert* arguably plays an especially prominent role, measurable differences were slight. *See id.* at 24–25. At bottom, the authors concluded, there was "very little evidence that adoption of the *Daubert* trilogy has any systematic effect on who is offered as an expert in state court disputes." *Id.* at 27.

Reconciling the Studies

How can we reconcile the Rand study's findings, which reflected closer judicial scrutiny of expert evidence in post-*Daubert* federal courts, with the lackluster results in state courts analyzed by Cheng and Yoon and Helland and Klick? Cheng and Yoon proposed a possible answer: perhaps *Daubert*'s impact lay not in the actual standards it imposed on admission of expert testimony, but in its warning that trial judges had grown lax in policing courthouse doors against junk science and its purveyors. That message perhaps pervaded the legal landscape, making *all* judges, federal and state, more vigilant against charlatans masquerading as learned experts. *See* Cheng & Yoon, *supra*, 91 VA. L. REV. at 506. The result in federal courts was more frequent rejection of proffered expert evidence and consequently more grants of summary judgment, as the Rand study observed. And as state judges across the land heard *Daubert*'s message to take seriously their role as gatekeepers, differences between *Frye* and *Daubert* states melted away. Cheng and Yoon and Helland and Klick, having gone in search of those differences, therefore found them wanting.

Taken together, these three studies leave critical questions unresolved: Has *Daubert* proved more or less hospitable than *Frye* to expert scientific evidence?—and what will its longer-term impact be? For now, at least in federal courts, the evidence suggests that standards are stricter and the bar against scientific expertise higher. The later history of *Daubert* itself hints as much. For after the Supreme Court returned *Daubert* to the Ninth Circuit for a newly liberal review of the plaintiffs' proposed evidence, the judges of that court responded with something less than enthusiasm for Justice Blackmun's opinion—and with no more liberality than before:

DAUBERT V. MERRELL DOW PHARMACEUTICALS, INC.

43 F.3d 1311 (9th Cir.), *cert. denied*, 516 U.S. 869 (1995).

■ KOZINSKI, CIRCUIT JUDGE. On remand from the United States Supreme Court, we undertake "the task of ensuring that an expert's testimony both rests on a reliable foundation and is relevant to the task at hand." Daubert v. Merrell Dow Pharmaceuticals, Inc., 509 U.S. 579 (1993).

I

Two minors brought suit against Merrell Dow Pharmaceuticals, claiming they suffered limb-reduction birth defects because their mothers had taken Bendectin, a drug prescribed for morning sickness to about 17.5 million pregnant women in the United States between 1957 and 1982. This appeal deals with an evidentiary question: whether certain expert scientific testimony is admissible to prove that Bendectin caused the plaintiffs' birth defects.

For the most part, we don't know how birth defects come about. We do know they occur in 2–3% of births, whether or not the expectant mother has taken Bendectin. Limb defects are even rarer, occurring in fewer than one birth out of every 1000. But scientists simply do not know how teratogens (chemicals known to cause limb-reduction defects) do their damage: They cannot reconstruct the biological chain of events that leads from an expectant mother's ingestion of a teratogenic substance to the stunted development of a baby's limbs. Nor do they know what it is about teratogens that causes them to have this effect. No doubt, someday we will have this knowledge, and then we will be able to tell precisely whether and how Bendectin (or any other suspected teratogen) interferes with limb development; in the current state of scientific knowledge, however, we are ignorant.

Not knowing the mechanism whereby a particular agent causes a particular effect is not always fatal to a plaintiff's claim. Causation can be proved even when we don't know precisely how the damage occurred, if there is sufficiently compelling proof that the agent must have caused the damage somehow. One method of proving causation in these circumstances is to use statistical evidence. If 50 people who eat at a restaurant one evening come down with food poisoning during the night, we can infer that the restaurant's food probably contained something unwholesome, even if none of the dishes is available for analysis. . . .

It is by such means that plaintiffs here seek to establish that Bendectin is responsible for their injuries. They rely on the testimony of three groups of scientific experts. One group proposes to testify that there is a statistical link between the ingestion of Bendectin during pregnancy and limb-reduction defects. These experts have not themselves conducted epidemiological (human statistical) studies on the effects of Bendectin; rather, they have reanalyzed studies published by other scientists, none of whom reported a statistical association between Bendectin and birth defects. Other experts proffered by plaintiffs propose to testify that Bendectin causes limb-reduction defects in humans because it causes such defects in laboratory animals. A third group of experts sees a link between Bendectin and birth defects because Bendectin has a chemical structure that is similar to other drugs suspected of causing birth defects.

The opinions proffered by plaintiffs' experts do not, to understate the point, reflect the consensus within the scientific community. The FDA—an agency not known for its promiscuity in approving drugs—continues to approve Bendectin for use by pregnant women because "available data do not demonstrate an association between birth defects and Bendectin." Every published study here and abroad—and there have been many—concludes that Bendectin is not a teratogen. In fact, apart from the small but determined group of scientists testifying on behalf of the Bendectin plaintiffs in this and many other cases, there doesn't appear to be a single scientist who has concluded that Bendectin causes limb-reduction defects.

It is largely because the opinions proffered by plaintiffs' experts run counter to the substantial consensus in the scientific community that we affirmed the district court's grant of summary judgment the last time the case appeared before us. . . . We found that the district court properly applied [the *Frye*] standard, and affirmed. The Supreme Court reversed, holding that *Frye* was super[s]eded by Federal Rule of Evidence 702, and remanded for us to consider the admissibility of plaintiffs' expert testimony under this new standard. . . .

II

A. Brave New World

Federal judges ruling on the admissibility of expert scientific testimony face a far more complex and daunting task in a post–*Daubert* world than before. The judge's task under *Frye* is relatively simple: to determine whether the method employed by the experts is generally accepted in the scientific community. Under *Daubert*, we must engage in a difficult, two-part analysis. First, we must determine nothing less than whether the experts' testimony reflects "scientific knowledge," whether their findings are "derived by the scientific method," and whether their work product amounts to "good science." Second, we must ensure that the proposed expert testimony is "relevant to the task at hand," i.e., that it logically advances a material aspect of the proposing party's case. The Supreme Court referred to this second prong of the analysis as the "fit" requirement.

The first prong of *Daubert* puts federal judges in an uncomfortable position. . . . [W]e are largely untrained in science and certainly no match for any of the witnesses whose testimony we are reviewing. . . . The task before us is more daunting still when the dispute concerns matters at the very cutting edge of scientific research, where fact meets theory and certainty dissolves into probability. As the record in this case illustrates, scientists often have vigorous and sincere disagreements as to what research methodology is proper, what should be accepted as sufficient proof for the existence of a "fact," and whether information derived by a particular method can tell us anything useful about the subject under study.

Our responsibility, then, unless we badly misread the Supreme Court's opinion, is to resolve disputes among respected, well-credentialed scientists about matters squarely within their expertise, in areas where there is no scientific consensus as to what is and what is not "good science," and occasionally to reject such expert testimony because it was not "derived by the scientific method." Mindful of our position in the hierarchy of the federal judiciary, we take a deep breath and proceed with this heady task.

B. *Deus ex Machina*

. . . How do we figure out whether scientists have derived their findings through the scientific method or whether their testimony is based on scientifically valid principles? Each expert proffered by the plaintiffs assures us that he has "utilized the type of data that is generally and reasonably relied upon by scientists" in the relevant field and that he has "utilized the methods and methodology that would generally and reasonably be accepted" by people who deal in these matters. The Court held, however, that federal judges perform a "gatekeeping role"; to do so they must satisfy themselves that scientific evidence meets a certain standard of reliability before it is admitted. This means that the expert's bald assurance of validity is not enough. Rather, the party presenting the expert must show that the expert's findings are based on sound science, and this will require some objective, independent validation of the expert's methodology.

While declining to set forth a "definitive checklist or test," the Court did list several factors federal judges can consider in determining whether to admit expert scientific testimony under Fed. R. Evid. 702. . . . We read these factors as illustrative rather than exhaustive; similarly, we do not deem each of them to be equally applicable (or applicable at all) in every case.[4] Rather, we read the Supreme Court as instructing us to determine whether the analysis undergirding the experts' testimony falls within the range of accepted standards governing how scientists conduct their research and reach their conclusions.

One very significant fact to be considered is whether the experts are proposing to testify about matters growing naturally and directly out of research they have conducted independent of the litigation, or whether they have developed their opinions expressly for purposes of testifying. That an expert testifies for money does not necessarily cast doubt on the reliability of his testimony, as few experts appear in court merely as an eleemosynary gesture. But in determining whether proposed expert testimony amounts to good science, we may not ignore the fact that a scientist's normal workplace is the lab or the field, not the courtroom or the lawyer's office.

That an expert testifies based on research he has conducted independent of the litigation provides important, objective proof that the research comports with the dictates of good science. . . . For one thing, experts whose findings flow from existing research are less likely to have been biased toward a particular conclusion by the promise of remuneration; when an expert prepares reports and findings before being hired as a witness, that record will limit the degree to which he can tailor his testimony to serve a party's interests. Then, too, independent research

4. Two of the four factors mentioned by the Supreme Court would be difficult or impossible to apply to the expert testimony in this case. Only one of plaintiffs' experts has done original research. Dr. Crescitelli mentions that he "specifically performed studies" on Bendectin and its antihistamine component, but does not explain the nature of those studies or the methodology employed. The others have examined the available literature and studies within their respective fields and drawn different conclusions than the scientists who performed the original work. As to such derivative analytical work, it makes little sense to ask whether the technique employed "can be (and has been) tested" or what its "known or potential rate of error" might be.

carries its own indicia of reliability, as it is conducted, so to speak, in the usual course of business and must normally satisfy a variety of standards to attract funding and institutional support. Finally, there is usually a limited number of scientists actively conducting research on the very subject that is germane to a particular case, which provides a natural constraint on parties' ability to shop for experts who will come to the desired conclusion. That the testimony proffered by an expert is based directly on legitimate, preexisting research unrelated to the litigation provides the most persuasive basis for concluding that the opinions he expresses were "derived by the scientific method."

We have examined carefully the affidavits proffered by plaintiffs' experts, as well as the testimony from prior trials that plaintiffs have introduced in support of that testimony, and find that none of the experts based his testimony on preexisting or independent research. While plaintiffs' scientists are all experts in their respective fields, none claims to have studied the effect of Bendectin on limb-reduction defects before being hired to testify in this or related cases.

If the proffered expert testimony is not based on independent research, the party proffering it must come forward with other objective, verifiable evidence that the testimony is based on "scientifically valid principles." One means of showing this is by proof that the research and analysis supporting the proffered conclusions have been subjected to normal scientific scrutiny through peer review and publication. *See* PETER W. HUBER, GALILEO'S REVENGE: JUNK SCIENCE IN THE COURTROOM 209 (1991) (suggesting that "the ultimate test of [a scientific expert's] integrity is her readiness to publish and be damned").

Peer review and publication do not, of course, guarantee that the conclusions reached are correct; much published scientific research is greeted with intense skepticism and is not borne out by further research. But the test under *Daubert* is not the correctness of the expert's conclusions but the soundness of his methodology. That the research is accepted for publication in a reputable scientific journal after being subjected to the usual rigors of peer review is a significant indication that it is taken seriously by other scientists.... If nothing else, peer review and publication "increase the likelihood that substantive flaws in methodology will be detected." *Daubert*, 509 U.S. at 593.

Bendectin litigation has been pending in the courts for over a decade, yet the only review the plaintiffs' experts' work has received has been by judges and juries, and the only place their theories and studies have been published is in the pages of federal and state reporters. None of the plaintiffs' experts has published his work on Bendectin in a scientific journal or solicited formal review by his colleagues. Despite the many years the controversy has been brewing, no one in the scientific community—except defendant's experts—has deemed these studies worthy of verification, refutation or even comment. It's as if there were a tacit understanding within the scientific community that what's going on here is not science at all, but litigation.

Establishing that an expert's proffered testimony grows out of pre-litigation research or that the expert's research has been subjected to peer review are the two principal ways the proponent of expert testimony can show that the evidence satisfies the first prong of Rule 702. Where such evidence is unavailable, the proponent of expert scientific testimony may attempt to satisfy its burden through the testimony of its own experts. For such a showing to be sufficient, the experts must explain precisely how they went about reaching their conclusions and point to some objective source—a learned treatise, the policy statement of a professional association, a published article in a reputable scientific journal or the like—to show that they have followed the scientific method, as it is practiced by (at least) a recognized minority of scientists in their field.

Plaintiffs have made no such showing. As noted above, plaintiffs rely entirely on the experts' unadorned assertions that the methodology they employed comports with standard scientific procedures.... We've been presented with only the experts' qualifications, their conclusions and their assurances of reliability. Under *Daubert*, that's not enough.

This is especially true of Dr. Palmer—the only expert willing to testify "that Bendectin did cause the limb defects in each of the children." In support of this conclusion, Dr. Palmer asserts only that Bendectin is a teratogen and that he has examined the plaintiffs' medical records, which apparently reveal the timing of their mothers' ingestion of the drug. Dr. Palmer offers no tested or testable theory to explain how, from this limited information, he was able to eliminate all other potential causes of birth defects, nor does he explain how he alone can state as a fact that Bendectin caused plaintiffs' injuries. We therefore agree with the Sixth Circuit's observation that "Dr. Palmer does not testify on the basis of the collective view of his scientific discipline, nor does he take issue with his peers and explain the grounds for his differences. Indeed, no understandable scientific basis is stated. Personal opinion, not science, is testifying here." Turpin v. Merrell Dow Pharmaceuticals, Inc., 959 F.2d 1349, 1360 (6th Cir. 1992). For this reason, Dr. Palmer's testimony is inadmissible as a matter of law under Rule 702.

The failure to make any objective showing as to admissibility under the first prong of Rule 702 would also fatally undermine the testimony of plaintiffs' other experts, but for the peculiar posture of this case. Plaintiffs submitted their experts' affidavits while *Frye* was the law of the circuit and, although they've not requested an opportunity to augment their experts' affidavits in light of *Daubert*, the interests of justice would be disserved by precluding plaintiffs from doing so....

Were this the only question before us, we would be inclined to remand to give plaintiffs an opportunity to submit additional proof that the scientific testimony they proffer was "derived by the scientific method." *Daubert*, however, establishes two prongs to the Rule 702 admissibility inquiry. We therefore consider whether the testimony satisfies the second prong of Rule 702: Would plaintiffs' proffered scientific evidence "assist the trier of fact to . . . determine a fact in issue"?

C. No Visible Means of Support

In elucidating the second requirement of Rule 702, *Daubert* stressed the importance of the "fit" between the testimony and an issue in the case: "Rule 702's 'helpfulness' standard requires a valid scientific connection to the pertinent inquiry as a precondition to admissibility." 509 U.S. at 591–92. Here, the pertinent inquiry is causation. In assessing whether the proffered expert testimony "will assist the trier of fact" in resolving this issue, we must look to the governing substantive standard, which in this case is supplied by California tort law.

Plaintiffs do not attempt to show causation directly; instead, they rely on experts who present circumstantial proof of causation. Plaintiffs' experts testify that Bendectin is a teratogen because it causes birth defects when it is tested on animals, because it is similar in chemical structure to other suspected teratogens, and because statistical studies show that Bendectin use increases the risk of birth defects. Modern tort law permits such proof, but plaintiffs must nevertheless carry their traditional burden; they must prove that their injuries were the result of the accused cause and not some independent factor. In the case of birth defects, carrying this burden is made more difficult because we know that some defects—including limb-reduction defects—occur even when expectant mothers do not take Bendectin, and that most birth defects occur for no known reason.

California tort law requires plaintiffs to show not merely that Bendectin increased the likelihood of injury, but that it more likely than not caused their injuries. In terms of statistical proof, this means that plaintiffs must establish not just that their mothers' ingestion of Bendectin increased somewhat the likelihood of birth defects, but that it more than doubled it—only then can it be said that Bendectin is more likely than not the source of their injury. Because the background rate of limb-reduction defects is one per thousand births, plaintiffs must show that among children of mothers who took Bendectin the incidence of such defects was more than two per thousand.

None of plaintiffs' epidemiological experts claims that ingestion of Bendectin during pregnancy more than doubles the risk of birth defects. . . . While plaintiffs' epidemiologists make vague assertions that there is a statistically significant relationship between Bendectin and birth defects, none states that the relative risk is greater than two. These studies thus would not be helpful, and indeed would only serve to confuse the jury, if offered to prove rather than refute causation. A relative risk of less than two may suggest teratogenicity, but it actually tends to disprove legal causation as it shows that Bendectin does not double the likelihood of birth defects.[17]

With the exception of Dr. Palmer, whose testimony is inadmissible under the first prong of the Rule 702 analysis,[18] the remaining experts proffered by plaintiffs were equally unprepared to testify that Bendectin caused plaintiffs' injuries; they were willing to testify only that Bendectin is "capable of causing" birth defects. Plaintiffs argue "these scientists use the words 'capable of causing' meaning that it does cause. This is an ambiguity of language.... If something is capable of causing damage in humans, it does." Tape of Oral Arg. Mar. 22, 1994. But what plaintiffs must prove is not that Bendectin causes some birth defects, but that it caused *their* birth defects. To show this, plaintiffs' experts would have had to testify either that Bendectin actually caused plaintiffs' injuries (which they could not say) or that Bendectin more than doubled the likelihood of limb-reduction birth defects (which they did not say).

As the district court properly found below, "the strongest inference to be drawn for plaintiffs based on the epidemiological evidence is that Bendectin could possibly have caused plaintiffs' injuries." ... Plaintiffs do not quantify this possibility, or otherwise indicate how their conclusions about causation should be weighted, even though the substantive legal standard has always required proof of causation by a preponderance of the evidence. Unlike these experts' explanation of their methodology, this is not a shortcoming that could be corrected on remand; plaintiffs' experts could augment their affidavits with independent proof that their methods were sound, but to augment the substantive testimony as to causation would require the experts to change their conclusions altogether. Any such tailoring of the experts' conclusions would, at this stage of the proceedings, fatally undermine any attempt to show that these findings were "derived by the scientific method." Plaintiffs' experts must, therefore, stand by the conclusions they originally proffered, rendering their testimony inadmissible under the second prong of Fed. R. Evid. 702.

CONCLUSION

The district court's grant of summary judgment is *Affirmed*.

---

17. The Supreme Court recognized that the "fit" requirement "goes primarily to relevance," but it obviously did not intend the second prong of Rule 702 to be merely a reiteration of the general relevancy requirement of Rule 402. In elucidating the "fit" requirement, the Supreme Court noted that scientific expert testimony carries special dangers to the fact-finding process because it "'can be both powerful and quite misleading because of the difficulty in evaluating it.'" Federal judges must therefore exclude proffered scientific evidence under Rules 702 and 403 unless they are convinced that it speaks clearly and directly to an issue in dispute in the case, and that it will not mislead the jury.

18. Dr. Palmer's testimony would easily meet Rule 702's fit requirement, were it not rendered inadmissible by the total lack of scientific basis for his conclusions. *See supra*. Dr. Palmer's testimony thus illustrates how the two prongs of Rule 702 work in tandem to ensure that junk science is kept out of the federal courtroom.

Judge Rules Breast Implant Evidence Invalid

Gina Kolata

NEW YORK TIMES, Dec. 19, 1996, at 1

A Federal judge who is overseeing breast implant cases in Oregon has ruled that lawyers cannot introduce evidence saying that implants cause disease, because such evidence is not scientifically valid. . . .

The judge dismissed 70 claims, and his ruling, if upheld on appeal, would stop scores of others from reaching the courts. Never before, experts say, has a science hearing of this kind affected so many claims all at once. Legal experts said that the ruling, if upheld, is likely to have a major impact on the tens of thousands of breast implant cases awaiting trial across the country, encouraging other judges to look more closely at the scientific foundation of the evidence that plaintiffs' lawyers want to introduce in court.

In his decision, Federal District Court Judge Robert E. Jones made clear that he was mindful of the scope of his opinion, which, he wrote, "goes further in evaluating and eliminating plaintiffs' claims than any other opinion in breast implant litigation pending in this country."

The ruling has significance beyond breast implant litigation, said Bert Black, a Dallas lawyer who is chairman of the American Bar Association's section on science and technology. "It's also an important example to other courts on how to handle scientific issues," Mr. Black said.

Some legal experts said the ruling was a stunning blow to plaintiffs' lawyers who had argued that breast implants cause disease. "This is absolutely critical," said Michael Green, a law professor at the University of Iowa in Iowa City. "The plaintiffs' lawyers have got to be devastated by this ruling," he added. . . .

As many as a million American women had silicone breast implants and, in the past decade, tens of thousands of them have sued implant manufacturers claiming that silicone leaked from the devices, oozed throughout their bodies, and made them ill. The diseases ranged from classic auto-immune diseases, like lupus or scleroderma, to what the women said was a new disease, with symptoms like fatigue, headache, and muscle aches and pains.

In cases that have gone to court, women have won verdicts as high as $25 million. But many more cases were settled out of court for undisclosed amounts. The vast amount of litigation was so overwhelming to the major implant manufacturer, Dow Corning Corporation, that it declared bankruptcy. Three other makers of silicone implants, Bristol–Myers Squibb, Minnesota Mining and Manufacturing, and Baxter International, negotiated a plan in Federal court in Alabama that may result in a total settlement of $2 to $3 billion.

Judge Jones was responsible for all of the Oregon silicone breast implant cases that were filed in Federal district court. In considering about 70 of those cases, he asked the lawyers for the plaintiffs and the defense to provide him with a list of expert witnesses that they would call. In July, the companies that are being sued, Baxter Healthcare and Bristol–Myers, asked the judge to exclude the scientific testimony from the plaintiffs' witnesses on the grounds that it was not based in science.

In 1993, in *Daubert v. Merrell Dow Pharmaceuticals,* . . . the Supreme Court instructed courts to aggressively screen out what they found to be ill-founded or speculative scientific theories.

"The Supreme Court charged district courts with the duty to act as 'gatekeepers' to insure that any and all scientific testimony or evidence admitted is not only relevant but reliable," Judge Jones wrote in his opinion. . . .

Judge Jones decided to ask a panel of disinterested scientists to advise him on the plaintiffs' evidence. After screening dozens of potential candidates, he finally selected "four totally unbiased and uncommitted experts in the necessary fields," he wrote. The experts were Dr. Merwyn R. Greenlick, an immunologist, Dr. Robert F. Wilkens, a rheumatologist, Dr. Mary Stenzel–Poore, an immunologist and toxicologist, and Dr. [Ronald] McClard, a polymer chemist.

He asked the scientists to study the scientific papers and documents submitted by the plaintiffs and then he held a hearing. It "spanned four intense days" in August, Judge Jones wrote, during which 12 experts for the plaintiffs and the defense were questioned by lawyers for both sides, by the court, and by the panel of scientists. Finally, the scientists provided their assessments of the plaintiff's scientific evidence. In his opinion, released late Tuesday, Judge Jones concluded that none of it was of sufficient quality to be presented in court.

While Judge Jones was deliberating, Federal Judge Samuel Pointer of Alabama, who is overseeing implant cases there, appointed a science panel of his own to advise him of the worthiness of plaintiffs' evidence that implants were harmful. His decision is not expected for about a year.

John McGoldrick, general counsel for Bristol–Myers, said he sees the decision as a "major blow to false science in this area." . . .

Susan Haack

An Epistemologist in the Bramble–Bush: At the Supreme Court with Mr. Joiner

26 J. HEALTH POL. POL'Y & L. 217 (2001)

"Judges Become Leery of Expert Witnesses," ran a headline in the *Wall Street Journal* a couple of years ago; they are "Skeptical of Unproven Science"—the "Testimony of Dilettantes." Intrigued, I began to struggle through thickets of details of exploding tires, allegedly poisonous perfumes, leaking and bursting breast implants, contaminated insulating oil, etc., etc., and through legal developments from *Frye* through the Federal Rules of Evidence to *Daubert,* until eventually I found myself at the U.S. Supreme Court . . . eavesdropping as the justices—for all the world like a conclave of medieval logicians—disagreed among themselves about whether there is a Categorical Distinction between methodology and conclusions. . . .

Legal efforts to winnow decent scientific evidence from the chaff, I shall argue, have often been based on false assumptions about science and how it works. . . . [If] the standards of strong evidence and well-conducted inquiry that apply to the sciences are the very same standards that apply to empirical inquiry generally, doesn't it follow that a lay person should be able to judge the worth of scientific evidence as well as a scientist? Unfortunately, no—far from it; for every area of science has its own specialized vocabulary, dense with theory, and judgments of the worth of evidence depend on substantive assumptions. Very often, the only alternative to relying on the judgment of scientists competent in the relevant field is to acquire a competence in that field yourself.

When a lay person (or even a scientist from another specialty) tries to judge the quality of evidence for a scientific claim, he is liable to find himself in the position of the average American asked to judge . . . a crossword puzzle where . . . the solutions are all in Turkish. . . . Similarly, to know what kinds of precaution would be adequate to ensure against experimental error requires substantive knowledge of what kinds of thing might interfere. To judge the likelihood that you are not dealing with a real phenomenon but with an artifact of the instrumentation requires substantive knowledge of how the instrument works. And so on. . . .

Unlike the *Frye* test, the Federal Rules as interpreted in *Daubert* require the trial judge to make determinations about scientific methodology in his own behalf. But what the *Daubert* Court has to offer by way of advice about how to make such determinations is—well, a little embarrassing.

[Justice Blackmun wrote in *Daubert* that " '[s]cientific methodology today is based on generating hypotheses and testing them to see if they can be falsified,' " and he referred for support to Karl Popper and Carl G. Hempel.] The justices are apparently unaware that Popper gives "falsifiable" a very narrow sense, "incompatible with some basic statement" (a basic statement being defined as a singular statement reporting the occurrence of an observable event at a specified place and time); and that according to Popper no scientific claim or theory can ever be shown to be true or even probable, but is at best "corroborated." In Popper's mouth, this is not equivalent to "confirmed," and does not imply truth or probable truth, but means no more than "tested but not yet falsified." If Popper were right, no scientific claim would be well-warranted. In fact, it is hard to think of a philosophy of science less congenial than Popper's to [*Daubert's*] relevance-and-reliability approach (or to the admissibility of psychiatric evidence, but that is a whole other can of worms). And if the reference to Popper is a *faux pas*, running Popper together with Hempel—a pioneer of the logic of confirmation, an enterprise the legitimacy of which Popper always staunchly denied—is a *faux pas de deux*.

In and of itself, of course, the *Daubert* Court's mixing up its Hoppers and its Pempels is just a minor scholarly irritation. A more serious problem is that neither Popper's nor Hempel's philosophy of science will do the job they want it to do. Popper's account of science is in truth a disguised form of skepticism; if it were right, what Popper likes to call "objective scientific knowledge" would be nothing more than conjectures which have not yet been falsified. And, though Hempel's account at least allows that scientific claims can be confirmed as well as disconfirmed, it contains nothing that would help a judge decide either whether evidence proffered is really scientific, or how reliable it is.

And the most fundamental problem is that the *Daubert* Court . . . is preoccupied with specifying what the method of inquiry is that distinguishes the scientific and reliable from the nonscientific and unreliable. There is no such method. There is only making informed conjectures and checking how well they stand up to evidence, which is common to every kind of empirical inquiry; and the many and various techniques used by scientists in this or that scientific field, which are neither universal across the sciences nor constitutive of real science.

The *Daubert* Court runs together (1) the tangled and distracting questions of demarcation and scientific method with (2) the question of the degree of warrant of specific scientific claims or theories and (3) the question of the reliability of specific scientific techniques or tests—which is different again. . . . Unlike determining whether a claim is falsifiable, however, determining whether a scientific theory . . . is well warranted, or whether a scientific test . . . is reliable, requires substantive scientific knowledge. Justice Rehnquist is right: the reference to falsifiability is no help, and judges are indeed being asked to be amateur scientists.

Furthermore, despite the majority's reassuring noises to the effect that juries can handle scientific evidence well enough, and can always be directed by the judge if they look like going off the rails, one is left wondering: if judges need to act as gatekeepers to exclude scientific evidence which doesn't meet minimal standards of warrant because juries may be taken in by flimsy scientific evidence, how realistic is it to expect juries to discriminate the better from the worse among the half-way decent? . . .

Which takes us back to that old worry of Justice Rehnquist's . . . [that] judges are neither trained [nor] qualified to do this kind of thing. . . . [True, there have] been some efforts to educate judges scientifically. In April 1999 about two dozen Massachusetts Superior Court judges attended a two-day seminar on DNA at the Whitehead Institute for Biomedical Research. A report in the *New York Times* quotes the director of the institute: in the O.J. Simpson trial lawyers "befuddle[d] everyone" over the DNA evidence; but after this program, "I don't think a judge will be intimidated by the science." Judges will "understand . . . what to allow in the courtroom." . . .

Not that educating judges about DNA or whatever mightn't do some good. But a few hours in a science seminar will no more transform judges into scientists competent to make subtle and sophisticated scientific determinations than a few hours in a legal seminar would transform scientists into judges competent to make subtle and sophisticated legal determinations. ("This kind of thing takes a lot of training," as Mad Margaret sings in *Ruddigore*.) And, to be candid, the *New York Times* report has me a little worried about the danger of giving judges a false impression that they *are* qualified to make those "subtle and sophisticated determinations." . . .

No wonder scientific evidence provides so many opportunities for opportunism! Often, we are trying to arrive at justice on the basis of imperfect and imperfectly understood information; and not so rarely, we are trying to create justice out of ignorance. . . .

b. A FOCUS ON POLYGRAPH EVIDENCE

This section on scientific evidence began with *Frye*'s rejection of a primitive lie detector. It is only fitting, in the aftermath of *Daubert*, to return where we began. How does polygraph evidence fare under *Daubert*'s relevance-and-reliability analysis? These materials attack that question in an era verging on post-polygraph technology.

D. Michael Risinger

Navigating Expert Reliability: Are Criminal Standards of Certainty Being Left on the Dock?

64 Alb. L. Rev. 99 (2000)

. . . So what do we see when we [look at] the universe of *Daubert*-citing opinions from July 1, 1993, to August 2, 1999 (the reference set) . . . ?

The Polygraph Cases

. . . Defendants proffered polygraph evidence fifty-three times in the reference set, losing all but four.[118] This accounted for 40% of the rejections of defense-proffered expertise in the reference set. The avalanche of polygraph cases seems, at least in part, to have resulted from hopes raised by *Daubert*'s rejection of the *Frye* test, coupled with the failure of criminal defense attorneys to understand a fundamental reality when it comes to polygraph evidence and other technological means of assessing witness veracity: judges will instinctively demand a level of reliability for such evidence that is much higher than with regard to any other expert evidence, *and it's a good thing too.*

The lie detector literature is vast, but surprisingly scant attention has been paid to the practical impact that the acceptance of any lie detector evidence would have. The furthest people usually go is to note that lie detector evidence would be prejudicial in the individual case if juries accepted it at face value when, in fact, it was subject to substantial error rates. But that is not the half of it. . . . [I]ts systemic impact is what makes lie detector evidence a potential nightmare. Acceptance of any lie detector evidence as admissible would change the entire litigation system in ways that would be drastic and unpredictable. Veracity is a relevant issue wherever there is to be live testimony, which is in virtually every litigated matter, civil and criminal. If polygraphs are good enough to be admissible, they would seem *a fortiori* good enough to be demanded of every witness as part of discovery. And if this is not the case, by what standards

118. *See* United States v. Cordoba, 104 F.3d 225, 228 (9th Cir. 1997) (holding that . . . *Daubert* "effectively overruled [the] per se rule . . . against admission of unstipulated polygraph evidence"); United States v. Posado, 57 F.3d 428, 434 (5th Cir. 1995) (rejecting a per se rule against the admissibility of polygraph evidence because polygraph testing had become "more standardized" and had been "subjected to extensive study"); United States v. Galbreth, 908 F.Supp. 877, 896 (D.N.M. 1995) (admitting polygraph evidence on the condition that the test is properly conducted "by a highly qualified, experienced, and skillful examiner"); United States v. Crumby, 895 F. Supp. 1354, 1365 (D. Ariz. 1995) (admitting polygraph evidence for the limited purpose of impeaching or corroborating the defendant's testimony). *Cordoba* and *Posado* involved the rejection of a per se rule of exclusion coupled with a remand for reconsideration of the admissibility of the polygraph with no guarantee of admission.

would we distinguish between those witnesses who are to be required to submit to this relevant and dependable process and those who are not? Or would there be a blanket rule that says these substantially accurate determiners of veracity could never be compelled? And, if so, could the refusal to submit to a polygraph voluntarily be commented upon to the jury? Remember, I am not speaking exclusively, or even largely, of criminal defendants now, but of every witness whatsoever who is to testify in any case. Could any rule limiting compellability of witness polygraphs withstand a due process challenge by criminal defendants who were being deprived of the opportunity to obtain such relevant and dependable evidence of the untruthfulness of the testimony against them, and therefore of their (claimed) innocence? A polygraph for every cop witness in every case? Would the government have to pay for defense polygraphs of witnesses, and if not, why not, if the stuff is good enough to be admissible? . . . Though it is now criminal defendants who proffer polygraphs most often (in the subset of cases where they pass one with the polygrapher of their choice), the large volume of litigation and the relatively small number of polygraphers would immediately give the government and well-heeled civil litigants the advantage were the results of the process generally admissible, most especially in regard to non-party witnesses. Most importantly, there is the question of whether any established reliability of the polygraph under test conditions is robust enough to withstand the expectancy pressures on polygraphers resulting from employment by litigants in an adversary system.

Polygraph evidence is probably already more dependable under ideal conditions than some evidence which is presently routinely admitted.[122] This, coupled with a reading of *Daubert* that was inconsistent with *any* per se rule of exclusion, was probably what was behind the few victories defendants achieved in regard to polygraph admission in the mid 1990s. This boomlet appears to have disappeared after the Supreme Court's decision in *United States v. Scheffer*, 523 U.S. 303 (1998) [page 825 below], that a per se exclusion of defense unstipulated polygraphs does not violate any Constitutional right, even though the case did not deal directly with FRE 702, and even though five justices had reservations about the wisdom of a per se rule of exclusion. However, I believe judges do properly intuit that declaring polygraphs sufficiently dependable for normal admissibility in any context is likely to lead to profound alterations in the entire litigation system, alterations which cannot be predicted and which may not be desirable once they are played out. . . . For these

122. The system's willingness to accept stipulated polygraphs is some evidence of this. While the admissibility of stipulated polygraphs may be dominantly a manifestation of a "trial-by-combat, fair fight" instinct rather than a "search for truth" principle, and, while one can argue that the conditions of a stipulated polygraph are more likely to approach the ideal conditions necessary for accuracy of the process than are unstipulated polygraphs, it is hard to imagine the system accepting the admissibility of stipulated astrology readings.

reasons, no technological means of assessing veracity is likely to become generally admissible unless it is so overwhelmingly dependable that failing to allow its entry into the courtroom would become a scandalous joke. . . .

United States v. Scheffer: *Case Note*

In the great majority of American jurisdictions, polygraph evidence remains inadmissible unless both parties stipulate to its admission. But what if a criminal defendant wishes to offer polygraph results that show his denials of guilt to be truthful? Could he claim under *Chambers v. Mississippi*, 410 U.S. 284 (1973) (page 718 above), and similar cases that either the Due Process Clauses of the Fifth and Fourteenth Amendments or the Compulsory Process Clause of the Sixth Amendment secure him the right to offer such evidence?

Under *Chambers* the defendant would have to show that the polygraph results were "critical to [his] defense" and supported by "persuasive assurances of trustworthiness." In a case in which the defendant had little evidence to offer beyond his own denials of guilt, a court might readily label the test results "critical." But the requirement of "trustworthiness" would seem to require an assessment of the reliability of polygraph examinations—and as you know, this matter is far from settled.

In *United States v. Scheffer*, 523 U.S. 303 (1998), the Supreme Court considered—and rejected—a claim that a criminal defendant (or, in this case, the accused in a court-martial proceeding) has a right under the Compulsory Process Clause to offer polygraph evidence. *Scheffer* turned on the absolute exclusion imposed by Military Rule of Evidence 707: "Notwithstanding any other provision of law, the results of a polygraph examination, the opinion of a polygraph examiner, or any reference to an offer to take, failure to take, or taking of a polygraph examination, shall not be admitted into evidence."

Eight Justices agreed that *Chambers* and later rulings under the Compulsory Process Clause do not guarantee a right to present such evidence. On this point, only Justice Stevens dissented. Writing for the rest of the Court, Justice Thomas noted that "the scientific community remains extremely polarized about the reliability of polygraph techniques." 523 U.S. at 309.

> [T]here is simply no way to know in a particular case whether a polygraph examiner's conclusion is accurate, because certain doubts and uncertainties plague even the best polygraph exams. Individual jurisdictions therefore may reasonably reach differing conclusions as to whether polygraph evidence should be admitted.

Id. at 312. Specifically rejecting the defendant's constitutional claims, Justice Thomas wrote that the military's exclusionary rule "is neither arbitrary nor disproportionate" under *Rock v. Arkansas*, 483 U.S. 44 (1987), and that "*Chambers* ... does not stand for the proposition that the accused is denied a fair opportunity to defend himself whenever a state or federal rule excludes favorable evidence." 523 U.S. at 309, 316.

In a portion of his opinion joined only by Chief Justice Rehnquist and Justices Scalia and Souter, Justice Thomas argued that polygraph evidence is alien to the principles of our adjudicatory system:

> It is equally clear that Rule 707 serves a second legitimate governmental interest: Preserving the jury's core function of making credibility determinations in criminal trials. A fundamental premise of our criminal trial system is that "the *jury* is the lie detector." ...
>
> By its very nature, polygraph evidence may diminish the jury's role in making credibility determinations.... Unlike other expert witnesses who testify about factual matters outside the jurors' knowledge, such as the analysis of fingerprints, ballistics, or DNA found at a crime scene, a polygraph expert can supply the jury only with another opinion, in addition to its own, about whether the witness was telling the truth. Jurisdictions, in promulgating rules of evidence, may legitimately be concerned about the risk that juries will give excessive weight to the opinions of a polygrapher, clothed as they are in scientific expertise and at times offering, as in respondent's case, a conclusion about the ultimate issue in the trial. Such jurisdictions may legitimately determine that the aura of infallibility attending polygraph evidence can lead jurors to abandon their duty to assess credibility and guilt.

Id. at 312–14.

In a concurring opinion joined by Justices O'Connor, Ginsburg, and Breyer, Justice Kennedy endorsed the Court's concerns about the reliability of polygraph tests, but made it clear that state and other federal jurisdictions should feel free not to follow the military's lead in banning polygraph evidence outright:

> [Given the] continuing, good-faith disagreement among experts and courts on the subject of polygraph reliability ... I agree the [military's] rule of exclusion is not so arbitrary or disproportionate that it is unconstitutional.
>
> I doubt, though, that the rule of *per se* exclusion is wise, and some later case might present a more compelling case for introduction of the testimony than this one does. Though the considerable discretion given to the trial court in admitting or excluding scientific evidence is not a constitutional mandate, *see Daubert v. Merrell Dow Pharmaceuticals, Inc.*, there is some tension between that rule and our holding today. And, as Justice Stevens points out, there is much

> inconsistency between the Government's extensive use of polygraphs to make vital security determinations and the argument it makes here, stressing the inaccuracy of these tests.

Id. at 318 (Kennedy, J., concurring in part and in the judgment).

In dissent, Justice Stevens endorsed the defendant's argument under the Compulsory Process Clause: "A rule that bars him 'from introducing expert opinion testimony to bolster his own credibility' unquestionably impairs any 'meaningful opportunity to present a complete defense'; indeed, it is sure to be outcome-determinative in many cases." 523 U.S. at 331 (Stevens, J., dissenting) (quoting *Crane v. Kentucky*, 476 U.S. 683, 690 (1986)). And Justice Stevens disputed the majority's conclusions about the relative unreliability of polygraph evidence:

> There are a host of studies that place the reliability of polygraph tests at 85% to 90%. While critics of the polygraph argue that accuracy is much lower, even the studies cited by the critics place polygraph accuracy at 70%. Moreover, to the extent that the polygraph errs, studies have repeatedly shown that the polygraph is more likely to find innocent people guilty than vice versa. Thus, exculpatory polygraphs—like the one in this case—are likely to be more reliable than inculpatory ones.

Id. at 333. In fact, Justice Stevens wrote, a good deal of the evidence routinely admitted in court is far less reliable than polygraph results:

> Expert testimony about a defendant's "future dangerousness" to determine his eligibility for the death penalty, even if wrong "most of the time," is routinely admitted. Studies indicate that handwriting analysis, and even fingerprint identifications, may be less trustworthy than polygraph evidence in certain cases. And, of course, even highly dubious eyewitness testimony is, and should be, admitted and tested in the crucible of cross-examination.

Id. at 334–35.

Justice Stevens also rejected Justice Thomas's contention that "the aura of infallibility attending polygraph evidence can lead jurors to abandon their duty to assess credibility and guilt." He noted that "research indicates that jurors do not 'blindly' accept polygraph evidence," *id.* at 337 n.26, and pointed for support to a 1980 behavioral study by Ann Cavoukian and Ronald J. Heslegrave. Cavoukian and Heslegrave presented 150 experimental jurors with a murder case in which the defendant claimed he falsely confessed to police. The defendant called two psychiatric witnesses who testified on the basis of several psychological tests that the defendant's deranged personality prompted the false confession. One-third of the jurors heard no other defense evidence concerning the confession. One-third of the jurors also learned that a polygraph examination showed the defendant had truthfully denied the killing. And one-third heard all this evidence plus a cautionary instruction from the judge advising them that polygraphs are about eighty percent accurate—a figure Cavoukian and Heslegrave thought reasonable in light of existing research. All 150 jurors were then asked whether they believed the defendant guilty or not guilty. *See* Ann Cavoukian & Ronald J. Heslegrave, *The Admissibility of Polygraph Evidence in Court*, 4 Law & HUM. BEHAV. 117, 119–22 (1980).

The authors found that the polygraph evidence significantly reduced the odds of a guilty verdict, but the judge's cautionary instruction shrank the influence of the polygraph evidence by half:

TABLE 1
DISTRIBUTION OF VERDICTS
(Percentages)

	Condition		
Verdict	*No Evidence of Polygraph*	*Polygraph*	*Polygraph and Judge's Caution*
Guilty	52%	28%	40%
Not guilty	48%	72%	60%

Id. at 123. "These results could be regarded as desirable," the authors concluded, "since they suggest that people had, in accordance with the judge's instruction, weighted the polygraph evidence with greater reservation. . . ." *Id.* at 124.

In a second, similar experiment, Cavoukian and Heslegrave asked the experimental jurors "how accurate they thought polygraphs were relative to other psychological tests used by psychologists and psychiatrists." On a nine-point scale, where 5 was labeled "about the same," the mean response was 4.98. The authors found it "interesting . . . that subjects did not think that polygraph tests were very accurate, despite the fact that three of the groups [in this experiment] were told the accuracy rate was about 80%." Supplying Justice Stevens with the support he needed, they concluded, "This suggests that polygraph tests are generally not blindly accepted or even carry a great deal of weight relative to other psychological tests, which are presently admissible in court." *Id.* at 129. So while the sort of evidence Scheffer hoped to present in his defense "may serve to raise a *reasonable* doubt," Cavoukian and Heslegrave determined that "such evidence would not . . . raise an *unreasonable* doubt." *Id.* at 131.

Justice Stevens's final argument operated independently of such empirical evidence about the polygraph's reliability or the jurors' malleability. Focusing on a point that drew no comment from the rest of the Court, he emphasized the defendant's interest in showing his consciousness of innocence. Here he quoted Judge Newman's opinion for the Second Circuit in *United States v. Biaggi*, 909 F.2d 662 (2d Cir. 1990) (excerpted above at page 138): "[E]vidence of [the defendant's] innocent state of mind is 'critical to a fair adjudication of criminal charges.'" 523 U.S. at 331–32 & n.19 (quoting *Biaggi*, 909 F.2d at 691–92). Although Justice Stevens did not say so, when a defendant offers evidence that he consented to a polygraph examination to show his consciousness of innocence, the reliability of the examination becomes a far less pressing issue. What matters is only that the defendant *thought* at the time he consented to the test that it would detect any deception on his part and that, if the test showed deception, the authorities would learn of it.

Henry T. Greely & Judy Illes

Neuroscience–Based Lie Detection: The Urgent Need for Regulation

33 AM. J.L. & MED. 377 (2007)

* * *

In the early 1970s, improved detection of weak magnetic fields produced by ion currents within the body enabled the recording of brain signals in the form of extracranial electromagnetic activity for the first time. . . .

In the early 1990s, academic medicine witnessed the discovery of a much more powerful technique for measuring brain activity using magnetic resonance imaging (MRI) principles. Using functional MRI (fMRI), researchers can assess brain function in a rapid, non-invasive manner with a high degree of both spatial and temporal accuracy. . . .

III. LIE DETECTION AND fMRI

* * *

A. Non-fMRI Lie Detection

. . . Polygraphy is the best-established method of lie detection, but other methods exist or are under development. . . . This article focuses on fMRI because it is the most explored and, apparently, the most advanced, but . . . other methods will be briefly described.

a. Electroencephalography

... EEGs measure electric currents generated by the brain. One particular kind of EEG measurement claimed to be useful in detecting lies is the "P300"—a wave of electrical signal, measured at the scalp, that occurs approximately 300 milliseconds after a subject receives a stimulus. The analysis of the timing and shape of this waveform has some meaning, but ... [less than] the hype given it by its leading proponent, Lawrence Farwell.

Farwell ... [has] argued that human P300 waves can be used as a "guilty knowledge" test, to determine whether, for example, a suspect has ever seen the site of a crime.... [His] company's website claims that in more than 175 tests, the method has produced inconclusive results six times and has been accurate every other time. Farwell's work, however, has not been substantially vetted in the peer-reviewed literature. Apparently, the only article he has published on his technology in a peer-reviewed journal is a 2001 on-line article in the *Journal of Forensic Science* where he and a co-author reported on a successful trial of his method with six subjects. He has not revealed any further evidence to support his claims of high accuracy....

c. Facial Micro-expressions

Berkeley psychologist Paul Ekman ... claims that careful analysis of fleeting "micro-expressions" on subjects' faces can detect lying with substantial accuracy. *See* Paul Ekman & Maureen O'Sullivan, *From Flawed Self-Assessment to Blatant Whoppers: The Utility of Voluntary and Involuntary Behavior in Detecting Deception,* 24 BEHAV. SCI. & L. 673, 684 (2006).

Ekman has done substantial research on using facial micro-expressions to detect lying, but he has not published much of the research in peer-reviewed literature; he has said that this is because of his concern about the information falling into the wrong hands. As a result, Ekman's methods and results have not been subject to much public analysis, making their value hard to assess. If effective, they would have the advantage of not requiring any obvious intervention with the subject—subjects would not have to have various sensors attached to them, as with polygraphs [or] EEGs, ... or be inserted into a machine, as with fMRI. This technique could quite plausibly be used surreptitiously, through undetected videotaping of the subject's face during questioning....

B. fMRI–Based Lie Detection—The Businesses

The most interesting of these new lie detection technologies is fMRI.... [I]t has been the subject of significant peer-reviewed literature from several laboratories, and ... is already commercially available to the general public from one firm, with another company poised to enter the market.

No Lie MRI apparently started offering its fMRI-based lie detection services in August 2006. This start-up firm has licensed its technology from the University of Pennsylvania, based on a patent application filed by the University based on work by Professor Daniel Langleben. . . . [I]t claims a "current accuracy" of 93%, with an expected *99%* accuracy "when development of the product is complete." . . . [The company's website] states that the firm "is presently working to have its testing allowed as evidence in U.S. and state courts."

It is hard to know what to make of No Lie MRI. The firm has received a great deal of publicity, but there is little evidence that its services are actually being used. . . .

A second firm has also announced that it will offer fMRI-based lie detection services. CEPHOS Corporation . . . uses technology developed by Dr. Frank A. (Andy) Kozel. . . . Steven Laken, the founder and chief executive officer of the firm, is a scientist with a Ph.D. in molecular and cellular biology from Johns Hopkins University. CEPHOS claims greater than 90% accuracy for its technology. . . . [The firm] says, "CEPHOS continues to test and validate the technology with the goal of achieving 95% accuracy. Based on valid clinical results in 2006, the company intends to offer this service in the first half of [2007]." . . .

In addition to these two companies, other firms are exploring fMRI-based lie detection with less visibility. A search through publicly accessible databases of Department of Defense websites for small business funding reveals research and development projects with the same technology and . . . security-related market. . . .

C. fMRI–Based Lie Detection—The Research

Through early February 2007, twelve peer-reviewed scientific articles have been published that describe experiments with fMRI-based lie detection. Three have come from the laboratory of Daniel Langleben of the University of Pennsylvania, whose technology has been licensed to No Lie MRI. Another three have been published by Andy Kozel, formerly at the Medical University of South Carolina and now at the University of Texas Southwestern Medical Center, whose technology is being developed by CEPHOS Corporation. The remaining six have come from laboratories all around the world. Of the twelve papers, only three (two by Langleben and one by Kozel) attempt to assess differences in truthful and deceptive responses within an individual; all the others look only at averaged group data. We will focus on the Langleben and Kozel reports, as those are the basis for the methods being used by the two known commercial firms. . . .

. . . We find very little in the peer-reviewed literature that even suggests that fMRI-based lie detection might be useful in real-world situations and absolutely nothing that proves that it is.

1. Studies by Langleben and Colleagues

Langleben's first paper on fMRI-based lie detection appeared in early 2002 in *NeuroImage. See* Daniel D. Langleben et al., *Brain Activity During Simulated Deception: An Event–Related Functional Magnetic Resonance Study,* 15 NEUROIMAGE 727 (2002). This article reported a study of eighteen subjects, all recruited from the University of Pennsylvania "community." The experiment used three playing cards as targets: the two of hearts, the five of clubs, and the ten of spades. Ten other cards were included in the experiments but were not targets. While in the scanner, the subjects were shown the pictures of cards, one at a time, through a mirrored reflection of a screen at their feet. The three target cards were displayed a total of sixteen times each; the ten non-target cards were each displayed twice. The cards were presented for three seconds each with twelve seconds between cards, so the total time of the trial was twenty-two minutes. At the top of the image for all the cards except the ten of spades was the question "Do you have this card?" Above the ten of spades was the question "Is this a Ten of Spades?"

Before the scanning started, each subject was asked to choose one of three sealed envelopes. Each envelope contained a five of clubs and a twenty-dollar bill. Subjects were told to lie about having the card they found in the envelope, but were told that they could keep the money *unless* they lied about any other card they saw. Thus, they were to report accurately that they did not have any of the cards other than the five of clubs, to answer falsely that they did not have the five of clubs, and to say honestly that the ten of spades was, in fact, a ten of spades. The goal was to look for differences in brain activation patterns between when the subjects honestly said they did not have the two of diamonds, and when they dishonestly said they did not have the five of clubs. . . .

When the researchers averaged the results of all eighteen subjects, they found two [brain] regions with statistically significant increases in activation when the subjects were lying about the five of clubs. No areas showed greater activation when telling the truth about the two of diamonds. . . .

Langleben reported on another experiment in a paper published in *Human Brain Mapping* in 2005. *See* Daniel D. Langleben et al., *Telling Truth from Lie in Individual Subjects with Fast Event–Related fMRI,* 26 HUM. BRAIN MAPPING 262, 262 (2005). . . . This study was done with twenty-six right-handed male undergraduates. . . . The experiment also presented the subjects with pictures of playing cards while being scanned with a promised twenty-dollar reward for "success." . . .

. . . The researchers . . . looked at individual results, using a logistic regression model. They used regions of interest identified in the group study to create a model that . . . was 78% accurate . . . at being able to tell, for an individual subject, when he was lying and when he was telling the truth. . . .

In 2005, *NeuroImage* published another lie detection paper from the Langleben lab.... *See* C. Davatzikos et al., *Classifying Spatial Patterns of Brain Activity with Machine Learning Methods: Application to Lie Detection,* 28 NEUROIMAGE 663 (2005). The paper uses the same brain scan results from ... the second Langleben article discussed above, but it uses a different method of data analysis.... Using this statistical method, [the researchers] report being able to distinguish when the individual subjects were lying or telling the truth just under 90% of the time....

In summary, Langleben's peer-reviewed publications report on two experiments, both of which involve lying about a playing card. The experiments involved exactly forty-four subjects, the majority of them male undergraduates....

2. Studies by Kozel and Colleagues

Kozel also has three peer-reviewed publications ... [on fMRI-based lie detection. The most recent] was published in *Biological Psychiatry* in 2005. *See* F. Andrew Kozel et al., *Detecting Deception Using Functional Magnetic Imaging,* 58 BIOLOGICAL PSYCHIATRY 605 (2005).... [T]he researchers recruited thirty healthy unmedicated adults from the local university community, between the ages of eighteen to fifty, to be part of the "model building group." ... The subjects were taken to a room and told to "steal" either a ring or a watch from a drawer. When scanned, they were asked whether they had taken the ring or had taken the watch, along with two control questions. Each of the four questions was asked twenty times. The subjects were instructed to deny taking either object. They were told they would receive an extra fifty dollars if their lie was not detected.

The experimenters first tested thirty subjects whose results were used to build a model that would distinguish, for those individuals, who was lying and who was telling the truth. They then tested thirty-one different subjects, with the same test, and applied the initial model. The subjects were more diverse than in many of the previous experiments. Only about 20% of them were students and a substantial number (six in the model building group and twelve in the testing group) were African–American. On average, they had completed over sixteen years of education and all of them had at least completed high school.

Group analysis in the model-building group showed significant increased activation when lying in seven clusters of brain regions.... When the researchers looked at activation in ... three [of those] clusters combined, they were able to determine accurately which object twenty-eight of the thirty subjects in the model-building group had taken. When they applied the same model to the thirty-one subjects in the model-testing group, they were able to detect lying just over 90% of the time....

D. fMRI–Based Lie Detection—Evaluating the Research

These . . . peer-reviewed articles establish fMRI-based lie detection as a promising technology. They do not prove that it is currently effective as a lie detector in the real world, at *any* accuracy level, let alone the 80 to 90% levels being claimed. . . .

. . . [One] problem is the lack of replication of the results by any other laboratories. . . . [E]ach laboratory tried its own experiments and used its own analytical methods. . . . A good rule . . . is to never believe a result until at least one investigator from outside the original group confirms it. Lie detection through fMRI does not pass this test.

[Another] concern is the number and diversity of subjects. The experiments used healthy young adults, almost all right-handed, with little gender or ethnic diversity. No one tested children, the middle-aged or elderly, those with physical or mental illnesses, or those taking drugs, either as medication or illicitly.

[Third], . . . the relevant experiments report finding activation of various regions of the brain . . . without strong consistency among the experiments, except when brain regions are very broadly defined. . . . This diversity casts some doubt on the accuracy of any particular method of lie detection.

A [fourth] problem, and perhaps the greatest, is the artificiality of the deceptive tasks. Most of the experiments involved subjects lying about something unimportant—what card they held or whether they could remember a three-digit number. Only the Kozel paper, involving an instructed "theft" of a ring or a watch from a room, and [one other study by a different researcher involving a] gun firing, seemed close to more typical real-world lie detection situations. Of course, in those cases, as in every other experiment, the subject telling a "lie" was following an instruction to tell a lie (and, in the Kozel experiment, the subjects "stealing" the objects were following instructions to "steal" them, knowing it was part of an experiment and not a real theft). Sometimes the subjects were told which lie to tell, other times they got to choose which of two conditions to lie about, but always they were acting not just with permission to lie, but under a *command* to do so. It is not clear how this difference from the more usual lie detection settings would affect the results. Although the researchers often told the subjects, falsely, to believe that their success in lying would earn them more money (in fact, researchers with that design paid all the subjects the "extra" money), it is also not clear that this apparent monetary incentive would affect the subjects the same way as the more common—and more powerful—incentives for lying, such as avoiding arrest.

The context points to a deeper problem with the artificiality of the situation—the researchers assume that whatever kind of "lie" they are having the subjects tell is relevant to the kinds of lies people tell in real life. But those lies vary tremendously. Are lies about participation in a crime the same as lies about the quality of a meal or the existence of a "prior engagement"? Do lies about sex activate the same regions of the brain as lies about money, lies to avoid embarrassment, or lies about the five of clubs? Do lies of omission look the same under fMRI as lies of commission? We do not know the answers to these, or many other questions—and neither do the researchers who published these papers. This is not a criticism of the researchers, as scientists have to start somewhere and a well-defined situation is essential for analysis. It is likely to be difficult, and perhaps even impossible, to create good tests of real-world lies. This is a criticism of any attempt to apply this research to the real world without a great deal more work.

All of the concerns discussed so far are reasons to doubt that these experiments did, in fact, prove that one can detect real world lies through fMRI. The last concern is slightly different. Even if the studies had proven that proposition, they did not begin to prove that the method could actually be effective because they did not exclude the very real possibilities that subjects could use countermeasures against fMRI-based lie detection.

The use of countermeasures to polygraphy has been discussed substantially in the past and has even been the subject of some limited research. The National Academy panel on the polygraph spent ten pages on countermeasures. The panel concluded:

> If these measures are effective, they could seriously undermine any value of polygraph security screening. Basic physiological theory suggests that training methods might allow individuals to succeed in employing effective countermeasures. Moreover, the empirical research literature suggests that polygraph test results can be affected by the use of countermeasures.

COMM. TO REVIEW THE SCIENTIFIC EVIDENCE ON THE POLYGRAPH, THE POLYGRAPH AND LIE DETECTION 151 (2003).

Countermeasures to fMRI-based lie detection could use a wide range of methods. . . . [Muscle movements] will introduce new areas of brain activation, muddying the underlying picture. Even less visibly, simply thinking about other things during a task may activate other brain regions in ways that interfere with the lie-detection paradigm.

If, as some think, lying is detectable because it is harder than telling the truth and thus requires the activation of more or different areas of the brain, a subject could try doing mental arithmetic or memory tests while giving true answers, thus, perhaps, making true answers harder to distinguish from false ones. Similarly, a well-memorized lie may not activate those additional regions and may look like a truth. . . .

. . . [I]f the countermeasures are easy enough, "training" may be as simple as a quick search of the Internet. A quick Google search of "polygraph countermeasures" already turns up many sites offering information on beating the polygraph, some free and some for payment, including one former polygrapher who charges $59.95 (plus shipping) for his manual plus DVD. If fMRI-based lie detection becomes common, efforts to beat fMRI-based lie detection will, no doubt, also become common....

IV. Regulation of fMRI–Based Lie Detection

* * *

A. Existing Regulation of Lie Detection

* * *

2. Judicial Admissibility

... As a general matter, no American judicial system routinely allows polygraph evidence to be introduced except New Mexico's. The New Mexico Supreme Court has adopted a rule of evidence generally allowing polygraph evidence under some conditions.[159] ...

... Interestingly, in spite of the almost universal conclusion that polygraph evidence does not meet the standards for admissibility of scientific evidence, it can still be admitted in many jurisdictions under several circumstances. First, many jurisdictions allow evidence of the results of a polygraph examination to be admitted if all the parties agree to its admission. Second, in some jurisdictions the results of a polygraph test can be used to corroborate or to impeach a witness's claims on the stand that are consistent or inconsistent with the polygraph test results. Third, at least one federal appellate court has held that a defendant has a constitutional right to have polygraph evidence admitted in the penalty phase of a death penalty case. *See Rupe v. Wood*, 93 F.3d 1434 (9th Cir. 1996). Finally, several federal courts have opened the door to the possible broader admissibility of polygraph evidence as a consequence of *Daubert*, finding that *Daubert* makes untenable any previous *per se* exclusions of polygraph evidence.[176]....

[Today, companies] are marketing the age-old dream of lie detection coupled with the high-tech mystique (and beautiful color graphics) of brain scanning. The combination may prove irresistible to many, but with so little evidence that the method is accurate, the result may be ... [that]

159. *See* N.M. R. Evid. 11–707(c) (allowing the opinion of the polygraph examiner to be admitted into evidence at the discretion of the trial judge). *See* Lee v. Martinez, 136 N.M. 166 (2004) (discussing when to allow polygraph evidence in court).

176. United States v. Cordoba, 104 F.3d 225 (9th Cir. 1997); United States v. Posado, 57 F.3d 428 (5th Cir. 1995). But see United States v. Prince–Oyibo, 320 F.3d 494 (4th Cir. 2003) (maintaining the Fourth Circuit's per se rule against the admissibility of polygraph evidence in spite of *Daubert*).

people may be treated unfairly based on negative tests; dishonest people may go free. . . .

UNITED STATES V. SEMRAU

693 F.3d 510 (6th Cir. 2012).

■ JANE B. STRANCH, Circuit Judge. Dr. Lorne Semrau appeals his conviction of three counts of healthcare fraud in violation of 18 U.S.C. § 1347. Among other issues, Dr. Semrau argues—on a matter of first impression in any jurisdiction—that results from a functional magnetic resonance imaging ("fMRI") lie detection test should have been admitted to prove the veracity of his denials of wrongdoing. . . .

I. BACKGROUND

Dr. Semrau, who holds a Ph.D. in clinical psychology, was president, owner, and CEO of two companies that provided follow-up psychiatric care to nursing home patients in Tennessee and Mississippi. These companies, Superior Life Care Services, Inc. and Foundation Life Care Services, LLC, offered services through contracting psychiatrists who submitted records describing their work to the companies. At Dr. Semrau's direction, Superior and Foundation billed these services to Medicare and/or Medicaid through private health insurance carriers CIGNA in Tennessee and CAHABA in Mississippi.

In order to facilitate processing of the millions of healthcare claims submitted each year, rendered services are categorized into various five-digit Current Procedural Terminology ("CPT") codes. . . . The Centers for Medicare and Medicaid Services ("CMS") . . . set[s] reimbursement levels for each code. . . . The fee schedules are submitted by CMS to carriers so that they may reimburse providers the appropriate amount depending on which CPT code is submitted. . . .

Submission of Medicare claims through a carrier requires providers to submit a [form] that includes . . . a notice stating: "Anyone who misrepresents or falsifies essential information to receive payment from federal funds requested by this form may upon conviction be subject to fine and imprisonment under applicable federal laws." . . .

In late 2002, CIGNA began an audit of Superior's billing practices in Tennessee and concluded that Superior had been billing at a higher rate than could be justified by the services actually performed, a practice known as "upcoding." In a letter to Superior dated January 23, 2003, CIGNA detailed its conclusion that Superior had overbilled fourteen of the eighteen claims reviewed at 90862 when it should have instead billed at 99311, which had a lower reimbursement amount. Code 90862 is for "psychiatric" treatments whereas 99311 is for "evaluation and management" services and generally describes a "basic follow-up nursing home visit" for a stable patient lasting about fifteen minutes. . . .

In January 2003, Superior began billing a new, higher code in Tennessee: 99312. . . . On July 1, 2003, Medicare reduced its Mississippi payment for code 90862 from $37 per claim to $23 per claim. Twenty days later, Superior began billing the higher code 99312 for the first time for its Mississippi claims. Because 99312 paid $45 per claim in Mississippi, Superior's change to this code resulted in an increased payment of $8 per claim from the previous 90862 rate instead of a reduced [payment] of $14 per claim at the new 90862 rate, for a net gain of $22 per claim. . . . On August 8, 2003, Dr. Semrau instructed his billing staff to bill all services indicated as 90862s as 99312s. . . .

For the next year and a half, nearly every service indicated as 90862 on the log sheets completed by the physician performing the service was billed at the higher 99312 rate in both Tennessee and Mississippi. . . . This practice continued until four days after a grand jury subpoena was served on Dr. Semrau and his companies on December 17, 2004, after which time code 90862 was billed when indicated on the log sheets.

[Dr. Semrau was charged] with sixty counts of healthcare fraud . . ., twelve counts of money laundering . . ., and one count of criminal forfeiture. . . . [In his defense he claimed that] . . . any improper billing was unintentional and despite his good faith attempts to be compliant because of the complicated and confusing nature of the codes. . . . He testified that he relied on advice from CIGNA's toll-free provider support phone line, which confirmed that his billing decisions were legitimate. To corroborate this claim, he unsuccessfully attempted to introduce . . . results of a fMRI lie detector test that found he was generally truthful when, during the test, he said his billing decisions were made in good faith and without an intent to defraud.

After a twelve-day jury trial, Dr. Semrau was convicted of three counts of healthcare fraud. . . . He was sentenced to concurrent eighteen-month terms of imprisonment and . . . ordered to pay $245,435 in restitution. Dr. Semrau timely appealed his conviction. . . .

II. DISCUSSION

A. Admissibility of fMRI Tests

Dr. Semrau argues that the district court erred in excluding opinion testimony from Dr. Steven Laken, who would have testified that fMRI testing indicated that Dr. Semrau was generally truthful when he said he attempted to follow proper billing practices in good faith. The admissibility of fMRI lie detection testing in a criminal case is an issue of first impression for any jurisdiction in the country, state and federal.[1] . . .

1. A New York state court considered the admissibility of fMRI lie detection technology in a civil case. *Wilson v. Corestaff Servs. L.P.*, 900 N.Y.S.2d 639 (Sup. Ct. 2010).

1. *Background*

a. fMRI *Science*

Dr. Steven J. Laken, Ph.D., is the President and CEO of Cephos Corporation, a company he founded in Tyngsboro, Massachusetts, in 2004. Cephos markets itself as a company that provides ... lie detection/truth verification using fMRI.... Cephos holds a patent on a version of an fMRI-based lie detection method, which identifies Dr. Laken as its inventor.

At the heart of Dr. Laken's lie detection method is fMRI imaging. An fMRI enables researchers to assess brain function "in a rapid, non-invasive manner with a high degree of both spatial and temporal accuracy." Henry T. Greely & July Illes, *Neuroscience–Based Lie Detection: The Urgent Need for Regulation*, 33 AM. J.L. & MED. 377, 379 (2007). When undergoing an fMRI scan, a subject lies down on a bed that slides into the center of a donut-shaped magnet core. *See* Teneille Brown & Emily Murphy, *Through a Scanner Darkly: Functional Neuroimaging as Evidence of a Criminal Defendant's Past Mental States*, 62 STAN. L. REV. 1119, 1139 (2010). As the subject remains still, he or she is asked to perform a task while magnetic coils in the scanner receive electric current and the device gathers information about the subject's Blood Oxygen Level Dependent ("BOLD") response. By comparing the subject's BOLD response signals with the control state, small changes in signal intensity are detectable and can provide information about brain activity.

Dr. Laken began working closely with a small group of researchers in this field in or around 2003 and conducted a series of laboratory studies to determine whether fMRI could be used to detect deception. Generally, these studies involved a test subject performing a task, such as "stealing" a ring or watch, and then scanning the subject while he or she answered questions about the task. The subjects were usually offered a modest monetary incentive if their lie was not detected. Dr. Laken agreed during cross-examination that he had only conducted studies on such "mock scenarios" and was not aware of any research in a "real-life setting" in which people are accused of "real crimes." He also testified that his studies examined only subjects between the ages of eighteen and fifty, although "we don't see any decreasing or increasing or any changes across accuracy rates in those individuals." Dr. Semrau was sixty-three years old at the time he underwent testing.

Based on these studies, as well as studies conducted by other researchers, Dr. Laken and his colleagues determined the regions of the brain most consistently activated by deception and claimed in several peer-reviewed articles that by analyzing a subject's brain activity, they were able to identify deception with a high level of accuracy. During direct examination at the *Daubert* hearing, Dr. Laken reported these studies found accuracy rates between eighty-six percent and ninety-seven percent. During cross-examination, however, Dr. Laken conceded that his 2009 "Mock Sabotage Crime" study produced an "unexpected" accuracy decrease to a rate of seventy-one percent. *See* F. Andrew Kozel et al., *Functional MRI Detection of Deception After Committing a Mock Sabotage Crime*, 54 J. FORENSIC SCI. 220, 228 (2009).

Dr. Laken testified that fMRI lie detection has "a huge false positive problem" in which people who are telling the truth are deemed to be lying around sixty to seventy percent of the time. One 2009 study was able to identify a "truth teller as a truth teller" just six percent of the time, meaning that about "nineteen out of twenty people that were telling the truth we would call liars." Another study expressed concern that "accuracy rates drop by almost twenty-five percentage points when a person starts becoming fatigued." Dr. Laken also explained that a person can become sufficiently fatigued during testing such that results are impacted after about two "scans" because "[t]heir brain starts kind of going to sleep." Similarly, inadequate sleep the night before a test could cause such fatigue.

b. *Testing Conducted on Dr. Semrau*

In late 2009, Dr. Semrau's attorney, J. Houston Gordon, contacted Dr. Laken to inquire about having an fMRI-based lie detection test conducted on Dr. Semrau in hopes of bolstering the defenses that Dr. Semrau lacked intent to defraud and undertook actions to ensure proper billing compliance. Dr. Laken agreed to test Dr. Semrau and testify about his results at no cost. Dr. Laken decided to conduct two separate fMRI scans on Dr. Semrau, one involving questions regarding the healthcare fraud charges discussed above and the other involving questions regarding charges that he improperly billed for Abnormal Involuntary Movement Scale ("AIMS") tests.

Prior to the scheduled test date, Dr. Laken developed a set of twenty neutral questions and twenty control questions that would be asked during the scanning. The neutral questions—such as "Is today Tuesday?"—provided Dr. Laken with the "baseline" for the results to improve accuracy. The control questions—such as "Have you ever used illegal drugs?" and "Have you ever lied to a court?"—are included "just to fill up empty space" and do not directly contribute to the final analysis. Attorney Gordon and Dr. Laken co-developed Specific Incident Questions ("SIQs") directly relating to the upcoding and AIMS charges. The SIQs for the first scan included questions such as "Did you ever receive varying instructions or guidance regarding which codes to bill, including being told that 99312 would be the appropriate code to use instead of 90862?" and "Did you bill CPT Code 99312 to cheat or defraud Medicare?" The SIQs for the second scan included questions such as "Did you know that AIMS tests performed by psychiatrists [were] not a necessary service that could be separately billed?" The prosecution was not notified that Dr. Semrau was going to take the deception test and thus lacked an opportunity to submit its own questions to Dr. Laken for use during the test or to observe the testing procedures.

Dr. Semrau traveled to Massachusetts to undergo the fMRI tests with Dr. Laken on December 30, 2009. After they met at the scanner at 6:00 a.m. that morning, Dr. Laken explained the fMRI testing procedure to Dr. Semrau, had him review the questions,[7] and conducted several preliminary tests to ensure he was a suitable test candidate. In each fMRI scan, Dr. Semrau was visually instructed to "Lie" or to tell the "Truth" in response to each SIQ. He was told to respond truthfully to the neutral and control questions. Dr. Semrau practiced answering the questions on a computer prior to the scans. Dr. Laken observed Dr. Semrau practice until Dr. Laken believed that Dr. Semrau showed sufficient compliance with the instructions, responded to questions appropriately, and understood what he was to do in the scanner.

Once this preparation was completed, Dr. Semrau was placed in the scanner and a display was positioned over his head that flashed the questions. The order of the questions was made random and each response was recorded. Each scan took around sixteen minutes. During a brief break between scans, Dr. Semrau expressed some fatigue but did not request a longer break. After the second scan, however, Dr. Semrau complained about becoming "very fatigued" and having problems reading all the questions.

On January 4, 2010, Dr. Laken analyzed the scans using his fMRI testing protocol and found that Dr. Semrau answered an appropriate number of questions, responded correctly, and had no excess movement. From the first scan, which included SIQs relating to upcoding, the results showed that Dr. Semrau was "not deceptive." However, from the second scan, which included SIQs relating to AIMS tests, the results showed that Dr. Semrau was "being deceptive." Dr. Laken's report noted, however, that "testing indicates that a positive test result in a person reporting to tell the truth is only accurate 6 percent of the time and may be affected by fatigue."[8] Based on his findings for the second test, Dr. Laken suggested that Dr. Semrau be administered another fMRI test on the AIMS tests topic, but with shorter questions and conducted later in the

7. Dr. Laken explained that telling subjects the questions before the test is important for two reasons. First, it allows the subject to determine if a question might lead to a misleading response in the brain by reminding the subject of a similar, but unrelated, thought or occurrence. Second, it reduces the "surprise factor" because the brain responds differently to new things.

8. Dr. Laken acknowledged on cross-examination that the fatigue Dr. Semrau expressed after the first scan could mean that test was also inaccurate.

day to reduce the effects of fatigue. Dr. Laken developed the revised set of SIQs for the third scan.

The third scan was conducted on January 12, 2010, at around 7:00 p.m. According to Dr. Laken, Dr. Semrau tolerated it well and did not express any fatigue. Dr. Laken reviewed this data on January 18, 2010, and concluded that Dr. Semrau's brain activity showed he was "not deceptive" in his answers. He further testified that, based on his prior studies, the third test was "more valid" because Dr. Semrau "didn't have fatigue" and the data produced "has a very high probability of being correct." In fact, Dr. Laken's report stated that "a finding such as this is 100% accurate in determining truthfulness from a truthful person."

During cross-examination at the *Daubert* hearing, Dr. Laken agreed that the test results do not indicate whether Dr. Semrau responded truthfully as to any specific question but rather show only whether he was generally truthful as to all of his answers collectively. Accordingly, Dr. Laken conceded that it is "certainly possible" that Dr. Semrau was lying on some of the particularly significant questions. Dr. Laken was unable to state the percentage of questions on which Dr. Semrau could have lied while still producing the same result. He also acknowledged that the scan results only show whether someone believes what he is saying at the time of the test rather than what his mental state was at the time of the events discussed, and that there is no research on the effect of a "long-term lie." . . .

3. *Admissibility Under Rule 702*

a. *Applicable Law*

. . . Shortly after *Daubert* was decided, the Sixth Circuit applied that new test in *United States v. Bonds*, 12 F.3d 540 (6th Cir. 1993), and held that DNA test results, a new type of forensic evidence, could be admitted in court. *Id.* at 565–67. In advocating for the admissibility of fMRI lie detection results, Dr. Semrau relies heavily upon some of the broader language in *Bonds* and its willingness to consider cutting-edge scientific evidence. *See id.* at 561 ("[N]either newness nor lack of absolute certainty in a test suffices to render it inadmissible in court. Every useful new development must have its first day in court."

b. *Analysis*

The magistrate judge's R & R [Report and Recommendation], which was adopted by the district court, weighed several factors in Dr. Semrau's favor: "[T]he underlying theories behind fMRI-based lie detection are capable of being tested, and at least in the laboratory setting, have been subjected to some level of testing. It also appears that the theories have been subjected to some peer review and publication." The Government does not appear to challenge these findings, although it does point out that the bulk of the research supporting fMRI research has come from Dr. Laken himself.

The magistrate judge determined that Dr. Semrau could not satisfy the rate of error and controlling standards factor: "While it is unclear from the testimony what the error rates are or how valid they may be in the laboratory setting, there are no known error rates for fMRI-based lie detection outside the laboratory setting, i.e., in the 'real-world' or 'real-life' setting." . . . Dr. Peter Imrey, a statistician, testified: "There are no quantifiable error rates that are usable in this context. The error rates [Dr. Laken] proposed are based on almost no data, and under circumstances [that] do not apply to the real world [or] to the examinations of Dr. Semrau." Dr. Imrey also stated that the false positive accuracy data reported by Dr. Laken does not "justify the claim that somebody giving a positive test result . . . [h]as a six percent chance of being a true liar. That simply is mathematically, statistically and scientifically incorrect."

Based on Dr. Imrey's testimony, there was a reasonable and objective basis for the magistrate judge to reject Dr. Laken's stated error rates. Moreover, the magistrate judge qualified his conclusion by specifying such rates are unknown specifically for fMRI-based lie detection in the "real world" as opposed to the "laboratory." Thus, Dr. Semrau's argument on this point is merged with his second argument, that the magistrate judge erroneously "created" a distinction between "laboratory" and "real world" testing.

A review of the record demonstrates the laboratory/real world distinction was not "created" by the magistrate judge. As Magistrate Judge Pham recognized, federal courts have long appreciated that certain kinds of analyses may have different rates of error depending on the setting because of the difficulties of simulating realistic conditions. More importantly, studies by Dr. Laken and other fMRI researchers have recognized this distinction and expressed caution about it. For example, the "Mock Sabotage Crime" article stated:

> This study has several factors that must be considered for adequate interpretation of the results. Although this study attempted to approximate a scenario that was closer to a real-world situation than prior fMRI detection studies, it still did not equal the level of jeopardy that exists in real-world testing. The reality of a research setting involves balancing ethical concerns, the need to know accurately the participant's truth and deception, and producing realistic scenarios that have adequate jeopardy. . . . Future studies will need to be performed involving these populations.

Kozel et al., Mock Sabotage Crime, supra, at 228. Other articles have similarly highlighted the difference between laboratory and real world testing while stressing the need for more testing.

More significantly, there are concerns with not only whether fMRI lie detection of "real lies" *has* been tested but whether it *can* be tested. *See Daubert v. Merrell Dow Pharmaceuticals, Inc.*, 509 U.S. 579, 593 (1993) (page 794 above). Dr. Laken testified that "the issue that one faces with lie detection, is what is the real world baseline truth[?]" In this case, for example, only Dr. Semrau knows whether he was lying when he denied intentional wrongdoing, so there is no way to assess with complete certainty the accuracy of the two results finding he was "not deceptive" (not to mention the one finding that he *was* deceptive). The same is presumably true for many other "real world" scenarios in which a person may be trying to conceal something which is not already known or easily verifiable.

Due to the recognized lack of real world testing, this same laboratory/real world distinction applies to the other facet of the third factor, the existence and maintenance of standards, as well as the fourth factor, general acceptance. There was simply no formal research presented at the *Daubert* hearing demonstrating how the brain might respond to fMRI lie detection testing examining potential deception about real world, long-term conduct occurring several years before testing in which the subject faces extremely dire consequences (such as a prison sentence) if his answers are not believed. *See* FED. R. EVID. 702(c) (requiring expert testimony to be the "product of reliable principles and methods").

There were also aspects of Dr. Semrau's particular tests that differed from those employed in the studies discussed at the hearing. Most obviously, at sixty-three years of age, he was significantly older than the eighteen- to fifty-year-old subjects who participated in the studies.[10] Also problematic was Dr. Semrau's participation in a third study after the first two yielded different results, a tactic that does not appear to have been followed in any of the studies performed or cited by Dr. Laken. As the magistrate judge observed, Dr. Laken's "decision to conduct a third test begs the question whether a fourth scan would have revealed Dr. Semrau to be deceptive again." The decision to conduct an fMRI "best-two-out-of-three re-test" as to the AIMS charges suggests testing on Dr. Semrau was itself part of Dr. Laken's research to refine and better understand how the brain can reveal deception and truthfulness. Particularly troubling was Dr. Laken's explanation of why the initial "deceptive" result was untrustworthy—"the chances of calling a truth teller a truth teller was only roughly six percent"—because this "huge false positive problem" could potentially justify continual re-testing on anyone until a "not deceptive"

10. Dr. Laken testified that he "made the assumption that there wasn't going to be an age effect on the scans ... because we didn't see any age effect" in the research. However, he also stated that the application of fMRI technology to a sixty-three-year-old is "unknown." *See also Kozel et al., Mock Sabotage Crime, supra*, at 228 ("[W]hether fMRI deception testing would work is unknown for participants who are ... outside the 18–50 year age range. Future studies will need to be performed involving these populations.").

result is obtained. *See* FED. R. EVID. 702(d) (requiring expert testimony to have "reliably applied the principles and methods to the facts of the case").

Although Dr. Laken offered various plausible-sounding explanations and theories for why these distinctions from his prior studies should be irrelevant, the record reveals uncertainty from the relevant scientific community as to whether and to what extent the distinctions may, in fact, matter. It is likely that jurors, most of whom lack advanced scientific degrees and training, would be poorly suited for resolving these disputes and thus more likely to be confused rather than assisted by Dr. Laken's testimony. *See* FED. R. EVID. 702(a) (requiring expert testimony "will help the trier of fact to understand the evidence or to determine a fact in issue"). Accordingly, we conclude that the district court did not abuse its discretion in excluding Dr. Laken's testimony about Dr. Semrau's fMRI lie detection results under Rule 702.

4. *Admissibility Under Rule 403*

The magistrate judge's R & R, as adopted by the district court, also excluded Dr. Laken's testimony under Federal Rule of Evidence 403, which permits a court to exclude relevant evidence if its probative value is substantially outweighed by a danger of confusing the issues or misleading the jury, among other things. "A district court has 'very broad' discretion in making this determination." *United States v. Smithers*, 212 F.3d 306, 322 (6th Cir. 2000). . . .

The magistrate judge recommended excluding the fMRI evidence under Rule 403 for three reasons. First, the test was unilaterally obtained without the Government's knowledge, so the Government had no supervision of the testing and Dr. Semrau risked nothing because the results would never have been released had he failed. Second, this court has held that the use of lie detection test results "solely to bolster a witness' credibility is 'highly prejudicial,' especially where credibility issues are central to the verdict." *United States v. Sherlin*, 67 F.3d 1208, 1217 (6h Cir. 1995); *see also United States v. Scheffer*, 523 U.S. 303, 313–14 (1998) ("[J]urisdictions may legitimately determine that the aura of infallibility attending polygraph evidence can lead jurors to abandon their duty to assess credibility and guilt.").[11] Finally, a jury would not be assisted by hearing that Dr. Semrau's answers were truthful "overall" without learning which specific questions he answered truthfully or deceptively.

. . . Dr. Semrau relies on our holding in *Bonds* that DNA evidence was admissible pursuant to Rule 403. *See* 12 F.3d at 567–68. *Bonds* does not address the unique legal issues stemming from lie detection evidence. *See Scheffer*, 523 U.S. at 313 ("Unlike other expert witnesses who testify about

11. Although *Sherlin* involved polygraph tests rather than fMRI tests, the magistrate judge concluded that the concerns are the same regardless of the technology employed.

factual matters outside the jurors' knowledge, such as the analysis of . . . DNA found at a crime scene, a polygraph expert can supply the jury only with another opinion, in addition to its own, about whether the witness was telling the truth."); *see also* Julie A. Seaman, *Black Boxes*, 58 EMORY L.J. 427, 488 (2008) ("[W]ere an accurate lie detector developed, the jury's unique role in determining witness credibility would be called into question.").

We hold that the district court did not abuse its discretion in excluding the fMRI evidence pursuant to Rule 403 in light of (1) the questions surrounding the reliability of fMRI lie detection tests in general and as performed on Dr. Semrau, (2) the failure to give the prosecution an opportunity to participate in the testing, and (3) the test result's inability to corroborate Dr. Semrau's answers as to the particular offenses for which he was charged.[12] . . .

III. CONCLUSION

For the reasons stated above, Dr. Semrau's conviction is AFFIRMED.

Problem 9.15
Polygraph Consent II

Two months before the defendant's murder trial, his lawyer hired a polygraph expert to quiz him about the day of the crime. The examination took place in defense counsel's office. Only the defendant, his lawyer, and the polygraph examiner were present. Two weeks later, defense counsel notified the prosecutor that she would seek to call the polygraph examiner as an expert witness at trial. The prosecutor filed a motion to bar the examiner's testimony, and after a *Daubert* hearing, the trial judge ruled that the polygraph examination was insufficiently reliable. The court excluded all testimony about the results of the test.

At trial, defense counsel called the polygraph examiner as a witness. Over the prosecutor's repeated objections, the judge permitted the examiner to testify as follows: At the beginning of

12. The prospect of introducing fMRI lie detection results into criminal trials is undoubtedly intriguing and, perhaps, a little scary. *See* Daniel S. Goldberg, *Against Reductionism in Law & Neuroscience*, 11 HOUS. J. HEALTH L. & POL'Y 321, 324 n.6 (2012) (reviewing literature that "challenges the very idea that fMRI or other novel neuroimaging techniques either can or should be used as evidence in criminal proceedings."). There may well come a time when the capabilities, reliability, and acceptance of fMRI lie detection—or even a technology not yet envisioned—advances to the point that a trial judge will conclude, as did Dr. Laken in this case: "I would subject myself to this over a jury any day." Though we are not at that point today, we recognize that as science moves forward the balancing of Rule 403 may well lean toward finding that the probative value for some advancing technology is sufficient.

her meeting with the defendant, she explained the polygraph equipment and her methodology. She told the defendant that in the past she had achieved a very high degree of success in detecting deceit on the part of her subjects. Then, adhering to her usual protocol in preparing a subject for an examination, she asked the defendant if he wished to proceed. He responded, "Go ahead, Doc, hook me up." The examiner testified that the defendant spoke these words "firmly and unhesitatingly." She said this entire exchange took place before the polygraph examination. She did not testify about the examination itself.

How should the court have ruled on the prosecutor's objection that this testimony constituted improper opinion evidence and must be excluded?

5. Assessing the Reliability of Non-Scientific Expertise

a. THE DOCTRINE

Kumho Tire Company v. Carmichael

526 U.S. 137 (1999)

■ BREYER, J. . . . On July 6, 1993, the right rear tire of a minivan driven by Patrick Carmichael blew out. In the accident that followed, one of the passengers died, and others were severely injured. In October 1993, the Carmichaels brought this diversity suit against the tire's maker and its distributor, whom we refer to collectively as Kumho Tire, claiming that the tire was defective. The plaintiffs rested their case in significant part upon deposition testimony provided by an expert in tire failure analysis, Dennis Carlson, Jr., who intended to testify in support of their conclusion.

Carlson's depositions relied upon certain features of tire technology that are not in dispute. A steel-belted radial tire like the Carmichaels' is made up of a "carcass" containing many layers of flexible cords, called "plies," along which (between the cords and the outer tread) are laid steel strips called "belts." Steel wire loops, called "beads," hold the cords together at the plies' bottom edges. An outer layer, called the "tread," encases the carcass, and the entire tire is bound together in rubber, through the application of heat and various chemicals. The bead of the tire sits upon a "bead seat," which is part of the wheel assembly. That assembly contains a "rim flange," which extends over the bead and rests against the side of the tire:

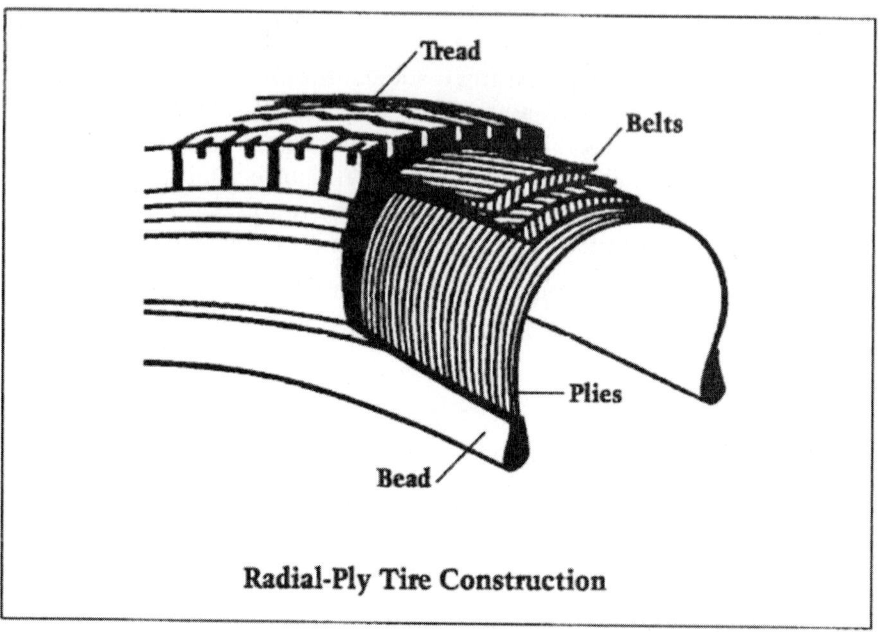

A. Markovich, How To Buy and Care For Tires 4 (1994).

Carlson's testimony also accepted certain background facts about the tire in question. He assumed that before the blowout the tire had traveled far. (The tire was made in 1988 and had been installed some time before the Carmichaels bought the used minivan in March 1993; the Carmichaels had driven the van approximately 7,000 additional miles in the two months they had owned it.) Carlson noted that the tire's tread depth, which was 11/32 of an inch when new, had been worn down to depths that ranged from 3/32 of an inch along some parts of the tire, to nothing at all along others. He conceded that the tire tread had at least two punctures which had been inadequately repaired. Despite the tire's age and history, Carlson concluded that a defect in its manufacture or design caused the blow-out. He rested this conclusion in part upon three premises which, for present purposes, we must assume are not in dispute: First, a tire's carcass should stay bound to the inner side of the tread for a significant period of time after its tread depth has worn away. Second, the tread of the tire at issue had separated from its inner steel-belted carcass prior to the accident. Third, this "separation" caused the blowout.

Carlson's conclusion that a defect caused the separation, however, rested upon certain other propositions, several of which the defendants strongly dispute. First, Carlson said that if a separation is not caused by a certain kind of tire misuse called "overdeflection" (which consists of underinflating the tire or causing it to carry too much weight, thereby generating heat that can undo the chemical tread/carcass bond), then, ordinarily, its cause is a tire defect. Second, he said that if a tire has been subject to sufficient overdeflection to cause a separation, it should reveal certain physical symptoms. These symptoms include (a) tread wear on the tire's shoulder that is greater than the tread wear along the tire's center; (b) signs of a "bead groove," where the beads have been pushed too hard against the bead seat on the inside of the tire's rim; (c) sidewalls of the tire with physical signs of deterioration, such as discoloration; and/or (d) marks on the tire's rim flange. Third, Carlson said that where he does not find at least two of the four physical signs just mentioned (and presumably where there is no reason to suspect a less common cause of separation), he concludes that a manufacturing or design defect caused the separation.

Carlson added that he had inspected the tire in question. He conceded that the tire to a limited degree showed greater wear on the shoulder than in the center, some signs of "bead groove," some discoloration, a few marks on the rim flange, and inadequately filled puncture holes (which can also cause heat that might lead to separation). But, in each instance, he testified that the symptoms were not significant, and he explained why he believed that they did not reveal overdeflection. For example, the extra shoulder wear, he said, appeared primarily on one shoulder, whereas an overdeflected tire would reveal equally abnormal wear on both shoulders. Carlson concluded that the tire did not bear at least two of the four overdeflection symptoms, nor was there any less obvious cause of separation; and since neither overdeflection nor the punctures caused the blowout, a defect must have done so.

Kumho Tire moved the District Court to exclude Carlson's testimony on the ground that his methodology failed Rule 702's reliability requirement. The court agreed with Kumho that it should act as a *Daubert*-type reliability "gatekeeper," even though one might consider Carlson's testimony as "technical," rather than "scientific." [*See* Daubert v. Merrell Dow Pharm., Inc., 509 U.S. 579 (1993).... And] the court agreed with the plaintiffs that *Daubert* should be applied flexibly, that its four factors were simply illustrative, and that other factors could argue in favor of admissibility. It conceded that there may be widespread acceptance of a "visual-inspection method" for some relevant purposes. But the court found insufficient indications of the reliability of "the component of Carlson's tire failure analysis which most concerned the Court, namely, the methodology employed by the expert in analyzing the data obtained in the visual inspection, and the scientific basis, if any, for such an analysis." It consequently ... declar[ed] Carlson's testimony inadmissible and grant[ed] the defendants' motion for summary judgment.

The Eleventh Circuit reversed.... It noted that "the Supreme Court in *Daubert* explicitly limited its holding to cover only the 'scientific context,' " adding that "a *Daubert* analysis" applies only where an expert relies "on the application of scientific principles," rather than "on skill-or experience-based observation." It concluded that Carlson's testimony, which it viewed as relying on experience, "falls outside the scope of *Daubert*," that "the district court erred as a matter of law by applying *Daubert* in this case," and that the case must be remanded for further (non-*Daubert*-type) consideration under Rule 702.

. . . We granted certiorari in light of uncertainty among the lower courts about whether, or how, *Daubert* applies to expert testimony that might be characterized as based not upon "scientific" knowledge, but rather upon "technical" or "other specialized" knowledge.

II

A

In *Daubert*, this Court held that Federal Rule of Evidence 702 imposes a special obligation upon a trial judge to "ensure that any and all scientific testimony . . . is not only relevant, but reliable." The initial question before us is whether this basic gatekeeping obligation applies only to "scientific" testimony or to all expert testimony. We, like the parties, believe that it applies to all expert testimony.

For one thing, [Unrestyled] Rule 702 itself says:

> "If scientific, technical, or other specialized knowledge will assist the trier of fact to understand the evidence or to determine a fact in issue, a witness qualified as an expert by knowledge, skill, experience, training, or education, may testify thereto in the form of an opinion or otherwise."

This language makes no relevant distinction between "scientific" knowledge and "technical" or "other specialized" knowledge. It makes clear that any such knowledge might become the subject of expert testimony. In *Daubert*, the Court specified that it is the Rule's word "knowledge," not the words (like "scientific") that modify that word, that "establishes a standard of evidentiary reliability." Hence, as a matter of language, the Rule applies its reliability standard to all "scientific," "technical," or "other specialized" matters within its scope. We concede that the Court in *Daubert* referred only to "scientific" knowledge. But as the Court there said, it referred to "scientific" testimony "because that was the nature of the expertise" at issue.

Neither is the evidentiary rationale that underlay the Court's basic *Daubert* "gatekeeping" determination limited to "scientific" knowledge. *Daubert* pointed out that Federal Rules 702 and 703 grant expert witnesses testimonial latitude unavailable to other witnesses on the "assumption that the expert's opinion will have a reliable basis in the knowledge and experience of his discipline." *Id.* at 592 (pointing out that experts may testify to opinions, including those that are not based on firsthand knowledge or observation). The Rules grant that latitude to all experts, not just to "scientific" ones.

Finally, it would prove difficult, if not impossible, for judges to administer evidentiary rules under which a gatekeeping obligation depended upon a distinction between "scientific" knowledge and "technical" or "other specialized" knowledge. There is no clear line that divides the one from the others. Disciplines such as engineering rest upon scientific knowledge. Pure scientific theory itself may depend for its development upon observation and properly engineered machinery....

Neither is there a convincing need to make such distinctions. Experts of all kinds tie observations to conclusions through the use of what Judge Learned Hand called "general truths derived from ... specialized experience." Hand, *Historical and Practical Considerations Regarding Expert Testimony*, 15 HARV. L. REV. 40, 54 (1901). And whether the specific expert testimony focuses upon specialized observations, the specialized translation of those observations into theory, a specialized theory itself, or the application of such a theory in a particular case, the expert's testimony often will rest "upon an experience confessedly foreign in kind to [the jury's] own." *Ibid.* The trial judge's effort to assure that the specialized testimony is reliable and relevant can help the jury evaluate that foreign experience, whether the testimony reflects scientific, technical, or other specialized knowledge.

We conclude that *Daubert*'s general principles apply to the expert matters described in Rule 702. The Rule, in respect to all such matters, "establishes a standard of evidentiary reliability." 509 U.S. at 590. It "requires a valid ... connection to the pertinent inquiry as a precondition to admissibility." *Id.* at 592. And where such testimony's factual basis, data, principles, methods, or their application are called sufficiently into question, *see* Part III, *infra*, the trial judge must determine whether the testimony has "a reliable basis in the knowledge and experience of [the relevant] discipline." 509 U.S. at 592.

B

The petitioners ask more specifically whether a trial judge determining the "admissibility of an engineering expert's testimony" may consider several more specific factors that *Daubert* said might "bear on" a judge's gate-keeping determination. These factors include:

- Whether a "theory or technique ... can be (and has been) tested";
- Whether it "has been subjected to peer review and publication";
- Whether, in respect to a particular technique, there is a high "known or potential rate of error" and whether there are "standards controlling the technique's operation"; and

- Whether the theory or technique enjoys "general acceptance" within a "relevant scientific community."

Emphasizing the word "may" in the question, we answer that question yes.

. . . As the Solicitor General points out, there are many different kinds of experts, and many different kinds of expertise. *See* Brief for United States as Amicus Curiae 18–19, and n.5 (citing cases involving experts in drug terms, handwriting analysis, criminal modus operandi, land valuation, agricultural practices, railroad procedures, attorney's fee valuation, and others). Our emphasis on the word "may" thus reflects *Daubert*'s description of the Rule 702 inquiry as "a flexible one." *Daubert* makes clear that the factors it mentions do not constitute a "definitive checklist or test." And *Daubert* adds that the gatekeeping inquiry must be " 'tied to the facts' " of a particular "case." We agree with the Solicitor General that "the factors identified in *Daubert* may or may not be pertinent in assessing reliability, depending on the nature of the issue, the expert's particular expertise, and the subject of his testimony." The conclusion, in our view, is that we can neither rule out, nor rule in, for all cases and for all time the applicability of the factors mentioned in *Daubert*, nor can we now do so for subsets of cases categorized by category of expert or by kind of evidence. Too much depends upon the particular circumstances of the particular case at issue.

Daubert itself is not to the contrary. It made clear that its list of factors was meant to be helpful, not definitive. Indeed, those factors do not all necessarily apply even in every instance in which the reliability of scientific testimony is challenged. It might not be surprising in a particular case, for example, that a claim made by a scientific witness has never been the subject of peer review, for the particular application at issue may never previously have interested any scientist. Nor, on the other hand, does the presence of *Daubert*'s general acceptance factor help show that an expert's testimony is reliable where the discipline itself lacks reliability, as, for example, do theories grounded in any so-called generally accepted principles of astrology or necromancy.

At the same time, and contrary to the Court of Appeals' view, some of *Daubert*'s questions can help to evaluate the reliability even of experience-based testimony. In certain cases, it will be appropriate for the trial judge to ask, for example, how often an engineering expert's experience-based methodology has produced erroneous results, or whether such a method is generally accepted in the relevant engineering community. Likewise, it will at times be useful to ask even of a witness whose expertise is based purely on experience, say, a perfume tester able to distinguish among 140 odors at a sniff, whether his preparation is of a kind that others in the field would recognize as acceptable.

We must therefore disagree with the Eleventh Circuit's holding that a trial judge may ask questions of the sort *Daubert* mentioned only where an expert "relies on the application of scientific principles," but not where an expert relies "on skill- or experience-based observation." We do not believe that Rule 702 creates a schematism that segregates expertise by type while mapping certain kinds of questions to certain kinds of experts. Life and the legal cases that it generates are too complex to warrant so definitive a match.

. . . [W]e conclude that the trial judge must have considerable leeway in deciding in a particular case how to go about determining whether particular expert testimony is reliable. That is to say, a trial court should consider the specific factors identified in *Daubert* where they are reasonable measures of the reliability of expert testimony.

C

The trial court must have the same kind of latitude in deciding *how* to test an expert's reliability, and to decide whether or when special briefing or other proceedings are needed to investigate reliability, as it enjoys when it decides *whether* that expert's relevant testimony is reliable. Our opinion in [*General Electric Co. v.*] *Joiner* makes clear that a court of appeals is to apply an abuse-of-discretion standard when it "reviews a trial court's decision to admit or exclude expert testimony." General Electric Co. v. Joiner, 522 U.S. 136, 138–39 (1997). That standard applies as much to the trial court's decisions about how to determine reliability as to its ultimate conclusion. Otherwise, the trial judge would lack the discretionary authority needed both to avoid unnecessary "reliability" proceedings in ordinary cases where the reliability of an expert's methods is properly taken for granted, and to require appropriate proceedings in the less usual or more complex cases where cause for questioning the expert's reliability arises. . . .

III

We further explain the way in which a trial judge "may" consider *Daubert*'s factors by applying these considerations to the case at hand, a matter that has been briefed exhaustively by the parties and their 19 amici. The District Court did not doubt Carlson's qualifications, which included a masters degree in mechanical engineering, 10 years' work at Michelin America, Inc., and testimony as a tire failure consultant in other tort cases. Rather, it excluded the testimony because, despite those qualifications, it initially doubted, and then found unreliable, "the methodology employed by the expert in analyzing the data obtained in the visual inspection, and the scientific basis, if any, for such an analysis." After examining the transcript in "some detail," and after considering respondents' defense of Carlson's methodology, the District Court determined that Carlson's testimony was not reliable. It fell outside the range where experts might reasonably differ, and where the jury must decide among the conflicting views of different experts, even though the evidence is "shaky." *Daubert*, 509 U.S. at 596. In our view, the doubts that triggered the District Court's initial inquiry here were reasonable, as was the court's ultimate conclusion.

For one thing, and contrary to respondents' suggestion, the specific issue before the court was not the reasonableness in general of a tire expert's use of a visual and tactile inspection to determine whether overdeflection had caused the tire's tread to separate from its steel-belted carcass. Rather, it was the reasonableness of using such an approach, along with Carlson's particular method of analyzing the data thereby obtained, to draw a conclusion regarding the particular matter to which the expert testimony was directly relevant. That matter concerned the likelihood that a defect in the tire at issue caused its tread to separate from its carcass. The tire in question, the expert conceded, had traveled far enough so that some of the tread had been worn bald; it should have been taken out of service; it had been repaired (inadequately) for punctures; and it bore some of the very marks that the expert said indicated, not a defect, but abuse through overdeflection. The relevant issue was whether the expert could reliably determine the cause of this tire's separation. Nor was the basis for Carlson's conclusion simply the general theory that, in the absence of evidence of abuse, a defect will normally have caused a tire's separation. Rather, the expert employed a more specific theory to establish the existence (or absence) of such abuse. Carlson testified precisely that in the absence of at least two of four signs of abuse (proportionately greater tread wear on the shoulder; signs of grooves caused by the beads; discolored sidewalls; marks on the rim flange) he concludes that a defect caused the separation. And his analysis depended upon acceptance of a further implicit proposition, namely, that his visual and tactile inspection could determine that the tire before him had not been abused despite some evidence of the presence of the very signs for which he looked (and two punctures).

For another thing, the transcripts of Carlson's depositions support both the trial court's initial uncertainty and its final conclusion. Those transcripts cast considerable doubt upon the reliability of both the explicit theory (about the need for two signs of abuse) and the implicit proposition (about the significance of visual inspection in this case). Among other things, the expert could not say whether the tire had traveled more than 10, or 20, or 30, or 40, or 50 thousand miles, adding that 6,000 miles was "about how far" he could "say with any certainty." The court could reasonably have wondered about the reliability of a method of visual and tactile inspection sufficiently precise to ascertain with some certainty the abuse-related significance of minute shoulder/center relative tread wear differences, but insufficiently precise to tell "with any certainty" from the tread wear whether a tire had traveled less than 10,000 or more than 50,000 miles. And these concerns might have been augmented by Carlson's repeated reliance on the "subjectiveness" of his mode of analysis in response to questions seeking specific information regarding how he could differentiate between a tire that actually had been overdeflected and a tire that merely looked as though it had been. They would have been further augmented by the fact that Carlson said he had inspected the tire itself for the first time the morning of his first deposition, and then only for a few hours. (His initial conclusions were based on photographs.) . . .

Finally, the court, after looking for a defense of Carlson's methodology as applied in these circumstances, found no convincing defense. Rather, it found (1) that "none" of the *Daubert* factors, including that of "general acceptance" in the relevant expert community, indicated that Carlson's testimony was reliable; (2) that its own analysis "revealed no countervailing factors operating in favor of admissibility which could outweigh those identified in *Daubert*"; and (3) that the "parties identified no such factors in their briefs." For these three reasons taken together, it concluded that Carlson's testimony was unreliable.

. . . As we said before, the question before the trial court was specific, not general. The trial court had to decide whether this particular expert had sufficient specialized knowledge to assist the jurors "in deciding the particular issues in the case." 4 J. McLAUGHLIN, WEINSTEIN'S FEDERAL EVIDENCE ¶ 702.05[1], p. 702–33 (2d ed. 1998). . . . The particular issue in this case concerned the use of Carlson's two-factor test and his related use of visual/tactile inspection to draw conclusions on the basis of what seemed small observational differences. We have found no indication in the record that other experts in the industry use Carlson's two-factor test or that tire experts such as Carlson normally make the very fine distinctions about, say, the symmetry of comparatively greater shoulder tread wear that were necessary, on Carlson's own theory, to support his conclusions. Nor, despite the prevalence of tire testing, does anyone refer to any articles or papers that validate Carlson's approach. Indeed, no one has argued that Carlson himself, were he still working for Michelin, would have concluded in a report to his employer that a similar tire was similarly defective on grounds identical to those upon which he rested his conclusion here. Of course, Carlson himself claimed that his method was accurate, but, as we pointed out in *Joiner*, "nothing in either *Daubert* or the Federal Rules of Evidence requires a district court to admit opinion evidence that is connected to existing data only by the *ipse dixit* of the expert." 522 U.S. at 146.

. . . [The District Court] explicitly recognized that the relevant reliability inquiry "should be 'flexible,' " that its " 'overarching subject [should be] . . . validity' and reliability," and that "*Daubert* was intended neither to be exhaustive nor to apply in every case." And the court ultimately based its decision upon Carlson's failure to satisfy either *Daubert*'s factors or any other set of reasonable reliability criteria. . . . [T]hat conclusion was within the District Court's lawful discretion.

In sum, Rule 702 grants the district judge the discretionary authority, reviewable for its abuse, to determine reliability in light of the particular facts and circumstances of the particular case. The District Court did not abuse its discretionary authority in this case. Hence, the judgment of the Court of Appeals is

Reversed.

■ JUSTICE SCALIA, with whom JUSTICE O'CONNOR and JUSTICE THOMAS join, concurring. . . .

■ JUSTICE STEVENS, concurring in part and dissenting in part. . . .

RULE 702
Public Comments on 2000 Amendment

In 2000, Congress amended FRE 702 to add the italicized language:

> **Rule 702. Testimony by Experts.** If scientific, technical, or other specialized knowledge will assist the trier of fact to understand the evidence or to determine a fact in issue, a witness qualified as an expert by knowledge, skill, experience, training, or education, may testify thereto in the form of an opinion, or otherwise *if (1) the testimony is based upon sufficient facts or data, (2) the testimony is the product of reliable principles and methods, and (3) the witness has applied the principles and methods reliably to the facts of the case.*

The amendment embraced *Daubert*'s notion that the trial judge should act as gatekeeper, guarding against unreliable expert evidence. And it embraced *Kumho Tire*'s conclusion "that *Daubert*'s general holding—setting forth the trial judge's general 'gatekeeping' obligation—applies not only to testimony based on 'scientific' knowledge, but also to testimony based on 'technical' and 'other specialized' knowledge."

In the course of vetting the proposed amendment before its adoption, the Advisory Committee sought public comment. A great number of practitioners, judges, academics, and concerned parties offered their views. Here is a sampling:

> . . . Hon. D. Brock Hornby, Chief Judge of the United States District Court for the District of Maine, argues that the proposed amendment to Evidence Rule 702 will impose substantial litigation costs due to "the proliferation of motions to preclude expert testimony and voir dire hearings held in advance of trial that the growing elaborateness of the gatekeeping rules entails." Judge Hornby asks: "Where is the evidence that lawyers are not able to cross-examine effectively and show whatever limitations there are on the bases for expert opinion testimony that is not scientific?" . . .

Kevin J. Dunne, Esq., supports the proposal to amend Evidence Rule 702. In his view, complaints that the proposal deprives the jury of its role in assessing the weight of the evidence are unfounded. He states: "The phrase, 'it goes to the weight,' has become synonymous with laissez-faire judging and a license for admissibility of junk science. Indeed, this ... argument can be used to eliminate all rules of evidence ..."

Thomas E. Carroll, Esq., opposes the proposed amendment insofar as it would embody the principles of *Daubert*. He contends that *Daubert* has "tripled the cost of litigation in matters involving significant issues of expert testimony." ...

The Chemical Manufacturers Association, the Defense Research Institute, the Federation of Insurance and Corporate Defense Counsel, the International Association of Defense Counsel, Lawyers for Civil Justice, the National Association of Manufacturers, and the Product Liability Advisory Council "fully support" the proposed amendment to Rule 702. ...

Alan Voos, Esq., opposes the proposed amendment to Evidence Rule 702. He states that "[r]ather than codifying *Daubert* the Committee should formulate a rule which does away with *Daubert* and allows new, cutting edge, but reliable scientific expert testimony to assist triers of fact in civil trials." ...

Problem 9.16
Hedonics

Consider the facts of *Ayers v. Robinson*, 887 F. Supp. 1049, 1051–53 (N.D. Ill. 1995), in which Lillian Ayers sought damages for the wrongful shooting death of her son, Lenardo, by a Chicago police officer:

> At trial Lillian would hope to introduce into evidence expert testimony by Professor Stan Smith on the issue of hedonic damages. In Smith's book ... *(Economic/Hedonic Damages: The Practice Book for Plaintiff and Defense Attorneys (1990))*, the hedonic value of life is defined as "the value of the pleasure, the satisfaction, or the 'utility' that human beings derive from life, separate and apart from the labor or earnings value of life." ... Smith claims to be able to put a dollar figure on those intangibles. ...
>
> ... [T]he principles and methodology upon which Smith relies—the so called "willingness-to-pay" approach to

valuing human life—are reported in a number of articles in addition to *Hedonic Damages*. . . .

For current purposes the most useful explication of willingness-to-pay methodology is set forth in the sample testimony [of an expert economist] in Chapter 11 of *Hedonic Damages*. . . .

> *Q:* Are you saying that economists have made measurements of the value of life beyond lost earning capacity?
>
> *A:* Yes they have. . . . First, economists have examined the value of life expressed by consumers in their expenditures on safety. . . . Assume that a person purchases a safety device for $700 and that device reduces the probability of his death from 7 in 10,000 to 5 in 10,000. By reducing his chance of dying by 2/10,000ths, or one chance in 5,000, at a cost of $700, economists would say that he valued his life at $3,500,000.

Smith is prepared to testify that this analysis, adjusted to account for Lenardo Ayers's age and other factors, would put the hedonic value of Ayers's life at about $2 million.

Should the court admit the evidence? How should it go about deciding?

---

b. A FOCUS ON SYNDROME EVIDENCE

Holly Hogan

The False Dichotomy of Rape Trauma Syndrome

12 CARDOZO J.L. & GENDER 529 (2006)

* * *

II. BACKGROUND

After conducting a year-long study of rape victims in a Boston emergency room in 1974, Ann Burgess and Lynda Holmstrom found enough consistency among the victims' emotional and physical reactions to identify a syndrome called Rape Trauma Syndrome ("RTS"). *See* Ann Wolpert Burgess & Lynda Lytle Holmstrom, *Rape Trauma Syndrome*, 131 AM. J. PSYCHIATRY 981 (1974). RTS explains the behavior of a victim immediately after the rape, as well as the long-term impact of the rape on the victim....

The syndrome manifests itself in two response phases. In the first phase, immediately following the attack until several hours after it, victims display one of two reactions: "emotional excitement" or "emotional flatness." Fifty percent of rape victims display "emotional excitement," demonstrated by crying, anxiety, and inappropriate smiling. The other half exhibit "emotional flatness," remaining subdued, calm, and non-emotional. The physical symptoms for both reactions are the same, ranging from soreness and bruising, to tension headaches, sleeplessness, fatigue, stomach pains, and genitourinary disturbance....

The second response stage is a long-term reorganization process that all victims experience, regardless of whether they fell into the "emotional flatness" or "emotional excitement" categories during the first phase. The timing of the onset of the second stage varies, and can occur even years after the rape. Symptoms include sexual fears, nightmares, and phobic reactions....

The specific behavioral and emotional symptoms that a particular victim exhibits in the two response stages are influenced by various factors, including the personality of the victim, the nature of the rape, the life experience of the victim, the support system that the victim possesses, and the victim's relationship with the offender....

... RTS has identified many victim behaviors that are counterintuitive. The controlled response, for example, is a clear counterintuitive behavior. Some will assume that a rape did not occur because the victim is not crying and hysterical, but rather calm and subdued. Without more knowledge about the response stages, and the controlled and expressive reactions, one might assume that rape victims consistently behave hysterically after such a traumatic event. The fact that many victims behave in exactly the opposite way is an example of a counterintuitive behavior that RTS helps explain.

Denying that a rape occurred illustrates another counterintuitive behavior. One might expect a rape victim to contact the police immediately after an attack, just as victims often do in other crimes. The Layman study, however, identified a large number of unacknowledged rapes—rapes in which the victims do not believe that they were raped when circumstances indicate otherwise. *See* Melissa J. Layman et al., *Unacknowledged Versus Acknowledged Rape Victims: Situational Factors and Posttraumatic Stress*, 105 J. ABNORMAL PSYCHOLOGY 124, 125–28 (1996). A victim's acknowledgement that a rape occurred is correlated with the level of violence during the rape because many people incorrectly believe that rape only occurs when the rapist injures the victim or threatens to do so. Although a high level of violence often exists when victims are raped by a family member, generally, more violence occurs in stranger rapes. Hence, victims of acquaintance rapes are less likely to experience violence when raped, and because the level of violence is correlated with the level of acknowledgement, acquaintance rape victims are less likely to acknowledge that a rape occurred. Not acknowledging that a rape occurred leads to further counterintuitive behaviors. While only ten percent of acknowledged rape victims in the study had sexual intercourse with the offender after the incident, thirty-two percent of the unacknowledged victims did so.

Victims' memory of the rape can also be counterintuitive. The Koss study found that memories of rape "were less clear and vivid, were less likely to occur in a meaningful order, were less well remembered, and were less thought and talked about" than other types of unpleasant memories. Mary P. Koss et al., *Traumatic Memory Characteristics: A Cross–Validated Mediational Model of Response to Rape Among Employed Women*, 105 J. ABNORMAL PSYCHOLOGY 421, 428 (1996). Moreover, the Mechanic study found that women who were victims of acquaintance rape were more likely than victims of stranger rape to report significant levels of amnesia about the rape. Minday B. Mechanic et al., *A Comparison of Normal Forgetting, Psychopathology, and Information–Processing Models of Reported Amnesia for Recent Sexual Trauma*, 66 J. CONSULTING & CLINICAL PSYCHOLOGY 948, 953 (1998). These studies demonstrate that rape victims may have trouble remembering and may even give inconsistent statements about the rape, which may be counterintuitive behavioral responses to some who believe that one would never forget such a traumatic experience. . . .

These counterintuitive behaviors can devastate a victim's credibility because in many non-rape contexts, such behavior would be interpreted as strong evidence that the victim is lying. The controlled response is counterintuitive to an expectation that the rape victim should be crying hysterically, denial that a rape occurred is counterintuitive to an expectation that the rape victim should be quick to seek justice after an attack, and inconsistent memories about the rape are counterintuitive to an expectation that the rape victim should never forget the details of such a traumatic event. Therefore, RTS testimony plays a vital role in rape trials by providing much-needed knowledge about these behaviors to the factfinder so that he or she is better informed to determine the credibility of the victim.

III. COURTROOM FUNCTIONS

A. Offensive RTS Testimony

First, the State may utilize RTS in its case-in-chief to prove that a rape occurred. In other words, after an expert diagnoses the victim with RTS, the State may argue that because the victim suffers from RTS, she must have been raped. Courts categorize this diagnostic testimony as offensive testimony, even though a diagnosis may be introduced in the prosecution's case-in-chief either offensively without any credibility attacks by the defendant, or defensively in response to attacks on the victim's credibility during cross-examination. Note that despite this testimony, the question of who raped the victim will, arguably, remain open. . . .

. . . [T]his admission of diagnostic testimony is atypical among jurisdictions in the United States.

B. Defensive RTS Testimony

Second, the State may introduce RTS in its case-in-chief and/or rebuttal to rehabilitate the victim's credibility after attack by the defense, but not to specifically diagnose the particular victim in the case as suffering from RTS. The courts categorize this non-diagnostic, rehabilitative testimony as defensive. . . . Defensive RTS expert testimony explains counterintuitive behaviors generally, and hence rehabilitates the victim's credibility without a diagnosis. . . .

STATE v. KINNEY

Supreme Court of Vermont.
171 Vt. 239 (2000).

■ DOOLEY, J. Defendant Steven Kinney was convicted by a jury on charges of kidnapping, aggravated sexual assault, and lewd and lascivious behavior. . . . On appeal he argues that . . . the trial court erred in admitting expert testimony about rape trauma syndrome. . . .

According to the testimony presented at trial, defendant committed the offenses during the night of October 9, 1998. He began drinking with friends around 6:00 p.m. . . . Defendant admitted during cross-examination that "[his] faculties would have been fairly clouded given the amount of coke, alcohol and pot [he] had consumed over the course of the evening."

At some time after 1:00 a.m., defendant and three friends drove to the home of Lucas Sweetser, hoping to buy some more cocaine. When they arrived, defendant went into the home and emerged a short time later, carrying the victim over his shoulder. He put her in the back seat of the car, and they drove away. The testimony as to what happened inside the house is conflicting. Defendant claims he found Sweetser and the victim asleep in bed. The victim happened to wake up, and they began to talk. The victim said she might be able to help him find some drugs to buy. When his friends pressed him to leave, defendant picked up the victim, put her over his shoulder, and carried her to the car. According to defendant, the victim was giggling, and went in the car willingly.

The victim testified that she did not go with defendant willingly. She testified that when defendant woke her, he asked her to come with him, but she refused. Defendant then pulled her out of bed and threw her over his shoulder. She resisted, but defendant carried her out of the house and put her in the backseat of the car. According to the victim, she repeatedly said she did not want to go with them and asked to be let out of the car.

Once they were all back in the car, defendant and his friends gave up on finding more cocaine. Instead, they went back to the house where they had been earlier, and all five people, including the victim, drank more beer and smoked marijuana. Defendant and one of his friends testified that the victim got out of the car and walked into the house ahead of them, of her own volition. The victim testified that defendant pulled her into the house by her arm, and another of defendant's friends testified that defendant dragged her into the house "like a puppy dog." The victim also testified that she drank the beer and smoked the marijuana because she did not want defendant and his friends to think she was scared.

Eventually, the party broke up, and the victim went with defendant to his house, where he lived with his parents, because he offered to drive her home from there. According to defendant's testimony, he planned to ask his parents to drive her home, but when they got there, he decided it was too late to wake his parents. He and the victim got into bed, where "one thing led to another," and they had consensual sex. The victim, on the other hand, testified that when they got to defendant's house, he took her to his room and raped her. Afterwards, she fell asleep. In the morning when she woke up, she asked to be taken home, and he arranged for a friend to give her a ride. . . .

The State called Dr. Jan Tyler to testify about rape trauma syndrome and the characteristics and conduct of rape victims. The admissibility of this testimony was first contested in pretrial proceedings when the State made an offer of proof indicating Dr. Tyler would testify about rape trauma syndrome and "the behavioral patterns of victims of sexual assault." The State noted that the expert witness would have no contact with the victim and would not offer an opinion on whether the victim was raped by defendant. Defendant challenged the evidence as inadmissible under Daubert v. Merrell Dow Pharmaceuticals, Inc., 509 U.S. 579 (1993). The court orally rejected the challenge on the first day of trial, and followed up with a written decision after the trial.

Dr. Tyler testified that rape trauma syndrome is associated with post-traumatic stress disorder [PTSD]—that is, it is a set of behaviors and symptoms experienced by victims of trauma. She explained that victims of severe trauma commonly experience symptoms such as nightmares, anxiety, and fear as a result of the trauma. Victims of rape, in particular, may experience symptoms such as difficulty in interpersonal relationships, guilt, shame, and sexual dysfunction.

Dr. Tyler also testified that studies have shown that victims of rape are more likely to resist their attacker by making verbal protests than by struggling or screaming, and that victims are less likely to resist if force is used or threatened. Furthermore, she said that it is not unusual for victims to delay in reporting a rape, especially if the attacker is an acquaintance, and that a rape victim may be more likely to report to a friend first, rather than to someone with whom she is having an intimate relationship. This delay in reporting is related to the feelings of guilt and shame experienced due to the trauma of the rape. Dr. Tyler then testified to statistics regarding the rate of false reporting of rape. Finally, she testified that, although she had no statistics, she thought it would not be unusual for a victim of rape to fall asleep immediately after the assault, due to the physical exertion and psychological responses to the trauma such as denial and withdrawal.

Defendant objected at the outset of the trial to the reliability and relevancy of Dr. Tyler's testimony and contended that it would impermissibly bolster the credibility of the complainant. Defendant renewed his objection to its reliability during a break in Dr. Tyler's testimony. Finally, the day after Dr. Tyler's testimony concluded, defendant objected to her testimony regarding the rate of false reports of rape. In this Court, defendant makes three arguments: (1) the court failed to conduct a proper *Daubert* inquiry; (2) the expert's evidence was not admissible under *Daubert* and State v. Streich, 163 Vt. 331 (1995) [which adopted *Daubert* as Vermont law]; and (3) the expert's testimony on the rate of false reporting improperly bolstered the credibility of the victim.

At the outset we point out that most of the evidence offered by the expert, not including that about the rate of false reporting, is of the type we have found admissible in State v. Catsam, 148 Vt. 366 (1987), and its progeny, with respect to child sexual abuse. *Catsam* involved expert evidence describing post-traumatic stress disorder suffered by child victims of sexual assault. We held such evidence was admissible to help the jury understand the evidence because "the unique psychological effects of sexual assault on children place the average juror at a disadvantage in understanding the behavior of the victim." *Catsam,* 148 Vt. at 369. We amplified on the theory of admissibility in State v. Gokey, 154 Vt. 129, 133–34 (1990):

> "Profile or syndrome evidence is evidence elicited from an expert that a person is a member of a class of persons who share a common physical, emotional, or mental condition. The condition must be one that is generally recognized in the field." Profile evidence is typically admitted in evidence to assist the jury in understanding "superficially bizarre behavior" of a putative victim, such as a child's ambiva-

> lence about pursuing a sexual abuse complaint, or a child's recantation of an earlier accusation. . . .

Once we ruled such evidence is admissible in *Catsam*, and followed with decisions defining the outside contours of admissibility, PTSD evidence involving child victims became admissible in the trial courts. Trial judges can take judicial notice of the admissibility of such evidence.

The admissibility standard continues despite the intervening issuance of the *Daubert* decision, and the adoption of its holding in . . . *Streich.* . . . Largely because we had adopted F.R.E. 702 as V.R.E. 702, we adopted the *Daubert* standard as our own.

We affirmed the admission of PTSD evidence in *Catsam* under V.R.E. 702 using a flexible standard of admissibility that is fully consistent with *Daubert*. Our emphasis in *Catsam* was on whether the expert evidence of PTSD, and related explanations of the typical behavior of child sexual assault victims, would "assist the trier of fact to understand the evidence." V.R.E. 702. We also drew on decisions from other states to show the evidence was reliable.

We recognize that *Daubert*, and the more recent decision in Kumho Tire Co. v. Carmichael, 526 U.S. 137 (1999), emphasized the gatekeeper function of the trial court to determine that . . . [expert opinion] evidence is sufficiently reliable and relevant before it is admissible. This is simply an example of the traditional role of the court to determine that evidence presented to the fact-finder is admissible, *see* V.R.E. 104, and the gatekeeper can perform this function in a number of ways. In many cases, like this one and *Catsam*, the issue is whether a certain category of evidence is admissible, often in particular types of cases that are recurring. In some cases, both the trial court and this Court can fully evaluate the reliability and relevance of the evidence generally based on the decisions of other appellate courts. In this way, we can avoid conducting our own lengthy and expensive evidentiary hearing aimed at establishing, or attacking, the foundation for the disputed expert testimony.

We are not suggesting that the new standard for admissibility has somehow become general acceptance among appellate courts. Irrespective of the decisions of other courts, the responsibility for determining the admissibility of evidence in Vermont courts remains with our trial judges, and on appeal with this Court. However, scientific or technical evidence which is novel to us is frequently not novel to many other state and federal courts. To the extent the evaluation of these courts is complete and persuasive, we can affirmatively rely upon it in reaching our own decision.

We have explained the application of *Daubert* in cases like *Catsam* because much of defendant's argument is that the trial court in this case failed to comply with the procedural requirements of *Daubert*—that is, that it failed to exercise its gatekeeping function by determining the reliability and relevance of Dr. Tyler's testimony based on foundational evidence presented to the court in this case. We acknowledge that we have never explicitly ruled upon the admissibility of evidence of rape trauma syndrome and the common behavior of adult rape victims, as we discuss below. Thus, the trial court was required to evaluate the admissibility of Dr. Tyler's testimony, beyond her qualifications to provide such testimony, and the result of this evaluation was not clearly dictated by a decision of this Court. This does not mean, however, that the State was obligated in this case to present independent evidence that Dr. Tyler's methodology could be tested, was subject to peer review and publication, had a known and measurable error rate, and was generally accepted in the relevant scientific community, the factors suggested in *Daubert*.[2] Nor was the trial court required to make findings on each of these factors. It could find the evidence admissible because its reliability equals that of other technical evidence we have given trial courts the discretion to admit and the evaluation of other courts allowing admission of the evidence is complete and persuasive. This is the analysis the trial court conducted, and we affirm its decision that Dr. Tyler's testimony was admissible, except for the testimony on the rate of false reporting.

We concur with the trial court that expert evidence of rape trauma syndrome and the associated typical behavior of adult rape victims is admissible to assist the jury in evaluating the evidence, and frequently to respond to defense claims that the victim's behavior after the alleged rape was inconsistent with the claim that the rape occurred. As with child sexual abuse victims, the jury may be at a loss to understand the behavior of a rape victim. For example, the defense made much of the fact that defendant's parents were close by when the sexual contact took place but heard no signs of a struggle, that the victim appeared to be sleeping peacefully in defendant's bed the next morning, and that she failed to immediately tell her boyfriend she had been raped. Dr. Tyler's testimony explained why a rape victim might exhibit these behaviors.

For the purpose the evidence was used here, it is sufficiently reliable to be admitted. Rape trauma syndrome is professionally recognized as a type of post-traumatic stress disorder, and the behavioral characteristics of rape victims [have] been the subject of numerous professional studies. As the trial court noted in this case, Dr. Tyler was prepared to address

2. We cite the *Daubert* factors as illustrative. As the Court stated in *Kumho Tire*, "*Daubert's* list of specific factors neither necessarily nor exclusively applies to all experts or in every case." We recognize that the State has urged us to hold that *Daubert* does not apply at all to psychological trauma syndrome evidence because it does not involve hard science capable of reliability testing by the scientific method. V.R.E. 702 applies, however, to "scientific, technical, or other specialized knowledge" and does not distinguish between those categories. *See Kumho Tire*.

The nature of the expert testimony may affect the factors to be examined bearing on reliability and relevancy; it does not change the need for such an inquiry where the scientific, technical or specialized knowledge is novel.

some of the studies that formed the bases for her opinions if the defendant raised them in cross-examination. We note that the evidence here was of a type that the danger of improper usage or excessive prejudice was at a minimum. The expert never interviewed the victim and offered no opinion whether the victim suffered from rape trauma syndrome or exhibited any of the behavior of a rape victim.[4] Thus, there was little risk that Dr. Tyler would be seen as a truth detector.

We do not, however, have the same view of the expert's testimony about the incidence of false reporting by rape victims. The prosecutor asked Dr. Tyler whether "there are any data on the issue of false reporting that you are aware of?" She answered:

> False reporting, the percentages are very low. About two percent. That's about the same as any other crime that's committed. In other words, the number of people who would report a burglary that didn't happen is about the same as people who would report a rape, with one difference. The statistics for the rape include those reports that are made and then either withdrawn by the victim for whatever reason, either they were false or there's a fear of going through the legal system, or they're being pressured by other persons. Those also include reports that the police will not arrest on because they don't feel they have enough evidence. And they also include those that don't get to trial because the prosecutor feels it's not a winnable case. So when you get down to literal false reporting of this really never happened, it's very small.

In short, Dr. Tyler testified that at least 98% of the rapes reported actually occurred....

[I]n *Catsam,* we found inadmissible an expert's opinion that child victims of sexual abuse do not make up stories of the abuse. As in this case, the evidence was offered as part of the expert's explanation of the typical behavior of victims. We concluded that the expert testimony was tantamount to an expert opinion that the victim was telling the truth and that it invaded the proper role of the jury.

4. In a twist, defendant suggests that Dr. Tyler's testimony was inadmissible because she did not address whether the victim suffered from the syndrome.... We reiterate the point of State v. Wetherbee, 156 Vt. 425, 433 (1991), that the opinions of experts who have examined the victim are much more likely to be seen as vouching for the victim's story than the opinions of experts who have never examined the victim.

Moreover, the common behaviors of rape victims are directly related to the rape trauma syndrome in the sense that the stress reaction creates a profile. This testimony has been the least controversial of the expert evidence related to rape trauma syndrome. Some courts and commentators have concluded that rape trauma syndrome evidence should be admissible solely for this purpose. *See* K.W. Gaines, *Rape Trauma Syndrome: Toward Proper Use in the Criminal Trial Context*, 20 AM. J. TRIAL ADVOC. 227, 251 (1997).

Dr. Tyler's testimony on the rate of false reporting clearly went over the line as explained in ... *Catsam*. The jury could infer from her testimony that scientific studies have shown that almost no woman falsely claims to have been raped and convict defendant on that basis.

[T]he evidence of the incidence of false reporting of rape accusations was inadmissible and prejudicial.... [Because the defendant made no specific objection to this testimony, however, and because the trial court did not commit "plain error" as defined by Vermont case law in admitting the evidence, the defendant's conviction is]

Affirmed.

William M. Grove & R. Christopher Barden

Protecting the Integrity of the Legal System: The Admissibility of Testimony from Mental Health Experts Under **Daubert/Kumho** *Analyses*

5 PSYCHOL. PUB. POL'Y & L. 224 (1999)

* * *

CONTROVERSIAL DIAGNOSES (PTSD AND MPD/DID)

We consider just two diagnoses here: PTSD [post-traumatic stress disorder] and MPD [multiple personality disorder], now called DID [dissociative identity disorder] in the *Diagnostic and Statistical Manual of Mental Disorders* (American Psychiatric Association, 4th ed. 1994) (*DSM–IV*). First, we note that PTSD and MPD are *labels*, not theories. This is a critical distinction—some experts have misled courts to believe falsely that the existence of a diagnostic label in *DSM–IV* somehow proves general acceptance of the existence of the described disorder as well as acceptance of proposed causal mechanisms for the etiology of such a disorder. This is a very serious error of logic and method. The *DSM–IV* is simply an agreed upon set of terms and descriptions—a catalog. It does not provide, and was not intended to provide, documentation of the general acceptance of the existence of disorders. Furthermore, the *DSM–IV* is not in any way documentation of general acceptance of the etiology (cause) of a disorder. To clarify with an example: The word *unicorn* is in the dictionary and we all agree on the concept and description of a unicorn, but this surely does not document the existence of unicorns.

DSM labels, considered only as labels, may not be generally accepted, even though they make it into the manual (just as the Volstead Act [the National Prohibition Act of 1919] stayed on the books years after public support for it had eroded). With regard to the *DSM*, the manual's cautionary statement describes the categories and criteria as a "consensus" position. However, this must not be understood to imply any general polling to establish consensus. Indeed, the manual's introductory explanation of the *DSM* revision process makes clear that no polling was involved. Instead, specialty subcommittee (e.g., there was a subcommittee on dissociative disorders) members were assigned to review aspects of the literature relating to certain categories.... Analyses of existing data sets were sometimes undertaken. These reviews were then critiqued by others, chosen by Task Force members. Subcommittees then voted for revised labels (or criteria), and the Task Force voted whether to accept a subcommittee's recommendation. This procedure is defensible, but it is not completely explicit, repeatable, or tied to polling representative samples of scientists.

P.R. McHugh explained the distinction between *DSM* category inclusion and category validation in a *Daubert* hearing:

Q: ... [I]s the fact that the term "dissociative amnesia" is found in the *DSM* any evidence at all of the scientific validity of the condition?

A: No, it's not. *DSM–IV* is an attempt to ... develop reliability among psychiatrists about what they are observing. It is not intended to say that they are claims for the existence of a particular condition as confirmed by its enclosure within *DSM–IV*. It's a question of reliability versus validity.*

Psychiatry is the only discipline that runs itself on a catalog, and the reason it did that was that back in the 19—late 1960s and early 1970s, it was discovered that they couldn't do much research in psychiatry because they couldn't get agreement on what they were observing, let alone what they were calling things. So a patient with a set of symptoms called schizophrenia in Baltimore was called manic depressive in London and demoralized in San Diego. It was the decision of the American Psychiatric Association and of the American psychiatric community that we should build a catalog of reliability, not of validity, so that we could do research. So that when we said these patients are showing these symptoms that we are going to call Dissociative Disorder or schizophrenia, we could have a common language. After that, we could discover whether they had, in fact, anything like dementia, or whether they were behaving in a particular way for other reasons. So when I'm saying this [*DSM*] is a book of reliability, I'm saying this gives you a code ... whereby you can describe people [who] you say will be given—

* [On the distinction between "reliability" and "validity," see note 9 of *Daubert*, at page 797.—GF]

> will satisfy the criteria in this book [*DSM*] for Dissociative Disorder, but whether Dissociative Disorder exists in itself is not proven or even claimed in this book [*DSM*].

In use, *DSM* diagnoses of MPD (or PTSD) generally are linked to accompanying theories of etiology: namely, that these psychological disorders are caused, in whole or in large part, by psychological trauma. In the case of PTSD, this includes a wide range of upsetting events; for MPD, the cause is purported to be early, severe (and almost always repressed) abuse, chiefly sexual abuse. The following *Daubert* features are related to admissibility for PTSD.

1. The concept of PTSD, simply as a diagnostic label, is testable in principle. However, to obtain a test placing such a diagnosis at risk of falsification, one would need a benchmark for accuracy. Because many, even most, forensic PTSD evaluations now use structured interviews and claim to adhere to *DSM* criteria, validity studies seldom have a benchmark better than the forensic diagnosis itself. . . .

Testing the theory that PTSD is caused by exposure to trauma is also possible: Compare people who have been exposed to an objectively verified, naturally occurring traumatic event with people who have not been exposed, and find out whether the traumatized group gets PTSD more often then the unexposed group does. (Ethical principles preclude a direct experimental test.)

2. Has the causal theory of PTSD been tested? Yes, but the tests have been weak because of ethical and practical problems. Tests to date have yielded variable, mostly weak confirmations demonstrating the unreliable nature of the concept. For example, McFarlane found that just 9% of individuals' symptoms could be accounted for by exposure to a disastrous fire, whereas Galante and Foa found no relationship between proximity to an earthquake and children's behavioral disturbances. By contrast, preexisting symptoms may predict as much as half of the variance in posttrauma symptoms. Only for those exposed to the severest, most prolonged traumas (e.g., prisoners of war) does the rate of PTSD rise to one-half or more. In a review of 45 studies Kendall–Tackett, Williams, and Finkelhor reported that abused children displayed more symptoms than nonabused children, with abuse accounting for 15% to 45% of the variance, but they did not analyze rates of PTSD diagnoses.

One might argue that if any PTSD-type symptoms are significantly associated with trauma, this makes PTSD testimony probative and hence admissible. However, this ignores the difference between scientific and legal concepts of causation. An expert usually has to testify as to whether a specific trauma was a "substantial factor" in creating the disorder, because causation in the "but for" sense is typically out of the question in trauma cases. As research shows that traumas usually account for only a minority of symptoms, an expert may have difficulty opining that a specific trauma is a substantial factor in causing symptoms. . . .

Psychological causation is seldom so straightforward. Correlational studies relating traumas to symptoms often show that third variables (such as other adversity, preexisting symptoms, or coping styles) can account for much of the apparent trauma-symptom connection. If this is so, then theories like "PTSD is caused by trauma" cannot be fairly characterized as having survived strong risks of falsification. In sum, the causal connection between trauma and PTSD appears too unreliable to survive a thorough *Daubert/Kumho* analysis.

3. Is the theory of PTSD generally accepted? The label is more controversial than some (e.g., mania) but less so than others (e.g., MPD). We believe that the syndrome is generally, but by no means universally, accepted.

However, as noted above, acceptance of the label need not imply acceptance of the causal theory. PTSD positively invites misunderstanding on this score; its diagnostic requirement of a trauma event invites experts to commit the *post hoc ergo prop[t]er hoc* fallacy, assuming that the trauma caused the PTSD. The very name *posttraumatic stress disorder* seems to imply what the criteria do not state, namely causality.

If we consider an analogy from the depressive disorders, the fallacy is clarified. If *DSM–IV* erected a "reactive depression" category, with diagnostic criteria requiring a negative life event plus certain depressive symptoms, would this justify the conclusion that the negative event caused the symptoms? Of course not. In fact, negative life events have little proven relation to depression and "neurotic" ailments.

4. What is the known or potential error rate of a PTSD diagnosis? A relevant error rate would seem to be the frequency with which a court would err, if it equated a PTSD diagnosis with proof of traumatic causation.... Because we do not know the true rate of trauma exposure suffered by plaintiffs, it is fair to say that the error rate is unknown. Such uncertain and potentially very high error rates clearly should not survive thorough *Daubert/Kumho* scrutiny.

5. A major problem with standards in diagnosing *DSM–IV* PTSD is the vagueness of its "A" criterion:

> The person has been exposed to a traumatic event in which both of the following were present: (1) the person experienced, witnessed, or was confronted with an event or events that involved actual or threatened death or serious injury, or a threat to the physical integrity of self or others; and (2) the person's response involved intense fear, helplessness, or horror.

The inclusion of the phrase "threat to the physical integrity of self or others" may allow a biased or careless "expert" to overdiagnose PTSD. Moreover, criterion A(2) is obviously quite subjective, as are most of the symptoms of PTSD.* Malingering these symptoms would not be difficult. Even though a PTSD diagnosis requires actual (not just claimed) trauma, it has been the authors' observation that many forensic clinicians do not even attempt to corroborate the trauma claim or make the PTSD diagnosis conditional on a court's determination of the accuracy of the trauma claim. This standards problem is especially striking given that, in many PTSD claims, it seems that the parties dispute all or part of the trauma claim. . . .

6. With regard to peer review, many studies of the relationship between trauma and psychiatric symptoms have been published in mainstream journals (e.g., *Archives of General Psychiatry*) as well as in specialty journals (e.g., *Journal of Traumatic Stress, Child Maltreatment,* and *Child Abuse and Neglect*). As mentioned above, however, many of these studies report only weak support for the trauma-illness connection. . . .

Summary and Recommendations

. . . In our view, experts have an affirmative ethical duty to refuse to give testimony that would not reasonably be expected to pass *Daubert/Kumho* scrutiny. This is true even if opposing counsel do not challenge its admissibility. In addition, experts have a similar duty to accurately report to judges and juries the kind of research we have summarized. This is true even if opposing counsel does not introduce such research. We say this because professionals are bound by their oath to tell the whole truth; trying to "slip one by" opposing counsel is hardly that. Moreover, unethical testimony inevitably brings the profession into disrepute. . . .

Case Notes on Syndrome Evidence

Perhaps predictably, some courts have attached far more significance to a syndrome's listing in the *Diagnostic and Statistical Manual of Mental Disorders* (4th ed. 1994), or *DSM–IV*, than Drs. Grove and Barden would approve. Other courts seem to have heeded the cautions voiced by Grove and Barden and other experts about the misuse of *DSM–IV* as an investigative manual. Compare these excerpts from rulings by the New Mexico and Louisiana Supreme Courts in cases alleging sexual conduct with minors:

* [In the fifth edition of the *Diagnostic and Statistical Manual of Mental Disorders*, to be known as DSM–5 and set for publication in May 2013, Criterion A (past exposure to traumatic events) reportedly will be more specifically put, and assessment of an individual's emotional response at the time (present criterion A2) will be abandoned.—GF]

State v. Alberico

116 N.M. 156, 173–76 (1993)

. . . *DSM III–R* [the predecessor to *DSM–IV*] is specialized literature that specifically catalogues the symptoms of mental disorders and prescribes the method by which the psychological evaluation should take place. *DSM III–R*, according to the State's experts, is widely used in courtrooms. . . . PTSD is generally accepted by psychologists and psychiatrists as a valid technique for evaluating patients with mental disorders. The existence of *DSM III–R* and its general acceptance in psychology indicate that PTSD has been exposed to objective scientific scrutiny and empirical verification.

Furthermore, the PTSD diagnosis appears to be grounded in basic behavioral psychology. *DSM III–R* accumulated the symptoms of mental disorders by examining human reactions to certain events or stimuli. The theory behind PTSD is that a severe traumatic experience impacts upon the human psyche and exhibits itself in certain identifiable symptoms that are linked to a specific stressor or cause. In evaluating an alleged victim of sexual abuse, the psychologist compares her symptoms with known reactions to sexual abuse and attempts to correlate the victim's symptoms with the known causes of behavioral patterns that have been categorized. . . .

. . . [S]everal jurisdictions that have disallowed PTSD testimony on the issue of whether sexual abuse occurred emphasized that psychologists could not pinpoint the cause of the PTSD although they could diagnose the symptoms. In the present cases, however, the experts testified that psychologists can isolate the cause of the symptoms because different stressors manifest themselves in different symptoms. . . .

All of the expert testimony in these two cases establishes that victims of sexual abuse may exhibit identifiable symptoms that have been catalogued in *DSM III–R*. . . . Thus, testimony regarding a complainant's PTSD symptoms has the tendency to show that she might have been sexually abused. . . .

. . . [B]ecause PTSD evidence is both valid and probative and because it is not unduly prejudicial, it is admissible for establishing whether the alleged victim exhibits symptoms of PTSD that are consistent with rape or sexual abuse. . . .

We hold that expert testimony concerning RTS [Rape Trauma Syndrome] is inadmissible mainly because it is not part of the specialized manual *DSM III–R* [as] PTSD is, even though there is evidence in the record that RTS is generally accepted by psychologists just [as] PTSD is. . . .

[*See also Chapman v. State*, 18 P.3d 1164, 1171–72 (Wyo. 2001) (quoting and relying on *Alberico* to establish the significance of the *DSM* listing in demonstrating the evidentiary reliability of testimony about PTSD).—GF]

State v. Chauvin

846 So. 2d 697, 706–08 (La. 2003)

. . . The State of Maryland's highest court has considered the issue of whether expert testimony that the alleged victim was suffering from PTSD as a result of being sexually abused was admissible to prove that the sexual abuse occurred. *See* Hutton v. State, 339 Md. 480 (1995). We find their analysis helpful and quote with approval their scholarly comments on this aspect of PTSD:

> PTSD may be experienced by persons who have been in combat, natural disasters, automobile or airplane accidents, or raped, among other traumatic events. Thus, there is no particular stressor that triggers PTSD; it can be caused by any number of stressful experiences. The symptoms characteristic of PTSD may become apparent shortly after the traumatic event or they may not appear until several months or even years later. [*DSM–III* at 237]. Moreover, determining from the symptoms that PTSD is the proper diagnosis ordinarily does not answer the question of what traumatic event caused it; the symptoms, in other words, are not reliable identifiers of the specific cause of the disorder. . . .

We are concerned about the use of PTSD evidence as substantive evidence that sexual abuse has occurred, when such evidence is not limited to explaining "superficially bizarre" reactions common to victims of child sexual abuse but which are uncommon to the experience of jurors. First, the psychiatric procedures used in developing the diagnosis of PTSD are designed for therapeutic purposes and are not reliable as fact-finding tools to determine whether sexual abuse has in fact occurred. And secondly, the potential for prejudice looms large because the jury may accord too much weight to expert opinions stating medical conclusions which were drawn from diagnostic methods having limited merit as fact-finding devices.

Although PTSD is widely accepted among professionals as an anxiety disorder attributable to some type of trauma, it has not been proven to be a reliable indicator that sexual abuse is the trauma underlying the disorder or that sexual abuse has even occurred. . . .

The *DSM–IV* adds the following general observation: "nonclinical decision makers should also be cautioned that a diagnosis does not carry any necessary implications regarding the causes of the individual's mental disorder or its associated impairments. . . ." *DSM–IV* at xxxiii. The psychiatric diagnosis of PTSD was not designed to determine sexual abuse, and the threshold criteria for the diagnosis of PTSD are not specific to child sexual abuse. Furthermore, there are a variety of stressors in a child's life that can produce PTSD-type symptoms, and there is no baseline data about the presence of PTSD-type symptoms in nonabused and otherwise nonstressed children. In short, there is not a sufficient consensus within the mental health community that there are certain behavioral symptoms that can lead a mental health professional to a conclusion of "consistent with child sexual abuse." . . .

. . . [W]e find expert testimony of PTSD is inadmissible for the purpose of substantively proving that sexual abuse occurred.

RTS and CSAAS

In *Kinney* the Vermont Supreme Court permitted evidence about rape trauma syndrome (if only for limited purposes), while in *Alberico* the New Mexico Supreme Court barred any reference to RTS. Other state courts differ on this question, as they do about whether testimony about Child Sexual Abuse Accommodation Syndrome (CSAAS) is admissible. As the Maryland Court of Appeals has written, in cases charging rape or child abuse "[t]he use of such terms may themselves be prejudicial." *Hutton v. State*, 339 Md. 480, 492 n.9 (1995) (citing similar holdings by other state courts). *See also* D. Michael Risinger, *Navigating Expert Reliability: Are Criminal Standards of Certainty Being Left on the Dock?* 64 ALB. L. REV. 99, 118–19 (2000) (canvassing cases). Testimony about post-traumatic stress disorder (PTSD) has proved far less controversial.

Problem 9.17

Separation Violence

On December 11, 1996, Green River Police officers found Keri Ryan shot to death in her home. Her estranged husband, Roy Dale Ryan, was charged with her murder. Ryan denied any involvement. Consider the facts as reported by the Wyoming Supreme Court:

> Ryan and Keri had a turbulent marriage punctuated by Ryan's physical abuse of his wife. . . . [T]he State produced witnesses who stated that Ryan controlled and isolated Keri. Ryan would not allow Keri to go anywhere without his permission, and he demanded to know where she was and who she was with at all times. . . . Ryan called [Keri] at work ten times or more during her shifts to check up on her. . . . Ryan had attempted to commit suicide in Keri's presence. . . . [He] emotionally abused Keri through constant criticism. . . . He often accused Keri of having extramarital affairs with the customers she spoke with at work. . . .

Keri left Ryan in early November of 1996 and had a family violence protection order issued against Ryan on November 5, 1996.... During the separation period, Keri expressed her desire to return to school; she began dating another man and suggested that Ryan begin dating other women. For his part, Ryan did not handle the separation well. He became depressed and had noticeable weight loss....

[The state called Rosemary Bratton as an expert witness.] Bratton has extensive experience working with both battered and battering spouses and has previously testified as an expert on the subject of Battered Woman Syndrome (BWS). BWS experts generally attempt to explain the ... behavior of battered spouses, such as seeking withdrawal of a protective order or continually returning to an abusive spouse....

At trial, Bratton began by explaining the now familiar characteristics of BWS to the jury. She explained the cyclical pattern of violence often present in abusive relationships and then went on to describe a phenomen[on] termed "separation violence":

> *Q.* Now, is there any particular phase of this cycle of violence which tends to be more dangerous than another?
>
> *A.* Yes. And we actually term it now as separation violence.... [T]he time that the victim is planning to leave or has left this relationship is the time of the greatest danger. That's the time more homicides are committed, ... and it happens because perpetrators of domestic violence who need to maintain power and control over their partner become extremely upset ... when they feel that they are losing that control.... [I]t becomes far more dangerous for the victim, because the violence will escalate to whatever it takes to prevent this person from actually leaving....

Bratton added that the majority of the women involved in [a study she described] were killed with guns. She ... testified that batterers tend to control and isolate their spouses by such means as constant calls to their place of employment, demanding to know where they are, who they are with, and when they will return; ... [they] often threaten to commit suicide in order to force their partner to remain in the relationship; ... [they] abuse their spouses emotionally through constant criticism; ... [and they] exhibit pathological jealousy often accusing their spouses of having adulterous affairs with random strangers.

The prosecutor argued, and the district court agreed, that separation violence is a logical extension of BWS....

Ryan v. State, 988 P.2d 46 (Wyo. 1999). Should the trial judge have admitted Bratton's testimony over Ryan's objection? Is this case just like *Kinney*?

---

6. ASSESSING THE RELIABILITY OF THE FORENSIC SCIENCES

THE FATE OF THE FORENSIC SCIENCES

The old *Frye* test had proved especially flimsy when deployed to govern admission of the several forms of forensic expertise. In such realms as handwriting analysis, fingerprint identification, fiber analysis, and ballistics, the relevant scientific community consisted largely or entirely of the cadre of courtroom practitioners of the questioned technique. Depending for their bread on the challenged field of study, these practitioners hardly rushed to lock the gates against admission of junk forensics. Professor Jennifer Mnookin made the point with pith:

> We would hardly expect polygraph examiners to be the most objective or critical observers of the polygraph, or those who practice hair identification to argue that the science was insufficiently reliable. When there is [a] challenge to the fundamental reliability of a technique through which the practitioners make their living, there is good reason to be especially dubious about "general acceptance" as a proxy for reliability.

"*Daubert*, then, made it imaginable," Mnookin concluded, "that courts would revisit a long-accepted technique that was clearly generally accepted by the community of practitioners." Jennifer L. Mnookin, *Fingerprint Evidence in an Age of DNA Profiling*, 67 BROOK. L. REV. 13, 63 (2001).

*The Early Post–*Daubert *Years*

In *Daubert*'s first years prosecutors and other advocates often sought to elude its seemingly stringent regime by insisting that a challenged forensic science was not a "science" at all. Recall Chief Justice Rehnquist's pointed question: "Does all of this *dicta* apply to an expert seeking to testify on the basis of 'technical or other specialized knowledge'—the other types of expert knowledge to which Rule 702 applies—or are the 'general observations' limited only to 'scientific knowledge'?" (Page 802.) Justice Blackmun's opinion for the Court left the question unaddressed. Purveyors of doubtful techniques, as Professor Michael Saks has written in the context of handwriting identification, exploited this uncertainty to duck all but the barest quality control:

> [M]ost of the post–*Daubert* decisions by federal courts considering the admissibility of the long-asserted scientific expertise of handwriting identification followed this reasoning: Forensic handwriting examination flunks the *Daubert* test. Because it flunks *Daubert*, it is not science. Because it is not science, it need not pass the *Daubert* test. A much looser "test" of soundness applies. Under this test, it is admissible.

The irony, Saks argued, is that an asserted expertise "that has been more casually developed and is less readily shown to be dependable (and probably is less dependable) was admitted with far less scrutiny than expertise from fields that have passed the more rigorous muster of the scientific method." So practitioners of the "weakest fields, [those] with the most tenuous commitment to real science, offered to recategorize [their fields] as nonsciences. They discovered that the easiest way to remain expert witnesses in a post–*Daubert* world was to admit—indeed, to insist—that they are not the science they long pretended to be." Michael J. Saks, *The Aftermath of* Daubert: *An Evolving Jurisprudence of Expert Evidence*, 40 Jurimetrics J. 229, 237 (2000).

Here Professor Saks wrote from firsthand knowledge, for he took a star turn in an early post–*Daubert* case concerning handwriting analysis. A prominent federal conspiracy prosecution, *United States v. Starzecpyzel*, 880 F. Supp. 1027 (S.D.N.Y. 1995), turned on the genuineness of two signatures the government alleged were forged. In a bid to exclude the government's forensic document examiner (FDE), who was to testify about the genuineness of the signatures, the defendants argued that the "alleged expertise [of forensic document examination] has never been validated as credible scientific or technical knowledge and does not comport with the requirements of evidentiary reliability articulated by the Supreme Court in *Daubert*." At a pretrial *Daubert* hearing held to determine the reliability of the FDE's expert methods, the government presented the vice president of the American Board of Forensic Document Examiners. The defendants presented a professor of exercise science and Professor Saks, whose field is law and psychology.

The trial judge's ruling took precisely the form that prompted Professor Saks's ire. The judge began by noting that the defendants had prevailed on points:

> The *Daubert* hearing established that forensic document examination, which clothes itself with the trappings of science, does not rest on carefully articulated postulates, does not employ rigorous methodology, and has not convincingly documented the accuracy of its deter-

> minations. The Court might well have concluded that forensic document examination constitutes precisely the sort of junk science that *Daubert* addressed.

Id. at 1028. The judge acknowledged moreover that he "originally considered *Daubert* to be controlling as to the admissibility of the forensic testimony at issue. . . ." And yet, having all but declared the government's proposed expert a hawker of junk science, the court handed the government victory:

> [T]he Court now concludes that *Daubert,* which focuses on the "junk science" problem, is largely irrelevant to the challenged testimony. . . . FDE expertise is not properly characterized as scientific, but as practical in character. In a nutshell, over a period of years, FDEs gradually acquire the skill of identifying similarities and differences between groups of handwriting exemplars. The Court therefore treats forensic document expertise under the "technical, or other specialized knowledge" branch of Rule 702, which is apparently not governed by *Daubert.*

And if *Daubert* did not apply, there was no reason to demand of FDEs that they "articulate and justify the theoretical bases underlying their practice, . . . expose their techniques to a larger community of practitioners through peer-reviewed publication, or . . . subject those techniques to extensive testing." *Id.* at 1028–29.

As forensic document examination survived challenge precisely because it is *not* a science, the trial judge aimed to demystify the discipline for the jury. He worried that although "FDE expertise is purely practical in nature, jurors might well view FDEs as experimental *scientists,* placing more weight on their testimony than was justified by the government's showing at the *Daubert* hearing." *Id.* at 1048 (emphasis added). This risk that the jury would regard too highly the expert's discipline and the certainty of his conclusions was a form of unfair prejudice policed by Rule 403. Hence "the jury will be instructed, in advance of any forensic document testimony [and again at the close of the trial], that FDEs offer practical, rather than scientific expertise," so their skill "does not have the demonstrable certainty that some sciences have." The judge also reserved the option at trial to forbid the government's FDE to use a numerical scale smacking of science to describe his confidence in his conclusions. *Id.* at 1049–50. And the court voiced its belief that jurors' ability "to perform the crucial visual comparisons relied upon by handwriting experts [would cut] against the danger of undue prejudice from the mystique attached to 'experts.' " *Id.* at 1044 (internal quote marks omitted). Able to examine for themselves both the challenged signatures and signatures known to be genuine, jurors were unlikely to be gulled by an expert asking them to disbelieve their own eyes.

Kumho Tire: *Game Change?*

Kumho Tire's shift in the legal ground rules soon made fossils of *Starzecpyzel* and cases like it. If all realms of expertise, whether sciences or not, must meet Rule 702's "standard of evidentiary reliability" and must have "a valid . . . connection to the pertinent inquiry" (page 851), forensic experts no longer could shield their fields from *Daubert*–style scrutiny by denying their status as sciences. For Professor Saks the ruling was heartening. "Perhaps the best reason for extending *Daubert* beyond 'sciences,'" he wrote, is that "[m]any fields, perhaps most notably the forensic identification sciences, will do whatever it takes to satisfy the courts and little more." These fields no longer would be "excuse[d] . . . from testing the validity of their claims." Saks, 40 JURIMETRICS at 240–41.

Yet the enduring lesson of *Starzecpyzel* is how deftly many forensic sciences have dodged the sort of close judicial scrutiny to which *Daubert* subjects classically scientific fields. Despite occasional flashes of judicial mettle, most forensic fields have evaded the extensive self-testing that Professor Saks sought. As in *Starzecpyzel* they have done so in part by being no less precise than they promise and by making their methods transparent to jurors. That jurors can look over experts' shoulders and assess for themselves the soundness of their methods continues to set judges at ease.

To see this dynamic at work, let's turn from handwriting expertise to fingerprint identification. In the early years after *Daubert* and again after *Kumho Tire*, the defense bar launched a raft of challenges to what many once viewed as forensic science's gold standard. Although almost all such challenges to the reliability of fingerprint identification failed, one found a fleeting sunray of success. Early in 2002 U.S. District Judge Louis H. Pollak ruled that while fingerprint identification experts are free to highlight the various similarities between the defendant's known fingerprints and the crime-scene prints, those experts may not opine that the suspected prints are in fact the defendant's. For this purpose, Judge Pollak held, fingerprint identification failed to satisfy the usual *Daubert* factors.

The difficulty did not turn on whether a person's fingerprints are unique or typically remain unchanged through life—both facts Judge Pollak deemed true "beyond reasonable dispute." *United States v. Llera Plaza*, 188 F. Supp. 2d 549, 551 (E.D. Pa. 2002) (summarizing earlier rulings). The difficulty instead was the widely used ACE–V technique of fingerprint examination, a four-step process consisting of analysis, comparison, and evaluation followed by verification by a second examiner. Measured against the standard *Daubert* factors, the ACE–V technique fell short. Only with regard to general acceptance did Judge Pollak pronounce himself satisfied, and then only "marginally" so. That was not enough to save the ACE–V technique. Having failed four of five *Daubert* factors, it could not support the conclusion that the questioned prints were the defendant's.

Predictably "delight[ing] defense lawyers and alarm[ing] law enforcement officials," Pollak's ruling did not last long. Andy Newman, *Judge Who Ruled Out Matching Fingerprints Changes His Mind,* N.Y. TIMES, Mar. 14, 2002, at A27. Barely two months later he reversed himself after experts from the FBI and Scotland Yard testified at length at a *Daubert* hearing held on the government's motion to reconsider. This time Judge Pollak emphasized *Kumho Tire*'s counsel that "the test of reliability is 'flexible,' and *Daubert*'s list of specific factors neither necessarily nor exclusively applies to all experts or in every case." 188 F. Supp. at 562. His strategy, however, was not to abandon the five *Daubert* factors, but to apply them forgivingly wherever fingerprint examination with the ACE–V technique came up short.

Despite earlier reservations on the question of peer review, Judge Pollak now declared his doubts resolved. He allowed that "fingerprint specialists are not 'scientists,' and hence ... the forensic journals in which their writings on fingerprint identification appear are not 'scientific' journals in *Daubert*'s peer review sense...." But the nature of the journals, he said, does not make fingerprint identification less reliable. Nor did he discount general acceptance just because the community of fingerprint examiners who accepted the ACE–V technique lacked " 'scientific ... knowledge,' and hence [were] not what *Daubert* termed a 'scientific community.' "

On the matter of standards, Judge Pollak and the experts met each other halfway. For its part the FBI, which conducted the fingerprint examinations at issue, presented impressive testimony of its tough qualification demands. Certification as an FBI fingerprint examiner required a bachelor's degree, two years of in-house training, a three-day certification exam, and annual proficiency tests. *See id.* at 555–56 & n.2. For his part Judge Pollak dropped his earlier complaint that the FBI's standards for claiming a fingerprint "match" had no numerical component. In his earlier opinion he had highlighted the British standard, which demanded sixteen points of similarity, termed Galton points, to declare a match between a crime-scene print and a suspect's known print. The Australian standard required twelve Galton points, though the Canadian system imposed no numerical minimum. The FBI's standard, which likewise imposed no minimum, fell well behind the leaders, prompting Pollak to rule it could not satisfy *Daubert*'s standards factor. *See id.* at 555 (reviewing earlier ruling). In his later ruling, however, he reported that the British standard had changed and now imposed no numerical minimum. Finding more company in the FBI's camp, he ruled that the Bureau's protocol met *Daubert*'s grade. *See id.* at 568–70.

Having yielded on standards, Pollak likewise papered over problems in the FBI's testing regimen for fingerprint examiners. He did not dispute a former Scotland Yard examiner's testimony that the FBI's proficiency tests, which generated an error rate of less than one percent, were absurdly simple. "[I]f I gave my experts these tests," the examiner said, "they'd fall about laughing." *Id.* at 556–57. "I concluded in [my earlier] opinion that *Daubert*'s testing factor was not met," Pollak wrote, "and I have found no reason to depart from that conclusion." Yet he added that "the defense witnesses offered not a syllable to suggest that certified FBI fingerprint examiners . . . have not achieved at least an *acceptable* level of competence." *Id.* at 564–65. And with that lukewarm endorsement, he abandoned his concerns regarding testing.

Finally as to error rate, Judge Pollak found himself bound by his complacency concerning tests. Absent good tests, fingerprint examiners could not generate meaningful error rates. Pollak therefore avoided the question, noting only that he had found "no evidence that the error rate of certified FBI fingerprint examiners is unacceptably high." *Id.* at 566.

In the end Judge Pollak relented and permitted FBI examiners to opine that the crime-scene prints matched the defendant's. In this he was remarkable only in first having ruled that fingerprint identification, when used to declare a match between a crime-scene print and a suspect's known print, could not satisfy *Daubert*'s standards. When this contrarian burst faded and Pollak fell in line with the FBI's experts, he took his place alongside almost every judge in the country, for fingerprint identification almost always has survived challenge. The rare exceptions to this judicial complacency, such as two trial court rulings in New Hampshire and Maryland, have faced an unfriendly reception in other courts. The New Hampshire Supreme Court slapped down the wayward trial court in that state. And the Maryland trial court's ruling that ACE–V is "subjective, untested, [and] unverifiable" did not merit even a citation when a Maryland appellate court ruled the next year that "[g]iven the longstanding consensus that fingerprint evidence is reliable . . . and the lack of any reported decision holding that the ACE–V method is unreliable," trial judges may take judicial notice of ACE–V's reliability. *See Markham v. State*, 189 Md. App. 140, 159–60, 163 (2009); *State v. Langill*, 157 N.H. 77, 88–90 (2008); *State v. Rose*, 2008 WL 2914326 (Md. Cir. Ct. 2008). Nor did the Maryland trial court persuade a U.S. District Court that later ruled on the same question in a case arising from the same facts. The federal judge concluded that "the ACE–V methodology is generally accepted in the relevant scientific community, has a very low incidence of erroneous misidentifications, and is sufficiently reliable to be admissible under Fed. R. Evid. 702 generally and specifically in this case." *United States v. Rose*, 672 F. Supp. 2d 723, 726 (D. Md. 2009).

The National Academy of Sciences Report

In 2005, prompted in part by a spate of convict exonerations, Congress commissioned the National Academy of Sciences (NAS) to undertake a study of the state of the forensic sciences in America. The task fell to a Committee on Identifying the Needs of the Forensic Sciences Community, cochaired by Judge Harry T. Edwards of the U.S. Court of Appeals for the D.C. Circuit and Constantine Gatsonis, a Brown University biostatistics professor. Years in the making, the committee's 300–page report appeared with some fanfare in 2009. *See* NATIONAL ACADEMY OF SCIENCES, STRENGTHENING FORENSIC SCIENCE IN THE UNITED STATES: A PATH FORWARD (2009) ("NAS Report").*

Sweeping across the forensic landscape, the NAS Report scrutinized more than a dozen forensic fields, from nuclear DNA analysis at one end of the reliability spectrum to such imprecise methods as bite mark and tire tread analysis at the other. The report aimed to tackle the "law's greatest dilemma"—whether and to what extent "there is *science* in any given forensic science discipline." *Id.* at 8. With the prominent exception of nuclear DNA analysis, which won praise for its scientific methods and the precision of its results, the forensic "sciences" largely proved unworthy of that label. *See id.* at 41.

Though the identified shortcomings varied from field to field, several criticisms recurred throughout:

- the field lacked a formal, standardized training program for its practitioners;
- practitioners often lacked an understanding of the scientific principles that underlay their work;
- testing facilities lacked accreditation and often were operated by law-enforcement agencies;
- no standardized protocols governed investigative tests;
- nor did standardized criteria guide analysis of results; and
- judges and lawyers often lacked the scientific training needed to evaluate the reliability of the resulting evidence.

Taken together, these factors almost ensured that analysis, interpretation, and conclusion would devolve into highly subjective enterprises. A corollary of subjectivity was the risk of biased results, which analysts could shape to suit the interests of their employers, their clients, or allied agencies. That risk was especially great because "[t]he majority of forensic science laboratories are administered by law enforcement agencies, such as police departments, where the laboratory administrator reports to the head of the agency." *Id.* at 183.

Nuclear DNA analysis emerged in the Academy's report as the "preeminent" forensic science, "the standard against which many other forensic ... techniques are judged." Its practitioners could boast that their procedures were scientifically rooted, backed by sound numerical

* My thanks to Mark Menzies, one of my research assistants, who assembled the background materials on the National Academy's report and tracked its reception in the courts.

data, and guided by widely known protocols for declaring a "match." True, DNA labs "can make errors ... such as mislabeling samples ... or misinterpreting the data." But "absent fraud or an error in labeling or handling, the probabilities of a false positive are quantifiable and often miniscule." And the results of DNA analysis can be reproduced by others in the field and by the opposing party's experts. *See id.* at 100–01, 114–15, 130 (detailing the FBI's Quality Assurance Standards for Forensic DNA Testing Laboratories).

Fingerprint identification, perhaps the most accurate of the remaining identification sciences, fell far short. Although the FBI's protocols had proved demanding enough to satisfy Judge Pollak, procedures in place in many state and local agencies did not meet the FBI's grade—nor did the FBI's protocols satisfy the NAS. Again the problem was not the premise that a person's fingerprints are unique. Like Judge Pollak, the NAS allowed that "[s]ome scientific evidence supports the presumption that friction ridge [i.e., fingerprint] patterns are unique to each person and persist unchanged throughout a lifetime." *Id.* at 43, 143–44. Instead the difficulties were the lack of objective criteria for finding a match and the poor quality of many latent (crime-scene) prints.

At least the first of these problems should prove soluble. The NAS complained that

> [t]he fingerprint community continues to assert that the ability to see latent print detail is an acquired skill attained only through repeated exposure to friction ridge impressions. In their view, a lengthy apprenticeship (typically two years, at the FBI Laboratory) with an experienced latent print examiner enables a new examiner to develop a sense of the rarity of features and groups of features....

"Clearly," the Academy countered, "the reliability of the ACE–V process could be improved if specific measurement criteria were defined." Without such objective criteria, ACE–V "does not guarantee that two analysts following it will obtain the same results." But those criteria cannot consist of a mere count of Galton points: "A simple point count is insufficient for characterizing the detail present in a latent print; more nuanced criteria are needed...." Though the Academy did not suggest what those criteria might be, it insisted they "likely can be determined." *Id.* at 140–42.

The second obstacle to more certain conclusions—the poor quality of many crime-scene prints—surely is not the fault of fingerprint analysts. But the Academy faulted fingerprint analysts for speaking with certainty on the basis of uncertain data. Here it quoted Professor Mnookin's condemnation of the practice:

> [F]ingerprint examiners typically testify in the language of absolute certainty. Both the conceptual foundations and the professional norms of latent fingerprinting prohibit experts from testifying to identification unless they believe themselves certain that they have

> made a correct match. Experts therefore make only what they term 'positive' or 'absolute' identifications—essentially making the claim that they have matched the latent print to the one and only person in the entire world whose fingertip could have produced it ... Given the general lack of validity testing for fingerprinting; the relative dearth of difficult proficiency tests; the lack of a statistically valid model of fingerprinting; and the lack of validated standards for declaring a match, such claims of absolute, certain confidence in identification are unjustified....

"Therefore, in order to pass scrutiny under *Daubert*," Mnookin concluded, "fingerprint identification experts should exhibit a greater degree of epistemological humility." *Id.* at 142 (quoting Jennifer L. Mnookin, *The Validity of Latent Fingerprint Identification: Confessions of a Fingerprinting Moderate*, 7 LAW, PROBABILITY & RISK 127, 139 (2008).) As we will see shortly, many courts have proved ready to demand epistemological humility—and to forbid experts to overstate the certainty of their conclusions.

Response in the Courts

Even before release of the Academy's report, rumors of its harsh evaluation of forensic practices had prompted optimistic observers to predict corrective judgments in the courts. In its first, pre-publication account of the report, the *New York Times* quoted an anonymous source with access to the text: "I'm sure that every defense attorney in the country is waiting for this report to come out. There are going to be challenges to fingerprints and firearms evidence and the general lack of empirical grounding. It's going to be big." Solomon Moore, *Science Found Wanting in Nation's Crime Labs*, N.Y. TIMES, Feb. 5, 2009, at A1. Barry Scheck, cofounder of the Innocence Project, announced, "This is a major turning point in the history of forensic science in America." Jason Felch & Mara Dolan, *The Science Behind Many Courtroom Claims About Forensic Evidence Is Lacking, a National Panel Says*, L.A. TIMES, Feb. 19, 2009, at A9.

Within months the NAS Report secured a space in the annals of evidence law when Justice Scalia spotlighted its findings to support his opinion for the Court in *Melendez-Diaz v. Massachusetts*, 557 U.S. 305, 318–21 (2009) (pages 646, 648–49 above). The Justices ruled that admission of an absent state lab chemist's report against a criminal defendant violated his confrontation right. Answering the prosecution's argument that reports of "neutral scientific testing" will prove reliable, Justice Scalia quoted the Academy's concern that many lab analysts are employed by the state and therefore " 'sometimes face pressure to sacrifice appropriate methodology for the sake of expediency.' " *Id.* at 318 (quoting NAS Report, *supra*, at 23–24).

Today, with the benefit of a few years' hindsight, it appears the report's influence on admission of forensic testimony in the nation's courtrooms may be slim. Many courts have cited the NAS Report when ruling on the admissibility of an analyst's testimony, and some have discussed the report at length. *See, e.g., United States v. Aman*, 748 F. Supp. 2d 531, 540 (E.D. Va. 2010); *United States v. Love*, 2011 WL 2173644 (S.D.

Cal. 2011), at 10–11, 13, 22, 28; *United States v. Rose, supra*, 672 F. Supp. 2d at 725–26. Yet one finds few prominent courts acting to exclude forensic expertise because of the Academy's criticisms or for any other reason. Instead, when faced with a challenge to the admissibility of forensic evidence, courts have nodded to the insights of the NAS Report—and especially to its worry that experts speak with certainty even when describing inherently uncertain results—and then have justified admission of the questioned evidence.

Let us focus on one such ruling, a case in which Professor Mnookin took the witness stand and channeled the Academy's criticisms, many of which she had voiced for years. In *United States v. Council*, 777 F. Supp. 2d 1006 (E.D. Va. 2011), the trial court weighed the defendant's motion in limine to exclude the testimony of the government's latent print examiner, a forensic scientist with the Virginia Department of Forensic Sciences (VDFS), who stood ready to say that a latent palm print on a discarded gun tied the gun to the defendant. At a *Daubert* hearing on the defendant's motion the examiner testified that she had compared the latent print with the defendant's known palm print and had found "no unexplainable differences" and "several points in common." A second VDFS latent print examiner testified that she had verified the first examiner's work by comparing the latent print with the defendant's known print. She found between seventeen and twenty points of comparison.

The defendant then presented Professor Mnookin, who testified as an expert in the scientific foundations of print analysis. She characterized the ACE–V technique not as a scientific method, but as a mere exercise in " 'careful looking.' " Largely unbound by objective criteria, ACE–V "relies almost entirely on the experience and intuition of the examiner." Nor have studies "shown that ACE–V is consistently successful or demonstrated its error rate." *Id.* at 1010 (quoting or paraphrasing Mnookin's testimony). In these ways, the court noted, "Dr. Mnookin's criticisms of ACE–V's scientific validity track the conclusions offered by the [NAS] report." *Id.*

Yet with seemingly little hesitation, the court concluded that "in light of *Daubert*'s recommended considerations," the ACE–V technique "is sufficiently reliable to permit a jury to hear testimony on it." Quickly the court turned aside Professor Mnookin's criticisms. Resisting her suggestion that ACE–V gave free rein to examiners' subjective judgments, the court replied without specifics that the examiner's "subjective judgments were cordoned off by objective standards shared by virtually the entire community of friction ridge analysts." And replying to Mnookin's assessment of ACE–V as an exercise in "careful looking," the court wrote that this description "unfairly suggests that a layperson not subject to those standards could effectively perform the same task." *Id.* at 1012. The court made no mention of Professor Mnookin's testimony that "absolutely, examiners do have expertise in looking closely at similarities and differences" and "can clearly do that with more expertise than lay people."

When the court turned to the several *Daubert* factors, it followed Judge Pollak's lead in his second ruling in *Llera Plaza* and applied those factors with a notably light hand. This complacency showed starkly when the court addressed testing. Though the judge began with the frank admission that this factor was "least helpful in establishing the reliability of [the examiner's] testimony under rule 702," he then grabbed a branch held out by a decision of the Tenth Circuit Court of Appeals. For a hundred years, the Tenth Circuit had written, fingerprint analysis " 'has been subject to testing . . . in the world of criminal investigation, court proceedings, and other practical applications, such as identification of victims of disasters.' " *Id.* at 1013 (quoting *United States v. Baines*, 573 F.3d 979, 990 (10th Cir. 2009)). Such "testing," however, tells us little about the accuracy of fingerprint analysis unless we already know the "correct" answer. Criminal courts look to fingerprint examiners for answers and cannot check those answers against some hidden answer key revealing the perpetrator's true identity. In the words of a critic quoted in the NAS Report, the "silly statement" that fingerprinting has been "tested by the adversarial process over the last one-hundred years" shows how incomprehensible courts find the prospect of excluding fingerprint evidence. The very idea has "stilled their critical faculties." 1 D. L. FAIGMAN ET AL., MODERN SCIENTIFIC EVIDENCE: THE LAW AND SCIENCE OF EXPERT TESTIMONY § 1:1, at 4 (2007–2008), *quoted in* NAS Report, *supra*, at 103. Maligned as it may have been among scholars, the *Council* court's treatment of testing inspired imitation in other courts. *See, e.g.*, *United States v. Gutierrez–Castro*, 805 F. Supp. 2d 1218, 1232 (D.N.M. 2011).

The *Council* court likewise forgave the absence of peer review and publication supporting ACE–V's reliability because in the "verification" stage of the ACE–V technique, a second print examiner from the Virginia Department of Forensic Sciences had reviewed the work of the first. *See Council*, 777 F. Supp. 2d at 1012. Though the court emphasized that the second review was "blind" in the sense that the second examiner did not know the results reached by the first, verification by an employee of the same state agency hardly seems to meet the *Daubert* Court's image of "submission to the scrutiny of the scientific community." (Page 799.)

The court's ruling with regard to error rate, the third *Daubert* factor, seems on somewhat firmer ground. Even "harsh critics . . . suggest an error rate of three percent," the court wrote, deeming this figure "within the boundary of acceptability for purposes of admission under Rule 702." *Id.* at 1013. Indeed most evidence of print analysis suggests that the rate of false positives—the most troubling sort of error because it carries the risk of wrongful accusation and conviction—is well less than one percent in ideal testing-room conditions. *See United States v. Love, supra*, at 13–14 (reviewing studies); *United States v. Rose, supra*, 672 F. Supp. 2d at 726 (same). Though crime-scene error rates may be higher, the *Council* court ruled they were not so high as to justify exclusion and should go merely to the weight of the examiners' testimony and not to its admissibility.

To their credit both VDFS examiners testified at the *Daubert* hearing "that friction ridge analysis was susceptible to some error rate, since it is possible for a human examiner to misapply ACE–V." *Council*, 777 F. Supp. 2d at 1013. That is, neither examiner made the claim that so troubled the authors of the NAS Report—that the ACE–V technique had a zero error rate, a claim the report deemed "not scientifically plausible." It is true that the NAS study found that ACE–V *itself* was flawed—"[t]he method, and the performance of those who use it, are inextricably linked, and both involve multiple sources of error. . . ." NAS Report, *supra*, at 143. But in admitting the risk of human error, the VDFS examiners gave more ground than had others before them. And having made that admission at the *Daubert* hearing, the examiners could be held to it at trial. *Council*, 777 F. Supp. 2d at 1013.

Advancing to standards, the fourth *Daubert* factor, the court wrote dismissively that "*Daubert* requires trial judges to ensure that [the fingerprint] examination was reliable. *Daubert* does not, however, demand of expert testimony 'such an extremely high degree of intellectual purity' that an underlying procedure must be 'truly scientific in an intellectual, abstract sense' in order to be admitted." *Id.* at 1012 (quoting *Baines, supra*, 573 F.3d at 989).

Having construed narrowly *Daubert*'s notion of standards, the court then construed very broadly the relevant community in which to seek general acceptance, sweeping in not only Professor Mnookin herself but countless *non-expert* law-enforcement officials. The court began with the obvious proposition that ACE–V is generally accepted among fingerprint examiners. "But even widening the circle to include commentators such as Dr. Mnookin and the members of the committee that drafted the [NAS] report barely changes the balance of opinion. Adding those commentators to the equation does not outweigh the acceptance friction ridge analysis has gained from numerous forensic experts and law enforcement officials across the country." *Council*, 777 F. Supp. 2d at 1011.

At every turn, then, the *Council* court chipped at *Daubert*'s already rounded corners and reached the same result endorsed by almost every other judge facing the question: the NAS Report notwithstanding, evidence of fingerprint matching is admissible. As was true in the days before the NAS Report, the few courts that have excluded or sharply constrained testimony of fingerprint examiners stand out from the norm. Hence when a Miami–Dade trial judge recently reserved the right at trial to bar an examiner from testifying that a latent print "matched" the defendant's, the decision proved newsworthy. *See State v. Borrego*, Nos. F12–101, F12–7083 (Fla. Cir. Ct. Oct. 25, 2012); David Ovalle, *Miami–Dade Judge Rules Fingerprint Evidence Should be Restricted*, MIAMI HERALD, Oct. 28, 2012, *available at* http://www.miamiherald.com/2012/10/28/3071658/miami-dade-judge-rules-fingerprint.html.*

* I thank Professor Joelle Moreno, who pointed me to this case.

A U.S. District Judge in New Mexico likewise raised eyebrows when he ruled that "[t]he United States may not [offer its fingerprint examiner] as an expert witness in the jury's presence, the Court will not certify [him] as an expert witness in the jury's presence, and the jury instructions will not refer to [him] as an expert witness." The judge did not wish to "put its imprimatur on him as an expert witness in the jury's presence." *United States v. Gutierrez–Castro*, 805 F. Supp. 2d at 1235. The judge's reticence had the endorsement of both the advisory committee and the ABA. In its Note to the 2000 amendment to Rule 702, the advisory committee had written that "there is much to be said for a practice that prohibits the use of the term 'expert' by both the parties and the court at trial. Such a practice 'ensures that trial courts do not inadvertently put their stamp of authority' on a witness's opinion, and protects against the jury's being 'overwhelmed by the so-called "experts."' " (ACN to 2000 Amendment to FRE 702, RB 175 (quoting Hon. Charles Richey, *Proposals to Eliminate the Prejudicial Effect of the Use of the Word "Expert" Under the Federal Rules of Evidence in Criminal and Civil Jury Trials*, 154 F.R.D. 537, 559 (1994)).) And in February 2012 the ABA House of Delegates adopted a resolution urging judges and advocates "to consider . . . [w]hether the court should prohibit the parties from tendering witnesses as experts and should refrain from declaring witnesses to be experts in the presence of the jury." ABA Criminal Justice Section, Report No. 101C (Feb. 6, 2012) (as revised).

But perhaps the most common restriction courts have placed on fingerprint examiners in the wake of the NAS Report is to bar them from claiming a zero error rate. As U.S. District Judge Catherine C. Blake observed in 2009, "[a]ny claim of a 'zero' error rate for fingerprint identification that does not acknowledge the possibility of examiner error would be misguided." *United States v. Rose, supra*, 672 F. Supp. at 726. And there is reason to think that few fingerprint examiners will dare venture out on this limb. In the aftermath of the NAS Report, even the Scientific Working Group on Friction Ridge Analysis, Study and Technology (SWGFAST), composed largely of fingerprint specialists from local, state, and federal law-enforcement agencies, rejected claims of a zero error rate as "not scientifically plausible." SWGFAST Position Statement (Aug. 3, 2009). A 2012 report of the National Institute of Standards and Technology (NIST) likewise declared that testimony tracing a latent print to one and only one person is "needlessly strong, not yet adequately supported by fundamental research, and impossible to validate solely on the basis of experience." National Institutes of Justice, *Latent Print Examination and*

Human Factors: Improving the Practice Through a Systems Approach (Feb. 2012); *see* Gabriel A. Fuentes, *Toward a More Critical Application of* Daubert *in Criminal Cases: Fingerprint Opinion Testimony After the National Academy of Sciences Report*, 92 CRIM. L. REP. 135 (2012) (collecting sources).

Recall in this light the trial judge's ruling in *United States v. Starzecpyzel*: he reserved the option to forbid the government's forensic document examiner to use a numerical scale to describe his confidence in his conclusions. Of the many troublesome aspects of forensic expertise, trial judges have proved most willing to condemn claims of certainty when describing inherently uncertain results.

A Glance at Other Forensic Sciences

As harsh as the NAS Report was in its assessment of ACE–V and the state of research on fingerprint identification, it proved even less forgiving of hair and fiber analysis. With seeming approval the authors noted that some courts "have recognized that testimony linking microscopic hair analysis with particular defendants is highly unreliable." When hair samples yield DNA, identification can be highly precise, but "microscopic studies alone are of limited probative value." The authors "found no scientific support for the use of hair comparisons for individualization in the absence of nuclear DNA." They cited an FBI study of eighty hair comparisons "associated" through microscopic examination. DNA testing later proved that nine of them—or 12.5 percent—came from different sources. NAS Report, *supra*, at 161. Because analysis of fibers other than hair can employ analytical chemistry to discern one strand from another, some comparisons can achieve greater precision. Still, fiber analysts agree that neither microscopic nor chemical analysis "is suitable for individualizing fibers (associating a fiber from a crime scene with one, and only one, source) and that fiber evidence can be used only to associate a given fiber with a class of fibers." *Id.* at 161.

The lesser reliability of hair and fiber analysis has not prevented courts from admitting such evidence. Typically, however, courts have not permitted analysts to testify to a "match" between a questioned fiber and an individual source, but only to a "class association." In the NAS Report's words, experts may say "only that the hair could have come from any person whose hair exhibited—within some level of measurement uncertainties—the same microscopic characteristics, but [the hair] cannot uniquely identify one person." NAS Report, *supra*, at 156. Experts therefore often hedge their testimony with such phrases as "is consistent with" and "could have the same source as."

Consider for example the reasoning of the Eleventh Circuit Court of Appeals in *United States v. Barnes*, 88 Fed. R. Evid. Serv. 1018 (11th Cir. 2012) (unpublished). Charged with bank robbery, the defendant had sought to exclude three government experts—one concerning boot prints, another concerning hairs and fibers, and a third concerning adhesives. The boot print expert was prepared to say that prints left at the bank "corresponded to" the boots the defendant was wearing when caught later the same day—that is, they were the same size and bore matching patterns and wear marks. But the expert admitted he could not link them "definitively, 100 percent." The hair analyst offered to testify that hairs found on a fake beard linked with the crime "were consistent with" those found on the backseat of a patrol car that transported the defendant after his arrest. But she admitted that hair is "not a means of positive identification to one individual to the exclusion of all others." And the adhesive expert would testify that she had analyzed a black, latex-like substance found in both the front seat of the getaway car and in the backseat of the patrol car and had determined on both visual examination and chemical analysis that they were "physically consistent" and "comparable . . . in chemical composition" to "the black material on the fake beard." But because the adhesive was common rubber cement, or polyisoprene, she allowed that she could not say all the samples came from the same source. *Id.* at [9–16].

Having lost both his pretrial motions to exclude the experts' testimony and the trial that followed, the defendant argued on appeal that the experts' opinions should have been excluded as unreliable because they "r[an] afoul of the scientific requirement of at least some degree of quantification." The Eleventh Circuit held, however, that there was no such requirement. Because the "experts did not express probabilistic or quantitative opinions"—they did not say "how likely it was" that the boot prints or hairs or adhesive came from the same source—the government had no need to present quantifiable data in support. *Id.* at [22–26].

In a second bank robbery case that also involved hair analysis, the Sixth Circuit showed similar deference toward an expert who claimed no more precision than his technique could offer. This time the hair came from a makeshift ski mask worn by one of the robbers. And this time the technique in question was mitochondrial DNA (mtDNA) analysis. Analysis of the DNA found in the mitochondria outside a cell's nucleus cannot deliver the astronomical, one-in–390–quadrillion precision achieved by nuclear DNA analysis. Because only one's mother contributes to mtDNA, there is far less variation among offspring. Still, mtDNA testing is particularly useful in hair analysis because nuclear DNA, although present in living hair roots, is absent from hair shafts, where mtDNA is plentiful. *See United States v. Beverly*, 369 F.3d 516, 528–29 (6th Cir.), *cert. denied*, 543 U.S. 910 (2004); NAS Report, *supra*, at 131 (describing mtDNA testing).

The defendant argued that the risk that the jury would attribute the precision of nuclear DNA analysis to the mtDNA evidence in his case was a form of unfair prejudice justifying exclusion under Rule 403. The appeals court disagreed, as the government's expert had "made clear to the jury that this type of evidence could not identify individuals with the precision of conventional DNA analysis." Yet the technique is plenty precise to be probative. "The statistical evidence at trial showed that, at most, less than 1% of the population would be expected to have this mtDNA pattern." *Id.* at 531.

Consider finally firearms analysis, an identification technique based on the distinctive marks that firing hammers and spiraled gun barrels leave on shells and bullets when a shot is fired. *See* NAS Report, *supra,* at 150–55. Here again the NAS Report warned that an analyst's judgment "remains a subjective decision based on unarticulated standards and no statistical foundation for estimation of error rates." Moreover, the " 'uniqueness and reproducibility of firearms-related toolmarks [have] not yet been fully demonstrated.' " Nor will we cross this threshold soon. "A significant amount of research would be needed to scientifically determine the degree to which firearms-related toolmarks are unique or even to quantitatively characterize the probability of uniqueness." *Id.* at 153–54 (quoting NATIONAL RESEARCH COUNCIL, BALLISTIC IMAGING 3 (2008)).

The most prominent protocol guiding firearms analysis hardly instills confidence in the reliability of results. The Association of Firearm and Tool Mark Examiners (AFTE) advises practitioners to declare an identification only "when the unique surface contours of two toolmarks"—say the marks on a crime-scene bullet and on a test-fired bullet—"are in 'sufficient agreement.' " As a guiding standard in a critical forensic science, "sufficient agreement" is badly wanting in precision. And it remains imprecise even after the AFTE Theory of Identification adds, "Agreement is significant when it exceeds the best agreement demonstrated between toolmarks known to have been produced by different tools and is consistent with agreement demonstrated by toolmarks known to have been produced by the same tool." *United States v. Taylor,* 663 F. Supp. 2d 1170, 1177 (D.N.M. 2009) (quoting AFTE Theory) (internal quote marks deleted); NAS Report, *supra,* at 153.

Courts' response to this imprecision has *not* been to exclude testimony by firearms experts. Rather, as with handwriting examiners, fingerprint examiners, and hair and fiber examiners, courts have acknowledged the inadequacies of the discipline as amplified by the NAS Report's critique. Then, emphasizing the subjective and hence imprecise results generated by the experts' technique, courts have required that these shortcomings be made known to the jury and have permitted the experts to testify with that caveat.

Hence in *United States v. Taylor, supra,* the court launched its analysis with a withering review of AFTE's guidance:

> The AFTE Theory, thus, does not provide any uniform numerical standard examiners can use to determine whether or not there is a match.... Instead, the AFTE theory is circular. An examiner may make an identification when there is sufficient agreement, and sufficient agreement is defined as enough agreement for an identification.

Taylor, 663 F. Supp. 2d at 1177. "The conclusion that there is a match between a recovered bullet and a particular gun," the court continued, "is, therefore, necessarily a subjective one, 'held in the mind's eye of the examiner and . . . based largely on training and experience in observing the difference between known matching and known non-matching impression toolmarks.' " *Id.* (quoting Richard Grzybowski et al., *Firearm/Toolmark Identification: Passing the Reliability Test Under Federal and State Evidentiary Standards*, 35 AFTE J. 209, 213 (2003)).

The consequence of the court's cutting review of firearms identification evidence was not exclusion. Rather the court deemed the evidence admissible, but carefully hedged what the examiner could say:

> [The examiner] will be permitted to give to the jury his expert opinion that there is a match between [a recovered rifle] and the bullet believed to have killed [the victim]. However, . . . [the examiner] will not be permitted to testify that his methodology allows him to reach this conclusion as a matter of scientific certainty. [He] also will not be allowed to testify that he can conclude that there is a match to the exclusion . . . of all other guns. He may only testify that, in his opinion, the bullet came from the suspect rifle to within a reasonable degree of certainty in the firearms examination field.

Taylor, 663 F. Supp. 2d at 1180. Likewise, in *United States v. Cerna*, 2010 WL 3448528 (N.D. Cal. 2010), the court rejected the defendants' motion in limine to exclude testimony by the government's firearms examiners. At the same time the court limited the certainty with which those experts could express evidence of a "match" to a "reasonable degree of certainty in the ballistics field." *Id.* at 4–5, 14–15.

Not all courts have regarded firearms analysis as warily as the *Taylor* and *Cerna* courts. In *United States v. Otero*, 849 F. Supp. 2d 425 (D.N.J. 2012), the government supplied studies showing the rate of false positives among trained firearms examiners hovered between 0.9 percent and 1.0 percent, and a government witness put the rate at around one or two percent. As the firearms examiner challenged by the defendants proposed to testify of "such a positive identification of the guns recovered from Defendants as the origin of the bullet and shells recovered from the crime scene," the rate of false positives was the critical figure. *Id.* at 433–34.

Acknowledging the authority of the NAS Report, the *Otero* court allowed "that the toolmark identification procedures discussed in this Opinion do indeed involve some degree of subjective analysis and reliance upon the expertise and experience of the examiner. The Court further recognizes, as did the [NAS Report], that claims for absolute certainty as to identifications made by practitioners in this area may well be somewhat overblown." But *Daubert* does not charge trial courts with "determining whether or not the procedures utilized are sufficient to satisfy scientists that the expert opinions are virtually infallible." Rather the court must do "a flexible reliability analysis and leave questions about the strength of evidence to the jury." Without specific qualification, therefore, the court permitted the government's examiner to testify that the guns recovered from the defendants were the source of the crime-scene bullets and shells. *Id.* at 438.

A Last Thought

Over and over throughout this unit a similar plotline has unfolded: Defendants have challenged a claimed forensic "science" as unreliable under *Daubert* and *Kumho Tire.* Courts have recognized widely the discipline's shortcomings and the imprecision of its results. Then they have admitted the evidence anyway as long as the government and its experts do not advertise it as better than it is.

When the shortcomings of the questioned techniques are apparent to jurors—and especially when jurors can look at the challenged evidence and assess it themselves—courts express confidence that jurors won't be gulled into giving an expert's opinion more weight than it warrants. Recall the confidence of the trial judge in *United States v. Starzecpyzel,* 880 F. Supp. 1027 (S.D.N.Y. 1995), when admitting evidence of handwriting identification. Jurors' ability "to perform the crucial visual comparisons relied upon by handwriting experts [cuts] against the danger of undue prejudice from the mystique attached to 'experts.'" *Id.* at 1044 (internal quote marks omitted). When assisted by magnified courtroom images, jurors can review for themselves almost all of the evidence discussed in this unit—handwriting, fingerprints, hairs and fibers, boot prints, and bullet markings. Untrained visual inspection will not, however, assist jurors in interpreting polygraph or DNA data. So it is maybe unsurprising that courts typically have excluded polygraph results and have held DNA evidence to the strict standards of a true science.

The overarching lesson of the forensic sciences, then, is that evidence must be as good as it purports to be. That is likewise the lesson of Rule 901 and our study of authentication, which we take up next.

CHAPTER 10

Authentication, Identification, and the "Best Evidence Rule"

A. Authentication and Identification

Focus on FRE 901 & 902

Introduction

The problem of authentication, often knotty in its details, reduces at bottom to a simple question: Is this exhibit what its proponent says it is? The question takes on different meanings depending on the nature of the exhibit and the proponent's purpose in offering it.

In a typical cocaine possession case, proper authentication demands proof that a nondescript package of white powder offered by the prosecution is the same package seized from the defendant and later shown by chemical analysis to contain cocaine. In a case alleging threats sent by mail, authentication normally requires evidence that the defendant wrote the threatening letter. If the threats instead were made by phone, authentication will turn on proof that the voice at the other end of the line was the defendant's. And authentication of a photograph or videotape demands evidence that the photo or tape accurately depicts the thing or events it is offered to prove.

Each of these authentication recipes omits one important detail: By what standard must the proponent prove that the exhibit is what she says it is? Rule 901(a) declares that "[t]o satisfy the requirement of authenticating or identifying an item of evidence, the proponent must produce *evidence sufficient to support a finding* that the item is what the proponent claims it is." (Emphasis added.) The rule therefore embraces the same standard applied by Rule 104(b) when the relevance of a piece of evidence turns on some other condition of fact. Rule 901(a)'s echo of Rule 104(b) is no accident—authentication is in fact a matter of conditional relevance. Evidence of white powder, even if proved to contain cocaine, has no relevance absent evidence the defendant once possessed it. And evidence of a call or letter, no matter how threatening, normally has no relevance absent evidence the defendant authored the threat.

The Supreme Court's elaboration of Rule 104(b)'s standard in *Huddleston v. United States*, 485 U.S. 681, 688 (1988), presumably applies in this context as well. Hence proper authentication demands that the proponent produce sufficient evidence that "the jury could reasonably find . . . by a preponderance of the evidence" that the exhibit is what its proponent claims. *See Huddleston* at page 205, above.

The balance of this unit develops the various techniques by which a litigant might satisfy this standard. Rule 901(b) supplies a helpful list of authentication techniques that "satisfy[y] the requirement" of the rule. The rule writers emphasize that they offer this list as "examples only" and not to limit the litigant's options. A lawyer therefore may crib together an authentication technique from several of the examples given in Rule 901(b). Or she may ignore that list altogether and strike out on her own. No matter what tack she takes, at the end of the day the question will be whether she has offered "sufficient [evidence] to support a finding" that the evidence is what she says it is.

Meeting that standard does not ensure admission of the evidence. Even after the proponent properly authenticates a document, the opponent may claim it contains hearsay or improper opinion evidence or risks unfair prejudice. And even after the court admits the challenged evidence, the opponent remains free to contest authenticity before the jury, and the jury remains free to reject the exhibit as a fraud.

Note that Rule 902 designates several categories of documents as "self-authenticating." The rule rests on the theory that when a document meets the conditions of one of these categories, "practical considerations reduce the possibility of unauthenticity to a very small dimension." (ACN to FRE 902, RB 298.) Newspapers, addressed in Rule 902(6), are a good example. Because it is hard to mimic a newspaper's familiar appearance and easy for others to detect forgeries simply by comparing the fake with one of many genuine copies, the risk of an inauthentic newspaper is vanishingly small. Newspapers and other self-authenticating documents are therefore admitted as "prima facie genuine." (ACN to FRE 901, RB 291.) Still, the advisory committee took pains to note that "[i]n no instance is the opposite party foreclosed from disputing authenticity." (ACN to FRE 902, RB 298.)

Proof of Chain of Custody

Rule 901(b)'s list of authentication techniques proves most helpful when seeking to authenticate documents or phone calls. The next two cases, *United States v. Stelmokas* and *State v. Small*, apply the principles of the rule in those two contexts. Then, in *Simms v. Dixon* and *Wagner v.*

State, we turn to authentication of photographs and videotapes, a topic that has been left largely to common law rulemaking.

But we begin with a subject that falls in a category of its own: proving the chain of custody of physical evidence. Authentication generally poses little difficulty when an exhibit is unique on its face. Guns, for example, often bear a unique serial number. To prove that a gun presented in court is the same gun a police officer took from the defendant's glove compartment and the same gun a ballistics expert determined to be the murder weapon, a prosecutor often can rely simply on the weapon's serial number. If the police officer made a record of the number at the time he seized the gun and if the ballistics expert made such a record at the time she tested it, the serial number normally suffices for authentication.

Authenticating a small packet of white powder, on the other hand, can challenge a litigant's creativity and industry. Such packets are endlessly common and monotonously alike. How can a prosecutor prove *this* packet is the same packet the police seized from the defendant and a chemist determined to contain cocaine?

By far the most common authentication technique for drugs or other fungible evidence is proof of "chain of custody." The notion is simple: Proof of a "perfect" chain of custody requires testimony by each person who had custody of the item from the moment it was seized from the defendant until its delivery to the courtroom. In *United States v. Collado*, 957 F.2d 38, 39 (1st Cir. 1992), the First Circuit summarized the prosecution's evidence:

> Providence Police officer Michael Wheeler saw Collado drop the bag and directed Officer Venditto to seize it. Venditto took the evidence to the police station, completed a seizure report, and turned the evidence over to the Special Investigations Bureau ("SIB"). . . .
>
> . . . Detective Purro, the SIB officer responsible for processing drug evidence, testified to the standard operating procedure for depositing seized drugs at the police station between midnight and 8:00 a.m. when the SIB office is closed. The procedure required that Venditto deposit the evidence in a "mail slot" leading into a locked safe, fill out the seizure report, and place the report on top of the SIB safe. Detective Purro further testified that at 9:00 a.m. the following morning, he found Venditto's seizure report on top of the SIB safe, opened the safe, and retrieved a clear plastic bag whose contents precisely matched those described in Venditto's testimony as having been seized from appellant. Other testimony established an uninterrupted chain of custody, commencing with Purro's retrieval of the evidence from the SIB safe and concluding with its presentation at trial. There was no indication that the proffered evidence had been altered in any way.

As you already know, however, a chain of custody need not be perfect. The final arbiter of authentication is Rule 901(a), and it demands only that the chain of custody be good enough "to support a finding that the item is what the proponent claims it is." The absence of one or more of the exhibit's custodians will not always—or even usually—keep out the evidence. As Mueller and Kirkpatrick write, "Although serious gaps may raise enough doubt to require exclusion, a break in the chain is not necessarily fatal to admissibility. . . ." MUELLER & KIRKPATRICK, EVIDENCE § 9.5, at 1092 (5th ed. 2012). The usual slogan is that as long as the chain is strong enough to satisfy Rule 901(a), any defect goes to weight, not admissibility.

Normally a chain of custody is good enough if it supports a finding that the item in question is the *same item* and is in *substantially the same condition*. The first requirement—that of sameness—is obvious enough. The significance of the item's condition will vary from one sort of evidence to another and from case to case. With a packet of white powder, it is critical to know that nobody added anything to the packet between its seizure from the defendant and the chemist's determination that it contains cocaine. Hence proof of chain of custody must be sufficient to support a finding that no such tampering took place.

In the case of a gun, in contrast, the significance of condition may be far less. If the prosecution alleges only that the defendant brandished the gun in the course of a robbery, and if proof of the crime requires only that the defendant have displayed something that looked like a gun, it matters little whether the exhibit has been kept tamper-proof. On the other hand, if the prosecution's case turns on evidence that the gun was fired at the time of the crime, maintaining the gun's condition may be critical, as gunpowder residue can be wiped away or—by firing the gun—added.

In the end, the judge must decide case by case whether the chain of custody is sufficiently complete to satisfy Rule 901(a)'s standard in the context at hand.

---

1. DOCUMENTS

Problem 10.1
"To Send Money"

In *United States v. Vigneau*, 187 F.3d 70 (1st Cir. 1999), *cert. denied*, 528 U.S. 1172 (2000), which we took up in Chapter 7 (see page 556), the appeals court ruled that evidence of Western Union "To Send Money" forms used to transmit funds cross-country was wrongly admitted against Patrick Vigneau. Whoever filled out the forms had identified the "sender" of the money as Vigneau. The court held that this statement was hearsay and that the trial court was wrong to admit this information under the business records exception to the hearsay rule. But the appeals court added:

> . . . Whoever wrote the name "Patrick Vigneau" on the "To Send Money" forms was stating in substance: "I am Patrick Vigneau and this is my address and telephone number." Of course, if there were independent evidence that the writer was Patrick Vigneau, the statements would constitute party-opponent admissions and would fall within an exception to the rule against hearsay, Fed. R. Evid. 801(d)(2)[(A)]. . . . However, the government [lacked such independent evidence].

One of the government's difficulties in *Vigneau* was that most of the "To Send Money" forms no longer survived—at trial the government offered Western Union's computer records of the destroyed forms instead. Assume that the forms in fact survived and were secured from Western Union by the government. By what means could prosecutors authenticate the forms as having been filled out by Vigneau himself? (Several answers are available.)

Problem 10.2

Handwriting Opinion

Samet and Hollender were charged in March 2001 with participating in a racketeering enterprise in violation of the Racketeer Influenced and Corrupt Organizations Act (RICO). The government alleged that over the years the enterprise had engaged in many fraudulent schemes and money laundering. At trial the prosecutor sought to introduce a number of documents used to advance those schemes.

To authenticate certain documents as written by Hollender, the prosecutor called as a witness U.S. Postal Inspector Patricia Thornton. The appeals court summarized Thornton's trial testimony:

> . . . Thornton became involved with the investigation of Samet and Hollender in June 1999, and, with the exception of a five-month hiatus, spent eighty percent of her time over the next three years on the case. She testified that, during that time, she became familiar with Hollender's handwriting by viewing documents such as his passport, driver's license,

> post-arrest documents, and a check register for an account in his name. She offered her lay opinion that certain signature and handwriting samples shown to her at trial were written by Hollender. . . .
>
> . . . [O]n direct examination she was able to identify at least twenty-one samples as having been written by Hollender. . . . [O]n cross examination, she identified an additional sample of Hollender's handwriting, and two more on redirect.

Hollender challenged admission of the documents shown to Thornton, arguing they were not sufficiently authenticated as written by him. What were Hollender's best arguments? What were the government's best arguments in response? How should the trial court have ruled? *See United States v. Samet*, 466 F.3d 251, 254–57 (2d Cir. 2006).

UNITED STATES v. STELMOKAS

100 F.3d 302 (3d Cir. 1996), *cert. denied*, 520 U.S. 1242 (1997).

■ GREENBERG, CIRCUIT JUDGE. . . . Defendant Jonas Stelmokas appeals from a final judgment entered August 2, 1995, . . . revoking Stelmokas's citizenship and ordering him to surrender his certificate of naturalization. . . .

In its complaint, the government alleged that Stelmokas was born in Moscow, Russia, and resided in Lithuania commencing in 1930. . . . The complaint [further] alleged that in June 1941 the armed forces of Nazi Germany occupied Lithuania, which occupation continued until August 1944. During the occupation, the Germans organized armed Lithuanian units known as Schutzmannschaft. . . . The Lithuanian Schutzmannschaft in Kaunas assisted the Germans in confining and murdering Jews. The government contended that Stelmokas was a voluntary member and officer of the Schutzmannschaft and advocated, assisted, participated, and acquiesced in the murder and persecution of Jews and other unarmed civilians in Lithuania. Around August 1944, at the time the German occupation of Lithuania ended, Stelmokas entered the German Air Force (Luftwaffe) in the 91st Light Flak Replacement Unit.

The complaint further alleged that in July 1949 Stelmokas sought a determination from the United States Displaced Persons Commission ("DPC") that he was a displaced person as defined in the Displaced Persons Act of 1948 and therefore was eligible to immigrate to the United States. In connection with his application, a DPC analyst interviewed Stelmokas. He did not inform the analyst that he had served in the Schutzmannschaft or the Luftwaffe. Rather, Stelmokas falsely claimed that he had been a teacher in Seda, Lithuania, from July 1940 until

August 1943. He claimed that he then was unemployed in Kaunas until July 1944, and was a laborer in Dresden, Germany, from 1944 until March 1945. The complaint alleged that in 1949 the DPC regarded the Schutzmannschaft to be "inimical" to the United States, meaning it was a hostile movement.

The complaint further stated that, in reliance on Stelmokas's misrepresentations, the DPC analyst concluded that Stelmokas was eligible for displaced person status, and that the DPC so certified him on July 8, 1949. . . .

The [district] court conducted a bench trial from February 27, 1995, until March 3, 1995. . . . [T]he government . . . called four witnesses, two experts on the Holocaust, Dr. Raul Hilberg and Michael MacQueen, and two survivors of the Holocaust in Lithuania, David Levine and Abe Malnik. . . . The court pointed out that Hilberg was a particularly credible witness with a remarkable knowledge of the documents placed into evidence.

The court noted that many of the documents in evidence had been stored in the archives of the former Soviet Union. While Stelmokas argued that the documents were not trustworthy, the court rejected this contention because Hilberg's and MacQueen's testimony established that they were authentic. Indeed, Hilberg testified that he was not aware of a single World War II Soviet Union archival document that was a forgery. The court concluded that the government "amply established the authenticity and trustworthiness of the documents in evidence." . . .

. . . The court found that on July 28, 1941, Stelmokas voluntarily enlisted in the Schutzmannschaft and was appointed platoon commander in the 7th Company. The court traced Stelmokas's various assignments in the Schutzmannschaft, a process made possible by the meticulous record keeping of the Schutzmannschaft units, which court opinions demonstrate was consistent with the Germans' practice during World War II of recording their murderous conduct in specific detail. By August 30, 1944, Stelmokas had been transferred to Germany, where he served in the 91st Light Flak Replacement Unit of the Luftwaffe. The records in evidence show that Stelmokas was in a military hospital in Germany on February 12, 1945.

The court found that on September 15, 1941, Stelmokas was a guard commander at Vilijampole, which was the ghetto in Kaunas. The evidence showed clearly, unequivocally, and convincingly, that Stelmokas served as the commander of the ghetto guard for at least a 24–hour period commencing on September 16, 1941, at 1:00 p.m., and, accordingly, that he participated in confining the Jews to an area in which they were regularly subjected to extreme deprivation, brutality, and arbitrary shootings. The court then found, through a painstaking analysis of the Schutzmannschaft records, that Stelmokas's battalion took part in the Grosse Aktion of October 28 and October 29, 1941, which involved the murder of precisely 9,200 Jews, and that Stelmokas was on duty at that time. Levine and Malnik, who were children in the ghetto at the time, supported the documentary evidence with eye-witness testimony. While Levine and Malnik did not identify Stelmokas, both testified that armed Lithuanians took part in the murders. . . .

II. DISCUSSION

. . . Stelmokas focuses his objection on two groups of documents, principally those recovered from the records of the Lithuanian Schutzmannschaft that were located at Vilnius, the Lithuanian capital, and secondarily those recovered from German records found at other locations. While Stelmokas recognizes that Germans or Lithuanians purportedly wrote the Schutzmannschaft documents, he observes that the Vilnius documents were kept from public inspection by the Soviet Union until 1990. Though he also acknowledges that the government did not have to demonstrate a strict chain of custody for the documents to be admitted, in his view the documents cannot be treated as authentic because it is unclear how they were moved to the Vilnius archives. Thus, he argues that the documents were not found in a place where, if authentic, they "would likely be" as set forth in Fed. R. Evid. 901(b)(8).

Stelmokas further argues that the documents are suspicious because the Germans destroyed many documents demonstrating their criminal conduct, but "preserved evidence of Lithuanian misconduct." Furthermore, he regards the documents as questionable because they came from Soviet sources, and he claims that it was Soviet policy to discredit the Baltic states. Finally, he argues, though with less particularity, that the government did not establish the chain of custody and authenticity of the second group of documents, i.e., those from German sources.

. . . [Unrestyled] Federal Rule of Evidence 901(a) provides that the requirement of "authentication . . . as a condition precedent to admissibility is satisfied by evidence sufficient to support a finding that the matter in question is what its proponent claims." Rule 901(a) is written, of course, in general terms, but is followed by Rule 901(b) which includes examples of methods by which to authenticate evidence. Rule 901(b)(8) provides that authentication of an ancient document may be supplied by a demonstration that a document is in such condition as to create no suspicion concerning its authenticity, was in a place where, if authentic, it likely would be, and has been in existence 20 years or more at the time it is offered. Ancient documents are admissible into evidence as an exception to the hearsay rule. [*See* FRE 803(16).]

. . . Initially, we observe that Stelmokas's argument in part is self-defeating because his contention that the Germans destroyed documents demonstrating their own criminal conduct, but preserved documents incriminating the Lithuanians, supports rather than undermines the district court's conclusions that the documents incriminating him were legitimate. Furthermore, the documents were certified by competent Lithuanian archival personnel. Hilberg, who has testified in many cases regarding eastern European Holocaust records and whose expertise cannot be doubted, testified that the documents he examined were authentic and that the documents found in Soviet possession are as reliable as documents from western countries. He said that he found the documents to be reliable and not to be forgeries. He also testified that one would expect to find documents relating to the Lithuanian Schutzmannschaft in Vilnius, the Lithuanian capital.

MacQueen testified that he personally searched archives in Lithuania and that the documents he found were authentic and reliable. In particular, he had found Schutzmannschaft records implicating Stelmokas in Vilnius, which is where they were likely to be found. Stelmokas simply has not produced any evidence or forwarded any reason to impeach the validity of the documents.

We also point out that German records demonstrate that while Stelmokas was in the Luftwaffe, he was hospitalized in Germany. We cannot conceive that any rational person would believe that someone set out to incriminate Stelmokas and planted fake documents in widely scattered places for that purpose. If anyone created the documents to injure Stelmokas, the fabricator most peculiarly placed the bulk of the documents in a location where they were not accessible to the public and from which, in fact, they were not released for decades. There certainly is no evidence in the record that anyone hatched such a bizarre plot. Indeed, Stelmokas does not explain what motivation any person would have had to fabricate documents so as to attribute responsibility to him for the atrocities in Lithuania or how that could have been accomplished. Stelmokas was hardly a prominent figure in the war and it is difficult to conceive why someone would go to the lengths he suggests in order to frame him. Stelmokas's attack on the authenticity of the documents is not substantial....

III. CONCLUSION

After a careful examination of this matter, we have concluded that the district court made no errors of law and that the record fully supports and, in fact, compels the district court's conclusion that Stelmokas did not qualify for admission to this country as a displaced person. Thus the district court correctly revoked his citizenship and ordered him to surrender his certificate of naturalization. While many years have passed since his admission to the country and his obtaining of citizenship, it is not too late to remedy the wrong done when he was admitted. Accordingly, we will affirm the judgment of August 2, 1995.

■ STAPLETON, J., concurring....

■ ALDISERT, CIRCUIT JUDGE dissenting....

Problem 10.3

Anonymous Note

Consider the facts of *United States v. Mitchell*, 145 F.3d 572, 574–75 (3d Cir. 1998):

> [B]etween 9:00 a.m. and 9:15 a.m. on September 12, 1991, two men waited in a check cashing store . . . when an armored truck made a delivery of currency to the store. The assailants . . . attacked the delivery man as he entered the store, robbing him of currency in excess of $20,000. The two men fled the scene in a beige car driven by a third person. . . .
>
> At 10:00 a.m., . . . police officers found the beige [getaway car, which had been abandoned]. . . . A search by FBI agents recovered . . . [an anonymous note] from the front seat. . . . [The note] stated: "Light green ZPJ–254. They changed cars; this is the other car." A check on the light green car [with license plate number ZPJ–254] revealed that it was a green 1978 Buick registered to Anita Young, then fiancée and later wife of defendant Mitchell.
>
> That afternoon, an FBI agent . . . observed Mitchell park the green Buick and enter Young's house. He exited shortly thereafter and drove away, with the agent following him. When the agent had grounds for a stop because of traffic violations, he searched Mitchell who was carrying $1,400 dollars in small bills. . . .

At Mitchell's trial, the prosecutor sought to admit the note found on the seat of the beige getaway car. Her theory was that a bystander saw the robbers switch cars and, hoping to help the police catch the robbers without becoming involved in the case, left the anonymous note. Assume that a fingerprint expert, handwriting expert, and chemist all testified that they examined the note and discovered no means of identifying who wrote it. On the defendant's objection that the note was insufficiently authenticated, how should the court have ruled? (Please ignore any objection the defendant might have raised under the hearsay rule or Confrontation Clause.)

2. Phone Calls

Problem 10.4
"Star 69"

Consider these (slightly modified) facts of *Pounds v. State*, 1994 WL 543466 (Tex. App. 1994):

> . . . On the morning of October 30, 1993, a [bearded] man arrived [at] the Pizza Hut store at Wirt Road and Long Point Boulevard before the store opened. The man, wearing a Pizza Hut uniform, asked for the manager by name and persuaded employees to let him in. When the manager arrived, he told her he was there for training and handed her an application folder. Inside the folder was a note bearing the message, "Just give me the money and you won't get shot." The manager complied with the man's request. As he was leaving, the manager asked the man about his gun. He opened his apron and showed her the handle of a gun tucked into his pants. After the man left, she called police and her regional manager. Shortly after they arrived, the man called the store to make sure the manager was all right and to find out whether anyone had been fired over the incident. The store's telephone had a "Star 69" feature that allowed redial of the last number to call. By using this feature, police were able to determine that the call came from the South Shepard Pizza Hut store.
>
> Minutes later at the South Shepard store, police found a man fitting the description of the robber [except for the absence of a beard] and arrested him. Appellant [was] a 10–year employee of the pizza chain. . . . Pursuant to a warrant, police searched appellant's car and recovered Pizza Hut employment applications and employee manuals, lists of store locations and manager's names, a .380 handgun and [$284] in currency. . . .

Assume that the employees and manager of the first Pizza Hut proved unable to identify the defendant as the robber and that there was no evidence the defendant customarily wore a beard. Assume as well that the manager had not counted or marked the money she handed the robber. At trial, when the prosecutor asked the manager to relate the words she heard over the phone, defense counsel objected on the grounds that the call had not been properly authenticated. By what means could the prosecutor have authenticated the call as having been made by the defendant? (Several answers are available.)

STATE V. SMALL

Court of Appeals of Ohio.
2007 Ohio 6771 (2007).

■ BRYANT, J.... By indictment filed on March 17, 2006, [Dean D. Small] was charged with one count of aggravated murder in ... the death of Robel Medhin.... [O]n February 8, 2005, Medhin's body was discovered lying on the ground near an apartment building; Medhin died from a single gunshot wound to the mouth....

... [At Small's trial, his wife] testified [he] was angry with Medhin because Medhin owed defendant money. One of Medhin's friends, Tesfalem Ellos, testified Medhin so believed his life was in danger because of a $900 debt that Medhin asked Ellos for a gun....

Ellos did not know to whom Medhin owed the money, but on the night of the murder Medhin made a phone call on Ellos' phone and told the person who answered that he did not have the money. After learning of Medhin's death, Ellos retrieved the phone number and called it. The person who answered the phone had a Jamaican accent and said his name was Dominique, a name that [Small's wife] testified defendant used. [Defendant is of Jamaican descent.] Ellos and Dominique discussed arrangements under which Ellos would repay Medhin's debt....

... [On appeal following his murder conviction, Small] alleges the trial court violated the hearsay rules in admitting testimony from Ellos concerning statements of [the] individual calling himself Dominique.... The state urges the testimony was admissible as a party opponent admission under Evid. R. 801([d])(2)([A])....

To render the statement admissible under Evid. R. 801([d])(2)([A]), the state first needed to authenticate that the person to whom Ellos spoke on the phone was defendant: that defendant is "Dominique." A piece of evidence is sufficiently authenticated or identified to pass the threshold of admissibility when "evidence [is] sufficient to support a finding that the matter in question is what the proponent claims." *See* EVID. R. 901[unrestyled].*

Several methods exist for authenticating a telephone conversation.... Evidence that a call was made to the number the telephone company assigned at that time to a particular person can satisfy the authentication requirement, if the circumstances, including self-identifica-

* [Has the court stated the proper standard of proof? Problem 10.5, which lies just ahead, poses this question again.—GF]

tion, show the person answering to be the one called. EVID. R. 901([b])(6). The method is unavailable in the present case, as the record does not disclose whether the number Ellos dialed was a number assigned to defendant's phone. Similarly, voice identification, under Evid. R. 901([b])(5), does not apply, as Ellos' testimony did not indicate he could identify Dominique's voice as that of defendant.

Evid. R. 901([b])(4), however, relies upon "distinctive characteristics" and contemplates that a caller may be identified because only he could utter the speech under the circumstances. "A letter or a voice over the telephone may be related to a particular person by the very fact that the matters set forth in the letter or the telephone conversation were known peculiarly to a particular person." EVID. R. 901([b])(4), Staff Notes [Ohio's equivalent of Advisory Committee's Notes]. Even so, the party seeking admission must produce "direct and circumstantial evidence which reasonably identifies the defendant as a party to a telephone conversation." The mere fact that a caller identified himself as the defendant is insufficient. Rather, the contents of the conversation, the characteristics of the speech itself, or the circumstances of the call, must render it improbable that the caller could be anyone other than the person the proponent claims him to be....

The telephone conversation between Ellos and "Dominique" ... contains sufficient evidence to identify defendant as Dominique. "Dominique's" Jamaican accent and claim that Medhin owed him money, coupled with the testimony of [defendant's wife] that defendant was known as "Dominique," had a Jamaican accent, and was owed money by Medhin, make it highly improbable that the person answering the phone was anyone other than defendant. Adding to identification reliability is the evidence the phone call originated with Ellos, who testified he did not know defendant [or defendant's wife]. The chance an imposter also would have a Jamaican accent and would respond to an unexpected phone call in a manner tending to incriminate defendant is very slim; the evidence presented suffices to meet the requirements of Evid. R. 901([a]).

As the state's evidence authenticates defendant as "Dominique," the statements made to Ellos during the telephone conversation constitute party opponent admissions and are admissible.... [T]he trial court did not err in allowing Ellos to testify about the statements....

Judgment affirmed.

Problem 10.5

Calling Small

Consider again this paragraph of *Small* (page 905):

To render the statement admissible under Evid. R. 801([d])(2)([A]), the state first needed to authenticate that the

> person to whom Ellos spoke on the phone was defendant: that defendant is "Dominique." A piece of evidence is sufficiently authenticated or identified to pass the threshold of admissibility when "evidence [is] sufficient to support a finding that the matter in question is what the proponent claims." *See* EVID. R. 901[unrestyled].
>
> Did the court state the proper standard of proof?*

Rulings in Simpson Trial Fuel Second–Guessing

Carey Goldberg

NEW YORK TIMES, Dec. 9, 1996, at B12

LOS ANGELES. The E-mail exchanges among evidence experts have escalated. The legal pundits have gone into analytical overdrive. And the betting has begun on whether grounds have already been created for a possible third O.J. Simpson trial—a retrial should Mr. Simpson lose the current [civil trial]. . . .

Judge [Hiroshi] Fujisaki "is coming close to the line," said Norman Garland, a professor at the Southwestern University School of Law. "Any one of these recent decisions could tip the scales against him." . . .

One ruling allowed a lawyer for the plaintiffs to . . . have a counselor for battered women testify about a call she got from a frightened woman who identified herself only as "Nicole." . . .

[T]he judge allowed Nancy Ney, the counselor, to describe a phone call she took on June 7, 1994, five days before Mrs. Simpson and [Ronald] Goldman were slashed and stabbed to death. Mr. Simpson was acquitted of their murders in his criminal trial last year.

The caller identified herself only as "Nicole," Ms. Ney said, but her description of herself seemed to fit Mrs. Simpson. Ms. Ney said the woman's frightened voice matched that of Mrs. Simpson in recordings of calls she had made to 911 complaining of threats and abuse by Mr. Simpson. The woman said her husband was stalking her, Ms. Ney said, and had threatened to kill her. . . .

"I'd say most people are outraged about the ruling" to allow Ms. Ney's testimony, said Professor Garland, a member of a national on-line chat group of professors of evidence. . . .

Why were the professors "outraged"? Should they have been?

---

* My thanks to Professor Tanina Rostain, whose inquiry prompted this problem.

3. PHOTOGRAPHS

SIMMS v. DIXON

District of Columbia Court of Appeals.
291 A.2d 184 (D.C. 1972).

■ FICKLING, J. This case arises from a collision between automobiles driven by appellant Cheryl Simms and appellee Herbert Dixon. Appellant contends that the trial judge erred in refusing to admit into evidence six photographs of appellant's automobile taken after the collision. We agree and, therefore, reverse.

During the trial there was an irreconcilable conflict between the testimony of appellant and appellee. Appellee testified that the collision occurred when appellant, suddenly and without warning, turned her vehicle into and across the path of his automobile. He specifically testified that his automobile struck appellant's automobile on the right hand side of her vehicle, "[right] in the center. It was a four-door car, with the posts coming up through the center, and right in about where the posts come up, in the center." Appellant testified, however, that after having properly signaled her intention to turn right from the curb lane and while entering the turn, her vehicle was struck in the rear of the right side by appellee's automobile.

During direct examination of appellant, her counsel attempted to introduce six photographs of appellant's vehicle taken after the collision. Counsel informed the trial court that his reason for introducing the photographs was to show where the impact occurred to appellant's vehicle and that he could lay the proper foundation through the appellant. The trial court refused to consider the admissibility of the photographs unless the person who actually took them first testified as to how the photographs were taken and opposing counsel was given an opportunity to cross-examine the photographer. However, the photographer could not be located and the trial court repeated its ruling that appellant's testimony would not be sufficient to lay a proper foundation for the admission of the photographs. . . .

. . . Professor McCormick has stated the guidelines for determining admissibility as follows:

> [The] prime condition on admissibility is that the photograph be identified by a witness as a portrayal of certain facts relevant to the issue, and verified by such a witness on personal knowledge as a correct representation of these facts. *The witness who thus lays the foundation need not be the photographer nor need the witness know anything of the time or conditions of the taking.* It is the facts represented,

> the scene or the object, that he must know about, and when this knowledge is shown, he can say whether the photograph correctly portrays these facts.... [C. MCCORMICK, EVIDENCE § 181, at 387 (1954).]

Other authorities agree that the photographer is not necessary to lay a proper foundation for the admissibility of the proffered photographs. The essential test is whether the photographs accurately represent the facts allegedly portrayed in them. 3 WIGMORE, EVIDENCE § 794(3) (Chadbourn Rev. 1970); 2 C. SCOTT, PHOTOGRAPHIC EVIDENCE § 1141, at 608–15 (2d ed. 1969)....

In the case at bar, the trial court examined the photographs but made no finding that they did not accurately represent the relevant facts or that he had some question as to their accuracy. Rather, apparently out of a sense of caution because of the obvious importance of the photographs in determining whether the vehicle was struck on the right rear or in the center of the right side, the court simply required that the photographer testify. Dimensions and perspective were not critical to the admissibility of these photographs. In the absence of a finding that the proffered foundation by appellant was not [sufficient to show that the photographs were] an accurate representation of the vehicle immediately following the accident, it was reversible error to deny admission of the photographs....

Reversed and remanded for a new trial.

Problem 10.6

Staged Photo

In *State v. Kelley*, 46 S.C. 55 (1896), the defendants were convicted of having shot C. L. Jenkins through a window of his house with the intent to kill him. Jenkins, though injured, survived. Consider these facts:

> The defendants ... [claim] it was error to allow the witness, M. A. Helm, ... [to testify about a] photograph he had made the next morning after Mr. Jenkins was shot, of the window through which [Jenkins] was shot, and also of Mr. Jenkins in the position in the bed he was in when shot, and also to exhibit the photograph to the jury.... [The following examination of Helm preceded the prosecution's introduction of the photograph:]
>
> "What was your business in Hartsville?" *Answer:* "Taking pictures, sir."

> "Did you take any for Mr. Jenkins?" *Answer:* "I took some for him the morning [after] he was shot. . . ."
>
> "Do you mean his own picture?" *Answer:* "Yes, sir. . . . I took a picture of the window where he was shot, he sitting by it in the position he was in when he was shot." . . .
>
> "Where were your instruments when you took this, inside or outside the house?" *Answer:* "It was outside." . . .
>
> "Where was Mr. Jenkins at the time you took that picture?" *Answer:* "He was sitting near about where he was when he was shot."
>
> The [prosecutor] here offered to introduce the picture in evidence. Defendants' counsel objected. . . .

Helm testified he was in the room with Jenkins when Jenkins was shot. If the prosecutor offered Helm's photograph to prove both Jenkins's position at the time he was shot and the shooter's view from outside the house, what was the defendant's best argument for excluding the photo? How should the court have ruled?

Problem 10.7
Serge *Animation*

Recall the facts of *Commonwealth v. Serge*, 586 Pa. 671, *cert. denied*, 549 U.S. 920 (2006) (page 49), in which the prosecution presented its theory of the fatal shooting through a computer-generated animation (CGA). The Pennsylvania Supreme Court defined a CGA as a series of drawings "created by a computer that . . . depict[] the previously formed opinion of a witness or witnesses, in this case the Commonwealth experts. . . ." (Page 50 n.1.) The prosecution offered the CGA "to illustrate the expert opinions of its forensic pathologist, Gary W. Ross, M.D., and crime scene reconstructionist, Trooper Brad R. Beach. The CGA showed the theory of the Commonwealth based upon the forensic and physical evidence, of how Appellant shot his wife first in the lower back and then through the heart as she knelt on the living room floor of their home." (Page 50.)

How should the prosecution have gone about authenticating its CGA? *See Serge*, 586 Pa. at 686–90.

WAGNER V. STATE

District Court of Appeal of Florida.
707 So. 2d 827 (Fla. Dist. Ct. App. 1998).

■ LAWRENCE, J. . . . The facts of this case are as follows. Officer Duncan, an investigator with the Special Investigations Division of the Bay County Sheriff's Office, on December 15, 1995, enlisted the aid of a female confidential informant to make drug purchases. The informant made the purchases from an automobile equipped with a hidden video camera which provided a view of the driver's window. Officer Duncan gave a detailed explanation as to the installation and operation of the camera. He explained the manner in which he mounted a Sony recording device in the trunk of a county-owned vehicle, attached by wire to a camera and microphone positioned on the rear window tray of the vehicle. The camera and lens were covered by a blanket containing a small hole through which the camera lens protruded. He further testified that he tested the apparatus and that it was in good order and was working properly during the time of the drug investigation.

. . . Officer Duncan then gave the informant twenty dollars, turned on the video recorder, verbally recorded the date and time, and sent the informant to the purchase area along 16th street. Officer Duncan followed the informant in a separate vehicle, but when approaching [defendant Arthur] Wagner's area on 16th street, he diverted his vehicle to a course on 17th street, parallel with the informant's vehicle. He observed the informant during most of her travel to and from the purchase area, but did not observe the actual transaction for fear of being detected. The videotape showed that the informant stopped the car and remained seated when Wagner approached her and conversed with her through the driver's window. Wagner, within a few seconds of his approach, handed the informant something and she handed him what appeared to be United States currency. The informant, upon return to a prearranged location, presented Officer Duncan with a twenty-dollar rock of cocaine. Officer Duncan then turned off the video camera. . . .

Officer Duncan retrieved the videotape from the recording device and kept it in his exclusive custody and control until he presented it to the trial judge at the appropriate time for viewing. There was no evidence that the tape had been altered, edited, or tampered with in any way.

The jury, at trial, was permitted to view the . . . videotape. . . . A witness for the State identified the person on the videotape as Wagner.

The informant was unavailable and did not testify.[2] The jury found Wagner guilty of ... sale of cocaine within 1000 feet of a school....

ADMISSIBILITY OF VIDEOTAPE

... Wagner argues that the videotape was not properly authenticated because there was no "pictorial testimony" offered. He argues that it was incumbent upon the State to offer testimony of the informant or some other witness who could testify that, based upon his or her personal knowledge, the tape fairly and accurately portrayed the incidents reflected thereon.

Authentication under the "pictorial testimony" theory is one means of authenticating a photograph or videotape; it is not however the exclusive means of authentication. Under the "silent witness" theory, photographic evidence may be admitted upon proof of the reliability of the process which produced the photograph or videotape. As Professor Wigmore explains:

> With later advancements in the art of photography, however, and with increasing awareness of the manifold evidentiary uses of the products of the art, it has become clear that an additional theory of admissibility of photographs is entitled to recognition. Thus, even [if] no human is capable of swearing that he personally perceived what a photograph purports to portray (so that it is not possible to satisfy the requirements of the "pictorial testimony" rationale) there may nevertheless be good warrant for receiving the photograph in evidence. Given an adequate foundation assuring the accuracy of the process producing it, the photograph should then be received as a so-called silent witness or as a witness which "speaks for itself."

3 WIGMORE, EVIDENCE § 790, at 219–20 (Chadbourn rev. 1970); *see also* 2 MCCORMICK ON EVIDENCE § 214, at 15 (4th ed. 1992). The Florida Supreme Court ... has adopted the "silent witness" theory of admissibility, but has not elaborated on the procedure to be followed for authentication under this theory.

We find the treatment of the "silent witness" theory by the courts of other states instructive. The Court in Litton v. Commonwealth, 597 S.W.2d 616 (Ky. 1980), in a pharmacy burglary case, approved the admission into evidence of three photographs taken by an automatic camera while the burglary was in progress. The court held that the photographs were properly authenticated based on the pharmacy owner's testimony that the burglary alarm system was activated upon closing the business and that the camera could be started by a number of magnetic switches connected to a motion detector. The pharmacy owner

2. The informant apparently had absconded and at the time of trial a warrant was outstanding for her arrest on charges unrelated to the instant case.

also identified the background in the photographs as being an accurate representation of his store.

The court in State v. Bunting, 187 N.J. Super. 506 (1983), held that a film from a surveillance camera, depicting the robbery of a store, was properly authenticated where the state introduced testimony describing the installation and view of the camera, operation of the camera, testing of the camera, removal of the film, and the chain of custody of the film after removal. . . .

. . . The testimony in the instant case concerning the installation and operation of the video camera, the identification of Wagner on the videotape, a clear indication of the time and date on which the tape was made, together with the absence of any evidence concerning tampering or editing, provide the indicia of reliability required to authenticate a videotape for purposes of the "silent witness" theory.

We thus hold that relevant photographic evidence may be admitted into evidence on the "silent witness" theory when the trial judge determines it to be reliable, after having considered the following:

(1) evidence establishing the time and date of the photographic evidence;

(2) any evidence of editing or tampering;

(3) the operating condition and capability of the equipment producing the photographic evidence as it relates to the accuracy and reliability of the photographic product;

(4) the procedure employed as it relates to the preparation, testing, operation, and security of the equipment used to produce the photographic product, including the security of the product itself; and

(5) testimony identifying the relevant participants depicted in the photographic evidence.

The record in this case establishes that evidence was presented to the trial judge on all of the enumerated factors. Moreover, the record supports the judge's decision to admit the videotape into evidence. We find no abuse of discretion on this point. . . .

B. THE "BEST EVIDENCE RULE"

Focus on
FRE 1001, 1002, 1003, & 1004

INTRODUCTION

The best evidence rule causes a degree of confusion out of all proportion to its importance. Much of that confusion stems from its name. Both its slang tag (the "best evidence rule") and its formal title (the "requirement of original") can greatly mislead.

The "Best Evidence Rule"

The law no longer demands that litigants produce the "best evidence" on any particular point. Blackstone's day, when "the best evidence the nature of the case will admit of shall always be required," is done. 3 WILLIAM BLACKSTONE, COMMENTARIES ON THE LAWS OF ENGLAND 368 (1765). It is not that the system no longer prefers better evidence to worse. Rather, the system presumes that most litigants will want to produce the most compelling evidence they can.

Assume, then, that the defendant has been charged with armed robbery at knifepoint. A police officer will be permitted to testify that when she arrested the defendant minutes after the robbery, he had a knife in his sock. Although the knife itself might be the "best" evidence of its existence, the prosecutor need not show the knife to the jury. He may if he prefers show the jury a photograph of the knife instead. He may even choose to rely on the officer's testimony describing the knife and offer no physical evidence of the knife at all. But he would be foolish to withhold the knife if he can produce it. For the defense lawyer very likely will argue to the jury, "If there really was a knife, *where is it?*"

As it turns out, the best evidence rule says nothing at all about the admissibility of knives—or of guns or drugs or most other kinds of physical evidence. And it says nothing about the quality of oral testimony. As embodied by Rule 1002, the best evidence rule applies only to "writing[s], recording[s], or photograph[s]"—all as defined by Rule 1001. Behind the rule lies a belief that when a case turns on the content of a writing, recording, or photograph, a litigant must present such evidence in the most precise form possible. Even within this rather narrow scope, however, Rule 1002 is not all it appears to be.

The "Requirement of Original"

Rule 1002, titled "Requirement of Original," states that "[a]n original writing, recording, or photograph is required in order to prove its content unless these rules or a federal statute provides otherwise." One might guess that a rule requiring production of "the original" would forbid substitution of a copy. Yet the word "original," as defined by Rule 1001(d), includes many things we think of as copies. The negative of a photograph is an "original," as is a new print made from the old negative or a new printout of stored computer data. The Advisory Committee's

Note tells us that even a "carbon copy" is an "original" (RB 304)—and the carbonless copy of a credit card receipt qualifies as well.

What is more, Rule 1003 states that in most circumstances "[a] duplicate is admissible to the same extent as the original." And the definition given the word "duplicate" by Rule 1001(e) is broader than one might expect. A photograph or photocopy of a document is a "duplicate," as is a re-recording of an old tape or a photographic print made from another print. In fact, just about any mechanical reproduction of a writing, recording, or photograph fits within Rule 1001(e)'s definition of "duplicate," as long as the reproduction process excludes the possibility of human transcription error. "Copies subsequently produced manually, whether handwritten or typed, are not within the definition." (ACN to 1001(e), RB 305.)

This concern with the possibility of human error hints at the true meaning of the best evidence rule. The rule aims to bar litigants from presenting *human recollections* of the content of writings, recordings, or photographs in place of the physical item itself. Hence the rule is not much concerned with the distinction between an "original" and a mechanical reproduction of the original—for both originals and duplicates typically inform the jury of the exact content of a writing, recording, or photograph.

The best evidence rule aims to assure that whenever possible, the jury has access to an original or duplicate if a case turns on the content of a writing, recording, or photograph. In the words of Rule 1002, the litigant must supply an original or duplicate *"to prove [the] content"* of these items. (Emphasis added.) Unfortunately, that simple phrase—"to prove [the] content"—turns out to be unexpectedly tricky.

Proof of Content

Let's begin with an example of what does *not* constitute proof of content. Assume that a bank has been robbed and that the bank's hidden security camera captured the robbery on videotape. At trial the prosecution is perfectly free to present a teller's testimony about what he saw during the robbery *without ever presenting the videotape.* The rule does not forbid the prosecutor to substitute the teller's very human memory for the camera's precise mechanical recording, even though most people would agree that the videotape is usually *better* evidence. That is because the prosecutor is not trying to prove *the content of the recording,* but rather *the fact of the robbery.* The teller is not telling the jury what is on the tape, but rather what he remembers of the event. Put differently, if the prosecutor manages to convince the jury that what the teller says about the robbery is true, the government will win the case—even if the jury never hears anything about what is on the tape. True, the videotape happens to capture "the content" of the teller's testimony. That does not mean, however, that the prosecutor is trying to prove the content of the tape.

Now consider a different scenario: During the bank teller's testimony, the prosecutor shows the videotape of the robbery. If the teller testifies that the videotape fairly and accurately depicts the robbery as he remembers it, the videotape may now be admitted. Yet it still is not being admitted "to prove [its] content," but only to illustrate the teller's testimony. In a sense, the witness "adopts the [videotape] as his testimony." (ACN to FRE 1002, RB 306.)

So when *does* a litigant "prove the content of a writing, recording, or photograph"? The advisory committee tells us the rule applies in two contexts. (RB 306.)

The first is where the writing, recording, or photograph *is itself at issue* in the litigation. In most copyright infringement lawsuits, for example, the question is whether a writing published by the defendant says substantially the same thing as a writing copyrighted by the plaintiff. Most libel actions concern whether a writing published by the defendant alleges damaging falsehoods about the plaintiff. Many privacy infringement lawsuits and child pornography prosecutions turn on whether a photograph depicts the plaintiff in a private situation or shows a child in a sexual scene. In each of these cases, the plaintiff or prosecutor must prove the content of the writing or photograph to make out her case. Rule 1002 therefore requires her to produce either the original writing or photograph or a duplicate of it. Only if the original has been lost or destroyed or is otherwise inaccessible—contingencies addressed by Rule 1004—may she substitute human testimony describing the content of the writing or photograph.

The second circumstance in which a litigant is "prov[ing] the content of a writing, recording, or photograph" is analytically very different. Consider again the bank robbery mentioned earlier. Now assume that in the months since the robbery, both the teller and the security guard, who were the only witnesses to the crime, have died. If the prosecutor attempts to prove the robbery through the videotape's recording of the event, she will be "prov[ing] the content" of the tape. True, the prosecutor's ultimate objective remains proof of the robbery, just as before. Now, though, the prosecutor will be trying to prove that event *by proving the content of the tape*. As the advisory committee writes, the tape has attained "independent probative value." (RB 306.) Rule 1002 therefore requires that the prosecutor show the jury the tape or a duplicate of it. Unless the tape is lost or destroyed or otherwise inaccessible, the prosecutor may not replace the tape with an imperfect human substitute—such as a police detective's testimony about what she saw when she watched the tape.

Or take another example: A litigant may wish to offer evidence that a business shipped a particular truckload of goods on a particular day. She could call various employees of the business to testify to that fact. Or instead she could offer the records of the business if they satisfy Rule 803(6) and are properly authenticated under Rule 901 or 902(11). If the litigant chooses the latter course and relies on the records to prove the events they recite, she will be proving their content and will be bound by Rule 1002. In this instance, as in the previous example, the records have independent probative value in showing that the goods were shipped. They are *not* being offered simply to illustrate or enhance a witness's memory of the shipment, for no such witness takes the stand.

In these two circumstances—when the writing, recording, or photograph is itself at issue in the case and when it has "independent probative value"—the best evidence rule generally demands that the proponent produce the original or a duplicate *instead of a human reconstruction in the form of testimony or otherwise.* Often courts refer to such human reconstructions as "secondary" evidence of content—and generally the rule bans secondary evidence.

At bottom, the best evidence rule rests on four propositions. Writings, recordings, and photographs are, first of all, far more detailed and nuanced than many other forms of evidence. Second, differences in fine details of language often sway the outcome of a case. Third, proving such details with the needed precision is particularly hard because writings, recordings, and photographs are susceptible to forgery. And fourth, even when forgery and fraud are not issues, the human memory simply fails in the task of reproducing a writing, recording, or photograph with the precision of the thing itself. *Cf.* MUELLER & KIRKPATRICK, EVIDENCE § 10.1, at 1161 (5th ed. 2012).

As you examine the rest of the materials in this unit, consider whether these rationales adequately explain the odd borderlines of this quirky doctrine.

Problem 10.8

Perjury Trial

At the trial of Bennett Meyers for suborning the perjured testimony of Bleriot Lamarre, the government called William P. Rogers to the stand. Rogers had been present at an earlier proceeding at which, according to the government, Lamarre lied under oath at Meyers's instigation. Assume that when the prosecutor asked Rogers to relate Lamarre's earlier testimony, Meyers objected, claiming (in substance) that the best evidence rule required the government to prove Lamarre's earlier testimony with the official stenographic transcript made at the time.

How should the trial judge have ruled? *See Meyers v. United States*, 171 F.2d 800 (D.C. Cir. 1948), *cert. denied*, 336 U.S. 912 (1949). Why do you think the government failed to rely on the transcript? Will this situation come up often?

Problem 10.9

Alice's Restaurant II

Late on a February night, the Partridge Restaurant was gutted by fire. An arson investigator arrived at the restaurant soon after the fire. A neighbor who lived across the street told the investigator that she had seen a man break the restaurant's front window and pour something from a gasoline can into the restaurant. Then he lit a match, dropped it through the window, and raced away in a white car. The neighbor said she immediately wrote the license plate number of the car on the back of a business card. She gave that card, bearing the number "9PPF994," to the investigator.

The investigator determined that license plate number 9PPF994 was registered to Michael Akker. At Akker's trial on arson charges, the neighbor related the same facts she told the arson investigator. When the prosecutor asked her the license plate number of the white car, she testified from memory—and over Akker's objection—that the number was 9PPF994.

If Akker's counsel argues on appeal that the best evidence rule required the prosecutor to introduce the card on which the neighbor wrote the license plate number, how should the court rule?

SEILER V. LUCASFILM: *Prequel*

March 17, 1981

Mr. George Lucas

Lucasfilms, Ltd.

Dear Mr. Lucas:

This is a somewhat difficult letter for me to write. As a lifelong science-fiction fan and film maker, I greatly admire your films. It was quite a shock, therefore, when my friends told me that certain concepts and illustrations of mine appeared in your latest film, "The Empire Strikes Back." I went to see the picture with the expectation that they would turn out to be wrong, but they weren't. The sequence involving the Imperial forces and rebels on the planet Hoth is indeed based on my concepts and on illustrations of my walking invasion machines. I enclose several examples of my published materials as well as Xerox copies of [Lucasfilm] illustrations that are clearly copied or derived from my work.

According to what I've read about you, you are an honorable person, who always tries to do what is fair. I, too, try to be fair in my dealings with others. I suggest, therefore, that you and I get together to resolve this matter in an amicable manner.

Please let me hear from you at your earliest convenience.

Cordially,
Lee M. Seiler

Seiler v. Lucasfilm, 613 F. Supp. 1253 (N.D. Cal. 1984) (attached as Exhibit 1 to Plaintiff's Notice of Taking Deposition) (June 7, 1983).

May 23, 1981

Mr. Lee M. Seiler

Cliffridge Publishing

Dear Mr. Seiler:

This office represents Lucasfilm Ltd. I am in receipt of your letter of March 17, 1981. We have investigated the claim made by you and find that it has no merit and consequently we reject same. The concepts, illustrations and special effects for "The Empire Strikes Back" were original with well-respected artists and special effects personnel in the industry who were employed in connection with the above picture.

Very truly yours,
A. Fredric Leopold

Seiler v. Lucasfilm, 613 F. Supp. 1253 (N.D. Cal. 1984) (attached as Exhibit 2 to Plaintiff's Notice of Taking Deposition) (June 7, 1983).

"THE SPRINTER" AO-785/2

EXHIBIT"D"

Seiler's "Garthian Sprinter." *Seiler v. Lucasfilm*, 613 F. Supp. 1253 (N.D. Cal. 1984) (attached as Exhibit D to Complaint for Damages) (Feb. 14, 1983).

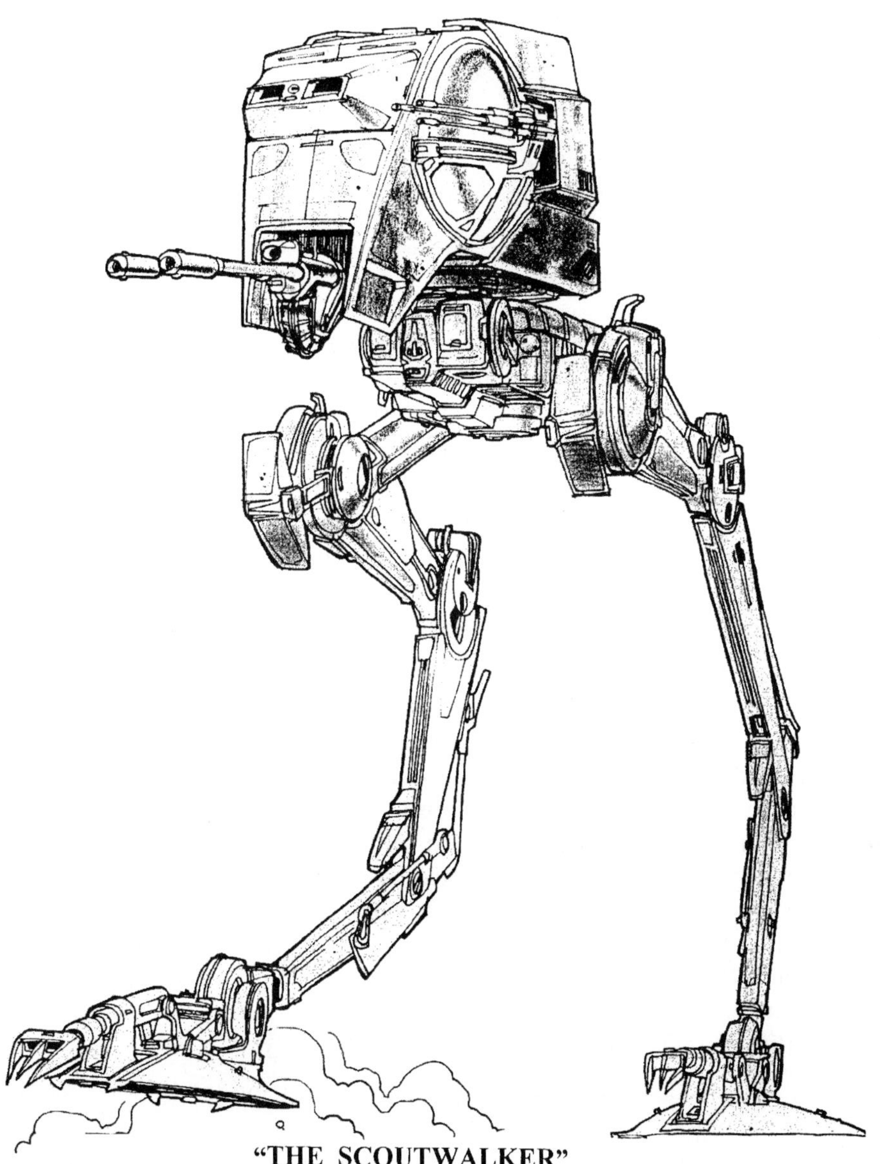

"THE SCOUTWALKER"

EXHIBIT "E"

Lucasfilm's "Scoutwalker." *Seiler v. Lucasfilm*, 613 F. Supp. 1253 (N.D. Cal. 1984) (attached as Exhibit E to Complaint for Damages) (Feb. 14, 1983). From the Lucasfilm Archives, reprinted by permission.

SEILER V. LUCASFILM

808 F.2d 1316 (9th Cir. 1986), *cert. denied*, 484 U.S. 826 (1987).

■ FARRIS, CIRCUIT JUDGE: Lee Seiler, a graphic artist and creator of science fiction creatures, alleged copyright infringement by George Lucas and others who created and produced the science fiction movie "The Empire Strikes Back." . . .

Seiler contends that he created and published in 1976 and 1977 science fiction creatures called Garthian Striders. In 1980, George Lucas released The Empire Strikes Back, a motion picture that contains a battle sequence depicting giant machines called Imperial Walkers.* In 1981 Seiler obtained a copyright on his Striders, depositing with the Copyright Office "reconstructions" of the originals as they had appeared in 1976 and 1977.

Seiler contends that Lucas' Walkers were copied from Seiler's Striders. . . . Lucas responds that Seiler did not obtain his copyright until one year after the release of The Empire Strikes Back and that Seiler can produce no documents that antedate The Empire Strikes Back.

Because Seiler proposed to exhibit his Striders in a blow-up comparison to Lucas' Walkers at opening statement, the district judge held an evidentiary hearing on the admissibility of the "reconstructions" of Seiler's Striders. Applying the "best evidence rule," Fed. R. Evid. 1001–1008, the district court found at the end of a seven-day hearing that Seiler lost or destroyed the originals in bad faith under Rule [1004(a)] and that consequently no secondary evidence, such as the post-Empire Strikes Back reconstructions, was admissible. In its opinion the court found specifically that Seiler testified falsely, purposefully destroyed or withheld in bad faith the originals, and fabricated and misrepresented the nature of his reconstructions. The district court granted summary judgment to Lucas after the evidentiary hearing.

On appeal, Seiler contends . . . that the best evidence rule does not apply to his works. . . .

DISCUSSION

. . . The best evidence rule embodied in Rules 1001–1008 represented a codification of longstanding common law doctrine. Dating back to 1700, the rule requires not, as its common name implies, the best evidence in every case but rather the production of an original document instead of a copy. Many commentators refer to the rule not as the best evidence rule but as the original document rule.

* [Garthian Striders and Imperial Walkers are versions of the many walking machines involved in this suit.—GF]

[Unrestyled] Rule 1002 states: "To prove the content of a writing, recording, or photograph, the original writing, recording, or photograph is required, except as otherwise provided in these rules or by Act of Congress." Writings and recordings are defined in [unrestyled] Rule 1001 as "letters, words, or numbers, or their equivalent, set down by handwriting, typewriting, printing, photostating, photographing, magnetic impulse, mechanical or electronic recording, or other form of data compilation." . . .

We hold that Seiler's drawings were "writings" within the meaning of Rule [1001(a)]; they consist not of "letters, words, or numbers" but of "their equivalent." To hold otherwise would frustrate the policies underlying the rule and introduce undesirable inconsistencies into the application of the rule.

In the days before liberal rules of discovery and modern techniques of electronic copying, the rule guarded against incomplete or fraudulent proof. By requiring the possessor of the original to produce it, the rule prevented the introduction of altered copies and the withholding of originals. The purpose of the rule was thus long thought to be one of fraud prevention, but Wigmore pointed out that the rule operated even in cases where fraud was not at issue, such as where secondary evidence is not admitted even though its proponent acts in utmost good faith. Wigmore also noted that if prevention of fraud were the foundation of the rule, it should apply to objects as well as writings, which it does not. 4 WIGMORE, EVIDENCE § 1180 (Chadbourn rev. 1972).

The modern justification for the rule has expanded from prevention of fraud to a recognition that writings occupy a central position in the law. When the contents of a writing are at issue, oral testimony as to the terms of the writing is subject to a greater risk of error than oral testimony as to events or other situations. The human memory is not often capable of reciting the precise terms of a writing, and when the terms are in dispute only the writing itself, or a true copy, provides reliable evidence. To summarize then, we observe that the importance of the precise terms of writings in the world of legal relations, the fallibility of the human memory as reliable evidence of the terms, and the hazards of inaccurate or incomplete duplication are the concerns addressed by the best evidence rule.

Viewing the dispute in the context of the concerns underlying the best evidence rule, we conclude that the rule applies. McCormick summarizes the rule as follows:

> In proving the terms of a writing, where the terms are material, the original writing must be produced unless it is shown to be unavailable for some reason other than the serious fault of the proponent.

MCCORMICK ON EVIDENCE § 230, at 704. The contents of Seiler's work are at issue. There can be no proof of "substantial similarity" and thus of copyright infringement unless Seiler's works are juxtaposed with Lucas' and their contents compared. Since the contents are material and must be proved, Seiler must either produce the original or show that it is unavailable through no fault of his own. Rule [1004(a)]. This he could not do.

The facts of this case implicate the very concerns that justify the best evidence rule. Seiler alleges infringement by The Empire Strikes Back, but he can produce no documentary evidence of any originals existing before the release of the movie. His secondary evidence does not consist of true copies or exact duplicates but of "reconstructions" made after The Empire Strikes Back. In short, Seiler claims that the movie infringed his originals, yet he has no proof of those originals.

The dangers of fraud in this situation are clear. The rule would ensure that proof of the infringement claim consists of the works alleged to be infringed. Otherwise, "reconstructions" which might have no resemblance to the purported original would suffice as proof for infringement of the original....

Seiler argues that the best evidence rule does not apply to his work, in that it is artwork rather than "writings, recordings, or photographs." He contends that the rule both historically and currently embraces only words or numbers. Neither party has cited us to cases which discuss the applicability of the rule to drawings....

A creative literary work, which is artwork, and a photograph whose contents are sought to be proved, as in copyright, defamation, or invasion of privacy, are both covered by the best evidence rule. *See* Advisory Committee's Note to Rule 1002. We would be inconsistent to apply the rule to artwork which is literary or photographic but not to artwork of other forms. Furthermore, blueprints, engineering drawings, architectural designs may all lack words or numbers yet still be capable of copyright and susceptible to fraudulent alteration. In short, Seiler's argument would have us restrict the definitions of Rule [1001(a)] to "words" and "numbers" but ignore "or their equivalent." We will not do so in the circumstances of this case.

Our holding is also supported by the policy served by the best evidence rule in protecting against faulty memory. Seiler's reconstructions were made four to seven years after the alleged originals; his memory as to specifications and dimensions may have dimmed significantly. Furthermore, reconstructions made after the release of the Empire Strikes Back may be tainted, even if unintentionally, by exposure to the movie. Our holding guards against these problems....

Affirmed.

Problem 10.10

GPS Data

Authorities spotted and boarded Vincent Bennett's boat as he sailed north in U.S. waters off the California coast, just north of the U.S.–Mexico border. After a search revealed over 1500 pounds of marijuana in a hidden compartment, Bennett was charged with illegally importing marijuana from outside the U.S. The prosecution's trial witnesses included U.S. Customs Officer Malcolm Chandler, who testified over Bennett's objection "that he discovered a global positioning system ('GPS') while searching Bennett's boat and that the GPS revealed that Bennett's boat had traveled from Mexican waters"—a fact essential to the prosecution's proof of illegal importation. The court of appeals elaborated:

> . . . A GPS device uses global positioning satellites to track and record the location of the device and, therefore, the location of any object to which it is attached. The GPS came with a "backtrack" feature that graphed the boat's journey that day. Chandler testified that the backtrack feature mapped Bennett's journey from Mexican territorial waters off the coast of Rosarito, Mexico, to the Coronado Islands and then north to San Diego Bay. . . .
>
> [T]he government did not produce the GPS itself—or a printout or other representation of such data. . . . When asked on cross-examination to produce the GPS or its data, Chandler . . . testified [that he had not taken possession of the GPS device and] that "there was no need to" videotape or photograph the data. . . . Moreover, the government has not offered any record evidence that it would have been impossible or even difficult to download or print out the data on Bennett's GPS.

United States v. Bennett, 363 F.3d 947, 952–54 (9th Cir.), *cert. denied*, 543 U.S. 950 (2004).

(a) How should the trial court have ruled on Bennett's objection that Chandler's testimony about the GPS data violated the best evidence rule?

(b) Assume instead that the only trial witness who saw the GPS data was an accomplice of Bennett who joined the boat's crew in U.S. waters shortly before authorities boarded the boat. The accomplice noted that the GPS data revealed the boat's passage from Mexican to U.S. waters. To eliminate evidence, he purged the GPS of all data before agents discovered the device.

> Later the accomplice agreed to plead guilty and testify for the government in exchange for leniency. How should the trial court have ruled on Bennett's objection that the accomplice's testimony about the GPS data violated the best evidence rule?

UNITED STATES V. JACKSON

488 F. Supp. 2d 866 (D. Neb. 2007).

■ BATAILLON, J. . . . [T]he Federal Bureau of Investigation and the Douglas County Sheriff's Office participated in an investigation involving the defendant which centered around online chats during the summer of 2001. An agent of the Postal Investigation Service, David Margritz (Margritz), known as "k8tee4fun," identified himself to defendant as a fourteen-year-old girl. The officers set up a meeting with the defendant. . . . [On August 14, 2001,] defendant drove to a park, apparently with his daughter, but instead of stopping, he returned home. Officers then went to defendant's home, arrested him, and seized his computers. . . . Assistant United States Attorney Robert Kokrda was first assigned to handle the case on November 3, 2002, but he did not do anything on it prior to his retirement on October 1, 2004. On September 28, 2004, Assistant United States Attorney Michael Norris was assigned to handle the case. On February 24, 2005, a grand jury indicted defendant for using a computer to knowingly attempt to persuade, induce, and entice a minor to engage in sexual activity. . . .

DISCUSSION

a. *The testimony*

In his current motion in limine, defendant seeks an order prohibiting the government from introducing [a] cut-and-paste document of alleged online chat conversations . . . into evidence at trial. . . .

The evidence at issue involves certain "instant message" or "chat" conversations conducted via computer between . . . k8tee4fun and the defendant, using the screen name gnesta18. . . . The parties agree that there are no original transcripts of the conversations, either because computers are missing or because instant-message conversations were not maintained or archived on the computers. The parties also agree that there are no longer original electronic computer printouts or copies on floppy discs or hard drives or disc drives capturing the computer conversations between Margritz and the defendant during that period of time. None of the conversations were saved. It appears from the testimony of Margritz that he wiped his computer clean during a routine upgrade a couple of years after this investigation. Consequently, the government is attempting to introduce copy-and-paste notes taken by Margritz from the online chats and saved into a Microsoft Word document. Defendant objects to the admissibility of this evidence.

Margritz testified . . . that, at the end of each chat session, he saved the conversations between k8tee4fun and gnesta18 by clicking and dragging to highlight the complete conversation from start to finish. He then copied and pasted the entire selection into a word processing document in Microsoft Word. He testified that he saved each conversation chronologically in an ongoing log. He further testified that immediately after he copied and pasted the conversations into Word, he made another copy for himself and added certain notes and edits to that copy. He acknowledged that it was possible to leave out words if they were not properly highlighted and dragged, but stated that there was no human error in this case because he took "great pains" to look back at the screen and make sure he captured everything accurately before closing the chat window. He further testified that he never modified the document in any way. . . .

Kevin H. Peden, a computer forensics expert, also testified at the hearing. He stated that he had seventeen years of law enforcement, had background experience investigating crimes involving children, and he had a computer engineering degree from Spokane Community College. He received training at the computer forensic boot camp, and he attended the NTI school of forensics. . . . He testified that he has conducted over 100 investigations and worked on fifteen child pornography cases. He testified that he always produced a bit-stream image of the hard drive, which was the forensic copy of the hard drive and is the best way to confirm the chat. Peden testified that the bit stream image would be the only way to see the evidence exactly as it appeared during the conversations. . . . Peden testified that the cut-and-paste method employed by Margritz was the least effective way to capture the chat log. . . .

Peden testified at great length regarding the multiple errors that he believes exists in the cut-and-paste version of the exhibit offered by Margritz. He . . . attributed them to operator errors. Peden testified that there are numerous missing offline messages [and several instances of selective cutting and pasting, time-sequence errors, and missing data, as well as a four-minute gap in one conversation]. Margritz admits that not all of the offline messages appear in the cut-and-paste document. . . .

b. *Admissibility of the cut-and-paste document*

. . . The government attempts to introduce the editorialized version of the cut-and-paste document [because the first cut-and-paste document was destroyed during the upgrade to Margritz's computer]. However, the court finds the evidence offered by Peden is credible and supportable. Peden testified about a number of methods that could have been utilized to accurately capture the chats, but none of these methods were used. . . .

The court finds that this document does not accurately represent the entire conversations that took place between the defendant and Margritz. The defendant argues that his intent when agreeing to the meeting was to introduce his grandniece to the fourteen-year-old girl. . . . Defendant alleges that such information was excluded from the cut-and-paste document or from a lost audiotape of a phone conversation between him and Margritz. . . .

[D]efendant argues that the cut-and-paste document is not admissible as it is not the best evidence. This rule [generally requires] an original writing or recording to prove the truth of the contents. FED. R. EVID. 1002. A computer printout is considered the original if it accurately reflects the data. FED. R. EVID. [1001(d)]. The same is true of a duplicate. FED. R. EVID. [1001(e)], 1003. . . . [T]he cut-and-paste document offered by the government is not an accurate original or duplicate, because . . . it does not accurately reflect the entire conversations between the defendant and Margritz. In addition, Margritz changed this document by including his editorial comments. . . . Accordingly, . . . the court . . . finds the cut-and-paste document inadmissible. In that same regard, the court finds the document is inadmissible under Fed. R. Evid. 1004 (allows for . . . secondary evidence when original is destroyed). It is clear that the proposed document does not accurately reflect the contents of the original.

. . . Defendant . . . contends the missing evidence, either on the actual computer log or on the missing auditory tape, would contain exculpatory evidence. . . . No hard drive is available, and because of the delay in prosecuting Jackson, the government's electronic records have been erased, the first copy made by Margritz is missing, the audiotape is missing, and the defendant cannot verify the accuracy of Margritz's cut-and-paste job. . . .*

. . . [T]he fact that the file languished on the desk of Mr. Kokrda for two years is significant and very intentional. There was an intentional decision not to make this a priority case, not to preserve evidence, and not to prosecute this case. . . . The court finds that if the charges had been promptly and properly filed against the defendant, reliable evidence would likely have been available and not destroyed. . . . The court finds that this conduct by the government which caused the four-year delay was at the very least extremely reckless. . . .

THEREFORE, IT IS ORDERED that defendant's motion in limine . . . [be] granted. . . .

* [In this paragraph and the next, the district judge was addressing a different point of law, not the best evidence rule. I have included these paragraphs here because they address the government's arguable bad faith in the loss of the original conversations and hence complete the court's reasoning under Rule 1004(a).—GF]

UNIT III: PRIVILEGES

CHAPTER 11

PRIVILEGES: GENERAL PRINCIPLES

A. RULE 501'S ORIGINS AND APPLICATION

Focus on **FRE 501**

FEDERAL RULE OF EVIDENCE 501: *Historical Prelude*

Buried in the back of your rulebooks, under the ominous heading, "Deleted and Superseded Materials," are Proposed Rules 501 through 513. These thirteen never-enacted rules would have established several general principles of privilege law and nine specific evidentiary privileges. Some of these specific privileges, such as the lawyer–client, psychotherapist–patient, and clergy–penitent privileges, survive today at federal common law. Others, such as the privilege for marital testimony, survive only in greatly altered form. None of the proposed privilege rules is law.

These thirteen rules proved to be the most controversial component of the slate of evidence rules transmitted by the Supreme Court to Congress in 1973. The firestorm they sparked highlights the odd place of privilege rules in our law, straddling the procedural niceties of evidence and the substantive concerns of social policy. Privileges are of course evidence rules—they act to limit the flow of information to the jury. Yet unlike the rules we have studied so far, they exclude evidence that suffers from no suspicion of irrelevance or unreliability. Privileges serve entirely different social goals—and implicate more complex political interests.

February 1973, when the proposed federal rules reached Congress, was hardly a time of American social harmony. Just as the nation's involvement in Vietnam was drawing to a close, public attention shifted to the brewing Watergate scandal. Enlisting Congress at that moment to negotiate the conflicting demands of evidence and privilege, truth-seeking and privacy, federalism and states' rights asked too much. In the end, Congress threw up its hands and replaced the entire set of proposed privilege rules with a single rule, Rule 501, which abdicates the whole matter of privileges to the courts.

The Fate of State Privilege Law

The controversy generated by the proposed privilege rules gelled largely around two issues. The first concerned the force of state privilege law. As originally proposed, Rule 501 commanded that federal privilege law should govern even in diversity actions otherwise controlled by state substantive law.

This choice-of-law controversy was a product of the pseudo-substantive nature of privilege rules. Whereas most evidence rules are considered "procedural" in the sense that they serve mainly to guide the truth-seeking process, privilege rules advance substantive social policies. A privilege that protects doctor–patient communications, for example, expresses a social judgment that the worth of doctor–patient confidentiality occasionally exceeds that of relevant and reliable evidence. On such judgments, the various states were reluctant to yield to the views of Congress. "[B]y failing to recognize state-created personal testimonial privileges," one commentator charged, "the [proposed rules] seriously impair the important capacity of the states to enlarge the enjoyment and protection of personal liberty." Thomas G. Krattenmaker, *Testimonial Privileges in Federal Courts: An Alternative to the Proposed Federal Rules of Evidence*, 62 GEO. L.J. 61, 102 (1973). Moved by such appeals, Congress chose to pay greater deference to state privilege law. Representative Dennis explained the change during House hearings:

> Now, it seems to me that those are pretty substantive matters for the law of the State to determine and I just wonder whether . . . the State's policy should be nullified simply because they sue me in Federal court instead of my own State court.

See EDWARD J. IMWINKELRIED, THE NEW WIGMORE § 4.2.2, at 179 (2002) (quoting from House hearings).

Under Rule 501 as enacted, federal privilege law controls in all federal criminal actions and in civil actions in federal court insofar as federal law supplies the rule of decision. But when state law supplies the rule of decision, as in diversity actions, state privilege law controls. In such cases, Congress concluded that "the State nature of the issues renders deference to State privilege law the wiser course. . . ." (Report of the Senate Judiciary Committee, RB 99.) Not surprisingly, this ungainly division of authority has spawned vexing choice-of-law issues, especially where state and federal claims are joined. *See* MUELLER & KIRKPATRICK, EVIDENCE § 5.7, at 313–15 (5th ed. 2012). As the Senate Judiciary Committee predicted, the rule has proved to be "pregnant with litigious mischief." (RB 100.)

Missing Privileges

The second perceived flaw of the proposed rules was their failure to protect communications between wife and husband,* doctor and patient, and reporter and source. These omissions probably reflected the advisory committee's general disapproval of broad evidentiary privileges. One committee member, Judge Jack B. Weinstein, reported the committee's consensus that privileges were " 'hindrances' which should be curtailed." *See* IMWINKELRIED, *supra,* § 4.2.1, at 153 (quoting Weinstein). Testifying before a House subcommittee in his role as the committee's reporter, Professor Edward W. Cleary noted Wigmore's opinion that many privileges simply protect the *privilege* of powerful professions and argued that privileges often act as "blockades" to the discovery of truth. *See id.* (quoting Cleary).

Harnessing their considerable rhetorical talent to defeat the proposed privilege rules, various commentators took aim at the omission of a marital confidences privilege. The advisory committee had argued that the privilege would do nothing to facilitate marital communications because spouses "in all likelihood are unaware" of the privilege. (ACN to Proposed Rule 505(a), RB 353.) To this "unsupported assertion," Professor Thomas Krattenmaker replied, "it might be sufficient simply to argue that a poll be taken, and dare the Committee to wager on the outcome." Krattenmaker, *supra,* at 91. Professor Charles Black likewise chided the Supreme Court, which formally promulgated the evidence rules, for its disregard of marital privacy. How odd, he said, that the Court so "staunchly defended" a privacy-based right to marital contraception in *Griswold v. Connecticut,* 381 U.S. 479 (1965), yet approved a set of evidence rules that abandoned the privacy of marital conversation. And Black ridiculed the advisory committee's distinction between the marital confidences privilege (omitted) and the lawyer–client, psychotherapist–patient, and clergy–penitent privileges (included).* The committee justified the distinction, Black noted,

> on the ground forsooth, that those other relations are "essentially and almost exclusively *verbal* in nature, quite unlike marriage." [Emphasis supplied.] Does this mean, *can* it be meant, that the marriage relation is entitled to less protection because its parties sleep together, found and maintain a home together, raise children together, besides talking to each other? But if not that, what *is* meant?

Charles L. Black, Jr., *Marital and Physician Privileges—A Reprint of a Letter to a Congressman,* 1975 DUKE L.J. 45, 48–49. That the committee included a privilege for "trade secrets" but none for marital secrets was, in Black's view, "sordid." *Id.* at 52.

Turning his ire next on the absence of a physician–patient privilege, Black again contrasted the Supreme Court's concern for some aspects of privacy with its unconcern for others:

* Proposed Rule 505 did provide for a spousal testimonial privilege. As we will see in Chapter 13, the spousal testimonial privilege, unlike the marital confidences privilege, is not specifically concerned with protecting marital privacy.

> In *Rochin v. California*, 342 U.S. 165 (1952), the late Mr. Justice Frankfurter, for the Court, condemned as utterly indecent the forced pumping of a man's stomach to get criminal evidence. Does not the forced revealing of every medical and personal fact, stomach contents and all, learned by the doctor of a person . . ., just to serve the convenience of any litigant, partake at least a little of the same indecency?

Id. at 50. "[A] human being ought to be able to consult any kind of a doctor," Black continued, "without by that act . . . rendering himself vulnerable to being stripped to and below the skin in public." *Id.* at 51. And he scorned the protections the committee gave lawyer–client confidences in Proposed Rule 503 while abandoning the privacy interests of doctors, patients, and spouses:

> [A]s a lawyer, I own I find it embarrassing that a group of lawyers, having so summarily dealt with the privacies of marriage and medicine, proceed, without any satisfactory explanation of the vast difference, to shield our own profession so amply. I wonder what kind of Rules we would have gotten if the doctors had drawn them.

Id.

In the end, of course, Professor Black and his fellow critics won the day. Congress abandoned the proposed privilege rules, largely withdrew from the task of lawmaking in this area, and committed the problem to the courts. Rule 501, the sole privilege rule enacted by Congress, left the law of privileges where it was and directed federal courts to enforce and develop privileges according to "[t]he common law—as interpreted by United States courts in the light of reason and experience."

As for the rejected privilege rules, they survive in more than mere memory. "[T]he action of Congress," the Senate Committee wrote, "should not be understood as disapproving any . . . of the enumerated privileges contained in the Supreme Court rules," but simply as "reflecting the view that . . . privileges should be determined on a case-by-case basis." (RB 101.) The proposed rules stand today, therefore, as reflections of the common law and as the work of the leading evidence scholars of their day. Having once borne the imprimatur of the Supreme Court, they retain substantial authoritative cachet. Both state and federal courts look to them for guidance.

As we will see in Chapter 13, Professor Black has prevailed on the issue that seemed to matter to him most. The Supreme Court has continued to recognize the common law privilege for marital confidences. On the other hand, the Court never did create a physician–patient privilege, nor have lower federal courts generally recognized one. *See United States v. Bek*, 493 F.3d 790, 801–02 (7th Cir.), *cert. denied*, 552 U.S. 1010 (2007); MUELLER & KIRKPATRICK, EVIDENCE § 5.34, at 424 (5th ed. 2012). As the next case shows, the Supreme Court instead used Rule 501's implicit grant of rulemaking authority to formulate a psychotherapist–patient privilege of the sort embodied by Proposed Rule 504. No doubt Black would have found this state of affairs unsettling. He thought it "preposterous" that a patient's disclosure of an embarrassing ailment to a doctor would be unprivileged, while the same disclosure by the same patient to his psychotherapist would be privileged. "It is a case," he wrote, "of the tail ceasing to wag the dog, and continuing to wag in place after the dog has gone away." Black, *supra*, at 51.

Focus on
Proposed FRE 504

JAFFEE v. REDMOND

518 U.S. 1 (1996).

■ JUSTICE STEVENS delivered the opinion of the Court. After a traumatic incident in which she shot and killed a man, a police officer received extensive counseling from a licensed clinical social worker. The question we address is whether statements the officer made to her therapist during the counseling sessions are protected from compelled disclosure in a federal civil action brought by the family of the deceased. Stated otherwise, the question is whether it is appropriate for federal courts to recognize a "psychotherapist privilege" under Rule 501 of the Federal Rules of Evidence.

I

. . . On June 27, 1991, [Mary Lu] Redmond was the first officer to respond to a "fight in progress" call at an apartment complex. As she arrived at the scene, two of [Ricky] Allen's sisters ran toward her squad car, waving their arms and shouting that there had been a stabbing in one of the apartments. . . . Before Redmond reached the building, . . . [two] men then burst out of the building, one, Ricky Allen, chasing the other. According to Redmond, Allen was brandishing a butcher knife and disregarded her repeated commands to drop the weapon. Redmond shot Allen when she believed he was about to stab the man he was chasing. Allen died at the scene. Redmond testified that before other officers arrived to provide support, "people came pouring out of the buildings," and a threatening confrontation between her and the crowd ensued.

Petitioner [the administrator of Allen's estate] filed suit in Federal District Court alleging that Redmond had violated Allen's constitutional rights by using excessive force during the encounter at the apartment complex.... At trial, petitioner presented testimony ... that Redmond drew her gun before exiting her squad car and that Allen was unarmed when he emerged from the apartment building.

During pretrial discovery petitioner learned that after the shooting Redmond had participated in about 50 counseling sessions with Karen Beyer, a clinical social worker licensed by the State of Illinois.... Petitioner sought access to Beyer's notes concerning the sessions for use in cross-examining Redmond. Respondents vigorously resisted the discovery. They asserted that the contents of the conversations between Beyer and Redmond were protected against involuntary disclosure by a psychotherapist–patient privilege. The district judge rejected this argument. Neither Beyer nor Redmond, however, complied with his order to disclose the contents of Beyer's notes....

In his instructions at the end of the trial, the judge advised the jury that the refusal to turn over Beyer's notes had no "legal justification" and that the jury could therefore presume that the contents of the notes would have been unfavorable to respondents. The jury awarded petitioner $45,000 on the federal claim and $500,000 on her state-law claim.

The Court of Appeals for the Seventh Circuit reversed and remanded for a new trial. Addressing the issue for the first time, the court concluded that "reason and experience," the touchstones for acceptance of a privilege under Rule 501 of the Federal Rules of Evidence, compelled recognition of a psychotherapist–patient privilege. 51 F.3d 1346, 1355 (7th Cir. 1995). "Reason tells us that psychotherapists and patients share a unique relationship, in which the ability to communicate freely without the fear of public disclosure is the key to successful treatment." As to experience, the court observed that all 50 States have adopted some form of the psychotherapist–patient privilege. The court attached particular significance to the fact that Illinois law expressly extends such a privilege to social workers like Karen Beyer....

The Court of Appeals qualified its recognition of the privilege by stating that it would not apply if "in the interests of justice, the evidentiary need for the disclosure of the contents of a patient's counseling sessions outweighs that patient's privacy interests." Balancing those conflicting interests, the court observed, on the one hand, that the evidentiary need for the contents of the confidential conversations was diminished in this case because there were numerous eyewitnesses to the shooting, and, on the other hand, that Officer Redmond's privacy interests were substantial. Based on this assessment, the court concluded that the trial court had erred by refusing to afford protection to the confidential communications between Redmond and Beyer....

II

Rule 501 ... did not freeze the law governing the privileges of witnesses in federal trials at a particular point in our history, but rather directed federal courts to "continue the evolutionary development of testimonial privileges." Trammel v. United States, 445 U.S. 40, 47 (1980)....

The common-law principles underlying the recognition of testimonial privileges can be stated simply. " 'For more than three centuries it has now been recognized as a fundamental maxim that the public ... has a right to every man's evidence. When we come to examine the various claims of exemption, we start with the primary assumption that there is a general duty to give what testimony one is capable of giving....' " United States v. Bryan, 339 U.S. 323, 331 (1950) (quoting 8 J. WIGMORE, EVIDENCE § 2192, p. 64 (3d ed. 1940)). Exceptions from the general rule disfavoring testimonial privileges may be justified, however, by a " 'public good transcending the normally predominant principle of utilizing all rational means for ascertaining the truth.' " *Trammel*, 445 U.S. at 50....

III

Like the spousal and attorney–client privileges, the psychotherapist–patient privilege is "rooted in the imperative need for confidence and trust." *Trammel*, 445 U.S. at 51. Treatment by a physician for physical ailments can often proceed successfully on the basis of a physical examination, objective information supplied by the patient, and the results of diagnostic tests. Effective psychotherapy, by contrast, depends upon an atmosphere of confidence and trust in which the patient is willing to make a frank and complete disclosure of facts, emotions, memories, and fears. Because of the sensitive nature of the problems for which individuals consult psychotherapists, disclosure of confidential communications made during counseling sessions may cause embarrassment or disgrace. For this reason, the mere possibility of disclosure may impede development of the confidential relationship necessary for successful treatment....

Our cases make clear that an asserted privilege must also "serve public ends." Upjohn Co. v. United States, 449 U.S. 383, 389 (1981). Thus, the purpose of the attorney–client privilege is to "encourage full and frank communication between attorneys and their clients and thereby promote broader public interests in the observance of law and administration of justice." *Ibid*. And the spousal privilege, as modified in *Trammel*, is justified because it "furthers the important public interest in marital harmony," 445 U.S. at 53. The psychotherapist privilege serves the public interest by facilitating the provision of appropriate treatment for individuals suffering the effects of a mental or emotional problem. The mental health of our citizenry, no less than its physical health, is a public good of transcendent importance.[10]

10. This case amply demonstrates the importance of allowing individuals to receive confidential counseling. Police officers engaged in the dangerous and difficult tasks associated with protecting the safety of our communities not only confront the

In contrast to the significant public and private interests supporting recognition of the privilege, the likely evidentiary benefit that would result from the denial of the privilege is modest. If the privilege were rejected, confidential conversations between psychotherapists and their patients would surely be chilled, particularly when it is obvious that the circumstances that give rise to the need for treatment will probably result in litigation. Without a privilege, much of the desirable evidence to which litigants such as petitioner seek access—for example, admissions against interest by a party—is unlikely to come into being. This unspoken "evidence" will therefore serve no greater truth-seeking function than if it had been spoken and privileged.

That it is appropriate for the federal courts to recognize a psychotherapist privilege under Rule 501 is confirmed by the fact that all 50 States and the District of Columbia have enacted into law some form of psychotherapist privilege. We have previously observed that the policy decisions of the States bear on the question whether federal courts should recognize a new privilege or amend the coverage of an existing one.... [G]iven the importance of the patient's understanding that her communications with her therapist will not be publicly disclosed, any State's promise of confidentiality would have little value if the patient were aware that the privilege would not be honored in a federal court. Denial of the federal privilege therefore would frustrate the purposes of the state legislation that was enacted to foster these confidential communications....

The uniform judgment of the States is reinforced by the fact that a psychotherapist privilege was among the nine specific privileges recommended by the Advisory Committee in its proposed privilege rules.... In rejecting the proposed draft that had specifically identified each privilege rule and substituting the present more open-ended Rule 501, the Senate Judiciary Committee explicitly stated that its action "should not be understood as disapproving any recognition of a psychiatrist–patient ... privilege contained in the [proposed] rules."

Because we agree with the judgment of the state legislatures and the Advisory Committee that a psychotherapist–patient privilege will serve a "public good transcending the normally predominant principle of utilizing all rational means for ascertaining truth," *Trammel*, 445 U.S. at 50, we hold that confidential communications between a licensed psychotherapist and her patients in the course of diagnosis or treatment are protected from compelled disclosure under Rule 501 of the Federal Rules of Evidence.

risk of physical harm but also face stressful circumstances that may give rise to anxiety, depression, fear, or anger. The entire community may suffer if police officers are not able to receive effective counseling and treatment after traumatic incidents, either because trained officers leave the profession prematurely or because those in need of treatment remain on the job.

IV

All agree that a psychotherapist privilege covers confidential communications made to licensed psychiatrists and psychologists. We have no hesitation in concluding in this case that the federal privilege should also extend to confidential communications made to licensed social workers in the course of psychotherapy. The reasons for recognizing a privilege for treatment by psychiatrists and psychologists apply with equal force to treatment by a clinical social worker such as Karen Beyer. Today, social workers provide a significant amount of mental health treatment. Their clients often include the poor and those of modest means who could not afford the assistance of a psychiatrist or psychologist. . . . Perhaps in recognition of these circumstances, the vast majority of States explicitly extend a testimonial privilege to licensed social workers. We therefore agree with the Court of Appeals that "drawing a distinction between the counseling provided by costly psychotherapists and the counseling provided by more readily accessible social workers serves no discernible public purpose."

We part company with the Court of Appeals on a separate point. We reject the balancing component of the privilege implemented by that court and a small number of States. Making the promise of confidentiality contingent upon a trial judge's later evaluation of the relative importance of the patient's interest in privacy and the evidentiary need for disclosure would eviscerate the effectiveness of the privilege. As we explained in *Upjohn*, if the purpose of the privilege is to be served, the participants in the confidential conversation "must be able to predict with some degree of certainty whether particular discussions will be protected. An uncertain privilege, or one which purports to be certain but results in widely varying applications by the courts, is little better than no privilege at all." 449 U.S. at 393.

These considerations are all that is necessary for decision of this case. A rule that authorizes the recognition of new privileges on a case-by-case basis makes it appropriate to define the details of new privileges in a like manner. Because this is the first case in which we have recognized a psychotherapist privilege, it is neither necessary nor feasible to delineate its full contours in a way that would "govern all conceivable future questions in this area." *Id.* at 386.[19]

V

The conversations between Officer Redmond and Karen Beyer and the notes taken during their counseling sessions are protected from

19. Although it would be premature to speculate about most future developments in the federal psychotherapist privilege, we do not doubt that there are situations in which the privilege must give way, for example, if a serious threat of harm to the patient or to others can be averted only by means of a disclosure by the therapist.

compelled disclosure under Rule 501 of the Federal Rules of Evidence. The judgment of the Court of Appeals is affirmed.

It is so ordered.

■ JUSTICE SCALIA, with whom THE CHIEF JUSTICE joins as to Part III, dissenting. The Court has discussed at some length the benefit that will be purchased by creation of the evidentiary privilege in this case: the encouragement of psychoanalytic counseling. It has not mentioned the purchase price: occasional injustice. That is the cost of every rule which excludes reliable and probative evidence—or at least every one categorical enough to achieve its announced policy objective. In the case of some of these rules, such as the one excluding confessions that have not been properly "Mirandized," *see* Miranda v. Arizona, 384 U.S. 436 (1966), the victim of the injustice is always the impersonal State or the faceless "public at large." For the rule proposed here, the victim is more likely to be some individual who is prevented from proving a valid claim—or (worse still) prevented from establishing a valid defense. . . .

I

The case before us involves confidential communications made by a police officer to a state-licensed clinical social worker in the course of psychotherapeutic counseling. Before proceeding to a legal analysis of the case, I must observe that the Court makes its task deceptively simple by the manner in which it proceeds. It begins by characterizing the issue as "whether it is appropriate for federal courts to recognize a 'psychotherapist privilege,'" and devotes almost all of its opinion to that question. Having answered that question (to its satisfaction) in the affirmative, it then devotes less than a page of text to answering in the affirmative the small remaining question whether "the federal privilege should also extend to confidential communications made to licensed social workers in the course of psychotherapy."

Of course the prototypical evidentiary privilege analogous to the one asserted here—the lawyer–client privilege—is not identified by the broad area of advice-giving practiced by the person to whom the privileged communication is given, but rather by the professional status of that person. Hence, it seems a long step from a lawyer–client privilege to a tax advisor–client or accountant–client privilege. But if one recharacterizes it as a "legal advisor" privilege, the extension seems like the most natural thing in the world. That is the illusion the Court has produced here: It first frames an overly general question ("Should there be a psychotherapist privilege?") that can be answered in the negative only by excluding from protection office consultations with professional psychiatrists (i.e., doctors) and clinical psychologists. And then, having answered that in the affirmative, it comes to the only question that the facts of this case present ("Should there be a social worker–client privilege with regard to psychotherapeutic counseling?") with the answer seemingly a foregone conclusion. . . .

Relegating the question actually posed by this case to an afterthought makes the impossible possible in a number of wonderful ways. For example, it enables the Court to treat the Proposed Federal Rules of Evidence developed in 1972 by the Judicial Conference Advisory Committee as strong support for its holding, whereas they in fact counsel clearly and directly against it. The Committee did indeed recommend a "psychotherapist privilege" of sorts; but more precisely, and more relevantly, it recommended a privilege for psychotherapy conducted by "a person authorized to practice medicine" or "a person licensed or certified as a psychologist," PROPOSED R. EVID. 504, which is to say that *it recommended against the privilege at issue here*. . . .

. . . [Hence] the Court's very methodology—giving serious consideration only to the more general, and much easier, question—is in violation of our duty to proceed cautiously when erecting barriers between us and the truth.

II

. . . Effective psychotherapy undoubtedly is beneficial to individuals with mental problems, and surely serves some larger social interest in maintaining a mentally stable society. But . . . are [these values] of such importance, and is the contribution of psychotherapy to them so distinctive, and is the application of normal evidentiary rules so destructive to psychotherapy, as to justify making our federal courts occasional instruments of injustice? . . .

When is it, one must wonder, that *the psychotherapist* came to play such an indispensable role in the maintenance of the citizenry's mental health? For most of history, men and women have worked out their difficulties by talking to, *inter alios*, parents, siblings, best friends and bartenders—none of whom was awarded a privilege against testifying in court. Ask the average citizen: Would your mental health be more significantly impaired by preventing you from seeing a psychotherapist, or by preventing you from getting advice from your mom? I have little doubt what the answer would be. Yet there is no mother–child privilege.

How likely is it that a person will be deterred from seeking psychological counseling, or from being completely truthful in the course of such counseling, because of fear of later disclosure in litigation? And even more pertinent to today's decision, to what extent will the evidentiary privilege reduce that deterrent? The Court does not try to answer the first of these questions; and it cannot possibly have any notion of what the answer is to the second, since that depends entirely upon the scope of the privilege, which the Court amazingly finds it "neither necessary nor feasible to delineate." If, for example, the psychotherapist can give the patient no more assurance than "A court will not be able to make me disclose what you tell me, unless you tell me about a harmful act," I doubt whether there would be much benefit from the privilege at all. . . .

Even where it is certain that absence of the psychotherapist privilege will inhibit disclosure of the information, it is not clear to me that that is an unacceptable state of affairs. Let us assume the very worst in the circumstances of the present case: that to be truthful about what was troubling her, the police officer who sought counseling would have to confess that she shot without reason, and wounded an innocent man. . . . [T]he officer would of course have the absolute right not to admit that she shot without reason in criminal court. But I see no reason why she should be enabled . . . to deny her guilt in the criminal trial—or in a civil trial for negligence—while yet obtaining the benefits of psychotherapy by confessing guilt to a social worker who cannot testify. It seems to me entirely fair to say that if she wishes the benefits of telling the truth she must also accept the adverse consequences. . . .

The Court suggests one last policy justification: since psychotherapist privilege statutes exist in all the States, the failure to recognize a privilege in federal courts "would frustrate the purposes of the state legislation that was enacted to foster these confidential communications." This is a novel argument indeed. A sort of inverse pre-emption: the truth-seeking functions of federal courts must be adjusted so as not to conflict with the policies of the States. . . . If furtherance of state policies is the name of the game, rules of privilege in federal courts should vary from State to State, a la *Erie*. . . .

The Court concedes that there is "divergence among the States concerning the types of therapy relationships protected and the exceptions recognized." To rest a newly announced federal common-law psychotherapist privilege, assertable from this day forward in all federal courts, upon "the States' *unanimous judgment* that some form of psychotherapist privilege is appropriate," is rather like announcing a new, immediately applicable, federal common law of torts, based upon the States' "unanimous judgment" that some form of tort law is appropriate. In the one case as in the other, the state laws vary to such a degree that the parties and lower federal judges confronted by the new "common law" have barely a clue as to what its content might be.

III

Turning from the general question that was not involved in this case to the specific one that is: The Court's conclusion that a social-worker psychotherapeutic privilege deserves recognition is even less persuasive. In approaching this question, the fact that five of the state legislatures that have seen fit to enact "some form" of psychotherapist privilege have elected not to extend *any form* of privilege to social workers, ought to give one pause. So should the fact that the Judicial Conference Advisory

Committee was similarly discriminating in its conferral of the proposed Rule 504 privilege....

... A licensed psychiatrist or psychologist is an expert in psychotherapy—and that may suffice (though I think it not so clear that this Court should make the judgment) to justify the use of extraordinary means to encourage counseling with him, as opposed to counseling with one's rabbi, minister, family or friends. One must presume that a social worker does not bring this greatly heightened degree of skill to bear, which is alone a reason for not encouraging that consultation as generously. Does a social worker bring to bear at least a significantly heightened degree of skill—more than a minister or rabbi, for example? I have no idea, and neither does the Court. The social worker in the present case, Karen Beyer, was a "licensed clinical social worker" in Illinois, a job title whose training requirements consist of "master's degree in social work from an approved program," and "3,000 hours of satisfactory, supervised clinical professional experience." ILL. COMP. STAT., ch. 225, § 20/9 (1994).... With due respect, it does not seem to me that any of this training is comparable in its rigor (or indeed in the precision of its subject) to the training of the other experts (lawyers) to whom this Court has accorded a privilege, or even of the experts (psychiatrists and psychologists) to whom the Advisory Committee and this Court proposed extension of a privilege in 1972. Of course these are only Illinois' requirements for "social workers." Those of other States, for all we know, may be even less demanding....

In its consideration of this case, the Court was the beneficiary of no fewer than 14 amicus briefs supporting respondents, most of which came from such organizations as the American Psychiatric Association, the American Psychoanalytic Association, ... and the National Association of Social Workers. Not a single amicus brief was filed in support of petitioner. That is no surprise. There is no self-interested organization out there devoted to pursuit of the truth in the federal courts. The expectation is, however, that this Court will have that interest prominently—indeed, primarily—in mind. Today we have failed that expectation, and that responsibility. It is no small matter to say that, in some cases, our federal courts will be the tools of injustice rather than unearth the truth where it is available to be found. The common law has identified a few instances where that is tolerable. Perhaps Congress may conclude that it is also tolerable for the purpose of encouraging psychotherapy by social workers. But that conclusion assuredly does not burst upon the mind with such clarity that a judgment in favor of suppressing the truth ought to be pronounced by this honorable Court. I respectfully dissent.

Problem 11.1
Relayed Threats

> [John] Auster, a retired New Orleans police officer, has been receiving workers' compensation benefits since 1989. Cannon Cochran Management Services, Inc. ("CCMSI"), manages Auster's benefit claim. Auster is treated for paranoia, anger, and depression and has threatened various individuals over the years. He often makes his threats during sessions with his two [psycho]therapists, [Dr. Fred] Davis and Dr. Harold Ginzburg, and his therapists then relay—pursuant to their "duty to warn" [imposed by local law]—his threats to their targets. Auster admits that he is aware that his threats are communicated in that way....
>
> In September 2006, CCMSI informed Auster that it would stop paying a portion of his benefits beginning on October 1, 2006. On September 13, Auster discussed the pending partial termination of benefits with Davis, specifically threatening CCMSI personnel, city authorities, and police officials. Davis sent Keith Smith, a CCMSI employee responsible for Auster's claim, a letter warning that it was Auster's position that if "CCMIS [sic] persists in their position," that would "serve as a provocation for him to carry out his plan of violent retribution against a list of persons he feels have caused him injury." Davis alerted CCMSI that Auster had stated that he possessed "stockpiles of weapons and supplies to provide the basis for his actions." October 2 was marked as the date of "violent retribution." ...
>
> ... [A federal] grand jury indicted [Auster for extortion in that he] "attempt[ed] to obtain property of CCMSI ... by the wrongful use of threatened force, violence and fear, in that the defendant did communicate to CCMSI, via his treating psychotherapist," his threat of violence if his benefits were reduced.

United States v. Auster, 517 F.3d 312, 313–15 (5th Cir.), *cert. denied*, 555 U.S. 840 (2008). In a pretrial motion, Auster argued to the district judge that the threats he relayed to Davis were protected by Auster's psychotherapist–patient privilege and therefore should be excluded. His lawyer conceded that Auster "was in fact on occasion told [by his therapist] that his threats of violence would be communicated to CCMSI." The district judge found that Auster "knew, when he made the September 13 threat, that it would be forwarded to CCMSI."

Was the trial judge right to rule that Auster's threats toward CCMSI, as relayed to Davis during private therapy sessions, were privileged? What were the best arguments for the prosecution and defense?

IN RE: GRAND JURY SUBPOENA, JUDITH MILLER

397 F.3d 964 (D.C. Cir.), *cert. denied*, 545 U.S. 1150 (2005), *reissued*, 438 F.3d 1141 (2006).

■ Before: SENTELLE, HENDERSON and TATEL, CIRCUIT JUDGES.

■ SENTELLE, CIRCUIT JUDGE. An investigative reporter for the New York Times; the White House correspondent for the weekly news magazine Time; and Time, Inc., the publisher of Time, appeal from orders of the District Court for the District of Columbia finding all three appellants in civil contempt for refusing to give evidence in response to grand jury subpoenas served by Special Counsel Patrick J. Fitzgerald. Appellants assert that the information concealed by them, specifically the identity of confidential sources, is protected by a reporter's privilege arising from the First Amendment, or failing that, by federal common law privilege. . . .

I. BACKGROUND

. . . [T]he controversy giving rise to this litigation began with a political and news media controversy over a sixteen-word sentence in the State of the Union Address of President George W. Bush on January 28, 2003. In that address, President Bush stated: "The British government has learned that Saddam Hussein recently sought significant quantities of uranium from Africa." . . . On July 6, 2003, the New York Times published an op-ed piece by former Ambassador Joseph Wilson, in which he claimed to have been sent to Niger in 2002 by the Central Intelligence Agency in response to inquiries from Vice President Cheney to investigate whether Iraq had been seeking to purchase uranium from Niger. Wilson claimed that he had conducted the requested investigation and reported on his return that there was no credible evidence that any such effort had been made.

On July 14, 2003, columnist Robert Novak published a column in the Chicago Sun–Times in which he asserted that . . . "two senior administration officials" told him that Wilson's selection was at the suggestion of Wilson's wife, Valerie Plame, whom Novak described as a CIA "operative on weapons of mass destruction." After Novak's column was published, various media accounts reported that other reporters had been told by government officials that Wilson's wife worked at the CIA monitoring weapons of mass destruction, and that she was involved in her husband's selection for the mission to Niger. One such article, published by Time.com on July 17, 2003, was authored in part by appellant Matthew

Cooper. . . . The Department of Justice undertook an investigation into whether government employees had violated federal law by the unauthorized disclosure of the identity of a CIA agent. *See, e.g.*, 50 U.S.C. § 421 (criminalizing, *inter alia*, disclosure of the identity of a covert agent by anyone having had authorized access to classified information). As the investigation proceeded, . . . the Deputy Attorney General . . . appointed Patrick J. Fitzgerald . . . as Special Counsel. . . .

In cooperation with Special Counsel Fitzgerald, . . . the grand jury issued a . . . subpoena to Cooper seeking "any and all documents . . . [relating to] conversations between Matthew Cooper and official source(s) prior to July 14, 2003, concerning in any way: former Ambassador Joseph Wilson; the 2002 trip by former Ambassador Wilson to Niger; Valerie Wilson Plame, . . . and/or any affiliation between Valerie Wilson Plame and the CIA." An August 2, 2004 subpoena to Time requested [related materials] . . . Cooper and Time . . . moved to quash the subpoenas, and on October 7, 2004, the District Court denied the motion. The two refused to comply with the subpoenas, and on October 13, 2004, the District Court held that their refusal was without just cause and held both in contempt.

In the meantime, . . . grand jury subpoenas were issued to Judith Miller, seeking documents and testimony related to [the Plame controversy]. . . . Miller refused to comply with the subpoenas and moved to quash them. The District Court denied Miller's motion to quash. Thereafter, the court found that Miller had refused to comply without just cause and held her in civil contempt of court also. She also has appealed. . . .

II. ANALYSIS

A. *The First Amendment Claim*

In his opinion below, the Chief District Judge held that "a reporter called to testify before a grand jury regarding confidential information enjoys no First Amendment protection." . . . In Branzburg v. Hayes, 408 U.S. 665 (1972), the Highest Court considered and rejected the same claim of First Amendment privilege on facts materially indistinguishable from those at bar.

. . . The named petitioner, Branzburg, had been held in contempt in . . . proceedings, arising from [an] extended task of investigative journalism. The [controversy] arose from an article published by his employer, a daily newspaper, describing his observation of two Kentucky residents synthesizing hashish from marijuana as part of a profitable illegal drug operation. . . . A Kentucky grand jury subpoenaed the journalist, who "refused to identify the . . . persons he had seen making hashish from marihuana." Branzburg claimed privilege . . . under the First Amendment of the United States Constitution. . . . [He] claim[ed] "that if he were forced to go before the grand jury or to answer questions regarding the identity of informants . . . , his effectiveness as a reporter would be greatly damaged." . . .

In rejecting the claim of privilege, the Supreme Court . . . recognized that "the grand jury's authority to subpoena witnesses is not only historic . . . but essential to its task." The grand juries and the courts operate under the "longstanding principle that 'the public has a right to every man's evidence,' except for those persons protected by constitutional, common law, or statutory privilege." . . . In language as relevant to the alleged illegal disclosure of the identity of covert agents as it was to the alleged illegal processing of hashish, the Court stated that it could not "seriously entertain the notion that the First Amendment protects a newsman's agreement to conceal the criminal conduct of his source, or evidence thereof, on the theory that it is better to write about a crime than to do something about it." . . .

. . . [T]he High Court went on to recognize that "there remain those situations where a source is not engaged in criminal conduct but has information suggesting illegal conduct by others." As to this category of informants, the Court was equally adamant in rejecting the claim of First Amendment privilege:

> We cannot accept the argument that the public interest in possible future news about crime from undisclosed, unverified sources must take precedence over the public interest in pursuing and prosecuting those crimes reported to the press by informants and in thus deterring the commission of such crimes in the future.

. . . While the Court recognized the right of the press to abide by its agreements not to publish information that it has, the Court stated unequivocally that "the right to withhold news is not equivalent to a First Amendment exemption from an ordinary duty of all other citizens to furnish relevant information to a grand jury performing an important public function."

We have pressed appellants for some distinction between the facts before the Supreme Court in *Branzburg* and those before us today. They have offered none. . . . [T]here is no First Amendment privilege protecting journalists from . . . providing evidence to a grand jury. . . . The Highest Court has spoken and never revisited the question. Without doubt, that is the end of the matter. . . .

B. *The Common Law Privilege*

Appellants argue that even if there is no First Amendment privilege protecting their confidential source information, we should recognize a privilege under federal common law, arguing that regardless of whether a federal common law privilege protecting reporters existed in 1972 when *Branzburg* was decided, in the intervening years much has changed. . . . [This] Court is not of one mind on the existence of a common law privilege. Judge Sentelle would hold that there is no such common law privilege for reasons set forth in a separate opinion. Judge Tatel would hold that there is such a common law privilege. Judge Henderson believes that we need not, and therefore should not, reach that question. However, all believe that if there is any such privilege, it is not absolute and may be overcome by an appropriate showing. All further believe, for the reasons set forth in the separate opinion of Judge Tatel, that if such a privilege applies here, it has been overcome. Therefore, the common law privilege, even if one exists, does not warrant reversal. . . .

III. CONCLUSION

For the reasons set forth above, the judgment of the District Court is affirmed.

■ SENTELLE, CIRCUIT JUDGE, *concurring*: . . . I would hold that reporters refusing to testify before grand juries as to their "confidential sources" enjoy no common law privilege beyond the protection against harassing grand juries conducting groundless investigations that is available to all other citizens. . . .

I base my rejection of the common law privilege theory on foundations of precedent, policy, and separation of powers. As to precedent, I find *Branzburg* to be as dispositive of the question of common law privilege as it is of a First Amendment privilege. . . . [T]he *Branzburg* Court repeatedly discussed the privilege question in common law terms as well as constitutional. Indeed, the majority opinion by Justice White includes the phrase "common law" no fewer than eight times. More significant . . . is what the Court had to say about [the common law]: "at common law, courts consistently refuse to recognize the existence of any privilege authorizing a newsman to refuse to reveal confidential information to a grand jury." 408 U.S. at 685 (collecting cases).

. . . I think it therefore indisputable that the High Court rejected a common law privilege in the same breath as its rejection of such a privilege based on the First Amendment. Especially is this so when we consider that it makes little sense to assume that the Court first reached out to take a constitutional question it would not have needed to answer had there been such a common law privilege, and then proceeded to answer that question in such a fashion as to reach a result upholding contempt citations. . . .

[Appellants' argument] that we would have the power to adopt such a privilege in the face of the *Branzburg* precedent . . . begins with the Federal Rules of Evidence. Rule 501, enacted by Congress in the Federal Rules of Evidence in 1975, three years after *Branzburg*, rejected an enumeration of specific federal privileges and provided that privileges in federal criminal cases "shall be governed by the principles of the common law as they may be interpreted by the courts of the United States in the light of reason and experience." Although the rules became effective after *Branzburg*, Rule 501 does not effect any change in the authority of federal courts to adopt evidentiary privileges. Before the enactment of the Federal Rules of Evidence, the authority of the federal courts to adopt common law privileges was governed by case law.... Indeed, the language of the rule is drawn directly from case law governing at the time of *Branzburg*. The Supreme Court expressly held in *Wolfle v. United States*, 291 U.S. 7 (1934), that "the rules governing the competence of witnesses in criminal trials in the federal courts are ... *governed by common law principles as interpreted and applied by the federal courts in the light of reason and experience.*" *Id.* at 12 (emphasis added).... Thus, the enactment of Rule 501 cannot by itself work any change in the law which should empower us to depart from the Supreme Court's clear precedent in *Branzburg*.

Appellants persist, however, that the state of the common law has changed sufficiently to warrant a new approach. By appellants' count, at the time of the *Branzburg* decision, only seventeen states had enacted what appellants refer to as "shield laws" to protect journalists from forced disclosure of confidential sources or newsgathering materials, while today, thirty-one states (plus the District of Columbia) have such statutes....

... [E]ven if we are authorized to [create a common law privilege] reasons of policy and separation of powers counsel against our exercising that authority.... I find the adoption of the privilege by the legislatures of the states instructive as to how the federal government should proceed, if at all, to adopt the privilege. The [state] statutes differ greatly as to the scope of the privilege, and as to the identity of persons entitled to the protection of the privilege....

The Supreme Court itself in *Branzburg* noted the difficult and vexing nature of [defining the group of protected persons], observing that applying such privilege would make it

> necessary to define those categories of newsmen who qualify for the privilege, a questionable procedure in light of the traditional doctrine that liberty of the press is the right of the lonely pamphleteer who uses carbon paper or a mimeograph just as much as of the large metropolitan publisher who utilizes the latest photocomposition methods.

The Supreme Court went on to observe that "freedom of the press is ... not confined to newspapers and periodicals. It necessarily embraces ... every sort of publication which affords a vehicle of information and opinion." Are we then to create a privilege that protects only those reporters employed by Time Magazine, the New York Times, and other media giants, or do we extend that protection as well to the owner of a desktop printer producing a weekly newsletter to inform his neighbors, lodge brothers, co-religionists, or co-conspirators? Perhaps more to the point today, does the privilege also protect the proprietor of a web log: the stereotypical "blogger" sitting in his pajamas at his personal computer posting on the World Wide Web his best product to inform whoever happens to browse his way? If not, why not? How could one draw a distinction consistent with the Court's vision of a broadly granted personal right? If so, then would it not be possible for a government official wishing to engage in the sort of unlawful leaking under investigation in the present controversy to call a trusted friend or a political ally, advise him to set up a web log (which I understand takes about three minutes) and then leak to him under a promise of confidentiality the information which the law forbids the official to disclose?

The state legislatures have dealt with this vexing question of entitlement to the privilege in a variety of ways. Some are quite restrictive.... Arkansas's legislature has declared the privilege applicable to "any editor, reporter, or other writer for any newspaper, periodical, or radio station, or publisher of any newspaper or periodical, or manager or owner of any radio station...." Ark. Code Ann. § 16–85–510.... Presumably, states [with similar laws] would provide the privilege only to the "established" press.

Others are quite inclusive. The Nebraska legislature, for example, has declared:

> (1) That the policy of the State of Nebraska is to insure the free flow of news and other information to the public, and that those who gather, write, or edit information for the public or disseminate information to the public may perform these vital functions only in a free and unfettered atmosphere; (2) That such persons shall not be inhibited, directly or indirectly, by governmental restraint or sanction....

Neb. Rev. Stat. § 20–144. To that end, it protects any "medium of communication" which term "shall include, *but not be limited to*, any newspaper, magazine, other periodical, book, pamphlet, news service, wire service, news or feature syndicate, broadcast station or network, or cable television system." *Id.* § 20–145(2) (emphasis added).... Presumably, then, Nebraska ... protects the pamphleteer at the rented printer, and the blogger at the PC, as well as the giant corporation with its New York publishing house.

... If the courts extend the privilege only to a defined group of reporters, are we in danger of creating a "licensed" or "established" press? If we do so, have we run afoul of the breadth of the freedom of the press ... ? Conversely, if we extend that privilege to the easily created blog, or the ill-defined pamphleteer, have we defeated legitimate investigative ends of grand juries in cases like the leak of intelligence involved in the present investigation? ...

... [If] a decision requires the resolution of so many difficult policy questions, many of them beyond the normal compass of a single case or controversy such as those with which the courts regularly deal, doesn't that decision smack of legislation more than adjudication? ... The creation of a reporter's privilege, if it is to be done at all, looks more like a legislative than an adjudicative decision....

■ HENDERSON, CIRCUIT JUDGE, concurring: I write separately to emphasize that adherence to the principle of judicial restraint ... would produce a better result.... Because my colleagues and I agree that any federal common-law reporter's privilege that may exist is not absolute and that the Special Counsel's evidence defeats whatever privilege we may fashion, we need not, and therefore should not, decide anything more today than that the Special Counsel's evidentiary proffer overcomes any hurdle, however high, a federal common-law reporter's privilege may erect....

... I am far less eager a federal common-law pioneer than Judge Tatel as I find less comfort than he in riding *Jaffee v. Redmond* 518 U.S. 1 (1996), into the testimonial privilege frontier.... [W]e should proceed as cautiously as possible "when erecting barriers between us and the truth," *id.* at 21 (Scalia, J., dissenting), recognizing that the Legislature remains the more appropriate institution to reconcile the competing interests—prosecuting criminal acts versus constricting the flow of information to the public—that inform any reporter's privilege to withhold relevant information from a bona fide grand jury.

Because *Jaffee* sits rather awkwardly within a jurisprudence marked by a fairly uniform disinclination to announce new privileges or even expand existing ones, and even though it enjoyed the support of an overwhelming majority, I am hesitant to apply its methodology to a case that does not require us to do so....

■ TATEL, CIRCUIT JUDGE, concurring in the judgment: This case involves a clash between two truth-seeking institutions: the grand jury and the press.... On the one hand, the grand jury ... holds "broad powers" to collect evidence through judicially enforceable subpoenas. "Without thorough and effective investigation, the grand jury would be unable either to ferret out crimes deserving of prosecution, or to screen out charges not warranting prosecution." On the other hand, the press, shielded by the First Amendment, "has been a mighty catalyst in ... exposing corruption among public officers and employees and generally informing the citizenry of public events...." ...

Because I agree that the balance in this case, which involves the alleged exposure of a covert agent, favors compelling the reporters' testimony, I join the judgment of the court. I write separately, however, because ... I believe that the consensus of forty-nine states plus the District of Columbia—and even the Department of Justice—would require us to protect reporters' sources as a matter of federal common law were the leak at issue either less harmful or more newsworthy....

II.

... In 1975—three years after *Branzburg*—Congress enacted Rule 501 of the Federal Rules of Evidence.... Given *Branzburg*'s instruction that

"Congress has freedom to determine whether a statutory newsman's privilege is necessary and desirable and to fashion standards and rules as narrow or broad as deemed necessary to deal with the evil discerned," Rule 501's delegation of congressional authority [to courts] requires that we look anew at the "necessity and desirability" of the reporter privilege—though from a common law perspective.

Under Rule 501, that common lawmaking obligation exists whether or not, absent the rule's delegation, Congress would be "the more appropriate institution to reconcile the competing interests ... that inform any reporter's privilege to withhold relevant information from a bona fide grand jury." *Supra* (Henderson, J., concurring). As the Supreme Court has explained, "Rule 501 was adopted precisely because Congress wished to leave privilege questions to the courts rather than attempt to codify them." Thus, subject of course to congressional override, we must assess the arguments for and against the claimed privilege, just as the Supreme Court has done in cases recognizing common law privileges since 1975. *See, e.g., Jaffee v. Redmond.*

In this case, just as *Jaffee v. Redmond* recognized a common law psychotherapist privilege based on "the uniform judgment of the States," I believe that "reason and experience" dictate a privilege for reporters' confidential sources—albeit a qualified one....

Existence of the Privilege

Under *Jaffee*, the common law analysis starts with the interests that call for recognizing a privilege.... Like psychotherapists, as well as attorneys and spouses, all of whom enjoy privileges under Rule 501, reporters "depend[] upon an atmosphere of confidence and trust," *Jaffee*, 518 U.S. at 10. If litigants and investigators could easily discover journalists' sources, the press's truth-seeking function would be severely impaired. Reporters could reprint government statements, but not ferret out underlying disagreements among officials; they could cover public governmental actions, but would have great difficulty getting potential whistleblowers to talk about government misdeeds; they could report arrest statistics, but not garner first-hand information about the criminal underworld. Such valuable endeavors would be all but impossible, for ... sources who fear identification [would] avoid revealing information that could get them in trouble.

Because of these chilling effects, "without a privilege, much of the desirable evidence to which litigants ... seek access ... is unlikely to come into being." *Id.* at 12. Consequently, as with other privileges, "the likely evidentiary benefit that would result from the denial of the privilege is modest." *Id.* at 11. At the same time, although suppression of some leaks is surely desirable (a point to which I shall return), the public harm that would flow from undermining all source relationships would be immense. For example, appellant Judith Miller tells us that her Pulitzer

Prize-winning articles on Osama bin Laden's terrorist network relied on "information received from confidential sources at the highest levels of our government." (Miller Aff. at 10.) Likewise, appellant Matthew Cooper maintains that his reports for "*Time*'s four million-plus readers about White House policy in Iraq . . ." would have been impossible without confidentiality. (Cooper Aff. at 21.) Insofar as such stories exemplify the press's role "as a constitutionally chosen means for keeping officials . . . responsible to all the people whom they were elected to serve," "reason and experience" support protecting newsgathering methods crucial to their genesis. . . .

Turning next, as did *Jaffee*, to the consensus among states, I find support for the privilege at least as strong for journalists as for psychotherapists. Just as in *Jaffee*, where "the fact that all 50 states and the District of Columbia have enacted into law some form of psychotherapist privilege" favored an exercise of federal common lawmaking, so here undisputed evidence that forty-nine states plus the District of Columbia offer at least qualified protection to reporters' sources confirms that " 'reason and experience' support recognition of the privilege," *Jaffee*, 518 U.S. at 12–13. Indeed, given these state laws, "denial of the federal privilege . . . would frustrate the purposes of the state legislation" by exposing confidences protected under state law to discovery in federal courts. *Id.* at 13. . . .

Making the case for a privilege here even stronger than in *Jaffee*, federal authorities also favor recognizing a privilege for reporters' confidential sources. . . . [W]e ourselves have limited discovery of reporters' sources in both civil and criminal litigation, as have other federal courts. . . .* In addition, the Justice Department guidelines . . . establish a federal policy of protecting "news media from forms of compulsory process, whether civil or criminal, which might impair the news gathering function." 28 C.F.R. § 50.10. Denial of the privilege, then, would not only buck the clear policy of virtually all states, but would also contradict regulations binding on the federal government's own lawyers. . . .

. . . [T]he shift in favor of the privilege since [the time of *Branzburg*]—from seventeen states with statutory privileges then to thirty-one plus D.C. today, with another eighteen providing common law protection— . . . [means that] this court must assess the reporters' claim in light of "reason and experience" today.** As *Branzburg* itself observes in describ-

* [Here Judge Tatel cites cases from the First, Second, Third, and Tenth Circuit Courts of Appeals. The Fourth, Fifth, Ninth, and Eleventh Circuits also have recognized a reporter–source privilege of greater or lesser scope. The Sixth and Seventh Circuits have denied such a privilege. The Eighth Circuit has not ruled definitively on the question. *See* Jeffrey S. Nestler, *The Underprivileged Profession: The Case for Supreme Court Recognition of the Journalist's Privilege*, 154 U. PA. L. REV. 201, 224–25 nn.103–115 (2005); *U.S. Dept. of Educ. v. NCAA*, 481 F.3d 936, 938 (7th Cir. 2007).—GF]

** [The lone state without either a statutory or common-law reporter–source privilege is Wyoming. *See* Nestler, *supra*, 154 U. PA. L. REV. at 226 n.124.—GF]

ing Congress's powers, privilege rules may require "refashioning . . . as experience from time to time may dictate." Bestowing that refashioning power on the federal courts, Rule 501 evidences an "affirmative intention not to freeze the law of privilege," but rather "to leave the door open to change." Trammel v. United States, 445 U.S. 40, 47 (1980). . . . [Hence] . . . the omission of a reporter privilege from the Judicial Conference Advisory Committee's draft rules submitted to Congress in 1972 (and ultimately replaced by Rule 501) need not dictate the outcome here. . . .

. . . Nor does it matter that unconventional forms of journalism—freelance writers and internet "bloggers," for example—may raise definitional conundrums down the road. As *Jaffee* makes clear, "[a] rule," such as Rule 501, "that authorizes the recognition of new privileges on a case-by-case basis makes it appropriate to define the details of new privileges in a like manner." 518 U.S. at 18. . . . Here, whereas any meaningful reporter privilege must undoubtedly encompass appellants Cooper and Miller, full-time journalists for Time magazine and the New York Times, respectively, future opinions can elaborate more refined contours of the privilege—a task shown to be manageable by the experience of the fifty jurisdictions with statutory or common law protections.

In sum, "reason and experience," as evidenced by the laws of forty-nine states and the District of Columbia, as well as federal courts and the federal government, support recognition of a privilege for reporters' confidential sources. To disregard this modern consensus in favor of decades-old views, as the special counsel urges, would not only imperil vital newsgathering, but also shirk the common law function assigned by Rule 501 and "freeze the law of privilege" contrary to Congress's wishes, *see Trammel,* 445 U.S. at 47.

Scope of the Privilege

. . . I agree with the special counsel that protection for source identities cannot be absolute. Leaks similar to the crime suspected here (exposure of a covert agent) apparently caused the deaths of several CIA operatives in the late 1970s and early 1980s. . . . Other leaks—the design for a top secret nuclear weapon, for example, or plans for an imminent military strike—could be even more damaging, causing harm far in excess of their news value. In such cases, the reporter privilege must give way. Just as attorney–client communications "made for the purpose of getting advice for the commission of a fraud or crime" serve no public interest and receive no privilege, *see United States v. Zolin,* 491 U.S. 554, 563 (1989), neither should courts protect sources whose leaks harm national security while providing minimal benefit to public debate.

Of course, in some cases a leak's value may far exceed its harm, thus calling into question the law enforcement rationale for disrupting reporter–source relationships. For example, assuming Miller's prize-winning

Osama bin Laden series caused no significant harm, I find it difficult to see how one could justify compelling her to disclose her sources, given the obvious benefit of alerting the public to then-underappreciated threats from al Qaeda. . . . "[T]he approach in every case must be to strike the proper balance between the public's interest in the free dissemination of ideas and information and the public's interest in effective law enforcement and the fair administration of justice." 28 C.F.R. § 50.10(a). . . .

. . . Specifically, the court must weigh the public interest in compelling disclosure, measured by the harm the leak caused, against the public interest in newsgathering, measured by the leaked information's value. That framework allows authorities seeking to punish a leak to access key evidence when the leaked information does more harm than good, such as in the nuclear weapon and military strike examples, while preventing discovery when no public interest supports it, as would appear to be the case with Miller's Osama bin Laden articles. Though flexible, these standards (contrary to the special counsel's claim) are hardly unmanageable. Indeed, the Supreme Court employs a similar requirement of "legitimate news interest," meaning "value and concern to the public at the time of publication," in assessing restrictions on government employee speech. *See City of San Diego v. Roe,* 543 U.S. 77 (2004) (per curiam). . . .

. . . [A]ppellants insist that a qualified privilege fails to provide the certainty their work requires because sources are unlikely to disclose information without an advance guarantee of secrecy. In particular, they argue that journalists cannot balance a leak's harm against its news value until they know what information the source will reveal, by which time it is too late to prevent disclosure. True enough, but journalists are not the ones who must perform the balancing; sources are. Indeed, the point of the qualified privilege is to create disincentives for the source—disincentives that not only promote the public interest, but may also protect journalists from exploitation by government officials seeking publication of damaging secrets for partisan advantage. Like other recipients of potentially privileged communications—say, attorneys or psychotherapists—the reporter can at most alert the source to the limits of confidentiality, leaving the judgment of what to say to the source. While the resulting deterrent effect may cost the press some leads, little harm will result, for if the disincentives work as they should, the information sources refrain from revealing will lack significant news value in the first place.

In any event, although *Jaffee* said that "making the promise of confidentiality contingent upon a trial judge's later evaluation . . . [will] eviscerate the effectiveness of the privilege," the clash of fundamental interests at stake when the government seeks discovery of a reporter's sources precludes a categorical approach. . . .

In short, the question in this case is whether Miller's and Cooper's sources released information more harmful than newsworthy. If so, then the public interest in punishing the wrongdoers—and deterring future leaks—outweighs any burden on newsgathering, and no privilege covers the communication. . . .

III.

Applying this standard to the facts of this case, . . . I have no doubt that the leak at issue was a serious matter. . . . [Plame's] exposure . . . not only may have jeopardized any covert activities of her own, but also may have endangered friends and associates from whom she might have gathered information in the past. Acting to criminalize such exposure of secret agents, *see* 50 U.S.C. § 421, Congress has identified that behavior's "intolerable" consequences: "the loss of vital human intelligence which our policymakers need, the great cost to the American taxpayer of replacing intelligence resources lost due to such disclosures, and the greatly increased risk of harm which continuing disclosures force intelligence officers and sources to endure." S. Rep. No. 97–201, at 10–11 (1981).

The leak of Plame's apparent employment, moreover, had marginal news value. To be sure, insofar as Plame's CIA relationship may have helped explain her husband's selection for the Niger trip, that information could bear on her husband's credibility and thus contribute to public debate over the president's "sixteen words." Compared to the damage of undermining covert intelligence-gathering, however, this slight news value cannot, in my view, justify privileging the leaker's identity. . . . While requiring [these reporters] to testify may discourage future leaks, discouraging leaks of this kind is precisely what the public interest requires. . . .

Reporter Jailed After Refusing to Name Source

Adam Liptak

New York Times, July 7, 2005, at A1

Washington.—Judith Miller, an investigative reporter for The New York Times, was sent to jail on Wednesday after a federal judge declared that she was "defying the law" by refusing to divulge the name of a confidential source.

Another reporter who faced jail in the case, Matthew Cooper of Time magazine, was spared after announcing a last-minute deal with a confidential source that he said would allow him to testify before a grand jury.

Before being taken into custody by three court officers, Ms. Miller said she could not in good conscience violate promises to her sources. "If journalists cannot be trusted to guarantee confidentiality," she told Judge Thomas F. Hogan, "then journalists cannot function and there cannot be a free press."

Judge Hogan held the two reporters in civil contempt in October for refusing to cooperate with a federal prosecutor's investigation into the disclosure of the identity of a covert operative of the Central Intelligence Agency. The prosecutor's efforts produced the most serious confrontation between the government and the press since the Pentagon Papers case in 1971. The Supreme Court refused to hear appeals from the reporters last week. . . .

After listening to Ms. Miller, the judge ordered her sent to "a suitable jail . . ." until she decided to talk or until the term of the grand jury expired in October. . . .

In her statement in court, Ms. Miller said . . . , "The freest and fairest societies are not only those with independent judiciaries, . . . but those with an independent press that works every day to keep government accountable by publishing what the government might not want the public to know." . . .

[Special Counsel Patrick J.] Fitzgerald said the law now requires her to testify. "The law says the grand jury is entitled to every man's evidence," he said. "We're doing our honest best to get to the bottom of whether a crime has been committed." . . .

In a statement, Arthur Sulzberger Jr., the publisher of The Times, said . . . , "I sincerely hope that now Congress will move forward on federal shield legislation so that other journalists will not have to face imprisonment for doing their jobs." . . .

House Extends Law to Protect Reporters

The Legislation Passes in a Landslide, Garners Enough Bipartisan Support to Override Bush's Promised Veto.

Noam N. Levey

LOS ANGELES TIMES, Oct. 17, 2007, at A9

WASHINGTON.—Setting up a potential confrontation with the Bush administration over press freedoms, the House on Tuesday overwhelmingly passed legislation to extend new protections to journalists and their confidential sources.

The so-called shield law would for the first time establish standards that limit the power of federal authorities to compel reporters to testify or to disclose documents and unidentified sources they have used in their reporting.

The bill passed, 398 to 21. . . . With 176 Republicans joining 222 Democrats, the measure far exceeded the two-thirds needed to override a veto.

"In recent years, the press has been under assault," said House Judiciary Committee Chairman John Conyers Jr. (D–Mich.). "It's . . . Congress' responsibility to ensure that the press is able to perform its job adequately. . . . This measure balances the public's right to know against the legitimate and important interests society has in maintaining public safety."

A similar bill attracted broad bipartisan support when the Senate Judiciary Committee approved it, 15 to 2, earlier this month.

Even if the federal shield law wins Senate passage, it faces staunch opposition from the White House, which warned Tuesday that the law "would produce immediate harm to national security and law enforcement" by encouraging leaks and hampering the government's ability to prosecute terrorism cases. The administration warned of a veto if it is sent to the president. . . .

Tuesday's House vote comes after a more than 30–year campaign by media organizations for a law to prevent journalists from being forced to divulge their sources in federal court. . . . [R]ecent high-profile showdowns between journalists and the federal courts over confidential sources reinvigorated the legislative campaign.

Two years ago, a federal judge sent New York Times reporter Judith Miller to jail for refusing to disclose her source in the investigation of the leaked identity of covert CIA operative Valerie Plame. She spent 85 days in jail. In San Francisco, another federal judge threatened to jail two San Francisco Chronicle reporters for refusing to disclose a source in their investigation of steroid use in Major League Baseball.

Media groups also softened their demands, agreeing to exceptions that would allow a federal judge to compel disclosure of documents or sources if it would prevent an act of terrorism or if a source would be "critical" to resolving a criminal case.

Responding to criticism from the Bush administration, the sponsors also added an exception Tuesday to allow a judge to order disclosure if it is "essential" to the investigation or prosecution of a leak of classified information. The exception requires a judge to find that the unauthorized leak "has caused or will cause significant and articulable harm to the national security."

And in a concession to business groups that had opposed the bill, the measure allows a judge to order the disclosure of individuals who have divulged trade secrets or private medical records protected by federal law.

The measure also seeks to resolve a longstanding debate about who should be considered a journalist and afforded the protections in the law. It limits protections to people who "regularly" gather and report news "for a substantial portion of the person's livelihood or for substantial financial gain." . . .

Department of Justice officials, noting how rarely the government has sought information from journalists, testified at hearings that federal prosecutors are better equipped than judges to assess when a reporter should be required to reveal a source.

"Department guidelines require prosecutors to seek to subpoena journalists and media organizations only when it is necessary to obtain important, material evidence that can't reasonably be obtained through other means," [a spokesperson said]. . . .

Tuesday, House Speaker Nancy Pelosi (D–San Francisco) came to the floor to urge passage of the measure. Democratic lawmakers cited the work of newspapers in recent years in uncovering scandals, including the administration's use of warrantless wiretaps and secret CIA detention centers in its campaign against international terrorism.

Many Republicans also were unwilling to accept the administration's assurances. "As a conservative who believes in limited government, I believe the only check on government power in real time is a free and independent press," [Indiana Rep. Mike] Pence said on the House floor Tuesday. "The concentrations of power should be subject to investigation."

Shield Law

Who is covered: "A person who regularly gathers, prepares, collects, photographs, records, writes, edits, reports, or publishes news or information that concerns local, national, or international events or other matters of public interest for dissemination to the public for a substantial portion of the person's livelihood or for substantial financial gain."

How it would work: Federal authorities may not compel a reporter to testify or reveal a source unless a court determines disclosure would:

- Provide critical information in a criminal case.
- Prevent an act of terrorism.
- Prevent imminent death.
- Reveal the identity of someone who has revealed a trade secret or private health information.
- Help authorities investigate the unauthorized leak of classified information that would cause "significant and articulable harm" to national security.

(Source: H.R. 210[2], the Free Flow of Information Act.)

***Postscript to* In re: Grand Jury Subpoena, Judith Miller:** As public concern for Judith Miller's plight faded, so too did congressional enthusiasm for a reporters' shield law. The House bill just described (H.R. 2102) claimed no progress in the Senate past a few supportive speeches. The parallel Senate bill (S. 2035), sent to the full Senate on October 14, 2007, likewise stalled.

In September 2011 Representative Mike Pence of Indiana introduced yet again the Free Flow of Information Act, the same legislation he had cosponsored in 2005, 2007, and 2009. *See* Free Flow of Information Act of 2011 (H.R. 2932), 112th Cong., 1st Sess. (2011); J.C. Derrick, *Federal Shield Law Introduced in House Once More*, Reporters Committee for Freedom of the Press (Sept. 19, 2011), available at http://www.rcfp.org/node/98369.

That bill died. As this book goes to press late in 2012, Mike Pence has abandoned his House seat and is the new governor-elect of Indiana.

B. Witnesses' Privileges vs. Defendants' Need for Evidence

Problem 11.2
Right Meets Privilege

Consider the facts of *State v. King*, 2000 WL 697454 (Ohio Ct. App. 2000), *cert. denied*, 532 U.S. 994 (2001):

> On November 20, 1997, the [grand jury] indicted [Kenneth D.] King on one count of rape . . . and one count of gross sexual imposition . . . for committing those crimes on a young girl named "Y.E." who was under thirteen years of age at the time of the abuse. . . .
>
> Mr. King sought, by way of defense, to have a young boy named "B.R." testify that he, rather than Mr. King, committed the crimes. However, B.R. refused to testify based upon his Fifth Amendment rights. Mr. King then sought to have Dr. Ann Carden, B.R.'s psychologist, testify that B.R. had admitted to Dr. Carden doing the acts for which Mr. King was being tried. However, although B.R.'s mother had waived the psychologist–patient privilege at one point, and hence, Dr. Carden had disclosed B.R.'s statements to Mr. King's defense counsel, the trial court allowed B.R. to assert the psychologist–patient privilege and ruled that Dr. Carden could not testify. . . .
>
> B.R.'s mother admitted to the trial court that a conflict of interest might exist between her interests and those of her son. At that point, the trial court indicated that it might be appropriate for a guardian *ad litem* to be appointed to protect B.R.'s interests, as is required . . . when a conflict of interest is present. The [court] appointed B.R.'s attorney as his guardian *ad litem*, [who] then asserted the psychologist–patient privilege before the trial court. . . .

What are the best arguments for and against admission of Dr. Carden's testimony? How should the court rule?

Focus on
Proposed FRE 506 & 511

Jail Notes Led to Revelation

Rev. Waited 12 Years to Bare Slay Confession

Devlin Barrett, Bridget Harrison, Jessie Graham and Denise Buffa

NEW YORK POST, July 18, 2001, at 4

... For 12 years, [Father Joseph] Towle remained silent about a conversation he had with Jesus Fornes, a gang member who admitted to the priest that he and two others killed Jose Rivera in 1987.

Fornes told "Father Joe" that he, Peter Ramirez and Ramirez's uncle Carlos Ocasio killed Rivera in a park, and that the two men convicted of the crime, [Ruben] Montalvo and Jose Morales, were innocent.

Believing the conversation confidential, Towle kept quiet, but wrote to Montalvo in 1995: ... "You have been sent to jail for something I know you did not do.... It is just like Jesus Christ, who was innocent and still was put to death.... God knows you did not do the thing you are accused of." ...

"I will help you in any way I can that does not oblige me to speak of things I know only in confidence as a priest," he said.

After the exchange, even Montalvo seemed to struggle with the priest's restrictions.

"I know you know what happened, and if it wasn't shared with you under the cloak of the Priesthood, I'm ... hoping you'd be willing to share it with a court so I can try to get my life back on track," he wrote....

In Court, a Priest Reveals a Secret He Carried for 12 Years

Jim Dwyer

NEW YORK TIMES, July 17, 2001, at B1

... Yesterday, in a collision of sacred and secular obligations, Father [Joseph] Towle went to court and testified about his conversation with [Jesus] Fornes, who died in 1997....

... "He was asking me what he should do," Father Towle said of Mr. Fornes. "I told him that if he had the courage and the heart to do it, that he should go to the court and that he should acknowledge that he was responsible and the others were not."

On the day the other men were to be sentenced in 1989, Mr. Fornes did go to court, and poured his story of remorse and guilt to a lawyer for one of the young men, but it came too late: both men, Jose Morales and Ruben Montalvo, were sentenced to a minimum of 15 years. The courts in New York State have rejected their appeals. Mr. Fornes's direct testimony was never heard by a jury.

... The priest said that after Mr. Fornes was killed in Upper Manhattan in 1997, he ... began to reconsider the nature of his meeting with Mr. Fornes eight years earlier, and he wondered as he went about his life running a small middle school if he might be able to share his secret.

Eventually, he submitted an affidavit that became part of a habeas corpus petition now pending before Judge Denny Chin of Federal District Court in Manhattan that says the convictions of the men were constitutionally flawed.

In papers filed with the court, Allen P. W. Karen, an assistant district attorney, argued that the statement made by Mr. Fornes to Father Towle would be inadmissible as a matter of law and impermissible under church teaching. "Had Reverend Towle consulted the New York Archdiocese, he would not have been permitted to reveal this information," Mr. Karen wrote.

A spokesman for the archdiocese said last night that Father Towle had in fact cleared his court appearance. "Father Towle, given the circumstances as we understand it, was not violating any church law by testifying," said Joseph G. Zwilling, the archdiocese's spokesman. "It was not a sacramental confession, in which confidentiality would be absolute." ...

Father Towle went to some pains yesterday to revisit the circumstances of his meeting with Mr. Fornes.

"What did you understand Mr. Fornes to be doing?" Judge Chin asked. "He asked you to come to his home. Was he confessing, was he having a heart-to-heart talk with you?"

Father Towle replied: "I am very careful about the use of the word 'confession'; that can be used in many different ways. It was a heart-to-heart talk where he was feeling very badly that two of his friends had been accused and convicted of something which he had done and it was his desire to do something to make the truth appear."

The priest said confession was a matter between a "person and God," with the priest acting as an intermediary. Such confidences could never be revealed, Father Towle said. "Formal confession is when a person comes and confesses his sins with no public purpose," he said. "He came to me precisely with a public purpose. From the beginning, it had that intention."

Nevertheless, Father Towle said, he granted Mr. Fornes absolution for his sins at the end of their meeting. "It was kind of tacked on," he said.

By the end of the day, the secular credibility of Father Towle's account was backed by another source who also enjoyed a special relationship of confidentiality with Mr. Fornes: his former lawyer, Stanley Cohen.

Back in 1989, Mr. Fornes went to the Bronx office of the Legal Aid Society and was assigned to Mr. Cohen, who was then working as a Legal Aid lawyer.

Mr. Fornes "was very clear he had committed murder and these other men had not," Mr. Cohen testified. "He said, 'I'm here because I can't sleep, I can't eat, I can't live with myself.' "

Unlike the priest, however, Mr. Cohen said he had advised his young client to keep quiet. "He was going to throw his whole life away by going to court and saying he did it"....

MORALES v. PORTUONDO

154 F. Supp. 2d 706 (S.D.N.Y. 2001).

■ CHIN, DISTRICT JUDGE.... Petitioner Jose Morales and his co-defendant, Ruben Montalvo, were convicted of murder in the Supreme Court of the State of New York, Bronx County, almost thirteen years ago. They have been in prison ever since.

... Just days after the trial, as Morales and Montalvo were about to be sentenced, another teenager, Jesus Fornes, told at least four individuals—a priest, Montalvo's mother, Morales's attorney, and a Legal Aid attorney—that he and two other individuals had committed the murder and that Morales and Montalvo were innocent.

Fornes's statements were never heard by a jury. Fornes invoked his Fifth Amendment privilege against self-incrimination and refused to testify at a post-trial hearing on a motion to set aside the verdict. The priest from whom Fornes had sought spiritual guidance did not reveal the statements because they were made as part of an informal confession. The Legal Aid attorney from whom Fornes had sought legal advice did not reveal the statements because he was prohibited by the attorney–client privilege from doing so. Although Fornes's statements to Montalvo's mother and Morales's attorney were presented to the state court at a hearing on the motion to set aside the verdict, the state court denied the motion, refusing to order a new trial because it concluded that Fornes's statements were inadmissible hearsay.

Fornes was killed in an unrelated incident in 1997. The priest and the Legal Attorney have now come forward and publicly disclosed what Fornes said to them....

STATEMENT OF THE CASE

A. The Facts

1. *The Murder*

On September 28, 1987, Jose Antonio Rivera was murdered in the Bronx. At approximately 11 p.m., Rivera, Jennifer Rodriguez, and Rodriguez's eleven-year-old son, Cesar Montalvo ("Cesar"), were walking along a street near Kelly Park. They saw a group of teenagers, at least one of whom was carrying a baseball bat or stick. There had previously been an incident between Rivera and one of the teenagers, and the teenagers approached the family.

Rivera ran. Members of the group chased and caught him. Someone struck him in the head with a stick or bat.... As he lay on the ground, others stabbed him and hit him again....

2. *Morales Is Indicted, Tried, and Convicted*

No one was arrested at the scene of the murder. A few days later, Morales, who was then only 18 years old, appeared at a police station for questioning. He did so voluntarily and denied any involvement in the murder. He was placed in a lineup. Rodriguez, who had watched as her common-law husband was murdered, identified Morales as one of the assailants.

Morales was thereafter indicted, together with Montalvo and Peter Ramirez, for Rivera's murder. Morales was offered a plea bargain that would have required a prison term of only one to three years, but he rejected the offer and insisted on going to trial. In December 1988, Morales and Montalvo went to trial. In the meantime, Ramirez had committed suicide.

On December 22, 1988, the jury returned a verdict finding both Morales and Montalvo guilty of murder in the second degree.

3. *Fornes Comes Forward*

Shortly after Montalvo and Morales were convicted but before they were sentenced, another teenager from the neighborhood, Jesus Fornes, asked to speak to Father Joseph Towle. Fornes was approximately 17 years old at the time. Towle, a Roman Catholic priest who worked in the Hunts Point section of the South Bronx, visited Fornes in his home. Fornes told him that he was upset because two members of his group had been convicted of a murder ... and that he and two others had actually committed the murder. Fornes said that one of the other two individuals was Peter Ramirez.... Fornes asked Towle what he should do, and Towle told him that "if he had the courage and heart to do it, that he should go to the court and that he should acknowledge that he was responsible and the others were not." At the end of the conversation, Towle granted Fornes absolution, "offering him pardon in the name of God for the things that he had done wrong." ...

5. *Fornes Seeks Legal Advice*

... Accompanied by Father Towle and a family member, Fornes went to the Legal Aid offices.... There, he met with Stanley Cohen, Esq.... Towle told Cohen that this was a "young man" who "felt horrible" and "had something he needed to get off his chest." Cohen then met with Fornes alone.

After Cohen explained the attorney–client privilege to him, Fornes told Cohen that he and two other individuals had killed someone and that the two individuals who had been convicted of the murder had not been involved. Fornes also told Cohen that he had been to court earlier that day and had spoken to a lawyer for one of the defendants....

... Cohen discussed Fornes's "exposure" with him. He told Fornes that he could "conceivably be throwing [his] life away" by coming forward to admit the crime, but Fornes "didn't care. He said I did it, they didn't. I should be there, not them." Cohen then advised Fornes as follows:

> I said, look, you are 17, 18 years old, you have your entire life ahead of you. If you feel guilt, you have the priest here, you can feel guilt with the priest. It is not in your best interests to go any further....
>
> I said one of the problems that you have here is [that] by going forward [you may] not end up clearing the gentlemen who have been convicted ... but what you may end up doing is putting yourself in the middle of the case, you would end up being prosecuted, the other two who you tell me didn't do anything would not necessarily end up being released....
>
> I just said I thought it was—he should not step forward, he should not answer questions and he should invoke the Fifth Amendment.

Cohen agreed to represent Fornes. He thereafter had conversations with defense attorneys and the District Attorney's Office. He became further convinced that because the District Attorney believed that more than two persons had committed the murder, it was conceivable that Fornes could implicate himself by coming forward without helping the two individuals who had been convicted. Hence, he continued to urge Fornes not to come forward. He also explained that it was "very, very, very difficult" to upset a verdict after trial.

6. *Fornes Takes the Fifth*

Eventually, Fornes accepted Cohen's advice. At some point, Cohen spoke to both defense counsel [for Morales and Montalvo] and the District Attorney's Office, advising them that he was representing Fornes and instructing them not to speak to Fornes.

Morales's attorney moved to set aside the verdict and a hearing was held on the motion in March 1989. Fornes followed Cohen's advice and invoked his Fifth Amendment privilege, refusing to answer questions. [The trial court denied the motion.]

7. *Father Towle Breaks His Silence*

In 1997, Fornes was killed in an incident unrelated to this case.

In May 2000, Father Towle executed an affidavit in which he described the statements that Fornes had made to him some 11 or 12 years earlier. He had been corresponding with Morales in prison, and Morales had described the efforts he was making to overturn his conviction. Towle began to consider whether there was some way, "within the framework of Catholic practice," for him to reveal Fornes's statements. Upon rethinking the matter, Towle concluded that the conversation was not a "formal confession" and that consequently, in the unique circumstances of this case, he was permitted to disclose the statements. If the conversation had constituted a formal confession, Towle would never have been able to reveal any portion of it, even after Fornes's death....

B. Prior Proceedings

... On March 25, 1997, proceeding pro se, Morales filed his petition for a writ of habeas corpus in this Court.... I conducted an evidentiary hearing on July 16, 2001. Morales called five witnesses [including Father Towle and Cohen]....

... Morales contends that he ... was denied due process because he was not permitted to present evidence of Fornes's statements in his defense, evidence that he maintains constitutes proof of actual innocence....

C. The Merits

1. *Applicable Law*

... In Chambers v. Mississippi, 410 U.S. 284 (1973), the Supreme Court recognized that a defendant's right to present evidence at trial is a matter of due process.... *See also* Washington v. Schriver, 255 F.3d 45, 56 (2d Cir. 2001) (the "right to call witnesses in order to present a meaningful defense at a criminal trial is a fundamental constitutional right secured by both the Compulsory Process Clause of the Sixth Amendment and the Due Process Clause of the Fourteenth Amendment").

The right to present a defense, of course, is not absolute, as defendants in criminal cases "must comply with established rules of procedure and evidence designed to assure both fairness and reliability." *Washington,* 255 F.3d at 56 (quoting *Chambers,* 410 U.S. at 302). On the other hand, state rules of evidence may not be "inflexibly applied" so that they deprive a defendant of a fundamentally fair trial. Indeed, the Supreme Court held in *Chambers* that "where constitutional rights directly affecting the ascertainment of guilt are implicated, the hearsay rule may not be applied mechanistically to defeat the ends of justice."

Because the right to present a defense necessarily implicates state evidentiary rulings, federal courts considering evidentiary claims on habeas review must be careful to differentiate between mere errors of state law and those of constitutional dimension. Habeas relief ... is unavailable for mere errors of state law, and "erroneous evidentiary rulings rarely rise to the level" of a constitutional violation. Nonetheless, habeas courts confronting a Due Process claim must examine state evidentiary rulings to determine whether those rulings deprived petitioner of a fundamentally fair trial.

To obtain habeas relief on these grounds, a petitioner "must demonstrate first that the [trial court's evidentiary] ruling was erroneous and, second, that the erroneous ruling 'so infected the proceedings as to have rendered the trial fundamentally unfair.'" Even if the state court's evidentiary ruling is technically correct, and the evidence would otherwise be inadmissible under the state's rules of evidence, a petitioner may nonetheless be entitled to introduce such evidence if exclusion of the evidence would render his trial fundamentally unfair. *See Chambers*, 410 U.S. at 302–03....

In People v. Robinson, 89 N.Y.2d 648 (1997), the New York Court of Appeals, citing the due process requirements described in *Chambers v. Mississippi*, permitted a criminal defendant to introduce the exculpatory grand jury testimony of an unavailable witness. Acknowledging that the evidence was inadmissible under New York's "prior testimony" exception to the rule against hearsay, the Court of Appeals held that the grand jury testimony could nevertheless be admitted at trial because it "met certain standards of admissibility": (1) the testimony was "vital" to the defense; (2) the witness who gave the testimony was unavailable; and (3) the testimony bore sufficient indicia of reliability....

2. *Application*

... The admissibility issue raises several layers of inquiry: whether the requirements of an exception to the hearsay rule are met; whether Fornes's statements bore sufficient indicia of reliability; whether Fornes's statements to Father Towle are blocked by the priest–penitent privilege; and whether Fornes's statements to Cohen are blocked by the attorney–client privilege.

i. *The Technical Requirements*

... Fornes's statements to Father Towle and Cohen do not qualify as declarations against penal interest, for he was not aware, when he made the statements to them, that the statements would be against his penal interest. To the contrary, he fully expected that both Father Towle and Cohen would keep his conversations with them confidential. [Nonetheless,] the statements to both Father Towle and Cohen ... are admissible under ... *Robinson* and its progeny: (1) Fornes's statements to Father Towle and Cohen are "vital" to Morales's defense; (2) Fornes was unavailable then because he invoked his privilege against self-incrimination and he is unavailable now because he is deceased; and (3) the statements bear sufficient indicia of reliability.

ii. *The Indicia of Reliability*

Perhaps the most critical issue presented is whether Fornes's statements were trustworthy—whether he was telling the truth when he stated that he had committed the murder and that Morales and Montalvo were not involved. I conclude that Fornes's statements bore sufficient indicia of reliability and trustworthiness to make them admissible.

First, Fornes made the statements to at least four different people in four different circumstances: to Father Towle in a heart-to-heart talk of a religious nature; to Maria Montalvo [Ruben Montalvo's mother] in her home; to Anthony Servino [one of Morales's lawyers] at the courthouse on the scheduled date of sentencing; and to Cohen at the offices of the Legal Aid Society. As the New York courts have noted, the fact that a declarant has made numerous confessions to different individuals is an "independent circumstance attesting to the trustworthiness and reliability" of declarant's statements.

Second, the circumstances in which Fornes made the statements strongly suggest that he was telling the truth because he had no motive to lie. . . . He had no reason to lie to Father Towle and Cohen because he was seeking their advice and guidance, and he had every reason to believe that his conversations with them would be kept completely confidential.

Third, the circumstances also strongly suggest that Fornes was telling the truth because he genuinely felt remorse and guilt over the fact that two friends had been unjustly convicted of a crime that he had committed. Unlike a co-defendant "confessing" to authorities in the hopes of receiving a lenient sentence, Fornes "was [not] using the system" here for his own gain; rather, he was "unburdening his conscience, the linchpin" of a declaration against penal interest. . . .

Fourth, Fornes's statements were corroborated by other, independent evidence. For example, Ramirez told his mother and his attorney that he was involved in the murder and that Morales and Montalvo were not present. . . .

I conclude that sufficient indicia of reliability and trustworthiness exist to qualify Fornes's statements for admission into evidence under the exceptions to the hearsay rule [as interpreted in *Robinson* in light of *Chambers v. Mississippi*]. In short, there is ample evidence to show that Fornes was telling the truth. . . .

iii. *The Priest–Penitent Privilege*

Even assuming Fornes's statements to Father Towle fall within an exception to the hearsay rule, the issue remains as to whether the statements are nonetheless privileged as confidential communications to a member of the clergy and thus inadmissible at trial.

Under New York law, a minister, priest, or other member of the clergy may not disclose, at trial, "a confession or confidence made to him in his professional character as spiritual advisor," absent a waiver of the privilege by the confessing person. N.Y. C.P.L.R. § 4505. Although the clergy–penitent privilege derives from the Catholic practice of confession, it encompasses statements made to clerics of any denomination, so long as the "communication in question was made in confidence and for the purpose of obtaining spiritual guidance." As the statute indicates, the privilege may be waived by the person who made the confession. . . .

In the instant case, Fornes's statements to Father Towle arguably qualified as privileged communications under C.P.L.R. § 4505, for Fornes spoke to Father Towle "in confidence and for the purpose of obtaining spiritual guidance." Nonetheless, I hold that the statements are not rendered inadmissible by virtue of § 4505.

First, Father Towle has concluded that his conversation with Fornes was not a "formal confession," but that it was a "heart-to-heart" talk. After much deliberation, he has concluded that he was free, after Fornes died, to disclose the conversation. The Archdiocese has agreed that Father Towle acted properly in disclosing the conversation. Indeed, the Archdiocese permitted Father Towle to testify in this case and to repeat his disclosures. . . .

Second, even assuming Fornes's statements were covered by § 4505, Fornes waived the privilege. Following his conversation with Father Towle, he disclosed at least portions of his conversation to three different people—Maria Montalvo, Servino, and Cohen. Moreover, Fornes spoke to Father Towle precisely about whether he should reveal his involvement in the crime to exculpate Morales and Montalvo. Towle told him that "if he had the courage and heart to do it, that he should go to the court and that he should acknowledge that he was responsible and the others were not." Fornes tried to do precisely that. Under these circumstances, Fornes acted in a manner "inconsistent with any desire to maintain a priest–penitent privilege," and thus he "effectively waived that privilege." Accordingly, the statements to Father Towle are admissible.

iv. *The Attorney–Client Privilege*

Likewise, even if Fornes's statements to Cohen fall within an exception to the hearsay rule, the issue remains as to whether the statements are barred by the attorney–client privilege.

. . . Once an attorney–client relationship is established, the privilege precludes the attorney from disclosing any "confidential communication[s]" made to the attorney for the purpose of obtaining legal advice or services, in the absence of a waiver by the client. Such a waiver may be found where the client voluntarily discloses the communications to another party, or the communications are made in the known presence of a third party in whom the client could have no "reasonable expectation of confidentiality."

The attorney–client privilege is personal to the client, and thus "may not be waived by the attorney after the client's death." *See* People v. Modzelewski, 611 N.Y.S.2d 22, 22 (2d Dep't 1994) (affirming, on privilege grounds, trial court's decision to preclude defendant from calling attorney to testify regarding potentially exculpatory statements of deceased client); *see also* Swidler & Berlin v. United States, 524 U.S. 399, 410 (1998) ("It has been generally, if not universally, accepted, for well over a century, that the attorney–client privilege survives the death of the client in a case such as this").[10]

Here, Fornes's statements to Cohen were made in the course of a privileged conversation; Fornes clearly was seeking advice from Cohen as a criminal defense lawyer. Cohen specifically advised Fornes that anything he said to him would be kept confidential, and Fornes disclosed his involvement in Rivera's murder to Cohen with that understanding. Moreover, Fornes did not engage in any conduct subsequent to speaking with Cohen that could be construed as a waiver of the privilege: once Cohen advised him to invoke the Fifth Amendment, Fornes apparently stopped telling others about the murder. The fact that Fornes has died does not alter the privileged nature of the conversation, as the privilege survives his death.

Nonetheless, under the authority of *Chambers v. Mississippi*, I conclude that Fornes's statements to Cohen are admissible. As the Supreme Court held in *Chambers*, even if the evidence would otherwise be inadmissible under the state's rules of evidence, a defendant in a criminal case may nonetheless be entitled to introduce the evidence if its exclusion would render his trial fundamentally unfair. *See Chambers*, 410 U.S. at 302–03.

Fornes spoke to Cohen to obtain legal advice, but he was merely repeating what he had already told three other people, including Morales's lawyer and Montalvo's mother. Fornes wanted to continue to help Morales and Montalvo, but Cohen advised him that he would probably only hurt himself without helping Morales and Montalvo at all. Fornes was undoubtedly speaking the truth when he told Cohen that he had committed the murder and that Morales and Montalvo were not present. Fornes has been deceased for some four years now, while two apparently innocent men have spent nearly thirteen years in prison for a crime that he committed. Under these remarkable circumstances, the attorney–client privilege must not stand in the way of the truth. Fornes's statements to Cohen are admissible. . . .

10. For one commentator's argument that a criminal defendant's Due Process rights should override the attorney–client privilege in cases where a deceased client has confessed to the crime, see Tyson A. Ciepluch, *Comment, Overriding the Posthumous Application of the Attorney–Client Privilege: Due Process for a Criminal Defendant*, 83 MARQ. L. REV. 785 (2000).

The *Chambers* case is remarkably similar to this case. . . . In *Chambers*, the defendant was convicted of murder. At trial, the court refused to allow him to call three witnesses, each of whom would have testified that another individual, McDonald, admitted on separate occasions that he actually committed the murder. . . .

The Supreme Court reversed, holding that the statements, while hearsay, were made under circumstances that provided "considerable assurance of their reliability." 410 U.S. at 300. . . . The Court reasoned that the exclusion of the testimony contributed to a denial of the defendant's right to "a trial in accord with traditional and fundamental standards of due process." *Id.* at 302.

Likewise, here, Morales was denied "a trial in accord with traditional and fundamental standards of due process." Accordingly, his petition for a writ of habeas corpus must be granted. . . .

So ordered.

MORALES V. PORTUONDO: *Afterthoughts*

In the compelling circumstances of this case, it is hard to contest Judge Chin's ruling that Jose Morales's right to present a full defense should prevail over Jesus Fornes's posthumous privileges. But one should not conclude from *Morales* that a criminal defendant's claim under *Chambers v. Mississippi* or the Compulsory Process Clause always will defeat a witness's assertion of privilege. After all, the claims of privilege in this case were unusually weak. A "heart-to-heart talk" does not constitute a clergy–penitent confession, Judge Chin held, and Fornes's death and disclosures weakened (though they did not dissolve) his lawyer–client privilege.

Had Fornes's claims of privilege been full force, they might well have prevailed over Morales's rights under *Chambers v. Mississippi*. In *Washington v. Texas*, 388 U.S. 14 (1967), the first case in which the Supreme Court applied the Compulsory Process Clause to defeat a state evidence rule, the Court said, "Nothing in this opinion should be construed as disapproving testimonial privileges. . . ." *Id.* at 23 n.21 (1967). And in the many lower-court opinions that have considered a criminal defendant's demand for privileged evidence under *Chambers* or the Compulsory Process Clause, results have varied according to the defendant's need for the evidence and the weightiness of the witness's claim of privilege.

Applying Chambers *to Evidentiary Privileges*

Chambers addressed Mississippi's hearsay law and in particular the exception for statements against interest. (*See Chambers*, excerpted in

Chapter 8 at page 718.) The two-factor analysis employed by the Supreme Court, which focused on the defendant's "critical" need for the evidence and the existence of "persuasive assurances of trustworthiness," was well suited to the hearsay context. Because the hearsay rule aims to exclude *unreliable* evidence, Mississippi arguably had little reason to exclude, on hearsay grounds, evidence that "bore persuasive assurances of trustworthiness"—particularly when that evidence was critical to the defendant's case.

Evidentiary privileges, in contrast, often exclude perfectly reliable evidence to serve other social goals. So a defendant cannot undermine a witness's claim of privilege simply by showing that the excluded evidence bears "persuasive assurances of trustworthiness." When applying *Chambers* to Fornes's potential claims of privilege, therefore, Judge Chin rightly looked beyond the two-factor analysis of *Chambers*. After noting Morales's "vital" need for Fornes's privileged statements and the "ample evidence ... that Fornes was telling the truth," the judge weighed the interests protected by Fornes's privileges against Morales's need for the evidence. *See* Robert Weisberg, Note, Defendant v. Witness: *Measuring Confrontation and Compulsory Process Rights Against Statutory Communications Privileges*, 30 STAN. L. REV. 935, 964–73 (1978) (advocating a similar weighing test). That Fornes was both dead and careless with his confidences diminished the weightiness of his claims of privilege. That Morales was serving time for a murder Fornes said Morales did not commit intensified Morales's need for the privileged statements.

To assess the weightiness of a witness's privilege, a judge must identify and evaluate the goals privileges serve. Here judges enter contested territory. In one camp are those traditionalists who, following Wigmore, hold that privileges serve broad social goals. To survive Wigmore's utilitarian scrutiny, a privilege "*must be essential* to the full and satisfactory maintenance of" a relationship "which in the opinion of the community ought to be sedulously *fostered*." 8 WIGMORE, EVIDENCE § 2285, at 527 (McNaughton rev. 1961) (emphasis in original). No privilege is justified, Wigmore wrote, unless "[t]he *injury* that would inure to" a socially valued relationship by disclosing confidential communications is "*greater than the benefit* thereby gained for the correct disposal of litigation." *Id.*

In another camp are those commentators who reject Wigmore's narrow focus on social goals and instead regard "confidentiality [as] an end in itself," protecting the broader, humanist concerns of "honor, conscience, and privacy." Weisberg, *supra*, at 943–44 (characterizing others' views). Recall the comments of Charles Black, who worried that the lack of a federal physician–patient privilege would render a person "vulnerable to being stripped to and below the skin in public." (*See* page 933, above.) David Louisell likewise hailed privileges as protecting "a right to be let alone, a right to unfettered freedom, in certain narrowly prescribed relationships, from the state's coercive or supervisory powers. . . ." David W. Louisell, *Confidentiality, Conformity and Confusion: Privileges in Federal Court Today*, 31 TUL. L. REV. 101, 101 (1956).

Given these starkly differing views of the values privileges serve, and given the endless variety of factual circumstances in which claims of privilege arise, one cannot expect courts to be of one mind when resolving contests between a witness's privilege and a defendant's claims under *Chambers* or the Compulsory Process Clause. And in fact, when settling conflicts between a witness's lawyer-client privilege and a defendant's claimed right to present evidence, the conflict Judge Chin faced in *Morales*, courts have come down on both sides of the question. On the one hand, the Tenth Circuit and other courts have held that the witness's lawyer-client privilege must prevail. *See, e.g., Valdez v. Winans*, 738 F.2d 1087, 1090 (10th Cir. 1984); *Browning v. State*, 134 P.3d 816, 834–35 & n.49 (Okla. Crim. App.), *cert. denied*, 549 U.S. 963 (2006). The Tenth Circuit explained:

> The hearsay rule [which was at issue in *Chambers*] serves to exclude potentially unreliable evidence. . . . [In contrast, p]rivileges are designed to promote relationships and interests outside the courtroom by permitting witnesses to keep even reliable evidence secret. Therefore, *Chambers* does not support the notion that the right to compulsory process overrides the attorney–client privilege.

Valdez, 738 F.2d at 1090 (citation and quotation marks omitted). Other courts have proved readier to override a witness's assertion of attorney–client privilege. One federal district judge recently held that "[t]he nature and content of the privileged evidence must be weighed against the purposes served by the attorney–client privilege to determine whether any of the [privileged] documents are of such value as to require [the privilege holder's] rights under the attorney–client privilege to yield to the individual Defendants' Sixth Amendment right to present evidence." *United States v. Grace*, 439 F. Supp. 2d 1125, 1142–43 (D. Mont. 2006), *aff'd on other grounds*, 526 F.3d 499 (9th Cir. 2008). Other courts have taken a similar stance. *See State v. Hoop*, 134 Ohio App. 3d 627, 641 (1999); *United States v. Romano*, 46 M.J. 269, 274 (1997); *In re Kozlov*, 79 N.J. 232, 243 (1979).

Clashes between other evidentiary privileges and a defendant's compulsory process claims arise less often. Witnesses in criminal cases are after all far more likely to assert the lawyer–client privilege than any other communications privilege. The few courts that have addressed contests between a witness's psychotherapist–patient or marital confidences privilege and a defendant's claim under *Chambers* or the Compulsory Process Clause have gone both ways. Some have held that the witness's claim of privilege trumps the defendant's claim of need. The Seventh Circuit reached this result in the context of the marital confidences privilege, *see United States v. Lea*, 249 F.3d 632, 643 (7th Cir. 2001), as have other courts in the context of the psychotherapist–patient privilege, *see United States v. Doyle*, 1 F. Supp. 2d 1187, 1190–91 (D. Ore. 1998); *Commonwealth v. Patosky*, 440 Pa. Super. 535, 540–42 (1995). Other courts have concluded that the defendant's constitutional demand for evidence must prevail. Hence a Massachusetts appeals court held that the marital confidences privilege must yield, *see Commonwealth v. Sugrue*, 34 Mass. App. Ct. 172, 175–78 (1993), while several courts have ruled that the psychotherapist–patient privilege must give way, *see United States v. Alperin*, 128 F. Supp. 2d 1251, 1253–55 (N.D. Cal. 2001); *Commonwealth v. Barroso*, 122 S.W.3d 554, 563 (Ky. 2003); *State v. L.J.P.*, 270 N.J. Super. 429, 439, 442–43 (1994).

In one context, however, courts seem to be of one mind. Overwhelmingly courts have ruled that a defendant's compulsory process claim must yield in the face of a witness's Fifth Amendment privilege against self-incrimination. *See, e.g., United States v. Highgate*, 521 F.3d 590, 593 (6th Cir. 2008); *United States v. Jones*, 512 F.3d 1007, 1008–09 (8th Cir. 2008); *United States v. Serrano*, 406 F.3d 1208, 1213–16 (10th Cir.), *cert. denied*, 546 U.S. 913 (2005); *State v. Crawford*, 729 N.W.2d 346, 350 (S.D. 2007). A few courts have sought middle ground, commanding that "when balancing the Sixth Amendment right of the accused and the Fifth Amendment right of the witness, 'the trial judge must make an appropriate inquiry into the basis of the privilege claimed by the witness, and may not permit the witness to refuse to testify where a narrower privilege will adequately protect him.'" *United States v. Thornton*, 733 F.2d 121, 125 (D.C. Cir. 1984); *accord United States v. Vavages*, 151 F.3d 1185, 1191–92 (9th Cir. 1998) (same, quoting *Thornton*). But if there is no way to reconcile the witness's Fifth Amendment privilege with the defendant's need for her testimony, the privilege apparently prevails, and the defendant must mount his defense without her evidence.

No doubt this exalted position of the Fifth Amendment privilege, virtually immune to criminal defendants' Sixth Amendment claims of compulsory process, owes a great deal to its explicit constitutional stature. Other privileges can stake an inferential claim to constitutional lineage—the lawyer–client privilege under the Sixth Amendment right to counsel, the clergy–penitent privilege under the First Amendment right to free exercise of religion, and the marital and psychotherapist–patient privileges under the privacy rights recognized in *Griswold v. Connecticut*, 381 U.S. 479 (1965), and its progeny. *See* Weisberg, *supra*, at 944–45 n.40. But as the Constitution supports such claims (if at all) only by implication, these privileges may yield more readily to a defendant's claim of need under the Compulsory Process Clause.

CHAPTER 12

THE LAWYER–CLIENT PRIVILEGE AND THE PRIVILEGE AGAINST SELF-INCRIMINATION

Jeremy Bentham

RATIONALE OF JUDICIAL EVIDENCE

(London: Hunt & Clarke 1827)
Vol. 5, at 302–10 (Book 9, Ch. 5, § 2)

. . . When, in consulting with a law adviser, attorney or advocate, a man has confessed his delinquency, or disclosed some fact which, if stated in court, might tend to operate in proof of it, such law adviser is . . . neither to be compelled, nor so much as suffered, to betray the trust thus reposed in him. Not suffered? Why not? Oh, because to betray a trust is treachery; and an act of treachery is an immoral act. . . .

But if such confidence, when reposed, is permitted to be violated, . . . the consequence will be, that no such confidence will be reposed. Not reposed?—Well: and if it be not, wherein will consist the mischief? The man by the supposition is guilty; if not, by the supposition there is nothing to betray. . . . [That] no such confidence will be reposed, is natural enough: the first thing the advocate or attorney will say to his client, will be,—Remember that, whatever you say to me, I shall be obliged to tell, if asked about it. What, then, will be the consequence? That a guilty person will not in general be able to derive quite so much assistance from his law adviser, in the way of concerting a false defence, as he may do at present. . . .

"A counsel, solicitor, or attorney, cannot conduct the cause of his client," (it has been observed) "if he is not fully instructed in the circumstances attending it: but the client" (it is added) "could not give the instructions *with safety*, if the facts confided to his advocate were to be disclosed." Not with safety? So much the better. To what object is the whole system of penal law directed, if it be not that no man shall have it in his power to flatter himself with the hope of safety, in the event of his engaging in the commission of an act which the law, on account of its supposed mischievousness, has thought fit to prohibit? The argument

employed as a reason against the compelling such disclosure, is the very argument that pleads in favour of it....

A. Scope of the Lawyer-Client Privilege

Common Elements of the Professional Privileges

Jeremy Bentham's cynicism toward the lawyer–client privilege may call to mind Justice Scalia's views of the psychotherapist–patient privilege, expressed in *Jaffee v. Redmond* (at page 941, above):

> I see no reason why [Officer Redmond] should be enabled ... to deny her guilt in [a] criminal trial ... while yet obtaining the benefits of psychotherapy by confessing guilt to a social worker who cannot testify. It seems to me entirely fair to say that if she wishes the benefits of telling the truth she must also accept the adverse consequences....

No other member of the Court joined Justice Scalia in these sentiments. Nor have legal authorities in general flocked to Bentham's ranks in advocating the demise of the lawyer–client privilege.

Although judges rarely question the validity of long-established privileges, courts do take to heart Wigmore's admonition "that the public ... has a right to every man's evidence." Federal judges therefore have been slow to exercise their implied authority under Rule 501 to establish new privileges "in the light of reason and experience." Today only three professional privileges are generally recognized in federal courts—the psychotherapist–patient, clergy–penitent, and lawyer–client privileges. *Jaffee* and *Morales v. Portuondo* have introduced each of these and have given you some sense of their shape. Now we need to focus in more detail on the lawyer–client privilege, surely the most prominent of the three. It is the oldest and the most frequently asserted professional privilege and has given rise to the most developed caselaw. It will serve as our model for the structure of professional privileges in general.

Although the precise contours of the professional privileges vary somewhat from privilege to privilege and across jurisdictions, most professional privileges share four elements. The first of these—that the privilege is the client's and may be waived only by her consent—arose in passing in *Morales*. The remaining three elements offer a rough roadmap of the next three sections of the book:

(1) The privilege is the *client's*. Only the client—or the professional on her behalf—may assert the privilege. The professional's authority to claim the privilege for the client is presumed in absence of contrary evidence. "It is assumed that the ethics of the profession will require him to do so except under most unusual circumstances." (ACN to Proposed Rule 503(c), RB 345.) Because the privilege is the client's, only the client may waive it—though again, the professional may do so on the client's authority and in certain other customary situations. (*See* Proposed Rules 503(b), (c); 504(b), (c); 506(b), (c).) Despite these general principles, some states permit clergy members to assert the clergy–penitent privilege on their own behalf.

(2) The privilege protects only those confidential communications *made to facilitate professional services.* Like Jesus Fornes's "heart-to-heart talk" with Father Towle, friendly chats do not qualify. Nor do communications made to a lawyer acting as a lobbyist or business agent, for example, not as a law advisor. (*See* Proposed Rules 503(b); 504(b); 506(b); *People v. Gionis*, 9 Cal. 4th 1196 (1995) (next page).)

(3) The privilege protects only *confidential* communications. A communication is "confidential" if the client intended that it be confidential and that it stay confidential. Precautions taken against eavesdropping bear on the reasonableness of the client's intent. No privilege attaches if, at the time of the communication, the client plans to disclose it to persons outside the privilege or knows her lawyer plans to do so. But persons reasonably necessary to the lawyer's services may be present during the communication and may be told of it, as may persons needed to transmit the communication. As the privilege is the client's, she waives its protection if she voluntarily discloses or consents to disclosure of any significant part of the communication to a person outside a privileged relationship. (*See* Proposed Rules 503(a)(3), (a)(4); 504(a)(3); 506(a)(2); 511; ACN to Proposed Rule 503(a)(4), RB 343–44.) In many jurisdictions a lawyer's carelessness in mistakenly disclosing a privileged communication to an adversary can, together with other circumstances, waive the client's privilege. (*See* FRE 502(b); *Howell v. Joffe*, 483 F. Supp. 2d 659 (N.D. Ill. 2007); *Williams v. District of Columbia*, 806 F. Supp. 2d 44 (D.D.C. 2011), (page 985 below).)

(4) The privilege protects only confidential *communications*. The *communication*, not the facts communicated, is privileged. If you tell your lawyer a *fact* and you are later asked about that fact in court, you may not answer, "That's privileged—I told it to my lawyer." But if asked, "What did you tell your lawyer?" you may properly assert the privilege. By the same principle, you would not waive your privilege in a confidential communication by revealing the facts communicated to someone else. To waive the privilege, you would have to disclose the "the communication itself." (ACN to Proposed Rule 511, RB 369.) Absent such a waiver, if your lawyer is asked *what you told her*, she likewise may and should decline to answer on grounds of privilege. Moreover, if she knows something only because you told it to her, she may decline to answer a question about that fact. (*Cf.* Proposed Rules 503(b); 504(b); 506(b); *In re Osterhoudt*, 722 F.2d 591 (9th Cir. 1983) (discussed at 998–99, below).)

The rest of this unit explores the contours and limits of these general principles.

---

1. THE NATURE OF LEGAL SERVICES

Focus on
Proposed FRE 503

PEOPLE V. GIONIS

Supreme Court of California.
9 Cal. 4th 1196 (1995).

■ BAXTER, J. . . .

I. FACTUAL AND PROCEDURAL BACKGROUND

Defendant [Thomas Gionis], a doctor, and Aissa Marie Wayne, daughter of the late movie actor John Wayne, were married in 1986. In February 1987, defendant and Wayne had a daughter named Anastasia.

Soon after the baby was born, the marriage began to deteriorate. Defendant twice threatened to kill Wayne if she got in the way of his relationship with Anastasia. . . . Despite these threats, Wayne left defendant in June 1987, taking Anastasia with her. . . .

John Lueck was an attorney who referred clients to defendant for medical evaluations. In May or June 1987, Lueck received a telephone call from defendant asking him to come to defendant's home. Defendant was in tears. He said he had just been served with divorce papers, and he needed somebody to talk to because he was upset. Although Lueck initially declined to go to defendant's home, he ultimately agreed to meet defendant after making it clear that he would not be willing to have any involvement as a lawyer in defendant's dissolution case. Lueck refused to represent defendant because he knew both defendant and Wayne.

When Lueck arrived at defendant's home, defendant said he was upset about the circumstances of the separation and about the fact that Wayne had taken the baby. Defendant displayed very wide mood swings, alternating between tears and anger. At one point during the visit, defendant showed Lueck a declaration by Wayne in support of an order to show cause, and indicated he would like to change venue from Orange County to Los Angeles County because Wayne was the daughter of one of Orange County's most famous residents; the county airport was his namesake. Lueck, speaking as defendant's friend, said he thought a change of venue might be appropriate, but did not offer to do it. Lueck also told defendant to quickly retain a good attorney.

While in one of his very angry moods, defendant showed Lueck some holes in a wall, as well as a closet door off its track in the bedroom. Defendant said that the altercation which resulted in the holes in the wall was nothing relative to what he was capable of doing. He also told Lueck that Wayne "had no idea how easy it would be for him to pay somebody to really take care of her."

After hearing defendant make these statements, Lueck commented that if something were to happen to Wayne during the dissolution or a child custody dispute, defendant would certainly be the primary suspect. Defendant replied ... that if he were to do something, he "would wait until an opportune time and circumstances [*sic*] so that suspicion wouldn't be directed towards him." ...

On a Friday in October 1987, defendant showed up at Lueck's office, apparently upset with some papers that had been prepared by his counsel in his dissolution case. Defendant appeared desperate. He told Lueck that Wayne was trying to prevent him from having Anastasia at her baptism, that his attorney was unavailable, and that something had to be done immediately because people were leaving Greece that Friday afternoon for the baptism. Defendant pleaded with Lueck to go to court on an ex parte basis. Lueck agreed, but when he went to court, an irate judge told him that arrangements had already been made.... Lueck was paid $750 for the court appearance.

During January and February 1988, Wayne began a romantic relationship with Roger Luby.... On the morning of October 3, 1988, Wayne and Luby [were attacked at Luby's residence. The defendant was prosecuted on the theory that he had hired the attackers.] The jury found defendant guilty ... [of] conspiracy to commit an assault [and other charges]....

The Court of Appeal reversed defendant's convictions, finding that defendant was prejudiced by ... the trial court's erroneous admission of defendant's statements to John Lueck in violation of the attorney–client privilege.... We granted the People's petition for review.

II. DISCUSSION

... Under [California Evidence Code] section 954, a client holds a privilege to prevent the disclosure of confidential communications between client and lawyer. As pertinent here, a "client" includes a person who "consults a lawyer for the purpose of retaining the lawyer or securing legal service or advice from him in his professional capacity" (§ 951), while "confidential communications" include "information transmitted between a client and his or her lawyer in the course of that relationship and in confidence" (§ 952). . . .

To further its purposes, the attorney–client privilege does not require that the attorney actually be retained. "[W]here a person seeks the assistance of an attorney with a view to employing him professionally, any information acquired by the attorney is privileged whether or not actual employment results." The rationale for this rule is compelling: "no person could ever safely consult an attorney for the first time with a view to his employment if the privilege depended on the chance of whether the attorney after hearing his statement of the facts decided to accept the employment or decline it." Estate of Dupont, 60 Cal. App. 2d 276, 288–89 (1943).

Although the attorney–client privilege is essential to our system of justice, it can and does result in the withholding of relevant information from the fact finder. Therefore, "[t]he party claiming the privilege carries the burden of showing that the evidence which it seeks to suppress is within the terms of the [privilege]." . . .

The trial court determined below that the statements attributed to defendant by Lueck were not protected by the attorney–client privilege. According to the record, Lueck . . . was defendant's friend and had been to defendant's home approximately 15 times. The two [also] shared a business relationship in which Lueck referred between 100 and 200 clients to defendant. . . .

In ruling that the trial court erred, the Court of Appeal placed heavy emphasis on other evidence in the record indicating that issues of a legal nature were discussed during Lueck's visit to defendant's home. . . . [Lueck testified] that defendant showed him some papers from the dissolution action, including a declaration by Wayne, which apparently contained assertions that defendant physically assaulted Wayne. Lueck read the declaration and asked defendant: "Is this true?" When defendant replied that most of it was, Lueck told defendant to retain capable counsel quickly. In addition, the subject of venue was brought up at some point, with Lueck commenting that a change of venue might be appropriate. . . .

We cannot endorse the Court of Appeal's apparent view that the attorney–client privilege applies whenever issues touching upon legal matters are discussed with an attorney. That has never been the law. Significantly, a communication is not privileged, even though it may involve a legal matter, if it has no relation to any professional relationship of the attorney with the client. Moreover, it is not enough that the client seek advice from an attorney; such advice must be sought from the attorney "in his professional capacity."

. . . [T]his is not a situation in which an individual disclosed information while exploring the possibility of retaining the lawyer. . . . [D]efendant was told in no uncertain terms, prior to making any of the challenged communications, that Lueck wanted no involvement in the legal proceedings concerning defendant and Wayne. . . . [N]either the relevant statutory provisions nor California decisional law suggests that the privilege extends to disclosures made after the attorney refuses to undertake representation. . . .

[A]uthorities in other jurisdictions appear to uniformly hold that the attorney–client privilege does not protect statements made after an attorney declines employment. As the Washington Supreme Court reasoned in State v. Hansen, 122 Wn. 2d 712 (1993), once the attorney refused to represent the defendant and explained that he might be better off finding another attorney, there was no basis for the defendant to form a reasonable belief that an attorney-client relationship existed.

. . . In Wigmore's words, "if the client continues his communication after the attorney's refusal to act for him, or if a person knowingly attempts to retain one who is already retained by the opponent and therefore was not retainable by the consultant, he does not need or deserve the protection of the privilege." 8 WIGMORE, EVIDENCE (McNaughton ed. 1961) § 2304, at 587. . . .

. . . There is no evidence indicating that, at the time of Lueck's visit to [defendant's] home or when he made the incriminating statements, defendant did not understand Lueck's position. Defendant's insistence on talking with Lueck, despite Lueck's clear and reiterated unwillingness to act as defendant's lawyer or to have any involvement in defendant's legal dispute with Wayne, gives rise to the reasonable inference that defendant sought to speak with Lueck in his capacity as a friend, not as an attorney. . . .[9] That Lueck agreed some four or five months later to represent defendant on a one-time emergency basis, and that the disclosures surrounding this emergency matter were found to be privileged by the trial court, fail to undermine the conclusion that the earlier communications were unprivileged. . . .

The judgment of the Court of Appeal is [therefore] reversed. . . .

■ KENNARD, J., Concurring and Dissenting. . . . I agree with the majority that in the conversation at issue defendant was not consulting Lueck for "the purpose of" retaining him. This conclusion, however, does not dispose of the question whether any of defendant's conversation with Lueck was privileged. For Evidence Code section 951 [defining "client"] also provides that an attorney–client relationship arises when "a person . . . consults a lawyer for the purpose of . . . securing advice from him in

9. Lueck's trial testimony also supported the reasonable inference that defendant, who was distraught over having been served with divorce papers, simply wanted a shoulder to cry on and did not seek to speak with Lueck in his professional capacity as a lawyer. In Lueck's words, defendant "was in tears" and told Lueck "that he was very upset and he needed somebody to talk to because of the fact that he was upset." . . .

his professional capacity." California cases have not analyzed the meaning of the phrase "professional capacity," as used in Evidence Code section 951, and the majority never directly addresses the issue of whether an attorney–client relationship arose between Lueck and defendant within the meaning of this statutory term. . . .

The determination whether an individual is seeking advice from an attorney in the attorney's "professional capacity" requires a close analysis of the facts in each case: "In view of the frequency with which some persons seek to obtain informally and gratuitously valuable legal advice, and the lamentable frequency with which attorneys submit to such an imposition . . . , it is often difficult to determine whether the consultation is a professional one, within the privilege. The local habits of life, and the circumstances of the case, must largely determine the ruling." 8 WIGMORE, EVIDENCE (McNaughton ed. 1961) § 2303, at 584. Wigmore explains: "[T]he mere circumstance that the advice is given gratuitously does not nullify the privilege."

In this case, Attorney Lueck testified that, in response to a specific inquiry by defendant regarding the advisability of asking the trial court to transfer the case from Orange County to Los Angeles County, he told defendant it might be appropriate to do so. In rendering this legal advice, Lueck was acting in his "professional capacity" as an attorney, thus triggering the attorney–client privilege as to this aspect of the conversation.

I now turn to those portions of the conversation in which defendant made inculpatory statements to Lueck. . . . None of these inculpatory statements had any bearing on defendant's inquiry of Attorney Lueck regarding the legal advisability of requesting a change of venue. Nor does the evidence show that defendant made any of these statements while seeking Lueck's professional advice on any other legal matter. The statements were simply blunt observations by defendant that he was capable of, and contemplating the commission of, a violent assault on Wayne, either by himself or by hired thugs. Therefore, the attorney–client privilege did not attach to these inculpatory statements by defendant. . . .

Although, for the reasons I have given, the trial court erred in ruling that no part of the conversation between defendant and Attorney Lueck was protected by the attorney–client privilege, I conclude that the privileged portion of the conversation, in which defendant and Lueck discussed the legal advisability of seeking a motion for a change of venue in defendant's divorce case, was irrelevant to the criminal charges in this case. [Its admission was therefore harmless.] . . .

■ MOSK, J., Dissenting. . . . [T]he existence of the privilege does not depend on whether an attorney accepts or refuses employment, but rather "hinges upon the client's belief that he is consulting a lawyer in that capacity and his manifested intention to seek legal advice." 1 MCCORMICK ON EVIDENCE (4th ed. 1992) § 88, at 322....

According to the attorney's own testimony ..., his relationship with defendant was more one of business than of personal friendship. He referred some of his clients to defendant. As he stated: "It was the kind of relationship where favors are frequently traded." Lueck strongly suggested in [his] testimony that he was providing defendant with a free legal consultation in exchange for services defendant had previously rendered him. As he stated in reference to defendant's request to meet with him on the occasion in question: "I didn't feel imposed on at that point because there were many times that I had asked him for" help of an unspecified type....

[I]t is obvious that defendant did not call on Lueck because he needed a good friend in whom to confide: by Lueck's own admission, he and defendant did not have that kind of close relationship. It is, rather, evident that from defendant's perspective the predominant reason he asked Lueck to come to his house was to review, and to give advice on, the legal papers with which he had just been served. Above and beyond any of the specific questions defendant asked about change of venue and the like, he was plainly inquiring in an open-ended manner for Lueck's opinion, as a lawyer, of those legal documents. And defendant had a reasonable expectation that the lawyer would render gratuitous legal advice, despite the latter's refusal of employment, because their relationship "was the kind ... where favors are frequently traded."

The nature of the relationship between defendant and Lueck is further illuminated by the latter's consent to represent defendant in an ex parte court appearance some four months later.... On this occasion, defendant called on the attorney to do more than engage in an informal consultation: Lueck drafted the necessary papers and made the ex parte appearance, for which he was paid. But their relationship at that time was fundamentally as it was on the prior occasion: defendant looked to Lueck for emergency legal assistance, and received it from him. Whether formally hired or not, it is clear that defendant viewed Lueck not as his regular counsel but as a lawyer to whom he could turn in times of crisis for legal service and advice.... And ... nothing that defendant said during his meeting with Lueck or subsequently indicated that he intended any of his statements to be anything but confidential....

The other cases cited by the majority involve situations in which the attorneys not only refused employment, but made clear that they represented a client or interest that was adverse to the parties attempting to assert the privilege. In such cases, it is surely unreasonable to believe that statements made to an attorney who represents a conflicting interest are protected by the attorney–client privilege. In this case, Lueck never claimed to be representing an adverse party and, as explained above, defendant reasonably believed that Lueck would function, and Lueck did in fact function, as his ad hoc legal consultant. He was therefore a "client" consulting with Lueck to "secure legal service or advice" within the meaning of Evidence Code section 951.

Nor do I agree with the concurring and dissenting opinion herein that Lueck's role as legal adviser and as friend can or should be separated once it is established that an attorney–client relationship existed between them on the occasion in question. There is no basis either in precedent or policy for making such a separation. Indeed, an attorney is often called upon to listen to client communications that are not strictly law-related. As one commentary has stated: "It must often occur to the lawyer as he listens to his client's problems that the client is less interested in legal redress than he is in purging himself emotionally by telling 'his side of the story' and using the lawyer as sounding board and general counselor. One could argue that these communications should not be protected by the attorney–client privilege because not made to a 'professional legal adviser in his capacity as such.' Frequently, however, client and lawyer would be unable to distinguish between personal and legal matters." Note, *Functional Overlap Between the Lawyer and Other Professionals: Its Implications for the Privileged Communications Doctrine,* 71 YALE L.J. 1226, 1251 (1962). This inextricable connection between the attorney's role as legal adviser and his role as "sounding board and general counselor" is nowhere more true than in the area of family law, the subject on which defendant consulted Lueck, where legal issues are often also deeply personal.

For this reason, courts do not distinguish between privileged and nonprivileged communications between an attorney and a client made in the same consultation, except perhaps when it is manifest that the client intended certain communications to be nonconfidential, . . . or when the statement falls within one of the statutory exceptions to the privilege. A crabbed view of the attorney–client privilege that would differentiate between privileged and nonprivileged statements according to whether the statements contained the requisite "legal content" would impossibly burden the free flow of communication between lawyer and client that the privilege is designed to promote. . . .

I conclude, therefore, that the trial court committed error in permitting Lueck to testify over defendant's objection. . . .

---

2. MAINTAINING CONFIDENTIALITY

Focus on
FRE 502

Problem 12.1
Eavesdropped

Thomas Blackmon stood trial for having tried to steal a snowmobile. During a brief recess in the proceedings, his lawyer directed him to a corner of the courtroom farthest from a state police trooper, the only other person present. The trooper was keeping guard of Blackmon, who was in custody.

Blackmon and his lawyer stood with their backs to the trooper about twenty-five feet away and spoke in a whisper. The trooper heard only these nine words of their conversation: To the lawyer's question, "Why did you leave?" Blackmon answered, "I couldn't get it started." As he spoke, Blackmon made a motion with his arm as if pulling an engine's starter cord.

The trooper told the prosecutor of these events. When court reconvened, the prosecutor called the trooper as a witness and asked him about the overheard conversation. Blackmon objected that the conversation was privileged.

How should the trial judge have ruled? (Assume current federal privilege principles apply.) Does it change your answer if, as the state argued, there was a private lawyer–client conference room just outside the courtroom that Blackmon's lawyer often had used when conferring with other clients? *See Blackmon v. State*, 653 P.2d 669 (Alaska Ct. App. 1982).

Problem 12.2
Dumpster Diving

The facts of *McCafferty's, Inc. v. Bank of Glen Burnie*, 179 F.R.D. 163 (D. Md. 1998):

> [This case] involves a sexual harassment claim against certain high ranking management officials of BGB [Bank of Glen Burnie].... In connection with this dispute, [Attorney] Neil Serotte ..., hired to represent BGB in connection with the sexual harassment claim, prepared a memorandum discussing certain aspects of the claim. On February 27, 1998, Serotte faxed a draft of this memorandum to Ms. Rebecca Joyner, director of human resources at BGB.... Joyner did not show the draft memorandum to anyone else, and after reading and revising it, she discarded it in a trash can

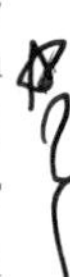

located in her office. Joyner does not recall whether she tore up the memo before throwing it away.

At the end of that business day, Joyner's trash can was emptied by custodial staff into a large plastic bag containing other trash from BGB employees. The plastic bag was then placed in a dumpster with other bags of trash. The dumpster is located on BGB property and displays a three-foot square sign which states: "This container is for the exclusive use of the Bank of Glen Burnie. Unauthorized use will be prosecuted to the fullest extent of the Law." The parking lot where the dumpster is located is for the exclusive use of BGB employees, and there are six three-foot-by-one-foot signs on the lot which state: "Parking only for employees of the Bank of Glen Burnie. Violators will be towed at owner's expense."

On March 2, 1998, at 5:00 a.m., a private investigator employed by [plaintiff] removed numerous bags of trash from BGB's dumpster while engaged in what counsel for [plaintiff] describes . . . as "the lawful art of dumpster diving." According to this investigator, the dumpster was not secure, its doors were open, and the trash bags within were visible. The investigator further states that trash from other businesses was found within the dumpster. . . . [T]he Serotte memorandum . . . had been torn into 16 pieces.

If the plaintiff seeks at trial to offer the memorandum in evidence against BGB and BGB objects, citing its lawyer–client privilege, how should the court rule? Assume current federal evidence principles control.

Williams v. District of Columbia

806 F. Supp. 2d 44 (D.D.C. 2011).

■ Colleen Kollar-Kotelly, J.* In this action, Plaintiff Christina Conyers Williams claims that Defendant the District of Columbia (the "District") retaliated against her in violation of the District of Columbia Whistleblower Protection Act for testimony that she provided before the District of Columbia Council. The action is currently in the pretrial stage of litigation and there is now a single motion before the Court: the District's Renewed Motion to Exclude Plaintiff's Exhibit 9A, through which the District seeks

* [Professor Ann Murphy kindly called this case to my attention.—GF]

to preclude Williams from using a purportedly privileged communication at trial on the basis that it was inadvertently produced in discovery....

I. BACKGROUND

On or about June 27, 2008, the District responded to Williams's first set of document requests. Included with the District's response was what it described as a "recommendation to terminate packet," which consisted of approximately 104 pages of documents pertaining to the termination of Williams's employment with the District. Within the first ten pages of the packet was a two-page e-mail communication involving the then-Deputy General Counsel for the District's Department of Health, discussing certain matters relating to Williams's proposed termination.[2]

Subsequently, the District realized that it had produced the communication and sought its return.[3] On November 22, 2008, the District wrote Williams as follows:

> As we briefly discussed over the telephone, I write pursuant to Fed. R. Civ. P. 26(b)(5)(B) to request that you return a document that was inadvertently produced as part of the District of Columbia's responses to Plaintiff's Request for Production of Documents....
>
> As provided by Rule 26(b)(5)(B), we ask that you return this document to counsel for the District of Columbia at once. You must not use or disclose this information until, if necessary, this issue is resolved by the Court.

It is undisputed that Williams never responded to the notice, favorably or unfavorably. It is similarly undisputed that the District never followed up on its letter—for example, it never asked whether Williams had destroyed or sequestered the communication when it was not "return[ed] ... at once" as the District had requested. Neither party promptly brought the matter to the Court's attention; in fact, in the succeeding two years and eight months, the parties proceeded as if nothing had happened at all. Nor was it for a lack of opportunity: discovery did not close until January 31, 2009; in January and February 2009, the parties filed a series of discovery-related motions; in July 2009, the parties cross-moved for

2. In its written responses, the District included boilerplate assertions of privilege. However, Williams asserts that the District failed to produce a privilege log as required by Rule 26(b)(5)(A) of the Federal of Rules of Civil Procedure, and that assertion is left uncontested by the District. Regardless, it is undisputed that the District did not assert a claim of privilege specifically with respect to the communication at issue until long after the document had been produced.

3. The District speculates that the error was discovered close in time to November 22, 2008—the date that it notified Williams of the alleged error. *See* Def.'s Mem. at 5 ("The timing of the District's letter seems to indicate that [former] counsel discovered the error when preparing to transfer the file [to new counsel]."). However, even though it is presumably the only party that could have firsthand knowledge of the matter, the District is unable to say with certainty when the error was actually discovered.

summary judgment; and, in July 2010, the parties filed a round of motions *in limine*. At no point during these extensive proceedings did the parties bring the matter to the Court's attention.

The matter was revived when the parties began preparing in earnest for the trial in this action. In or about July 2011, the parties exchanged revised proposed exhibit lists. Williams's exhibit list identified her "Exhibit 9A" as "Johnson email re Williams," which the parties agree is a reference to the purportedly privileged communication at issue. On July 20, 2011, the District filed a Motion to Exclude Plaintiff's Exhibit 9A.

During a Status Hearing on July 22, 2011, the Court . . . set an appropriate briefing schedule and the parties were directed to address, *inter alia*:

(a) [W]hether [the District] took reasonable steps to protect the information from inadvertent disclosure, and

(b) whether [the District] took reasonable steps to rectify the inadvertent disclosure once discovered. . . .

II. LEGAL STANDARD

In this Circuit, it used to be the case that virtually any disclosure of a communication protected by the attorney–client privilege, even if inadvertent, worked a waiver of the privilege. However, Congress partially abrogated this relatively strict approach to waiver by enacting Rule 502(b) of the Federal Rules of Evidence,[5] which addresses the extent to which a waiver may be found based upon an inadvertent disclosure in a federal proceeding. Specifically, Rule 502(b) provides:

> When made in a federal proceeding . . . , the disclosure [of a communication or information covered by the attorney–client privilege or work-product protection] does not operate as a waiver in a federal or state proceeding if:
>
> (1) the disclosure is inadvertent;
>
> (2) the holder of the privilege or protection took reasonable steps to prevent disclosure; and
>
> (3) the holder promptly took reasonable steps to rectify the error, including (if applicable) following Federal Rule of Civil Procedure 26(b)(5)(B).

5. Congress enacted Rule 502 on September 19, 2008, and in so doing expressly directed courts to apply the Rule in all proceedings pending on that date "insofar as is just and practicable." Offering no meaningful analysis, Williams contends that the District cannot lay claim to the protections of Rule 502 in this case because the production at issue occurred prior to Rule's effective date, even though the discovery of the error and the efforts that the District undertook to rectify the error post-dated enactment. In reply, the District offers no rejoinder to this argument. Nonetheless, for purposes of resolving the pending motion, the Court will assume, without deciding, that Rule 502 applies in this case. . . .

FED. R. EVID. 502(b). The party claiming that its disclosure was inadvertent bears the burden of proving that each of the three elements of Rule 502(b) has been met. Even if the document at issue is privileged and inadvertently disclosed, if the "disclosure is not excused by the application of Rule 502, then the privilege protecting it from production is gone." *Amobi v. D.C. Dep't of Corrections*, 262 F.R.D. 45, 51 (D.D.C. 2009).

III. DISCUSSION

The Court's discussion here proceeds in two parts. . . .[6]

A. The District Has Failed to Show That It Took Reasonable Steps to Prevent Inadvertent Disclosure

Notwithstanding the easing of the waiver doctrine brought about by the enactment of Rule 502(b), the Rule "does not remove the parties' responsibility to take reasonable precautions against [the] disclosure of privileged documents." *Amobi*, 262 F.R.D. at 51. In order to invoke the protections of Rule 502(b), the holder of the privilege bears the burden of establishing that it "took reasonable steps to prevent disclosure" in the first place. FED. R. EVID. 502(b)(2). In this regard, the District's showing is woefully deficient.

As a threshold matter, the District relies exclusively on the unsworn averments of its counsel, who is almost certain to lack personal knowledge of the circumstances that surrounded the District's review and production of the communication at issue because she was yet to be assigned to this matter. The District has failed to support its arguments with an affidavit or declaration from its prior counsel or the paralegal who is claimed to have reviewed the documents. This failure is both inexplicable and unacceptable and constitutes sufficient grounds to deny the District's motion outright. Nonetheless, even crediting the unsupported statements by the District's counsel, those statements fall far short of establishing that the District took reasonable steps to prevent the disclosure in the first place.

First, and most importantly, the District has utterly failed to explain its "methodology" for review and production. *Amobi*, 262 F.R.D. at 54. The District explains only that "[p]rior to production, this material was

6. The Court will assume, without deciding, that the communication at issue would be protected by the attorney–client privilege were it not for the disclosure to Williams, a matter which the parties dispute. A copy of the communication has been reviewed *in camera*, and while it is certainly arguable that at least some aspects of the communication reflect non-legal advice, the Court agrees that other aspects may fall within the ambit of the privilege. . . . The Court will also assume that the District's disclosure of the communication to Williams was inadvertent, in the sense that it was an "unintended." Given the nature of the communication and the nature of the District's response, the Court finds it difficult to imagine that the disclosure was anything but unintended, notwithstanding Williams's speculation to the contrary.

reviewed by an experienced litigation paralegal under the supervision of an attorney." It should go without saying that this sort of conclusory statement is patently insufficient to establish that a party has discharged its duty of taking "reasonable steps" to guard against the disclosure of privileged documents. Indeed, were courts to accept conclusory statements of this kind, it is difficult to imagine circumstances when Rule 502(b) would *not* apply so long as the disclosing party conducted *any* privilege review, no matter how cursory or unreasonable. In this case, the District does not indicate when its review occurred, how much time it allocated to the review of documents, the nature of the reviewer's experience, the extent of the alleged supervision of an attorney, whether it conducted multiple rounds of review, how it segregated privileged documents from non-privileged documents, and other basic details of the review process. The general statement that a privilege review was performed, without any supporting details, is completely uninformative.[7]

Second, the District has failed to provide a concrete sense of the total number of documents that it reviewed and produced. The parties agree that the "recommendation to terminate" packet that was produced to Williams consisted of slightly over a hundred pages—a relatively *de minimis* production—and the District does not contest Williams's assertion that the two-page e-mail communication at issue here appeared within the first ten pages of the packet. Beyond this, the District claims that "[s]ix other sets of document[s] were also produced to [Williams] that day," but the District fails to provide any further details of the scope of the overall production. So far as the Court is concerned, these additional documents could have consisted of eight pages, eighty pages, eight-hundred pages, or eight-thousand pages. The District's assertions are hopelessly generic, reducing to the unilluminating contention that the communication at issue was part of "a larger production" that ranged somewhere between one-hundred pages and infinity. The District has provided no factual basis for the Court to conclude, as the District suggests, that the error was "reasonable given the size of the production." *Id.* Indeed, based on the record created by the District, the Court can only conclude that the overall size of the production was *de minimis.*

Third, the District offers no clear picture of the demands placed upon it by virtue of Williams's document requests and the timetable of production. Altogether absent from the District's moving papers is any sense of

7. Indeed, the District appears to recognize that there are issues with its factual showing, claiming that the passage of time and changes in counsel "make[] it infinitely harder to supply the type of detail plaintiff argues should be required." Def.'s Reply at 3. The rejoinder to this argument is two-fold. First, regardless of these circumstances, it is the District's burden to establish the applicability of Rule 502(b), and demonstrating that it took reasonable steps to guard against inadvertent disclosure is an essential element of that burden. Second, the District cannot absolve itself of its burden by citing the passage of time; nothing prevented the District from petitioning this Court for relief *years* ago, and indeed it should have.

how many documents it reviewed relative to its overall production, the complexity of the review required, and the time it had to gather, review, and produce responsive documents. This leaves important questions unanswered. Since the total size of the District's production appears to have been small, the Court cannot assume that Williams's demands were particularly onerous or burdensome. Since it appears that the records were all produced in hard copy format, the Court cannot assume that the District was required to sort through a significant amount of electronically stored information. Since Williams's assertion that the District failed to produce any privilege log is left uncontested by the District, the Court cannot assume that the District was required to expend significant time and resources on an exhaustive privilege review. At bottom, the only thing that the Court *can* assume is that Williams served document requests on the District and that the District had at least thirty days to respond to those requests.

The Court does not intend to suggest a party seeking to invoke the protections of Rule 502(b) must always address all, or even necessarily most, of the considerations described above in order to secure relief. However, these are the sort of considerations that one would expect to be relevant, and not one is addressed with any meaningful measure of detail in the District's moving papers. The District bears the burden of establishing . . . that it "took reasonable steps to prevent disclosure." FED. R. EVID. 502(b)(2). In the final analysis, the District's showing is so cursory and incomplete that there simply is no foundation for this Court to evaluate the reasonableness of the precautions taken to guard against inadvertent disclosure. Because . . . the District has failed to discharge [its] burden, the Court will deny the District's Motion to Exclude on this basis.

B. The District Has Failed to Establish That It Took Reasonable Steps to Rectify the Error Once Discovered

Even where the holder of the privilege can show that it took reasonable precautions to guard against disclosure, the holder bears the further burden of showing that it "promptly took reasonable steps to rectify the error" once discovered. FED. R. EVID. 502(b)(3). In this case, the District has taken the position that all it was required to do was to notify Williams of the inadvertent disclosure and to request the return of the communication in accordance with Rule 26(b)(5)(B) of the Federal Rules of Civil Procedure. That Rule provides, in relevant part:

> If information produced in discovery is subject to a claim of privilege or of protection as trial-preparation material, the party making the claim may notify any party that received the information of the claim and the basis for it. After being notified, a party must promptly return, sequester, or destroy the specified information and any copies it has; must not use or disclose the information until the claim is resolved; must take reasonable steps to retrieve the information if the party disclosed it before being notified; and may promptly

> present the information to the court under seal for a determination of the claim.

FED. R. CIV. P. 26(b)(5)(B). Notably, even though the Court expressly instructed the District to support its argument that compliance with Rule 26(b)(5)(B) is sufficient to discharge its obligation under Rule 502(b) to "promptly take reasonable steps to rectify the error," the District cites to no authority in support of its position. The Court can only assume that there is none.

The Court does not doubt that there will be circumstances where a party's compliance with Rule 26(b)(5)(B) will constitute "reasonable steps to rectify the error," FED. R. EVID. 502(b), but this is not such a case. Here, the District notified Williams of its error in a letter dated November 22, 2008, requesting that the communication be "return[ed] ... at once." When Williams did not promptly return the communication or otherwise respond to the District's letter, the District was on notice that further action was required. Nonetheless, the District waited approximately *two years and eight months* before it filed a motion seeking the Court's intervention. *Cf. Amobi*, 262 F.R.D. at 54 (noting that characterizing attempts to rectify the error 55 days after discovery as a "prompt effort" was a "debatable proposition"). Which is not to say that the District was required to seek the Court's intervention immediately on the heels of its letter to Williams. In appropriate circumstances, a producing party may be justified in waiting a reasonable period of time to see if the receiving party will "sequester" the document and "present the information to the court under seal for a determination of the claim." FED. R. CIV. P. 26(b)(5)(B). Alternatively, a producing party may, and in fact should, attempt to meet-and-confer with the receiving party in a good faith attempt to resolve the dispute and obviate the need for the district court's intervention. Here, the District took no further action, electing instead to wait *years* while a privileged communication remained in the hands of a third party to the communication. This sort of indifference is fundamentally at odds with the principle that the attorney–client privilege "must be jealously guarded by the holder of the privilege lest it be waived." *In re Sealed Case*, 877 F.2d 976, 980 (D.C. Cir. 1989).

Under these unique circumstances, the District's mere compliance with Rule 26(b)(5)(B), without more, did not constitute "reasonable steps to rectify the error." FED. R. EVID. 502(b). Accordingly, the Court will deny the District's Motion to Exclude on this separate, independent basis.

IV. CONCLUSION

... The Court finds that there is no injustice to denying the District the protections of Rule 502(b). Here, "the only 'injustice' in this matter is that done by defendant[t] to [itself]." *Amobi*, 262 F.R.D. at 55. The District's failure to make reasonable efforts to guard against the disclosure in the first place and to rectify its error once discovered is fatal to its reliance on Rule 502(b). . . .

Problem 12.3
Uncradled Phone

. . . [Andrew] Howell's complaint allege[d] that between 1976 and 1979, when he was a child, defendant William Joffe . . . sexually abused him. At that time, Joffe was a priest associated with St. Mary's [School, also a defendant in the lawsuit]. Howell also alleges that [Ellen] Lynch, an agent or employee of Hinshaw [& Culbertson, LLP, which represented the Diocese], contacted him in April of 2004 along with [Monsignor David] Kagan. Howell contends that Kagan and Lynch left him a voicemail message with "rude, derogatory, inflammatory, and inappropriate comments" about Howell and about "other victims who had experienced sexual assault and abuse" by Joffe. Howell allege[d] that as a result of this voicemail he suffered severe emotional distress. He . . . brought numerous claims, including claims for negligent and intentional infliction of emotion distress caused by the voicemail message. . . .

[In the phone message] Lynch states that she is "getting back" to Howell and asks him to call her. At this point, a "clicking" sound is heard on the recording. Lynch then converses with [Kagan]. . . . Lynch and Kagan comment about the characteristics of Howell's voicemail recording and Kagan expresses an opinion about Howell's vocal characteristics. The two then discuss how Howell compares to other people who have made allegations of abuse against the Diocese. Finally, Kagan expresses an opinion about the type of victims that Joffe allegedly targeted. . . . The recording then ends.

. . . [D]efendants have submitted an affidavit from Kagan and an affidavit from Lynch. In Kagan's affidavit he avers that in 2004 he was an ordained priest in the Diocese. As part of his duties he analyzed complaints or allegations of misconduct against individuals associated with the Diocese, and met with the Diocese's legal counsel (at that time Lynch) to discuss legal claims against the Diocese. In evaluating sexual misconduct claims, Kagan avers that he would "consider the similarities, if any, between the claims made by various claimants concerning the same person" and would "ask Diocesan Counsel for input and impressions concerning similarities, if any." According to his affidavit, on April 27, 2004, he heard Lynch leave a message for Howell, and after he believed that Lynch had hung up the tele-

> phone receiver, he "voiced his impressions about [Howell's] vocal characteristics and other aspects of the message, including the music in the background of the message." Then, Kagan avers Lynch "provided her impressions about the similarities, if any, in the claims for sexual misconduct alleged to have been committed by the same person against minors who were now reporting such conduct as adults." . . .
>
> In Lynch's affidavit, she states that . . . [o]n April 27, 2004, . . . she had a meeting with Kagan to discuss claims. . . . [Lynch] avers that after she left a telephone message for Howell she intended to end the call, but the telephone connection did not disconnect because she had unknowingly placed the receiver on the phone incorrectly. At that time, she conversed with Kagan "in evaluation of [Howell's] allegations including responding to [Kagan's] comments and impressions about the type of boy the accused priest might have targeted based on the similarities between [Howell] and other victims of the accused priest". . . . [Lynch's] affidavit further states that she was unaware that the line was still connected during the call until August 9, 2004, when Howell's counsel contacted her and told her that he had an audiotape of the conversation. She says that the same day she contacted Howell's counsel, told him that the conversation was protected by attorney–client privilege, and demanded the return of any copies of the conversation.

Howell v. Joffe, 483 F. Supp. 2d 659, 660–62 (N.D. Ill. 2007). In response to the defendants' motion in limine to exclude evidence of the recording and its contents on grounds of lawyer-client privilege, how should the court rule? Assume current federal evidence principles apply.

Inside Straight

Clawback Agreements—An Oft-Missed Tack

Mark Herrmann*

Abovethelaw.com (June 11, 2011), available at:
http://abovethelaw.com/2011/06/inside-straight-clawback-agreements/#more-75424
Reprinted by permission.

I recently heard a panel of judges speak about e-discovery issues. Their opinions on several subjects varied, but on one subject they

* [Again I owe Professor Ann Murphy for this citation.—GF]

agreed unanimously: Clawback provisions under Federal Rule of Evidence 502 are valuable tools in most significant litigation, but they remain rarely used.

This piqued my interest, so I asked several in-house litigators . . . whether they routinely seek FRE 502 clawback provisions in their cases. The in-house lawyers do not. And I asked whether outside counsel routinely recommend seeking those provisions. Not surprisingly (because the in-house folks aren't using them), outside counsel do not.

The judges think clawback provisions are a good idea; in most situations, it strikes me that the judges are right. So what are FRE 502 clawback provisions, and why are inside and outside counsel routinely missing this trick?

In a nutshell, FRE 502 now provides that the disclosure of attorney–client or work product information in a federal proceeding does not waive either privilege, so long as (1) the disclosure was inadvertent, (2) the holder of the privilege took reasonable steps to prevent the disclosure, and (3) the holder promptly took reasonable steps to rectify the error. The Advisory Committee Notes explain that Rule 502 "contemplates enforcement of 'claw-back' and 'quick peek' arrangements as a way to avoid the excessive costs of pre-production review for privilege and work product." [RB 110.] Under a clawback agreement, the parties can agree (and a court can order) that, if a party inadvertently produces a privileged document, the receiving party must return it. This eliminates the need for the producing party to take "reasonable steps" (or, in some cases, any steps) to prevent the disclosure of the privileged information. If a privileged document is inadvertently disclosed, the document must be returned, period.

If a federal court enters a clawback order, FRE 502(d) provides that the order can prevent the inadvertent disclosure from being a waiver not just between the parties to the agreement, but also "in any other federal or state proceeding." Thus, for maximum effect, parties should typically ask federal courts to enter clawback orders to give the broadest protection to the attorney–client and work product privileges in case of inadvertent disclosure.

Naturally, the need to enter these orders will occasionally raise controversies. In asymmetrical litigation—where one party possesses few electronic documents, and the other side possesses many—the party less concerned with inadvertently producing privileged documents may oppose entering a clawback order. But that shouldn't stop the player with voluminous e-documents from applying to a court for help.

Indeed, one of the judges on the panel that I attended suggested that a law firm's failure to request a clawback agreement (or order) might someday be used as evidence of malpractice if the firm later inadvertently disclosed a privileged, and highly sensitive, document. . . .

Why do many litigators frequently miss the clawback trick? Perhaps because the clawback provisions appear in the Federal Rules of Evidence, rather than the Federal Rules of Civil Procedure. Before folks trot down to court for a Rule 16 pretrial conference, they look at Rule 16, think about initial disclosures and the scope of discovery, negotiate the required deadlines, and do the other stuff mandated by Rule 16. But clawback provisions are hidden in the Federal Rules of Evidence, so the Rules of Civil Procedure never force litigators to focus on them during the pretrial process.

Outside lawyers should stop missing this trick. They ought to add "consider a clawback provision" to the standard lists of items—jurisdiction, venue, affirmative defenses—that they consider in every case. And inside lawyers should do the same....

Someday, when you inadvertently disclose a privileged document, you'll be glad that you put Rule 502 clawback provisions on your list of items to consider in every case.

Errant E-Mail

Inadvertent Disclosure of Confidential Material Poses Dilemma

Barry R. Temkin

NEW YORK LAW JOURNAL, Oct. 14, 2003, at 5

... Assume you are embroiled in a complex commercial litigation when you receive an e-mail from adversary counsel that is sent apparently in error. While the message bears your e-mail address, the text suggests it is addressed to your adversary's client or co-counsel....

The errant e-mail is a virtual template to your adversary's case, a battle plan ... that could enable you to win your client's case decisively. While there are no disclaimers or confidentiality warnings on the e-mail, it appears evident from the start that it was not intended for your eyes. What are your ethical duties?

ZEALOUS ADVOCACY

The question highlights a tension between an attorney's duty of zealous advocacy on behalf of the client ... [and] duties of courtesy and professionalism to adversaries.... The duty of zealous advocacy has been called "the fundamental principle of the law of lawyering." ...

Professor Monroe Freedman, in a short but influential article, has argued that an inadvertently disclosed fax should be exploited for the benefit of the recipient's clients. He suggests that the "current vogue for professionalism" should not cause us to "sacrific[e] our clients' interests to protect opposing counsel from embarrassment or a malpractice action."

Indeed, several state bar associations have opined that the beneficiary of inadvertently produced confidential materials should be able, with some qualifications, to exploit the materials to the benefit of their clients.

Moreover, Mr. Freedman queries, what about those situations in which adversary counsel has waived the privilege or confidentiality protection as a matter of substantive law? Should principles of courtesy and professionalism override an adversary's waiver of these privileges?. . . .

THE ABA POSITION

The American Bar Association, in two formal ethics opinions and a recent amendment to its Model Rules of Professional Conduct, has resolved the inadvertent disclosure dilemma in favor of professionalism and confidentiality concerns.

In ABA Formal Opinion 92–368, the Committee on Ethics and Professional Responsibility wrote: "A lawyer who receives materials that on their face appear to be subject to the attorney–client privilege or otherwise confidential, under circumstances where it is clear they were not intended for the receiving lawyer, should refrain from examining the materials, notify the sending lawyer, and abide by the instructions of the lawyer who sent them."

The ABA opinion was based on principles of substantive law, which evinced "an unwillingness to permit mere inadvertence to constitute a waiver," and considerations of reciprocity. As the ABA Committee observed: "While a lawyer today may be the beneficiary of the opposing lawyer's misstep, tomorrow the shoe could be on the other foot." . . .

In 2002, the ABA amended its Model Rules of Professional Conduct to include a provision obligating a lawyer who knowingly receives an inadvertently sent confidential missive promptly to notify the sender.

ABA Model Rule 4.4(b) provides: "A lawyer who receives a document [or electronically stored information] relating to the representation of the lawyer's client and knows or reasonably should know that the document [or electronically stored information] was inadvertently sent shall promptly notify the sender."*

The Rule's Commentary explains that the lawyer's duty of advocacy on behalf of the client "does not imply that a lawyer may disregard the rights of third persons." . . .

The "Oops" Factor

Latest Model Rule Leaves Wiggle Room for Lawyers Receiving Misdirected Materials

Eileen Libby

92 A.B.A. J. 26 (February 2006)

THE ABA HAS EASED UP ON ITS expectations of what a lawyer should do upon receiving materials that he or she was never intended to have.

The ABA first addressed the issue in 1992 when the Standing Committee on Ethics and Professional Responsibility issued Formal Opinion

* [The bracketed language was added by amendment in 2012.—GF]

92–368 (Inadvertent Disclosure of Confidential Materials)....

The ABA opinion came in for its share of criticism, particularly on grounds that, even when a lawyer receives a document that could win a client's case, the opinion would require the lawyer to give more weight to a careless adversary's obligation of confidentiality than to the lawyer's own obligation of zealous representation....

Some Questions Remain

In 2002, the ABA House of Delegates ... amend[ed] Model Rule 4.4 (Respect for Rights of Third Persons). The amendment essentially reversed Formal Opinion 92–368.

Amended Rule 4.4 requires a lawyer who receives materials sent inadvertently only to notify the lawyer who sent them. The amended rule does not prohibit the recipient lawyer from reviewing the materials, nor does it require the lawyer to abide by the sending lawyer's instruction as to disposition of the materials.

And on Oct. 1, the ethics committee formally withdrew its 1992 opinion (Formal Opinion 05–437).

In essence, lawyers who receive materials they weren't intended to see—including faxes, e-mails and other electronic transmissions—have no ethical obligation other than to inform the sender.

But there is some wiggle room. The comment to amended ABA Model Rule 4.4 states that some issues, such as whether a lawyer must return the materials or whether the privileged nature of the materials is waived, are "questions of law beyond the scope of the rule" that lawyers should decide as "a matter of professional judgment ordinarily reserved to the lawyer."

Meanwhile, no uniform rule regarding the treatment of materials that are inadvertently sent to opposing counsel has evolved at the state level. The best solution may be to be very careful before hitting the "send" button.

---

3. Defining Communications: Source of Fees and Client's Identity

Courts generally regard neither the client's fee arrangements nor her identity to be facts *communicated* in confidence to the professional. True, many clients *want* their fee arrangements or identities to stay hidden. Some worry that by paying legal fees in cash, they risk suspicion as drug sellers or bribe takers or bookies—or that if a "friend" pays the tab, police will suspect a criminal enterprise. Other clients worry that even by seeking a lawyer's aid, they give prosecutors or plaintiffs grounds for suspicion and therefore prefer that their status as clients be confidential.

But the lawyer–client privilege does not protect against disclosure of all *incriminating* information. It safeguards only confidential *communications*. Courts generally do not regard fee payments as communications, even if the form of payment reveals evidence of guilt. It is true that clients often *communicate* their identities to lawyers. But even if a client tells a lawyer her name in confidence, the law generally does not regard the disclosure as a confidential communication. That is in part because most people—even most criminals—do not regard their names as secrets. And in part it's because the law regards disclosure of one's identity to be a step in *forming* the lawyer–client relationship, not something that occurs *in the course of* that relationship. The Supreme Court stated the principle long ago in noting that a lawyer could not treat as privileged a person's status as his client:

> The fact [of representation] is preliminary, in its own nature, and establishes only the existence of the relation of client and counsel, and therefore, might not necessarily involve the disclosure of any *communication* arising from that relation, after it was created.

Chirac v. Reinicker, 24 U.S. (11 Wheat.) 280, 294–95 (1826) (emphasis added).* This reasoning also helps explain why fee arrangements are almost never privileged. Even when a client must *communicate* fee terms to counsel, that communication is arguably preliminary to the lawyer–client relationship, not a confidence conveyed within that relationship.

The leading modern case in this realm is *In re Osterhoudt*, 722 F.2d 591 (9th Cir. 1983). *Osterhoudt* is often misunderstood and taken to stand for principles it specifically declares unsound. Read carefully, *Osterhoudt* confirms the general rule that neither the manner of payment nor the client's identity is privileged. It then states one important—but narrow—proviso: A client's identity may be privileged if "in the circumstances of the case disclosure of the identity of the client [is] in substance a disclosure of the confidential communication in the professional relationship between the client and the attorney." 722 F.2d at 593. To illustrate this principle, the *Osterhoudt* court cited the facts of *Baird v. Koerner*, 279 F.2d 623 (9th Cir. 1960). Baird was a tax lawyer jailed by a district judge for refusing to disclose "who employed [him] in connection with his transmittal of a cashier's check in the sum of $12,706.85 to the Director of Internal Revenue." In transmitting the check to the IRS, Baird had written, "This represents additional amounts due from one or more taxpayers for some past years." Earlier Baird had "discussed with [an IRS agent] in detail the facts and circumstances of the case." Until Baird came forward the government apparently had not discovered the underpayment(s) and had launched no audit or investigation. *Id.* at 625–26; 635.

The *Osterhoudt* court recognized that in these circumstances Baird properly claimed his clients' privilege in refusing to disclose their identities. Still, the court stayed faithful to the general rule that the lawyer–client privilege protects only confidential *communications*. The communications in question were not the clients' names, but their sources of income

* There is, however, some authority for privileging the patient's identity in the context of the psychotherapist–patient privilege. *See* MUELLER & KIRKPATRICK, EVIDENCE § 5.35, at 430 & n.22 (5th ed. 2012).

and their failure to pay taxes owed. Baird already had disclosed some of these privileged facts in the course of representing his clients. By revealing their identities too, he would have enabled authorities to link their past communications to their names, effectively "disclos[ing] . . . confidential communication[s] in the professional relationship between the client[s] and the attorney." *Osterhoudt*, 722 F.2d at 593.

Consider Problems 12.4 through 12.7 in this light.

Problem 12.4

Unknown Driver

Consider the facts of *Dietz v. Doe*, 131 Wash. 2d 835 (1997):

> Morgan Dietz was killed in an automobile accident on May 24, 1989, on Highway 101 west of Port Angeles when his car collided with a dump truck that lost control while allegedly trying to avoid another car making an unsafe left turn. The driver of the car that made the unsafe left turn has never come forward, and the authorities do not know the driver's identity.
>
> Within a week of the accident the following news article appeared in a local newspaper:
>
> > PORT ANGELES—An attorney is now handling the case of a motorist sought for questioning in connection with a fatal traffic accident which occurred last week, the State Patrol said Tuesday.
> >
> > The man's identity has not been released and it is unknown whether he has talked with Patrol troopers.
> >
> > Port Angeles attorney Craig Ritchie acknowledged Tuesday that the man had retained his services but had no further comment.
> >
> > The Patrol wanted to question the motorist who reportedly turned left in front of a dump truck on Highway 101 west of Port Angeles Wednesday. . . .
>
> There is nothing in the record as to how the writer of this article obtained the information in it. Based on the newspaper article, the attorney for the Dietz family members and estate contacted attorney Craig Ritchie in an attempt to discover the name of the person who had retained him. Ritchie refused to divulge the information, asserting attorney–client privilege. The Dietzes undertook an investi-

gation to discover the person's name, to no avail. The wife, children, and estate of Morgan Dietz filed the present action on May 22, 1992, for wrongful death and loss of consortium against the unknown driver, whom they have named John Doe. . . .

Assume that Washington's lawyer–client privilege is similar to the federal privilege. If Ritchie is called to testify in connection with the Dietzes' suit and again invokes the privilege in the face of questions about his client's identity, should the court sustain the claim of privilege?

Problem 12.5

Stolen Typewriter

Hughes v. Meade, 453 S.W.2d 538 (Ky. Ct. App. 1970), concerned the trial of one Williams on a charge of stealing an IBM typewriter. The prosecution called a local lawyer, Henry Hughes, as a witness because Hughes had delivered the typewriter in question to the Lexington Police Department. Hughes did not represent Williams at trial. During his testimony, Hughes and the prosecutor had this exchange:

> *Q.* Would you tell the jury the circumstances and how you happened to deliver that typewriter?
>
> *A.* Well, a certain party called me and employed me because of, first of all, my relationship with the Lexington Police Department, which is very good, and I do entirely criminal law and know all of the policemen and members of the Police Department, and asked me if I could get some property returned. . . .
>
> So I called Morris Carter, who was then either assistant chief or a major. I know Morris well, and I asked him, I said, "Morris, are you all interested in getting some stolen property back?" And he said "Yes we are," and he said, "What is it?" I said "I don't know, I have no idea." . . . He said, "All right, how is it going to be delivered?" And I said, "Well, I'm watching the cartoons." It was Saturday morning, and I said, "Somebody is going to leave it on my front porch," and the shades were down and I heard a car come up and left, and I called Morris back and I said "Morris, it's out here," and he said, "Okay I'll send somebody out to get it."
>
> . . .

[Hughes testified that Officer Sparks arrived at his home and found a taped box containing an IBM typewriter on Hughes's porch.]

Q. You didn't want to see who it was [who left the typewriter]?

A. No, that's right.

Q. You say that the certain party called you and employed you to do what you have just described and said you did, is that correct?

A. Yes, sir.

Q. Was this the extent of your employment?

A. Yes, sir.

Q. Have you been paid for that service?

A. Yes, sir.

Q. And I'll ask you now if you will tell us the name of the individual who employed you?

A. I refuse to answer.

Hughes asserted the lawyer–client privilege on behalf of the secret caller. Should the trial judge have sustained the claim of privilege? Is this case just like *Dietz v. Doe*, excerpted in the previous problem?

Problem 12.6
Counterfeit Bill

Consider the facts of *Alexiou v. United States*, 39 F.3d 973 (9th Cir. 1994), *cert. denied*, 514 U.S. 1097 (1995):

> Mr. Alexiou, an attorney, deposited money in his law firm bank account. The deposit included a $100 bill which turned out to be counterfeit. The Secret Service eventually contacted him, asking for the identity of the person who passed the bill. Mr. Alexiou . . . [refused to] respond to the inquiry. . . . In a letter to the Assistant United States Attorney on the case, Mr. Alexiou explained that:
>
> > Lastly, the client simply retained us to represent him, paying a modest retainer for modest events. All violations were traffic with the exception of a misdemeanor assault charge. The client made no disclosure as to the source of the money to us. From what the bank has advised, there was one questionable bill amongst

> the amount paid which now is decidedly counterfeit and that is all I can tell you. . . . [W]e are bound to make no disclosure at this time.

Later, a federal grand jury issued a subpoena directing Alexiou to produce documents that would identify this client. If Alexiou declines and the government seeks an order compelling him to comply with the subpoena, how should the court rule?

Problem 12.7

Handwriting

In the course of her representation of Martin Stone, attorney Elaine Koh received several handwritten letters from him divulging various facts in confidence. Otherwise, Koh has never seen Stone's handwriting. At Stone's criminal trial on unrelated charges, at which he is represented by a different lawyer, the prosecutor calls Koh as a witness. He shows Koh a document purportedly written by Stone—but unrelated to Koh's representation of him—and asks Koh whether the handwriting in the document is Stone's. May she refuse to answer on the grounds that her knowledge of Stone's handwriting results from confidential lawyer–client communications?

---

4. DURATION OF THE PRIVILEGE

Foster Was Shopping for Private Lawyer, Probers Find

Michael Isikoff

WASHINGTON POST, Aug. 15, 1993, at A20

In the days before he committed suicide, deputy White House counsel Vincent W. Foster Jr. began efforts to hire a private lawyer to advise him in connection with inquiries into the firing of seven White House travel office employees, investigators probing Foster's death recently discovered.

While Republicans on the House Judiciary Committee were pushing a "resolution of inquiry" to force a congressional investigation into the travel office affair, Foster consulted ... with James Hamilton, a former deputy counsel to the Senate Watergate committee and a key legal adviser to the Clinton transition team....

White House counsel Bernard Nussbaum said in an interview that it would have been "prudent" for Foster to seek outside legal advice given the prospect that he might be questioned in the course of Justice Department, congressional and General Accounting Office inquiries.

... Nussbaum added: "Vince was not concerned that he did anything wrong in connection with the travel office.... If there is any implication that he was worried about personal liability, that's just totally wrong and unfair."

Hamilton, who now represents Foster's family, declined to comment.

Foster's concern about the travel office issue was evident in the handwritten note discovered in his briefcase after his death and released by the Justice Department last week. In the note, Foster wrote, "I did not knowingly violate any law or standard of conduct," and contended that the FBI had "lied" in its report to Attorney General Janet Reno on its dealings with the White House counsel's office on the travel office affair....

... A Justice Department spokesman confirmed the conduct of White House officials in connection with the travel office remains under review by the department's criminal division.

SWIDLER & BERLIN V. UNITED STATES

524 U.S. 399 (1998).

■ CHIEF JUSTICE REHNQUIST delivered the opinion of the Court.... This dispute arises out of an investigation conducted by the Office of the Independent Counsel into whether various individuals made false statements, obstructed justice, or committed other crimes during investigations of the 1993 dismissal of employees from the White House Travel Office. Vincent W. Foster, Jr., was Deputy White House Counsel when the firings occurred. In July 1993, Foster met with petitioner James Hamilton, an attorney at petitioner Swidler & Berlin, to seek legal representation concerning possible congressional or other investigations of the firings. During a 2–hour meeting, Hamilton took three pages of handwritten notes. One of the first entries in the notes is the word "Privileged." Nine days later, Foster committed suicide.

In December 1995, a federal grand jury, at the request of the Independent Counsel, issued subpoenas to petitioners Hamilton and Swidler & Berlin for, *inter alia*, Hamilton's handwritten notes of his meeting with Foster. Petitioners filed a motion to quash, arguing that the notes were protected by the attorney client privilege.... The District

Court, after examining the notes *in camera*, concluded they were protected from disclosure . . . and denied enforcement of the subpoenas.

The Court of Appeals for the District of Columbia Circuit reversed. While recognizing that most courts assume the privilege survives death, the Court of Appeals noted that holdings actually manifesting the posthumous force of the privilege are rare. Instead, most judicial references to the privilege's posthumous application occur in the context of a well recognized exception allowing disclosure for disputes among the client's heirs. It further noted that most commentators support some measure of posthumous curtailment of the privilege. The Court of Appeals thought that the risk of posthumous revelation, when confined to the criminal context, would have little to no chilling effect on client communication, but that the costs of protecting communications after death were high. It therefore concluded that the privilege was not absolute in such circumstances, and that instead, a balancing test should apply. It thus held that there is a posthumous exception to the privilege for communications whose relative importance to particular criminal litigation is substantial. While acknowledging that uncertain privileges are disfavored, Jaffee v. Redmond, 518 U.S. 1, 17–18 (1996), the Court of Appeals determined that the uncertainty introduced by its balancing test was insignificant in light of existing exceptions to the privilege. . . .

. . . One state appellate court, Cohen v. Jenkintown Cab Co., 238 Pa. Super. 456 (1976), . . . [reached a similar result]. In *Cohen*, a civil case, the court recognized that the privilege generally survives death, but concluded that it could make an exception where the interest of justice was compelling and the interest of the client in preserving the confidence was insignificant. 238 Pa. Super. 462–64.

But other than these two decisions, cases addressing the existence of the privilege after death—most involving the testamentary exception—uniformly presume the privilege survives, even if they do not so hold. Several State Supreme Court decisions expressly hold that the attorney–client privilege extends beyond the death of the client, even in the criminal context. In John Doe Grand Jury Investigation, 408 Mass. 480, 481–83 (1990), for example, the Massachusetts Supreme [Judicial] Court concluded that survival of the privilege was "the clear implication" of its early pronouncements that communications subject to the privilege could not be disclosed at any time. The court further noted that survival of the privilege was "necessarily implied" by cases allowing waiver of the privilege in testamentary disputes. . . .[2]

2. About half the States have codified the testamentary exception by providing that a personal representative of the deceased can waive the privilege when heirs or devisees claim through the deceased client (as opposed to parties claiming against the estate, for whom the privilege is not waived). These statutes do not address expressly the continuation of the privilege outside the context of testamentary disputes, although many allow the attorney to assert the privilege on behalf of the client

Indeed, in Glover v. Patten, 165 U.S. 394, 406–08 (1897), this Court, in recognizing the testamentary exception, expressly assumed that the privilege continues after the individual's death. The Court explained that testamentary disclosure was permissible because the privilege, which normally protects the client's interests, could be impliedly waived in order to fulfill the client's testamentary intent.

The great body of this caselaw supports, either by holding or considered dicta, the position that the privilege does survive in a case such as the present one. Given the language of Rule 501, at the very least the burden is on the Independent Counsel to show that "reason and experience" require a departure from this rule.

The Independent Counsel contends that the testamentary exception supports the posthumous termination of the privilege because in practice most cases have refused to apply the privilege posthumously. He further argues that the exception reflects a policy judgment that the interest in settling estates outweighs any posthumous interest in confidentiality. He then reasons by analogy that in criminal proceedings, the interest in determining whether a crime has been committed should trump client confidentiality, particularly since the financial interests of the estate are not at stake.

But the Independent Counsel's interpretation simply does not square with the caselaw's implicit acceptance of the privilege's survival and with the treatment of testamentary disclosure as an "exception" or an implied "waiver." And the premise of his analogy is incorrect, since cases consistently recognize that the rationale for the testamentary exception is that it furthers the client's intent, *see, e.g., Glover, supra.* There is no reason to suppose as a general matter that grand jury testimony about confidential communications furthers the client's intent.

... Undoubtedly, as the Independent Counsel emphasizes, various commentators have ... urg[ed] that the privilege should be abrogated after the client's death where extreme injustice would result, as long as disclosure would not seriously undermine the privilege by deterring client communication. But even these critics clearly recognize that established law supports the continuation of the privilege and that a contrary rule would be a modification of the common law.

Despite the scholarly criticism, we think there are weighty reasons that counsel in favor of posthumous application. Knowing that communications will remain confidential even after death encourages the client to communicate fully and frankly with counsel. While the fear of disclosure, and the consequent withholding of information from counsel, may be

apparently without temporal limit.... California's statute is exceptional in that it apparently allows the attorney to assert the privilege only so long as a holder of the privilege (the estate's personal representative) exists, suggesting the privilege terminates when the estate is wound up. *See* CAL. CODE EVID. ANN. §§ 954, 957 (West 1995). But no other State has followed California's lead in this regard.

reduced if disclosure is limited to posthumous disclosure in a criminal context, it seems unreasonable to assume that it vanishes altogether. Clients may be concerned about reputation, civil liability, or possible harm to friends or family. Posthumous disclosure of such communications may be as feared as disclosure during the client's lifetime....

Without assurance of the privilege's posthumous application, the client may very well not have made disclosures to his attorney at all, so the loss of evidence is more apparent than real. In the case at hand, it seems quite plausible that Foster, perhaps already contemplating suicide, may not have sought legal advice from Hamilton if he had not been assured the conversation was privileged.

The Independent Counsel additionally suggests that his proposed exception would have minimal impact if confined to criminal cases, or, as the Court of Appeals suggests, if it is limited to information of substantial importance to a particular criminal case.[3] However, there is no case authority for the proposition that the privilege applies differently in criminal and civil cases, and only one commentator ventures such a suggestion, *see* MUELLER & KIRKPATRICK, 2 FEDERAL EVIDENCE § 199, at 380–81 (2d ed. 1994). In any event, a client may not know at the time he discloses information to his attorney whether it will later be relevant to a civil or a criminal matter, let alone whether it will be of substantial importance. Balancing *ex post* the importance of the information against client interests, even limited to criminal cases, introduces substantial uncertainty into the privilege's application. For just that reason, we have rejected use of a balancing test in defining the contours of the privilege. *See Jaffee*, 518 U.S. at 17–18.

In a similar vein, the Independent Counsel argues that existing exceptions to the privilege, such as the crime-fraud exception and the testamentary exception, make the impact of one more exception marginal. However, these exceptions do not demonstrate that the impact of a posthumous exception would be insignificant, and there is little empirical evidence on this point.[4] The established exceptions are consistent with the

3. Petitioner, while opposing wholesale abrogation of the privilege in criminal cases, concedes that exceptional circumstances implicating a criminal defendant's constitutional rights might warrant breaching the privilege. We do not, however, need to reach this issue, since such exceptional circumstances clearly are not presented here.

4. Empirical evidence on the privilege is limited. Three studies do not reach firm conclusions on whether limiting the privilege would discourage full and frank communication. Alexander, *The Corporate Attorney Client Privilege: A Study of the Participants*, 63 ST. JOHN'S L. REV. 191 (1989); Zacharias, *Rethinking Confidentiality*, 74 IOWA L. REV. 352 (1989); Comment, *Functional Overlap Between the Lawyer and Other Professionals: Its Implications for the Privileged Communications Doctrine*, 71 YALE L.J. 1226 (1962). These articles note that clients are often uninformed or mistaken about the privilege.... Two of the articles conclude that a substantial number of clients and attorneys think the privilege enhances open communication, Alexander, *supra*, at 244–46, 261, and that the absence of a privilege would be detrimental to such communication, Comment, 71 YALE L.J., *supra*, at 1236.

purposes of the privilege, while a posthumous exception in criminal cases appears at odds with the goals of encouraging full and frank communication and of protecting the client's interests. A "no harm in one more exception" rationale could contribute to the general erosion of the privilege, without reference to common law principles or "reason and experience."

Finally, the Independent Counsel, relying on cases such as United States v. Nixon, 418 U.S. 683, 710 (1974), and Branzburg v. Hayes, 408 U.S. 665 (1972),* urges that privileges be strictly construed because they are inconsistent with the paramount judicial goal of truth seeking. But both *Nixon* and *Branzburg* dealt with the creation of privileges not recognized by the common law, whereas here we deal with one of the oldest recognized privileges in the law. And we are asked, not simply to "construe" the privilege, but to narrow it, contrary to the weight of the existing body of caselaw.

It has been generally, if not universally, accepted, for well over a century, that the attorney–client privilege survives the death of the client in a case such as this. While the arguments against the survival of the privilege are by no means frivolous, they are based in large part on speculation—thoughtful speculation, but speculation nonetheless—as to whether posthumous termination of the privilege would diminish a client's willingness to confide in an attorney. In an area where empirical information would be useful, it is scant and inconclusive.

[Unrestyled] Rule 501's direction to look to "the principles of the common law as they may be interpreted by the courts of the United States in the light of reason and experience" does not mandate that a rule, once established, should endure for all time. But here the Independent Counsel has simply not made a sufficient showing to overturn the common law rule embodied in the prevailing caselaw. Interpreted in the light of reason and experience, that body of law requires that the attorney client privilege prevent disclosure of the notes at issue in this case. The judgment of the Court of Appeals is

Reversed.

The third article suggests instead that while the privilege is perceived as important to open communication, limited exceptions to the privilege might not discourage such communication, Zacharias, *supra*, at 382, 386. Similarly, relatively few court decisions discuss the impact of the privilege's application after death. This may reflect the general assumption that the privilege survives—if attorneys were required as a matter of practice to testify or provide notes in criminal proceedings, cases discussing that practice would surely exist.

* [In *Nixon* the Court recognized an executive privilege, but held it "must yield to the demonstrated, specific need for evidence in a pending criminal trial." 418 U.S. at 710. In *Branzburg*, as we saw in Chapter 11 in the context of the *Judith Miller* case, the Supreme Court declined to create a constitutional newsperson's privilege.—GF]

■ JUSTICE O'CONNOR, with whom JUSTICE SCALIA and JUSTICE THOMAS join, dissenting. Although the attorney–client privilege ordinarily will survive the death of the client, I do not agree with the Court that it inevitably precludes disclosure of a deceased client's communications in criminal proceedings....

We have long recognized that "the fundamental basis upon which all rules of evidence must rest—if they are to rest upon reason—is their adaptation to the successful development of the truth." Funk v. United States, 290 U.S. 371, 381 (1933). In light of the heavy burden that they place on the search for truth, *see* United States v. Nixon, 418 U.S. 683, 708–10 (1974), "evidentiary privileges in litigation are not favored, and even those rooted in the Constitution must give way in proper circumstances," Herbert v. Lando, 441 U.S. 153, 175 (1979)....

I agree that a deceased client may retain a personal, reputational, and economic interest in confidentiality. But, after death, the potential that disclosure will harm the client's interests has been greatly diminished, and the risk that the client will be held criminally liable has abated altogether. Thus, some commentators suggest that terminating the privilege upon the client's death "could not to any substantial degree lessen the encouragement for free disclosure which is [its] purpose." 1 J. STRONG, MCCORMICK ON EVIDENCE § 94, at 350 (4th ed. 1992). This diminished risk is coupled with a heightened urgency for discovery of a deceased client's communications in the criminal context. The privilege does not "protect[] disclosure of the underlying facts by those who communicated with the attorney," Upjohn Co. v. United States, 449 U.S. 383, 395 (1981), and were the client living, prosecutors could grant immunity and compel the relevant testimony. After a client's death, however, if the privilege precludes an attorney from testifying in the client's stead, a complete "loss of crucial information" will often result.

As the Court of Appeals observed, the costs of recognizing an absolute posthumous privilege can be inordinately high. Extreme injustice may occur, for example, where a criminal defendant seeks disclosure of a deceased client's confession to the offense. In my view, the paramount value that our criminal justice system places on protecting an innocent defendant should outweigh a deceased client's interest in preserving confidences. Indeed, even petitioner acknowledges that an exception may be appropriate where the constitutional rights of a criminal defendant are at stake. An exception may likewise be warranted in the face of a compelling law enforcement need for the information. "Our historic commitment to the rule of law ... is nowhere more profoundly manifest than in our view that the twofold aim of criminal justice is that guilt shall not escape or innocence suffer." *Nixon, supra,* at 709. Given that the complete exclusion of relevant evidence from a criminal trial or investigation may distort the record, mislead the factfinder, and undermine the central truth-seeking function of the courts, I do not believe that the attorney–client privilege should act as an absolute bar to the disclosure of a deceased client's communications. When the privilege is asserted in the criminal context, and a showing is made that the communications at issue contain necessary factual information not otherwise available, courts should be permitted to assess whether interests in fairness and accuracy outweigh the justifications for the privilege.

A number of exceptions to the privilege already qualify its protections, and an attorney "who tells his client that the expected communications are absolutely and forever privileged is oversimplifying a bit." In re Sealed Case, 124 F.3d 230, 235 (D.C. Cir. 1997). In the situation where the posthumous privilege most frequently arises—a dispute between heirs over the decedent's will—the privilege is widely recognized to give way to the interest in settling the estate. This testamentary exception, moreover, may be invoked in some cases where the decedent would not have chosen to waive the privilege. For example, "a decedent might want to provide for an illegitimate child but at the same time much prefer that the relationship go undisclosed." 124 F.3d at 234. . . . Nor are other existing exceptions to the privilege—for example, the crime-fraud exception or the exceptions for claims relating to attorney competence or compensation—necessarily consistent with "encouraging full and frank communication" or "protecting the client's interests." Rather, those exceptions reflect the understanding that, in certain circumstances, the privilege " 'ceases to operate' " as a safeguard on "the proper functioning of our adversary system." *See* United States v. Zolin, 491 U.S. 554, 562–563 (1989). . . .

Moreover, as the Court concedes, there is some authority for the proposition that a deceased client's communications may be revealed, even in circumstances outside of the testamentary context. California's Evidence Code, for example, provides that the attorney–client privilege continues only until the deceased client's estate is finally distributed, noting that "there is little reason to preserve secrecy at the expense of excluding relevant evidence after the estate is wound up and the representative is discharged." Cal. Evid. Code Ann. § 954, and comment, § 952, at 232 (West 1995).* And a state appellate court has admitted an attorney's testimony concerning a deceased client's communications after "balancing the necessity for revealing the substance of the [attorney–client conversation] against the unlikelihood of any cognizable injury to the rights, interests, estate or memory of [the client]." *See* Cohen v. Jenkintown Cab Co., 238 Pa. Super. 456, 464 (1976). The American Law

* [In 2009 the California legislature amended the California Evidence Code to clarify whether and when the lawyer–client privilege survives the client's death. As amended, the evidence code declares that a deceased's "personal representative," including one appointed by the court for purposes of later estate administration, is a "holder of the privilege." The amendment has received little or no attention in published caselaw, and its impact is not wholly clear. A 2009 report of the California Law Revision Commission, which recommended the law change, suggested its intent was not to change the duration of the privilege as described above in Justice O'Connor's opinion. *See* Cal. Evid. Code § 953, *as amended*, 2009 Cal. Stat. ch. 8, § 1 (eff. Jan. 1, 2010); *Attorney-Client Privilege After Client's Death*, 38 Cal. L. Revision Comm'n Reports 163, 166, 175–80, 195, 198 (2008) (Recommendation, February 2009) (recommending the new law and exploring its meaning).—GF]

Institute, moreover, has recently recommended withholding the privilege when the communication "bears on a litigated issue of pivotal significance" and has suggested that courts "balance the interest in confidentiality against any exceptional need for the communication." RESTATEMENT (THIRD) OF THE LAW GOVERNING LAWYERS § 127, at 431, Comment d; *see also* 2 C. MUELLER & L. KIRKPATRICK, FEDERAL EVIDENCE, § 199, at 380 (2d ed. 1994) ("If a deceased client has confessed to criminal acts that are later charged to another, surely the latter's need for evidence sometimes outweighs the interest in preserving the confidences").

Where the exoneration of an innocent criminal defendant or a compelling law enforcement interest is at stake, the harm of precluding critical evidence that is unavailable by any other means outweighs the potential disincentive to forthright communication. In my view, the cost of silence warrants a narrow exception to the rule that the attorney–client privilege survives the death of the client. . . .

With respect, I dissent.

B. THE CRIME–FRAUD EXCEPTION

Problem 12.8
Custody Dispute

Elsa Newman and her husband, Arlen Slobodow, had two sons, Lars and Herbie. As the couple's marriage broke down in 1999, they began divorce and custody proceedings. Newman filed formal complaints against Slobodow alleging he sexually abused the children. In August 2001 she met privately with Stephen Friedman, whom she hired to represent her in an upcoming custody hearing. At that meeting Newman mused: "You know, I don't have to kill both children. I only need to kill Lars because I can save Herbie, and then Arlen will go to jail [for killing Lars] and get what he deserves because he is a criminal, and I can at least save Herbie." Friedman replied, "You cannot involve me in a murder case, and you need to convince me that you are just frustrated . . . [and] upset [and not serious]."

Several days later Friedman disclosed Newman's remark to a county court judge. He did so under a state ethics rule, common to many jurisdictions, that permits lawyers to reveal otherwise confidential communications "to the extent the lawyer reasonably believes necessary . . . to prevent the client from committing a criminal or fraudulent act that the lawyer believes is likely to result in death or substantial bodily harm. . . ." *Cf.*

Model Rules of Professional Conduct R. 1.6(b)(1). The court restricted Newman to supervised visits with her children.

In January 2002 a friend of Newman's broke into Slobodow's house and shot and wounded him. The intruder brought with her pornographic materials, apparently intending to plant them in Slobodow's home as evidence he molested the children. Two days later authorities charged Newman with conspiracy to murder.

At a pretrial motion *in limine*, at which another lawyer represented Newman, the state sought an order to compel Friedman to testify at trial about Newman's August 2001 statement. The state resisted Newman's claims of privilege, arguing first that Friedman's earlier disclosure had waived the privilege and second that Newman's statement was subject to the crime-fraud exception to the lawyer–client privilege.

How should the trial court have ruled on each of the state's arguments? Assume federal evidence principles control. See *Newman v. State*, 384 Md. 285 (2004).

United States v. Zolin

491 U.S. 554 (1989).

■ Justice Blackmun delivered the opinion of the Court. This case arises out of the efforts of the Criminal Investigation Division of the Internal Revenue Service (IRS) to investigate the tax returns of L. Ron Hubbard, founder of the Church of Scientology (the Church), for the calendar years 1979 through 1983. We granted certiorari, to consider . . . the testimonial privilege for attorney–client communications and, more particularly, the generally recognized exception to that privilege for communications in furtherance of future illegal conduct—the so-called "crime-fraud" exception. The specific question presented is whether the applicability of the crime-fraud exception must be established by "independent evidence" (*i.e.*, without reference to the content of the contested communications themselves), or, alternatively, whether the applicability of that exception can be resolved by an *in camera* inspection of the allegedly privileged material. . . .

I

In the course of its investigation, the IRS sought access to 51 documents that had been filed with the Clerk of the Los Angeles County Superior Court in connection with a case entitled *Church of Scientology of*

California v. *Armstrong*. The *Armstrong* litigation involved, among other things, a charge by the Church that one of its former members, Gerald Armstrong, had obtained by unlawful means documentary materials relating to Church activities, including two tapes. Some of the documents sought by the IRS had been filed under seal. . . .[4] . . .

Respondents asserted the privilege as a bar to disclosure of the tapes. The IRS argued, among other things, however, that the tapes fell within the crime-fraud exception to the attorney–client privilege, and urged the District Court to listen to the tapes in the course of making its privilege determination. In addition, the IRS submitted to the court two declarations by Agent [Steven] Petersell. In the first, Petersell stated his grounds for believing that the tapes were relevant to the investigation. In the second, Petersell offered a description of the tapes' contents, based on information he received during several interviews. Appended to this declaration—over respondents' objection—were partial transcripts of the tapes, which the IRS lawfully had obtained from a confidential source. In subsequent briefing, the IRS reiterated its request that the District Court listen to the tapes *in camera* before making its privilege ruling. . . .

Turning to the tapes, the District Court ruled that respondents had demonstrated that they contain confidential attorney–client communications, that the privilege had not been waived, and that "[t]he 'fraud-crime' exception to the attorney–client privilege does not apply. The quoted excerpts tend to show or admit past fraud but there is no clear indication that future fraud or crime is being planned." On this basis, the court held that the Clerk "need not produce its copy of the tapes pursuant to the summons." The District Court denied the IRS' motion for reconsideration, rejecting the IRS' renewed request that the court listen to the tapes *in toto*. . . .

[Before the Court of Appeals for the Ninth Circuit], the IRS contended that the District Court . . . should have listened to the tapes before ruling that the crime-fraud exception was inapplicable. Respondents contended, in contrast, that the District Court erred in the opposite direction: they argued that it was error for the court to rely on the partial transcripts, because "[i]n this Circuit, a party cannot rely on the communications themselves—whether by listening to the tapes *or reviewing excerpts or transcripts of them*—to bear its burden to invoke the exception but must bear the burden by independent evidence." (Emphasis added.)

The panel of the Court of Appeals agreed with respondents that . . . "the Government's evidence of crime or fraud must come from sources independent of the attorney–client communications recorded on the tapes". . . . The Court of Appeals then reviewed "the Government's

4. The current Clerk of the Superior Court, Frank S. Zolin, is a named respondent in this case, but did not participate in briefing or argument before the Court of Appeals or before this Court. We use the term "respondents" to refer to Mary Sue Hubbard and the Church, the only active respondents in this Court.

independent evidence." That review appears to have excluded the partial transcripts, and thus the Court of Appeals implicitly agreed with respondents that it was improper for the District Court to have considered even the partial transcripts. On the basis of its review of the "independent evidence," the Court of Appeals affirmed the District Court's determination that the IRS had failed to establish the applicability of the crime-fraud exception....

III

... The attorney–client privilege must necessarily protect the confidences of wrongdoers, but the reason for that protection—the centrality of open client and attorney communication to the proper functioning of our adversary system of justice—"ceas[es] to operate at a certain point, namely, where the desired advice refers *not to prior wrongdoing*, but to *future wrongdoing*." 8 Wigmore, § 2298, at 573 (emphasis in original)....

[T]he initial question in this case is whether a district court, at the request of the party opposing the privilege, may review the allegedly privileged communications *in camera* to determine whether the crime-fraud exception applies. If such *in camera* review is permitted, the second question we must consider is whether some threshold evidentiary showing is needed before the district court may undertake the requested review....

A

(1)

At first blush, two provisions of the Federal Rules of Evidence would appear to be relevant. Rule 104(a) provides: "Preliminary questions concerning the qualification of a person to be a witness, *the existence of a privilege*, or the admissibility of evidence shall be determined by the court.... In making its determination it is not bound by the rules of evidence *except those with respect to privileges*." (Emphasis added.) Rule 1101(c) provides: "The rule with respect to privileges applies at all stages of all actions, cases, and proceedings." Taken together, these Rules might be read to establish that ... attorney–client communications cannot be considered by the district court in making its crime-fraud ruling: to do otherwise, under this view, would be to make the crime-fraud determination without due regard to the existence of the privilege.

Even those scholars who support this reading of Rule 104(a) acknowledge that it leads to an absurd result.

> "Because the judge must honor claims of privilege made during his preliminary fact determinations, many exceptions to the rules of privilege will become 'dead letters,' since the preliminary facts that give rise to these exceptions can never be proved. For example, an exception to the attorney–client privilege provides that there is no privilege if the communication was made to enable anyone to

commit a crime or fraud. There is virtually no way in which the exception can ever be proved, save by compelling disclosure of the contents of the communication; Rule 104(a) provides that this cannot be done." 21 C. WRIGHT & K. GRAHAM, FEDERAL PRACTICE & PROCEDURE: EVIDENCE § 5055, at 276 (1977).

We find this Draconian interpretation of Rule 104(a) inconsistent with the Rule's plain language. The Rule does not provide by its terms that all materials as to which a "clai[m] of privilege" is made must be excluded from consideration. In that critical respect, the language of Rule 104(a) is markedly different from the comparable California evidence rule, which provides that "the presiding officer may not require disclosure of information *claimed to be privileged* under this division in order to rule on the claim of privilege." CAL. EVID. CODE ANN. § 915(a) (West Supp. 1989) (emphasis added). There is no reason to read Rule 104(a) as if its text were identical to that of the California rule.

Nor does it make sense to us to assume, as respondents have throughout this litigation, that once the attorney–client nature of the contested communications is established, those communications must be treated as *presumptively* privileged for evidentiary purposes until the privilege is "defeated" or "stripped away" by proof that the communications took place in the course of planning future crime or fraud. . . .

. . . We thus shall not adopt a reading of Rule 104(a) that would treat the contested communications as "privileged" for purposes of the Rule, and we shall not interpret Rule 104(a) as categorically prohibiting the party opposing the privilege on crime-fraud grounds from relying on the results of an *in camera* review of the communications.

(2)

Having determined that Rule 104(a) does not prohibit the *in camera* review sought by the IRS, we must address the question as a matter of the federal common law of privileges. *See* Rule 501. We conclude that a complete prohibition against opponents' use of *in camera* review to establish the applicability of the crime-fraud exception is inconsistent with the policies underlying the privilege.

We begin our analysis by recognizing that disclosure of allegedly privileged materials to the district court for purposes of determining the merits of a claim of privilege does not have the legal effect of terminating the privilege. Indeed, this Court has approved the practice of requiring parties who seek to avoid disclosure of documents to make the documents available for *in camera* inspection, and the practice is well established in the federal courts. Respondents do not dispute this point: they acknowledge that they would have been free to request *in camera* review to establish the fact that the tapes involved attorney–client communications, had they been unable to muster independent evidence to serve that purpose.

Once it is clear that *in camera* review does not destroy the privileged nature of the contested communications, the question of the propriety of that review turns on whether the policies underlying the privilege and its exceptions are better fostered by permitting such review or by prohibiting it. In our view, the costs of imposing an absolute bar to consideration of the communications *in camera* for purpose of establishing the crime-fraud exception are intolerably high.

"No matter how light the burden of proof which confronts the party claiming the exception, there are many blatant abuses of privilege which cannot be substantiated by extrinsic evidence. This is particularly true . . . of . . . situations in which an alleged illegal proposal is made in the context of a relationship which has an apparent legitimate end." Note, *The Future Crime or Tort Exception to Communications Privileges*, 77 HARV. L. REV. 730, 737 (1964). A *per se* rule that the communications in question may never be considered creates, we feel, too great an impediment to the proper functioning of the adversary process. This view is consistent with current trends in the law.

B

We turn to the question whether *in camera* review at the behest of the party asserting the crime-fraud exception is *always* permissible, or, in contrast, whether the party seeking *in camera* review must make some threshold showing that such review is appropriate. . . .

Our endorsement of the practice of testing proponents' privilege claims through *in camera* review of the allegedly privileged documents has not been without reservation. This Court noted in United States v. Reynolds, 345 U.S. 1 (1953), a case which presented a delicate question concerning the disclosure of military secrets, that "examination of the evidence, even by the judge alone, in chambers," might in some cases "jeopardize the security which the privilege is meant to protect." Analogizing to claims of Fifth Amendment privilege, it observed more generally: "Too much judicial inquiry into the claim of privilege would force disclosure of the thing the privilege was meant to protect, while a complete abandonment of judicial control would lead to intolerable abuses." . . .

A blanket rule allowing *in camera* review as a tool for determining the applicability of the crime-fraud exception, as *Reynolds* suggests, would place the policy of protecting open and legitimate disclosure between attorneys and clients at undue risk. There is also reason to be concerned about the possible due process implications of routine use of *in camera* proceedings. Finally, we cannot ignore the burdens *in camera* review places upon the district courts, which may well be required to evaluate large evidentiary records without open adversarial guidance by the parties.

There is no reason to permit opponents of the privilege to engage in groundless fishing expeditions, with the district courts as their unwitting (and perhaps unwilling) agents. . . . Indeed, the Government conceded at oral argument (albeit reluctantly) that a district court would be mistaken if it reviewed documents *in camera* solely because "the government beg[ged it]" to do so, "with no reason to suspect crime or fraud." We agree.

In fashioning a standard for determining when *in camera* review is appropriate, we begin with the observation that "*in camera* inspection . . . is a smaller intrusion upon the confidentiality of the attorney–client relationship than is public disclosure." We therefore conclude that a lesser evidentiary showing is needed to trigger *in camera* review than is required ultimately to overcome the privilege. . . .

We think that the following standard strikes the correct balance. Before engaging in *in camera* review to determine the applicability of the crime-fraud exception, "the judge should require a showing of a factual basis adequate to support a good faith belief by a reasonable person," Caldwell v. District Court, 644 P.2d 26, 33 (Colo. 1982), that *in camera* review of the materials may reveal evidence to establish the claim that the crime-fraud exception applies.

Once that showing is made, the decision whether to engage in *in camera* review rests in the sound discretion of the district court. The court should make that decision in light of the facts and circumstances of the particular case, including, among other things, the volume of materials the district court has been asked to review, the relative importance to the case of the alleged privileged information, and the likelihood that the evidence produced through *in camera* review, together with other available evidence then before the court, will establish that the crime-fraud exception does apply. The district court is also free to defer its *in camera* review if it concludes that additional evidence in support of the crime-fraud exception may be available that is *not* allegedly privileged, and that production of the additional evidence will not unduly disrupt or delay the proceedings. . . .[12]

D

In sum, we conclude that a rigid independent evidence requirement does not comport with "reason and experience," FED. RULE EVID. 501, and we decline to adopt it as part of the developing federal common law of

12. In addition, we conclude that evidence that is not "independent" of the contents of allegedly privileged communications—like the partial transcripts in this case—may be used not only in the pursuit of *in camera* review, but also may provide the evidentiary basis for the ultimate showing that the crime-fraud exception applies. We see little to distinguish these two uses: in both circumstances, if the evidence has not itself been determined to be privileged, its exclusion does not serve the policies which underlie the attorney–client privilege.

evidentiary privileges. We hold that *in camera* review may be used to determine whether allegedly privileged attorney–client communications fall within the crime-fraud exception. We further hold, however, that before a district court may engage in *in camera* review at the request of the party opposing the privilege, that party must present evidence sufficient to support a reasonable belief that *in camera* review may yield evidence that establishes the exception's applicability. Finally, we hold that the threshold showing to obtain *in camera* review may be met by using any relevant evidence, lawfully obtained, that has not been adjudicated to be privileged.

Because the Court of Appeals employed a rigid independent-evidence requirement which categorically excluded the partial transcripts and the tapes themselves from consideration, we vacate its judgment on this issue and remand the case for further proceedings consistent with this opinion. . . .

It is so ordered.

■ JUSTICE BRENNAN took no part in the consideration or decision of this case.

C. GOVERNMENT LAWYERS

IN RE: GRAND JURY INVESTIGATION [ROWLAND]

399 F.3d 527 (2d Cir. 2005).

■ Before: WALKER, CHIEF JUDGE, JACOBS and LEVAL, CIRCUIT JUDGES.

■ JOHN M. WALKER, JR., CHIEF JUDGE: . . .

BACKGROUND

On February 19, 2004, in the course of investigating possible criminal violations by Connecticut public officials and employees, . . . a federal grand jury subpoenaed the testimony of Anne C. George, former chief legal counsel to the Office of the Governor of Connecticut. George served in that position from August 2000 to December 2002 and before that as deputy legal counsel. During the period leading up to issuance of the subpoena, the U.S. Attorney's Office ("the Government") had been investigating, in particular, whether Governor Rowland and members of his staff had received gifts from private individuals and entities in return for public favors, including the favorable negotiation and awarding of state contracts. The Government had sought, through direct contact with

Governor Rowland, to gain access to specified communications between Rowland, his staff, and legal counsel, all to no avail. The Government had also asked George herself to submit to a voluntary interview. She declined, however, after the Office of the Governor notified her that it believed that the information the Government was seeking was protected by the attorney–client privilege.

On March 3, 2004, prior to George's appearance before the grand jury, the Government moved in the district court to compel George to testify about the contents of confidential communications between George and Governor Rowland and members of his staff. The district court withheld decision pending George's actual appearance and assertion of the privilege before the grand jury.

On April 7, 2004, when George appeared before the grand jury, she testified that in her capacity as legal counsel to the Governor she had engaged in numerous conversations with Rowland and other members of his staff on the subject of the receipt of gifts and the meaning of related state ethics laws. George also stated that she had spoken with Rowland's former co-Chief of Staff about a practice of state contracts being sent to the Governor's Office for approval. She testified, however, that because all of these conversations were in confidence and conducted for the purpose of providing legal advice, the Office of the Governor was of the view that they were protected by the attorney–client privilege, which it declined to waive. Accordingly, asserting the privilege on behalf of her client, George refused to answer questions pertaining to the content of the conversations.

On April 26, 2004, the district court entered an order compelling George's testimony. After noting that it was "undisputed that the grand jury need[ed] the information it [sought] to obtain from Ms. George," the district court concluded that "reason and experience dictate that, in the grand jury context, any governmental attorney–client privilege must yield because the interests served by the grand jury's fact-finding process clearly outweigh the interest served by the privilege." The district court distinguished the "governmental" attorney–client privilege from the privilege in the context of a private attorney–client relationship, by explaining that "unlike a private lawyer's duty of loyalty to an individual client, a government lawyer's duty does not lie solely with his or her client agency," but also with the public.

Both the Office of the Governor and Rowland, as interested parties, appealed the district court's decision. . . .

On June 21, 2004, one day prior to oral argument, Governor Rowland announced that he would resign as Governor, effective July 1, 2004. At argument, we asked the parties to address the question of whether Rowland's resignation would affect our disposition of the appeal. The Government subsequently informed us that it had asked Rowland's successor, Governor M. Jodi Rell, to consider waiving the privilege insofar as the privilege was held by the Office of the Governor, and requested that we defer our disposition of the appeal pending Governor Rell's decision. On August 6, 2004, the newly appointed counsel to the Office of the Governor informed us that Governor Rell declined to waive the privilege. . . .

DISCUSSION

Federal Rule of Evidence 501 governs the nature and scope of a privilege claimed in proceedings before a federal grand jury. . . . [In applying that rule], while we may draw on the law of privilege as it has developed in state courts, we are not bound by it. In criminal cases, Rule 501 plainly requires that we apply the federal law of privilege.

Although there is little case law addressing the application of the attorney–client privilege in the specific circumstances presented here, we are nonetheless dealing with a well-established and familiar principle. . . . [C]ourts have by reason and experience concluded that a consistent application of the privilege over time is necessary to promote the rule of law by encouraging consultation with lawyers, and ensuring that lawyers, once consulted, are able to render to their clients fully informed legal advice.

In light of the common-law roots of the attorney–client privilege and the attendant principle (evident in case law stretching back at least a century, *see Hunt v. Blackburn*, 128 U.S. 464, 470 (1888)) that safeguarding client confidences promotes, rather than undermines, compliance with the law, we believe it best to proceed cautiously when asked to narrow the privilege's protections in a particular category of cases. We are aware, of course, that even existing privileges are not to be "expansively construed," as they "are in derogation of the search for truth," *United States v. Nixon*, 418 U.S. 683, 710 (1974), and that the attorney–client privilege, in particular, "applies only where necessary to achieve its purpose," *Fisher v. United States*, 425 U.S. 391, 403 (1976). But this admonishment does not invite a wholesale reassessment of the privilege's utility whenever it is invoked under previously unexplored circumstances. Instead, our application of the privilege in a "new" context remains informed by the longstanding principles and assumptions that underlie its application in more familiar territory.

There is no dispute in this case that these principles and assumptions apply to government lawyers and their clients under certain circumstances. The Government concedes, for instance, both that a governmental attorney–client privilege exists generally, and that it may be invoked in the civil context. (Gov't Brief at 33). Ample authority supports both propositions. In 1972, the Supreme Court promulgated Federal Rules of Evidence setting forth nine specific categories of privileges, including an attorney–client privilege. Proposed Federal Rule 503, defining the privilege, included public officers and public entities within its definition of "client," *see* PROPOSED FED. R. EVID. 503(a)(1); commentary accompanying the proposed rule, moreover, provided that the "definition of 'client' includes governmental bodies." While Proposed Rule 503 was not adopted by Congress, courts and commentators have treated it as a source of general guidance regarding federal common law principles. *See, e.g., In re Grand Jury Subpoena Duces Tecum*, 112 F.3d 910, 915 (8th Cir. 1997) ("*Grand Jury*") ("We have described [Proposed Rule 503] as 'a useful starting place' for an examination of the federal common law of attorney–client privilege."); 3 JACK B. WEINSTEIN & MARGARET A. BERGER, WEINSTEIN'S FEDERAL EVIDENCE § 503.02, at 503–10 (2d ed. 1997) ("[Proposed Rule 503] restates, rather than modifies, the common-law lawyer–client privilege. Thus, it has considerable utility as a guide to the federal common law."). . . . While these authorities are not conclusive as to the existence at common law of a governmental attorney–client privilege, they demonstrate that serious legal thinkers, applying "reason and experience," have considered the privilege's protections applicable in the government context.

The case law, as well, while not extensively addressing the issue, generally assumes the existence of a governmental attorney–client privilege in civil suits between government agencies and private litigants. *See, e.g., In re Lindsey*, 158 F.3d 1263, 1268 (D.C. Cir. 1998) ("*Lindsey*") ("Courts, commentators, and government lawyers have long recognized a government attorney–client privilege in several contexts."). The privilege has arisen in a number of these cases in the context of Exemption 5 of the Freedom of Information Act, which allows a federal government agency to withhold from requests under the Act "inter-agency or intra-agency memorandums or letters which would not be available by law to a party other than an agency in litigation with the agency." Courts have construed Exemption 5 as covering materials protected by the attorney–client privilege and, in doing so, have assumed that such a privilege attaches when the attorney is a government lawyer and the client a government entity.

There is, then, substantial authority for the view that the rationale supporting the attorney–client privilege applicable to private entities has general relevance to governmental entities as well. The Government argues that while this authority may establish a privilege of some kind, recent case law in other circuits supports its view that the attorney–client privilege in the government context is weaker than in its traditional form. It cites *In re Witness Before the Special Grand Jury 2000–2*, 288 F.3d 289 (7th Cir. 2002) ("*Ryan*"), *Lindsey*, and *Grand Jury* for the proposition that the "governmental" attorney–client privilege must give way where a federal grand jury seeks access to otherwise privileged statements in order to further a criminal investigation. While *Lindsey* and *Grand Jury* involved applications of the privilege to communications by a *federal* executive, and thus involved statutes and considerations unrelated to this case, all three decisions broadly questioned the relevance of the traditional rationale supporting the privilege to the government context.

Drawing on these decisions, the Government contends that the reasons for the traditional attorney–client privilege do not apply with the same force in the circumstances presented by this case: a federal grand jury investigation into potentially criminal government conduct. It argues, first, that George, as a government attorney, has a fundamentally different relationship with her client, the Office of the Governor, than does a private attorney representing a private individual. George's client is a public entity, accountable to the general citizenry. As the Office of the Governor serves the public, the Government argues, so too must George as counsel to that office. Her loyalty to the Governor, the Government contends, must yield to her loyalty to the public, to whom she owes ultimate allegiance when violations of the criminal law are at stake. Accordingly, the Government argues that the privilege should not be used as a shield to permit George, as a government attorney, to withhold client confidences, when revealing them would be in the public interest. Implicit in the Government's argument is the presumption that the public interest in the present circumstances lies with disclosure and the furtherance of the "truth-seeking" function of the grand jury. "To allow the Governor's Office to interpose a testimonial privilege 'as a shield against the production of information relevant to a federal criminal investigation,'" the Government concludes, "'would represent a gross misuse of public assets.'" (Gov't Brief at 23 (quoting *Grand Jury*, 112 F.3d at 921)).

We cannot accept the Government's unequivocal assumption as to where the public interest lies. To be sure, it is in the public interest for the grand jury to collect all the relevant evidence it can. However, it is also in the public interest for high state officials to receive and act upon the best possible legal advice. Indeed, the people of Connecticut have deemed the latter interest more important than the former: if *state* prosecutors had sought to compel George to reveal the conversations at issue, there is little doubt that the conversations would be protected. The Connecticut legislature has enacted a statute specifically providing that "in any civil or criminal case or proceeding . . ., all confidential communications shall be privileged and a government attorney shall not disclose any such communications unless an authorized representative of the public agency consents to waive the privilege and allow such disclosure." CONN. GEN. STAT. § 52–146r(b). The people of Connecticut, then, acting through their representatives, have concluded that the public interest is advanced by upholding a governmental privilege even in the face of a criminal investigation. We do not suggest, of course, that federal courts, charged with formulating federal common law, must necessarily defer to state statutes in determining whether the public welfare weighs in favor of recognizing or dissolving the attorney–client privilege. But we cite the Connecticut statute to point out that the public interest is not nearly as obvious as the Government suggests. One could as easily conclude, with the Connecticut legislature, that the protections afforded by the privilege ultimately promote the public interest, even when they might impede the search for truth in a particular criminal investigation.

We believe that, if anything, the traditional rationale for the privilege applies with special force in the government context. It is crucial that government officials, who are expected to uphold and execute the law and who may face criminal prosecution for failing to do so, be encouraged to seek out and receive fully informed legal advice. Upholding the privilege furthers a culture in which consultation with government lawyers is accepted as a normal, desirable, and even indispensable part of conducting public business. Abrogating the privilege undermines that culture and thereby impairs the public interest. *See* 1 PAUL R. RICE, ATTORNEY-CLIENT PRIVILEGE IN THE UNITED STATES § 4:28, at 4 (2d ed. 1999) ("If the government attorney is required to disclose [internal communications with counsel] upon grand jury request, it is sheer fantasy to suggest that it will not make internal governmental investigations more difficult, to the point of being impossible.... To the extent that the protection of the privilege is justified in any corporate context, the need within the government is equal, if not greater.").

We are aware, of course, that the relationship between a government attorney and a government official or employee is not the same as that between a private attorney and his client. For one, in the government context, the individual consulting with his official attorney may not control waiver of the privilege. Even if he does control waiver during his time in government, the possibility remains that a subsequent administration might purport to waive the privilege exercised by a predecessor.[3] Thus, some commentators (and presumably the Government, here) question whether application of the attorney–client privilege in the government context will in fact encourage public officials and employees to confide in counsel. While encouraging little in the way of legal consultation and disclosure, their argument goes, the privilege engenders significant costs by frustrating the "search for truth."

Whatever merit there is to this reasoning, we think it insufficient to jettison a principle as entrenched in our legal tradition as that underlying the attorney–client privilege. Such reasoning amounts to little more than speculation over the way in which the privilege functions in the government context. *Cf. Swidler & Berlin v. United States*, 524 U.S. 399, 410 (1998) ("A 'no harm in one more exception' rationale could contribute to the general erosion of the privilege, without reference to common-law principles or 'reason and experience.'"). We also reject the idea that because government employees can confer with private counsel to represent their own, individual interests, the privilege is somehow less important when applied to government counsel. The privilege serves to promote the free flow of information to the attorney (and thereby to the client entity) as

3. We express no view of the effectiveness of such a waiver.

well as to the individual with whom he communicates. The government attorney requires candid, unvarnished information from those employed by the office he serves so that he may better discharge his duty to that office.

Having determined that the attorney–client privilege applies to the communications at issue in this case, we decline to fashion a balancing test, or otherwise establish a rule whereby a "generalized assertion of privilege must yield to the demonstrated, specific need for evidence. . . ." *Nixon*, 418 U.S. at 713 (establishing balancing test with regard to executive privilege). The Supreme Court has instructed that, where the attorney–client privilege applies, its protections must be reliably enforced in order to effectuate its goal of promoting compliance with the law. *See Swidler*, 524 U.S. at 409 ("Balancing *ex post* the importance of the information against client interests, even limited to criminal cases, introduces substantial uncertainty into the privilege's application. For just that reason, we have rejected use of a balancing test in defining the contours of the privilege."). We see no persuasive reason to abandon that logic here. Of course, nothing we hold today derogates from traditional doctrines, such as the crime-fraud exception, that apply to the private attorney–client relationship and that courts have developed, through reason and experience, to limit egregious abuses of the protections that the privilege affords.

In arguing that we ought not "extend" the attorney–client privilege to the present situation, the Government asks us, in essence, to assign a precise functional value to its protections and then determine whether, and under what circumstances, the costs of these protections become too great to justify. We find the assumptions underlying this approach to be illusory, and the approach itself potentially dangerous. The Government assumes that "the public interest" in disclosure is readily apparent, and that a public official's willingness to consult with counsel will be only "marginally" affected by the abrogation of the privilege in the face of a grand jury subpoena. Because we cannot accept either of these assumptions, we decline to abandon the attorney–client privilege in a context in which its protections arguably are needed most.[4] In the end, we do not view the question before us as whether to "extend" the privilege to the government context, and our decision today does no such thing. Rather, we have simply refused to countenance its abrogation in circumstances to which its venerable and worthy purposes fully pertain.

Conclusion

For the foregoing reasons, we REVERSE the order of the district court.

---

4. Our decision is in conflict with the Seventh Circuit's decision in *Ryan*, and is in sharp tension with the decisions of the Eighth *(Grand Jury)* and the D.C. Circuits (*Lindsey*). We are mindful that uniformity among the circuits fosters predictability in the invocation of the privilege and suppresses forum shopping. *See also Boren v. Sable*, 887 F.2d 1032, 1038 (10th Cir. 1989) ("The Federal Rules of Evidence are intended to have uniform nationwide application. . . ."). We are in no position, however, to resolve this tension in the law.

D. THE LAWYER–CLIENT PRIVILEGE AND THE PRIVILEGE AGAINST SELF-INCRIMINATION

1. GENERAL PRINCIPLES

A GUIDE THROUGH THE DOCTRINAL THICKET

Fisher v. United States, 425 U.S. 391 (1976), confronted the Supreme Court with this rather tricky question: What privilege (if any) protects the confidentiality of documents given by clients to their lawyers? The answer to this question depends on the boundaries of the lawyer–client privilege and of the privilege against self-incrimination. *Fisher* therefore can serve as a transition, completing our exploration of the lawyer–client privilege and guiding us into the realm of the Fifth Amendment privilege. *United States v. Doe*, 465 U.S. 605 (1984), succeeded *Fisher* and filled important gaps in its analysis. After examining the reasoning of *Fisher* and *Doe*, we turn to *United States v. Hubbell*, 530 U.S. 27 (2000) (page 1034). *Hubbell* takes us beyond the specific problem addressed in *Fisher* and *Doe* and pursues in more depth the scope of the Fifth Amendment's protection of documents demanded by the government.

Though closely reasoned, *Fisher* is unusually difficult to follow. That's largely because the question it tackles—whether any privilege protects documents given by clients to their lawyers—is so hard. As you will see, the Supreme Court's conclusion turns ultimately on a judgment that the Fifth Amendment privilege protects against only *compelled testimonial self-incrimination.*

Assume, then, that a client has given documents to her lawyer. For the moment, assume (as was true in *Fisher*), that the client's accountant prepared the documents. Assume finally that a prosecutor has issued a subpoena to the lawyer to compel production of the documents. The answer to the question whether any privilege protects against compelled disclosure derives from the following four propositions. As *Doe* later made clear, the same propositions govern if the client, rather than the client's accountant, prepared the documents.

(1) The lawyer–client privilege protects against disclosure of *communications* between lawyer and client, but not against disclosure of the *underlying facts*.

As you know, a person cannot privilege a *fact* by disclosing it to her lawyer. Let's say that I tell my lawyer in confidence and for the purpose of getting legal help that my business has been losing money. If my lawyer is subpoenaed to testify about the health of my business, she may (and ethically she must) decline to reveal what she learned in our confidential conversation. If I am asked on the stand what I said to my lawyer, I may also decline to answer. If I am asked about the health of my business, however, the lawyer–client privilege gives me no grounds to refuse to answer. *See Upjohn Co. v. United States*, 449 U.S. 383, 395 (1981) ("The privilege only protects disclosure of communications; it does not protect disclosure of the underlying facts by those who communicated with the attorney.").

The same principles apply if I give my lawyer a document. If I wrote the document to communicate facts to her and to assist her in representing me and if I delivered it to her in confidence, the document is privileged just as a similar conversation would be. But if that document contains facts recorded for some other purpose, I cannot privilege either the document or its contents by handing it to my lawyer. The document and its contents have no greater protection from compelled production in my lawyer's hands than in my hands. As the Supreme Court of Wisconsin has noted, "a party cannot conceal a fact merely by revealing it to his lawyer, nor may he secrete a preexisting document merely by giving it to his attorney." *State ex rel. Dudek v. Circuit Court*, 34 Wis. 2d 559, 580 (1967).

Proposition (1) does not come from *Fisher*. It is part of the common law of the lawyer–client privilege.

(2) The client's Fifth Amendment privilege does not protect the client's documents against compelled production when they are in the lawyer's hands.

The Supreme Court made this point clearly in *Couch v. United States*, 409 U.S. 322, 328 (1973): "The Constitution explicitly prohibits compelling an accused to bear witness 'against himself'; it necessarily does not proscribe incriminating statements elicited from another." This proposition is a corollary of the fourth proposition, below. The reasoning behind it will be discussed in more detail there.

3. *If* (a) **the client's Fifth Amendment privilege would have protected the documents against disclosure when they were in the client's hands,**

and (b) **the client has transferred the documents to the lawyer in confidence and to get legal advice,**

then **the lawyer–client privilege protects the documents against compelled production when they are in the lawyer's hands.**

This proposition is the holding of Part III of *Fisher*. The Court reasoned simply: "Where the transfer [of the documents] is made for the purpose of obtaining legal advice, the purposes of the attorney–client privilege would be defeated unless the privilege is applicable." *Fisher*, 425 U.S. at 404. That is, "if the client knows that damaging information could more readily be obtained from the attorney following disclosure than from himself in the absence of disclosure, the client would be reluctant to confide in his lawyer and it would be difficult to obtain fully informed legal advice." *Id.* at 403.

So now we must answer another question: *Would* the client's Fifth Amendment privilege protect against compelled production of the documents when they are in the client's hands?

(4) The client's Fifth Amendment privilege protects against only compelled testimonial self-incrimination.

It is easy to find in the pages of United States Reports stirring statements of the high aims of the Fifth Amendment privilege. The most famous appears in *Murphy v. Waterfront Commission*, 378 U.S. 52, 55 (1964):

> The privilege against self-incrimination ... reflects many of our fundamental values and most noble aspirations: our unwillingness to subject those suspected of crime to the cruel trilemma of self-accusation, perjury or contempt; our preference for an accusatorial rather than an inquisitorial system of criminal justice; our fear that self-incriminating statements will be elicited by inhumane treatment and abuses; our sense of fair play which dictates "a fair state-individual balance by requiring the government to leave the individual alone until good cause is shown for disturbing him and by requiring the government in its contest with the individual to shoulder the entire load"; our respect for the inviolability of the human personality and of the right of each individual "to a private enclave where he may lead a private life"; our distrust of self-deprecatory statements; and our realization that the privilege, while sometimes "a shelter to the guilty," is often "a protection to the innocent."

These "noble aspirations" arguably inform the Supreme Court's jurisprudence on the Fifth Amendment privilege. But they do not—and perhaps they could not—dictate the shape of the privilege's protection. When defining the privilege's scope, the Court has relied instead on a close reading of the language of the Fifth Amendment.

The Fifth Amendment states that "[n]o person ... shall be *compelled* in any criminal case* to be a *witness against himself*." (Emphasis added.) In Parts II and IV of *Fisher*, the Supreme Court interpreted this language to

* Don't construe the words, "in a criminal case," too strictly. A person may not *in any proceeding* be compelled to give testimonial evidence that would tend to incriminate that person in a criminal case.

mean that the privilege is violated only when a person is *compelled* to provide *testimonial self-incrimination. See also United States v. Hubbell,* 530 U.S. 27, 34 (2000) ("The word 'witness' in the constitutional text limits the relevant category of compelled incriminating communications to those that are 'testimonial' in character.").

All three of these elements—compulsion, testimonial evidence, and self-incrimination—must be present at more or less the same moment. If only two of the three elements are present, there is no violation of the privilege. Consider the following examples:

- *Testimonial self-incrimination,* but no *compulsion*: "[U]nder appropriate safeguards private incriminating statements of an accused may be overheard and used in evidence, if they are not compelled at the time they were uttered. . . ." *Fisher,* 425 U.S. at 404. That is, if the defendant confesses her involvement in a crime to a friend at a lunch counter, a police officer who overhears the remark may testify about it.
- *Compelled testimony,* but no *self-incrimination*: "[D]isclosure of private information may be compelled if immunity removes the risk of incrimination." *Id.* The prosecutor, by guaranteeing that the witness's testimony will not be used against him (or that the witness will not be prosecuted for any of the underlying events), can compel testimony that otherwise would incriminate the witness.
- *Compelled self-incrimination,* but no *testimonial evidence*: The Supreme Court has "declined to extend the protection of the privilege to the giving of blood samples; to the giving of handwriting exemplars; voice exemplars; or the donning of a blouse worn by the perpetrator." *Id.* at 408 (citations omitted). The Court suggested that these are all examples of *nontestimonial* evidence.

How can we distinguish testimonial from nontestimonial evidence? *Crawford v. Washington* and *Davis v. Washington,* which we studied in Chapter 8, do not directly bear on this question. In the Fifth Amendment context, *testimonial* takes a slightly different—or at least a differently expressed—meaning than in the Sixth Amendment context. Here the critical factor is whether the witness is being asked "to disclose the contents of his own mind." *Curcio v. United States,* 354 U.S. 118, 128 (1957). By this definition, " '[t]he vast majority of verbal statements . . . will be testimonial.' " *Hiibel v. Sixth Judicial District Court of Nevada,* 542 U.S. 177, 194 (2004) (Stevens, J., dissenting) (quoting *Doe v. United States,* 487 U.S. 201, 213 (1988)).

A good shorthand for this inquiry is to ask, "Could the witness lie about this fact?" A witness who is asked whether she robbed a bank of course could lie and say no. Such evidence is testimonial. But if asked to provide a fingerprint or a blood sample, a witness could not very well lie (or tell the truth for that matter). Such evidence is nontestimonial. True, a witness who is asked to give a voice or handwriting exemplar or to try on a piece of clothing could disguise his voice or his handwriting or try to make it appear that the clothing does not fit. But such contortions rarely succeed. And true, a witness could lie and say she does not know how to write. To that extent, the provision of a handwriting exemplar *is* testimonial. The Court deals with this problem by saying it is a "near truism" that the witness can write. *Fisher*, 425 U.S. at 411. The disclosure of that fact therefore is not very *incriminating*.

If you accept the Court's conclusion that the Fifth Amendment privilege protects against only compelled testimonial self-incrimination, the basis for the second proposition above becomes clear. The client's Fifth Amendment privilege does not protect against compelled production of documents in the lawyer's hands because, when the lawyer is ordered to produce those documents, " 'the ingredient of personal compulsion against an accused is lacking.' " *Id.* at 397 (quoting *Couch*).

But the reasoning of *Fisher*—and in particular, proposition three above—required the Court to decide whether the Fifth Amendment protects against compelled production of the documents from the *client's* hands. The Court held that the Fifth Amendment offers no such protection for two reasons. First, the documents "were not prepared by the taxpayer [the client], and they contain no *testimonial* declarations *by him*." *Id.* at 409 (emphasis added). Second, "the preparation of all of the papers sought in these cases was wholly voluntary" and hence not *compelled*. *Id.* at 409–10.

By eliminating one of these two bases of decision, the facts of *United States v. Doe* required the Court to focus its reasoning. In *Doe* the person claiming the Fifth Amendment privilege had prepared the documents himself. They therefore contained "testimonial declarations by him." The Court held, however, that "[w]here the preparation of business records is voluntary, no compulsion is present." *Doe*, 465 U.S. at 610. That is, even though production of the documents was compelled, there was no compulsion *at the time the incriminating words were written.* The Fifth Amendment offers no protection, it seems, unless compulsion, testimonial evidence, and self-incrimination are present in the same act.

Although the reasoning of *Doe* implies that the Fifth Amendment offers no protection for the contents of a private diary, the Justices seemed to split on this question. Justice O'Connor's concurrence made "explicit what is implicit in the analysis of [Justice Powell's majority opinion in *Doe*]: that the Fifth Amendment provides absolutely no protection for the contents of private papers of any kind." *Doe*, 465 U.S. at 618 (O'Connor, J., concurring). Justice Marshall responded that "the documents at stake here are business records which implicate a lesser degree of concern for privacy interests than, for example, personal diaries." *Id.* at 619 (Marshall, J., concurring in part and dissenting in part). Lower courts have reached no consensus on this question, and the

Supreme Court has not reexamined it. *See Barrett v. Acevedo*, 169 F.3d 1155, 1167–68 (8th Cir. 1999) (listing the conflicting caselaw of several federal circuit courts); Lenora Ledwon, *Diaries and Hearsay: Gender, Selfhood, and the Trustworthiness of Narrative Structure*, 73 TEMP. L. REV. 1185, 1221–26 (2000).

ACT OF PRODUCTION

The *act of production* refers to a person's *delivery* of existing documents to the government. In both *Fisher* and *Doe*, the Court acknowledged that the compelled production of documents, even if those documents were voluntarily prepared, would violate the Fifth Amendment if the *act of producing* them is testimonial and incriminating. In that event, all three elements—compulsion, testimonial evidence, and self-incrimination—would be present in the same act.

The Court reasoned that the act of production could disclose three facts: "the existence of the papers demanded," "their possession or control by the [defendant]," and "the [defendant's] belief that the papers are those described in the subpoena." *Fisher*, 425 U.S. at 410. Each of these facts amounts to testimonial evidence (one could lie about each of them). The question is whether, in any particular case, these facts are sufficiently incriminating that their compelled disclosure would violate the Fifth Amendment. The Court held in *Fisher* that the resolution of this issue may "depend on the facts and circumstances of particular cases." *Id.* The Court reasoned that under the facts presented there, the "existence and location of the papers are a foregone conclusion and the [defendant] adds little or nothing to the sum total of the Government's information by conceding that he in fact has the papers." *Id.* at 411. That is, the disclosure was not very *incriminating*.* And "[a]s for the possibility that responding to the subpoena would authenticate the workpapers, production would express nothing more than the [defendant's] belief that the papers are those described in the subpoena." *Id.* at 412–13. The point, again, is that disclosure was not very incriminating.**

In contrast, the trial court in *Doe* found that under the facts of that case, "the act of producing the documents would involve testimonial self-incrimination." *Doe*, 465 U.S. at 613. The trial court therefore held, and the

* The *Fisher* Court suggested that the question was *not* whether disclosure of the existence and possession of the papers was sufficiently *incriminating*, but rather whether such disclosure rose "to the level of *testimony*." *Fisher*, 425 U.S. at 411 (emphasis added). But the Court's insistence that the existence and location of the papers were "a foregone conclusion" suggests otherwise. If I tell the police a fact they already know, I still do something testimonial. But if I tell the police something they already know, I normally do not incriminate myself (much).

** The Court's treatment of the authentication issue is not very convincing. "[T]he statement of the subpoenaed party as to his belief that documents in his possession were those prepared by another would appear to be admissible evidence in establishing authenticity. . . ." W. LAFAVE & J. ISRAEL, CRIMINAL PROCEDURE 441 (2d ed. 1992).

Supreme Court agreed, that the "act of producing the documents . . . is privileged and cannot be compelled without a statutory grant of *use immunity.*" *Id.* at 617 (emphasis added). I will return to the problem of use immunity in a few pages. As we will see, the scope of the privilege's protection determines how broad the grant of immunity must be.

Before moving on, I should emphasize that the rather narrow bounds traced by the Supreme Court around the Fifth Amendment privilege have no effect on other constitutional and evidentiary safeguards. Hence the Fourth Amendment protects against unreasonable searches and seizures, the First Amendment and other constitutional doctrines shield various private realms and modes of expression, and the lawyer–client privilege shelters confidential communications in aid of legal services. Confronted with a governmental demand for papers or testimony, a person may have recourse to any of these protections.

Problem 12.9

Guilty Knowledge

Traditional polygraph techniques have involved analysis of a subject's answers as either truthful or deceptive. Early in this century a team of prominent researchers advocated use of the "guilty knowledge test" (or GKT) instead. They described the test this way:

> For a prototypical GKT, a series of questions is prepared, which could pertain to various aspects of the crime. The idea is that each question should focus on a detail that can be known only to someone . . . who has actually been at the scene of the crime or involved in it. . . . Sample questions could be: . . .
>
> Your getaway car was [a]:
>
> Nissan; Honda; Toyota; Ford; Chrysler
>
> Usually, examinees are instructed to say "no" to all possibilities (although other procedures, such as allowing the suspect to remain silent, . . . also exist). The suspect's physiological responses to the correct details are compared to those elicited by the incorrect ones. The physiological measures typically monitored . . . include: changes in electrodermal activity (e.g., skin conductance responses), changes in the pattern of respiration, . . . and changes in . . . blood pressure and heart rate. . . . A pattern of consis-

> tently stronger responses elicited by the correct details . . . is interpreted as an indication [of guilt].

Gershon Ben–Shakhar, et al., *Trial by Polygraph: Reconsidering the Use of the Guilty Knowledge Technique in Court*, 26 LAW & HUM. BEHAV. 527, 529 (2002) (© 2002 by the American Psychological Association). (Compare the EEG-based lie-detection technique discussed by Greely and Illes on page 830, above.)

Assume that a particular polygraph examiner uses the version of the guilty knowledge test that involves asking the subject to remain silent throughout the test. Would compelling a criminal suspect to undergo such an examination violate her Fifth Amendment privilege? *See Schmerber v. California*, 384 U.S. 757, 764 (1966); *id.* at 775 (Black, J., dissenting); Sarah E. Stoller & Paul Root Wolpe, *Emerging Neurotechnologies for Lie Detection and the Fifth Amendment*, 33 AM. J.L. & MED. 359, 365–74 (2007).

Problem 12.10

Spell Check

Consider these facts from *United States v. Pheaster*, 544 F.2d 353 (9th Cir. 1976), *cert. denied*, 429 U.S. 1099 (1977):

> At approximately 9:30 p.m. on June 1, 1974, Larry Adell left a group of his high school friends in a Palm Springs restaurant. . . . Larry never returned to his friends in the restaurant that evening, and his family never saw him thereafter. . . .
>
> At about 2:30 a.m. on June 2, 1974, Larry's father was telephoned by a male caller who told him that his son was being held and that further instructions would be left in Larry's car. . . . Those instructions included a demand for a ransom of $400,000 for the release of Larry. . . .
>
> Before the kidnappers finally broke off communications on June 30, 1974, Mr. Adell had received a total of ten letters from the kidnappers, nine of which were typed in a "script" style and one of which was handwritten. . . .
>
> Pheaster argues that the somewhat unorthodox method of obtaining and utilizing exemplars of his handwriting violated his Fifth Amendment right against self-incrimination. The agent who obtained the handwriting exemplars from Pheaster testified that the normal practice for obtaining such exemplars is to have the suspect copy from materials placed before him. In the instant case, the agent dictated the material that Pheaster was to write. The reason that this

modified procedure was followed is quite clear. The notes from the kidnappers included a number of rather unusual spelling mistakes, and the material dictated to Pheaster included those words. The fact that a number of the same spelling mistakes appeared both in the notes and in the exemplars was introduced into evidence at the trial....

Assume that the trial court had ordered Pheaster to produce handwriting exemplars as directed by the agent. Did this "somewhat unorthodox method" of obtaining exemplars in fact violate Pheaster's Fifth Amendment right against compelled self-incrimination? *Cf. United States v. Campbell*, 732 F.2d 1017, 1020–22 (1st Cir. 1984).

Problem 12.11

"I Consent"

In *Doe v. United States*, 487 U.S. 201 (1988)—a different case from *United States v. Doe*, discussed above—a grand jury was investigating possible income tax evasion. The grand jury issued subpoenas to three banks located in Bermuda and the Cayman Islands demanding records of any accounts held by the defendant. The banks refused to comply, citing their governments' bank-secrecy laws, which barred release of bank records absent the customer's signed consent. The government then asked the District Court to order the defendant to sign the following form:

> I, ______, ... do hereby direct any bank or trust company at which I may have a bank account of any kind ... to disclose all information and deliver copies of all documents of every nature in your possession or control which relate to said bank account to Grand Jury 84–2, ... sitting in the Southern District of Texas, ... and this shall be irrevocable authority for so doing. This direction has been executed pursuant to that certain order of the United States District Court for the Southern District of Texas issued in connection with the aforesaid investigation.... This direction is intended to apply to the Confidential Relationships (Preservation) Law of the Cayman Islands, and to any implied contract of confidentiality between Bermuda banks and their customers ..., and shall be construed as consent with respect thereto....

The court ultimately ordered the defendant to sign the form. He refused, arguing that being compelled to do so violated his Fifth Amendment privilege. Was he right?

2. The Problem of Use Immunity

Use and Transactional Immunity

The Supreme Court held in *United States v. Doe* that if the act of producing documents is testimonial and incriminating, it "cannot be compelled without a statutory grant of use immunity." (*Doe*, 465 U.S. at 617.) That is, if the prosecutor wants to demand production of the documents, she first must promise to make no *use* of the testimonial aspects of the act of production. At trial, the prosecutor would be barred from offering evidence that the defendant had produced the documents. She would not, however, be barred from offering the documents themselves, as long as the government had independent proof of the three testimonial aspects of the act of production: that the documents existed, that the defendant possessed them, and that the documents produced are the ones the government demanded (i.e., that they are authentic).

In theory, such a grant of use immunity would eliminate the incriminating potential of the act of production. The jury would not learn that by producing the documents, the defendant had disclosed their existence, his possession of them, or his belief that they were the ones described in the subpoena. And the jury would not learn anything that the prosecutor may have discovered as a result of these testimonial disclosures.

As the Court notes in *United States v. Hubbell*, excerpted below, the type of immunity needed is "use and derivative-use" immunity. (Pages 1037–39.) The prosecutor must not *use* the act of production against the defendant. And because the point of a grant of immunity is to render harmless any testimony the defendant is compelled to give, the prosecutor must not use any evidence *derived from* the testimonial aspects of the defendant's immunized act of production. That is, the prosecutor must not use any evidence that is a fruit of the defendant's disclosures that the documents exist, that he has them, and that he believes them to be the ones demanded. The required immunity therefore is sometimes called "use-plus-fruits" immunity. It must be broad enough to purge the incriminating force, direct or derived, of any testimonial disclosure the defendant is compelled to make. The prosecutor need *not* grant the defendant *transactional* immunity—immunity from prosecution for the underlying acts. In most cases, a grant of transactional immunity would render pointless the whole exercise of getting the documents.

In practice, immunizing the act of production presents some tricky questions. The hardest question arises when the government did not know that a particular document existed before the defendant produced it. In that event, the government's *knowledge of the existence of the document* would be a fruit of the immunized act of production. A grant of "use and derivative-use" immunity therefore might immunize the defendant against *any* use of the document, including any use of its contents, because *any* use would be a fruit of the disclosure that the document exists. *See* W. LAFAVE & J. ISRAEL, CRIMINAL PROCEDURE 443 (2d ed. 1992). The Supreme Court wrestles with the consequences of this reasoning in *Hubbell.*

UNITED STATES V. HUBBELL

530 U.S. 27 (2000).

■ JUSTICE STEVENS delivered the opinion of the Court. The two questions presented concern the scope of a witness' protection against compelled self-incrimination: (1) whether the Fifth Amendment privilege protects a witness from being compelled to disclose the existence of incriminating documents that the Government is unable to describe with reasonable particularity; and (2) if the witness produces such documents pursuant to a grant of immunity, whether 18 U.S.C. § 6002 [which provides for use and derivative-use immunity] prevents the Government from using them to prepare criminal charges against him.

I

This proceeding arises out of [an inquiry conducted] by the Independent Counsel appointed in August 1994 to investigate possible violations of federal law relating to the Whitewater Development Corporation [a failed Arkansas land venture in which Bill Clinton and Hillary Rodham Clinton invested]. . . .

In October 1996, while respondent [Webster Hubbell] was incarcerated, the Independent Counsel served him with a subpoena *duces tecum* calling for the production of 11 categories of documents before a grand jury sitting in Little Rock, Arkansas. *See* Appendix, *infra* [at pages 1040–41]. On November 19, he appeared before the grand jury and invoked his Fifth Amendment privilege against self-incrimination. In response to questioning by the prosecutor, respondent initially refused "to state whether there are documents within my possession, custody, or control responsive to the Subpoena." Thereafter, the prosecutor produced an order, which had previously been obtained from the District Court . . . , directing him to respond to the subpoena and granting him immunity "to the extent allowed by law." Respondent then produced 13,120 pages of documents and records and responded to a series of questions that established that those were all of the documents in his custody or control that were responsive to the commands in the subpoena, with the exception of a few documents he claimed were shielded by the attorney–client and attorney work-product privileges.

The contents of the documents produced by respondent provided the Independent Counsel with the information that led to this ... prosecution. On April 30, 1998, a grand jury in the District of Columbia returned a 10–count indictment charging respondent with various tax-related crimes and mail and wire fraud. The District Court dismissed the indictment relying, in part, on the ground that the Independent Counsel's use of the subpoenaed documents violated § 6002 because all of the evidence he would offer against respondent at trial derived either directly or indirectly from the testimonial aspects of respondent's immunized act of producing those documents. Noting that the Independent Counsel had admitted that he was not investigating tax-related issues when he issued the subpoena, and that he had " 'learned about the unreported income and other crimes from studying the records' contents,' " the District Court characterized the subpoena as "the quintessential fishing expedition." 11 F. Supp. 2d 25, 37 (D.D.C. 1998).

The Court of Appeals vacated the judgment and remanded for further proceedings. The majority concluded that the District Court had incorrectly relied on the fact that the Independent Counsel did not have prior knowledge of the contents of the subpoenaed documents. The question the District Court should have addressed was the extent of the Government's independent knowledge of the documents' existence and authenticity, and of respondent's possession or control of them. It explained:

> "On remand, the district court should hold a hearing in which it seeks to establish the extent and detail of the Government's knowledge of Hubbell's financial affairs (or of the paperwork documenting it) on the day the subpoena issued. It is only then that the court will be in a position to assess the testimonial value of Hubbell's response to the subpoena. Should the Independent Counsel prove capable of demonstrating with reasonable particularity a prior awareness that the exhaustive litany of documents sought in the subpoena existed and were in Hubbell's possession, then the wide distance evidently traveled from the subpoena to the substantive allegations contained in the indictment would be based upon legitimate intermediate steps. To the extent that the information conveyed through Hubbell's compelled act of production provides the necessary linkage, however, the indictment deriving therefrom is tainted." 167 F.3d 552, 581 (D.C. Cir. 1999).

In the opinion of the dissenting judge, the majority failed to give full effect to the distinction between the contents of the documents and the limited testimonial significance of the act of producing them. In his view, as long as the prosecutor could make use of information contained in the documents or derived therefrom without any reference to the fact that respondent had produced them in response to a subpoena, there would be no improper use of the testimonial aspect of the immunized act of production. In other words, the constitutional privilege and the statute conferring use immunity would only shield the witness from the use of any information resulting from his subpoena response "beyond what the prosecutor would receive if the documents appeared in the grand jury room or in his office unsolicited and unmarked, like manna from heaven." 166 F.3d at 602.

On remand, the Independent Counsel acknowledged that he could not satisfy the "reasonable particularity" standard prescribed by the Court of Appeals and entered into a conditional plea agreement with respondent. In essence, the agreement provides for the dismissal of the charges unless this Court's disposition of the case makes it reasonably likely that respondent's "act of production immunity" would not pose a significant bar to his prosecution. . . . [W]e granted the Independent Counsel's petition for a writ of certiorari in order to determine the precise scope of a grant of immunity with respect to the production of documents in response to a subpoena. We now affirm.

II

. . . It is clear [after *Fisher* and *Doe*] that respondent Hubbell could not avoid compliance with the subpoena served on him merely because the demanded documents contained incriminating evidence, whether written by others or voluntarily prepared by himself.

On the other hand, we have also made it clear that the act of producing documents in response to a subpoena may have a compelled testimonial aspect. . . . Moreover, as was true in this case, when the custodian of documents responds to a subpoena, he may be compelled to take the witness stand and answer questions designed to determine whether he has produced everything demanded by the subpoena.[20] The answers to those questions, as well as the act of production itself, may certainly communicate information about the existence, custody, and authenticity of the documents. . . .

[We also note that] the phrase "in any criminal case" in the text of the Fifth Amendment might have been read to limit its coverage to compelled testimony that is used against the defendant in the trial itself. It has, however, long been settled that its protection encompasses compelled statements that lead to the discovery of incriminating evidence

20. Thus, for example, after respondent had been duly sworn by the grand jury foreman, the prosecutor called his attention to paragraph A of the Subpoena Rider (reproduced in the Appendix [see page 1041, below]) and asked whether he had produced "all those documents."

even though the statements themselves are not incriminating and are not introduced into evidence.... It is the Fifth Amendment's protection against the prosecutor's use of incriminating information derived directly or indirectly from the compelled testimony of the respondent that is of primary relevance in this case.

III

Acting pursuant to 18 U.S.C. § 6002, the District Court entered an order compelling respondent to produce "any and all documents" described in the grand jury subpoena and granting him "immunity to the extent allowed by law."* In Kastigar v. United States, 406 U.S. 441 (1972), we upheld the constitutionality of § 6002 because the scope of the "use and derivative-use" immunity that it provides is coextensive with the scope of the constitutional privilege against self-incrimination.

... In [*Kastigar*], we stressed the importance of § 6002's "explicit proscription" of the use in any criminal case of " 'testimony or other information compelled under the order (or any information directly or indirectly derived from such testimony or other information).' " 406 U.S. at 453. We particularly emphasized the critical importance of protection against a future prosecution " 'based on knowledge and sources of information obtained from the compelled testimony.' " 406 U.S. at 454.

... [W]e concluded [in *Kastigar*] that a person who is prosecuted for matters related to testimony he gave under a grant of immunity does not have the burden of proving that his testimony was improperly used. Instead, we held that the statute imposes an affirmative duty on the prosecution, not merely to show that its evidence is not tainted by the prior testimony, but "to prove that the evidence it proposes to use is derived from a legitimate source wholly independent of the compelled testimony." 406 U.S. at 460. Requiring the prosecution to shoulder this burden ensures that the grant of immunity has "left the witness and the Federal Government in substantially the same position as if the witness had claimed his privilege in the absence of a grant of immunity." 406 U.S. at 458–59.

The "compelled testimony" that is relevant in this case is not to be found in the contents of the documents produced in response to the subpoena. It is, rather, the testimony inherent in the act of producing those documents. The disagreement between the parties focuses entirely on the significance of that testimonial aspect.

IV

The Government correctly emphasizes that the testimonial aspect of a response to a subpoena *duces tecum* does nothing more than establish

* [Although the District Court entered the order granting immunity, it had power to do only on the motion of the United States Attorney, as provided in 18 U.S.C. § 6003.—GF]

the existence, authenticity, and custody of items that are produced. We assume that the Government is also entirely correct in its submission that it would not have to advert to respondent's act of production in order to prove the existence, authenticity, or custody of any documents that it might offer in evidence at a criminal trial; indeed, the Government disclaims any need to introduce any of the documents produced by respondent into evidence in order to prove the charges against him. It follows, according to the Government, that it has no intention of making improper "use" of respondent's compelled testimony.

The question, however, is not whether the response to the subpoena may be introduced into evidence at his criminal trial. That would surely be a prohibited "use" of the immunized act of production. But the fact that the Government intends no such use of the act of production leaves open the separate question whether it has already made "derivative use" of the testimonial aspect of that act in obtaining the indictment against respondent and in preparing its case for trial. It clearly has.

It is apparent from the text of the subpoena itself that the prosecutor needed respondent's assistance both to identify potential sources of information and to produce those sources. *See* Appendix, *infra*. Given the breadth of the description of the 11 categories of documents called for by the subpoena, the collection and production of the materials demanded was tantamount to answering a series of interrogatories asking a witness to disclose the existence and location of particular documents fitting certain broad descriptions. The assembly of literally hundreds of pages of material in response to a request for "any and all documents reflecting, referring, or relating to any direct or indirect sources of money or other things of value received by or provided to" an individual or members of his family during a 3–year period, Appendix, *infra,* is the functional equivalent of the preparation of an answer to either a detailed written interrogatory or a series of oral questions at a discovery deposition. Entirely apart from the contents of the 13,120 pages of materials that respondent produced in this case, it is undeniable that providing a catalog of existing documents fitting within any of the 11 broadly worded subpoena categories could provide a prosecutor with a "lead to incriminating evidence," or "a link in the chain of evidence needed to prosecute."

Indeed, the record makes it clear that that is what happened in this case. The documents were produced before a grand jury sitting in the Eastern District of Arkansas [investigating a largely unrelated matter].... The use of those sources of information eventually led to the return of an indictment by a grand jury sitting in the District of Columbia.... What the District Court characterized as a "fishing expedition" did produce a fish, but not the one that the Independent Counsel expected to hook. It is abundantly clear that the testimonial aspect of respondent's act of producing subpoenaed documents was the first step in a chain of evidence that led to this prosecution. The documents did not magically appear in the prosecutor's office like "manna from heaven." They arrived there only after respondent asserted his constitutional privilege, received a grant of immunity, and—under the compulsion of the District Court's order—took the mental and physical steps necessary to provide the prosecutor with an accurate inventory of the many sources of potentially incriminating evidence sought by the subpoena. It was only through respondent's truthful reply to the subpoena that the Government received the incriminating documents of which it made "substantial use . . . in the investigation that led to the indictment." Brief for United States 3.

For these reasons, we cannot accept the Government's submission that respondent's immunity did not preclude its derivative use of the produced documents because its "possession of the documents [was] the fruit *only* of a simple physical act—the act of producing the documents." *Id.* at 29. It was unquestionably necessary for respondent to make extensive use of "the contents of his own mind" in identifying the hundreds of documents responsive to the requests in the subpoena. *See* Curcio v. United States, 354 U.S. 118 (1957). The assembly of those documents was like telling an inquisitor the combination to a wall safe, not like being forced to surrender the key to a strongbox. The Government's anemic view of respondent's act of production as a mere physical act that is principally nontestimonial in character and can be entirely divorced from its "implicit" testimonial aspect so as to constitute a "legitimate, wholly independent source" (as required by *Kastigar*) for the documents produced simply fails to account for these realities.

In sum, we have no doubt that the constitutional privilege against self-incrimination protects the target of a grand jury investigation from being compelled to answer questions designed to elicit information about the existence of sources of potentially incriminating evidence. That constitutional privilege has the same application to the testimonial aspect of a response to a subpoena seeking discovery of those sources. Before the District Court, the Government arguably conceded that respondent's act of production in this case had a testimonial aspect that entitled him to respond to the subpoena by asserting his privilege against self-incrimination. On appeal and again before this Court, however, the Government has argued that the communicative aspect of respondent's act of producing ordinary business records is insufficiently "testimonial" to support a claim of privilege because the existence and possession of such records by any businessman is a "foregone conclusion" under our decision in *Fisher v. United States,* 425 U.S. at 411. This argument both misreads *Fisher* and ignores our subsequent decision in *United States v. Doe,* 465 U.S. 605 (1984).

. . . *Fisher* involved summonses seeking production of working papers prepared by the taxpayers' accountants that the IRS knew were in the possession of the taxpayers' attorneys. *Fisher,* 425 U.S. at 394. In rejecting the taxpayers' claim that these documents were protected by the Fifth Amendment privilege, we stated:

> "It is doubtful that implicitly admitting the existence and possession of the papers rises to the level of testimony within the protection of the Fifth Amendment. The papers belong to the *accountant*, were prepared by him, and are the kind usually prepared by an accountant working on the tax returns of his client. Surely the Government is in no way relying on the 'truthtelling' of the *taxpayer* to prove the existence of or his access to the documents.... The existence and location of the papers are a foregone conclusion and the taxpayer adds little or nothing to the sum total of the Government's information by conceding that he in fact has the papers." 425 U.S. at 411 (emphases added).

Whatever the scope of this "foregone conclusion" rationale, the facts of this case plainly fall outside of it. While in *Fisher* the Government already knew that the documents were in the attorneys' possession and could independently confirm their existence and authenticity through the accountants who created them, here the Government has not shown that it had any prior knowledge of either the existence or the whereabouts of the 13,120 pages of documents ultimately produced by respondent. The Government cannot cure this deficiency through the overbroad argument that a businessman such as respondent will always possess general business and tax records that fall within the broad categories described in this subpoena. The *Doe* subpoenas also sought several broad categories of general business records, yet we upheld the District Court's finding that the act of producing those records would involve testimonial self-incrimination. 465 U.S. at 612–14.

Given our conclusion that respondent's act of production had a testimonial aspect, at least with respect to the existence and location of the documents sought by the Government's subpoena, respondent could not be compelled to produce those documents without first receiving a grant of immunity.... As we construed § 6002 in *Kastigar*, such immunity is co-extensive with the constitutional privilege. *Kastigar* requires that respondent's motion to dismiss the indictment on immunity grounds be granted unless the Government proves that the evidence it used in obtaining the indictment and proposed to use at trial was derived from legitimate sources "wholly independent" of the testimonial aspect of respondent's immunized conduct in assembling and producing the documents described in the subpoena. The Government, however, does not claim that it could make such a showing....

Accordingly, the indictment against respondent must be dismissed. The judgment of the Court of Appeals is affirmed.

It is so ordered.

APPENDIX TO OPINION OF THE COURT

On October 31, 1996, upon application by the Independent Counsel, a subpoena was issued commanding respondent to appear and testify before the grand jury of the United States District Court for the Eastern

District of Arkansas on November 19, 1996, and to bring with him various documents described in a "Subpoena Rider" as follows:

> "A. Any and all documents reflecting, referring, or relating to any direct or indirect sources of money or other things of value received by or provided to Webster Hubbell, his wife, or children from January 1, 1993, to the present, including but not limited to the identity of employers or clients of legal or any other type of work. . . .
>
> "K. Any and all documents related to work performed or to be performed for or on behalf of Lippo Ltd. (formerly Public Finance (H.K.) Ltd.), the Lippo Group, the Lippo Bank, Mochtar Riady, James Riady, Stephen Riady, John Luen Wai Lee, John Huang, Mark W. Grobmyer, C. Joseph Giroir, Jr., or any affiliate, subsidiary, or corporation owned or controlled by or related to the aforementioned entities or individuals, including but not limited to correspondence, retainer agreements, contracts, time sheets, appointment calendars, activity calendars, diaries, billing statements, billing memoranda, telephone records, telephone message slips, telephone credit card statements, itineraries, tickets for transportation, payment records, expense receipts, ledgers, check registers, notes, memoranda, electronic mail, bank deposit items, cashier's checks, traveler's checks, wire transfer records and/or other records of financial transactions."

■ Chief Justice Rehnquist dissents and would reverse the judgment of the Court of Appeals in part, for the reasons given by Judge Williams in his dissenting opinion in that court, 167 F.3d 552, 597 (D.C. Cir. 1999).

■ Justice Thomas, with whom Justice Scalia joins, concurring. Our decision today involves the application of the act-of-production doctrine, which provides that persons compelled to turn over incriminating papers or other physical evidence pursuant to a subpoena *duces tecum* or a summons may invoke the Fifth Amendment privilege against self-incrimination as a bar to production only where the act of producing the evidence would contain "testimonial" features. I join the opinion of the Court because it properly applies this doctrine, but I write separately to note that this doctrine may be inconsistent with the original meaning of the Fifth Amendment's Self-Incrimination Clause. A substantial body of evidence suggests that the Fifth Amendment privilege protects against the compelled production not just of incriminating testimony, but of any incriminating evidence. In a future case, I would be willing to reconsider the scope and meaning of the Self-Incrimination Clause. . . .

United States v. Hubbell: *Afterthoughts*

Does the result in *Hubbell* render moot the dispute between Justices Marshall and O'Connor about whether the Fifth Amendment protects the contents of one's private diary from disclosure? (*See* pages 1028–29, above.) In his separate opinion in *Fisher*, written a quarter-century before *Hubbell*, Justice Marshall predicted the result in *Hubbell* and declared victory (in advance) on the issue of a diary's privacy:

> The Court recognizes, as others have argued, that the act of production can verify the authenticity of the documents produced. But the promise of the Court's theory lies in its innovative discernment that production may also verify the documents' very existence and present possession by the producer. This expanded recognition of the kinds of testimony inherent in production . . . seems to me to afford almost complete protection against compulsory production of our most private papers.
>
> . . . Since the existence of corporate record books is seldom in doubt, the verification of their existence, inherent in their production, may fairly be termed not testimonial at all. On the other hand, there is little reason to assume the present existence and possession of most private papers. . . . Indeed, there would appear to be a precise inverse relationship between the private nature of the document and the permissibility of assuming its existence. Therefore, under the Court's theory, the admission through production that one's diary . . . exist[s] would ordinarily provide substantial testimony. The incriminating nature of such an admission is clear, for while it may not be criminal to keep a diary, . . . the admission that one does and that [it is] still available may quickly—or simultaneously—lead to incriminating evidence. . . . [That is enough] to make such testimony subject to the claim of privilege. . . .
>
> The Court's theory [of the testimonial aspects of the act of production] will also limit the prosecution's ability to use documents secured through a grant of immunity. If authentication that the document produced is the document demanded were the only testimony inherent in production, immunity would be a useful tool for obtaining written evidence. So long as a document obtained under an immunity grant could be authenticated through other sources, as would often be possible, reliance on the immunized testimony—the authentication—and its fruits would not be necessary, and the document could be introduced. The Court's recognition that the act of production also involves testimony about the existence and possession of the subpoenaed documents mandates a different result. Under the Court's theory, if the document is to be obtained the immunity grant must extend to the testimony that the document is presently in existence. Such a grant will effectively shield the contents of the document, for the contents are a direct fruit of the immunized testimony—that the document exists—and cannot usually be obtained without reliance on that testimony. . . .

Fisher v. United States, 425 U.S. at 432–34 (Marshall, J., concurring in the judgment).

CHAPTER 13

FAMILIAL PRIVILEGES

A. THE MARITAL PRIVILEGES

1. THE SPOUSAL TESTIMONIAL PRIVILEGE

TILTON v. BEECHER

2 Abbott's Repts. at 49, 87 (N.Y. 1875).

* * *

Mr. Evarts, arguing for the plaintiff:

The common law has said ... the administration of justice was made for society, not society for the administration of justice; and there are certain institutions of society lying at the base of our civilization, sustaining the whole fabric of its prosperity, its purity, its dignity, and its strength, which must not be undermined, or corrupted, or disfigured, or defiled, under the notion that in the administration of justice the truth must be sought in every quarter and from every witness.... When the common law says that a man and his wife are one, or, in Lord Coke's language, "two souls in one person"—it is said no man shall put asunder those who are thus joined together, and, least of all, in the name of law, shall the administration of justice pull and tear asunder this conjugal relation by the step of the sheriff or the precept of the judge that compels one to come and betray the other.

Mr. Beach, arguing for the defendant:

I agree ... that there is much of beauty and sacredness in the idea of unity attached to the marriage relation.... But are we to forget that in what is called the progress of civilization that idea has been mangled and defaced? ... Now she may get out into the world and barter and trade and tussle with the energies of commercial and business life. Once her true sphere was in the domestic circle and around the hearthstone, cultivating those tender sentiments and qualities which were at once her grace and glory, but today by the voice and power of legislation she is ushered into the busy scenes of life, and becomes an active and independent actor in all its struggles. The counsel says this idea of unity, this consecration of the domestic circle, can not be torn by the rude hand of the law. Sir, it *has been* mangled and torn! . . .

Focus on
Proposed FRE 505

TRAMMEL V. UNITED STATES

445 U.S. 40 (1980).

■ MR. CHIEF JUSTICE BURGER delivered the opinion of the Court. We granted certiorari to consider whether an accused may invoke the privilege against adverse spousal testimony so as to exclude the voluntary testimony of his wife. This calls for a re-examination of Hawkins v. United States, 358 U.S. 74 (1958).

I

On March 10, 1976, petitioner Otis Trammel was indicted . . . for importing heroin into the United States from Thailand and the Philippine Islands and for conspiracy to import heroin. . . . The indictment also named six unindicted co-conspirators, including petitioner's wife, Elizabeth Ann Trammel.

According to the indictment, petitioner and his wife flew from the Philippines to California in August 1975, carrying with them a quantity of heroin. . . . Elizabeth Trammel then traveled to Thailand where she purchased another supply of the drug. On November 3, 1975, with four ounces of heroin on her person, she boarded a plane for the United States. During a routine customs search in Hawaii, she was searched, the heroin was discovered, and she was arrested. After discussions with Drug Enforcement Administration agents, she agreed to cooperate with the Government.

Prior to trial on this indictment, petitioner . . . advised the court that the Government intended to call his wife as an adverse witness and asserted his claim to a privilege to prevent her from testifying against him. At a hearing on the motion, Mrs. Trammel was called as a Government witness under a grant of use immunity. She testified that she and petitioner were married in May 1975 and that they remained married.[1] She explained that her cooperation with the Government was based on

1. In response to the question whether divorce was contemplated, Mrs. Trammel testified that her husband had said that "I would go my way and he would go his."

assurances that she would be given lenient treatment.[2] She then described, in considerable detail, her role and that of her husband in the heroin distribution conspiracy.

After hearing this testimony, the District Court ruled that Mrs. Trammel could testify in support of the Government's case to any act she observed during the marriage and to any communication "made in the presence of a third person"; however, confidential communications between petitioner and his wife were held to be privileged and inadmissible....

At trial, Elizabeth Trammel testified within the limits of the court's pretrial ruling; her testimony, as the Government concedes, constituted virtually its entire case against petitioner. He was found guilty on both the substantive and conspiracy charges....

In the Court of Appeals petitioner's only claim of error was that the admission of the adverse testimony of his wife, over his objection, contravened this Court's teaching in *Hawkins v. United States, supra,* and therefore constituted reversible error. The Court of Appeals rejected this contention....

II

The privilege claimed by petitioner has ancient roots. Writing in 1628, Lord Coke observed that "it hath been resolved by the Justices that a wife cannot be produced either against or for her husband." 1 E. COKE, A COMMENTARIE UPON LITTLETON 6b (1628). This spousal disqualification sprang from two canons of medieval jurisprudence: first, the rule that an accused was not permitted to testify in his own behalf because of his interest in the proceeding; second, the concept that husband and wife were one, and that since the woman had no recognized separate legal existence, the husband was that one. From those two now long-abandoned doctrines, it followed that what was inadmissible from the lips of the defendant-husband was also inadmissible from his wife.

Despite its medieval origins, this rule of spousal disqualification remained intact in most common-law jurisdictions well into the 19th century.... Indeed, it was not until 1933, in Funk v. United States, 290 U.S. 371, that this Court abolished the testimonial disqualification in the federal courts, so as to permit the spouse of a defendant to testify in the defendant's behalf. *Funk,* however, left undisturbed the rule that either spouse could prevent the other from giving adverse testimony. The rule thus evolved into one of privilege rather than one of absolute disqualification.

2. The Government represents to the Court that Elizabeth Trammel has not been prosecuted for her role in the conspiracy.

The modern justification for this privilege against adverse spousal testimony is its perceived role in fostering the harmony and sanctity of the marriage relationship. Notwithstanding this benign purpose, the rule was sharply criticized. Professor Wigmore termed it "the merest anachronism in legal theory and an indefensible obstruction to truth in practice." 8 J. WIGMORE, EVIDENCE § 2228, at 221 (McNaughton rev. 1961). The Committee on Improvements in the Law of Evidence of the American Bar Association called for its abolition. 63 AMERICAN BAR ASSOCIATION REPORTS 594–95 (1938). In its place, Wigmore and others suggested a privilege protecting only private marital communications, modeled on the privilege between priest and penitent, attorney and client, and physician and patient.[5]

These criticisms influenced the American Law Institute, which, in its 1942 Model Code of Evidence, advocated a privilege for marital confidences, but expressly rejected a rule vesting in the defendant the right to exclude all adverse testimony of his spouse. In 1953 the Uniform Rules of Evidence, drafted by the National Conference of Commissioners on Uniform State Laws, followed a similar course; it limited the privilege to confidential communications and "[abolished] the rule, still existing in some states, and largely a sentimental relic, of not requiring one spouse to testify against the other in a criminal action." Several state legislatures enacted similarly patterned provisions into law.

In Hawkins v. United States, 358 U.S. 74 (1958), this Court considered the continued vitality of the privilege against adverse spousal testimony in the federal courts. There the District Court had permitted petitioner's wife, over his objection, to testify against him. With one questioning concurring opinion, the Court held the wife's testimony inadmissible; it took note of the critical comments that the common-law rule had engendered, but chose not to abandon it. Also rejected was the Government's suggestion that the Court modify the privilege by vesting it in the witness-spouse, with freedom to testify or not independent of the defendant's control. The Court viewed this proposed modification as antithetical to the widespread belief, evidenced in the rules then in effect in a majority of the States and in England, "that the law should not force or encourage testimony which might alienate husband and wife, or further inflame existing domestic differences."

Hawkins, then, left the federal privilege for adverse spousal testimony where it found it, continuing "a rule which bars the testimony of one spouse against the other unless both consent." *Id.* at 78. *Accord* Wyatt v.

5. This Court recognized just such a confidential marital communications privilege in Wolfle v. United States, 291 U.S. 7 (1934), and in Blau v. United States, 340 U.S. 332 (1951). In neither case, however, did the Court adopt the Wigmore view that the communications privilege be substituted *in place of* the privilege against adverse spousal testimony. The privilege as to confidential marital communications is not at issue in the instant case; accordingly, our holding today does not disturb *Wolfle* and *Blau*.

United States, 362 U.S. 525, 528 (1960).[7] However, in so doing, the Court made clear that its decision was not meant to "foreclose whatever changes in the rule may eventually be dictated by 'reason and experience.' " 358 U.S. at 79.

III

A

The Federal Rules of Evidence acknowledge the authority of the federal courts to continue the evolutionary development of testimonial privileges in federal criminal trials "in the light of reason and experience." FED. R. EVID. 501. The general mandate of Rule 501 was substituted by the Congress for a set of privilege rules . . . [that] includ[ed] a husband–wife privilege which would have codified the *Hawkins* rule and eliminated the privilege for confidential marital communications. *See* proposed FED. R. EVID. 505. In rejecting the proposed Rules and enacting Rule 501, Congress manifested an affirmative intention not to freeze the law of privilege. Its purpose rather was to "provide the courts with the flexibility to develop rules of privilege on a case-by-case basis," 120 CONG. REC. 40891 (1974) (statement of Rep. Hungate), and to leave the door open to change.

Although Rule 501 confirms the authority of the federal courts to reconsider the continued validity of the *Hawkins* rule, the long history of the privilege suggests that it ought not to be casually cast aside. That the privilege is one affecting marriage, home, and family relationships—already subject to much erosion in our day—also counsels caution. At the same time, we cannot escape the reality that the law on occasion adheres to doctrinal concepts long after the reasons which gave them birth have disappeared and after experience suggests the need for change. This was recognized in *Funk* where the Court "[declined] to enforce . . . ancient [rules] of the common law under conditions as they now exist." For, as Mr. Justice Black admonished in another setting, "[when] precedent and precedent alone is all the argument that can be made to support a court-fashioned rule, it is time for the rule's creator to destroy it."

B

Since 1958, when *Hawkins* was decided, support for the privilege against adverse spousal testimony has been eroded further. Thirty-one jurisdictions, including Alaska and Hawaii, then allowed an accused a privilege to prevent adverse spousal testimony. The number has now declined to 24.[9] In 1974, the National Conference on Uniform State Laws

7. The decision in *Wyatt* recognized an exception to *Hawkins* for cases in which one spouse commits a crime against the other. 362 U.S. at 526. This exception, placed on the ground of necessity, was a longstanding one at common law. It has been expanded since then to include crimes against the spouse's property, and in recent years crimes against children of either spouse. Similar exceptions have been found to the confidential marital communications privilege. *See* 8 WIGMORE § 2338.

9. Eight States provide that one spouse is incompetent to testify against the

revised its Uniform Rules of Evidence, but again rejected the *Hawkins* rule in favor of a limited privilege for confidential communications.[10] . . . The trend in state law toward divesting the accused of the privilege to bar adverse spousal testimony has special relevance because the laws of marriage and domestic relations are concerns traditionally reserved to the states. Scholarly criticism of the *Hawkins* rule has also continued unabated.

C

Testimonial exclusionary rules and privileges contravene the fundamental principle that "'the public ... has a right to every man's evidence.'" As such, they must be strictly construed and accepted "only to the very limited extent that permitting a refusal to testify or excluding relevant evidence has a public good transcending the normally predominant principle of utilizing all rational means for ascertaining truth." Elkins v. United States, 364 U.S. 206, 234 (1960) (Frankfurter, J., dissenting). Here we must decide whether the privilege against adverse spousal testimony promotes sufficiently important interests to outweigh the need for probative evidence in the administration of criminal justice.

It is essential to remember that the *Hawkins* privilege is not needed to protect information privately disclosed between husband and wife in the confidence of the marital relationship—once described by this Court as "the best solace of human existence." Those confidences are privileged under the independent rule protecting confidential marital communications. Blau v. United States, 340 U.S. 332 (1951); *see* n.5, *supra*. The *Hawkins* privilege is invoked, not to exclude private marital communications, but rather to exclude evidence of criminal acts and of communications made in the presence of third persons.

No other testimonial privilege sweeps so broadly. The privileges between priest and penitent, attorney and client, and physician and patient limit protection to private communications.* These privileges are rooted in the imperative need for confidence and trust. . . .

The *Hawkins* rule stands in marked contrast to these three privileges. Its protection is not limited to confidential communications; rather it

other in a criminal proceeding. Sixteen States provide a privilege against adverse spousal testimony and vest the privilege in both spouses or in the defendant-spouse alone. Nine States entitle the witness-spouse alone to assert a privilege against adverse spousal testimony. The remaining 17 States have abolished the privilege in criminal cases. . . .

10. In 1965, California took the privilege from the defendant-spouse and vested it in the witness-spouse, accepting a study commission recommendation that the "latter [was] more likely than the former to determine whether or not to claim the privilege on the basis of the probable effect on the marital relationship." *See* CAL. EVID. CODE ANN. §§ 970–973 (West 1966 and Supp. 1979). . . .

* [Note, however, that most federal courts have not recognized a general physician–patient privilege. *See* MUELLER & KIRKPATRICK, EVIDENCE § 5.34, at 424 (5th ed. 2012).—GF]

permits an accused to exclude all adverse spousal testimony. As Jeremy Bentham observed more than a century and a half ago, such a privilege goes far beyond making "every man's house his castle," and permits a person to convert his house into "a den of thieves." 5 RATIONALE OF JUDICIAL EVIDENCE 340 (1827). It "secures, to every man, one safe and unquestionable and ever ready accomplice for every imaginable crime." *Id.* at 338.

The ancient foundations for so sweeping a privilege have long since disappeared. Nowhere in the common-law world—indeed in any modern society—is a woman regarded as chattel or demeaned by denial of a separate legal identity and the dignity associated with recognition as a whole human being. Chip by chip, over the years those archaic notions have been cast aside so that "[no] longer is the female destined solely for the home and the rearing of the family, and only the male for the marketplace and the world of ideas." Stanton v. Stanton, 421 U.S. 7, 14–15 (1975).

The contemporary justification for affording an accused such a privilege is also unpersuasive. When one spouse is willing to testify against the other in a criminal proceeding—whatever the motivation—their relationship is almost certainly in disrepair; there is probably little in the way of marital harmony for the privilege to preserve. In these circumstances, a rule of evidence that permits an accused to prevent adverse spousal testimony seems far more likely to frustrate justice than to foster family peace.[12] Indeed, there is reason to believe that vesting the privilege in the accused could actually undermine the marital relationship. For example, in a case such as this, the Government is unlikely to offer a wife immunity and lenient treatment if it knows that her husband can prevent her from giving adverse testimony. If the Government is dissuaded from making such an offer, the privilege can have the untoward effect of permitting one spouse to escape justice at the expense of the other. It hardly seems conducive to the preservation of the marital relation to place a wife in jeopardy solely by virtue of her husband's control over her testimony.

IV

Our consideration of the foundations for the privilege and its history satisfy us that "reason and experience" no longer justify so sweeping a rule as that found acceptable by the Court in *Hawkins*. Accordingly, we conclude that the existing rule should be modified so that the witness-spouse alone has a privilege to refuse to testify adversely; the witness

12. It is argued that abolishing the privilege will permit the Government to come between husband and wife, pitting one against the other. That, too, misses the mark. Neither *Hawkins*, nor any other privilege, prevents the Government from enlisting one spouse to give information concerning the other or to aid in the other's apprehension. It is only the spouse's testimony in the courtroom that is prohibited.

may be neither compelled to testify nor foreclosed from testifying. This modification—vesting the privilege in the witness-spouse—furthers the important public interest in marital harmony without unduly burdening legitimate law enforcement needs.

Here, petitioner's spouse chose to testify against him. That she did so after a grant of immunity and assurances of lenient treatment does not render her testimony involuntary. Accordingly, the District Court and the Court of Appeals were correct in rejecting petitioner's claim of privilege, and the judgment of the Court of Appeals is

Affirmed.

■ MR. JUSTICE STEWART, concurring in the judgment. . . .

CONSIDER the next article together with that by Robert Tharp in Chapter 8 (page 614). As under the Confrontation Clause, a law change triggered greater pressure on women to testify against alleged abusers:

Athlete and Legal Issue on Trial

Sam Howe Verhovek

NEW YORK TIMES, Feb. 19, 1996, at A8

RICHMOND, Tex. When Warren Moon, the star National Football League quarterback, went on trial on assault charges this week, his wife, Felicia, was by his side. They held hands on the way into the courthouse. During breaks, they embraced and bowed their heads in prayer.

But then, on Friday, prosecutors called Mrs. Moon to the stand. And over her repeated protests that she was dismayed charges had been brought and was testifying to avoid the threat of jail, the prosecutors started questioning the woman they say was the victim of Mr. Moon's assault last summer: Felicia Moon.

Mrs. Moon was being forced to testify under a new law that took effect in Texas just last fall, echoing similar legal changes already made in most other states in the past several years, and one that represents a controversial revision of the longstanding legal principle that spouses should never be compelled to testify against each other.

While the principle, known as the spousal immunity privilege, still holds for most crimes, the new Texas law made an exception for crimes of domestic abuse.

And so, even as Mrs. Moon implored prosecutors to "leave me, my privacy and the sanctity of my marriage alone," she avoided a possible contempt citation and jail term by taking the stand. She recounted details of an altercation in the Moons' suburban home one afternoon last July that she once told the police had left her "so that I couldn't talk or breathe" and in fear for her life.

Mrs. Moon, 39, testified this week that the scratches and abrasions shown in photographs to jurors came when Mr. Moon, also 39 and a 10–year marquee player with the Houston Oilers, restrained her only after she became enraged and physically abusive during an argument....

The Moon case ... affords a window on ... what many legal scholars say is a striking collision of two very different sets of women's rights.

Prosecutors ... hail the removal of spousal immunity in such cases as an important tool to secure convictions and overcome the threats that many violent men use to make their wives afraid to press charges.

But many lawyers argue that the change, far from empowering a woman, actually represents a perversion of her right to decide for herself whether she is a victim.

"There's a real paternalistic attitude at work here" in the new law, said Betty Blackwell, an Austin lawyer who frequently lectures on domestic abuse. "It's, 'We know what's best for women.' "

And to make the matter yet more clouded, many legal scholars argue that the fundamental concept of spousal immunity in any case—whether domestic abuse, murder of a third party or petty shoplifting—should be considered obsolete.

It dates hundreds of years to a time when women were considered property of their husbands and could not testify against them even if they wanted to. More recently, it was transformed into a privilege, under which marriage was considered so sacrosanct that married people should never be forced to testify against each other.

Prosecutors here in Fort Bend County insist that they had evidence an assault had occurred and are simply using the law to seek justice.

But Rusty Hardin, Mr. Moon's lawyer and a former Houston prosecutor, says that prosecutors have turned a private matter into a nightmare for the Moon family, including the couple's four children. "Prosecutors now have the right to destroy the village to save it," said Mr. Hardin....

When the Texas Legislature was considering changes in the spousal immunity law last spring, it seemed clear from testimony that the typical case most everybody had in mind was that of a battered woman so shell-shocked or terrified that she could not decide whether to press charges against an abusive husband.

Prosecutors in Texas and elsewhere say that while the threat behind the law is an effective means of persuading a battering victim to testify, it has extremely rarely resulted in a case where such a person has been jailed for refusing to testify.

But just months after the law took effect, along came the Moon case and its alleged victim, Mrs. Moon, who once served on the board of a local women's center that runs a shelter for battering victims.

"The present situation—an independent, strong-minded, college-educated woman who wants the state to stay out of her bedroom—is one that the Legislature recognized and was reassured would not occur," said a lawyer for Mrs. Moon, Bobbi Blackwell, in an unsuccessful motion to throw out the subpoena that compelled her client to testify. . . .

Of course, just whether Mrs. Moon will actually help the state's case against her husband . . . remains to be seen. In July, she told the police that Mr. Moon had choked her so hard during an argument that she "saw black and could not breathe." . . .

But on Friday, Mrs. Moon said the altercation was precipitated by her throwing a heavy candlestick holder at her husband. . . .

Mrs. Moon once said she would not testify against her husband by invoking her Fifth Amendment rights against self-incrimination. Under the new Texas law, prosecutors were able to compel testimony by granting her immunity from prosecution. . . .

THE TWO MARITAL PRIVILEGES: *Overview*

Tilton, *Trammel*, and *Moon* all concern the "spousal testimonial privilege." As Chief Justice Burger noted in *Trammel*, this is one of two distinct marital privileges. The *Trammel* Court did not have to consider the "marital confidences privilege" because the trial judge had not permitted Elizabeth Trammel to testify about confidential communications between her and her husband, and neither party appealed this ruling. *See Trammel*, at pages 1045, 1046 n.5.

All fifty states and the District of Columbia recognize the marital confidences privilege. *See* Mikah K. Story, *Twenty-First Century Pillow-Talk*, 58 SANTA CLARA L. REV. 275, 281 & n.40 (2006). Some thirty-one states and the District of Columbia also respect the spousal testimonial privilege. *See* R. Michael Cassidy, *Reconsidering Spousal Privileges after* Crawford, 33 AM. J. CRIM. L. 339, 364 & n.192 (2006). The federal courts respect both.

The boundaries and mechanics of the two privileges vary somewhat from jurisdiction to jurisdiction, but one rule is common to both privileges and almost every jurisdiction: Absent a lawful marriage, civil union, or domestic partnership, there is no privilege. Other intimate relationships do not qualify. *See* MUELLER & KIRKPATRICK, EVIDENCE § 5.31, at 413–14 (5th ed. 2012). Today at least sixteen states and the District of Columbia permit same-sex couples to claim a legal status that affords them the evidentiary privileges of heterosexual spouses.* But same-sex couples

* Same-sex marriage is lawful in Connecticut, Iowa, Massachusetts, New Hampshire, New York, and Vermont, as well as in the District of Columbia. *See* CONN. GEN. STAT. ANN. § 54–84a (2012); *Kerrigan v. Commissioner of Pub. Health*, 289 Conn. 135, 957 A.2d 407 (2008); *Varnum v. Brien*, 763 N.W.2d 862 (Iowa 2009); *Goodridge v. Department of Public Health*, 440 Mass. 309, 312, 342, 798 N.E.2d 941 (2003); N.H. REV. STAT. § 457:1–a (2012); N.Y. DOM. REL. LAW § 10–a (2012); 15 VT. STAT. ANN. § 8 (2012); D.C. CODE § 46–401(2012).

In November 2012 voters in Maine, Maryland, and Washington approved referenda making same-sex marriage lawful. Those actions take effect on January 5, 2013, in Maine; January 1, 2013, in Maryland; and December 9, 2012, in Washington.

Delaware, Hawaii, Illinois, New Jersey, and Rhode Island extend to partners in civil unions all the rights and privileges of spouses. *See* DEL. CODE ANN. tit. 13, § 212 (2012); HAW. REV. STAT. § 572B–9 (2012); 750 ILL. COMP. STAT. 75/20 (2012); N.J. STAT. ANN.

enjoy no marital privilege in federal courts. The federal Defense of Marriage Act confines "marriage" for federal purposes to a union between one woman and one man. And it permits states that have not recognized same-sex unions to refuse to grant them evidentiary privileges available to heterosexual spouses. *See* Pub. L. No. 104–199, 110 Stat. 2419 (1996) (codified at 1 U.S.C. § 7 (2008); 28 U.S.C. § 1738C (2008)); Maria A. La Vita, *When the Honeymoon Is Over*, 33 NEW ENG. J. ON CRIM. & CIV. CONFINEMENT 243, 244, 255–56 (2007). As this book goes to press toward the end of 2012, the Defense of Marriage Act has been declared unconstitutional by several federal courts on various grounds. The Supreme Court has granted review in two of these cases and is expected to decide the Act's constitutionality in late spring 2013.

The Spousal Testimonial Privilege

"This spousal disqualification sprang from two canons of medieval jurisprudence," Chief Justice Burger wrote in *Trammel*, "first, the rule that an accused was not permitted to testify in his own behalf because of his interest in the proceeding; second, the concept that husband and wife were one, and that since the woman had no recognized separate legal existence, the husband was that one."

This thumbnail history of the spousal testimonial privilege was perhaps a bit unfair to the common law. The Chief Justice may have been mistaken, first of all, to assume that the spousal testimonial privilege evolved from the old disqualification that made spouses incompetent to testify for or against each other. Wigmore believed the privilege existed first. Whereas he could not trace the spousal disqualification back before 1628, the privilege made its first recorded appearance in 1580. *See* 8 WIGMORE, EVIDENCE § 2227, at 221–23 (3d ed. 1940).

But beyond this historical quibble, Chief Justice Burger arguably cast the spousal disqualification in an unduly unflattering light. Even in its very earliest manifestation, the rule rested on more than the supposed identity of wife and husband—a theory Jeremy Bentham dismissed as the "grimgribber nonsensical reason" for the rule. 5 JEREMY BENTHAM, RATIONALE OF JUDICIAL EVIDENCE 344 (London, Hunt & Clarke 1827). Writing in the early seventeenth century, Lord Coke held that a wife may not testify

§ 37:1–31 (2012); R.I. GEN. LAWS § 15–3.1–6 (2012).

California, Nevada, and Oregon grant domestic partners all the rights and privileges of spouses. *See* CAL. FAM. CODE § 297.5 (2012); NEV. REV. STAT. § 122A.200 (2012); OR. REV. STAT. § 106.340 (2012). Moreover, Washington's privilege law confers both a testimonial privilege and a confidential communications privilege on both spouses and domestic partners. *See* WASH. CODE § 5.60.060 (2012).

Wisconsin's privilege law applies to both spouses and domestic partners. The privilege it confers is an odd hybrid of a testimonial and a confidential communications privilege: "A person has a privilege to prevent the person's spouse or former spouse or domestic partner or former domestic partner from testifying against the person as to any private communication by one to the other made during their marriage or domestic partnership." WIS. STAT. ANN. § 905.05 (2012).

I thank Gabriel Schlabach and Justin Barnard, who scoured the law books in compiling this list.

either for or against her husband because they are two souls in one body ("*quia sunt duae animae in carna una*"). But he then added that such testimony "might be a cause of implacable discord and dissention between the husband and the wife." SIR EDWARD COKE, COMMENTARY UPON LITTLETON 6b (1628). This concern with marital "discord and dissention" is of course the same rationale Chief Justice Burger cited (without attribution to Coke) for the modern form of the privilege.

The Chief Justice also implied that the spousal disqualification barred only wives from the witness stand. It is true that Coke's rhetoric focused on a wife's testimony against her husband, but the rule was not as one-sided as that—or at least it was not that one-sided for long. Barely more than half a century after Coke's statement of the rule, Lord Chief Justice Jeffreys maintained that "[b]y the law the husband cannot be a witness against his wife, nor a wife against her husband, to charge them with anything criminal." *Lady Ivy's Trial*, 10 HOW. ST. TR. 555, 644 (1684). Jeffreys added that "[t]his is so known a common rule that I thought it could never have borne any question or debate." *Id.* Likewise, Jeffrey Gilbert, who wrote his famous evidence treatise sometime around the turn of the eighteenth century, applied the rule to both spouses. "Husband and Wife cannot be admitted to be Witnesses for or against each other," Gilbert declared, "for if they swear for the Benefit of each other, they are not to be believed, because their Interests are absolutely the same, and therefore they can gain no more Credit when they attest for each other, than when any Man attests for himself." [JEFFREY GILBERT], THE LAW OF EVIDENCE 135–36 (London, Henry Lintot 1756).*

Today, the spousal testimonial privilege usually takes one of two forms. In most jurisdictions, it permits witnesses at criminal proceedings to refuse to testify against their spouses. In a few, it permits criminal defendants to prevent their spouses from testifying against them. The critical distinction is whether the witness-spouse or the defendant-spouse holds the privilege. Because in Washington defendants hold the privilege, Michael Crawford was able to bar his wife's testimony—and then complain that his inability to cross-examine her violated his confrontation right. *See Crawford v. Washington*, pages 595–96, 597 n.1 (above). A third, less common form of the spousal testimonial privilege bars spousal testimony against criminal defendants unless both spouses consent. *See* Cassidy, *supra*, at 365 & nn.195–97.

While proposed Rule of Evidence 505 would have placed the privilege in the hands of the defendant-spouse, the *Trammel* Court unanimously rejected this approach. It does seem odd to put the privilege in the defendant's control. The Chief Justice quoted the cutting rhetoric Bentham aimed at this aspect of the old rule:

* Gilbert, who died in 1726, wrote his treatise several decades before it was first published.

> Let us, therefore, grant to every man a license to commit all sorts of wickedness, in the presence and with the assistance of his wife: let us secure to every man in the bosom of his family . . . a safe accomplice: let us make every man's house his castle; and . . . let us convert that castle into a den of thieves.

5 BENTHAM, *supra*, at 340. Even Wigmore, hardly a progressive hero on relations between the sexes, saw no sense in permitting the defendant-spouse to claim the privilege:

> [I]f Doe has committed a wrong against Roe, and Doe's wife's testimony is needed for proving that wrong, Doe, the very wrong-doer, is to be licensed to withhold it and thus to secure immunity from giving redress, because, forsooth, Doe's own marital peace will be thereby endangered—a curious piece of policy, by which the wrongdoer's own interests are consulted in determining whether justice shall have its course against him.

8 WIGMORE, *supra*, § 2228, at 227.

But since all privileges sometimes shield criminals from the law, the Court must have had a different reason to withdraw the spousal testimonial privilege from defendant-spouses. The real problem with letting defendant-spouses claim the privilege is that doing so perhaps did little to protect marriages. Chief Justice Burger made the point pithily: "When one spouse is willing to testify against the other in a criminal proceeding—whatever the motivation—their relationship is almost certainly in disrepair; there is probably little in the way of marital harmony for the privilege to preserve."

Yet less than a quarter-century earlier, when explaining its decision in *Hawkins v. United States* to permit both spouses to claim the privilege, the Supreme Court had taken a different view of marital squabbles. The Justices offered the fatherly wisdom that "not all marital flare-ups in which one spouse wants to hurt the other are permanent." 358 U.S. 74, 77 (1958).

Of course, those marital flare-ups in which one spouse wants to put the other in prison may be more permanent than most. In any event, it is clear that something changed the Court's outlook between *Hawkins* and *Trammel*. Perhaps the Justices' newly sanguine view of marital breakups reflected the increasing frequency and decreasing stigma of divorce in American society. Or perhaps, as Justice Stewart suspected, the Court's change of heart said more about the Court than it did about American culture: "[T]here is reason to believe that today's opinion . . . will be of greater interest to students of human psychology than to students of law." *Trammel*, 445 U.S. at 54 (Stewart, J., concurring in the judgment).

Beyond the question of who may claim it, the spousal testimonial privilege takes more or less the same form from jurisdiction to jurisdiction. Whether the privilege belongs to the witness-spouse or the defendant-spouse, it may be asserted only during the marriage. In most jurisdictions, persons who are now married may assert the privilege as to events that took place before the marriage. Proposed Rule 505(c)(2), however, would have restricted the privilege to events that occurred during the marriage. As the advisory committee explained, "[t]his provision eliminates the possibility of suppressing testimony by marrying the witness." (RB 354.)

Although in many states, including California, Michigan, and Pennsylvania, the privilege applies in both criminal and civil proceedings, in most states and in federal courts it seems to apply only in criminal cases, including grand jury proceedings. *See* MUELLER & KIRKPATRICK, *supra*, § 5.31, at 411; Pamela A. Haun, *The Marital Privilege in the Twenty–First Century*, 32 U. MEM. L. REV. 137, 158 nn.148–149 (2001) (listing jurisdictions). And it applies only in those criminal proceedings in which one spouse is the defendant. Moreover, the spousal testimonial privilege usually bars only *adverse* testimony. When a criminal defendant seeks favorable testimony from a spouse, the spouse usually has no testimonial privilege to refuse.

Some courts—though not most—refuse to recognize the privilege in cases involving crimes committed jointly by the two spouses. *See* MUELLER & KIRKPATRICK, *supra*, § 5.31, at 415–16. In most jurisdictions, the privilege does not apply in cases "in which one spouse is charged with a crime against the person or property of the other or of a child of either." Proposed FRE 505(c)(1); *see Trammel*, page 1047 n.7; Cassidy, *supra*, at 367–68 & nn.206–207. As one court reasoned, though it is true that one spouse's testimony against the other endangers family peace, "a serious crime against a child is an offense against that family harmony and to society as well." *United States v. Allery*, 526 F.2d 1362, 1366 (8th Cir. 1975).

The Marital Confidences Privilege

In its traditional form, the marital confidences privilege permits either spouse to refuse to reveal—and to prevent the other from revealing—confidential communications made between the spouses during their marriage. Aided perhaps by its analogy to the lawyer–client privilege, which also exalts confidential communications, the marital confidences privilege has rarely attracted the sort of ridicule sometimes aimed at the spousal testimonial privilege. As one group of experts concluded in 1853, the two privileges stand on "very different ground":

> So much of the happiness of human life may fairly be said to depend on the inviolability of domestic confidence that the alarm and unhappiness occasioned to society by invading its sanctity and compelling the public disclosures of confidential communications between husband and wife would be far a greater evil than the disadvantages which may occasionally arise from the loss of light which such revelations might throw on questions in dispute.

COMM'RS ON COMMON LAW PROCEDURE, SECOND REPORT 13 (1853), *quoted in* 8 WIGMORE, *supra*, § 2332, at 636.

In some respects, as Mueller and Kirkpatrick note, the marital confidences privilege has a narrower scope than the testimonial privilege. The marital confidences privilege protects only confidential communications between spouses. It does not, as does the testimonial privilege, authorize either spouse to refuse to testify against the other, nor does it enable either spouse to bar the other from testifying adversely. But in several ways, the marital confidences privilege is broader than the testimonial privilege. In federal and most state courts, it applies in both criminal and civil cases. It applies even if neither spouse is a party. And even if the marriage ends, the privilege continues to protect confidential communications that took place during the marriage. *See* MUELLER & KIRKPATRICK, *supra*, §§ 5.31–5.32, at 411–13, 416, 419; Cassidy, *supra*, at 366 & nn.199–202; *Pereira v. United States*, 347 U.S. 1, 6 (1954).

In most jurisdictions, the privilege protects only *communications*. It extends to communicative conduct, but not to one spouse's observations of the other's appearance or noncommunicative conduct. *See* MUELLER & KIRKPATRICK, *supra*, § 5.32, at 416, 419–20. Moreover, the privilege protects only *confidential* communications. At federal common law, "marital communications are presumptively confidential." *Blau v. United States*, 340 U.S. 332, 333 (1951). But this presumption may be rebutted by evidence that communications were "obviously not intended to be confidential." *Wolfle v. United States*, 291 U.S. 7, 14 (1934). Hence the privilege generally does not extend to statements made in the presence of a third person or in the expectation that they would be shared with others. Communications in front of *young* children may be deemed confidential. And the privilege protects only confidential *marital* communications. This is a temporal—not a subject-matter—limitation. The marital confidences privilege protects *any* confidential communication made between spouses during their marriage. It does not protect communications that took place before or after the marriage. *See* MUELLER & KIRKPATRICK, *supra*, § 5.32, at 419, 420–21.

A few jurisdictions grant the privilege exclusively to the communicator-spouse and extend no privilege to the listener-spouse. *See id.* at 401–02 (disapproving the minority rule); Cassidy, *supra*, at 366 & n. 203. Although the Supreme Court has not directly addressed this issue, it has upheld a claim of privilege made by a listener-spouse—"[w]e have no doubt that he was entitled to claim his privilege"—suggesting that the Court would permit either spouse to claim the privilege and to bar the other from revealing marital confidences. *Blau*, 340 U.S. at 333–34; *accord United States v. Montgomery*, 384 F.3d 1050, 1058–59 & n.1 (9th Cir. 2004) (citing dicta from the First, Third, Fourth, Sixth, Seventh, Eighth, and Tenth Circuits as well as the laws of thirty-three states suggesting that even the listener-spouse may assert the privilege).

Almost all federal circuit courts refuse to extend the privilege to communications concerning ongoing or future crimes committed jointly by the spouses. *See* MUELLER & KIRKPATRICK, *supra*, § 5.32, at 421–22. And some courts have refused to enforce the privilege when it would prevent criminal defendants from presenting evidence in their defense. (*See* pages 972–73, above.)

In federal and most state courts, the marital confidences privilege does not apply in cases in which one spouse is charged with an offense against the person or property of the other or a child of either. *See Trammel*, page 1047 n.7; Cassidy, *supra*, at 368 & n.213. In 2006, as part of the Adam Walsh Child Protection and Safety Act, Congress ordered a study of the "desirability of amending the Federal Rules of Evidence to provide that the confidential marital communications privilege and the adverse spousal privilege shall be inapplicable" in federal prosecutions of a spouse for a crime against a child of either spouse. Pub. L. No. 109–248, § 214, 120 Stat. 587, 617 (July 27, 2006). The evidence advisory committee recommended against any such amendment. None is needed, the committee reasoned, as there is only one reported federal case involving a crime against a spouse's child in which a court upheld a marital privilege claim. And the court in that case, *United States v. Jarvison*, 409 F.3d 1221 (10th Cir. 2005), ruled "without actually analyzing the issue . . . and without citing or recognizing two previous cases with the opposite result, including a case in its own circuit." Judicial Conference Committee on Rules of Practice and Procedure, *Report on the Necessity and Desirability of Amending the Federal Rules of Evidence to Codify a "Harm to Child" Exception to the Marital Privileges* (June 15, 2007).

As you know, the Proposed Federal Rules of Evidence omitted a privilege for marital confidences. (See the Advisory Committee's Note, RB 353, for an explanation.) Nonetheless, as the *Trammel* Court noted, such a privilege survives at federal common law as it does in the law of every state. *See Trammel*, page 1046 n.5. Professor Charles Black's worst fear therefore never came to pass—that "however intimate, however private, however embarrassing may be a disclosure by one spouse to another, . . . that disclosure or fact can be wrung from the spouse under penalty of being held in contempt of court, if it is thought barely relevant to the issues in anybody's lawsuit for breach of contract to sell a carload of apples." Charles L. Black, Jr., *Marital and Physician Privileges—A Reprint of a Letter to a Congressman*, 1975 DUKE L.J. 45, 48.

---

2. THE MARITAL CONFIDENCES PRIVILEGE

Problem 13.1
Office Emails

Philip Etkin, a New York State Police (NYSP) investigator, faced trial on a federal extortion charge. He brought a pretrial motion *in limine* to bar the prosecution from introducing an email Etkin wrote to his wife. Police seized a printout of the email from Etkin's car at the time of his arrest. Etkin argued that the email is a privileged marital communication.

The prosecution alleged that this text from the email showed Etkin's intent to commit extortion:

> Also on another note, i finally got "T" last night. Hes now in jail for parole violation. I had a talk with him last night and told him to deliver by no later than March 31, a brand new PSP to the Sheriff Dept. He's facing a parole hearing on 4/6, and if he doesnt come through, he's done and will go by by for 3 yrs on parole violation alone. Lets see what happens dont tell evan, just in case it doesnt come through, but im sure it will.

The government offered evidence that Etkin sent the email from his work computer, owned by the NYSP. A flash-screen notice appeared each time Etkin logged on to his work computer:

> For authorized use only. The system and all data are the property of the New York State Police.... Any use of the NYSP computer systems constitutes express consent for the authorized personnel to monitor, intercept, record, read, copy, access and capture such information for use or disclosure without additional prior notice. Users have no legitimate expectation of privacy during any use of this system or in any data on this system.... By logging into this system, you are agreeing that you have read, and accepted the above terms and conditions.

To continue past this notice, a user had to click on "OK" or hit "Enter." There was no evidence authorities in fact monitored office email, and the defendant claimed he never read the disclosure. *United States v. Etkin* (S.D.N.Y., No. 07–CR–913, Feb. 20, 2008).

Was the email a privileged marital communication? What are Etkin's and the prosecution's best arguments? Would the result be different if Etkin's wife sought to bar admission of the email against her husband on the grounds that its disclosure would violate her marital confidences privilege?

Problem 13.2

Kitchen Counter Note

James Montgomery and his sister, Mary Lou O'Connor, were charged in federal court with mail fraud and a related conspiracy. The alleged fraud took form after O'Connor joined Montgomery and his wife, Louise, at the family's property-management business. Louise Montgomery suspected that O'Connor was defrauding property owners of their legitimate rental income. The court of appeals described the consequence:

> . . . [Louise Montgomery] expressed her concerns in a [handwritten] letter she left for [her husband] on the kitchen counter of their residence. She wrote that she would not "be part of a dishonest operation," would not prepare owners' statements unless his "sister stops stealing," and would not solicit new owners because they "will probably be cheated." . . .
>
> [T]he letter begins, "Dear Jimmy," and ends, "Love, Louise." . . . The letter states, "If you can't stop [O'Connor] or if we can't stop her together I am going to write to her or talk to her."

Later Louise Montgomery joined the conspiracy and began omitting one-night rentals from property owners' statements, denying them overnight rental income. Still later, IRS agents lawfully searched the Montgomery residence, which James and Louise shared with their children, and seized the letter from the couple's bedroom. *United States v. Montgomery*, 384 F.3d 1050, 1053–57 (9th Cir. 2004).

Louise Montgomery agreed to cooperate with the government and testify against her husband and O'Connor. At his trial, James Montgomery objected to admission of the letter, which the prosecution offered to prove James's knowledge of O'Connor's fraudulent conduct. How should the trial court have ruled on James Montgomery's claim that the letter was a privileged marital communication?

UNITED STATES V. RAKES

136 F.3d 1 (1st Cir. 1998).

■ BOUDIN, CIRCUIT JUDGE. . . . Stephen and Julie Rakes were married in 1978 and engaged in various business ventures together. In 1983, with the help of their attorney, John Sullivan, the Rakes couple established a corporation named Stippo's, Inc., as their jointly owned company to operate a liquor store business at a site on Old Colony Avenue in South Boston. The store opened shortly before Christmas 1983.

The government believes that not long thereafter, the Rakeses were threatened by unnamed people in South Boston who were angry that the Rakeses were underpricing competitors. Then, in early January 1984, the government believes that James "Whitey" Bulger visited Stephen Rakes at home while Julie was at the liquor store and threatened to kill Stephen unless Bulger or his associates were made partners in the liquor store. By May 1984, again with the assistance of Sullivan, the Rakeses had transferred Stippo's, Inc., to another individual, who[] the government believes was associated with Bulger, for a fraction of what the government says was its real value.

In May 1991, the government summoned Stephen Rakes before a federal grand jury in Massachusetts investigating extortion, racketeering and money laundering. The government questioned Rakes about the transfer of Stippo's, Inc., to the alleged Bulger associate. Rakes testified that he had sold the store to make a profit and because it was too much work, and said that no one had threatened him to make him sell the store. In September 1995, Stephen Rakes gave similar testimony before a second federal grand jury....

In May 1996, the grand jury indicted Stephen Rakes, charging him with five counts of perjury based on his grand jury testimony and two counts of obstruction of justice....

Asserting the privilege for confidential marital communications, Stephen Rakes moved [before trial] to suppress evidence of conversations in December 1983 and January 1984 between him and Julie Rakes [from whom he is now divorced] concerning alleged threats and the sale of Stippo's....

In April 1997, the district court granted Stephen Rakes' motion with one exception: it denied the motion as to one conversation between Stephen and Julie Rakes, apparently because it took place in the presence of a third party.... The government then brought this interlocutory appeal.

We will assume *arguendo* the relevance of the suppressed conversations to the government's prosecution. At the same time, most of the formal requisites for the ... marital communications privilege[] are clearly met; the government's main claim is that the [privilege was] waived or forfeited. In a federal criminal case, privileges take their content from the common law as it may be altered from time to time in the light of reason and experience. FED. R. EVID. 501.

No brief version of ... the marital communications ... privilege can be both complete and accurate. But, broadly stated and subject to exceptions, the . . . privilege permits an individual to refuse to testify, and to prevent a spouse or former spouse from testifying, as to any confidential communication made by the individual to the spouse during their marriage.[2] . . .

The communications suppressed by the district court between Stephen and Julie Rakes were made in the absence of third parties and in the course of their marriage; that the Rakeses later divorced is irrelevant, and the government properly makes nothing of the possibility that one of the conversations occurred in the presence of their infant children. . . .

Both the content and context of the communications support the implicit finding by the district judge that Rakes intended his conversations . . . with his wife . . . to be confidential. Further, if Stephen Rakes had been threatened, as the government alleges, he had ample reason over and above any ordinary interest in privacy to want them to be kept confidential. We reserve for discussion below the government's claim that later disclosures by Stephen Rakes undermine the claim of confidentiality.

The government suggests that some general rule deprives spousal conversations of the privilege if they relate to financial matters. . . . The marital communications privilege contains no such limitation: the cases say, at most, that a discussion of financial matters between husband and wife may not be intended to be confidential. In this case, however, the subject was manifestly sensitive, albeit not for the usual reasons.

Nor do we agree with the government's suggestion that communications were not privileged insofar as Stephen Rakes may have been relating to his wife events that occurred prior to the communication. It is true that "communications" privileges typically prevent inquiry into communications and not into the underlying facts, Upjohn Co. v. United States, 449 U.S. 383, 395–96 (1981), although the subject is more complicated than this generalization suggests.[4] But the district court's suppression order was directed to communications, not to facts, and that is enough for present purposes.

This brings us to the main thrust of the government's argument, namely, that "the suppressed communications are not privileged because they occurred during an ongoing extortion scheme." A crime of extortion, says the government, extends from the initial threat through the actual obtaining of the property. Here, the government says that the crime extended from the first alleged threat in December 1983 through the

2. The separate marital privilege—to refuse to testify against a spouse in a criminal case—is not pertinent here. Trammel v. United States, 445 U.S. 40 (1980).

4. Where an attorney knows facts only because they were confidentially communicated by the client, the government cannot circumvent the privilege by asking the attorney about "the facts." *See* Upjohn Co. v. United States, 449 U.S. 383, 395 (1981). The same rule applies to the marital communications privilege.

completion of the property transfer in May 1984, a period embracing all but one of the communications that the government seeks to use.

No general rule withdraws the privilege from communications that occur in the same time frame as criminal act conduct. But [the marital confidences privilege is] subject to some type of crime-fraud exception.... [I]t is expressed in somewhat different terms in different jurisdictions.[5] However, we will assume for present purposes—favorably to the government—that the privilege for marital communications would be lost to Stephen Rakes if he made the communications in question to Julie for the purpose of carrying out a crime.

The government concedes that Stephen and Julie Rakes were the "victims" of an extortion scheme. But to invoke the crime-fraud exception, the government also says ... that "the communications suppressed by the District Court occurred while the Rakeses were participating in carrying out the [extortion] scheme and covering it up, and while Stephen was persuading Julie to do so." This, says the government, entails loss of the privilege.

Yet, on the government's own version of events, the Rakeses were not participants in the extortion in any capacity other than that of victim. The Rakeses were participants only in the very specialized sense that the victim of a robbery "participates" by handing over his wallet under threat of violence, or the victim of a rape "participates" by offering no further resistance when resistance appears futile or dangerous. This is not the kind of participation in an offense that, in our view, vitiates the privilege.

It is no accident that the government's case law is remote from the present facts and consists of cases where one spouse enlisted a second spouse in a criminal venture, or a wife knowingly assisted a husband in criminal conduct. Here, even the government shrinks from flatly asserting that the Rakeses were criminally liable for extortion.

We have considered the government's further suggestion that Stephen Rakes engaged in misconduct by inducing his wife not to report the threat against him. It is enough to say that the fragments of evidence cited do not even approach misprision of felony or accessory after the fact. The government's theory would make a criminal of anyone who, as the victim of a crime or faced with a criminal threat, resisted a spousal suggestion that the police be called.

The government's underlying notion may be that the privilege is lost for any communication that plays a functional role in a crime—regardless of whether the parties to the communication are entirely innocent and otherwise protected by the privilege. On this view, the parents of a kidnapped child could be compelled to testify after the event about their

5. In federal courts, the marital communications privilege typically is forfeited only where both husband and wife are jointly engaged in criminal activity or where the victim is the other spouse or some other family member.

intimate conversations with each other concerning the kidnapping and possible payment of a demanded ransom. It is not an attractive picture, and it is hard to believe that the suggestion is seriously intended.

In all events, it is not the law. Under the crime-fraud exception, we think that it takes wrongful complicity by the privilege holder, not innocent or involuntary action, to forfeit the privilege. This is so even though, as with many applications of privilege, law enforcement may be hampered in the interest of other values. The victims of kidnapping or extortion have problems enough; loss of otherwise applicable privileges is not part of the package.

The government's remaining argument is that Stephen Rakes himself disclosed the alleged threats to others, most importantly, to one Brian Burke. According to the government, Rakes had promised to pay Burke for construction and related work on the liquor store and owed him a substantial sum. When in early 1984 Burke called about the debt, the government says that Rakes told Burke in dramatic terms that he (Rakes) had been forced out of the business. This, says the government, shows that the information was never confidential, and, in any event, the disclosure waived the privilege.

The disclosure to Burke is weak, and to us wholly unpersuasive, evidence that the communications suppressed by the district court were never intended to be confidential. For reasons already indicated, there is every reason to think Stephen Rakes' conversations with Julie Rakes ... were intended to be confidential. The limited disclosure to Burke, however dramatic, was obviously made to ward off a debt collection effort and not because Stephen Rakes had any interest in broadcasting information that might endanger his life.

The waiver issue is more complicated. Ordinarily, deliberate disclosure of a privileged communication, where no privilege protects this further disclosure, waives a communications privilege. The restriction is directed against selective disclosures by reserving protection for only those communications that the privilege holder himself is prepared to keep confidential. The restriction is one of public policy, and applies regardless of the privilege holder's subjective intent [regarding the scope of waiver].

As already noted, the privileged communication and the facts recounted within it are two different things. *Upjohn*, 449 U.S. at 395. Thus, a client does not normally lose the privilege as to communications with his attorney merely because he testifies at trial to the same events discussed with his lawyer. Here, there is no suggestion that Stephen Rakes ever told Burke or anyone else about his communications with Julie....

... We ... agree with the district court that the suppressed communications were originally privileged, and that there was no later loss of the privilege as claimed by the government.

The government's arguments are, as is usual in this district, presented with skill, and its zeal to pursue an alleged extortionist is understandable. But skill and zeal are to be harnessed by common sense. The notion that the Rakeses could properly be treated as participating in their own extortion is Orwellian. An appeal for which such a proposition had to be the linchpin ought never to have been brought.

Affirmed.

Problem 13.3

Poisoned Deadstock

Brian Lea owned a "deadstock" (or dead animal) removal business. For many years, he did business with National By–Products (NBP), which produced animal food from Lea's deadstock. In 1996 NBP started its own deadstock collection business, which eventually drove Lea into bankruptcy. The court of appeals reported what happened next:*

> On December 28, 1996, the Berlin Police Department received an anonymous letter ... recounting an act of sabotage against the NBP Berlin plant. Enclosed with the letter was a sample of the contaminant used by the perpetrator [to contaminate NBP's deadstock]....
>
> [T]he investigation into the contamination initially focused on former NBP employees. On January 15, 1997, one such individual, Barry Werch, was questioned by the United States Food and Drug Administration ("FDA") agent handling the matter. In that interview, Werch described the working conditions at NBP, relating that giant ants crawled from the ceiling of the NBP plant....
>
> On May 14, 1997, a second letter was received by the Berlin Police Department in which the author claimed responsibility for an additional contamination of NBP materials. That message [complained that] ... "giant ants crawl the walls and ceilings [of the NBP plant] and the stench is so bad that you can cut it with a knife." ...
>
> On January 30, 1997, Heidi Werch met with Agent Hejny of the FDA.... Heidi recalled to the agent that one day during the course of their marriage, Barry had ... informed Heidi that a grinder at the plant had broken down

* [I've altered the facts somewhat to make them slightly less nauseating.—GF]

and that he had been required to go in and fix it. While inside the grinder, Barry said, there were giant ants dropping all over him.

[Lea was eventually indicted and charged with poisoning NBP's deadstock. The theory of his defense was that Barry Werch was the saboteur.] At trial, Lea sought to call Heidi to testify to the statements made by Barry concerning the giant ants at the NBP plant. . . . Barry Werch's counsel invoked the marital communications privilege, and the court instructed Heidi not to respond to any of Lea's questions. Lea [was convicted and] argues on appeal that the decision of the district court to allow Barry Werch to invoke that privilege was in error. Lea asserts that Barry Werch waived the privilege during an interview with the FDA, wherein he mentioned giant ants at the NBP plant. . . .

Is Lea right that Werch waived his marital communications privilege by telling the FDA agent about conditions at the plant? What are Lea's strongest arguments that Werch should not have been allowed to prevent his ex-wife's disclosure of their conversation? How should the court rule? *See United States v. Lea*, 249 F.3d 632 (7th Cir. 2001).

B. A PARENT-CHILD PRIVILEGE?

IN RE GRAND JURY PROCEEDINGS

103 F.3d 1140 (3d Cir.), *cert. denied*, 520 U.S. 1253 (1997).

■ GARTH, CIRCUIT JUDGE: Three appeals presenting the same critical issue are before us. One appeal originated in the District Court of the Virgin Islands. . . . The other two appeals pertaining to the same Delaware defendant originated in the District Court of Delaware. . . . [T]hey raise[] the same question—should this court recognize a parent–child privilege? . . .

I.

. . . In the Virgin Islands case, the grand jury sitting in St. Croix subpoenaed the father of the target of the grand jury investigation as a witness. . . . At the time of the alleged transactions [being investigated by the grand jury], the son was eighteen years old.

. . . The father, a former FBI agent, lived with his wife and son in St. Croix. On April 17, 1995, based on his belief that the grand jury intended to question him about conversations that he had had with his son, the father moved to quash the subpoena, asserting that those conversations were privileged from disclosure under Fed. R. Evid. 501.

The father testified, at a hearing before the district court, that he and his son "had an excellent relationship, very close, very loving relationship." He further testified that if he were coerced into testifying against his son, "[their] relationship would dramatically change and the closeness that [they] have would end. . . ." . . .

> I will be living under a cloud in which if my son comes to me or talks to me, I've got to be very careful what he says, what I allow him to say. I would have to stop him and say, "you can't talk to me about that. You've got to talk to your attorney." . . .

On June 19, 1995, the district court entered its order denying the father's motion to quash. . . .

. . . In the Delaware case, a sixteen-year-old minor daughter was subpoenaed to testify before the grand jury, as part of an investigation into her father's participation in an alleged interstate kidnapping of a woman who had disappeared. . . . [A] motion to quash subpoena was made by counsel for the daughter and her mother, as well as by separate counsel for the father.

The motion sought to bar the testimony of the daughter claiming a parent–child privilege. . . . "The privilege [was] claimed for confidential communications as well as for protection against being compelled to testify in a criminal proceeding."

The district court [denied] the motion to quash and order[ed] the minor daughter to testify before the grand jury. . . . Pursuant to the court order, the daughter appeared at court (in an ante-room to the grand jury courtroom) in the evening of September 10, 1995. She refused to testify and was found in contempt. The district court then stayed the imposition of sanctions during the pendency of these appeals. . . .

III.

. . . Appellants argue that recognition [of a parent–child privilege] is necessary in order to advance important public policy interests such as the protection of strong and trusting parent–child relationships; the preservation of the family; safeguarding of privacy interests and protection from harmful government intrusion; and the promotion of healthy psychological development of children. . . .

Although legal academicians appear to favor adoption of a parent–child testimonial privilege, no federal Court of Appeals and no state supreme court has recognized such a privilege. We too decline to recognize such a privilege for the following reasons:

(1) The overwhelming majority of all courts—federal or state—have rejected such a privilege.

(a) Eight federal Courts of Appeals have rejected such a privilege and none of the remaining Courts of Appeals have recognized such a privilege.

(b) Every state supreme court that has addressed the issue has rejected the privilege, and only four states have protected parent–child communications in some manner.[13] . . . *

(2) No reasoned analysis of Federal Rule of Evidence 501 or of the standards established by the Supreme Court or by this court supports the creation of a privilege.

(3) Creation of such a privilege would have no impact on the parental relationship and hence would neither benefit that relationship nor serve any social policy.

(4) Although we have the authority to recognize a new privilege, we believe the recognition of such a privilege, if one is to be recognized, should be left to Congress. . . .[15]

B. The Standards Prescribed by Federal Rule of Evidence 501 Do Not Support the Creation of a Privilege.

. . . It is true that Congress, in enacting Fed. R. Evid. 501, "manifested an affirmative intention not to freeze the law of privilege. Its purpose rather was to 'provide the courts with the flexibility to develop rules of privilege on a case-by-case basis,' and to leave the door open to change." Trammel v. United States, 445 U.S. 40, 47 (1980). . . . [But] we are admonished that privileges are generally disfavored; that " 'the public . . . has a right to every man's evidence' "; and that privileges are tolerable "only to the very limited extent that permitting a refusal to testify or excluding relevant evidence has a public good transcending the normally predominant principle of utilizing all rational means for ascertaining truth." *Trammel*, 445 U.S. at 47 (internal quotation omitted).

In keeping with these principles, the Supreme Court has rarely expanded common-law testimonial privileges.[19] Following the Supreme

13. . . . Idaho and Minnesota are the only states which have recognized a variant of the parent–child privilege through statute. It is important to note that neither statute is rooted in the common law.

Massachusetts law prevents a minor child from testifying against a parent in a criminal proceeding. However, the . . . Massachusetts statute does not create a testimonial privilege; rather it is best described as a witness-disqualification rule. . . .

* [Connecticut has joined the short list of states with statutory privileges, granting a parent or guardian of an accused juvenile a privilege not to testify unless the case concerns the child's violence against the parent or guardian. *See* CONN. GEN. STAT. § 46b–138a (2007); Hillary B. Farber, *Do You Swear to Tell the Truth, the Whole Truth, and Nothing but the Truth Against Your Child?*, 43 LOY. L.A. L. REV. 551, 554 n.8 (2010).—GF]

15. New York's inferior courts are the only state courts which have judicially recognized a parent–child privilege. The privilege so recognized is essentially derived from New York's constitution. The New York Appellate Division explained that the privilege it recognized was rooted in the constitutional right to privacy. *See* In re A & M, 403 N.Y.S.2d 375, 381 (App. Div. 1978). . . .

19. *See, e.g., Trammel*, 445 U.S. at 53 (narrowing husband–wife privilege and

Court's teachings, other federal courts, including this court, have likewise declined to exercise their power under Rule 501 expansively.

C. Creating a Parent–Child Privilege Would Be Inconsistent with the Teachings of the Supreme Court and of This Court.

1. *Supreme Court*

... The *Jaffee* Court ... instructed that a federal court should look to the "experience" of state courts.... Notably, in recognizing a psychotherapist–patient privilege, the Supreme Court relied on the fact that all fifty states had enacted some form of a psychotherapist privilege.... Here, by contrast, only four states have deemed it necessary to protect from disclosure, in any manner, confidential communications between children and their parents....

The *Jaffee* Court also relied on the fact that the psychotherapist–patient privilege was among the nine specific privileges recommended by the Advisory Committee on Rules of Evidence in 1972.... [T]he parent–child privilege ... was not....

2. *Third Circuit*

... In In re Grand Jury Investigation, 918 F.2d 374 (3d Cir. 1990) (Becker, J.), we adopted a clergy–communicant privilege. We did so, however, only after examining the state and federal precedents addressing the issue of a clergy–communicant privilege and after determining that these precedents, on balance, weighed in favor of recognizing such a privilege.... Judge Becker, writing for a unanimous panel, noted that "virtually every state has recognized some form of a clergy–communicant privilege." *Id.* at 381 & n.10 (listing state statutes).

... Judge Becker then concluded that "the inclusion of the clergy–communicant privilege in the proposed [federal] rules ... strongly suggests that [the] privilege is, in the words of the Supreme Court, 'indelibly ensconced' in the American common law." Judge Becker also ... detailed ... the historical development of the clergy–communicant privilege, stressing that common-law tradition ... supported recognition of such a privilege.

In contrast, the parent–child privilege sought to be recognized here is of relatively recent vintage, *see* United States v. Ismail, 756 F.2d 1253,

holding that witness-spouse may testify over the objections of the other spouse); University of Pa. v. EEOC, 493 U.S. 182, 189 (1990) (declining to recognize a privilege for academic peer review proceedings); United States v. Arthur Young & Co., 465 U.S. 805, 817–19 (1984) (rejecting an accountant work-product privilege); United States v. Gillock, 445 U.S. 360, 367–68 (1980) (expressly refusing to recognize a privilege for state legislators in federal court); United States v. Nixon, 418 U.S. 683, 709 (1974) (rejecting [an absolute] privilege for confidential communications between the President and the President's high-level advisors); Couch v. United States, 409 U.S. 322, 335 (1973) (rejecting an accountant–client testimonial privilege).

1257–58 (6th Cir. 1985) ("The parent–child privilege did not exist at common law"), and is virtually no more than the product of legal academicians. . . .

Furthermore, an analysis of the four Wigmore factors, which Judge Becker used to buttress this court's disposition in *In re Grand Jury Investigation,* does not support the creation of a privilege. Dean Wigmore's four-factor formula requires satisfaction of all four factors in order to establish a privilege:

(1) The communications must originate in a *confidence* that they will not be disclosed.

(2) This element of *confidentiality must be essential* to the full and satisfactory maintenance of the relation between the parties.

(3) The *relation* must be one which in the opinion of the community ought to be sedulously *fostered.*

(4) The *injury* that would inure to the relation by the disclosure of the communications must be *greater than the benefit* thereby gained for the correct disposal of litigation.

At least two of Wigmore's prerequisite conditions for creation of a federal common-law privilege are not met under the facts of these cases. We refer to the second and fourth elements of the Wigmore test.

First, confidentiality—in the form of a testimonial privilege—is not essential to a successful parent–child relationship. . . . [I]t is not clear whether children would be more likely to discuss private matters with their parents if a parent–child privilege were recognized than if one were not. It is not likely that children, or even their parents, would typically be aware of the existence or non-existence of a testimonial privilege covering parent–child communications. On the other hand, professionals such as attorneys, doctors and members of the clergy would know of the privilege that attends their respective profession, and their clients, patients or parishioners would also be aware that their confidential conversations are protected from compelled disclosure.[21]

Moreover, even assuming *arguendo* that children and their parents generally are aware of whether or not their communications are protected from disclosure, . . . the existence . . . [of such a privilege] is probably one of the least important considerations in any child's decision as to whether

21. Notably, the Advisory Committee on the Rules of Evidence reached a similar conclusion with respect to a marital communications privilege. The Advisory Committee explained:

> [Proposed Rule 505] recognizes no privilege for confidential communications [between spouses]. . . . [It cannot] be assumed that marital conduct will be affected by a privilege for confidential communications of whose existence the parties in all likelihood are unaware. The other communication privileges, by way of contrast, have as one party a professional person who can be expected to inform the other of the existence of the privilege. [RB 353.]

to reveal some indiscretion, legal or illegal, to a parent. [And] it is unlikely that any parent would choose to deter a child from revealing a confidence to the parent solely because a federal court has refused to recognize a privilege protecting such communications from disclosure.

Finally, the proposed parent–child privilege fails to satisfy the fourth condition of the Wigmore test. As explained above, any injury to the parent–child relationship resulting from non-recognition of such a privilege would be relatively insignificant. In contrast, the cost of recognizing such a privilege is substantial: the impairment of the truth-seeking function of the judicial system and the increased likelihood of injustice resulting from the concealment of relevant information. . . .

An even more compelling reason for rejecting a parent–child privilege stems from . . . the unique duty owing to the child from the parent. A parent owes the duty to the child to nurture and guide the child. . . .

If, for example, a fifteen-year-old unemancipated child informs her parent that she has . . . been using or distributing narcotics, and this disclosure has been made in confidence while the child is seeking guidance, it is evident to us that, regardless of whether the child consents or not, the parent must have the right to take such action as the parent deems appropriate in the interest of the child. That action could be commitment to a drug rehabilitation center or a report of the crime to the juvenile authorities. This is so because, in theory at least, juvenile proceedings are undertaken solely in the interest of the child. We would regard it intolerable in such a situation if the law intruded in the guise of a privilege, and silenced the parent because the child had a privilege to prevent disclosure. . . .

In sum, neither historical tradition, nor common-law principles, nor Wigmore formulations, nor the logic of privileges, nor the "reason and experience" of the various states supports creation of a parent–child privilege.

D. Recognition of a Parent–Child Privilege Should Be Left to Congress.

Although we, and our sister courts, obviously have authority to develop and modify the common law of privileges, we should be circumspect about creating new privileges based upon perceived public policy considerations. This is particularly so where there exist policy concerns which the legislative branch is better equipped to evaluate. To paraphrase Justice Scalia, writing in dissent in *Jaffee*, and referring to the psychotherapist privilege:

> The question before us today is not whether there should be an evidentiary privilege for [parent–child communications]. Perhaps there should. But the question before us is whether (1) the need for that privilege is so clear, and (2) the desirable contours of that

> privilege are so evident, that it is appropriate for this court to craft it in common law fashion, under Rule 501.

Jaffee v. Redmond, 116 S. Ct. 1923, 1940 (1996) (Scalia, J. dissenting).

The legislature, not the judiciary, is institutionally better equipped to perform the balancing of the competing policy issues required in deciding whether the recognition of a parent–child privilege is in the best interests of society. Congress ... is also better suited for the task of defining the scope of any prospective privilege. Congress is able to consider, for example, society's moral, sociological, economic, religious and other values without being confined to the evidentiary record in any particular case.... These considerations are also relevant to determining whether the privilege, if it is to be recognized, should extend to adult children....

Among additional factors that Congress could consider are ... [whether] "parent" [should] include step-parent or grand-parent? ... Should the privilege extend to siblings? Furthermore, if another family member is present at the time of the relevant communication, is the privilege automatically barred or destroyed? ...

V.

In short, if a new privilege is deemed worthy of recognition, the wiser course in our opinion is to leave the adoption of such a privilege to Congress....

■ MANSMANN, J., concurring and dissenting. I write separately because I am convinced that the testimonial privilege issue raised by the Virgin Islands appeal is substantially different from that presented in the Delaware appeals[28] and should be resolved in favor of the targeted son. The Virgin Islands appeal ... requires that we confront an issue of first impression in our circuit: should we make available to a parent and child an evidentiary privilege which could be invoked to prevent compelling that parent to testify regarding confidential communications made to the parent by his child in the course of seeking parental advice and guidance? It appears that this precise question is one of first impression in the federal courts....

I.

... I am convinced that this is an appropriate case in which to recognize and set parameters for a limited privilege. Doing so is critical to several important public policy interests such as the "protection of strong and trusting parent–child relationships and the preservation of the sanctity of the family...." The recognition of a parent–child privilege is

28. In the Virgin Islands appeal, a father has been subpoenaed to testify regarding communications made to him by his teenaged son. In the Delaware appeals, on the other hand, a teenaged daughter has been subpoenaed to give testimony, based on her own knowledge, which could implicate her father in a crime; confidential communications between parent and child are not alleged in the Delaware appeals....

essential to "the healthy psychological development of children and to the development of society as a whole"; compelling a parent to testify adversely to a child is "'repugnant to social sensibilities'...." Wendy Meredith Watts, *The Parent–Child Privilege: Hardly a New or Revolutionary Concept*, 28 Wm. & Mary L. Rev. 583, 611–13 (1987).

These and other related public policy arguments have been advanced in a spate of articles by academicians and other legal commentators who, virtually uniformly, favor incorporating a parent–child testimonial privilege into the fabric of the law. The courts, however, federal and state, have been reluctant to make these policy arguments the foundation for a "new" privilege. In the circumstances presented here, I do not share that reluctance....

II.

* * *

B.

... I stress that the privilege which I would recognize is a limited one, applying only to compelled testimony concerning confidential communications made to a parent by his child in the course of seeking parental advice.[32] Although this case might have been more compelling had the son been a minor at the time of his statements to his father, I would not adopt a bright-line rule applicable only to those who have not reached legal majority. In order to advance the policy interests which the targeted son articulated, I would prefer to leave the particular factors to be considered in determining application of the privilege to development on a case-by-case basis. I expect that these factors would include such variables as age, maturity, whether or not the child resides with the parents, and the precise nature of the communications for which the privilege is claimed. The privilege would apply to situations in which it is invoked by both parent and child; this case does not require that we confront applicability of the privilege where it is invoked by the parent or the child alone.

32. ... Dean Wigmore has suggested a four-part test for determining whether or not a particular testimonial privilege should be recognized.... [*See* page 1070 above.] I part company with the majority in the application of this test.... The first condition ... is satisfied in that the parent–child relationship is one which naturally gives rise to confidential communication. Second, confidentiality underlies the parent–child relationship; mutual trust encourages children to consult parents for guidance with the expectation that the parent will, in appropriate circumstances, honor the confidentiality of those statements. Third, the family unit is the building block of our society and the parent–child relationship is at the core of that family unit. Finally, ... I am convinced that the damage resulting from compelling a parent to testify against his child, in most if not all cases, outweighs the benefit associated with correct disposal of the litigation.

The goal in recognizing this limited privilege would not be to guarantee confidentiality per se but to shield parent–child relationships from the devastating effects likely to be associated with compelled testimony. As one commentator has written:

> To conceive of . . . privileges merely as exclusionary rules, is to start out on the wrong road and, except by happy accident, to reach the wrong destination. They are, or rather by chance of litigation may become, exclusionary rules; but this is incidental and secondary. Primarily they are a right to be let alone, a right to unfettered freedom, in certain narrowly prescribed relationships, from the state's coercive or supervisory powers. . . .

Louisell, *Confidentiality, Conformity, and Confusions: Privileges in Federal Court Today*, 31 TUL. L. REV. 101, 110–11 (1956). An effective parent–child relationship . . . [is one] of mutual trust where the child has the right to expect that the parent will act in accordance with the child's best interest.[33] If the state is permitted to interfere in that relationship by compelling parents to divulge information conveyed to them in confidence by their children, mutual trust, and ultimately the family, are threatened.

While I am aware that the availability of even this limited parent–child privilege may, in some rare circumstances, complicate a criminal fact-finding proceeding, I am convinced that the risk is one well worth bearing. . . . This is especially true where, as here in the Virgin Islands case, the parent is not a co-defendant or a co-witness to a criminal act, and is not alleged to be hiding the instrumentality or the fruits of a criminal act.

. . . I am convinced, as was the district court, that "youngsters today are increasingly faced with excruciatingly dangerous and difficult situations" and that "the law ought to do everything possible to encourage children to confide in their parents and turn to [them] in times of trouble."

C.

The spousal privilege is the only testimonial privilege based on a familial relationship to have received general acceptance in the federal

33. While it is true, as the majority says, that few children are likely to be aware of a privilege per se, there is, in any event, a certain expectation that this information will not be disclosed.

As the majority points out, there may be circumstances in which a parent, having heard communications from a child, decides that it is in the child's best interest that those communications be divulged. The privilege which I advocate would not interfere with that parental judgment. Presumably, if the parent is indeed acting in the child's best interest, disclosure will not ultimately threaten the family relationship which I seek to protect. Furthermore, if the parent is willing to disclose information which may harm the child, the relationship is already beyond the need for protection.

courts. In arguing that we should uphold the father's claim of privilege in this case, I am motivated by many of the same concerns which underlie the spousal privilege.[35] ...

> Ideally, the child–parent relationship encompasses aspects of the marital relationship—mutual love, affection, and intimacy ..., the parent providing emotional guidance and the child relying on him for help and support.... As in the marital ... relationship, this optimal child–parent relationship cannot exist without a great deal of communication between the two....

Comment, *The Child–Parent Privilege: A Proposal,* 47 FORDHAM L. REV. 771, 781 (1979)....

D.

The parent–child privilege is not a novel or radical concept. "Both ancient Jewish law and Roman law entirely barred family members from testifying against one another based on a desire to promote the solidarity and trust that support the family unit. The Napoleonic Code also prevented the disclosure of confidences between family members." The civil law countries of Western Europe including France, Sweden, and the former West Germany also recognize a privilege covering compelled testimony from family members.

Three states (Idaho, Massachusetts and Minnesota) have adopted some variant of the parent–child privilege by statute,[37] and one state,

35. Some commentators have sought to analogize the parent–child privilege to the more widely recognized professional testimonial privileges such as that between attorney and client, priest and penitent, and physician and patient:

> ... As the professional exercises his skill in the delicate relationship with his client, the parent plays a unique and sensitive role in the life of his "client," the child. In fulfilling this role, the parent must assume many of the same responsibilities as professionals. The parent, for example, often must serve as the child's legal advisor, spiritual counselor, and physical and emotional health expert. The necessity for confidentiality is comparable to that within the professional relationships. Like the attorney, priest, or psychiatrist, parents must establish an atmosphere of trust to facilitate free and open communication.

Gregory W. Franklin, Note, *The Judicial Development of the Parent–Child Testimonial Privilege: Too Big for Its Britches?* 26 WM. & MARY L. REV. 145, 151 (1984).

37. The Idaho statute limits the privilege to communications by minors to their parents. It provides in relevant part:

> Any parent, guardian or legal custodian shall not be forced to disclose any communication made by their minor child or ward to them concerning matters in any civil or criminal action to which such child or ward is a party. Such matters so communicated shall be privileged and protected against disclosure....

Idaho Code § 9-203(7) (1990 & Supp. 1995)....

Minnesota also recognizes a limited parent–child (minor) privilege:

> A parent or the parent's minor child may not be examined as to any communication made in confidence by the minor to the minor's parent. A communication is confidential if made

New York, has judicially recognized the privilege. Furthermore, our review of the caselaw convinces us that although a number of courts have declined to recognize a parent–child privilege in one form or another, the vast majority of those cases, indeed all of the federal cases, are distinguishable, on significant grounds, from the case before us.

Most cases discussing the availability of a parent–child privilege have done so in the context of whether a child should be compelled to testify against a parent. As the court of appeals acknowledged in In re Grand Jury Proceedings (Starr), 647 F.2d 511, 513 n. 4 (5th Cir. 1981), cases involving testimony by a child regarding activities of or communications by a parent are not as compelling as cases "involving confidential communications from the child to the parent" because the former do not implicate "the desire to avoid discouraging a child from confiding in his parents." A similar theme is echoed in Three Juveniles v. Commonwealth, 390 Mass. 357 (1983), *cert. denied sub nom* Keefe v. Massachusetts, 465 U.S. 1068 (1984): "Because a parent does not need the advice of a minor child in the same sense that a child may need the advice of a parent, the case for a testimonial privilege as to confidential communications from parent to child seems weaker...." This distinction separates the Virgin Islands and Delaware appeals.

A second set of cases refusing to recognize a parent–child privilege involve children who were significantly older than the son in this case and did not implicate communications seeking parental advice and guidance.... Finally, a number of cases rejecting the parent–child privilege involved defendants who sought to bar voluntary testimony offered by their parents. These cases do not present the threat to the family relationship posed in the case before us....

IV.

I am convinced that the public good to be derived from a circumscribed parent–child testimonial privilege outweighs the judicial system's interest in compelled parental testimony. I would, therefore, recognize a privilege which could be invoked by a parent and child together to bar compelled testimony concerning confidential communications made to that parent by his child in the course of seeking parental advice and guidance....

out of the presence of persons not members of the child's immediate family living in the same household. Minn. Stat. § 595.02(1)(i) (1988 & Supp. 1996).

Conclusion

Evidence Law and Jury Mistrust

A familiar cliche is that evidence law expresses our mistrust of juries—that it serves to control and rationalize the otherwise untethered and irrational process of jury factfinding. Like most cliches, this one has some truth. How else can we explain, for example, the law's reluctance to trust jurors with emotionally freighted evidence? In *State v. Bocharski*, 22 P.3d 43 (Ariz. 2001), which we studied in Chapter 1, Justice Martone criticized the majority's apparent belief that we can't count on jurors to weigh gruesome photographs dispassionately: "I do not believe that jurors need to be protected from themselves. . . . I do not believe that we should be paternalistic with our jurors." 22 P.3d at 64 (Martone, J., concurring in the judgment) (pages 47–48, above). But Justice Martone wrote alone—the rest of the court apparently thought a dose of paternalism just right.

Several evidence doctrines betray similar mistrust of jurors' discernment and good sense:

> *Rule 404:* The bar against character evidence flags concern that jurors will either punish defendants for the wrong crime or assign too much weight to past acts when judging the defendant's guilt. Surely no judge would hire a law clerk or babysitter without checking character references. Yet judges worry that such references will lead a jury astray.
>
> *Rule 802:* The hearsay rule reveals suspicion that jurors cannot assess witnesses' truthfulness without facial cues and a lawyer's probing cross-examination. Though there are many exceptions to the hearsay ban, they rest not on episodic faith in jurors' lie-detecting skills, but on the theory that in some circumstances we can be fairly confident that the declarant told the truth.
>
> *Rule 702:* And the system's careful screening of expert testimony, commanded by Rule 702 as interpreted in *Daubert*, responds to fears that if judges do not act as gatekeepers, jurors will be at the mercy of quacks and charlatans, unable to distinguish true science from junk.

At bottom, with the possible exception of Rule 401 and the privilege rules, every rule we have studied could give rise to a theory of jury mistrust. And yet there is a competing theory. At the outset of the book, I suggested that evidence law may express the system's rather reckless *faith* in the jury. The Supreme Court's decision in *Tanner v. United States*, 483 U.S. 107 (1987) (page 8), reaffirmed a centuries-old rule generally banning juror testimony about shortcomings in the deliberation process. Evidence rules may be a necessary function of our traditional reluctance to oversee jury deliberations. Having no way to control what jurors do with the evidence we give them, we perhaps have to impose strict controls on the evidence itself.

The story is of course more complicated than either the no-faith or full-faith interpretation suggests. Evidence rules have not been static over the years, and the ways they have changed may reflect our changing assessment of jurors' fact-finding powers. In at least one area—the determination of witness credibility—the system's confidence in jurors surely has grown.

Consider what is probably the most striking difference between evidence law today and evidence law two centuries ago. At the turn of the nineteenth century, a strict code of competency rules barred all likely liars from the witness stand. Neither parties, nor spouses of parties, nor felons, nor atheists, nor anyone with a financial interest in the outcome could take an oath and testify before the jury. These rules rested at least in part on the belief that jurors could not be trusted to discern and disregard a liar.

Yet rule by rule, this cardhouse of competency rules came down. The last to go was the bar against testimony by criminal defendants, seen as the likeliest liars of all. In 1867, just as the first, daring American states opened their witness stands to the accused, one judicial observer predicted a "fearful and overpowering temptation to perjury." Seth Ames, *Testimony of Persons Accused of Crime*, 1 AM. L. REV. 443, 446 (1867). In England, where the rule against defendant testimony persisted decades longer, legislators fretted over a "habitual spectacle of this wholesale perjury" and "perjury upon a gigantic scale." Joel N. Bodansky, *The Abolition of the Party–Witness Disqualification: An Historical Survey*, 70 KY. L.J. 91, 109 n.74, 110 (1981–1982) (quoting Parliamentary debates).

Lawyers of the day saw that permitting parties to testify demanded far greater faith in jurors' lie-detecting powers. One Massachusetts lawyer commented on the new order in 1861:

> [T]he admission of parties imposes new and grave trusts on jurymen, and makes their position more difficult and responsible than before. They are now called upon to decide between conflicting testimony . . . and this, we hardly need say, requires the exercise of more than average judicial faculties.

[George S. Hillard], *Review of John Appleton*, The Rules of Evidence Stated and Discussed, 92 N. AM. L. REV. 515, 524 (1861). Another observer agreed that with "the admission of parties to give evidence . . . the temptation to perjury is thereby increased, and the task of the jury will be often rendered more difficult and delicate . . . and [will] require more than usual caution and intelligence on their part." WILLIAM FORSYTH, HISTORY OF TRIAL BY JURY 380–82 (1878).

Beyond letting even likely liars testify, the system has resolved in other ways to trust jurors' power to sniff out lies. You know from *State v. Batangan*, 71 Haw. 552 (1990), that expert witnesses, prolific in so many other areas, generally may not comment on a witness's credibility. "The common experience of a jury," the court wrote, "in most cases, provides a sufficient basis for assessment of a witness' credibility." 71 Haw. at 556 (page 767). And even after *Daubert* consigned *Frye* to history's dust heap, *Frye*'s rejection of lie-detection technology survives in almost every American court unless parties stipulate to its use. *United States v. Semrau*, 693 F.3d 510 (6th Cir. 2012) (page 837), simply confronted fMRI lie detection with the same suspicion with which earlier courts had greeted standard polygraphs. "Were an accurate lie detector developed," wrote Professor Julie Seaman in a passage quoted by the *Semrau* court, "the jury's unique role in determining witness credibility would be called into question." (Page 846.)

Hovering just outside the boundaries of evidence law is another sign of the system's growing faith in jurors' lie-detecting powers. In the course of the nineteenth century, trial judges in the great majority of American jurisdictions lost their discretion to comment freely on the evidence when instructing the jury. *See* Kenneth A. Krasity, *The Role of the Judge in Jury Trials: The Elimination of Judicial Evaluation of Fact in American State Courts from 1795 to 1913*, 62 U. DET. MERCY L. REV. 595, 595 (1985). The most forbidden realm is judicial instruction on a witness's credibility. Some 75 years ago, one federal trial judge dared advise a jury how it could tell that the defendant had lied:

> And now I am going to tell you what I think of the defendant's testimony. You may have noticed ... that he wiped his hands during his testimony. It is rather a curious thing, but that is almost always an indication of lying. Why it should be so we don't know, but that is the fact. I think that every single word that man said, except when he agreed with the Government's testimony, was a lie.

Quercia v. United States, 289 U.S. 466, 468 (1933). Reversing the defendant's conviction, a unanimous Supreme Court declared that " '[i]t was for the jury to test the credibility of the defendant as a witness, giving his testimony such weight under all the circumstances as they thought it entitled to, ... uninfluenced by [the judge's] instructions....' " *Id.* at 471 (quoting *Allison v. United States*, 160 U.S. 203, 207 (1895)).

Today almost no American trial judge would presume to tell the jury her pet theory of credibility. Even the boilerplate instructions on assessing a witness's credibility no longer include much substance. California judges once advised juries that when weighing a defendant's testimony, they should consider "the *consequences* to him relating from the results of this trial and the *inducements* and stipulations which would ordinarily influence a person in his situation." *People v. Morrow*, 60 Cal. 142, 147 (1882). Today, California trial judges, like most American judges, intone that "[y]ou alone, must judge the credibility or believability of the witnesses. . . ." 1–200 CALCRIM 226 (2008); *see United States v. Gaines*, 457 F.3d 238, 242 (2d Cir. 2006) (vacating a conviction because of the trial judge's instruction that "[o]bviously, the defendant has a deep personal interest in the result of his prosecution. This interest creates a motive for false testimony. . . .").

In the end, the question whether evidence law reflects trust or mistrust in the factfinding powers of jurors does not readily reduce to a legal cliche. Evidence law has grown haphazardly over the centuries, shaped by the needs and prejudices of passing generations. Even if each individual rule can claim a sensible rationale, it is unlikely that any single theme can unite the whole. Evidence law may not be, in Justice Jackson's words, a "grotesque structure," but neither is it a model of precision and symmetry. Generalizing it along any dimension is difficult—generalizing its entire reason for being may be impossible.

Haphazard and ungainly, evidence law can be hard for legal artisans to admire. Still, I hope you have taken a certain liking to its awkward form.

Hearsay Quiz

Suggested Answers and Explanations

[For the problems, please refer to pages 403 to 406.]

1. *Hearsay:* That the declarant is repeating her own out-of-court words does not take her past statement out of the realm of hearsay. The advisory committee explained its decision to include past statements of testifying witnesses as hearsay in its Note to Rule 801(d)(1), at RB 198–99. For criticism of this approach, see the Morgan excerpt at pages 432 to 435. (Although hearsay, this evidence may very well be admissible under Rule 801(d)(1)(C) as long as the witness testifies from her present memory about the fact of the robbery or the prosecutor proves the fact of the robbery in some other way. That is, a statement of identification under Rule 801(d)(1)(C) extends only to the question of identification, not to past events generally.)

2. *Hearsay:* "[N]onverbal conduct of a person, if it is intended by the person as an assertion," also qualifies as a "statement" under Rule 801(a). (As in the last problem, the evidence may be admissible under Rule 801(d)(1)(C), if the owner testifies, or under Rule 803(2).)

3. *Not hearsay:* It is very unlikely that the owner, in chasing the other man, was intending to communicate anything to anyone. Without communicative intent, there is no assertion—and therefore no hearsay.

4. *Not hearsay:* It is a simple fact of life that only cars registered in Wyoming lawfully bear Wyoming license plates. We need not rely on the truthfulness or other testimonial capacities of the car's owner or the plate's maker or anyone else to prove the car came from Wyoming. We know it is likely to have come from Wyoming because it had to be registered in Wyoming to be issued this plate. Now, if someone stole a Wyoming plate and fixed it to this car to suggest to police that the car, actually from someplace else, was from Wyoming, the plate would bear the communicative intent of the plate's thief. Still the evidence probably would not be hearsay because the prosecutor, under these facts, probably would not be trying to prove that the car came from Wyoming. Hence the evidence would not be offered "to prove the *truth* of the matter asserted."

5. *Not hearsay:* The tape cannot be hearsay because, as both Rules 801(a) and 801(b) make clear, hearsay requires an out-of-court statement *of a person*. After all, a videotape typically presents no problem of memory loss or insincerity. And to the extent we are worried about the camera's perception or recording capacities, we normally can examine the camera or seek the testimony of someone who inspected the camera at or near the time of the event. Alternatively, the prosecutor could present an

eyewitness to testify that the videotape fairly and accurately depicts what the witness saw during the robbery.

6. *Hearsay:* The store-owner's reenactment is an assertion about what he did at the time of the robbery: He is trying to communicate what he did, even if not in words. Note that a nonverbal assertion qualifies as a "statement" under Rule 801(a)(2).

7. *Not hearsay:* The defendant's words constitute a "verbal act." That is, his words *are* a threat. Because the defendant has *made*—and not *asserted*—a threat, we need not rely on any of his testimonial capacities to know that he threatened the store-owner. See the discussion of verbal acts at pages 381 to 382.

8. *Not hearsay:* Take the testimony of the store-owner and his wife separately. The store-owner's testimony that he saw the robber flee the store is of course not hearsay because the store-owner is on the witness stand and subject to cross-examination. His testimony that he called his wife about a minute later is not hearsay for the same reason. What he said to his wife is irrelevant. The significance of the store-owner's phone call is only that it establishes when the robber fled the store. If the store-owner had testified that he called his wife after the robber fled and said, " 'Hi,' " the testimony would not be hearsay (because "Hi" does not assert anything). Likewise, if his wife then took the stand and testified, "My husband called me a little after ten o'clock and said, 'Hi,' " this testimony would not be hearsay either. Yet their accounts, taken together, would suffice to prove when the robber fled the store.

9. *Hearsay:* This is an example of an "indirect assertion." It is similar to the hypothetical about the statement, "I just spent all morning with the architect planning my retirement home," discussed at pages 397 to 398. Here, the immediate fact (that the store-owner did not ring up a single sale all night) is a necessary link in a chain of inferences leading to the intermediate fact (that there had been few customers all night), which in turn leads to the ultimate fact (that the store was probably empty of customers at the time of the robbery). The statement, "I never rang up a single sale all night," therefore *is* being offered to prove what it asserts—what the store-owner meant to communicate—and is hearsay.

10. *Not hearsay:* There is no reason to think that the silent citizens of Oakdale meant to *assert*, by not calling the police, that they had not been robbed.

11. *Not hearsay:* It is very unlikely that the defendant, by stuttering and hyperventilating, meant to assert that he was nervous.

12. *Not hearsay:* This problem is quite similar to Problem 4, concerning the Wyoming license plate. Why would anyone *except* the Oakdale Quik–Stop have plastic coffee stirrers bearing the store's name and logo? That is, we need not rely on the truthfulness or other testimonial capacities of the store-owner, the coffee stirrer's maker, or anyone else to

prove that someone carrying one of these coffee stirrers recently was in the Quik–Stop.

13. *Not hearsay:* As a simple definitional matter, the defendant's lie is not being offered "to prove the truth of the matter asserted." On the contrary, the significance of the defendant's self-identification is precisely that it was false. We need not rely on the defendant's sincerity—or on his perception or (except marginally) on his memory—to use his statement to prove his guilty state of mind. (Whether hearsay or not, this evidence would be admissible under Rule 801(d)(2)(A), as the statement of a party-opponent.)

14. *Hearsay:* At first glance, the defendant's statement that he is Jesse James does not look like hearsay (and some evidence authorities would say it is not). After all, it is not being offered to prove he *is* Jesse James. But if the theory of defense counsel's insanity claim is that the defendant *believes* he is Jesse James, this evidence is hearsay. In that case, defense counsel's intended chain of inferences is: The defendant said he is Jesse James; therefore he thinks he is Jesse James; therefore he is insane. The defendant's statement, "I am Jesse James," *means* that he thinks he is Jesse James—these two statements are fundamentally equivalent. Therefore his words are being offered to prove what he meant to communicate. See the material on implied and indirect assertions at pages 397 to 398. (Though hearsay, this evidence might be admissible under Rule 803(3).) *See also* Michael H. Graham, *"Stickperson Hearsay": A Simplified Approach to Understanding the Rule Against Hearsay*, 1982 U. ILL. L. REV. 887, 919.

15. *Not hearsay:* This problem presents facts very much like those of *Wright v. Tatham*, discussed at pages 398 to 399. The sister's words are not hearsay for the same reason the letters to the testator in *Wright v. Tatham* were not hearsay. Her words *manifest* her belief in her brother's sanity and good judgment—but there is no suggestion she meant to communicate that belief to him.

16. *Not hearsay:* Whether or not the wife's statement to the defendant was *true*, her words gave him a motive to rob *so long as he believed them.* Hence this example falls outside the definition of hearsay at the very first branch of the hearsay flowchart at page 383. The significance of the wife's words is not their truthfulness, but rather their effect on the listener.

17. *Not hearsay:* In saying to his friend, "Here's the ten grand I owe you," the defendant did not mean to communicate to his friend that he owed such a debt, for his friend surely knew that already. The words are simply a verbal act, *making* the money repayment on the debt, rather than communicating any fact to the friend. See the discussion of verbal acts at pages 381 to 382. Note that the analysis would be different had the debt been of ten dollars rather than ten thousand. If the defendant had owed his friend ten dollars, he very well might have felt the need to remind his

friend of the debt. Hence if the prosecutor sought to prove that the debt existed, she would be offering the defendant's words to prove what he intended to assert. The difference is that (most) friends don't forget loans of ten thousand dollars. In making repayment, one rarely feels the need to remind one's creditor of a debt of that size.

18. *Not hearsay:* This problem is similar to that dealing with bets made to a suspected gambling den. (See pages 401 to 402.) The friend's claim to have some spare ammunition, whether or not true, expressed his belief that the defendant had a .45–caliber weapon. But the friend surely felt no need to *communicate* to the defendant that the defendant had such a weapon. (It's not the sort of thing the defendant would have forgotten.) So the statement is not offered to prove anything it asserts.

19. *Not hearsay:* The defendant's statement is not being offered to prove that the Guinness really is shelved between the Sam Adams and the Becks. After all, no one in this litigation really cares how the beer is stocked, and if anyone did, there are more straightforward ways to prove it. Rather, his statement is offered as circumstantial evidence that the defendant has been in the store before: How else could he have known how the beer is stocked? Note that when the statement is offered for this purpose, we do not care about the defendant's testimonial capacities. He could not possibly have been lying about where the Guinness is shelved—unless he is a clairvoyant liar—because he was exactly right about something that is hard to guess exactly. And we are not worried that he may have misperceived or misremembered or misnarrated where the beer is shelved, because the perfect correlation between what he said and the beer's actual location shows the accuracy of his statement—and proves he was in the store before. This problem is similar to *Bridges v. State*, 247 Wis. 350, 363–67, 19 N.W.2d 862 (1945), discussed at pages 399 to 400.

Whether hearsay or not, this evidence of course would be admissible under Rule 801(d)(2)(A), as the statement of a party-opponent.

20. *Hearsay:* Evidence that the defendant has a reputation for peacefulness merely summarizes various out-of-court statements by his neighbors that he is peaceful or has behaved peacefully in various contexts. Because the factfinder is being asked to infer from evidence of the defendant's reputation that he is indeed peaceful, the evidence is being offered to prove what it asserts. (Note that Rule 803(21) creates an exception for this form of hearsay.)

21. *Not hearsay:* This problem bears some similarity to Problem 15 and *Wright v. Tatum*. The wife's words *manifest* her confidence that she has the means to pay. But there is no suggestion that her purpose in speaking was to communicate her ability to pay. Alternatively, you may consider her words a verbal act. (See the discussion of verbal acts at pages 381 to 382.) Though her words took the form of an assertion ("I'd like to buy . . ."), their operative force was to *request* from the store-owner a TV

and four speakers. In the normal course of events, the store-owner will arrange delivery of these items to the customer and will demand payment from her. Few of us would walk into a store and set in motion this very predictable chain of events unless we had the means to pay. Hence we need not rely on anything the wife *asserted* to conclude that she had the means to pay.

22. *Not hearsay:* The explanation of this problem is very similar to that of Problem 19. The answer here is somewhat easier, because in this case there is no reason to think the defendant meant to assert *anything* by uttering, "Thomas Barrington O'Toole."

23. *Not hearsay:* As in Problem 16, the significance of the store-owner's warning (and of the defendant's threat nested within it) is the impact those words had on the *listener*—the police officer. This example falls outside the definition of hearsay at the first branch of the hearsay flowchart at page 383.

24. *Not hearsay:* This problem is similar to the last one. The manager's out-of-court warning is not being offered to prove that there really had been several robberies in the neighborhood, but rather that the store-owner was *on notice* that this was a dangerous neighborhood. Note that the factfinder does not care whether the manager was lying about the neighborhood crime statistics or misperceived or misremembered them or simply misspoke. All the factfinder cares about is what the store-owner heard.

25. *Hear*say: If the assistant himself were on the witness stand testifying about the warning he gave to the store-owner, we would have Problem 24 all over again, with the same result. But the manager's testimony *about what the assistant told her* does present hearsay. We have to believe the assistant's out-of-court report that he gave warning to the store-owner to conclude that the store-owner was on notice of the risk of being robbed.

INDEX

References are to pages.

†